T0368189

"Nuestros Antepasados"
(Our Ancestors)

"Nuestros Antepasados" (Our Ancestors)

Los Nuevo Mexicanos del Condado de Lincoln
(Lincoln County's History of its New Mexican Settlers)

By

ERNEST S. SANCHEZ & PAUL R. SANCHEZ

Edited by

Reynel Martinez

authorHOUSE

AuthorHouse™
1663 Liberty Drive
Bloomington, IN 47403
www.authorhouse.com
Phone: 1 (800) 839-8640

Published by AuthorHouse 09/11/2015

ISBN: 978-1-5049-2751-2 (sc)
ISBN: 978-1-5049-2750-5 (e)

Library of Congress Control Number: 2015912708

Print information available on the last page.

This book is printed on acid-free paper.

Table of Contents

Dedication

"para mi familia"

Acknowledgements

First and foremost I would like to acknowledge and thank my grandson Paul Sanchez for his hard work, long hours, and heart he put into this book. I could not have written this book without him. To my sons Ernest and James, daughter Janice, who contributed and supported me through this process. To all the families that provided their family history and helped with this endeavor…thank you. To Reynel Martinez for helping with the editing, compilation and support. Most of all to my loving wife Oralia, who gave up her dining room table all those years for my research and without her this book would not have been possible.

Foreword

Through the years, my people have been referred by many different labels such as; Spanish, Mexican, Chicano, Hispanic, and eventually Latino. These labels have been imposed upon my people to describe who we were, who we are, and who we will be. Regardless of which label has been put upon us, one thing is for certain. A great travesty, and injustice has been imposed upon us. Our culture has been pillaged, and our history has been watered down, and even forgotten by many people.

It is often said that the truth can be found somewhere between two differing points of view. The point of view that receives the most exposure becomes the truth that the masses accept. The point of view that receives the least amount of exposure is eventually lost with the passing of time. Like the truth, history can sometimes be biased by the perceptions of those who write it, and blindly accepted by people who don't know any better.

History is often dictated by the drama that accompanies human tragedy. It is often written for those who are bold enough to instill fear and awe into the human psyche, by senseless acts of lawlessness, atrocities committed against the human spirit and violence as a means of establishing control. Yet there is a softer side to history that is just as important, but not as glamorous and often goes untold. What may be considered important to my history may not be considered important to others' history.

Nowhere, are these statements I've made, more evident than by the history that has been written about Lincoln County, New México. In particular, the events that led up to the Lincoln County War. It is in this history where my ancestors are often referred to as, "Mexicans". They are the many people without names, without a sense of purpose as perceived by many historians. My ancestors have been relegated to second-class status, even though we had played a part in the history of New México for over 350 years.

This book is the final result of a lifetime of research. What started out as a passing interest into the genealogy of my family, led me on a journey of discovery about the lives of the people that would make up several different communities spread throughout all of Lincoln County. I've spent countless hours conversing with hundreds of different people, taking notes of their stories, their parents' stories, and their grandparents' stories.

This book is about the original settlers in the Ruidoso and Hondo Valley, Plaza de San José, later called Missouri Bottom, El Berendo, now named Roswell, New México, which were all in what later became Lincoln County. The information was obtained from descendants of the original settlers and verified from legal documents, church records, US Census, homesteads, land patents and publications. Some of the records do not correspond with other records as to dates, but they are proof of a family's existence and their place of residence at the time. Some of the original settlers were descendants of the first colonists that came to Nueva España, which is now México, and came north in 1598, with the first conquest and named the country, Reyno de Nuevo Méjico, not because of the country of México, as the colonists had been in Nuevo México for two hundred and twenty years before México got it's independence from España in the 1820's.

J. Ernesto S. Sánchez

Chapter One:
Los Sánches: Las Colonias, La Reconquista y el Río Abajo, 1663-1777

La Colonia

Nuevo México had been mentioned by name as early as 1563 by Francisco de Ibarra who was seeking his fortune by scouting potential sites for gold mining.[1] The name for this region became official from about 1581 to 1582 during the Gallegos expedition. The name Nuevo México was used in reference to all the lands north of Nueva Vizcaya that Gallegos and his men had explored. Thus El Reyno de Nuevo México and or La Provincia de Nuevo México was the given name from 1582 on.[2]

Although Don Juan de Oñate and 400 other *pobladores* (settlers) first established San Juan de los Caballeros, on July 11, 1598[3] the direct descendants for many of Los Sánches came to the northern colonies at a later time. Jacinto Sánchez de Iñigo, the progenitor of many families who carry the Sánchez name in present day New México, was born during a very tumultuous time in its early history. At the root of the turbulence were the Church, the provincial civil government, the pobladores, and the indigenous people that all had called the Río del Norte Valley home. To better understand the complexities of that forgone time, one has to understand the social structure of that society.

In El Reyno de Nuevo México the Spanish caste system was instituted for the purpose of identifying *Los Cristianos viejos de pureza de sangre Española* (The old Christians of pure Spanish blood). The degree of purity was dependent on the bloodlines of the person or families in question. Those people who were born in España and had immigrated to *Las Américas* were known as *Peninsulares*. Those people who had pure Spanish blood but were born in Las Américas were known as *Criollos*. Those people who didn't have Jewish or Moorish blood were known as *Un Cristiano Viejo*. Peninsulares and Criollos were the ones who were more likely to obtain the most revered positions in the civil government and a higher social standing.

The widely embraced system of *castas* was an early attempt to categorize those people with mixed blood. Often times, illustrators were commissioned to create visual representations of the offspring of mixed marriages or couples. Although there were many categories to describe the offspring of mixed marriages, there were a few that were more prevalent in El Reyno de Nuevo México.

Color quebrado (Broken color) was a generic term used to describe any person of mixed blood. Its usage was more prevalent during the early colonial times. There were more specific categorizations that aimed to label those with mixed blood. *Mestizos* were people who had a Spanish and Native American bloodline. The term *Coyoté* also signified a Spanish and Native American bloodline, but the terminology was more prevalent in El Reyno de Nuevo México. *Indios* were pure blood Native Americans that were neither Puebloan or perceived to be civilized. *Mulatos* were born of Spanish and African blood.

As was the case before the Españoles had arrived in the Río del Norte Valley, some of the Native American tribes were often at war with each other. Those captured during times of war were sometimes forced to perform hard labor. The arrival of the Españoles created a new demand for manual intensive labor. The term *genízaros* was used to categorize those Native Americans who were captured during a time of tribal warfare and consequently sold or bartered to the Españoles.

Genízaros would often adopt the name of the Spanish families that they served. Many converted to Catholicism. Over time, the term also became synonymous with those Native Americans who were perceived as being civilized.[4]

Being of pure blood or of mixed blood was a big determinant of one's social stratification, but was not the sole determinant. One's trade also played an important role in their influence and prestige. The upper political echelon consisted of the *Gobernador* (Governor) and their highest appointed officials and highest-ranking officers in the presidio. The Franciscan friars were also held in high regard, even though they were trained to serve a life of humility. Next were the *labradores* (farmers) and artisans. The third tier included the common people whom owned no land and were relegated to working for the people in the upper echelons. Remarkably, many of the low ranking soldiers from the presidios were considered members of the lower echelon of social stratification.

The majority of pobladores were labradores who spent the better part of their lives farming on their *estancias* (ranching establishments). Amongst the labradores, there was very little need for any formal education. The boys of the family learned to work the farm. In some instances, the boys would become an artisan and learn a trade such as being a carpenter, a blacksmith, a lumberjack, or even an adobé maker. The girls learned to become homemakers.

A formal education was often reserved for the children of the wealthiest members of society. Obtaining an education usually meant that the child would be sent south to the larger population centers of Nueva España. If and when an educator was present in the Río del Norte Valley, they often served as tutors for the children of wealthy families.[5]

The government hierarchy of El Reyno de Nuevo México was set up to establish Spanish control over the pobladores, and the indigenous people of the *Pueblos*. Through his Devine Right to govern, the King of España exercised his authority over all claimed lands, and their inhabitants. The King would appoint a viceroy who oversaw the Spanish rule over the Américas. The viceroy in turn would appoint a Gobernador to oversee the province in their charge.[6]

The Gobernador of El Reyno de Nuevo México was bestowed with many duties and responsibilities, some of which were to defend the Estancias, the Pueblos, and the Missions from an internal revolt, or attacks from neighboring indigenous tribes. They also ensured that neither the Church nor the pobladores exploited or abused the indigenous people of the Pueblos. They were empowered to issue the administration of justice, for all matters dealing with civil laws. They commanded the military, and ensured that their troops were sufficient enough to protect the province, and administer justice when called upon.[7]

The Gobernador was given the authority to issue decrees and ordinances over the citizens of their respective province. They authorized the establishment of new estancias for settlement, in which they also oversaw the assignment of land and water rights. They wielded the power to divide the province into *jurisdicciónes* (jurisdictions), which usually consisted of several *villas* (townships), and estancias. They also had the right to judge those who broke the provincial civil laws, and administer justice in a manner they saw fit.[8]

The Gobernador had the authority to appoint prominent citizens of their provinces to the title of *Alcalde Mayor* (Chief Judge). The Alcalde Mayor became the liaison of their respective jurisdicción and acted on behalf of the Gobernador. Below the Alcalde Mayor was the *Alcalde*, who was responsible for the respective villa or Pueblo within the jurisdicción. All disputes within the villa or Pueblo would be brought before the Alcalde, who often administered justice on a more localized level. If there was no satisfactory resolution to a dispute, it would then be brought before the Alcalde Mayor who would issue an opinion. If the Alcalde Mayor's opinion did not resolve the dispute, then an appeal was sent before the Gobernador who would ultimately resolve the dispute. For better or for worse, the Gobernador had the final and deciding opinion in the matter of solving any dispute reaching their office.[9]

As was the practice of El Reyno de Nuevo México's early colonization by the **Españoles**, the Gobernador strongly encouraged the settlement of the lower Río del Norte Valley by approving both privately held, and church held estancias. By 1665, it was estimated that there were roughly 2,000 Españoles living in the Río del Norte Valley. Most of them lived on estancias, with only about 100 living in the villa of Santa Fé.[10]

There were many ordinances in place that were provided as a means of protecting the rights of the Puebloan people. An Español could not claim ownership of any Puebloan product unless they had legally purchased that product. They could not establish a settlement within 9 miles of a Pueblo. Españoles could employ the labor of the indigenous people only if they could pay them a daily wage, a practice referred to as **repartimiento**.[11]

The Gobernador had the authority to appoint **encomenderos**, who were given the right to collect tributes, a practice called **encomienda**, from the Pueblos in exchange for military protection. Encomenderos usually obtained the privilege of encomienda by serving as a soldier in the military. The tributes they often received were in the form of agricultural goods such as corn; and cloth such as blankets, furs, and leather hides. Additionally, the encomenderos often acquired some degree of control over the lands that were in their charge, which were not being used by the Pueblos. Through the years the encomenderos had become increasingly vital to the economic success of El Reyno de Nuevo México. By having the rights to encomienda they controlled the Pueblos, which were a major source of wealth for a few Españoles. [12]

The use of labor as a form of encomienda was prohibited by the King of España because of the gross abuses of the indigenous people during the early colonization of Nueva España. To circumnavigate this prohibition, the Gobernador, Franciscans, and encomenderos used the lawful provision of repartimiento as a means of forcing the Puebloans into indentured servitude. Although the ordinance required that they should be paid a daily wage, in many instances they were not compensated for their labor.[13]

A limit of thirty-five encomenderos was established by the government as a means of keeping some control over the practice of encomienda. The intent was to ensure that the Puebloan resources were not stretched too thin, which could lead to conflict amongst competing Españoles. Furthermore, the privilege of encomienda could be passed down to their heirs for three generations. The practice of encomienda grew exponentially as the encomenderos' families grew from one generation to the next.[14]

The encomenderos often settled on an estancia in close proximity to their encomienda. As a condition of being named an encomendero, one had to have the ability to muster a militia in the event an army was needed. The encomenderos often recruited their militias through the ranks of the pobladores who settled on estancias within their controlled region. They often used the militia as a means of supplementing their income. This practice resulted in a growing relationship of interdependence between the encomenderos and the pobladores.[15]

Santa Custodia de la Conversión de San Pablo de Nuevo México

The Catholic Church's primary objective was to convert the indigenous people to the Christian faith. Their secondary objective was to bring the European lifestyle to the people of the Pueblos by offering a means of teaching them agricultural techniques, and civil morality, which they felt were absent from their lives.

In El Reyno de Nuevo México the ecclesiastical headquarters was established in Santo Domingo. From Santo Domingo the Franciscans were administered throughout the region referred to as **Santa Custodia de la Conversión de San Pablo de Nuevo México** (Holy Custodia of the Conversion of Saint Paul of New México). Santo Domingo was administered by the **provincial** (chief administrator), which was based in Ciudad de México. The provincial would appoint a **custodio** (custodian) for the Custodia. The custodio oversaw members of a **difinitorio**, which was a clerical governing committee that helped in the administration of all Church affairs in the Custodia. On an annual basis, from amongst their peers, committee members were elected during the yearly chapter meetings held in Santo Domingo, and later in San José de Giusewa, which was near Pueblo de Jémez.

The chapter meetings were held in late summer and were open to all Franciscans of the Custodia. Many Franciscans however, were not able to make the journey to attend the meetings. In many instances, the meetings were attended only by the custodio and the difinitorio. During these meetings the establishment of new missions was discussed and approved. The assignment of Friars to a mission was also administered. New Friars often were sent to an established mission, whereas those friars with seniority had the option to remain at their current mission or move to another mission of their choice.[16]

The process in which the Puebloan people were converted to Christianity was called a **misión**. The misión usually fell into two categories a **conversión**, which encompassed a single tribe within the Pueblo, or a **reducción**, which brought several different tribes together within the Pueblo.

The Pueblo became a conversión when one or more tribes within the Pueblo agreed in principle, to allow the Friar to build a mission church, and to help with its construction. If the friar decided to take up residence within a Pueblo, a **convento** was also built next to the church. Those churches that had a resident friar were referred to as **cabeceras**. For those churches that did not have a resident friar they were referred to as **visitas**. In the case of a visita, a friar from the cabecera would make regular visits to the Pueblos. Often times, the status of a mission could change based on whether a friar decided to take residence within a Pueblo. The number of friars in any given convento was dependent on two factors, the amount of friars in the Custodia, and the importance of the convento.[17] By 1626, the Catholic Church had established 43 churches and missions that ranged as far north as Pueblo de Taos, as far south as Guadalupe del Paso, as far east as the Río Pecos, and as far west as the Hopi and Zuñi Pueblos.

Although the Church was independent of the Spanish crown, it often had been used as an agent to promote pacification amongst the indigenous people. As a result, both the Church and the civil government demanded obedience and labor from the citizens of the Pueblos as a payment of homage. Furthermore, when the encomenderos collected their tributes, it was often at the expense of the Pueblo's ability to provide sustenance for itself. In many instances the Puebloans went hungry because of this practice.[18]

In the early colonial years of El Reyno de Nuevo México, many of the missions were often built in relative isolation from the Spanish villas. This posed a problem when matters of civil law had to be dealt with. As a result, the viceroy in Ciudad de México had decreed that the Franciscan friars would be given the authority to serve judgment on matters of civil law, as well as the Church's Christian teachings.

Over time, the authority given to the Franciscans ultimately came into conflict with the Gobernadores, who had felt it was their responsibility to oversee all matters of civil law. In an attempt to subvert the Franciscans authority, the Gobernadores restricted them to pass judgment only on Church matters. Defiantly, the Franciscans continued to serve justice in the manner in which they had grown accustomed to. Furthermore, the Franciscans threatened the Gobernadores with their powers of excommunication, and their willingness to withhold sacraments from the pobladores.[19]

Tensions between the Civil Government and the Church

Tensions between the civil government and the Church became more evident when on February 21, 1639 the Santa Fé town council signed a declaration to the viceroy condemning the treatment of the Puebloans by the Franciscan Friars. The Franciscan Friars, in turn, made accusations that Gobernador Rosas was falsely persecuting them.[20]

The allegations centered on the widely accepted practice of repartimiento, and encomienda that Puebloan citizens were often subjected to. However, both the civil government and the Franciscan Friars were alternately subjecting them to the same types of practices. Furthermore, many people within the Pueblos became resentful of the Españoles' unwillingness to allow them to practice their own religion. In many instances, the consequences of practicing their own religion resulted in whippings or imprisonment.[21]

In 1643, the Jémez and Navajo plotted to drive out the Español invaders. The attempt failed, as the Españoles thwarted their efforts. Again in 1650, the Jémez, Ysleta, Alameda, San Felipé, Cochití, and Apaché plotted to drive out the Español occupiers. As was the case in the first attempt to liberate their lands from Español control, the stronger fighting force prevailed. In both instances the leadership and participants of both uprisings were hanged, imprisoned, or sold into slavery, by the Españoles.[22]

Between 1659 and 1662 Gobernador Bernardo Lópes de Mendizábal contested the limits of ecclesiastical jurisdiction, which gave the Franciscans the authority to force the Pueblos to comply with Church doctrine. It was the Franciscans interpretation that the friars could force physical punishment as a means of penance. This included forced labor for farming, construction, and grazing without repartimiento. Gobernador Lópes de Mendizábal looked upon the Puebloan citizens as the subjects of civil law, and therefore should be judged as such. It was his assertion that the friars were only responsible for conducting mass and administering the holy sacrament, and nothing else.[23]

The legal status of the Pueblos came into contention during the conflict. It was the Gobernadores' position that by 1640, all Pueblos with a convento or a visita had legally become a ***doctrina*** per the decree of the government of Nueva España based in the capital of Ciudad de México. A doctrina had established the right of the Pueblo to govern itself, and therefore an alcalde would be appointed. By default, the friar would be responsible only for the spiritual guidance of their parishioners.

As was the standard practice for many conquered indigenous people in Nueva España, taxes would usually be paid to the crown, and tithes would be given to the bishop, while its citizens would become subject to civil laws and judgment like any other villa. The viceroy however, later complicated matters by decreeing that no bishop would be placed over El Reyno de Nuevo México because it was too isolated from the rest of the Episcopal Authority, and that no taxes or tithes needed to be paid because tributes were already being given to the encomenderos who already paid tithes to the Franciscans.

Without a bishop, and being isolated from the rest of Nueva España, the Franciscans continued to operate their Pueblos like conversiónes. They continued to pass judgment for both civil laws and Church doctrines. On the other hand, the government invoked their authority under the doctrina. What complicated the conflict further was the fact that the government in Ciudad de México was reevaluating the laws governing encomienda and the status of all conquered indigenous people. The ambiguity of the laws had led to neither a compromise nor any reconciliation between the Church and the government. As a result of the impasse, the Puebloan people were the ones who suffered the most.[24]

Jacinto Sánches de Iñigo

Jacinto Sánches de Iñigo was born in El Reyno de Nuevo México in about 1663.[25] He along with his brother Pedro are regarded as some of the first settlers that had passed the Sánchez surname to many of their descendants that now live throughout New México, and more specifically to many of those who later settled in what was to become Lincoln County.

Jacinto's mother was Juana Lópes de Aragón who was the daughter of Francisco Lópes de Aragón and Ana Baca. There has been a great deal of speculation as to who Jacinto's father was. At the root of the speculation is the absence of a known father listed as a husband to Juana Lópes de Aragón and in the prenuptial of Jacinto's second marriage. Furthermore, in the prenuptials of his brother Pedro and, sister Francisca, a father also was not listed.[26]

In his struggle with the Church, Gobernador Lópes de Mendizábal had encouraged many of his citizens to come forward and report any scandalous behavior committed by any of the Franciscan friars. During the inquisition, there were several allegations that many friars had indeed had sexual affairs and had fathered children with Española and Puebloan women.

As Inquisition officials in Ciudad de México examined the evidence, they had concurred that there was enough testimony to prove that some friars had indeed lived scandalously. In one such incident, upon further review of the Inquisition by officials, it was discovered that in August of 1663 in the Pueblo de San Ildefonso, Capitán Diego Pérez Romero, identified Fray Francisco Muños as one whom, *"vivido siempre muy escandolosamente"* ("always lived very scandalously.") It was alleged that he had an affair with Doña Juana Lópes de Aragón and her first cousin, the daughter of Capitán Diego de Trujillo.

Interestingly enough, Ana Baca and her daughter Juana Lópes de Aragón were living on their estancia christened, El Alamo, which was about four leagues (~14 miles) from **La Villa Real de la Santa Fé de San Francisco de Asis** (The royal township of the Holy Faith of Saint Francis of Assisi). Their estancia could have been settled at the foot of present day Ortiz Mountain in close proximity to Alamo Creek just northwest of Santa Fé. If so, then Padre Francisco Muños and Juana Lópes de Aragón had lived within 15 miles of each other at the time of Jacinto's birth.

Francisco Muños was born in Puebla de los Ángeles, Nueva España in about 1629. He was baptized on October 22, 1629. His father's name was Jacinto Muños and his mother's name was Madalena Sánches de Iñigo. He became a friar in Ciudad de México on December 20, 1646, when he was 18 years of age. He had already migrated north to El Reyno de Nuevo México by September of 1660.[27]

It is not definitive that Francisco Muños Sánches de Iñigo is the real father to Jacinto, his brother Pedro, and his sister Francisca, but the evidence is very compelling. The one constant, concerning Jacinto and his siblings' father was that many people may have known who their father was, but there were painstaking efforts to conceal his identity. If there were any validity to the allegations that Fray Francisco Muños was their father, they would have carried the stigma of their parents' sins for their entire lives.

Pueblo Revolt of 1680

For several generations, the Puebloans and other indigenous people had been subjected to encomienda, repartimiento, oppression to practice their religion, and disease, which served to be the most fatal of all. All other prior attempts to overthrow the Español invaders were met with defeat.

In 1675 Gobernador Juan Francisco de Treviño made an attempt to further suppress the religious practices of the Puebloan people. Their religions were viewed in the minds of the clergy and the government as witchery and thus would no longer be tolerated. Treviño claimed that Fray Andrés Durán, his brother, his brother's wife, and a genízaro interpreter named Francisco Guíter were bewitched by a group of Puebloan *hechiceros* (medicine men).

The allegations led to the arrest of forty-seven Tewas. Four of the forty-seven had admitted to being hechiceros, and were condemned to death. Three of the four condemned to death were hanged, while the fourth committed suicide. The other forty-three Tewas served their punishment either by imprisonment or public lashings. One of the Tewas who received lashings and then was released was Po-Pé. After being released Po-Pé's hatred for the Españoles only grew more intense.[28]

In the following years, Po-Pé had gathered the chiefs of the many nations and conspired to revolt against the foreign invaders. He understood that success can only come if the majority of the nations fought as one force. Being that the leaders from all of the nations spoke a different language, it is believed that he communicated with them by using visual representations of what needed to be done. On August 9, 1680 runners were sent in different directions to all the pueblos carrying knotted cords made of yucca fiber. The cords carried a message from Po-Pé announcing the day the revolt would start. Two youths named Catua and Omtua ran all day from Tesuqué to San Marcos Pueblo, a distance of twenty-five miles. The *opi* or war chief along with the *cacique* or headman of San Marcos along with several village leaders and shamans listened as the runners explained the cords. Untie one knot each day, when no knots remained, attack. Po-Pé decreed that if San Marcos failed to join in the assault, Puebloans would descend from the north and kill every villager. The runners returned to the trail running south, carrying the message of the knotted cord to the other pueblos. Within the hour the cacique headed north to Santa Fe, fifteen miles distant, who had ties with the Gobernador. He was not the only turncoat that betrayed the plot to Gobernador Antonio de Otermín. Alerted by his loyalist he had the runners, Catua and Omtua seized, tortured and interrogated. With the plot leaked the various pueblos launched their attack.

Finding Refuge

On the eve of August 10, 1680 Gobernador Antonio de Otermín was apprised of an impending revolt, which was about to imperil his province. He diligently dispatched messengers to notify his Lieutenant General Alonso García, of the Río Abajo, and all of his alcaldes mayores so that they could prepare for the revolt. It was his intention to gain assistance from the soldiers who were living in the Río Abajo region. Tragically, Lt. General García had never received the Governor's orders. Of the three men he dispatched, none had reached the ear of García. One messenger was killed, and the other two had not made it pass Santo Domingo.

As the cool breeze softly sifted through the trees of the early morning on August 10, 1680, the silence of the dawn was abruptly interrupted by the terror filled screams of chaos, brutality and slaughter, which were then silenced by death. From the furthest settlements near Pueblo de Taos to those as far south as Pueblo de Ysleta, the blood of the Españoles flowed unto the earth at the hands of the enraged warriors of the people of the various Tewa, Navajo, and Apaché nations.

The first waves of the revolt hit the Pueblo de Tesuqué, which was about four miles due north of La Villa de Santa Fé. Padre Juan Bautista Pío was killed as he knelt before the altar while in prayer. After his death, the Tesuqueños destroyed all of the religious artifacts within the church as a show of retaliation, which was symbolic of what the Church had previously done to their own religious artifacts.

In the Pueblo de Jémez, Padre Juan de Jesús was stripped naked and paraded through the cemetery. He then was mounted upon a pig and viciously flogged while the Jémez people mocked his religious beliefs. Bloodied and pleading for mercy as he prayed, the Jémez viciously attacked him with sticks until the life had left his body.

Similar uprisings and murders were evident in many of the Pueblos as the friars were specifically targeted. In all, twenty-one priests had lost their lives during the revolt. The warriors didn't just murder the priests; they also killed about 400 pobladores and genízaros. The victims of the slaughter were young and old; men, women, and children. Among some of the dead were Jacinto, Pedro and Francisca's grandmother, Ana Ortiz Baca who was killed near the Pueblo de Taos. She was about 49 years of age upon her death. Their aunt, Juana de Aragón was also killed near the Pueblo de Taos.

Having received no correspondence from Lt. General García by August 13th, Gobernador Otermín had figured that either many of the pobladores on the Río Abajo had perished, or that they had sought refuge from the attacks. Those Españoles and genízaros that were fortunate enough to escape with their lives, found refuge within La Villa de Santa Fé and Pueblo de Ysleta. El Gobernador took leadership of the refugees in Santa Fé, while Lieutenant General Alonso García took leadership of the refugees in Ysleta. Of the approximately 1,000 people that had sought refuge in Santa Fé; Juana Lópes de Aragón and her children Jacinto, Pedro, and Francisca were amongst them. Padre Francisco Muños and four soldiers had sought refuge in Ysleta after narrowly escaping their murders in Pueblo de Zía, which was due northwest. Padre Muños was amongst the approximately 1,500 refugees at Ysleta.

The Refugees at Pueblo de Ysleta[29]

Lt. General García and the members of his leadership hierarchy had to appraise the situation of the 1,500 refugees before they decided what actions they should take in regards to the revolt. Many of the refugees had escaped to Ysleta without horses, nor food. Many of them, mostly women and children were barefoot and only partially clothed. Even worse, hunger was soon to set in, and there was very little food to meet the needs of all the people, and animals.

It was widely unknown whether the people to the north had all perished or if any had found refuge and thus remained alive. This was a serious issue of contention amongst the Lt. General's ad hoc council. Unwilling to risk any further life to assess the situation further north, the council decided it was in the best interest of the 1,500 refugees in their charge that they move to flee the revolt.

Lt. General García and several of the *maestre del campo*; Thomé Domíngues de Mendosa, Juan Domíngues de Mendosa, Francisco Gómes Robledo, and Diego de Trujillo, all had signed a religious proclamation indicating that they would retreat to El Paso del Norte on the southern fringes of El Reyno de Nuevo México, with the presumption that they would eventually re-conquer the lands to the north. Sixteen Sargentos Mayores and Capitánes in his company further validated the statement.

On August 14, 1680, Lt. General García and the 1,500 refugees set off due south for El Paso del Norte. Shortly after embarking on their retreat, the Lt. General had recalled that Gobernador Otermín had petitioned for a supply-train to be sent to La Villa de Santa Fé almost a year prior. He had come to know that Pedro de Leiva was charged with escorting the supply-train. García wrote a letter in which he described the gravity of the revolt, and the fate, which he believed had befallen the northern settlements. Padre Diego de Mendosa also had written a similar letter to his superior. Both letters were dispatched to Pedro de Leiva and Padre Francisco de Ayeta respectively.

The refugees had reached Sevilleta by August 20, 1680, where the Piros tribe had opted to join the ranks of the refugees. Although it meant more mouths to feed, Lt. General García felt it was strategically beneficial to the refugee caravan. By August 20, 1680 Sebastian de Herrera and Fernando de Cháves had met up with the refugee encampment in Pueblo del Alto, just north of Socorro. Both men had recently arrived from the jurisdicción de Taos, where the Españoles had been decimated by the slaughter.

On their way from Taos they happened across the siege that was taking place in La Villa de Santa Fé. Hidden from sight, they watched in horror as the warriors set houses, la Iglesia de San Miguel, and other government buildings afire. Shortly thereafter they heard the echoes of artillery, and saw the warriors retreat into the distance, to the safety of the llanos, setting all of the houses afire as they moved out of the range of the rifle fire. The two men left at that point, not wanting to be discovered, captured, and killed.

The Lt. General and his council thus were faced with a problematic dilemma. Having found out that the people to the north were still alive, and fighting for their lives, what were they to do? The people in their charge were starving, severely dehydrated and unable to withstand any onslaught from marauding bands of Apaché warriors that routinely made their presence emphatically known from a distance. Their munitions were severely depleted, which compromised their defensive capabilities. Furthermore, they were several days travel from the capital.

In the interest of the people in their charge, García and the men in his council decided it was more prudent to press on to Pueblo de Socorro where they would regroup deep within the confines of the Piros nation. They arrived at the pueblo on August 24, 1860. After realizing that the Piros had every intention of remaining in their charge, the Lt. General was inclined to fortify their position within the pueblo.

At this point the council convened yet again to discuss the matter of dispatching soldiers to the north to help their besieged brethren. García had previously dispatched a letter to Pedro de Leiva who was escorting a supply train from Nueva España, which included 30 troops and sufficient munitions to re-supply their soldiers. They had surmised that the supply-train should be in close proximity of the pueblo. Once meeting with the supply-train, he would fortify the town with a garrison, and take the other soldiers up north to assist the refugees.

Hastily, the Lt. General was making preparations to move forward with his plans when suddenly confusion thwarted his urgency to act upon them. It had come to his attention that the munitions on hand were severely inadequate to mount any successful rescue effort. All was not well amongst the Piros either, as it was discovered that some within their ranks had secretly harbored hostility towards the Españoles. A scout from one of the northern tribes had infiltrated the refugee ranks. Some of the members of the Piros had hid him from capture for three days. There was a brewing sentiment amongst the Piros that could compromise the security of the Español and genízaro refugees.

A junta, consisting of all the officers, was called before the council to discuss the matter in greater detail. The first to speak was Thomé Domíngues de Mendosa who described the events of the revolt and their current situation. He continued by stating that even with Sebastian de Herrera and Fernando de Cháves' accounts, the current fate of the people to the north still was unknown. Domíngues de Mendosa continued by making it known before the council, that he did not want the caravan to be divided but rather they should meet up with the supply-train first, and then send a contingent of troops north to the capital. In all, there were sixteen officers who spoke before the council in favor of Domíngues de Mendosa's proposal. There was only one officer, Capitán Don Fernando Durán y Cháves, who had expressed that the troops should promptly go to La Villa de Santa Fé to assist the northern refugees. It was unanimous though, that the refugees would continue pushing south until they met up with the supply-train.

Padre Francisco de Ayeta had received the letter sent by Padre Diego de Mendosa and immediately dispatched a letter notifying the Lt. General that Pedro de Leiva would be leaving El Paso del Norte on August 30, 1680 with the supply-train in tow. Upon reception, the news must have been refreshing for the refugees, and surely lifted their overall morale.

By September 04, 1680 the Ysleta refugees had reached the community of Fray Cristóbal, which was about 55 miles south of Pueblo de Socorro and 197 miles north of El Paso del Norte. Later in the day, García had also received a letter from his Gobernador instructing him to rendezvous with him and the Santa Fé refugees at Pueblo de Senecú. The Lt. General thus mounted his horse, and accompanied by six other men, set off to meet up with the northern refugees in Senecú. By September 13, 1680 the Santa Fé refugee caravan had finally caught up with the Ysleta refugee caravan.

The Refugees at La Villa de Santa Fé [30]

On August 13, 1680 Gobernador Antonio de Otermín could hear the war cries of the warriors from the Tanos, Pecos, and Queres nations. He and approximately 1,000 other refugees had found safety within the confines of the casas reales in the heart of La Villa de Santa Fé. El Gobernador was soon informed that one of the attacking warriors had previously taken up residence within the capital prior to the revolt. Gobernador Otermín dispatched some soldiers to summon the genízaro ensuring him safe passage for the purpose of extending diplomacy. Upon hearing the Gobernador's petition to talk, the genízaro came before the Español leader to discuss the reasons for the revolt and their intentions for all of the refugees.

The genízaro explained to Otermín that he had been elected to serve as the warriors' Capitán. He continued by showing two banners, one red, and the other white. The genízaro then explained to El Gobernador that he would have to choose between the two banners. If he were to choose the white banner, it would signify that the Españoles sought peace, and that they would have to leave the lands of the Río Arriba, and Río Abajo. If he were to choose the red banner, it would signify that the Españoles had sought war, and that all of the refugees would thus meet their deaths.

El Gobernador contemplated his options, giving each some thought. He looked into the eyes of the Puebloan Capitán and countered by saying, that as a Catholic, how did he and all of those who had accepted Catholicism expect to live without their adopted religion. He continued by explaining, that as an acting liaison between the indigenous peoples and the Españoles, the genízaro had a duty to foster a peaceful resolution to the conflict. He further challenged his counterpart to speak on his behalf, thus explaining to the Puebloan, Navajo and Apache leaders that all would be forgiven of all atrocities if they left peacefully and without any further incidents. The Capitán promptly left and upon coming before the leaders of the many nations, he relayed to them the Gobernador's opinion.

A short time after, the Capitán returned with a reply from the leaders of the revolt. The leaders had asked for all of the genízaros and any other indios in the service of the Españoles to immediately be released. The liaison continued by demanding that his own wife and children be released unto him. Then he demanded that all Apachés who had been captured during previous battle campaigns be released to their brethren. He stated that his leaders and their warriors were unwilling to leave the outskirts of the capital because they were awaiting the arrival of the Pecurís, Taos, and Teguas nations. He concluded by saying that if their demands were not met, the warriors would wage war upon the Españoles.

Gobernador Otermín looked at the genízaro with suspicion as he had come to realize that they didn't have any captive Apachés in their company. He had figured that it was a ruse meant to gain custody of his wife and children, while at the same time, stalling for the arrival of further reinforcements from the northern nations. All the while, the warriors were looting, and destroying the houses, and misiónes within La Villa de Santa Fé, and other communities throughout El Reyno de Nuevo México. The Español leader rebuked the offer, telling the genízaro to return to his leaders so that he may tell them that if they didn't stop the looting, and disperse, he would order his soldiers to march upon them.

The Puebloan Capitán thus left, returning to his leaders to inform them of El Gobernador's decision. After recounting what Otermín had said, the warriors erupted in a thunderous war cry. The sound was enough to send a cold chill down the spines of all the Españoles and genízaros that were trapped behind the walls of the casas reales. The soldiers readied their weapons, while the huddled masses recanted their prayers. Children cried to their parents as the echoes of war began to drown out their thoughts.

Many of the warriors continued to pillage and destroy the villa as they advanced further into the villa. Otermín thus ordered his soldiers to march upon the warriors to thwart their attempt to capture their position of refuge. The soldiers marched forward, killing many warriors and thus sending them to find cover within the adobé houses, and the convento. Gun fire erupted for the better part of the day, the soldiers intermittently fired their rifles upon the warriors who returned fire with their rifles and bows and arrows.

On the morning of August 14, 1680 Otermín was scouring the perimeter and had noticed that a large contingent of warriors were making their way down the mountainside. Becoming alarmed, he gathered his meager troops together and rode out to meet the war party. The warriors had seen the Español leader and his troops and quickly took cover amongst the sabinos and within the arroyos. After securing their positions, they let out a war cry, as if daring their oppressors to initiate an attack.

A brief standoff took place, in which neither side initiated an attack. After some time, the warriors sought cover closer to the mountainside, as they repositioned themselves near the former residence of the maestre del campo, Francisco Gómes. Here they remained without initiating an attack upon Otermín's forces. The remainder of the day remained free from battle, as both factions contemplated their strategies.

On the next day, in an attempt to stall the Españoles from escaping the capital, the warriors again descended upon the villa. El Gobernador had become wise to the warriors' tactics, knowing that they were stalling for time so that the other revolting nations could reinforce their numbers. Once all of the forces joined together, they would surely engage in a massive attack, in an attempt to overcome the refugees' defenses.

Several firefights erupted throughout the day, but the warriors remained content to hold their positions. Otermín and his council had surmised that the warriors had a tactical advantage, having the high ground, which ensured that they could not be dispersed. The refugees were thus at the mercy of God, they couldn't do anything to prevent their oncoming fate.

Under the cover of the night, the Jémez, Pecurís, Queres, and Taos nations had finally arrived to join the other nations encamped on the outskirts of the villa. Upon their arrival, the warriors' war cry echoed through the darkness. From a distance, the refugees could see the large bonfires reaching for the heavens, as the sound of drums and chanting stirred through the darkness. The Sánches de Iñigo children huddled with their mother as a chill permeated through the air.

The morning of August 16th had witnessed an impressive army of 2,500 warriors who had gathered upon the outskirts of the capital. They descended upon the Español stronghold, fortifying their positions within the adobés, and behind building walls. The soldiers fired upon the warriors as they attempted to dam the ***acequia*** (water ditch), thus preventing the water from flowing into the casas reales. To no avail, there were too many warriors, and the acequia was ultimately dammed. The attackers proceeded to set fire to the church, and many other residences throughout the villa. The refugees were relegated to watching in disbelief as the warriors chaotically destroyed structure after structure.

The warriors were so audacious that they were dashing towards the doors of the casas reales and attempting to set them afire. Otermín was deeply concerned about the likelihood that the stronghold would be torched. He and his soldiers gallantly marched upon the placita with no cover in an attempt to stop the advances of their brazen attackers. Throughout the afternoon several firefights raged on, in which several soldiers were either killed or seriously wounded. As night had descended, there was a slight reprieve from the battle that raged earlier in the day. With the utmost diligence, the remaining soldiers kept a watchful eye for any enemy movements.

With the acequia being dammed up, the water supplies were rapidly diminishing and thirst was setting in for many of the refugees and all of the livestock. The stench of raw sewage permeated through the air. Food inventories were greatly diminished even though many people were sustaining themselves off of meager rations. Morale was suffering as the frightened refugees, many mostly women and children, were resolving themselves to a potentially horrible demise. They congregated in prayer and reflection, in the hope that they may escape their hell on earth. Thus went the night, as many had surely felt it could be their last moments of life.

As the dawn broke on the 17th, the Puebloan warriors marched closer to the casas reales and further fortified their positions. They fired upon the refugees with rifle shots, arrows and stones. They taunted their hostages, by proclaiming that they could not escape and that their deaths were imminent. They informed the Españoles and genízaros that the feared Apachés were en route, as they had summoned them to join the battle.

Mental and physical fatigue had taken their toll on the refugees as the day wore on. The battle raged on for the better part of the day. The warriors attempted to commandeer the two canons stationed near the doors of the casas reales. In a defensive measure, Otermín had his men bring the canons in and he was resolved to losing the two stations to the enemy's capture. Once conceding the canon stations, the warriors reacted with a deafening roar. They chanted of victory as they continued to set the remaining structures on fire.

The mental anguish of seeing their beloved villa being destroyed was too much to bear for many of the refugees. Many of the animals harbored within the casas reales were beginning to die of starvation and dehydration. The threat of disease hung in the air as the stench of rotting, uneaten animal carcasses grew stronger under the increasing heat of the sun. The people were deeply concerned that many of the horses would soon perish, or become too weak to be useful. Many of the people were also succumbing to the pains of thirst.

In the darkness of night, the fire embers of war had cast an eerie glow upon the destroyed structures. The immense smoke columns filled the air with a slowly drifting, suffocating haze. Again, like many previous nights, many people had to contemplate whether this would be their final stand. The refugee leader had surmised that most of his people would begin to die if he didn't take drastic action. Hence, it was determined that on the next morning he and his soldiers would mount an attack upon the Puebloans within the villa.

In a final act of desperation, El Gobernador was resolved to initiating an offensive attack upon the warriors. At his request, the friars held a special mass at dawn, with the hope that their last stand would lead to salvation. Shortly after mass, he his soldiers mounted their horses. Those who didn't have a horse served as foot soldiers. Those genízaros who pledged their loyalty to the Españoles would go into battle with their bows and arrows.

The doors to the casas reales were thrown open, and from within, the mounted men valiantly charged out. Initially catching their enemies off guard, the first wave of the besieged was launched with resounding success. Several Puebloans had drawn their last breath at that moment.

The second wave of foot soldiers charged through the door. A barrage of deafening gunfire ensued with many of the bullets finding their marks. The Españoles and genízaros continued to relentlessly attack the people who had held them hostage, killing many of them without pity or remorse. The battle raged on until their adversaries' courage had been overtaken with trepidation. Their rivals hastily retreated with the soldiers in close pursuit. While in retreat, many warriors had been overtaken and killed mercilessly. After expelling their captors, the refugee fighting force had regrouped within the confines of the casas reales.

With soldiers at the ready, the refugees were quick to quench their thirst, drinking the precious lifesaving liquid. After restocking their barrels, the livestock was allowed to drink from the acequia. Otermín had already decreed that by the next morning, the refugees would push southward toward El Paso del Norte. On the way, they would stop in Pueblo de Ysleta to ascertain the fate of their brethren.

Exiled from El Reyno de Nuevo México[31]

On Monday, August 19, 1680 the Santa Fé refugees had departed from their beloved villa. As they passed through the town they bore witness to the destruction of their capital. Without any provisions to feed themselves except their livestock, their journey south had begun. On the way out they scavenged for any provisions that they could gather. Many of the approximately one thousand exiles were embarking on their journey on foot.

On August 23rd the Santa Fé refugees briefly halted their exile procession near the Pueblo de San Marcos. A scouting party consisting of Sargento Mayor, Bernabé Marqués, and eight other soldados brought a captive Tewa before Gobernador Otermín. While he was being interrogated by the refugee leader, it came out that his name was Antonio and that he was the Sargento Mayor's indentured servant. He was originally one of the refugees seeking the protection within the casas reales.

When questioned as to how he was caught so far from the refugee column, Antonio claimed that he escaped only after he resolved himself to the fact that the Españoles were forced to leave the country. He further indicated that he did not want to leave the lands of his ancestors so he had chosen to desert his master. A day after making his escape he returned to La Villa de Santa Fé to find that it had been abandoned by the Españoles and it was still being pillaged by many Puebloans. He was told by one of the rebels named Roqué that several warriors were going to set an ambush for the refugees near Cristóbal de Anaya's hacienda. At that point he left and sought refuge at his master's estancia, where he was later found in hiding.

On August 24th the Santa Fé refugee caravan had reached Pueblo de Santo Domingo. During their procession they had come across Puebloan rebels perched upon some mesas in the distance. The rebels kept to themselves, choosing to avoid any confrontation. Within the pueblo the bodies of dead priests and several of its citizens were found strewn about.

On the morning of August 25th while the soldiers were preparing to break camp, it was discovered that a few rebels were congregating on the other side of the river. Being diligent however, it was discovered that it was only a ruse meant to bring the soldiers into an ambush. There was posturing between both adversaries but no bloodshed. Several warriors had crossed the river and followed the refugees from a safe distance. It was an obvious attempt to intimidate the exiled people. Later in the day the caravan had arrived at an abandoned Pueblo de San Felipé. By that evening a few Puebloans were spotted making a camp atop one of the mesas in the distance.

As the caravan broke camp the following day and proceeded on southward, it had become very apparent that they were being mirrored by several groups of indigenous people along the way. As they approached Cristóbal de Anaya's hacienda, Otermín had prepared his soldiers for an ambush. He further indicated to the refugees that they needed to be ready to protect themselves in the event that they were attacked. As they passed from one estancia to the other, the bodies of murdered people lay in plain sight.

They finally arrived at Pueblo de Sandía and had noted many of the atrocities committed against person and property. The Puebloans had set the church on fire but the fire must have burned itself out, it was hardly damaged. In the distance they could see a large contingent of rebels gathered around a herd of cattle. The enemy tried to intimidate the refugees by making threatening gestures, and even firing upon them with their **arcabuz** (muzzle-loaded firearm). In a show of force, El Gobernador ordered fifty of his soldiers to repel the threat. Once their foes saw the soldiers coming towards them, herding their rustled cattle retreated into the safety of the mountains. Before continuing south, the soldiers were ordered to set fire to the whole pueblo.

As their progress continued to carry them further south, the devastation of the raids were evident from one hacienda to another. It wasn't until they had passed Los Gómes that they had finally captured a Puebloan, named Pedro Nanboa, riding his horse on the road. The captive indicated that Lt. General Alonzo García and those refugees in his company had already abandoned Pueblo de Ysleta. El Gobernador was greatly disheartened by the news. He was hopeful that he could reinforce his troops to better protect the refugees. As it was, he and his travel weary exiles had to push on.

The Santa Fé refugees had traveled as far south as the hacienda of Francisco de Valencia. From here, Otermín promptly dispatched Padre Francisco Farfán and four soldiers to overtake his Lt. General and give him the message that he and his refugees needed to stop where they were at, and wait until the Santa Fé refugees could reach them. He also requested that carts and horses also be sent to him to help those who were traveling on foot.

The travel worn people had arrived in Alamillo, a community slightly north of Pueblo de Socorro on September 6th. It was here that Lt. General Alonso García and his men were finally reunited with their Gobernador. Very little pleasantries were exchanged as Otermín promptly had his Lt. General arrested for abandoning his jurisdicción and initiating a retreat from the provincia without his permission. Furthermore, García would remain imprisoned until he could explain his reasoning and thus clearing his name.

García made a compelling case, showing his superior his **autos** (personal journals) since the Pueblo Revolt. He showed the opinions of his council created at Pueblo de Ysleta and at Pueblo de Socorro. He showed his movements, which he carefully recorded. He concluded by proclaiming his allegiance to the crown by his life's long service to his majesty, the King of Spain. Otermín didn't pass judgment immediately but rather reserved that right until after he had read the autos. He did ensure his General that justice would be served.

As the procession continued southward a large cloud of dust could be made out in the distance. Initially it was thought that it could be the enemy coming to attack the exiles before they reunited with their brethren further south. As it turned out, it was Pedro de Leiva who was leading forty soldiers and four padres. Fearing that the Santa Fé refugees had perished during the revolt, the fresh troops were overjoyed to discover them alive.

The hopes and morale of many of the refugees had drastically increased. Suddenly, there was a sliver of hope that many of them would make it through the journey and survive the atrocities of the past several weeks. This euphoric feeling must have played to the good nature of Otermín because he soon absolved his Lt. General of all guilt for abandoning his jurisdicción. García was a free man and had his good name restored.

September 7th had arrived with a new and invigorating hope for the people. After arriving in Pueblo de Socorro, their leader had surmised that they needed more provisions if they were to make it through the lands controlled primarily by the Apaché. His refugees were mostly surviving on meager rations of roasted corn. Thus, he ordered a few of his soldiers to ride to El Paso del Norte, find Padre Ayeta, and request that he promptly send them a shipment of provisions.

On this same day he had also received correspondence from the Ysleta refugees. Within the letter Padre Diego de Parraga had asked for more provisions given that the people had exhausted the rations that they had brought with them. If no provisions could be sent he would then ask for permission to continue moving south from Fray Cristóbal, in order to receive provisions sooner rather than later. After reading the letter El Gobernador thought it was odd that Thomé Domíngues de Mendosa had not written the letter himself. Thomé, after all, was the man who was left in charge of the Ysleta refugees.

On September 8th he responded to the letter detailing his own circumstances of gravity and misfortune. He indicated that the chain of command had not been followed; being that he has not received any correspondence from Thomé Domíngues de Mendosa. He stated that if the Padre wanted to leave Fray Cristóbal he was free to do so, however, the refugees were to remain behind until the northern contingent were reunited with those from the south.

On September 13th the Santa Fé refugee caravan finally had united with the Ysleta refugee camp in Fray Cristóbal. Gobernador Otermín called a council which included his officers, those civilians of prestige and those from the religious order; for the purpose of brainstorming a plan that would bring them through the Apaché Nation.

The religious order had decreed that they would follow the wishes of the council. Each maestre del campo was in agreement of pushing further south until they reached El Paso del Norte. Once the exiles were settled and their safety was assured, they would devise a strategy of the reconquest of El Reyno de Nuevo México. They had determined that such action would be difficult given that the indigenous people were well armed and better organized. Sixteen Sargento Mayores, Capitánes and high-ranking soldiers signed off on the agreement, as did the Cabildo de La Villa de Santa Fé.

El Gobernador had received a correspondence from Padre Ayeta. Within the letter the padre indicated that there was some confusion as to the timing of when the supply train should be sent northward. He indicated that although he received a letter from Lt. General García, he had not heard from his Excellency regarding the matter. He thus requested to meet with Otermín personally to clear any doubts that he had.

Meeting with Padre Ayeta had taken precedent over all matters, and as such, it was imperative that he leave immediately. Otermín thus postponed his decision on the opinions of his council. He ordered for twelve soldiers to accompany him to meet up with the Padre. In his stead, he left Francisco Gómes and Alonso García in charge of the refugee camp.

On September 18th El Gobernador had finally reached Padre Ayeta in La Salineta. The Padre had already started moving the supply train of twenty-four wagons northward in an attempt to reach the refugees sooner. His progress was slowed by the persistent rains that flooded many of the rivers and streams. The weight of the wagons also made traveling through the thick mud nearly impossible.

When Otermín had come upon the Padre, he and his men were trying to cross the flooded river. It was determined later that the wagons would not be able to make it across. Instead, the provisions would have to be carried by horse.

At the request of Padre Ayeta, Otermín stayed behind at the Monastery of Guadalupe so that he may help take an inventory of it provisions. After taking an inventory, El Gobernador sent men to buy additional provisions from any town within an eighty league radius of El Paso del Norte.

The governor had anticipated that many refugees may try to flee the exile colony. To ensure the safety and integrity of the community, an edict was enacted that prohibited refugees from leaving El Paso del Norte. Any persons allowed to leave could do so only if they received permission by obtaining a license from the governor. By September 24th he petitioned Bartolomé de Estrada y Ramíres, the Gobernador of El Reyno de Nueva Vizcaya, to help in capturing and returning deserting refugees. Gobernador de Estrada y Ramíres in turn ordered his Alcalde Mayores and his Capitánes to arrest any deserter under the threat of the penalty of death.

El Paso del Norte (Guadalupe del Paso)

On September 29th the exiles had finally arrived in La Salineta. Otermín found it imperative to make a record of the survivors and their plight. As such, each family passed before him so that an inventory could be made. Such things mentioned in the report would be; how many surviving children were in the family, those family members who were killed or lost during the revolt, the number of surviving servants and the number of servants that were killed. Also included in the report were the number and condition of their livestock and their firearms and munitions. In all there were 1,946 refugees in the exile colony. It was determined that of those, 155 were able to bear arms. Furthermore, Francisco Xavier had made the refugees aware of the edict concerning the matter of deserting the exile colony.[32]

Over the next several days it was discovered that some families had indeed left La Salineta and had gone to the Monastery of Guadalupe. From there a few of those people had managed to escape further south into El Reyno de Nueva Vizcaya. To stem the flow of refugees from leaving, Otermín had made another request to Joseph Lópes de Gracia a Lieutenant to the Alcalde Mayor of San Antonio de Casas Grandes, to arrest any refugee attempting to flee.

Most of the exiles had arrived in La Salineta destitute, losing all that they had during the uprising. A few of the more prominent, entrepreneurial families were able to turn their misfortunes around. Juan Domíngues de Mendosa and Pedro Durán y Cháves were brokering the trade of grain and cattle between Padre Ayeta and many of the refugees. Later they were trading with other communities throughout Nueva Viscaya and Sonora.[33]

The living conditions in the refugee colonies of Guadalupe de los Mansos, Real de San Lorenso de la Toma, Real de San Pedro de Alcántara and Real del Santísimo Sacramento were deplorable. Most of the people were poverty stricken, malnourished, didn't have adequate clothing and didn't have access to any means of viable transportation. Many of the refugees fled to Casas Grandes, Parral, Río del Sacramento and other villas throughout Nueva Viscaya, even though there was an edict in place. [34] Those that remained behind were subjected to repeated raids from the Apaché and Mansos. By October of 1681, so many men with families had left the refugee colonies that Otermín noted that he didn't have enough men to muster an army.[35]

The First Attempt at Reconquest[36]

At about 18 years of age, Jacinto Sánches de Iñigo enlisted to serve as a soldier for the Spanish Crown, passing muster in September of 1681 and again in April of 1687.[37] During his service he advanced to the rank of Capitán.[38] Shortly after he enlisted in 1681, Otermín led a campaign of reconquest in the northern expanse of El Reyno de Nuevo México. By November 04, 1681, he had moved his men of 146 Españoles and 112 indios from Real de San Lorenzo de la Toma to El Paso del Norte. The Gobernador remarked that his troops were young and inexperienced.

On November 7th Juan Domíngues de Mendosa was named the Lieutenant General of the cavalry. Shortly thereafter, the army rode north to the lands from which they were exiled. With great expedience they had arrived in Pueblo de Senecú by November 26th. The deserted pueblo was burned to the ground.

By the next morning the force had come upon Pueblo de Ysleta. There were several small skirmishes that were quickly diffused after the pueblo's inhabitants had come to the realization that they were fighting the Españoles and not bands of Apachés. From here, Otermín ordered his Lt. General to take sixty men further north to find and confront enemy forces.

It was mid December and the Lt. General was coming upon the pueblos of La Alameda, Puaray and Sandía. Each was abandoned yet their storage rooms were well stocked with beans and corn. Rather than destroying the pueblos, Domíngues de Mendosa opted to save them from destruction in the hope that it could lead to peaceful negotiations with the Puebloans. This decision was in direct violation of the governor's orders. As such, he made the suggestion that Otermín should come and set up his base of operations further north.

The Lt. General pressed on, visiting the pueblos of Cochití, Santo Domingo and San Felipé. Near the Pueblo de Cochití they had come upon a force of rebels led by Alonso Catití. The two sides were amicable towards each other. There were subtle peace offerings and preliminary talk of rectifying the wrongs committed by both parties. Puebloan messengers were sent out to bring together several other leaders. A messenger from the south brought news that Otermín and his troops were moving northward, setting fire to all the pueblos he had come across. At that point the peace negotiations were over.

The first attempt of reconquista had come to an end. It was decided by Otermín and his top officers that it wasn't practical to try and subdue the Puebloans. Upon their return to El Paso del Norte, El Gobernador accused Lt. General Juan Domíngues de Mendosa of failing to obey a direct order and the dereliction of his duties during the peace negotiations held in Pueblo de Cochití.

Deserting El Paso del Norte[39]

There were several attempts by the exiles to abandon the refugee colonies between the years of 1684 and 1685.[40] Sucessive droughts and repeated raids from the Apaché ensured that most of the people were on the brink of starvation. It had become so dire that many people nourished themselves with herbs and roots.

There was great discord within the refugee communities and most people found fault in Gobernador Otermín. Jacinto had allied himself with Juan Domínges de Mendosa, who had aspirations of one day becoming Gobernador of El Reyno de Nuevo México. He was under the command of the Lt. General and surely must have shared similar thoughts about the reconquest of the lands he was exiled from.

Domíngues de Mendosa must have felt slighted at not being offered the Gobernador's position when Otermín made it known that he was stepping down. Instead, the office went to Jironza Petríz de Cruzate who had arrived in the Américas from España just 36 months prior. Realistically though

Juan was embattled with several legal problems and stood little chance at gaining the coveted office. None the less, the new Gobernador looked upon Juan to carry out several explorations into Téjas.

On September 27, 1685 Jacinto Sánches de Iñigo left the colony but was apprehended, brought into custody and stood before Gobernador y Capitán General Don Domingo Jironza Petríz de Cruzate. The charge set before him was the attempt to desert the refugee colony with Maestre de Campo Juan Domíngues de Mendosa. Under oath, he indicated that he was aware of the edict concerning the desertion from the refugee colonies and the penalties of disobeying it. He continued by telling of the events that took place before being seized.

Jacinto testified that he was riding on horseback and had come to pass Juan Domíngues de Mendosa's house. He was sitting near the door and called upon the young man to approach him. As the two started talking, the Maestre de Campo shared that it was his intention to leave the colony. He indicated that Padre Nicolás Lópes had written him a letter claiming that he had a business proposition in Ciudad de México. The Padre called upon his prospective associate to join him. He informed Jacinto that he had already recruited the services of Alonso Raél de Aguilar, Juan de Anaya, Baltasar Domíngues, Diego Lucero de Godoy, and Lásaro de Misquía. After some deliberation Jacinto agreed to accompany Juan Domíngues de Mendosa.

Domíngues de Mendosa indicated to Jacinto that he was waiting for Francisco Gómes to give the seal of the cabildo so that he could take some dispatches to Padre Lópes. Francisco however, was reluctant to give the dispatches a seal. As a result of this inaction their departure would thus be delayed. He assured his new recruit that as soon as everything was in order they would promptly leave for Ciudad de Mexico. When asked about the route they would take, the Maestre de Campo indicated that they would most likely travel along the coast to escape detection and capture. Another possible route would be through Parral.

A short time thereafter, he was instructed by Padre Pedro Gómes to procure three mules and a horse from the King's herd. He brought the livestock to Pueblo de Ysleta where he handed the livestock over to the Padre. There were two men, one named Juan de Anaya and the other named Matías Luján who immediately took possession of the animals for the journey.

Alonso Raél de Aguilar instructed Padre Gómes to pay Maestre de Campo Alonso García a visit for the purpose of securing more horses for the trip. The Maestre de Campo was boarding several horses that belonged to Raél de Aguilar's father-in-law and he knew which ones in the herd were the strongest and healthiest. The Padre, in turn, delegated this duty by directing Jacinto to go in his stead. Jacinto showed great trepidation, anticipating that he may come across someone and therefore refused to carry out the order.

Somewhat perturbed by Jacinto's unwillingness, Padre Gómes wrote a letter to Raél de Aguilar detailing the youngster's insubordination. Fearing some type of repercussion from his inaction, he reluctantly went about delivering the letter. As he passed Maestre de Campo Juan Domíngues de Mendosa's house he noticed that his wife was standing outside and appeared to be upset.

They talked briefly and during their discussion she informed Jacinto that the news of her husband's intention to leave the colony had gone beyond his inner circle. Fearing that he and his recruits would soon be apprehended, they hurriedly left to avoid capture. As such, there wasn't enough time for her husband to notify his newest recruit of his intentions. When he asked about the dispatches, she replied that her son, Baltasar had them in hand. Filled with alarm, Jacinto handed her the letter and then excused himself.

A New Lease on Life

About three years after trying to desert the refugee colony, Jacinto found greater purpose and more stability when he married Isabel Telles Jirón in about 1688. He started a family in the refugee colony of Real de San Lorenso de la Toma and he had one son that he named José. He also had two daughters that he named Ana Juana Isabel and Gertrudis. His love for his family was unquestioned, but the young father had another love, one he longed to be with again. The lands to the north were always calling to him to return home. Surely he had reminisced with his neighbors of the enchanted lands of his youth and how he was tragically uprooted from them and forced into exile.

The anticipation of one day returning to his native soil was short-lived. On September 14, 1692 Don Diego de Vargas Zapata y Luxán Ponzé de León claimed victory over the Puebloans to the north. He proclaimed the reconquest of those lands in the name of the King of Spain.[41] As the news had spread through the refugee colonies it was met with mixed emotions. Although several refugees had sought to return to their lands of the north, many more of them had no desire to return.

On October 13, 1693; Jacinto, his brother Pedro, his sister Francisca, and their immediate families had accompanied Don Diego de Vargas in his re-colonization party. The anticipation of seeing their home was only thwarted by their two-month journey to reach La Villa de Santa Fé. Their dream of returning home was finally realized on December 16, 1693.[42]

The threat of starvation followed the pobladores back to the northern frontier. Many women and children died from malnourishment and exposure to the harsh, unforgiving winter. Several of the Puebloans still harbored an extreme resentment towards the Españoles. Furthermore, there was no shelter to accommodate the mass of people. The Españoles thus made the acquisition of food and securing housing a priority.

On December 28th a battle ensued between the Españoles and the Puebloans. To the victor, the prize would be La Villa de Santa Fé. For two days the adversaries had fought. Upon its conclusion, the Españoles had prevailed. The Puebloans had lost nine during the skirmish while their counterparts had lost only one. Afterward, seventy Puebloans were executed and two others had taken their own lives. The cold and malnutrition had claimed another twenty-two Reconquistas by the end of the confrontation.[43]

Jacinto was quick to realize that he would have to start his life all over. Life in his homelands would be drastically different. Unlike when he was an adolescent growing up, he now had the responsibility of his family. He had to provide food, shelter, and safety for them. Like many of the other families making the journey north, his family had to be resourceful to survive. During this time, Isabel gave birth to two more sons whose names were Pedro and Joaquín.

As fate would have it, Jacinto would not be able to live the remaining years of his life with his beloved Isabel. She tragically died in La Villa de Santa Fé shortly after giving birth to their son Joaquín in 1695. The brutal reality of being a widower with five children compelled him to search for another wife, even as he mourned the loss of his first love. Such was the life of many of the pobladores. It may have come across as lacking in empathy, being callous, and even living a loveless lifestyle, but it was essential to the survivability of the bloodlines.

On March 30, 1696, the widower married María Rodarte de Castro Xabalera in La Villa de Santa Fé.[44] She was born in Sombrerete, Nueva España. The region she came from was also known as El Reyno de Nueva Galicia, Provincia de Los Zacatecas. At the time, Sombrerete and several other communities in the region relied heavily on mining as their primary industries. María and several other people from the villas of Sombrerete and Nuestra Señora de los Zacatecas were recruited by

Juan Páez Hurtado, under the orders of Don Diego de Vargas, to help re-colonize El Reyno de Nuevo México in 1695. This group of new pobladores finally arrived in the capital in July of 1695.

The muster roll of this group of pobladores was found to contain many fraudulent discrepancies intentionally created by Juan Páez Hurtado. It was his intent to maximize the amount of monies received from the Spanish crown by deceptively creating fictitious families. The Spanish crown awarded each family 300 pesos, and if the family was unusually large, they were awarded an additional 40 pesos for each additional family member over the given threshold. In many instances it was declared that the older children of the larger families were married hence creating the illusion of another family. To compound the deception some of the younger children were listed under the fictitious families.

María Rodarte de Castro Xabalera was a member of one of the fraudulent families. She was the daughter of Miguel de Castro Xabalera and Juana Guerrero. The muster rolls list Juana Guerrero as the widow of Miguel Rodarte. Listed under her were her children Bernabé and Catalina. Bernabé later attempted to flee La Villa de Santa Fé in 1695, was immediately caught and subsequently executed for desertion.

In 1697 there was a cattle distribution in the capital, where Juana Guerrero stated that she had originally enlisted with seven children, who were placed in different groups to make up the fictitious families. María testified in 1697 that she had enlisted alone and was single at the time. She concurred with her mother's story claiming that she was listed as the wife of Felipé de Soría. Felipé repeated that he too was single at the time but that he was instructed to claim María as his wife and his natural brother as their own son.[45]

As he matured, Jacinto's aspirations for greater notoriety and influence became increasingly evident. He had applied for a grant for some land situated on the banks of the Río del Norte, just east of the Pueblo de Cochití.[46] The land in question was originally owned by Cristóbal Fontes before the Pueblo Revolt of 1680. Gobernador Pedro Rodrígues Cubero approved the grant but Jacinto later lost the grant.

Not to be discouraged, he applied again for another grant. Gobernador Diego de Vargas diligently approved the grant over objections from the people living in Pueblo de Cochití on December 23, 1703. There was contention over which land belonged to the grant petitioner and which land belonged to the people of Cochití. There were also accusations that Jacinto had become increasingly abusive and even threatening towards his neighbors across the river. This fact was brought to the Gobernador's attention by means of a letter written by Padre Juan Álvares on behalf of the people of Cochití. The Gobernador addressed their concerns by stipulating to the accused that his grant applied only to those lands originally owned by Cristóbal Fontes and that he could not cause any harm to any of the people from Cochití. The added decree was dated January 11, 1704.[47]

As with any land grant, Jacinto had to establish that he was improving, working and living on the land. The mutual contempt he must have felt towards the people of Cochití surely gave him a rather bitter disposition. Like many communities and estancias along the Río del Norte, a great deal of his resources had to go towards defending against Apaché and Navajo raids. It would've most likely brought about the question of whether it was even worth the trouble to have possession of the land.

It was like any other spring day, when Jacinto heard the news that Don Diego de Vargas had died on April 08, 1704, in Bernalillo. He must have been dumbfounded by the news of his untimely death. Don Diego had contracted a severe illness while leading his soldiers and some Puebloan scouts against the Apachés who had been raiding various settlements in and around the Rio Abajo.[48] Like many other people in the region, he honored his leader with a prayer and a day of remembrance.

Within ten year's time of gaining the land grant, Jacinto was offered the office of Alcalde for the Villa de Santa Cruz de la Cañada in 1713.[49] It must have been one of his greatest accomplishments, something that he was long aspiring for. Maybe he felt that his fortunes were changing, and that he was finally being noticed by the politicos. He may have questioned whether he would ever be accepted into their fraternity.

During this time of good fortune he also conducted a few real estate deals. On May 09, 1713 he conveyed both his house and land near La Villa de Santa Fé to Juan García de la Rivas.[50] On November 09, 1716 he conveyed a plot of land near the capital to Petrona Gómes.[51]

Jacinto had a difficult time upholding the integrity of his office. He was in the process of investigating the murder of Catalina Valdés by her husband. Gobernador Juan Ignacio Flores Mogollón directed him to cease the investigation, indicating that he did not have judicial authority. Mogollón then placed Juan Páez Hurtado in charge of the investigation.[52] Furthermore, the governor questioned his leadership abilities, stating that he was incompetent in his duties.

After his failed attempt as Alcalde, Jacinto tempered his adventurous spirit by requesting for a permit to venture outside of the El Reyno de Nuevo México, in 1715. He and his son Francisco Sánches went on the expedition together. Upon his return, he eventually settled in the Rio Abajo region. his last attempt at notoriety came in 1728 when he led a small, unauthorized expedition into the Moquí country, west of the Pueblo de Jémez. He eventually died on December 14, 1734 in Alburquerque, seven months after his wife María had died.[53]

Pedro Sánches de Iñigo[54]

Pedro Sánches de Iñigo was born in El Reyno de Nuevo México, Nueva España in about 1673. His parents were Francisco Muños and Ana Juana Lópes. He fled to the refugee colony of Reál de San Lorenso after the Pueblo Revolt of 1680. He was about eighteen years old when he married Leonor Baca on January 07, 1692. His wife was about thirteen years of age on her wedding day. Her parents, Ignacio Baca and Juana Anaya de Almazán did not indicate that they had any objections with the marriage. Before long, he may have mustered into the King's army under the name of Pedro Lópes de Yñigues.

He and his family accompanied Don Diego de Vargas during the reconquest of 1693. Having arrived in December, the Nuevo México winter was quickly overtaking the land. After procuring food and shelter from the Puebloans, who had occupied La Villa de Santa Fé, the Españoles went about their business of reestablishing their missions in the adjacent Pueblos. They also repeatedly sent soldiers to commandeer food from the Puebloans to feed most of the malnourished pobladores.

Life in the re-established capital was communal in nature. All the food that was gathered and harvested was stored in a centralized location. There was an official that administered the rationing of clothing, food, medicine and other basic necessities to all of the pobladores. For shelter many people would live in adobé huts. Often times, there would be more than one family living in one structure.[55]

By 1695 most of the Pueblos had fallen under the siege of the Españoles. The task of restoring the missions had begun. Trade between the indigenous and the Spanish people increased as life was becoming more settled. On April 19, 1695 it was proclaimed that the Villa Nueva de Santa Cruz de Españoles Mexicanos del Rey Nuestro Señor Carlos Segundo would be established. The villa would later be known as Santa Cruz de la Cañada. The purpose of the villa was to help protect all of the missions to the north and to help promote settlement along the northern tier of the Río del Norte.

Persistant hunger continued to plague the citizens, which led to discord not only amongst civilians but also many soldiers. In some instances, people were said to be eating domesticated animals such as cats, dogs and horses. The soldiers meanwhile, were looting houses and causing disturbances throughout the kingdom.

The problems within Spanish society had emboldened many of the Puebloans that still held contempt for their oppressors. Their intentions had become apparent to many of the friars throughout the region. Several letters were sent to the governor seeking military assisstence. He in turn pleaded his case to officials in Ciudad de México but no troops were sent to help protect the floundering kingdom.

In early June of 1696 another revolt was beginning as five padres were killed and their churches were set on fire. El Gobernador systematically moved his troops from one Pueblo to another, subduing the rebels and quelling the threat. Once the threat of the rebellion was over twenty-one civilians had lost their lives. Of those lost; Leonor, her mother Juana, one of her brothers and two of her children could be counted as some of the casualties. They were killed near the Pueblo de San Yldefonso.

Pedro had lost his wife and two children but he managed to save his infant son, also named Pedro. In response to the tragedy that befell his family, he mustered into the army to help protect his people from any other Puebloan rebellions. In about January of 1698 he married María Juana Luján. She was the daughter of Matías Luján and Francisca Romero. He and his family moved to the Río Arriba region, near Santa Cruz de la Cañada. He died sometime before 1720.

Francisco Sánches

Francisco Sánches was born near Atrisco, El Reyno de Nuevo México, Nueva España, in about 1705. His parents were Jacinto Sánches de Iñigo and María Rodarte de Castro Xabalera.[56] The farming community he was from was in close proximity to a villa newly founded in 1706. The villa was christened, ***Villa de Alburquerque de San Francisco Xavier del Bosque***, in honor of Francisco Fernándes de la Cueva Enríques, also known as the Duke of Alburquerque, who was the Viceroy of Nueva España. Gobernador Francisco Cuervo y Valdés approved the founding of the villa and 35 families in total, which included a complement of 10 soldiers and their families, settled in the new community. In total there were approximately 252 souls living in the settlement. Later, the name was changed, by royal decree to ***Villa de San Felipé de Alburquerque***.[57]

On September 16, 1712 the *cabildo de la Villa de Santa Fé* (Santa Fé city council), made a proclamation instituting La Fiesta de Santa Fé. The fiesta was to become an annual celebration that would be held every September, and would commemorate the reconquest of El Reyno de Nuevo México in 1692. The proclamation indicated that a mass, a sermon, and vespers were to be held as a tribute to God. People from all the surrounding communities would converge upon the capital to join in the festivities.

In 1715, at the young age of about ten, Francisco had accompanied his father on a trip outside of the provincia de Nuevo México. Upon their return he continued to live near the community of Atrisco. He labored upon the land for the greater part of his youth. As such, he was developing the skills and knowledge needed to eventually work his own farm.

Although Francisco didn't have to endure the tragedies that his father had experienced, he was indirectly affected by events that were taking place thousands of miles away. In 1719, the war between España and France had provoked the fear that the French would eventually invade El Reyno de Nuevo México from the north and east. On June 14, 1720 Capitán Pedro Villasur had left LaVilla de

Santa Fé with an expedition to scout the movements of the French upon its northernmost frontier, in the Pawnee country. Upon reaching the Platte River in central Nebraska, Villasur and 44 of his men were killed by the Pawnee, who were being armed by French traders. Only 13 survivors from the expedition had escaped the massacre.[58]

By 1723 the governing body in El Reyno de Nuevo México forbade trade with the French. Furthermore, trade with the indigenous people was limited to the Taos and Pecos communities. This mandate eventually fostered the highly anticipated and successful annual trade fair held in Taos. The Comanchis and Kiowas would arrive from the east. The Hopís, Navajos and Zuñis would arrive from the west. The *Utas* (Utes) would arrive from the north. Many of the Puebloans and southern Apachés would arrive from the south.[59]

By 1725, Francisco had married Josefa de Cháves in Villa de San Felipé de Alburquerque. Josefa was the daughter of Don Pedro Durán y Cháves and Juana Montoya de Ynojos, who were one of the twelve founding families of what is now Alburquerque, New Mexico when he was garrisoned and living in the villa.[60] In the early 1740s, Francisco eventually moved further south in the Rio Abajo district to Thomé. In 1765 Don Francisco Sanchez was a Lieutenant Alcalde Mayor and who also had been Capitan of War (Capitan Mayor de Guerra de la Jente) of the jurisdiction of the Villa de Canada and Lieutenant of Militia in Soledad. It is believed that Francisco died shortly before 1769.

Juan Cristóbal Sánches

Juan Cristóbal Sánches was born in Villa de San Felipé de Alburquerque on September 21, 1726. His parents were Francisco Sánches and Josefa de Cháves. With the end of the French and Indian War, France ceded much of the territory west of the Mississippi River to España. This helped facilitate greater commerce between the French, Native American, and Spanish traders. In 1739 the Mallet brothers and a few other French traders entered into El Reyno de Nuevo México, which helped usher in new trading routes by way of the Missouri, Platte, Canadian, and Arkansas rivers.[61]

La Villa de San Felipé de Alburquerque had seen its population steadily grow between its founding through the 1730s. As more families migrated to the burgeoning villa, more stress was placed on its natural resources. Ideal farming conditions had become increasingly difficult due to the higher population densities. The population increase had aggravated the hardships for all its citizens, but in 1739 twenty-nine genízaro families, who had especially been detrimentally affected, had petitioned the Alcalde Mayor for the right to establish their own settlement. The Alcalde Mayor promptly sent their petition to Gobernador Gaspar Domingo de Mendosa who promptly approved their petition for a land grant and the families established the *Villa de Nuestra Señora de la Concepcíon de Thomé Domíngues* on July 30, 1739.

The village of Thomé was established on a previous estancia initially destroyed during the Pueblo Revolt of 1680. Its original founder was Thomé Domíngues de Mendosa. After the reconquest of 1693, neither Thomé Domíngues de Mendosa nor his family had returned to El Reyno de Nuevo México. What made this particular land grant unique was the fact that genízaros had petitioned for the land grant, and were subsequently approved.

In 1740 thirty-eight families under the leadership of Capitán Don Diego de Torres petitioned for the Belén land grant. Don Gaspar Domingo de Mendosa granted the petition thus enabling the settlement of *Nuestra Señora de Belén*. After the establishment of Belén, the population in the area grew exponentially. People were drawn to the area because of its fertile lands and its proximity to the Río del Norte.

Although many families were moving south, including his father, Juan Cristóbal was content in staying in Atrisco for the time being. He soon fell in love and married Juana Tomasa Durán y Cháves in Villa de San Felipé de Alburquerque on September 24, 1758. Captain Juan Cristóbal Sánches was alcalde mayor of Alburquerque from 1766-68 and then again in 1779. After marriage and fathering several children, the lure of the southern frontier weighed heavily on Juan Cristóbal's mind. It is believed that he, his wife and some of his children migrated just north of Thomé to the villa of *Los Chábes* sometime in the early- to mid- 1770s. Juan Cristóbal Sánches died at *Los Chábes*, south of Alburquerque on February 27, 1798.

On August 17, 1773 the Spanish Viceroy, Antonio Bucareli, had created one of the most ambitious mandates, which empowered his northern governors to issue common lands to any pobladores who wished to settle on the frontier, long deemed too dangerous or hostile for previous colonization. The intent of this mandate was to further establish a buffer against some of the more hostile tribes. Many pobladores took advantage by settling on lands far beyond the traditional borders.

With the expansion of Spanish settlements beyond the long honored traditional boundaries, numerous conflicts between the pobladores and the indigenous people continually flared up. The attacks on the new villas and estancias by the Apachés, Comanchis, Navajos, and the Utas became more frequent and more violent in nature. In turn, the attacks on those tribes by the Españoles had also increased in frequency and violence.

Chapter Two:
Migration to the Salinas Basin 1777- 1820

José Gregorio de la Trinidad Sánches

José Gregorio de la Trinidad Sánches was born in Los Chábes on November 19, 1777. His parents were Juan Cristóbal Sánches and Juana Tomasa Durán y Cháves. He lived at an exciting time in El Reyno de Nuevo México's history. The frontier was about to open up to traders from both the north and the east.

The Comanche Campaign of 1779

Gobernador Juan Bautista de Anza[1] had arrived in La Villa de Santa Fé in 1778. He had conducted a thorough expedition of the Alta California coast and had founded the Presidio de San Francisco two years prior, in 1776. Upon his arrival, he had surmised that something had to be done about the marauding bands of Comanchis to the north and east. They threatened the sustainability of several northern villas and Pueblos. He had figured that a show of force would be the only manner in which he could assure the safety of his citizens.

The new Gobernador's initial concern was with their newly ascended Cuchanec Comanchis chief, Cuerno Verde whose real name was Tabivo Naritgant (Dangerous Man). The legend that was to become "Cuerno Verde" was created by the tradition of successive chiefs that wore the elaborate headdress adorned with two buffalo horns. It was described that one of the horns had a green tint to it. Each chief that wore the headdress took the name of Cuerno Verde.

Tabivo Naritgant's vicious, and bloody raids were a result of his contempt and hatred towards the Españoles. He had faulted them for the death of his father during the Comanchis' raid of Ojo Caliente. His father was the Chief Cuerno Verde at the time of the attack. Legend has it that the fallen chief's family swore an oath of vengeance against the Spanish and later their Native American allies.

Anza's primary objective was to eliminate Cuerno Verde and in doing so he felt that it would break the warrior chief's power and influence upon his people. Once accomplished, it was thought that peace and commerce would again find favor within the region. It would also promote further settlement to the lands on the northern frontier.

On August 15, 1779, the governor departed the capital with a contingent of 600 troops. Five days later another 200 Apachés and Utas allies joined his forces. They proceeded north through an unnamed valley under the cover of the full moon. His army eventually set camp near a *ciénega* (marshy spring) that he named San Luís (later known as the San Luís Valley in southern Colorado). He continued to march past the ***Río San Augustín*** (later named South Arkansas River) and the ***Río Nepestle*** (later named the Arkansas River). He and his army pushed as far north as the imposing mountain he named ***La Sierra del Almagre*** (later named Pike's Peak). He passed through El Puerto de la Sierra Almagre (later known as Ute Pass) until he came to ***Río Sacramento*** (later known as Fountain Creek).[2]

It was near Río Sacramento where Anza's soldiers and allies discovered an encampment of Comanchis on August 31, 1779. A battle ensued and several warriors had lost their lives. Cuerno

Verde was not among those in the camp. He had taken a contingent of warriors to mount an attack upon Taos.

The citizens of Taos were able to refortify their community and thus Cuerno Verde's attack was rendered unsuccessful. He headed back to his encampment and on September 03, 1779 he came upon his decimated encampment. De Anza and his men were laying in wait but rather than attacking the travel worn warrior chief, he used the ploy of a retreat to lure the enemy into a trap. Once they realized their impending fate, Cuerno Verde and many of his best warriors fought to the death. Cuerno Verde, his first-born son and apparent heir, four of his trusted chiefs, and a spiritual advisor had all perished. With his death the Comanchis threat was mostly subdued. A peace treaty between the Comanchis and El Reyno de Nuevo México was made many years later in 1786.[3]

In 1780 the resolve of the pobladores and the Puebloans was severely tested by a smallpox epidemic. To compound the misery of the survivors of the epidemic, the entire area suffered a severe drought, famine, and pestilence. In all about 5000 souls were lost in the Pueblos alone.[4]

With much of the Spanish territory west of the Mississippi River still inaccessible, the problem of creating economic, political and social opportunities were often left for the traders that found their way into the region. In 1787, Pedro (Pierre) Vial was officially dispatched to find a route from San Antonio in the Provincia de Téjas, to Santa Fé. Other trails from El Reyno de Nuevo Mexico to the east were established afterwards, but none of them had found their way to St. Louis in the Spanish controlled Louisana territory. Pedro Vial was again called upon to discover a corridor from Santa Fé to St. Louis on May 21, 1792.[5]

The Louisiana Purchase of 1803, compelled many eastern foreigners to migrate westward in search of greater opportunities. This was a cause of great concern for the government of Nueva España because many feared that it would mean a greater influx of émigrés to El Reyno de Nuevo México and the Provincia de Téjas. This steady migration into Spanish controlled lands would eventually lead to continued conflicts.

On June 05, 1805 José Gregorio de la Trinidad Sánches married María Rita Baca in Belén. His beautiful bride was the daughter of Don Bartolomé Baca and Dona Maria de la Luz Chaves. Don Baca was a man whose influence was growing within the social and political ranks. She was well versed in etiquette, and always presented herself as a proper lady. Although her husband could never offer her the type of life that she had become accustomed to, neither of them were any worse off after their marriage. Bartolomé was a fair and righteous man, providing his son-in-law the opportunity to assist with the Baca family's sheep ranching operations.

For many Nuevo Mexicanos the events that were unfolding on the northern fringes of *la frontera* (the border) did not directly concern them, yet the subtle intrusion by U.S. American expansionism would soon change many lives throughout El Reyno de Nuevo México. On March 02, 1807 it was discovered that Lieutenant Zebulon M. Pike had erected a small stockade and patriotically raised the U.S. flag on Spanish territory. The stockade was constructed about 5 miles north on the Río Conejos just west of the Río del Norte. Gobernador Joaquín Alencastre dispatched a platoon to arrest the lieutenant. Upon his arrest, Pike was then promptly sent to Chihuahua, Nueva España. He was later released and escorted back to the Louisiana frontier.[6] To further deter the advancement of U.S. interests into El Reyno de Nuevo México, Alencastre instituted policies that would either expel or imprison those traders who attempted to enter the Spanish territories.[7]

Several years later, the Treaty of 1819, was signed by both the U.S. and Spanish governments, which outlined the boundaries between both of the countries. This was an attempt to further institute the sovereignty of the Spanish claims, thus preventing U.S. citizens from encroaching into the region of El Reyno de Nuevo México and the Provincia de Téjas.

On September 16, 1821 La República de México had officially declared its independence from España. The leaders of the newly formed country were very eager to establish its trade and diplomatic relations with several foreign countries but focused their attention mainly with the United States. This had greatly affected Nuevo México because it had already established trade routes to the north and east.

In 1822, William Becknell of Missouri pioneered one of the first successful trade routes, which had already been mapped out previously by Pedro Vial. He had traversed the vast plains and had arrived in Santa Fé with several wagons loaded full of goods. The route he had followed soon became known as the Santa Fé Trail.[8] The next two years saw a tremendous amount of trade between Missouri of the U.S. and Santa Fé of La República de México.

Los Hermanos Penitentes

With La República de México declaring its independence, many of the missions, and churches in Nuevo México had lost the financial support of the king of España. Furthermore, many of the friars were also forced to leave the missions and churches. With few priests to serve many of the growing communities, the spiritual needs of the faithful were unfortunately neglected. The lack of funding had forced the remaining priests to try to make ends meet. Thus in many instances, the rites of baptism, confirmation, matrimony, the anointing of the sick, and burial all had carried exorbitant fees. These suspect conditions had enabled the growth of ***Los Hermanos Penitentes*** (The Penitent Brothers) originally thought to have formed in the 1790s.[9] The Penitentes were a secretive fraternity of men, complete with their own rules and rituals. They had practiced their faith in relative isolation which was separate from the Catholic Church.

In many communities throughout northern and central Nuevo México, *moradas* were being constructed as the rituals of the Penitentes became more ingrained into the cultural lifestyle of the people. When a morada was built, it was often constructed in an inconspicuous location away from the village. The morada would serve as a house of worship, and a gathering place in which community conflicts were often resolved.

Through the years an organizational hierarchy was developed, in which the ***Hermano Mayor*** would serve as the spiritual leader. This office was usually elected on an annual basis and with it; the individual would carry a higher social status within the community. It was his responsibility to oversee the operations of the morada. Some of his duties would include the scheduling of all meetings and religious observations; delegate amongst his brothers the tasks that needed to be done, and to have an active role in the community. On occasion, a ***Hermano Segundo*** would be selected to assist the Hermano Mayor.

There were other officers that were annually elected to conduct specific duties within the brotherhood. These officers often had already gone through five years of penance, and thus were considered cleansed of impurity. Those officers were:

El Celador had the responsibility of maintaining order amongst the brothers. He determined the methods of punishment amongst the brotherhood.

El Secretario had the responsibility of keeping the morada's records. He also read from the rulebook whenever conflict or rules needed to be clarified.

El Mandatorio had the responsibility of collecting alms. He also instructed novios (new members), and notified the brotherhood of meetings and ceremonies.

El Maestro de Novios had the responsibility of examining the petitions for novios. He also oversaw the Mandatorio's instruction of the novios to ensure that it was precise according to the rules.

El Sangredor had the responsibility of whipping the novios when they were preparing for penitential exercises.

El Rezador had the responsibility of reading prayers, rituals, and other orders of service.

El Cantador had the responsibility of leading all hymns.

El Pitero had the responsibility of playing a flute for various services.

El Coadjutor had the responsibility of washing the whips, and attending to the wounds of his brothers performing penance.

El Enfermero had the responsibility of taking care of sick brothers.[10]

Many of the rituals that Los Hermanos Penitentes were noted for were:

La Cuaresma (Lent), in which every Friday during Lent, Los Hermanos would meet and privately conduct flagellant processions, as well as take part in fasting.

La Semana Santa (Holy Week), in which Los Hermanos spend most of their time in the morada, conducting their ceremonies. Many of the ceremonial activities included serving penance, praying, singing, sleeping, and eating those meals brought in by the ayudantes (helpers).

Los Ejercicios (Exercises), in which the Hermano Mayor supervised acts of penance, such as self-flagellation. Other forms of more severe penance included bearing the crucifix, which entailed the carrying of a wooden crucifix about seven feet in length and weighing up to two hundred pounds upon the shoulder. Dragging the death cart, which was a cart filled with rocks. A rope would be wrapped across the chest of a brother like a harness and he would have to drag the cart behind him for a predetermined distance. Other forms of penance included bearing a smaller crucifix, wearing a crown of thorns, and the use of cactus during self-flagellation. In some extreme acts of devotion, some Penitentes would play the role of Christ and would willingly enact the crucification. Most of the time, a rope would be used to attach the brother to the cross. On rare occasions a brother would be affixed to the cross using a rope and large nails would be tacked through his wrists.

Ceremonies during death often entailed the use of *descansos* (piles of stones), in which mourners bearing the coffins of Hermanos, that were to be brought to *el campo santo* (cemetery), would rest, sing, and say a prayer. Afterwards the mourner would place another rock upon the pile and continue to el campo santo.[11]

Bartolomé Baca

Bartolomé Baca was born in about 1767 in Belén, El Reyno de Nuevo México, Nueva España. His parents were Diego Domingo Baca and María Antonia Montoya. Los Bacas were some of the most prominent families in the Río Abajo region many of whom owned large acreages of land. As such, Bartolomé was afforded a formal education unlike few in the area would ever have. He was an astute individual that understood the importance of an education, and the need for proper etiquette. His parents continually impressed upon him those characteristics he would need to become a future leader.

By the age of about twenty-three Bartolomé had married María de la Luz Cháves on May 02, 1790. Together they both raised a family in the Belén and Thomé regions. Much like himself, his children were also afforded the opportunity to have a formal education. His daughters were groomed to be proper ladies, and his sons were groomed to be future leaders. When his sons had come of age, they helped their father operate the family sheep ranching business.

Bartolomé was a patriotic young man and served in the military to protect the lives of his family, his people, and Español lands. He was quickly promoted to the rank of Capitán in one of the companies from the Santa Fé presidio originally organized in 1808. Capitán Baca did not hesitate at the thought of risking his life to serve El Rey de España. For him, he accepted it as an honor, and appreciated the fact that his superiors thought so highly of his abilities.

On September 04, 1808 Capitán Baca was dispatched by Don Lorenzo Gutiérres, the Alcalde of the Villa de Alburquerque, to track down and bring to justice sixteen Apachés who had killed nineteen men and women near the Pueblo de Ysleta. He followed the Apachés through the Sierra Magdalena. He and his soldiers were unsuccessful in capturing them, and he reluctantly returned to notify the Alcalde of their escape.[12]

Capitán Baca had led many campaigns against bands of Apaché and Navajo during his time as a military officer. He led major campaigns Against the Gila Apachés in October of 1809 and the Navajos at Cebolleta in August of 1816. On July 09, 1821 he was stationed at Cebolleta and had sent correspondence to Gobernador Facundo Melgares that questioned the Navajo Nation's desire for peace. He asked that a contingent of troops be made ready for a retaliatory strike in the event it was necessary. Never doubting Capitán Baca's wisdom, El Gobernador ordered a detachment of forty armed men with extra munitions to fortify Cebolleta.[13]

His dedication to duty did not go unnoticed; several of his superiors, including many of the Gobernadores he had served held him in very high esteem. When it came time for Bartolomé to collect on some political favors, he was met with little or no opposition.

When Don Bartolomé Baca had mustered out of the military he made a living as a respected politician, a businessman, and was considered one of the most influential men of his time. Even his contemporaries did not easily rival his prominence in status. During different times he was appointed as the Alcalde for both Thomé and Belén. He held these terms of office for many years. As a businessman, he employed hundreds of people. Later, he would claim ownership of more than a million acres east of the Sierra Abó (later re-named Sierra Manzano).

In an effort to re-colonize the Salinas Basin, Gobernador Alberto Maynez encouraged the eventual settlement of the villa of Manzano in 1815. Many of the pobladores living in the Belén/ Thomé region were intrigued with the idea of settling the basin. They had known of previous settlements east of the Sierra Abó Mountains before the Pueblo Revolt of 1680. The stories of its vast expanse and fertile soil had become somewhat the legend of lore. The only deterrent that stood between them and the land were the bands of Apachés and Navajos who were notorious for fiercely defending their lands.[14]

El Torreón Land Grant

In 1819, Don Bartolomé Baca had petitioned for the El Torreón land grant, claiming about 500,000 to 1.5 million acres in the Salinas Basin east of the Sierra Abó.[15] Gobernador Facundo Melgares allegedly approved his petition on July 02, 1819. This was the first attempt to re-colonize east of the Sierra Abó since it's abandonment in 1673 by José Nieto, who originally had an estancia in El Torreón from 1650 until its eventual abandonment. Don Bartolomé continued to live in Thomé but used the land within the grant to graze livestock. He also constructed a hacienda, which served as a base of operations for the resident herders. He thus was able to claim the land while satisfying the requirements of his petition's acceptance. El Torreón served as the catalyst for further re-colonization of the Salinas Basin.[16]

The *llanos* (plains) were prime grazing lands for Bartolomé's sheep ranching operations, which were estimated to number over 500,000 head. He had left his flocks in the charge of his **mayordomo** who in turn supervised 700 shepherds who tended to the flocks. The shepherds were equipped with muskets for the purpose of protecting the flocks from predatory animals and Apaché and Navajo raids.[17]

The sheep supported a large wool based economy in the region. Some of the wool would make its way to the Navajo, who were excellent weavers of beautiful blankets. Wool also found its way into the U.S. and La República de México.

The Battle at Ojo de la Estancia[18]

Shortly after Bartolomé's death, his heirs sold the El Torreón land grant to the Otero family. Subsequently in 1845, some nine years after Bartolomé's death, Antonio Sandoval had petitioned for a land grant, which was platted within the boundaries of the land grant. Gobernador Manuel Armijo had approved the Estancia Land grant, which consisted of 300,000 acres. Sandoval had passed on and his nephew inherited the newly established land grant. In the early 1880s, the nephew decided that he wanted to sell the land. He sold the land to Joel and James Whitney, two wealthy brothers from Boston, Massachusetts.

The sale of the Estancia land grant did not sit well with either of the two Otero brothers, Manuel and Miguel. They questioned the legality of the Estancia land grant completely. The two Whitney brothers countered with their own claims. The matter would thus have to be brought before the court to find a resolution.

The Whitney brothers were eager to start a new life in the west, and didn't command the patience necessary to see their legal matters through the long legal processes. James, the younger of the two, hastily headquartered their base of ranching operations in a dwelling at Ojo de la Estancia. After which, he proceeded to hire a group of cowboys and ordered them to remove the resident sheepherders off of their land.

This enraged the two Otero brothers to no end. In August of 1883 Manuel Otero made haste in riding to Ojo de la Estancia to confront the foreigners. On the way he had come across a local who had warned him on a threat that James Whitney had made. Fearing the worst, Manuel readied himself for an armed confrontation.

Upon arriving, Manuel Otero, his cousin Carlos Armijo, and his brother-in-law, Dr. Henríques dismounted their horses. They made their way to the headquarters and forced their way inside. Everyone drew their pistols and commenced firing. After all was done, Alexander Fernándes, James' brother in law, lay dead. Injured in the gun battle were James and Dr. Henríques. Manuel was mortally hit and he stumbled out of the door.

Dr. Henríques placed both Otero and Whitney on a wagon and set off for the long journey home to Los Lunas. Henríques had known that his brother-in-law wasn't going to make it therefore they sent a rider ahead to Manzano to seek the services of a priest. The priest had met the party around sun down, but by then Manuel had already died.

In April of 1884, James Whitney was brought to trial and acquitted of murder. The evidence brought before the court had shown that both men were culpable of being armed. In an ironic twist of fate, both the Torreón and Estancia land grants were found to be invalid when brought before the courts.

Bergere v. U.S., 168 U.S. 66 (1897)

In a case brought before the U.S. Supreme Court one of Bartolomé's direct descendants, Bergere and the heirs of Manuel Antonio Otero and Miguel Antonio Otero, who she also was also representing, was trying to prove that their claim to the El Torreón land grant was legitimate. Of the 500,000 to 1.5 million acres in contention, the government saw the judgment of confirmation for only 11 square leagues pursuant under subdivision 7, section 13 of the act of Congress of March 03, 1891 (26 Stat. 854, c. 539) which states:

> 'No confirmation of any claims or lands mentioned in section six of this act, or in respect of any claim or title that was not complete and perfect at the time of the transfer of sovereignty to the United States as referred to in this act, shall in any case be made or patent issued for a greater quantity than eleven square leagues of land to or in the right of any one original grantee or claimant, or in the right of any one original grant to two or more persons jointly, nor for a greater quantity than was authorized by the respective laws of Spain or Mexico applicable to the claim.'

The courts had determined that the lands granted to Bartolomé Baca were imperfect at the time of cession from La República de México to the United States by the Treaty of Guadalupe Hidalgo. Bergere had taken the position that the prior courts should have confirmed the entire acreage, whereas the government's counsel had the position that no part of the grant should be honored. During the trial Bergere produced documentation written in Spanish to the courts that would substantiate her claims.

The Petition

The document of petition stated that Don Bartolomé Baca had in his possession a substantial number of sheep, horned cattle, and horses for which he did not have any legitimate lands to sustain them on. At the time of his petition, his livestock were roving upon the countryside and were susceptible to Apaché, Navajo, and Comanche raids. He had petitioned for a land grant so that his livestock could graze and be watered. He also wanted the shepherds, cattle and horse herders to adequately protect his livestock.

Bartolomé had identified the vast, but vacant lands to the east of the Sierra Abó known as El Torreón, as the lands he was petitioning for. He mentioned that the boundaries for the land grant would be to the north, the Monte de Cibolo, to the south, Ojo de Cuervo, to the east, Ojo de la Estancia, and to the west, the Sierra Abó.

Bartolomé continued by assuring that it was his intention to establish a rancho or a hacienda for the purpose of caring for his livestock. He would thus employ many people to tend to his livestock in his stead. He would arm his shepherds and herders with weapons for the purpose of protecting his interests from enemy incursions. It was also his intention to cultivate the lands, either through irrigation, or by the fate of the seasons.[19]

The Approval

A second document was provided to the court, which was a response to Don Bartolomé Baca's land grant petition. The document stated that as of July 02, 1819, the Judge Don José García de la Mora who was commissioned by Gobernador Facundo Melgares was going to accompany Bartolomé to the said vacated lands east of the Sierra Abó. José García de la Mora further alluded to the fact that he was accompanying Bartolomé as a reward for his many services for both majesties. The document continues by stating that José García de la Mora was acting on behalf of the King of España.

The document proceeds to describe the boundaries of the land grant as such. To the south the boundaries stretched from Ojo del Cuervo to Ojo del Chico, to the east to Cerro de Pedernal, to the north, the Ojo de Cibolo, and to the west, Altura de la Sierra (summit of the mountain range). Upon traversing the lands Don Bartolomé Baca was noted as giving thanks to the King of España, Don Fernando VII. The document concluded by laying out the conditions of the approval per Don Bartolomé's petition.

José García de la Mora and two assisting witnesses, José Andrés Callér, and Franco Galís signed the document. The full signature of the Gobernador was torn; therefore the only legible part of the signature was "elgares".[20]

The U.S. Supreme Court Opinion & Methodology

The U.S. Supreme Court ruled against Bergere and the heirs of Manuel Antonio Otero and Miguel Antonio Otero because they could not substantiate their case on the grounds that it was imperfect at the time of cession from the department of New México to United States by the Treaty of Guadalupe.

It was the Supreme Court's opinion that there was no proof that Gobernador Melgares had approved the petition on the document signed by José García de la Mora and his two assisting witnesses. In the torn portion of the document there was nothing that could substantiate that an approval was given for the land grant. The court continued by proclaiming that surely there must have been other paperwork that could substantiate their claims.

It was also noted that José García de la Mora actually gave more land to Bartolomé than what he had originally petitioned for. The discrepancy in the amount of land wouldn't have gone unnoticed by the Gobernador. Therefore, the court insisted that other documents should exist as evidence that Melgares had acknowledged this fact. In the Supreme Court's opinion, he would most certainly not have approved such a discrepancy in the total land to be awarded without some type of supporting documentation.

One of his grandsons countered that the documents that had been submitted to the Supreme Court, were originally in the possession of his grandfather. He continued by explaining that the documents in question were delivered on behalf of Melgares, and therefore it served as evidence that the grant was approved. The Supreme Court's rebuttal was that it was being asked of them, by the claimants, to presume that the papers were delivered on behalf of the Gobernador, and that the presumption did not support actual facts. None the less, they stood by their opinion that regardless of whether the documents were in Bartolomé's personal possession or not, there was still no proof of a legitimate approval.

The Supreme Court then questioned the validity of the papers, claiming that there were too many inconsistencies concerning the legality of the document of approval. The documents were torn, with Melgares' signature mostly missing. The documents shouldn't have been in Bartolomé's possession because of their importance as legal documents. The grant approval wasn't written in a manner, which was consistent with its contemporaries. Therefore, the claimants were unable to prove without a doubt, the legality of the papers. If the documents had been legal they would have been placed in the government archives. The Supreme Court added that it should have been duly noted if the document of approval in the petitioner's possession was used as a legal document in place of the more traditional ***testimonio*** (legal approval).

On the issue of whether Don Bartolomé had actually lived on the said property, the Supreme Court's opinion found the following to be true. After the petitioner had received the said property by the authority of José García de la Mora, he had constructed several small buildings on a portion of the land that served to house the herders and his other servants whom had the charge of looking after the sheep, cattle, and horses. The said lands were also being used to graze his livestock. Bartolomé however, had not actually resided on El Torreón land grant.

Subsequently, and prior to Don Bartolomé's death in 1834, several other families had settled upon the land. The Supreme Court acknowledged that in all likelihood he had known about, and even approved of many of the families settling on his El Torreón land grant because their settlement provided a degree of protection against Apaché and Navajo, raids. Also during the time of ownership, several other land grants had been petitioned for and approved within the boundaries of the Torreón land grant. Many of those land grants were actually approved by Bartolomé Baca himself when he was appointed as Gobernador. Many of the families who settled on El Torreón attempted sparingly to cultivate the land.

Several witnesses that settled El Torreón had acknowledged the lands as belonging to Don Bartolomé Baca during life and even after death. The Supreme Court questioned who these witnesses were considering none of them had been named. They were perceived as being ignorant to the stipulations and the size of the land grant. Again, the court maintained its position that none of the evidence supported that the petition for the land grant was approved.

On the issue of grazing his livestock on said lands, the Supreme Court's opinion indicated that although he grazed his livestock on the land, it didn't signify ownership. The court cited the previous case of Whitney vs. U. S., 167 U.S. 529, 546, 17 S. Sup. Ct. 857, 863 to justify their opinion.

The Supreme Court did not find evidence of exclusive ownership under a claim of right or title, and therefore the possession of the grant could therefore be disputed. They then questioned whether Bartolomé had ever acknowledged that he had a rightful claim to El Torreón land grant. They based this on the fact that he had never mentioned the ownership of the land grant in his will, nor did he claim any title to the land grant. They pointed out that all his other real and personal properties were described in detail in his will. As such, it was surmised that he had known that he did not own the land because Gobernador Melgares never approved those actions of José García de la Mora.

The Supreme Court continued by stating that, although the court of private land claims had deemed the grant to be imperfect and therefore gave judgment for 11 square leagues; it was their finding that there was actually no grant, perfect or imperfect in existence at the time. What this meant was that the judgment of the 11 square leagues to the petitioner could no longer be sustained. The judgment of the court of private land claims was reversed on the appeal of the United States

Gobernador Bartolomé Baca

The culmination of Bartolomé's political ascension was realized when he was appointed as Gobernador of La Provincia de Nuevo México between 1823 and September 1825 shortly after La República de México had declared its independence from Spain. Under Gobernador Baca's leadership, Nuevo México would become one of La República de México's springboards into foreign trade with the French Canadians and the United States.

On December 20, 1823 Santiago Montoya had reported to Gobernador Baca that El Calletano, one of the chiefs from a band of Navajos, and El Chato another Navajo had entered Santa Fé. Upon their arrival they told him that about 45 foreign traders had entered their country looking to trade. Santiago had good reason to believe them because many of the Navajos entering the city as of late were wearing strange jewelry, thought to have come from beyond the provincia's borders. He continued by relaying to Gobernador Baca that the Navajos had told him the foreigners were also trading weapons and ammunition.[21] Gobernador Baca was rightfully alarmed with the news so he asked many of his Alcaldes on *la frontera* (the border) to be vigilant. If they were to meet or see any foreign trader they should report that to him immediately.

Sometime in December of 1823 several Nuevo Mexicano representatives acting on behalf of La República de México had met with the leaders of the Navajo Nation to discuss the terms of a peace treaty. The meeting was held in Pueblo de Ysleta and Gobernador Baca was leading the discussions. The deliberations were long, and both sides debated for terms that would be advantageous towards their own interests. After all of the negotiations fourteen terms were agreed upon between La República de México and the Navajo Nation.

The conditions of the treaty were that all Españoles that had become captives of the Navajos would be released. All Navajos that had become captives of the Españoles would be released on the condition that they wanted to return to the Navajo Nation. Citizens from either nation would be held accountable for any theft of property, and be forced to return stolen property to the accuser if they were found guilty. The Navajos would elect captains that would ensure that grievances were handled properly. Furthermore, those tribal chiefs who were not in attendance at the meetings would be encouraged to join the greater Navajo Nation. Once the peace treaty was ratified, members of the Navajo Nation would cease hostilities against the people of Nuevo México. All past grievances against the Navajo Nation would be forgiven. Lastly the Navajo Nation was strongly encouraged to embrace Christianity. On January 20, 1824 in Jémez, Gobernador Baca had finalized the treaty with his signature. Also in attendance were José Antonio Vizcarra and Antonio El Pinto, the general of the Navajo Nation, both of whom had signed the treaty.[22]

As Gobernador one of Don Bartolomé's duties was to aggressively promote the settlement of areas previously deemed too hostile towards colonization. He approved several land grants during his office as Gobernador. He approved the Ojo del Río de las Gallinas grant, which totaled 318,699 acres, of which the U.S. Land Claims later confirmed all of the 318,699 acres of the grant. He approved the Agua Negra grant, which totaled 17,361 acres, of which the U.S. Land Claims later confirmed only 4,447 of the 17,361 acres of the grant. He approved the Tecolote grant, which totaled 48,123 acres, of which the U.S. Land Claims later confirmed all of the 48,123 acres of the grant. He approved the Vallecito de Lovato grant, which totaled 114,000 acres, of which the U.S. Land Claims later confirmed none of the 114,000 acres of the grant.[23]

A law had passed prohibiting all foreigners from trapping beaver within the northern lands claimed by La República de México. Failure to comply with the law meant that, if caught trapping, those foreigners would have their pelts confiscated. Gobernador Baca however, had identified that there were very few of his countrymen who had possessed the skills to trap beaver. He realized that the fur trade was a very lucrative market, and he wanted to promote trapping within the provincia. He thus enacted a policy in which foreign trappers would be issued a permit, which enabled them to trap in Nuevo México with the condition that they would teach Nuevo Mexicanos the trade.[24]

Although the policy had the best of intentions, it wasn't without its flaws. In many instances those who accompanied the foreign trappers didn't get the appropriate training to learn the trade. In most cases, they were used more like hired help. Often times, the foreigners would use a local to get a permit, then they would buy it off of them, and the two would go their separate ways. Sometimes, the foreign trapper would allow their local apprentice to tag along, just in case an official approached him.

Policing the foreigners was proving to be extremely difficult because the trade entailed a mostly nomadic lifestyle. There weren't enough resources to try and find the trappers to ensure that they were abiding by the conditions of having a permit. In most instances, catching someone without one would be a chance encounter.

In an unusual incident concerning Francois "Francisco" Robidoux, the trapper had all of his merchandise confiscated by the Alcalde of Taos upon his arrival. Francois was angry and confused because the Alcalde hadn't given him a reasonable explanation. Over the next several weeks, it had been discovered that the trapper may have been trading weapons with several Native Americans. It was also discovered that he did not have a permit to trap.

The matter was resolved in March of 1825 when Gobernador Baca sent correspondence to the Alcalde of Taos. In the letter he ordered the Alcalde to return all of Francois' merchandise on the condition that the Canadian not trade any weapons with the Native Americans. He proclaimed that Francois or any other foreign trapper would not be detained for trading with the Native Americans if all trade were deemed legitimate. Furthermore, the Gobernador issued a trapping permit to Francois.[25]

Gobernador Baca helped usher in a new era of foreign relations and international trade between La República de México and the United States. It was during his tenure as governor that the Santa Fé and Cimmarón trails had their beginnings. He greatly encouraged their usage, which lead to great prosperity for numerous families.

Manzano

The villa of Manzano, which was situated in the Estancia Valley, was already an established settlement as early as 1823. The petitioners of the Casa Colorada land grant, many of whom would later call the Estancia Valley home, made reference to the villa.[26] At the time of its founding, Don Jacinto Sánchez who was *el Presidente del Ayuntamiento de Thomé* (the president of Thomé's territorial assembly), was overseeing the administration of the villa because it fell under his jurisdicción.

On September 22, 1829, Don Jacinto was presented with a petition for a land grant on behalf of José Manuel Truxillo and seventy-five other pobladores. The petition indicated that the lands would be used as communal pastures and subsistence farming. The land grant was situated on lands already said to be owned by Don Bartolomé Baca and Don Antonio José Otero. [27]

On September 25, 1829, Don Jacinto Sánchez had indicated that he saw no apparent obstacles to granting the land to the petitioners. The only foreseeable objection would be those lands which were already owned by Don Bartolomé Baca. The ex-governor however indicated that although he would not be residing on said lands he would retain the right to cultivate and improve upon those lands that were recognized as being his. Furthermore, he indicated that he would reserve the right to purchase lands owned by grantees[28] Don Jacinto thus promptly forwarded the petition to the Territorial Deputation for its approval. On September 28, 1829 the land grant was approved. The total land area claimed in the petition would be 17,360 acres.[29]

The Locals indicated that there were two churches built in Manzano. The first was built in about 1824 and was later abandoned. A second church was constructed near the old church, which they consecrated in 1835. They christened the church *Nuestra Señora de los Dolóres* (Our Lady of Sorrows). Los Hermanos Penitentes had built a morada and their own campo santo atop a hill just west of the villa. Many of the patrónes also built an *oratorio*, which was more for family use rather than for the greater community.

Members of the community worked diligently on constructing a *torreón* (tower) as a defensive measure against attacks primarily from the marauding bands of Apachés and Navajos that frequently raided the communities throughout the Estancia Valley. The torreón was incorporated into a small two to three room fortress. The structure was built on the southern fringes of the placita.[30]

The villa was plotted in a manner, which enabled its citizens to easily defend themselves against raids. They constructed a wall made of large timber logs around the placita. There were three entrances into the placita. Each had a fortified gate and a sentinel station. Each station would always be manned by a trained individual who would warn the community of an impending attack.[31]

A small militia calling themselves "Los Vigilantes" were trained and always prepared to go to war if they were called upon. They were the ones primarily responsible for protecting the villa when it came under attack. They were also responsible for retaliatory strikes against those bands of Apachés and Navajos who had attacked them. They often would retaliate by raiding the enemy's encampments to regain lost property.

Much of the folkloric tales amongst the Manzaneños, as they often identified themselves as, involved their warfare with the Apachés and Navajos. Legend had that on some occasions Los Vigilantes would come back with the scalps of their enemies. Whether there was any truth to this is a matter of much debate. It was in all likelihood that much of the tales dating back from the original pobladores was meant to create a sense of unity and pride within the community.[32]

With the torreón complete, the citizens of the villa focused their energies on agriculture and grazing sheep. The villa itself was situated at the base of the Sierra Manzano near a natural spring, which the original pobladores named ***Ojo del Gigante*** (Giant Spring). They also constructed a system of acequias that carried the water to their respective farms. To help buffer against systematic droughts in the area, they eventually built an earthen dam near the torreón. The first apple orchard was planted during Manzano's earliest years.[33]

Situated at an elevation of 6,857 feet, the growing season in Manzano was relatively short. Most of the families would pray to San Ysidro with the hope that there wasn't a late freeze towards the start of the growing season, or an early freeze towards the end of the growing season. In the event that such freezes were also coupled with a drought, the crop yields could be devastatingly low.

Many families in the region raised sheep by trade, and therefore would be away from their homes for weeks, if not months at a time. Many would choose to live in their campitos out on the llanos rather than come home. The herders would only come into the villa if they needed provisions. After obtaining their provisions, they would stop by the house before returning to the llanos.

Sheep ranching was an extremely dangerous trade because there was always the constant threat of marauding bands of Apachés and Navajos. Mostly, they would raid the herds with little incident, but in some instances where there was significant resistance, either the shepherds or the warriors would instigate a firefight, which could lead to serious wounds or even death.

Not all contact between the people of the community and the bands of Apachés and Navajos were violent in nature. There were many instances in which trade had occurred amongst each other. In fact, for every violent conflict between the Españoles and the Native Americans, there were many more peaceful encounters. It was also a common practice for bands of warriors, mostly Apaché, to enter the village and trade their captured enemies, mostly Navajo, for provisions such as food, weapons, ammunition, and livestock. Many of their captured enemies would thus become ***peónes*** (indentured servants) of the patrónes.

In the early 1800's the Catholic Church initially was reluctant to accept the practice of indentured servants, but was convinced that it was the best alternative between two evils. Their reasoning was that, had the patrónes not taken them in trade, their captors would surely have killed them, or used them as slaves themselves. Furthermore, it gave them an opportunity to convert many of the indentured servants into Catholics.

Most of the peónes took the last name of their patrón, and in many instances became acculturated. Many of them had married into Español families, had embraced the Catholic religion, and spoke in the Spanish language. As such, many Manzaneños could claim mixed blood.

It cannot be denied that the culture of Manzano was largely influenced by its warlike and peaceful relationships with the Apachés and Navajos. Almost every aspect of life up until the mid 1870's was dependent on their relationships with the two nations. The warlike environment and the repeated raids may have been one of the reasons that so many of its citizens opted to leave Manzano after Fort Sumner and Fort Stanton were commissioned.

Filomeno "El Patrón" Sánchez[34]

Tomás Sánchez was born in about 1770. It is unclear exactly where Tomás was from, but there was some speculation that he may have come from a region near the Jémez Mountains. He married María Rita Juliana Lucero. He was listed as one of the original 75 petitioners of the Manzano land grant.[35]

Filomeno "El Patrón" Sánchez was born in San Rafael del Guiqué, El Reyno de Nuevo México, Nueva España on July 05, 1819. He was the son of Tomás Sánchez and María Rita Juliana Lucero. He married Victoriana Sánchez in about 1845. He and his wife were some of the original settlers of Manzano.

Filomeno Sánchez was held in high esteem within the community of Manzano. As an adult he was often known as "El Patrón", because he had amassed a fortune as a freight trader. It was believed that he operated several freight wagons that traversed the entire region. His most lucrative route however, was to Ciudad Chihuahua, La República de México. Later, after the Province of Nuevo México came under the control of the United States, he had trade routes to Leavenworth, Kansas and he even drove livestock to California during the 1849 gold rush.

Filomeno "El Patrón" had between twenty to thirty *peónes* (indentured servants) that worked for him. He provided them with a wage that was equivalent to about three pesos a month. He also provided them with food, water, clothing materials, and shelter. During the day the servants would work the fields, load the wagons, or herd the sheep. At night, they were allowed to fashion their own clothes and entertain themselves in the manner in which they chose. Filomeno had a degree of compassion for his workers, and they in turn looked upon him favorably.

Filomeno had constructed an oratorio in an apple orchard near his house. Here, he would give sermons and lead prayer vigils. He often encouraged his servants and other family members to use the oratorio for prayer, meditation, and self-reflection. Filomeno being a God-fearing man had also traveled to La República de México to purchase and bring back a new *campana* (bell) for the Church. The campana thus was baptized as Filimena, Manuela, Victoria y Dolóres in honor of the wives of the donors.

On March 02, 1867 the United States Congress passed a bill that abolished the practice of peonage or debt servitude.[36] Filomeno and many other Español families thus were inclined to release all of their indentured servants. Of those that were released by Filomeno, five males and four females, all of whom were Navajo in origin, were adopted into Filomeno's family. Those boys who became his sons were Eugenio, Julian, Manuel, Rafael, and another unknown Navajo. Those girls who became his daughters were Bartola, Cruz, María, and Tomasita.[37]

Being that Filomeno was a very wealthy man, he was often the target of schemes and even theft. As a result, as the local stories go, it was believed that he hid his money in a box, and he placed this box in a small compartment under one of the stairs that led to the front door of his house. His secret compartment was discovered by one of his servants who had inadvertently walked over the plank and noticed that it sounded hollow below. The servant investigated and pried the wooden plank open, only to discover Filomeno's hidden treasure. From time to time, the Navajo servant would return to the compartment and take a coin or two, and go into town and purchase items for his family.

One day, Filomeno was in town and he had noticed that his servant was purchasing items at the general store. Suspecting that something was a foul, he diligently found a new hiding place for his money. As the story goes, it was widely believed that he had hid his money in a couple of barrels out on the llano. His adopted son, Eugenio was believed to have found the barrels, but when he opened the barrels, he found nothing but old rags.

The town of Manzano mourned Filomeno's death, and much of his life has now become legend. One thing is for sure; he was widely revered as a compassionate and loving man, even by those Navajos who were his indentured servants. His life has become the material of folklore and speculation.

Chapter Three:
Mauricio de la Trinidad Sánches, 1820-1892

Life under three Ruling Countries

Mauricio de la Trinidad Sánches, christened José Mauricio de la Trinidad Sánches, was born in San Fernandes on September 22, 1820. His parents were José Gregorio de la Trinidad Sánches and María Rita Baca. Although Mauricio was born a subject of El Reyno de Nueva España, he soon became a citizen of La República de México on September 16, 1821 when it declared its independence from España.

By 1828, the Treaty of 1819 was ratified by La República de México thus re-affirming the borders between the U.S. and the Mexican held provinces of Nuevo México and Téjas. By the fall of 1834 Nuevo México's first printed newspaper, **El Crepúsculo de la Libertad** (The Dawn of Liberty) went into circulation in Santa Fé.[1]

On August 03, 1837 an uprising carried out by disenchanted Nuevo Mexicanos led to the assassination of Gobernador Albino Pérez. At the root of the discord was the imposition of taxes, which many in the region had never been subjected to. They were also disgruntled with the newly revised Mexican constitution, and the centralization of power away from Santa Fé.[2] Following Albino Pérez's assassination the people elected José Gonzáles as the new Gobernador. This illegitimate office did not last long. On January 28, 1838 Genéral Manuel Armijo marched upon Santa Fé and overthrew Gonzáles thus re-establishing the Mexican government's authority over the provincia. Armijo named himself as Gobernador and remained in power until 1846. The only time that Armijo was not Gobernador was from April 28, 1844 and November of 1845.[3]

By 1841 Téxas sought to expand their borders to the Río Grande. Initially under the guise of commerce, but knowing that there was a great deal of tension between the Nuevo Mexicanos and the Mexican government, the Tejanos may have tried to induce Nuevo México to cede from La República de México. Genéral Armijo was wise to their intentions, and upon entering Nuevo México, many members of the Téxas-Santa Fé trade expedition were arrested and subsequently sent to prisons in La Ciudad de México, while those members showing the greatest resistance were shot during the altercation. The Mexican government however, was receiving a great deal of diplomatic pressure from Téxas, the United States, and British governments and buckled under the pressure and eventually released the prisoners. Following their release the prisoners told of the deplorable conditions, and the manner in which they were mistreated while in captivity. This further incensed the strained relations between the Mexican and U.S. governments.[4]

It was during this great upheaval that Mauricio had found love, and soon wed his beloved Jesúsita Gonzáles, who was christened María Candida de Jesús Gonzáles, in Tomé on June 02, 1843. Shortly after marrying his wife, the family moved from San Fernando to Torreón in 1844. Torreón was just north of Manzano, the villa that his grandfather Bartolomé Baca had helped establish about 15 years prior.

Mauricio de la Trinidad Sánches
(photograph has not been autheticatd)

Amadita Sánchez (Daughter of Juan Rafaél Berceló Sánches and Besita Sánchez),
"Jesúsita" María Candida de Jesús Gonzáles de Sánches (Wife of Mauricio de la Trinidad
Sánches), María Sánchez (Daughter of Donaciano Sánchez and Adela Vigil).

On May 13, 1846 President Polk of the United States signed a declaration of war against La República de México. By August 15, 1846 General Stephen W. Kearney had entered Las Vegas via Ratón from the north. Upon his arrival into Las Vegas he declared himself governor and proclaimed that all citizens of Nuevo México would no longer have any allegiance to the Mexican government. By August 18, 1846 General Kearney marched upon and occupied Santa Fé with very little resistance from Genéral Armijo. After absolving the Nuevo Mexicanos of Mexican rule, he promptly started to erect Fort Marcy on August 23, 1846. It was the first U.S. military fort in Nuevo México, and was constructed just northeast of Santa Fe.[5]

After creating a new government for Nuevo México, with Charles Bent as its civil governor, and Donaciano Vigil as its secretary, General Kearney left for California. In his stead he left Colonel Alexander W. Doniphan in charge of the military, with orders to march south to Chihuahua, La República de México. Before Colonel Doniphan could march on Chihuahua, he had to quell the Navajo raids. He thus marched into northwestern Nuevo México and forced the Navajos to sign a treaty at Bear Spring on November 22, 1846. After the treaty with the Navajo, Colonel Doniphan and his soldiers proceeded to march south towards Chihuahua.[6]

With both leaders of the military on other campaigns, local revolutionaries had plotted against the occupying government before its control and influence became too entrenched. The date set for the overthrow attempt was December 19, 1846 at the midnight hour. The plot unraveled as the Americans became aware of the revolutionaries' intentions. Once the plot was discovered the leaders of the insurgency either fled or were imprisoned.[7]

On December 25, 1846 Colonel Doniphan's forces had met resistance at Brazito, which was the only battle during the Mexican War that was actually fought on Nuevo México soil. The resistance was minimal as his forces quickly claimed victory over the revolutionaries. On December 28, 1846 Doniphan's troops quickly took El Paso del Norte with barely any military resistance. After resting and re-supplying the troops, they continued their march on Chihuahua on February 08, 1847.[8]

On January 19, 1847 numerous Nuevo Mexicanos and some allies from the Pueblo de Taos again plotted to overthrow the United States government. During the Taos Revolt, Governor Bent and several of his officials were assassinated. Many other foreigners' homes were destroyed and looted.[9]

Colonel Price, who was left in charge in Colonel Doniphan's absence, promptly led 350 troops north to Taos. He reached Taos on February 03, 1847 and set camp outside the Pueblo. The following morning his troops surrounded the Taos Pueblo and proceeded to fire upon the revolutionaries who were holed up in the church. The threat of revolt was eliminated as the revolutionaries surrendered thus confirming the United States' control over the Nuevo México.[10]

On February 02, 1848 the Mexican War was officially over, with the signing of the Treaty of Guadalupe Hidalgo. The conditions that had to be met were: that La República de México would cede all the recognized provinces of Nuevo México, Alta California, and any lands claimed east of the Río Grande. The United States would thus compensate in the amount of $15,000,000 for those lost territories. All people living within the ceded territories would become United States citizens unless they chose to move back to La República de México or that they stated within a year their intention to remain Mexican citizens. These new US citizens would be admitted with the promise of having all of the rights of a US citizen bestowed upon them.[11]

As was the case prior to the Mexican War, Téxas had made its intentions known as they laid claim to the lands up to the east banks of the Río Grande. Additionally it was their intent to introduce slavery into Nuevo México. On October 10, 1848, delegates from around the territory gathered in Santa Fé to protest those measures. Concurringly they petitioned the US Congress for the expedient organization of a civil territorial government. Congress however, did not act upon the petition and preferred to opt for the status quo.[12]

Successive constitutional conventions were held to promote the admission of Nuevo México as a state. The petitions to become a state were repeatedly rejected by Congress on September 24, 1849, May of 1850, and again on September 9, 1850 with the passage of the Organic Act of the Territory of New México. The Organic Act established the Territory of New México complete with a civil government. Also included in the act was the resolution to the dispute between the Territory of New México and Téxas concerning lands extending east from the Río Grande.[13]

The Apaché Nation [14]

Although the United States had subdued the threat of a revolt from the citizens of Nuevo México, they had not been so successful to contain the repeated attacks, and raids from the Apachés. Within the Apaché nation there were several different tribes that had called the southern Territory of New México, and the north-central fringes of La República de México their home. Some of those tribes were the Chiricahua, Coyotero, Gila, Jicarilla, Lipan, Mescalero, Mimbreño, and Mogollón to name a few. Within each tribe, there were several bands, which were led by a chief, and his most revered warriors.

The social structure of the Apaché Nation was decentralized in nature, and therefore, it was nearly impossible for the United States to make one all-encompassing treaty, that all tribes and tribal bands would willingly accept. The first such attempt occurred in July 1852 when Colonel E. V. Sumner and John Greiner negotiated with several leaders of the Apaché tribes. Those Apaché leaders in attendance were Blanquito, Capitán Simón, Capitán Vuelta, Cuentas Azules, Mangas Coloradas, and Negrito.

The terms of the treaty were such that the Apaché Nation would now fall under the jurisdiction of the United States. As a condition of peace, the Apachés were forbidden to continue their raids into the northern fringes of La República de México. As a result of accepting this treaty the United States would thus be able to construct forts within the Apaché Nation, trading outposts would also be established, and all who went through their lands would be free from raids and attacks. If all of the conditions were met, the United States promised to provide assistance such as farming equipment, livestock, and other material rewards.

The one objection that several of the leaders had was the condition that they could not raid into the northern fringes of La República de México. It was Mangas Coloradas assertion that the Mexican's often killed their brethren in cold blood, and now the U.S. wanted them to stop protecting them. Mangas Coloradas continued by describing how some of his own people were invited into Sonora to share in some festivities. Soon the Sonorans brought out a barrel of ***aguardiente*** (type of alcoholic beverage) and after all of his people had become intoxicated, fifteen of them were bludgeoned to death.

Even with the one objection, all parties present had agreed to the treaty. The United States Senate later ratified the treaty on March 23, 1853. Shortly thereafter, there were incidents in which several bands of Apachés had defied the spirit of the treaty. In one of the largest raids in the winter of 1853, some of Chief Delgadito's band of warriors was accused of rustling 132 head of cattle and four horses. The winter of 1853 turned out to be exceptionally brutal for many of the Apaché tribes, as many of them were malnourished and some were starving to death. Rustling cattle had become the only means of survival.

On numerous occasions several tribal or bandleaders such as Cuchillo Negro, Delgadito Genéro, Delgadito Grande, Itán, Josecito, José Nuevo, Poncé, and Sargento had ridden to Fort Webster seeking food for their people. In most cases the U.S. Army obliged them, giving them just enough to satisfy their peoples' hunger temporarily.

By April 1853, William Carr Lane attempted to offer a treaty to the Mimbreño tribe. Achieving peace was easier said than done for in November of that year; Chief Cuentas Azules and some of his warriors were traveling from Fort Fillmore to Doña Ana. As they set up camp, the chief was lured away, and he was bludgeoned to death. The Apachés waited to see the white man's system of justice bring the murderer to trial. Their expectations of justice were dashed when the perpetrator could not be apprehended. Needless to say, the white man's incompetence in finding Cuentas Azules' killer, taught them one thing. There was no sense of justice in the white man's system.

Mescalero

The mighty Mescalero commanded the entire south-central area of the territory. Its western boundary was the Río Grande, its northern border stretched from Manzano to Anton Chico, its eastern border followed the Río Pecos, and its southern border stretched through Téxas' Big Bend region and into the northern fringes of La República de México. The Mescalero had shown some of the the greatest resistance towards American and Spanish colonization of their homelands.

In July 1849 a detachment of the U.S. Army was dispatched from Santa Fé to investigate a reported murder in the community of Placer. Their investigation took them into the heart of the Mescalero country in the southern region of the Sierra Sacramento. They had come upon two different bands of Mescalero, but they continued without further incident.

In April 1851, several leaders of the Mescalero lead by Head Chief Francisco Chacon, Lobo, Guerro, and Josecito all had come to Santa Fé seeking a peace treaty. The Mescalero leaders represented many of the bands that lived east of the Río Grande. For several months after the treaty, a semi-peaceful period existed between the Anglos, the Spanish, and the Mescalero. During this time several Apaché tribes would visit the communities of Manzano and Anton Chico and conduct trade. After conducting their business, they would meet with members of other tribes near Bosque Redondo.

By 1853, the U.S. was working with the Mescalero in an attempt to get them to accept an agricultural lifestyle. Josecito had already been planting crops over the past three growing seasons and he had already hinted that he wanted to settle near the Río Bonito. It was the United States' ultimate desire to keep the Mescalero from living a nomadic life. In general though, most bands of the Mescalero resisted the idea of settling down, and growing crops.

In July 1854 the Mescalero reportedly rustled 5,000 head of sheep from the farming community of Anton Chico. Three caravans traveling westward were also raided as they passed through Cañon Blanco. There were also reports from the southern region that California émigrés were habitually being harassed. The U.S. saw these transgressions as a direct violation of the treaties that had been signed in years past.

In August Captain Chandler was dispatched from Fort Craig to the Sierra Blanca region. On the way, his troops were reinforced with others from Fort Fillmore. Chandler's first contact with the Mescalero was with Chief Pluma, who denied that his band had anything to do with such crimes. Rather, he put the onus on Chief Santana's band of warriors. Chandler informed that he couldn't distinguish between the tribal bands and that if there were any further depredations, he would hold any Mescalero accountable.

Chief Santana was regarded as one of the most cunning and feared chiefs among the Mescalero. He was a worthy adversary who had given all of the foreign invaders of his people's lands a most difficult time. To achieve peace, the U.S. Army would have to contend with Chief Santana and his fierce warriors.

On January 18, 1855 at about 3:00 p.m. Captain R. S. Ewell and Captain Henry W. Stanton were encamped near the Sierra Blanca. Under the cover of the thick forest, Santana and his warriors had positioned themselves for an attack on the unsuspecting U.S. soldiers. Captain Ewell diligently sent Captain Stanton a contingent of men to investigate a small valley a short distance from their encampment.

Captain Stanton had spotted some of Santana's warrior's movements and quickly gave chase. As he rode up the steep hillside, he became separated from his men. Once he was able to rally his troops they gave chase again. He rode until he and his men were satisfied that the Santana's warriors had retreated from capture.

As Captain Stanton retired the chase, he and his men made their return to their encampment. About ¾ of a mile from camp Stanton and his men had come upon a narrowing of the valley. As he passed through the narrows, Santana and his warriors were waiting in ambush. At the right moment the Mescalero warriors attacked the unsuspecting U.S. soldiers firing upon them.

One of Stanton's men was instantly killed. Stanton then ordered his men to take cover amongst the trees but the Santana's warriors were too great. A volley of shots rang out between the U.S. soldiers and the Mescalero. When the gun battle was over 15 Mescalero and several U.S. soldiers were killed. Captain Stanton had taken a bullet to the head and died instantly. The Mescalero warriors claimed that Santana and one of his sons were among the dead.[15]

With Santana confirmed dead by his own warriors, several Mescalero Chiefs had sought peace with the U.S. Army. In April 1855 the following chiefs; Barilla, Blanco, Copas, Huelta, José Piño, Josecito, Llanero, Negrito, and Venancio were present. Together, they felt with Santana's death, there was a real chance to forge peace amongst the Mescalero and the Americans. Colonel D. S. Miles informed the chiefs that their offer of peace was noted, but that a treaty couldn't be offered until after it was taken to task by the proper authorities.

During this time, the U.S. Army was constructing a fort in the heart of Mescalero country. As was expected, the Mescalero had taken great exception to the fort being built on the Río Bonito. None the less, on May 04, 1855, the fort was commissioned as Fort Stanton, in honor of Captain Henry W. Stanton, who was killed in a battle with Santana and his warriors.

Migration to El Bonito

There was much debate amongst the American military, and politicos whether the newly established Territory of New México had any value to the United States. There was the contention that the cost to protect the Territory of New México far outweighed the economic benefits that would be afforded to the United States. In 1852 Colonel Edwin Voss Sumner had submitted an official report to the U.S. Congress with the recommendation that the Territory of New México should be returned to the Mexicans and Indians.[16]

The Missouri freight traders, American homesteaders, or the Téxas cattle barons who foresaw profits and a new beginning in the vast expanses of the Territory of New México's southeastern plains did not share these sentiments. Although the land was sparsely populated, the adventure of becoming a pioneer stoked the imaginations of many American homesteaders.

In conjunction with the American settlers, many Españoles from the Salinas Basin also started to migrate further south to establish their estancias. There were two primary migration patterns, the first forked southeast, following the Río Pecos and the second forked southwest into the Sierra Blanca, the Sierra Sacramento and the Sierra Capitán mountain ranges.

Many of those people who migrated southeast via the Río Pecos established the farming community of *El Berendo* just north of present day Roswell. Upon their arrival, it was discovered that there was already a farming community slightly further to the south. It had been settled by families that had migrated north from La República de México. The Mexicanos had claimed that they had come north from Chihuahua via the Río Pecos[17] and were already using the *Ojo del Norte* (North Spring) for farming but that they were having problems with their acequia. Apparently the water in the acequia would seep into sand and cause the water to flow to a trickle.

Many of the El Bonito's earliest settlers had indicated that Andricus Trujillo had initially established *La Placita del Río Bonito* sometime during the 1840s. Andricus had built the three-story torreón in an attempt to defend against repeated attacks by the Mescalero. These attacks not only instilled fear amongst the the newly arrived pobladores, but it also resulted in the deaths of many farmers, sheep ranchers and sheepherders throughout the valley.[18] Andricus was said to have been a penitente and he also helped construct a morada and a campo santo about two miles northwest of town just to the north side of the Río Bonito.[19] By 1851 the Spanish-speaking people that settled in the Sierra Blanca, the Sierra Sacramento and the Sierra Capitán mountains had already named the river that forked northwest, *El Río Bonito*. The river that forked due west was named *El Río Ruidoso*. The junction of these two rivers formed the source of *El Río Hondo*, which flowed into the Río Pecos southeast of El Berendo.[20]

There were two events that helped promote further settlement into the Sierra Blanca and the Sierra Capitán. The first was the enactment of United States land laws by Congress on July 22, 1854,[21] and the other was the commissioning of Fort Stanton. The small agricultural villa of *La Junta* was soon established in 1855 by several families at the junction of the Río Ruidoso and the Río Bonito. A second wave of families had settled La Junta and they were; José Cháves, Santiago Gonzáles, José Gutiérres, Cresencio Sánchez, Elisandro Torres, and Ignacio Torres. La Junta later became known as *Hondo*, when the first post office opened on February 06, 1900.

Jose Mauricio de la Trinidad Sánches Migrates South

Mauricio had heard many stories about the endless sea of llano near El Berendo. He also had heard about how the U.S. government was opening up land to those individuals who wanted to settle, farm, and improve the land. This was much more alluring than the communal lands which he and his ancestors had grown accustomed to. The lure of owning his own piece of land, and the wide sea of grazing lands continually wore heavily on his mind.

His only concerns were spawned from the stories he had often heard about the repeatedly violent attacks by the Apachés in general, and the Mescalero in particular. His apprehensions were rested when he heard that the soldiers at Fort Stanton had mostly subdued the Apaché threat in the region. His indecision finally broke when in 1862 he and his family had finally made the move from Manzano to El Berendo. He brought with him about 10,000 head of sheep. When migrating from one region to another, it was a common practice for several families to travel together. This ensured the safety of the caravan, by providing a sufficient defense against marauding Apachés.

As was the way of many sheep ranchers, Mauricio de la Trinidad Sánches and his family lived primarily a nomadic life. They never really settled in one place for an extended period of a time. They had lived in many different communities depending on where the grazing was best. By 1862, Mauricio had already settled in the Ojo del Norte/ El Berendo area. In the coming years, they would also have settled in Tularoso, *Tres Ritos* (Three Little Rivers) and in the Río Ruidoso valley.

While living in El Berendo, Mauricio and his sons Estolano, Antonio, and José Toribio helped a small enclave of Mexicanos build a more sophisticated and sturdy acequia to irrigate their farms. The acequia drew its water from the Río Berendo and flowed well enough to water their fields. Returning the favor, many of the Mexicanos helped Mauricio build the acequia that would supply his farm with water. Thus the beginnings of mutually beneficial relationships were being developed during El Berendo's early years.

La Plaza de San José

By 1867 Mauricio, and several other families from El Berendo, had already abandoned the lands they were squatting on and migrated southwest and helped establish a new villa, which they named ***La Plaza de San José.*** Family legend indicates that Mauricio was the one who named the settlement. It was located about 15 miles west of El Berendo, where the Twin Rivers Dam is now situated. About 40 families families had established themselves on the north bank of the Río Hondo. They farmed about 200 acres on the south bank of the river. A wagon trail separated the villa, which on the south side, a row of adobés was constructed. Built on the north side of the wagon trail were the *corrales* (barnyard), a stockade, and a blacksmith.[22] By 1869 ***El Oratorio de San José*** had been constructed within the villa. The oratorio was where the Catholic parishioners had often gathered to celebrate their faith. The oratorio was built within a house, where the padre would come to stay while he gave mass.

While campaigning as a delegate for Congress in 1867, José Francisco Cháves had stopped in La Plaza de San José for the evening, while en route to La Plaza del Río Bonito. Intrigued with the bustling villa, José Francisco Cháves asked some of the residents where they had come from. Many of the residents replied that they were from the Manzano region.

When asked why they had established the villa, many of the men told the candidate that they were traveling merchants by trade. They continued by telling him that they brought freight to and from St. Joseph, Missouri, sometimes stopping in Kansas. Other residents cultivated crops for the purpose of selling their produce in Fort Stanton and Fort Sumner. [23]

La Plaza de San José had become an important trading outpost for the freight traders from both the Territory of New México and Missouri. The trade route had become profitable and encouraged further emigration of Missourians into the area. In the following years La Plaza de San José became known as ***La Plaza de Misúri,*** which reflected the growing importance of the villa as a Missourian trading outpost.[24]

With increased competition with the cattle barons, for prime grazing pastures, many of the sheep ranching operations either moved elsewhere, or ceased to exist. Mauricio had come to the realization that his operations were being squeezed. He had labored over his dilemma and had finally come to the conclusion that he would have to expand the scope of his business. He had decided that he would try to supplement his sheep ranching operations by also becoming a freighter.

As a freighter, Mauricio had primarily made trips to Las Vegas, Fort Sumner, and Fort Stanton. On occasion he would make the long journey to St. Joseph, Missouri. His eldest sons Estolano, Antonio, José Toribio, and Francisco helped their father with his freighting operations. On occasion they would accompany their father on the long trips to Missouri. As was the case most of the time, they would stay behind and work the sheep ranching operations.[25]

Life for the settlers in La Plaza de Misúri, which later became known as Missouri Bottom, had become increasingly difficult as the water flow in the Río Hondo continued to diminish. The water from the river was aggressively being diverted to irrigate farms further up in the mountain valleys. By 1872, most of the people chose to abandon their homes at Missouri Bottom, opting to move further up the Río Hondo, to the Río Ruidoso and Río Bonito valleys. Through the years Missouri Bottom had become one of the rest stops for travelers between Roswell, Lincoln, the Rio Hondo and the Rio Ruidoso valleys.[26]

On January 16, 1869 the Territory of New México passed legislation, which established Lincoln County. The lands that fell under its jurisdiction encompassed the entire southeastern Territory of New México. Lincoln County was about 27,000 square miles and was a 180-mile journey from north to south and a 160-mile journey from east to west. It would take several days on horseback or wagon to travel the expanse from each of its borders.[27]

The first election for the newly created county was held on April 19, 1869 in which the first sheriff and the Probate Judge had run for office. Jesús Sandoval y Sena was elected as the first sheriff of Lincoln County but he failed to take office because he failed to secure the performance bond money. Governor H.H. Heath thus appointed Mauricio de la Trinidad Sánches as interim sheriff until another election could be held on September 6, 1869. Mauricio thus became Lincoln County's first active sheriff for all of six months.[28] Florencio Gonzáles and Sabino Gonzáles y Castillo secured his bond as sheriff of Lincoln County.[29]

A sheriff's bond served as a form of insurance, in the event that the sheriff couldn't perform his legal duties in a competent manner. At the time, those duties included the collection of taxes and keeping law and order within the county. The amount of the bond was a hefty $2,000, which could serve as a barrier for those sheriffs that could not raise the necessary money before being sworn into office.

Sheriff José Mauricio de la Trinidad Sánches (Sheriff Mauricio Sánches as he was commonly known) had often made the trip to the county seat in Lincoln (formerly La Placita del Río Bonito) several times a week. Sometimes his eldest sons would make the trip with him to Lincoln. In his brief stint as the sheriff, Mauricio didn't encounter the degree of lawlessness that would eventually lead up to the famed Lincoln County War.

Las Angosturas

Mauricio Sánchez eventually squatted on a tract of land just northeast of present day Ruidoso. He built a permanent residence out of adobé about two hundred feet off the south bank of the Rio Ruidoso. At the time, the river flowed along the northernmost side of the mouth of the narrow canyon. Over the eons, the river had cut into the mountainside, creating a large crevasse that resembled a rudimentary cave,[30] now known as Fox Cave.

Mauricio and several of the other families that settled in the area referred to the area as **Las Angosturas** (The Narrows). The farming community followed the Río Ruidoso, eastward for about two miles. At that time the river ran from the crevasse through the mouth of the canyon, which was situated between two mountainsides that could barely accommodate a horse and wagon alongside the river.

The crevasse had become a focal point of the tiny community. Mauricio had often hosted several bailes for weddings, anniversaries, birthdays and other community events. The crevasse was a natural attraction and the soothing sound of the river created an atmosphere of romance and tranquility. Often times, one could see people from the community swimming in the waterhole that was situated adjacent to the cave. A small manzano grove and other types of fruit trees helped create an Eden-like atmosphere.

Some of the other families that had also settled in the area were, Mauricio de la Trinidad's children Antonio and Manuel. Other families that settled the area were Santiago García, Roberto Cháves, and Juan Rafael Barceló Sánchez.

Mauricio de la Trinidad Sánches' later years

Mauricio and Jesúsita visited Manzano only once after migrating to Lincoln County. They most likely returned to Manzano to attend their daughter, Visita's wedding in 1875. When they arrived in Manzano, all their relatives and old friends had come to pay them a visit, to hear the news about

Lincoln County. Mauricio referred to the lands of his new home as **Bonito**. They inquired about the challenges of living amongst the Tejanos and the Mescalero. Mauricio was more than obliged to tell his kinfolk of his perception of the foreigners. He told them all of his stories of adventure and wonderment. After returning to Lincoln County, neither Mauricio or Jesúsita ever returned to Manzano.

Both Mauricio and Jesúsita had become respected citizens of the Rio Ruidoso valley. They were both heralded for their medicinal knowledge of yerbas, and other natural remedies. Both were considered *curanderos* (healers). It is said that they healed many people from otherwise grave illnesses. Some had even said that God had blessed them so that they could heal the sick.

In November of 1892, Mauricio de la Trinidad Sánches passed away in Las Angosturas. On January 11, 1899 Jesúsita Gonzáles de Sánches paid 200 pounds of maíz to La Capilla de San Patricio for the purpose of having her husband buried in the campo santo.[31] He lies within one of the many unmarked graves that scatter the sacred grounds. His final resting spot is most likely memorialized by a rock that serves as his headstone. Jesúsita also rests within the same campo santo and she too lies in an unmarked grave.

The adobé that Mauricio and his wife had built stood vacant for several decades after they both had passed away. In the late 1960's the adobé had fallen into such disrepair that the owners of the property had it demolished. It wasn't until the late 1970's that one of his granddaughters had reminisced about the long forgotten community of Las Angosturas. It was then, that the true history of the community had been told.

Several adobé-like cabins were built in its place. Little did the owners realize that they had in their possession, one of the older and more significant adobés in the region, which was owned by one of its most respected men. Maybe if they had known the history of the structure, they would have made an attempt at keeping it.

Chapter Four:
Los Comunidades del Valle (Communities of the Valley)

The Spanish-speaking population had originally named many of the communities throughout the valleys of the northern Sierra Sacramento, Sierra Blanca, and Sierra Capitán. The names of these communities were derived either from the original ranchitos that dotted the landscape, the geological landmarks, or a description of an event that occurred at that location.

Rebentón

Rebentón was named as such by its founders because the area was always subject to fast moving storms. It was also known as Reventón and Rabentón. Often times, one could hear the thunderous roar, and see the flashes of lightning as a storm approached over the mountains. The town was established at the foot of what is now known as Patos Mountain. Most of the housing in the community was constructed of adobé. To the east, there were widespread llanos that stretched as far as the eye could see. To the southeast, one could see the splendor of the Sierra Capitán, which rose from the llanos like an impenetrable wall.

The community was first settled in about 1855, and it was situated about 18 miles north of Fort Stanton.[1] It was initially a ranching community, but eventually it became the center of commerce for a region, which saw several sheep ranching operations. Since the llanos had no fences at the time, the area was considered open rangeland. Thus everybody had the right to use the lands for grazing.

Several different families had settled in the community of Rebentón. At one time, the community had boasted a general store, a church, a school, and a post office. The first post office was established on February 26, 1896 and Davíd Lueras was the first postmaster. Elsie Kimbrell's first teaching job was at the Rebentón primary elementary school just before it shut down in the late-1930s.

The community flourished for several decades but a series of events occurred which lead to its eventual abandonment shortly during the late-1930s. First, there was a severe drought that made it almost impossible to graze sheep. Second, with the onset of the Great Depression, several families were forced to leave the area. Third, large tracts of land were being fenced off by large-scale ranching operations making it increasingly more difficult for smaller sheep operations to remain profitable.

By September 29, 1928 the post office had closed down completely.[2] Most of the families that lived in or near the town had moved to Carrizozo. The remnants of old abandoned ruins are all that exists of Rebentón today. Most of the adobé walls have fallen to the ground, which has hidden almost any evidence that the town had even existed. Tulips still grow in flower gardens that look more like the surrounding terrain. Broken dishes and abandoned furniture can be found within the dirt from time to time. The abandoned town is inaccessible to the public because it lies within a private ranch still owned by the late Leandro Vega Jr.'s family.

Patos

Patos was another community originally settled by several families in about 1855. The family of Aurelio Sánchez and Anastacia Aragón were one of several families that lived in the small community which was nestled at the foot of Patos Mountain about one mile from Rebentón. The community was named as such because it was established next to a small naturally occurring pond. During the summer, ducks would often frequent the pond. It was fed by a natural spring, which flowed throughout the year.

Patos, like Rebentón, was primarily a ranching community. Most of its inhabitants also had sheep ranching operations. A chapel was built on the eastern edge of the community, which was named Nuestra Señora de Guadalupe. A modest campo santo surrounded the chapel. Most of the standing ruins indicate that Patos' inhabitants chose to construct their buildings with rock rather than adobé. The ruins that remain are far more pronounced and have stood thus far, to the test of time.

The fates of the two sister communities were interwoven with each other. As such, Patos was also abandoned during the late-1930s. The abandoned community is also inaccessible to the public because it lies within a private ranch.

La Voquilla

With the advent of continued migration into the Río Bonito, Río Ruidoso and Río Hondo valleys, several farming communities were established. One such settlement was *La Voquilla,* on the Río Hondo, which was originally settled by Juan Maés and his family. In La Voquilla, a fortified placita was constructed to guard against Apaché raids and Tejano outlaws. Their compound housed scouts that kept a watchful eye in all directions. It was widely rumored at the time that there was a rudimentary tunnel system that connected many of the buildings together within the compound.

Juan Maés and his brothers José de Jesús, Paz, and Juanito, had become the ringleaders of a band of notorious horse thieves based in Lincoln County. Their primary target was often John Chisum's herds. Family legend was that their days of rustling were in response to being victimized by Tejano rustlers themselves. The brothers had figured that it was an eye for an eye. After stealing enough horses, the Maés brothers would drive the herd to Chihuahua and then sold the horses to willing buyers.

In December of 1875 they killed Oliver Thomas in Lincoln. After the killing, the 9th Calvary (the Buffalo Soldiers) out of Fort Stanton was dispatched to break up the ring of horse thieves. Upon descending on La Voquilla, the Calvary was met with significant resistance. After the battle six members, including two of the Maés brothers had either been captured or killed. Those that had escaped with their lives or capture moved their operations to Puerto de Luna on the Río Pecos.[3]

La Plaza de San Patricio

A land surveyor had made reference to the community of La Plaza de San Patricio as early as October of 1867,[4] but several Spanish-speaking families had settled the area shortly after Fort Stanton was commissioned. Many of the families that lived slightly east of La Plaza de San Patricio referred to the area as *Rancho Libertad* (Liberty Ranch). The families of the original settlers continued to call that area Libertad, for many years to come. The name was still in use by some of the old-timers as late as the 1970's.

As was the custom, the region around La Plaza de San Patricio was referred by many different names, depending on which rancho one was at. Aniseto Lucero had a rancho adjacent to Rancho Libertad, which he named *Rancho de Patos,* which was also referred to as *Las Arenales* (The Sands), because of the small sandy beaches that lined the banks of the river. Ysidro Sisneros owned some land he named the *Rancho Trinidad* (Trinity Ranch). Whichever name was used, the citizens of the community were brought together at La Plaza de San Patricio, which had become the epicenter of the Rio Ruidoso Valley.

Many of the communities in the region were always under the constant threat of a Mescalero raid, and La Plaza de San Patricio was no different. After the original settlers of the community had built their houses, and planted their crops, they came together to build a torreón that was centrally located. Although the whereabouts of the torreón remain a mystery, the old-timers claimed that it was built near the first church constructed in the community.

As an added defensive measure, several men within the community volunteered to keep a vigilant eye out for potential danger of a Mescalero, or an outlaw attack. The volunteers would rotate their watch schedules so that there was an eye on the valley at all times. Each man thus would have to climb a strategic peak and serve as the community's sentinel. From the vantage point at the top of the peak, the sentinel could see from one end of the valley to the other. It was thus the sentinel's responsibility to warn the community below, of any impending danger. This peak eventually was named ***La Sentinela*** in honor of the many sentinels that kept watch upon it.[5]

An influx of settlers coming into La Plaza de San Patricio brought about opportunities for commerce. Soon a small general store had opened, a cantina (White Cat Bar) and salón de baile was built, and then Ygnacio Olguín opened up a pool hall. The pool hall was often the place where all the gamblers would congregate with the hope that they could make some quick money.

Later, La Plaza de San Patricio had become known more simply as San Patricio. The community of San Patricio extended six miles in either direction within the valley. It encompassed several ranchos from La Junta on the east to Las Angosturas on the west. Hence, when somebody said they were from San Patricio, they were talking about the valley between La Junta and Las Angosturas rather than the Plaza at the center of the community.

Some of the original families that chose to settle La Plaza de San Patricio were; Merijildo Chávez, Hilario Gallegos, Lucas Gallegos, Cruz Herrera, Juan Lucero, Tranquelino Montoya, José Ygnacio Olguín, Pablo Salas, Esiquio Sánchez, Francisco Sánchez, Calixtro Sedillo, Cosmé Sedillo, José Miguel Sedillo, Manuel Silva, Ysidro Sisneros, Bonifacio Trujillo, Francisco Trujillo, Juan de Dios Trujillo, Juan Ulibarrí, and Santiago Lucero y Ulibarrí.

Las Chosas

There were two small communities that many of the locals referred to as Las Chosas. The more prominent of the two was situated about seven miles east of La Placita del Rio Bonito. José Miranda and his brother Felipé Miranda had migrated to Las Chosas in the late 1850s. Cleto Chávez had also settled the area and had married José's daughter Prudencia Miranda.

The other community was situated about two miles west of La Plaza de San Patricio near La Capilla de San Patricio and situated up against the base of the mountains. There are two ditches, Las Chosas north and Las Chosas south that owe their names to this forgotten community.

The Horse Races near San Patricio.

La Aguilita

The community of La Aguilita encompassed an area stretching from the Río Ruidoso on the south and up through the Cañon de Diablo on the north. The name of the community was later changed to Eagle's Creek, Devil's Canyon, and Glencoe.

Analla[6]

The community of Analla was originally named for the Rancho Analla. José Analla, Pedro Analla and their families were some of the first people to settle in this ranching community. The first post office was established on April 27, 1903. It was incorporated within the mercantile that the Analla family had built and operated. Isidro Analla was named as its first postmaster, and held that position for about seven months. Pedro Analla then took over the postmaster duties for about two months. Sallie A. Murray eventually took over the post master duties on January 08, 1904.

In 1906 the Raymond family had purchased the mercantile from Analla and had petitioned to change the name of the post office, in honor of their daughter, Tinnie. Nearly everyone from the community had signed the petition for the name change. On April 05, 1909 the name of the post office, and the surrounding community was changed from Analla to Tinnie. Later the Tinnie Silver Dollar Restaurant served fine dining for many people, tourists and locals alike.

Las Palas [7]

One of the first people to settle at the base of Sierra Capitán was Casimiro Barela (Also spelled Varela) who had come to the area in about 1880. The area eventually encompassed the communities of *Las Palas* (The Shovels), *Las Tablas*, and *Agua Azul* (Blue Water). Legend has it that the community was named for several shovels that were discovered lying next to a hole dug by some gold prospectors that had left their supplies behind. Casimiro constructed his first jacal near *El Ojo de Las Palas* (The Shovel Spring). He built a small wooden fence around the spring, which served as the source of a small stream that meandered through the center of town. The stream served as the main water supply for all the settlers who came to the area later. The stream enabled the community to cultivate the land in the immediate vicinity.

By about 1900 Cornelio Lucero's family and some members of his extended family migrated from southern Colorado to the area. Others that settled in the area were the families of Jesúsito and Querino Maés who were also originally from southern Colorado. Anselmo Pacheco and his family migrated to Las Palas from La Polvadera de San Lorenzo, Territory of New México via Lincoln.[8] Others that settled in the area were Juan Quintana, Selso Gallegos, Juan José Durán, A.H. Rue, Patrick McTiegue, and Andy Richardson to name a few.

Over time, the names of the communities have changed. The community of Las Palas was changed to Arabela when the town received its first post office on February 15, 1901.[9] It is thought that the name "Arabela" originated from a young woman named Arabela Quintana who eventually married Tomás Richardson. Many of the original settlers of the area continued to refer to the community as Las Palas even after the name change. Las Palas was still in use up through the 1920 Census. The community of Las Tablas was changed to Richardson when the community received its first post office on April 03, 1895.[10] The newly named town was in honor of the Richardson family that settled in the area. Several of the old-timers often referred to the region around Richardson as Carolita.[11] The community of Agua Azul was later changed to Blue Water.

By about 1913 the first schoolhouse was constructed in Arabela. It was originally constructed of wooden logs. The schoolhouse was a one-room rectangular structure. Long wooden benches were provided for the children to sit on during class. Several years later the original schoolhouse was abandoned when a second schoolhouse was constructed nearby.

Las Palas had become a lively community. There were two cantinas in town and another in Agua Azul. There was also a general store owned and operated by Leopoldo Pacheco. Elerdo Chávez owned a salón de baile in **Los Cordova**. There were two other salón de bailes in the community, one of which was owned by Manuel Carrillo. People from all over the region converged on the town to listen to the three orchestras that played at the salón de bailes. Elerdo Chávez, Ramón Torres, and Andalecio Sabedra were accomplished fiddlers that supplied the rhythms.

The first capilla was built in the center of town, near the general store. It was a simple jacal but it served its purpose. The Reverend Enríque Herman would travel from Lincoln to the chapel about once a month to preside over mass, perform baptisms if needed, and conduct weddings. The townsfolk would always be on the lookout for the two white horses that pulled the priest's buggy into town. Casimiro Barela would always provide lodging for the priest when he came to town.

La Plaza de Picacho

By the mid 1860's several pioneering families had settled on lands adjacent to the Río Hondo. The agricultural and ranching community was about mid-way between La Plaza de San José and La Placita del Río Bonito and was situated amongst jagged hills, which sharply sloped down to the river. The community later became known as La Plaza de Picacho, in reference to the small peaks that surrounded the community.

Some of the pioneering families that settled in La Plaza de Picacho were Francisco Romero, José Antonio Romero, Juan Romero, and Vicente Romero. All of the Romero were brothers who had come from Manzano. Other families that settled the area were Torivio Avila, Martín Chávez, Pablo Fresquez, Los Gallegos, George Kimbrell, José Miguel Lucero, Los Miranda, José Montaño, Camilo Núñez, Francisco Pacheco, Cresencio Salas, Los Serrano, Juan Silva, and Francisco Vigil.

In the fall of 1867, Robert A. Casey had migrated from Téxas to a farm in the Río Hondo Valley. He had purchased some land from Leopold Chene. Casey had claimed that there were only two other families in the immediate area. The other families were identified as David Warner and Elias Hughes, both of whom were married to Spanish-surnamed women.[12] Warner was married to Predicanda Sánchez and Hughes was married to Antonia Luján. A third family, who had already been living in the area for a year and was headed by Heiskell Jones, had just moved to La Aguilita before Casey's arrival. Jones was a butcher by trade and was supplying meat to the Mescalero. Casey had migrated to Picacho with his wife Ellen Evelyn Schellenberger.

Agua Azul[13]

Severino Apodaca and his wife Juanita had emigrated from La República de México in 1871. Their long travels brought them to La Plaza de Picacho near the Río Hondo. They remained there for a few months before they finally decided to settle in the community of Agua Azul in 1872. The community was named for **El Ojo del Agua Azul** (Blue Water Spring), which fed the community's irrigation system.

One chilled New Year's Eve day in 1873, Marciál Rodríguez, had traveled to his compadre Severino Apodaca's house so that the two could go hunting. The two wanted to bag a deer before the New Year. They woke up at daybreak and rode towards the mountains, stopping periodically on the llano to search for fresh tracks.

Dotting the landscape at the base of the mountains were many **sabinos** (junipers), whose tree limbs grew outward from the ground up. It made for an extremely difficult hunt as one could seldom see through the thicket. Further up in the mountains, tall pine trees dotted the landscape. The foliage was thick and difficult to navigate through. As the two men ventured further into the mountains they had unwittingly come across a band of Mescalero.

Alarmed by the two unsuspecting hunters, and taking advantage of their camouflaged position, the Mescalero ambushed the two men. Marciál was shot in the back and Severino was shot in the leg. The two of them quickly took cover and held their attackers at bay for the better part of the day. An exchange of periodic fire between the two factions broke the silence of the day. Marciál had killed a few warriors, as did his friend but there were still many more, surrounding their position.

Night was drawing near and Marciál was growing weaker. His blood loss was pulling him in and out of a state of consciousness. Marciál called to his wounded friend and told him to make a break for the arroyo, and flee to safety. Severino initially had no desire to leave his friend to die, but Marciál had already accepted his fate and he didn't want his friend to suffer the same consequence. Reluctantly, Severino left his friend behind to die alone under the cold stillness of the darkening skies. He made a quick dash towards the arroyo and started running for his life. The Mescalero followed close behind losing Severino in the shadows of the darkness.

In a calculated attempt to protect Juanita, who was with child, he chose to lead his attackers away from his adobé. God willing, maybe the Mescalero would leave the premises thus ensuring the safety of his beloved. He had made his escape, but he did not take his luck for granted. He hobbled through the night until he came across Robert Casey's rancho.

In a raspy and parched voice, he called out to Casey's ranch hands for help. He explained what had happened up on the llano near the base of the mountain, and that he had left his compadre Marciál behind to fend for himself. Casey and his men rounded up a posse, sending word up the valley for all willing and able bodied men to meet in Agua Azul. At daybreak they headed up the llano towards Severino's adobé house.

Severino's worst nightmare had become a horrid reality as he frantically searched for his wife. He called out to her, screaming in the hopes that she could hear his voice. All he heard were the echoes of his voice disappearing into the cold breeze. Juanita was gone, accosted by the Mescalero. Despondent, Severino motioned to leave, so that they may continue the search for his attackers, and maybe he could find his wife and their unborn child still alive.

They followed the trail which led them to the site were the battle had initially taken place. Lying on the ground in a pool of dried, blackened blood was Marciál Rodríguez. His right arm was severed and his scalp had been removed. The men said a prayer and buried him where he lay.

They continued through the llano and found a band of Mescalero at the west end of the Sierra Capitán. A short battle ensued, where many Mescalero met their death. Juanita, however, was nowhere to be found. The posse scoured the mountainside looking for any indication that she was still alive. They finally found her in the company of two squaws who were trying to lead her up the mountainside.

They rode in pursuit in an attempt to assist Juanita. The two squaws saw their pursuers and in an attempt to stall them, they struck a heavy blow to Juanita's skull with an axe, splitting her head open. Upon reaching Juanita, she already lay unconscious, covered with blood and dying. Severino ran to his dying wife and held her in his arms, screaming to the heavens.

Miraculously, Juanita was no longer with child. She had given birth to a son. They found the abandoned child some distance from his now dead mother. They brought the child to Severino and he christened his son, José Apodaca. The tragedy of his wife's death was too much for Severino to bear, and he didn't know the first thing about taking care of a child. He brought his son to Tulia Gurulé Stanley. About a year later, in 1875, Severino was killed by Tejanos while he was taking a load of wheat to Dowlin's Mill up on the Río Ruidoso.

Chapter Five:
Los Hijos de Mauricio de la Trinidad Sánches

Francisco Sánchez

From left to right: Unknown, Alejandro Gallegos, Francisco Sánchez, Unknown.

Francisco Sánchez, christened José Panfilo Francisco Sánchez, was born in Torreón, Territory of New México in 1853. His parents were Mauricio de la Trinidad Sánches and María Candida de Jesús Gonzáles. Many of his friends and compadres had known him as Pancho or Don Pancho, which were some of the nicknames for Francisco. He also went by the name, Francisco Sánchez y Gonzáles.

Francisco, his parents and his siblings had all migrated first to El Berendo, and then to La Plaza de San José, before finally settling in the Río Ruidoso valley in the community of Las Angosturas. In his youth he helped his father raise sheep, and in many instances, he accompanied his father on freight runs to Las Vegas.

As Francisco grew into a young man, he had become very handsome and imposing. He was a giant amongst his peers, standing about 6' tall. He had a strong, stern gaze that exuded confidence and seriousness. Yet, he had an endearing playful nature that showed a softer side to those who knew him best. He was a complex man, who was very difficult to read. His personality suited him well because Francisco had gained a reputation as an avid and cunning gambler. Family legend was that Francisco had acquired most of the land that he eventually would own in La Plaza de San Patricio, by means of gambling.

His passion for gambling also brought him into frequent contact with the likes of William H. Bonney, Fernando Herrera, Charles Bowdre, Josiah "Doc" Scurlock, and several of the other Regulators. Most people knew William H. Bonney from his more infamous alias, Billy the Kid. Many Nuevo Mexicanos knew him as ***Chivato***, or ***Billito***.

Robert Casey's missing livestock [1]

On April 01, 1869 Francisco had arrived at Robert Casey's rancho for the purpose of purchasing one oxen for $125. Francisco had become acquainted with the Casey's a few years prior when they had come to pass through La Plaza de San José. His father and Robert had come to know of one another. When he inquired about the oxen, a young boy named Juan de Dios Romero, was instructed to go to the pasture to herd the livestock back to the corral, so Francisco could choose which one he wanted.

Juan de Dios returned and whispered something into his Tío, Pablo Romero's ear. Pablo quickly, but quietly, glanced over at Francisco and excused himself from the room. The hurried gentleman and his *sobrino* (nephew) then proceeded to leave the house, in which they were gone for about half an hour. The two returned and explained to Francisco that all of the livestock was gone and it was assumed that the Mescalero had most likely raided the herd. Francisco laughed, thinking it was a joke, and asked them to fess up. Pablo had a look of seriousness on his face, and Francisco's amusement soon turned to concern.

Francisco was quickly brought outside to the pasture, where they discovered a trail that led off into the distance. Mixed in with the hoof prints were those of several men. By this time, Juan de Dios' other uncle, Vicente Romero, had been apprised of the situation and he had quickly made his way to the rancho. It was late afternoon, and Francisco had conferred with Vicente and the others and it was decided that it was best to track the livestock trail, the following day.

Early the next morning, Francisco, Vicente, and another man named Neco had followed the trail up into the hills. About two and a half miles up, they came across two arrows that had been left behind. Francisco closely inspected the arrows and he had concluded that they were made by a Mescalero. They had figured that there must have been six or more men who were driving the cattle. Within the rudimentary encampment, they found mescal, and a buck skin.

The three followed the trail for about another quarter of a mile before they had decided to turn back. To them it had become apparent that a group of Mescalero had raided the livestock and herded them in the direction of Sierra Blanca. They didn't want to pursue the matter any further because they were ill equipped to do anything in the event that the Mescalero took exception to their accusations. They weren't about to get into any type of armed conflict with the Mescalero over eleven to twelve head of livestock. Thus the three men returned to the Casey's ranch and diligently explained to Robert what they had discovered.

The matter was left with no incident for well over twenty years. It was revisited in the Court of Claims in December of 1893. At that time, Ellen Casey had claimed that eight cows and three yoke cattle had been rustled. Francisco was one of the witnesses that gave testimony to the incident. Ellen Casey's claim was never honored and she never received any reimbursement for the stolen livestock.

Francisco had grown fond of a beautiful, young woman who lived nearby. Her name was Concepción Trujillo. She had a beautiful fair complexion, long wavy red hair, and root beer brown colored eyes. She had the misfortune of contracting a disease that had robbed her of the gift of eyesight when she was but a child. Oddly enough, her mother Aucención Trujillo was also blind. Her disability didn't deter Francisco from pursuing a love relationship. On May 19, 1873, Francisco Sánchez had married Concepción Trujillo in La Plaza de San Patricio, Territory of New México. In all they had nine children together, seven sons and two daughters.

The Horrell War

The Horrell brothers were known outlaws that had escaped persecution from the law in Lampasas County, Téxas. They had migrated and eventually settled on the Río Ruidoso. They had an intense hatred for any "Mexican" that crossed paths with them. Sometimes this hatred lead to acts of intimidation, and sometimes it ended in murder.

On December 01, 1873 several of the Horrells had congregated in Lincoln and eventually met up with Dave Warner, the ex-sheriff Jack Gylam, Zachariah Crumpton, and Jerry Scott. The bunch took to drinking heavily and soon became disorderly.[2]

Knowing that the Horrells had a reputation of becoming violent while intoxicated, Constable Juan Martín (Martínez) had approached Ben Horrell, Warner, Gylam and the others, asking them for their weapons in an attempt to preserve the peace. The men reluctantly forfeited their weapons and continued drinking. As the night progressed, they managed to re-arm themselves. In a drunken stupor, the unruly men threatened to commandeer their confiscated weapons from Jacinto Gonzáles, whom they believed had been holding their guns.

Finding their way out of the cantina, the impaired men traversed through town, in search of their weapons. Gun shots disturbed the night as the men discharged their newly acquired weapons in all directions. Screaming insults and threats, Constable Martín's hand was forced. Martín sought the assistance of several men. Those that he had assembled were Juan Patrón, José Montaño, Juan Gonzáles, Serafino Trujillo, Joe Haskins, and William Warnick who served as their interpreter. The Constable and his men proceeded to find the Horrells and their rag tag gang of drunkards.

Constable Martín then asked Warnick to interpret for him, but before Warnick could finish, the Constable was inexcusably shot by David Warner. As the Constable fell dead to the ground, his men opened fire on the Horrells, killing David Warner. In the melee that ensued, both Ben Horrell, and Jack Gylam had made their escape. Juan Patrón, Serafino Trujillo, Juan Gonzáles, and several others were in close pursuit. As they caught up to Ben and Jack, they mercilessly shot and killed both men. Ben Horrell was shot nine times and his accomplice was shot thirteen times.[3]

The news of the killings quickly spread throughout town, and all of Lincoln's citizens had a cause for concern. In anticipation of some type of retaliation by the Horrells, Justice of the Peace Manuel Gutiérrez had petitioned the commanding officer at Fort Stanton, for protection. Major John Sanford Mason denied the JP's request citing that his troops could only be used against a Mescalero attack.

An enraged bunch, members of the Horrell family traveled to Lincoln and demanded that the murderers of their brother, Ben and his two accomplices, Dave Warner and Jack Gylam, be brought to justice. Their demands were rejected as the lawmen and their posse cited that his brother and both of his accomplices were resisting arrest when they were killed. Disenchanted with the outcome, the Horrells took matters into their own hands. Two days later, Serafino Trujillo and one of his laborers were killed under the guise that they were rustling some of the Horrell's herd.

The Spanish-speaking community was incensed by the murders and there were rumblings by some extremists that all those violent and disruptive newcomers should be either killed or run out of the area. Juan Gonzáles had traveled to Tularosa to assemble a posse for the very purpose of a decisive retaliatory attack against the Horrells and any of their supporters. Led by Gonzáles and the just recently appointed sheriff Alexander "Ham" Mills, the posse descended upon the Horrell's ranchito on Eagle Creek. An eventless firefight ensued throughout the day, with no bloodshed from either faction. Eventually the posse left the Horrell's ranchito.

It was December 20, 1873 and many people from in Lincoln were celebrating a wedding. A baile was being held in honor of the bride and groom. The Horrell's had happened to come across the baile about midnight, and quickly put an end to the festivities by shooting up the house. They indiscriminately shot into the house, spreading the revelers out, in fear for their lives.

The senseless violence claimed the lives of Juan Patrón's father Isidro, Marío Balazán, Isidro Padilla, and José Candelaria. Polonia García was shot in the knee, blowing off her kneecap, which crippled her for the rest of her life. Pilar Candelaria and Mario Balazán's nephew were also seriously injured during the shooting.[4]

Juan Patrón had hastily left for Santa Fé with the intent of petitioning Governor Marsh Giddings to protect the citizens of Lincoln County from the Horrell brothers. By December 26th, Probate Judge Lawrence Murphy, Justice of the Peace Manuel Gutiérrez, and Jacinto Gonzáles signed and dispatched a letter to the Governor also petitioning for help.

On January 07, 1874 the Governor offered a reward of $100 each, for the capture of three of the Horrell brothers, Zachariah Crumpton, and Jerry Scott. Sheriff Alexander Mills assembled a large posse for the purpose of arresting the Horrells. Upon arriving at the Horrell ranchito, they had discovered that it had already been abandoned.

The Horrells moved most of their livestock south near Missouri Bottom where they eventually sold out to Charles Miller. By January 30th they opted to return upriver, intent on settling the score with Murphy, Dolan, Patrón, Juan Gonzáles and several others they had taken exception to.

Their plans were deterred after they spoke with Robert Casey who had persuaded them to leave the area. The Horrells thus split into two groups. As the Horrells left Lincoln County, they continued to subject its citizens to random acts of senseless violence, intimidation, and murder. One Horrell associate, Edward "Little" Hart murdered Deputy Sheriff Joseph Haskins at Picacho, New Mexico because he was married to a Hispanic woman. Upon coming across five Nuevo Mexicano freighters that were bringing corn to John Chisum's rancho, the Horrells indiscriminately killed them all, with no empathy or regard for human life. Thus the Horrells left Lincoln County in a blaze of violence.

The Black Smallpox of 1877

In 1877 an epidemic of the black smallpox had spread throughout the valley, killing numerous people, and permanently disabling many more. Most of those who died were either infants or the elderly.[5] Many of the religious people had interpreted the illness as a penance that was bestowed upon the people of the valley by God. Lawlessness was running rampant throughout the valley, and acts of theft and murder were being committed.

Many of the people in the region were deeply religious and very superstitious. Those that subscribed into the paranoia had felt that if someone was inflicted with the disease, either they or someone in their family was not living a righteous life. Communities were torn apart as people allowed their fear to overcome their sense of rationality. Those families that had infected members were often times isolated from the rest of the community. Many people reinvigorated their passion for their faith in the hope that they and their loved ones would be spared God's wrath. Francisco's family had escaped the tragedies of the outbreak that had befallen so many families in the area.

The Regulators

Francisco had ridden with the Regulators from time to time. In one such instance, a posse assembled by a member of the Murphy and Dolan faction had attempted to apprehend William H. Bonney, and those that rode with him. There was a fandango being held in El Berendo, and several of the Regulators were in attendance. Of those who were in attendance were; Bonney, José Chávez y Chávez, Fernando Herrera, Francisco Sánchez, Jesús Saíz, Candelario Hidalgo, Francisco Trujillo, Juan de Dios Trujillo, Charles Bowdre, John Middleton, Jim French, and several others. They had been forewarned that the Murphy and Dolan's posse was looking for them, and that it would be prudent for them to make their escape, or risk being caught.

The men agreed and rode westward towards the Sierra Capitán. Once arriving at Agua Negra, the men dismounted and rested. The men were all sitting around the fire discussing what they were going to do. McSween had pleaded with some of the men a day earlier, at South Spring, to accompany him back to Lincoln. McSween was fearful that some of Murphy and Dolan's men would apprehend him and that he would surely be hung.

Bonney had suggested that the men should draw to see who would accompany McSween to Lincoln. After each man took their draw, the task fell upon Charles Bowdre, Jim French, and John Middleton. After it was decided who would accompany McSween, everybody in the group went to their respective homes. Francisco Sánchez however had some business to attend to in Lincoln the following day, so he opted to head over to Lincoln for the evening.

At about eleven o'clock that next morning, Francisco was at the general store in Lincoln when Bonney and some of his men ambushed and gunned down Sheriff Brady.[6] Francisco had heard the shots and he quickly sought cover once he realized there was a gun battle raging in town. He wasn't quite sure what was going on, but he had known that Bonney and some of his men were somewhere in town. He peered out the window, but couldn't see anything, so he kept his head down until the gunshots ceased.

The Lincoln County War had erupted and violence and thievery had exploded to all parts of the county. The newly appointed sheriff George Pippin deputized the notorious outlaw John Kinney, and his gang of hired outlaws who had victimized the citizens of Lincoln County on several occasions. A campaign of terror was waged against all of the McSween sympathizers within the community. Francisco had enough of the barbaric manner in which Dolan's henchmen had ransacked La Plaza de San Patricio, and threatened the lives of its citizens.

A *junta* (meeting) was called in La Plaza de San Patricio, at the home of Juan de Dios Trujillo, and many of the able bodied men had chosen to stand up and fight against the Dolan faction. Francisco had become a staunch supporter of the cause. He offered to carry arms against those who brought such misery to his home, and those of his neighbors. Thus Francisco had come to participate in "The Five Days Battle", also known as the "Big Killing". Although he had never gained any notoriety for his participation in the Lincoln County War, he did have a small part in it.

With the Lincoln County War coming to an end, after the death of Alexander McSween, the lawlessness within the county persisted. Capitán Juan B. Patrón had come knocking on Francisco's door, with the hope that he could recruit him into the Lincoln County Mounted Riflemen. Francisco didn't deliberate the thought much, he was a man who wanted peace, and he diligently offered his services, and his guns, in an attempt to bring harmony back to the Río Ruidoso. Francisco was hell bent on wanting to bring those outlaws who terrorized his community to justice.

After order was finally restored to the region, Francisco returned to his life as a farmer and a gambler. Concepción had died sometime before 1910 while living with her grandson, Patricio Sánchez. She was buried in an unmarked grave in the cemetery of La Capilla de San Patricio. Francisco then married a twenty-year-old woman whose name was Virginia Padilla on November 16, 1910. Francisco and Virginia had three children, two sons and a daughter. These children were never really accepted into the family by their preceding brothers and sisters. Rather they were alienated from the rest of the family.

Eventually he either sold or gave most of his land holdings in San Patricio to his children. Most of Francisco's children remained in San Patricio where many of their descendants still live. He opted to trade some of his land in San Patricio for some land owned by Cosmé Sedillo en El Berendo.

Later in life Francisco lost his eyesight and became bedridden with a severe illness. He could often be found sleeping in his son Davíd's living room. Thus, he lived the rest of his days with his son Davíd until his death. He died a poor man in Roswell, and was buried in a cemetery just north of present day Roswell. His grave was unmarked, but it had a cast iron fence situated around it. One of Francisco's sons, Conrado Sánchez, confirmed that the cast iron fence marked his father's final resting spot. Eventually, the cast iron fence was taken from the grave and now all that remains is a cemetary filled with weeds and rocks between two roads.

Juan Sánchez

Juan Sánchez, christened Juan Rafael Sánchez was born in 1855 in Torreón, Territory of New México. His parents were Mauricio de la Trinidad Sánches and Jesúsita Gonzáles de Sánches. He often went by the nickname Juanguerro during the days when he allegedly rode with the Regulators. Juan married Evarista Gonzáles on May 09, 1877 in Tularoso.

Trouble in Tularoso[7]

Mauricio's entrepreneurial nature had compelled him to open livery stables in the small villa of Tularoso, which was about forty miles southwest of his seasonal home in Las Angosturas. Both of his sons, José Antonio, and Juan were living, and had been married in Tularoso by 1877. José Antonio, known as Antonio was the oldest son in the family, he was 32 years of age. Juan was about 21 years of age.

The two brothers oversaw the operations of the stables for most of the year. Mauricio and his family would come down from Las Angosturas for months at a time to help oversee its operations. It was speculated that the Sánchez brothers had also worked with Patrick "Pat" Coghlan who was referred to as the "King of Tularoso". Family legend claimed that Juan had ridden with Billy the Kid on several occasions.

Another family legend has it that Mauricio had come from Las Angosturas to oversee the operations of the livery stables. He was inside the adobé, seeking refuge from working under the intense heat of the sun. His youngest daughter Amada was quietly playing outside. Amada noticed a strange man discretely casing the premise, attempting to see if there was anybody present. He didn't notice the youngster and after he was satisfied that there was nobody around, he approached one of the stables. He proceeded to lead one of the horses out of the stable.

Amada quietly, but quickly made her way to the adobé where she told her father what she had just witnessed. Mauricio hurriedly and with angry feet, stomped out of the door and confronted the thief. He shouted out vulgarities in Spanish, startling the stranger who quickly drew his gun and intently aimed the gun at Mauricio's chest. Cold stares were exchanged between the two men as an eerie silence filled the unbearably hot air.

While the would-be-thief contemplated his next move, Juan snuck up from behind him and disarmed the unsuspecting man by pistol-whipping the assailant's arm. The gun fell harmlessly to the ground. Juan then rose his own pistol, aimed it at the back of the stranger's neck, and without hesitation he pulled the trigger. In an instant, as the shot echoed in the distance, the thief instinctively grabbed for his neck as he fell dead to the ground.

Juan looked at his father, emotionless and unfazed at what he had just done. Mauricio didn't condemn his son's actions, because more than likely, his son had just saved his life. Juan then told his father, that maybe it was best that he left, until after the law had come to investigate, and the situation was settled. As it turns out, the man that Juan had killed was James "Jim" B. Reese, a member of the Dolan Faction.

Trouble on the Río Hondo[8]

Juan had eluded the law for several years since the killing at his father's livery stable, by moving around the region, and never staying in one place for too long a time. Juan was staying with his brother-in-law Pablo Chávez who was married to his sister Amada. Juan and Amada's mother Jesúsita was also living in the Chávez house, which was about ½ mile east of La Junta.

Juan was inside of the house, when he and several others noticed a posse riding up to the house. As the men approached closer, they recognized one of the men as Deputy José Gonzáles. The deputy and his men were looking for Juan, because he had been working for Patrick Coghlan, who had an ongoing dispute with Albert Fountain, a lawyer who was well respected within the Spanish-speaking community. Fountain and his nine-year-old son Henry had mysteriously disappeared on January 31, 1896. The deputy and the rest of the posse were looking for answers, fearing that foul play was the reason for their disappearance.

Juan turned to his family members and professed, "Those men are looking for me." Juan's mother looked at her son and told him that he should run out the back door, and hide in the cornfield, or run to the river, and that she or the others would take food to him later in the night. Juan rejected his mother's pleas, stating that he was tired of living life on the run. He knelt before his mother and asked for her blessing because he was going before the men that were looking for him.

After his blessing, Juan gathered his rifle in one hand, and his pistol in the other. He confidently and courageously walked out the door to face the posse. Jesúsita went into her room, and she came out with a rifle. She sat by the window and watched her son walk towards Deputy Gonzáles. As her son approached the deputy she trained the rifle at his chest.

As Juan stood before the deputy, who was still mounted on his horse, he spoke out for all to hear, "Who are you looking for?"

Gonzáles looked at Juan, who had his weapons in hand, and then he looked towards the house and he could make out Jesúsita at the window, with a rifle aimed at him. There was a momentary silence before the deputy answered, "We're looking for Juan Sánchez."

Juan defiantly retorted, "I'm Juan Sánchez."

The deputy looked into Juan's eyes, and paused for a moment. "No, you're not the Juan Sánchez we're looking for," Gonzáles yelled out for all the posse men to hear. The deputy then turned his horse around and left Pablo Chávez's property, with his posse in tow.

After the posse had left, Juan took a deep breath and turned back towards the house. He walked into the house and was greeted with playful bantering. Juan looked at his mother and said, "See mamá, if I hadn't come out, I would have had to keep hiding for the rest of my life."

Jesúsita held her arms out and embraced and kissed her son, and whispered into his ear, "Si mi hijo, Dios siempre estaba contigo." (Yes, my son, God has always been with you.)

Jesúsita Amada Sánchez de Chávez

(Top row from left to right): Lilia Blea, Armalinda, Unknown, Paula Blea,
Ermando Chávez, John Blea, (Bottom row from left to right): Amy Blea, (Sitting)
Pablo Chávez, **Jesúsita Amada Sánchez de Chávez**, Homer Blea.

Amada Sánchez, christened Jesúsita Amada Sánchez was born on December 02, 1870 in La Plaza de San José, Territory of New México. She was the youngest child of Mauricio de la Trinidad Sánches and María Candida de Jesús Gonzáles de Sánchez. Shortly after her birth, her parents, and siblings all migrated to the Río Ruidoso valley, near the farming community of Las Angosturas.

Amada had fallen in love, and married a gentleman by the name of Pablo Chávez, on July 20, 1883 in Las Angosturas. With Amada being so young, both her parents had to approve of her marriage. The two were married, and had their baile at her father's adobé situated a few hundred feet from the Río Ruidoso in an area now known as Fox Cave located east of Ruidoso Downs.

Pablo Chávez[9]
José Chávez

Family legend was that Pablo's father; José Chávez's real name was actually Joseph Lamar. Joseph's father was thought to have originally come from the east. Joseph's father was a freighter who traveled from Los Lunas to Chihuahua, La República de México. When Joseph's father went on his freight trips, he would leave his son with one of the Chávez families in Los Lunas.

On one such trip, Joseph's father failed to return from Chihuahua. The Chávez's had feared the worst, suspecting that their friend had met his death at the hands of a band of Apachés, or ruthless outlaws. The Chávez family adopted young Joseph into their family, and he became known as José Chávez.

José had married a woman by the name of Avrora Sánchez. They had two known children, both of whom were sons, Cleto and Desiderio. José Chávez eventually migrated to Torreón where he lived for a short period of time. While in Torreón, Avrora had succumbed to illness, and she died. José and his children then migrated from Torreón to Rancho Torres on the Río Bonito. He farmed some land for about two years before he finally migrated to La Plaza de San Patricio. He bought some land from

Joe Kline. This transaction however was not deemed legal, so José lost the land, and he was forced to move to La Junta, where he squatted on some land. José later married María Francisca Luna.

José had owned several Arabian horses, which he was very fond of. On September 28, 1878 tragedy had struck the family as several members of The Rustlers murdered two of the children, Cleto and Desiderio, after they refused to let the outlaws steal their father's prized horses. After the two boys were killed, the outlaws took their horses and rode off.

Pablo Chávez

Pablo Chávez was born sometime in 1857. It is believed that he may have been born somewhere near Los Lunas, Territory of New México. Pablo's parents were José Chávez and Avrora Sánchez.[10] Shortly after marrying Amada Sánchez, he and his wife moved to La Junta to live on his father's farm. Over the years, Pablo Chávez and his sons had applied for several homesteads, amassing over 320 acres of prime farmland along the Río Hondo.

Every fall during the harvest Amada's brother, Francisco Sánchez, would come from El Berendo to help out the family. Francisco would often spend the winter in La Junta before he returned to El Berendo in the spring. Ermando, who was Pablo's son, recalls that there were no trees between his parent's house and the community of Analla. The entire family would often keep a watchful eye for their Tío Francisco. Every time they would see someone coming around the bend they would drop what they were doing, in anticipation of meeting their tío. When he finally arrived, the whole family rejoiced that tío was with them again.

Pablo and Amada had lost their land, when one of their sons had mortgaged the property to a merchant from Capitán. The son had forged his parent's signatures and borrowed $5,000 against the land. The merchant was fully aware that the signatures were forged but he continued with the transaction. A few months later, when the loan was not paid, the merchant sent a collector, whose last name was Freeman, to collect on the loan. Both Pablo and Amada had no idea what their son had done, and they didn't have the money to pay off the debt.

The merchant offered Pablo and Amada a deal. If they both would sign a bill of sale to him, he would not have their son sent to prison on the charge of forgery. Feeling obligated to keep their son out of prison they both signed the bill of sale. Shortly thereafter Pablo, Amada, and their family had moved off the farm and returned to José Chávez's farm. A few years later, the merchant had died of a stroke and he was found face first in a sack of rice.[11]

Estolano Sánchez

Estolano Sánchez was born in about 1847 in Torreón, Nuevo México, La República de México. He was the second oldest son of Mauricio de la Trinidad Sánches and María Candida de Jesús Gonzáles. He married Cornelia Pacheco on July 21, 1871 in La Placita del Río Bonito, Territory of New México. Cornelia was a beautiful yet rugged looking woman. She had deep blue eyes and a fair complexion. She was the daughter of Francisco Pacheco and "Nana" Romula Saavdera who was of Apache or Navajo ancestry.

Cornelia Pacheco wife of Estolano Sánchez. (Ernest Sanchez collection)

"Nana" Romula Savedra-Pacheco. Died 1912 at 110 years of age. This photograph was reproduced through the courtesy of Abraham P. Sanchez who had an old reproduction from the original copper plate. Taken sometime between 1870-1880 in Lincoln, N.M. (Courtesy of George Sanchez)

Eventually he and his wife moved to La Junta, Territory of New México where he built an L-shaped adobé. All of the bedrooms were constructed on the elongated portion of the house. The room jutting out from the main living space was a storage room, where all of the children's beds were kept. The children would sleep in the storage room rather than the bedrooms because their mother reserved the bedrooms for her guests. Cornelia always had guests over at the house, whether it was her own grown children, her grandchildren, siblings or friends. She was very accommodating, compassionate and a gracious host.

Like his father before him and several of his siblings, Estolano made a living as a sheep rancher. His chosen trade meant that he lead a predominantly nomadic life. He and usually his oldest sons never stayed in one particular area for too long a period of time. Although most of his family lived in La Junta, he seldom saw them while he was grazing his sheep.

Estolano was recruited by Juan B. Patrón to serve as a Lincoln County Mounted Rifleman. He also rode alongside the Regulators and participated in the Five Days battle during the Lincoln County War. That being said, like many other Nuevo Mexicanos, he seldom uttered a word concerning the matter. The events of the Lincoln County War were best left unspoken.

By 1900 he and most of his family were living in Rebentón, Territory of New México. By this time he had retired from ranching opting to act as an owner while his sons took over the family business. He died on June 20, 1907 in San Patricio, Territory of New México. His estate included 3,039 head of sheep and 13,080 pounds of wool.

Felipé E. Sánchez

Front row from left to right: Cornelia Sánchez, Paublita Sánchez, Sipio Sánchez. –
Middle row and sitting from left to right: Candelaria Padilla de Sánchez, Felipé E. Sánchez. –
Back row: Antonio Sánchez. (White Oaks NM, ~1903) Felipé Sánchez was the son of
Estolano Sánchez and Cornelia Pacheco de Sánchez. Candelaria Padilla was the daughter
of Andalesio Padilla and Paublita Mariño de Padilla. (Courtesy of George Sanchez)

Felipe Sanchez with horsemen (Courtesy of George Sanchez)

Felipé E. Sánchez was born on January 20, 1874 near La Placita del Río Bonito, Territory of New México. His parents were Estolano Sánchez and Cornelia Pacheco. He married Candelaria Padilla the daughter of Andalesio Padilla and Paublita Marino. The Padilla family migrated from Los Padillas near Albuquerque to Three Rivers. Candelaria was born in February 1879 in Three Rivers. They had the following children; Antonio Sanchez, Paublita Sanchez, Sipo Sanchez, Cornelia Sanchez, Emilano Sanchez, Abran Sanchez, Renaldo Sanchez, Cledonia Sanchez, Benito Sanchez, Onecimo Sanchez.

Felipe died January 15, 1954 and Candelaria on March 13, 1956. They are both buried in Tularosa, New Mexico.

Antonio Sanchez

Antonio Sanchez
(Courtesy of Sam Sanchez)

    Antonio Sanchez was born May 17, 1897 in Tres Ritos. He married Martina Salsberry who died in childbirth with their first child. He later married Juanita Alvarado and had eleven children. They were Paublina, Cecilia, Elisa, Luisa, Tony, Efrin, Samuel, Lucila, David, Rufina, Benjamin and had two other children out of wedlock Eileen and Reynel Martinez.

Back row left to right: Senaida Sánchez, Lupita Sánchez, María de Jesús (Jesúsita) Sánchez, Manuel Sánchez, Josefa (Jennie) Gill de Sánchez who is holding her daughter, Virginia Sánchez, Solomon Sánchez, Danois Sánchez. -Sitting: Telesfora Mirabal de Gonzáles, Prospero Gonzáles. -Front row left to right: Porfirio Gonzáles, Rubén Gonzales, María Arcenia Gonzáles. (San Patricio NM, Taken about 1903) These children of Sánchez were the children of Antonio Sánchez and Telesfora Mirabal and they were the grandchildren of Mauricio de la Trinidad Sánches and María Candida de Jesús Gonzáles de Sánches.

Chapter Six:
La Vida Díara (Daily Life)

Chosas, Jacales y Adobé

Many single American émigré and foreign immigrant men had found companionship and marriage amongst the Spanish-speaking women. In many such instances the men had adopted the language, culture and religion of their wives, friends and acquaintances. Some raised their children to speak only Spanish, and attend Catholic churches. In some instances, they changed the pronunciation and spelling of their names to reflect their acceptance of the predominant language. The name Warner was known as Juana or Guana. The name Salsberry was known as Solsberéte. The name Randolph was known as Randolfo.

Many of the first settlers initially claimed their lands under squatters' rights. Since there were no building materials readily available, and for lack of money, many of the people became resourceful by using what the land had provided. Many of them simply dug a hollowed hole into the side of a hill and fashioned a rudimentary roof out of sticks, mud and straw. The one room dugout was very modest, being just big enough for two people to live in it. This type of dwelling was called a *chosa*.

Usually after building a chosa, the family would take the task of building a *jacal*. A sturdy frame for the jacal would be anchored by large posts that were placed in each respective corner of the dwelling. The anchors would be set about three feet into the ground. Eight-foot long posts made of branches would be gathered from *piñon* and *sabino* (juniper) trees. The posts measured anywhere from four to six inches in diameter. The tops of the posts would be shaved until there was a dull point, which had the appearance of a spear. The posts were then placed within the ground, with the sharpened edges facing up, so that they all lined up together. About every three to four feet, a studier post about one foot in diameter would be planted into the ground. Sometimes thin rope or wire was used to keep the posts together for additional support. This would serve as the framing of the outside wall of the jacal.

A post, usually about one foot in diameter, would have a two-inch deep triangular tract cut along its entire length. This post would then be placed upon the sharpened points of the sticks. The posts were long enough that they would stick out about one foot on either side of the walls. This served as a support to keep the wall from toppling over. After the support beams were in place, the roof would be set in place. The roof consisted of long posts of varying diameters.

After the shell of the jacal was constructed, mud would be placed over the posts. This served to fill in any of the gaps between the posts. The mud was often mixed with straw, to help create a stronger bond. After the first coat of mud had dried, several other coats would be applied. This process was done several times until the walls were adequately insulated. After the numerous layers of mud had dried on the roof, about one foot of dirt would be spread out to help soak up any precipitation.

The window did not have any glass therefore its purpose was to let the air circulate within the jacal, and to allow the occupants to see outside. A doorframe would be constructed about one foot off the ground. This served three purposes the first was to help keep floodwaters from entering the jacal. The second was to help discourage the snakes and rodents from coming in. The third was to help keep small, crawling infants from leaving the jacal. The door was constructed from wood planks and was hinged to the doorframe with leather straps. The flooring was usually made of dirt. Each day, the floor would be sprinkled with water to prevent it from cracking and to lessen the effects of dust.

After becoming more established, almost every family built a modest two-room *adobé*. The adobé bricks were made with a mixture of mud and straw. The mud was packed into rectangular molds and left out in the sun to dry. Each dried brick would weigh about twenty-five pounds, and would be as solid as a rock. Once dry, the bricks were used to construct the walls of the house. The bricks were placed such that they overlapped one another for greater stability. When the house's walls were completed a mixture of mud and straw was plastered to the outdoor walls. The mud served as a weathering buffer from the harsh elements. Whenever it was needed, the outside stucco had to be reapplied to keep the adobé from weathering down.

To create a smoother indoor wall surface, gypsum was ground into a fine powder and water was later added to create a thick paste. This paste was applied with sheepskin to the indoor walls to enhance the adobé's weatherproofing. Several layers would be applied to achieve the desired effect. The ceiling was built from wood planks and the gabled roof was usually constructed from corrugated metal or wood. Rather than a dirt floor, most adobés had wood plank floors, built about one or two feet off the ground. The windows were made of glass and the wood doors were factory built with metal hinges. The crawlspace under the floor was often used to store perishables.

The average family consisted of about seven to ten family members. The living arrangements would require a great deal of resourcefulness. The sons would sleep in a barn, a corral, or a storage room if available. The daughters would usually sleep in the house. Usually the barns would have a bunkhouse, where several bed slots would be provided for the children. In some instances, the children would also sleep up in the attic of the adobé.

After building a dwelling, the settlers focused their attention on improving the land in which they had settled. The first order of business was to clear the land of brush and trees. Their next task was to clear the topsoil of large rocks, and to till the dirt until it was sufficiently soft enough to take a seed, or sapling.

There was no running water in the chosas, jacales, and adobés, therefore, all of the water had to be carried in buckets for bathing, laundering, cooking, and cleaning dishes. Also because of a lack of plumbing an outhouse was usually built about one hundred yards from the house. There were four widely accepted methods of gathering water.

The first was to get the water directly from the river. Due to the threat of flash flooding, the adobés had to be built far enough from the river to ensure one's safety. Gathering water in this manner was inefficient and exhausting, yet many families did it this way. The second was to gather the water from an acequia. This was safe and efficient and thus had become a common method of determining where one should build their adobé. The third was to dig a well in close proximity to the house. During the 1850's the underground water table was rather high so a family could expect to dig about 15' to 25' before hitting water. The fourth was to gather rainwater in a cisterna.

Many of the people had to be resourceful, and often made everything that they used. There was no electricity and the primary source of light came from a wood stove, candles, or laterns. Families made their own candles from tallow, and animal fat. Soap was also made from tallow and bones. They boiled the bones until they dissolved into the water, and they used this to keep the soap together. Meat came from their own livestock and their vegetables and fruit came from their own gardens and small orchards.

Acequias y Agua (Ditches and Water): The Lifeblood of the Community

For generations of Nuevo Mexicanos, water has always been the lifeblood of the community. Acequias have also played a vital role in the distribution of water to all of the ranchitos within the community. Water was the primary reason that several communities were able to flourish within the Rio Ruidoso, Rio Bonito, and Rio Hondo valleys. Without a sustainable water source, many foregone communities were eventually abandoned.

Many of the laws enacted into legislation since 1851 by the New Mexico territorial government were adopted from the acequia laws, which had been in effect by the Españoles for hundreds of years.[1] The laws enabled property owners, also known as members, to obtain "ditch rights", and to govern over those rights in accordance with the law.

Organizational structure and delegation of duties

If three or more members shared a common acequia, they had the ability to form an association. Every year, on the first Monday of December, members of the acequia association would elect three commissioners and a mayordomo. Only those members who were current with the association's ditch dues were able to vote, those who were delinquent at the time of the vote were exempted from voting. Each member's vote was proportional to the amount of "water rights" owned.[2] Each member had the right to vote by proxy. The elected officers would serve their respective terms on the first Monday of January.

If a special election was held, that did not coincide with the first Monday of December, and a period of five days' notice must be given to the association members. No fewer than six notices were posted along the ditch. For many associations, it was easier to satisfy the notification requirement by posting the intent to call a special election in the local newspaper.

Among the commissioners the three would decide upon who would act as the chairman, the secretary, and the treasurer. After the election of all the officers, the commissioners were tasked with setting a bond limit for the mayordomo and the treasurer. The bond was needed in order to hold both the mayordomo and treasurer accountable for the collection of funds, expenditures of those funds, and performing their obligations to the association.

The commissioners oversaw and managed the overall operation of their association's acequia. They adopted by-laws, in accordance with state laws, which were passed on to all of their members. They imposed and collected dues, which were used to fund any expenditure to the irrigation system. They reviewed and approved all expenditures related to the upkeep of the acequia. They ensured that the flow of water was not impeded by repairing any damages or removing any obstructions.

The mayordomo served to manage the acequia under the direction of the commissioners. His primary responsibility was to regulate the flow of water to each respective member of the association in proportion of their allotted water rights. Usually the logistics of who received what and when was dictated by a schedule of watering that made it easier to manage. This helped diffuse any minor disputes that may have arisen between members because the responsibility of water usage rested solely on the mayordomo. He had the authority to prosecute any member that obstructed the flow of water, or was caught illegally diverting water from the acequia.

It was the mayordomo's responsibility to ensure that all of the projects approved by the commissioners were completed in a timely manner. He was responsible for managing the labor needed to complete the work on the acequia. He had the authority to collect monies from members in lieu of *trabajo* (working on the acequia). He also had the authority to fine and collect from those members who refused his request to work on the acequia.

The mayordomo had the right to collect from the members, all costs associated with large project expenditures in proportion to their water rights. Thus those members with more water rights incurred a greater expense of the project than those members with less water rights. If a member failed to pay his portion of the costs of the project, the mayordomo had the right to refuse that member the use of the water until the monies were collected.

The mayordomo was required to create at least two reports a year detailing the monies he had collected, the costs associated with all projects, and any other relevant information as requested by the commissioners. The commissioners in turn would review the reports and either approved or rejected them. The reports would then be filed and kept for a state approved audit.

The treasurer ensured the accountability of all collections and distributions of monies. He would be responsible for the safeguard of all monies and would serve to help control costs. The secretary ensured that the minutes for all meetings were properly recorded and filed. He was also tasked with keeping on file, all paperwork that could be used during a state audit.

It was the responsibility of the association members to provide the labor required for the annual maintenance, improvements, or any other major repairs of the acequia. The annual maintenance usually entailed ensuring an unobstructed flow of water, which dictated cleaning up the ditch of debris and mud. Association members were usually responsible for cleaning up the section of the acequia that passed through their own property. Major infrastructure improvements consisted of building dams, bridges, and increasing water flow capacity. Major repairs were usually evident after a catastrophic flood had made the acequia unusable.

State law indicated that if any property owner did not use their water rights for a period of four consecutive years, they would forfeit or "lose" those rights for future use. At that point, the State Engineer had to submit in writing that failure to use one's water rights within the next year would result in losing those rights. The property owner was protected from losing their water rights only if circumstances beyond their control prohibited the use of water. Such circumstances could be a prolonged drought or a catastrophic flood.

Water rights could be sold, leased or transferred to another property as long as they did not have any adverse effects to the water rights of other users. If the property owner wanted to sell their property's water rights they had to file a form for "Change of Ownership of Water Right" with the office of the State Engineer. The form would include a description of the property, the amount of water rights, the priority date of those water rights, and the names of those who committed to sell and those who committed to buy.

In the event that a property owner wanted to transfer their water rights to another property they had to file an application to the office of the State Engineer. A notice of the transfer had to be published in the local newspaper once a week for three consecutive weeks. The office of the State Engineer had to receive any objections or protests against the application no later than ten days after the last week of the publication. The State Engineer had the authority to approve or disapprove of the application. If all parties interested were not satisfied with the State Engineers decision, they had the option to appeal to the District Court. Once the water rights had been transferred, the use of irrigation on the old property was not allowed.

A property owner could lease all or part of their water rights for a period no greater than ten years. During the lease, the property owner had to reduce the amount of water they could use by the amount that was being leased. The lease could become effective for immediate or future uses, but couldn't be accumulated or incrementally increased in a manner that would cause adverse effects on the water rights of the other property owners. The individual, municipality, or business entity had to file an application with the office of the State Engineer. The notice of the lease had to be published in the local newspaper once a week for three consecutive weeks. Any objections or protests had to be filed within ten days after the last week of the publication.

Building the Acequia infrastructure

Many of the property owners with water rights had built a series of rudimentary dams that extended the length of the Río Bonito, the Río Hondo, and the Río Ruidoso. The dams were built about every two to three miles apart starting in Ruidoso, going through Hondo, Picacho and on to La Plaza de San José. Many of the dams were constructed from *ramas* (large tree branches), *jarrales* (smaller sticks), *tierra* (clay and dirt), and *piedras* (large and medium-sized rocks). In other parts of the river where the banks were shallow, the ditches extended off directly from the river without the use of a dam.

Each acequia was distinguished by its own name, which usually took the name of the property owner for whom it was originally constructed. Some examples of the names are; Acequia de Leopoldo Gonzáles dating back to 1865, Acequia de Pablo Chávez dating back to 1866, Acequia de Francisco Sánchez dating back to 1866, Acequia de las Chosas (North, Middle, and South) all are dating back to 1867, Acequia de Fernando Herrera dating back to 1868.[3] The oldest known acequias that were constructed in the region were in La Plaza del Rio Bonito. They were named Acequia de la Providencia, the H. Fritz Spring, and the E. Fritz Spring; all are dating back to 1853.[4]

Water as a source of conflict

Being that water was a very scarce resource, it had often become a matter of contention and ongoing conflict. In most cases concerning water rights, they would be solved through litigation. In a minority of the conflicts the nature of the dispute took a more serious and sometimes violent nature such as the Tularoso Ditch War.

The Tularoso Ditch War had strong, racially motivated overtones that pitted Hispanos from the village of Tularoso against the Anglo farmers that irrigated their lands from the Rio Tularoso. The farmers, most of who had settled around Blazer's Mill had constructed a dam that nearly cut off the flow of water from reaching Tularoso. Fed up with the farmer's unwillingness to let more of the water down the river, a contingent of angry Tularoso vigilantes ascended upon the dam in May of 1873 and destroyed the dam. Defiantly the farmers reconstructed the dam. The vigilantes destroyed the dam a second time.

Lawrence Murphy, Dr. Joseph Hoy Blazer, and several other farmers petitioned the U.S. military at Fort Stanton for assistance. Captain Chambers McKibben sent one of his lieutenants and five cavalrymen to quell the uprising. En route the soldiers encountered armed vigilantes and a firefight ensued. One of the vigilant men was killed. The soldiers were forced to retreat to Blazer's Mill though, for lack of better numbers, where they were joined by several of the farmers. The Tularoso vigilantes' continued attack was cut short though as Captain McKibben and more cavalry drove them back to the village. The threat of continued violence was abated as Captain McKibben threatened to destroy the town if hostilities did not cease.

A Dialect of the Spoken Language

Most schools that teach the Spanish language throughout the western hemisphere, instruct their students in the widely spoken Castellano (Castilian) dialect. The original dialect of Spanish spoken in Lincoln County and many other parts of Nuevo México and the rural areas of northern México was, and still is slightly different. Much of what made Nuevo México so unique linguistically was that it had become isolated from Spanish and later Mexican influences for such a long period of time that it was able to retain the original archaic Spanish dialect, as it was spoken hundreds of years ago.

Many of the non-traditional Spanish words that New Mexicans used (and still are using) had been adopted from some of the Native Americans that had lived amongst them. Other words that came into use were Spanish slang that was regionally unique. Still other words were a combination of English and Spanish more commonly known today as Spanglish.

The use of –ado is very familiar to today's Spanish speakers. However in many parts of New México and northern México, the –ado is replaced with –ao (as in how). For example: lado would be spoken as lao, mojado would be spoken as mojao, embrujado would be spoken as embrujao, and borrachado would be spoken as borrachao. The use of the word *para* is also slightly different in that it is abbreviated. Instead it would be spoken as pa'. When pa' is used with el it becomes pal'

Often times, words would be condensed as such that they would be almost unrecognizable to today's common Spanish speaker. For example one that would say, *"Más para alla, para el otro lado"* (More over there, on the other side) would be spoken as *"Más paya, pa'lotro lao"*. *"Voy para el otro lado"* (I'm going to the other side) would be spoken as *"Voy pa'lotro lao."* Another example would be *"Comé y Callate"* ("Eat and be quiet") would be spoken as *"Comécalla"*.

Some of the words used may be a derivative of a mispronunciation. For example: *estomago* (stomach) would be spoken as *estogamo*. The usage of interchangeable spellings may also attribute to a difference in language, which may sound the same. For example: Cháves could also be spoken as Chábes, Feliz could be spoken as Felix, or Felis, Baca could be spoken as Vaca, Trujillo could be spoken as Truxio or Trujio, Sánchez could be spoken as Sánches, Sedillo could be spoken as Sedio or Cedillo, and so on.

There are many words in the New Mexican Spanish dialect, which may be spoken differently than the more common use of Castellano. To go through an analysis of the similarities and differences would be an entirely different study. The rest of the language is basically the same as in many of the other parts of the Spanish-speaking world.

La Fé (The Faith)

Religion Before the Clergymen Arrived

Los Hermanos Penitentes had filled a large spiritual void during the early years of settlement within the region. They had built their morada just north of La Placita del Río Bonito. The morada had been built close to La Placita because it stood at the center of all the outlying communities. Los Penitentes had members from as far north as Rebentón, as far south as La Plaza de Picacho, as far west as Ruidoso, and as far east as the communities of the Sierra Capitán. Los Penitentes had remained the sole organized religious institution for many years.

As a result of their isolation, most people from Nuevo México had to improvise when it came to practicing their catholic faith. Almost every family had built a *santuario* (small family shrine) within the house, or in close proximity to the house. Since many of the people had a limited means of income, they often hand carved, out of wood, their *bultos* (representations of saints) that would often adorn their santuario. They also painted pictures of saints, the Holy Trinity, and Jesus on wood placards, which were known as *retablos*.

Every santuario had *La Santa Cruz* (The Holy Cross), *santitos* (the same as bultos), retablos, *oraciónes* (prayer books), *rosarios* (rosaries), and *velas* (candles). *La Biblia* (the Bible) would prominently be shown for all to see. If a family would have the fortune of having their Biblia or Santa Cruz blessed by a priest, it would be the talk of the community.

Religious heirlooms were the most prized possessions within the family. Often times, religious family heirlooms would be passed down from one generation to the next. The most sought after heirlooms would be La Biblia, and La Santa Cruz. Each son or daughter would receive a piece of the santuario to add to their own, upon the death of one or both of their parents.

There was never the question of whether the people in the community had practiced their faith as opposed to whether they were living their faith. Practicing ones' faith implied that they went through the motions of being a good Catholic. They went to church consistently. They did good deeds from time to time. They would often pray.

Living one's faith implied that God was the binding force that kept family, friends, and the whole community together. Their faith in God was unwavering and interwoven in everything that they had done. Whether it was going on a long trip to a relatives' house, tilling ones' farm, the weather, disease, or any multitude of events, God had a hand in everything that happened. So as not to offend God, they offered praise in so many different ways.

Many individuals offered their hospitality freely and willingly even though they were poverty stricken, and more than likely would have been heavily burdened for their acts of compassion. They would offer food and lodging for those in need, simply because it was the Christian thing to do.

When a storm was coming in over the mountains, the mother of the household would grab a pinch of salt and walk to the doorway and make the sign of the cross as she threw the salt into the air. This gesture was meant to safeguard the house and its occupants from any harm that could be brought upon them from flash floods, heavy winds, or hailstones.

The manner in which they spoke to one another was also evidence of their undying devotion to their faith. It was common to hear a greeting of, *"Buenos días le de Dios."* If someone was leaving they were sent on their way with, *"Vaya con Dios!"* (Go with God) or *"Qué Dios lo protega."* (So that God will protect you) or *"Qué Dios lo ayude"* (So that God will help you). If someone was going to bed one would say, *"Dios te bendiga"* (God bless you). If someone was talking about the plans they had for the next day, or sometime in the near future they would say, *"Si Dios quiere"* (If God wants). If someone had finished work for the day, or reached a goal they had set for themselves they would thank God by saying, *"Gracias a Dios."*

There is a little story that has been told concerning the women when they prayed at night before going to bed. The women would end their prayers with, *"Con Dios me acuesto, con Dios me levanto"* (With God I go to bed, with God I get up). Upon finishing her prayers, the wife would catch a glimpse at her husband and she would see him with a huge grin on his face because he jokingly teased that his wife had referred to him as a God. Then she would respond, *"¡Ay qué chivo, no lo pienses!"* (What a scoundrel, don't even think about it!")

Before the first chapel was built, people would often show their worship of God by holding a devotional. This was their personal one-on-one time with the Lord and they could do it at any point of the day, or night. They did this in lieu of going to see a priest. Sundays were traditionally a day of rest. The only people that would work on Sundays were the sheep herders that were watching their flock up in the mountains.

As was the tradition, congregations of people would often meet on Sundays to share in worship. They usually met at a designated neighbor's house. The congregation would rotate from one house to the other until all had hosted worship and then the cycle would repeat itself. Everyone would sit, or kneel, before the santuario, and they would pray a rosario. The rosario usually consisted of recanting *oraciónes* (prayers) and singing a few *canticos* (church hymns). After their worship, the host would prepare *café* (coffee), and serve *galletas* (cookies). While drinking their café and eating their galletas, they would socialize. At times, some conversations would extend well into the night.

Bautizos (Baptisms) were a very important sacrament to many parishioners. The *Padrinos* (Godparents) were chosen very carefully. The Padrinos to the child would become *compadres* with the parents. In many instances the Padrinos would take care of the child rather than the child's own parents. *Bodas* (weddings) were also a very important sacrament. Bodas brought the entire community together, because it was a time of festivity. Both bautizos and bodas were conducted by a priest when one was readily available.

Religion After the Clergymen Arrived

Padre Jean Baptiste Railliére from Tomé had made many a journey to Manzano and on rare occasion he would venture to the Río Bonito. By December of 1860 Padre Railliére had ventured south to La Placita del Río Bonito. Once in La Placita, Padre Railliére had baptized several children.[5] In the early summer of 1866, Bishop Jean Baptiste Lamy had made a visit to his flocks at Fort Stanton and the surrounding region.[6]

With the arrival of the Bishop, the Catholics on the Río Bonito were inspired to start construction on a new capilla. Sometime in 1867, Antonio Torres y Marquez had constructed a capilla, which was named *La Capilla del Señor Antonio Torres*. The capilla was later re-named to *Nuestra Señora del Pueblito* (Our Lady of the little Pueblo). By July 02, 1868 Padre Jean Baptiste Francois Boucard had become the resident priest in *La Parroquia del Río Bonito* (The Río Bonito Parrish) for about ten months. On January 24, 1870 Padre Pierre Lassaigne was assigned to *La Parroquia del Tularoso* thus relegating Nuestra Señora del Pueblito back to a mission church.[7]

By January of 1870, La Capilla de San Francisco had become the first chapel to be constructed in La Plaza de San Patricio, on land, which was later owned by Aniseto Lucero and Lucas Gallegos. Because of the isolation of the region, a priest was seldom on hand to perform the sacraments of marriage, and baptism. On occasion, Padre Pedro Lassaigne from La Parroquia de Tularoso would venture between La Plaza de San Patricio, La Placita, and La Plaza de San José to conduct mass and other sacraments. In what had become a common occurrence, the people of the valley would be lucky to have mass at least once a month. Many families would coordinate their weddings and baptisms with the arrival of the priest. However, the accepted practice was that the people would have to make a special trip by wagon or on horseback, to either Tularoso or Manzano to get married or have their baby baptized by the Church.

The Catholic community in the Río Ruidoso Valley region continued to grow and it was becoming increasingly apparent that the services of a priest were needed. By March 04, 1876 Archbishop Lamy had assigned Padre José Sambrano Tafoya, a native of Nuevo México, to La Parroquia del Río Bonito. Padre Sambrano was a man of great faith, perseverance, and unwavering conviction. He had accepted the challenge of administering the faith in an area that was extremely isolated and he was held in very high esteem by all of the communities in the valley.[8]

On November 13, 1878 Padre Sambrano and a business partner, Francisco Antonio Vigil y Valdéz had reached an agreement with Stephen Stanley to purchase his ranch of 160 acres, thus increasing their land holdings to 320 acres. The ranch later became known as ***El Rancho del Padre*** and was situated about two miles east of Analla. Here on the rancho, Padre Sambrano grazed sheep and sold their wool. He used the proceeds of his operations to help fund his parroquia's growth and maintenance.[9]

All was not well on El Rancho del Padre when on April 29, 1879 Ellen E. Casey had filed a lawsuit seeking to take possession of the dwelling both Padre Sambrano and Antonio Vigil were living in. She also had sought $2,000 in damages. The lawsuit stemmed from the fact that both men were living in a residence on three acres that had originally belonged to the Casey's. Neither man however, had thought twice about living in the house because the Casey's were occupying three acres of their land. This arrangement had originally taken place while the Stanley's had ownership of the property.

Ellen Casey, her son William, and a hired hand broke into Padre Sambrano's house and stole about $4,800 in currency, some jewelry, and important papers. The documents suggested that Ellen Casey had entered into an agreement with Padre Sambrano to buy El Rancho del Padre. She later reneged on their deal. Justice of the Peace John B. Wilson issued a warrant for the arrest of the three responsible for the burglary.

Later, on June 28, 1879 Padre Sambrano had become a victim of an intimidation crime, which ultimately led to him being beaten, shot at, and subsequently wounded. Francisco Vigil, Ramón Vigil, Felix Vigil, Anselmo Juárez and José Baca were witness to the incident. They implicated Ellen Casey, Adam Casey, W.A. Alexander, and the brothers John and William Jones.

On November 07, 1880 the district court had motioned to dismiss Ellen Casey's lawsuit for failure to appear. On November 13, 1880 the grand jury charged Ellen Casey and her cohorts responsible for the assault on Padre Sambrano, with premeditated murder. On November 17 Ellen Casey, William Casey and their hired hand were charged with theft. In the end, District Attorney Simon B. Newcomb had dropped all the charges against Ellen Casey.[10]

By 1883, Padre Sambrano had become the first Catholic Priest to do missionary work on the Mescalero Reservation. In May of 1883 Padre Sambrano was in negotiations with all of the persons who owned the lands to Nuestra Señora del Pueblito and La Capilla de San Francisco. It was Padre Sambrano's task to have the lands in which the capillas and campo santos were situated, deeded over to the archdiocese in the name of the Archbishop. Antonio Torres y Marquez and his wife Juana had graciously deeded the land to the Church without hesitation.

Aniseto Lucero had patented the land in which La Capilla de San Francisco was situated and Lucas Gallegos had patented the land that served as the campo santo.[11] Aniseto Lucero rebuked the idea of deeding any part of his land to the Church, but offered a compromise by allowing the capilla to remain. He also was willing to make the concession of allowing the people of La Plaza de San Patricio to use the capilla as a place of worship. Lucas Gallegos also refused to deed any part of his land to the Church for the use as a campo santo.

The negotiations had stalled and the discussions had become rather impassioned. From the Church's perspective the building was considered a "House of God" if it did not have title to the land whereas, it would be considered a "Home of God" if the Church had title to the land. The difference between the two was that communion could only be kept within a home of god.

After reaching an impasse, the parishioners reserved themselves to abandoning the fledgling capilla. They began dismantling the capilla's doors and windows. They also took all of the pews, and other furniture. Many citizens of La Plaza de San Patricio later alleged that Padre Sambrano had excommunicated both Lucas Gallegos and Aniseto Lucero.[12]

Tragedy had struck Padre Sambrano on June 01, 1884, while en route to Candelario Griego's house. While he was driving a horse carriage, he was in a horrific accident, which caused severe trauma to his head. There were many stories surrounding the manner in which the accident had occurred but all of them were unfounded. On June 08, 1884 Padre Sambrano had drawn his last breath. After his death, many of the local residents referred to the canyon where he had the accident, Cañon del Padre Sambrano and Cuesta del Padre, (now known as Priest's Canyon). He was buried next to the *Oratorio de Santo Niño*, which he himself had established at El Rancho del Padre.[13]

Prior to Padre Sambrano's death, in the spring of 1883, construction had commenced on a new capilla but work had abruptly stopped by November of 1883 and it was only partially finished.[14] Shortly thereafter, construction of a third, new capilla commenced in 1884 on land, which was mostly owned by Feliz Trujillo. Part of the campo santo also fell on land, which was owned by Francisco Sánchez who had graciously donated it to the Church. Tranquelino Montoya served as the general contractor of the capilla. The citizens of La Plaza de San Patricio provided the labor to construct La Capilla de San Patricio. Ysidro Sisneros provided most of the building materials that went into its construction. By 1885 construction of La Capilla de San Patricio was complete. Missing from the capilla was a wooden floor, and the steeple.

The capilla measured about 40' long and 20' wide. The walls were constructed entirely from adobé. The inside walls were covered with gypsum. The outside walls were covered with mud. Large vigas supported the ceiling which was raised about 20' from the dirt floor. Román Barragán had donated La Capilla de San Patricio's *campana* (bell), which was baptized "La Barragána".[15] Since there was no steeple, the campana was placed on two wooden blocks resting on a platform above the ground and two men would ascend atop the platform and ring the bell to call mass into service. Lorenso Mendoza was one of the men that always rang the bell, while the other man was someone who usually offered to help him.

Shortly thereafter Eusevio Torres built a steeple and hoisted the bell 35' to its resting spot. The bell tower started to lean away from the wall, and Bernabé Lara reinforced the steeple by attaching it to the main building. A wooden floor was also built and La Capilla de San Patricio had finally been completed. On May 19, 1886 Feliz Trujillo and Natividad Olguín de Trujillo had deeded the land that La Capilla de San Patricio was situated on to the archdiocese on behalf of the Archbishop Salpointe.[16]

La Capilla de San Patricio

Curanderos

There were no doctors to take care of the sick and injured. Parteras (midwives) were prevalent within the communities. They helped deliver almost all of the babies born throughout the valley. There were also the curanderos, who took care of those who fell ill. Curanderos had great knowledge of the healing powers of *yerbas* (herbs). When using yerbas, the curanderos would use the roots, leaves or seeds to manufacture broths, ointments, powders, pastes and teas. These in turn would be given to the one who sought a remedy.

The practice of using yerbas for medicinal purposes had been passed down from one generation to the other. Some of the healing properties of yerbas were learned from the Native Americans while the knowledge of other types of yerbas were brought from España and México. Curanderos would often collect their yerbas throughout the year. The following are just a few of the more popular remedial herbs.

Anemia

Chicoria was also known as Dandelion root were used to thicken and purify the blood. The roots were boiled into a tea and ingested. Chicoria was used for anemia, liver ailments, urinary tract, and kidney infections.

Aspirin

The bark of the *Álamo* tree was a popular remedy because of its properties that resembled aspirin once it was digested by the body. The bark was used to make tea for ingestion, or it was manufactured into a powder and made into a paste for external uses. *Jarita* also had medicinal properties similar to aspirin. Boiling the bark into a tea helped alleviate the symptoms associated with colds and fevers. With higher dosages either through ingestion or added to a hot water bath, it could help relieve pain due arthritis and even hemorrhoids.

Asthma and breathing allergies

Cañutillo was boiled in water and served warm or cold to help with the symptoms of congestion due to allergies. *Punchéon*, also known as Mullein, was ingested as a tea, which helped to remedy the symptoms of asthma, and other breathing ailments. An oil extract of the herb was used to remedy earaches. *Yerba Santa* was used to remedy lung ailments. The leaves were boiled and used for the treatment of bronchitis, laryngitis and a sore throat.

Colds and Influenza

Altamisa was commonly used for colds and fevers. *Manstranso* was also known as Horehound and was used to treat the symptoms of colds and influenza. When Manstranso was added to honey it worked as a cough suppressant. *Oshá* was used as an all-purpose remedy for a variety of ailments. The root of the herb was chewed in its raw form to help alleviate sore throats and gum disease. When the herb was boiled into a tea it was used to treat the symptoms of colds, influenza, and helped loosen phlegm. When the *Rosa de Castilla* was made into a tea, it was believed that it helped remedy gas and nausea. When the petals were eaten it was believed to relieve colds and coughing.

Detoxifying the body

Chamiso Heidondo was also known as sagebrush and it was noted as having a pungent smell to it. The herb was boiled into a tea. The Native Americans used the herb during their sweat bathing rituals to cleanse the body of toxins that exuded through their pours during perspiration.

Digestive remedies

Alhucema was also known as lavender and was originally brought to Nuevo México from España. It was used for stomach ailments, migraine headaches, and minor congestion. *Manzanilla* was also known as Chamomile and was commonly used as a gastric remedy. When boiled into a tea Manzanilla helped with diarrhea, gas, heartburn, and even menstrual cramping. Oil extracts of the herb were used as a remedy for arthritis and gout. *Salvia* was also known as sage and when ingested as a tea would help with digestive disorders, and was also thought to expel digestive worms. *Té de Sena* was used as a laxative that cleansed the intestines. *Yerba Buena* was also known a Mint. When Yerba Buena was ingested as a tea it remedied digestive ailments, colic and constipation. It was also used a breath freshener when the leaves were chewed.

Increase in stamina and energy

Alfalfa was used as a tonic to help restore energy because of its high mineral and vitamin content.

Miracle remedies

Comfe is also known as Comfrey Root and was thought to have incredible healing properties when applied to slight tissue damage, sprains, and fractured or broken bones. The root was chopped up, boiled and could be served as a tea.

Muscle aches, Arthritis and joint pain

Maravilla was used as an ointment for sore muscles and inflamed joints. Yerba Mansa was also known as Swamp Root. *Yerba Mansa* was made into an ointment that helped relieve the pain of arthritis and rheumatism. When the herb was crushed into a powder it was mixed in with an ointment and was believed to remedy cuts and even hemorrhoids.

Personal hygiene

Amolé which was produced from the yucca root was first used by the Native Americans. It was used in shampoo and detergent. The pulp of the root was made into a tea and ingested for the purpose of treating arthritis and rheumatism. *Poñil* was often used as a shampoo to stimulate stronger and healthier hair. *Yerba de la Negrita* was used as a shampoo because of its properties to help stimulate hair growth.

Skin ailments

Lantén was also known as Broad Leaf Plantain and was used to treat rashes, bee stings and other types of skin irritation. Many Native Americans also used lantén for snakebites. *Malva* was also known as a Mallow Plant and was used as an all-purpose remedy for rashes, and insect bites or stings. When made into a tea it would help with coughing and sore throats. *Romerillo* was also known as Silver Sage and could be used to remedy dry and itchy skin.

Plumajillo was also known as Yarrow and was primarily used for healing cuts and bruises. When ingested as a tea the herb could remedy stomach ailments. The herb also had anti-inflammatory properties, which made it useful in reducing pain and swelling in rheumatism and hemorrhoids. The leaves of the **Punche** were often used to remedy burns and cuts. Ointments made from the herb were also used to help relieve arthritis, and muscle aches. **Trementina de Piñon** was often used to pull out **espinas** (cactus spines) and wood splinters imbedded within the skin.

Curanderos didn't only cure the physical ailments of the people they also cured the spiritual ailments that they believed were inflicted upon society. Many people believed in the powers of the supernatural and often sought the services of a curandero if they felt **embrujado** (bewitched) by a **bruja** (witch). The power of the **ojo** (evil eye) was enough for the people to seek the curative abilities of a curandero. As such, curanderos were held in high esteem amongst the people and all respected their god given abilities.

Brujas were feared for their ill-fated intentions. Brujas also had a great knowledge of the effects of yerbas, but rather than use them for their curative abilities, they often used them to make one ill. It was often believed that they took the form of owls, rats, snakes, wolves, and crows. Often times, a social outcast would be labeled a bruja even if they had never practiced witchery. Once someone was labeled a bruja, they would carry that stigma for the rest of their lives. In many instances even their families and children were perceived to be mal-intentioned.

Death was often a community affair. The news of someone's death spread throughout the valley rather quickly. Once it was confirmed that somebody had died, the church bells would be rung to let the entire community know what had happened. The church had two bells, a larger one that was loud with a heavy boom, and a smaller one, which had softer yet distinct ring. If an adult had passed on, the larger bell would be rung. If it were a child that had passed on the smaller bell would be rung.

Since there were no funeral homes at the time, the **velorio** (wake) was held in the residence of the person who had died. Family members, or close friends of the family would come together to build a coffin. Once the deceased was placed in the coffin, the coffin was then placed upon some benches in middle of the room. Chairs were positioned around the coffin and benches were lined up against the walls. Relatives and close friends were allowed to come in and pray for the soul of the departed. The velorio would last through the night until the next day's first sunlight.

Most of the women would wear black **tápalos** (shawls), which were a symbol of mourning and was customary for any woman to wear in the event of a death in the family, or of a close friend. The tápalos were usually worn over the shoulder so as to cover the entire face, except one's eyes. The garment would cover the woman from her head to her ankles. The practice of wearing a tápalo had originally come from Spain, a tradition that had probably been started by the Moors during their occupation of Spain.

During the velorio the women would offer **requiebros** (endearing expressions), which were meant to express their mourning. Usually a wife would proclaim her undying love for her deceased husband and ask what was to become of her, now that he had left her alone. Interspersed between requiebros the women would cry, shout or wail. The tápalo would be used to cover their faces, and therefore hide their dismay.

Café and **pasteles** (sweet rolls) were provided for the **dolientes** (mourners) to help keep them awake throughout the night. It was a common tradition, that if an unwitting passerby stopped to ask who had passed on, a common reply would be, *"¡Ya Don José colgó los chopos!"* (Don José hung up his slippers! The cultural vernacular meant that Don José had died.) If any of the elders had overheard the children speak in such a manner, the children would have received a tongue lashing because that type of talk was considered disrespectful. They were reminded that to show respect for the departed they needed to say, *"¡Ya Don José falleso!"*

The men usually paid their last respects, offered their prayers for the deceased, gave their condolences to the spouse and the children, and quietly made their exit outside to take in the fresh air. Once several men gathered outside, they would build a bonfire and talk amongst each other for the remainder of the night. The women would stay inside, reciting the rosario, recanting oraciónes, and singing canticos. From time to time, the spouse of the deceased would cry with their children and the other women would give them their show of support.

The following morning some of the men would ride to the campo santo to begin digging the grave by pick and shovel. It was the custom to dig the grave the day of the burial, because it wasn't supposed to remain open through the night. Once the grave was dug, the pallbearers would ready the coffin for the procession to the campo santo. The coffin was often loaded onto a cart or a buggy. The length of the procession was dependent on how far the house was from the campo santo. The procession of people threw their arms into the air, allowing the sun to hit their faces as they prayed for the spirit of the deceased to ascend into heaven. The procession first took the dolientes to the church where more prayers were offered. After a special mass, the procession proceeded to the campo santo, where the deceased would be laid to rest.

It was widely speculated that people who were held in high esteem within the church were buried the closest to the church. Those who were Catholic by name, but did not regularly attend mass, nor gave alms would be buried further from the church. There was also a section in the campo santo for non-Catholics and those Catholics that had died in sin.

How far a person was buried from the Church was very important to the living. In many instances, one could see the deceased's *compadre* kneeling next to the grave, wiping their tears from their face. If one were to ask, "*¿Qué pasa compadre?*" ("What's the matter compadre?") The compadre of the deceased would respond, "*¡Pero mira! Está aquí en la oria como si fuera nada.*" ("Just look where they buried him, here at the end as if he were nothing.")

Bailes, Fiestas y Fandangos

The people were always looking for a reason to celebrate. When there was a boda they came to the reception. When there was a *cumpleaños* (birthday), they held a *baile* (dance). They celebrated different Patron Saints' days such as *El Día de San Juan*, which was in June, *El Día de Santiago*, which was July 25th, and *El Día de Santa Ana*, which was on July 26th.[17] These celebrations consisted of *gran fiestas* where people could play games, eat food, and dance late into the night. One of the great attractions was the horse races that were run on the *llano* (flat plain) just outside of San Patricio.

One of the local traditions that took place on special occasions pitted a team of men usually from two different communities within the Rio Ruidoso Río Bonito, and Rio Hondo Valleys. The locals referred to the competition as *El Gallo* (The Roster). The object of the friendly but intense competition was for each team to race their horses upon a long track. At the midpoint there was a hole that was dug into the ground. A rooster was placed within the hole and the bird was buried up to its neck in dirt so that only its head was raised just above the brim of the hole. To keep the rooster from escaping its feet were tied together.

The competing teams would thus race their horses from each starting line at opposite ends of the track, towards the midpoint. As they came upon the rooster they would attempt to capture the bird by its head. A great deal of skill and agility was required because the task of capturing the rooster was extremely difficult. The competitors had to lean down from their saddles to grab at the roosters head. Sometimes the rider would fall from the horse; sometimes the rooster would duck its head just out of the reach of the competitor's outstretched hand.

Once a rider from either of the teams was able to capture the rooster, it was off to the races towards the finish line. The competing team would chase after the individual who had captured the rooster and attempt to steal it from him. Frequently the men would receive a good beating as each tried to wrestle the bird away. Sometimes the individual with the bird would hit their opponents with the rooster to fend them off. The locals referred to this as ***dando gallazo*** (getting roostered). The individual who crossed the finish line with the rooster in hand would be declared the victor. The community that he represented would be rewarded with a baile that was sponsored by the loosing team's community. Needless to say, the poor rooster was always killed when it was plucked from the ground. The rooster however, was always used in the ***caldo*** (soup) made in honor of the victorious. The tradition of El Gallo took place up until about 1915.

The people needed a place for recreation to conduct meetings, celebrate fiestas, and dance therefore they built a salón de baile (Dance hall). It was usually constructed in a manner in which the benches were placed along the walls. A stage was built to one side of the hall. Once built, the local musicians, and traveling musicians would stop and play for the people, and they would all dance well into the late night. Some people would travel a whole day on horseback or buggy to attend the bailes.

Attending any celebration whether it was a boda, fiesta or baile, was a grand occasion. Women wore their best dresses, and men wore their finest attire. One could travel from house to house and see the men's white shirts hanging on the clothesline, and a few trousers that had been lightly brushed with kerosene set out to dry. Boots would be shined with kitchen grease mixed with stove soot and a little spit, and then they would be conveniently placed next to the door. They would brush their teeth and refresh their breath with baking soda. The women would gather white dirt, yellow dirt, and red dirt to use on their facial skin as a powder base. The men would apply hair oil so that they could style it in place.

The horses were washed, brushed, and their horseshoes would be replaced if needed. The buggies were readied for the trip. People from all over the valley would make their way to the baile in San Patricio every Saturday night. They would come on horseback, by buggy, and some even walked the whole distance. This was an occasion for the entire family, even the babies made the trip because there was nobody at home to take care of them.

Blankets were often taken to the bailes to provide a cushion for the benches. As the night wore on and the children tired from playing and dancing, they would lie under the benches, fall asleep, and the parents would cover them with the blankets. While the children slept, the parents would go out on the dance floor and ***tirando chancla*** (throwing shoes), slang for dancing up a storm.

The people loved to listen to the ***conjuntos***, which usually consisted of band members who played a fiddle, an accordion, a guitar, a clarinet, and a drum. They loved to dance to ***corridos***, ***cumbias***, ***taquache***, ***quadrillas***, polkas square dances and ***el mambo***. Sometimes, they danced to waltzes, but the most anticipated dance was ***el baile de la cilla***.

The men could be found dancing for a while and then walking outside for some fresh air. Once outside they would find a compadre with a gallon of ***mula*** (moonshine), and commence with the drinking and talking. Mula was the liquor of choice and was easy to make. It was made from fermented corn. Mula had a powerful kick, and usually made the men ***mucho boracho*** (really drunk).

There was a story that was often told concerning a dance from a long time ago. It was said that a child who had fallen asleep under a bench was awoken by all of the noise. As he looked out onto the dance floor he noticed a man who was dancing without any shoes. He was frightened when noticed that the man's feet were hoofed, like that of a goat. The child quickly got up and looked for his father, who was also dancing.

Upon finding him, he stated, "Papi, there is a man dancing without any shoes!"

The father thought to himself for a while and looked at his son and replied, "Well maybe his shoes were hurting his feet and he took them off."

The boy quickly exclaimed to his father, "But Papi, the man had the feet of a goat." With that the father didn't know whether he should sober up or go outside and help his compadre finish off the gallon of mula. If mass was being held the next day, it was a sure bet that those people who were the most inebriated were also the ones sitting in the first pew. The moral of the story insinuated that if one could not behave, they could end up dancing with the devil.

El baile de la cilla was similar to musical chairs in that the chairs would be positioned in the center of the dance floor. The amount of chairs positioned would always be one less than the number of participants in the dance. Everyone would dance around the chairs while the conjunto played a *canción* (song). When the music stopped, everyone had to sit down on a chair. The odd one out who didn't have a chair would then have to say a *dicho* (saying), an *adivinanza* (riddle), or a biblical proverb. Those who were witty enough to come up with something were allowed to remain in the dance. Those who couldn't, would retire from the dance and the music would play again and everyone would get up and start dancing until the music stopped. This dance continued until there was only one person left. The dance usually lasted for about an hour or so, and everybody had a great deal of fun with it.

Dichos (Sayings)

Dichos were very popular with the people both young and old. In many instances the dichos were specific to certain regions or even families. In most cases they served as a form of educational entertainment. Sometimes dichos were used to remember important dates or important events. Most dichos were meant to rhyme, and some were silly in nature. The meaning of the dicho is often lost in the English translation, which takes away from the fun of trying to create one.

"Por aquí sale el sol, por aquí se mete, cuando llueve hay mucho soquete" The English translation is as follows: "The sun comes out on this side, and it goes down on the other side, when it rains there is a lot of mud."

"Febrero loco. Marzo hay groso (airoso), Abríl lluvioso. Sacan Mayo florido y hermoso." The English translation is as follows: "February is crazy. March it is windy. April showers, bring Mayflowers. This dicho was used to describe the monthly weather patterns in the region.

Adivinanzas[18]

Adivinanzas were a means in which the adults would often interact with both the children and other adults. It a form of entertainment meant to pass the time. Many were passed down from one generation to the other. In many cases they could only be understood if one was familiar with the regional culture. There were many different types of adivinanzas, some were a play with words where the answer was masked within the riddle, some were a reference to daily life, and others pertained to the Catholic faith. In many instances the meanings are lost during the English translations.

Adivine mi adivinanza...

1. Plata no es, oro no es. ¿Qué es?

2. En un llano muy llano, vaca blanca se acostó. Se hizo vaca pinta, y luego se paró.

3. ¿Cuál es la santa más olorosa?

4. ¿Cuál es el ave que no tiene pansa?

5. Espera amigo, espera te digo. Si no lo adivines, no vas conmigo.
Espera amigo, esperara te digo.

6. Su nombre es Juan. Su apellido es Goche. ¡Si no lo adivines, duermes conmigo esta noche!

7. Tú de arriba y yo de abajo, y hacemos el mismo trabajo.

8. Lana sube, lana abaja

9. Ya ves que claro es, el que no adivina, vien tonto es.

Guess my riddle...

It isn't silver, it isn't gold. What is it?

A white cow lay down on a flat plain. The cow becomes spotted, and later gets up.

Which is the saint that smells the best?

Which is the bird that has no belly?

Wait friend, wait I tell you. If you don't guess it, you can't go with me.
Wait friend, wait I tell you.

Your name is Juan. Your last name is Goche. If you can't guess it, you will sleep with me tonight!

You are above, and I am below and we do the same job.

Lint rising, lint going down

You see how clear it is, the one who can't guess it, becomes a fool.

Answers:

1. Una plátano es. / It's a banana.
2. Es una tortilla. / It's a tortilla.
3. Santa Rosa
4. Ave María
5. Es Pera / A pear
6. Es un guangoche / It's a gunnysack.
7. Es tijeras / It's scissors.
8. La navaja/ The knife
9. Llaves/ Keys

The Children

The children! What about the children? It was a must, that all of the family would sit together at the table for every meal if possible. Some times because of the morning rush, or at noon, because of their work or the kids at school it was not possible, but for dinner some one had to give thanks to God for the food that they were about to receive, and it was a time for conversation.

Dinner was the most important meal of the day because it enabled the whole family to come together and discuss the events of the day. The mother and the eldest daughters would start preparing for dinner at about 5:00pm. The main staple was beans, chili, vegetables and tortillas, but on occasion they would have meat from a slaughtered livestock. Before eating dinner, the family would give thanks by praying to God.

The parents would then initiate the conversation by talking about the work or whom they had met during the day. Children never interjected into the conversation unless they were spoken to. Only the eldest children were allowed to discuss adult matters. The children's opportunity to talk usually came after dinner. the children would talk about their school activities and who got to stay in at recess for having spoken in Spanish, (yes the teachers would penalize the students for saying a word in Spanish) and yet it is said that New México had a law then, that in order to be a teacher, they would have to be able to sign their name, as payroll checks were coming in endorsed with an X.

The students would tell of which ones got spanked. But would not say a word if they themselves got spanked, because if the parents found out that the kids had been in trouble, they would get another spanking at home. *Pero no era mi culpa*! (but it was not my fault!) I am sure that you were not spanked because you were a (santa) saint. Girls were discouraged from going to school, but they could go up to the eighth grade. But then the girls would marry young, some of them at the age of fourteen.

My father would say that when he was going to school, (about 1912), he either had to walk or ride a horse to school. When they got school buses, the kids had to get off the bus to push it up a hill. The first thing that the teacher had him do when he got to school, was to send him to the river to bring an armload of *jaras* (willow branches) and clean all the limbs off the main branch so that the teacher would have a supply of sticks to paddle the kids with.

My father never spoke of him being whipped, but he would have a smirk on his face when he talked about that, as though it reminded him of something. If the kids asked him if he ever got whipped, he would say, *eso, no se dice* (that is not said). When it snowed, the elders would wrap gunnysacks around the child's feet to keep them warm and from getting wet. Every one in the home had their chores to be done after school and on weekends.

Each year before school started, each boy would get three pair of pants, three shirts, three pair of socks, one pair of shoes and one coat. The girls would get three dresses, three blouses, three pair of cotton stockings, one pair of shoes and one coat each. The underclothes would usually be made at home out of cotton sacks where flour came in. If the child wore out their clothes or shoes before the next school term, they better know that they were going to go in rags or bare footed for the rest of the year.

A typical day usually started at daybreak with ***desayuno*** (breakfast), which consisted of a cup of café. After desayuno, the cows or goats would be milked, and fed. All the other livestock would also be fed, and their pens would be cleaned. Once all the animals were taken care of, attention would be focused on tending to the crops. About mid-morning ***almuerso*** (lunch) would be served. This meal was very important in that it provided the necessary energy to carry one through the day. The remainder of the day would be spent on tending to the crops, the orchard, or the livestock.

Chapter Seven: Florencio Gonzáles

Florencio Gonzáles
(Photo courtesy of Juan Montoya and Eva Gonzáles-Montoya).

Before Lincoln County

Florencio Gonzáles, christened José Florencio Gonzáles, was born on November 07, 1843 in Los Corrales, Nuevo México, La República de México. His parents were Santiago Gonzáles and María Manuela Aragón. He lived with his family in Los Corrales, Territory of New México until he was about ten. Family legend had that in his youth he had become an acquaintance of Aleksander Grzelachowski, more commonly known to many Nuevo Mexicanos as Padre Alejandro Polaco. At the time, Padre Polaco was living in Peña Blanca, which was near Santiago Gonzáles' farm.

Padre Polaco must have made quite an impression on the youngster because he initially had a desire to become a priest. As a boy, he had been taught at the Catholic School in Santa Fé. He was sent to attend several courses at the Seminary at Clermont-Ferrand in France. By 1854 he was noted as returning to Santa Fé with Archbishop Jean Baptiste Lamy.[1] He continued to attend the Catholic School in Santa Fé up through 1860.[2]

Florencio's aspirations of becoming a priest were deterred as the American Civil War broke out to the east, and the threat of a Confederate Army invasion into the Territory of New México became a possibility. He enlisted as a Second Lieutenant on November 19, 1861 in Perea's Battalion Militia, fighting for the Union Army.[3] He had mustered out of the Union Army on February 28, 1862. By March 28, 1862 the Battle of Glorieta Pass had driven the Confederate Army out of the Territory of New México. A few years after the civil war, he had decided to move to the vast expanse of the southeastern quadrant of the Territory of New México.

Together with his brother Ignacio, the two set forth east of the Manzano region. During his travels he met a beautiful young woman named Reimunda Cigismunda Sánchez. She was the daughter of Don Mauricio de la Trinidad Sánches. They eventually married in Manzano and established a life on the Río Bonito where he and his brother Ignacio promptly entered into a contract on March 01, 1867 with George Kimbrell to purchase land about three miles east of La Placita del Río Bonito.[4] The farm was adjacent on the west by land eventually owned by William Brady.

On June 12, 1869, he had applied under squatters rights for the land he had possession of since 1867. He had been farming and making other improvements on the land that was in close proximity to Lincoln (formerly La Placita del Río Bonito). On the petition he signed his name as Florencio Gonzáles y Aragón. The family remained on this farm for several years to come.

Running for Office

Florencio was a well-educated man for his time. His many years of schooling, first at the Seminary in France, and then the six years in Santa Fé had served him well. He knew how to read and write in both Spanish and English. He also could speak Portuguese, Latin, and some French. He was eloquent, well mannered, and carried himself with great confidence. Many people within the community held him in the highest esteem for those reasons alone.

He was a man filled with a great sense of humility though. This was a characteristic that was engrained in him over the many years he studied to become a priest. He was a natural born leader and he wasn't afraid to be the voice of reason when so many people were fearful of expressing their own opinions. He understood his people, and his people trusted his judgment.

Florencio had become concerned about the friction that was developing between the Spanish-speaking populace, the newly arrived settlers from America and the European immigrants. This was a sentiment shared by many other native New Mexicans throughout the Sierra Blanca, the Sierra Capitán, and the Sierra Sacramento. He was encouraged by his popularity among the people and had the support of several high profile citizens in the region. He had a great desire to temper the friction that was developing and he decided to run for the office of the Territorial House of Representatives.

Being that Lincoln County encompassed over 27,000 square miles of land, and having only three voting precincts, each candidate had to travel extensively to run an effective campaign. For the first election, one congressman, two territorial legislators, and six county officials would be elected. On September 06, 1869, Florencio who had run unopposed was elected to the Territorial House of Representatives for Lincoln County. Lawrence G. Murphy was elected as the Probate Judge, and William Brady was elected as Lincoln County Sheriff. He was unable to serve his term because the Territory of New México couldn't appropriate the required funds for the office, and therefore he did not attend the 1869 legislature.[5]

With the threat of Mescalero raids mostly subdued, life on the Río Bonito was fairly tranquil for many of the people. This peace was relatively short lived though, as more Eastern U.S. Americans and foreign immigrants continued to migrate into the Río Bonito, Río Hondo, and Río Ruidoso valleys. Whereas many of the previous waves of foreign settlers to the region had shared a mutual respect for the Nuevo Mexicanos, many of the more recent ones did not share those same values.

In 1871 Florencio ran for the Territorial House of Representatives again. He was encouraged with his odds considering he had won the office in 1869. He ran against William Brady who had the support from many of the Americans and the immigrants. Brady also had some support from the hispanos, considering he had married María Bonifacia Cháves, and had children who could speak the Spanish language. Furthermore, he was in good standing with the Spanish-speaking people because he often socialized amongst them. After a highly contested campaign against each other, Brady would easily claim victory over Gonzáles for the highly coveted office. Brady tallied 215 total votes to Gonzáles' 67 votes. Other winners of the elections were; Murphy for Probate Judge and L.G. Gylam for sheriff.[6]

Lawrence G. Murphy

Lawrence G. Murphy emigrated from Ireland to the United States during the great Potato famine in 1845. He enlisted in the military and was stationed in the western territories. He fought alongside Kit Carson during the civil war. Soon thereafter, he served as a post trader for Fort Stanton. On June 03, 1874 Lawrence G. Murphy, Emil Fritz, and James Dolan opened the L.G. Murphy & Co. store in the town of Lincoln.[7] Shortly after the completion of the store, Emil Fritz returned to Stuttgart, Germany where he died on June 26, 1874.[8]

The building that they constructed was very impressive for a town of Lincoln's size. It towered over all of the other structures in town, rising two stories in the air. The first floor housed the store while the second floor housed the living quarters. The building and those who lived within it were referred to as "The House".[9]

The House served more as a commodity brokerage house that supplied Fort Stanton and the Mescalero Reservation with beef and grains, rather than a store. Since there were no other commodity suppliers for over two hundred miles, many contractors both small and large had to do business through the House. This became a very lucrative business for the House and very few people could challenge its dominance.

Furthermore, Murphy had also established a lucrative banking business, which provided agricultural equipment, seeds, common house wares, and canned fruit, that would be delivered on credit when needed. Being that most people in Lincoln County did not have money, it could be said that most people were indebted to the House. The credit terms usually meant that the farmer and or families would deliver an agreed upon amount of goods or services to satisfy the debt. Failure to meet the terms usually meant that Murphy would repossess the equipment and in some cases, he would foreclose on their property.[10]

Over the years the House had gained a reputation as being hard-nosed and exploitive. The prices the House charged for goods sold were unreasonably high, and the amount the House paid for goods received was unreasonably low. It became increasingly difficult for the farmers throughout the region to meet the credit terms. With such unscrupulous business practices, many people held the House in low esteem, yet they had no choice in the matter of doing business with anybody else.

To further enhance Murphy's stranglehold on Lincoln County's citizens, he was elected to the office of Probate Judge. He often used his office to further his economic ambitions. Since he had significant control over the interpretation of the laws and those who served as lawmen, he could intimidate citizens with very little repercussion.

Alexander McSween

Alexander McSween had emigrated from Kansas to Lincoln County with his wife Sue in March of 1875. McSween was a lawyer by trade and found his employment with none other than the House. McSween served as the House's legal enforcer in which he sued the debtors, and taking a hefty 10%

fee for his services. McSween's services would eventually be called upon with the death of Murphy's business partner, Emil Fritz about a year and a half prior. At stake was a $10,000 life insurance policy that Fritz had taken out on himself.

An unfortunate turn of events had occurred simultaneously upon Fritz's passing. First, Murphy had failed to open probate of Emil Frtiz's estate because he was fearful that the debts he owed into the estate would be discovered. Fritz had re-invested a large percentage of his money back into the business and Murphy sought to conceal the amount of those investments. He was successful in hiding the estate's assets for almost a year.

Secondly, Murphy had assigned the insurance proceeds to Spiegelberg Brothers as a partial payment of the House's debts owed to them. However, he did not have the authority to do so. Lastly, The Merchants Life Insurance Company of New York had become insolvent during which Spiegelberg Brothers had become the receiver. Spiegelberg Brothers refused to pay the claim on account that Murphy had used the proceeds to settle his debts owed to them. Because Florencio had come in during the transition of the claim between insurer and receiver, he was powerless to settle any dispute.

The administrator of Fritz's estate, William Brady, thus hired McSween to travel to New York for the purpose of resolving the matter. Shortly after, William Brady was elected as the Sheriff of Lincoln County he resigned his position as administrator to Charles Fritz and Emile Fritz Scholand who were his siblings.

McSween negotiated a settlement with Spiegelberg Brothers that would release the claim for a one-time $700 payment. McSween secured the $700 by agreeing to a deal with the banking company of Donnell, Lawson & Co. The bank, in turn, would receive a fee for providing the capital to secure the claim. After all fees were paid, the amount of the claim had been reduced to approximately $6,000. After brokering the deal, McSween returned to Lincoln without the benefit of any money in hand, and was promptly excused from his duties as the House's lawyer in December of 1876.[11]

John Henry Tunstall

John Henry Tunstall was an Englishman who had come to America to invest his father's money in potentially profitable business endeavors. Tunstall was enamored with the prospect of doing business in the west, because it exacted a degree of mental toughness that he aspired to achieve. His travels brought him to Santa Fé, where he met Alexander McSween. McSween played upon Tunstall's adventurous spirit and encouraged his new acquaintance to accompany him back to Lincoln.

Tunstall was a savvy businessman and within a short period of time he had already analyzed the profit potential of doing business in Lincoln County. In March of 1877, he sent correspondence to his father detailing the manner in which the federal government purchased goods for military and reservation consumption. Tunstall, helped by McSween's council, had fashioned his business model similar to that of the House. Tunstall's persuasiveness tipped his father's interest because the purse strings were soon opened. Tunstall and McSween were soon in business, and they were in direct competition with The House.[12]

Tunstall who was the consummate entrepreneur wanted to establish a cattle ranch and was looking for prime grazing land to support his newest endeavor. McSween had advised his business partner about some land on the Río Felix (pronounced Feliz). Robert Casey who had been murdered in 1875 originally settled the land. Ironically, before Casey's murder, he had publicly denounced Lawrence G. Murphy during a town meeting.[13] Casey had never filed a claim on the land thus it was considered public domain. Tunstall diligently filed a claim against the land under the Desert Lands Act. In all, Tunstall laid claim to thousands of acres while paying very little for it.[14]

Shortly after Casey's murder, the House filed a judgment, for debts owed, against the property now owned by Casey's widow, Ellen E. Shellenbarger-Casey. Sheriff William Brady executed the judgment by seizing over 200 head of cattle. The livestock seized eventually would be auctioned off in order to settle the debt owed to the House. The auction for her cattle was forthcoming and it was her intention to regain ownership of the herd. To Ellen Schellenberger-Casey's disbelief, Tunstall outbid her when her cattle were put up for auction. Ellen Casey held Tunstall in low esteem after she had nearly lost everything to him.[15]

Probate Judge, Florencio Gonzáles

In 1875 Probate Judge Lawrence G. Murphy was being investigated by a Lincoln County grand jury. As a result, it was discovered that $20,000 worth of tax deductions had gone missing. Although Murphy was not indicted, he was forced to resign his office in September of 1875. Florencio gained the judgeship through a special election that was held to replace the deposed Murphy.[16] His election to Probate Judge ultimately shifted the balance of power within the county. It was widely known that the new Probate Judge did not hold any favor towards the Murphy/ Dolan faction. This was attributed to the fact that he was often subjected to shady business practices by the House, and therefore he held great contempt for the man and his associates.[17]

Probate Judges held the highest elected judgeships in the territory. As a Probate Judge, he often judged over territorial conflicts between the territorial legislators and the federal politicians. He also had control of the county treasury, supervised trade with the Mescalero, and he also served as the court of appeals. All appeals by the five Justices of the Peace of Lincoln County were brought before him. His judgment was final and there were no other appeals after his opinion was given.[18] It was his untimely task to regain the citizens' confidence in the office of the Probate Judge during a time of great lawlessness within Lincoln County.

In the November 1876 general elections, Florencio Gonzáles ran for the office of Probate Judge and with no opposition he was elected to serve another term. Elected as the county commissioners were Juan Patrón, Francisco Romero y Lueras, and William Dowlin. William Brady defeated Saturnino Baca, the incumbent sheriff.[19]

During the spring of 1877, Murphy had finally succumbed to the error of his ways. He was a chronic alcoholic, who was incapable of running his business efficiently. He sold his stake in the business he founded to Jimmy Dolan and John Riley. The name of the company was appropriately renamed to J.J. Dolan & Co. Murphy retreated to his rancho on the llanos known as *Carrizo* (reed grass), which was later renamed Carrizozo.[20]

In the summer of 1877 Charles Fritz and Emile Fritz Scholand petitioned Florencio to initiate an order that would allow them to collect on Emil Fritz's life insurance policy. McSween had already surmised that it was Charles Fritz's intent to use the money to pay his debt to "The House". McSween expressed his grievances to the Probate Judge but to no avail. On August 01, 1877, Florencio wrote a request to Donnell, Lawson & Co. to deposit the insurance monies into Fritz's account at the First National Bank of Santa Fé. As it happened, the letter was received after Donnell, Lawson & Co. had already deposited the monies into McSween's bank account in St. Louis in the amount of $7148.49.[21]

After receiving the insurance claim proceeds, McSween promptly petitioned Florencio to oversee the distribution of the monies amongst the administrators of the estate, namely Charles Fritz and Emile Scholand. McSween was reluctant to move forward until he had received direction from the

Probate Court. Unfortunately McSween would have to wait another five months, in January of the next year, before the Probate Court would reconvene.[22]

Thomas Catron, a US Attorney for the Territory of New México, and an unlikely player in the events that led up to the Lincoln County War, had a vested interest in the events that were unfolding in Lincoln. As the principal owner of the First National Bank of Santa Fé, he had done business with the House on numerous occasions. The House was indebted to Catron for a significant amount of money, and their business was being decimated by Tunstall's business. Catron was a shrewd businessman, and he knew his way around the law. He thus conspired to bring down the House's chief competitor, Tunstall, by going after his business partner, McSween.[23]

On December 07, 1877 Charles Fritz filed a petition with the Probate Judge requesting that McSween pay the insurance monies to the court for the purpose of distributing it to the rightful heirs.[24] McSween however, had already petitioned the Probate Court, which wouldn't reconvene until January of 1878. Having already known this, McSween had planned to travel to St. Louis on a business trip over the Christmas Holiday. In a proactive maneuver, McSween had sent correspondence to several people including Judge Bristol and Judge Newcomb, detailing the nature of his business in St. Louis.[25]

As McSween, his wife, and John Chisum headed for St Louis they were abruptly denied passage as they rode through Las Vegas in San Miguel County. Catron had already notified the San Miguel County Sheriff that they would be traveling through the area, and he wanted them arrested. Upon crossing paths with the Sheriff, McSween was promptly apprehended on a warrant for his arrest issued by Judge Warren Bristol from Mesilla. The warrant was issued based on an affidavit by Emile Fritz Scholand. In the affidavit she accused McSween of embezzling $10,000 from the estate of Emil Fritz.[26]

Emile's allegations did not completely make sense when one looked at the actual amount that was purportedly embezzled. The amount transferred into his account by Donnell, Lawson & Company was $7,148.46. Factoring in McSween's 10% fee and travel expenses further reduced the amount. There was also the issue of the amount of money McSween was owed by the Fritz estate for collecting all outstanding debts prior to him going to New York City. After all his fees were deducted from the insurance claim monies, the amount that was in dispute was about $2,000. McSween was hoping that Judge Bristol had enough sense to figure it out and that he wouldn't risk his integrity for $2,000.

Tunstall, being wise to the events that were unfolding, attempted to turn the tables on J. Dolan and his men by divulging their questionable relationship with Sheriff William Brady. The sheriff was bestowed with the authority to collect taxes from the citizens of Lincoln County for the Territory of New México. Sheriff Brady had collected about $2,500 in taxes for the 1877 fiscal year. Sheriff Brady in turn, gave the money to the House, possibly with the thought that they would send the money to Santa Fé. The House used $1,500 of the tax money to issue a business loan to two gentlemen for the purpose of buying cattle. J. Dolan, meanwhile, was inclined to rebuke the allegations by stating Tunstall, McSween, and Chisum were conspiring to destroy his business.[27]

The environment in Lincoln County was becoming toxic but that didn't deter Florencio from moving from his farm on the Río Bonito. On January 11, 1878 his wife Reimunda purchased land from José Rafael Gutiérrez near La Plaza de San Patricio.[28] After purchasing the property he and his family discreetly moved from Lincoln to their new, fertile lands. The move wasn't that far from their previous land holdings, the move was no more than seven miles away.

On January 28, 1878 McSween and Deputy Barrier left for Mesilla. Accompanying him on the trip was John Tunstall, Justice of the Peace John Wilson, and McSween's brother-in-law David Shield.

On February 02, 1878 McSween was brought before Judge Bristol and District Attorney William L. Rynerson in Mesilla. Both the Judge and the DA appeared to have been extremely prejudiced against McSween. A few days later, on February 04, 1878 Judge Bristol tried to get McSween and Tunstall to admit that they were partners. Tunstall knowing of the implications to admitting he was McSween's partner denied the assertion. Judge Bristol then ordered McSween to be sent to the underground jail in Lincoln and be placed on $8,000 bail, subject to DA Rynerson's approval.[29]

While McSween and Tunstall were in Mesilla, Judge Bristol had served an attachment to their properties on behalf of Emile Scholand and Charles Fritz. Upon their return to Lincoln, Sheriff Brady had already seized their properties. He had seized Tunstall's property under the presumption that Tunstall had admitted under oath to being McSween's business partner.[30] In essence, the $8,000 owed by McSween could also be collected from Tunstall.

On the evening of February 13, 1878 Deputy U.S. Marshall Rob Widenmann had met with John Tunstall. Widenmann revealed that both Jacob "Billy" Mathews, who was a deputy sheriff and William Morton, J. Dolan's ranch foreman, were recruiting men for the purpose of taking Tunstall's cattle by force to satisfy the attachment on McSween's $8000 bond. Both Mathews and Morton had agreed that they would meet at Turkey Springs on the evening of February 16, 1878. Upon hearing this bit of information, Tunstall opted to leave his ranch on the Río Felix the next morning. He asked Billy, Fred Waite who was from the Choctaw tribe, and Widenmann to remain so that they may keep an eye on his ranch.[31]

On February 16, 1878 George Washington, a retired Buffalo Soldier, had tipped Tunstall to the fact that Mathews and Morton had raised a posse that was 43 men strong. Tunstall became very concerned for his men that he had asked to remain on the ranch. He made haste on his return to the ranch for the purpose of asking them to make their escape, fearing that a violent and deadly confrontation may ensue.

Tunstall arrived at his ranch on the evening of February 17, 1878. He was successful in persuading his men to abandon the ranch and opting to leave his cattle exposed to capture by Mathews and Morton's posse. He figured that the matter of assessing the value of the relinquished property was better suited for the court to settle. After much deliberation Tunstall and his men decided that they would dispatch a message to Mathews with William McCloskey. The message indicated that they intended to allow them to gather the value of the cattle in the amount of the $8000 attachment without putting up a fight. Before making their exit, Tunstall had asked Old man Gauss if he could stay behind and oversee the transfer of the cattle.[32]

Tunstall and his men promptly abandoned the ranch at about 8:00am on the morning of February 18, 1878 and headed for Lincoln. In Tunstall's company were William H. "Billy the Kid" Bonney, Waite, Widenmann, Richard Brewer, and John Middleton. Mathews and Morton arrived at the ranch with their posse about two hours after Tunstall's departure. After they discovered that the farm had been abandoned, they came across Gauss who told them that Tunstall and his party had already left and that he thought they might have been headed either to Lincoln or Brewer's ranch. Realizing that Tunstall and his men were gone Morton and his posse followed in pursuit.[33]

At about 5:00pm and just ten miles due south of Lincoln, Tunstall and his men had abruptly come across a flock of wild turkeys gathered at the junction of the trail and the Río Ruidoso. Widenmann, after offering a weaponless Tunstall his pistol, made for the turkeys and commenced shooting at them. Billy the Kid and Middleton, who were riding at the rear, had come upon the crest of the hill. From that vantage point they caught a glimpse of Morton's posse riding at full speed towards them.

Billy and Middleton quickly rode forward warning the others of the oncoming posse. As Billy approached Widenmann and Brewer, shots rang out as the posse quickly came into view. Tunstall's men promptly rode into the hills and took cover behind some large outcroppings of rocks. Middleton hurriedly rode past Tunstall all the while screaming to take cover. In the mass of confusion Tunstall couldn't make out what Middleton was screaming. Middleton proceeded to ride into the hills to take cover.

All the while, Morton's posse was firing a slew of shots that pierced the cold evening air. Lost in his confusion, Tunstall only began to realize that the posse had caught up to him with bloodlust coursing through their veins. Tunstall valiantly led his horse up a steep embankment but it was too late to make his escape as Morton and his men had him directly in their sights. In a matter of minutes, three more shots rang out and Tunstall had drawn his last breath.[34]

After discovering that Tunstall had been murdered, McSween had dispatched a note to John Newcomb, who lived near La Plaza de San Patricio, for the purpose of retrieving the corpse and returning it to Lincoln for burial. Newcomb sought out the services of Florencio, Patricio Trujillo, Lázaro Gallegos, and Román Barragán to accompany him in the search for Tunstall's body. They set out following the Río Ruidoso with Newcomb's wagon in tow to the purported murder site. After diligently searching, Román Barragán finally found the body lying upon a steep and winding trail next to some bushes. They couldn't maneuver the wagon up the steep slope so they improvised by strapping Tunstall's body to a horse and led it down the trail. Once reaching the wagon, they transferred the body and set off for Lincoln.[35]

Lieutenant Daniel M. Appel conducted the autopsy on Tunstall's corpse, in which he had reported that there were two wounds as a result of carbine bullets. Florencio gave testimony that contradicted the autopsy's report. In his testimony he stated that there were three discernible wounds to the corpse. A rifle or carbine bullet that had entered through the chest created the first wound. The second was that of a pistol's bullet that had entered through the back of the head. The third was an exit wound, which was a result of being shot from the back of the head.[36]

Immediately following the murder, the Dolan faction had taken the position that Morton and some of his men had shot and killed Tunstall in self-defense. William Morton alleged that while he was issuing the writ, Tunstall turned his horse around, had drawn his pistol and shot at him. Morton and those men in his company drew their weapons in response and returned the fire.[37]

During Special Agent Angel's inquiries of the events that took place during Tunstall's death, several inconsistencies in their stories were discovered. Furthermore, Wallace Olinger and Sam Perry had detracted from the story. Both had claimed that they thought Tunstall's pistol had two rounds unloaded after his death by William Morton, Tom Hill, or Jesse Evans. A third member of the posse, George Kitt, had a conversation with Albert Howe stating that Morton had shot Tunstall in the chest, Hill had shot him in back of the head, and another member of the posse had shot Tunstall's horse. According to Kitt, Tunstall had never fired a shot.[38]

On February 19, 1878, Justice of the Peace John B. "Juan Bautista" Wilson conducted an inquiry of John Tunstall's murder. He later declared their guilt and proceeded to issue the arrest warrants for Jesse Evans, Frank Baker, Thomas Hill, George Hindemann, J. Dolan, and William Morton. Upon discovering that Sheriff William Brady and his deputies had knowingly taken hay from Tunstall's store, Wilson also issued an arrest warrant for Brady and his deputies. Constable Anastacio Martínez was tasked with the duty of serving the warrants.

Widenmann on the other hand, had asked for assistance from Captain George A. Purington, at Fort Stanton, to assist in the arrest of Evans, Baker, Hill, and George Davis, all of whom were implicated in stealing government livestock. Widenmann now with U.S. troops in tow proceeded to J. Dolan's ranch house for the purpose of apprehending Evans, Baker, Hill, and Davis. They ransacked the house but didn't find the men they were looking for. Widenmann proceeded to Tunstall's store, looking for the men, but found nobody.

Constable Martínez had assembled a posse, which included Ignacio Gonzáles, Román Barragán, Jesús Rodríguez, Esiquio Sánchez, Josiah "Doc" Scurlock, Billy the Kid, Richard Brewer, Fred Waite, Frank McNab, Frank Coe, George Coe, George Washington, George Robinson, John Middleton, and several others.[39]

Concurrently while Widenmann was searching stores in Lincoln, Constable Martínez, and his posse were impatiently waiting for Widenmann to depart so that they could conduct their own search. Constable Martínez eventually found two deputies that Brady had posted at Tunstall's store along with John Long, Charley Martin, and an ex Buffalo Soldier named John Clark. With no resistance they apprehended the five men and took them to jail. The name of the first deputy was James Longwell and the other's name was George Peppin. [40]

With Longwell, Peppin and the other three men in hand, Constable Martínez, Billy, and Waite took to the task of searching for Sheriff Brady. They did not have to search for long. Sheriff Brady and some of the men for which he had an arrest warrant were quickly found at the entrance to the House. Upon stepping up to Brady, the sheriff and his men trained their rifles upon the Constable, and his men. Martínez and his men knew there was no chance for them to escape with their lives if they chose to fight thus they gave up their weapons. After Brady disarmed the three who sought him out, he arrested them and detained them in the underground county jail.[41]

Sheriff Brady had already anticipated a degree of lawlessness by those citizens loyal to the McSween/ Tunstall faction. On February 18, 1878 he diligently dispatched a letter to Captain Purington, of Fort Stanton, seeking military assistance. In the letter Brady had conveyed his concern that he was not able to muster enough armed men to help him execute his duties as sheriff. He requested one officer and fifteen soldiers to attend Tunstall's burial for the sole purpose of keeping the peace.[42]

Tunstall's untimely death was weighing heavily on the minds of many men and women who had come to pay their last respects on February 22, 1878. After Tunstall's body had been laid to rest, many of them had congregated at McSween's house to reminisce amongst each other. Their mourning gradually turned to agitation and finally anger as they relived the events that had led to his murder.

The crowd was bewildered that Tunstall's murderers remained free from incarceration and furthermore, they were shielded from due justice by Sheriff William Brady. They were disenchanted with Constable Anastacio Martínez's inability to apprehend those responsible for his death. Although Martínez was soon released from his incarceration, both Billy the Kid and Fred Waite had remained in jail. The crowd grew increasingly restless with the sentiment that a great injustice was being served.

In an attempt to temper the crowd's increasing displeasure, it was decided that Florencio Gonzáles, José Montaño, John Newcomb, and Isaac Ellis would serve as an ad hoc committee that would voice the crowd's grievances to Sheriff Brady. The committee steadily made their way from McSween's house to the Dolan store. As the four men passed through the door's threshold, they were greeted by the eerie silence of Sheriff Brady's cold stare.

Florencio broke the silence by offering his first grievance, which questioned the reasoning of the unwarranted incarceration of Constable Martínez and the members of his posse. Brady arrogantly replied that he did it because he had the authority to do so. Feeling no satisfaction with Brady's nonchalant disposition on the matter, but not deterred from his objective, The stern spokesman offered his second grievance. He had explained to Brady that it was the committee's position to satisfy the bond by offering twice the value of McSween and Tunstall's attached property.

Sheriff Brady deliberated the idea briefly before resoundingly rejecting the spokeman's proposition. Brady's primary objective wasn't to satisfy the bond requirements but rather to break up the McSween faction. The committee resigned themselves to discussing the value of the property that had already been attached to the bond. Brady showed his objection to any further deliberations by promptly asking the group of men to leave his office.[43]

Brady was fully cognizant that the fair value of the attached property greatly exceeded the $8000 bond that District Attorney Rynerson had authorized. Admitting to that fact would reveal that there was no justification behind sending Morton and his men after Tunstall's livestock. Upon the committee's forced departure, Brady had time to evaluate the gravity of the situation. In an attempt to appease the general populace's disenchantment with his office, he set both Bonney and Waite free later in the day.[44]

Florencio left for La Plaza de San Patricio with the news of the events that led up to his meeting with Sheriff Brady. It was a widely accepted practice for many men in and around the community to gather together and discuss political matters or the current events with one another. Discussions as such were referred to as *juntas* (gatherings) and they were often very loosely organized. Only in the most dire of circumstances was a meeting actually called to order. Some of the more notable people who often attended such juntas were Mauricio de la Trinidad Sánches, his sons Estolano Sánchez and Francisco Sánchez. Others who could be found attended these juntas were Román Barragán, Fernando Herrera, Esiquio Sánchez, Ignacio Gonzáles, Jesús Rodrígues, Vicente Romero, Martín Cháves, and Francisco Trujillo just to name a few. The juntas were often held at Francisco Trujillo's brother, Juan de Dios Trujillo's house. On this evening Florencio had a wondrous story to tell.

Biased by his contempt for Dolan and the sheriff, he was placed in a precarious predicament. Florencio was a highly dignified man, who relied on his integrity to perform his duties as the Probate Judge. His core values were challenged, however, due to the fact that Tunstall's murder had become a personal matter for him.

As such, his dislike for the Dolan faction was evident as he discussed the affairs of the day with several other men in the junta. He didn't have to persuade any of those in attendance, because many of them had also been victimized, first by Lawrence Murphy, and then by the Dolan faction. The one common bond between many of them was that they wanted Dolan and his henchmen out of their lives, and therefore, out of Lincoln County.

In the following days, discontent began to brew throughout the ranching community and throughout the rest of the Río Ruidoso, Río Hondo, and Río Bonito valleys. The people grew restless as it became apparent that Tunstall's killers were still roaming as free men. Some men became openly vocal of Sheriff Brady and the Dolan faction. The people wanted justice and justice was not being served.

On March 01, 1878, in an act of defiance, Justice Wilson swore in Richard "Dick" Brewer as a deputy constable, for the sole purpose of bringing Tunstall's murderer's to justice. Sheriff Brady was so enraged by the news he promptly moved to arrest many in the McSween/ Tunstall faction that had come looking for him and his men just after Tunstall's murder.

Many of those who were arrested were from La Plaza de San Patricio, and the Río Ruidoso valley. Some of the men arrested were Ignacio Gonzáles, Román Barragán, Esiquio Sánchez, and Jesús Rodriguez. Also arrested were Widenmann, Billy the Kid, John Middleton, Josiah "Doc" Scurlock, Frank McNabb, George Washington, Frank Coe, and George Coe. Brady contended that

Widenmann and the other men were arrested because they were inciting a riot that previously had led to the apprehension of two of his deputies on February the 19th. It was more a case of one-upmanship as opposed to a matter of law. [45]

By arresting so many McSween/ Tunstall sympathizers under the false pretense of quelling a riot, Brady had further polarized the majority of Dolan's enemies. Born of this contempt were a vigilante group known as the Regulators. Some of those who were arrested by Brady for participating in the supposed riot accompanied Deputy Constable Brewer in his attempt to apprehend Tunstall's murderers.

It didn't take the Regulators long to catch William Morton and Frank Baker on March 06, 1878. The vigilantes gave chase on the banks of the Río Pecos for a few miles and finally caught the two desperados after their horses had come up lame. Morton and Baker surrendered without any further incident, to the dismay of some in the group who had wanted to kill them both. Once apprehended, they took their two captives to John Chisum's ranch before heading north to Lincoln. On March 09, 1878 both Morton and Baker were killed. The captors concurred that they shot them only after they had killed William McCloskey in an attempt to escape their captors.[46] There were some suspicions that their captors were looking for any excuse to kill them as a means of avenging the murder of John Tunstall.

To further exasperate the crisis that was unfolding in Lincoln County, Governor Axtell, while visiting Lincoln on March 09, 1878, had pronounced that John Wilson's office as Justice of the Peace was illegal and thus would be made void. He also notified that Widenmann's office as U.S. Marshal was being revoked. He proclaimed that by order of the United States President, that the military would be used to assist, the lawful territorial civil officers, in maintaining the peace. The governor continued by encouraging all those who bore arms, to lay them down and return to their houses as a gesture of peace.[47] It was no wonder that Governor Axtell had shown partiality towards the members of the House, as it turns out John H. Riley had loaned them money in the amount of $1,800 sometime in 1876.[48]

Obviously it was the Governor's intention to vilify all the members of the Regulators. To a degree he was saying that anybody who took the position of the McSween faction was an outlaw. It was a bold, but an ignorant move considering the majority of the constituents he was condemning as being lawless were the very people who held such contempt for Dolan and his bunch of desperados. It was tragically apparent to Florencio, that the Governor had slighted the people.

Disillusioned by the events that had unfolded over the past month, many people had to do some deep soul searching. Several questions arose when one had to contemplate how they fit into the bigger picture. Do I want to be the activist, or the pacifist? Am I willing to lay down my life for something I truly believe in? Am I willing to take a life for the sake of my convictions? Am I willing to live with the lawlessness of the newcomers and of *mi gente* (my people)? What will happen to my wife, my children, my land, or my livestock? These questions and many more weighed heavily on the minds of many men.

Although many within the community chose the path of peace and passivity, there were several who chose to fight the corruption, lawlessness, and violence. They were a bigger force than the Regulators. They didn't get the sensationalist headlines. They often accompanied the core members that history has so elegantly enshrined. Their allegiance to the McSween faction, although true, was loosely bonded, as their ranks often fluctuated from week to week. The core of the Regulators was well documented. This core group consisted of Billy the Kid, Fred Waite, Josiah "Doc" Scurlock,

Charlie Bowdre, José Chávez y Chávez, Frank Coe, George Coe, Henry Brown, Tom O'Folliard, Jim French, and Frank MacNab.

Another member of Morton's posse, whom the Regulators were after, had finally met his fate on March 14, 1878. Tom Hill and Jesse Evans had come across a sheepherder by the name of John Wagner and his Cherokee driver just southwest of Tularoso. They proceeded to rob Wagner of his horses and looked for any monies that he might have had. During the robbery attempt a scuffle ensued, and the Cherokee shot Hill, dropping him dead in his boots. The Cherokee shot at a fleeing Evans, hitting and shattering his wrist. After several days, Evans was forced to ride to Fort Stanton seeking a doctor that could help heal his wound. Evans was promptly arrested upon his arrival at Fort Stanton.[49]

Dolan on the other hand had escaped the vigilante vengeance by suffering a broken leg during a freak accident. Fortunately to his detriment, he was recuperating in Santa Fé. The Regulators had basked in the glory of bringing down those who were primarily responsible for Tunstall's murder.[50]

The jury duty notices clearly stated that a grand jury would be held at the Lincoln County courthouse on April 01, 1878. Unbeknownst to the jurors, a clerical error had been made because the actual court date should have been a week later. Sheriff Brady had the unfortunate task of having to explain to the jurors that court was not going to be held until the following week. In his company were George Peppin, George Hindemann, Billy Mathews, and John "Jack" Long. After talking with the jurors for a few moments, Brady and his men made their way back to the House, from whence they came.[51]

The morning silence was eerily broken as gunshots rang out from all directions. A slew of bullets had found their mark, dropping Brady to the ground. With one last gasp for life he let out an agonizing scream before death finally came upon him. Hindemann was also hit and he quickly fell to the ground. As he bled upon the earth, he grew thirsty, but nobody was willing to help him as the echo of gunshots pierced the air. Hindemann soon found peace as death crawled in his direction. Peppin, Mathews, and Long quickly found cover, and started spraying bullets in an attempt to find a mark.

Suddenly Billy the Kid sprung from the adobé corral, and hastily ran to Sheriff Brady. He dropped to his knees and grabbed the rifle that Sheriff Brady had commandeered during his arrest several weeks earlier. As he stood up to take cover, the Kid was hit in the thigh by one of the deputies' bullets. He escaped death by finding cover in the corral.

All six Regulators that partook in Sheriff Brady's assassination had made their escape. Bonney's escape, however, came only after Dr. Ealy had tended to his leg wound. At this point he was being hunted down by Brady's deputies and had made his getaway only after he had cunningly hid from them.[52]

On April 13, 1878, Judge Bristol had unassumingly made his way to Lincoln, unannounced and in fear of his life. He knew all too well, that Lincoln County justice was often served at the end of a barrel of a gun. Once convening court, he made painstaking efforts to vilify McSween, Tunstall, and the vigilantes. He stated that the administrators of Emil Fritz's estate had legitimate grounds for accusing McSween with embezzling the $10,000 in insurance proceeds. He tried to convince the jurors that Tunstall had implicated himself as a willing partner of McSween while under oath, thus legitimizing the attachment to Tunstall's property.

After hearing several testimonies from people from around the county, the grand jury issued their opinion. The jury did not find enough testimony that implicated McSween for the alleged charges. The jury thus exonerated McSween from any wrongdoing. The jury also had harsh words for Governor Axtell claiming that his partiality in the matter was partly responsible for the loss of many lives in Lincoln County.

Concerning members of the Dolan faction, the grand jury found Jesse Evans, Frank Rivers, and Miguel Segovia guilty in Tunstall's murder. They also indicted Dolan, and Billy Mathews as accessories to murder. Concerning the members of the McSween faction, the grand jury found Bonney, Waite, Middleton, and Brown guilty of Brady's murder. Charlie Bowdre was indicted for the murder of Andrew Roberts during a confrontation at Blazer's Mill.[53]

In the following weeks, the House was dissolved, and ceased to exist as a business in Lincoln County. The citizens had their final say, first during the grand jury, and second during a town meeting that was called by Juan Patrón on April 24, 1878. Florencio was nominated as the president and primary speaker. The Vice Presidents were Saturnino Baca and José Montaño. The Secretaries were Alexander McSween and Isaac Ellis.

Juan Patrón called for order as he commenced the meeting by calling forward, the Probate Judge. Florencio looked into the crowd with a grin of satisfaction upon his face. He waited for the clamoring crowd to quiet down. In a dignified voice, he gave a spirited speech that went over the events that had transpired over the past several months, the senseless killings, and the outcome of the grand jury. He continued by addressing what direction the community should take in the near future. His words touched many people and his positively charged speech was often interrupted by widespread applause from the crowd.

The meeting addressed the demise of the House, and the condemning of Governor Axtell's partiality towards the House. It also aimed to cease any further hostilities between the native New Mexicans and the newcomers. There was the hope that the many different cultures could share mutual respect and understanding for one another. For many, the war between the two factions was over, and peace was thus temporarily restored to Lincoln County.[54]

Even so, hostilities and distrust between the Hispanos, the Americans and the immigrants still persisted. The truce as accepted by the politicos did little to temper the human nature of many of the people in the valley. People were still divided, and that was something a piece of paper, or a proclamation could not change. The racial tension was still evident although somewhat subdued.

On May 28, 1878 Governor Axtell had appointed George Peppin as the new sheriff of Lincoln County.[55] Sheriff Peppin promptly sought out the services of John Kinney and his band of outlaws. He hastily swore in Kinney and his men as deputy sheriffs of Lincoln County for the sole purpose of serving warrants to the members of the Regulators.[56]

John Kinney's notoriety stemmed from his participation in the El Paso Salt Wars, where he and his men committed numerous atrocities against the Mexican people, as deputized Texas Rangers. During the Salt Wars his men raped the Mexican women and murdered many other Mexicans who showed resistance. His acts of terror led many citizens within the El Paso community to abandon their homes as they reluctantly returned to México or moved elsewhere into the Territory of New México.

Kinney lead a band of thieves and murderers who had come to be known as the Río Grande Posse. His operation was based in La Mesilla, Doña Ana County. The "Río Grande Posse" was 30 men strong and they all carried the same savage disposition as their leader.[57]

As the word spread of the arrival of John Kinney and his bunch of deputized outlaws, many Spanish-speaking citizens opted to briefly leave their homesteads behind. They had heard about the atrocities he and his men had committed during the El Paso Salt Wars. They didn't want to have any part of his type of vicious injustice.

Florencio and several other citizens of the region responded by sending a petition to Governor Axtell requesting the removal of Sheriff Peppin. He had been made aware that he had been black listed, and that Kinney and his men would serve him their kind of justice. Upon hearing of the new threat, by June 14, 1878 both he and Juan Patrón had sought refuge at Fort Stanton. Many of the Regulators and their supporters fled to the safety of the hills in and around La Plaza de San Patricio.[58]

In the following months Kinney and his men had unleashed a reign of terror upon the people of Lincoln County. The fear they created stopped only after some of the brave men from La Plaza de San Patricio and the surrounding communities banded together and launched an assault of their own on the town of Lincoln, which came to be known as the "Five Days Battle" or "The Big Killing". After Five Days Battle was over, the Lincoln County War had come to an end but the lawlessness and violence continued to disrupt people's lives.

In response to the continued violence, newly appointed Governor Lew Wallace had arrived in Lincoln on March 05, 1879 for the purpose of shaking out all of the outlaws in Lincoln. The Governor launched an assault specifically on Shedd's ranch in San Augustín, Beckwith's ranch, and the Seven Rivers region. He wanted to round up as many cattle rustlers as possible.

The Governor continued by forwarding Captain Carroll a list of all the registered cattle brands in Lincoln County. He mandated that any livestock not compliant would thus be confiscated. He tasked Captain Carroll with this duty and gave him specific instructions to turn over all the unbranded, and presumed to be stolen, cattle to the Probate Judge Florencio Gonzáles. He would then turn all the cattle over to John Newcomb, who had been appointed by the Governor to become their ward.[59]

Once a semblance of peace returned to the valley, Florencio was able to re-focus his energies into a more tranquil living. He grazed cattle on his rancho in La Plaza de San Patricio where there were several people in his employment. Sharecroppers helped with the crops while vaqueros helped with his cattle. He also bought into a share of a White Oaks newspaper called "The Lincoln County Leader". By October 25, 1883 he, along with José Montaño, George D. Dasher, and Samuel R. Corbett, sold their interest in the newspaper to William Caffrey.[60]

Florencio died at a relatively young age, he was 54 years old when he had finally passed away on December 18, 1897. He was buried at La Capilla de San Patricio, in what can be considered one of the more distinguished gravesites in an otherwise unappreciated campo santo. After his death, Reimunda married again, to Ambrocio Chávez. Ironically, when Reimunda passed away, she wasn't buried next to her first husband, but rather in an unassuming grave.

Florencio Gonzáles and Reimunda Sánchez de Gonzáles' legacy however lives on through their descendants. Many of their descendants still live on the lands they once owned in the tiny community of San Patricio.

Chapter Eight: Fernando Herrera

From left to right: Fernando Herrera, Estela Gill, Epifania Muños (Photo courtesy of Fred Flores)

Fernando Heads South

Fernando Herrera, christened José Fernando de Herrera, was born on July 02, 1836 in Santa Cruz de la Cañada, Nuevo México, La República de México. His parents were Pedro Alcantar de Herrera and María Celedonia Archuleta. Los Herrera were sheep ranchers, who lived a mostly nomadic life. They had large land holdings near the Pueblo de San Juan, and the Villa de **Ojo Caliente** (Hot Springs). The family also had lived near Fernando de Taos (more commonly known as Taos), and the Río Colorado (Red River) region near the northern New México and southern Colorado border.

He married María Juliana Martín in Santa Cruz de la Cañada, Territory of New México on October 13, 1856. His wife was also known as Juliana Martínes, and was listed as such on some church documents. Juliana (also known affectionately as Julianita) gave her husband nine children before she died sometime after their daughter Celedonia was born.

Fernando was an adventurous, enterprising young man and he sought to expand his world beyond all that he had known in the Taos region. The young man had heard many stories about the southeastern frontier opening up for settlement and he was intrigued with what it may have had to offer. Sometime in late 1866 or early 1867, he packed a wagon and headed towards El Bonito with the hope that he could provide a better life for himself and his family.

As the young pioneer left for new lands, his wife and children all remained behind in the Río Colorado precinct, north of Taos. In all likelihood, he would have accompanied a caravan, rather than going by himself because the travel was long, arduous and extremely dangerous. There had been numerous attacks by the Apachés, and outlaws, therefore it was always safer to travel in numbers.

He squatted on lands near the Sierra Blanca on the Rio Ruidoso. Here he built a jacal, and proceeded to construct a rudimentary acequia. It was during 1867 that he obtained priority over the water rights that eventually fed both of his acequias of which, one ran to the north and the other ran to the south of his farm. The original names of the ditches are referred to as the Herrera Ditch, north and south. The north ditch irrigated all of his fields north of the river and the south ditch irrigated his fields south of the river. He did not petition for a homestead immediately, but rather he continued to squat on the land. He named the area *San Juanito*, in honor of the lands to the north from whence he had originally come from.[1]

As Fernando continued to make improvements on the land he was squatting on, his thoughts would often drift back to his family living up north. Although he greatly missed his family, he knew that there was a high probability that he might lose his land if he were to abruptly return to them. The new *vecinos* (neighbor) cultivated relations with several of the other squatting settlers nearby. Once he developed mutual friendships where he had become comfortable and trusting with his neighbors, he opted to return to the north to visit with his family. The visit was short lived though, as he had to return to his Rancho de San Juanito. Over the next few years, he continued to visit with his family up north. Soon thereafter, his eldest son Andrés would accompany his father in San Juanito to help make improvements to the land. This arrangement continued for well over three years.

Shortly after 1870, when Fernando and his son had finished constructing an adequate adobé and had cleared the farmlands for cultivation, they returned once more to finally move the family south to Bonito. As the family was making preparations for the move, a close family friend, Juanita Bojórque approached him about raising his daughter Manuelita, who had fallen gravely ill and couldn't make the arduous journey south. The patriarch and his wife deliberated the idea for several days before they had finally agreed to let Juanita raise their daughter. The decision to leave one of their own was difficult, but they never second-guessed their decision. The entire family packed all of their belongings into two wagons and then set off for El Rancho de San Juanito.[2]

When the first settlers moved to the Río Ruidoso, everyone occupying any land in Township 11 south range 14 east of principal meridian, at the time was doing so under squatter's rights. Then pursuant to an Act of Congress, approved on May 20, 1862, to secure homesteads to those settlers on public domain, Fernando Herrera and several others promptly applied for their homesteads. Each applicant could petition for 160 acres.

To the south of Fernando's homestead was a natural water spring that flowed from the base of the mountain. He fittingly named the spring Ojo de San Juanito (which later became known as Hale Spring). From the spring, the remnants of an ancient acequia jutted northeast down the side of the mountain towards the valley below. He often commented that the acequia was built before he had arrived in San Juanito. He had speculated and often told others that *"Los Ancianos"* (The Ancients), which he believed to be an ancient Native American tribe, had initially constructed it.

The acequia resembled a rock wall that traversed upon the curvatures of the downward slope of the hills. The base was built higher on lower ground and appeared to have been dug deeper on higher ground. A noticeable concave indentation was seemingly constructed upon the top of the wall for the purpose of carrying water to the valley below.[3] In more modern times, after further investigation, the rock wall was found to be a natural occurring formation made from the minerals and mud found in the spring water. At the time, Fernando wouldn't have had enough information to think otherwise.

Tragedy greets the family

After the birth of their son Teodoro in April of 1873, Julianita fell gravely ill. As she was struggling with her illness, she developed severe complications. To the entire family's horror, she lost the battle, succumbed to her illness, and died. The suddenness of her death threw the family into disbelief. Fernando buried his wife on the land in what would eventually become the family cemetery.

He had to condition himself to focus his energies on preparing his family move forward without their matriarch. It was difficult, but he managed to keep his family focused on what needed to be done.

A few years after the death of his beloved wife, he had sought the comfort of a woman by the name of Marta Rodríguez who was believed to be a sister of his compadre, Jesús Rodríguez. Eventually he would take Marta as his wife and she had helped raise his younger children. Although Marta was trying to fill in as a loving mother, many of the older children refused to embrace her as their mother, which led to a very strained relationship for many within the family.

Once again, tragedy had struck the family one fateful day as a quick moving thunderstorm passed overhead. Two of his children, his son Macedonio, and his daughter Seledonia were playing next to a wood stove inside of the house. The two children were inseparable, as they did everything together. An intense flash of light lit up the rooms within the adobé house. Then an eerie crackling and thunderous roar shook the house. Lightning had struck the chimney of the wood stove and had traveled down the chute and inside the house. Both children were instantly killed as the lightning traveled through their bodies. Their bodies fell to the ground, limp and smoldering.

An eerie sensation filled the room as the hair on everybody's bodies wildly stood on end. Everybody was forcefully knocked to the ground. Filled with alarm, Fernando quickly sprung up. He was horrified to see his youngest children both lying on the ground next to the wood stove they were playing around. A slight waft of pungent smoke was filtering into the air from their burnt, electrocuted bodies. He ran over to them and threw himself upon his knees, he took both of his babies into his arms and he screamed up towards the heavens. God had taken his babies. Some of the other children gathered around their father, their brother and sister. There they cried for their tragic losses. A few days later, the distraught father buried his children on the north bank of the Río Ruidoso next to their mother.[4]

Don Fernando Herrera

Fernando was a well-respected man in El Bonito. His opinion carried a great deal of weight concerning matters that affected the community. Like many other people in the valley, he was a farmer first and foremost. He was a loving father, and an even a more compassionate man when it came to extending his hospitality to other people.

The dicho, *"Mi casa es su casa"* (My house is your house) literally described his unselfish character. That was evident by the fact that both Josiah "Doc" Scurlock and Charles Bowdre lived on his farm for the better part of two years. Although Scurlock and Bowdre had purchased some land from Paul Dowlin on section 21, they continued to live on their friend's farm.[5] In time, another frequent visitor to Don Fernando's house would be Billy the Kid, who closely associated himself with both Scurlock and Bowdre.

Fernando had become more than just a very good friend to the three young men. He had become somewhat of a father figure for them. They admired his wisdom, his strength, his fortitude, his compassionate demeanor, and his sense of justice. He was a reserved man, who didn't like to boast of his deeds. His humility was the one characteristic that had drawn the admiration of his peers.

Scurlock, who was born in Tallapoosa, Alabama on January 11, 1850, had taken a liking to his friend's daughter. Scurlock later married Antonia Miguela Herrera, who was 16 at the time, on October 19, 1876 at *La Iglesia de San Juan* in Lincoln. He and his wife chose to remain living on his father-in-law's farm. Their first daughter, María Elena, and second daughter, Viola Inéz were both born in San Juanito. The son-in-law earned his keep by helping to work the Herrera farm.

Holan Miller, who had brought two hundred head of cattle to the Río Ruidoso, had leased a small tract of land from A. N. Blazer. The land could not sustain his herd so he sought Don Fernando's help in the matter. The two men worked out a mutually beneficial arrangement.[6] Fernando was already grazing two hundred head of cattle up in the mountains just south of his land and it wouldn't have been too much trouble to graze both herds together.

There were about 400 head of cattle grazing further up Turkey Canyon on lands that were considered public domain. Don Fernando was compelled though, to bring the herd back to his homestead after a band of Mescalero successfully raided his herd on several different occasions. He mustered a small posse together and headed up Turkey Canyon. Accompanying him was his son Andrés Herrera, Billy the Kid, Manuel Silva, and George Washington.

About half way up the canyon, near Turkey Springs, they came across the chief named Kamisa and twenty-five of his Mescalero warriors. Fernando and Kamisa had crossed paths on numerous occasions beforehand and therefore felt a mutual respect for one another. While he talked with Kamisa about the repeated raids, the Mescalero warriors surrounded the posse in an attempt to intimidate them. Many of them suggested to Kamisa that their accusers should be put to death without any further deliberation.

Being wise to the gravity of their situation Billy dismounted his horse and tightened up the front cinch of his saddle. He then yelled to his compadres telling them that they should do the same and follow his lead. He mounted his horse again, with a six-shooter in each hand. He began whooping and hollering and fired a couple of shots in the air as he made his way towards the warriors. The others followed Bonney's lead, shooting their six-shooters in the air as they made a dashing escape passed the Mescalero. Startled by their brazen act of defiance, they didn't pursue their accusers. The men were able to round up some cattle and drive them down to San Juanito.

The next day Kamisa, accompanied by a small attachment of his warriors, had paid a visit to Don Fernando. The chief indicated that if his friend were to butcher three beeves for them, that they would be indebted to him, and therefore, would cease all raids upon his cattle. The cattleman saw the benefits of complying with the request. Having the peace of mind of not being raided was worth it to him. This decision ended up being highly beneficial because Kamisa and his warriors honored their words by refraining from raiding his cattle herds. The two men remained in good standing for as long as they were associated with each other.[7]

Don Fernando was an expert marksman, who had learned the art of the hunt in the mountains of El Bonito. He often had hunted on the Llano Estacado to the east to hunt *cibola* (buffalo). His marksmanship had become legendary in the valley. Sometimes, his hunting exploits could be heard in the *cuentos* (stories) that were told next to a campfire. His skills would be put to the test in the months to come.

War!

A Campaign of Terror is launched against La Plaza de San Patricio

After Sheriff Peppin had sworn in John Kinney and his Río Grande Posse as deputies of Lincoln County, many people, mostly native New Mexicans, chose to temporarily leave their homesteads in a preemptive measure to safeguard their lives and personal property. Those that remained had become the subjects of Kinney's disregard for justice. In an attempt to garner more support from the Spanish-speaking community, Sheriff Peppin also deputized José Chávez y Baca.[8]

It was well known that La Plaza de San Patricio was a stronghold for the Regulators because many of its citizens either supported the vigilantes, or often rode with members of the group. The Regulators often found refuge amongst family or friends. Having unwillingly lost the support of Probate Judge Florencio Gonzáles and Juan Patrón whom had found refuge at Fort Stanton, it was left to the community at large to discuss the events that were unfolding and how to resolve the challenges that they would soon face.

McSween was a charismatic man who had found favor with many people within El Bonito's Hispanic community. Some of his biggest Anglo supporters such as Billy the Kid, Josiah "Doc" Scurlock and Charles Bowdre had either married into a native New Mexican family, or had fallen in love with a Nueva Mexicana. Bonney had been known to fancy many señoritas, and although he spoke English primarily, he often preferred to speak Spanish to impress upon all of them.

Many of the Nuevo Mexicanos had several different other motives to band together in opposition to Dolan and his henchmen. They were appalled with his strong-arm tactics, and disregard for person and property. The corrupt politicians and lawmen that refused to serve fair justice also disillusioned them. They felt a degree of hatred towards those who had murdered and maimed their family members and friends. They grew tired of living in terror every day, as the lawlessness spiraled out of control. Most of all, they were disenchanted by the fact that they hadn't empowered themselves to put an end to it.

Billy, Josiah "Doc" Scurlock, Charlie Bowdre, and many other Anglos who formed the core of the Regulators, along with McSween had found friends with Bonito's Spanish-speaking citizens. The Spanish community reciprocated the gesture by accepting them into their homes. With Peppin, Kinney and the Río Grande Posse hunting them down, the Regulators definitely needed all the support they could muster.

Sheriff Peppin had become wise to the progress that McSween was making in assembling a vigilante militia. He must have received word about the juntas in La Plaza de San Patricio because he implemented a plan that aimed to put a stop to it. Peppin wanted to thwart any attempt at a possible insurgency therefore he dispatched Deputy Jack Long and Kinney to the community on June 27, 1878. Leading the column into the community was Kinney who was hoping for trouble.

Women and children ran in terror as they saw Kinney and his ruffians riding through the community. McSween and his men had already been tipped off and they had taken their leave seeking refuge in the surrounding hills. Kinney and his men had managed to flush out George Washington, a sympathizer, and forced him to confess everything he knew about the Regulators and their whereabouts. Going off of what Washington had told them, Jack Long told Kinney to remain in town while he and five other men would investigate John Newcomb's ranch just up the Río Ruidoso.

Long and his men went to Newcomb's ranch but had discovered nothing out of the ordinary so they opted to head back to the plaza. On their way back they came across a band of Regulators. A small exchange of fire ensued, in which Long's horse was hit. The band included McSween, Billy, Scurlock, Bowdre, Fernando Herrera, Martín Chávez, and five others, who promptly made their escape into the hills.[9]

Upon hearing of the gun battle and McSween's narrow escape, Colonel Nathan Dudley became concerned with their unwillingness to be apprehended. He called upon the services of Captain Henry Carroll to lead a platoon of 35 soldiers to La Plaza de San Patricio to restore civility amongst the people. As Captain Carroll rode through town, all appeared tranquil. There was no evidence that an altercation had even taken place earlier in the day. None the less, Captain Carroll took pursuit of the vigilantes searching them out for well over 45 miles. Captain Carroll's pursuit abruptly ended upon receiving a hurried dispatch from Colonel Dudley that their actions were deemed illegal by the Posse Comitatus Act, which had previously and unknowingly been passed into law by Congress.[10]

In an attempt to save face, for Kinney's transgressions, Sheriff Peppin had dispatched Deputy José Chávez y Baca to La Plaza de San Patricio to arrest several members of the Regulators and their sympathizers. It was the sheriff's hope that a fellow native New Mexican would be able to succeed whereas others had failed in apprehending the vigilantes. On July 03, 1878 Deputy Chávez y Baca was dispatched to do the sheriff's dirty deeds. As Deputy Chávez y Baca rode into town with a contingent of the Río Grande posse, he received neither support nor respect from his people.

He explained to the residents that once the Regulators were brought to justice, they would live in peace. They weren't buying his lies, they knew better than to trust Sheriff Peppin, Kinney, Dolan, or the Governor. They looked upon Chávez y Baca as a puppet and a traitor to his people. Their resistance infuriated Chávez y Baca and he gave the order to seek out the vigilantes.

Chávez y Baca and his posse rode through the community stopping at each house. They busted the door's down even as the women and children screamed in terror. With tears falling from their eyes the women and children watched as the intruders ransacked the houses leaving nothing unturned. The intrusive men proceeded to cast disparaging remarks towards the women, and threatened them with bodily harm if they didn't fess up to the whereabouts of the Regulators. If the man of the house was present, he was interrogated with the threat of bodily injury or even death if he didn't divulge any information.[11]

The community as a whole kept their loyalties to the Regulators, and refused to cooperate. Disgusted with the lack of progress, Deputy José Chávez y Baca and his men begrudgingly retired back to Lincoln. Sheriff Peppin's wildcard had turned out to be a disaster. Furthermore, this only polarized the people who initially chose the path of passivity. They now were more inclined to support their brethren who chose to support the McSween faction.

Failing miserably in his duties to bring McSween and his men to justice, Sheriff Peppin was frantic to get results. He launched yet another assault upon the community of La Plaza de San Patricio. On July 10, 1878 Sheriff Peppin, Dolan, and the Río Grande Posse entered the town with an angry disposition.

Sheriff Peppin and his outlaw deputies had shot and killed many horses while riding through the community. Some of his men were so brazen as to steal the horses that weren't shot. They broke into houses, stealing anything of value under the tearful watch of terrified occupants. They broke doors, windows, and furniture. The deputies proceeded to the Dow Brothers' store where they commenced to loot the store, and destroy the roof of the building. They terrorized the people working in the fields by firing their guns upon them. The citizens in the fields scattered towards the Río Ruidoso seeking refuge from the bullets. They became belligerent with the women casting disparaging remarks about them as they sought refuge.

Before leaving the terrified citizens, John Kinney yelled out that he had the authority to do what he was doing because he was in the service of the Territorial Governor. He continued by stating that if the citizens wanted him out of Lincoln County that they should assist him and his men in arresting the Regulators. The deputized outlaws thus left the town in shambles again.[12]

On July 11, 1878 twenty-seven people from the ransacked community had signed a petition, which sought the protection of the soldiers from Ft. Stanton. Several women had walked to Ft. Stanton to personally hand Col. Dudley the petition. Unfortunately, Col Dudley declined their offer because he did not have the authority to do so. Instead, he offered the protection of the fort to any citizen who chose to take up residence within its boundaries. Some of the most notable names to appear on the petition were from the following families: Chávez, García, Gutiérrez, Jaramillo, Lucero, Miranda, Sánchez, Sedillo, and Trujillo.[13]

Although many of the townsfolk were obviously traumatized by the day's events, they weren't about to bend to the will of Kinney and his band of deputized outlaws. The people weren't about to turn in their own family and friends to satisfy the bloodlust of a bunch of barbarians. Rather, they came together that evening, at Juan de Dios Trujillo's house, and had one of the largest organized juntas they had ever held.

McSween's Regulators were in attendance, as were many of the people from all of the surrounding communities. The ex-sheriff, Don Mauricio de la Trinidad Sánches looked on as the people filed in. His sons Francisco and Estolano were also in attendance. Don Fernando Herrera stood next to his son in laws, Josiah "Doc" Scurlock, and Charles Bowdre, discussing the events that took place during the day. Martín Chávez had finally arrived with great fanfare. The atmosphere was somewhat chaotic, and it took a while for order to finally take hold of the emotionally charged mob.

As the room quieted down the people were encouraged to tell their stories of the events that took place over the past several weeks. In every story the same tragedy played out in a more detailed manner. From time to time the horror of the crowd was pierced with an angry voice stating that something should be done. The crowd would erupt in feverous agreement, and the stories would have to wait until the wave of emotion dissipated.

Obviously the fervor was playing into the hands of McSween and his Regulators. Kinney and his men, under the direction of J. Dolan had almost completely polarized the Hispanic community throughout the region against them. With each enraged tale to be told, the ranks of McSween's supporters grew. A militia of some 50 to 60 men thus was mustered up to fight for the cause of the Regulators. Their intent was to seek retribution against J. Dolan, Sheriff Peppin, and the deputized outlaws, better known as John Kinney and the Río Grande Posse.

The Five Days Battle

The people had grown weary of the repeated raids upon their communities. Many of those men throughout the region had volunteered to join the ranks of the Regulators under the leadership of Martín Chávez. On July 14, 1878, under the stealth of the night, the mob, who claimed well over fifty vigilantes, had descended upon Lincoln. They fortified themselves in three strategic positions. The first was at Ellis' store, which provided cover from the east. The second was at McSween's house, which was in middle of town. The third was at the Montaño store, which was situated between McSween's house and Ellis' store.

Fortunately for Sheriff Peppin, Kinney and most of the Río Grande posse, they were roaming about Lincoln County in search of the rogue Regulators. Deputy John "Jack" Long and a few members of the Río Grande Posse that had remained in Lincoln were none the wiser of the vigilante's movements into town. They were holed up in El Torreón, and were preoccupied with other matters.

McSween and his men had identified the strategic importance of El Torreón and had made haste in planning to commandeer it. Next to El Torreón was a house whose residents were Captain Saturnino Baca and his family. Being that both the house and El Torreón rightfully belonged to McSween, it was his purpose to take them back. He extended the courtesy of asking Baca to leave the house in a maneuver that would relieve him of prosecution in the event some tragedy should befall the Baca family during the attempt to take El Torreón. Baca perceived the matter in a different light, and fearing for his family, he diligently dispatched correspondence to Lieutenant Colonel Nathan Dudley seeking his assistance.[14]

Colonel Dudley promptly responded to Baca's plea for assistance by sending the Post Surgeon, Dr. Daniel Appel, to investigate and ascertain the situation that was developing in Lincoln. Colonel Dudley chose Dr. Appel deliberately as a means of showing McSween and his supporters that his intentions were not hostile. Dr. Appel proceeded into town and met with McSween and other members of the Regulators.

McSween explained to Appel his intentions, and had agreed that once vacated of the House's men, Dudley's soldiers would be allowed to take control of it. Scurlock added, that the Regulators would allow the House's men to leave without any further provocation. John Long, however, did not want to vacate El Torreón realizing its importance. As Dr. Appel left Lincoln to report back with Colonel Dudley in Fort Stanton, he crossed paths with Kinney and his men who were steadfastly returning to Lincoln.[15]

After it was apparent that Kinney and his men were greatly outnumbered by McSween supporters, Dolan sent dispatch pleading with the Seven Rivers Warriors for assistance. The Seven Rivers Warriors responded to Dolan's call, but even so, they were still greatly outnumbered by their counterparts. Sheriff Peppin was desperate to increase his odds of subduing the lawless mob but could only call upon the services of the U.S. military from Fort Stanton.

Colonel Dudley was faced with a most precarious dilemma. The Posse Comitatus Act prohibited the use of the U.S. military as a posse except in the event that an armed insurrection was developing. In other words, the act prohibited him from participating in the matter unless there was substantial evidence that would place his soldiers in harm of an insurgency. Colonel Dudley dispatched correspondence back to Peppin, of his duties to obey the law, with Private Barry Robinson.

Upon Private Robinson's arrival into Lincoln, shots were fired and the bullets whizzed by him. Important to note was the fact that there were intermittent shots fired throughout the day between the Regulators and the Río Grande posse. None of the shots between the two factions had hit their respective marks. Private Robinson had happened to arrive into Lincoln during such an exchange of shots. Peppin took advantage of the situation, by alleging in a letter to Colonel Dudley, that McSween's men had attempted to shoot Private Robinson while he rode into town.[16]

Upon Private Robinson's return to Fort Stanton, he confirmed Peppin's allegation. Colonel Dudley now had reasonable cause to justify any aggressive tactics used to preserve the peace in the region. At this point he ascertained that since one of his men had been fired upon while performing his military duties, he could lawfully ride into Lincoln and assist Sheriff Peppin in subduing the Regulator militia's insurgency.

By July 17, 1878 three uneventful days had passed since the Regulators had taken Lincoln siege, and neither faction could claim a kill. The sweltering heat was becoming unbearable, and had brought about a great deal of discomfort for many of the men. Intermittently, shots would be fired to break up the silence, and create a degree of excitement amongst the men. One man would think they saw enemy movement and proceed to shoot. Then everyone else would follow suit, firing at the unconfirmed target.

Lucio Montoya, Charles Crawford, and three other men had been sent by Sheriff Peppin to ascend the hillside south of town to cover his men's positions. They positioned themselves behind an outcropping of rocks, periodically shooting down into town. During one of the forays one of the bullets found its way into the Montaño store, hitting Martín Chávez's crucifix and deflecting harmlessly elsewhere.[17] Chávez made the sign of the cross thanking God for saving his life as several of the other men responded with return fire as the bullets from the opposing force continued striking the side of the walls. Eventually they fortified their positions by stacking bags of flour around the windows.

Fernando continued to diligently look through his field glasses in an attempt to make their attackers position. After painstakingly scouring the hillside, he could barely make out the heads of his enemy peering from behind the rocks as they sprayed gunfire down on the Montaño store. Patiently he attempted to figure out their tendencies. He was waiting for the opportunity of one of them making a mistake. As such, his mind was preoccupied from boredom well into the night.

The next morning Crawford, Montoya and the other men scouted the area for possible hostiles. They couldn't see nor hear anything as they scoured the rooftops, windows, and doorways in the early morning light. Presuming that the hostiles had left the Montaño's store, Crawford and Montoya proceeded to descend the side of the mountain. Both men had carelessly exposed themselves from behind the outcropping of rocks, to the vigilant marksman who had made their position from well over 500 yards away. Some say that the actual distance may have been 900 yards. Whichever the distance, his marksmanship could never be questioned.

Martín Chávez and the other men silently watched Fernando as he steadied his rifle. Once he had Crawford in his sights he took a deep breath and gently pulled the trigger. As the shot rang out, piercing the stillness of the morning air, the bullet quickly sought its target. The bullet initially missed its target, hitting a rock outcropping. It ricocheted, hitting Crawford's rifle, deflecting the bullet in through his stomach, and shattering his spinal cord. He fell to the ground writhing in agony. The other men nearby looked at each other in disbelief. They looked at their comrade, who was begging for help, but did nothing to help him. They weren't going to expose themselves to the man who had just taken him out. Lucio Montoya quickly ran down the hillside, dodging fire from the other men in Montaño's store.

Under the intense heat of the sun, the wounded man lay there bleeding and dying while his companions listened to his groans of intense agony. The men could clearly see that he was dying but their attempt to save him was repelled by the repeated shots fired from within the Montaño store.

Dr. Appel had heard about Crawford's plight and decided to ascend the hillside to assist the downed man. He asked for assistance from another officer and two other soldiers. As they climbed the hillside, the men within Montaño's store commenced firing but none of the shots had found their marks. Upon reaching Crawford, they saw him lying in a pool of blood, which had stained the ground with a blackened color. Dr. Appel and the others promptly took Crawford to Fort Stanton, where he died a week later. Fernando had broken the stalemate, being credited for the first kill from either faction. [18]

In another act of carelessness, this time by a member of a McSween supporter, Ben Ellis left his position to water and feed his mule. A shot rang out and he felt the sting of the bullet as it grazed his neck. He stumbled to the ground remaining motionless. Two of his comrades had bravely sought out the services of Dr. Ealy who was holed up with his family at Tunstall's store. Under cover by the darkness of night, the doctor left with the two men to tend to Ellis' wounds. The attempt was unsuccessful however, because the men could not get to him. The next day, the doctor walked through the center of town, with his baby in hand and his daughter, Ruth in tow. Long and his men holed up in El Torreón saw this and showed restraint. He dressed Ellis' wounds and the wounded man survived death. [19]

On July 19, 1878 Colonel Dudley and forty of his soldiers had made their entrance into Lincoln. In his company he also brought a Howitzer and a Gatling gun as a means of subduing the vigilante threat. Colonel Dudley and his men came under the pretense that they were in Lincoln to protect the women and children.

Colonel Dudley paraded his weapons through town so that all the McSween supporters could see what they were up against. He strategically parked the Howitzer near the Montaño store and proceeded to take aim. He called out to the occupants inside that the women and children had better leave. Señora Montaño and her children quickly vacated the premises. The men, who hadn't flinched with Sheriff Peppin and his men soon lost their nerve while staring down the barrel of the howitzer and quickly took flight out the back door of the Montaño store. With their heads covered with cloth to conceal their true identities Chávez, Herrera, and all the others scattered about, some of them seeking refuge within Ellis' store while the rest found refuge within the mountains.[20] The Colonel and his men didn't give chase.

Seeing what he had accomplished, Colonel Dudley must have been rather amused with the ease in which he had vacated Montaño's store. He methodically marched his Howitzer over to Ellis' stored and took aim. Again, the men took flight, not wanting to meet their demise.

Martín Chávez and several of the Regulators who had made their escape out of town briefly returned later that evening. Finding adequate cover behind the summit of the hills outside of town, they commenced to fire upon Dolan's posse who had surrounded the McSween house. Again their attempts were thwarted, as they had to disperse because the howitzer was trained on their position.

The men had resolved themselves to the fact that they had little power to help out their compadres that were holed up in the McSween house. They had thus left their fate in the hands of God. Some of the more noted Regulators who had escaped Lincoln that day were Josiah "Doc" Scurlock, Charles Bowdre, Martín Chávez, Fernando Herrera, Francisco Sánchez, Estolano Sánchez, Jesús Rodríguez, Román Barragán, and John Middleton.[21]

The lone holdouts were at McSween's house. Inside the house were McSween, his wife Sue McSween, a teacher named Susan Gates, Harvey Morris who aspired to practice law, Sue's sister, Elizabeth Shield and her children. Those Regulators who were holed up in the house were Bonney, Jim French, Yginio Salazar, José Chávez y Chávez, Ignacio Gonzáles, Vicente Romero, Francisco Zamora, José María Sánchez and Tom O'Folliard.[22]

Colonel Dudley was a devious but insightful man. He had come to realize that those people who were in McSween's house had their backs up against the wall. They weren't going to come out peacefully for the reason that Peppin and his men were ready to commit a massacre. Colonel Dudley had schemed to force Justice of the Peace John Wilson into issuing an illegal arrest warrant for the assault on Private Robinson. Wilson rebuked Colonel Dudley's demand, claiming that a warrant could be issued only if there was probable cause, which had to be supported by affirmation while under oath. Colonel Dudley hastily called upon three of his officers to give testimony under false pretense.

Wilson countered by claiming that the matter fell out of his jurisdiction because it was a federal offence. Peeved by Wilson's unwillingness to cooperate, Colonel Dudley demanded that Wilson serve the arrest warrant. Feeling pressure to comply with Dudley's demands, Wilson reluctantly issued the arrest warrant for all those who were in the McSween house.[23]

After McSween and Colonel Dudley exchanged correspondence with one another, Sue McSween aimed to challenge the stalemate by leaving the relative safety of the house. It was her intention to discuss the matter with the colonel. On her way to talk with him she noticed that two of her servants were stacking wood against the house. She had surmised that they were ordered by either Sheriff Peppin and Colonel Dudley, or both, to do so for the purpose of burning down the house. She called out upon the sheriff, who was holed up in El Torreón, asking him why they were going to burn down the house. He stoutly replied that the standoff was going to end that day, one way or another.

Upon reaching the colonel, Sue discussed what she had seen and was told by the sheriff. Dudley denied that he knew anything of the matter, and that he took an impartial stance in the stalemate between the two factions. After sparring with one another, he grew impatient with her confrontational manner, and became outright disrespectful towards her concerns.

As the day wore on, there were two separate attempts to start the house on fire. The first attempt was thwarted, but the second attempt was successful. At this point, all the women and children escaped to Tunstall's store. The fire spread from one room to the other, all the while the remaining men scuttled to escape the heat of the flames and the noxious fumes of the smoke.

The sun had already set and darkness was descending upon Lincoln. At that point some of the men from within made a break out of the house. First out of the back door were Billy Bonney, José Chávez y Chávez, Jim French, and Harvey Morris. They were greeted with a hail of bullets. They frantically made their way to the Río Bonito and threw themselves into the cover of the foliage. Morris however, was not so lucky; he was hit one time and fell dead upon the ground.

McSween was trapped and he knew it. The ferocious fire had McSween's back and Kinney's men had his front. After some deliberation, McSween finally called out to announce his intention to surrender. As McSween stepped out with Francisco Zamora, and Vicente Romero, deputy Beckwith approached them in an attempt to issue the arrest warrant. Kinney and his men had other ideas though.

They showered McSween and his men with bullets. McSween fell dead being hit five times, Zamora had been hit eight times, and Romero had been hit three times.[24] One of McSween's men fired upon Beckwith, hitting him in the eye, he fell dead on the spot. Fifteen-year-old Yginio Salazar made a mad dash to escape and was shot, he fell hard to the ground, but he was not dead. Ignacio Gonzáles and Tom O'Folliard promptly made their escape into the brush of the Río Bonito as the chaos continued to unfold.[25]

Andy Boyle approached Salazar, and had proceeded to kick the boy who at this moment was acting as if he was deceased. Boyle was going to place another bullet into the battered boy's skull, but Milo Pierce told him not to waste the bullet, because he had already passed. Kinney and his men left, and celebrated with whiskey. Finally, having been left for dead, Salazar crawled his way to his sister-in-law's house.[26]

With McSween dead, the last remnants of the Lincoln County war were at hand. Many of the supporters who had swelled the ranks of the vigilante mob had silently returned to their farms. Many of those who participated in the standoff in Lincoln chose not to associate themselves with the Regulators for fear that it would attract negative attention. Don Fernando and both his son-in-laws had briefly returned to their farms in San Juanito.[27]

Over the next few weeks, it was becoming increasingly apparent that certain members of the Dolan faction were not content with McSween's demise. Many in the Dolan faction had made it clear that their jobs were not done until the remaining Regulators were apprehended and brought to justice. The code of justice in Lincoln County however, usually meant death by lynching.

After The Five Days Battle, the core of the Regulators had devised a plan to elude capture from the vigilantes that had remained in Lincoln County for the purpose of hunting them down. On August 05, 1878 Billy Bonney, Charlie Bowdre, Fernando Herrera, Esiquio Sánchez, Anastacio Martínez, Ignacio Gonzáles, Jim French, John Middleton, and Henry Brown rode to The Mescalero Reservation in search of fresh horses. They were looking for the fastest horses for the sole purpose of outrunning any hostile posse that they may have encountered. Fernando and the mexicanos proceeded further into the reservation as Bonney and the other gringos decided to rest their horses. Fernando knew Chief Kamisa, and both had remained in good terms with each other. As fate would have it, Fernando and his men happened across the Mescalero Reservation clerk, Morris Bernstein. Ill-fatedly Bernstein questioned the men as to their purpose for being on the reservation. Fearing that their hasty escape would be thwarted, Anastacio Martínez pulled his gun and shot Bernstein through the heart. Without any further hesitation, they men proceeded further into the reservation in an attempt to search for horses.[28]

Life after the Lincoln County War

Hard times had soon befallen the Regulators. They existed in principal, to protect one another from the dangers they faced from other bands of outlaws. The most formidable were the Rustlers who filled the void left by the Dolan faction. It is thought that many of the Rustlers were actually members of the now defunct Río Grande Posse.[29] The "Wrestlers" also known as the "Rustlers", like the Río Grande Posse were outlaws who thrived on stirring up trouble with the locals.

On August 18, 1878 members from the newly formed Rustlers had stolen 200 head of cattle on the Río Felix that had once belonged to the late John Tunstall. Bonney and a few of his compadres had taken exception to the thievery and had vowed to make the matter right.

Scurlock and Bowdre had thought better of it, and they had no desire to remain in Lincoln County. By September 01, 1878 they had left for good and headed north for Fort Sumner. Bonney and the others accompanied Scurlock and Bowdre to Fort Sumner.

Shortly thereafter, Frank and George Coe migrated to the San Juan River basin in northern New México. Josiah "Doc" Scurlock and Charlie Bowdre took jobs at the Maxwell Ranch. Others who had left the ranks of the Regulators were John Middleton, Fred Waite, and Henry Brown. The Regulators, now just a rag tag bunch, had finally disbanded. [30]

Bonney and cohorts in essence had become a brutish gang of cattle rustlers themselves. Initially it was their intention to get Tunstall's cattle back, but if they couldn't they would've found the means to replace what was taken from Tunstall's stock. On September 06, 1878 they made good on their claim by raiding the Fritz ranch, stealing 15 horses and 150 head of cattle.[31] Billy and his men thus had resorted to thievery as a means of living, often taking what they rustled to the Téxas panhandle.

With no semblance of law enforcement in Lincoln County, and the Regulators leaving abruptly, the Rustlers were left to instill their will upon the citizens. In late September of 1878 members of the Rustlers initiated a campaign of terror in which they continually roved the region. They destroyed people's houses, stole people's personal property, stole their horses, and even raped two young Hispana women. [32]

On September 28, 1878 several members of the Rustlers had shot and killed four boys while attempting to steal their father's prized Arabian horses. The outlaws had come across Desiderio Chávez y Sánchez, Cleto Chávez y Sánchez, Lorenzo Lucero, and Gregorio Sánchez who was only 14 years old, all of whom were harvesting hay in the fields. The two Chávez y Sánchez brothers were shot down because they had refused to give up their horses.[33] Gregorio Sánchez was riddled with bullets as he was handing a melon over to some of the men.

The outlaws had always made it a point to terrorize the people throughout the El Berendo. In one such incident 20 outlaws had descended upon farming community and proceeded to pillage its citizens of livestock and personal property. After taking their fill, the outlaws held their pistols in the direction of several Nuevo Mexicanos and demanded that all of the "Mexicans" should return to where they came from. They were neither wanted nor desired and furthermore if they were still in El Berendo upon their return, they would kill them all.[34]

After the outlaws took their leave, many within the Spanish-speaking community became enraged. They had gathered that evening and discussed what they should do. Many within the infuriated bunch wanted to retaliate against the gringo newcomers that lived in the immediate area. Some had even suggested killing all of the newcomers.

Some of the more rational folk thought better of it and stood out as the voices of reason, explaining to the others that the newcomers they sought vigilantism against were not the ones who were responsible for the atrocities committed against their person earlier in the day. Therefore, as Christians they should exercise restraint because it might lead to another deadly uprising, like the one in Lincoln.

The Arrival of Governor Lew Wallace

With the arrival of Lew Wallace as the new Territorial Governor on October 02, 1878, one of his first actions was to ascertain the Lincoln County threat. Wallace had initially encouraged President Rutherford B. Hayes to impose martial law in Lincoln County. President Hayes opted rather, to provide amnesty to those citizens who returned to live a peaceful life by October 13, 1878. After receiving confirmation that Lincoln County had indeed become more peaceful, Governor Wallace thus pardoned all those involved in the civil lawlessness that took place between February 01, 1878 and October 13, 1878. Those people who were waiting pending prosecution however, were exempt from amnesty.

On February 18, 1879, ironically on the anniversary of John Tunstall's death, Bonney had returned to Lincoln seeking a truce of peace between himself, J. Dolan, and Jesse Evans. They mutually agreed to stop the fighting. Also, the agreement between the men forbade any of them to implicate one another, in a court of law, of the events that happened during the Lincoln County War. Reneging on the truce meant sure death for the betrayer. [35]

On March 15, 1879, Governor Lew Wallace was forced to make his presence felt in Lincoln two weeks after Billy Campbell and J. Dolan had murdered an inebriated citizen named Huston Chapman in cold blood. His body had remained where he was killed for more than twenty-four hours before soldiers from Ft. Stanton had finally recovered it in the middle of the street. When he was found, it had appeared as if his face had been burned, possibly from being shot at close range.[36] Chapman was a tenacious lawyer, from Las Vegas, who was hired by Sue McSween to implicate those people she felt, were responsible for her husband's death. Chapman had continually antagonized Colonel Dudley and at times questioned Governor Wallace's motives in an attempt to serve justice in the McSween murder.

Governor Wallace remained in Lincoln for about a month to show Lincoln County's citizens that he intended to reinstitute peace. He listened intently as Lincoln's residents shared their grievances with him. After some thought and deliberation, Governor Wallace suggested that a volunteer militia should be organized for the purpose of keeping order in Lincoln County.

Governor Wallace promptly compiled a list of 35 desperados who were fleeing justice. Among the most notorious on the list were, Bonney, Jesse Evans, J. Dolan, Billy Campbell, and Tom O'Folliard. He later named Juan Patrón as the Captain of the newly created, Lincoln County Mounted Riflemen. He also instructed the new commander of Fort Stanton, Henry Carroll to assist Patrón and his men in order to bring to justice the 35 men on the list.[37]

Wallace's 35 Most Wanted List [38]

1. John Slaughter
2. Andrew Boyle
3. John Selman
4. Tom Selman
5. Gus Gildea
6. James Irwin
7. Reese Gobles
8. Roscoe Bryant
9. Robert Speakes
10. John Beckwith
11. Hugh Beckwith
12. Jim French
13. Josiah Scurlock
14. William H. Bonney
15. Tom O'Folliard
16. Charles Bowdre
17. Henry Brown
18. John Middleton
19. Fred Waite
20. J.B. Mathews
21. Jesse Evans
22. Jimmy Dolan
23. George Davis
24. Frank Rivers
25. John Jones
26. William Jones
27. James Jones
28. Marion Turner
29. Caleb Hall
30. Heiskell Jones
31. Joseph Hall
32. Buck Powell
33. James Highsaw
34. Jake Owens
35. FrankWheeler

Juan B. Patrón was tasked with recruiting the members of his militia. Fernando Herrera was one of the first men that Patrón had approached. Patrón also solicited the services of Mauricio de la Trinidad Sánches' two sons, Estolano Sánchez and Francisco Sánchez. Patrón recruited 34 men in all. The following is a list of all those who he recruited to serve in the Lincoln County Rifleman.

Lincoln County Mounted Rifleman Roster [39]

1. Captain Juan B. Patrón
2. Ben H. Ellis (1st Lieutenant)
3. Martín Sánchez (2nd Lieutenant)
4. Fernando Herrera
5. Camilo Núñez
6. Esiquio Sánchez
7. Ramón Montoya
8. Estolano Sánchez
9. Trinidad Vigíl
10. Jesús Rodríguez
11. Juan Pedro Torres
12. Martín Chávez
13. José Chávez y Chávez
14. Maximiano Chávez
15. Romaldo Fresquez
16. Gregorio Girón
17. T.B. Longworth
18. Eugenio Maldonado
19. Pablo Miranda
20. Manuel Martín
21. Santiago Maés
22. Martín Montoya
23. Senon Mora
24. Trinidad Romero
25. Manuel Romero
26. Crescencio Sánchez
27. José María Sánchez
28. Elias Gray
29. Francisco Sánchez y Gonzáles
30. Yginio Salazar
31. José Salazar
32. J.C. Wilkins
33. George Washington
34. Alex Rudder
35. Florencio Chávez
36. Ramon Vigil

Many of the Lincoln County Mounted Riflemen had conflicting perspectives on the capture of the thirty-five men Governor Wallace had sought to bring to justice. Many of the men had no objections to bringing members of the Dolan faction to justice. For the men who were staunch supporters of the Regulators, they were reluctant to pursue those they considered friends.

Fernando was especially conflicted when it came time for the Lincoln County Mounted Riflemen to bring in his two son-in-laws from Fort Sumner. The Riflemen made the long and arduous journey north. Charlie Bowdre had eluded capture by hiding out but Josiah "Doc" Scurlock had been apprehended. Scurlock was brought back to Fort Stanton and thrown into the guardhouse, which was becoming increasingly overcrowded and somewhat chaotic.[40]

Sometime later, Billy Bonney sent Governor Wallace correspondence seeking a pardon in exchange for testifying against the men he had struck a peace treaty with. Governor Wallace who had become intrigued with the young outlaw had requested his audience. Billy agreed to meet with Wallace in order to discuss further, the terms of his potential pardon. As fate would have it, Evans and Campbell had escaped incarceration from Fort Stanton with the help of an accomplice named Texas Jack. Suddenly, the deal didn't have the same luster it once did. Governor Wallace called the Lincoln County Riflemen into action and offered a $1,000 reward for the capture of the fugitives.[41]

(From left to right): Manuel Mirabal-Sanchez and Peter Hale in Lincoln.

A more Peaceful Life

Fernando's life had become more peaceful after the departure of his son-in-law, Bonney, and a few of the other fellows from the Regulators. They had decided to leave Lincoln County behind, and sought a new life elsewhere. Lost to him were his daughters, Antonia Miguela and Manuelita who accompanied the party to Ft Sumner. Eventually he would learn that his friend Charles Bowdre had married his daughter Manuelita.

Don Fernando Herrera still commanded a great deal of respect amongst his peers. He was the *patrón* to many in the community. He achieved this status because of his gracious disposition, which he often freely extended to many within the Río Ruidoso valley. Many a person who had fallen on hard times had called upon Fernando and he always seemed to come through for them.

Jesús Rodríguez

One such person was Pedro M. Rodríguez whose father was gunned down in Lincoln. Pedro's father was Jesús Rodríguez, Fernando's compadre and a fellow member of the Lincoln County

Mounted Riflemen. Jesús had a daughter, Rosario Rodríguez, who was married to his compadre's oldest son, Andrés Herrera.

Jesús Rodríguez was also a former Private in Captain William Brady's Company A, First Regiment Cavalry stationed in Fort Stanton. His first year in Lincoln County was spent subduing the Mescalero threat that prevailed throughout the region. Jesús had enlisted his services from October 27, 1864 through October 27, 1865.

Jesús had a very angry disposition in general which was exasperated during his drinking binges. That was when all of the pain in his life would seep through his toughened exterior. Much of his anger stemmed from the tragic death of his brother, Marciál Rodríguez, at the hands of a band of Mescalero on New Year's Eve day in 1873. Jesús despised all Native Americans for that very reason. Some of his anger stemmed from the days that he rode with the Regulators.

The family story is that Jesús had been arrested and incarcerated by Constable Amado Chávez for disorderly conduct after successive days of binge drinking. During his drunken stupor Jesús had repeatedly threatened to kill the constable. On the night of Jesús' incarceration, he was not thrown into the pit, which served to hold the more hardened outlaws, but rather he was left unattended in the one room adobé that was constructed near the pit. By some unknown means, Jesús managed to escape from his captivity and went to his house to gather his pistols.

Still in a drunken stupor, Jesús meandered through Lincoln in search of his captor. He finally had come across the constable who was visiting Demetrio Pérez, at Pérez's mother's house. Impaired by the alcohol, he proceeded to the door and upholstered his pistol and began hitting the door with the butt of the gun. He began screaming for Chávez to come out and fight him.

Filled with liquor, and having very little inhibitions, Jesús stepped up his threats. The constable cautioned, asking that Jesús calm down, and that he would have to take him back to the jail until he sobered up. He continued to pound upon the door, this further enraged him, and his threats became even more severe as he threatened to kill the constable. Inebriated, irrational, and becoming increasingly violent, Chávez was forced to pull his weapon and fired upon the man on the other side of the door. He fell to the ground, bleeding profusely, and soon thereafter he died.

Pedro was about nine years old when his father was killed. Pedro's mother, Francisca Sánchez, soon left Lincoln and migrated to San Juanito to live on Don Fernando's farm. Tragically, Francisca died three years later and Fernando took Pedro in and raised him as one of his own. Pedro always referred to his guardian and his wife Marta as his ***aguelitos***, and never thought twice about that fact.[42]

Fernando's Later Years

Don Fernando had a penchant for showering many people with his unconditional love. Through the years he had brought several people under his wing, and even in old age he still had the heart to care for people who desperately needed help. His passion for giving to others ultimately would lead to him losing everything he owned in his beloved San Juanito.

It was told by his grandchildren that he had agreed to allow someone to work his land. The sharecropper, as many others in the valley had done, purchased all his goods on credit. Unbeknownst to Don Fernando, he had racked up a great amount of debt. Knowing that he couldn't repay the debt, he had left the region never to be heard from again. The land owner didn't think much of it until the creditors came to him to receive payment. He refused to pay the creditors the money owed because it was not his own debt. The creditors in turn, filed a lawsuit and the court ruled against him.

His grandchildren, the children of his daughter Altagracia and her husband William Gill also had filed a lawsuit against him. Their contention was that he misappropriated funds meant for them, and instead squandered their money for himself. The courts ruled in favor of the children with a judgment of $1,131.58 after he was unable to provide sufficient evidence to prove otherwise.[43]

Soon thereafter, he was forced to leave the lands that he had lived on since 1867. Many of his grandchildren who were under his guardianship had already left his care. The only child under his guardianship was Estela Gill. After the judgments Fernando moved to Alamogordo in a neighborhood known as "Chihuahuita". He remained there until he died in 1915. It is thought that he was buried in an unmarked grave at an old Catholic cemetery. It's not a very fitting memorial to a man who had given so much of himself to so many different people.

To say that Fernando was a perfect father or even a perfect man would be somewhat misleading. He had lived in a very turbulent time in Lincoln County's early history, in which one was forced to resort to violence as a means of keeping the peace. The memories of people he had either killed, or witnessed being killed, were something he carried with him to his grave. In life he didn't much want to talk about the days when he rode with Billy the Kid and the Regulators. It was too painful, he had lost too much. Maybe if he had, his legacy in the Lincoln County War would have warranted him a decent headstone.

María Altagracia Herrera

Altagracia Herrera, christened María Altagracia Herrera, was born in Santa Cruz de la Cañada on April 15, 1857. She was the daughter of Fernando Herrera and María Juliana Martín. Altagracia married William James Gill on November 15, 1880. William Gill was originally from Pennsylvania before he headed out west. He had enlisted in the military on August 30, 1864 and had served his country for three years. He served as a Private with Company F, Regiment 1, of the California Infantry. He was stationed out of Fort Stanton at the time he had met Altagracia. During his three years of service, Gill had been shot in the right leg.[44]

Gill had a homestead further up in the mountains near the source of the Río Ruidoso. He was cattle ranching at the time, and lived in a humble one-room log cabin.[45] Being the consummate entrepreneur, he was seeking business propositions that would further advance his earning potential. He bought the American mine in Nogal, which was due north of the Río Ruidoso Valley.[46] On March 02, 1884 he purchased the Vanderbilt Lead & Deposit mine at the head of Dry Gulch in Nogal from Frank Lesnett. On September 06, 1884 he purchased the Edith Placer claim situated on the Gill Gulch from Frank Lesnett.[47] On December 21, 1885 he decided to sell his holdings in the American Vanderbilt Mining Co. to John Rae who promptly named the new claims The Helen Rae.[48]

After William Gill's untimely death on April 11, 1889 it was discovered that he had left no will pertaining to his real estate holdings or any of his personal property. Fernando and his daughter had petitioned the court on numerous occasions to name himself as the administrator of Gill's estate. On May 09, 1889 the court had appointed Altagracia as the guardian of her children, and the administrator of her previous husband's real estate and other personal property.[49]

Over the next few months Altagracia had met Antonio Valensuela and bore him a daughter out of wedlock. They named their daughter Rosalía, but life for their baby was presumably short lived because nothing else has ever been mentioned about her again.

Fernando was displeased with his daughter's indiscretions but was even more incensed with Antonio because he had taken advantage of her obvious vulnerabilities. He viewed Antonio as nothing more than an opportunist, who sought his daughter's inheritance. He accused Antonio Valensuela of squandering all of his previous son-in-law's money. He charged that Antonio was greatly influencing his daughter to the entire family's detriment. This was an accusation that Antonio had whole-heartedly denied.

Although Altagracia knew of her father's objections to Antonio, she still married him on July 27, 1892. Fernando reserved himself to the fact that he had no choice but to accept Antonio into the family. By March 1893 Altagracia bore Antonio another child, a son they named Benancio. Tragically a few months later, on June 26, 1893 Altagracia had died at the age of thirty-six.

Nicolasa Herrera

Nicolasita Herrera, christened María Nicolasa Herrera was born in Santa Cruz de la Cañada on December 08, 1862. She was the daughter of Fernando Herrera and María Juliana Martín. Nicolasita had spent most of her young life helping her sisters, Manuelita, and Altagracia to raise their children. She was well loved by all of those she had brought under her care. Her unconditional love for her sobrinos may have been largely due to the fact that she didn't have any children of her own. After her sister Altagracia had passed away, Nicolasita had pledged to raise all of her sister's children as her own.

Although the patriarch didn't particularly care for Antonio's previous misdeeds, he allowed him and his son to remain on the rancho out of respect of the memory of Altagracia. Don Fernando wouldn't have been able to live with himself knowing that he had abandoned one of his grandchildren with a man of questionable motives and character.

Unbeknownst to Fernando, Antonio had been manipulating Nicolasita over the next several years. She and her sobrino Benancio had developed a very special bond with one another. Antonio was wise to this and he continually pressured her to marry him. Nicolasita was reluctant for many years to give in to Antonio's demands. It wasn't until after he threatened to take Benancio away with him that Nicolasita finally gave in to Antonio's repeated requests for marriage. On October 17, 1902 the two were married to her father's dissatisfaction.

To say that Nicolasita had only married Antonio because of his threat of leaving with his son is somewhat misguided. In truth, she had grown to love Antonio over a period of several years. Her father's objections were of little concern to Nicolasita who was a few months shy of forty years old. She was weary of living a life without a husband. She was lonely, and desperately sought the love and attention of a man.

Her desire for a husband betrayed her though, as Antonio had succumbed to alcoholism. In his drunkenness, Antonio had become very abusive towards Nicolasita. On many occasions he would pull his shaving knife out and threaten her life. On a few occasions he would be riding his horse and he would lasso her as she tried to run away. To her horror her husband would then drag her behind his horse as he roared out in laughter.[50]

The physical and mental abuse had both taken their toll on Nicolasita. The horror that became her life was short lived as Antonio had eventually left. One can only speculate on whether Fernando had intervened on his daughter's behalf. Nicolasita on the other hand was never able to bring herself to marry another man. She continued to find solace in taking care of her sobrinos until her last days of life. The love that she couldn't find with a man, she had found with her adoptive children.

Chapter Nine: Manuelita Herrera

Front row (left to right): Fernando Salsberry, Enrique (Henry) Salsberry, José Portio (holding guitar), Eduvijen Sánchez, Augustín Salsberry (holding fiddle), Florinda Salsberry (holding doll). Back row (left to right): Santiago (James) Salsberry 2nd, Martina Salsberry, Antonio Sánchez, Manuela Herrera de Salsberry, Venancio Valenzuela, Nicolasita Herrera, Tomasita Salsberry, Dorotea Salsberry, Elena Corona. Circa 1915 at Cañon de Salsberry (Salsberry Canyon) in San Juanito (Ruidoso Downs), Territory of New México.

Manuelita Herrera, christened María Manuela Herrera, was born on April 20, 1866 in Santa Cruz de la Cañada, Territory of New México. She was the daughter of Fernando Herrera and María Juliana Martín. She was baptized on August 22, 1866. Her Padrinos were Don Encarnación Martín and Doña María Rafaela Bustos.

About a year after her birth, her father had migrated to the southeast territory to Bonito with the hope of securing some land for his family. From time to time he would periodically return to see his family. Several years had passed and shortly after 1870 her father had returned for the purpose of moving his family to his rancho on the Río Ruidoso.

As her parents were finalizing the preparations for the move, Manuelita had fallen gravely ill. It was so severe that there was a high probability that she would not survive the journey south. A close family friend, Juanita Bojórque, paid the two anguished parents a visit. She was a single woman with so much love to give, but nobody to give it to. She approached them and offered to take care of Manuelita. She loved the child as if she was her own daughter, which was not lost upon them. She had helped Julianita raise the child since she was born. After much deliberation, lasting the better part of a week, the two finally agreed that the best thing for their infant daughter was to charge Juanita with her care.

A few days later the two reluctant parents visited Juanita with their daughter in hand. They both looked into Juanita's eyes nodding their heads with approval. As tears fell from the corner of their eyes they showered their daughter with kisses and continually told her that they loved her so very much. Fernando led Manuelita to Juanita and he forced out a smile. He looked deep into Juanita's eyes and he explained how important it was that Manuelita was to be brought up like a proper lady. After he was done talking, he left without once looking back. Julianita continued looking back, sobbing uncontrollably.

The family packed all of their belongings onto two wagons. Together with their children, they commenced with their journey to El Rancho de San Juanito. Less one sister, the family quietly thought to themselves if they would ever see her again. Surely the initial elation of a prospective new home was tempered by the bittersweet thought of leaving their baby sister behind.

Juanita Bojórque is somewhat of an enigmatic woman. It is unknown if there was any familial relations between herself and either Fernando or Julianita. She was not Manuelita's **Madrina** (godmother), so she was not bound or obligated to care for her. Obviously both parents felt comfortable enough to leave their daughter behind with Juanita. Manuelita was young enough that she wouldn't have remembered her family leaving her behind.

Sometime around the fall of 1875 Manuelita and Juanita had decided to migrate to El Rancho de San Juanito to be closer to the family. Upon arriving, a sense of excitement and mystery shrouded the entire family. The reunion was somewhat bittersweet, being that the matriarch of the family had recently passed on. Furthermore, Fernando had since re-married and most of the children didn't embrace his new wife.

Manuelita was still very young, rather immature and had a great deal of difficulty adjusting to the emotions of coming into such a large family. Her mind knew that she was among her brothers and sisters but her heart acknowledged that they were all strangers to her. It was hard to cope with all of the changes while having to integrate back into the family. She was somewhat of an outcast, at first, feeling a degree of alienation. It took several months for the family to fully integrate her into everyday life. It wasn't until that point, that the critical bonds between the family and her developed.

Manuelita had many questions concerning the manner in which her parents left her behind in Santa Cruz de la Cañada. Her first instinct was to ask her father why they had left her, but it was impolite, and improper of her to question her parents' motives. Even as she saw her father on a daily basis, she had suppressed the impulse to seek out the answers. Often an opportunity to talk would pass by, as she failed to seek out the answers to her questions.

Manuelita attempted in her own way to reach out to her father. She didn't hate him for leaving her behind but she didn't trust in his love for her either. He was a stranger to her, and she desperately wanted to replace that mistrust with the feeling of love. She would always try to please him, by keeping herself busy. She always wanted to make herself visible to him, so that he could see how much she did for him. She wanted to remind him with her presence that she was indeed his daughter. She wanted his acceptance, his love, his affection.

Seeing Manuelita struggle to gain her father's affection must have been very difficult for Juanita to witness. She had vowed to protect her from the pain of being left behind; therefore she always made it a point to be near to her. It was painful for both of them as they realized that gaining her father's affection would be a long time in coming.

Charles Bowdre

Charles Bowdre and wife Manuelita Herrera

Also finding a home on Fernando Herrera's farm were two men, Charles Bowdre and Josiah "Doc" Scurlock who had previously met in Arizona. Upon arriving on the Río Ruidoso in the spring of 1876, Scurlock and Bowdre had secured a loan from the House and used the proceeds to buy a farm from Paul Dowlin.[1] Although they had their own farm, both Scurlock and Bowdre chose to remain living on their amigo's ranchito for some time. Scurlock had taken a liking to Fernando's daughter, Antonia Miguela and married her on October 19, 1876.

Being almost ten years old, Manuelita didn't think much about what her future had in store for her. She did start to develop bonds with some of her siblings but she had always had the insecurities of being somewhat of an outcast. Over time, a rather unlikely relationship was developing between Charles Bowdre and herself, as she felt inclined to seek comfort in his presence. What made their relationship so unusual was that Charles didn't have a great command of the Spanish language, and therefore sometimes it became difficult for the two to communicate effectively.

Charles Bowdre was more preoccupied with the events that were occurring during the Lincoln County War rather than developing a relationship with an infatuated woman child. Manuelita however was searching for the love of a father figure, which she was yearning for, and had unwittingly sought to claim Bowdre's attention. Her persistence had paid off as Bowdre began noticing her in a womanly manner. Her father either didn't have any obvious objections, or wasn't cognizant of their budding relationship because there were no confrontations on the matter.

By September 01, 1878 Charles Bowdre and Manuelita had left Lincoln to escape the chaos that had ensued after The Five Days Battle. Together with Josiah "Doc" Scurlock and his wife Antonia Miguela they headed to Fort Sumner due northeast.[2] Bonney and several other members of the

Regulators had accompanied Bowdre and Scurlock on their move. Shortly after arriving and settling in, Charles Bowdre had married Manuelita Herrera who was believed to be almost thirteen years of age at the time. San Miguel County Probate records indicate that Charlie Bowdre had married a Manuela Gonzáles, the daughter of Fernando Herrera.[3] Why she either gave her name as such, or whether it was recorded incorrectly is still a mystery. Both Scurlock and Bowdre eventually found employment at Don Pedro (Pete) Maxwell's rancho.[4]

Manuelita had established a very close, friendly relationship with Billy the Kid. She felt more comfortable talking to him because they could carry on a conversation in Spanish. Often times, she felt she had more in common with Bonney, than she did with her own husband, because he didn't have a good command of her language. She always appreciated The Kid's company, and he in turn always enjoyed her cooking.[5]

Shortly after rustling 150 head of cattle and 15 horses away from Chas Fritz, Bonney and his men returned to Fort Sumner. Bowdre joined his friends as they drove the cattle North, up the Río Pecos. They raided Alejandro Polaco's ranch in Alamo Gordo, and several other farms at Juan de Dios. In all they rustled another 35 to 40 head of cattle. As they drove the cattle due east, Bowdre opted to sell his interest in the herd and he returned to Fort Sumner. After selling the stolen herd, and parting ways with Fred Waite, John Middleton, and Henry Brown, Bonney and O'Folliard returned to Fort Stanton and lived with Bowdre and Scurlock for a brief period.[6]

On December 12, 1878 Scurlock had accompanied Bonney, French and O'Folliard back to Lincoln to plead their case for amnesty, which had been offered to the participants of the Lincoln County War and those who chose to return to a life of civility. Upon hearing of their arrival into Lincoln, Sheriff Peppin became unnerved and asked for a military escort into Lincoln; as he was due to appear before the Probate Court. Lieutenant James H. French was assigned to escort the sheriff.[7]

Court had adjourned for the day and would reconvene the next morning. The sheriff was still apprehensive and had asked Lt. French to remain with him. Lt. French agreed and thus accompanied Peppin to Montaño's store where they would quarter for the night. Inside the store, they had come upon the company of Florencio Gonzáles, and José Montaño who were inclined to invite them to an evening of conversation. The men continued to talk and drink until about 9:00pm, in which Gonzáles and Montaño had finally taken their leave.

During the conversation, it was brought to Peppin's attention that Bonney and his men had been periodically visiting Lincoln as they pleased. Furthermore, they did so with very little fear of being apprehended. Taken aback, the sheriff was compelled to discuss the matter further with the lieutenant. French had asked if he was going to attempt to capture Boney and his men. Peppin indicated that he didn't want to have any part of them at that moment. The lieutenant, being rather cavalier and very drunk, had offered his services if the sheriff were to deputize him. Inexplicably, and foolhardily, Peppin willingly agreed to deputize Lt. French for the purpose of serving the arrest warrants to the fugitives.

In his search to apprehend the fugitives Lt. French first went to Maximiano Guevara's house. He knocked on the door and upon Guevara coming to greet his potential guest, the lieutenant unsuspectingly pushed his way into the house and pulled out the arrest warrants. Disrespectfully he demanded that the flabbergasted occupant fess up if he had any knowledge as to Scurlock's whereabouts. Guevara indicated to the intruder that he did not know what he was talking about and that he had no right barging into his house. The inebriated lieutenant became irate and belligerent as he threatened to kill him for not cooperating. Getting nothing out of an increasingly angered Maximiano, he finally left the house without any further incident.

The debacle continued into the night as Lt. French eventually crossed paths with Huston Chapman, who earlier had been falsely arrested. Still inebriated, he threatened to fight Chapman, who had only one arm. The captive had rebuked the idea of fighting the lieutenant. After bungling through town for several hours, Lt. French had never found the men that he was looking for. [8]

Unfortunately for Bonney, Scurlock, French and O'Folliard, none of them had received the amnesty that they had sought. Scurlock returned to Fort Sumner to be with his family and returned to work on the ranch. Bonney and the others went about their own business.

By the summer of 1879 Charles Bowdre had found new employment as a ranch hand at Thomas Yerby's rancho in Las Cañaditas. Scurlock and his family remained in Fort Sumner. Bonney also remained in the region, roving around between Fort Sumner, Anton Chico, and Puerto de Luna. The outlaw and his men continued to rustle cattle and gamble away their proceeds in Las Vegas, Territory of New México.

Bowdre and Scurlock continued to associate themselves with Bonney and his men, and were alleged to have rustled about 118 head of cattle from Bosque Grande that had belonged to John Chisum.[9] Shortly thereafter, at the insistence of Antonia Miguela, Scurlock had finally decided to move his family away from the Territory of New México, to Tascosa, Téxas in an attempt to distance himself from his outlaw buddies. The move occurred sometime in either October or November of 1879.

Before they left, Antonia Miguela had visited with her younger sister to warn her of the dangers of keeping company with Billy the Kid and his kind. The elder sister strongly suggested to the younger, that she keep her husband from consorting with such men or else there would be grave consequences associated with it. Manuelita was rightfully conflicted with her sister's advice because she had come to know Billy very well and she considered him a dear friend. After much discussion, Manuelita assured Antonia Miguela that she would take her concerns into great consideration.

After Scurlock's departure, Bowdre continued rustling with Bonney and his men. In May of 1880 he helped his partner in crime steal 44 head of cattle from the Téxas panhandle and drove them down to White Oaks. The outlaws repeatedly rustled cattle and livestock in Lincoln County and drove them to the Téxas panhandle, and vice versa. The thievery continued and the newly appointed sheriff, George Kimbrell, did not have the needed deputies to combat the situation. In an attempt to put a stop to the lawlessness, John Chisum and Joseph Lea approached a Fort Sumner resident by the name of Pat Garrett and encouraged him to move to Lincoln for the purpose of becoming Lincoln County's new sheriff elect.[10]

Pat Garrett took them up on their offer and he was elected as Lincoln County's new sheriff. Since sheriff-elect Garrett couldn't be sworn in until January 01, 1881, Sheriff Kimbrell had deputized him so that he could go after the outlaws that were wreaking havoc and terrorizing the ranchers of Lincoln County.[11]

Sheriff Pat Garrett was relentless in his pursuit of Bonney and his men. By November of 1880 he had assembled a posse of twenty able bodied men, to pursue the fugitives of justice. Garrett had known of the outlaw's many strategic hideouts and was constantly hunting after his prey, which resulted in the apprehension of several of Bonney's cohorts. In each instance though, Bonney, Bowdre, O'Folliard, and a newly recruited member, Dave Rudabaugh, were always one step ahead of the lawmen.

After apprehending two of Bonney's men, Sheriff Garrett, A. Lawton and G.W. Mitchell received a tip. They promptly headed north to Las Cañaditas hoping they could catch up to the fugitives. On the way they spotted the young Tom O'Folliard in the distance and had given chase. O'Folliard spotted them and raced off towards Yerby's rancho. O'Folliard kept his pursuers at bay by firing several shots at them as he made his hasty escape.

Garrett and his men had finally arrived at Bowdre's house and they cautiously approached it fully expecting trouble. They discovered that Manuelita and Juanita Bojórque were the only ones there. Although their intended targets were nowhere to be found, they did come across several head of stolen livestock. As the men were gathering the livestock, Manuelita noticed the commotion outside and was startled by their presence. Unsure of what their intentions were, both women came running out of the house and proceeded to shout at the sheriff and his men. Manuelita asked what they were doing there and subsequently demanded that they all leave. The men continued rounding up the livestock as Garrett informed both women that he was taking the stolen livestock. Before leaving, Garrett approached Bowdre's young wife and left her a message to tell her husband that they were there. Soon thereafter, all of the men left without further incident.[12]

Charles Bowdre was growing weary of being a fugitive on the run and he was forced to reflect on the error of his ways. He had come to realize that his association with his good friend was ultimately going to lead to either his death or a lifetime in prison. He had to do something for the sake of his wife, if he intended on living any normal life. Manuelita, remembering the prophetic words of her sister, was at her wits end, and didn't want to continue living the life she had hoped to have already left behind in Lincoln County.

On December 05, 1880 Bowdre had sought an audience with Sheriff Garrett for the purpose of talking about the conditions of his surrender. The two men had decided to rendezvous at the junction of the road just two miles outside of Fort Sumner. Sheriff Garrett had shown Bowdre a letter that he had received from Joseph Lea that stated that if he (Bowdre) were to sever his relations with William H. Bonney and his men, that he might be able to post bail and redeem himself of his lawlessness. Bowdre however wasn't too convinced that his freedom was assured. He left Sheriff Garrett with little resolution to his concerns of freedom and even more questions he had to ask of himself.[13]

On December 15, 1880, Charles Bowdre had written a letter to Joseph Lea explaining that he was no longer at Thomas Yerby's rancho because he felt it was his duty to keep Yerby out of the mess he and his outlaw associates had created. He continued by saying that if he wasn't cleared of the charges brought against him, it was his intention to leave the Territory of New México by winter.

He didn't want the violence anymore because the circumstances were different from those during the Lincoln County War. He indicated that both Bonney and Billy Wilson also had intentions of leaving the territory. He expressed his displeasure with the fact that his lawlessness was not pardoned by the Governor. He asked if Lea would speak on his behalf to the Governor so that the District Attorney may throw out his case without him having to appear in court. Bowdre had expressed reservations because he was fully aware that a posse was after him, and he feared for his life. He professed that he was innocent in many of the alleged crimes that he was accused of committing. He concluded by stating that his life experiences were a stern teacher, and that he had learned his lesson, and from that day forward, he would keep to his own.[14]

Although Bowdre had resolved himself to the thought of surrendering, this notion had not been brought to the attention of Sheriff Garrett. On the same day that Bowdre had written the letter, Garrett and several of his men continued their hunt for the outlaws. First, they attempted to apprehend the outlaws in Fort Sumner, but the fugitives had made their leave to the Wilcox-Brazil rancho prior to Garrett's arrival.

Pat Garrett then conspired with José Valdéz to pass a message on to Bonney that, he and his men were returning to Roswell. Garrett and his posse however were actually attempting to set a trap for the outlaws. Garrett had figured that the young outlaw would return to Fort Sumner to celebrate yet another escape.

Bonney had received the news of Sheriff Garrett's devious plot though, and made a plan of his own. It was decided that he and his men would come into Fort Sumner under the pretense that Garrett and his posse were gone. However, they were going to steal their horses and make yet another great escape. The youngster's plan backfired as an intense shootout between the two factions ensued. After all the smoke had dispersed, Tom O'Folliard lay dead, while his compadres made their escape. The sheriff and his men thus followed the outlaws' trail in the snow.[15]

On December 21, 1880 Sheriff Pat Garrett and his posse arrived at an old abandoned rock house in **Ojo Hediondo** (Stinking Springs). The fugitives' horses were tied to a pole just outside the door. Bonney, Bowdre, Rudabaugh, and Wilson were inside sleeping. Pat Garrett and his men quietly positioned themselves on the brow of a hill just within earshot of the house. They had a direct view plane of the doorway. There they waited for daybreak to make their move.[16]

As the sun began to rise over the horizon, they could hear the men waking up and talking amongst themselves. Charlie Bowdre was the first to step from the entryway. In his hand he held a nosebag filled with feed for his horse. As Bowdre was placing the nosebag around his horse's snout, Garrett and his men raised to their knees, taking aim of the unsuspecting fugitive.

Without warning Sheriff Pat Garrett pulled the trigger and his men followed his lead. One slug hit Bowdre in the leg, and two others found their marks deep within his body. Stunned with utter terror, Bowdre stumbled towards the doorway where his good friend, Billy the Kid, caught him by the belt strap.

From inside the house you could hear Wilson shout out that they had killed Charlie and that he was ready to surrender his arms. Bonney countered by drawing Bowdre's gun and pointing it out the door. The youngster shouted that they had murdered Charlie but before he died he should kill some of those sons of bitches. Billy then placed the gun in Bowdre's hand and nudged him out the door.

Bowdre stumbled away from the door, with his pistol in hand and with both arms raised in the air. As he walked towards the posse, he recognized Sheriff Garrett. He walked towards him with blood spitting from his mouth. Bowdre uttered, "I wish… I wish… I wish…" Bowdre paused for a few seconds before whispering his last words, "I'm dying!" Bowdre fell over as the sheriff caught him and laid him upon some blankets, and there upon he soon passed on.[17]

Bonney then called out, "Is that you Pat?" Garrett acknowledged him with a response. He then challenged Garrett to fight fairly, but the sheriff rebuked at the idea. The young fugitive and his men then attempted to make a dashing escape by trying to grab their horses and mount them inside the house. Garrett and his men prevented them from exiting the house by shooting one of the horses in front of the door. In doing so, they made it almost impossible to escape.

For the better part of the day, Bonney and the others were trapped inside the house. The lawman and his posse patiently waited outside. Finally, Dave Rudabaugh broke the stalemate by coming out of the house with his hands raised in the air. He approached Garrett and told him that Billy had every intention to surrender under the condition that they would be transported safely to the Santa Fé jail. The sheriff agreed after some thought on the matter.[18]

The sheriff sent for a cart, and loaded his prisoners and Bowdre's body onto it, and then trudged through the snow with the cart in tow back to Fort Sumner. Garrett and his men had arrived in Fort Sumner early in the morning on Christmas Eve day. Manuelita had seen them approaching the house and she was mortified at the sight of her dead husband. The tears welled up in her eyes as she instinctively made her way out of the door, to be next to her husband. Filled with despair and hatred, she approached Garrett and unleashed a fury of punches and kicks as she screamed at him.

Some of the other men had to come to Garrett's aid, pulling Manuelita off of him. Jim East was carrying Bowdre's body towards the house at the time of the fracas. Somehow Manuelita was able to escape their hold, grab onto a branding iron and proceeded to pummel East with it, hitting him over the head with such force that he dropped Bowdre's body at her feet. Overwhelmed with grief and fatigue Manuelita dropped to her knees next to her dead husband's side.

The sheriff approached the grieving woman and told her to look for a decent suit in which to bury her husband in. He told her that he would pay for its cost. He also offered to pay for his burial. Garrett's gestures did little to make up for the fact that her husband's dead corpse was brought to her one day before Christmas.[19] The lawman, his posse, and their prisoners continued on to Padre Polaco's house where they all had dinner that Christmas Eve night.

For Manuelita, the violence and terror that had consumed the last two years of her life had tragically come to an end. Her husband's indecision and reluctance to leave his friends ultimately cost him his life. She was left alone yet again, and she was forced to pick up the pieces of her shattered life. She and her loving guardian, Juanita soon made their leave back to the Río Ruidoso. It was in San Juanito, where Juanita finally met her future husband. She had married Gregorio Ybarra. After their marriage, both she and Manuelita had moved onto her husband's ranchito.

Maximiliano Corona

On February 25, 1884 Manuelita married Maximiliano Corona in Tularoso at la Iglesia de San Francisco de Paula. Maximiliano was originally from Casas Grandes, La República de México. After the two married, they lived on Gregorio Ybarra's ranchito. Maximiliano fathered three children with Manuelita, one son and two daughters. Their names were Manuel, Dorotea and Elena.

Their marriage was a turbulent affair, in which both sought to separate from one another due to irreconcilable differences. There had been a great deal of speculation within the community concerning the manner of their marital problems, but neither was willing to discuss the matter among friends. Eventually the marriage failed and they divorced. Maximiliano thus left Manuelita and their three children, as he migrated to Alamogordo, where he later married Josefina Maéstas on April 03, 1903.

Manuel Corona

Manuel Corona had become the most prominent of the three siblings as he held several political offices in Lincoln County. He served as a Constable in the San Patricio community. He served as Lincoln County's Probate Judge from 1933 to 1936. He served as a Lincoln County Commissioner, a school board member, and a Democratic political party chairman.[20] He even owned and operated a small grocery store in San Patricio. Although Manuel had served in the public office for many years, his one true passion was as a farmer. After his public life, he spent most of his time working his ranchito in San Patricio.

On July 17, 1966 Manuel's illustrious life had tragically come to an abrupt end as he was attempting to walk across the highway. He was waiting for a car to pass, and as it passed he proceeded to walk across. Unbeknownst to Manuel, the car had made a U-turn and quickly raced back towards him. The driver of the car didn't see Manuel and hit him head on. Manuel was thrown to the side of the road, where he died of the severe trauma to his head and body.

José Portio

About a year after Maximiliano and Manuelita had divorced, she gave birth to a son, José Portio, on December 03, 1893. José had light brown eyes, with reddish, wavy hair and a slightly freckled face. He had a very stern look about himself most of the time, and rarely flashed a smile. He married Julianita Ybarra on January 05, 1922 in San Patricio, New México. He had three children, two sons and a daughter.

In much the same manner as his mother, José was a reserved individual. Although his siblings loved and adored him, he usually preferred to keep to himself. He often lost himself in his thoughts, but when approached, he wouldn't shy away. He loved to express himself though music, in which he had a talent. In his youth, one could often see him strumming his guitar, and singing songs with his Salsberry siblings.

Although he didn't discuss the issue much, it was widely believed that he had an inclination of who his biological father was. He may have pursued the matter in his own way, but he never made it known whether he had ever approached his father. He often visited the Portillo family in Tularoso and acknowledged that many of them were *gente* (family). Maybe he had shared the knowledge of who his biological father was with his own children. Whatever the case, he lived his life with dignity and respect. He was embraced by his younger siblings in the Salsberry family.

His staunchness was a result of him enlisting in the Army. He was a World War One veteran, one of the few Spanish-surnamed men from Lincoln County that had enlisted into the military to serve their country during its time of need. He wore his uniform proudly, and he commanded a great amount of respect from his siblings and the rest of the community. His sense of patriotic duty was passed on to his sons and some of his grandchildren. He vigorously encouraged them to enlist into the military and serve their country as he had done.

From left to right: Manuel Corona, (Sitting in the background) Antonio
Sánchez, José Portio, Hilario Gómez, Augustín Salsberry.

Front row from left to right: Susana Corona, Martina Salsberry, Nicolasa Herrera, Enríque (Henry) Salsberry, Manuelita Herrera de Salsberry, Florinda Salsberry, Suzie Hale. The women in the back row are unknown as is the woman who is holding the child. This photo was taken in Ruidoso on July 03, 1915.

James R. Salsberry

James R. Salsberry (Ernest Sanchez collection)

James Wesley Saulsberry

The 1820 U.S. Census indicates that John H. Soesberry was living in Jefferson, Adams County, Ohio. He had married Delilah Hayslip and they had ten known children, seven sons and three daughters. James Wesley Saulsberry was their third eldest son and was born in about 1825 in Jefferson, Adams County, Ohio.

James W. Saulsberry married Harriet Clifton and they had seven known children, three sons and four daughters. Soon after their son Joseph Joel Pinkerton Saulsberry was born they emigrated from the township of Jefferson, Ohio to Illinois where their daughter, Nancy was born in 1866. By 1868 they had emigrated from Illinois to Iowa, where they had a son named James R. Salsberry. By 1870 they had emigrated from Iowa to Richland, Missouri. By 1880 they had emigrated from Richland, Missouri to Elk Horn Missouri.

The upheaval of constantly being on the move must have been rather difficult for the family, especially the children, because it was not conducive to establishing long-term relationships. While the family was traveling from Ohio to Missouri, James W. Saulsberry was ordained as a Baptist Minister.[21] This may have been one of the factors that drove the family to live a mostly nomadic life. As a minister, he may have wanted to continue to spread the word of God.

The patriarch had come to hear about the many opportunities in the Territory of New México. He and his family had packed their belongings once again and headed to Roswell. Two of their daughters, however had married and would not be accompanying them. The trip was long and arduous but they had finally arrived in about 1882.[22] Once in Roswell, he established a new ministry.

By 1883 Joseph Joel Pinkerton Saulsberry had migrated to the Río Ruidoso. He squatted on some land and he soon found employment, working for Lowel Hale. Joseph soon became acquainted with his boss' daughter, Mary Rebecca Hale, whom he eventually married by 1885. Soon thereafter, his parents and his younger brother, James R. Salsberry had also arrived in Ruidoso. The 1885 New México Territorial Census indicates that the James W. his wife and James R. were living with Joseph and his wife. It is believed that James W. Salsberry died in about 1887 in Ruidoso.

James Wesley's daughter, Lavinia Saulsberry, had also migrated to the Río Ruidoso valley, where she eventually became acquainted with a civil war veteran whose name was George Taylor. She eventually married her beau on July 01, 1888 in Lincoln. Taylor was a private in Company E, in the 5th California Infantry. He served from August 25, 1861 to January 1863, and enlisted again in January 1863, and served until September 25, 1866, when he mustered out in Silver City, Territory of New México. After his service in the military, Taylor became a stagecoach driver, and a caretaker at Fort Stanton.

On May 24, 1888 Joseph P. Salisbury applied for a homestead on the Río Ruidoso on sections 14 and 15 in township 11 south, range east, which was adjacent to James P. Conner's homestead on the north, and Henry C. Brown's homestead on the south.[23] He built a small house near the river and cultivated the land. There was a canyon nearby, which they named Saulsberry Canyon. He never stayed in any one place for an extended period of time because he eventually moved to La Aguilita, then to Nogal, then to La Luz, before he finally settled down in Alamogordo where he owned and operated a small business. By the time he had died he had acquired several businesses, which his son Harvey Hartsel later managed.

El Vaquero

Shortly after arriving in Ruidoso, James R. Salsberry had found employment with the Cree on the VV Ranch, which was based in Alto and had a beautiful vista of Sierra Blanca. The ranch was big, covering many sections atop the mountains and sprawling towards San Patricio. As a ranch hand, he usually spent most of his nights sleeping in a tent. Under the dark, starry night, and sitting next to a crackling fire, the men would drink, tell stories and sing well into the late night. Often times, one of the men would take out a guitar, and James would take out his fiddle or his harmonica and they all would sing traditional New Mexican folk songs or one of his favorites, "Buffalo Gals".

Many native New Mexicans found employment with the VV Ranch. They were the *vaqueros* who worked the ranch and went on cattle drives. It was with the vaqueros that James had learned the Spanish language and grew to appreciate their culture and customs. Many of his compadres knew him as Jimmy or Santiago. He felt a strong kinship with many of them.

130 |

James went on several cattle drives that took him east to Kansas, and Texas. He often told the stories of some of the events that took place while he and the other vaqueros were away from Lincoln County. He recalled that during a violent thunderstorm, the cattle were becoming quite unsettled. He claimed that he was able to calm their nerves by playing his harmonica and thus preventing a stampede.

He told the story about how he and his compadres had camped just outside of a small town. They had come across some of the townsfolk who were headed for a dance. He had asked them if he and some of his friends could partake in the festivities. Being that most of the men in his company were "Mexican", they were advised that it would be best if they all would refrain from going to town. This didn't sit very well with James and his compadres and several of them rode into town.

As they approached the dancehall, they were stopped and told that they were not dressed appropriately. He and his compadres were wearing dirtied chaps, spurs and they had the smell of five days travel upon them. He explained that they didn't have anything else to wear, but that they all loved to dance. After some discussion and deliberation, they were allowed to enter the dancehall.

Manuelita and James

From time to time, James would pass near El Rancho de San Juanito to visit his brother Joseph, who lived about two miles downstream. In many instances he came across Manuelita, who often could be seen working in the fields, or taking care of the livestock. Many a time he would stop and converse with her. She was impressed with his ability to speak Spanish, which she found very endearing. One could say that he reminded her of Billy, a close friend she had lost to tragedy.

James had become captivated by Manuelita's beauty, and he anticipated the moments that he could share with her. Being that James was extremely shy, it was a wonder that he garnered enough gumption to approach her and to talk to her as much as he did. Over time, the two grew smitten with each other and they initiated an informal courtship.

As the relationship continued to mature, James found himself wanting more than a courtship. Manuelita, having dealt with two prior marriages and a recently failed relationship, was somewhat reluctant to pursue something more meaningful. Her past love interests had all ended very badly and because of that, she developed a defensive mechanism to protect herself from being overly vulnerable. James was persistent though and he continued to try and win her favor. Gradually, she lowered her defenses and allowed her love for James to blossom.

Although the two were falling in love, many of James' Anglo peers were adamantly against their relationship. Some had taken exception to their forbidden love for many different reasons. First, they questioned Manuelita's character. It was in their opinion that she carried a tarnished reputation. Second, they didn't approve of her father and all of his misdeeds that he committed during the Lincoln County War. Third, they didn't approve of him falling in love with a "Mexican". They didn't accept the fact that he could embrace their language, culture and religion. They often ridiculed him, and later they ridiculed their children.

Although no records have been found of their marriage, it is believed that they were married sometime between 1894 and 1895. They had eight children, four sons and four daughters. His family was large but the patriarch sparingly saw them, because as a ranch hand, he was often away from home. The marriage was somewhat unusual in that both spouses had become accustomed to being separated from each other for long periods of time. Manuelita always had a strong and independent nature. She was a take-charge type of person. She had learned to rely on her independence as a means of survival. She must have conditioned herself to suppress the loneliness she must have felt over the course of many years.

Although Manuelita had an estranged relationship with her father, she had always made it a point to give birth to her children at his house. All of her children were born there except Florinda and Enríques (Henry), who were born on the Rancho Salsberry near at the mouth of Cañon de Salsberry (Saulsberry Canyon). The house they were born stands in a small grove of trees that mark where James, Manuelita, and their children lived.

The house was situated on land, which was originally homesteaded by his brother. On January 19, 1910 Joseph sold his 160 acre homestead and another 400 acres owned by his deceased wife, Mary Rebecca Hale. He sold his lands to S.M. Johnson for $180.[24]

Although the land was sold to S.M. Johnson, he was generous enough to allow James and his family to live in the house for several years thereafter. In about 1917 his family moved to San Patricio, where they lived with her son, Manuel Corona for a short period of time. He soon found employment, working for Mauricio Sánchez, who was a local farmer and sheep rancher.

James and Manuelita eventually bought about ½ acre of land from Manuel Silva, in San Patricio. They both lived at their new house but the living conditions were cramped considering there were only two rooms, and several children. When Mauricio Sánchez offered him a place to stay, he quickly jumped at the opportunity.

Manuelita took it upon herself to purchase most of the provisions for the house. As was the case, she often had to hitch the horse to the buggy. She would travel about twelve miles to Tinnie to purchase all that she needed. Sometimes she would take her daughter Florinda, who would help her stock the buggy. She would also make an annual trip to Elisa "Alice" Hale's house, to do her canning for the winter. Alice was her niece and she was married to Peter Hale.

James consciously chose not to speak English with his children and grandchildren. Papá Jimmy, as his grandchildren affectionately knew him, weren't even aware he knew a language other than Spanish. By chance, two of his grandchildren, Ernesto Sánchez and Augustín Salsberry, were walking down the street in Capitán when they had happened to come across two men speaking in a foreign language and laughing boisterously within the general store. They recognized the voice and the laughter, but couldn't understand the words being spoken. Curiously they walked into the store to investigate. To their amazement they saw their grandfather speaking in English with the shopkeeper. When their grandfather saw them, he acknowledged them with a smile and briefly continued talking before the three of them made their exit from the general store.

After learning that their grandfather could speak English, the grandchildren often asked him to teach them a few words from time to time. He refused to speak to them in English and he never gave them a legitimate reason why. He assured them that the Spanish language was much more pleasant to the ear and rolled off the tongue much easier. Although he spoke the language fluently, and his pronunciation was rather impressive, he talked with a slight accent. Even the pronunciation of his surname had changed so that it was easier to say in Spanish. Many in the New Mexican community knew him as Jimmy Solsberete because they couldn't pronounce his English given name.

James seldom associated himself with his Anglo peers. Being that he was married to Manuelita, his children were of New Mexican descent. He perceived that many of the newcomers who were migrating into Lincoln County were prejudiced against anybody with "Mexican" blood. He resented the fact that some people looked down upon his family because they spoke Spanish and they lived a predominantly New Mexican lifestyle. Like many of the other Anglo men and women who married into New Mexican families, he had adopted the language, customs, and beliefs of his spouse.

Over time, he became aware of how his adopted people were perceived by the Anglo newcomers. He was cognizant that some of them were opportunistic and that they would sometimes take advantage of the New Mexicans' lack of knowledge of the English language and U.S. laws. As a consequence, he often would tell his children and grandchildren that many of the Anglo newcomers could not be trusted.

Once James had formed an opinion about someone, very seldom did he ever change his mind about that person. He lived in a world of absolutes, in which either you were with him or you were against him. If someone were to cross him in the wrong manner, he would have held it against them either for the remainder of their lives, or for a very long time. Maybe this had become a defensive mechanism, which was a result of being alone most of his life. Whatever the reason, he would soon as cease having a relationship with somebody rather than try to communicate with them to resolve any conflict.

James was a *vaquero* at heart, and he had always lived as one. He was quite reserved, and very seldom did he ever speak a word if he didn't have to. When his own children would come to visit him at his daughter Florinda's house, he often took a walk to the river. Augustín and Santiago (James) often paid their father a visit. Looking for him, they would ask their sister where he was. She would tell them that he was last seen walking towards the river. Either Augustín or Santiago would then walk down to the river to see their father.

James always liked to trade personal mementoes with either Augustín or Santiago every time they came to visit. Usually it was a buck knife, a pocket watch, or any other little trinket of sentimental value. They referred to the gesture as *ojo tapado*, in which neither of the two had any idea what the other was going to trade. After trading, the ice would be broken between the two and they would begin to talk.

James liked to talk about the days when he worked for the Cree on the VV Ranch. He would talk about sleeping under the starry night, or how they would sing and tell stories into the early morning. Sometimes he would pull his harmonica from his pocket and he would do a rendition of some of the songs that they had sung. He always seemed to have a twinkle in his eyes when he was reminiscing about those days.

He never really cared much for picking apples, irrigating the orchards, or maintaining the acequias. Rather, he was impassioned about gathering and chopping wood. He could spend hours each day chopping and stacking the wood and making *palitos* (kindling). The wood was stacked uniformly and he always kept it well stocked. Often times one could find him shaving sticks with his buck knife, making palitos for the next morning's fire.

James spent an unusual amount of time each day shaving his face with a straight edge blade. He would shave, feel his face to make sure it was smooth, and then he would shave yet again. Sometimes he shaved so much that his face would turn red, and small beads of blood would collect upon his broken skin.

He always wore two sets of clothing. He wore his long johns and two pair of pants, and two pairs of shirts. This may have been a habit that he picked up while being a ranch hand. Often times, the nights would become bitterly cold, and extra clothing had always come in handy during those cold nights. It was always easier to take clothing off during the day.

During the summer months, James would pitch a tent outside of his daughter Florinda's house, under the large cottonwood trees, and invite his favorite *nieto* (grandson), Ernesto Sánchez, to sleep in the tent with him. Within the tent, he would place a trunk, which contained most of his personal belongings at one side. The two would spend hours talking to each other, telling stories before retiring for the night. Thus the two would sleep in the tent every night, for the entire summer.

Whenever James could make it to the general store, he had an unusual manner in which he paid for the items he wished to purchase. He would gather several items and place them on the counter, and then he would pay for each item separately. After receiving his change for the prior item, he would place his next item before the shopkeeper so that he could pay for it. He did this until he had paid for all of the items he wanted to buy.

Ernesto remembers that his abuelo had a trunk filled with most of his personal belongings. Every night, he would take out his clothes from within the trunk and lay them out about the room. He would then look at all his clothes, closely inspecting them. After about thirty minutes or so, he would fold his clothes and neatly place them back into the trunk.

James had covered all of the windows of the house so that the sunlight could be blocked out. This was a good way to keep the adobé cooler in the summer months. He found peace of mind within his adobé it was his sanctuary from the rest of the world. He didn't mind spending his time keeping to himself and his absence often added to the mystery of this man. One thing was for sure; he had passionately valued his personal privacy, and allowed only a few people into his private world. His nieto, Ernesto, was able to understand him better than anybody else.

Manuelita Herrera de Salsberry lived the remainder of her life in San Patricio. She died on February 13, 1939 and was buried in the campo santo de La Capilla de San Patricio. She now rests in a marked grave. Papá Jimmy also lived the remainder of his life in San Patricio with his daughter Florinda and her husband Román Sánchez. He died on April 14, 1947 and was buried in the campo santo de La Capilla de San Patricio. He rests in an unmarked grave where only his nieto, Ernesto knows of its location.

Manuelita Herrera de Salsberry, Unknown Child, Florinda Salsberry
de Sánchez, Unknown child (Ernest Sanchez collection)

Chapter Ten:
Other Pioneering Families

The Original Español Settlers

In addition to the US soldiers stationed at Fort Stanton, the 1860 US Census indicates that there were several families that had settled in the region that would be known to many throughout the Territory of New México as Bonito. The US Census referred to the precinct as Río Bonito, Socorro County, Territory of New México. Following is a list of the Hispanic families, but not all the people that settled the area.

Pablo Alderete and his wife Miquela settled with their five children. José de la Cruz Aragón and his wife María had settled with no children. Teodosio Aragón and his wife Nicolasa settled with their six children. Francisco Fajardo and his wife Juliana settled with their five children. Juan José García and his wife María had settled with their eight children. Sabino Gonzáles and his wife Encarnación settled with their two children. Tomás Gonzáles and his wife Francisca settled with one daughter and two grandchildren. Román Griego settled with two of his children. Juan Jaramillo and his wife Dolóres settled with their two children. Pascual Jojola and his wife Josefa settled with their two children. Jesús Lucero and his wife Ysabel settled with their four children. Felipé Miranda and his wife Dolóres settled with one child. José Miranda and his wife María settled with their four children. Casimiro Moya and his wife María settled with their three children. José Miguel Peña and his wife Pabla settled with their four children. Juan José Romero and his wife María settled with their three children. Tomás Sandoval and his wife Samana settled with their four children. José Silva and his wife Marta settled with their two children. Santiago Silva and his wife Marcelina settled with one child.

Los Analla

José Analla

José Analla, also known as José Pedro Nonato Analla, was born about June of 1830. Some of his descendants believe that he was born in San Pedro, Chihuahua, La República de México. His parents were Ysidoro Analla and Dolóres Gallegos. The 1860 U.S. Census has him and his wife María Cedillo, and their family living in Punta de Agua, Valencia County, Territory of New México. By 1869 he and his family had migrated to La Plaza de San José. Shortly thereafter they had settled in an area, which they named Rancho Analla. It is speculated that he also named the Picacho hills.

The 1870 U.S. Census indicates that José and his brother Pedro were living next to one another. Their sister María Andrea Analla de Sánches was living further up the valley, in the community of La Plaza de San Patricio. José made a living as a sheep rancher while his brother made his living as a freighter. They continued to live next to one another until María Cedillo de Analla's untimely death on August 12, 1875.

It didn't take very long for José to re-marry. By 1876 he had married Paula Galindro. They were living near María Andrea in La Plaza de San Patricio.[1] Together they had three children, two sons and one daughter. By 1885 the family had returned to Analla.[2] On October 17, 1887, José married

Dulcesnombres Montoya. They had three children together, two sons and one daughter. José died in Analla on March 24, 1899. His last wishes were that he be buried in a sheet, without a coffin, and that he be bare-footed.[3]

There was a family legend claiming that José had been captured by a band of Apachés when he was about 6 years old. He remained a captive for almost 12 years before he had planned his escape. It was speculated that during his escape, he had killed 8 of his captors and he was able to make off with a cache of valuables. Whether there is any truth to the story is up to much deliberation.

What can't be debated is his entrepreneurial spirit. He started out as a very successful sheep rancher. He further expanded his enterprise by opening up a general mercantile store. Throughout his life he was able to amass a tremendous amount of wealth. Rather than putting his money in the bank, he opted to keep his cash on hand. After several failed robbery attempts he hid his money in the hills around his house. Even upon his deathbed he refused to tell his family where he had hidden all of the money. Months later, one of his grandchildren claimed that he had found one of the hidden caches. He backed up his claim by producing a can filled with $20 gold pieces.[4]

Don Pedro was reluctant to embrace the English-speaking newcomers from the United States. He didn't understand the English language and didn't fully understand their new laws. Much of the lands that he used, to graze his large flock of sheep, were being patented out to other settlers. His livelihood was being squeezed and legally there was nothing that he could do to stop their encroachment on what he perceived to be rightfully his lands. As he continued to lose more land, he was forced to sell more of his sheep. At some point he had to abandon his operations because it was no longer profitable. In one instance he had come before a crowd at the Lincoln County courthouse and denounced the civic leaders for their lack of leadership.

Los Baca

Juan Baca

Juan Baca was born in about 1842. It is believed that he was originally from the region near Manzano, Territory of New México. He married Gabina Chávez y Torres who also was from Manzano, Territory of New México. The 1880 US Census indicates that Juan and his family were living in Lincoln, Territory of New México. Many of Juan's descendants continue to live in Lincoln County.

Saturnino Baca

Saturnino Baca was born on November 30, 1836 in Sebollita, Nuevo México, La República de México. He married Juana Chávez in about 1856. The 1850 US Census indicates that Saturnino lived in Cubero, Territory of New México. The 1870 US Census indicates that Saturnino and his family had migrated to Lincoln County, Precinct 1, Territory of New México.

Saturnino was an ambitious man, opting to throw his weight into the political arena. In 1868 he was elected to the New México Territorial House of Representatives. In September of 1870, he ran for the same office against William Brady and lost by three votes. In April of 1872 he and William Brady both ran for County Probate Judge, in which Saturnino won unanimously.[5] In 1875, he was appointed by Territorial Governor Giddings the new Lincoln County Sheriff. He replaced Alexander Mills who had been relieved of his duties. In November of 1876 both Baca and Brady ran for the office of Lincoln County Sheriff. Brady had unanimously won the vote of the people.[6]

During the Lincoln County War, Saturnino attempted to take a neutral stance. As with many people in Lincoln County, it was a hard situation not to have an opinion one way or another. It was widely held that he tended to favor Dolan's position considering that Sue McSween had accused him of sending a posse to San Patricio to find and kill her husband. This accusation, he denied claiming that it wasn't any concern of his.[7] In another instance, several members of The Regulators had begrudged Saturnino for his part in bringing Coronel Dudley to Lincoln. They threatened to burn his house down as a means of retaliation for the tragic fire that burned McSween's house down during the Five Days Battle.[8]

Los Barragán

Román Barragán[9]

Román Barragán was a tall man, with reddish hair, a fair complexion, and strikingly blue eyes. He was born in Chihuahua, La República de México in February of 1847. It was rumored that he was of Basque origin, but he had never really talked much about his ancestry. He was a passionate man who wasn't afraid to speak what was on his mind. He was held in high esteem by many of the other New Mexicans in the San Patricio community. On occasion, he had participated on some of the campaigns with the Regulators, most notably the Five Days Battle. Most of his contributions however where not at the end of a gun but rather through the words that he spoke.

Román owned 160 acres of land about four miles west of San Patricio. He had acquired the land that stretched on both sides of the Rio Ruidoso from Esiquio Sánchez. The farm was situated between El Rancho Gonzáles to the east and the Coe Ranch to the west. He made an honest living as a farmer, but most of his life was devoted to the 1,500 head of sheep he owned. He grazed his sheep on open rangelands just south of his farm. He often could be seen riding his horse from his farm up into the mountains so that he could tend to his sheep almost on a daily basis. Román enjoyed the land, and could spend the entire day up in the mountains. Sometimes he would set up a campito in the hills and stay there for a couple of days as he tended to his sheep.

Román and his wife Andrea Torres de Barragán did not have any children of their own. They were however, Padrinos to Delfinia Romero, the daughter of Juan de Dios Romero and Cristina Castillo de Romero. They took Delfinia into their home and raised her as their own daughter. After Delfinia married Mauricio Sánchez, the newlyweds continued to live at Rancho Barragán. Mauricio and Delfinia's eldest son was named in Román's honor. Hence Román Sánchez was Román Barragán's *tocallo* (namesake). Román Barragán also baptized Román Sánchez. Mauricio and Delfinia's family of seven children continued to live on Rancho Barragán even after both had passed on.

Andrea Torres de Barragán was said to have had mestizo features. She had caramel colored skin, dark hair and brown eyes. She often filled a large basket with about ten dozen eggs and then placed the basket upon her head. She would walk up Cañon de Flores and on to Lincoln so that she could sell the eggs by stopping from house to house on the way.

On the southern border of Rancho Barragán, from the south bank of the Río Ruidoso to the mountainside, there lies a small llano that stretches at the base of the mountain. This llano used to be a Mescalero camp where one could find small fragments of pottery and arrowheads strewn about. Further up into the mountains, one could find fossils of ancient seashells, fish, and other sea creatures that used to roam within an ancient sea that covered the entire area over 65 million years ago. One could also find fossils of ancient ferns that grew in the area when it had a wetter climate.

Román had a brother, Antonio Barragán, who had also migrated from Chihuahua, La República de México to La Plaza de San Patricio. Antonio had lived with his brother briefly before he decided to make a life for himself in Lincoln. Antonio remained in Lincoln for many years before he finally moved to Carrizozo. The irony was that the two brothers had not kept in contact with one another and Román Barragán had presumed that his brother had eventually returned to México.

Maximiliano "Maque" Sánchez, Román Barragán (sitting), María Sánchez (Ernest Sanchez collection)

Los Benavides

The Benavides like many other families had spelled their names in many different ways. Some of the spellings were as such; Benavides, Benavidez, Venavides, Benabides and Venabides. There were several different and unrelated families that settled throughout Lincoln County. Some of the families that settled in Lincoln County were Santiago Benavides and his wife Antonia Moya. José Benavides and his wife Trenidad Madrid also settled the region. José Benabides and his wife Petra Archuleta settled near Lincoln in the late 1870's.

Santiago Benavides

Miguel Benavides, christened Juan Miguel Benavides was born on December 14, 1794 in San Fernando, El Reyno de Nuevo México, Nueva España. His parents were Marcial Torres and María Gertrudis Toledo Venavides. He took the name of his mother rather than that of his father. Church records indicate that he had been born over a year before Marcial and Gertrudis were married. He married María Manuela Jaramillo and they had eleven known children, seven sons and four daughters.

Santiago Benavides, christened José Santiago Benavides was born in about 1841 near Tomé, Nuevo México, La República de México. His parents were Miguel Benavides and Manuela Jaramillo.

He had married Antonia Moya in Tomé on August 23, 1861. She was the daughter of Manuel Moya and María Teresa Montoya. They had seven known children, three sons and four daughters.

Santiago's tío, Mariano Torres had migrated to Lincoln County sometime in the late 1860's. When visiting his family and friends back in Punta de Agua and Manzano, Mariano often told of El Bonito's beauty and potential. His stories of adventure on the frontier enticed the young lad's imagination.

By the early 1870's Santiago and his wife migrated and settled in an area near Lincoln. Their son Juan Augustín was baptized on October 28, 1873 in Lincoln County. The 1880 US Census indicates that he and his family had finally settled near Las Tablas, Territory of New México. Many of Santiago's descendant's continue to live in Lincoln County.

José Benavides

José Benavides was born in about March of 1856. The 1900 and 1910 US Census indicated that he was born in the Territory of New México. The 1920 Census however, indicated that he was born in Téxas. He married Trenidad Madril in about 1880. Shortly thereafter he and his wife migrated to an area near Ruidoso, Territory of New México. Their first daughter, Marillita Benavides, christened María Josefa Benavides was born on March 19, 1885 in Ruidoso, Territory of New México.

Trenidad died sometime after the birth of her last daughter in 1892. She was not listed in the 1900 US Census. After his wife's death, José never remarried. He continued living with his children until his death on March 20, 1923. Upon his death he was living with his daughter Teofila and her husband Pedro Núñes Salas. Several of José's descendents continue to live throughout Lincoln County.

Back row from left to right: Apolonia Benavides-Trujillo, Teofila Benavides-Salas, Marillita Benavides-Montoya, Guillermo Benavides. Front row from left to right: A sister of José Benavides, Nasario Montoya, José Benavides. (Ernest Sanchez collection)

Los Candelaria

Ábran Candelaria

Ábran Candelaria was born in about 1848 in Barelas, Territory of New México. His parents were Pedro Candelaria and María Petra de Jesús Apodaca. Sometime in the early to mid 1870's he migrated to the Apishapa River Valley near Trinidad in the Territory of Colorado. He met a beautiful young woman named Josefa Maés whom he married sometime before 1875. She was the daughter of José de Jesús Maés and María Margarita Galves. Shortly thereafter they had a daughter named Antonia.

By the late 1870's Ábran and his father-in-law both moved their respective families to Arroyo Seco, Lincoln County, Territory of New México. Near the base of the Sierra Capitán the two families ranched for a living. They supplemented their income by gathering wood and selling it in Roswell.

Problems between Ábran and Josefa slowly began to surface over time. As the rift between the two continued to grow, their relationship came under increasing pressure. It is unclear as to the events that occurred over the following years, which led to their untimely separation.

A new family had recently arrived from Colorado and they settled in Las Palas, Territory of New México. Cornelio Lucero, his wife Noberta and all of their children were excited to settle in a strange, new land. Ábran had received word of the new family and he set forth to greet them. Being that he himself had lived a short time in Colorado, he wanted to reminisce about the far off land. Over many conversations with the Lucero family he was gradually overtaken with infatuation by one of their daughters named Benina.

The two spent a great deal of time together. Surely there was some hesitation on Benina's part to become romantically involved with an older gentleman. But as the power of love slowly enveloped her, she succumbed to its intoxicating affects. She had become pregnant and on November 16, 1883 she gave birth to a son. Ábran and Benina named their son José Candelaria.

Not much else is known about Ábran after the birth of his son. It appears that he may have died sometime between 1885 and 1893. Benina eventually married Andrew McNeely Richardson on June 15, 1893. Andrew Richardson thus helped raise his stepson, José Candelaria. Josefita died on December 14, 1929 in Belén, New México. Her death records indicated that her husband's name was Ábran Candelaria, which leads me to believe that she had never re-married. If she had married, there is no record of it.

Antonia Candelaria had married Felipé Sánchez y Raél on October 09, 1889. He was the son of Antonio Sánchez and Juanita Raél. They continued to live in Las Palas for many years. By 1920 they had moved to Belén. Most of Felipé an Antonia's descendents continue to live in the Belén region.

José Candelaria had first married Dominga Pacheco on March 29, 1906. He then married Rebecca Villescas on December 16, 1908. They had five known children, four sons and a daughter. He then married Isidra Sánchez on November 22, 1921. They had five known children, three sons and two daughters. Many of José's descendents continue to live in the San Patricio, Ruidoso region. Several have moved to other cities throughout New México.

Los Chávez

Cleto Chávez[10]

Cleto Chávez had lost his father, Mauricio Chávez when he was about six months old. He lost his mother, Pabla Lucero when he was about twelve years old. Becoming an orphan, he made a living for himself by working numerous odd jobs. He had happened to come into the acquaintance of George Neblett, who owned a sawmill operating out of Mescalero. In about 1870 he migrated to Mescalero to work in the saw mill.

It wasn't long thereafter that Cleto had come to learn of the dangers of living and working near the Mescalero. The Mescalero were still resisting a life on the reservation and from time to time they would form raiding parties that would traverse the surrounding region. Sometimes they would rustle livestock, other times they would destroy buildings, and on rare occasions someone would be killed.

On one occasion George had come to know that a raiding party was heading in the direction of Tularoso. Cleto was called upon to ride swiftly to Tularoso, warning all of those he came across about the potential danger. He came across Mariano Ruíz, who was heading into the mountains to gather wood. Mariano ignored the warning and continued into the mountains. He also came across Benito Montoya, but couldn't reach him fast enough. Benito being astute though had heard the raiding party approach and quickly found cover within the ***tules*** (reeds). As Cleto had figured, Mariano was killed and a search party did fine Mariano's body the next day.

By March of 1872 Cleto had left his employment at the saw mill and had moved to Picacho where he worked on William Casey's farm. He had worked at Casey's over the summer and up through October of 1872. He then started working for Jack Price. By 1874 Cleto had married Prudencia Miranda.

José Chávez

José Chávez was also known as José Chávez y Montoya. The 1860 US Census shows that José, his wife Apolinaria "Polonia" López and their children were living near Manzano, Territory of New México. Ambrocio, one of José's sons claimed that he was Martín Chávez's cousin. José and his family had migrated to Lincoln in about 1869.

José often drove freight wagons from Fort Stanton to Las Vegas and back. On average it took about twenty days to make a round trip, weather permitting. The route most used followed a path through Nogal and on to White Oaks. From White Oaks they continued through the Patos Mountains and on to Las Vegas. As with most other freight routes that traversed long distances, there was always the threat of a Mescalero attack. José and his son Ambrocio however, never came into any danger while running freight.[11]

Los Domínguez

Nicanor Domínguez was born in about 1850 in La República de México. He was married to Octaviana Fuentes who was also born there. He and his wife had immigrated to the United States in about 1880. They eventually settled in San Patricio, Territory of New México. Many of Nicanor's descendants continue to live in Lincoln County.

Los Dutchover

Anton Diedrick is the progenitor of most of the Dutchover's that have settled throughout southern New México, and in the Big Bend region of Téxas. He was born in about July 1819 in Antwerp, Belgium. He was described as having blonde hair and blue eyes.

In 1842, at the age of about 23, Anton had happened to witness a murder, as he was walking the city streets of Antwerp. Fearing what Anton had seen, the perpetrators set an ambush as the young man attempted to elude capture. Once he was caught, the killers sold Anton to the crew of a ship. It was upon this ship that the terrified young man had remained a virtual slave and prisoner. Over several years' time, he eventually earned the trust of his captors. In doing so, the ship's crew became somewhat unguarded, which worked to Anton's benefit. By 1845 as the ship docked in the port of Galveston, Téxas, he made his escape.[12]

In a very foreign country, with hunger setting in, Anton set out to find some food and shelter. Being that he could only speak Flemish, the dominant language of Belgium, he had a difficult time communicating with the people he happened to come across. He had happened to cross a pair of military recruiters, seeking to sign up volunteers for the Mexican War. They insisted that if he were to join, the U.S. Government would provide him with food and lodging. Finally convinced though aggressive coercion and a need to feed his hunger, he unwittingly agreed to volunteer his services. When asked what his name was, Anton had a difficult time trying to communicate, therefore one of the recruiters hastily remarked, "He looks Dutch all over." Hence his name was recorded on the rosters as Diedrick Dutchallover.[13] Later the name was condensed to Dutchover.

There is some speculation as to how the name Dutchover came into existence. A similar name, Duytschaever, does exist in Belgium. It's pronunciation in Belgium is very similar to the way we would say it here in the United States. It would require further research to determine whether this assumption holds any merit. So, was this an instance where a man's name was invented and changed, or misspelled?

After the Mexican War the man formally known as Anton, but in the United States was commonly known as Diedrick, found residence in San Antonio, Téxas. He learned a trade as a frontier scout. By 1850 W.A. "Big Foot" Wallace had approached him about escorting a mail run from San Antonio to El Paso. Diedrick continued working for the stage line for another two years before he finally decided to settle in Fort Davis, Téxas. He started operating a sheep ranching operation in Limpia Canyon. Later he acquired cattle and often conducted business with the fort. By 1861 he had married a young Mexican woman by the name of Refugia Cora Salcido.

During the civil war, Diedrick maintained a neutral stance opting to continue his sheep ranching operation regardless of which side was occupying the fort. He provided food for the troops at the fort. He remained with the fort when U.S. Federal Troops of the 8th Infantry left for the war in 1861. Soon thereafter the Confederate troops had come upon the abandoned fort. When the undermanned confederate troops vacated the fort, Diedrick was left in charge. While the fort remained abandoned for the second time, Apaché Chief Nicolás attacked the vulnerable settlement. Diedrick, a Mexican woman with two children, and four Americans hid up on the roof of the fort for three days as the Apachés looted the settlement and fort. Finally, Diedrick and the others, less one American who died of natural causes, escaped and made the long journey to Presidio. It took four rigorous days to complete their escape.

Diedrick eventually returned to Fort Davis where he continued his ranching operation. He had ten children to help him with his ranch. He died in Fort Davis on March 12, 1904. Many of his children and his grandchildren were born in Fort Davis, Téxas. In all, almost all of the Dutchover remained in the region often referred to as Big Bend. A few had migrated to New México and others to northern California.

His grandson, José de Jesús Dutchover, was one of the first to leave Téxas for New México. During the mid-1920's José, his wife Anita and their children migrated to several ranching communities in Cháves County, New México. José's daughter Evalina "Eva" Dutchover married Heraldo Modesto Chávez and lived most of her adult life in San Patricio, New México. Several of the other Dutchover continue to live in Roswell, New México. Although the Dutchover are not one of the founding families in the Rio Ruidoso valley, their descendants have lived there for over eighty years.

Los Fresquez

Vicente Fresquez was born near Arroyo Seco, Taos County on July 01, 1835. He married his wife María Antonia Tafoya and they had Pablo, María Elena, Rumaldo, and Pedro in Arroyo Seco. By 1870 the family had migrated to Punta de Agua in Valencia County. By 1880 the family had migrated and settled in La Plaza de Picacho. They remained there for several generations. The descendants of Porfirio Fresquez and María Sedillo still own some property in Picacho. Many of the Fresquez, however, have since left the ranch and Lincoln County.

Los Gallegos

Hilario Gallegos
Hilario Gallegos was born in about 1832. He was married to Josefita Chávez. By 1870 Hilario and his family had settled in La Plaza de San Patricio, Territory of New México. After his first wife died, Hilario married Josefa Sánchez. Many of Hilario's descendants continue to live in Lincoln County.

Lázaro Gallegos
Lázaro Gallegos was born in about 1848 in Sabinal, Territory of New México. He married Antonia Molina in about 1889. The 1880 Census indicates that he and his family were living in La Plaza de San Patricio. By 1900 he and his family had settled in Agua Azul, Territory of New México. Many of Lazaro's descendants continue to live in Lincoln County.

Lucas Gallegos
Lucas Gallegos was born in about 1842 and he was married to Francisca García. The 1870 US Census indicates that he was living in La Plaza de San Patricio, Territory of New México.

Lucas was no stranger to controversy; he carried with him a quick temper and an unwavering stubbornness. A small adobé church was constructed on a piece of land adjacent to his property. The Catholic Church wanted him to deed a part of his land for their campo santo. He refused to deed a part of his land to the Catholic Church and in doing so it is believed that he was excommunicated from the Church. He later used the abandoned adobé structure as a corral. Eventually the corral was taken down eliminating any evidence that the church even existed.[14]

Lucas was acquainted with a dubious group of men. At times, he could be found riding with Billy the Kid and his Regulators. In one instance, Billy, Lucas and several other men sprung a group of prisoners free in a daring jailbreak in Lincoln. Shortly thereafter, as they made their escape, Billy and Lucas came across two brothers, Francisco Trujillo and Juan Trujillo. The two men were forcibly stopped and Billy had taken their weapons and a saddle.[15]

Lucas' penchant for trouble had culminated during a violent dispute with his nephew. As tempers continued to flare between the two, Lucas killed his nephew, shooting him in the back. He was caught, tried, and sentenced to serve one year in prison.[16] It is believed that the dispute was over his nephew's unwillingness to pay on a debt owed to his uncle.

Los Gómez

Felipé Gómez[17]

Felipé Gómez was born in Lincoln, Territory of New México on February 09, 1869. He was the son of Francisco Gómes and Ignacia Rodrígues. He lived most of his childhood near the Río Bonito between Fort Stanton and Lincoln. He had one known sister named Guadalupe. His father had died before he turned ten years of age. At 22 years of age, he married Miquela Lucero on March 01, 1891. They had one son, Hilario Gómez who was born on January 14, 1892. Tragically, Miquela died shortly after giving birth to her son.

Almost five years later, Felipé Gómez married Beatríz Sedillo on January 04, 1897. She was originally from Picacho. They had twelve children, seven sons and five daughters. They lived in Lincoln with their children until about 1913. Shortly after the birth of their son, Francisco "Frank" Gómez, the family had moved to a community which later became known as Hollywood. They built a log cabin on the eastern side of their property. They lived there for a brief time. They farmed the land and grazed sheep for a living.

Eventually, the family moved to the Gómez farm near Glencoe, where Felipé first built a jacal. Eventually he and his family improved the land by planting crops, and building an adobé house. Many of the children attended school in a one-room adobé, built about two miles east of their family farm. The school was eventually knocked down in about 1936 when the first paved highway was built through the valley. Felipé was a vaquero and worked on the VV Ranch owned by the Cree. It was common for him to make cattle runs to Dodge City, Kansas and Amarillo, Téxas.

After Felipé and his family had established themselves on the farm, his father-in-law, Calixtro Sedillo and his wife Carmelita had moved from their farm in Las Angosturas, to the Gómez family farm. Calixtro built a jacal and lived there until he died. One could always see him riding his horse down to the Río Ruidoso, where he often sat for hours, listening to the soothing sound of the running water.

Many of the Felipé's children eventually attended a new school that was built behind the grocery store in San Patricio. The grocery store eventually became the White Cat Bar. The new school was centrally located and thus enabled all the children from Hondo to Glencoe to gather in one school, rather than several little schools throughout the valley.

Hilario Gómez served in the U.S. military during World War I. He married María Romero on June 25, 1917. Eventually he and his wife settled in San Patricio where he became a farmer. Although farming was his primary trade, he was also an active member of the community. He served as a Lincoln County Commissioner, a member of the school board, and also as a school bus driver.

Hilario and his wife had become gracious hosts. Their house often came to life when they sponsored family gatherings or some type of community event. The smell of food and sound of music always brought the people of the community together. Often times, their fiestas would last late into the evenings, and some of their guests would stay at their house overnight.

Los Gutiérres

José Manuel Gutiérres was born in about 1807. His parents were José Antonio Gutiérres and Barbara Lucero. He first married Juana Gertrudis Lópes in Socorro, Nuevo México, La República de México on December 06, 1828. Gertrudis died sometime before 1848. He later re-married Juana María Salas in Socorro, Territory of New México on April 23, 1848.

They had nine known children, eight sons and one daughter. Each son carried the name of José. There was José Manuel, José Rafael, José Tornino, José Dolóres, Juan José, José Damian, José Francisco, José Florentino, and the daughter Josefita. All of the Gutiérres boys were more commonly known by their second given names rather than their first given names of José. This was not unusual in that many children of the time had "José" as a part of their Christian names.

The 1860 U.S. Census indicates that he was living in Lemitar, Territory of New México. It is believed that the family migrated to La Luz; Territory of New México in about 1864 after large floods damaged much of their land and prompted them to seek a fresh start near the Sierra Sacramento. The family eventually built a home on their rancho in about 1869, which later became a state registered historical building, and is known as the Juan José Gutierrez House.[18]

Most of the family had migrated from La Luz to the Río Ruidoso valley. The 1870 U.S. Census indicates that they were living near La Plaza de San Patricio. One of the siblings who made his home near La Junta was Francisco Gutiérres. Family legend was that when Billy the Kid first arrived in Lincoln County, William Brady brought him over to Francisco's rancho. He offered Bonney a job and the kid was enthusiastic about the prospect of working. Billy worked on the rancho for a short time before he moved on. Bonney never forgot Francisco's hospitality and often stopped by his house for a visit. It was also said that Albert Fountain and his son had stayed the night at Juan José's house before they mysteriously disappeared.

Los Gutiérrez had owned three separate landholdings in the region. In 1876, they had sold one of their ranchitos in La Plaza de San Patricio to Florencio Gonzáles and his wife Reimunda Sánchez de Gonzáles. Tornino Gutiérrez had a rancho in Quemado near Socorro. Over several decades, Los Gutiérrez had amassed a large rancho near La Junta that was spread over several sections. They operated one of the larger ranching operations in the valley at the time. There are several descendants that still live in the area.

Los Lucero

Cornelio Lucero

Cornelio Lucero's ancestors had originated in a region near the Pueblo de Cochití. His grandfather, Pedro Antonio Lusero had married María Francisca Maese on September 23, 1779 in Cochití. Shortly thereafter, the family migrated to an area between the villas of Abiquiu and Ojo Caliente. Cornelio's father, José de la Concepción Lusero was born on November 28, 1806 near Ojo Caliente. José then married María de la Luz Sena.

Cornelio Lucero was born in about 1830 in Arroyo Hondo, Nuevo México, La República de México. He was the son of José Francisco de la Concepción Lusero and María de la Luz Sena. The 1860 U.S. Census indicates that he and his family were living in Conejos, Taos County, Territory of New México. This area later became a part of southern Colorado. By 1870 he and his family had migrated to Cucharas, Territory of Colorado. By 1880 the family was living near the Apishapa River

Valley in Las Animas County, Colorado. Sometime shortly after 1880, Cornelio and his family migrated to Las Palas, Territory of New México.

Many of Cornelio's descendants continue to live throughout Lincoln County and New México. Some of the families that can trace their family ancestry to the Lucero are those of Abrán Candelaria, Severo Gallegos, Edward Patrick McTeigue, Andrew McNeely Richardson, and Amos Herman Rue.

Juan Lucero

Juan Lucero christened Juan de Jesús Lusero was born in about 1828 in Tomé, Nuevo México, La República de México. His parents were Pablo de Jesús Romero and María Tomasa Salas. He married Marcelina Jaramillo in Tomé, Nuevo México, La República de México on May 08, 1843. The 1860 U.S. Census indicates that they lived in Arroyo Colorado, Territory of New México.

The family migrated to La Plaza de San Patricio sometime in the mid 1860's. Juan's son, Aniseto Lucero gained notoriety by refusing to deed a part of his land for the first Catholic Chapel built in San Patricio. Many of Juan's descendants continue to live in Lincoln County.

Los Mendoza

Dionisio Mendoza was born in México in April of 1848. He first married María de la Luz Moriel who was also born in México. They had three children, all of who were born near Ysleta, Téxas. Sometime before 1896 Luz Moriel had passed away and Dionisio had married Rosenda Montoya who was born in Téxas in January of 1874. Rosenda already had two children from a previous marriage, Lorenzo and Pedro, both of whom were born in San Patricio, Territory of New México. Being that they were both very young, they both took the name of their stepfather. Dionisio and Rosenda had three children.

Dionisio and Rosenda Mendosa had a 160-acre homestead on the south banks of the Rio Ruidoso in San Patricio. To date most of Dionicio Mendoza's descendants have migrated from the Rio Ruidoso Valley. There are however, a few of his descendants that continue to live in the valley.

Los Miller[19]

Holan "Julian" Miller

Holan Miller was born in Canada in 1834. He eventually migrated to the Territory of New México where many of the local New Mexicans knew him as Julian Miller. He had eventually made his way and briefly settled in Manzano. Once there he met a beautiful young woman by the name of Manuelita Herrera y Carrillo. The two were soon married in 1869. They had six known children, three sons and three daughters.

Soon thereafter, Holan and his family moved to Springer, Territory of New México, where he set up a blacksmith shop. He also took two hundred head of cattle to run on shares and he built up the herd until he had one hundred head of his own. After living in Springer for some time, Holan decided he wanted to move his cattle operations further south.

The family eventually left Springer in two covered wagons. Each wagon was drawn by a team of six oxen. They drove their cattle and traveled mostly by night in an attempt to avoid any confrontation with the Navajos and Apachés. Their trip took about two weeks to complete before arriving at Fort

Sumner where Holan set up a blacksmith shop. During their time in Fort Sumner, their cattle herd continued to flourish growing to about two hundred and seventy five head.

Manuelita's brother, Patricio Carrillo, was the only vaquero that helped protect the herd and keep it together. Holan and his brother-in-law always kept their six shooters visible, holstered to their belts. As added protection both also holstered a Winchester rifle upon their saddle. Patricio Carrillo would often offer his sobrino, Ábran Miller, to ride with him when he was tending to the herd. The youngster would be strapped to his tío's waist so that he would not fall off the horse saddle. The family remained living in Fort Sumner for an extensive period of time. Eventually in 1874, Holan decided to move on to Fort Stanton, in Lincoln County.

The family left Fort Sumner, crossing the Río Pecos and continued on towards Fort Stanton. Shortly after settling in their new home, Holan set up his blacksmith's shop. Soon thereafter he and his wife had a son and they named him Adolfo. Their infant fell ill and as a consequence, he died from complications. They buried him in the Fort Stanton cemetery.

Although Holan enjoyed his trade as a blacksmith, his intentions were to raise cattle on his own lands. He had realized that there were greater profits to be made in cattle. He leased a small piece of land from A.N. Blazer near the Mescalero Reservation, and moved into a two-room log cabin. He opened up his own blacksmith shop to supplement his income, and planted about twenty acres of corn. The land that he was leasing was too small to sustain his herd of about two hundred head of cattle, so he approached a local farmer, Fernando Herrera, and conveyed his situation. The two men worked out a deal in which Fernando would incorporate Holan's herd with his own.

It was like any other year, Holan was making preparations for the annual corn harvest and he needed assistance. He had a son named Ábran, who was living with his Tío Patricio elsewhere on the Mescalero Reservation. He sent a dispatch to his son, calling upon him to help out with the harvest. Ábran, always willing to work beside his father, accepted the invitation.

While the two men were working and talking, Holan unexpectedly made it known that he was going to pass his blacksmith shop over to Ábran. The father continued by telling his son that he was going to be leaving, and for him to take care of his mother. Dumbfounded at his father's inexplicable decision, he asked why he would want to leave his whole family. The elder offered no rational reason but continued by saying that he would not be coming back. After talking in length, Holan mounted his horse and rode off, leaving his son in disbelief.

Holan sought out Fernando Herrera and the two men talked in length. Holan explained that he was looking to leave the area and that he would need his cattle to be rounded up as quickly as possible. Fernando was caught off guard with his friend's request but he agreed to do it without any further discussion. It took a couple of days to complete the request. Once the herd was separated, the two men drove the cattle over to the Dowlin Mill where Holan sold them to Paul and Will Dowlin. After conducting their business, the two men talked again briefly, shook hands and parted ways.

Ábran Miller

Ábran found work as a ranch hand, punching cows for the Murphy/Dolan Company at their ranch in Carrizo Flats. His mother moved to the Salado Flats, about one mile west of the village of Capitán. He was provided with room and board, which enabled him to send his mother forty dollars a month. He married Juanita Romero on February 12, 1881. They had five known children; two sons and three daughters.

About four years had passed and Ábran was about to give up on the notion of ever hearing from his father again. One routine day however, he received a letter from his father. Within the letter,

Holan indicated that he was living near Belén in a village named Casa Colorada. He implored his son to pay him a visit and that they could catch up on each other's lives.

Ábran had much to deliberate and sought the council of his mother, wife and siblings. All had much to say, most of it not good, but it was agreed that he would serve as the ambassador of the family and accept his father's invitation. Before he left, he received his mother's **bendición** (blessing). He had much to think about en route to Casa Colorada. He thought about what he would tell his father and how he would say it. He wanted to be civil, yet direct.

Upon arriving he was greeted by his father. There was an elusive tension in the air as Ábran dismounted. He offered to shake his father's hand rather than give him a hug. His father invited him into the house where the two had talked at length about superficial things. Ábran was becoming increasingly perturbed as the nature of the conversation danced around the real reason that he was there, to get answers. Finally he abruptly stopped the conversation and sternly asked his father why he was invited to come for a visit.

There was a slight hesitation, a solemn look, and then a response. Holan first started by indicating that he wanted to give his son his prized black stallion. He continued by offering to give his son the blacksmith shop. Ábran had heard this type of talk before. His father was maneuvering towards something more sinister. The son came out with a sharp tongue, forcing his father's hand. Finally, the father announced that he would be leaving the territory and that he would never see nor keep in contact with anybody from the family. After parting ways, Holan was never heard from, or seen by anybody in the family, from that day on.

Ábran and Billy the Kid

Ábran had minimal contact with Billy the Kid on two separate occasions. The first time, was when Bonney and his gangly bunch had come across his Tío Patricio's shack while riding through the reservation. Ábran and his friend Lucio Montoya were watching over the cattle which were almost ready to be butchered for the Mescalero. The young Regulator asked the two if they could spare anything to eat. Ábran invited his guests into the shack and offered them anything that they wanted to eat as long as they cooked for themselves. They ate heartedly and upon leaving, they thanked their gracious host for his hospitality. They mounted their horses and rode off toward Elk Canyon. Neither youngster knew it at the moment, but they found out later, that they had unwittingly helped and met Billy the Kid and some of the Regulators.

The second time that Ábran and Billy the Kid had met was when he was visiting with his mother in Salado Flats. As fate would have it, Bonney was passing through and had recognized Ábran from their first encounter. He rode up to Manuelita's house and asked if she could offer him something to eat. Initially, she did not want to feed the vagabond. Her son interjected, telling of their first encounter and how pleasant he and his buddies were. After further discussion, she invited Billy into her home, offering food and lodging for the night.

The next day several men were seen riding on horseback towards the house. Ábran had just gone outside to gather some wood for the stove. Manuelita and Billy had also seen the men approaching and she quickly hid her guest inside a homemade packing crate. The men were searching for the outlaw because he had recently been implicated in the death of Mescalero Reservation Clerk, Morris Bernstein. The youngster was a fugitive, but Manuelita was compassionate enough to hide him. As the men drew closer, she recognized that it was Sheriff Peppin, Florencio Chávez, and two other men she didn't know.

The group of men dismounted their horses and asked if they could search the premise. She didn't have any objections, and allowed them to enter her home. The men looked around the house, showing respect by not ransacking the place. She astutely looked on, with her son by her side the whole time. Her heart beat rapidly as she wondered if they would find the fugitive she was hiding. To her relief, the men passed over the crate several times. After they were satisfied that Bonney wasn't on the premise, they thanked her and quickly rode away.

Billy remained at the house until it had become dark. Ábran's mother wanted her son to let the youngster borrow his black horse, as long as he returned it to them. Her son was reluctant to let his favorite horse go, fearing that he would never see it again, but Bonney made good on his word. About ten days later the horse with the saddle was tied up in the corral.

Shortly after Morris Bernstein was killed, L. Murphy dispatched Ábran to Santa Fé to take a message to the governor. He was directed to go to Fort Stanton first, to see the commanding officer. He arrived at the fort at about three in the morning and the commanding officer gave him another message and a fresh horse. He started for Santa Fé, riding to Pinos Altos on the north side of the Gallinas Mountains that first night and stayed at Marío Payne's place. Marío provided the youngster with a fresh horse and sent him on his way. He arrived in Santa Fé by the third day and delivered the message. The governor was concerned because they had sent such a young kid. He sent a letter back with Ábran directing Murphy to give his young rider three hundred dollars for his troubles, of which Murphy did.

Los Miranda

José Miranda, Felipé Miranda

José Miranda was born in San Acasio, Nuevo México, La República de México in about 1822. He was the son of Pedro Miranda and María Encarnación Sánches. He was the brother of Felipé Miranda. He married María Leonarda Fajardo on December 12, 1847 in Socorro, Territory of New México. They had eleven known children, four sons and seven daughters.

Felipé Miranda was born in San Acasio, Nuevo México, La República de México in about 1831. He was the son of Pedro Miranda and María Encarnación Sánches. He was the brother of José Miranda. He married a woman named Dolóres. They had six known children, two sons and four daughters.

José, Felipé and their respective families had migrated to Bonito in the late 1850s. They routed their migration through the Gallinas Mountains with 15 ox driven wagons. On their journey other wagons had joined the caravan to protect against Mescalero raids. As with many caravans before them and many thereafter, when they camped for the night, the wagons would be configured in a circle to serve as a defense against attacks. Usually several men would stand guard throughout the night.

Although they came across a band of Mescalero, their journey went without incident. The migration from San Acasio to Río Bonito Valley took about two weeks. Upon arriving, they settled in an area about seven miles east of La Placita del Rio Bonito. The area was known as Las Chosas, named for the numerous Chosas that were built into the hillsides.

Los Montoya

Francisco Montoya

Francisco Montoya was born in about 1830 and he lived most of his life in San Miguel County, Territory of New México. He was married to Francisca Maéstas. The 1870 US Census indicates that he and his family were living near Las Colonias and that he was a freighter.

Four of Francisco's sons had migrated to Lincoln County. The 1900 US Census indicates that Antonio, Avelino, Felipé and José Bernardo had all settled in Las Tablas, Territory of New México. Like their father, they were also freighters. Many of the descendants of Francisco Montoya continue to live in Lincoln County.

Juan Montoya

Juan Montoya was born in about October 1850 and was married to Porfiria Aragón. The 1880 U.S. Census indicates that he and his family were living in San Tomás, Doña Ana County, Territory of New México. By the 1900 US Census he and many of his children had migrated to Picacho, Territory of New México. Many of Juan's descendants continue to live in Lincoln County.

Avrora Sánchez, Mauricio Montoya. Mauricio Montoya was the son of Felipé Montoya and Paul Mares García. Avrora Sánchez was the daughter of Eugenio Sánchez and Rosa Griego. (Ernest Sanchez collection)

Tranquelino Montoya

Tranquelino Montoya was born in about 1847 in Tomé, Nuevo México, La República de México. He married María de Jesús Trujillo. It is believed that he and his family had migrated to the Río Bonito in the mid to late 1860's. The 1870 US Census indicates that he and his family were living near La Plaza de San Patricio, Territory of New México.

Family legend has it that Tranquelino's son, Áron Montoya, was a Federal US Marshall. In one instance, he was called upon to apprehend a fugitive and his orders were to capture him dead or alive. It was brought to Áron's attention that the man he was looking for had been seen at one of the local cantinas in Las Palas. He was also made aware that two of his sons were passing the time in another local cantina.

Áron entered the bar, made his presence known to the fugitive, and that it was his intention that he was going to take him in. The fugitive showed staunch resistance, threatening to kill Áron if he pursued the matter any further. Áron countered by informing the belligerent fugitive that his orders were to take him in, preferably alive but dead all the same. Not taking kindly to the marshal's words the man hastily made his way towards the door. Keeping vigilance, the marshal kept a wary eye on his prize while clutching the gun in its holster.

Upon stepping outside, the fugitive made a move for his horse, grabbed his rifle and attempted to aim it at his captor. A shot rang out; echoing throughout Las Palas and the fugitive fell dead. Instinctively, Áron had shot at and hit his target in the head. Figuring that word would quickly come to the two sons, of their father's death, Áron and several of the townsfolk readied themselves for further trouble. After sometime though, trouble never came as the two sons left town with their father's body in hand.[20]

Los Olguín

Ygnacio Olguín

Ygnacio Olguín, christened José Ygnacio Olguín was born in about 1813 in La Merced de los Quelitos, El Reyno de Nuevo México, Nueva España, which was near La Villa de Atrisco. His parents were José Vicente Olguín and María Dolóres García. He married María Brigida Gutiérres in Alburquerque, Nuevo México, La República de México on November 01, 1827. He later married María Dolóres Cedillo in Albuquerque, Territory of New México on January 29, 1855. Dolóres was born in La Cañada de los Apachés, which was just east of La Villa de Santa Fé.

Ygnacio and his family migrated from Atrisco to Bonito in the early 1860s. They settled and helped established the community of La Plaza de San Patricio. As with many other families who settled the area, life was always a struggle. The biggest and most immediate threat to their survival was the ability to repel the repeated raids by the Mescalero. Ygnacio and his son Ramón had helped construct the torreón, which served as the single greatest defense against an attack.

Ramón Olguín

Ramón Olguín, christened José Ramón Olguín was born in San Lorenzo de Pulvidero, Nuevo México, La República de México on December 24, 1842. He was the son of Ygnacio Olguín and María Brigida Gutiérres. He married Lorencita Cedillo.

Family legend has it that Ramón Olguín and his family was returning home from a trip and had been caught up in a severe thunderstorm. As they approached La Plaza de San Patricio they had come upon the Río Ruidoso. A torrent of muddied water had snaked its way down through the valley and had rose above its banks. The family was looking for a section of the river that ran wide, with the assumption that it would not be too deep to cross. They eventually found a section that appeared to be safe. As they guided their wagon across the river, it became bogged down in the mud.

As they prompted the panicked horses to pull the wagon harder, the suction of the mud became stronger, almost vice-like. The restless horses began to jostle in their attempts to escape the water's current, thus violently shaking the wagon. During this turbulence two of their young sons were knocked out of the wagon and the river's current unmercifully swept them downstream. Lorencita screamed out for her children as they struggled to keep their heads above the unforgiving water. Ramón ran the banks of the river, but he soon lost them in the thick of the brush. By the time the family had found them, they both had drowned. It is said that these two children were the only people buried at La Capilla de San Francisco; the very first chapel built in La Plaza de San Patricio.

After the fledgling community had become more established, Ramón had opened its first cantina. It was said that the cantina also served as a gambling establishment where many people from around the region would play games of chance. Sometimes the games were such high stakes that land was used as collateral for betting. Such was the luck of Francisco "Pancho" Sánchez, one of the better gamblers in the area, who is believed to have acquired much of his land holdings in such a manner.

During the Lincoln County War the cantina had become a favorite hangout for many of the Regulators. On any given day one could hear the heated discussions concerning water rights, politics, social injustices, and Regulator strategy. In essence, it had become the focal point of the community. It was a place for fiestas as well as a place for tragedy.

After the Lincoln County War, Los Olguín focused their energies on farming and other entrepreneurial endeavors. From June 18, 1904 to June 10, 1909, Román's son Ygnacio was appointed as San Patricio's first postmaster. The years during the Great Depression prompted almost all of the Olguín to migrate out of Lincoln County; most of them had resettled in Albuquerque and Belén. The few family members who remained in San Patricio eventually married into other families. There are not many people if any, in the valley, who carry the Olguín surname.

Los Pacheco

Francisco Pacheco[21]

Francisco Pacheco, christened José Francisco Silva, was born near La Plaza de Pulvidera, Nuevo México, La República de México, in about 1824. Family historians indicate that his father's surname was Silva and his mother was Petra Dominga de Silva.

Family legend tells a story that the family had fallen victim to Apaché raids on numerous occasions. Usually food and livestock would be taken under the cover of darkness without any violent confrontations. On one fateful evening however, Francisco's father had become alarmed by a loud noise that came from outside the house. He grabbed his rifle and quickly made his way outside. As he approached the coral he could make out the silhouettes of several men trying to steal his prized black stallion. He felt that the element of surprise was the best course of action. He steadied his rifle as he aimed for a kill shot.

The father's nerves must have overcome him because as he pulled the trigger, the shot went wide, missing its target. Alarmed, the thieves quickly took notice, and mounted their horses. As they were retreating, they aimed their rifles in their assailant's direction. Several shots rang out and as the bullets flew, a few of them had found their mark. On this evening, Francisco's father had drawn his last breath. He died shortly after in his wife's arms, and with his son standing next to him.

Petra Dominga eventually married a gentleman by the name of Manuel Antonio Pacheco. He was a kind, loving man who had embraced his new family. Being that Francisco was still a child, he had adopted his stepfather's *apellido* (surname), and loved him as if he were his own biological father.

Manuel operated a large sheep ranching operation and he had taught his stepson all about the business. The sheep usually didn't range too far from the Río Grande because of the Apaché threat. After his stepfather had died, Francisco took control of the sheep ranching operation.

Francisco eventually married Romula Isabela Saavedra shortly before 1850. Ironically, it is believed that she was of Native American descent, possibly an Apaché. They had four known children, two sons and two daughters. After Fort Stanton was commissioned he had expanded the range of grazing beyond the Río Grande. He often brought his sons with him to help watch over the sheep as they grazed farther eastward. They would graze the herd as far east as the Carrizo region. Needless to say, sheep ranching was still very dangerous because the Apaché raids continued for many years after Fort Stanton had been commissioned.

Francisco and his family migrated to Lincoln via Tres Ritos during the spring of 1870. Although the family continued to graze sheep, their operations were significantly smaller as they focused their energies on other business ventures. Francisco continued to live in Lincoln until he died on February 02, 1892.

Anselmo Pacheco

Ancelmo Pacheco (Photo courtesy of Orlando Pacheco)

Anselmo Pacheco was born near San Lorenzo de Pulvidero, Territory of New México on March 16, 1849. His parents were Francisco Pacheco and Romula Isabela Saavedra. He married Teresita Gallegos on February 13, 1874. Teresita's father was a full-blooded Apaché. It was said that her father could always be seen wearing his hair in long braids. For many that didn't know him, he seemed like a very intimidating man. [22]

Anselmo migrated to Lincoln with his father, mother and siblings, where he helped out with the sheep ranching operation.[23] Unlike his father though, he had resisted the notion of being a sheep rancher for the rest of his life. He had become an astute entrepreneur, opting to become a merchant instead. In 1879, prospectors had discovered gold ore near the Carrizo and Patos Mountains. The township of White Oaks was established soon thereafter. What followed was a local gold rush, which swelled the town's population. By 1880 Anselmo and his family had settled in White Oaks. He took advantage of the mining boom by opening a general store there.[24]

Anselmo continued living in White Oaks for several years, but as the prospect of becoming wealthy continued to diminish over time, he decided to return to Lincoln. He then opened a saloon and oversaw its day to day operations. He continued as such up until Teresita died on April 01, 1910. He then had married Alice Trampton on May 11, 1912. He was married for a third time to Reyes F. Sisneros on September 05, 1919. Finally he was married for the last time to Inez Lucero on June 26, 1920. He died in Las Palas, Territory of New México on February 20, 1921.

Leopoldo Pacheco[25]

Leopoldo Pacheco was born in Lincoln, Territory of New México in about 1878. He was the son of Anselmo Pacheco and Teresita Gallegos. He married Felicita Luján on August 15, 1900. They had four children, three sons and a daughter. After Leopoldo's first wife passed away he married a widow, Paulita Fresquez, who had two children from a previous marriage. Paulita's children from her previous marriage were George F. Sisneros and Clofas Sisneros. Leopoldo and Paulita had one son of their own whose name was Paul Pacheco.

As a young man and while living in Las Palas, he worked as a ranch hand at the Block Ranch.[26] He saved most of his earnings, which he used to open up a bar. He continued working at the ranch for about three years while his father Anselmo and his brother-in-law Polonio Lucero managed the bar. He eventually decided that he wanted to take a more active interest in the daily operations of his bar so he eventually took over the management of his business.

Leopoldo had a keen business sense, and an entrepreneurial spirit that drove him to always seek better opportunities that added to his net wealth. He opened a general merchandise store that offered everything from groceries to household items. This endeavor was very successful and afforded him further business opportunities.

The major industry in Las Palas was the cutting and gathering of firewood. Leopoldo had served as a broker and freighter for many of the families throughout the region. He would transport and find a buyer for the firewood in Roswell for a fee. Furthermore, he discovered that he could lower his transportation costs if he scheduled the store supplies shipments to coincide with his firewood shipments. Hence, firewood shipments would be sent to Roswell and store supplies would return to Las Palas.

The Homesteaders Act of 1862 enabled many families to apply for 160, 320, and 640-acre tracts of grazing land in and around Las Palas. Many of these families that settled the area established a line of credit at Leopoldo's general merchandise store. Being that most families did not earn enough money to pay off their debts, they would settle their bill with payments of land. As more families sought jobs in Roswell, Artesia and elsewhere, they often settled by selling their homestead to Leopoldo at a favorable price less the amount of their debt owed. He thus was able to accumulate over 55 sections or approximately 35,200 acres in such a manner.

The community of Las Palas is recognized in the 1910 U.S. Census, and in the 1920 U.S. Census it is recognized as Los Palos. It wasn't until the opening of the U.S. post office in February 15, 1901 that the community was formally known as Arabela. Leopoldo served as the Postmaster from March 14, 1907 through April 30, 1928.[27]

Leopoldo had become one of the most prominent men in the region. He had one of the largest ranches in all of Lincoln County at the time. He died in Arabela in April of 1965. Upon his death his sons, Paul Pacheco and George Sisneros inherited his ranch. The majority of the ranch has since been sold to other parties.

Ignacia Gómez-Pacheco[28]

Ignacia Gómez was born in Lincoln, Territory of New México on May 09, 1909. Her parents were Felipé Gómez and Beatriz Sedillo. She married Fermín Pacheco in San Patricio, New México on August 29, 1932. They had three children, two sons and a daughter. Fermín was the son of Román Pacheco and Bonifacia Richardson. He had a twin brother named, Fernando who died in his infancy. He had spent the better part of his life ranching in Arabela, and then later he ranched in San Patricio.

Ignacia Gómez had achieved one of the most remarkable feats for a New Mexican woman in her time. She was one of the first women in the valley to complete twelve years of schooling and continued on to a higher education. This was a testament to her perseverance during a time when so many women were discouraged from even attending high school.

She started her elementary education near Las Angosturas. Several years later she transferred to a newly built elementary school near Glencoe. She had become an astute student and often times she would help out her Spanish-speaking peers with their English studies. Senon Chávez, one of her classmates, adamantly admits that had it not been for Ignacia, he never would have made it through school.

After finishing the eighth grade she attended high school in Lincoln for two years. Every Sunday afternoon, Ignacia, her younger brother Francisco and her older sister Estela would ride on horseback to Lincoln. The trip took only a couple of hours but the three of them always looked forward to a pleasant ride. Sometimes, during the summer, they would prepare themselves a little picnic.

Once in town, the two sisters settled into their dormitory. As had become the custom over the months, they sent their brother off with hugs, kisses, blessings, and prayers. The two sisters would remain in Lincoln for the entire week. Their brother would return to town on Friday to accompany the girls back to Glencoe. Upon their return, the two sisters always had plenty of stories to tell the rest of the family.

After two years of high school in Lincoln, she finished her junior and senior years at a high school in Roswell. She worked as a housekeeper to earn money to pay for her room and board. When she had finally graduated in 1928, she was one of only two New Mexican women to have completed twelve years of education in Roswell.

Ignacia wasn't satisfied with her high school education though. She had aspired to continue her education. Her passion for helping other students convinced her that she should become a teacher. She enrolled in the New Mexico Teachers College in Silver City. The summer after graduating she took several courses on teaching.

Upon completing her courses Ignacia returned to Lincoln County where she first taught in Arabela in 1929. Shortly thereafter, she substituted in Agua Azul. By 1942 she was teaching in the community of Richardson. Her next teaching job came in San Patricio. By the early 1960's they had consolidated all of the schools throughout the valley, into one school in Hondo. At different times throughout her career, she would return to college in Las Vegas, New México and in Portales, New México.

She finished her long and distinguished teaching career in Hondo. She had dedicated her whole life to teaching, and in doing so, offered many children an opportunity to advance their own life's ambitions. She gave hope to several generations by showing them the positive aspects of a proper education. She forged a path for many towards a brighter future.

Los Padilla

Andalesio Padilla

Andalesio Padilla was born in Atrisco, Territory of New México in about 1856. He was the son of Juan Ricardo Padilla and Rosalía Cháves. He married Paublita Mariño in Los Padilla, Territory of New México in about 1875. They had fourteen known children, eight sons and six daughters. Shortly after their marriage they had migrated to Tres Ritos, Territory of New México.

Most of Andalesio's children remained near Tres Ritos. Those who migrated to Lincoln County were Nestor Padilla who was living in Ancho during the 1930 US Census. Candelaria Padilla had married Felipé E. Sánchez who had lived in Rebentón, Ancho, San Elizario, Téxas, and finally Tularosa.

Andalesio Padilla, Paublita Mariño (Ernest Sanchez collection)

Jesús María Padilla

Jesús María Padilla was born in about 1824. The 1850 US Census has he and his wife Sostena Carrillo living in La Jolla, Territory of New México. By 1870 he and his family had migrated to Manzano. The 1880 Census indicates that he and his family were living in Lincoln. Many of his descendants continue to live in Lincoln County.

José Encarnación Padilla

José Encarnación Padilla was born on March 18, 1814 in San Fernando, El Reyno de Nuevo México, Nueva España. He married Polonia Herrera on October 31, 1852. The 1870 US Census indicates that José Encarnación and his family had migrated to Lincoln County, Precinct 1, Territory of New México. His daughter, Francisca Padilla married Emiliano McKinley. Many of his descendants continue to live in Lincoln County.

José León Padilla

José León Padilla was born in October 1853 in La Jolla, Territory of New México. He was the son of José Antonio Padilla and María Narcisa Carrillo. José León and his family had migrated to Las Norias, Lincoln County, Territory of New México. Many of his descendants continue to live in Lincoln County.

Los Polaco

Serafín Polaco and Altagracia Gonzáles de Polaco

The history of Los Polaco in Lincoln County is one of mystery and intrigue. Many people have asked where the name had originally come from. Some have said that Padre Alejandro Polaco was the progenitor of the name. Yet there is evidence that the name Polaco is also prevalent in the Caribbean islands of Puerto Rico and Cuba. There are also a few Polaco families in northern and central New México.

The story of the family begins in the ranching community of Los Corrales, Territory of New México. The 1860 U.S. Census indicates that Serafín Polacre was a young man who was born in Italy in about 1824.[29] He had recently immigrated to the United States in about 1849.[30] He was a man of significant means, having respectable real estate and personal property holdings. He had married María Altagracia Gonzáles on September 11, 1853. They had seven known children, four sons and three daughters.

Altagracia was the daughter of Santiago Gonzáles and Manuela Aragón. Her two most noted brothers were Florencio and Ignacio who would later become integral participants of the Lincoln County War. Los Polacre and Los Gonzáles lived adjacent to one another thus many of the children grew up together.

By 1866 Serafín and Altagracia had migrated from Los Corrales to La Plaza de San Patricio. They had a daughter, Altagracia who was baptized by one of the traveling priests from Tularoso. By this time the family was already using the Polaco name, as was evidenced from the baptismal records. [31]

The family didn't remain in Lincoln County for very long though. By 1870 Serafín and his family had moved to Las Vegas, Territory of New México where they were reunited with an old family friend. Aleksander Grzelachowski, known by the New Mexicans as Alejandro Polaco who was living in the lower Las Vegas district. The Polaco had moved to the upper Las Vegas district. The majority of the family remained in the Las Vegas area and many of their descendants still live in the region.

Elfigo Polaco

Elfigo Polaco was born in Los Corrales, Territory of New México in about 1863. He was the son of Serafín Polaco and Altagracia Gonzáles. Not much is known about him before he had decided to return to Lincoln County. Upon arriving, he settled on a plot of land owned by his tío Florencio near La Aguilita. His cousin, Prospero Gonzáles was also living and working the land. He brought with him his four sons, Serafín, Pedro, Teodoro, and Julian. His wife had died sometime before the family had migrated but her mother Librada Abeyta had accompanied the family.[32]

Elfigo was attempting to make a new life for himself. The tragedy of losing his wife was still fresh in his memory and he needed a change of scenery. While working for his tío, he had become reacquainted with many cousins that he hadn't seen in several years. There was one cousin in particular, the beautiful Aeropajita Gonzáles that he had grown very fond of. The relationship between the two progressed into something more prohibited, and as a result, Elfigo felt it was prudent to try to repress his evolving feelings for her. The attempt to temper his feelings for Aeropajita was met with conflicting emotions. He made a conscious effort to avoid seeing her. He kept himself busy enough that he wouldn't be tempted to pursue a more meaningful relationship with her. From time to time he would steal a glance at her as she passed him while he was working. All was going well until fate had brought them together again and afforded them an opportunity to re-establish a connection.

Over time, his feelings for her grew stronger and to further complicate the matter, she began to reciprocate those feelings. As their relationship continued to develop, Elfigo began to think irrationally. In an act considered brave and irresponsible at the same time, he approached his Tío Florencio to discuss his feelings for Aeropajita. In the conversation, he had conveyed how strong his feelings for her were.

Upon hearing this, Florencio had become enraged, and humiliated. He gave a cold hard stare into his sobrino's eyes and everything was silent between them. Then the elder broke the silence, scolding

Elfigo, first for loving Aeropajita unlike a first cousin, and then having the nerve to express those feelings about her. The fury within his tío's voice was more than enough to make any man cower but Elfigo didn't back down and tuck tail.

Florencio was a devout Roman Catholic, he had studied to become a priest, and he had known how the Church would view such a marriage. Furthermore, he was a pillar within the community, and he didn't want his name to be tarnished by scandalous gossip. After he had spoken his mind, he sent Elfigo on his way, and forbade him from coming near his daughter, warning him to quell his feelings.

Elfigo remained in the valley for a few more years after Florencio had died. He continued to honor his tío's wishes and never pursued a love relationship with Aeropajita. Soon thereafter, Elfigo's brother, Trancito had unexpectedly migrated from Las Vegas to San Patricio. The two brothers lived together helping to farm the land, which at one time belonged to their tío Florencio.

Shortly after 1900 Elfigo, his children, and his mother-in-law had finally left Lincoln County. It was widely speculated that he and Trancito had a falling out with each other. He and his family migrated north to Río Arriba County where several of his descendants still live.

Trancito Polaco

Trancito Polaco christened Francisco Trancito Polaco was born in Los Corrales, Territory of New México in about 1858. He was the son of Serafín Polaco and Altagracia Gonzáles. Not much is known about him before he had decided to return to Lincoln County. He continued to live with his father and mother near Las Vegas while his younger brother Elfigo chose to migrate to San Patricio.

Upon hearing the news of Florencio Gonzáles' death, the Polaco family traveled to San Patricio to pay their last respects. Trancito took the opportunity to reacquaint himself with his cousins and his younger brother. He had come to know that Elfigo was doing fairly well for himself with a nice plot of farmland he was working. This intrigued him as he thought about his own prospects. After much deliberation he approached his brother about helping him out with the farm until he could become established. The two brothers soon agreed on the terms of their partnership.

Trancito, like his brother Elfigo, had become enamored with Aeropajita. Unlike his brother, he didn't have to contend with his tío and thus was able to pursue a more meaningful relationship with her. Surely Elfigo had strongly objected to their courtship by advocating that it cease, recalling their tío's emphatic objections. Trancito however, did not listen to his brother and continued to woo his cousin.

Trancito to this point had still remained a very mysterious man to most people in the valley. His slate was clean, and the only one that really knew anything about him was his brother. Trancito never had a history of being married before, so he had no children. As such, on November 08, 1900 Trancito and Aeropajita were married. In the church record's marriage book dated November 08, 1900 Trancito had listed himself as Francisco Polaco. He claimed that his parents were Alejandro Polaco and Secundina Gallegos (deceased).[33]

Trancito had made the claim that both he and his brother were in fact ***huerfanos*** (orphans). He indicated that his biological father was Padre Alejandro Polaco, but being that his father was still in the priesthood, they were left in the charge of another family.

He had often talked about his father to many of the people in San Patricio. One story he mentioned was that his father had enlisted in the union army during the civil war. During this time, there was an incident that happened where his father and several soldiers were riding on horseback. One of the soldiers was fooling around with his sword, waving it through the air as if he was going to stab at his father.

Trancito's father asked the unruly soldier to stop playing around because it was becoming annoying, and it was fool-hearted. The other soldier defied him as he continued to teasingly stab at him. By this time his father was so irate, he threatened him. As he did so, the soldier made another stabbing motion and had accidentally cut into one of his father's fingers. Stunned by what had happened, the soldier pleaded for forgiveness. His father, enraged by the soldier's stupidity screamed, "Qué te perdone Dios!" Then his father drew his own sword and thrust it into the soldier's chest, killing him.[34]

Trancito and his family continued to live near Rancho Gonzáles on the land that his wife Aeropajita had inherited from her mother, Reimunda Sánchez de Chávez. Several of Trancito's descendants still live in Lincoln County.

Los Salas

Pablo Salas

Pablo Salas was born near Belén, Nuevo México, La República de México before January 24, 1830. His parents were Francisco Salas and Nicolasa Trujillo. He married Margarita Trujillo. They had two known children, a son named Teofilo and a daughter named Anita. Pablo died abruptly between 1869 and 1870, shortly after the birth of his daughter. Margarita remarried Francisco Trujillo, who raised both children as his own. Several of Pablo Salas' descendants continue to live in Lincoln County.

Los Salcido

Diego Salcido

Diego Salcido was born near San Pablo Meoqui, Chihuahua, La República de México in about 1844. His parents were Sixto Salcido and Rosalía Pareida. He married Miquela Baca on October 16, 1866 in Tomé, Territory of New México. By 1870 he and his family had migrated to La Junta, Territory of New México. Los Salcido remained there for several years before the family bought a ranch belonging to Alisandro Torres in Cañon de Alamo. The family continues to work the ranch to this day. Several, of the descendants of Diego Salcido continue to live in Lincoln County.

Los Sánchez

Esiquio Sánchez

Esiquio Sánchez was born in Punta de Agua, Territory of New México in about November of 1854. His parents were Juan José Sánchez and María Andrea Analla. He married María Isabel Analla on April 24, 1873. Although Esiquio and María Isabel were first cousins neither the church nor the families had any objections to the marriage. They had ten known children, four sons and six daughters.

It was said that María Andrea was a tall woman for her day, standing well above the other women in the community. Esiquio on the other hand was small in stature, standing no taller than five feet. His uncle, José Analla, often teased him because of his height, nicknaming him *Sitio, El Terrenato* (Close to the dirt). Although the teasing was in jest, he must have tired of it because he always carried a bad disposition. Coupling his temperament with his love for alcohol, he often found himself in the midst of trouble.

María Andrea's husband had passed on and she had married John Newcomb. He was a rather large man bordering on being obese. He was a bossy and somewhat antagonistic man. He tried to exert his authority over his stepson but the two always butted heads. Sometimes their confrontations would become so heated that they both threatened to cause harm to one another.

Esiquio took such great exception to his stepfather's lack of respect that he vowed one day he would serve John his comeuppance. The opportunity had presented itself when his nemesis was engrossed in work near the corral. The stealthy and light-footed stepson had managed to lasso the unsuspecting giant. He threw all his weight into the rope flipping his captive hard to the ground. As he reached for his knife the big man was able to free himself from the rope and make his escape. Needless to say, neither man attempted to be cordial to each other.

Esiquio owned a swath of prime, fertile farmland that spanned almost two and one half miles over its entire length and about one fifth of a mile in width. Its westernmost boundary was bordered by the Coe Ranch and its easternmost boundary was bordered by the Rancho Gonzáles. He had an estimated 160 irrigated acres that fronted the Río Ruidoso from both banks of the river.

El Terrenato was a vocal opponent of the injustices brought upon the people by members of The House. Sheriff William Brady had implicated him and several other men for creating a riot, when Constable Anastacio Martínez recruited him to help search for those who were responsible for John Tunstall's murder.

On occasion, Esiquio would ride with the Regulators. He had volunteered his services during the five days battle. After the Lincoln County War, he was recruited by Juan Patrón to serve as a member of the Lincoln County Mounted Riflemen. When the violence that had wreaked havoc upon the whole county finally settled, he returned to a farmer's life. As with many others who were active participants during the Lincoln County War, he seldom ever talked about what he had done, what he had seen, or whom he had rode with. He eventually sold a part of his property holdings on the Rio Ruidoso to Román Barragán. It is believed that he died sometime before 1904.

Eugenio Sánchez

Eugenio Sánchez was born in about September of 1856 to Navajo parents. As a child, the band of Navajos that he belonged to was raided by Apachés. He and several other children were captured during the raid. The Apachés subsequently sold the children to Español slave traders. Filomeno Sánchez, one of the more wealthy men in the community, had purchased several of the children for about five pesos each.[35] The young Navajo was one of about twenty to thirty *peónes* (indentured servants) working for El Patrón.

On March 02, 1867 the United States Congress passed a bill that abolished the practice of peonage or debt servitude.[36] Filomeno and the other patrónes released their indentured servants. Of those that he had released, four were males and four were females, all of who were Navajo in origin. All eight servants were adopted into his family. Those boys who became his sons were Eugenio, Julian, Manuel, and Rafael. Those girls who became his daughters were Bartola, Cruz, María, and Tomasita.[37]

Eugenio had married a *Manzaneña* (local Manzano woman) named Rosa Griego. The two were married in Manzano sometime in 1882. They had eleven known children, seven sons and four daughters. By the mid-1890s the family had migrated to the Río Ruidoso Valley and settled in an area known as Las Angosturas. By June 09, 1910 he had applied for a homestead.

The family cultivated their land for several years after their homestead was approved. Although the land was fertile and their crops were adequate, many within the family had expressed a desire to return to Manzano. After some deliberation Eugenio, his wife, and several of his children decided to return to their homeland.

Eugenio and Rosa's daughter, Avrora Sánchez married Mauricio Montoya in La Capilla de San Ysidro, Las Angosturas, Territory of New México on December 15, 1902. They had ten known children, six sons and four daughters. Five of their sons had enlisted into the military and served their country during World War Two. One of their sons that enlisted was Santiago Montoya who was killed during the war in 1945. The other four sons that enlisted were Flavio, Ysidro, Manuel, and Juan. All of Mauricio and Avrora's children have passed away except for Juan Montoya who still lives in San Patricio. Several of Mauricio and Avrora's descendants still live in the Río Ruidoso valley.

From left to right: Eugenio Sánchez, Unknown (Photo courtesy of Jerry Montoya)

Juan Rafael Barceló Sánchez

Rafael Sánches christened Juan Rafael Barceló y Sánches was born in Tomé, Territory of New México on November 21, 1847. His parents were Juan Rafael Fernando Sánches and María de la Luz Barceló. He was a distant cousin of Mauricio de la Trinidad Sánches. The common ancestor between the two men was Jacinto Sánches de Iñigo. Juan Rafael's ancestral lineage came from Jacinto's first marriage to Isabel Telles Jirón and their son José Sánches de Iñigo.

By 1850 the family had migrated to Tajiqué, Territory of New México. The 1850 and 1860 U.S. Censuses indicate that the patriarch was not living with the family. It is possible that he had died before they had moved to Tajiqué. [38] He and his older brothers worked as laborers while their mother kept house.

Juan Rafael married María de la Visitación Sánchez (known by her family as Besita) in Manzano, Territory of New México on August 29, 1875. She was the daughter of Mauricio de la Trinidad Sánches and María Candida de Jesús Gonzáles. The family moved to Lincoln County and settled in the farming community of La Aguilita between 1883 and 1887.[39] Many of Juan Rafael's descendants continue to live throughout Lincoln County.

From left to right: Rafael Sánches (Juan Rafael Barceló Sánches), Besita Sánchez (María de la Visitación Sánchez), Sofia Sánchez-Orozco, Bersabé Sánchez-Montoya, Victoria Sánchez-Trujillo, Manuel B. Sánchez, Augustina Ulibarrí-Sánchez, Conferina Sánchez, Marclofa Sánchez-Pacheco, Rita Sánchez-Gill, Reymundo Sánchez. (Ernest Sanchez collection)

Los Sedillo

The Sedillo name, like many other Spanish surnames was spelled many different ways. Sometimes the same person would have two or three different spelling variations on various types of documentation. Some of the different ways that the name was spelled was, Cedillo, Sedillo, Sedillos, Sedio, Sediyo, and Zedillo.

Pedro de Cedillo Rico de Rojas is widely regarded as the progenitor of many families that carry the Sedillo name throughout present day New México. In 1689 he was listed as a member of the ***La Confradía de Nuestra Señora del Rosario La Conquistadora*** (Conquistadora Confraternity). He had married Isabel López de Gracia and they had six known children, three sons and three daughters respectively.[40]

Three of Pedro's children figured prominently in the founding of La Villa de San Felipé de Alburquerque. Joaquín Cedillo Rico de Rojas, his wife María Varela y Lucero and their children were one of the families to settle the area. Casilda Cedillo Rico de Rojas and her husband Cristóval Varela Jaramillo were another founding family. Isabel Cedillo Rico de Rojas and her husband Juan Varela Jaramillo were the third family.[41]

Several families that carried the name had settled throughout Lincoln County. They settled in El Berendo, the valleys of the Rio Ruidoso, the Rio Hondo, and the Rio Bonito. They were an integral part in the settlement of various communities. The 1880 Census of Lincoln County shows concentrations of several families in Las Tablas, Lincoln, Rebentón, and La Plaza de San Patricio.

José Miguel Sedillo[42]

José Miguel Sedillo was born in Lemitar, Nuevo México, La República de México on February 24, 1842. He was the son of José Blás Sedillo and María Petra Sánches. He married María Ines García in Las Cruces, Territory of New México on April 08, 1860. He had become a lawyer by trade while living in Las Cruces. By about June of 1868 the family had migrated to La Plaza de San Patricio.

Family legend indicates that when he and his family had settled in Lincoln County he had befriended William Bonney alias "Billy the Kid". It is also believed that his daughter Angelita had fallen in love with

Billy. The two used to secretly meet in the orchard down by the river. Angelita's younger brother, Sixto Sedillos, often kept a look out for anybody that may have been coming. If anybody happened to wander to that part of the orchard the younger brother would cusp his hands together and let out a whistle.

José Miguel had come to know about the budding relationship between his daughter and his friend. Feeling somewhat betrayed by the two youngsters, he forbade them from seeing one another. Setting their friendship aside, he didn't want his daughter to associate herself with someone of Billy's character. It would just lead to tragedy and despair.

José Miguel thus arranged a marriage between Angelita and Benito Trujillo. Benito was a very old man, well into his sixties. His young bride bore him one child who died in its infancy. Shortly thereafter, the old man had also passed on. Angelita then married Francisco Gutiérrez in Lincoln County in about 1890.

Juan Sedillo

During the early 1860's catastrophic floods on the Río Grande had destroyed much of the towns of La Jolla and Savinál in Socorro County, which prompted many of the families in those areas to migrate to the lands of the southeastern Territory of New México. Juan Sedillo was born in La Jolla, Nuevo México, La República de México in May of 1834. He was the son of Camilo Sedillo and Rosaria Cháves. In about 1850 at the age of 16 he married his sweetheart María Cháves who was only 15 years of age. Soon thereafter their first son, Cosmé was born. In the following years they had two daughters, Francisca who was born in about 1852 and Genoveva who was born in about 1854.

Juan Sedillo's wife Josefa Fajardo was born in Savinál in September of 1852. They were some of the first Sedillo to migrate into the vast expanse of the llano. He and his wife had squatted on some land on the Río Berendo. During the 1860's and many decades thereafter, water had always flowed from the Sierra Capitán down to the Río Pecos all year long. The *carrizo* (tall grass) was said to have grown waist high and stayed green well into July. The land was fertile which made it perfect for agriculture and grazing livestock. Like several other New Mexican families in the area, Juan was a sheep rancher by trade, and a farmer second.

Once living in El Berendo, Los Sedillo came in contact with many of the other families that were migrating into the valleys of the Rio Hondo, Río Ruidoso and Río Bonito. They were *vecinos* (neighbors) for a short time with Mauricio de la Trinidad Sánches and his entire family before they migrated further west. By 1880 Juan Sedillo, Josefa and their daughters had migrated to La Plaza de San Patricio.

Cosmé Sedillo

According to the 1870 Census of Fort Stanton he was born in about 1852. His given name on the census was written as Hicozmes Sedillos. Cosmé Sedillo married Maxima Sánchez on November 05, 1873. They had eight known children, four sons and four daughters, most of who were born in El Berendo.

Cosmé Sedillo was appointed as the constable for Precinct 5 when Lincoln County was first created in 1869.[43] Eventually Cosmé and some of his children would migrate to La Plaza de San Patricio. One of his children who migrated to La Plaza de San Patricio was his son Martín who eventually married Tomasa Herrera on March 08, 1906. Martín and Tomasa had nine known children, five sons and four daughters. Some of their descendants still live in San Patricio. Both Martín and Tomasa are buried in El Campo Santo de la Capilla de San Patricio.

José Alberto Sedillo

Alberto Sedillo, christened José Alberto Sedillo was born near Thomé, El Reyno de Nuevo México, Nueva España in about March 28, 1820. He was the son of Pablo Sedillo and Rosalía

Sánches. He married María Filipa Samora and they had nine known children, five daughters and four sons. He and his family had migrated from Manzano to Lincoln County in the late 1870s.

Calixtro Sedillo, also spelled as Calistro, was born on October 20, 1859 in Manzano, Territory of New México. He was the son of José Alberto Sedillo and María Filipa Samora. Alberto, as he was commonly known and much of his family had migrated to Lincoln before 1880. Many of Calixtro's descendants continue to live in Lincoln County and Los Ángeles, California.

Los Torres

Mariano & Nicolás Torres

Mariano Torres was born The 1860 Census indicates that Mariano Torres and his brother Nicolás Torres were both living in Punta de Agua, Territory of New México. The two brothers migrated to La Plaza de San Patricio in about the mid 1860's.

Los Trujillo

José Manuel Trujillo

José Manuel Trujillo was married to María Dolóres Sánches in about 1842. The family was originally from the region near Tomé, Territory of New México. It is believed that the family first settled in La Plaza de San Patricio in the mid to late 1860's. Soon thereafter their daughter Refugia married Aniceto Lucero on May 26, 1870 in Lincoln County.

Front row left to right: Bonifacio Trujillo, Lorensita Silva de Trujillo, Lorensa Trujillo, Back row left to right: Rosa Trujillo, Rita Trujillo, Reymunda Trujillo, Susana Trujillo

Juan de Dios Trujillo

In the mid-1870s Juan de Dios Trujillo and his brother Francisco Trujillo had both migrated to La Plaza de San Patricio from the ranching community of La Polvadera de San Lorenzo. The two brothers farmed in Las Palas for a couple of years. They finally settled in La Plaza de San Patricio.

Juan was the Justice of the Peace of La Plaza de San Patricio during the Lincoln County War. His house was often a place where many of the Regulators would congregate to rest, and discuss strategies. Both Juan and Francisco were associated with the Regulators.

Los Ulibarrí

José Enríques de los Reyes is the progenitor of some of Los Ulibarrí that had eventually settled in Lincoln County. José Enríques de los Reyes was born in San Luís Potosi, Nueva España. He married María de Ynojos and they had at least two known sons. The eldest of the two was Juan de los Reyes and the younger was Antonio de los Reyes. The two brothers enlisted in the military and they both were recruited to accompany the Vargas reconquest of 1693. They settled near Santa Fé and lived at the presidio for some time.

By 1704 Juan had been promoted to Capitán and second in command at the Santa Fé garrison. By 1706 he had become the Procurator of the same garrison. In a campaign against the Apachés from 1706 to 1707, he was one of the men responsible for liberating the Picurís tribe from their captors in El Cuartelejo. Juan de Ulibarrí had married Juana Hurtado during this time. His name was also found on Inscription Rock.[44]

Antonio also was involved in several campaigns against the Native Americans. He was rewarded for his service by being appointed to Alcalde of the Pueblos of Laguna, Acoma, and Zuñi. By 1731 he was appointed as the Alcalde Mayor of Santa Fé. He had married María de Cháves but they had no known children.[45]

Juan de Ulibarrí and Juana Hurtado had a son they named Juan. He married Rosalía de Armijo on July 01, 1732 in Alburquerque, El Reyno de Nuevo México. Juan de Ulibarrí y Hurtado and his family eventually moved to Belén where many of his descendants still live. Four successive generations remained or were born in Belén until Santiago Ulibarrí y Lucero and his wife Juana Bernardina Romero y Gallegos became the first of Los Ulibarrí to migrate to Lincoln County during the mid 1860's.[46] Los Ulibarrí settled just west of La Capilla de San Patricio.

Although the Ulibarrí were some of the first pioneers to settle in La Plaza de San Patricio, their name no longer lives within the community. Over the past one hundred forty years, Los Ulibarrí de San Patricio had either migrated from the valley, or those that chose to remain saw the name disappear over time. Although there are some descendants of the Ulibarrí that still call the Río Ruidoso valley home, they do not carry the Ulibarrí name.

Los Vega[47]

José María de Vega was born in Morelia, Michoacán, La República de México, on March 19, 1843. In his youth he had migrated to Téxas in about 1860. Being of an industrious and entrepreneurial nature he established himself as a carpenter by trade. He married Esiquia Torres in Tom Greene, Téxas on January 17, 1878. She was the daughter of José de los Reyes Torres y Lucero and María Trinidad Cháves.

José Torres was a native of Manzano, Territory of New México. Here he had enlisted with the U.S. Army, and soon thereafter he was stationed in, Téxas. He moved his family and several of his extended family members to a foreign land, so far away from home. He, his family, and many of their relatives remained in Houston until his eventual discharge from the army in 1879. José Torres and his family thus made the long arduous journey back home to the Territory of New México. José María de la Vega and his wife had also accompanied the caravan.

José María and Esiquia had settled in the White Oaks area. At the time, White Oaks was a bustling center of commerce. Gold fever had swelled its population with prospectors. He had developed a business relationship with Teofilo Lalone who was an immigrant from Canada. The two had endeavored in prospecting for gold and each was handsomely rewarded for their persistence.

José María used his small fortune to purchase a tract of land near the Vera Cruz. His entrepreneurial spirit drove him to run livestock as a new means of making a living. His grit and determination grew into a thriving business. His successes allowed him to purchase additional tracts of land near the Vera Cruz Springs. His large tracts of acreage enabled him to expand his livestock holdings to include cattle, hogs and horses. The Rancho Vega was renowned for its professionalism and expertise in breaking horses. In many instances, they broke horses and sold them to the U.S. Cavalry in Fort Stanton.

As his business grew, so did his base of operations. He spared no expense in building Casa de Vega, a house with few equals in Lincoln County. He built corrals, barns and several other structures within his complex. He allowed several of the other ranchers in the area the use of his corrals and barns. His gratuitous nature was the stuff of legend, as many an old-timer would recall.

The Casa de Vega's exterior walls were constructed from adobé. The interior of the house was described as being very extravagant. The furnishings were some of the finest that money could buy. Even the silverware, finely handcrafted in México, was something most people who visited had often remarked about. Most of the furnishings and silverware were later sold to Román Maés and his wife, who were the owners of the Lincoln Museum.

José María and Esiquia's first child was a son whom they named Antonio. Family legend tells of a day when the toddler, Antonio had wandered off and went missing. Wrought with grief and fearful for their son's life, a search party was organized to find him. It has been told from one generation to the next that William H. Bonney had joined the search and had eventually found the young boy wandering the hillside. Although Antonio tempted fate that day he could not escape his destiny as he tragically died of an illness when he was about three years old.

José María and Esiquia had two more children, both daughters. They named their first daughter Elvira, whom like her older brother died a tragic death at three years of age. Their second oldest daughter, Alejandra also met the same fate as her two previous siblings, dying at two years of age. Although it seemed that both José María and Esiquia were destined to live a life without children, they put their faith in God and were blessed with three more children; Antonio, Florencio, and Margarita all of whom lived well into adulthood.

Esiquia must have felt that her children were more than just a blessing, and more like special gifts from God. She, her husband and their children were devout Catholics. The resolve of the family would be tested again as Esiquia fell ill to pneumonia. She valiantly fought for her life, so that she could remain with her husband and children, but she finally lost the battle in 1890. In many ways one could say that she joined her children in God's kingdom while José María took care of their children here on earth.

Although José María was still grieving, the harsh realities of life dictated that he continued to move on with his life. He was a single father with three children, a business to run, and not enough time to devote his attention to ensure that all matters were adequately taken care of. About a year later, in 1891, José María married Josefa Sandoval in an arranged marriage. Josefa was a beautiful young woman who happened to be the daughter of Esiquia's sister María Sandoval y Torres.

José María and Josefa had their first child, a daughter they named Antonia shortly after their marriage. They had three more daughters Petra, Rosa, and Susana. As the family continued to grow, José María and Esiquia's children were afforded the opportunity to attend some prestigious regional Catholic schools. Both Antonio and Florencio were sent to St. Michael's Catholic School in Santa

Fé. Margarita was sent to the Loreto Girls Catholic School in El Paso, Téxas. After attending their first semesters in school, Antonio, Florencio, and Margarita were all called to return to the Rancho Vega because their sister, Antonia had fallen ill. Shortly upon their arrival, young Antonia, not more than eight years of age, had succumbed to her illness.

José María surely must have thought that the land in which he and his family lived had cast a terrible curse upon his family. This was the fourth child that he had seen taken into God's kingdom well before their time. This reason alone may have prompted José María, Josefa and the rest of their family to leave the Rancho Vega. It was decided that the family would return to Morelia, Michoacán, La República de México. José María promptly sold about 300 head of cattle to William C. McDonald, who eventually would be elected to become New México's first governor from 1912 to 1916. Shortly thereafter the entire family left for México.

Their travels eventually took them to José María's birthplace. Surely the entire family was introduced to tíos and primos that they had never seen or even heard about. It also afforded the opportunity for José María to reacquaint himself with one of his entrepreneurial endeavors of the manufacture of steamer trunks. It has been said that his other business had fashioned many beautiful products. In all, the family remained in México through the winter and finally returned to the Rancho Vega the following summer.

Upon their return from México José María and Josefa had several more children; José, Leandro, Tranquelino, Nicolás and Martín As the family continued to grow so did the family business as José María continued to invest in cattle and other livestock. The family business was prosperous, and the Vegas were again one of the more prominent families in the region.

It had become somewhat of a family tradition that the Vega children would continue their education in some of the most prominent Catholic Schools in the region. Petra had enrolled into the Loreto Catholic Convent in Santa Fé. Misfortune, however, again struck the family as she fell ill to pneumonia and died shortly thereafter in 1910. Petra was buried in the Convent cemetery. José María and Josefa would eventually have another daughter whom they named Petra in honor of their first daughter.

Josefa had become a social butterfly in many respects. She enjoyed hosting bailes for the people in the area. When such an event was announced people from all over the region wanted to attend. Before such bailes, Josefa was diligent in that she had her children prepare the *sala* (great room) by rearranging the furniture such that there was a spacious dance floor. The bailes were always the talk of the people the next day.

The Rancho Vega had garnered an early reputation as an important place for both social events and politicking within Lincoln County. Governor William McDonald, who hailed from White Oaks, shared a mutual friendship with José María and his wife. It is believed that several discussions about New Mexico statehood took place within the walls of the Casa De Vega.

José María played an integral part in the incorporation of Carrizozo. He had become a member of the first board of trustees for the newly incorporated village. He used his influence to help establish a respectable municipal government. His insight was a valuable resource in Carrizozo's early beginnings.

José María had lived a prosperous and productive life. On February 09, 1919 he had drawn his last breath as he passed on after battling an illness. In his passing, he had left a legacy of prominence to all of his children. Many people from throughout the region attended his funeral to pay their last respects. José María was buried in the Evergreen Cemetery.

Josefa continued to have an interest in the Rancho Vega's overall operations but she relied heavily on her son Leandro S. Vega Sr. to run all of the daily operations. She eventually moved from the Casa

D Vega to a house she had built in Carrizozo in about 1925. She remained very active in local politics and continued to host social events for the people. Often times she would call upon Leandro Vega Sr. to ready the Casa D Vega for her events. By 1940 she had sold the Rancho Vega to the Duggar family. She continued to reside in Carrizozo until her death on March 08, 1949. She was laid to rest in the Evergreen Cemetery next to her husband.

The legacy handed down by José María and Josefa continued as many of their children and grandchildren remained politically active. Their son Antonio Vega served as Carrizozo's town marshal for several terms.

Nicolás Vega also served as a town marshal in 1939 and then as a Lincoln County Deputy Sheriff from 1940 through 1944. He was later elected as Sheriff of Lincoln County where he served two consecutive terms from 1945 to 1948. He also was appointed by Governor Mechem to serve as a New México State Alcohol Inspector.

Leandro Vega Sr. served as a Carrizozo town trustee from 1950 through 1966. He was elected as Carrizozo's mayor, which he served from 1966 through 1968. He was also appointed to serve as the Lincoln County Appraiser for the New México Bureau of Revenue. Leandro Sr. and his wife Narcisa operated several businesses such as the Vega Feed Store, a restaurant, a liquor store, a lumberyard, and a freight trucking company. They also continued to ranch near Nogal.

Leandro Vega Jr. was elected as the Lincoln County Sheriff and he served two consecutive terms from 1965 through 1968. He later served as Chief Deputy Sheriff before he was elected again as sheriff for two more consecutive terms from 1973 through 1976. After serving the Lincoln County Sheriff's Department, he was appointed to serve as the Chief Criminal Investigator for the Twelfth Judicial District. He served in this position until his eventual retirement in 2002. Soon thereafter, Leandro Vega Jr. passed away on September 02, 2002.

Leandro Vega Jr.'s legacy as a lawman didn't personify his true nature. Like his father before him, and grandfather José María Vega, he was a rancher at heart. He enjoyed working his ranch, which encompassed the ghost town of Rebentón. It was here that his love for the land was most evident. The ranch is still owned by the Vega family.

José María de Vega. (Courtesy of the Vega Family)

Chapter Eleven: Los Romero

Migration to Lincoln County

Los Romero had originally come to El Reyno de Nuevo México with the Conquistadores from España via Nueva España. Some came to the province during the Spanish Conquest of 1598, while others came with the reconquest of 1692. Some came as soldiers, some as Spanish Officials, but most were pobladores. Some of Los Romero came to the New World from Corral de Almaquer, east of Toledo, España.

The southeastern section of the Territory of New México had just opened up for settlement with the commissioning of Fort Stanton. Los Romero of Lincoln County had come to the Río Hondo valley and eventually settled the lands near Picacho, Analla, and Las Palas. They had come in a caravan that included several other families from the Manzano vicinity. They proceeded south with the utmost caution because roving bands of Mescalero Apachés were raiding the region on a frequent basis.

A Romero family legend told a story of one such migration in the early 1860s, in which several families gathered in Manzano. After several festive days and nights, friends and family finally said their emotional goodbyes. The travel was grueling and cumbersome. On a good day, the caravan would journey, on average, about fifteen miles. The terrain was rough, and hard on the wagons and oxen. It was imperative that the group stay intact for the reason of safety. Hence, when one wagon would break down, the whole cavalcade was forced to slow down, or even stop. Scouts often rode several miles ahead, looking for signs of danger and unforeseen problems with the road.

On one such reconnaissance, a band of Mescalero were spotted. They were mounted upon their horses and perched atop a hillside. The scout quickly rode back to the caravan to warn of the impending danger. As the procession passed within view, the Mescalero diligently kept a watchful eye upon the travelers. They followed the column of wagons for several miles.

After some deliberation, the guide, Miguel Lucero and the leadership of the group had decided to err on the side of caution by circling the wagons. Some men and women grabbed their rifles and positioned themselves. The children were gathered up and placed in a secure place. The two sides weighed their options over the next several hours while nothing of any significance happened.

In an attempt to break the stalemate, it was decided that one of the men who had a fair command of the Mescalero's language would venture out to speak with them. As he did, the representative had asked what their intentions were. They replied that they weren't looking for bloodshed that day and that they were only making their presence known. The Mescalero did allude that they would return the next day with more warriors, and that their intentions would be more threatening in nature.

The messenger returned to the group and told them what the Mescalero's intentions were. Several of the men gathered together and discussed their options. The headship had decided that it was safer to stay where they were at, for the remainder of the day, rather than coming under an ambush while the caravan was spread out. Thus the group fortified their position in the event of an attack. They prayed and waited for the Apaché onslaught. As it turned out they held their position for three days and there was no further sign of the Mescalero. Steadfastly, they set off for Bonito. The caravan continued to grow smaller as each family squatted on lands along the way.[1] Some of the families from the caravan had settled in El Berendo, while others settled in La Plaza de San José. Those families that continued up the Río Hondo would push on in search of more suitable lands.

Several successive caravans, often staged from Las Cruces, Manzano and Socorro, helped populate Bonito. Some of those families that arrived were Eugenio Baldonado, Martín Cháves, Vicente Fresques, Agapito Gallegos, Cayetano Jaramillo José Montaño, Camilo Núñes, and Trenidad Vigil. Many of the families had decided to settle on lands adjacent to the Río Hondo about mid-way between La Plaza de San José and La Plaza del Río Bonito. They christened their community, Picacho in reference to the mountain peaks that surrounded them. They initially held their religious services in the house of Trenidad Vigil, before Padre Sambrano came to Picacho.

Ygnacio Romero

Ygnacio Romero christened José Ygnacio Trifón Romero was born near Santa Fé, El Reyno de Nuevo México, Nueva España, on June 30, 1795. His parents were José Vicente Romero and María Tomasa Trujillo. He married Rafaela Lueras in Santa Fé, Nuevo México, La República de México on March 01, 1828. By 1860 Ygnacio and most of his family had migrated to the Manzano region.[2]

Life in the Estancia Valley wasn't what the family had expected. The region was becoming overcrowded with newly arrived settlers and the lands were being overgrazed. The word was rapidly spreading throughout the valley, that there were abundant grasslands and the promise of homesteads in Bonito. From the Gran Quivira, one could see Sierra Blanca on the horizon, towering over the landscape. Its snow-capped summit advertised an abundance of water that would last through the summer. The lure of the mountain continued to tug on Ygnacio's pioneering spirit.

It didn't take much deliberation to convince his family that a move to Bonito could lead to greater opportunities. Ygnacio, his wife Rafaela, and several of their children were part of the before mentioned caravan that set off from Manzano for the lands of the southeastern region of the territory. They had arrived in Lincoln County by the mid-1860s and settled in La Plaza de Picacho.[3] They were greeted by a large valley that disappeared into the rolling hills.

The patriarch was an older man, well into his late-sixties, but he still had the desire to improve his position in life. Although he could not work the land and graze his sheep, he heavily relied on the support of his sons to continue their ranching operations. As such, he and his wife helped raise many of their grandchildren.

Juan de Dios Romero

Juan de Dios Romero was born near Casa Colorada in about March of 1859. He was the son of José Antonio Romero and Cornelia Sisneros. His father died shortly after he was born. He and his mother were graciously taken in by his grandfather, Ygnacio Romero. By 1860 the family had migrated to the Manzano region. Once there, he and his mother were living next to his tío Francisco.[4]

His mother had met Martín García and they fostered a love relationship. By 1861 the two had married and shortly thereafter they had a daughter they named Lucía. With the decision that the Romeros would be settling in Bonito, Ygnacio had insisted that Cornelia and her husband accompany them. Martín rebuked the idea, indicating that he and his family would be returning to Casa Colorada to live with his parents.

Angered with Martín's reluctance to bring his family to Bonito, Ygnacio indicated that his grandson was not going to be raised as a García. Caught in the middle of the dispute, Cornelia had insisted that her entire family remain together. Being firm and unwavering, Ygnacio deliberated in length with his young ex daughter-in-law. After much discussion she finally succumbed to her father-in-law's demands. The two siblings were soon separated and the family was broken up as the Romeros migrated to Bonito.

Juan de Dios was raised by his abuelos, Ygnacio Romero and Rafaela Lueras in La Plaza de San José.[5] By October of 1868 at the age of about ten, he was already working and living on Robert Casey's rancho near La Plaza de Picacho. Casey had hired the youngster to herd his livestock. Since there were no fences, it was his responsibility to ensure that the livestock remained close to the house. The Casey's thus paid Juan de Dios' wages to his grandfather.

Cristina Castillo de Romero, Juan de Dios Romero (Ernest Sanchez collection)

The Stolen Livestock [6]

On April 01, 1869 a family friend of the Casey's, Don Francisco Sánchez, had entered into an agreement to purchase an ox for the amount of $125. When the gentleman had arrived, Juan de Dios was directed to fetch the most impressive specimen and bring it back to the corral.

The youngster ran out into the pastureland, and to his disbelief, he had discovered that all of the livestock had mysteriously disappeared. Juan frantically searched for the livestock and came across a trail that led off into the hills. As he examined the tracks, he noticed men's footprints in the dirt. Juan quickly ran back to the house, where he whispered into his tío Pablo Romero's ear, about what he had discovered.

Pablo looked into his nephew's eyes, and then quickly stole a glance towards Francisco, and promptly excused himself from the room. He accompanied his nephew as he ran to the tracks that were left behind. He crouched down and examined the human tracks and he quietly stood up looking out into the distance. He shook his head with displeasure, thinking aloud that the Mescalero had to be responsible for this raid. The two thus returned to the house where Francisco was informed of the situation.

As Francisco accompanied his compadre outside to investigate the scene, Juan de Dios was sent to inform his tío Vicente Romero, of what had happened. Vicente met with the others at the scene and they had decided that it was too late to go looking for the livestock. It thus would be better to look the following morning.

The next day Vicente, Francisco Sánchez, and another ranch hand had followed the trail into the hills. About two and a half miles up the canyon; they had come across an encampment, which had been recently abandoned. Francisco was able to conclude that the Mescalero were definitely responsible for the raid. Rather than confront them though, the men returned to Casey's rancho and informed him of their findings. It is believed that nothing else was done to resolve the matter.

More than twenty years later, Juan de Dios was called before the Court of Claims to tell his version of the events that took place. His testimony did little to help resolve the claim that was filed by Ellen Casey. She received no compensation for her loss, because the Court found no compelling evidence that would lead to a fair judgment.

Husband and Father

Rafael Castillo was one of the few people to settle in Bonito before 1860.[7] He was squatting on a substantial amount of land, which he was beginning to cultivate. His wife, María Lucero, and their three children were living with her parents near Punta de Agua while he built a house for them. It was his notion that the lands were livable for his family. He didn't want to endure the hardships of establishing the farm and raising his children without the support network of their respective families. It was a sacrifice he willingly made.

María's father, Miguel Lucero had lived most of his adult life near Punta de Agua. He often served as a guide for many of the caravans that traversed between Manzano and Bonito. She was always willing to travel with him to Bonito so that she could help her husband ready the adobé. She did this for a couple of years until both she and Rafael were satisfied that the family could live in relative comfort.

When the time came for María and her children to move to Bonito, it was somewhat of a bittersweet departure. Although her parents were excited for their daughter to begin her new life away from Punta de Agua, they had both grown very fond of their grandchildren. Miguel and his wife Luciana both opted to help their daughter with the move.

Working the land was a labor of love. From sun up to sun down, Rafael and María had kept themselves busy. Visits from neighbors were a common practice to build a greater sense of community. Sometimes they would help each other mend the houses or ready the lands for planting crops. The Castillos were beginning to feel comfortable in their new community.

Fate was cruel however, as Rafael was stricken with an illness that took his life. Devastated by the loss of her husband, the grieving widow and her children reluctantly returned to Punta de Agua. Upon arriving at her parents' house she was embraced by their love and compassion. The whole family continued to live in the Estancia Valley for several more years.

It wasn't more than a few years after the death of her husband that María had lost her mother to old age. At that point, she had implored her father, who was suffering from failing health, to return to Bonito with her. Together, her father and her children made one last caravan. Rather than guiding the trip, Miguel was merely a passenger.

Juan de Dios Romero continued to live with his grandparents almost up to the time that he wed Cristina Castillo sometime in 1880. Cristina's life experience was very similar to her husband's. Both had lost their fathers when they were very young. Each had lived with their grandparents almost their entire lives. Each had even mourned the loss of a sibling. Juan was separated from his half-sister and Cristina's brother had died unexpectedly. They shared so much in common that it almost seemed that fate had brought the two of them together.

Juan de Dios and Cristina had eleven known children, five sons and six daughters. Their first born son died at a very young age. Many of their subsequent children were raised by their compadres, or other family members. Jinio and Lola Guerra raised their daughters Merenciana and Carolina. Román

Barragán and Andrea Torres de Barragán raised their daughter Delfinia in San Patricio. José Alvarez and Lucia García de Alvarez raised their daughter Lupita in Socorro.

It wasn't until Lupita was an adolescent that she returned to Picacho. Her father and Mauricio Sánchez both traveled to Socorro, by wagon, to bring her back. They traveled through Carrizozo, north of the Mal País, and through the hills to the west. The journey was slow, and arduous as either one took turns to walk in front of the wagon to determine the best route to take.

Juan de Dios, like his grandfather and uncles had chosen to lead a sheep rancher's life. This often took him and his eldest sons away from the house. This might have explained why many of his oldest daughters had come to live with their respective Padrinos. This was an accepted way of life in the valley, which wouldn't have negatively reflected too much upon Juan de Dios or Cristina.

Juan de Dios had a homestead in Aguaje de Ruidoso, which was a meadow located up within El Cañon del Alamo. When it rained, the water would collect on the meadow, and run its course through the canyon and into the Río Hondo. Up on his homestead he grazed his flock of sheep until the effects of age finally made it too physically demanding to perform his duties.

Román Sánchez recounts that he was visiting with family in Roswell when he heard the news of his grandfather's death. Juan de Dios was working on the rancho just south of Picacho. It was there that he had suffered a massive stroke, and had died. He was driven to Picacho where he met up with his father. Together they hiked in the hills looking for the body. When they finally found his grandfather, they wrapped him up in a sheet and brought him back to San Patricio, where he was buried in the Campo Santo de la Capilla de San Patricio.

Vicente Romero

Vicente Romero christened José Vicente Romero was born in Sevilleta, Nuevo México, La República de México on April 20, 1846. His parents were Ygnacio Romero and Rafaela Lueras. He migrated to La Plaza de Picacho with his father and several of his siblings. He married María Romero and had fathered three known children.

During the Lincoln County War, Vicente had rallied behind Martín Cháves who was one of the most vocal citizens within the community. He often rode in the same circles as those who associated themselves with the Regulators. This decision had ultimately cost him his life.

Vicente was one of the men who had fortified himself within the McSween House during The Five Days Battle.[8] On the night of July 19, 1878, John Kinney's men gunned him down as he attempted to flee McSween's burning house. He had been hit by three rifle bullets, which had penetrated his body and leg, and thus had died shortly thereafter.[9]

Vicente's body, along with the others that were killed, was left undisturbed throughout the night. By the next morning, McSween's chickens were curiously pecking on the bodies. Flies were gathering on the corpses' bloodied wounds as rigor mortis was slowly settling in. The smell of death filled the air with a repugnant stench.

The news of Vicente's death had reached his family back in Picacho. Sheriff Peppin had rounded up some men to serve as a coroner's jury. John P. Wilson served as the jury's foreman while Maximiano Cháves, José García, Felipé Maés, Felipé Miranda, Octaviano Salas, and José Serna served as the other jurors. This was obviously a half-hearted attempt to make the killings seem legitimate. In their writ they concluded that McSween and his men were killed while resisting arrest.[10]

Vicente's two brothers Francisco and Juan were tasked with the solemn duty of retrieving his body in Lincoln. They covered his body and loaded it on the wagon and hastily set off for Picacho. Once arriving to Vicente's house, his despondent wife wept over his body.

Martín Cháves

Arrival of wool wagon train in Las Vegas, NM; R-L First wagon driver Trinidad Romero; on foot Martín Cháves; Second wagon driver Juan Dios Romero; Third wagon driver Juen Kimbrell (Courtesy of Elsie Kimbrell)

Martín Cháves christened José Martín Cháves was born in Tomé, Territory of New México sometime in 1853. He was orphaned as a child and was taken in by Padre José Sambrano Tafoya. Padre Sambrano raised the youngster, and taught him how to read and write at the church's school. Over the years, his student looked upon him as a father figure.[11]

As Martín grew into a young man, he had befriended many of the Romero from Manzano. He married Juanita Romero on August 16, 1875. She was the daughter of Francisco Romero and Andrea Sánches. When the family had decided to migrate to Bonito, he had decided to accompany them. He really didn't have any other familial ties in Manzano and he had endeared himself to their family. The lure of owning land was also very appealing to him. Martín had settled along the Río Hondo in La Plaza de Picacho.

As the people of the valley struggled to keep the Catholic faith alive, it was he who had initiated the search for a resident priest. Family legend was that Martín and Pablo Fresquez had gone searching for a cleric, and had specifically sought the services of Padre Sambrano, in Manzano.[12] It had been said that Pablo Fresquez was the priest's *sobrino* (nephew) and Martín was like a son to him. They must have made quite a compelling case because shortly thereafter, the Padre was assigned to La Parroquia del Río Bonito in March of 1876 as Lincoln County's first Catholic resident priest.

Padre Sambrano and Francisco Antonio Vigil y Valdéz had purchased some land that was adjacent to Martín's ranchito and raised sheep to help offset the costs of his parroquia. Family legend was that Martín had a two-story house in which he lived on the first floor, and the Padre held mass on the second floor.[13] Eventually, the cleric blessed the house and named it el Oratorio de San José.[14] In 1891, after Padre Sambrano's death, the people of the community came together and built a stone capilla in close proximity to Martín's house.

While living in La Plaza de Picacho, tensions between the Nuevo Mexicanos and the Tejanos were about to erupt into a state of anarchy. First, the Horrell brothers waged a campaign of terror that was largely directed towards the Spanish-speaking populace, and those Anglos who were married to them. Many innocent civilians had tragically lost their lives at the end of a gun held by a Horrell, or one of their henchmen.

Martín had become incensed by the senseless slaughter of his people and aimed to do something about it. On January 21, 1874 he stealthily positioned himself for an ambush of the Horrell clan as they made their way back to Téxas via the Río Hondo. As they passed his position he opened fire and killed Ben Turner, one of the Horrell's henchmen.[15] After the fracas, he had become somewhat of a folk hero in the eyes of many people within the community because he stood up to the feared Horrell clan.

Martín's influence among his people served him well as he aligned his support to the McSween faction during the Lincoln County War. He rendered his services to the Regulators who were fighting the injustices wrought by the Dolan faction. Since he was held in such high esteem among his people, his influence helped polarize many of their loyalties in favor of McSween's faction.

His rise to prominence, as one of the most celebrated New Mexican heroes of the Lincoln County War wasn't realized until he took over as their leader and spokesperson when Juan Patrón opted for a less visible role. Martín was young, educated, charismatic, and filled with contempt for the Dolan faction, or any other Tejano or foreigner that brought lawlessness to his homelands.

He rode with the regulators from time to time. He developed a close relationship with many of them, and he had often broken bread with them. His house was often used as a stopping point for the gangly bunch as they traversed between Lincoln, La Plaza de San Patricio and John Chism's rancho.

The Horse Race[16]

It was said that Martín and Billy the Kid had forged a friendship. On numerous occasions one would see the two hanging out with each another. In one such instance both men were discussing a gambling debt owed by a bunch of Tejanos who happened to be passing through the valley. After much talk, Billy had offered to assist his amigo in collecting the debt.

As the story goes, the Tejanos had set camp just outside of Picacho. They had heard of many rumors from the locals that Martín owned one of the fastest horses in the area. A meeting was set and the two parties met. Confident in their own racing horses, the Tejanos claimed that one of their horses had never been beat. After a cordial discussion and the terms of the wager were agreed upon, a date had been set for the race to take place. The loser would pay the price of three of their best beeves.

Many people throughout the valley had caught word of the pending race. On the day of the running, they had come to watch. There was a sense of excitement as their anticipation grew with each passing minute. Attention was called to the starting line as the two horses were lined up. With the blow of the horn, the horses and their jockeys took off. The crowd exalted in cheer and bliss as the horses passed by.

Martín's horse ran true and unwavering. His hooves, legs and muscles were acclimated to the contours of the ground. The terrain was familiar and it ran without fear or hesitation. The Tejano's horse on the other hand couldn't hit its full stride as the terrain jostled it about. Martín's horse had won the race by an extraordinary margin. Being that he didn't much care for Tejanos, Martín took the opportunity to gloat. The Tejanos took exception, became enraged and refused to make good on their bet.

Billy had heard about the race earlier in the day and decided to pay his friend a visit. Martín recounted the day's events, indicating that he had every intention of collecting the debt. The Kid was masterful in manipulating the situation. He had offered his services as a means of serving justice. Juanita however, was fearful that Billy's solution always led to some form of violent discontent. She didn't want any troubles from a bunch of Tejanos nor did she want anybody to get killed over the matter. The Kid laughed, assuring them that he could take care of himself. Hence he and his friend set out to collect on the gambling debt, against her wishes.

Billy rode into the camp and promptly shot three beeves. Initially the Tejanos became enraged, but their rage quickly turned to fear when he promptly introduced himself. He motioned to Martín to collect his prize. The Tejanos didn't waste much time in tempting their fate. They packed up their camp and rode off.

After The Lincoln County War

In March of 1879 Martín was recruited by Juan Patrón to join the Lincoln County Mounted Riflemen, to subdue the lawlessness that still persisted throughout Lincoln County. Without hesitation, he had volunteered his services. He was adamant about exacting justice upon the men responsible for the murder of his brother-in-law, Vicente Romero.

As life on the Río Hondo finally became more civilized he had settled down and became a successful rancher. He fathered three known children and raised one stepson on his ranchito on the Río Hondo. Upon Padre Sambrano's accidental death, he had paid $600 to his heirs for a 320-acre tract of land that lay adjacent to his own.

He thus lived the remainder of his life serving the community that he had grown to love, and the community in turn grew to love the **huerfano** (orphan). He passed away in his beloved Picacho sometime in 1931. Many of his descendants continue to live throughout Lincoln County and New México.

George Kimbrell

George Kimbrell was born in Huntsville, Arkansas on March 31, 1842. He had headed west during the Pike's Peak Gold Rush, in Colorado, before eventually succumbing to illness. He migrated south to Las Vegas, Territory of New México where he lived for a short period of time. By 1863, George had already migrated to Lincoln County where he became a scout for the U.S. government.[17]

While in Lincoln County he eventually squatted on some land in the community of La Plaza de Picacho. He married Pablita Romero in Tomé, Territory of New México on June 29, 1864. She was the daughter of Francisco Romero and Andrea Sánches. The Romero family grew very fond of George and graciously accepted him into their family. He embraced their culture, became fluent in the Spanish language, and accepted their customs. He had befriended many of the people throughout the valley, and thus he was held in high esteem.

Although George was largely impartial to the events that led up to the Lincoln County War, he was by no means immune to its atrocities. In late January of 1874, while accompanying several freighters en route to John Chism's rancho, their party was attacked by the murderous Horrell brothers who killed all five Hispanos, but miraculously spared Kimbrell's life. His family again was affected by the violence as his wife's tío, Vicente Romero, was gunned down in Lincoln during the Five Days Battle.

The county commissioners on January 01, 1879, appointed George Kimbrell as Lincoln County Sheriff shortly after Sheriff George Peppin had resigned his office. Kimbrell thus was tasked with an almost insurmountable duty. The lawlessness that was running rampant throughout the county, combined with its vastness, and a serious lack of resources made it almost impossible to keep the peace. Realizing this fact, Sheriff Kimbrell had unofficially petitioned the Post Commander for military assistance in serving all of the arrest warrants that were passed to him by the now deposed Sheriff Peppin. [18]

Shortly after Huston Chapman had been murdered, Sheriff Kimbrell again had solicited the help of the military for the purpose of helping to keep the peace. Soldiers from Ft. Stanton responded quickly by sending 20 troops to Lincoln under the command of Lieutenant Dawson.[19]

William H. Bonney had eventually entered into an agreement with Governor Wallace that he would turn himself in, to Sheriff Kimbrell, in a staged arrest, for the purpose of testifying against many in the Dolan faction. For his testimony, the young outlaw had sought a pardon from the Governor. Once in captivity, he divulged invaluable information about many of the Rustlers operations. During his time in captivity however, Governor Wallace had quietly left Lincoln. Realizing that the governor may have betrayed their agreement, Billy made his escape from his prison at Juan Patrón's house.

Sheriff Kimbrell had served his term until January of 1881, when new Sheriff elect, Pat Garrett replaced him. George continued to serve his community later in life by becoming the Justice of the Peace for the Picacho precinct for several years. All the while, he continued farming on his land. His youngest son, William Kimbrell also served Lincoln County for much of his life, as the County Clerk, the Deputy County Assessor, the County Assessor, and as a Probate Judge. George died in his beloved community of Picacho on March 25, 1924.

Lázaro Gallegos, Antonio Romero. Lázaro Gallegos was the son of Lazaro Gallegos and Antonia Molina de Gallegos. Antonio Romero was the son of Juan de Dios Romero and Cristina Castillo de Romero.

Chapter Twelve:
Los Sánchez, 1880-2008

Mauricio Sánchez

Delfinia Romero de Sánchez, Mauricio Sánchez (Ernest Sanchez collection)

Mauricio Sánchez was born in San Patricio, Territory of New México on October 31, 1880. His parents were Francisco Sánchez and Concepción Trujillo. He grew into a tall, imposing man who stood out in a crowd. While most men in the valley stood on average about 5' 8" tall, Mauricio stood about 6'3" tall. Several of the old-timers recalled that all of Francisco Sánchez's sons were tall men and that they often had to duck their heads to pass through the doorways of houses, which were built for people of a smaller stature.

Mauricio had auburn colored hair, blue eyes, and a fairly light complexion. As a young man he wore a long mustache but as he grew older he preferred to be clean-shaven. He took a great deal of pride in his personal appearance. He liked to be seen in nice clothes. When he visited friends and relatives or went to mass, he always made sure that he wore his best wardrobe. He took especially great care of his hat, ensuring that it always remained crisp, like new. He always carried a pipe with him and when he and his compadres would gather to discuss the current events they would do so in between long smoke-filled puffs.

Mauricio married Delfinia Romero, christened María Delfinia Virginia Romero, in San Patricio, Territory of New México on January 09, 1901. She was the daughter of Juan de Dios Romero and Cristina Castillo. They had six children, two sons and four daughters. She was 15 years of age by the time that she had married and she was 16 years of age when she had her first child. They lived with her padrino, Román Barragán until he had passed on. Upon his death, he had willed most of his lands to Delfinia Romero and Crecencia "Crita" Ybarra de Gonzáles.

Mauricio made a living as a sheep rancher. He grazed over 2000 head of sheep as far north as Rebentón and as far south as Cañon del Alamo. In 1916 he filed for a land patent for 320 acres near

Pajarito Mountain, next to the Mescalero Reservation. In 1927 he filed for another land patent for 320 acres, most of which was adjoining his property near Pajarito Mountain. He then purchased about 160 acres north of El Rancho Barragán from Miguel Sedillos.

On November 13, 1926 tragedy had struck the family as Delfinia contracted an illness and had passed away at the age of 40. Mauricio was devastated by the loss of his wife. Although he was feeling lost and numbed by her absence, he didn't have much time to grieve. He had to take care of his children, his rancho, and the sheep. His faith in God had carried him through one of the most heartbreaking moments of his life. The love he had for his children drove him to continue on.

On July 28, 1927 Mauricio married Clara Bartlett. Although they shared a wonderful life together, Mauricio often had been heard proclaiming that, "Nothing can compare to the love that I shared with my querida Delfinia. Not even a daughter's love can compare to what we had. She was my world. She was everything to me. I loved her so much."[1]

The importance of one's faith in God was instilled within Mauricio from a very young age. By the time he was an adolescent he had already acquired a great knowledge of the power of prayer. He had learned the various prayers he would need to live in harmony with his environment. As such, he also had grown into a very superstitious man. He believed that all men, women and children were walking amidst the spirits. Some of these spirits had good intentions, and some of them had evil intentions. Whenever he felt an evil presence he would pray to God for protection. Whenever he felt a blessed presence he would say a prayer thanking God.

Mauricio had a compulsion of talking about ***brujeria*** (witchcraft). He believed that those people who didn't have a strong faith in God were more susceptible of being seduced by the evil spirits. He firmly believed that if an evil spirit had possessed those people, they would become an instrument of evil. He also believed that those evil individuals, whom were known as ***brujas*** (witches), would cast evil spells upon God-fearing people to cause them harm and to bring about misfortune. In many ways he felt that he had an obligation to warn people of the dangers that lurked within the shadows.

He reiterated his convictions by giving a testimony of his own experience with a bruja. The story goes that one night he was sleeping in a jacal on his homestead, up in Cañon del Alamo. While in his slumber he felt a presence that gave him a very unnerving feeling. He awoke only to discover that an unknown woman was menacingly leaning over his bed.

Unfazed that he had suddenly awoken, she looked closely at his facial features, which were somewhat distorted by the moonlight. The shadow of her outstretched arms appeared to grasp at his throat. He had trouble breathing, and he grew restless, but he couldn't move his body because he was petrified with fear. She drew closer, looking deep into his eyes. Her gaze hypnotized him; it was as if she were taking his soul.

She let out a sinister smile and said, "You are the son of Francisco Sánchez, who is the son of Mauricio de la Trinidad Sánches." He nodded his head acknowledging her suspicions. "I was going to do you harm, but I know your father, and your father's father. Thus, I will let you be, and I will never seek to harm you."

The old woman quietly turned away from Mauricio, walked out the opened door, and disappeared into the shadows of the night. Short of breath he gasped for air. As he was inhaling he had a sudden urge to sneeze. He sneezed so hard that he felt something become dislodged from within his nose. He arose in his bed and looked for the object. As he searched his hand came across some leaves that were woven tightly together. He looked out the door, into the darkness and presumed that the woman who had intended to do him harm was a bruja.

That night he said several prayers, and thanked God for protecting him. He wondered what the old woman had meant concerning his father and his grandfather. He had never figured it out, but he had made it a point of telling the story to anybody who would listen to him. From that day on Mauricio had become a very superstitious man. He could never pass a fortuneteller without visiting, to have his fortune told. He was a very strong believer of the powers of the curanderos.

Over the years Mauricio had become a very accomplished storyteller. One of his favorite stories he told was that of **La Llorona** (The Weeping Woman). He also enjoyed telling jokes, and other funny stories that would bring laughter to the crowd. Whether it was a frightening story, or a funny joke, he enjoyed getting a reaction from the people he visited. He also enjoyed talking about his travels all over New México, Arizona and California. He was a very well-traveled man in his time.

Mauricio was the first person in San Patricio to own a car and he took great pleasure in showing it off to the rest of the community. He enjoyed visiting his children, brothers, sisters, uncles, aunts, cousins and friends. People would gather around when they heard his car drive up to their house.

Later in life Mauricio would travel between Belén, Carrizozo, and San Patricio to visit with his children. He never stayed in one place for too long of a time. The allure of traveling and visiting with people had always been an important part of his life. He was living with his daughter Suzie Sánchez-Silva when he had passed away in 1962. He was buried in the Tomé cemetery.

Román Sánchez

Roman Sanchez and family taken by Ernest Sanchez in 1947.
Backrow L-R: Orlando, Florinda, Roman, Delphina, Flora.
Front row L-R: Geraldine, Freddy, Brezel, Luvin.

Román Sánchez was born in San Patricio, Territory of New México on April 23, 1904. His parents were Mauricio Sánchez and Delfinia Romero. He was named after his Padrino, Román Barragán, who also was his mother's Padrino. He was only seven years old when New México became the 47th state on January 06, 1912.

Román was born and subsequently grew up during a time when mechanical and technical innovations continually improved the standards of living for so many people across the United States.

Many innovations however, where slow in being introduced to the people of San Patricio and many other communities throughout Lincoln County, for a multitude of reasons. Its relative isolation was the most common barrier of entry. Other barriers of entry were prohibitive costs, product practicality, and lack of adequate product information. In many instances, most of the communities throughout Lincoln County were behind the innovation curve.

Román had recalled that he had never ridden in an automobile until his grandfather Juan de Dios Romero had passed away in 1914. At the time, he was staying with his Tía Merenciana Romero de Torres in Roswell. He accompanied her as she and her husband drove to Picacho where he was reunited with his father. He was amazed that it took only a few hours to make the trip by car, as opposed to two days by a horse drawn wagon. He also had recalled that up until the mid-1930s, it was more common to see people riding horses rather than driving in automobiles.

When Román was about 10 years old, he had been given an opportunity to attend Saint Michael's Catholic School in Santa Fé, where he briefly received his education. He had attended the private school with two of his cousins, Godfrey Gonzáles and Epaminoandas Gonzáles. Epaminoandas had become very ill while attending St. Michael's and had to return to San Patricio. It had been rumored, by many in the family that he had become extremely homesick.

At St. Michael's, Román learned the etiquette of being a young gentleman. Once a week he would make sure that his clothes were all properly ironed. Every morning he would polish his shoes, dress himself in his uniform and put on a tie. He then would tidy up his sleeping area. Each morning he would attend mass, in which he would say his prayers. After mass he would eat breakfast with all of the other boys. Finally he would attend his daily classes.

Román would sometimes talk with his children about the other things he did while at Catholic School. He indicated to them that he had often accompanied the priests on their travels from house to house. He explained that the priests had always tasked him with opening the gates for them, and then closing the gates behind them. There, next to the gate, he would wait until their eventual departure.

The youngster was an astute pupil, and always made it a point to observe the priests because he was intrigued with their mannerisms. Living in San Patricio, the priest was often one of the most revered persons in the valley. Filled with curiosity, he would always ask the priests questions, and they in turn were delighted to oblige him with an answer. Thus, his early perceptions of the Church were molding him into the man that he would later become.

Román had become homesick, like his two other cousins, and he missed his family a great deal. Eventually he returned to San Patricio, where he continued his education in a one-room adobé structure. Initially, all of the children throughout San Patricio had to either walk, or ride a horse to get to school. Román vividly remembers that the first bus he rode in had very little horsepower. When the bus came upon a hill, all of the children would have to get off the bus and help push it up the hill. The children would then quickly get back on the bus until they came to the next hill. In many instances, it was easier to walk or ride a horse to school.

From time to time, before school came into session, Román was tasked by the **maestro** (instructor) to go to the river and gather willow branches. He would have to strip the branches of any **jaras** that were protruding out. He would bring the willow branches back to the maestro, in which he would place them upon his desk. The maestro thus would use them as a whip for any student that would misbehave. As was the case for all of the children in San Patricio and all of the other surrounding communities, Román completed his education only through the eighth grade. At the time, there weren't any higher levels of education offered in the immediate area.

Román, like his other brothers and sisters, spent most of his childhood living with his mother and his Padrinos, Román Barragán and Andrea Torres de Barragán. His father was often away from the house, tending to the sheep on the homestead up in Cañon del Alamo, or on grazing land near Rebentón. On occasion, he would accompany his father to help tend to the sheep but most of the time he did chores on his Padrino's ranchito.

Román married Florinda Herrera Salsberry on February 20, 1927 in Mescalero, New México. She was the daughter of James R. Salsberry and Manuelita Herrera. Together they had twelve children, two of whom had died while they were still infants. Usually a few weeks before Florinda was about to give birth to her children, she would keep with tradition and travel to her mother's house. She would remain there while her mother took care of her. When the time was about to come, Manuelita would send for a midwife to help with the birthing process.

After giving birth, she would remain in bed, at her mother's house for forty days and forty nights, as her mother took care of her newly born infant. At the time, this tradition was not the exception, but rather the accepted norm for most of the women of the valley. Román was allowed to visit his wife, and infant child, but he wasn't ever allowed to bring either of them home until after the forty days and nights.

Civilian Conservation Corps (CCC)[2]

A severe drought that lasted from the late-1920s through the mid- 1930s coupled with the Great Depression had prompted an end to the Sánchez family's sheep ranching operations. Román eventually enlisted and found work with the Civilian Conservation Corps (CCC), which was established by President Franklin D. Roosevelt on March 31, 1933 with the enactment of the Emergency Conservation Work Act. The goal of the CCC was to provide jobs for those who were poverty stricken, underemployed, and unemployed during the Great Depression, while at the same time focusing the nation's underutilized labor resources to help protect and restore its depleted natural resources.

Another benefit of the CCC was that it aimed to educate the millions of individuals who were illiterate. Many within the leadership ranks of the Corps did not support the initiative though, fearing that it would conflict with the deadlines, and ultimately the completion of their assigned projects. It was thus left in the hands of the Educational Advisor for each camp to ensure the success of the program.

President Franklin D. Roosevelt's premise was to recruit hundreds of thousands of the unemployed and enlist them into a peacetime army. The U.S. Army thus would manage the logistics between moving hundreds of thousands of men from the eastern U.S., where the bulk of the labor pool resided, to the western U.S., where most of the projects were located. The majority of the nation had overwhelmingly embraced the establishment of the CCC. The only opposition came from organized labor unions, which viewed the U.S. Army's involvement in an unfavorable manner.

Those who enrolled into the Corps received monthly $25 family allotment checks as compensation. For many families in the valley, this greatly increased their standards of living. Rather than waiting for the wool harvest each year, the families were bringing in a monthly income. Coupled with the eldest sons also working, the money brought into the family far exceeded what they would have gotten for wool.

The Corps was tasked with the responsibility of making improvements to millions of acres of federal and state lands. Important infrastructure projects such as roads, schools and telephone lines were built. Millions of trees were planted to help prevent erosion. The project was so successful that the President of the United States wanted to extend the program for another year. Through 1935, many of the camps throughout the nation were updated so that living conditions were greatly improved. Altogether, there were more than 500,000 men enlisted in the 2600 camps throughout the nation.

In an attempt to balance the budget during an election year, the leadership was told that there would be a huge reduction in its enlistment rolls. There was an outcry of protests from many of the nation's citizens and politicians alike. The President wanted to reduce the enlistment rolls to 300,000 men and operate 1,400 camps. With sustained pressure from politicians and their constituents, the President opted not to pursue such an unpopular initiative.

By June of 1942, the Civilian Conservation Corps had seen its best days behind it, and ultimately had succumbed to its fate. Popular support for the organization had significantly dwindled as potential enlistees found better jobs elsewhere. Congress also was wavering in its support of the Corps, and they refused any further funding in a 158 to 151 vote against it.

During the years in which Román had sought work in the CCC, he became a cook for the local camp based out of Cloudcroft. Many of the others from the valley worked on forest projects such as planting trees, building fire roads, and digging acequias. During the fire seasons, many of the men fought the blazes that often raged through the forests.

With so many families becoming dependent on work from the CCC, their ability to remain self-sufficient was put in serious jeopardy. Sheep ranching, which had been the staple industry in the region had succumbed to the devastating effects of both the prolonged drought and the Great Depression. Many families had fallen into debt and had to sell sections of their property. Many other families moved from the valley because they were evicted from their land. Furthermore, the crops had suffered from long-term neglect, and their yields had greatly diminished. Many families throughout the valley were forced out of necessity to seek work in towns and cities far from their homes.

Román and his family were no exception; they lived a seasonally nomadic life, traveling from town to town each year in search of work. Their travels brought them to El Paso, where he had worked in the smelters. In Las Cruces he and his family picked cotton. In Artesia he found work in the refineries as a security guard. In Cloudcroft, he had found employment in the logging industry, skinning the bark off of logs. In Dexter and Hagerman the family had picked cotton.

By the late 1930's several families from the valley had opted to migrate to other states to find work. Most had found jobs as migratory farm workers in Téxas, California, and Colorado, which enabled them to return to the valley after the summer harvesting season. It wasn't until after the declaration of World War II, on September 01, 1939 that many families from the valley had migrated en masse to California and Téxas seeking the jobs that were vacated by those men who had enlisted into the armed forces.

By the end of World War II a significant percentage of the families from the Río Ruidoso, Río Hondo, and Río Bonito valleys continued to migrate to other states, or other cities within New México in search of jobs. Unlike the previous migrations, many of these families opted to remain, and establish new lives, electing to return to the valley only to visit with friends and relatives.

Roman and his family opted to remain in San Patricio during World War II. He and several of the other families that remained in the valley had decided to grow apple orchards as a means of reclaiming their self-sufficiency. Growing the orchards was a time consuming process. It usually took at least five to seven years before the trees even produced enough apples to harvest. About 15 to 20 percent of the saplings would never make it through their second year of growth.

The unpredictable weather cycles made it difficult to maintain consistently productive yields. Sometimes a hard freeze in April could occur after the first blossoms were in bloom. To combat such freezes, many farmers would build several bonfires to heat their orchards. Sometimes they lost control of the fire and it would damage some of the trees or burn part of the orchard.

Violent thunderstorms could produce large hailstones that would further damage the trees. Some years a severe drought coupled with sweltering heat would produce smaller yields. Deer, elk, mice, rabbits, squirrels, and insects would also feed on the leaves, bark, and apples. Fungus and other diseases would further damage or even kill the trees.

The economic benefits of an apple orchard thus weren't immediately realized. It took the orchards about ten years to fully mature into consistent yielding crops. Until the maturation of the orchards, many of the families had to manage their time between tending to their orchards, and finding work for the season. During this process, several other families had opted to move from the valley.

Once abundant yields were being harvested, many of the farmers began selling their apples to independent truckers who would transport the apples from each farm to markets in El Paso, Téxas. In an attempt to create better economies of scale, and efficiency of distribution, all of the farmers formed a co-op. The co-op constructed several warehouses in Hondo where all the farmers brought their apples.

It had been said that some of the apple farmers had inadvertently made alcohol in their attempt to make apple cider. Since the economy was largely based on apples, it was common for the farmers to make the sweet juice. If the apple cider were left in the barrels for an extended period of time, it would ferment. As a result, the apple cider definitely had a strong alcoholic kick to it. There had been some speculation that the apple cider may have intentionally been left in the barrels to ferment, but nobody would have actually admitted any guilt of doing so.

County Commissioner Román Sánchez[3]

On June 04, 1946 Román Sánchez was listed on the Election Proclamation as representing the Republican ticket for District One. He was running against Democratic incumbent Fred McTiegue. The general election was held on November 05, 1946. After all the votes had been tallied, he had beaten Fred McTiegue 1350 votes to 1148 votes. He took his office in January of 1947, in which he would serve a two-year term.

He served his two-year term and announced his intention to run for the County Commissioner's seat again. He ran unopposed, and thus was elected and served another two years on the commission. After four years of public service, he had reached his term-limit. December of 1950 was the last month in which he served his office.

Román took politics very seriously, as did many other people in the valley. It was widely known that on Election Day, some of the valley's biggest fist fights would occur between the supporters of rival candidates. Needless to say, the former commissioner chose not to let his fists do the talking, but rather his words.

He was initially a registered Democrat as a youth, but his loyalties to the party changed when he found employment with the WPA (Works Progress Administration), under Franklin D. Roosevelt's New Deal. Román often referred to it as the "Dirty Deal". At the root of Román's discontentment was the manner in which people were hired at the regional job site. As a registered Democrat, he had no problem finding work. Many of his friends and family, those of which were registered Republicans, were denied employment, unless they opted to change their political affiliation.

Román was incensed that people that were poor and starving were being denied work simply because of their political affiliation. He didn't want to have anything to do with an organization that would let people starve. He opted to quit the job and promptly registered as a Republican in an act of defiant protest.

Struggling Economic Times

Finding continued employment was a difficult proposition in and around southern New México. With the encouragement of his son Ernesto, who was already living in California, he and the family had joined the scores of people from the valley that had migrated there in an attempt to find employment. They lived in Wilmington near the Port of Los Ángeles. He worked at the Port as a security guard.

The hope of long term economic stability was tempered by the realities of the menial, low paying jobs that were in great supply. Life in the city had proved to be a struggle for many large families. Román and his family had seen much of the beauty that was California. The novelty of a foreign land had slowly diminished as the economic hardships continued to arise. Coupled with the desire to be around familiar people and comfortable surroundings, it wasn't long before Román and Florinda became homesick.

By 1956, Román, his wife, and many of his children had decided to return to San Patricio. Although several other families had chosen to remain in the Los Ángeles metropolitan area, the vast majority opted to return to their homes and lands in Lincoln County. Upon their arrival they were greeted by mature apple orchards.

There was great enthusiasm about the orchards, which were starting to produce large harvests. For a brief period of time, the economic impact of the apple industry was allowing many families to be self-sufficient. This prosperous period didn't last very long. By the early 1960's, many of the markets in Téxas had begun contracting with large corporate-style apple orchards, thus putting a debilitating squeeze, on the smaller orchards. The apple economy throughout the valley eventually collapsed.

The late 1960's saw the beginning of another large-scale migration out of the valley, as the baby boom generation sought greater economic opportunities. Their destinations were mostly to other New Mexico cities such as, Albuquerque, Las Cruces, Roswell, and Alamogordo. A few sons and daughters migrated to other states such as California, Téxas, Arizona and Colorado. Unlike the previous migration during the 1940's through the 1950's, many of those who had left the valley had opted not to return. An estimated sixty percent of the baby boom generation had left their ancestral homes.

Of Román and Florinda's ten children, one had migrated to Dallas, Téxas, one had briefly migrated to Denver, Colorado, two had migrated to Roswell, two had migrated to Carrizozo, and four had remained in San Patricio. In an attempt to keep the family together, a yearly reunion was often held at the parent's house, under the large cottonwood trees.

Later in life, Román had suffered from debilitating arthritis. The joints within his hands were so inflamed that his fingers grew crooked. Walking had become so painful for him that he opted to sit in his chair, in his small living room, most of the day. Ironically, he had passed away in an automobile accident just outside of Ruidoso Downs on February 08, 1973.

Florinda had suffered from diabetes, and had to receive insulin injections on a daily basis. One of her sons Orlando, who lived with her, would give her the injections she needed. Her diabetes never discouraged her undying faith in God. She kept the faith by praying the rosary and other oraciónes every day. She would often teach her grandchildren and great grandchildren her favorite prayers.

Florinda had embraced life, and was somewhat fearful of death. One day she was talking to her grandson, Steve Sánchez about her fears of dying. Her young grandson took his grandmother's hand and held it. He looked into her eyes and he said, "We are all living on borrowed time. Life is a blessing bestowed unto us by the Lord. If the Lord shall call upon us to return to his kingdom, we should be honored. Fear not death, for if you have accepted the Lord into your heart and soul, death will lead to eternal life. I have embraced the Lord, and I do not fear death."

Shortly thereafter Steve had tragically died no further than four hundred feet from his parents' house, in an automobile accident, on January 08, 1978. Florinda who had been recently diagnosed with pancreatic cancer passed away three months later, on March 27, 1978. Was it merely a coincidence, or was it God's will? Only the Lord knows the reason behind the conversation, and the tragic turn of events that followed. Family lore says that Stevie would show his grandmother the path to heaven.

José Ernesto Sánchez

Ernesto S. Sánchez, christened José Ernesto Sánchez, was born in San Patricio, New México on April 09, 1928. His parents were Román Sánchez and Florinda Herrera- Salsberry. During Ernesto's childhood and through his adolescence, he chose to stay with his aguelo, James Salsberry, when his parents often left San Patricio to find work in other towns and cities throughout southern New México. Sometimes, he would accompany his parents and siblings where they found work. He would usually stay with them for a couple of weeks and then he would always return to San Patricio so that he could spend time with Papá Jimmy.

A typical day would see the two working the ranchito. Ernesto recalls hearing his abuelo humming the song "Buffalo Gals" as he toiled throughout the day. He also often heard his abuelo whistling any number of spirited tunes if he wasn't singing. After all of the day's chores were completed, the two would cook dinner and prepare for the evening. After dinner, Papá Jimmy would often play songs on a harmonica for his grandson. Sometimes the elder would recall a memory of his youth, of when he was a vaquero, or tell some fantastic story. Together the two would share the evening until they both fell asleep. Sometimes, to help sleep settle in, the youngster would look through a hole at the top of the tent and look at the stars until he fell into a slumber.

Ernesto attended school at a time when the use of Spanish was greatly discouraged by the teacher. Those students that were caught speaking Spanish were often disciplined. Disciplinary action usually was administered by keeping the child indoors, while the rest of the children played during recess. Often times, children would tattle on each other, in an attempt to get one another in trouble with the teacher.

When the children would come home and the family was eating dinner, the parents would discuss the events of the day. The children would contently listen without interrupting the adult's conversation. When the parents were done talking about the day's activities they would ask the children how their day was in school. If one of the children admitted that they were in trouble at school that day, they were most likely going to get disciplined after dinner by papá. Furthermore, the children couldn't lie because it was a good bet their siblings already knew who had been in trouble at school.

When the son or daughter realized they were going to get disciplined they would often cry out, *"Pero no era mi culpa*!" ("But it wasn't my fault!").

Papá would come back with, "I'm sure you didn't get in trouble because you were a santo."

On numerous occasions, Ernesto and his siblings would ask their father if he had ever been spanked as a young boy. Román would look at his children, and a slight smirk would escape the corner of his mouth. Maybe he was remembering his own spankings, maybe he was remembering the other children jumping and screaming as they were being whipped, but he would always respond, *"Eso, no se dice*." ("That is not to be said.")

Ernesto vividly recalls one of his childhood teachers, Señora Pacheco, as telling him that all of the students with Spanish surnames would have to study much harder than their Anglo counterparts. She continued by telling him that an Anglo didn't have to try to work as hard, or try as hard to get a promotion because that was the way in which the world functioned. She told him that he would have to work twice as hard, study twice as much, and still he wouldn't be afforded the same type of respect. In retrospect, he felt that maybe she was trying to motivate him to try harder, than he already was. Whatever the reason, her words inspired him to be the best that he could possibly be.

Many of the citizens throughout the Lincoln County were passionate about their politics. Ernesto often heard his father discussing politics with the other men from around the area. His father was initially registered as a Democrat in his youth but had changed his affiliation to a Republican after experiencing an injustice concerning a program known as the WPA. He often heard his father discussing those injustices and many other political issues, which concerned land, water, and various social programs that were being implemented by the government. He was strongly influenced by his father's passion and convictions thus he felt inclined to join a political youth group known as the Young Republicans.

The Young Republicans was an organization that sought to bring together those adolescents that desired to become active in politics. They promoted the Republican agenda by passing out literature and campaigning for various candidates. They were tasked with discussing the candidates' platforms within the community, recruiting citizens into the Republican Party, and sponsoring fundraising efforts for the candidates.

Ernesto had grown accustomed to working hard since he was a child. He worked several odd jobs in his adolescence. He worked as a farm hand in San Patricio, at a gas station in Ruidoso, and at a bowling alley in Cloudcroft. As was the custom with many of the children of so many families throughout the valley, he helped to support his parents and ultimately the rest of the family by giving them a portion of his wages.

Ernesto first traveled to California in 1947 with Luvín Chávez and Efraín Chávez, his future brother-in-laws and his friend Emiliano Villescas. Luvín and Efraín were already familiar with California because they had previously lived in numerous cities and towns throughout the state. They showed him around and took him to several different places that they thought he would like to visit. Ernesto had taken a liking to the lifestyle that California had to offer. It was the first time he had ever seen the ocean, the lights of the big city, and the faster pace of life.

Upon his return to San Patricio he had started constructing his parents' house next to the highway. He managed to complete the foundation of the house, the exterior frame of the house, the interior framing of the walls, and the part of the flooring. The house wasn't totally completed by the time he and his wife had decided to move to Los Ángeles, California. Román and his other older sons completed the remainder of the house.

On March 20, 1948 Ernesto married Oralia Sánchez Chávez. She was the daughter of Ysidro Chávez and Paublita Sánchez. He recalls that although he was getting married, he didn't have enough money to buy ten loaves of *pan* (bread) from the local grocery store. Instead he had bought the loaves on store credit. After marrying his querida, they lived with her parents for a few months. By December of 1948 they both sought to make a living in Los Ángeles, California.

Life in Los Ángeles was very difficult for the newlyweds. Ernesto found employment primarily doing odd jobs that never provided any steady financial stability. The two eventually moved to Roseville, California where they lived with his tío Augustín Salsberry. He worked in the icehouses, which were built next to the rail yards. The work was grueling, as he continuously lifted heavy blocks of ice into the rail cars. The work was seasonal though, lasting through the fall months.

After their first year in California, Ernesto and Oralia returned to San Patricio by October of 1949 to much fanfare. They had many stories to tell the people, of all of the places where they had been.

They remained in San Patricio through the winter, and returned to Roseville again in January of 1950. At that time, Oralia's brother-in-law, Francisco "Frank" Gómez had accompanied them to California.

On July 08, 1951, Ernesto and Oralia's first son, Ernest Sánchez Jr. was born in Long Beach, California. He was the first grandchild of Román and Florinda's family and as such everybody in the family dotted upon him. On October 29, 1953 their second son James Sánchez was also born in Long Beach, California. The two brothers were showered with attention, being that they were the only two grandchildren in the family for several years. Stephen (Steve) Sánchez and Janice Sánchez were later born in Ruidoso, New Mexico.

Later in the year Ernesto finally found permanent employment in Los Ángeles, working at the North American Aviation manufacturing plant. He continued working at the plant for nine years. While he was working at the plant he also studied to become an insurance agent. Eventually he became a certified insurance agent with the state of California and sold insurance to help supplement his income.

North American Aviation furloughed many of its team members and Ernesto was told that he no longer had a job. He was promised that he would have a position with the company once business picked back up. Selling insurance was proving to be difficult so he began studying to become a real estate agent. By 1959 he and his family had decided to return to San Patricio. North American Aviation had eventually called upon him and offered him his old job but he opted to decline their offer.

Ernest Sanchez Family Bottom Row L-R: Ernest Sanchez, Steven Sanchez, Oralia Sanchez. Baby Janice Sanchez. Top Row L-R: James Sanchez, Ernest Sanchez Jr. (Ernest Sanchez collection)

A 20-Year Career in Law Enforcement

By 1966 Ernesto was being heavily recruited by his brother-in-law, sheriff elect Leandro Vega Jr., to work for the Lincoln County Sheriff's Department. He seized the moment as he left the New México Bureau of Revenue and was hired as the Chief Deputy of Lincoln County for the Ruidoso and Hondo valleys. Leandro was elected to two consecutive, two-year terms, which he served from 1965 to 1968. Ernesto served as his Chief Deputy for the rest of the sheriff's tenure. After Leandro had finished his second term, Ernesto had campaigned to become the new sheriff elect of Lincoln County. He won the sheriff's office and served two consecutive two-year terms from 1969 to 1972.

Ernesto's first tenure as sheriff was difficult to say the least. The county had approved only two deputies to serve under him. He needed at least two more deputies to effectively cover the entire county, which the county commissioners wouldn't approve. He had one jailor who had worked 10 hours a day for seven days a week. He needed at least two more jailers, which the county commissioners wouldn't approve. He had two dispatchers working eight-hour shifts for six days a week. His wife performed the duties as a cook for all of the prisoners. She also washed the inmates' uniforms. Deputies were required to furnish their own service revolvers. Training programs offered by the state government agencies for the support staff was inadequate and couldn't meet the higher standards that were being implemented.

The sheriff was responsible for covering all the other shifts that his team could not cover. Additionally, he was responsible for transporting county prisoners from the jail to their court dates, state prisons, and psychiatric evaluations throughout the state. He and his deputies often had to serve as witnesses on prisoners' court dates. He and his deputies also served as the security for dances and other functions throughout Lincoln County. On Election Day his department was responsible for transporting the election boxes from all the precincts. Even though he was on call 24 hours a day, seven days a week, all year long; he often worked 18 hours a day.

No overtime was paid to any member of the sheriff's department regardless of the amount of hours worked in a given week. The average salary for a Lincoln County deputy was $325 per month. The wage rate was not a major concern however, because the officers that worked in the sheriff's department considered it an honor to serve in the capacity of a lawman. Furthermore, there was a higher degree of political and social status that was attached to working in the department. Those core values enabled the department to maintain a high level of morale even though there were many hardships that all the members faced on an everyday basis.

Sheriff Sánchez was highly respected by the other local law jurisdictions. He often depended on them to help keep order throughout Lincoln County. At the time, Carrizozo had one officer, Ruidoso had three officers, and Ruidoso Downs had one officer. The State Police also were called upon on numerous occasions. All of the local jurisdictions were more than willing to assist the sheriff and his deputies when they were needed.

After Ernesto served his two consecutive two-year terms as Lincoln County Sheriff, Leandro Vega Jr. was re-elected to the sheriff's office for another two terms from 1973 to 1976. Sheriff Vega again appointed Ernesto as his Chief Deputy Sheriff for both of his terms in office.

On February 01, 1975 County Commissioner William A. Hart (Ruidoso) and County Commission Chairman Román C. Núñez (Picacho) had formally took action to reject the issuance of bond to Chief Deputy Sánchez, thus ordering Sheriff Vega to dismiss him from the Lincoln County Sheriff's Department. The sole County Commissioner that objected to the motion was Bud Payne (Carrizozo) who was overruled. The premise behind the motion was based on Section 5-1-10 N.M.S.A (1953); which prohibited nepotism unless it was first approved by the officer, the board, the council or the commission whose duty it was to approve the bond.

It was Commissioner Payne's contention that Chief Deputy Sánchez was neither endorsed nor his bond approved by the two said commissioners primarily because he belonged to the Republican Party, whereas both Commissioners Hart and Núñez were Democrats. Commissioner Payne further supported Chief Deputy Sánchez by claiming that his experience and rapport with the citizens throughout the Ruidoso and Hondo valleys was invaluable and would be difficult to replace.

Sheriff Vega appeared before the commission stating that he wasn't consulted on the matter and that he hadn't known of their intentions until the day of the formal proceedings, which took place on February 1st. He was first approached about the matter when the County Manager informed him that Chief Deputy Sánchez would have to be dismissed from his duties per the action taken by the County Commission. Sheriff Vega continued by calling into question why he was never consulted even though the Commission had been deliberating the issue since January 02, 1975. He claimed that during his previous terms as sheriff, the Commission didn't have any objections concerning the appointment of his brother-in-law as the Chief Deputy Sheriff. He continued by giving several examples of nepotism, which didn't result in dismissal, for other jurisdictions throughout New México. He further concluded that the whole issue was one of politics and not based on merit nor job performance.[4]

Former Lincoln County Sheriffs Ernesto Sánchez and Leandro Vega Jr. (circa, 1968) Ernesto is accepting the responsibility of Chief Deputy Sheriff from Sheriff Leandro Vega Jr. (Ernest Sanchez collection)

On February 05, 1975 the Twelfth Judicial District Judge, George Zimmerman, had issued an order retroactive to January 01, 1975, that Sheriff Vega was able to hire his brother-in-law, as his Chief Deputy Sheriff. District Judge Zimmerman further commented that he had conferred with the District Attorney and had learned that he had the authority to approve the sheriff's bonds, and with that authority he reinstated Chief Deputy Sánchez, claiming that he was well qualified and a good lawman.

Chief Deputy Sánchez continued to serve under the new Sheriff-elect, Bill Elliot for almost one year through 1977.

The sheriff had already established an impressive law enforcement résumé since 1966. He was recognized for his tireless efforts on December 01, 1980 by being selected to serve as one of 31 New Mexico law enforcement representatives for a delegation to China under the People-to-People program. The People-to-People program was first implemented in 1956 by President Dwight D. Eisenhower and was intended to foster a better understanding between the people of the United States and the people of other nations.[5]

The delegation was set to leave on April 29, 1981 and return on May 13, 1981. They would be visiting and discussing all phases of their respective professions with their counterparts in Peking

(Beijing), Canton, Shanghai, and Tientsin. They would also spend two nights in Hong Kong, and one night in Tokyo, Japan. All of the delegates were responsible for paying their own way on the trip. The all-inclusive cost of the trip was $3,297. Unfortunately Sheriff Sánchez had to decline the offer because, had he left, Lincoln County would have been left without adequate law enforcement coverage. It was a decision that he never regretted because he felt his first duty was to the people of his county.

He was selected to serve on the Drug Education Advisory Committee for New México's State Board of Education. He helped organize and implement the Lincoln County Search and Rescue. He was a member of the New México Sheriffs' and Police Association. He continued the modernization of the Lincoln County Sheriff's Department, a project that was initially championed by Leandro Vega Jr. He was successful in gaining the approval for Lincoln County's ability to house federal prisoners. He was a member of the local chapter of the Salvation Army. He served as a board member for the Southeastern New México Economic Development District. He also served as Chief of Police for the city of Tularosa, New Mexico from 1983 through 1987.

His impressive record as a lawman did not go unnoticed as he was often invited for social functions amongst many of the politicos in Santa Fé and elsewhere throughout the state. It was an honor befitting a man of his caliber, but he was a modest man who didn't want all of the attention. Rather he took pride in upholding the law.

Deputy Thomas Bedford Jr.[6]

Deputy Thomas Bedford Jr., age 30, was an ambitious man who had dedicated most of his adult life to law enforcement. He had previously served with the Cháves County Sheriff's Department for one and a half years, and the Ruidoso Police Department, before he accepted a position as a deputy of the Lincoln County Sheriff's Department. He had been with the department for three months. He had a great deal of respect for the responsibilities that came with the job as a deputy sheriff. He was a loving husband and the proud father of two young children. He had moved his family to the quaint town of Capitán. Life seemed to be progressing perfectly for the deputy.

On October 08, 1979 Deputy Thomas Bedford Jr. was responding to a dispatched call concerning several burglaries near Nogal Canyon. En route he came across two individuals who were walking alongside the road. One of the individuals was a juvenile; the other was a much older man. The elder man was carrying a small camping bedroll under his arm, which had a concealed rifle. As the deputy approached the two suspicious individuals, he noticed that they matched the APB descriptions of two men suspected of auto theft in Albuquerque and other thefts involving several weapons in the Estancia area. He diligently radioed the dispatcher stating that he had come across two hitchhikers, and thought they were possibly armed, and needed immediate backup.

Two other deputies answered the call. While en route, one of them had car trouble, in which a tire blew out. The second had come across the first, picked him up and they both promptly went to their comrade's aid. During that time of tragic circumstances, which delayed his backup, Bedford was mercilessly gunned-down by the elder, Robert Cox. The young deputy was shot five times with mortal wounds to his face, throat, chest, and one of his hands. About a half an hour after his initial call for backup, the two deputies finally came upon him. The scene was a grisly one, in which Deputy Bedford was bleeding out.

Word of Bedford's murder quickly spread throughout Lincoln County, and the surrounding region. A massive manhunt was organized to find the two fugitives. More than 200 search and rescue volunteers and local law enforcement officers canvassed the region. On Tuesday, October 09, 1979, the 16-year-old accomplice to the murder was apprehended as he surrendered himself to the local authorities at the Nogal picnic area. By Thursday, October 11th the District Judge had filed charges against the juvenile of aiding and abetting Robert Cox.

The adolescent, who had escaped from the Boys' School in Springer, New México, gave an account that he had met Cox several days prior in Albuquerque. He gave a detailed account about the auto theft in Albuquerque. He indicated that after Deputy Bedford's murder, the two had immediately gone their separate ways. He continued, fearing that he would be sought out and eventually killed. The youngster claimed that the elder fugitive had several weapons, which included a .35 caliber semi-automatic rifle, two .22 caliber rifles, and a .22 caliber pistol.

In a proactive measure to safeguard the case, Sheriff Sánchez had the juvenile transported and detained in the Alamogordo City Jail. He cited that with the sensitivity of the case, he did not want to take the chance that the adolescent could convince a jury that a Lincoln County officer had abused or mistreated him.

The search for the remaining fugitive was suspended on Thursday, October 11th. Sheriff Sánchez assured the public that although the manhunt was called off, his officers, as well as the state police would still patrol the area in search of the killer, whom he thought was still in the area. The sheriff asked that any citizen witnessing any suspicious individual, or activity should report it to the Sheriff's Department.

Robert Cox was a habitual felon who had served time in the state prison system and was also housed in the minimum-security facility at Camp Sierra Blanca near Fort Stanton. In 1976 he was temporarily housed in the Lincoln County jail for violating protocol at the camp. Other previous convictions included larceny, fraud, and unlawful entry. He had received paramilitary training and was an accomplished survivalist. He was familiar with the region being that he worked in Capitán, and also served as a guide in the area. Sheriff Sánchez had fully expected that the fugitive may elude capture for several more days.

On Friday, October 12, 1979 three officers who were investigating a tip given by a citizen in the town of Corona, apprehended the killer without incident. The three officers found him walking alongside a dirt road. On his person he had a pistol and a hunting knife. Cox thought better of dueling it out with the three officers and gave himself up without resistance.

The three officers disarmed their captive, taking his weapons and unwittingly placed them in a hat. Upon arriving at the Lincoln County jail, as the officers were transporting their prisoner from the car to a jail cell, the hat accidentally fell upon the ground. The force generated by hitting the ground caused the pistol to discharge. The bullet hit Deputy Donn Dose in the left leg. Fearing that Cox had somehow fired upon him with a concealed weapon, Deputy Dose spun around, braced himself and returned fire. He shot three rounds from his .44-caliber Magnum. Two rounds found their mark, hitting Cox in the leg and the hip. Both men were promptly transported to the Alamogordo Hospital.

Cox was eventually sentenced to life in prison. He was eligible for parole after ten years. Thomas Bedford's mother-in-law championed several campaigns to prevent her son's killer from being released on parole. After her death, Bedford's son, Michael championed the campaign against his father's murderer.[7]

Lincoln County Sheriffs 1869-2008

Jesús Sandoval y Sena	1869-1869	Porfirio Chávez	1913-1916
Mauricio de la Tri. Sánchez	1869-1869	C. Walker Hyde	1917-1918
William Brady	1870-1871	R. A. Durán	1919-1920
L.G. Gylam	1872-1873	Ed W. Harris	1921-1924
Alexander Mills	1874-1875	S. W. Kelsey	1925-1928
Saturnino Baca	1875-1876	J. E. Brady	1929-1932
William Brady	1877-1878	A.S. McCamant	1933-1936
John S. Copeland	1878-1878	S. E. Greisen	1937-1940
George Peppin	1878-1878	A.L. Stover	1941-1944
George Kimbrell	1879-1880	Nick S. Vega	1945-1948
Pat Garrett	1881-1882	S. M. Ortiz	1949-1952
John Poe	1883-1886	William Glen Bradley	1953-1956
James R. Brent	1887-1888	S. M. Ortiz	1957-1960
O.C. Nowlin	1889-1890	William Glen Bradley	1961-1964
D. W. Roberts	1891-1892	Leandro Vega Jr.	1965-1968
George Curry	1893-1894	Ernesto Sánchez	1969-1972
George Sena	1895-1896	Leandro Vega Jr.	1973-1976
Emil Fritz	1896-1896	Bill Elliot	1977-1978
Emil Lutz	1897-1898	Ernesto Sánchez	1979-1982
Demetrio Perea	1899-1900	Tom Sullivan	1983-1986
Alfredo Gonzáles	1901-1902	Don W. Samuels	1987-1988
R. D. Armstrong	1903-1904	James C. McSwane	1989-1996
John W. Owen	1905-1908	Tom Sullivan	1997-2004
C. A. Stevens	1909-1912	Ricky Virden	2005-2008

Chapter Thirteen: Los Chávez

Jesús Cháves

Jesús Cháves, christened Ygnacio de Jesús Cháves, was born on August 02, 1833 in Valencia, Nuevo México, La República de México. His parents were Manuel Antonio de los Reyes Cháves and María Nicolasa Rafaela Montoya. His parents migrated from the Valencia region to the Tajiqué region sometime in the early 1840's. His family moved near two other recently arrived families, those being of Vicente Luna and José María Aragón. These three families would remain inter-connected for several decades to come.

On January 20, 1854 he had married María Paula Aragón in Tomé, Territory of New México. They had two children, a daughter named Teofila and a son named Feliciano. After his first wife had died he married a second time. On August 08, 1860 he had married María Paula's sister, Nicolasa Aragón in Tomé, Territory of New México.

By 1860 Jesús was living on his own in a house that was adjacent to his mother's house. His father had since passed away and he was working with two other brothers to make ends meet. They all worked as farm laborers and between the three of them, they were able to provide for the entire family.

Roberto Cháves was born in about 1862 near Chililí, Territory of New México. His parents were Jesús Cháves and Nicolasa Aragón. He never knew his father because he died when he was very young. It is believed that his father had died sometime around 1863. His older sister, Teofila may have also died, was raised by another family or may have married into another family. By the 1870 US Census neither of them is mentioned by name. Jesús would have been in his mid-30s while Teofila would have been in her early teens.

Roberto was living with his stepfather Jesús Luna and his mother. His older brother Feliciano was living with their aguelita, Dolóres Aragón. By 1880 the family had migrated to Valencia, Territory of New México. Sometime in the mid 1880's the family had finally settled in the Río Ruidoso Valley. Roberto had married Lucía Weldon in Ruidoso, Territory of New México on February 11, 1888. She was the daughter of James Weldon and Angelita Sánches. They had three children, Angelita, Ysidro, and Manfor.

Ysidro Chávez & Paublita Sánchez

Ysidro Chávez[1]

Ysidro Chávez was born on April 13, 1892 in Ruidoso, Territory of New México. His parents were Roberto Cháves and Lucía Weldon. His father had settled on the banks of the Río Ruidoso in Las Angosturas before La Capilla de San Ysidro was constructed. He married Senaida Sánchez in Ruidoso, Territory of New México on April 29, 1909. They were both very young, he was 17 years old and she was about 14 years of age. The marriage did not last long and they were soon divorced. Senaida later married John Samora Mackey on February 01, 1912.

Ysidro's father had lived next to Felipé Sánchez and he had a very young, beautiful daughter named Paublita. As she was growing into a young woman, she had caught Ysidro's eye. It was often said that the two youngsters would steal a kiss, or go on long walks along the river at night. On August 04, 1913 Ysidro had married Paublita Sánchez in La Capilla de San Juan Bautista, in Lincoln. She had just turned 15 years old when she married her husband. Her father had to give his consent for her to marry at such a young age.[2] One of the conditions of their marriage was that Ysidro had to provide a doll for the new bride because she still enjoyed dolls. Paublita had to grow up really quick though because nine months after her marriage, she gave birth to her first daughter, Greselda (Grace) on May 13, 1914. In all, Ysidro and Paublita had sixteen children, two of which died when they were infants. They also raised two of Paublita's *sobrinos* (a nephew and a niece), who were the children of her brother Antonio Sánchez.

Ysidro had made a living, raising goats and sheep up in the hills where he had a homestead near Pajarito, which was about two miles southwest of San Patricio. In his youth, he helped raise his father's 400 head of goats, which he eventually inherited upon Roberto's death. The patriarch, his wife, and his oldest children had built a *campito* (camp) complete with a *cuartito* (little shack) and corrales on a small llano, where they would tend to their flocks. During the winter, spring, and fall one of the parents would return to La Aguilita with their three children Greselda, Amarante (Jack), and Senon so that they could attend school, while the other parent remained up in the campito to tend to the sheep.

Paublita, still in her adolescence, often had to spend the winter months up at the campito, alone. There were many nights that she would huddle amongst the sheep to keep warm as she tried to sleep. She had to remain diligent though, because she and her flock were always under the constant danger from predatory mountain lions, bears, packs of wild dogs, or even wolves. Occasionally she would be blessed with the company of her children and her husband over the weekend. She often told her children that during those days, she felt more secure amongst the sheep, rather than in the cuartito.

The Chávez, like many other families in the valley were self-sufficient because there were no markets in the immediate area. Many different crops would be planted on one's farm. Whether it would be vegetables, wheat, fruit trees, or hay, all of the families planted similar types of crops. As recently as the 1920's many of the people from the valley would load their wheat onto wagons, or a motorized truck (if they had one), and would travel to Ruidoso so their wheat could be ground into flour at the mill.

Ysidro had a truck, but he seldom used it because he couldn't get the truck up the side of large hills. Sometimes his children would have to jump out of the truck and push the truck to the top of the hill and then they would quickly jump back in until they came upon the next hill. For many families in the valley, there were no realized benefits of having a motorized vehicle except on long trips to Roswell. Thus, many people still preferred to ride horses as a means of everyday transportation.

Each day after school, the children would come home and immediately start their daily chores. Some would help mamá make dinner. Others would help in the garden, weeding, watering, or picking vegetables and fruit. The most important chore though was tending to the goats. During the day the goats would often venture into the mountains to graze, but they always came down from the mountains in the late afternoon to drink. Sometimes, if the goats hadn't come down by a certain time, the eldest children were tasked with herding them back down the mountain.

The baby goats were housed in a large corral until they had matured enough to graze up in the hills. Each kid had a wooden plaque inscribed with a number attached to its neck, which corresponded to a number painted in red upon the *pansa* (belly) of its mother. The children would have to herd the billies into chutes so that they could be paired with their mothers. After doing so, the babies would suckle their mother's milk.

After several years, Ysidro had come to the realization that it was more profitable to ranch sheep, rather than goats. He sold most of his goats and focused his energies on sheep. The children were still tasked with matching the mothers with the babies. His eldest sons, those who were still living at the home, often found it more convenient to live up at the campito. Senon, Emiliano, and Efraín, often would spend their summers up in the hills tending to their flock.

Every March, Ysidro and his family would gather his 500 head of sheep at the corral, and they would shear the sheep of their wool. After removing the wool, the sheep would be immersed in a water-based solution that would rid the animal of parasites such as fleas and ticks. The wool would be placed in large gunnysacks, and loaded onto wagons.

Once the wagons were loaded, Ysidro and his oldest sons would make a trip to Roswell to sell their wool. The trip took about three days in total. During the evenings, they would set up camp with some of the other sheep ranchers they came across along the way. Once they arrived to market, they would unload their cargo and an inventory would be taken. Once the price was set, the family would return to San Patricio and they would wait until their lot was sold. The merchandise would usually be purchased within three weeks of being brought to market. Once the wool was bought, an employee from the market was dispatched to inform the respective sheep ranchers from the area to come and pick up their money.

Often times, the wool harvest was the sole source of income for many families. That only accentuated the importance of growing one's flock through birthing, and ensuring that the flocks were well protected from predators. A loss of just a few sheep would seriously compromise the ability to make it through the year. As was often the case, the welfare of the family was placed in the able hands of the children.

Spring was always a very busy time of the year. After sheering the sheep, the money would be used to purchase shoes and clothing for the family, seed for the crops, and the payment of debts to the general mercantile. Large fifty-pound flour sacks were purchased for the purpose of making tortillas, and biscuits.

Paublita would always make it a point of purchasing an ample supply of bulk cloth so that she could fashion clothes for her family. She would spend the entire spring measuring her children and making two sets of clothes for each. The children seldom wore their shoes around the house because they had already known that they would only get one pair for the entire year. They saved their shoes for school, church, and bailes. Shoes, in essence were the most important belongings a child had, besides their clothing.

The entire family would ready the land for planting the seeds for the coming year's harvest. The ground would be tilled using a plow pulled by a horse. The process was very slow and very tedious because sometimes the horse didn't want to cooperate. One could always hear the men screaming at their horses and cursing the rocks that were strewn about the ground. Sometimes tilling the ground took an entire month or more to finish.

The acequias had to be cleaned out on an annual basis. Weeds, leaves, mud and rock that had accumulated over the past year had to be removed for a better water flow. The banks of the ditch had to be refortified if any weaknesses were discovered. After the cleanup, the acequias would be tested. High spots and depressions upon the land were usually discovered with the first watering. It was a good barometer for leveling out the land for the greatest irrigation efficiency.

The crops were planted after the tilling, and cleaning of the acequias. The main staples were *maíz* (corn), chile, cabbage, *frijoles* (beans), *calabazas* (squash), *zanahorias* (carrots), and *papas* (potatoes).

The family tended to the gardens on a daily basis; irrigating, weeding, and picking the vegetables so that they can be canned.

The canning process was tedious and time consuming. The goal for Paublita and her daughters was to can 1,000 jars for the coming year. The jars came in quart and gallon sizes. The vegetables, fruit, and even meat would be placed into the jars. After the jars were filled, a two-piece lid would be placed on top. First the round lid plate would be fitted in place and then the cover that screwed onto the jar would be set in place. The jars would be placed in a pressure cooker with boiling water for about 45 minutes. The heat created a vacuum that would seal the jar tightly shut. The jars would then be placed in a *soterano* (cellar) which could usually be found near the house, or an unused chosa. This kept the canned foods a little cooler during the late summers.

Many people in the valley often built a *cisterna* (cistern) to collect water. It was usually built to a depth of about 10 to 15 feet. After the hole was dug, its walls, floor and ceiling would be covered with cement and rocks, to protect the water from the hot rays of the sun. A single hole in the ceiling was left open to allow for the collection of water and so that the water could be retrieved when needed. The water would stay cold for most of the year. Since there were no electricity or ice boxes, many people would fill buckets with crème or butter and lower it into the cisterna, thus keeping it cool and edible for a longer period of time.

Paublita Sánchez de Chávez[3]

Paublita had lived a very hard and demanding life, yet she never allowed that to damper her love of it. She was a very jolly woman who could often be heard whistling, or singing canticos as she diligently worked each day. She was a petite yet a very strong woman who had naturally wavy black hair, and rosy cheeks.

She was an exceptional cook who had made some of the best biscuits and *arroz dulce* (sweet rice pudding) in the valley. She was also very fond of baking pies, sometimes making half a dozen at a time. When one passed la casa de Chávez, they could smell the sweet aroma of her delicious pies. She would often take her pies over to her comadres' houses and give them a pie as they talked amongst each other, sometimes for hours. Her comadres in turn would give her something they had baked thus she never came back home empty handed.

Christmas was the biggest holiday of the season and one could see Paublita, and many other women, making bags of goodies for all of the children. It was a widespread custom for all of the children of the valley to go from house to house and wish its occupants "*feliz navidad*" (merry Christmas). The children would then sing a song and be rewarded with a bag of goodies.

Las Posadas was also a very large event, in which the annual pageant would be held to much fanfare. The re-enactment of Christ's birth would be followed by a procession to the church. Positioned around the church were *luminarias*, which were large piles of sticks that were set afire. The procession would encircle the church, as people sang canticos, and recited prayers.

Paublita, like many of the other New Mexican women in the valley, was a very resourceful woman when it came to utilizing all that was at her disposal. She often made her children's under garments from the flour sacks. Sometimes, if the girls were lucky, their parents would buy the brand Harina de Flor, which had pretty little flowers imprinted on the sack. The boys on the other hand didn't want flowers on their under garments.

Paublita would gather black walnuts from the river and bring them back to the house. She would place all that she had gathered into heated water, until the water turned jet black. After the water cooled down, she would take a toothbrush, dip it in the water, and apply the black liquid to her hair. The water solution acted like a dye, which kept her from having grey hair.

To color her lips, she would crush berries into a juice. She would place the juice into a bottle and sip from it periodically to redden her lips. Sometimes you could see her gathering different colors of dirt, which she would crush into a very fine powder. She used the fine powder to give her face more color. To curl her hair, she used strips of a tin can, wrapped in paper. She would wrap the tin in her hair, and fold the ends to keep the strips in place.

She always mixed a bowl of honey with powdered sulfate. She used this concoction to place on her face, which function was similar to that of a facial mask. In doing so, her complexion was always kept clear. Like her mother before her, Paublita taught these same beauty secrets to her own daughters.

To ward off sickness during the winter, she would take each of her children to the acequia, break the ice from the top, and would gather the cold water and place it upon the back of the necks of her children. Her children hated having to go through such an ordeal, but they were subjected to it on a weekly basis. Whether there were any true benefits from doing so is a matter of debate but the children seldom became sick.

Paublita washed clothes once a week, using the water from either the cisterna or from the acequia. After cleaning the clothes she would hang them out to dry. After the clothes had dried, she used a *plancha* (steel iron) made of solid cast-iron to straighten out the creases. She would place the plancha onto a wood stove until it was hot enough to use.

Angelita Sánchez de Montes

Angelita Sánchez was born in Mesilla, Territory of New México in about 1858. Her parents were Santiago Sánches and Mariana Perea. While she was still an infant, her parents had taken her north to Tomé, where she was baptized. By 1860 the family had migrated to Torreón where they lived for several years. By 1869 they had passed through La Plaza de San José before settling on the Río Ruidoso. By 1880 the family was living in Tularoso.

At about 15 years of age her parents had arranged for her to be married to an Englishman named James Weldon. She had one known child with her husband, who she named Lucía. Shortly after her daughter's birth, her husband mysteriously disappeared without a trace. Angelita had speculated that he might have died during an altercation.

It wasn't until several months later that she discovered he was living in Lincoln. She was notified by the county assessor that he was attempting to sell his business and that he needed her approval before he could complete the transaction. As such, after signing the document, he left and was never heard from again.

Soon thereafter, she married Alejo Montes in Lincoln County on August 15, 1881. He had come from a family recently arrived from La República de México. His parents were Bacilio Montes and Jesúsita Ronquillo. Together they had nine children, six sons and three daughters. Of her nine children three of them had died when they were very young.

Angelita was a very petite woman, who stood slightly over 4' tall. Although she was small in stature, she had a gruff voice. If one didn't know her, they would have to do a double take because it was hard to believe that a voice like hers would come from somebody so small. She had beautiful blue eyes that could just melt a person's heart. She always wore a *gorro* (hat without a visor), with ruffles that hung from the brow.

Her bed was made of several mattresses stacked one on top of another. When she went to bed at night she often had to use the height of a box to get into it. Once she was in bed she would say her prayers. She always prayed for all of the men who were in the military and fighting a war. Sometimes she cried because she wanted everybody to be safe from harm. She had already lost two great grandchildren, Oziel Chávez and Aveslín Chávez, to the war.

Angelita had contracted a severe case of the influenza, which had robbed her of her sight. Although she became blind, she never allowed this tragedy to affect her good nature, or her ability to interact with her environment. She had adjusted well to compensate for her disability by using strings as a means of guiding her around the house. She also remained an accomplished cook and still did simple chores such as washing clothes, and cleaning around the house.

Having lost the gift of sight, her first husband and three of her children and several great grandchildren, she found solace in the humor life had to offer her, rather than dwelling on the negativity. She adored her great-grandson Luvín, and her great-granddaughter Oralia. Every time they came over to visit her, she would open up a trunk, pull out a trinket and give it to them as a keepsake. Many times, as Luvín and Oralia returned home, they would take the keepsakes and bury them, as if they were treasure.

Although Angelita had lost the blessing of sight, she was blessed with good health, which enabled her to live to be about 104 years old. In her old age, she had no regrets, and wouldn't have changed anything. Even at that age she still was blessed with purity of thought and could still talk vividly about her youth.

Life during and after the Great Depression

Back row from left to right: Adela, Inez, Ysidro, Paublita, Senon, Greselda, Amarante. –Front row from left to right: Efraín, Onfré, Luvín, Melvin, Danny, Oralia, Ramona, Josie. (Courtesy of the Chavez family)

Initially with the onset of the Great Depression during the 1930's, many of the families from the valley weren't so adversely affected as those who had lived in the cities, or towns. One of the reasons that many didn't see a dramatic decrease in their living standards was because most families were self-sufficient, and they were living in severe poverty to begin with.

Their major source of income, the wool industry, however was affected by the great depression. To make ends meet, many of the New Mexican families from the valleys were faced with an unusual dilemma. They had to choose between trying to ride the great depression out, or they had to find a source of income outside the comforts of the valley. Eventually for many families, finding adequate jobs had become a necessity because they were purchasing most of their seeds, and other goods on credit from the general store. Often times, their land became the collateral, which was used to pay their debts. Many New Mexican families lost many acres of land in such a manner.

Los Chávez, like so many other families focused their energies on migrating to where the jobs where. In towns such as Hagerman and Dexter Ysidro, Paublita and their oldest children worked in the fields picking cotton. One of their daughters, Oralia who was nine years old at the time, was charged with the care of her younger siblings. Senon and Emiliano would stay behind in San Patricio and tend to the sheep.

The family was housed in a quaint residence that was provided by the farmer. Oralia remembers watching her mother come into the house after working in the fields all day and started to prepare dinner for her large family. Paublita always seemed so exhausted, but she never complained, and she whistled and sang as she made dinner. She would smile and thank those of her children who offered to help.

One day, Oralia took the initiative and grabbed the necessary ingredients to make tortillas and took them to her **Madrina** (Godmother), Senaida Montoya de Sánchez's residence, which was nearby. She asked her Madrina if she could teach her how to make the **masa** (dough) for tortillas. After making the masa she quickly headed back home and made about three-dozen tortillas for her mother, father, brothers, and sisters. When her mother walked through the door, she could smell the aroma of freshly prepared tortillas.

Paublita held her young daughter in her arms, giving her kisses and thanking her for making the tortillas. The matriarch was able to relax a little that day and many other days thereafter. From that day on, Oralia continued to help her mother prepare tortillas. In time, she would learn to become a very accomplished cook and baker just like her mother.

After the summer harvesting season was over, many of the families from the valley would return to their homes for the fall, winter and spring. The children would return to school while the parents would continue working on their farms. Life would return to normal until the next summer.

Oralia had memories of a particular rooster that would attack her every day after coming home from school. In one such incident, the bird had attacked her so viciously that it cut her on her arms and legs. Her older brother Luvín, seeing what had happened to his sister had approached her and told her that one day he was going to kill that rooster. He then picked up a rock and threw it at the bird and hit it on the head. It squawked as it fluttered its feathers, jumping about in the air before falling over dead. The two children ran over to the dead rooster and looked at it for a while. Luvín looked at Oralia in great surprise, and commented, "Mamá is going to kill us if she finds out I killed her rooster." Thus he picked up the rooster and leaned it against the base of the tree.

Throughout the afternoon and evening, Paublita would look out the window from time to time and she had noticed that the rooster didn't move from under the tree. Luvín and Oralia, feeling guilty, and fearful that their mother would soon discover their misdeeds, quietly kept their distance. Later in the evening, they heard their mother say, "There is something wrong with my rooster, it hasn't moved from that spot the entire afternoon." Their mother soon went out to investigate the matter and discovered that her rooster was dead. Then the children heard her cursing, "What happened to my rooster!"

The late 1930's had seen many of the eldest Chávez children opt to find jobs in the growing cities of southern California. Amarante was one of the first to venture to Los Ángeles, where he found work in the shipping docks near San Pedro. Soon thereafter, in the early 1940's, many other families from Lincoln County had migrated to California in search of work. Like Amarante, many of the people had found jobs working in the shipping yards, the aircraft manufacturing plants, or the refineries.

Many of the families chose to live in Wilmington, Long Beach, and Torrance, which was directly north of the shipping yards. Here they were exposed to an entirely different way of life. English was the predominant language, and now the New Mexican families were in the minority. The children attended large schools with hundreds of students. Culture shock had set in for many New Mexicans, and it took a long time to adjust to the new way of life. Ysidro, Paublita, and many of their children, longed to return to New México. This sentiment was reflective of many other New Mexican families that found it difficult to adjust to the lifestyle, and culture of California.

During the summer, many of the New Mexican families had opted to work in the fruit and vegetable fields north in the San Joaquín Valley region. The families could make more money picking produce because the younger children could help out, whereas in the cities, they were too young to work and had to attend school.

One of Oralia's memories concerning her father Ysidro was that he always used to get after his children for picking green tomatoes. As it turned out, he was as guilty as some of his children because he was colorblind. This fact wasn't discovered until later in life. Maybe he had known about it all along, but he wasn't going to admit to it because it was easier to blame his children.

The work in the fields was migratory, and often times they would travel from farm to farm. The living conditions were often deplorable. Substandard housing was often the rule rather than the exception, by today's standards. Many of the New Mexicans didn't complain though, because it really wasn't much different from their homes back in Lincoln County. After the summer growing season, many of the families would return to Los Ángeles to work. Thus the cycle of migratory work had continued for several years before many of the New Mexican families had finally returned back to Lincoln County.

Chapter Fourteen: The Patriots

The Civil War

When the United States first came to power over those lands, which had originally belonged to España, and later La República de México, there was a question of whether the "Mexicans" would have any allegiance for their new country. This assumption would be overwhelmingly debunked as the U.S. Territorial Governor; Henry Connelly called upon New Mexicans to defend their lands from the Confederate Army on September 09, 1861. More than 4,000 New Mexican volunteers, most of whom only spoke Spanish, answered the call to duty.

The majority of the New Mexican volunteers were ill equipped for battle. They were provided with substandard, and often times, outdated weaponry. They were not afforded the proper military training. Many of the volunteers were subjected to prejudice and discrimination by many of their American counterparts. Through all of the adversity, American military officers such as Colonel Christopher "Kit" Carson held the New Mexican volunteers in high esteem. He had proclaimed that the "Mexican" troops were some of the best soldiers during battle.

The strategic importance of the Territory of New Mexico to both the Confederates and the Union often is overlooked because the two decisive battles that were fought paled in comparison to those battles fought in other parts of the country. At stake was the Confederates ability to mobilize its forces in the expansive American Southwest. Had the Confederates been able to take the American Southwest, one can only imagine what might have happened.

The Battle of Valverde[1]

The first significant battle to take place in the Territory of New Mexico was waged about 30 miles south of Socorro. Five regiments of New Mexico volunteers were dispatched to Fort Craig to stop the advancement of Confederate troops from Fort Fillmore, which was just south of Las Cruces. On February 21, 1862 both the Confederate Army, led by Brigadier General Henry H. Silby, and the Union Army, led by Colonel Edward R.S. Canby, had waged battle against one another in Valverde. The Confederate's goal was to cut off Federal communications between Fort Craig and the Union Army's military HQ in Santa Fé.

Under Brig. General Henry H. Silby's command were 2,500 troops. Colonel Edward R.S. Canby commanded 3,000 troops. The Confederate Army was strategically positioned and had stopped the Union Army's advancement. During battle the Union Army suffered 202 casualties while the Confederate Army suffered 187 casualties. More importantly the Confederate Army was able to capture six artillery canons during a strong frontal charge. In doing so, the Union Army was ordered to retreat, giving the Confederate Army a strategic victory.

After losing the battle the Union Army was forced to retreat. The Confederate Army continued to march northward, arriving in Alburquerque on March 02, 1862. By March 13th the Confederate Army had arrived in Santa Fé. While the Confederates were marching northward toward Fort Union, the Union Army's 1st Colorado Regiment was marching southward from Denver.

The Battle of Glorieta Pass[2]

In March of 1862 two to three hundred Confederate Army troops, led by Major Charles L. Pyron, had encamped at the mouth of Cañoncito de los Apachés just east of Santa Fé. On March 26th four hundred troops of the Union Army, led by Major John M. Chivington, had descended upon their Confederate enemies from atop Rowe Mesa.

The Union Army had defeated the Confederate Army at Cañoncito and continued the battle further east as they discovered a stronger force further in the cañon. Here they were met with a flurry of artillery fire and were forced back. After regrouping, Major Chivington flanked the Confederates on either side, hitting them with relentless cross-fire. This forced Major Pyron and his men to refortify their defensive positions. Again Major Chivington's troops had flanked the Confederates on either side forcing them to retreat again. While in retreat, the Union Army was able to capture the Confederate's rearguard.

The next day saw no fighting as both sides waited for further reinforcements. The Confederates claimed 1,100 troops after reinforcements while the Union gained 900 more troops. On March 28th both sides went into battle again. The Confederates held their positions with a barrage of attacks and counterattacks, which lasted throughout the day. The Union Army was repeatedly held at bay and they eventually retreated to the east of the cañon at Kozlowski's Ranch.

During the battle Major Chivington and his troops were able to destroy the 80-wagon supply train at Johnson's Ranch, which consisted of ammunitions, food, and clothing. With no supplies, the Confederate Army was forced to retreat. By May 01, 1862 the Confederates had abandoned their New México campaign. During the Battle of Glorieta Pass there were 142 Union casualties and 189 Confederate casualties.

The Civil War and its effects on the Sierra Blanca Region

The Civil war had a profound effect on the citizens of the Río Bonito, Rio Ruidoso, and Río Hondo valleys. In August of 1861 the Union Army abandoned Fort Stanton as the Confederate Army continued its push northward. Although the Union Army attempted to destroy the fort by setting it on fire, a torrential rainstorm quickly extinguished the fire thus preserving it. Once the Fort was abandoned, many American, New Mexican, and Apachés had fought amongst each other in an attempt to plunder the fort.[3]

Without the protection of the Union Army, many New Mexican and American settlers in the region chose to leave the area, for the safety of the villas from which they had originally come from. By October 1862, after the Confederate threat was expelled, Colonel Christopher "Kit" Carson was placed in command of Fort Stanton. Shortly after his return, he led a campaign against the Mescalero, Gila, and Navajo to re-establish a sense of security in the region. Once he established a degree of safety, the settlers slowly started to migrate back.

World War One

In 1915 German U-boats sank the British passenger ship, Lusitania, killing 128 Americans aboard. Even as this tragedy had unfolded, President Woodrow Wilson still preferred to take an isolationist approach to the war in Europe. He further demanded that the Germans cease their attacks on U.S. merchant and passenger ships. The Germans complied with his demands for a short time. In January of 1917 Germany resumed its attacks on U.S. merchant ships, destroying seven of them.

On January 16, 1917 the Foreign Secretary of the German Empire, Arthur Zimmerman, had dispatched a coded telegram to the German Ambassador in México. Britain's secret cryptography group, known as Room 40, had captured and decrypted the German diplomatic code. It was discovered that Germany was asking México to become its ally. It continued by suggesting that México should also ally with Japan for the purpose of declaring war against the United States. The Germans had offered financial support to México for the purpose of regaining Arizona, New México, and Téxas.

Strategically, Germany needed México to provide a war front in the Americas to keep the United States from entering the war in Europe. México however had no desire to commit to a war with the United States. Initially there was some skepticism pertaining to the telegram's authenticity. The skepticism was dispelled when Arthur Zimmerman confirmed the legitimacy of his telegram during a speech he had given on March 29, 1917.

On April 06, 1917 the United States of America formally declared war against Germany. Furthermore they allied themselves with the Allied forces. By the time World War I was over it is estimated that 116,708 U.S. troops had died during the war. Of those 53,402 died while in combat, 63,114 were listed as other deaths, and the U.S. Coast Guard listed 192 deaths. There were also 205,690 wounded troops.[4] World War One was also known as the "Great War".

World War One and its Effects on Lincoln County

Hundreds of Lincoln County's finest men had answered the call to duty during World War One. Provided is a list of some of the men that had enlisted into the military. The list is not totally representative of all of the great men who enlisted and served in the war. Most of the men on this list are from the Río Ruidoso, Río Hondo, and Río Bonito valleys and most of them are of New Mexican descent.

To further clarify some of the verbiage, Killed in Action signifies that the veteran in question was killed while in combat. Other Death signifies that the veteran had died due to some other illness, disease, or non-combat related accident. In all, there were about 16 men from Lincoln County who had lost their lives during World War One.

World War One Veterans[5]

Name	Township	Discharged From	Date of Discharge
Pedro Analla	Tinnie	Other Death	1918
Esequiel Chávez	Tinnie	Camp McArthur, Texas	December 20, 1918
Daniel A. Sánchez	Tinnie	Fort Bliss, Texas	July 22, 1919
Manuel T. Benavides	Hondo	Fort Bliss, Texas	May 23, 1919
Nicodemo Chávez	Hondo	Camp Travis, Texas	February, 10,1918
Juan E. Chávez	Hondo	Camp Fremont, CA	December 09,1918
Esequiel Gustamante	Hondo	Morrison, Virginia	December 10, 1918
Elfido Salas	Hondo	Camp Bowie, Texas	December 31, 1918
Mauro Sánchez	Glencoe	Camp Pike, Arkansas	December 14, 1918
Lewin D. Perry	Glencoe	Presidio de San Fran	October 22, 1919
Luís B. Torres	Patos	Camp McArthur, Texas	November 22, 1918
Antonio Baldonado	Picacho	Camp Owen, Texas	April 18, 1919
Julio Vigil	Picacho	Fort Bliss, Texas	May 23, 1919
Estanislado Cardona	Picacho	Camp Travis, Texas	February 20, 1919
Manuel Saíz	Picacho	Camp Bowie, Texas	April 23, 1919
Lupe G. Lueras	White Oaks	Camp Bowie, Texas	June 02, 1919
John B. Light	Mescalero	Other Death	1918
Pablo Montoya	Mescalero	Camp Cody, NM	December 13, 1918
Fred Montoya	Isleta	Fort Bliss, Texas	July 23, 1919
Nestor Padilla	Tres Ritos	Camp Kearny, CA	February 24, 1919
Robert J. Haggee	Alto	Other Death	1918
José Portio	Ruidoso	Camp Fremont, CA	October 07, 1918
Lino Herrera	Ruidoso	Camp Travis, Texas	January 21, 1919
Alfred E. Hale	Ruidoso	Fort Bliss, Texas	July 22, 1919
Alejandro Trujillo	San Patricio	Camp Travis, Texas	December 07, 1918
Rumaldo Chávez	San Patricio	Mitchell Field, NY	July 07, 1919
Vicente Domíngues	San Patricio	Camp Cody, NM	December 13, 1918
Lázaro Gallegos	San Patricio	Camp Cody, NM	December 13, 1918
Teodoro Montoya	San Patricio	Camp Owens, Texas	April 18, 1919
Susano Sánchez	San Patricio	Other Death	1918
Nestor Aguilar	Lincoln	Camp Cody, NM	December 09, 1918
Conley Gobble	Lincoln	Killed in Action	1918
Esidoro Gutíerrez	Lincoln	Fort Bliss, Texas	July 09, 1919
Roy Hamilton	Lincoln	Killed in Action	1918
Eusevio Sedillo	Lincoln	Fort Bliss, Texas	July 08, 1919
Nestor Trujillo	Lincoln	Fort Bliss, Texas	July 31, 1919
Candelario Zamora	Lincoln	Camp Travis, Texas	October 30, 1918
Esequiel García	Arabela	Camp Funston, Kansas	May 28, 1919
Louis Moya	Arabela	Other Death	1918
Edward Richardson	Arabela	Fort Bliss, Texas	June 04, 1919
Isabel Aldaz	Capitán	Camp Dodge, Iowa	October 27, 1919
George Coe	Carrizozo	Camp Kearny, CA	October 27, 1919
Harvey Hughes	Carrizozo	Other Death	1918
Fred M. Lindsey	Carrizozo	Other Death	1918
Richard Morgan	Carrizozo	Other Death	1918
Glander White	Carrizozo	Other Death	1918
Antonio Sedillo	Rebentón	Camp Kearny, CA	November 28, 1917
Blas Domínguez	Santa Rosalía, México	Fort Logan, CO	February 27, 1919

Conrado Sánchez

Conrado Sánchez was born on July 15, 1894 in San Patricio, Territory of New México. He was the son of Francisco Sánchez and Concepción Trujillo. He married Josefita Padilla on January 20, 1912. Later he enlisted and served in the military during World War One. After the war he and his wife moved to Roswell, and lived on his father's farm in the farming community of El Berendo.

While living in El Berendo, he would often visit his brothers and sisters living in San Patricio. During the summer months, he would bring baskets of watermelons, chili, and vegetables to the valley to sell. During the 1940's Conrado and his wife had moved to several different communities. They first moved to Manzano, then Las Cruces, and finally they moved to Casa Grande, Arizona. Although Conrado made a living elsewhere, his heart was always in San Patricio. Each summer, for three months, he and his wife would return to visit with family.

From left to right: Esquipulo Gonzáles, Alejandro Sánchez, Unknown, Conrado Sánchez (Ernest Sanchez collection)

World War Two

Lincoln County World War II Deaths

Name	Grade	Cause of Death
Santiago Analla	Private	Killed in Action
Moises Arellano	Private First Class	Killed in Action
José Beltran	Private	Killed in Action
Robert Bigger	Private First Class	Died Non-Battle
Hoyt Bivens	Private First Class	Killed in Action
Robert Bowlin	Private First Class	Died Non-Battle
Fredric Bridges	Staff Sergeant	Died Non-Battle
Weslie Brown	Staff Sergeant	Finding of Death
Albert Chase	First Lieutenant	Killed in Action
William Chase	Second Lieutenant	Died Non-Battle
Abeslín Chávez	Private First Class	Killed in Action
Oziel Chávez	Private	Died Non-Battle
Leet Forbus	Technician Fourth Grade	Killed in Action
Rafael Gonzáles	Private	Killed in Action
Charlie Hergett	Sergeant	Killed in Action
Aubrey Hines	First Lieutenant	Killed in Action
Elliot Jones	Captain	Died Non-Battle
John Lee	Private First Class	Killed in Action
Ben Leslie	Private	Killed in Action
Filbert Martínez	Private	Killed in Action
Eloy Montes	Private First Class	Killed in Action
José Montes	Private	Killed in Action
Jake Montoya	Sergeant	Killed in Action
Ramón Peña	Private	Died Non-Battle
Kemp Pepper	Private First Class	Died Non-Battle
Howard Porter	Private	Killed in Action
Tony Regalado	Private First Class	Died Non-Battle
Edward Richardson	Technical Sergeant	Killed in Action
Walter Robinson	Technical Sergeant	Killed in Action
Frederick Sherman	Captain	Died non-Battle
Sam Swan	Private First Class	Killed in Action
George Torres	Private	Died Non-Battle
Mervin Williams	Corporal	Killed in Action
Gladney Zumwalt	Technical Sergeant	Died Non-Battle

World War II had broken out, and many of Lincoln County's sons had answered the call to duty and enlisted in the U.S. armed forces. Many of Ysidro Chávez's sons enlisted to serve their country. Those who enlisted were: Senon, Emiliano, Efraín, Luvín, and Onfré (Humphrey). Upon looking at the discharge records for Lincoln County, one could not doubt the patriotism of many of its New Mexican heroes. There was not a single family in the Río Ruidoso, Río Hondo, and Río Bonito valleys that didn't have a family member actively participating in the war.

Senon Chávez

Senon Chávez was born at his parents' adobé in Glencoe, New México on March 03, 1917. His parents were Ysidro Chávez and Pablita Sánchez. He was the third oldest child in a family that had sixteen children. He and his older sister Greselda "Grace", and older brother Amarante "Jack" were raised near, and attended elementary school, in La Aguilita.

He had never really taken a liking to school. As a youth he resisted the instructor's attempts to teach him English. He figured that Spanish was his first and true language and that it was the only language he was going to speak. He was so bold as to say that nobody was going to tell him any differently. Senon vividly recalled that a fellow classmate, Inez (Ignacia) Gómez had tutored him throughout school. She helped him learn the English language. He swore that if it weren't for her help he never would have been able to get through school.

When the instructor threw him out of class for failing to obey her commands, he became so irate he impulsively and irrationally sat in the middle of an ant pile. There, he was repeatedly bitten until large red welts formed all over his body. Afterwards he became extremely sick, contracting a high-grade fever for almost a week. Needless to say, he didn't have to attend school while he was sick.

Senon had continued his schooling up to the eighth grade and chose not to continue any further. The fact that he never went pass the eighth grade didn't necessarily mean that he wasn't an intelligent man. On the contrary, he had done most of his learning through real life experiences, and in many instances was more adept at learning those tasks that would ensure self-preservation. These life experiences were all things that would play a vital role later on in his life.

As a juvenile, Senon was the adventurous type who liked to tempt fate. At the age of about 12, he and his cousin Gabriel Chávez would go into the hills and hunt for rattlesnakes. They would search every crevasse and listen for the sound of the snakes' rattles shaking in excitement. Once the two boys had found one, Senon would wrap his entire hand in cloth and would reach into the crevasse and pull out the rattlesnake. Once in their possession, one of the two boys would cut the rattles from the tail and release the snake. Afterwards, they would make a necklace or a bracelet with the rattles attached.

In the summers Senon with the rest of his family would move up to a homestead where they had a goat camp at the Parajito. It was located about two miles southwest of the ranchito where Melvin now lives.

Luvin remembers Senon formed a boxing club in the valley and all his friends would hold boxing events. He rode his horse everywhere in the valley. Riding his horse he would pull out his Bull Durham sack of tobacco, roll a cigarette one-handed never taking his eyes off the surrounding countryside. He was so in tune with his surroundings that he never missed anything. He would be the first one to spot a deer, be off his horse and have the deer shot before his companions could process the thought of doing so. Senon loved the country and the wide-open spaces. He loved his campitos and his coffee. God help the man that washed his coffee cup and worse his coffee pot!

There are lots of stories about Senon's athletic abilities and nimbleness. At the family reunions he would tie a rope into a tree and climb the rope daring the teenagers to have a go at it. Climbing trees were his specialty. Leroy Gomez recalls one inicident that happened close to his house by the river. The river was at flood stage and climbing a tree that overhung the river, Senon jumped onto another tree on the opposite bank thus crossing the river. Melvin says; "I remember Senon doing back flips into his late sixties. He was a good man and brother. Generous to all, he befriended everyone he met and would have given you the shirt off his back if you had asked for it. His nieces and nephews loved him. I loved him...God Bless you Senon".

Senon Chavez Picture taken after returning from serving with Darby's Rangers and as a POW. The two Ranger scrolls are visible with First Ranger Bn. scroll on right shoulder and 3rd Ranger Bn. On left shoulder. (Courtesy of Reynel Martinez)

World War II, Darby's Rangers[6]

Senon wasn't a big man, he stood about 5' 4" from head to toe, and couldn't have weighed more than 135 lbs. What he lacked in size was compensated by his unnerving strength and fortitude. On June 13, 1941, at the age of 24, Senon volunteered to serve his country by signing up for the U.S. Army. While in training he volunteered to serve in the U.S. Army Rangers that were newly forming up.

On January 28, 1943 PFC Senon S. Chávez joined the First Ranger Battalion in Arzew, Algeria. He arrived with 7 officers and 101 enlisted men from Ft. Devin, Mass. Referred to as "Darby's Rangers", Senon and his brother Rangers were assigned some of the most dangerous missions in World War II. They spearheaded all the major amphibious landings in the invasions of North Africa, at Arzew, Algeria; Gela and Licata in Sicily, Salerno and Anzio in Italy. The Rangers spearheaded the land attacks in the major battles of Dernia Pass, El Guettar in Tunisia; Gela, Licata, Porto Empedocle, Butera, Messina, in Sicily; and onto the mainland of Italy, Chiunzi Pass at Salerno, Venafaro, San Pietro, and ending at Cisterna. Darby's Rangers were awarded the Presidential Unit Citation for distinguished action in the battles of El Guettar in Tunisia and Chiunzi Pass at Salerno, Italy. The Rangers always led the way against incredible odds, and Senon Chavez had been with them all the way.

Because of pending plans for the invasion of Sicily, General Patton instructed Darby to come up with plans for the formation of two additional Ranger battalions. After approval from General Marshall, (Chief of Staff) Darby visited all replacement centers for volunteers for the formation of the two additional units. Darby, using his veterans from the First Ranger Battalion as cadre, organized the Third and Fourth Ranger Battalions on 20 May 1943 in North Africa. With all three Ranger battalions known as Force Ranger, and Darby commanding the First Ranger Battalion and in overall command of Force Ranger, Sicily awaited the Rangers.

Senon as a combat veteran of the First Ranger Battalion was shifted over to the Third Ranger Battalion and commanded by Major Herm Dammer. Senon remembers that while with the First they would say; "there goes Darby with his four hundred thieves," and when he was with the Third the saying would go; "here comes Dammer and his four hundred goats!"

With 1943 quickly coming to an end, the American Fifth Army, and the American Eighth Army were unsuccessful in capturing a strategic position in the Liri Valley in Italy. The town of Cassino had become an enemy stronghold that anchored the Gustav Line, which had become an impenetrable line of defense that utilized the Garigliano and Rapido Rivers as natural barriers.

The Allied strategic command had identified the town of Anzio as a launching pad for an assault on the German's southern lines. The 40,000 troops, which made up the U.S. VI Corps, would constitute the invading force, which would attack the Gustav Line. From their position at Anzio they could outflank the German's southern lines as they pushed towards the Colli Laziali. Once the frontlines from the south fell, the Fifth Army would be able to take Rome.

OPERATION SHINGLE
ANZIO-NETTUNO AND CISTERNA di LITTORIA

Senon and his Rangers had received their orders. They were going to make an amphibious landing on the shores of Anzio. The First and Fourth Ranger Battalions would subdue all of the beach defenses, establish a defensive perimeter, and make a strong push towards Nettuno, clearing the area of the enemy. Senon and the Third Battalion would land ashore two hours after the First and Fourth Ranger battalions and push ahead of the Fourth and clear the town of Anzio of the enemy. With their mission briefing in hand, Senon and his unit boarded the Ulster Monarch on January 20, 1944, and set sail the next day.

The First and the Fourth Ranger Battalions landed at 0200 hours. Senon and the Third Rangers landed an hour later and promptly made their push towards the northwest side of town, where they captured a four-gun battery of 100mm howitzers. About ninety minutes into the assault, Senon who was covering point saw a German scouting jeep. Under the cover of darkness, he opened fire killing two soldiers, while the third hastily made his escape. Senon and Lt. Palumbo commandeered the vehicle and continued scouting the area for the enemy. After canvassing the area for a brief period of time they proceeded back to the beach.

An attack on the Gustav Line by the Fifth Army, which had preceded the Anzio amphibious landings, had failed. The plan was for the Fifth Army and Darby's Rangers to eventually form into a solid front. The attack on Anzio however didn't divert German troops from the Gustav Line. After hearing the news of the Allied forces' movements to the south, the German's fortified their positions with 20,000 troops. It was their intent to hold the southern front at all costs.

On January 23rd, the Rangers pushed their patrols several miles north of Anzio. By January 24th they had pushed just two miles south of Carrocetta. German air strikes increased in frequency and their intensity. Over the next four days Senon and the other Rangers were involved in several firefights, but they held their positions. By January 28th Senon and the Third Ranger Battalion were replaced by British troops. That night, Darby's Rangers were repositioned to the northeast flank of the beachhead along with the Third Division.

The Allied strategic command had to re-evaluate their strategy because the U.S. VI Corps was being held back. Major General John Lucas was forced to withhold his invasion for yet another 24 hours. During this time General Lucas had devised a strategy that would have the Third Division push from the eastern flank towards Cisterna, and the British First Infantry Division would push from the western flank towards Albano. The First Armored Division would thus move upon Colli Laziali from Campoleone, from the west.

Darby's Rangers were tasked with leading the attack on Cisterna with the Third Division at 0100 hours. The First and Third Battalions would lead the charge through the Fosso di Pantano, which was an extension of the Mussolini Canal. The Pantano followed a path that led it to a point just 1½ mile south of Cisterna. From that point, the landscape was open terrain, where several ditches were interspersed throughout the fields thus providing minimal cover for the Rangers. It was imperative though that the Rangers infiltrate Cisterna under the cover of darkness, and avoid being detected by the Germans while making their push. The Fifth Division would follow behind at 0200 hours, clearing the way of mines and enemy positions.

Senon had spent almost the entire day of January 29th preparing for the night ahead. He diligently cleaned his Thompson submachine gun, sharpened the blade of his knife, gathered sticky grenades, and a few rounds of rocket rounds for the bazooka teams. He then proceeded to eat until his belly was full, and filled his canteen with water. He prayed that afternoon, as he had done every day. He reflected upon everything that was important to him. Even though his mind was filled with thoughts he attempted to get some sleep. During this time, while Senon and his brethren were preparing for battle, the Germans had amassed in excess of 71,000 troops to protect its southern lines.

At 2100 hours, Senon and the First and Third Ranger battalions had made their way towards the canal. They gathered there, in the bitter cold of the night. On January 30th at 0100 hours the 767 men that made up the First and Third Ranger battalions made their push into the Pantano ditch forming a single file line. The First battalion went in first, followed by the Third battalion.

Senon, who was with B Company in the Third Ranger battalion, had been marching for a few hours. Suddenly the eerie silence of the night exploded into turmoil as the Fourth Ranger battalion had engaged German hostiles. The crackling of machine gun fire pierced the night. Flares went off, Senon and his brethren took cover to conceal their positions.

The flashes of gunfire erupted as the Germans began firing from either side of the ditch, raining bullets upon the Fourth Ranger Battalion who were attacking Feminimorta, killing and maiming many of the men. The men from the Fourth had to resort to using grenades and bayonets as they fought the Germans closest to their positions. After failing to penetrate the enemy line, those remaining men that withstood the onslaught of death were forced to seek cover within a shallow ditch.

Meanwhile, the First and Third battalions had been separated from each other during the march, and there was no means of communicating with each other. Major Dobson, who commanded the First battalion, was forced to split his command. He took the front while Captain Charles Shunstrom took the rear. He sent a runner to meet up with the Third battalion to communicate what was happening. Major Dobson continued to push towards Cisterna.

Senon was amazed that his position hadn't yet been compromised, and that he and those in close proximity weren't taking any fire. He could hear the cracking of shots being fired from his rear flank. Word had traveled from one man to the other that the First Battalion had resorted to fighting the enemy in hand-to-hand combat. They were resorting to killing the enemy with their knives. Senon figured that the calm before the storm was about to end, so he gathered his wits and focused on the task at hand. All the while, progress pushing forward was slowed to a crawl because enemy flares kept lighting up the darkness. Senon and his brethren were forced to crawl on their stomachs to avoid detection.

Just before the crack of dawn, Senon and the Third Battalion had reached a tree-lined road, which they stealthily crossed, and quickly found cover within another ditch. Pushing onward toward Cisterna, the men passed many German artillery positions. As yet undetected, Senon could hear the Germans speaking to each other. Without provocation, or any shots fired, he continued a slow push forward.

Senon could hear screaming from the front. The shrill sound of the screams raised the hair on Senon's neck. He could hear death creeping up on him and his brethren. Adrenalin had kept him focused, and time didn't matter any more. This had become a matter of survival and Senon didn't have the luxury to let his mind wander.

The First Battalion had come within 600 yards of Cisterna before coming across the German bivouac area. Upon being discovered by a German soldier who had just climbed out from within a foxhole, the soldier screamed a warning to his comrades. A slew of German soldiers rushed out from their foxholes, and a melee ensued in which approximately 100 of the enemy met their deaths at the end of a Ranger's knife or a bayonet. The First battalion pushed forward another 400 yards before being stopped by intense artillery fire. They re-grouped at a road just outside of Cisterna that afforded very little cover.

The German's counterattacked from their rear flank, with 17 tanks and armored self-propelled guns. The Ranger's hit the first wave with everything that they had, disabling 15 of them. The Ranger's pushed forward, under the intense artillery attack.

Senon had just pushed across the highway and had come upon an irrigation ditch as the sun's rays had peaked over the eastern horizon. He spotted a farmhouse about 50 yards ahead to his left. He quickly took cover in the ditch as the Germans opened fire from either side. The thunderous booms of a flak-wagon, which was firing at point blank, drowned out the sounds of repeated machine gun fire. Dirt was flying all about him, as the bullets pierced the earth. Suddenly, he heard the whizzing of a bazooka rocket, and shortly thereafter an explosion, as the flak-gun was destroyed.

Senon and several other men had to continue crawling on their bellies, wise to the fact that if they lifted their heads above the ditch they might get a bullet in the head. As he pushed forward, he had to crawl over many of his injured and dead comrades. The ditch, which had very little water, was beginning to flow with blood. The stench of death and dying filled his nostrils. The cry of dying men's last words pierced his ears. The sight of so much death, so much blood and gore would forever haunt his mind. He became covered in the blood of dead and wounded men.

Senon's rifle had become compacted with mud, from crawling on his belly. He spotted a ditch that cordoned off towards a small shed. He called out to his friend and asked him if he wanted to go to the shed, and clean their Thompsons. His friend refused the offer so Senon continued towards the shed by himself.

Once inside the shed, Senon cleaned his weapon and collected his thoughts. He reached into his pocket to grab a piece of cheese he had stashed and upon pulling it out he had discovered that there was a bullet hole in it. He pulled his canteen out to take a drink and discovered that it also had a bullet hole in it. Senon felt that he had been blessed because neither bullet had found their mark.

After a brief moment cleaning his Thompson, Senon left the shed and made his way back through the irrigation ditch. He saw his friend up ahead and he called out to him, saying that he should have come with him to the shed. There was no reply in the deafening barrage of artillery fire. As he approached closer, he saw his friend with his eyes wide open, emptily looking upon him with a deathly stare. Upon closer inspection, Senon had noticed a red bullet wound on his forehead. His friend had been possibly hit with a sniper's bullet and killed instantly. Senon thought, "Oh, you should have gone with me."

Senon met up with some of his men and partook in an attack upon a farmhouse where they killed some ten to twelve Germans, and commandeered their machine guns. From the rear they could see a contingent of infantry, tanks, armored guns, and flak-wagons moving in on the Rangers. The battle could be seen everywhere and everything seemed like such a blur to Senon.

The Rangers were fighting for their lives, and during combat, they used anything they could find to continue the fight. They picked up weapons from dead or injured soldiers, both allies and the enemy. Senon had heard the news that his battalion commander had been killed, but the fight raged on. Senon didn't have time to reflect on his commander, Major Miller, but he thought very fondly of him later in life.

The Germans had surrounded the Rangers, cutting off any means of escape back to the Allied lines. The Rangers continued the battle with the slightest of hope that reinforcements would be able to break their way through the lines to the south. These hopes were soon shattered with the sight of so many of the enemy, and so few friendly faces.

The Germans had captured some members from E Company and proceeded to march them to an area that the Rangers were sufficiently defending. The Germans used them as hostages and as a means of negotiating the surrender of the fortified Rangers position. Initially, there was some reluctance on the part of the Rangers to surrender. A small firefight ensued in an attempt to give the Rangers of E Company a chance to escape, in which several Germans were killed, however the German captors retaliated by killing some of their hostages. The Rangers thought better of it, not willing to sacrifice any other Rangers from E Company, and surrendered themselves.

Senon remembers that by noon he ran out of ammo. Everyone had run out of ammo. He had picked up an M-1 and had what was left of a full clip in the rifle. He recalled; "In my mind I didn't want to give up. I had worked my way into a vineyard that was on a slight slope about forty yards from the ditch and road. I was trying to figure a way to escape or play dead. I could see a bunch of tanks and Germans herding captured Rangers in front of them and heading our direction. They would shoot into ditches once in awhile and knew they were killing wounded Rangers. I noticed this one particular German. He stood out because he was kind of fat. About hundred yards away I had seen him bayonet two Rangers in the back. As they got closer, about sixty yards away I could hear him yelling in perfect English to these Rangers in a house to come out or he would kill the Rangers. Suddenly they started shooting these men. All that morning I had been killing Germans but I cannot recall any of it. I remember this one though."

To Senon's horror, he witnessed the German soldier as he shot his Rangers, killing them. Senon steadied his gun, aimed, and squeezed the trigger. The bullet flew straight and found its mark, dropping the fat German soldier dead where he stood. In Senon's words, "I shot him through the heart and he fell like a pig. He was fat and he dropped like a pig."

The echoes of the Germans shooting had masked the fatal shot that had come from Senon's rifle. The German's were unaware of where the shot had come from or surely Senon would have been killed. Some of the Rangers who had known Senon called out to him urging him to give himself up. Once resolved, Senon placed his fate in God's hands. He stood up and started walking towards the road. On the way, he picked up a dead Ranger's canteen and a pack of cigarettes. He was quickly apprehended by the enemy and thus had become a prisoner of war.

Of the 767 Rangers of the First and Third Battalions that had attacked Cisterna, six came back; according to the official history, the rest were either killed or captured. Senon was among the captured and spent the remainder of the war in prisoner of war camps. In the POW camps he was subjected to unfathomable brutality. He was tortured, and starved. He became gravely ill while in captivity and upon his return to the United States, it took him several months to recuperate back to health.

In the summer of 1944, a Western Union telegram was received by the Chavez family. It was dated June 17, 1944 and it read:

Mrs Paublita Chavez
22606 Meyler St
Torrance, California

Based on information received through the Provost Marshall General records of the War Department have been amended to show your son Technician Fifth Grade Senon S. Chavez is now a Prisoner of War of the German government. Any further information received, will be furnished by the Provost Marshall General.

Signed: ULIO The Adjutant General

Oralia, thirteen years old remembers the day the telegram arrived. On reading the telegram, Paublita started crying. For the following week Mama Paublita was upset, crying, and praying for her son. Not knowing how he was doing kept her in constant turmoil. She prayed to God and asked him "please show me a sign that he's alive." One evening she went outside of the house praying and asked the Lord to please show her a sign, that Senon was alive. Oralia remembers her mother entering back into the house and telling her family that God had given her a sign, that Senon was alive. She explained that as she was praying, out of the corner of her eye she seen a "bulto" (a bulk of a shadow). It was a large shadow of a man or being and instantly knew in her heart that her hijo was alive. It relived her turmoil but didn't diminish her concern.

Ramona and Melvin remembered the events leading to the return of their brother Senon. "It was the summer of 1946 and Melvin (age 8), Ramona (age 6), and Danny (age 5) were playing in a barn situated behind the home where they were living on Meyler St in Torrance. They had a rope tied to the loft of the barn and were swinging on it. In the loft, Ramona noticed a soldier was walking down the road with a duffle bag on his shoulder coming towards them. She shouted "ay viene un soldado!" Ramona ran into the house and told her mother Paublita that a soldier was coming down the street. Mama Paublita came running out of the house and down the street, with her children besides her. She was crying and screaming "hijo, mi hijo." The whole family was crying and were very emotional as they ran towards him. It was a very sweet reunion with the whole family joyously crying, infused in happiness and very emotional, hugging him, each other, on the return of their brother and son. The family hadn't received any information and didn't know if Senon was alive or dead." Paublita's prayers had been answered. She loved all her children and she dearly loved her son, Senon. She had suffered with him as only a mother can. They all say that it was one of the most memorable event that had happened in their lives.

Life after World War II had become enigmatic for Senon. He combated the horrors of war and Anzio by keeping to himself and drinking. Later in life, Senon was forced to give up alcohol; he became ill and eventually lost part of his stomach. Readjusting to a civilian's life had often eluded him. Post Traumatic Stress Disorder had settled in, and at the time, little was known about the affects that war had on the men who had fought in it. In many instances the veterans were either not diagnosed, or misdiagnosed. Being that Senon continued to live in the rural town of San Patricio, he did not receive the care he needed to cope with life after the war.

Senon never married, and chose to live a semi-secluded lifestyle. He enjoyed the outdoors and often camped in the mountains for weeks on end. He set up a small camper on a hillside overlooking San Patricio and the valley below. From there he could see St. Jude Catholic Church in the distance. He would call this small camper, his campito, his home, which was situated on the far side of a hill just east of his brother Melvin's house. The vista was serene, and it afforded him the opportunity to drown out the haunting images of war. He became one with the earth, as if his tierra maternal gave him life.

At one point, Senon was hauling old tires to his camper. He was constructing some type of expansion to his abode. It looked much like a fortified foxhole, with a small opening for a window that he would peer through. It rested atop his camper and was fastened to the surrounding trees for greater stability.

Although Senon often chose to remain semi-secluded most of the time, he did reach out to certain people. Senon was honored, and accepted the responsibility of becoming a Padrino to his brother Melvin's daughter, Jennifer Chávez. He embraced Jennifer as if she were his own daughter; she meant the world to him. The two of them spent a great deal of time together. In many ways Jennifer embraced his persona, and adopted many of his core values into her own life. She remembers Senon used to always tell her; "you see that mountain, you go over that mountain, and you will see another mountain, and you go over it, and you'll have another one to go over and over…" The two of them seemed almost inseparable at times.

Senon also became particularly close with Reynel "Rey" Martínez, whom Senon's father had accepted into the Chávez family as his own. Rey recalled: "I remember we had a five-year-old stud horse that roamed the range, and had bred mares. Never had a rope on him. A typical crazy stud horse and it was spring. The horses name was Alacran (Scorpion), in honor of his disposition.

Senon ran the horse with some mares into the corral, segregated the stud and with the help of some of the men in the valley got the stud hogtied and saddled. It was a big social event. Drinking wine was heavy then. They turned Senon loose into the open area in the orchard. It was a rodeo. Alacran unloaded him, Senon got back on. This went on through the morning, interspersed with hits of "La Copita", the wine the men favored. Senon was getting into it and so was Alacran. I was nine years old and I was impressed. Alacran, full of piss and vigor, was snorting, bucking, farting and shitting, all at the same time, and having a harder time unloading his tormenter as it went on. By sheer imposition of his will, Senon broke that stud from bucking and eventually into a good saddle horse. I never forgot that.

In the springtime we would roam the ranch on horses with a pack-horse, a week at a time, protecting the family herd of sheep from feral dogs. Senon became a mentor to me and taught me how to live in the outdoors, shooting skills, tracking and killing game, and how to ambush dogs. During those outings, Senon's persona would change, becoming more alive, more vibrant. He would teach me things and the manner was sometimes borderline hard nose. I remember him extensively concentrating on the subject of fear and how one should react to it. How one had to recognize, respect, and accept it and not let it over come you. Fear could get you in trouble, even killed, but it could also be a great motivator if harnessed properly. Some of the lessons evolved in the moment, like having to run our horses down a steep hill on a chase. "Don't draw back, stay balanced or you'll throw your horse off…quit being scared," were some of the words I would hear as we barreled down some insane hill! Words mostly spoken in Spanish sometimes in English. I remember one day vividly I was thirteen years old and we had come upon a pack of dogs that were tearing into some sheep. We heard them first so we tied our horses, grabbed our lever action 30-30's and crept up a little hill over looking them. We had a good day and shot three of them, a good ambush. That evening in a little camp we had made, after eating by our small fire, he brought out his wine bottle of "La Copita". I guess it was the combination of what had transpired that day and the wine. I don't know but it was different. I had heard little bits and pieces from him and others, about the war, some, but not a lot. I was a snot nosed kid and you didn't ask those kind of questions. But this was different in that he spoke in detail, about Rangers, about Darby's Rangers and far away places. Not war stories, but about men he had shared his life with, and adventures. He talked into the night. He had rolled a cigarette out of his Bull Durham sack, one handed, and was smoking it and continued talking. I had never ever heard him talk at length about this part of his life. Not about this. I felt privileged and special, excited to hear all of this. All of a sudden a word came out, Anzio and followed slowly, almost painfully in a whisper, Cisterna…and the words stopped…like we had gone over a cliff. The silence that followed spoke volumes, addressing things best not said, emotionally charged, and the countenance of his face held such sadness, such vulnerability, that in my young mind I could only look down in the fire out of respect or I would have started crying. The conversation ended and I never heard another word from Senon about Anzio or Cisterna. It would be years later that he would tell me the full story. The next day as we were riding we stopped our horses on a ridgeline, looking down on a vista and he turned to me and out of the blue said: "Reynee if you ever go to war, go be with the best, they will keep you alive." Not in the wildest of our dreams or imagination could we have known just how prophetic those words came to be. Seven years later, in a place called Vietnam I was newly arrived in country and heading to an infantry line company. Two squared away Ranger sergeants approached us new guys and asked if anyone was interested in volunteering for a Special Operations Ranger unit. I could hear Senon's words echoing in my mind as I slowly raised my hand".

Senon and Rey had always been close to one another, but became closer because they had both experienced the horrors of war. Inspired by Senon, Rey had also volunteered for the Rangers and served two tours of duty with the 101st Airborne Division Rangers from 1966-1968 in Vietnam. Rey went on to share Senon's account by writing an article for Behind the Lines, The Journal of U.S. Military Special Operations entitled, "I Died at Anzio, Senon Chávez: A Ranger's Story" He also wrote another book entitled, "Six Silent Men", depicting his experiences during the Vietnam War.

Sgt. Reynel Martinez May 1968 (Courtesy of Reynel Martinez)

LINCOLN COUNTY VIETNAM WAR DEATHS

NAME	GRADE	TOWN	CAUSE OF DEATH
Glen Alex Chávez	PFC/Army	Glencoe	Killed in Action
Chester Donald Dale	Quatermaster Two/Navy	Capitan	Killed in Action
Jerome Don Klein	PFC/Army	Ruidoso	Killed in Action
Robert Gonzales Montoya	PFC/Army	Ruidoso	Killed in Action
George "Dody" Henry Nunez	Specialist Four/Army	Picacho	Killed in Action
John Sanders Oldham	Major/USMC	Tinnie	Killed in Action
Russell Eugene Pesewonit	PFC/Army	Mescalero	Killed in Action
Willie J. Sandfer Jr.	Staff Sergeant/Army	Tinnie	Killed in Action
Bennie L West	Corporal/USMC	Ruidoso	Killed in Action
Wilmer J Willingham	Warrant Officer 1/Army	Corona	Killed in Action
Carlos Zamora Jr.	Specialist 5/Army	Carrizozo	Killed in Action

Senon lost a nephew Glen Alex Chávez during the Vietnam War who was the son of Emilano Chávez. Also his sister Ramona, lost her brother in law George "Dody" Nunez. Both Alex and Dody were close childhood friends of Reynel Martinez.

Senon had also become close with his nephew, Steven Chávez. After the terrorist attacks on September 11, 2001 he became so impassioned about his patriotism that he joined the U.S. Marines. Lance Corporal Steven Chávez was tragically killed while on tour in Iraq on March 14, 2007. Over a thousand people throughout the Valley attended Steven's funeral. The Hondo Gymnasium was packed, a standing room crowd. He died a hero and an inspiration to the many people he directly and indirectly touched. He paid the ultimate price for his patriotism and his service to his country. Patriotism has always run deep in the Chavez family and other families in Lincoln County. Steven's father Eddie Chavez, was a twelve year Army soldier whose career was cut short by a forced medical retirement. Steven's uncle Charles Chavez had multiple tours in Afghanistan/Iraq and retired as a Command Sergeant Major.

Senon seldom shared his experiences about the war. As he grew older though, he opened up the pandora's box and started to tell his stories to a select few people. Suddenly, all of the secrets he kept inside began to ebb out. He felt it was his responsibility to share some of the stories of his battles. His recollections were vivid, as if it had just happened the day before. He stated that he didn't want to dishonor the memories of his brothers who had fallen in combat. He couldn't forget them, and he often wondered why his life was spared. Even with life, Senon felt as if he had died in Anzio.

Senon's contagious smile and laughter faded, as he grew older. He died on January 18, 2000 some of his ashes released by his goddaughter Jennifer, on a hill over- looking his *campito* with his brothers Danny and Luvin, Rey, Ramona, nephews and nieces and others in attendance. The next day, in a small ceremony the rest of his ashes were buried. A small memorial was built at his campito by his brother Melvin, Prescilla, Jennifer, Ramona and Rey. He rests on a llano, overlooking the vista that he loved so much.

Chapter Fifteen:
A Time of Change 1928-2007

The Hondo Valley Educational System

Contrary to popular thought, many people within the valley did have the belief that an education was relatively important for their children. However, many of those people who believed in the merits of an education had also resisted an extensive education as a means of improving their lifestyle. Was it simply hypocrisy, or were there some compelling reasons for the conflict? Why did so many students drop out, or never attend school past the eighth grade between the late 1800's through the early 1930's? The answers to those questions are complex because so many variables played a roll on one's ability to actually complete school.

It has been said by many of the locals that up until the late 1890's, most of the families from the valley had discouraged their daughters from attending school. It was a widely accepted belief that most women would have been married by the age of sixteen or seventeen, and their primary responsibilities were to raise a family, tend to the house, as well as helping out on the farm. Thus the emphasis on an education was perceived as impractical, because it was often the mother's duty to teach her daughters how to keep their own houses. This mindset gradually started to change from the 1900's through the 1920's when it became more acceptable to allow one's daughter to attend a primary elementary school.

By 1891 a formal education was adopted by the Territory of New México. By 1909 the first high school course was offered in the community of Carrizozo. By 1912 the New México legislature had given its counties the authority to establish their own high schools. During that same year, Lincoln County High School opened in the community of Capitán.[1]

Most of the primary elementary schools, which were one and two-room adobes, were built in each respective community throughout the valley and usually offered schooling no higher than the eighth grade. Most schools had only one, maybe two maestros to teach all of the students. Since most of the communities were spread out over several miles, the logistics of getting the students to school was quite cumbersome. It was often left to the parents or the students to find a way to get to school. This led to high levels of truancy because it was viewed impractical to spend so much time of the working day taking the children to school.

Once in school, it had become evident that keeping the children's interest in learning was another formidable challenge for the maestros. The maestros had hinted that if the parents had shown an interest in their child's learning, maybe it would compel their children to remain in school. This assumption was impractical in that the parents were too busy working their farms, or they had too many children to care for, to take the time to address their children's educational needs.

The school system was also trying to implement a change in the mindset of the parents, most of whom had either no formal education, or a limited education. Therefore the parents were unable to help their children with their schoolwork. There was also the mindset that even though many of the parents had a limited education, they were still able to live a productive life without any significant problems. Initially the schools were largely unsuccessful in showing the community the benefits of an education.

The community's economy relied mostly on agriculture as a means of making an income. Therefore, it was more practical for the sons and daughters to help out with the crops, livestock, and other daily farm chores. In most cases it was a matter of survival for the family rather than choosing whether or not one should continue to attend school. For many families it was easier to teach their own children the skills necessary to operate a farm, or a rancho.

The costs associated with providing an education for students was also a barrier to finishing school. Often times, it was difficult for the parents to come up with enough money to get all of their children through the eighth grade. As a consequence, when many students opted to drop out of school, their parents didn't much mind, because it saved them money. The cost of school supplies was also a barrier because many families were barely making ends meet. If a family had numerous children in school, it made the task of an education a very expensive proposition.

The first Hondo Valley High School was built near the junction of the Río Ruidoso, Río Bonito, and the Río Hondo. The Hondo High School was inaugurated in 1923 where it offered a one-year course. By 1925 Hondo High School offered a two-year course. By 1931 Hondo High School offered a full four-year course. May 1931 saw Hondo's first senior graduating class.[2]

As the valley transitioned from a largely agriculturally based economy to a more service-oriented economy, so did the perceptions of the importance of an education. As more families became less self-sufficient and more dependent on other sources of employment, the importance of a quality education was becoming more pronounced. By the 1950's both boys and girls were actually strongly encouraged to attend and complete high school. The result was a generation, which saw the highest levels of educational attainment by its children at the time. By the 1960s the Hondo Valley School System was sending almost their entire graduating classes on to college.

Ballet Folklórico de Hondo *"The Hondo Fiesta Dancers"*

Hondo Fiesta Dancers. Photograph was taken at San Patricio
school where the Hondo Fiesta Dancers originated.

Fermin Montes and Cirenia Montes

Fermín S. Montes was a visionary, a man who knew the lasting benefits of a complete education. Through perseverance and determination he had overcome all of the obstacles to achieving his education. He earned a B.A. degree from the University of New Mexico, holding a major in Spanish and a minor in Business Administration. Later he would return to the University of New Mexico to get a M.A. degree in School Administration and Secondary Education. Fermín would see his career at Hondo Public Schools start in 1935 and last through 1970. Some of the titles he held during his tenure were Elementary School Principal (6 years), High School Superintendent (28 years), during which he also taught a Spanish class. [3]

Through the early years, Fermín Montes had come to recognize that there was a sense of disconnection between the community and education. He had identified that this disconnect was largely a cultural issue. As it was, the educational system in place did not address the needs of a predominantly Hispanic student body. In the early years of what would eventually become the Hondo Valley School System, there was a great deal of emphasis on assimilating the students into the American ideal. In doing so, much of the traditional New Mexican culture and the Spanish language were being lost.

Fermín challenged institutionalized thought by seeking a way to reconnect the students to their heritage, while improving the perception of the school system within the community. He, his wife Cirenia, and the foreign languages teacher, Ruby R. Douglass, had come up with the idea of teaching the student body traditional folk songs and dances that were performed by their own ancestors two generations removed. The idea was inspired by a group of students from the San Patricio school that were performing some of the dances a few years prior. After much practice, on April 7, 1948 the first "Hondo fiesta" was held in honor of the ancestors. [4]

Since its inception and many years thereafter, Cirenia had devoted a tremendous amount of her time to ensuring that the dances and songs were authentic in nature. Her attention to detail had become legendary in the valley. Practices were grueling, yet all of the students looked forward to learning the dances, and the songs. The results were astounding. Many, if not all of the students, performed the dances so well that they were often mistaken for professional dancers.

Each succeeding fiesta had its own theme, of which the student body was asked to bring the theme to life for the community. The fiesta often told a story, of the lives of their ancestors. There would be a narrator, *cantantes* (singers), and *bailadores* (dancers). The students would set up *mercados* (markets) to sell food and art. In many instances one could liken the fiestas to a musical production, unlike any other in the region. The community showed overwhelming support for the fiestas since its inception. The fiestas brought the people a great sense of pride.

Word of the Hondo Dancers had spread beyond the valley, and there were raving reviews to be heard by many. In 1949 the Hondo Dancers were invited to perform in Corona, El Paso, Ruidoso, and Santa Fé. In 1951 they were invited to perform at the Tucson Festival of Arts.[5] After the Tucson invite, the entire community had banded together, asking for the fiestas to continue. Fermín's vision was becoming a reality, as the community, the students and the school were coming together to share a common goal.

Although the fiestas had become widely popular amongst the people within the community, none would be performed over the next four successive years. Cirenia, who had become the heart and soul of the fiestas had to focus her energies on her family. It wasn't until the spring of 1956 when the fiestas returned once again to the valley. The return came with great fanfare.

In May 1959 the Hondo dancers were invited to perform in Nashville Tennessee. This invite was so successful, that New Mexican Governor, John Burroughs had taken the time to honor both Fermín and Cirenia, with a letter of gratitude. In the years that followed, the annual Hondo fiestas were beginning to draw people from around the entire state of New México.

In May 1966, the Hondo Dancers were invited to perform at a county fair being held in San Juan Capistrano, California. Two former residents from the valley had moved to San Juan Capistrano and had told the fair organizers of the Hondo Dancers. In May 1968 the Hondo Dancers performed in San Antonio Téxas.

By 1970, Fermín had announced his retirement from the Hondo Valley School System. For many years thereafter, until 1982, both Fermín and Cirenia continued to actively participate in the Hondo Fiestas. After 1982, both Fermín and Cirenia were no longer involved with the fiestas. Their departure has diminished the allure of the fiestas in the eyes of the community. Shortly after the 1986 fiestas, many of the students didn't appear to have the same passion to perform the dances. Gone were the cantantes, the mercados, and the narrators. The annual fiestas have transformed from a three-day festival into a one-day event. However, one astute pupil, Frank Herrera, has resurrected the old traditional dances by incorporating his knowledge and passions into the Ballet Folklórico de Roswell, which has become an annual event in its own right.

Ruidoso Downs

The village of Ruidoso Downs had its roots take hold in the 1860's with the arrival of settlers from around Nuevo México, other states, and other countries. By 1862 Congress had passed the homesteaders act, which enabled several squatters to apply for 160 acres of property. It wasn't until the early 1870's though that many of the squatters had applied for homesteads throughout the valley.

Fernando Herrera applied for 160 acres on sections 20 and 29 on December 9, 1876. Upon his arrival in about 1867, he had named his rancho San Juanito in honor of the lands in northern Nuevo México from which his family had operated one of their sheep ranches. San Juanito encompassed the ranchos owned by his son Andrés Herrera who had applied for land on section 29 on October 5, 1890, his son Augustín Herrera who had applied for land on sections 21 and 28 on January 20, 1896, and his son-in-law Adrian Muñoz who had applied for land on section 29 on August 15, 1890. The Ojo de San Juanito (later known as Hale Spring) was a natural spring that was located on Andrés

Herrera's homestead. Adrian Muñoz petitioned for the water rights from the spring. This spring was used to irrigate some of the lands below.

The other family that had significant land holdings on the upper Río Ruidoso were the Hales. Lower Hale applied for land on section 21 on January 25, 1883. He also applied for land on section 28 on August 8, 1883, and on section 20 on February 3, 1886. His son Joshua Hale applied for land on sections 11, 13, and 14 on January 19, 1883. Eventually the Hales purchased the water rights from Andrés Herrera and promptly changed its name to Hale Spring.

Paul Dowlin was the first to apply for land on section 30 on March 30, 1871. He also applied for land on sections 29 and 30 on December 4, 1876. This property eventually became the site where the Ruidoso Downs Race Track & Casino are presently located.

Other settlers who homesteaded in the region were; Henry G. Tidemann applied for land on section 14 and 15 on May 22, 1871, Agapito Gallegos applied for land on section 12 on December 13, 1880, Edwin Terrell applied for land on section 30 on March 8, 1884, James P. Conner applied for land on section 15 on March 10, 1884, S. Cowgill applied for land on section 12 on July 21, 1885, Isaac Ellis applied for land on sections 15, 21, and 22 on August 11, 1885, Chas F. Gifford and Brandon Kirby applied for land on sections 28 and 33 on August 12, 1885, Joel P. Salisbury applied for land on sections 14 and 15 on May 24, 1888, Henry C. Brown applied for land on section 22 on October 7, 1890, Andrés Najeres applied for land on section 14 on July 28, 1894, Manuel Silva applied for land on section 13 on January 11, 1895, Francisco Armera applied for land on section 20 on December 2, 1895, Felipé Montoya applied for land on section 21 on February 5, 1897, Nickolas Bastion applied for land on section 28 on March 18, 1898, B. Eaker applied for land on section 21 on December 7, 1899, Marlin Brown applied for land on section 30 on March 20, 1900, Lee McGehee applied for land on section 32 on May 31, 1902, Alejo Montes applied for land on section 12 on August 21, 1902, Eugenio Sánchez applied for land on section 12 on September 15, 1903.

The entire area continued to be known as San Juanito by the locals, even after Fernando Herrera and most of his children had migrated elsewhere, until Herrick V. Johnson platted and subdivided a part of section 28 and called the township Palo Verde in the summer of 1933. Herrick was in the process of selling lots and parcels of land when the county interjected because he had never filed with the Lincoln County Clerks Office. By October 26, 1942 Herrick had sold his remaining interest less those lots and parcels he had previously sold, to D.B Morgan Jr.

D.B. Morgan Jr. had the plat of Palo Verde surveyed on July 22, 1944. The survey showed the locations of all of the streets and any alleys for the prospective township. Both D.B. Morgan Jr. and his wife Ruby L. Morgan filed the plat with the Lincoln County Clerks office on August 8, 1944. Jane LaRue approved the plat on December 28, 1944.[6]

As Palo Verde continued to grow, the need for a post office was necessary to serve the residents of the community. In 1946 a petition was sent to Washington D.C. for a post office. After the Postal Inspector visited the community, it was determined that Palo Verde would indeed need its own post office. Dorothy Parnell was notified that she would be appointed as the acting postmaster. She was also advised that the name of the post office should be changed from Palo Verde to an English translation to prevent any confusion. Several other communities throughout the southwestern U.S. also were named Palo Verde. Thus the new post office, and the community was known as Green Tree.

In 1947 the New México Racing Commission had legalized organized horse races. Hollywood Park was soon developed, and horse racing found a foothold in the region. To many locals, the area was also known as Hollywood. As the lure of horse racing grew, the Ruidoso Downs Racetrack was developed on the land, which was originally owned by Paul Dowlin. As Ruidoso Downs grew in popularity, and its races began to hold more national appeal, the track sought to change the name of Green Tree to Ruidoso Downs. In February of 1958 the Green Tree council called a special election to rename village. The voters overwhelmingly supported the name change. On October 01, 1958 the name of the post office was thus changed to Ruidoso Downs.[7]

Demographic Trends

Self-identity

The concept of self-identity is a complicated subject that I want to briefly put into context. The issue of self-identity is one of evolution because we as the human race continually try to define who we are, how we see ourselves, and how we want to be perceived by others. Entire texts could be written on the subject, and have been written, and will continue to be written as we continue to evolve. My overly simplistic summation of the evolution of my own self-identity does not do the subject much justice.

Of great interest is how New Mexicans usually identified themselves, or to be more accurate, how the government classified its citizens. The 1850 census classified people based on the color of their skin hence many New Mexicans were "white". This was rather misleading because most Spanish surnamed people of the southwest were viewed as Mexicans. New Mexicans identified themselves simply as New Mexicans. It wasn't until the 1940 Census that the government tried to make the distinction between white people who spoke English, and white people who spoke Spanish.

The 1940's saw the beginning of the Mexican-American Civil Rights Movement, which sought to gain political empowerment and obtain social justice. This movement eventually led to the Chicano Movement in the 1960's. During this movement of empowerment many Mexican-Americans and other Spanish surnamed Americans were identified as Chicano.

The 1970 census first used the term "Hispanic" to classify Spanish speaking or Spanish surnamed citizens of the United States or those who were born in Spanish speaking countries. Even with the Hispanic categorization, many people still identified themselves as a Chicano and or Spanish surnamed. It wasn't until the 1980's that the categorization of, "Hispanic" became widely accepted amongst the Spanish surnamed or Spanish speaking people.

Even with its acceptance, the term Hispanic could not fully define the diversity of the people that it was meant to classify. Some Hispanics spoke English, some spoke Spanish, some spoke either language or even Spanglish. Some were of Spanish descent, Mexican descent, Central or South American descent, African descent, Native American descent, or Asian descent. Some had surnames such as Dutchover, Gill, McKinley, McTiegue, Salsberry, or Warner. In many instances the lines of distinction had been and still are blurred through intermarriage.

By the mid- 1990's the term "Latino" had been adopted by the Government, Corporate America and the mainstream media to define the people that were previously categorized as being Hispanic. It was widely accepted as being more politically correct because it better embraced the people emigrating from Latin America. By the 2000 Census the identifying categorization of Spanish speaking and or Spanish surnamed peoples of the United States was changed to Spanish/Hispanic/Latino. The debate concerning the usage of Hispanic versus Latino has many critics from both sides.

Lincoln County Historical Population Counts

Year	1900	1910	1920	1930	1940	1950	1960	1970
Population	4,953	7,822	7,823	7,198	8,557	7,409	7,744	7,560
% Change	-	57.92%	.01%	-7.99%	18.88%	-13.42%	4.52%	-2.38%

A statistical sampling of the 1900 and 1910 US census shows a dramatic shift in the demographics of Lincoln County. In 1900 it is estimated that Hispanics accounted for about 58% of the total population. By 1910 it is estimated that Hispanics accounted for about 40% of the total population. There were several contributing factors that led to the shift.

The 1910 US Census shows that between 1900 and 1910 the population of Lincoln County grew by 57.92%. The majority of this population growth was attributed to the construction of the railroad through Carrizozo. The railroad brought many new jobs to the area, most of which were filled by people from other states. Consequently, there was an increase in the number of New Mexican families that began to migrate out of Lincoln County as they searched for work. Coupled with a higher than average infant mortality rate for rural New Mexicans, the Hispanic population barely grew during the decade.

New Mexican families continued to steadily migrate out of Lincoln County well into the mid-1930's. The first mass migration began as the United States entered World War I in 1917. Many of the families that left, helped fill the labor shortages in agriculture. While several families returned to Lincoln County after the war, many families decided to settle where jobs were more abundant. Many of the families that remained in Lincoln County became migrant farm laborers, seeking seasonal work in Texas and southeastern New Mexico.

In conjunction with the Great Depression, an extended drought beginning in the late 1920's, decimated the agricultural industry in Lincoln County, prompting more New Mexican families to migrate from Lincoln County. Many of these families migrated to other cities in New Mexico, California, Texas, and Colorado. The creation of the Civilian Conservation Corps helped ebb the flow of migration out of Lincoln County. This led to a population growth of about 18.88%, most of which occurred from the mid- 1930's to 1940.

The population growth spurt was short lived as a third mass migration out of Lincoln County was prompted by the United States entering World War II. Again, many New Mexican families sought to fill the labor shortages created by those who went to war. Most of the families from the Rio Ruidoso, Rio Hondo, and Rio Bonito valleys migrated to California. The 1950 Census shows a 13.42% decline in population. At one point during the war, however, the decline in population was significantly higher.

The next twenty years saw very little growth, or negative growth as the county's youth sought economic opportunities elsewhere. The only growth industries in Lincoln County from the 1950's to the 1970's, was in the tourism and service sectors. The popularity of the Ruidoso Downs horse track and the Ski Apache ski resort provided seasonal employment for many of those who chose to remain behind.

The second dramatic demographic shift for Lincoln County occurred during the mid-1970's as Ruidoso became a popular vacation destination mostly visited by Texans. Ruidoso's appeal as a mountain community prompted many of these tourists to construct vacation homes, and eventually some of these "outsiders" became permanent residents. By 1980 Lincoln County had grown by 45.46%. Population growth was fueled by people emigrating in from other states. The 1980 Census also shows that only about 26.6% of the population was Hispanic.

It was during the 1980's that the political landscape also began to change. The Hispanic political power base that had endured for most of the 20th century had finally succumbed to the changing demographics of the county. Rather than being the majority of elected officials in office, they had become the minority. It would prove increasingly more difficult to elect any Hispanic into office. For the most part Hispanic political activism had diminished significantly.

	1980	1990	2000	2008 estimate
Total	10,997	12,219	19,411	20,793
Hispanic	2927	3,378	4,975	6,155
Non-Hispanic	8072	8798	14,436	14,638
% Hispanic	26.61%	27.64%	25.63%	29.60%
Speak Spanish	-	2,426	3,461	-
% Speak Spanish	-	19.85%	17.83%	-
Foreign born	-	498	1165	-

The 1990's saw growth for both the Hispanic and non-Hispanic populations. However, most of the Hispanic population growth was attributable to the foreign born from México. Many of the Mexican-born residents either worked in the service industry or as ranch hands.

The 1990's saw a boom in the growth of Lincoln County's population. The 1990 Census shows a population of 12,219. The 2000 Census shows a population of 19,411, while the 2008 population estimate shows a population of 20,793.

As of the 2000 US Census, about 53% of Lincoln County's population was born in another state. Most of those who were born out of state migrated to Lincoln County from 1970 to the present. About 25% of the population was Hispanic. About 6% of the population were foreign born, of which, 80% were born in México. About 18% of the population speaks Spanish in the home. The 2000 US Census shows how the demographics of Lincoln County have greatly changed.

EPILOGUE

This book represents forty plus years of patient, thorough and often exhausting research through the diligence of Ernest Sanchez. His grandson, Paul took the helm in writing and expressing the bulk of the story being told.

This story represents my ancestry fueling my personal interest in this accounting. It is the story of the conquest and settling of the American Southwest. The people in this history endured tremendous hardship, and often misrule, under the governments of Spain, Mexico and the United States, but produced what we have today, the state of New Mexico. The foundation and beginning of Spanish influence in the settlement of Nuevo Mexico is an extremely important part of the American experience.

The authors bring into focus the historical birth of our antepasados, and how our progeny evolved in the population and history of Nuevo Mexico. As invaders making claims on the lands and people for the Spanish crown, our ancestors, experienced a clash of civilizations with the indigenous natives of the American Southwest. With the encroachment of the Spaniards into Nuevo Mexico they brought their colonization principals to the bands of Pueblo, Apache and Navajo tribes. Based on conquest, subjugation and the enslavement of the indigenous people, their methods were undeniably harsh.

In order to better understand our ancestral history and the history of the makeup of the Nuevo Mexicanos as a group of people to this present day, it is essential we understand the integration of Spanish and indigenous blood (color quebrado/broken color). We must also understand the brutality of enslavement and underlying spiritual clash between the theology of Kachina and Catholicism that erupted in the Pueblo Revolt of 1680. This was brought to a climax by the injustices suffered by the Pueblo natives, perpetrated partly by the friars of the Catholic Church. The practices of repartimiento and encomienda that the Puebloan citizens were frequently subjected too---and also the unwillingness of the Espanoles to allow them to practice their own religion---often led to whippings, imprisonment or hanging. All of this led to the greatest insurrection of indigenous people and the only incident in the Americas where the invaders were successfully expelled.

The impact of this rebellion allowed the Puebloan to chart their course in history. In a sense the revolt was a profound success. Resuming control in the 1690's, the Spanish made major concessions to prevent further uprisings. Gone was the hated repartimiento and encomienda. The pueblos were allowed to self-govern by electing their own officials in a democratic system that persists to this day. Of most importance, the Puebloans were allowed to practice their Kachina religion. The syncretic faith that permeates the villages today is not so much the dogma imposed upon the natives by the friars but the picking and choosing of the Puebloans of which aspects of Catholicism were compatible with their traditional beliefs.

The re-conquest by De Vargas in 1692 brought into focus our ancestral lineage through Jacinto Sanches de Inigo and the migration into the Salinas Basin out of the Rio Ariba and Rio Abajo Rio Grande valleys. The impact of U.S American expansionism in the early 1800's changed many lives throughout El Reyno de Nuevo Mexico is told with vivid detail and great verve.

In the 1800's we view the undisputable historical proof of our antepasados through Mauricio de la Trinidad Sanches. Through him we see the migration and settlement of Condado de Lincoln. The history was rich with constant strife, fueled by the recent ending of the Civil War, the Mescalero Apache defending their nation and at war with everyone, and the lawlessness of arriving immigrants.

The influx of outside greed, jealousy and prejudice of Tejano immigrants and gangs brought on violence that spiraled out of control and made them the recipients of such violence. The history of Lincoln County has become one of the most exciting---and often misrepresented---stories in American history and folklore. This story brings into focus the Nuevo Mexicano version of the events that transpired in Lincoln County.

The story reveals the perseverance, integrity and moral character of our antepasados, as they dealt with these trying times. They offered a moral compass for their families, relatives and community to follow.

Today we have four generations of our ancestral family living in Condado de Lincoln. They and the others that migrated out of the county represent our antepasados, our history. Today, Lincoln County demographics display that the Hispanic population has increased in the 90's. This increase consists mostly of people born in Mexico. The greatest impact of the 1960's, and forward was that of education, especially higher education. This has produced a professional social class of lawyers, engineers, fighter pilots, teachers, county commissioners, and other professional people that have benefited from and contributed to the modern American dream.

The authors bring a new and unique focus, tracing our ancestral lineage from the past into the present. This book enhances and adds depth to the often over-looked history of the state of New Mexico. Knowing these ancestral histories give all of us the opportunity to personally connect with who we are, and where we came from.

Reynel Martinez

Index

Appendix: Genealogies

Genealogy of Ysidoro Analla

Generation No. 1

1. YSIDORO[1] ANALLA. He married DOLÓRES GALLEGOS.

Notes for YSIDORO ANALLA:
Also known as Ysidro Analla.

Notes for DOLÓRES GALLEGOS:
Also known as Dolóres Gayegos.

Children of YSIDORO ANALLA and DOLÓRES GALLEGOS are:
2.   i.   JOSÉ PEDRO[2] ANALLA, b. Abt. 1830; d. March 24, 1899, Analla, Territory of New México.
3.   ii.   PEDRO ANALLA, b. June 1835.
4.   iii.   MARÍA ANDREA ANALLA, b. Abt. 1836.

José Pedro Analla

Generation No. 2

2. JOSÉ PEDRO[2] ANALLA *(YSIDORO[1])[1]* was born Abt. 1830[2], and died March 24, 1899 in Analla, Territory of New México[3]. He married (1) MARÍA SEDILLO[3]. He married (2) PAULA GALINDRO, daughter of JUAN GALINDRO and NICOLÁSA TORRES. He married (3) DULCESNOMBRES MONTOYA[4] October 17, 1887 in Lincoln County, Territory of New México[5], daughter of JUAN MONTOYA and PORFIRIA ARAGÓN.

Notes for JOSÉ PEDRO ANALLA:
Also known as José Pedro Nonato Analla.
1860 Census: Living in Punto del Agua, Territory of New México. (Born 1834)
1869: Living in La Plaza de San José, Territory of New México.
1870 Census: Living in Lincoln, Precinct 3, Territory of New México. (Born 1830)
1880 Census: Living in Plaza de San Patricio, Territory of New México. (Born 1832)
1885 Territorial Census: Living in Analla, Territory of New México. (Born 1832)
1910 Census: Living in Tinnie, Territory of New México. (Born 1834)

Notes for MARÍA SEDILLO:
Buried in Picacho Cemetary.

Notes for PAULA GALINDRO:
Also known as Petra, Pabla.

Notes for DULCESNOMBRES MONTOYA:
Also known as Dulce Analla, Dulcesnombres Analla.
1910 Census: Living in San Patricio, Territory of New México. (Widow)

Children of JOSÉ ANALLA and MARÍA SEDILLO are:
5.   i.   TIMOTEO[3] ANALLA, b. August 23, 1854.
6.   ii.   JUAN ANALLA, b. January 1856.
7.   iii.   MARÍA ISABEL ANALLA, b. July 1859.
8.   iv.   JOSEFA ANALLA, b. March 1865.

Children of JOSÉ ANALLA and PAULA GALINDRO are:
       v.   ISABELA[3] ANALLA, b. Abt. 1874[6].
9.   vi.   FRANCISCO ANALLA, b. March 14, 1882, San Patricio, Territory of New México; d. July 02, 1947, Tulare, California.
       vii.   MANUEL G. ANALLA[7], b. June 1884[8]; d. 1916; m. MARIANA CARRILLO, December 30, 1901, Lincoln, Territory of New México[9].

Notes for MANUEL G. ANALLA:
    1900 Census: living with his brother-in-law, Paz Torres and his sister, Josefa Analla de Torres.

Pedro Analla

Children of JOSÉ ANALLA and DULCESNOMBRES MONTOYA are:

10.	viii.	PEDRO[3] ANALLA, b. November 10, 1890, Analla, Territory of New México; d. Abt. 1919, Capitán, New México.
11.	ix.	PAUBLITA ANALLA, b. Abt. 1894, Analla,Territory of New México.
	x.	ISIDRO ANALLA[10], b. June 06, 1896[11]; d. March 1985, Roswell, New México; m. MANUELITA GUTIÉRREZ.
	xi.	MANUEL MONTOYA, b. Abt. 1905[12]; Stepchild.
	xii.	DORA MONTOYA, b. Abt. 1909[12]; Stepchild.

3. PEDRO[2] ANALLA *(YSIDORO[1])* was born June 1835[13]. He married MARÍA DEL REFUGIO CHÁVES[14] Abt. 1855[15].

Notes for PEDRO ANALLA:
1870 Census: Living in Lincoln, Precinct 3, Territory of New México.
1880 Census: Living in Analla, Territory of New México. (Born 1834) His occupation is a freighter.
1885 Territorial Census: Living in Analla, Territory of New México. (Born 1831)

Notes for MARÍA DEL REFUGIO CHÁVES:
Also known as Refugio Cháves.
1900 Census: Lists her birth year as March 1843.

Children of PEDRO ANALLA and MARÍA CHÁVES are:

12.	i.	DOMINGO[3] ANALLA, b. Abt. 1861.
13.	ii.	NARCISO ANALLA, b. October 1864.
14.	iii.	BIDAL ANALLA, b. Abt. 1869; d. Tularosa, New México.
	iv.	TRINIDAD ANALLA, b. Abt. 1869[16].
15.	v.	ESCOLASTICA ANALLA, b. February 10, 1872, Picacho, Territory of New México; d. October 15, 1969, Roswell, New México.
	vi.	FRANCISCA ANALLA, b. Abt. 1875[17].
	vii.	CANDELARIA ANALLA, b. Abt. 1877[17].
	viii.	DOLÓRES ANALLA, b. Abt. February 1880[17].
	ix.	VIVIANA ANALLA, b. December 1883[18].

4. MARÍA ANDREA[2] ANALLA *(YSIDORO[1])* was born Abt. 1836[19]. She married (1) JUAN JOSÉ SÁNCHES, son of JUAN SÁNCHES and MARÍA CHÁVES. She married (2) JOHN NEWCOMB.

Notes for MARÍA ANDREA ANALLA:
Also known as María Antonia Anaya, María Andrea Analla, Andrea.

Notes for JUAN JOSÉ SÁNCHES:
Also known as José Chávez y Sánchez.
1850 Census: Living in Valencia, Territory of New México
1860 Census: Living in Punta de Agua, Territory of New México.

Child of MARÍA ANALLA and JUAN SÁNCHES is:

| 16. | i. | ESIQUIO[3] SÁNCHEZ, b. November 1854, Punta de Agua, Territory of New México; d. Bef. 1904. |

Generation No. 3

5. TIMOTEO[3] ANALLA *(JOSÉ PEDRO[2], YSIDORO[1])* was born August 23, 1854[20]. He married (1) AMADA MONTOYA[21] April 24, 1873 in Lincoln County, Territory of New México[22], daughter of JUAN MARTÍNES and PAULA MONTOYA. He married (2) EUFEMIA NAJERES October 03, 1907 in La Capilla de San Ysidro, Territory of New México[23], daughter of ANDRÉS NEJERES and ANTONIA MAÉS.

Notes for TIMOTEO ANALLA:
1885 Territorial Census: Living in Analla, Territory of New México.
1920 Census: Living in Las Palas, New México.

Notes for AMADA MONTOYA:
Also known as María Amada Montoya and Amalita Montoya.

Children of TIMOTEO ANALLA and AMADA MONTOYA are:
      i.   REFUGIA[4] ANALLA, b. December 16, 1880, San Patricio, Territory of New México[24].
17.   ii.   PEDRO NOBERTO ANALLA, b. July 18, 1884, Lincoln County, Territory of New México.
      iii.   NESTOR ANALLA, b. September 16, 1888, Analla, Territory of New México[25]; m. REYNALDA SALAZAR, September 28, 1907, Lincoln, Territory of New México[25].
      iv.   PANTALEÓN ANALLA, b. July 08, 1890[26].
      v.   PAUBLA ANALLA[27], b. March 1892[28].
      vi.   GUADALUPE ANALLA, b. August 1894[28].
18.   vii.   ANTONIA ANALLA, b. September 1898.

Children of TIMOTEO ANALLA and EUFEMIA NAJERES are:
      viii.   AUGUSTÍN[4] ANALLA, b. Abt. 1910[29].
      ix.   TRENIDAD ANALLA, b. Abt. 1913[29].
      x.   MARTILDA ANALLA, b. Abt. 1919[29].
      xi.   JOSÉ NAJERES ANALLA, b. October 12, 1908, Arabela, Territory of New México[30]; m. BERSABÉ S. RAMÍREZ, June 12, 1929, Carrizozo, New México[30].

6. JUAN[3] ANALLA *(JOSÉ PEDRO[2], YSIDORO[1])* was born January 1856[31]. He married (1) FLORIA LUNA[32]. He married (2) ROSARIA MIRELES Abt. 1895[33], daughter of SANTIAGO MIRELES and BRIGIDA GALINDRO.

Notes for JUAN ANALLA:
1880 Census: Living in La Plaza de Picacho, Territory of New México.
1900 Census: Living in Picacho, Territory of New México.

Child of JUAN ANALLA and FLORIA LUNA is:
19.   i.   JESÚSITA[4] ANALLA, b. July 1877.

Children of JUAN ANALLA and ROSARIA MIRELES are:
      ii.   REBECCA[4] ANALLA[34], b. February 12, 1905, Picacho, Territory of New México[35]; m. DANIEL SÁNCHEZ, December 18, 1919, Lincoln, New México[36].

Notes for DANIEL SÁNCHEZ:
1900 Census: Living with his grandfather, Pedro Analla and grandmother, María del Refugio Chávez de Analla.

      iii.   SANTIAGO ANALLA, b. June 1897, Picacho, Territory of New México[37].

7. MARÍA ISABEL[3] ANALLA *(JOSÉ PEDRO[2], YSIDORO[1])* was born July 1859[38]. She married (1) ESIQUIO SÁNCHEZ April 24, 1873 in Lincoln County, Territory of New México[39], son of JUAN SÁNCHES and MARÍA ANALLA. She married (2) ANTONIO CARASCO December 21, 1904[40].

Notes for ANTONIO CARASCO:
Immigrated to the U.S. in about 1894.
1910 Census: Living in Alamogordo, Territory of New México.

Children of MARÍA ANALLA and ESIQUIO SÁNCHEZ are:
      i.   JOSÉ ANALLA[4] SÁNCHEZ, b. Abt. 1874[41]; m. NESTORA FLORES, February 01, 1893, Lincoln County, Territory of New México[42].
      ii.   MIGUEL ANALLA SÁNCHEZ, b. Abt. 1876[43].
      iii.   NICOLÁSA ANALLA SÁNCHEZ, b. Abt. 1878[43].
      iv.   LYDIA SÁNCHEZ, b. Abt. 1879[43]; m. PEDRO VILLESCAS, December 04, 1895, Lincoln County, Territory of New México[44].
20.   v.   JOSEFA ANALLA SÁNCHEZ, b. August 27, 1881, Picacho, Territory of New México.

    vi.   ROSENDA SÁNCHEZ, b. March 1883, San Patricio, Territory of New México[45]; m. CELESTINO VIGIL, July 15, 1901[46].

    vii.   GERONIMO SÁNCHEZ, b. September 30, 1885, San Patricio, Territory of New México[47].

    viii. ESIQUIO SÁNCHEZ[48], b. April 15, 1887, San Patricio, Territory of New México[49]; m. CARMEN A. WILSON, September 26, 1938, San Patricio, New México[50].

    ix.   MALCLOVIA SÁNCHEZ, b. November 1892, San Patricio, Territory of New México[51].

    x.   VICTORIANA SÁNCHEZ, b. May 1900, San Patricio, Territory of New México[51].

8. JOSEFA[3] ANALLA *(JOSÉ PEDRO[2], YSIDORO[1])* was born March 1865[52]. She married PAZ TORRES Abt. 1881[52].

Notes for JOSEFA ANALLA:
1880 Census: Living in La Plaza de San Patricio, Territory of New México. (Born 1864)

Notes for PAZ TORRES:
1880 Census: Living in La Plaza de Picacho, Territory of New México.

Children of JOSEFA ANALLA and PAZ TORRES are:
    i.   CANDELARIA[4] TORRES, b. December 01, 1885, Picacho, Territory of New México[53].

Notes for CANDELARIA TORRES:
Baptized: January 7, 1886. Padrinos: Roberto Chávez, Trenidad Luna.

    ii.   CATARINA TORRES, b. April 1886, Picacho, Territory of New México[54].

    iii. SARA TORRES, b. May 1888, Picacho, Territory of New México[54].

    iv. JOSÉ ANALLA TORRES, b. February 1890, Picacho, Territory of New México[54].

    v.   DOLORES TORRES, b. November 1893, Picacho, Territory of New México[54].

    vi.   VIDAL TORRES, b. March 1895, Picacho, Territory of New México[54].

    vii. EDUARDO TORRES, b. October 1896, Picacho, Territory of New México[54].

    viii. LUGARDA TORRES, b. October 1898, Picacho, Territory of New México[54].

9. FRANCISCO[3] ANALLA *(JOSÉ PEDRO[2], YSIDORO[1])*[55] was born March 14, 1882 in San Patricio, Territory of New México[56], and died July 02, 1947 in Tulare, California. He married FLORENTINA PEÑA June 27, 1901[57].

Notes for FRANCISCO ANALLA:
1900 Census: Living with his brother-in-law, Paz Torres and his sister, Josefa Analla de Torres.
1910 Census: Living in San Patricio, Territory of New México.
1930 Census: Living in Arabela, New México. Analla?

Children of FRANCISCO ANALLA and FLORENTINA PEÑA are:
    i.   JOSÉ PEÑA[4] ANALLA[58], b. 1902; d. December 26, 1936, Lincoln, New México; m. SENAIDA MAÉS.

    ii.   SANTIAGO ANALLA, b. Abt. 1917[59].

10. PEDRO[3] ANALLA *(JOSÉ PEDRO[2], YSIDORO[1])* was born November 10, 1890 in Analla, Territory of New México[60], and died Abt. 1919 in Capitán, New México[61]. He married SOFIA TORRES December 25, 1911[62], daughter of JOSÉ TORRES and ROSA CHÁVEZ.

Children of PEDRO ANALLA and SOFIA TORRES are:
21.   i.   LUCÍA[4] ANAYA, b. September 20, 1912; d. August 02, 1967, Barstow, California.

      ii.   AVRORA ANAYA, b. Abt. 1914[63].

      iii. CARMEN ANAYA, b. Abt. 1918, Capitán, New México[63].

      iv. PABLA ANAYA, b. Abt. 1919, Capitán, New México[63].

      v.   DORA T. CHÁVEZ, b. July 12, 1927, Capitán, New México[64]; m. LUCIANO ARAGÓN OTERO, January 31, 1946, Carrizozo, New México[64].

Notes for LUCIANO ARAGÓN OTERO:
1930 Census: Living in Encinoso, New México.

      vi.   MANUEL FREEMAN, b. Private.

      vii. RICHARD TORRES, b. Private.

11. PAUBLITA[3] ANALLA *(JOSÉ PEDRO[2], YSIDORO[1])* was born Abt. 1894 in Analla,Territory of New México[65]. She married (1) DANIEL PÉREZ. She married (2) ELÍAS BACA October 07, 1920 in Arabela, New México[66], son of DAMACIO BACA and MARÍA BACA.

Notes for PAUBLITA ANALLA:
Also known as Pablita, Paulita and Panchita.
Marriage records indicate that she was born on January 25, 1897. (Book 5, Page 88)

Notes for ELÍAS BACA:
1930 Census: Living in Roswell, New México. Late 1940s: He was a special deputy sheriff for Lincoln County.

Children of PAUBLITA ANALLA and DANIEL PÉREZ are:
    i.   DILIA[4] PÉREZ, b. 1910.
    ii.   LORENZO PÉREZ, b. 1912.

Children of PAUBLITA ANALLA and ELÍAS BACA are:
22.   iii.   AVRORA[4] BACA, b. January 06, 1920, Arabela, New México.
    iv.   YSIDRO BACA[67], b. February 11, 1922.
    v.   LEANDRO BACA[67], b. March 13, 1924.
    vi.   BARBARITA BACA[67], b. January 20, 1926.
    vii. ADAM BACA.

12. DOMINGO[3] ANALLA *(PEDRO[2], YSIDORO[1])* was born Abt. 1861[68]. He married (1) JOSEFA GUTIÉRREZ[69]. He married (2) MANUELA ALMENDARES SÁNCHEZ September 08, 1895 in Lincoln County, Territory of New México[70], daughter of DOMINGO SÁNCHES and JUANITA ALMENDARES.

Notes for DOMINGO ANALLA:
Also known as Domingo Anaya.
1900 Census: Living in Alamogordo, Guadalupe County, Territory of New México.

Children of DOMINGO ANALLA and JOSEFA GUTIÉRREZ are:
    i.   ENCARNACIÓN[4] ANALLA[71], b. March 25, 1887[72]; d. December 1975, Roswell, New México.
    ii.   MARIANO ANALLA, b. December 1890[72].

Child of DOMINGO ANALLA and MANUELA SÁNCHEZ is:
    iii.   OFELIA[4] ANALLA, b. July 1897[72].

13. NARCISO[3] ANALLA *(PEDRO[2], YSIDORO[1])* was born October 1864[73]. He married ELENA BARTLETT October 01, 1885 in Lincoln County, Territory of New México[74], daughter of CHARLES BARTLETT and ADELA GALINDRO.

Children of NARCISO ANALLA and ELENA BARTLETT are:
    i.   AMELIA[4] ANALLA, b. August 1898[75].
    ii.   LUISA ANALLA, b. Abt. 1901[76].
    iii.   EUFANIA ANALLA[77], b. February 1906[78]; d. December 21, 1921, Roswell, New México.

Notes for EUFANIA ANALLA:
Also known as Epifania.

    iv.   CARLOS ANALLA[79], b. March 05, 1908, Picacho, Territory of New México[80]; d. July 21, 1920, Roswell, New México.
    v.   ALFREDO ANALLA, b. Abt. 1914[80].

14. BIDAL[3] ANALLA *(PEDRO[2], YSIDORO[1])* was born Abt. 1869[81], and died in Tularosa, New México. She married DONACIANO SÁNCHEZ[82] May 11, 1884 in Tularoso, Territory of New México[83], son of MAURICIO SÁNCHES and JESÚSITA GONZÁLES.

Notes for BIDAL ANALLA:
Also known as Vidal.

Notes for DONACIANO SÁNCHEZ:
1880-1920 Census: Living in Tularoso, Territory of New México.
Buried: Tularosa, New México.

Children of BIDAL ANALLA and DONACIANO SÁNCHEZ are:
    i.   JUAN BAUTISTA[4] SÁNCHEZ, b. December 05, 1885[84].

Notes for JUAN BAUTISTA SÁNCHEZ:
Baptized: January 3, 1885. Padrinos: Mauricio de la Trinidad Sánchez, María Candida de Jesús Gonzáles.

    ii.   DANIEL SÁNCHEZ, b. January 03, 1896, Analla, Territory of New México[85]; m. REBECCA ANALLA[86], December 18, 1919, Lincoln, New México[86].

Notes for DANIEL SÁNCHEZ:
1900 Census: Living with his grandfather, Pedro Analla and grandmother, María del Refugio Chávez de Analla.

15. ESCOLASTICA[3] ANALLA *(PEDRO[2], YSIDORO[1])*[87] was born February 10, 1872 in Picacho, Territory of New México[88], and died October 15, 1969 in Roswell, New México. She married DAMIAN MIRELES October 17, 1887[89], son of SANTIAGO MIRELES and BRIGIDA GALINDRO.

Notes for DAMIAN MIRELES:
1910 Census: Living in Las Palas, Territory of New México.
1930 Census: Living in Arabela, New México.

Children of ESCOLASTICA ANALLA and DAMIAN MIRELES are:
23.   i.   JUAN MIGUEL[4] MIRELES, b. November 19, 1889, Picacho, Territory of New México; d. October 1977, Dexter, New México..
24.   ii.   DOMITILIA MIRELES, b. January 23, 1905, Fort Sumner, Territory of New México; d. 1928-1932.

16. ESIQUIO[3] SÁNCHEZ *(MARÍA ANDREA[2] ANALLA, YSIDORO[1])* was born November 1854 in Punta de Agua, Territory of New México[90], and died Bef. 1904[91]. He married MARÍA ISABEL ANALLA April 24, 1873 in Lincoln County, Territory of New México[92], daughter of JOSÉ ANALLA and MARÍA SEDILLO.

Children of ESIQUIO SÁNCHEZ and MARÍA ANALLA are:
    i.   JOSÉ ANALLA[4] SÁNCHEZ, b. Abt. 1874[93]; m. NESTORA FLORES, February 01, 1893, Lincoln County, Territory of New México[94].
    ii.   MIGUEL ANALLA SÁNCHEZ, b. Abt. 1876[95].
    iii.   NICOLÁSA ANALLA SÁNCHEZ, b. Abt. 1878[95].
    iv.   LYDIA SÁNCHEZ, b. Abt. 1879[95]; m. PEDRO VILLESCAS, December 04, 1895, Lincoln County, Territory of New México[96].
20.   v.   JOSEFA ANALLA SÁNCHEZ, b. August 27, 1881, Picacho, Territory of New México.
    vi.   ROSENDA SÁNCHEZ, b. March 1883, San Patricio, Territory of New México[97]; m. CELESTINO VIGIL, July 15, 1901[98].
    vii.   GERONIMO SÁNCHEZ, b. September 30, 1885, San Patricio, Territory of New México[99].
    viii.   ESIQUIO SÁNCHEZ[100], b. April 15, 1887, San Patricio, Territory of New México[101]; m. CARMEN A. WILSON, September 26, 1938, San Patricio, New México[102].
    ix.   MALCLOVIA SÁNCHEZ, b. November 1892, San Patricio, Territory of New México[103].
    x.   VICTORIANA SÁNCHEZ, b. May 1900, San Patricio, Territory of New México[103].

Generation No. 4

17. PEDRO NOBERTO[4] ANALLA *(TIMOTEO[3], JOSÉ PEDRO[2], YSIDORO[1])*[104] was born July 18, 1884 in Lincoln County, Territory of New México[105]. He married CARLOTA CARILLO.

Notes for PEDRO NOBERTO ANALLA:
Draft registration card indicates that he was born on January 27, 1885.

Child of PEDRO ANALLA and CARLOTA CARILLO is:
      i.   ERNESTO[5] ANALLA[106], b. 1910; d. June 19, 1933, Las Vegas, New México.

18. ANTONIA[4] ANALLA *(TIMOTEO[3], JOSÉ PEDRO[2], YSIDORO[1])* was born September 1898[107]. She married (1) TIBURCIO BENAVIDEZ[108]. She married (2) MANUEL HORTON, son of WALTER HORTON and TERESA LÓPEZ. She married (3) CORNELIO LUCERO, son of AMARANTE LUCERO and REBECA DE LUCERO.

Notes for ANTONIA ANALLA:
Also known as Tonita.

Notes for TIBURCIO BENAVIDEZ:
Also known as Tivoricio.
1920 Census: Living in Las Palas, New México.

Children of ANTONIA ANALLA and TIBURCIO BENAVIDEZ are:
      i.   LEONOR[5] BENAVIDEZ, b. June 29, 1917, Arabela, New México[109]; m. GEORGE RUE, May 29, 1934, Arabela, New México[109].

Notes for LEONOR BENAVIDEZ:
Raised by Elías Baca and Pablita Analla de Baca.

Notes for GEORGE RUE:
Natural father was A. H. Rue.

      ii.   ANTONIO BENAVIDEZ, b. Abt. 1920[110].
      iii.   TIVORCIA BENAVIDEZ.

Notes for TIVORCIA BENAVIDEZ:
Raised by Elías Baca and Pablita Analla de Baca.

Child of ANTONIA ANALLA and MANUEL HORTON is:
      iv.   RAMÓN[5] HORTON[111], b. December 15, 1931, Roswell, New México; d. April 01, 1994, Sacramento, California.

Notes for RAMÓN HORTON:
Buried in South Park Cemetery, Roswell, New México.

Child of ANTONIA ANALLA and CORNELIO LUCERO is:
      v.   ARCENIA[5] LUCERO[112], b. 1934; d. May 18, 1934, Escondida, New México.

19. JESÚSITA[4] ANALLA *(JUAN[3], JOSÉ PEDRO[2], YSIDORO[1])* was born July 1877[113]. She married (1) PEDRO SALCIDO[114]. She married (2) PEDRO GUEBARRA RODRÍGUEZ May 06, 1902[115], son of MARGARITO RODRÍGUEZ and LUCÍA GUEBARA.

Child of JESÚSITA ANALLA and PEDRO SALCIDO is:
      i.   SUSANITA[5] SALCIDO, b. August 1891[116].

20. JOSEFA ANALLA[4] SÁNCHEZ *(ESIQUIO[3], MARÍA ANDREA[2] ANALLA, YSIDORO[1])* was born August 27, 1881 in Picacho, Territory of New México[117]. She married SEVERO PADILLA March 04, 1899[118], son of CENOBIO PADILLA and SATURNINA TORRES.

Child of JOSEFA SÁNCHEZ and SEVERO PADILLA is:
      i.   DELFINIA PADILLA Y[5] WEST, b. November 21, 1900, San Patricio, Territory of New México[119]; m. FIDEL CHÁVEZ[120], June 28, 1915, Lincoln, New México[121].

Notes for DELFINIA PADILLA Y WEST:
Also known as Delfinia Sánchez, Delfinia Sánchez y West.
Raised and adopted by John C. West.

Notes for FIDEL CHÁVEZ:
Lists his mother as Francisquita Luna.

21. LUCÍA[4] ANAYA *(PEDRO[3] ANALLA, JOSÉ PEDRO[2], YSIDORO[1])*[122] was born September 20, 1912, and died August 02, 1967 in Barstow, California. She married JAMES SALSBERRY March 26, 1927[123], son of JAMES SALSBERRY and MANUELITA HERRERA.

Children of LUCÍA ANAYA and JAMES SALSBERRY are:

    i.   BERTHA GRACE[5] SALSBERRY[124], b. October 13, 1928, Capitán, New México[125]; m. JOE M. BARELA, February 05, 1948, Carrizozo, New México[126].

    ii.   JAMES ANAYA SALSBERRY[127], b. March 16, 1930, Ruidoso, New México; d. November 26, 2009, Dulzura, California; m. (1) GLORIA SALSBERRY; m. (2) ALICIA ESPERANSA CARABAJAL, March 16, 1951.

    iii.   BETTY SALSBERRY, b. May 28, 1932, Capitán, New México; m. PATROCINIO GARCÍA, April 12, 1951.

    iv.   MARY ROSE SALSBERRY[128], b. March 02, 1934, Fort Stanton, New México; d. November 11, 1985, San Bernadino, California; m. MAX CÓRDOVA, September 30, 1956, Barstow, California.

    v.   PEDRO JOSÉ SALSBERRY, b. January 29, 1937, Capítan, New México; m. MARLYNE MARTÍNEZ, September 30, 1957, San Bernadino, California.

    vi.   ANTHONY SALSBERRY, b. June 10, 1939, Capítan, New México; m. (1) PATRICIA SANDOVAL, San Bernadino, California; m. (2) WANDA SALSBERRY.

    vii.   LUCY SOCORRO SALSBERRY[128], b. January 02, 1941, Capítan, New México; d. July 13, 1992, San Bernadino, California; m. (1) SULLIVAN COOK; m. (2) HENRY HESTER ANGLIN, July 19, 1960, San Bernadino, California[129].

    viii.   MANUEL SALOMON SALSBERRY, b. April 05, 1943, Fort Stockton, New México; m. LYDIA RAMOS, June 03, 1963, San Bernadino, California.

    ix.   CARMEN DORA SALSBERRY, b. November 15, 1945, Fort Stockton, New México; m. (1) ARNOLD CARLOS; m. (2) RONNIE C. LARA, October 02, 1965, San Bernadino, California.

    x.   DAVÍD JESÚS SALSBERRY, b. April 23, 1949, Roswell, New México; d. March 03, 1995, San Bernadino, California; m. (1) ANA LEE GUTIÉRREZ; m. (2) ELIZABETH MARTÍNEZ.

    xi.   LUPE SALSBERRY, b. June 15, 1951, Alamogordo, New México; m. RUBÉN JOE CHÁVEZ, April 07, 1975, San Bernadino, California.

    xii.   MARÍA BONITA SALSBERRY, b. September 1953, San Bernadino, California.

    xiii.   ELIZABETH SALSBERRY, b. February 02, 1956, San Bernadino, California; m. (1) ROBERT VITO COMITO; m. (2) DANNY ENRÍQUEZ, February 02, 1975, Las Vegas, Nevada.

22. AVRORA[4] BACA *(PAUBLITA[3] ANALLA, JOSÉ PEDRO[2], YSIDORO[1])*[130] was born January 06, 1920 in Arabela, New México[131]. She married RAFAEL GONZÁLES[132] June 05, 1936 in San Patricio, New México[133], son of EPAMINOANDAS GONZÁLES and ELVIRA GONZÁLES.

Children of AVRORA BACA and RAFAEL GONZÁLES are:

    i.   DOMINGO[5] GONZÁLES[134], b. Abt. 1937, San Patricio, New México; d. October 28, 1937, San Patricio, New México.

    ii.   ARMANDO GONZÁLES[135], b. Abt. 1940, San Patricio, New México; d. October 08, 1940, San Patricio, New México.

23. JUAN MIGUEL[4] MIRELES *(ESCOLASTICA[3] ANALLA, PEDRO[2], YSIDORO[1])*[136] was born November 19, 1889 in Picacho, Territory of New México[137], and died October 1977 in Dexter, New México.. He married ROSA MOYA June 12, 1913 in Arabela, Territory of New México[138], daughter of RUMALDO MOYA and CARLOTA MONTOYA.

Child of JUAN MIRELES and ROSA MOYA is:

    i.   ELOY[5] MIRELES[139], b. November 17, 1924, Arabela, New México; d. July 21, 2003, Dexter, New México.; m. ELISER LUCERO, November 22, 1943, Carrizozo, New México[140].

24. DOMITILIA[4] MIRELES *(ESCOLASTICA[3] ANALLA, PEDRO[2], YSIDORO[1])* was born January 23, 1905 in Fort Sumner, Territory of New México[141], and died 1928-1932. She married PAZ MOYA March 18, 1920 in Tinnie, New México[141].

Children of DOMITILIA MIRELES and PAZ MOYA are:

    i.   BEATRIZ[5] MOYA, b. Abt. 1925, Arabela, New México[142].

    ii.   JOSEFITA MOYA, b. Abt. 1928, Arabela, New México[142].

Genealogy of Juan Baca

Generation No. 1

1. JUAN[1] BACA was born Abt. 1842[1]. He married GABINA TORRES CHÁVEZ, daughter of JUAN CHÁVEZ and MARÍA TORRES.

Notes for JUAN BACA:
1870 & 1880 Census: Living in Lincoln, Territory of New México.

Notes for GABINA TORRES CHÁVEZ:
1860 Census: Living in Manzano, Territory of New México.

Children of JUAN BACA and GABINA CHÁVEZ are:

2.	i.	SYLVESTERE[2] BACA, b. January 01, 1863, La Placita del Río Bonito, Territory of New México; d. February 09, 1935, Carrizozo, New México.
3.	ii.	JOSÉ LEÓN BACA, b. Abt. 1865.
	iii.	TERESITA BACA, b. 1867.

Generation No. 2

2. SYLVESTERE[2] BACA *(JUAN[1])* was born January 01, 1863 in La Placita del Río Bonito, Territory of New México[2], and died February 09, 1935 in Carrizozo, New México[3]. He married (1) EULOJIA GALINDRO November 17, 1880 in Lincoln, Territory of New México[4]. He married (2) MARÍA CONCEPCIÓN PADILLA October 31, 1910 in Lincoln, Territory of New México[5], daughter of JOSÉ PADILLA and NESTORA SAMORA. He married (3) PULIDORA CHÁVEZ June 23, 1917 in Carrizozo, New México[6].

Notes for SYLVESTERE BACA:
Also known as Sylvestre, Silvestre.

Children of SYLVESTERE BACA and EULOJIA GALINDRO are:

	i.	ENCARNACIÓN[3] BACA, b. November 1881, Lincoln, Territory of New México[7]; m. ÁBRAN MORAGA, January 21, 1901[8].
4.	ii.	EUSEVIO BACA, b. March 06, 1883, Lincoln, Territory of New México; d. December 24, 1926, Carrizozo, New México.
	iii.	JUANITA GALINDRO BACA, b. March 18, 1886, Lincoln, Territory of New México[9]; m. MERIJILDO TORRES, September 26, 1907, Lincoln, Territory of New México[9].

Notes for JUANITA GALINDRO BACA:
Also known as Juana.

5.	iv.	GABINA BACA, b. June 1891, Lincoln, Territory of New México.

3. JOSÉ LEÓN[2] BACA *(JUAN[1])* was born Abt. 1865[10]. He married BEATRIZ CARRILLO December 22, 1888 in Manzano, Territory of New México[11], daughter of JOSÉ CARRILLO and NICANORA MÁRQUEZ.

Children of JOSÉ BACA and BEATRIZ CARRILLO are:

	i.	MARIVALA[3] BACA, b. October 1891[12].
	ii.	CARLOTA BACA, b. October 1892[12].
	iii.	JUAN BACA, b. May 1894[12].
	iv.	JOSEFA BACA, b. December 1895[12].
	v.	ENRÍQUES BACA, b. November 1898[12].

Generation No. 3

4. EUSEVIO[3] BACA *(SYLVESTERE[2], JUAN[1])[13]* was born March 06, 1883 in Lincoln, Territory of New México[14], and died December 24, 1926 in Carrizozo, New México[15]. He married REGINA BARRAGÁN June 06, 1904[16], daughter of ANTONIO BARRAGÁN and MARÍA HERRERA.

Notes for EUSEVIO BACA:
Also known as Eusebio.

Children of EUSEVIO BACA and REGINA BARRAGÁN are:
      i.   JUAN BAUTISTA[4] BACA, b. Abt. 1906[17]; m. VIVIANA LUERAS, November 22, 1924, Lincoln, New México[18].

Notes for VIVIANA LUERAS:
Also known as Biviana.

      ii.   ROSA BACA, b. Abt. 1912[19]; m. ALFREDO LÓPEZ, October 21, 1933, Carrizozo, New México[20].

Notes for ALFREDO LÓPEZ:
Immigrated to the U.S. in about 1908.

      iii.   SYLVESTRE BACA[21], b. October 20, 1913, Lincoln, New México[22].
      iv.   ANTONIO BACA, b. Abt. 1916[22].
6.   v.   EUSEBIO BACA, b. September 12, 1920, Lincoln, New México; d. April 30, 2010, Mescalero, New México.
      vi.   LUPITA BACA, b. 1919.

5. GABINA[3] BACA *(SYLVESTERE[2], JUAN[1])* was born June 1891 in Lincoln, Territory of New México[23]. She married GEORGE ARCHULETA August 17, 1910[24], son of JESÚS ARCHULETA and PABLA TORRES.

Notes for GABINA BACA:
Also known as Gavinita.

Children of GABINA BACA and GEORGE ARCHULETA are:
      i.   AMALIA[4] ARCHULETA, b. 1902.
      ii.   BEATRICE ARCHULETA, b. 1903.

Generation No. 4

6. EUSEBIO[4] BACA *(EUSEVIO[3], SYLVESTERE[2], JUAN[1])[25]* was born September 12, 1920 in Lincoln, New México[26], and died April 30, 2010 in Mescalero, New México. He married TERESA VIDAURRI October 05, 1952 in Carrizozo, New México[27].

Notes for EUSEBIO BACA:
Also known as Chevo.
He moved to California in 1966 but returned to Lincoln County in 1972. Worked for the Lincoln County Sheriff Department.

Children of EUSEBIO BACA and TERESA VIDAURRI are:
      i.   PAUL[5] BACA, b. Private.
      ii.   PETER BACA, b. Private.
      iii.   MARINA BACA, b. Private.

Genealogy of Mariano Baca

Generation No. 1

1. MARIANO[1] BACA[1]. He married MARÍA MONTAÑO[1].

Child of MARIANO BACA and MARÍA MONTAÑO is:

2.   i.   DAMACIO[2] BACA, b. August 20, 1851; d. August 07, 1934, Hondo, New México.

Generation No. 2

2. DAMACIO[2] BACA *(MARIANO[1])*[2] was born August 20, 1851, and died August 07, 1934 in Hondo, New México[3]. He married MARÍA LEANDRA LUNA BACA[4] Abt. 1875[5], daughter of JUAN BACA and DOLÓRES LUNA.

Notes for DAMACIO BACA:
1910 Census: Living in San Patricio, Territory of New México.
1920 Census shows that both Damacio and Maria as being 66 years old.
1930 Census: Living in Hondo, New México. Indicates that both Damacio and Maria as being 87 years old.

Notes for MARÍA LEANDRA LUNA BACA:
1860 Census: Living in Belén, Territory of New México.

Children of DAMACIO BACA and MARÍA BACA are:

3.   i.   DELFINIA[3] BACA, b. May 1880, San Patricio, Territory of New México; d. October 01, 1946, Roswell, New México.
4.   ii.   JACOBO BACA, b. 1885.
5.   iii.   ELÍAS BACA, b. May 15, 1893, Hondo, Territory of New México.
6.   iv.   CATARINA BACA, b. May 20, 1889, Hondo, Territory of New México; d. January 1979, Roswell, New México.

Generation No. 3

3. DELFINIA[3] BACA *(DAMACIO[2], MARIANO[1])* was born May 1880 in San Patricio, Territory of New México[6], and died October 01, 1946 in Roswell, New México. She married (1) IGNACIO MAÉS[7], son of JOSÉ MAÉS and MANUELITA LUCERO. She married (2) PRECILIANO TORRES[8] Abt. 1893[9], son of JUAN TORRES and LUGUARDITA CEDILLO.

Children of DELFINIA BACA and PRECILIANO TORRES are:

7.   i.   MARTÍN BACA[4] TORRES, b. January 13, 1895, Rebentón, Territory of New México.
8.   ii.   LUÍS BACA TORRES, b. October 11, 1897, Patos, Territory of New México; d. November 03, 1970, Roswell, New México.
9.   iii.   JOSÉ BACA TORRES, b. August 15, 1898, Hondo, Territory of New México; d. April 25, 1970, Roswell, New México.

4. JACOBO[3] BACA *(DAMACIO[2], MARIANO[1])* was born 1885[10]. He married JUANITA MIRANDA December 06, 1909 in Hondo, Territory of New México[11], daughter of PABLO MIRANDA and VICTORIANA GUTIÉRREZ.

Notes for JACOBO BACA:
1920 Census: Living in Hondo, New México.
1930 Census: Living in Roswell, New México.

Children of JACOBO BACA and JUANITA MIRANDA are:

       i.   ELISEO[4] BACA, b. December 05, 1910, Hondo, Territory of New México[12]; d. July 1975, Roswell, New México; m. AGAPITA BENAVIDEZ, July 23, 1934[13].

Notes for ELISEO BACA:
Also known as Elijio.

      ii.   FRANK BACA, b. 1915[14].
      iii.   MARGARITA BACA, b. Abt. 1918[14].

5. ELÍAS[3] BACA *(DAMACIO[2], MARIANO[1])* was born May 15, 1893 in Hondo, Territory of New México[15]. He married PAUBLITA ANALLA October 07, 1920 in Arabela, New México[15], daughter of JOSÉ ANALLA and DULCESNOMBRES MONTOYA.

Notes for ELÍAS BACA:
1930 Census: Living in Roswell, New México.
Late 1940s: He was a special deputy sheriff for Lincoln County.

Notes for PAUBLITA ANALLA:
Also known as Pablita, Paulita and Panchita.
Marriage records indicate that she was born on January 25, 1897. (Book 5, Page 88)

Children of ELÍAS BACA and PAUBLITA ANALLA are:
10.   i.   AVRORA[4] BACA, b. January 06, 1920, Arabela, New México.
      ii.   YSIDRO BACA[16], b. February 11, 1922.
      iii. LEANDRO BACA[16], b. March 13, 1924.
      iv. BARBARITA BACA[16], b. January 20, 1926.
      v.   ADAM BACA.

6. CATARINA[3] BACA *(DAMACIO[2], MARIANO[1])* was born May 20, 1889 in Hondo, Territory of New México[17], and died January 1979 in Roswell, New México. She met (1) CRECENCIO CARRILLO, son of CAYETANO CARRILLO and BERIGNA BARELA. She married (2) RAFAEL SALCIDO February 08, 1923[18], son of FAUSTINO SALCIDO and MARÍA CHÁVES.

Notes for CRECENCIO CARRILLO:
1880 Census: Living in Tularoso, Doña Ana County, Territory of New México.
1920 Census: Living in Lincoln, Territory of New México.
1930 Census: Living in Roswell, New México.

Child of CATARINA BACA and CRECENCIO CARRILLO is:
11.   i.   JUAN[4] BACA, b. August 01, 1914; d. March 20, 1995, Ruidoso Downs, New México.

Children of CATARINA BACA and RAFAEL SALCIDO are:
      ii.   ARCENIA[4] SALCIDO, b. March 22, 1922, Hondo, New México[19]; d. February 09, 2000, Roswell, New México; m. IGNACIO ORTIZ.
      iii. CARMELITA SALCIDO, b. Abt. 1923[19].
      iv. FLORINDA SALCIDO, b. Abt. 1925[19].
      v.   ISABEL SALCIDO, b. Abt. 1927[19].

Generation No. 4

7. MARTÍN BACA[4] TORRES *(DELFINIA[3] BACA, DAMACIO[2], MARIANO[1])* was born January 13, 1895 in Rebentón, Territory of New México[20]. He married (1) RITA VALLES February 05, 1915 in San Patricio, New México[21], daughter of FELIPA ORONA. He married (2) JUANITA CHÁVES[22] March 16, 1933[23], daughter of PLACIDO CHÁVES and TRENIDAD LUNA.

Children of MARTÍN TORRES and RITA VALLES are:
      i.   MANUEL VALLES[5] TORRES, b. Abt. November 1919[24].
      ii.   ERNESTO TORRES[25], b. February 14, 1922, Hondo, New México; d. April 21, 2010, Roswell, New México; m. MARIANA ALDAZ SÁNCHEZ[25].

8. LUÍS BACA[4] TORRES *(DELFINIA[3] BACA, DAMACIO[2], MARIANO[1])* was born October 11, 1897 in Patos, Territory of New México[26], and died November 03, 1970 in Roswell, New México[26]. He married AMANDA SÁNCHEZ November 30, 1927 in Tularosa, New México[27], daughter of MANUEL SÁNCHEZ and ESTELA GILL.

Notes for LUÍS BACA TORRES:
After selling the farm, he and his wife migrated to Roswell, New México.
August 26, 1918: Discharged WW I Veteran.

Children of LUÍS TORRES and AMANDA SÁNCHEZ are:
  i.   MAX[5] TORRES[28], b. October 12, 1928, Glencoe, New México; d. August 24, 2008, Willcox, Arizona; m. ESTER MENDOZA, October 25, 1952, Roswell, New México[29].
  ii. TERESITA TORRES[30], b. December 04, 1929, Glencoe, New México; d. December 28, 1997, Alburquerque, New México; m. JOHNNY MATA[30], December 28, 1950, Roswell, New México[31].
  iii. EPIFANIA TORRES, b. January 11, 1931, Glencoe, New México[32]; d. October 31, 1986, Roswell, New México[32]; m. JOSEPH THOMAS ATKINSON[32], November 25, 1952, Pecos, Texas[32].
  iv. CLARITA TORRES, b. June 04, 1932, Glencoe, New México[32]; m. BUDDY BAKER[32].
  v.   PRECILIANO SÁNCHEZ TORRES, b. April 27, 1935, Glencoe, New México[32]; m. MARY LOU MARRUJO[32], May 05, 1957, Roswell, New México[32].
  vi. ESTELLA JUANITA TORRES, b. May 04, 1936[32]; m. ROY BASCOM[32].
  vii. BILLY SÁNCHEZ TORRES, b. March 13, 1938, Glencoe, New México[32]; m. MARTHA MOYERS.
  viii. ANTONIO TORRES, b. November 18, 1944, Lake Arthur, New México[32]; m. PATRICIA GRZELACHOWSKI[32].
  ix. JOSÉ JESÚS TORRES, b. December 15, 1946, Glencoe, New México[32]; d. March 04, 2006, Edgewood, New México[32]; m. IRENE MARGARETE GRZELACHOWSKI.

9. JOSÉ BACA[4] TORRES *(DELFINIA[3] BACA, DAMACIO[2], MARIANO[1])*[33] was born August 15, 1898 in Hondo, Territory of New México, and died April 25, 1970 in Roswell, New México. He married EMILIA CHÁVEZ[33] December 30, 1918 in Lincoln, New México[34], daughter of ANTONIO CHÁVEZ and JUANA CARRILLO.

Children of JOSÉ TORRES and EMILIA CHÁVEZ are:
  i.   HILARIO CHÁVEZ[5] TORRES, b. Abt. 1922[35].
  ii. TOM CHÁVEZ TORRES, b. Abt. 1924[35].
  iii. MANUEL CHÁVEZ TORRES, b. Abt. 1926[35].
  iv. AMABLE J CHÁVEZ TORRES[36], b. June 19, 1928[37]; d. October 12, 1999, Roswell, New México.
  v.   JOE CHÁVEZ TORRES, b. Private.
  vi. MARY CHÁVEZ TORRES, b. Private.

10. AVRORA[4] BACA *(ELÍAS[3], DAMACIO[2], MARIANO[1])*[38] was born January 06, 1920 in Arabela, New México[39]. She married RAFAEL GONZÁLES[40] June 05, 1936 in San Patricio, New México[41], son of EPAMINOANDAS GONZÁLES and ELVIRA GONZÁLES.

Children of AVRORA BACA and RAFAEL GONZÁLES are:
  i.   DOMINGO[5] GONZÁLES[42], b. Abt. 1937, San Patricio, New México; d. October 28, 1937, San Patricio, New México.
  ii. ARMANDO GONZÁLES[43], b. Abt. 1940, San Patricio, New México; d. October 08, 1940, San Patricio, New México.

11. JUAN[4] BACA *(CATARINA[3], DAMACIO[2], MARIANO[1])*[44] was born August 01, 1914[45], and died March 20, 1995 in Ruidoso Downs, New México. He married JOSEFITA MONTOYA[46], daughter of DOROTEO MONTOYA and ALBINA SILVA.

Notes for JUAN BACA:
Social Security Death Index indicates that he was born on June 30, 1914. Raised with Crecencio Carrillo.

Notes for JOSEFITA MONTOYA:
Also known as Josephine.

Children of JUAN BACA and JOSEFITA MONTOYA are:
  i.   CRUCITA[5] BACA, b. May 03, 1946; m. (1) DANNY CHÁVEZ.
  ii. PETE BACA, b. Private.

Genealogy of Saturnino Baca

Generation No. 1

1. SATURNINO[1] BACA[1] was born November 30, 1836 in Sebollita, Nuevo México, La República de México[2], and died March 07, 1925 in Lincoln, New México. He married JUANA CHÁVEZ[3].

Notes for SATURNINO BACA:
Captain, Company E, 1st NM Calvary.
1850 Census: Cubero, Territory of New México.
1868: Elected to the Territorial House of Representitives.

Children of SATURNINO BACA and JUANA CHÁVEZ are:
2.   i.   BONIFACIO[2] BACA, b. April 26, 1857; d. January 19, 1913, Lincoln, New México.
         ii.   ISADORA BACA, b. Abt. 1858, Cubero, Territory of New México[4].
         iii.   RAMÓN BACA, b. Abt. 1862[5].
         iv.   JOSEFA BACA, b. Abt. 1864[5].
         v.   CARLOTA BACA, b. Abt. 1866[5]; m. JAMES R. BRENT, June 24, 1886[6].

Notes for JAMES R. BRENT:
1870 Census: Living in Scott, Virginia
         1900 Census: Living in Silver City, Territory of New México.

Generation No. 2

2. BONIFACIO[2] BACA *(SATURNINO[1])[7]* was born April 26, 1857, and died January 19, 1913 in Lincoln, New México. He married TELESFORA BACA August 30, 1882 in Lincoln, Territory of New México[8], daughter of MARTÍN BACA and GUADALUPE VALLES.

Children of BONIFACIO BACA and TELESFORA BACA are:
         i.   CARMEL[3] BACA, b. July 1887[9].
         ii.   SOFIA BACA, b. September 12, 1888, Lincoln, Territory of New México[10]; m. (1) JUAN REGALADO[11], September 11, 1905, Lincoln, Territory of New México[12]; m. (2) JUAN MIRABAL, September 11, 1905, Lincoln, Territory of New México[12].

Notes for JUAN REGALADO:
Also known as Juan Regalao.
1875: Emigrated from México.
1900 Census: Living in Rebentón, New
Buried: Rebentón, New México.

         iii.   MABEL BACA, b. April 20, 1890, Lincoln, Territory of New México[13]; m. SAMBRANO VIGIL, October 06, 1907, Lincoln, Territory of New México[13].
         iv.   JOSÉ BACA, b. April 15, 1894[14].
         v.   ANEDA BACA, b. March 1894[15].
         vi.   JUANITA BACA, b. May 1896[15].
         vii.   AVESLINO BACA, b. June 1898[15].
         viii.   JOSEFA BACA, b. January 1900[15].

Genealogy of Miguel Benavides

Generation No. 1

1. MIGUEL[1] BENAVIDES was born Abt. 1790[1]. He married MARÍA MANUELA JARAMILLO November 17, 1816 in Tomé, El Reyno de Nuevo México, Nueva España[2].

Children of MIGUEL BENAVIDES and MARÍA JARAMILLO are:
2.	i.	MARÍA BENTURA[2] BENAVIDES, b. Abt. 1826.
3.	ii.	JOSÉ FRANCISCO BENAVIDES, b. Abt. 1831.
	iii.	VICTORIA BENAVIDEZ, b. Abt. 1840[3].
4.	iv.	SANTIAGO BENAVIDES, b. Abt. 1841, Tomé, Nuevo México, La República de México; d. May 24, 1924, Carrizozo, New México.
	v.	MARÍA ANICETA DE JESÚS BENAVIDES, b. Abt. 1843[3].
	vi.	JOSÉ DE LA PAZ BENAVIDES, b. Abt. 1845[3].

Generation No. 2

2. MARÍA BENTURA[2] BENAVIDES *(MIGUEL[1])* was born Abt. 1826[4]. She married ANTONIO ROMERO.

Notes for ANTONIO ROMERO:
Also known as Antonio Romero y Baca.

Children of MARÍA BENAVIDES and ANTONIO ROMERO are:
	i.	JOSÉ DE JESÚS[3] ROMERO, b. Abt. 1841[4].
	ii.	MARCOS ROMERO, b. Abt. 1846[4].
	iii.	ROSA ROMERO, b. Abt. 1851[4].

3. JOSÉ FRANCISCO[2] BENAVIDES *(MIGUEL[1])* was born Abt. 1831[5]. He married MARÍA SESARIA ROMERO April 16, 1854 in Tomé, Territory of New México[6].

Notes for JOSÉ FRANCISCO BENAVIDES:
1850 Census: Living in Tomé, Territory of New México.
1860 Census: Living in Manzano, Territory of New México.
1870 Census: Living in Santa Clara, Mora County, Territory of New México.
1880 Census: Living in Hot Springs & Upper Las Vegas, Territory of New México.

Children of JOSÉ BENAVIDES and MARÍA ROMERO are:
	i.	MARÍA[3] BENAVIDEZ, b. Abt. 1854[7].
	ii.	ESTEFANA BENAVIDEZ, b. Abt. 1856[7].
	iii.	JUAN BENAVIDEZ, b. Abt. 1858[7].

Santiago Benavides

4. SANTIAGO[2] BENAVIDES *(MIGUEL[1])* was born Abt. 1841 in Tomé, Nuevo México, La República de México[8], and died May 24, 1924 in Carrizozo, New México. He married ANTONIA MOYA August 23, 1861 in Tomé, Territory of New México[9], daughter of MANUEL MOYA and MARÍA MONTOYA.

Notes for SANTIAGO BENAVIDES:
Also known as José Santiago Benavides.
1850 Census: Living in Tomé, Territory of New México. (Born 1841)
1880 Census: Living in Las Tablas, Territory of New México.

Notes for ANTONIA MOYA:
Also known as María Antonia Molla.
1900 Census: Living in Lincoln, District 64, Territory of New México. (Antonia Moya)
1920 Census: Living in Las Palas, New México. (Antonia Benavides, Widow, born 1855)

Children of SANTIAGO BENAVIDES and ANTONIA MOYA are:
5.   i.   VICTORIANA[3] BENAVIDEZ, b. January 1867; d. March 16, 1942, Lincoln, New México.
6.   ii.   JUANITA BENAVIDEZ, b. March 31, 1869; d. February 21, 1945, Hagerman, New México
       iii.   AUGUSTÍN BENAVIDEZ, b. Abt. 1872[10].
       iv.   TOMÁS BENAVIDEZ, b. Abt. 1877[10].
       v.   ANTONIO BENAVIDEZ[11], b. January 17, 1880[12].
7.   vi.   IGINIA BENAVIDEZ, b. January 11, 1885, Las Chosas, Lincoln County, Territory of New México.
8.   vii.   EMELIA BENAVIDEZ, b. July 1887, Lincoln, Territory of New México.

Generation No. 3

5. VICTORIANA[3] BENAVIDEZ *(SANTIAGO[2] BENAVIDES, MIGUEL[1])* was born January 1867[13], and died March 16, 1942 in Lincoln, New México[14]. She married ROMULO SALAZAR Abt. 1880[15].

Notes for ROMULO SALAZAR:
1880 Census: Living in Las Tablas, Territory of New México. He was living with his stepfather, Francisco Lerma and his mother, Pabla.

Children of VICTORIANA BENAVIDEZ and ROMULO SALAZAR are:
9.   i.   EMITERIA[4] SALAZAR, b. March 1885.
       ii.   ROMULO BENAVIDEZ SALAZAR, b. July 1888[16].
       iii.   GUADALUPE SALAZAR, b. December 1890[16].

6. JUANITA[3] BENAVIDEZ *(SANTIAGO[2] BENAVIDES, MIGUEL[1])*[17] was born March 31, 1869[18], and died February 21, 1945 in Hagerman, New México . She married (1) JACINTO LUCERO[19], son of JOSÉ LUCERO and MARÍA ALDERETE. She married (2) FRANCISCO LUCERO Abt. 1900[20], son of JOSÉ LUCERO and MARÍA ALDERETE.

Notes for FRANCISCO LUCERO:
1870 Census: Living in Precinct 3, Lincoln County, Territory of New México.
1910 Census: Living in Lincoln, Territory of New México.

Children of JUANITA BENAVIDEZ and JACINTO LUCERO are:
10.   i.   REBECCA[4] LUCERO, b. March 1885, Agua Azul, Territory of New México.
11.   ii.   SARA LUCERO, b. March 1892, Agua Azul, Territory of New México.
       iii.   LUCÍA LUCERO, b. December 1893, Agua Azul, Territory of New México[21].
       iv.   JULIANITA LUCERO, b. October 1894, Agua Azul, Territory of New México[21].
       v.   DAVÍD LUCERO, b. October 1895, Agua Azul, Territory of New México[21].
       vi.   JUAN LUCERO, b. May 1899, Agua Azul, Territory of New México[21].
       vii.   FELIPA LUCERO, b. March 1900, Agua Azul, Territory of New México[21].

Children of JUANITA BENAVIDEZ and FRANCISCO LUCERO are:
       viii.   FELICITA[4] LUCERO, b. Abt. 1900[22].
       ix.   UTILIA LUCERO, b. Abt. 1901[22].
12.   x.   MARTÍN LUCERO, b. July 1902; d. May 09, 1985, Alamogordo, New México.
       xi.   CARPÍO LUCERO, b. Abt. 1908[22].

7. IGINIA[3] BENAVIDEZ *(SANTIAGO[2] BENAVIDES, MIGUEL[1])*[23] was born January 11, 1885 in Las Chosas, Lincoln County, Territory of New México[24]. She married FLORENCIO MIRELES[25] August 03, 1898[26], son of SANTIAGO MIRELES and BRIGIDA GALINDRO.

Notes for FLORENCIO MIRELES:
1930 Census: Living in Carrizozo, New México.

Children of IGINIA BENAVIDEZ and FLORENCIO MIRELES are:

	i.	CLARA[4] MIRELES, b. Abt. 1907, Lincoln, Territory of New México[27]; Stepchild; m. WILLIAM BARTLETT, March 06, 1926[28].
13.	ii.	JACOBO MIRELES, b. March 16, 1900, Lincoln, Territory of New México; d. May 1986, Albuquerque, New México.
14.	iii.	SALOMÉ MIRELES, b. 1905; Stepchild.
	iv.	ALFREDO MIRELES, b. August 07, 1909, Carrizozo, Territory of New México[29]; m. MANUELITA GUTIÉRREZ, July 17, 1933, Carrizozo, New México[29].

Notes for ALFREDO MIRELES:
1930 Census: Living in Carrizozo, New México.

| | v. | JULIAN MIRELES, b. Abt. 1910[30]. |

8. EMELIA[3] BENAVIDEZ *(SANTIAGO[2] BENAVIDES, MIGUEL[1])[31]* was born July 1887 in Lincoln, Territory of New México[32]. She married ELERDO CHÁVEZ[33] March 02, 1902[34], son of CLETO CHÁVEZ and PRUDENCIA MIRANDA.

Notes for ELERDO CHÁVEZ:
Served as a Lincoln County Probate Judge for eight years. Served as a Justice of the Peace for Carrizozo.
1920 Census: Living in Las Palas, New México.

Children of EMELIA BENAVIDEZ and ELERDO CHÁVEZ are:

| | i. | DANIEL[4] CHÁVEZ, b. Abt. 1908[35]. |
| | ii. | ANTONIO CHÁVEZ, b. Abt. 1911[35]. |

Generation No. 4

9. EMITERIA[4] SALAZAR *(VICTORIANA[3] BENAVIDEZ, SANTIAGO[2] BENAVIDES, MIGUEL[1])* was born March 1885[36]. She married RAMÓN LUNA August 28, 1901[37], son of JOSÉ DE LUNA and MARÍA TORRES.

Notes for EMITERIA SALAZAR:
Also known as Victoria Salazar.

Notes for RAMÓN LUNA:
1870 & 1880 Census: Living in Lemitar, Territory of New México.
1910-1930 Census: Living in Lincoln, Territory of New México.

Children of EMITERIA SALAZAR and RAMÓN LUNA are:

15.	i.	SANTIAGO[5] LUNA, b. July 29, 1902, Lincoln, Territory of New México.
	ii.	JUAN LUNA, b. Abt. 1908[38].
	iii.	RAMÓN LUNA[39], b. August 02, 1911, Lincoln, Territory of New México[40]; d. July 11, 1997, Alamogordo, New México; m. CRUSITA SEDILLO[41].
	iv.	JOSEFINA LUNA, b. Abt. 1919, Lincoln, New México[42]; d. 1978.

10. REBECCA[4] LUCERO *(JUANITA[3] BENAVIDEZ, SANTIAGO[2] BENAVIDES, MIGUEL[1])* was born March 1885 in Agua Azul, Territory of New México[43]. She married DEMETRIO GONZÁLES Abt. 1904[44].

Notes for DEMETRIO GONZÁLES:
1920 Census: Living in Las Palas, New México.

Children of REBECCA LUCERO and DEMETRIO GONZÁLES are:

16.	i.	ELVIRA LUCERO[5] GONZÁLES, b. January 25, 1905; d. August 09, 1996, Socorro, New México.
17.	ii.	OFELIA GONZÁLES, b. October 28, 1907; d. April 28, 1984, Roswell, New México.
	iii.	JACINTO GONZÁLES, b. Abt. 1909[45].
	iv.	BEATIZ GONZÁLES, b. Abt. 1912[46].
	v.	ERMINIO GONZÁLES[47], b. April 09, 1919, Las Palas, New México[48]; d. May 16, 2006, Roswell, New México.

11. SARA[4] LUCERO *(JUANITA[3] BENAVIDEZ, SANTIAGO[2] BENAVIDES, MIGUEL[1])* was born March 1892 in Agua Azul, Territory of New México[49]. She married LUÍS SÁNCHEZ February 07, 1909[50], son of PREDICANDA SÁNCHEZ.

Notes for LUÍS SÁNCHEZ:
Raised by María Chávez de Sánchez after his mother Predicanda had died.

Children of SARA LUCERO and LUÍS SÁNCHEZ are:
     i.   JACINTO[5] SÁNCHEZ, b. 1909, Hondo, Territory of New México[51].
    ii.   DAVÍD LUCERO SÁNCHEZ[52], b. January 17, 1911, Hondo, Territory of New México[53]; m. ISIDORA BENAVIDEZ, November 24, 1936, Arabela, New México[54].
   iii. TOMÁS SÁNCHEZ, b. May 13, 1913, Lincoln, New México[55]; m. LOYOLA SÁNCHEZ, March 26, 1947, Carrizozo, New México[55].

Notes for TOMÁS SÁNCHEZ:
Also known as Tom, Tomasito.
1920 Census: Living in Hondo, New México.

    iv. BENJAMÍN SÁNCHEZ, b. 1915, Hondo, New México[56].
    v.   FERNANDO SÁNCHEZ, b. 1919, Hondo, New México[56].
    vi. DAN SÁNCHEZ, b. 1920, Hondo, New México[57].
   vii. CARPIO SÁNCHEZ, b. 1922, Hondo, New México[57].
  viii. CARLOS SÁNCHEZ, b. 1926, Hondo, New México[57].

12. MARTÍN[4] LUCERO *(JUANITA[3] BENAVIDEZ, SANTIAGO[2] BENAVIDES, MIGUEL[1])*[58] was born July 1902[59], and died May 09, 1985 in Alamogordo, New México. He married LUCÍA ORTEGA[60] April 23, 1923[61], daughter of SANTIAGO ORTEGA and MIQUELA ARAGÓN.

Notes for MARTÍN LUCERO:
1910 Census: Living in Lincoln, Territory of New México
1930 Census: Living in Roswell, New México.

Children of MARTÍN LUCERO and LUCÍA ORTEGA are:
     i.   CARPÍO[5] LUCERO[62], b. June 02, 1924, Carrizozo, New México[63].
    ii.   MIGUEL LUCERO, b. Abt. 1926[63].
   iii. VIOLA LUCERO, b. Abt. 1928[63].
    iv. LOLA LUCERO, b. Abt. 1930[63].

13. JACOBO[4] MIRELES *(IGINIA[3] BENAVIDEZ, SANTIAGO[2] BENAVIDES, MIGUEL[1])*[64] was born March 16, 1900 in Lincoln, Territory of New México[65], and died May 1986 in Albuquerque, New México. He married LORENZA OTERO.

Notes for JACOBO MIRELES:
1900 Census: Living in Lincoln, Territory of New México.

Child of JACOBO MIRELES and LORENZA OTERO is:
     i.   BEATRIZ[5] MIRELES, b. Abt. 1924.

14. SALOMÉ[4] MIRELES *(IGINIA[3] BENAVIDEZ, SANTIAGO[2] BENAVIDES, MIGUEL[1])* was born 1905[66]. She married FILIMON CASTILLO LÓPEZ September 22, 1928 in Carrizozo, New México[66], son of JUAN LÓPEZ and MARÍA SÁNCHEZ.

Notes for FILIMON CASTILLO LÓPEZ:
1900 Census: Living in Lincoln, Territory of New México. (Filomeno Castillo) He is listed as an adopted son.
1910 Census: Living in Lincoln, Territory of New México.

Children of SALOMÉ MIRELES and FILIMON LÓPEZ are:
  i.   BERNICE[5] LÓPEZ, b. Abt. 1918[67]; Stepchild.
  ii.   ESTER LÓPEZ, b. Abt. 1920[67]; Stepchild.
  iii. MARY LÓPEZ, b. Abt. 1924[67]; Stepchild.
  iv.   EUGENIA LÓPEZ, b. Abt. 1929[67].

Generation No. 5

15. SANTIAGO[5] LUNA *(EMITERIA[4] SALAZAR, VICTORIANA[3] BENAVIDEZ, SANTIAGO[2] BENAVIDES, MIGUEL[1])* was born July 29, 1902 in Lincoln, Territory of New México[68]. He married CHONITA SEDILLO March 17, 1926 in San Patricio, New México[68], daughter of GREGORIO SEDILLO and BENINA DE SEDILLO.

Notes for SANTIAGO LUNA:
Also known as Jim.
1930 Census: Living in Lincoln, New México.

Notes for CHONITA SEDILLO:
Also known as Benina.

Children of SANTIAGO LUNA and CHONITA SEDILLO are:
  i.   JOSEPHINE[6] LUNA, b. Abt. 1927[69].
  ii.   OCTAVIA LUNA, b. Private.

16. ELVIRA LUCERO[5] GONZÁLES *(REBECCA[4] LUCERO, JUANITA[3] BENAVIDEZ, SANTIAGO[2] BENAVIDES, MIGUEL[1])*[70] was born January 25, 1905[71], and died August 09, 1996 in Socorro, New México. She married PEDRO SÁNCHEZ[72] Abt. 1920[73], son of SAMBRANO SÁNCHEZ and GREGORIA DE SANCHEZ.

Children of ELVIRA GONZÁLES and PEDRO SÁNCHEZ are:
  i.   GREGORITA[6] SÁNCHEZ, b. Abt. 1921[74].
  ii.   ANNIE SÁNCHEZ, b. Private; m. ADAM DUTCHOVER.

Notes for ADAM DUTCHOVER:
WW II Veteran. Killed in Action. Buried in Brittany, France.

  iii. HENRY SÁNCHEZ, b. Private; m. AMADA CHÁVEZ.

Notes for AMADA CHÁVEZ:
    Also known as Amy.

17. OFELIA[5] GONZÁLES *(REBECCA[4] LUCERO, JUANITA[3] BENAVIDEZ, SANTIAGO[2] BENAVIDES, MIGUEL[1])*[75] was born October 28, 1907[76], and died April 28, 1984 in Roswell, New México. She married MARIANO MONTOYA, son of JOSÉ MONTOYA and EULALIA SÁNCHEZ.

Notes for OFELIA GONZÁLES:
Also known as Felia. Buried in Hagerman, New México.

Notes for MARIANO MONTOYA:
1930 Census: Living in Hagerman, New México.

Children of OFELIA GONZÁLES and MARIANO MONTOYA are:
  i.   CLAUDIO[6] MONTOYA[77], b. May 20, 1922[78]; d. November 09, 1991.
  ii.   WILFREDO MONTOYA, b. Abt. 1925[78].
  iii. SIGFREDO MONTOYA, b. Abt. 1927[78].

Genealogy of William Brady

Generation No. 1

1. JOHN[1] BRADY. He married CATHERINE DARBY November 08, 1928 in Cavan, Ireland[1].

Child of JOHN BRADY and CATHERINE DARBY is:

2.   i.   WILLIAM[2] BRADY, b. August 16, 1829, Cavan, Ireland; d. April 01, 1878, Lincoln, Territory of New México.

Generation No. 2

2. WILLIAM[2] BRADY *(JOHN[1])* was born August 16, 1829 in Cavan, Ireland[1], and died April 01, 1878 in Lincoln, Territory of New México. He married BONIFACIA CHÁVES November 16, 1862 in Los Corrales, Territory of New México[2], daughter of JABIEL CHÁVES and YLDEFONSA DE CHÁVES.

Notes for WILLIAM BRADY:
1851: Immigrated to United States of America.
July 11, 1851: Enlisted into th United States Army in New York.
April 01, 1878
Land Patent # NMNMAA 010814, on the authority of the Homestead Entry-Original (12 Stat. 392), May 20, 1862. Issued 160 acres.

Notes for BONIFACIA CHÁVES:
Also known as María Bonifacia Cháves.

Children of WILLIAM BRADY and BONIFACIA CHÁVES are:

      i.   TEODORA[3] BRADY, b. 1862, Los Corrales, Territory of New México.

Notes for TEODORA BRADY:
Also known as Teodorita.

3.   ii.   WILLIAM CHÁVES BRADY, b. 1864, Los Corrales, Territory of New México; d. 1923.
4.   iii.   ROBERT BRADY, b. November 08, 1866, La Placita del Rio Bonito, Territory of New México; d. November 23, 1945.
5.   iv.   JUAN CHÁVEZ BRADY, b. 1868, La Placita del Rio Bonito, Territory of New México.
6.   v.   PROMETIVO BRADY, b. Abt. 1869, La Placita del Rio Bonito, Territory of New México.
      vi.   LORENZO BRADY, b. 1870, Lincoln, Territory of New México.

Notes for LORENZO BRADY:
Also known as Lawrence.
1880: He was killed by a band of Mescalero Apachés. He was struck with a tomahawk.

7.   vii.   ANITA BRADY, b. Abt. 1877, Lincoln, Territory of New México.
      viii. JAMES BRADY, b. April 10, 1877, San Patricio, Territory of New México[3]; m. LOUISA GONZÁLES, May 14, 1906, Lincoln, Territory of New México[3].

Notes for JAMES BRADY:
Lincoln County marriage records show that James Brady was born on April 10, 1877.

8.   ix.   CATARINA BRADY, b. 1879, La Junta, Territory of New México; d. January 19, 1940, San Patricio, New México.

Generation No. 3

3. WILLIAM CHÁVES[3] BRADY *(WILLIAM[2], JOHN[1])*[4] was born 1864 in Los Corrales, Territory of New México, and died 1923. He married JOSEFITA SAÍZ[4] April 28, 1902 in Lincoln, Territory of New México[5].

Notes for WILLIAM CHÁVES BRADY:
Also known as Guillermo.
1920 Census: Living in Carrizozo, New México.

Children of WILLIAM BRADY and JOSEFITA SAÍZ are:
     i.   BONIFACIA[4] BRADY, b. Abt. 1903[6].
     ii.   WILLIAM SAÍZ BRADY, b. Abt. 1907[6].
     iii.   JOSEFINA BRADY, b. May 30, 1908, White Oaks, Territory of New México; m. VICTORIANO LÓPEZ, June 16, 1929, Carrizozo, New México.
     iv.   NATAVIDAD BRADY, b. Abt. 1910[6].
     v.   ANGELINA BRADY, b. Abt. 1919[6].

4. ROBERT[3] BRADY *(WILLIAM[2], JOHN[1])*[7] was born November 08, 1866 in La Placita del Rio Bonito, Territory of New México, and died November 23, 1945. He married MANUELA LUCERO[7] September 07, 1891[8], daughter of JUAN LUCERO and MARCELINA JARAMILLO.

Notes for ROBERT BRADY:
Also known as Roberto.

Notes for MANUELA LUCERO:
Also known as Manuelita Lucero de Torres.

Children of ROBERT BRADY and MANUELA LUCERO are:
9.   i.   WILLIAM LUCERO[4] BRADY, b. March 07, 1892, Lincoln, Territory of New México; d. March 11, 1968, Hondo, New México.
     ii.   FELIS BRADY, b. May 18, 1896, San Patricio, Territory of New México[9].
10.   iii.   JOHN LUCERO BRADY, b. December 03, 1899, Hondo, Territory of New México; d. December 26, 1936.

5. JUAN CHÁVEZ[3] BRADY *(WILLIAM[2], JOHN[1])* was born 1868 in La Placita del Rio Bonito, Territory of New México. He married MARÍA URBÁN August 03, 1895[10], daughter of PABLO URBÁN and PIADAD GONZÁLES.

Notes for JUAN CHÁVEZ BRADY:
Also known as John. Living in La Junta, Territory of New México at the time of his marriage.
1910 Census: Living in Roswell, Territory of New México.

Notes for MARÍA URBÁN:
Also known as Marillita.
Living in Lincoln at the time of her marriage.

Children of JUAN BRADY and MARÍA URBÁN are:
     i.   JOHN URBÁN[4] BRADY, b. Abt. 1892[11].
     ii.   LORENZO BRADY, b. August 10, 1894, Lincoln, Territory of New México[12]; m. BESSIE CHÁVEZ, September 25, 1915[12].
11.   iii.   GUADALUPE URBÁN BRADY, b. Abt. 1897.
     iv.   JAMES BRADY, b. Abt. 1902[13].
     v.   EMMA BRADY, b. Abt. 1905[13]; m. IGNACIO GARCÍA, Abt. 1925[14].
     vi.   ALFONSO BRADY, b. Abt. 1909[15].

6. PROMETIVO[3] BRADY *(WILLIAM[2], JOHN[1])* was born Abt. 1869 in La Placita del Rio Bonito, Territory of New México[16]. He married (1) JOSEFA GUTIÉRREZ, daughter of DAMIAN GUTIÉRREZ and JUANITA SÁNCHEZ. He married (2) MANUELITA OLGUÍN April 03, 1899[17], daughter of RAMÓN OLGUÍN and LORENSA SEDILLO.

Notes for PROMETIVO BRADY:
1910 Census: Living in Roswell, Territory of New México. Listed as P.S. Brady.

Notes for JOSEFA GUTIÉRREZ:
Also known as Josefita.

Notes for MANUELITA OLGUÍN:
Also known as Manuela, Manuelita Sedillo.
1900 Census: She was living with her brother-in-law, Sisto Sedillo, and her sister, Margarita Olguín de Sedillo.

Children of PROMETIVO BRADY and JOSEFA GUTIÉRREZ are:

    i.   ORLANDO[4] BRADY, b. Abt. 1909[18].
    ii.   CELIA BRADY, b. Abt. 1914[19].
    iii. PROMETIVO BRADY, b. Abt. 1918[19].
    iv. ROY BRADY, b. Abt. 1920[19].
    v.   ERVIN BRADY, b. Abt. 1922[19].
    vi. BONIFACIO BRADY, b. Abt. 1925[19].

7. ANITA[3] BRADY *(WILLIAM[2], JOHN[1])* was born Abt. 1877 in Lincoln, Territory of New México[20]. She married FEDERICO GARCÍA February 09, 1899[21], son of VICTOR GARCÍA and APOLONIA SÁNCHEZ.

Notes for ANITA BRADY:
Also known as Anne.

Notes for FEDERICO GARCÍA:
1910 Census: Living in Roswell, Territory of New México.

Child of ANITA BRADY and FEDERICO GARCÍA is:

    i.   MIGUEL[4] GARCÍA, b. Abt. 1900[22].

Frank Randolph

8. CATARINA[3] BRADY *(WILLIAM[2], JOHN[1])*[23] was born 1879 in La Junta, Territory of New México[24], and died January 19, 1940 in San Patricio, New México. She married FRANK LUCERO RANDOLPH January 30, 1893[25], son of JOSEPH RANDOLPH and ELENOR LUCERO.

Notes for CATARINA BRADY:
Also known as Catherine, Catalina.

Notes for FRANK LUCERO RANDOLPH:
Also known as José Francisco Randolfo. Many of the Spanish speaking locals often used Randolfo rather than Randolph.
1930 Census: Living in Hondo, New México.

Children of CATARINA BRADY and FRANK RANDOLPH are:

    i.   JOSEFITA[4] RANDOLPH[26], b. April 25, 1894, San Patricio, Territory of New México; d. April 16, 1920, Roswell, New México; m. YGNACIO OLGUÍN[26], August 19, 1911, San Patricio, Territory of New México[27].

Notes for JOSEFITA RANDOLPH:
Baptismal records indicate that she was born on August 27, 1895. (Microfiche# 0016754, Page 287)

Notes for YGNACIO OLGUÍN:
June 18, 1904 to June 10, 1909- Was selected as the first postmaster of San Patricio.
1910 Census: Living in San Patricio, Territory of New México.

12.   ii.   JOSÉ CANDELARIO RANDOLPH, b. September 15, 1898, San Patricio, Territory of New México; d. December 05, 1978, Ruidoso, New México.
13.   iii. WILLIAM RANDOLPH, b. January 31, 1900, San Patricio, New México; d. March 27, 1999, Ruidoso Downs, New México.
          iv. FRANCISQUITA RANDOLPH, b. Abt. 1905, San Patricio, New México[28]; m. PEDRO TORRES, September 27, 1920, San Patricio, New México[29].

Notes for FRANCISQUITA RANDOLPH:
Also known as Francis.

Generation No. 4

9. WILLIAM LUCERO[4] BRADY *(ROBERT[3], WILLIAM[2], JOHN[1])* was born March 07, 1892 in Lincoln, Territory of New México[30], and died March 11, 1968 in Hondo, New México[31]. He married ROSARIO SÁNCHEZ[32] February 19, 1912 in Lincoln, New Mexico[33], daughter of ESTOLANO SÁNCHEZ and CORNELIA PACHECO.

Notes for WILLIAM LUCERO BRADY:
Also known as Guillermo.

Notes for ROSARIO SÁNCHEZ:
Also known as Rosarita.

Children of WILLIAM BRADY and ROSARIO SÁNCHEZ are:
     i.   MAX[5] BRADY, b. June 01, 1913, Hondo, New México[34]; d. July 17, 1985[35].

Notes for MAX BRADY:
Also known as Maximiliano.
Major in the US Army. WW II Veteran.

     ii.   ERMILO BRADY[36], b. March 13, 1915, Hondo, New México[37]; m. PRESCILLA PÉREZ, November 10, 1936, San Patricio, New México[38].
     iii.   ELMO BRADY, b. October 30, 1917, Hondo, New México[39]; d. December 29, 2008, Ruidoso, New México[39]; m. GERALDINE KIMBRELL[40], 1946, California[41].

Notes for ELMO BRADY:
WW II Veteran.

     iv.   ORLIDIA BRADY, b. Abt. 1920[42]; m. ANDREW FRESQUEZ.
     v.   BARTOLA BRADY, b. Abt. 1922[42].
     vi.   WILLIAM SÁNCHEZ BRADY[43], b. April 12, 1924, Hondo, New México[44]; m. ORALIA HERRERA[45].
     vii.   PRESTINA BRADY[46], b. March 20, 1926, Hondo, New México; d. January 18, 1995, Hondo, New México.
     viii.   LEROY BENNETT BRADY, b. April 14, 1930[47].
     ix.   BILLY JOE BRADY, b. Private; m. PATSY SALCIDO.

10. JOHN LUCERO[4] BRADY *(ROBERT[3], WILLIAM[2], JOHN[1])*[48] was born December 03, 1899 in Hondo, Territory of New México, and died December 26, 1936. He married AMALIA GONZÁLES July 05, 1919 in Capitán, New México[49], daughter of JOSÉ GONZÁLES and MARÍA CHÁVEZ.

Notes for JOHN LUCERO BRADY:
Also known as J.E. Brady and Juan Brady.
Baptismal records indicate that he was born on October 01, 1894. (Microfiche# 0016754, Page 219)

Notes for AMALIA GONZÁLES:
Also known as Emelia, Emiliana.

Child of JOHN BRADY and AMALIA GONZÁLES is:
     i.   JOHN GONZÁLES[5] BRADY[50], b. Abt. 1922, Albuquerque, New México; d. August 05, 1922, Albuquerque, New México.

11. GUADALUPE URBÁN[4] BRADY *(JUAN CHÁVEZ[3], WILLIAM[2], JOHN[1])* was born Abt. 1897[51]. She married RAMÓN SEDILLO Abt. 1920[52], son of SISTO SEDILLO and MARGARITA OLGUÍN.

Notes for RAMÓN SEDILLO:
1930 Census: Living in Roswell, New México.

Children of GUADALUPE BRADY and RAMÓN SEDILLO are:
     i.   JUANITA[5] SEDILLO, b. Private, Roswell, New México.

Notes for JUANITA SEDILLO:
She was raised by her grandmother, Margarita Olguín.

       ii.   ONESIMA SEDILLO, b. Abt. 1921, Roswell, New México[52].
      iii.   MARÍA SEDILLO, b. Abt. 1922, Roswell, New México[52].
      iv.   VIOLA SEDILLO, b. Abt. 1924, Roswell, New México[52].
      v.   OLIVIA SEDILLO, b. Abt. 1926, Roswell, New México[52].
      vi.   SISTO SEDILLO, b. Abt. 1927, Roswell, New México[52].

12. JOSÉ CANDELARIO[4] RANDOLPH *(CATARINA[3] BRADY, WILLIAM[2], JOHN[1])*[53] was born September 15, 1898 in San Patricio, Territory of New México, and died December 05, 1978 in Ruidoso, New México[54]. He married VIRGINIA SÁNCHEZ[55] September 14, 1918 in Lincoln, New México[56], daughter of SALOMON SÁNCHEZ and JENNIE GILL.

Notes for JOSÉ CANDELARIO RANDOLPH:
Also known as Andelario, Andy.

Children of JOSÉ RANDOLPH and VIRGINIA SÁNCHEZ are:
      i.   JOSEPHINE[5] RANDOLPH[57], b. March 04, 1920, San Patricio, New México[58]; m. EDDIE SÁNCHEZ, November 04, 1939, Carrizozo, New México[59].
      ii.   AROPAJITA RANDOLPH, b. May 05, 1922, San Patricio, New México; d. September 12, 2007, Tularosa, New México.

Notes for AROPAJITA RANDOLPH:
Moved to Tularosa, NM in 1957.

      iii. ELMON RANDOLPH[60], b. March 14, 1926, San Patricio, New México; d. March 1986, Ruidoso Downs, New México; m. FEDELINA ROMERO, July 01, 1950, Carrizozo, New México[61].

Notes for ELMON RANDOLPH:
Also known as Elmer.

      iv. CATHERINE RANDOLPH, b. July 10, 1928[62].

Notes for CATHERINE RANDOLPH:
Also known as Catarina.

      v.   NORA S. RANDOLPH, b. December 05, 1930, San Patricio, New México[63]; m. CANDIDO CHÁVEZ[64], February 15, 1947, Carrizozo, New México[65].

Notes for CANDIDO CHÁVEZ:
Private First Class. World War II.

13. WILLIAM[4] RANDOLPH *(CATARINA[3] BRADY, WILLIAM[2], JOHN[1])*[66] was born January 31, 1900 in San Patricio, New México[67], and died March 27, 1999 in Ruidoso Downs, New México. He married DULCINEA POLACO July 09, 1920 in San Patricio, New México[68], daughter of TRANCITO POLACO and AROPAJITA GONZÁLES.

Notes for WILLIAM RANDOLPH:
Also known as: Willie, Guillermo and Billy.

Children of WILLIAM RANDOLPH and DULCINEA POLACO are:
      i.   FRANK POLACO[5] RANDOLPH, b. Abt. 1921[69].
      ii.   VIOLA RANDOLPH, b. Abt. 1923[69].
      iii. WILLIE POLACO RANDOLPH[70], b. 1926[71]; d. 1954.
      iv. KYSTER RANDOLPH, b. Abt. 1929[71].

Genealogy of Cayetano Carrillo

Generation No. 1

1. CAYETANO[1] CARRILLO was born Abt. 1840 in La República de México[1]. He married BERIGNA BARELA[2].

Notes for CAYETANO CARRILLO:
1870 Census: Living in Lincoln County, Precinct 4 (Tularoso), Territory of New México.
1880 Census: Living in Tularoso, Doña Ana County, Territory of New México.

Children of CAYETANO CARRILLO and BERIGNA BARELA are:

	i.	ROSITA[2] CARRILLO, b. Abt. 1869[3].
2.	ii.	PATROCINIO CARRILLO, b. Abt. 1872.
3.	iii.	CRECENCIO CARRILLO, b. Abt. 1880, Tularoso, Territory of New México.

Generation No. 2

2. PATROCINIO[2] CARRILLO *(CAYETANO[1])* was born Abt. 1872[4]. He married RAMONA LUCERO Abt. 1892[5].

Notes for PATROCINIO CARRILLO:
Also known as Patricio.
1880 Census: Living in Tularoso, Territory of New México.
1910 Census: Living in Tres Ritos, Territory of New México.
1920 & 1930 Census: Living in Tularosa, New México.

Notes for RAMONA LUCERO:
Was said to be from the Yaqui tribe.

Children of PATROCINIO CARRILLO and RAMONA LUCERO are:

	i.	PATROCINIO[3] CARRILLO, b. Abt. 1898[5].
	ii.	MERIJILDO CARRILLO, b. Abt. 1900[5].
	iii.	FEDENCIO CARRILLO[6], b. November 16, 1902, Richardson, Territory of New México[7]; d. March 1987.
	iv.	GEORGE CARRILLO[8], b. February 22, 1906[9]; d. December 11, 1993, Tularosa, New México; m. BEATRIZ MARRUJO[10].
	v.	EMMA CARRILLO, b. Abt. 1908[11].

3. CRECENCIO[2] CARRILLO *(CAYETANO[1])* was born Abt. 1880 in Tularoso, Territory of New México[12]. He met (1) CATARINA BACA, daughter of DAMACIO BACA and MARÍA BACA. He married (2) JUANA SÁNCHEZ April 21, 1902 in San Patricio, Territory of New México[13]. He married (3) NICOLASA CHÁVEZ February 16, 1905[14], daughter of ISSAC CHÁVEZ and ATILANA GUTIÉRREZ.

Notes for CRECENCIO CARRILLO:
1880 Census: Living in Tularoso, Doña Ana County, Territory of New México.
1920 Census: Living in Lincoln, Territory of New México.
1930 Census: Living in Roswell, New México.

Child of CRECENCIO CARRILLO and CATARINA BACA is:

4.	i.	JUAN[3] BACA, b. August 01, 1914; d. March 20, 1995, Ruidoso Downs, New México.

Children of CRECENCIO CARRILLO and NICOLASA CHÁVEZ are:

	ii.	BENITO[3] CARRILLO, b. Abt. 1905[15].
	iii.	ROSA CARRILLO, b. Abt. 1909[15].
	iv.	AURORA CARRILLO, b. Abt. 1910[15].

Generation No. 3

4. JUAN[3] BACA *(CRECENCIO[2] CARRILLO, CAYETANO[1])*[16] was born August 01, 1914[17], and died March 20, 1995 in Ruidoso Downs, New México. He married JOSEFITA MONTOYA[18], daughter of DOROTEO MONTOYA and ALBINA SILVA.

Notes for JUAN BACA:
Death index indicates that he was born on June 30, 1914. Raised by Crecencio Carrillo.

Notes for JOSEFITA MONTOYA:
Also known as Josephine.

Children of JUAN BACA and JOSEFITA MONTOYA are:
  i.   CRUCITA[4] BACA, b. May 03, 1946; m. (1) DANNY CHÁVEZ.
  ii.   PETE BACA, b. Private.

Genealogy of José Carrillo

Generation No. 1

1. JOSÉ[1] CARRILLO was born Abt. 1835[1]. He married NICANORA MÁRQUEZ[2].

Notes for JOSÉ CARRILLO:
1860 & 1870 Census: Living in Manzano, Territory of New México.
1880 Census: Living in Lincoln, District 18, Territory of New México.
Was known by many of the locals as Chief José Carrillo. Both José Carrillo and his wife Nicanora were Native Americans.

Notes for NICANORA MÁRQUEZ:
Was said to be a Native American woman. She was also known as María Nicanora Marquez.

Children of JOSÉ CARRILLO and NICANORA MÁRQUEZ are:
	i.	MANUELITA MÁRQUEZ[2] CARRILLO.
2.	ii.	JOSÉ MÁRQUEZ CARRILLO, b. Abt. 1855, Manzano, Territory of New México.
3.	iii.	DOROTEO CARRILLO, b. June 1859, Manzano, Territory of New México.
	iv.	MARIANO CARRILLO, b. Abt. 1862, Manzano, Territory of New México[3].
4.	v.	TERESA CARRILLO, b. August 1868, Manzano, Territory of New México.
5.	vi.	JUANA CARRILLO, b. May 1870, Manzano, Territory of New México.
6.	vii.	BEATRIZ CARRILLO, b. January 20, 1873, Lincoln, Territory of New México.
	viii.	BIRGINIA CARRILLO, b. Abt. 1875, Lincoln, Territory of New México[3].

Notes for BIRGINIA CARRILLO:
Also known as Virginia.

Generation No. 2

2. JOSÉ MÁRQUEZ[2] CARRILLO *(JOSÉ[1])* was born Abt. 1855 in Manzano, Territory of New México[4]. He married CRUSITA ARCHULETA April 15, 1905[5], daughter of JESÚS ARCHULETA and PABLA TORRES.

Notes for JOSÉ MÁRQUEZ CARRILLO:
Also known as José Espiradión Carrillo.
1860 Census: Living in Manzano, Territory of New México.
1910 Census: Living in San Patricio, Territory of New México. (Born about 1884)

Notes for CRUSITA ARCHULETA:
Also known as Cruz.

Children of JOSÉ CARRILLO and CRUSITA ARCHULETA are:
7.	i.	ANITA CARRILLO[3] ANALLA, b. July 26, 1905, Arabela, Territory of New México.
	ii.	ANTONIO CARRILLO[6].
	iii.	CAYETANO CARRILLO[6].

Notes for CAYETANO CARRILLO:
May have gone by Cayetano Bell.

	iv.	FERNANDO CARRILLO[6].
	v.	MELQUIDES CARRILLO[6].

3. DOROTEO[2] CARRILLO *(JOSÉ[1])* was born June 1859 in Manzano, Territory of New México[7]. He married FELICITA CHÁVEZ July 28, 1879 in Rancho Torres, Territory of New México[8].

Notes for DOROTEO CARRILLO:
1910 Census: Living in Roswell, Territory of New México.

Children of DOROTEO CARRILLO and FELICITA CHÁVEZ are:
      i.   ANTONIA[3] CARRILLO, b. May 1878, Rancho Torres, Territory of New México[9].

Notes for ANTONIA CARRILLO:
1910 Census: Living in Lincoln, Territory of New México.

8.   ii.   PEDRO JOSÉ CARRILLO, b. February 20, 1884, Roswell, Territory of New México; d. March 09, 1910, Tularosa, New México.
      iii.   MARGARITA CARRILLO, b. October 27, 1884, Rancho Torres, Territory of New México[10].

Notes for MARGARITA CARRILLO:
Also known as Marianita.

      iv.   MARIANO CARRILLO, b. October 1890, Rancho Torres, Territory of New México[11].
9.   v.   MANUEL CARRILLO, b. October 1893, Lincoln, Territory of New México.
      vi.   RAMONA CARRILLO, b. October 1898, Lincoln, Territory of New México[11].

4. TERESA[2] CARRILLO *(JOSÉ[1])* was born August 1868 in Manzano, Territory of New México[12]. She married GEORGE SENA[13] July 23, 1885[14], son of IGNACIO SENA and AGAPITA ORTIZ.

Notes for GEORGE SENA:
1900 Census: Living in Lincoln, Territory of New México.
Elected as Lincoln County Clerk. He later was elected as the Lincoln County sheriff.

Children of TERESA CARRILLO and GEORGE SENA are:
      i.   MANUELA[3] SENA[15], b. October 22, 1886, Lincoln, Territory of New México[16].
      ii.   VICENTA SENA, b. April 1889[16].
      iii.   SORAIDA SENA[17], b. December 21, 1889[18].
      iv.   IGNACIO CARRILLO SENA, b. May 1892[18].
      v.   ANACLETA SENA, b. January 1894[18].

5. JUANA[2] CARRILLO *(JOSÉ[1])* was born May 1870 in Manzano, Territory of New México[19]. She married ANTONIO CHÁVEZ February 14, 1885[20], son of JOSÉ CHÁVEZ and APOLINARIA LÓPEZ.

Notes for ANTONIO CHÁVEZ:
1900 Census: Living in Ruidoso, Territory of New México.
1910 Census: Living in Richardson, Territory of New México.

Children of JUANA CARRILLO and ANTONIO CHÁVEZ are:
      i.   VICTORIANA[3] CHÁVEZ, b. December 1885[21].
      ii.   GEORGE CARRILLO CHÁVEZ, b. December 1889[21].
      iii.   MARIANO CHÁVEZ, b. October 20, 1892, Lincoln, Territory of New México[22].

Notes for MARIANO CHÁVEZ:
1900 Census: Living in Lincoln, Territory of New México.

10.   iv.   EMILIA CHÁVEZ, b. April 05, 1898; d. September 1983, Alburquerque, New México.

6. BEATRIZ[2] CARRILLO *(JOSÉ[1])* was born January 20, 1873 in Lincoln, Territory of New México[23]. She married JOSÉ LEÓN BACA December 22, 1888 in Manzano, Territory of New México[24], son of JUAN BACA and GABINA CHÁVEZ.

Children of BEATRIZ CARRILLO and JOSÉ BACA are:
      i.   MARIVALA[3] BACA, b. October 1891[25].
      ii.   CARLOTA BACA, b. October 1892[25].
      iii.   JUAN BACA, b. May 1894[25].
      iv.   JOSEFA BACA, b. December 1895[25].
      v.   ENRÍQUES BACA, b. November 1898[25].

Generation No. 3

7. ANITA CARRILLO³ ANALLA *(JOSÉ MÁRQUEZ² CARRILLO, JOSÉ¹)²⁶* was born July 26, 1905 in Arabela, Territory of New México²⁷. She married (1) SENOVIO VILLESCAS, son of CASIMIRO VILLESCAS and EMILIANA TAFOYA. She married (2) GEORGE LUCERO²⁸ May 21, 1921 in Arabela, New México²⁹, son of APOLONIO LUCERO and ADELIA PACHECO.

Notes for ANITA CARRILLO ANALLA:
Anita often went by the name, Anita Analla, because she was raised with an Analla family in Arabela, New México. She was raised by the Analla family after her mother passed away when she was about four years old.
1910 Census: Lists her parents as José Carrillo and Crusita. Her listed name was Tonita.
1920 Census: Living with her cousin, Julio Vigil in Las Palas, Territory of New México.

Child of ANITA ANALLA and GEORGE LUCERO is:
      i.   ORLANDO⁴ LUCERO³⁰, b. July 18, 1923, Roswell, New México³¹; d. February 15, 2004; m. ERLINDA GONZÁLES, July 18, 1942, Carrizozo, New México³¹.

Notes for ORLANDO LUCERO:
     Private First Class. World War II.

8. PEDRO JOSÉ³ CARRILLO *(DOROTEO², JOSÉ¹)* was born February 20, 1884 in Roswell, Territory of New México³², and died March 09, 1910 in Tularosa, New México. He married (1) CLARA VIGIL, daughter of FRANCISCO VIGIL and ELENA FRESQUEZ. He married (2) ANTONIA GONZÁLES November 27, 1907 in Lincoln, Territory of New México³³.

Notes for PEDRO JOSÉ CARRILLO:
1900 Census: Living in Lincoln, Territory of New México.
Baptismal indicates he was born on June 10, 1873. (Microfiche# 0016754)

Child of PEDRO CARRILLO and ANTONIA GONZÁLES is:
      i.   MANUELITA GONZÁLES⁴ CARRILLO, b. Abt. 1908³⁴.

9. MANUEL³ CARRILLO *(DOROTEO², JOSÉ¹)* was born October 1893 in Lincoln, Territory of New México³⁵. He married DOROTEA DE CARILLO.

Notes for MANUEL CARRILLO:
1900 Census: Living in Lincoln, Territory of New México.
1920 Census: Living in Las Palas, New México.
1930 Census: Living in Arabela, New México.

Children of MANUEL CARRILLO and DOROTEA DE CARILLO are:
      i.   TEODORA⁴ CARRILLO, b. Abt. 1920³⁶.
     ii.   DELIA CARRILLO, b. Abt. 1922³⁶.
    iii.   VIOLA CARRILLO, b. Abt. 1925³⁶.
    iv.   VIOLETA CARRILLO, b. Abt. 1925³⁶.
     v.   GODFREY CARRILLO, b. Abt. 1927³⁶.

10. EMILIA³ CHÁVEZ *(JUANA² CARRILLO, JOSÉ¹)³⁷* was born April 05, 1898³⁸, and died September 1983 in Alburquerque, New México. She married JOSÉ BACA TORRES³⁹ December 30, 1918 in Lincoln, New México⁴⁰, son of PRECILIANO TORRES and DELFINIA BACA.

Notes for JOSÉ BACA TORRES:
About 1928: Moved to Roswell.

Children of EMILIA CHÁVEZ and JOSÉ TORRES are:

i. HILARIO CHÁVEZ[4] TORRES, b. Abt. 1922[41].
ii. TOM CHÁVEZ TORRES, b. Abt. 1924[41].
iii. MANUEL CHÁVEZ TORRES, b. Abt. 1926[41].
iv. AMABLE J CHÁVEZ TORRES[42], b. June 19, 1928[43]; d. October 12, 1999, Roswell, New México.
v. JOE CHÁVEZ TORRES, b. Private.
vi. MARY CHÁVEZ TORRES, b. Private.

Genealogy of Manuelita Herrera Carrillo

Holan Miller

Generation No. 1

1. MANUELITA HERRERA[1] CARRILLO was born Abt. 1845 in Manzano, Territory of New México[1]. She married (1) HOLAN WILLIAM MILLER 1869 in Manzano, Territory of New México[2]. She married (2) JOSEPH W. SWAN June 26, 1893 in Rebentón, Territory of New México[3].

Notes for MANUELITA HERRERA CARRILLO:
Also known as Manuelita Herrera.
1860 Census: Living in Rio Bonito, Socorro County, Territory of New México.
1870 Census: Living in Lincoln County, Precinct 1, Territory of New México.
1880 Census: Living in Fort Stanton, Territory of New México. Living with Joseph Swan.
1900-1920 Census: Living in Capitán, New México.

Notes for HOLAN WILLIAM MILLER:
Also known as; Holan, Hogan, William, Julian.
Migrated from Manzano, NM to Springer, NM then to Ft Stanton, NM.
1870 Census: Worked as a blacksmith.

Notes for JOSEPH W. SWAN:
1920 Census: Living in Capitán, New México.

Children of MANUELITA CARRILLO and HOLAN MILLER are:
  i. ADOLPHO[2] MILLER, b. Fort Stanton, Territory of New México; d. Fort Stanton, New México.

Notes for ADOLPHO MILLER:
Died young. Buried at Fort Stanton.

	ii.	DEBBIE MILLER, b. Fort Stanton, Territory of New México.
	iii.	LIBRADA MILLER, b. 1859, Fort Stanton, Territory of New México[4].
2.	iv.	ÁBRAN MILLER, b. May 1861, Fort Stanton, Territory of New México; d. May 29, 1942, Carrizozo, New México.
3.	v.	ELIZA MILLER, b. Abt. 1867, Fort Stanton, Territory of New México; d. September 15, 1939.
4.	vi.	WILLIE MILLER, b. April 11, 1873, Fort Stanton, Territory of New México.

Joseph Swan

Children of MANUELITA CARRILLO and JOSEPH SWAN are:

5.	vii.	ROBERT[2] SWAN, b. Abt. 1876, Fort Stanton, Territory of New México.
	viii.	EVALINA SWAN, b. June 1880, Fort Stanton, Territory of New México[5].

Generation No. 2

2. ÁBRAN[2] MILLER *(MANUELITA HERRERA[1] CARRILLO)*[6] was born May 1861 in Fort Stanton, Territory of New México[7], and died May 29, 1942 in Carrizozo, New México. He married JUANITA ROMERO February 12, 1881[8], daughter of JUAN ROMERO.

Notes for ÁBRAN MILLER:
Listed his mother as Manuelita Herrera.

Children of ÁBRAN MILLER and JUANITA ROMERO are:

6.	i.	ANDREA[3] MILLER, b. Abt. 1882, Tucson Mountain, Lincoln County, Territory of New México.
	ii.	LUCIO MILLER, b. December 13, 1885[9].
	iii.	VICENTA MILLER, b. Abt. 1886[10]; m. MELQUIDES GONZÁLES, July 06, 1910, Capitán, Territory of New México[10].

iv.   ANDRÉS MILLER[11], b. December 04, 1891, El Salado, Territory of New México[12]; d. November 1979, Ruidoso Downs, New México; m. ISAQUIA SÁNCHEZ[13], February 02, 1914, Lincoln, New México[14].
v.   BENITO MILLER, b. June 1894[15].
vi.   SUZIE MILLER, b. September 1899[15].
vii. MANUELA MILLER, b. August 28, 1901, Capitán,Territory of New México[16]; d. January 08, 1918[17]; m. DESIDERIO MÁRQUEZ, February 19, 1917, Lincoln, New México[18].

3. ELIZA[2] MILLER *(MANUELITA HERRERA[1] CARRILLO)*[19] was born Abt. 1867 in Fort Stanton, Territory of New México[20], and died September 15, 1939[21]. She married (1) MANUEL ARTIAGA Abt. 1880[22]. She married (2) PEDRO LÓPEZ March 11, 1902[23], son of LORENZO LÓPEZ and MANUELA TORRES. She married (3) BONIFACIO ZAMORA[24] March 23, 1907 in Picacho, Territory of New México[25].

Notes for MANUEL ARTIAGA:
1870 Census: Living in Manzano, Territory of New México. (Born about 1853) Living with Hilaria García.

Notes for BONIFACIO ZAMORA:
Also known as Boney.

Children of ELIZA MILLER and MANUEL ARTIAGA are:
7.   i.   VICTORIANO[3] ARTIAGA, b. March 23, 1881; d. 1915-1920.
      ii.   VICENTE ARTIAGA, b. Abt. 1894[26].

Notes for VICENTE ARTIAGA:
1910 Census: Listed as Bonifacio Zamora's step son.

      iii. RAMÓN ARTIAGA, b. March 01, 1896[27].

Notes for RAMÓN ARTIAGA:
1910 Census: Listed as Bonifacio Zamora's step son.
      iv.   SOLEDAD ARTIAGA, b. Abt. 1902[28].

Notes for SOLEDAD ARTIAGA:
1910 Census: Listed as Bonifacio Zamora's step daughter.

Children of ELIZA MILLER and BONIFACIO ZAMORA are:
      v.   AURORA[3] ZAMORA, b. Abt. 1907[28].
      vi.   BONIFACIO MILLER ZAMORA[29], b. December 02, 1908, Capitán, Territory of New México; d. July 26, 1991.

4. WILLIE[2] MILLER *(MANUELITA HERRERA[1] CARRILLO)* was born April 11, 1873 in Fort Stanton, Territory of New México[30]. He married FELIPA GUERRA January 13, 1896[31], daughter of SAVINO GUERRA and TONGINIA VARELA.

Notes for WILLIE MILLER:
Also known as: William or Julian.
Living in Salado at the time of his marriage.

Children of WILLIE MILLER and FELIPA GUERRA are:
8.   i.   MANUEL GUERRA[3] MILLER, b. May 08, 1898, Capitán, Territory of New México; d. September 05, 1987, Capitán, New México.
      ii.   JUAN MILLER, b. December 11, 1899[32]; m. TILLIE BROWN.

Notes for JUAN MILLER:
1910 Census: Listed as Francisco Durán's step son.

9.   iii. ELVIRA MILLER, b. November 10, 1901, Capitán, Territory of New México.
      iv.   JULIAN GUERRA MILLER, b. Abt. 1903[33]; m. ANDREA DE MILLER.

Notes for JULIAN GUERRA MILLER:
1910 Census: Listed as Francisco Durán's step son.

5. ROBERT[2] SWAN *(MANUELITA HERRERA[1] CARRILLO)* was born Abt. 1876 in Fort Stanton, Territory of New México[34]. He married MARÍA SWAN Abt. 1898[35].

Children of ROBERT SWAN and MARÍA SWAN are:
-   i.   ADOLFO[3] SWAN, b. Abt. 1900[35].
-   ii.   CAROLINA SWAN, b. Abt. 1901[35].
-   iii. AMADA SWAN, b. Abt. 1903[35].
-   iv.   MANUELITA SWAN, b. Abt. 1904[35].
-   v.   ROBERTO SWAN, b. Abt. 1905[35].
-   vi.   LIBRADA SWAN, b. Abt. 1907[35].
-   vii. ALEJANDRA SWAN, b. Abt. 1909[35].

Generation No. 3

6. ANDREA[3] MILLER *(ÁBRAN[2], MANUELITA HERRERA[1] CARRILLO)* was born Abt. 1882 in Tucson Mountain, Lincoln County, Territory of New México[36]. She married BONIFACIO PINO June 13, 1898[37], son of PABLO PINO and MARÍA CHÁVEZ.

Children of ANDREA MILLER and BONIFACIO PINO are:
-   i.   TOMASITA[4] PINO, b. Abt. 1905[38].
-   ii.   JUANITA PINO, b. June 12, 1907, Capitán, Territory of New México[39]; m. PERFECTO ROMERO, October 03, 1925, Carrizozo, New México[39].

7. VICTORIANO[3] ARTIAGA *(ELIZA[2] MILLER, MANUELITA HERRERA[1] CARRILLO)* was born March 23, 1881[40], and died 1915-1920[41]. He married DOLORES TORRES PADILLA[42] January 03, 1901[43], daughter of CENOBIO PADILLA and SATURNINA TORRES.

Notes for DOLORES TORRES PADILLA:
Also known as Lola.

Children of VICTORIANO ARTIAGA and DOLORES PADILLA are:
-   i.   RUFINA[4] ARTIAGA, b. Abt. 1902[44].
-   ii.   JULIANITA ARTIAGA, b. Abt. 1904[44].
-   iii. MANUEL ARTIAGA, b. Abt. 1906[44].
-   iv.   VICTORIANO PADILLA ARTIAGA, b. Abt. 1908[45].
-   v.   TRENIDAD ARTIAGA, b. Abt. 1915[45]; m. PABLO SANDOVAL, August 04, 1934[46].

8. MANUEL GUERRA[3] MILLER *(WILLIE[2], MANUELITA HERRERA[1] CARRILLO)*[47] was born May 08, 1898 in Capitán, Territory of New México[48], and died September 05, 1987 in Capitán, New México. He married ISABEL DURÁN[49] February 05, 1917 in Capitán, New México[50], daughter of FRANCISCO DURÁN and EUGENIA HERNÁNDEZ.

Notes for MANUEL GUERRA MILLER:
1910 Census: Listed as Francisco Durán's step son.

Children of MANUEL MILLER and ISABEL DURÁN are:
-   i.   IGNACIO LLOYD[4] MILLER, b. February 01, 1917, Capitán, New México[51]; m. PETRA OLGUÍN, February 13, 1943, Carrizozo, New México[51].

Notes for IGNACIO LLOYD MILLER:
1930 Census: Living in Lincoln, New México.

-   ii.   TITO MILLER[52], b. February 02, 1919, Capitán, New México[53].

Notes for TITO MILLER:
Also known as Pita.

    iii.   FELIPICITA MILLER, b. Abt. 1922[53].
    iv.   NILO MILLER[54], b. September 21, 1922, Fort Stanton, New México[55]; d. February 1980, Albquerque, New México; m. NATALIA L. SÁNCHEZ, December 28, 1947, Carrizozo, New México[55].

Notes for NILO MILLER:
US Navy, Machinist Third Class. World War II.

    v.   LILLIAN ELIZABETH MILLER[56], b. October 05, 1924, Capitán, New México; d. November 13, 2010, Capitán, New México; m. EFRAÍN CHÁVEZ.

Notes for EFRAÍN CHÁVEZ:
Social Security Death Index indicates that he was born on January 1, 1924.
WW II veteran.

    vi.   MANUEL DURÁN MILLER[57], b. October 22, 1927, Capitán, New México[58]; d. April 29, 2001, Capitán, New México.

Notes for MANUEL DURÁN MILLER:
EN 3, US Navy, Korea.

    vii.   BILLIE MILLER, b. Private, Capitán, New México.
    viii.   LLOYD MILLER, b. Private, Capitán, New México.
    ix.   TONY MILLER, b. Private, Capitán, New México.

9. ELVIRA[3] MILLER *(WILLIE[2], MANUELITA HERRERA[1] CARRILLO)* was born November 10, 1901 in Capitán, Territory of New México[59]. She married CLEMENTE PADILLA November 27, 1916 in Lincoln, New México[59], son of JESÚS PADILLA and ISAQUIA SANDOVAL.

Notes for ELVIRA MILLER:
Also known as Alvira
1910 Census: Listed as Francisco Durán's step daughter.

Children of ELVIRA MILLER and CLEMENTE PADILLA are:
    i.   EMMA MILLER[4] PADILLA, b. Abt. 1920[60].

Notes for EMMA MILLER PADILLA:
Also known as Emilia.

    ii.   CLARA PADILLA, b. Abt. 1922[60].
    iii.   CLEMENTE MILLER PADILLA, b. Abt. 1923[60].
    iv.   LUCIA PADILLA, b. Abt. 1924[60].
    v.   DOMINGO MILLER PADILLA, b. Abt. 1926[60].
    vi.   JULIAN PADILLA, b. Abt. 1928[60].
    vii.   ROMONSITA GONZÁLES, b. Private.
    viii.   TRENIDAD GONZÁLES, b. Private.
    ix.   BEATRICE PADILLA, b. Private.
    x.   BENJAMÍN PADILLA, b. Private.
    xi.   DAVÍD PADILLA, b. Private.
    xii.   DOLORES PADILLA, b. Private.
    xiii.   FRED MILLER PADILLA, b. Private.
    xiv.   HELEN PADILLA, b. Private.
    xv.   MARGARET PADILLA, b. Private.
    xvi.   TERESA PADILLA, b. Private.

Genealogy of José Cháves

Generation No. 1

1. JOSÉ[1] CHÁVES[1] was born Abt. 1830 in Tomé, Nuevo México, La República de México[2], and died in Hondo, Territory of New México. He married (1) AVRORA SÁNCHEZ. He married (2) MARÍA FRANCISCA LUNA November 02, 1846 in Belén, Nuevo México, La República de México[3].

Notes for JOSÉ CHÁVES:
1860 Census: Living in Torreón, Territory of New México.
1870 Census: Living in Lincoln County, Precinct 1, Territory of New México.
The family legend was that his real name was, Joseph Lamar. It is believed that he was adopted into a Chávez family near Los Lunas, Territory of New México.

Children of JOSÉ CHÁVES and MARÍA LUNA are:

      i.   DESIDERIO[2] CHÁVEZ[4], d. September 28, 1878.

Notes for DESIDERIO CHÁVEZ:
September 28, 1878: Killed by a group of men called The Rustlers.

2.   ii.   AMBROCIO LUNA CHÁVEZ, b. Abt. 1849; d. 1918, Hondo, New México.

      iii.   ANACLETO CHÁVEZ, b. Abt. 1850[5]; d. September 28, 1878.

Notes for ANACLETO CHÁVEZ:
Also known as Cleto.
September 28, 1878: Killed by a group of men called The Rustlers.

3.   iv.   PABLO CHÁVEZ, b. Abt. 1852, Los Lunas, Valencia County, Territory of New México; d. July 16, 1938, Hondo, New México.

      v.   MARÍA CHÁVEZ, b. Abt. 1856[5].

Notes for MARÍA CHÁVEZ:
Raised Luís Sánchez after his mother's death.

      vi.   TRENIDAD CHÁVEZ, b. Abt. 1858[5].

4.   vii.   SUSANITA CHÁVEZ, b. Abt. 1863.

      viii.   VICENTE CHÁVEZ, b. Abt. 1865[6].

5.   ix.   FRANCISCO LUNA CHÁVEZ, b. August 04, 1871, La Junta, Territory of New México; d. July 28, 1943, San Patricio, New México.

Generation No. 2

2. AMBROCIO LUNA[2] CHÁVEZ *(JOSÉ[1] CHÁVES)*[7] was born Abt. 1849[8], and died 1918 in Hondo, New México. He married (1) MIQUELA CHÁVEZ[9] Abt. 1882[10], daughter of NAVOR CHÁVEZ and GREGORIA TRUJILLO. He married (2) MARÍA TRUJILLO CHÁVEZ May 20, 1882[11], daughter of NAVOR CHÁVEZ and GREGORIA TRUJILLO.

Notes for AMBROCIO LUNA CHÁVEZ:
1870 Census: Living in Lincoln County, Precinct 1, Territory of New México. Birth year listed as 1849.
1900 Census: Living in Picacho, Territory of New México.

Notes for MIQUELA CHÁVEZ:
Also known as Miquelita.
1930 Census lists Miquela as the head of the household.

Notes for MARÍA TRUJILLO CHÁVEZ:
Death Records indicate that she died on November 07, 1933.

Children of AMBROCIO CHÁVEZ and MIQUELA CHÁVEZ are:
       i.   TOMÁS[3] CHÁVEZ, b. September 18, 1887, Hondo, Territory of New México[12]; d. September 1953[13].

Notes for TOMÁS CHÁVEZ:
Cemetery records indicate he was born in March 1887.
1900 Census: Living in Picacho, Territory of New México.

6.   ii.   GEORGE CHÁVEZ, b. April 20, 1892, Analla, Territory of New México; d. July 24, 1972.
       iii. JUAN JOSÉ CHÁVEZ, b. April 08, 1900, Picacho, Territory of New México[14].

Notes for JUAN JOSÉ CHÁVEZ:
1900 Census: Living in Picacho, Territory of New México.

       iv. OSCAR CHÁVEZ, b. Abt. 1906[15].
       v.   FRANCISQUITA CHÁVEZ[16], b. October 10, 1906[17]; d. January 03, 1983; m. ARISTOTEL ROMERO[18], 1936[19].

Notes for ARISTOTEL ROMERO:
NM Private, Med Dept, WWI

Pablo Chávez

3. PABLO[2] CHÁVEZ *(JOSÉ[1] CHÁVES)*[20] was born Abt. 1852 in Los Lunas, Valencia County, Territory of New México[21], and died July 16, 1938 in Hondo, New México. He married AMADA SÁNCHEZ July 20, 1883 in Las Angosturas (San Ysidro), Territory of New México[22], daughter of MAURICIO SÁNCHEZ and JESÚSITA GONZÁLES.

Notes for AMADA SÁNCHEZ:
Also known as Jesúsita Amada Sánchez.
Baptismal Padrinos: Juan Torres, Trinidad Chávez.
1880 Census: Living in Tularoso, Territory of New México.

Children of PABLO CHÁVEZ and AMADA SÁNCHEZ are:
       i.   AMADA[3] SÁNCHEZ[23], b. August 1886, La Junta, Territory of New México; Stepchild.
7.   ii.   TRANCITO CHÁVEZ, b. July 20, 1887, La Junta, Territory of New México; d. April 07, 1975, San Patricio, New México.
8.   iii. CANDIDO CHÁVEZ, b. April 12, 1889, La Junta, Territory of New México; d. May 20, 1979.
       iv. FLORINDA CHÁVEZ, b. July 08, 1891, La Junta, Territory of New México[24]; m. JUAN BLEA, July 03, 1908, Lincoln, Territory of New México[25].
9.   v.   OLYMPIA CHÁVEZ, b. 1894, La Junta, Territory of New México; d. Abt. 1911, Hondo, Territory of New México.
       vi. ADELAIDO CHÁVEZ[26], b. December 16, 1903, Hondo, Territory of New México; d. November 1984, San Patricio, New México; m. LUPE VALENSUELA[26], August 21, 1935, Picacho, New México[27].

Notes for ADELAIDO CHÁVEZ:
Land Patent # NMLC 0029127, on the authority of the Homestead Entry-Stock Raising (39 Stat. 862), December 29, 1916. Issued 610.88 acres on January 30, 1931.

10.   vii. LEOPOLDO CHÁVEZ, b. April 25, 1907, Hondo, Territory of New México.
11.   viii. RUMELIO CHÁVEZ, b. 1909, Hondo, Territory of New México; d. 1963.
12.   ix. ERMANDO CHÁVEZ, b. February 24, 1914, Hondo, New México; d. June 05, 2010, San Patricio, New México.

4. SUSANITA[2] CHÁVEZ *(JOSÉ[1] CHÁVES)* was born Abt. 1863[28]. She married SANTIAGO MAÉS January 20, 1883[29], son of QUIRINO MAÉS and CONCEPCIÓN SUAZO.

Notes for SANTIAGO MAÉS:
Maés was often spelled as Mez.

Child of SUSANITA CHÁVEZ and SANTIAGO MAÉS is:
       i.   CELESTINA[3] MAÉS, b. December 27, 1883, Junta de los Ríos (La Junta/ Hondo), Territory of New México[30].

5. FRANCISCO LUNA² CHÁVEZ *(JOSÉ¹ CHÁVES)³¹* was born August 04, 1871 in La Junta, Territory of New México, and died July 28, 1943 in San Patricio, New México. He married (1) ESLINDA GONZÁLES March 29, 1891 in Lincoln County, Territory of New México³², daughter of FLORENCIO GONZÁLES and RAYMUNDA SÁNCHEZ. He married (2) MARTINA PRUDENCIO³³ October 07, 1922³⁴, daughter of JOSÉ PRUDENCIO and VICTORIA FAJARDO.

Notes for FRANCISCO LUNA CHÁVEZ:
Also known as Frank.

Children of FRANCISCO CHÁVEZ and ESLINDA GONZÁLES are:

      i.   FIDEL³ CHÁVEZ³⁵, b. June 30, 1893, San Patricio, Territory of New México³⁶; d. August 29, 1937, San Patricio, New México; m. DELFINIA PADILLA Y WEST, June 28, 1915, Lincoln, New México³⁶.

Notes for FIDEL CHÁVEZ:
Lists his mother as Francisquita Luna.

Notes for DELFINIA PADILLA Y WEST:
Also known as Delfinia Sánchez, Delfinia Sánchez y West.
Raised and adopted by John C. West.

13.   ii.   ERMINDA CHÁVEZ, b. July 12, 1894, San Patricio, Territory of New México; d. November 01, 1956.
        iii.   PALMIRA CHÁVEZ, b. 1896³⁷; m. IGNACIO MAÉS³⁸.

Notes for IGNACIO MAÉS:
1900-1920 Census: Living in Picacho, New México.

      iv.   RAMÓN CHÁVEZ³⁹, b. February 12, 1897, San Patricio, Territory of New México⁴⁰; d. October 17, 1985, San Patricio, New México.
       v.   ENCARNACION CHÁVEZ, b. November 15, 1899⁴¹. Died young.

Children of FRANCISCO CHÁVEZ and MARTINA PRUDENCIO are:
      vi.   DOMINGO³ CHÁVEZ, b. Abt. 1922⁴².
      vii. DEMETRIA CHÁVEZ, b. Abt. 1924⁴³.

Generation No. 3

6. GEORGE³ CHÁVEZ *(AMBROCIO LUNA², JOSÉ¹ CHÁVES)⁴⁴* was born April 20, 1892 in Analla, Territory of New México⁴⁵, and died July 24, 1972. He married JULIA HERNÁNDEZ⁴⁶ February 04, 1920 in Tinnie, New México⁴⁷, daughter of EULOJIO HERNÁNDEZ.

Children of GEORGE CHÁVEZ and JULIA HERNÁNDEZ are:
      i.   AMBROCIO HERNÁNDEZ⁴ CHÁVEZ, b. Abt. 1920, Hondo, New México⁴⁸.
      ii.   MARÍA CHÁVEZ, b. Abt. 1921⁴⁸.
      iii.   JOSIE HERNÁNDEZ CHÁVEZ, b. Abt. 1923⁴⁸.
      iv.   AUGUSTÍN HERNÁNDEZ CHÁVEZ, b. Abt. 1925⁴⁸.
      v.   GEORGE HERNÁNDEZ CHÁVEZ⁴⁹, b. February 27, 1928, Hondo, New México⁵⁰.
      vi.   ALFONZO CHÁVEZ, b. Abt. 1929⁵⁰.
      vii. DANNY CHÁVEZ⁵¹, b. March 05, 1938, Hondo, New México; d. May 02, 2008, Douglas Flats, California.
      viii. OLOJIO CHÁVEZ⁵¹, b. Private.
      ix.   VICTORIO CHÁVEZ⁵¹, b. Private.
      x.   PHILIP CHÁVEZ⁵¹, b. Private.

7. TRANCITO³ CHÁVEZ *(PABLO², JOSÉ¹ CHÁVES)⁵²* was born July 20, 1887 in La Junta, Territory of New México, and died April 07, 1975 in San Patricio, New México. He married ANGELITA CHÁVEZ⁵³ April 15, 1907 in Lincoln, Territory of New México⁵⁴, daughter of ROBERTO CHÁVEZ and LUCÍA WELDON.

Notes for TRANCITO CHÁVEZ:
Buried: Hondo cemetary.
Land Patent # NMR 0025917, on the authority of the Homestead Entry-Enlarged (35 Stat. 639), February 19, 1909. Issued 320 acres on November 15, 1917.
Land Patent # NMR 003740, on the authority of the Homestead Entry-Stock Raising (39 Stat. 862), December 29, 1916. Issued 320 acres on July 17, 1924.

Notes for ANGELITA CHÁVEZ:
Also known as Angela.

Children of TRANCITO CHÁVEZ and ANGELITA CHÁVEZ are:

    i.   ARISTEO[4] CHÁVEZ[55], b. November 30, 1910, Hondo, New México[56]; d. August 21, 1993, San Patricio, New México; m. CRISTINA ROMERO[57], February 10, 1936, San Patricio, New México[58].

    ii.   ISMAEL CHÁVEZ[59], b. November 12, 1912, Hondo, New México; d. July 31, 1980, San Patricio, New México; m. ELISA MENDOSA[60].

    iii.   OZIEL CHÁVEZ, b. 1917, Hondo, New México[61]; d. August 19, 1942, Phillipines[62].

Notes for OZIEL CHÁVEZ:
Also known as Ouciel.
March 15, 1941: Enlisted into the Army, 200th Cavalry Regiment. Fought in the Southwest Pacific Theatre, Philippines. Died as a Prisoner of War during World War Two.

    iv.   AVESLÍN CHÁVEZ, b. 1920, Hondo, New México[63]; d. March 20, 1945, Phillipines[64].

Notes for AVESLÍN CHÁVEZ:
January 24, 1941: Enlisted into the Army. 158th Infantry Regiment. He was awarded a Purple Heart Medal and a Bronze Star Medal. He was killed on March 20, 1945.

    v.   HERALDO MODESTO CHÁVEZ[65], b. December 09, 1922, Hondo, New México; d. July 26, 1965, Hondo, New México; m. EVALINA MAE DUTCHOVER[66], February 11, 1946, Carrizozo, New México[67].

Notes for EVALINA MAE DUTCHOVER:
Also known as Eva Mae.
Lived in Lincoln County since 1946.

    vi.   EVA CHÁVEZ, b. February 05, 1925, Hondo, New México[68]; m. (1) CARLOS CHÁVEZ; m. (2) HARRY SÁNCHEZ, February 21, 1944, Carrizozo, New México[68].

Notes for HARRY SÁNCHEZ:
1930 Census: Living in San Patricio, New México.
1944 Marriage Records: Living in Artesia, New México.

8. CANDIDO[3] CHÁVEZ *(PABLO[2], JOSÉ[1] CHÁVES)*[69] was born April 12, 1889 in La Junta, Territory of New México, and died May 20, 1979. He married ESTELA LUCY WEST[70] October 31, 1910[71], daughter of JOHN WEST and MARÍA MONNET.

Notes for CANDIDO CHÁVEZ:
Buried: Hondo cemetery.
Land Patent # NMR 0029544, on the authority of the Homestead Entry-Enlarged (35 Stat. 639), February 19, 1909. Issued 240 acres on October 28, 1921.
Land Patent # NMLC 0037460, on the authority of the Homestead Entry-Stock Raising (39 Stat. 862), December 29, 1916. Issued 400 acres on August 7, 1925.

Notes for ESTELA LUCY WEST:
Also known as Estelle.
Baptismal Witnesses: Estelle Kaestler and George Ulricks.

Children of CANDIDO CHÁVEZ and ESTELA WEST are:
- i.   CECILIA[4] CHÁVEZ, b. Abt. 1912[72]; m. REFUGIO ROMERO.
- ii.   ETHAL CHÁVEZ[73], b. September 14, 1913[74]; d. January 18, 1970; m. MIGUEL MAÉZ[75].

Notes for MIGUEL MAÉZ:
Buried in Hondo, New México.

- iii.   CANDIDO CHÁVEZ[76], b. December 25, 1915, San Patricio, New México[77]; d. June 14, 1995; m. NORA S. RANDOLPH, February 15, 1947, Carrizozo, New México[77].

Notes for CANDIDO CHÁVEZ:
Private First Class. World War II.

- iv.   VIOLA CHÁVEZ, b. Abt. 1918[78].
- v.   ELIZABETH CHÁVEZ, b. Abt. 1922[78]; m. JAMES MACKEY.

Notes for ELIZABETH CHÁVEZ:
Also known as Libby.

Notes for JAMES MACKEY:
Also known as Jaime Mackey.

- vi.   CLIFFORD WEST CHÁVEZ, b. Private.
- vii.   DOROTHY CHÁVEZ, b. Private; m. LARRY TORREZ.
- viii.   JOHNNY CHÁVEZ, b. Private.
- ix.   WILLIE DEAN CHÁVEZ, b. Private.

9. OLYMPIA[3] CHÁVEZ *(PABLO[2], JOSÉ[1] CHÁVES)*[79] was born 1894 in La Junta, Territory of New México[80], and died Abt. 1911 in Hondo, Territory of New México. She married JOHN MACKEY April 26, 1909[81], son of PATRICK MACKEY and GUADALUPE SAMORA.

Notes for JOHN MACKEY:
Was Justice of the Peace in San Patricio.
Land Patent # NMR 0035308, on the authority of the Homestead Entry-Enlarged (35 Stat. 639), February 19, 1909. Issued 320 acres on May 01, 1922.

Child of OLYMPIA CHÁVEZ and JOHN MACKEY is:
- i.   OLYMPIA[4] MACKEY, b. June 05, 1910; d. Abt. 1912.

Notes for OLYMPIA MACKEY:
Died young.

10. LEOPOLDO[3] CHÁVEZ *(PABLO[2], JOSÉ[1] CHÁVES)* was born April 25, 1907 in Hondo, Territory of New México[82]. He married ALTAGRACIA POLACO May 24, 1930 in Carrizozo, New México[82], daughter of TRANCITO POLACO and AROPAJITA GONZÁLES.

Notes for ALTAGRACIA POLACO:
Also known as Grace.

Children of LEOPOLDO CHÁVEZ and ALTAGRACIA POLACO are:
- i.   BREZEL[4] CHÁVEZ[83], b. June 01, 1934; d. March 29, 1992; m. PABLITA HERRERA.
- ii.   RICHARD CHÁVEZ[83], b. October 07, 1938; d. March 24, 2003.
- iii.   LYDIA CHÁVEZ, b. Private; m. BOBBY CHÁVEZ.
- iv.   ROY CHÁVEZ, b. Private; m. CRUSITA SILVA.

11. RUMELIO[3] CHÁVEZ *(PABLO[2], JOSÉ[1] CHÁVES)*[84] was born 1909 in Hondo, Territory of New México, and died 1963. He married CECILIA OLGUÍN July 11, 1936[85], daughter of ESTANISLADO OLGUÍN and ANASTACIA CHÁVEZ.

Notes for CECILIA OLGUÍN:
Also known as Yselia.

Children of RUMELIO CHÁVEZ and CECILIA OLGUÍN are:
     i.   AMADA[4] CHÁVEZ, b. Private; m. HENRY SÁNCHEZ.

Notes for AMADA CHÁVEZ:
Also known as Amy.

     ii.   PABLO OLGUÍN CHÁVEZ, b. Private.

Notes for PABLO OLGUÍN CHÁVEZ:
Died at a young age.

     iii.   ÁBRAN OLGUÍN CHÁVEZ, b. Private.

12. ERMANDO[3] CHÁVEZ *(PABLO[2], JOSÉ[1] CHÁVES)*[86] was born February 24, 1914 in Hondo, New México[87], and died June 05, 2010 in San Patricio, New México. He married (1) MACLOVIA MARTÍNEZ[88] December 07, 1935 in Carrizozo, New México[89], daughter of ADENAGO MARTÍNEZ and ANITA GUTIÉRREZ. He married (2) ANEDA ULIBARRÍ SÁNCHEZ September 13, 1941 in Carrizozo, New México[90], daughter of RAYMUNDO SÁNCHEZ and AUGUSTINA ULIBARRÍ.

Notes for MACLOVIA MARTÍNEZ:
Buried: San Patricio.

Children of ERMANDO CHÁVEZ and MACLOVIA MARTÍNEZ are:
     i.   PABLO MOISES[4] CHÁVEZ[91], b. July 13, 1936, San Patricio, New México; d. May 28, 2009, Amarillo, Téxas.

Notes for PABLO MOISES CHÁVEZ:
Also known as Paul.

     ii.   BOBBY MARTÍNEZ CHÁVEZ[92], b. Private, San Patricio, New México.
     iii.   LOUIS CHÁVEZ[92], b. Private.
     iv.   LILLIAN CHÁVEZ[92], b. Private; m. DANNY GARCÍA[92].
     v.   LUCY CHÁVEZ[92], b. Private.
     vi.   VIOLA CHÁVEZ, b. Private.
     vii.   JEANE CHÁVEZ, b. Private.
     viii.   DANNY CHÁVEZ, b. Private.

Children of ERMANDO CHÁVEZ and ANEDA SÁNCHEZ are:
     ix.   ABRAHAM[4] CHÁVEZ[93], b. November 28, 1946, San Patricio, New México; d. October 30, 1998, San Patricio, New México.
     x.   OZIEL CHÁVEZ[94], b. Private.

13. ERMINDA[3] CHÁVEZ *(FRANCISCO LUNA[2], JOSÉ[1] CHÁVES)*[95] was born July 12, 1894 in San Patricio, Territory of New México, and died November 01, 1956. She married (1) EPIFANIO ULIBARRÍ[96] November 04, 1915 in Lincoln, New México[97], son of VICENTE ULIBARRÍ and MARÍA SEDILLO. She married (2) JOSÉ JÁQUEZ[98] May 17, 1950[99].

Notes for EPIFANIO ULIBARRÍ:
1900 Census: Approximate birthdate listed as May 1895.

Children of ERMINDA CHÁVEZ and EPIFANIO ULIBARRÍ are:
     i.   ANUNCIÓN[4] ULIBARRÍ[100], b. August 13, 1917, San Patricio, New México; d. September 13, 1917, San Patricio, New México.
     ii.   DIEGO ULIBARRÍ[101], b. February 20, 1920; d. April 15, 1994, Carrizozo, New México.

Genealogy of Navor Cháves

Generation No. 1

1. NAVOR[1] CHÁVES was born Abt. 1836 in La Polvadera de San Lorenso, Nuevo México, La República de México[1]. He married GREGORIA TRUJILLO in La Polvadera, Territory of New México[2], daughter of ASCENCIÓN TRUJILLO.

Notes for NAVOR CHÁVES:
1860 Census: Living in La Polvadera de San Lorenso, Socorro County, Territory of New México.
1870 Census: Living in Lincoln County, Precinct 1.

Notes for GREGORIA TRUJILLO:
Also known as María Gregoria Trujillo.

Children of NAVOR CHÁVES and GREGORIA TRUJILLO are:
2.   i.   MACARIO[2] CHÁVEZ, b. March 1852.
3.   ii.   PLACIDO CHÁVEZ, b. January 1862; d. June 21, 1935, Tinnie, New México.
4.   iii.   MIQUELA CHÁVEZ, b. Abt. 1863; d. September 12, 1943, Hondo, New México.
5.   iv.   SOSTENA CHÁVEZ, b. Abt. 1864.
6.   v.   MARÍA TRUJILLO CHÁVEZ, b. 1869; d. January 06, 1933.
        vi.   DOLÓRES CHÁVEZ, b. April 04, 1872, La Junta, Territory of New México[3].
7.   vii.   JOSEFA CHÁVEZ, b. June 1876.
8.   viii.   JUAN TRUJILLO CHÁVEZ, b. January 27, 1880, La Junta, Territory of New México.

Generation No. 2

2. MACARIO[2] CHÁVEZ *(NAVOR[1])* was born March 1852[4]. He married (1) FRANCISCA FRESQUEZ Abt. 1868[5]. He married (2) ELFIDA MONTOYA[6] December 07, 1902[7], daughter of TRANQUELINO MONTOYA and MARÍA TRUJILLO.

Notes for MACARIO CHÁVEZ:
1870 Census: Living in Manzano, Territory of New México.
1880 Census: Living in La Plaza de Picacho, Territory of New México.
1900 Census: Living in Las Tablas, Territory of New México.
1910 Census: Living in Richardson, Territory of New México.

Notes for ELFIDA MONTOYA:
Also known as Delfida.
November 30, 1833: Baptized. Padrinos: Francisco Trujillo, Margarita Trujillo.

Children of MACARIO CHÁVEZ and FRANCISCA FRESQUEZ are:
        i.   MARILLITA[3] CHÁVEZ.
        ii.   CONCEPCIÓN CHÁVEZ, b. Abt. 1872, Picacho, Territory of New México[8].
9.   iii.   ELFIDA CHÁVEZ, b. February 26, 1874; d. April 24, 1926.
        iv.   BEATRIZ CHÁVEZ, b. Abt. 1877, Picacho, Territory of New México[8].

Children of MACARIO CHÁVEZ and ELFIDA MONTOYA are:
10.   v.   PEDRO[3] CHÁVEZ, b. October 23, 1903, Lincoln, Territory of New México; d. December 27, 1995, San Patricio, New México.
        vi.   SALVADOR MONTOYA, b. Abt. 1910[9]; Stepchild.

3. PLACIDO[2] CHÁVEZ *(NAVOR[1])* was born January 1862[10], and died June 21, 1935 in Tinnie, New México[11]. He married TRENIDAD LUNA January 16, 1887 in La Junta, Territory of New México[12], daughter of JESÚS LUNA and NICOLASA ARAGÓN.

Notes for PLACIDO CHÁVEZ:
1910 Census: Living in San Patricio, Territory of New México.

Children of PLACIDO CHÁVEZ and TRENIDAD LUNA are:
    i.   NECUDEMO[3] CHÁVEZ[13], b. January 07, 1888, Hondo, Territory of New México[14]; d. November 13, 1960.

Notes for NECUDEMO CHÁVEZ:
Land Patent # NMLC 0028257, on the authority of the Homestead Entry-Stock Raising (39 Stat. 862), December 29, 1916. Issued 320 acres on October 29, 1930.

11.   ii.   JUAN EVANGELISTA CHÁVEZ, b. June 15, 1888, Hondo, Territory of New México.
    iii.   JUANITA CHÁVEZ[15], b. June 12, 1890[16]; m. (1) SEQUIEL GUSTAMANTE[17]; m. (2) MARTÍN BACA TORRES, March 16, 1933[18].

Notes for SEQUIEL GUSTAMANTE:
1920 Census: Living in Las Palas, New México.
1930 Census: Living in Cháves County, New México, Precinct 4.

    iv.   FRANCISQUITA CHÁVEZ, b. Abt. 1893.
12.   v.   ESEQUIEL CHÁVEZ, b. April 10, 1893, Analla, Territory of New México.
13.   vi.   CAROLINA LUNA CHÁVEZ, b. Abt. 1897, Analla, Territory of New México.
14.   vii.   ALVINO CHÁVEZ, b. December 16, 1898, Analla, Territory of New México.
15.   viii.   JACOBO CHÁVEZ, b. September 01, 1901; d. December 12, 1964.
    ix.   ANITA CHÁVEZ, b. Abt. 1904[19]; m. ANTONIO MONTANTES[20].
    x.   TOÑITA CHÁVEZ[21], b. June 13, 1906, Tinnie, Territory of New México[22]; m. BRAULIO GONZÁLES, August 26, 1929[23].

Notes for TOÑITA CHÁVEZ:
Also known as Antonia.

Notes for BRAULIO GONZÁLES:
Braulio and his wife immigrated to La República de México.

4. MIQUELA[2] CHÁVEZ *(NAVOR[1])*[24] was born Abt. 1863[25], and died September 12, 1943 in Hondo, New México. She married AMBROCIO LUNA CHÁVEZ[26] Abt. 1882[27], son of JOSÉ CHÁVEZ and MARÍA LUNA.

Notes for MIQUELA CHÁVEZ:
Also known as Miquelita.
1930 Census lists Miquela as the head of the household.

Notes for AMBROCIO LUNA CHÁVEZ:
1870 Census: Living in Lincoln County, Precinct 1, Territory of New México. Birth year listed as 1849.
1900 Census: Living in Picacho, Territory of New México.

Children of MIQUELA CHÁVEZ and AMBROCIO CHÁVEZ are:
    i.   TOMÁS[3] CHÁVEZ, b. September 18, 1887, Hondo, Territory of New México[28]; d. September 1953[29].

Notes for TOMÁS CHÁVEZ:
Cemetery records indicate he was born in March 1887.
1900 Census: Living in Picacho, Territory of New México.

16.   ii.   GEORGE CHÁVEZ, b. April 20, 1892, Analla, Territory of New México; d. July 24, 1972.
    iii.   JUAN JOSÉ CHÁVEZ, b. April 08, 1900, Picacho, Territory of New México[30].

Notes for JUAN JOSÉ CHÁVEZ:
1900 Census: Living in Picacho, Territory of New México.

    iv.   OSCAR CHÁVEZ, b. Abt. 1906[31].
    v.   FRANCISQUITA CHÁVEZ[32], b. October 10, 1906[33]; d. January 03, 1983; m. ARISTOTEL ROMERO[34], 1936[35].

Notes for ARISTOTEL ROMERO:
NM Private, Med Dept, WWI

5. SOSTENA[2] CHÁVEZ *(NAVOR[1])* was born Abt. 1864[36]. She married VICTORIO PERALES May 16, 1898[37], son of JULIAN PERALES and CATARINA PINO.

Notes for VICTORIO PERALES:
1900 Census: Living in Picacho, Territory of New México.
1910 Census: Living in San Patricio, Territory of New México.
1920 Census: Living in San Patricio, New México.

Children of SOSTENA CHÁVEZ and VICTORIO PERALES are:
17.   i.   BLASITA[3] PERALES, b. February 03, 1899, Abeline, Téxas; d. October 13, 1971, Roswell, New México.
        ii.   LAZARA PERALES, b. February 03, 1899, San Patricio, New México[38].
        iii.   GREGORIA PERALES, b. Abt. 1900[39].
        iv.   MIGUEL PERALES, b. Abt. 1905[39].

6. MARÍA TRUJILLO[2] CHÁVEZ *(NAVOR[1])* was born 1869[40], and died January 06, 1933[41]. She married (1) AMBROCIO LUNA CHÁVEZ[42] May 20, 1882[43], son of JOSÉ CHÁVEZ and MARÍA LUNA. She married (2) FAUSTINO BACA SALCIDO[44] January 10, 1898[45], son of DIEGO SALCIDO and MIQUELA BACA.

Notes for MARÍA TRUJILLO CHÁVEZ:
Death Records indicate that she died on November 07, 1933.

Notes for AMBROCIO LUNA CHÁVEZ:
1870 Census: Living in Lincoln County, Precinct 1, Territory of New México. Birth year listed as 1849.
1900 Census: Living in Picacho, Territory of New México.

Children of MARÍA CHÁVEZ and FAUSTINO SALCIDO are:
18.   i.   DIEGO[3] SALCIDO, b. December 19, 1898, Hondo, New México ; d. March 1966, Roswell, New México.
19.   ii.   RAFAEL SALCIDO, b. May 25, 1900, Hondo, Territory of New México.
20.   iii.   FAUSTINO CHÁVEZ SALCIDO, b. November 24, 1901; d. November 05, 1959, Hondo, New México.
        iv.   PEDRO SALCIDO[46], b. February 23, 1903, Hondo, Territory of New México[47]; d. May 29, 1988, Hondo, New México; m. FELIS SÁNCHEZ TORRES[48], October 24, 1928, Carrizozo, New México[49].
        v.   JOSÉ SALCIDO[50], b. May 17, 1904[51]; d. August 24, 1974, Hondo, New México
        vi.   SAFINA SALCIDO, b. 1910[53]; m. ELOY TORREZ. ; m. NARCISA MONTOYA[52].
21.   vii.   PROCESO SALCIDO, b. March 23, 1911, Hondo, Territory of New México; d. April 28, 1999, Hondo, New México
        viii. SYLVESTRE SALCIDO[54], b. December 31, 1913[55]; d. May 08, 1975, Hondo, New México ; m. ANGELITA MONTOYA[56].

7. JOSEFA[2] CHÁVEZ *(NAVOR[1])* was born June 1876[57]. She married JUAN BARTLETT May 13, 1892[58], son of CHARLES BARTLETT and ADELA GALINDRO.

Children of JOSEFA CHÁVEZ and JUAN BARTLETT are:
        i.   BONNEY[3] BARTLETT, b. November 24, 1894[59].
22.   ii.   WILLIAM BARTLETT, b. May 20, 1896, Lincoln, Territory of New Mexico.

8. JUAN TRUJILLO[2] CHÁVEZ *(NAVOR[1])* was born January 27, 1880 in La Junta, Territory of New México[60]. He married MARÍA AGUIDA PEÑA March 20, 1907 in Lincoln, Territory of New México[60], daughter of JUAN PEÑA and BEATRIZ MARTÍNEZ.

Children of JUAN CHÁVEZ and MARÍA PEÑA are:
        i.   DOMINGO[3] CHÁVEZ, b. April 30, 1916, Tinnie, New México[61]; m. BENICIA ARCHULETA, October 15, 1942, San Patricio, New México[61].

Notes for DOMINGO CHÁVEZ:
1930 Census: Living in Hondo, New México.

Notes for BENICIA ARCHULETA:
Also known as Bennie.

     ii.   BEATRIZ CHÁVEZ, b. 1918[62].
     iii.   GREGORIO CHÁVEZ[63], b. September 04, 1920, Tinnie, New México[64].
     iv.   CRUCITA CHÁVEZ, b. 1926[64].

Generation No. 3

9. ELFIDA[3] CHÁVEZ *(MACARIO[2], NAVOR[1])*[65] was born February 26, 1874[66], and died April 24, 1926. She married DANIEL TRUJILLO VIGIL[67] May 08, 1888 in Manzano, Territory of New México[68], son of JOSÉ VIGIL and MARÍA TRUJILLO.

Notes for DANIEL TRUJILLO VIGIL:
1900 Census: Living with his parents in Las Tablas.

Children of ELFIDA CHÁVEZ and DANIEL VIGIL are:
     i.   ANTONIA[4] VIGIL, b. September 15, 1889, Las Tablas, Territory of New México[69]; m. ÁRON MONTOYA, April 23, 1906, Las Tablas, Territory of New México[69].
     ii.   MILITÓN VIGIL[70], b. March 10, 1891[71]; d. December 1970, Albuquerque, New México.
     iii. FRANCISQUITA VIGIL[72], b. March 10, 1893, Lincoln, Territory of New México[73].
     iv. MARILLITA CHÁVEZ VIGIL, b. March 1895[73].
     v.   MACARIO CHÁVEZ VIGIL, b. September 1898[73].
     vi. SERILA VIGIL[74], b. July 09, 1901; d. January 24, 1939.
     vii. VENANCIO VIGIL, b. Abt. 1904[75].
     viii. DANIEL CHÁVEZ VIGIL, b. Abt. 1906[75].
     ix. BEATRICE VIGIL, b. Abt. 1908[75].

10. PEDRO[3] CHÁVEZ *(MACARIO[2], NAVOR[1])*[76] was born October 23, 1903 in Lincoln, Territory of New México, and died December 27, 1995 in San Patricio, New México. He married LORENCITA TRUJILLO[77] July 13, 1930 in Carrizozo, New México[78], daughter of BONAFICIO TRUJILLO and LORENSA SILVA.

Notes for PEDRO CHÁVEZ:
Also known as Pedro Chávez y Montoya.
Pedro was raised by his half sister's (Elfida Chavez) daughter, Marillita and her husband Julian Romero y Torres in Manzano, NM until he was 16 years old. He was re-united with his mother in Corona, NM.
Buried in San Patricio, NM.

Children of PEDRO CHÁVEZ and LORENCITA TRUJILLO are:
     i.   MARÍA CIRILIA[4] CHÁVEZ[79], b. Abt. 1937, San Patricio, New México; d. March 24, 1937, San Patricio, New México.
23.   ii.   MACARIO TRUJILLO CHÁVEZ, b. Private.
     iii. RAYMOND CHÁVEZ, b. Private.
     iv. RUFINA CHÁVEZ, b. Private; m. SIGISFREDO MONTOYA.

11. JUAN EVANGELISTA[3] CHÁVEZ *(PLACIDO[2], NAVOR[1])*[80] was born June 15, 1888 in Hondo, Territory of New México[81]. He married LEONOR CHÁVEZ PEÑA[82] January 08, 1925 in San Patricio, New México[83], daughter of LUÍS PEÑA and RAQUEL CHÁVEZ.

Children of JUAN CHÁVEZ and LEONOR PEÑA are:
     i.   LUÍS[4] CHÁVEZ, b. Private.
     ii.   MACEDONIO CHÁVEZ, b. Private.
     iii. FRANCISCO PEÑA CHÁVEZ, b. Private.
     iv. REBECA CHÁVEZ, b. Private. Died young.
     v.   MARTÍN CHÁVEZ, b. Private. Died young.
     vi. ANGELITA CHÁVEZ, b. Private. Died young.

12. ESEQUIEL[3] CHÁVEZ *(PLACIDO[2], NAVOR[1])* was born April 10, 1893 in Analla, Territory of New México[84]. He married TOÑITA HORTON October 19, 1916 in Picacho, New México[85], daughter of WALTER HORTON and TERESA LÓPEZ.

Child of ESEQUIEL CHÁVEZ and TOÑITA HORTON is:
    i.   VIOLA[4] CHÁVEZ, b. Private, Hondo, Territory of New México; m. MARTÍN PEÑA[86].

13. CAROLINA LUNA[3] CHÁVEZ *(PLACIDO[2], NAVOR[1])* was born Abt. 1897 in Analla, Territory of New México[87]. She married (1) LORENSO SAMBRANO[88]. She married (2) PRESILIANO HERNÁNDEZ[89] February 07, 1912[90].

Children of CAROLINA CHÁVEZ and PRESILIANO HERNÁNDEZ are:
    i.   MARÍA[4] HERNÁNDEZ, b. Abt. 1913[91].
    ii.   PEDRO HERNÁNDEZ, b. Abt. 1917[91].
    iii. PABLO HERNÁNDEZ[92], b. June 30, 1918, Tinnie, New México[93]; m. SOCORRO MENDOSA[94], June 19, 1940, Hondo, New México[94].
    iv. JENOSO HERNÁNDEZ, b. Abt. 1923[95].
    v.   MAXIMIANO HERNÁNDEZ, b. Abt. 1926[95].
    vi. ANA HERNÁNDEZ, b. Abt. 1928[96].
    vii. DORATITA HERNÁNDEZ, b. Abt. 1929[96].

14. ALVINO[3] CHÁVEZ *(PLACIDO[2], NAVOR[1])* was born December 16, 1898 in Analla, Territory of New México[97]. He married ERMINDA TRUJILLO March 13, 1935 in San Patricio, New México[97], daughter of FRANCISCO TRUJILLO and GENOVEVA MONTOYA.

Notes for ALVINO CHÁVEZ:
Also known as Albino.

Child of ALVINO CHÁVEZ and ERMINDA TRUJILLO is:
    i.   MODESTO TRUJILLO[4] CHÁVEZ, b. Private.

15. JACOBO[3] CHÁVEZ *(PLACIDO[2], NAVOR[1])[98]* was born September 01, 1901, and died December 12, 1964. He married ROSALÍA MENDOZA LARA September 08, 1927[99], daughter of BERNABÉ LARA and NESTORA MENDOZA.

Child of JACOBO CHÁVEZ and ROSALÍA LARA is:
    i.   NATALIA[4] CHÁVEZ[100], b. January 01, 1931, San Patricio, New México; d. November 06, 1995, Tucson, Arizona; m. FRANCISCO HERRERA[100].

16. GEORGE[3] CHÁVEZ *(MIQUELA[2], NAVOR[1])[101]* was born April 20, 1892 in Analla, Territory of New México[102], and died July 24, 1972. He married JULIA HERNÁNDEZ[103] February 04, 1920 in Tinnie, New México[104], daughter of EULOJIO HERNÁNDEZ.

Children of GEORGE CHÁVEZ and JULIA HERNÁNDEZ are:
    i.   AMBROCIO HERNÁNDEZ[4] CHÁVEZ, b. Abt. 1920, Hondo, New México[105].
    ii.   MARÍA CHÁVEZ, b. Abt. 1921[105].
    iii. JOSIE HERNÁNDEZ CHÁVEZ, b. Abt. 1923[105].
    iv. AUGUSTÍN HERNÁNDEZ CHÁVEZ, b. Abt. 1925[105].
    v.   GEORGE HERNÁNDEZ CHÁVEZ[106], b. February 27, 1928, Hondo, New México[107].
    vi. ALFONZO CHÁVEZ, b. Abt. 1929[107].
    vii. DANNY CHÁVEZ[108], b. March 05, 1938, Hondo, New México; d. May 02, 2008, Douglas Flats, California.
    viii. OLOJIO CHÁVEZ[108], b. Private.
    ix. VICTORIO CHÁVEZ[108], b. Private.
    x.   PHILIP CHÁVEZ[108], b. Private.

17. BLASITA[3] PERALES *(SOSTENA[2] CHÁVEZ, NAVOR[1])* was born February 03, 1899 in Abeline, Téxas[109], and died October 13, 1971 in Roswell, New México. She married (1) YSIDRO MONTOYA[110], son of MAURICIO MONTOYA and AVRORA SÁNCHEZ. She married (2) FILOMENO HERRERA[111] August 12, 1916 in San Patricio, New México[112], son of CRUZ HERRERA and REDUCINDA CARDONA.

Notes for YSIDRO MONTOYA:
New Mexico Private First Class 3263 Sig Service Co. Was a WW II veteran.

Child of BLASITA PERALES and YSIDRO MONTOYA is:
    i.   JOSPHINE[4] MONTOYA[113], b. May 03, 1935; d. April 1991, Roswell, New México.

Children of BLASITA PERALES and FILOMENO HERRERA are:
    ii.   ROSA[4] HERRERA, b. April 19, 1918; d. October 21, 1982.
    iii.   SOSTENA HERRERA[114], b. March 06, 1920; d. October 12, 1994, Roswell, New México; m. ANDRÉS GONZÁLES[114], July 22, 1936, Roswell, New México.
    iv.   MARÍA REYES HERRERA, b. January 06, 1922, Jones County, Texas; d. October 20, 2001, Las Cruces, New México; m. HENRY GONZÁLES, May 15, 1941, Roswell, New México.
    v.   LORENCITA HERRERA, b. Abt. 1923[115]; d. Abt. 1929, Abeline, Texas.
    vi.   EMMA HERRERA, b. July 05, 1925; d. June 04, 1997, Roswell, New México.

18. DIEGO[3] SALCIDO *(MARÍA TRUJILLO[2] CHÁVEZ, NAVOR[1])*[116] was born December 19, 1898 in Hondo, New México[117], and died March 1966 in Roswell, New México. He married PETRA ULIBARRÍ[118] November 06, 1922[119], daughter of VICENTE ULIBARRÍ and MARÍA SEDILLO.

Notes for PETRA ULIBARRÍ:
Buried in Roswell, New México.

Children of DIEGO SALCIDO and PETRA ULIBARRÍ are:
    i.   VICENTE[4] SALCIDO[120], b. May 05, 1924[121].
    ii.   MONICA SALCIDO[122], b. February 14, 1926, San Patricio, New México[123]; d. August 05, 1991, San Patricio, New México; m. ESTOLANO TRUJILLO SÁNCHEZ[124], January 10, 1945, Carrizozo, New México[125].
24.   iii.   MARY SALCIDO, b. April 23, 1934, Hondo, New México; d. March 10, 2001, Dexter, New México.
    iv.   DELLA SALCIDO[126], b. Private.
    v.   FITA SALCIDO[126], b. Private.
    vi.   NORA SALCIDO[126], b. Private.

19. RAFAEL[3] SALCIDO *(MARÍA TRUJILLO[2] CHÁVEZ, NAVOR[1])* was born May 25, 1900 in Hondo, Territory of New México[127]. He married CATARINA BACA February 08, 1923[128], daughter of DAMACIO BACA and MARÍA BACA.

Notes for RAFAEL SALCIDO:
1930 Census: Living in Hondo, New México.

Children of RAFAEL SALCIDO and CATARINA BACA are:
    i.   ARCENIA[4] SALCIDO, b. Abt. 1921[129].
    ii.   CARMELITA SALCIDO, b. Abt. 1923[129].
    iii.   FLORINDA SALCIDO, b. Abt. 1925[129].
    iv.   ISABEL SALCIDO, b. Abt. 1927[129].

20. FAUSTINO CHÁVEZ[3] SALCIDO *(MARÍA TRUJILLO[2] CHÁVEZ, NAVOR[1])*[130] was born November 24, 1901, and died November 05, 1959 in Hondo, New México. He married PREDICANDA WARNER[130] January 24, 1924[131], daughter of JUAN WARNER and EMILIA TORREZ.

Children of FAUSTINO SALCIDO and PREDICANDA WARNER are:
    i.   ALBERT W.[4] SALCIDO, b. October 25, 1925, Lincoln, New México[132]; m. NORA NÚÑEZ[133], November 16, 1946, Carrizozo, New México[134].
    ii.   DAVÍD SALCIDO[135], b. June 29, 1927, Hondo, New México[136]; d. October 03, 1958, Hondo, New México; m. MARTINA SILVA, December 13, 1950, Ruidoso, New México[137].
    iii.   AMELIA SALCIDO, b. Abt. 1929, Hondo, New México[138].

21. PROCESO[3] SALCIDO *(MARÍA TRUJILLO[2] CHÁVEZ, NAVOR[1])*[139] was born March 23, 1911 in Hondo, Territory of New México[140], and died April 28, 1999 in Hondo, New México. He married DOMINGA ULIBARRÍ[141] December 05, 1931[142], daughter of VICENTE ULIBARRÍ and MARÍA SEDILLO.

Child of PROCESO SALCIDO and DOMINGA ULIBARRÍ is:

    i.   CIRILIA OLYMPIA[4] SALCIDO[143], b. Abt. 1932, Hondo, New México; d. November 22, 1933, Hondo, New México.

22. WILLIAM[3] BARTLETT *(JOSEFA[2] CHÁVEZ, NAVOR[1])* was born May 20, 1896 in Lincoln, Territory of New Mexico[144]. He married (1) SARA ROMERO July 18, 1917 in Lincoln, New México[145], daughter of REFUGIO ROMERO and ROBERTA CHÁVEZ. He married (2) CLARA MIRELES March 06, 1926[146], daughter of FLORENCIO MIRELES and IGINIA BENAVIDEZ.

Children of WILLIAM BARTLETT and SARA ROMERO are:

    i.   ERMINIA[4] BARTLETT, b. Abt. 1922[147].
    ii.   WILLIAM ROMERO BARTLETT, b. Abt. 1923[147].
    iii.   JOHNNIE BARTLETT[148], b. February 1924, Lincoln, New México; d. June 27, 1924, Carrizozo, New México.

Generation No. 4

23. MACARIO TRUJILLO[4] CHÁVEZ *(PEDRO[3], MACARIO[2], NAVOR[1])* was born Private. He married TERESA GÓMEZ.

24. MARY[4] SALCIDO *(DIEGO[3], MARÍA TRUJILLO[2] CHÁVEZ, NAVOR[1])*[149] was born April 23, 1934 in Hondo, New México, and died March 10, 2001 in Dexter, New México. She married JERRY MARTÍNEZ[149] August 19, 1950[149].

Genealogy of Nicanor Dominguez

Generation No. 1

1. NICANOR[1] DOMINGUEZ was born Abt. 1850 in La República de México[1]. He married OCTAVIANA FUENTES[23], daughter of ANTONIO FUENTES and SENONA VASQUEZ.

Notes for NICANOR DOMINGUEZ:
Immigrated to the U.S. in about 1880.

Notes for OCTAVIANA FUENTES:
Also known as Ceferina.
Immigrated to the U.S. in about 1880.

Children of NICANOR DOMINGUEZ and OCTAVIANA FUENTES are:
2.	i.	GREGORIO FUENTES[2] DOMINGUEZ, b. 1882, Ciúdad Juárez, Chihuahua, La República de México.
3.	ii.	JESÚSITA DOMINGUEZ, b. Abt. 1884.
4.	iii.	PETRA DOMINGUEZ, b. Abt. 1886; d. May 07, 1933, San Patricio, New México.
	iv.	JOSÉ DOMINGUEZ[4], b. Abt. 1890; d. August 16, 1937, San Patricio, New México.
	v.	VICENTE FUENTES DOMINGUEZ, b. Abt. 1891[5].

Notes for VICENTE FUENTES DOMINGUEZ:
Land Patent # NMR 0044248, on the authority of the Homestead Entry-Original (12 Stat. 392), May 20, 1862. Issued 320 acres on October 20, 1924.
Land Patent # NMR 0050882, on the authority of the Homestead Entry-Stock Raising (39 Stat. 862), December 29, 1916. Issued 320 acres on October 20, 1924.

5.	vi.	TIVORCIO DOMINGUEZ, b. 1895, Téxas; d. December 11, 1927, San Patricio, New México.

Generation No. 2

2. GREGORIO FUENTES[2] DOMINGUEZ *(NICANOR[1])*[6] was born 1882 in Ciúdad Juárez, Chihuahua, La República de México[7]. He married DONICIA CARDONA February 16, 1910[7].

Notes for GREGORIO FUENTES DOMINGUEZ:
Both of his parents were born in México.

Children of GREGORIO DOMINGUEZ and DONICIA CARDONA are:
	i.	MANUEL[3] DOMINGUEZ, b. 1913[8].
	ii.	NICANOR DOMINGUEZ, b. 1916[8].
	iii.	REDUCINDA DOMINGUEZ, b. 1918[8].

3. JESÚSITA[2] DOMINGUEZ *(NICANOR[1])* was born Abt. 1884[9]. She married (1) MANUEL CORONA[10] January 26, 1905 in Lincoln, Territory of New México[11], son of MAXIMIANO CORONA and MANUELITA HERRERA. She married (2) CARMEL ORTEGA December 20, 1907[12], son of JOSÉ ORTEGA and BENINA REÁL.

Notes for JESÚSITA DOMINGUEZ:
She divorced Manuel Corona.

Child of JESÚSITA DOMINGUEZ and MANUEL CORONA is:
6.	i.	SARA[3] CORONA, b. December 17, 1905, Arabela, Territory of New México.

Children of JESÚSITA DOMINGUEZ and CARMEL ORTEGA are:
7.	ii.	GUADALUPE[3] ORTEGA, b. Abt. 1910.
	iii.	SUSANA ORTEGA, b. Abt. 1913[13].
	iv.	TONICIO ORTEGA, b. Abt. 1915[13].

4. PETRA[2] DOMINGUEZ *(NICANOR[1])* was born Abt. 1886[14], and died May 07, 1933 in San Patricio, New México[15]. She married CRUZ HERRERA March 02, 1905[16], son of SANTIAGO HERRERA and MARÍA ESCALANTE.

Notes for PETRA DOMINGUEZ:
1930 Census lists her as the head of the household.

Children of PETRA DOMINGUEZ and CRUZ HERRERA are:

	i.	MARIANA[3] HERRERA, b. San Patricio, New México.
8.	ii.	VICENTE HERRERA, b. January 22, 1906, San Patricio, Territory of New México; d. December 31, 1993, San Patricio, New México.
9.	iii.	SANTIAGO DOMINGUEZ HERRERA, b. May 01, 1915, San Patricio, New México; d. February 18, 1995, San Patricio, New México.
	iv.	MANUEL DOMINGUEZ HERRERA, b. Abt. 1917, San Patricio, New México[17].
	v.	ANTONIO HERRERA[18], b. August 29, 1919, San Patricio, New México[19].
	vi.	FRANCISCO HERRERA[20], b. April 02, 1921, San Patricio, New México[21]; d. November 15, 1994, Tucson, Arizona; m. NATALIA CHÁVEZ[22].

5. TIVORCIO[2] DOMINGUEZ *(NICANOR[1])*[23] was born 1895 in Téxas[24], and died December 11, 1927 in San Patricio, New México. He married DECIDERIA MONTOYA December 20, 1915 in Lincoln, New México[25], daughter of FELIPÉ MONTOYA and PAULA GARCÍA.

Notes for TIVORCIO DOMINGUEZ:
Death records indicate that his birth year was 1888.

Children of TIVORCIO DOMINGUEZ and DECIDERIA MONTOYA are:

	i.	ESTEVAN[3] DOMINGUEZ[26], b. December 26, 1916, Hondo, New México[27].

Notes for ESTEVAN DOMINGUEZ:
Private. World War II.

	ii.	MANUELITA DOMINGUEZ, b. 1918[27].

Generation No. 3

6. SARA[3] CORONA *(JESÚSITA[2] DOMINGUEZ, NICANOR[1])* was born December 17, 1905 in Arabela, Territory of New México[28]. She married JOSÉ MIGUEL ARCHULETA[29] March 01, 1924 in Arabela, New México[30], son of ANTONIO ARCHULETA and LUZ LUCERO.

Notes for JOSÉ MIGUEL ARCHULETA:
He was the adopted son of Antonio José Archuleta.

Children of SARA CORONA and JOSÉ ARCHULETA are:

	i.	ANTONIO[4] ARCHULETA, b. Private.

Notes for ANTONIO ARCHULETA:
Also known as Tony.

	ii.	GUILLERMO ARCHULETA, b. Private.
	iii.	FRANK ARCHULETA, b. Private.
	iv.	ORLANDO ARCHULETA, b. Private.
	v.	MELVIN ARCHULETA, b. Private.
	vi.	SERAFÍN ARCHULETA, b. Private.
	vii.	FELISITA ARCHULETA, b. Private.
	viii.	JOSEFINA ARCHULETA, b. Private.
	ix.	CECILIA ARCHULETA, b. Private.
	x.	ARABELA ARCHULETA, b. Private.

7. GUADALUPE[3] ORTEGA *(JESÚSITA[2] DOMINGUEZ, NICANOR[1])* was born Abt. 1910[31]. He married DORA CARRILLO.

Children of GUADALUPE ORTEGA and DORA CARRILLO are:
- i.   CARMEN CARILLO[4] ORTEGA, b. Private.
- ii.   CONNIE ORTEGA, b. Private.
- iii. STEVE ORTEGA, b. Private.
- iv.   STELLA ORTEGA, b. Private.
- v.   LUPITA ORTEGA, b. Private.
- vi.   EDNA ORTEGA, b. Private.
- vii. LOUISA ORTEGA, b. Private.
- viii. ARTHUR ORTEGA, b. Private.
- ix.   JOHNNY ORTEGA, b. Private.

8. VICENTE[3] HERRERA *(PETRA[2] DOMINGUEZ, NICANOR[1])*[32] was born January 22, 1906 in San Patricio, Territory of New México, and died December 31, 1993 in San Patricio, New México. He married CIPRIANA GONZÁLES[32] August 27, 1932 in San Patricio, New México[33], daughter of EPAMINOANDAS GONZÁLES and ELVIRA GONZÁLES.

Notes for VICENTE HERRERA:
Also known as Bisente.

Children of VICENTE HERRERA and CIPRIANA GONZÁLES are:
- i.   RUFINO[4] HERRERA[34], b. July 25, 1933, San Patricio, New México; d. January 17, 2006, San Patricio, New México; m. HELENA MONTOYA, April 04, 1957, San Patricio, New México.

Notes for RUFINO HERRERA:
Korean War Veteran

10.   ii.   BERTA HERRERA, b. Private, San Patricio, New México.

9. SANTIAGO DOMINGUEZ[3] HERRERA *(PETRA[2] DOMINGUEZ, NICANOR[1])*[35] was born May 01, 1915 in San Patricio, New México[36], and died February 18, 1995 in San Patricio, New México. He married GENOVEVA VIGIL[37] December 23, 1936 in Carrizozo, New México[38], daughter of CELESTINO VIGIL and SARA SÁNCHEZ.

Child of SANTIAGO HERRERA and GENOVEVA VIGIL is:
- i.   ROGER[4] HERRERA, b. Private.

Generation No. 4

10. BERTA[4] HERRERA *(VICENTE[3], PETRA[2] DOMINGUEZ, NICANOR[1])* was born Private in San Patricio, New México. She married FRED SÁNCHEZ, son of ROMÁN SÁNCHEZ and FLORINDA SALSBERRY.

Genealogy of Antonio Fresquez

Generation No. 1

1. ANTONIO[1] FRESQUEZ. He married MARÍA REYES SÁNCHEZ.

Children of ANTONIO FRESQUEZ and MARÍA SÁNCHEZ are:
2.   i.   VICENTE[2] FRESQUEZ, b. July 01, 1835; d. 1925.
       ii.   MARIA IGNACIA FRESQUEZ, b. Abt. 1841[1].
      iii.   MADALENA FRESQUEZ, b. Abt. 1843[1].

Generation No. 2

2. VICENTE[2] FRESQUEZ *(ANTONIO[1])*[2] was born July 01, 1835[3], and died 1925. He married MARÍA ANTONIA TAFOYA[4].

Notes for VICENTE FRESQUEZ:
Also known as José Vicente Fresquez.
1850 Census: Living in Taos County, Territory of New México.
1860 Census: Living in Arroyo Seco, Territory of New México.
1870 Census: Living in Punta de Agua, Territory of New México.
1880 Census: Living in La Plaza de Picacho, Territory of New México.

Children of VICENTE FRESQUEZ and MARÍA TAFOYA are:
3.   i.   PABLO[3] FRESQUEZ, b. Abt. 1853, Arroyo Seco, Taos County, Territory of New México..
       ii.   MARÍA ELENA FRESQUEZ, b. Abt. 1854, Arroyo Seco, Territory of New México.[5].
4.   iii.   RUMALDO FRESQUEZ, b. Abt. 1860, Arroyo Seco, Territory of New México..
       iv.   PEDRO FRESQUEZ, b. Abt. 1863, Arroyo Seco, Territory of New México.[6]; m. CANDELARIA LUCERO, January 28, 1883[7].
       v.   LUCINDA FRESQUEZ, b. Abt. 1867, Punta del Agua, Territory of New México[8].
       vi.   RAFAEL FRESQUEZ[9], b. Abt. 1870, Punta del Agua, Territory of New México[10].
5.   vii.   REYES FRESQUEZ, b. March 1873.
     viii.   MARTÍN FRESQUEZ, b. Abt. 1874[10]; m. LEANDRA GÓMEZ, July 05, 1900[11].
       ix.   ELIJA FRESQUEZ, b. Abt. 1876[12].
       x.   ADOLFO FRESQUEZ, b. Abt. 1877[12].

Generation No. 3

3. PABLO[3] FRESQUEZ *(VICENTE[2], ANTONIO[1])* was born Abt. 1853 in Arroyo Seco, Taos County, Territory of New México.[13]. He married EPIFANIA GARCÍA Abt. 1873[14].

Children of PABLO FRESQUEZ and EPIFANIA GARCÍA are:
       i.   DAVÍD[4] FRESQUEZ.

Notes for DAVÍD FRESQUEZ:
US Marshall for about 20 to 30 years.

       ii.   LUCÍA FRESQUEZ, b. Abt. 1873[15]; m. ROBERT CASEY, January 18, 1894, Picacho, Territory of New México[16].
      iii.   CLEOFAS FRESQUEZ[17], b. September 28, 1874[18]; d. August 10, 1894, Picacho, Territory of New México.
6.   iv.   CHON FRESQUEZ, b. March 25, 1878; d. March 11, 1950, Picacho, New México.
       v.   ENCARNACIÓN FRESQUEZ, b. March 1879[19].
       vi.   YSIDRO FRESQUEZ[20], b. May 15, 1880, Picacho, Territory of New México[21]; d. February 1968, Roswell, New México.
7.   vii.   PORFIRIO FRESQUEZ, b. January 12, 1885, Picacho, Territory of New México; d. January 26, 1978, Roswell, New México.
8.   viii.   LUTARIO FRESQUEZ, b. March 1887; d. 1946.

ix.   MANUEL GARCÍA FRESQUEZ, b. November 1890[21].

9.   x.   PAULITA FRESQUEZ, b. March 22, 1892, Picacho, Territory of New México; d. 1981.

xi.   EPIFANIO FRESQUEZ, b. February 1895[21].

xii.   RUMALDO FRESQUEZ[22], b. July 03, 1897[23]; d. March 1971, Roswell, New México.

Notes for RUMALDO FRESQUEZ:
1930 Census: Living in Spindle, New México.

4. RUMALDO[3] FRESQUEZ *(VICENTE[2], ANTONIO[1])* was born Abt. 1860 in Arroyo Seco, Territory of New México.[24]. He married TEOFILA RODRÍGUEZ[25].

Notes for RUMALDO FRESQUEZ:
Also known as José Rumaldo Fresquez.
1910 Census: Living in Las Palas, Territory of New México.

Children of RUMALDO FRESQUEZ and TEOFILA RODRÍGUEZ are:

10.   i.   SALOMON[4] FRESQUEZ, b. March 18, 1883, Las Palas, Territory of New México.

ii.   ALFREDO FRESQUEZ, b. Abt. 1885[26].

iii.   MANUEL RODRÍGUEZ FRESQUEZ, b. Abt. 1890[26].

11.   iv.   CLEOTILDE FRESQUEZ, b. April 04, 1893, Las Palas, Territory of New México.

v.   EMILIO FRESQUEZ, b. Abt. 1894, Las Palas, Territory of New México[27].

vi.   MARCOS FRESQUEZ[28], b. April 20, 1895, Las Palas, Territory of New México[29]; d. April 1975, Roswell, New México.

vii.   MARÍA REYES FRESQUEZ, b. June 21, 1897, Las Palas, Territory of New México[30].

viii.   ISABEL FRESQUEZ, b. Abt. 1904, Arabela, Territory of New México[31].

ix.   RUMALDO RODRÍGUEZ FRESQUEZ, b. Abt. 1907, Arabela, Territory of New México[31].

12.   x.   PABLO FRESQUEZ, b. January 15, 1899, Las Palas, Territory of New México.

5. REYES[3] FRESQUEZ *(VICENTE[2], ANTONIO[1])* was born March 1873[32]. She married TEOFILO SISNEROS Abt. 1886[32], son of YSIDRO SISNEROS and PETRA SISNEROS.

Notes for TEOFILO SISNEROS:
1910 Census: Living in San Patricio, Territory of New México.

Children of REYES FRESQUEZ and TEOFILO SISNEROS are:

13.   i.   PETRA FRESQUEZ[4] SISNEROS, b. December 29, 1896.

ii.   TEOFILO SISNEROS[33], b. May 14, 1903, San Patricio, Territory of New México; d. November 30, 1992, Roswell, New México.

14.   iii.   YSIDRO SISNEROS, b. April 16, 1904, San Patricio, New México; d. July 1978, Deming, New México.

iv.   DOLORES SISNEROS[33], b. May 09, 1916, San Patricio, New México; d. March 1983, Roswell, New México; m. LEOPOLDO CARRILLO[33].

Notes for DOLORES SISNEROS:
Also known as Lola.

Notes for LEOPOLDO CARRILLO:
1920 Census: Living in Picacho, Territory of New México.

Generation No. 4

6. CHON[4] FRESQUEZ *(PABLO[3], VICENTE[2], ANTONIO[1])*[34] was born March 25, 1878[35], and died March 11, 1950 in Picacho, New México. He married LUPITA DE FRESQUEZ.

Notes for CHON FRESQUEZ:
Died while clearing out brush from a ditch. He and others started a fire to burn the dead underbrush and it grew out of control. The fire overwhelmed Chon and he died from the fire.
1920 & 1930 Census: Living in Picacho, New México.

Notes for LUPITA DE FRESQUEZ:
Also known as Lupita

Children of CHON FRESQUEZ and LUPITA DE FRESQUEZ are:
   i.   BRAZEL[5] FRESQUEZ[36], b. December 04, 1918, Lincoln, New México[37].
   ii. EPEFANIA FRESQUEZ, b. Abt. 1921[37].

7. PORFIRIO[4] FRESQUEZ *(PABLO[3], VICENTE[2], ANTONIO[1])[38]* was born January 12, 1885 in Picacho, Territory of New México, and died January 26, 1978 in Roswell, New México. He married MARÍA S. DE FRESQUEZ[38] Abt. 1923[39].

Children of PORFIRIO FRESQUEZ and MARÍA DE FRESQUEZ are:
   i.   LUCÍA[5] FRESQUEZ, b. Abt. 1923[39].
   ii. ORLANDO FRESQUEZ[40], b. August 15, 1924, Roswell, New México[41].
   iii. ORFILA FRESQUEZ, b. August 24, 1927, Picacho, New México[42]; m. CARLOS ENRÍQUE RAMÍREZ, April 19, 1947, Picacho, New México[42].
   iv. ALVINO FRESQUEZ, b. Abt. 1928[43].
   v.   PRESTINA FRESQUEZ, b. Abt. 1929[43].

8. LUTARIO[4] FRESQUEZ *(PABLO[3], VICENTE[2], ANTONIO[1])[44]* was born March 1887[45], and died 1946. He married TERESITA DE FRESQUEZ[46] Abt. 1907[47].

Children of LUTARIO FRESQUEZ and TERESITA DE FRESQUEZ are:
   i.   ALMA[5] FRESQUEZ, b. Abt. 1910[47].
   ii. ANDREW FRESQUEZ[48], b. February 02, 1914[49]; d. April 03, 1995, Roswell, New México.

Notes for ANDREW FRESQUEZ:
Also known as Andrés

   iii. ESEQUIEL FRESQUEZ[50], b. July 07, 1917, Picacho, New México[51].

9. PAULITA[4] FRESQUEZ *(PABLO[3], VICENTE[2], ANTONIO[1])[52]* was born March 22, 1892 in Picacho, Territory of New México[53], and died 1981. She married (1) LEOPOLDO PACHECO[54], son of ANSELMO PACHECO and TERESITA GALLEGOS. She married (2) GEORGE SISNEROS[55] December 01, 1912 in Lincoln, New México[56], son of MANUEL SISNEROS and REBECCA SALAZAR.

Notes for GEORGE SISNEROS:
1900 Census: Living with his grandfather, Sipio Salazar, in Lincoln, Territory of New México.

Child of PAULITA FRESQUEZ and LEOPOLDO PACHECO is:
   i.   PAUL[5] PACHECO, b. Private.

Children of PAULITA FRESQUEZ and GEORGE SISNEROS are:
15.   ii. GEORGE[5] SISNEROS, b. May 21, 1918, Roswell, New México; d. October 13, 2010, Arabela, New México.
      iii. CLOFAS SISNEROS, b. Private; m. TOM MONTOYA.

10. SALOMON[4] FRESQUEZ *(RUMALDO[3], VICENTE[2], ANTONIO[1])* was born March 18, 1883 in Las Palas, Territory of New México[57]. He married CARMEN TRUJILLO[58] February 15, 1909[59], daughter of LUCIANO TRUJILLO and ROSARIO VIGIL.

Notes for CARMEN TRUJILLO:
Also known as Carmelita, Carmel.

Child of SALOMON FRESQUEZ and CARMEN TRUJILLO is:
16.   i.   JACOBO[5] FRESQUEZ, b. February 10, 1910; d. June 13, 1980, Tinnie, New México.

11. CLEOTILDE[4] FRESQUEZ *(RUMALDO[3], VICENTE[2], ANTONIO[1])*[60] was born April 04, 1893 in Las Palas, Territory of New México[61]. She married PEDRO ROMERO[62] April 07, 1913 in Lincoln, New México[63], son of TRENIDAD ROMERO and EUGENIA GONZÁLES.

Notes for CLEOTILDE FRESQUEZ:
Also known as Tillie.
Baptized on November 03, 1893. Padrinos: Esiquiel Vigil and Eliza de la Garza.

Notes for PEDRO ROMERO:
Baptized on February 04, 1892. Padrinos: Martín Chávez and Juanita Romero
1930 Census: Living in Arabela, New México.

Children of CLEOTILDE FRESQUEZ and PEDRO ROMERO are:
17.   i.   FRED[5] ROMERO, b. February 03, 1913, Picacho, New México.
18.   ii.   CLAUDIO ROMERO, b. February 18, 1914, Arabela, New México.
       iii.   ERMINIA ROMERO[64], b. 1920[65]; d. 1943.

12. PABLO[4] FRESQUEZ *(RUMALDO[3], VICENTE[2], ANTONIO[1])*[66] was born January 15, 1899 in Las Palas, Territory of New México[67]. He married EUFRACIA LUCERO January 10, 1920 in Arabela, New México[68], daughter of AMARANTE LUCERO and REBECA DE LUCERO.

Notes for PABLO FRESQUEZ:
1930 Census: Living in Arabela, New México.

Notes for EUFRACIA LUCERO:
Marriage records indicate that she was born on May 01, 1902. (Book of Marriages, Lincoln County. Book 5, Page 54)

Child of PABLO FRESQUEZ and EUFRACIA LUCERO is:
       i.   ELARIO[5] FRESQUEZ, b. Abt. 1928, Arabela, New México[69].

13. PETRA FRESQUEZ[4] SISNEROS *(REYES[3] FRESQUEZ, VICENTE[2], ANTONIO[1])* was born December 29, 1896[70]. She married PABLO GALLEGOS SALAS[71] November 14, 1910[72], son of TEOFILO SALAS and IGENIA GALLEGOS.

Children of PETRA SISNEROS and PABLO SALAS are:
       i.   TEOFILO SINEROS[5] SALAS, b. 1912, San Patricio, New México[73].
19.   ii.   FERMÍN SALAS, b. October 23, 1915, Hondo, New México; d. March 04, 1992.
       iii.   REYES SALAS[74], b. 1919, San Patricio, New México; d. September 29, 1943, Los Angeles, California.

Notes for REYES SALAS:
Died in Los Angeles, California but was burried in San Patricio, New Mexico on October 3, 1943.

       iv.   SOFIA SALAS, b. 1925, San Patricio, New México[75].

14. YSIDRO[4] SISNEROS *(REYES[3] FRESQUEZ, VICENTE[2], ANTONIO[1])*[76] was born April 16, 1904 in San Patricio, New México, and died July 1978 in Deming, New México. He married MANUELA CHÁVEZ[76] Abt. 1925[77].

Notes for YSIDRO SISNEROS:
1930 Census: Living in Cháves County, Precinct 4, Territory of New México.

Children of YSIDRO SISNEROS and MANUELA CHÁVEZ are:
       i.   ANDRÉS[5] SISNEROS, b. Abt. 1925[77].
       ii.   ADOLFO SISNEROS, b. Abt. 1928[77].
       iii.   REYES SISNEROS, b. Abt. 1929[77].

Generation No. 5

15. GEORGE[5] SISNEROS *(PAULITA[4] FRESQUEZ, PABLO[3], VICENTE[2], ANTONIO[1])* was born May 21, 1918 in Roswell, New México, and died October 13, 2010 in Arabela, New México. He married ROSE MARY THYRAULT.

16. JACOBO[5] FRESQUEZ *(SALOMON[4], RUMALDO[3], VICENTE[2], ANTONIO[1])*[78] was born February 10, 1910[79], and died June 13, 1980 in Tinnie, New México. He married SESARIA ARCHULETA[80] July 09, 1935[81], daughter of SEFARINO ARCHULETA and ANITA SEDILLO.

Notes for JACOBO FRESQUEZ:
Also known as Jake.

Notes for SESARIA ARCHULETA:
Also known as Suzie.

Child of JACOBO FRESQUEZ and SESARIA ARCHULETA is:
  i. JAKE[6] FRESQUEZ[82], b. March 23, 1935; d. December 26, 1997, Picacho, New México.

17. FRED[5] ROMERO *(CLEOTILDE[4] FRESQUEZ, RUMALDO[3], VICENTE[2], ANTONIO[1])* was born February 03, 1913 in Picacho, New México[83]. He married BEATRICE KIMBRELL[84] April 16, 1938 in Carrizozo, New México[85], daughter of JUAN KIMBRELL and DOMISINDA ORTEGA.

Child of FRED ROMERO and BEATRICE KIMBRELL is:
  i. MARTHA[6] ROMERO, b. Private; m. PABLO BENITO MONTOYA.

18. CLAUDIO[5] ROMERO *(CLEOTILDE[4] FRESQUEZ, RUMALDO[3], VICENTE[2], ANTONIO[1])* was born February 18, 1914 in Arabela, New México[86]. He married INEZ REGALADO July 24, 1935 in Carrizozo, New México[86], daughter of JOSÉ REGALADO and FRANCISCA MARRUJO.

Children of CLAUDIO ROMERO and INEZ REGALADO are:
  i. ALBERT[6] ROMERO, b. June 15, 1936, Arabela, New México[87]; m. ROSELLA M. GONZÁLES, December 05, 1959, Hondo, New México[87].
  ii. RALPH ROMERO, b. November 02, 1938, Arabela, New México[88]; m. MARY GARCÍA, June 27, 1959, Hondo, New México[88].
  iii. LORINA ROMERO, b. April 19, 1942, Arabela, New México[89]; m. MELVIN CHÁVEZ, January 03, 1959, Hondo, New México[89].
  iv. MINNIE ROMERO, b. December 03, 1945, Arabela, New México[90]; m. BREZEL ROBERT SÁNCHEZ, June 15, 1963, Hondo, New México[90].

Notes for MINNIE ROMERO:
Also known as Erminia Romero.

Notes for BREZEL ROBERT SÁNCHEZ:
Moved to Roswell, New México.

19. FERMÍN[5] SALAS *(PETRA FRESQUEZ[4] SISNEROS, REYES[3] FRESQUEZ, VICENTE[2], ANTONIO[1])* was born October 23, 1915 in Hondo, New México[91], and died March 04, 1992. He married LOUISA MARTÍNEZ October 21, 1939 in Hondo, New México[92], daughter of ADENAGO MARTÍNEZ and ANITA GUTIÉRREZ.

Notes for FERMÍN SALAS:
Buried: The family farm in Hondo, New México.

Notes for LOUISA MARTÍNEZ:
Buried: The family farm in Hondo, New México.

Genealogy of Charles Fritz

Generation No. 1

1. CHARLES[1] FRITZ was born Abt. 1831 in Wurtemburg, Germany[1]. He married CATHERINE FRITZ.

Children of CHARLES FRITZ and CATHERINE FRITZ are:

	i.	EMIL[2] FRITZ, b. Abt. 1859, Pennsylvania[1].
	ii.	CLARA FRITZ, b. Abt. 1863, Pennsylvania[1].
2.	iii.	HENRY FRITZ, b. Abt. 1865, Pennsylvania.
3.	iv.	CHARLES PHILLIP FRITZ, b. June 02, 1867, Pennsylvania; d. January 1917.
	v.	WILLIAM FRITZ, b. Abt. 1871, Pennsylvania[1].
	vi.	MATHILDA FRITZ, b. Abt. 1873, La Junta, Territory of New México[1].

Generation No. 2

2. HENRY[2] FRITZ *(CHARLES[1])*[2] was born Abt. 1865 in Pennsylvania[3]. He married MAUDE FRITZ Abt. 1897[3].

Notes for HENRY FRITZ:
1920 Census: Living in Capitán, New México.

Notes for MAUDE FRITZ:
Immigrated to the United States in about 1888.

Children of HENRY FRITZ and MAUDE FRITZ are:

i.	MARY[3] FRITZ, b. Abt. 1898[3].
ii.	CLARE FRITZ, b. Abt. 1901[3].
iii.	FRANCES FRITZ[4], b. June 15, 1903[5]; d. December 10, 1987; m. HENRY HALE[6], November 1927[7].
iv.	MAUDE FRITZ, b. Abt. 1907, San Patricio, New México[8].
v.	LOUISE FRITZ, b. Abt. 1910, San Patricio, New México[8].

3. CHARLES PHILLIP[2] FRITZ *(CHARLES[1])*[9] was born June 02, 1867 in Pennsylvania[10], and died January 1917. He married MANUELITA SISNEROS[11] March 11, 1891 in Picacho, Territory of New México[12], daughter of JUAN SISNEROS and GUADALUPE SÁNCHEZ.

Children of CHARLES FRITZ and MANUELITA SISNEROS are:

i.	CHARLES PHILLIP FREDERICK[3] FRITZ[13], b. May 27, 1892; d. October 31, 1948; m. TELESFORA SÁNCHEZ, July 24, 1926[14].

Notes for TELESFORA SÁNCHEZ:
July 04, 1891: Baptized in Socorro, Territory of New México.

ii.	TILLIE FRITZ, b. July 1897[15].
iii.	BESSIE FRITZ, b. November 08, 1899[16].

Notes for BESSIE FRITZ:
Baptized on December 05, 1899.
1900 Census: Living in San Patricio, Territory of New México.

iv.	CORA FRITZ, b. October 30, 1901[17]; d. 1902[18].

Genealogy of Juan Galindro

Generation No. 1

1. JUAN[1] GALINDRO was born Abt. 1830[1]. He married NICOLASA TORRES[2].

Notes for JUAN GALINDRO:
1860 Census: Living in La Polvadera de San Lorenzo, Territory of New México.
1870 Census: Living in Lincoln County, Precinct 1, Territory of New México.

Children of JUAN GALINDRO and NICOLASA TORRES are:

2.	i.	BRIGIDA[2] GALINDRO, b. Abt. 1842.
	ii.	JUAN GALINDRO, b. Abt. 1846[3].
3.	iii.	ADELA GALINDRO, b. Abt. 1856, La Polvadera de San Lorenzo, Territory of New México.
4.	iv.	PAULA GALINDRO, b. Abt. 1857, La Polvadera de San Lorenzo, Territory of New México.
	v.	MANUELA GALINDRO, b. Abt. 1859, La Polvadera de San Lorenzo, Territory of New México[3]; m. CHARLES BARTLETT, January 15, 1871[4].

Notes for CHARLES BARTLETT:
Buried in Lincoln Cemetary. No dates given.
> Land Patent # NMNMAA 010822, on the authority of the Homestead Entry-Original (12 Stat. 392), May 20, 1862. Issued 160 acres.

Generation No. 2

2. BRIGIDA[2] GALINDRO *(JUAN[1])* was born Abt. 1842[5]. She married (1) JUAN PACHECO[6]. She married (2) SANTIAGO MIRELES[7].

Notes for BRIGIDA GALINDRO:
1860 Census: Living in La Polvadera de San Lorenzo, Territory of New México.
1880 Census-1910 Census: Living in Lincoln, Territory of New México.
Land Patent # NMNMAA 010838, on the authority of the Homestead Entry-Original (12 Stat. 392), May 20, 1862. Issued 40.44 acres. (Brijida Pacheco)

Child of BRIGIDA GALINDRO and JUAN PACHECO is:

5.	i.	AMADA[3] PACHECO, b. Abt. 1882, Picacho, Territory of New México.

Children of BRIGIDA GALINDRO and SANTIAGO MIRELES are:

	ii.	RAMONA[3] MIRELES, b. Abt. 1860[8].
6.	iii.	DAMIAN MIRELES, b. November 1866.
	iv.	BEATRIZ MIRELES[9], b. March 05, 1872[10].
7.	v.	FLORENCIO MIRELES, b. April 21, 1874, Lincoln, Territory of New México; Stepchild.
8.	vi.	ROSARIA MIRELES, b. May 1875; Stepchild.
	vii.	SANTIAGO GALINDRO MIRELES, b. Abt. 1878[10]; Stepchild.

Charles Bartlett

3. ADELA[2] GALINDRO *(JUAN[1])* was born Abt. 1856 in La Polvadera de San Lorenzo, Territory of New México[11]. She married CHARLES BARTLETT[12].

Notes for ADELA GALINDRO:
1910 Census: Living in San Patricio, Territory of New México.

Notes for CHARLES BARTLETT:
Buried in Lincoln Cemetary. No dates given.
Land Patent # NMNMAA 010822, on the authority of the Homestead Entry-Original (12 Stat. 392), May 20, 1862. Issued 160 acres.

Children of ADELA GALINDRO and CHARLES BARTLETT are:
9. i.   JUAN[3] BARTLETT, b. June 28, 1873, Lincoln, Territory of New México.
10. ii. CLARA BARTLETT, b. December 09, 1878, Lincoln, Territory of New México.
    iii. LUISA BARTLETT, b. October 09, 1883, Lincoln, Territory of New México[13]; m. SIPIO GÓMEZ, November 12, 1906, Lincoln, Territory of New Mexico[13].
    iv. ANITA BARTLETT, b. April 12, 1890, Lincoln, Territory of New Mexico[14]; m. SIPIO SALAZAR, March 06, 1906, Lincoln, Territory of New México[14].

Notes for ANITA BARTLETT:
Also known as Annie.

Notes for SIPIO SALAZAR:
Also known as Serafino Salazar.
1880 Census: Living in Las Tablas, Territory of New México.

    v.   MARTÍN BARTLETT, b. February 02, 1897, Lincoln, Territory of New México[15]; m. (1) REBECCA GAMBOA, November 20, 1917, Lincoln, New México[16]; m. (2) RUFINA CARABAJAL[17], August 11, 1920, Lincoln, Territory of New México[18].

Notes for RUFINA CARABAJAL:
She was a twin.

11. vi. ELENA BARTLETT, b. April 1872.

4. PAULA[2] GALINDRO *(JUAN[1])* was born Abt. 1857 in La Polvadera de San Lorenzo, Territory of New México[19]. She married (1) JOSÉ PEDRO ANALLA, son of YSIDORO ANALLA and DOLÓRES GALLEGOS. She married (2) JOSÉ ANTONIO ROMERO August 25, 1873 in Lincoln County, Territory of New México[20], son of LORENZO ROMERO and LORENZA SILVA.

Notes for PAULA GALINDRO:
Also known as Petra, Pabla.

Notes for JOSÉ ANTONIO ROMERO:
Also known as Joseph Antonio Romero.

Children of PAULA GALINDRO and JOSÉ ANALLA are:
    i.   ISABELA[3] ANALLA, b. Abt. 1874[21].
12. ii. FRANCISCO ANALLA, b. March 14, 1882, San Patricio, Territory of New México; d. July 02, 1947, Tulare, California.
    iii. MANUEL G. ANALLA[22], b. June 1884[23]; d. 1916; m. MARIANA CARRILLO, December 30, 1901, Lincoln, Territory of New México[24].

Notes for MANUEL G. ANALLA:
1900 Census: living with his brother-in-law, Paz Torres and his sister, Josefa Analla de Torres.

Child of PAULA GALINDRO and JOSÉ ROMERO is:
    iv. FRANCISCO[3] ROMERO, b. Abt. October 14, 1874, Rio Bonito, Territory of New México[25].

Generation No. 3

5. AMADA[3] PACHECO *(BRIGIDA[2] GALINDRO, JUAN[1])* was born Abt. 1882 in Picacho, Territory of New México[26]. She married FREDERICO MONTOYA January 02, 1898[27], son of JUAN MONTOYA and PORFIRIA ARAGÓN.

Notes for FREDERICO MONTOYA:
1920 Census: Living in Picacho, Territory of New México.

Children of AMADA PACHECO and FREDERICO MONTOYA are:
13. i.   ADELINA[4] MONTOYA, b. July 22, 1900, Picacho, Territory of New México.

	ii.	MARGARITA MONTOYA, b. Abt. 1901, Picacho, Territory of New México[28].
	iii.	ANITA MONTOYA, b. Abt. 1905, Picacho, Territory of New México[28].
	iv.	FRANCISCO MONTOYA, b. Abt. 1908, Picacho, Territory of New México[28].
	v.	RAMONA MONTOYA, b. Abt. 1909[29].
	vi.	FEDERICO MONTOYA, b. Abt. 1913[29].
	vii.	GENOVEVA MONTOYA, b. Abt. 1914[29].
14.	viii.	JUAN PACHECO MONTOYA, b. January 22, 1916, Tinnie, New México; d. February 11, 2001, Roswell, New México.
	ix.	JOSÉ MONTOYA, b. Abt. 1919[29].
	x.	MARÍA MONTOYA, b. Private.
15.	xi.	DELFIDA MONTOYA, b. December 07, 1896, Analla, Territory of New México.

6. DAMIAN[3] MIRELES *(BRIGIDA[2] GALINDRO, JUAN[1])* was born November 1866[30]. He married ESCOLASTICA ANALLA[31] October 17, 1887[32], daughter of PEDRO ANALLA and MARÍA CHÁVES.

Notes for DAMIAN MIRELES:
1910 Census: Living in Las Palas, Territory of New México.
1930 Census: Living in Arabela, New México.

Children of DAMIAN MIRELES and ESCOLASTICA ANALLA are:

16.	i.	JUAN MIGUEL[4] MIRELES, b. November 19, 1889, Picacho, Territory of New México; d. October 1977, Dexter, New México..
17.	ii.	DOMITILIA MIRELES, b. January 23, 1905, Fort Sumner, Territory of New México; d. 1928-1932.

7. FLORENCIO[3] MIRELES *(BRIGIDA[2] GALINDRO, JUAN[1])*[33] was born April 21, 1874 in Lincoln, Territory of New México[34]. He married (1) IGINIA BENAVIDEZ[35] August 03, 1898[36], daughter of SANTIAGO BENAVIDES and ANTONIA MOYA. He married (2) JUANITA CHÁVEZ May 19, 1913[37].

Notes for FLORENCIO MIRELES:
1930 Census: Living in Carrizozo, New México.

Children of FLORENCIO MIRELES and IGINIA BENAVIDEZ are:

	i.	CLARA[4] MIRELES, b. Abt. 1907, Lincoln, Territory of New México[38]; m. WILLIAM BARTLETT, March 06, 1926[39].

Notes for WILLIAM BARTLETT:
Also known as Willie, Guillermo.
1930 Census: Living in Roswell, New México.

18.	ii.	JACOBO MIRELES, b. March 16, 1900, Lincoln, Territory of New México; d. May 1986, Albuquerque, New México.
19.	iii.	SALOMÉ MIRELES, b. 1905.
	iv.	ALFREDO MIRELES, b. August 07, 1909, Carrizozo, Territory of New México[40]; m. MANUELITA GUTIÉRREZ, July 17, 1933, Carrizozo, New México[40].

Notes for ALFREDO MIRELES:
1930 Census: Living in Carrizozo, New México.

	v.	JULIAN MIRELES, b. Abt. 1910[41].

Children of FLORENCIO MIRELES and JUANITA CHÁVEZ are:

	vi.	FLORENCIO CHÁVEZ[4] MIRELES, b. Abt. 1914[41].
	vii.	ELUTICIA MIRELES, b. Abt. 1916[41].
	viii.	VERONICA MIRELES, b. Abt. 1917[41].
	ix.	WILFREDO MIRELES, b. Abt. 1918[41].
	x.	TOMÁS MIRELES, b. Abt. 1920[41].
	xi.	SANTIAGO CHÁVEZ MIRELES, b. Abt. 1921[41].
	xii.	FLORIEN MIRELES, b. Abt. 1924[41].
	xiii.	ROSITA MIRELES, b. Abt. 1929, Carrizozo, New México[41].

8. ROSARIA[3] MIRELES *(BRIGIDA[2] GALINDRO, JUAN[1])* was born May 1875[42]. She married JUAN ANALLA Abt. 1895[43], son of JOSÉ ANALLA and MARÍA SEDILLO.

Notes for JUAN ANALLA:
1880 Census: Living in La Plaza de Picacho, Territory of New México.
1900 Census: Living in Picacho, Territory of New México.

Children of ROSARIA MIRELES and JUAN ANALLA are:
      i.   REBECCA[4] ANALLA[44], b. February 12, 1905, Picacho, Territory of New México[45]; m. DANIEL SÁNCHEZ, December 18, 1919, Lincoln, New México[46].

Notes for DANIEL SÁNCHEZ:
1900 Census: Living with his grandfather, Pedro Analla and grandmother, María del Refugio Chávez de Analla.

      ii.   SANTIAGO ANALLA, b. June 1897, Picacho, Territory of New México[47].

9. JUAN[3] BARTLETT *(ADELA[2] GALINDRO, JUAN[1])* was born June 28, 1873 in Lincoln, Territory of New México[48]. He married JOSEFA CHÁVEZ May 13, 1892[49], daughter of NAVOR CHÁVEZ and GREGORIA TRUJILLO.

Notes for JUAN BARTLETT:
Also known as John.
1900 Census: Living in Picacho.
Land Patent # NMLC 0027450, on the authority of the Homestead Entry-Stock Raising (39 Stat. 862), December 29, 1916. Issued 640.66 acres on March 20, 1929.

Children of JUAN BARTLETT and JOSEFA CHÁVEZ are:
      i.   BONNEY[4] BARTLETT, b. November 24, 1894[50].
20.   ii.   WILLIAM BARTLETT, b. May 20, 1896, Lincoln, Territory of New Mexico.

10. CLARA[3] BARTLETT *(ADELA[2] GALINDRO, JUAN[1])* was born December 09, 1878 in Lincoln, Territory of New México[51]. She married (1) DAVÍD GALLEGOS January 02, 1899[52], son of LUCAS GALLEGOS and FRANCISCA GARCÍA. She married (2) MAURICIO SÁNCHEZ July 28, 1927 in Hondo, Territory of New México[53], son of FRANCISCO SÁNCHEZ and CONCEPCIÓN TRUJILLO.

Notes for CLARA BARTLETT:
1880 Census: Listed as being born in about 1875.
Land Patent # NMLC 0035363, on the authority of the Homestead Entry-Stock Raising (39 Stat. 862), December 29, 1916. Issued 640 acres on September 1, 1933.

Notes for DAVÍD GALLEGOS:
Land Patent # NMR 0035918, on the authority of the Homestead Entry-Enlarged (35 Stat. 639), February 19, 1909. Issued 280 acres on May 1, 1922.

Children of CLARA BARTLETT and DAVÍD GALLEGOS are:
      i.   FRANCISCA[4] GALLEGOS, b. April 1900[54].
      ii.   MIGUEL GALLEGOS, b. 1902[55].
      iii.   PABLO GALLEGOS, b. 1904[55].
      iv.   VALENTIN GALLEGOS, b. 1907[55].
      v.   JUAN GALLEGOS, b. 1908[55].
      vi.   ELUGARDITA GALLEGOS, b. 1910[55].
      vii. FACUNDO GALLEGOS, b. 1919[55].

11. ELENA[3] BARTLETT *(ADELA[2] GALINDRO, JUAN[1])* was born April 1872[56]. She married NARCISO ANALLA October 01, 1885 in Lincoln County, Territory of New México[57], son of PEDRO ANALLA and MARÍA CHÁVES.

Children of ELENA BARTLETT and NARCISO ANALLA are:
      i.   AMELIA[4] ANALLA, b. August 1898[58].
      ii.   LUISA ANALLA, b. Abt. 1901[59].
      iii.   EUFANIA ANALLA[60], b. February 1906[61]; d. December 21, 1921, Roswell, New México.

Notes for EUFANIA ANALLA:
Also known as Epifania.

      iv.   CARLOS ANALLA[62], b. March 05, 1908, Picacho, Territory of New México[63]; d. July 21, 1920, Roswell, New México.
      v.   ALFREDO ANALLA, b. Abt. 1914[63].

12. FRANCISCO[3] ANALLA *(PAULA[2] GALINDRO, JUAN[1])*[64] was born March 14, 1882 in San Patricio, Territory of New México[65], and died July 02, 1947 in Tulare, California. He married FLORENTINA PEÑA June 27, 1901[66].

Notes for FRANCISCO ANALLA:
1900 Census: Living with his brother-in-law, Paz Torres and his sister, Josefa Analla de Torres.
1910 Census: Living in San Patricio, Territory of New México.
1930 Census: Living in Arabela, New México.Analla?

Children of FRANCISCO ANALLA and FLORENTINA PEÑA are:
      i.   JOSÉ PEÑA[4] ANALLA[67], b. 1902; d. December 26, 1936, Lincoln, New México; m. SENAIDA MAÉS.
      ii.   SANTIAGO ANALLA, b. Abt. 1917[68].

Generation No. 4

13. ADELINA[4] MONTOYA *(AMADA[3] PACHECO, BRIGIDA[2] GALINDRO, JUAN[1])* was born July 22, 1900 in Picacho, Territory of New México[69]. She married SANTIAGO CHÁVEZ GONZÁLES November 22, 1918 in Lincoln, New México[69], son of JOSÉ GONZÁLES and MARÍA CHÁVEZ.

Notes for SANTIAGO CHÁVEZ GONZÁLES:
Also known as Jim.
1930 Census: Living in Roswell, New México.

Children of ADELINA MONTOYA and SANTIAGO GONZÁLES are:
      i.   RAFAEL MONTOYA[5] GONZÁLES, b. Abt. April 1919[70].
      ii.   JOE GONZÁLES, b. Abt. 1921[71].
      iii.   JULIO GONZÁLES, b. Abt. 1922[71].
      iv.   FRED GONZÁLES, b. Abt. 1926[71].

Notes for FRED GONZÁLES:
Also known as Fredrick.

      v.   RAMONA GONZÁLES, b. Abt. 1928[71].
      vi.   FRANCIS GONZÁLES, b. Private.
      vii.   SONYA GONZÁLES, b. Private.

14. JUAN PACHECO[4] MONTOYA *(AMADA[3] PACHECO, BRIGIDA[2] GALINDRO, JUAN[1])*[72] was born January 22, 1916 in Tinnie, New México, and died February 11, 2001 in Roswell, New México. He married VIRGINIA MOODY May 24, 1966[72].

Notes for JUAN PACHECO MONTOYA:
Also known as John.

Children of JUAN MONTOYA and VIRGINIA MOODY are:
      i.   LORETTA RAY[5] MONTOYA, b. Private.
      ii.   JOHN F. MONTOYA, b. Private.

15. DELFIDA[4] MONTOYA *(AMADA[3] PACHECO, BRIGIDA[2] GALINDRO, JUAN[1])*[73] was born December 07, 1896 in Analla, Territory of New México[74]. She married GREGORIO SALAS[75] Abt. 1920[76], son of CRECENCIO SALAS and LUPITA VIGIL.

Children of DELFIDA MONTOYA and GREGORIO SALAS are:

   i. SANTIAGO[5] SALAS, b. Abt. 1918[77].
   ii. BELA SALAS, b. Abt. 1923[77].
   iii. ORALIA SALAS, b. Abt. 1925[77].
   iv. FRED SALAS, b. Abt. 1926[77].
   v. ANA SALAS, b. Abt. 1929[77].

16. JUAN MIGUEL[4] MIRELES *(DAMIAN[3], BRIGIDA[2] GALINDRO, JUAN[1])[78]* was born November 19, 1889 in Picacho, Territory of New México[79], and died October 1977 in Dexter, New México.. He married ROSA MOYA June 12, 1913 in Arabela, Territory of New México[80], daughter of RUMALDO MOYA and CARLOTA MONTOYA.

Child of JUAN MIRELES and ROSA MOYA is:
   i. ELOY[5] MIRELES[81], b. November 17, 1924, Arabela, New México; d. July 21, 2003, Dexter, New México.; m. ELISER LUCERO, November 22, 1943, Carrizozo, New México[82].

17. DOMITILIA[4] MIRELES *(DAMIAN[3], BRIGIDA[2] GALINDRO, JUAN[1])* was born January 23, 1905 in Fort Sumner, Territory of New México[83], and died 1928-1932. She married PAZ MOYA March 18, 1920 in Tinnie, New México[83].

Children of DOMITILIA MIRELES and PAZ MOYA are:
   i. BEATRIZ[5] MOYA, b. Abt. 1925, Arabela, New México[84].
   ii. JOSEFITA MOYA, b. Abt. 1928, Arabela, New México[84].

18. JACOBO[4] MIRELES *(FLORENCIO[3], BRIGIDA[2] GALINDRO, JUAN[1])[85]* was born March 16, 1900 in Lincoln, Territory of New México[86], and died May 1986 in Albuquerque, New México. He married LORENZA OTERO.

Notes for JACOBO MIRELES:
1900 Census: Living in Lincoln, Territory of New México.

Child of JACOBO MIRELES and LORENZA OTERO is:
   i. BEATRIZ[5] MIRELES, b. Abt. 1924.

19. SALOMÉ[4] MIRELES *(FLORENCIO[3], BRIGIDA[2] GALINDRO, JUAN[1])* was born 1905[87]. She married FILIMON CASTILLO LÓPEZ September 22, 1928 in Carrizozo, New México[87], son of JUAN LÓPEZ and MARÍA SÁNCHEZ.

Notes for FILIMON CASTILLO LÓPEZ:
1900 Census: Living in Lincoln, Territory of New México. (Filomeno Castillo) He is listed as an adopted son.
1910 Census: Living in Lincoln, Territory of New México.

Children of SALOMÉ MIRELES and FILIMON LÓPEZ are:
   i. BERNICE[5] LÓPEZ, b. Abt. 1918[88]; Stepchild.
   ii. ESTER LÓPEZ, b. Abt. 1920[88]; Stepchild.
   iii. MARY LÓPEZ, b. Abt. 1924[88]; Stepchild.
   iv. EUGENIA LÓPEZ, b. Abt. 1929[88].

20. WILLIAM[4] BARTLETT *(JUAN[3], ADELA[2] GALINDRO, JUAN[1])* was born May 20, 1896 in Lincoln, Territory of New Mexico[89]. He married (1) SARA ROMERO July 18, 1917 in Lincoln, New México[90], daughter of REFUGIO ROMERO and ROBERTA CHÁVEZ. He married (2) CLARA MIRELES March 06, 1926[91], daughter of FLORENCIO MIRELES and IGINIA BENAVIDEZ.

Notes for WILLIAM BARTLETT:
Also known as Willie, Guillermo.
1930 Census: Living in Roswell, New México.

Notes for SARA ROMERO:
Death records indicate that she was born in about 1893.

Children of WILLIAM BARTLETT and SARA ROMERO are:
    i.   ERMINIA[5] BARTLETT, b. Abt. 1922[92].
    ii.   WILLIAM ROMERO BARTLETT, b. Abt. 1923[92].
    iii.   JOHNNIE BARTLETT[93], b. February 1924, Lincoln, New México; d. June 27, 1924, Carrizozo, New México.

Genealogy of Hilario Gallegos

Generation No. 1

1. HILARIO[1] GALLEGOS was born 1832[1]. He married (1) JOSEFITA CHÁVEZ[2]. He married (2) JOSEFA SÁNCHEZ March 11, 1887[2], daughter of JUAN MEDINA and ROSALÍA SÁNCHEZ.

Notes for HILARIO GALLEGOS:
Also known as Ylario.
1870 Census: Living in Lincoln County, Precinct 2 (La Plaza de San Patricio), Territory of New México.
1880 Census: Living in Valles de Francisco, San Francisco, Socorro County, Territory of New México.

Notes for JOSEFITA CHÁVEZ:
Also known as Josefa.

Children of HILARIO GALLEGOS and JOSEFITA CHÁVEZ are:
2.	i.	ALEJANDRO[2] GALLEGOS, b. April 24, 1857; d. June 20, 1939, San Patricio, New México.
3.	ii.	MAGDALENA GALLEGOS, b. Abt. 1859.
	iii.	TAVIANA GALLEGOS, b. 1864[3].
4.	iv.	OCTAVIANO GALLEGOS, b. Abt. 1865; d. February 25, 1938, Arabela, New México.
	v.	TERESITA GALLEGOS, b. 1866[3]; m. MAXIMILIANO TORRES[4].
5.	vi.	IGENIA GALLEGOS, b. September 16, 1870, Ruidoso, Territory of New México; d. February 28, 1944, San Patricio, New México.
	vii.	MIGUEL GALLEGOS, b. May 10, 1873, Ruidoso, New México[5].

Generation No. 2

2. ALEJANDRO[2] GALLEGOS *(HILARIO[1])[6]* was born April 24, 1857, and died June 20, 1939 in San Patricio, New México. He married ANITA SALAS Abt. 1884[7], daughter of JUAN SALAS and MARGARITA TRUJILLO.

Notes for ALEJANDRO GALLEGOS:
1870 Census: Living in Lincoln County, Precinct 2 (La Plaza de San Patricio), Territory of New México. Listed birthyear as 1863.
1900 & 1910 Census: Living in San Patricio, Territory of New México.

Notes for ANITA SALAS:
Also known as Anita Trujillo.

Children of ALEJANDRO GALLEGOS and ANITA SALAS are:
	i.	FRANCISCO[3] GALLEGOS.
	ii.	MAXIMILIANO GALLEGOS.
6.	iii.	EULOJIO GALLEGOS, b. February 01, 1887; d. July 04, 1938.
	iv.	ROBERTO GALLEGOS, b. July 06, 1894, Ruidoso, Territory of New México[8].
7.	v.	MANUELITA GALLEGOS, b. May 14, 1899, San Patricio, Territory of New México.
	vi.	RAMONA GALLEGOS, b. Abt. 1910[9].
	vii.	ELISEO GALLEGOS[10], b. May 30, 1912; d. May 16, 1995, San Patricio, New México; m. ROSA MONTOYA[10].

3. MAGDALENA[2] GALLEGOS *(HILARIO[1])* was born Abt. 1859[11]. She married ALFONSO PERALTA Abt. 1878[12].

Notes for ALFONSO PERALTA:
1870 & 1880 Census: Living in La Joya, Territory of New México.
1900 Census: Living in San Acacia, Territory of New México.

Children of MAGDALENA GALLEGOS and ALFONSO PERALTA are:

    i.   MIGUELITA[3] PERALTA, b. September 1879, La Joya, Territory of New México[13].
    ii.   VIVIANA PERALTA, b. Abt. 1878, La Joya, Territory of New México[13].
    iii. PABLO PERALTA, b. Abt. 1880, La Joya, Territory of New México[13].
    iv. NATIVIDAD PERALTA, b. May 1883, La Joya, Territory of New México[14].
    v.   JUAN PERALTA, b. February 1895[14].
    vi. FELIPÉ PERALTA, b. July 1896[14].

4. OCTAVIANO[2] GALLEGOS *(HILARIO[1])*[15] was born Abt. 1865[16], and died February 25, 1938 in Arabela, New México. He married (1) ELOISA GONZÁLES[17]. He married (2) PILAR GUEBARA[18] September 21, 1908[19], daughter of JUAN GUEBARA and MARÍA MONTAÑO.

Notes for OCTAVIANO GALLEGOS:
Raised their sobrinas, Petra Trujillo and Altagracia Montoya.
1900, 1910, 1920 & 1930 Census: Living in Los Palos (Arabela), Territory of New México. He was not listed with his family in the 1900 Census.

Children of OCTAVIANO GALLEGOS and ELOISA GONZÁLES are:

    i.   EMILIA[3] GALLEGOS, b. August 31, 1892, Las Palas, Territory of New México[20].
    ii.   FRANCISCO ANTONIO GALLEGOS, b. July 11, 1894, San Patricio, Territory of New México[21].
    iii. JOSÉ GALLEGOS, b. November 1896[22].
    iv. ABEL GALLEGOS, b. August 1899[22].

Children of OCTAVIANO GALLEGOS and PILAR GUEBARA are:

    v.   MAURICIO[3] GALLEGOS, b. Abt. 1920[23].
    vi. JACOBO GALLEGOS, b. Abt. 1923[23].

5. IGENIA[2] GALLEGOS *(HILARIO[1])* was born September 16, 1870 in Ruidoso, Territory of New México[24], and died February 28, 1944 in San Patricio, New México[25]. She married TEOFILO TRUJILLO SALAS[26] January 09, 1887 in San Patricio, Territory of New México[27], son of JUAN SALAS and MARGARITA TRUJILLO.

Notes for IGENIA GALLEGOS:
Also known as Jinia and Higinia. Baptismal Padrinos: Juan Trujillo, Ana María Fajardo.
1920 Census: Listed as Virginia.
Land Patent # NMLC 0042337, on the authority of the Homestead Entry-Enlarged (35 Stat. 639), February 19, 1909. Issued 200 acres on October 13, 1936.

Children of IGENIA GALLEGOS and TEOFILO SALAS are:

8.   i.   PABLO GALLEGOS[3] SALAS, b. October 12, 1887, San Patricio, Territory of New México; d. June 29, 1948, San Patricio, New México.
9.   ii.   PELEGRINA SALAS, b. August 1894.
10.   iii. ELFIDO SALAS, b. March 13, 1897, Hondo, Territory of New México; d. November 30, 1973, Hondo, New México.
      iv. ELVIRA SALAS, b. Abt. 1898[28].
11.   v.   JACOBO SALAS, b. February 21, 1899, Hondo, Territory of New México; d. April 1973, Artesia, New Mexico.

Generation No. 3

6. EULOJIO[3] GALLEGOS *(ALEJANDRO[2], HILARIO[1])*[29] was born February 01, 1887[30], and died July 04, 1938. He married (1) LUGARDITA LUCERO March 12, 1908 in San Patricio, Territory of New México[31], daughter of ANISETO LUCERO and REFUGIA TRUJILLO. He married (2) VIVIANA CHÁVEZ[32] August 24, 1911[33], daughter of JUAN CHÁVEZ and TERESA HERRERA.

Child of EULOJIO GALLEGOS and VIVIANA CHÁVEZ is:
    i.   GENOVEVA[4] GALLEGOS, b. 1904[34].

7. MANUELITA[3] GALLEGOS *(ALEJANDRO[2], HILARIO[1])* was born May 14, 1899 in San Patricio, Territory of New México[35]. She married SIMÓN SAÍZ January 10, 1920 in San Patricio, New México[36], son of BRAULIO SAÍZ and LAZARA JARAMILLO.

Child of MANUELITA GALLEGOS and SIMÓN SAÍZ is:
    i.   ELIZABETH[4] SAÍZ, b. March 22, 1928, San Patricio, New México[37].

Notes for ELIZABETH SAÍZ:
Also known as Isabel.

8. PABLO GALLEGOS[3] SALAS *(IGENIA[2] GALLEGOS, HILARIO[1])[38]* was born October 12, 1887 in San Patricio, Territory of New México[39], and died June 29, 1948 in San Patricio, New México. He married (1) PETRA FRESQUEZ SISNEROS November 14, 1910[40], daughter of TEOFILO SISNEROS and REYES FRESQUEZ. He married (2) RUBY QUINTANA October 25, 1930 in Glencoe, New México[41], daughter of CAYETANO QUINTANA and FEDELINA SALAZAR.

Children of PABLO SALAS and PETRA SISNEROS are:
    i.   TEOFILO SINEROS[4] SALAS, b. 1912, San Patricio, New México[42].
12.   ii.   FERMÍN SALAS, b. October 23, 1915, Hondo, New México; d. March 04, 1992.
    iii.   REYES SALAS[43], b. 1919, San Patricio, New México; d. September 29, 1943, Los Angeles, California.

Notes for REYES SALAS:
Died in Los Angeles, California but was burried in San Patricio, New Mexico on October 3, 1943.

    iv.   SOFIA SALAS, b. 1925, San Patricio, New México[44].

9. PELEGRINA[3] SALAS *(IGENIA[2] GALLEGOS, HILARIO[1])* was born August 1894[45]. She married (1) RAFAEL MÁRQUEZ August 08, 1909 in Hondo, Territory of New México[46], son of FELIPÉ MÁRQUEZ and CONCEPCIÓN BARELA. She married (2) REFUGIO TORRES[47] January 16, 1911[48], son of IGNACIO TORRES and MANUELA LUCERO.

Notes for REFUGIO TORRES:
Land Patent # NMR 0036867, on the authority of the Homestead Entry-Enlarged (35 Stat. 639), February 19, 1909. Issued 320 acres on June 12, 1922.
Land Patent # NMLC 0041321, on the authority of the Homestead Entry-Stock Raising (39 Stat. 862), December 29, 1916. Issued 320 acres on April 27, 1936.

Children of PELEGRINA SALAS and REFUGIO TORRES are:
13.   i.   MAGGIE[4] TORRES, b. 1913.
    ii.   AMALIA TORRES[49], b. December 17, 1915, Hondo, New México; d. July 25, 1967; m. FIDEL SÁNCHEZ[49], February 12, 1934, San Patricio, New México[50].

10. ELFIDO[3] SALAS *(IGENIA[2] GALLEGOS, HILARIO[1])[51]* was born March 13, 1897 in Hondo, Territory of New México[52], and died November 30, 1973 in Hondo, New México[53]. He married MASIMIANA MONTOYA[54] February 13, 1924[55], daughter of MAURICIO MONTOYA and AVRORA SÁNCHEZ.

Notes for ELFIDO SALAS:
Also known as Elfigo, Delfido.
Land Patent # NMLC 0025968, on the authority of the Homestead Entry-Stock Raising (39 Stat. 862), December 29, 1916. Issued 611 acres on August 16, 1927.

Notes for MASIMIANA MONTOYA:
Also known as Maximiana.

Children of ELFIDO SALAS and MASIMIANA MONTOYA are:
     i.   YLARIO[4] SALAS[56], b. August 05, 1925, Hondo, New México[57]; d. October 11, 1973; m. STELLA WARNER[58], December 01, 1951, Ruidoso, New México[59].

Notes for YLARIO SALAS:
Private US Army. World War Two.

     ii.   PEDRO SALAS, b. 1926[60].
     iii.   REYNALDA SALAS, b. 1929[60].
     iv.   TERESA SALAS[61], b. July 23, 1932; d. October 01, 2005, Roswell, New México.
     v.   RAMONA SALAS[61], b. October 08, 1937, Hondo, New México; d. March 09, 1997[62].
     vi.   JUAN SALAS, b. Private.
     vii.   MADALENA SALAS, b. Private.
     viii.   RAMÓN SALAS, b. Private.
     ix.   TEOFILO MONTOYA SALAS, b. Private.

11. JACOBO[3] SALAS *(IGENIA[2] GALLEGOS, HILARIO[1])[63]* was born February 21, 1899 in Hondo, Territory of New México, and died April 1973 in Artesia, New Mexico. He married TOMASITA SALSBERRY January 14, 1920 in San Patricio, New México[64], daughter of JAMES SALSBERRY and MANUELITA HERRERA.

Notes for JACOBO SALAS:
Also known as Jake.

Children of JACOBO SALAS and TOMASITA SALSBERRY are:
     i.   PABLITA[4] SALAS[65], b. Abt. 1924, San Patricio, New México; d. April 17, 1924, San Patricio, New México.
     ii.   MARÍA SALAS[66], b. Abt. 1932, Hondo, New México; d. February 23, 1932, Hondo, New México.
     iii.   JOSEFA SALAS, b. December 27, 1936; d. March 28, 1999, Artesia, New Mexico.

Notes for JOSEFA SALAS:
Also known as Josefita Salas Durán.

     iv.   DOMINGO SALAS, b. Private; d. Artesia, New Mexico; m. SOFIA DE SALAS.
     v.   ROSA SALAS, b. Private; d. Artesia, New Mexico.
     vi.   RUBÉN SALAS, b. Private.
     vii.   WILLIE SALAS, b. Private.
     viii.   BESSIE LUISA JULIA SALAS[67], b. Abt. 1940, Hondo, New México; d. March 05, 1940, Hondo, New México.

Generation No. 4

12. FERMÍN[4] SALAS *(PABLO GALLEGOS[3], IGENIA[2] GALLEGOS, HILARIO[1])* was born October 23, 1915 in Hondo, New México[68], and died March 04, 1992. He married LOUISA MARTÍNEZ October 21, 1939 in Hondo, New México[69], daughter of ADENAGO MARTÍNEZ and ANITA GUTIÉRREZ.

13. MAGGIE[4] TORRES *(PELEGRINA[3] SALAS, IGENIA[2] GALLEGOS, HILARIO[1])* was born 1913[70]. She married FRED MONTES[71,72], son of JESÚS MONTES and TOMASITA ALDAZ.

Child of MAGGIE TORRES and FRED MONTES is:
     i.   HERALDA[5] MONTES[72], b. Abt. 1934, Hondo, New México; d. March 14, 1934, Hondo, New México.

Genealogy of Lucas Gallegos

Generation No. 1

1. LUCAS[1] GALLEGOS was born 1842[1]. He married (1) JOSEFITA CHÁVEZ. He married (2) FRANCISCA GARCÍA[2].

Notes for LUCAS GALLEGOS:
Lucas Gallegos was Hilario Gallegos' nephew.
1860 Census: Living in Fray Cristobal, Socorro County, Territory of New México
Land Patent # NMNMAA 010820, on the authority of the Homestead Entry-Original (12 Stat. 392), May 20, 1862. Issued 40 acres.

Notes for JOSEFITA CHÁVEZ:
Also known as Josefa.

Notes for FRANCISCA GARCÍA:
Also known as Encarnación.

Child of LUCAS GALLEGOS and JOSEFITA CHÁVEZ is:
      i.   FLORENCIO CHÁVEZ[2] GALLEGOS, b. Abt. 1855[3].

Children of LUCAS GALLEGOS and FRANCISCA GARCÍA are:
      ii.   CANUTA[2] GALLEGOS, b. 1859[3].
      iii.   PETRA GALLEGOS, b. 1862[3].
      iv.   MARÍA GALLEGOS, b. 1865[3].

2.   v.   SEVERO GARCÍA GALLEGOS, b. October 28, 1869, Rio Bonito, Territory of New México.
      vi.   AVRORA GALLEGOS, b. February 25, 1870, Ruidoso, Territory of New México[4].

3.   vii. DAVÍD GALLEGOS, b. April 1878, San Patricio, Territory of New México; d. September 25, 1921, Roswell, New México.

Generation No. 2

2. SEVERO GARCÍA[2] GALLEGOS *(LUCAS[1])* was born October 28, 1869 in Rio Bonito, Territory of New México[5]. He married (1) EMILIA ARCHULETA February 06, 1888[6], daughter of JESÚS ARCHULETA and JUANA PERALTA. He married (2) STABRANA LUCERO Abt. 1900[7], daughter of CORNELIO LUCERO and NOBERTA ARCHULETA. He married (3) ISADORA MARTÍNEZ December 22, 1915[8]. He married (4) ALVIRA LEA September 24, 1920[9]. He married (5) LEOLA DAY ENGLISH March 14, 1936[10].

Notes for SEVERO GARCÍA GALLEGOS:
1910 Census: Living in Las Palas, Territory of New México.

Notes for ISADORA MARTÍNEZ:
Also known as Ydadora.

Children of SEVERO GALLEGOS and EMILIA ARCHULETA are:
      i.   SANTIAGO[3] GALLEGOS, b. December 30, 1888, Lincoln, Territory of New México[11]; m. RUFINA SÁNCHEZ, June 01, 1913, Lincoln, New México[11].

Notes for SANTIAGO GALLEGOS:
Both Santiago and Rufina were living in Arabela at the time of their marriage. They were married at La Capilla de San Juan Bautista. Pedro Sánchez and Ramona C. Sánchez gave their consent. Padrinos were Juan Chábes and Saturnina Sánchez.

4.   ii.   ELVIRA ARCHULETA GALLEGOS, b. November 29, 1891, Las Palas, Territory of New México; d. December 1980, Belén, New México.
      iii. SEVERO ARCHULETA GALLEGOS, b. March 11, 1894, Las Chosas, Territory of New México[12].

Children of SEVERO GALLEGOS and STABRANA LUCERO are:

    iv.   MARGARITA³ GALLEGOS, b. Abt. 1900[13].
    v.   ROBERTO GALLEGOS, b. Abt. 1902[13].
    vi.   SMLE GALLEGOS, b. Abt. 1904[13].
    vii. DANIEL GALLEGOS, b. Abt. 1908[13].

3. DAVÍD² GALLEGOS *(LUCAS¹)* was born April 1878 in San Patricio, Territory of New México[14], and died September 25, 1921 in Roswell, New México[15]. He married CLARA BARTLETT January 02, 1899[16], daughter of CHARLES BARTLETT and ADELA GALINDRO.

Notes for DAVÍD GALLEGOS:
Land Patent # NMR 0035918, on the authority of the Homestead Entry-Enlarged (35 Stat. 639), February 19, 1909. Issued 280 acres on May 1, 1922.

Children of DAVÍD GALLEGOS and CLARA BARTLETT are:
    i.   FRANCISCA³ GALLEGOS, b. April 1900[17].
    ii.   MIGUEL GALLEGOS, b. 1902[18].
    iii. PABLO GALLEGOS, b. 1904[18].
    iv.   VALENTIN GALLEGOS, b. 1907[18].
    v.   JUAN GALLEGOS, b. 1908[18].
    vi.   ELUGARDITA GALLEGOS, b. 1910[18].
    vii. FACUNDO GALLEGOS, b. 1919[18].

Generation No. 3

4. ELVIRA ARCHULETA³ GALLEGOS *(SEVERO GARCÍA², LUCAS¹)*[19] was born November 29, 1891 in Las Palas, Territory of New México[20], and died December 1980 in Belén, New México. She married DOMINGO MAÉS[21] July 15, 1914 in Arabela, Territory of New México[22], son of JESÚS MAÉS and AMANDA MOLINA.

Notes for ELVIRA ARCHULETA GALLEGOS:
Buried in Hondo, New México.

Notes for DOMINGO MAÉS:
Marriage records indicate that he was born on May 12, 1894.
1920 Census: living in Las Palas, Territory of New México.

Children of ELVIRA GALLEGOS and DOMINGO MAÉS are:
    i.   EMILIA⁴ MAÉS, b. Abt. 1915, Las Palas, New México[23].
    ii.   EDUMENIO MAÉS[24], b. August 08, 1917, Agua Azul, New México[25]; d. July 29, 2009, Alamogordo, New México.

Notes for EDUMENIO MAÉS:
Private First Class. World War II.

Genealogy of Antonio García

Generation No. 1

1. ANTONIO[1] GARCÍA.

Child of ANTONIO GARCÍA is:
2.   i.   INEZ[2] GARCÍA, b. January 1855, Doña Ana County, Territory of New México.

Generation No. 2

2. INEZ[2] GARCÍA *(ANTONIO[1])* was born January 1855 in Doña Ana County, Territory of New México[1]. He married (1) LORENCITA MOLINA. He married (2) PABLA PEPPIN June 29, 1912 in Arabela, Territory of New México[2].

Notes for INEZ GARCÍA:
Also known as Chino.
1880 Census: Living in La Plaza de San Patricio.

Children of INEZ GARCÍA and LORENCITA MOLINA are:
     i.   TOMASA[3] GARCÍA, b. Abt. 1875, San Patricio, Territory of New México[3].
     ii.   PIUCITA GARCÍA, b. November 1879, San Patricio, Territory of New México[4].
     iii.   TERESITA GARCÍA, b. January 1880, San Patricio, Territory of New México[5]; m. JULIAN PADILLA, July 29, 1895[6].

Notes for JULIAN PADILLA:
1870 Census: Living in Albuquerque, Territory of New México.
1880 Census: Living in Anton Chico, Territory of New México.

3.   iv.   FLAVIO M. GARCÍA, b. February 04, 1882, San Patricio, Territory of New México; d. June 1972, Roswell, New México.
     v.   MIGUEL GARCÍA[7], b. May 08, 1885, Las Palas, Territory of New México[8]; d. February 1976, Capitán, New México.
     vi.   MANUEL GARCÍA, b. January 1888, Las Palas, Territory of New México[8].

Notes for MANUEL GARCÍA:
Land Patent # NMR 0042423, on the authority of the Homestead Entry-Original (12 Stat. 392), May 20, 1862. Issued 40 acres on September 20, 1923.
Land Patent # NMLC 0026643, on the authority of the Homestead Entry-Stock Raising (39 Stat. 862), December 29, 1916. Issued 120 acres on May 13, 1929.

4.   vii.   ANTONIO GARCÍA, b. May 10, 1894, Las Palas, Territory of New México; d. March 1976, Roswell, New México.
5.   viii.   ESIQUIEL GARCÍA, b. April 01, 1896, Las Palas, Territory of New México; d. September 1973, Roswell, New México.

Child of INEZ GARCÍA and PABLA PEPPIN is:
     ix.   PAUBLITA[3] GARCÍA, b. Abt. 1922[9].

Generation No. 3

3. FLAVIO M.[3] GARCÍA *(INEZ[2], ANTONIO[1])*[10] was born February 04, 1882 in San Patricio, Territory of New México[11], and died June 1972 in Roswell, New México. He married JOSEFITA GÓMEZ LUCERO[12] November 25, 1908 in Arabela, Territory of New México[13], daughter of VICTORIANO LUCERO and GUADALUPE GÓMEZ.

Notes for FLAVIO M. GARCÍA:
Also known as Flabio.
1920 Census: Living in Los Palos, New México.

Children of FLAVIO GARCÍA and JOSEFITA LUCERO are:
  i.   AEROPAJITA[4] GARCÍA, b. Abt. 1909[14].
  ii. ARCENIA GARCÍA, b. Abt. 1915[14].
  iii. ALEJO GARCÍA[15], b. Private.
  iv. LORENCITA LUCERO GARCÍA[15], b. Private.

4. ANTONIO[3] GARCÍA *(INEZ[2], ANTONIO[1])[16]* was born May 10, 1894 in Las Palas, Territory of New México[17], and died March 1976 in Roswell, New México. He married MANUELITA GUEVARA, daughter of CRUZ GUEBARA and SARA MONTOYA.

Notes for ANTONIO GARCÍA:
1900 Census: Living in Agua Azul, Territory of New México.

Children of ANTONIO GARCÍA and MANUELITA GUEVARA are:
  i.   INEZ GUEVARA[4] GARCÍA, b. November 19, 1930, Arabela, New México; d. September 15, 2006, Hondo, New México.
  ii.   ERMINIA GARCÍA, b. Private.
  iii. FLAVIO GARCÍA, b. Private.
  iv.   LORENCITA GARCÍA, b. Private.
  v.   MANUEL GARCÍA, b. Private.
  vi.   MIGUEL GARCÍA, b. Private.
  vii. ONOFRÉ GARCÍA, b. Private.

5. ESIQUIEL[3] GARCÍA *(INEZ[2], ANTONIO[1])[18]* was born April 01, 1896 in Las Palas, Territory of New México[19], and died September 1973 in Roswell, New México. He married LUISA ROMERO Abt. 1925[20], daughter of PORFIRIO ROMERO and AVRORA GONZÁLES.

Notes for ESIQUIEL GARCÍA:
1930 Census: Living in Arabela, Territory of New México.

Notes for LUISA ROMERO:
1910 Census: Living in Rebentón, Territory of New México.

Child of ESIQUIEL GARCÍA and LUISA ROMERO is:
  i.   PRISCILLA[4] GARCÍA[21], b. July 01, 1928, Arabela, New México[22]; m. FRANCISCO TRUJILLO[23], November 15, 1948, Carrizozo, New México[24].

Notes for FRANCISCO TRUJILLO:
New Mexico Private First Class US Army. WW II Veteran.

Genealogy of Encarnación Gavaldon

Generation No. 1

1. ENCARNACION[1] GAVALDON was born 1833. He married ANTONIA DE GAVALDON.

Children of ENCARNACION GAVALDON and ANTONIA DE GAVALDON are:

	i.	JOSÉ[2] GAVALDON, b. 1861.
2.	ii.	ERINEO FRANCISCO GAVALDON, b. 1867.
	iii.	LUCIA GAVALDON, b. Abt. 1880.

Generation No. 2

2. ERINEO FRANCISCO[2] GAVALDON *(ENCARNACION[1])* was born 1867. He married ELUTICIA SÁNCHEZ[1], daughter of ESTOLANO SÁNCHEZ and CORNELIA PACHECO.

Notes for ERINEO FRANCISCO GAVALDON:
1880 Census lists that he lived in Torreón, Valencia County, New México.

Notes for ELUTICIA SÁNCHEZ:
Also known as Luticia.
1900 Census: Eluticia and her children were living with her parents.
1930 Census: Living in Corona, New México.

Children of ERINEO GAVALDON and ELUTICIA SÁNCHEZ are:

3.	i.	ROSA[3] GAVALDON, b. January 1892.
	ii.	AVRORA GAVALDON[2], b. January 07, 1894[3]; d. January 17, 1986, Corona, New México; m. NARCISO MONTOYA[4], October 26, 1918[5].

Notes for NARCISO MONTOYA:
1920 Census: Living in White Oaks, New México.

4.	iii.	LUPE GAVALDON, b. August 20, 1897, Patos, Territory of New México.

Generation No. 3

3. ROSA[3] GAVALDON *(ERINEO FRANCISCO[2], ENCARNACION[1])* was born January 1892[6]. She married AVRELIO MARTÍNEZ[7] December 12, 1910 in Patos, New México[8], son of ATANACIO MARTÍNEZ and RAMONA DE MARTÍNEZ.

Notes for AVRELIO MARTÍNEZ:
Also known as Aurelio. He was raised by Leandro Pacheco.
1930 Census: Lived in Corona, New México.

Children of ROSA GAVALDON and AVRELIO MARTÍNEZ are:

	i.	GUILLERMO[4] MARTÍNEZ[9], b. December 24, 1911, Ruidoso, Territory of New México[10]; m. CAROLINA SEDILLO[11], February 26, 1934, Carrizozo, New México[11].

Notes for GUILLERMO MARTÍNEZ:
Also known as Billie.
1930 Census: Living in Corona, New México.

	ii.	SENAIDA MARTÍNEZ, b. Abt. 1914[12]; m. DOLÓRES MÁRQUEZ, September 30, 1933[13].
	iii.	MACARIO MARTÍNEZ, b. Abt. 1916[14].
	iv.	ERMINIO MARTÍNEZ[15], b. August 12, 1919, Rebentón, New México[16].
	v.	ARTURO MARTÍNEZ[17], b. March 04, 1921, Rebentón, New México[18]; d. March 27, 1987.

Notes for ARTURO MARTÍNEZ:
Private. World War II.

4. LUPE[3] GAVALDON *(ERINEO FRANCISCO[2], ENCARNACION[1])* was born August 20, 1897 in Patos, Territory of New México[19]. He married ELVIRA MÁRQUEZ August 13, 1921 in Rebentón, New México[20], daughter of MELCOR MÁRQUEZ and ALEJANDRA LUERAS.

Notes for LUPE GAVALDON:
Also known as Lupito, Guadalupe Gavaldon.
Patos, New México is located close to Rebentón, New México east of Sierra Capitán. Currently it is inaccesible because it is located on a private farm.
1930 Census: Living in Corona, New México.

Children of LUPE GAVALDON and ELVIRA MÁRQUEZ are:

    i.   ELIZA[4] GAVALDON, b. Abt. 1924[21].

    ii.   ERINEO GAVALDON[22], b. November 16, 1924, Rebentón, New México[23]; m. ANTONIA OLIVAS, November 15, 1947[24].

    iii.   ELUTICIA GAVALDON[25], b. September 28, 1927, Carrizozo, New México[26]; m. FRANCISCO D. VEGA, July 11, 1948, Carrizozo, New México[27].

    iv.   ORLANDO GAVALDON[28], b. August 09, 1929, Carrizozo, New México[29].

Genealogy of José Manuel Gutiérres

Generation No. 1

1. MIGUEL LORETO[1] GUTIÉRRES. He married MARÍA DE LA LUZ GONZÁLES[1].

Notes for MIGUEL LORETO GUTIÉRRES:
Also known as Miguel Lorenso Gutiérres.

Notes for MARÍA DE LA LUZ GONZÁLES:
Also known as María de la Cruz Gonzáles.

Children of MIGUEL GUTIÉRRES and MARÍA GONZÁLES are:
      i.   PEDRO[2] GUTIÉRRES, b. January 20, 1782[2]; m. MARIA LORENSA LUCERO, April 27, 1811, Tomé, El Reyno de Nuevo México, Nueva España[3].

Notes for PEDRO GUTIÉRRES:
Baptized in Sandia Pueblo, El Reyno de Nuevo México, Nueva España.

2.   ii.   JOSÉ ANTONIO GUTIÉRRES, b. March 28, 1783.

Generation No. 2

2. JOSÉ ANTONIO[2] GUTIÉRRES *(MIGUEL LORETO[1])* was born March 28, 1783[4]. He married BARBARA LUCERO[5].

Notes for JOSÉ ANTONIO GUTIÉRRES:
Also known as Juan Joseph Antonio Gutiérres. Baptized in Sandia Pueblo, El Reyno de Nuevo México, Nueva España.

Notes for BARBARA LUCERO:
Also known as María Barbara Lucero.

Children of JOSÉ GUTIÉRRES and BARBARA LUCERO are:
3.   i.   JOSÉ MANUEL[3] GUTIÉRRES, b. 1807.
      ii.   MARÍA BIBIANA GUTIÉRRES, m. JUAN BAUTISTA SILVA, March 31, 1823, Socorro, Nuevo México, La República de México[5].
      iii. JUAN GUTIÉRRES, m. MARÍA BARBARA TRUJILLO, May 15, 1841, Socorro, Nuevo México, La República de México[6].

Generation No. 3

3. JOSÉ MANUEL[3] GUTIÉRRES *(JOSÉ ANTONIO[2], MIGUEL LORETO[1])*[7] was born 1807[8]. He married (1) JUANA GERTRUDIS LÓPES December 06, 1828 in Socorro, Nuevo México, La República de México[9], daughter of ANTONIO LÓPES and MARÍA JARAMILLO. He married (2) JUANA MARÍA SALAS April 23, 1848 in Socorro, Territory of New México[10], daughter of FRANCISCO SALAS and NICOLASA TRUJILLO.

Notes for JOSÉ MANUEL GUTIÉRRES:
1870 Census: Living in Lincoln County, Precinct 2 (San Patricio), Territory of New México.

Child of JOSÉ GUTIÉRRES and JUANA LÓPES is:
4.   i.   MANUEL ANTONIO[4] GUTIÉRRES, b. Abt. 1832.

Children of JOSÉ GUTIÉRRES and JUANA SALAS are:
      ii.   TORNIO[4] GUTIÉRRES, b. La Luz, New México.

Notes for TORNIO GUTIÉRRES:
Also known as José Tornio.
Had a ranch in Quemado, NM.

      iii.   DOLÓRES GUTIÉRRES, b. 1847[11]; m. IRINEA MARTÍNES, April 14, 1874, Tularoso, Territory of New México[12].

Notes for DOLÓRES GUTIÉRRES:
Also known as José Dolóres.

      iv.   JUAN JOSÉ GUTIÉRRES, b. 1849, La Luz, New México[13]; m. LEONOR MARTÍNES, April 14, 1874, Tularoso, Territory of New México[14].
5.   v.   RAFAEL GUTIÉRRES, b. Abt. 1850.
6.   vi.   DAMIAN GUTIÉRRES, b. 1852.
7.   vii.   FRANCISCO GUTIÉRRES, b. 1855.
8.   viii.   FLORENTINO GUTIÉRRES, b. March 1861.
      ix.   JOSEFITA GUTIÉRRES, b. 1864, La Luz, New México[15].

Generation No. 4

4. MANUEL ANTONIO[4] GUTIÉRRES *(JOSÉ MANUEL[3], JOSÉ ANTONIO[2], MIGUEL LORETO[1])* was born Abt. 1832[15]. He married MARÍA ALTAGRACIA ROMERO December 30, 1850 in Socorro, Territory of New México[16], daughter of JOSÉ ROMERO and ESTEFANA MONTOLLA.

Notes for MANUEL ANTONIO GUTIÉRRES:
Also known as José Manuel.
1870 Census: Living in Lincoln County, Precinct 2, (San Patricio), Territory of New México.
Land Patent # NMNMAA 010815, on the authority of the Homestead Entry-Original (12 Stat. 392), May 20, 1862. Issued 160 acres.

Children of MANUEL GUTIÉRRES and MARÍA ROMERO are:
      i.   RAFAEL ROMERO[5] GUTIÉRREZ, b. Abt. 1849[17]; m. NICOLASA DURÁN, July 16, 1871[18].
      ii.   JUANA MARÍA GUTIÉRREZ, b. Abt. 1854[19].
      iii.   FELICITA GUTIÉRREZ, b. Abt. 1867[19].

5. RAFAEL[4] GUTIÉRRES *(JOSÉ MANUEL[3], JOSÉ ANTONIO[2], MIGUEL LORETO[1])* was born Abt. 1850[20]. He married ENCARNACIÓN PATRÓN December 06, 1873[21].

Notes for RAFAEL GUTIÉRRES:
Also known as José Rafael Gutiérrez.
1880 Census: Living in La Plaza de La Junta, Territory of New México.
Land Patent # NMLC 0025956, on the authority of the Homestead Entry-Stock Raising (39 Stat. 862), December 29, 1916. Issued 646.28 acres on November 15, 1926.

Children of RAFAEL GUTIÉRRES and ENCARNACIÓN PATRÓN are:
      i.   BIRGINIA[5] GUTIÉRREZ, b. Abt. 1876[22].
      ii.   MANUEL GUTIÉRREZ, b. Abt. 1878[22].

6. DAMIAN[4] GUTIÉRRES *(JOSÉ MANUEL[3], JOSÉ ANTONIO[2], MIGUEL LORETO[1])* was born 1852[23]. He married JUANITA SÁNCHEZ Abt. 1880[24], daughter of CRECENCIO SÁNCHEZ and MARÍA SÁNCHEZ.

Notes for DAMIAN GUTIÉRRES:
Also known as José Damian.

Children of DAMIAN GUTIÉRRES and JUANITA SÁNCHEZ are:

9.   i.   ROBERTO[5] GUTIÉRREZ, b. February 28, 1883, Hondo, Territory of New México; d. 1951, Hondo, New México.
      ii.   EPIMENIO GUTIÉRREZ, b. December 1887[25].
10.   iii.   JOSEFA GUTIÉRREZ, b. March 1892.
11.   iv.   ISABEL GUTIÉRREZ, b. April 02, 1893, Hondo, Territory of New México; d. November 01, 1993, Roswell, New México.
12.   v.   ANITA GUTIÉRREZ, b. Abt. 1895, Hondo, Territory of New México.
      vi.   CRESCENCIO GUTIÉRREZ, b. March 1900[25].
      vii.   VITERBO GUTIÉRREZ, b. March 1900[25].

7. FRANCISCO[4] GUTIÉRRES (*JOSÉ MANUEL*[3], *JOSÉ ANTONIO*[2], *MIGUEL LORETO*[1]) was born 1855[26]. He married ANGELITA DE GUTIÉRREZ Abt. 1890[27].

Notes for FRANCISCO GUTIÉRRES:
Also known as José Francisco.

Children of FRANCISCO GUTIÉRRES and ANGELITA DE GUTIÉRREZ are:
      i.   MANUELITA[5] GUTIÉRREZ, b. Abt. 1900, San Patricio, Territory of New México[27].
      ii.   RAMÓN GUTIÉRREZ, b. Abt. 1903, San Patricio, Territory of New México[27].

8. FLORENTINO[4] GUTIÉRRES (*JOSÉ MANUEL*[3], *JOSÉ ANTONIO*[2], *MIGUEL LORETO*[1]) was born March 1861[28]. He married ANGELITA MONTOYA November 01, 1886 in Tularoso, Territory of New México[29].

Notes for FLORENTINO GUTIÉRRES:
Also known as José Francisco.

Children of FLORENTINO GUTIÉRRES and ANGELITA MONTOYA are:
      i.   AMADO[5] GUTIÉRREZ, b. January 1893[30].
      ii.   RAFAEL GUTIÉRREZ, b. March 1895[30].
      iii.   JOSEFITA GUTIÉRREZ, b. July 1898[30].
13.   iv.   SARAFINA GUTIÉRREZ, b. 1900.

Generation No. 5

9. ROBERTO[5] GUTIÉRREZ (*DAMIAN*[4] *GUTIÉRRES, JOSÉ MANUEL*[3], *JOSÉ ANTONIO*[2], *MIGUEL LORETO*[1])[31] was born February 28, 1883 in Hondo, Territory of New México[32], and died 1951 in Hondo, New México. He married (1) REBECCA GARCÍA May 19, 1910 in Picacho, Territory of New México[32], daughter of JOSÉ GARCÍA and CARLOTA GARCÍA. He married (2) ANITA GONZÁLES[33] September 16, 1916 in Hondo, New México[34], daughter of JOSÉ GONZÁLES and MARÍA CHÁVEZ.

Notes for ROBERTO GUTIÉRREZ:
World War One Draft Registration Card indicates that he was born on July 18, 1882.
1930 Census: Living in Hondo, New México. His name is listed as Roberto Gonzáles.
Land Patent # NMR 0026686, on the authority of the Homestead Entry-Original (12 Stat. 392), May 20, 1862. Issued 151.71 acres on August 26, 1920.
Land Patent # NMR 0029140, on the authority of the Homestead Entry-Enlarged (35 Stat. 639), February 19, 1909. Issued 168.64 acres on October 18, 1923.
Land Patent # NMR 0036537, on the authority of the Homestead Entry-Stock Raising (39 Stat. 862), December 29, 1916. Issued 320 acres on April 20, 1925.

Notes for ANITA GONZÁLES:
Also known as Anne.

Children of ROBERTO GUTIÉRREZ and REBECCA GARCÍA are:
    i.   MANUEL[6] GUTIÉRREZ.
    ii.   LUCILA GUTIÉRREZ.

Children of ROBERTO GUTIÉRREZ and ANITA GONZÁLES are:
14.   iii. JOSÉ GONZÁLES[6] GUTIÉRREZ, b. July 07, 1917, Hondo, New México; d. August 13, 1997, Hondo, New México.
        iv. ROBERTO GONZÁLES GUTIÉRREZ[35], b. May 14, 1919, Hondo, New México[36]; d. September 1974, Hondo, New México.

Notes for ROBERTO GONZÁLES GUTIÉRREZ:
June 25, 1942: Enlisted into the Army. Corporal US Army, WW II. Wounded in Italy April 29, 1945.

        v.   FERNANDO GUTIÉRREZ[36], b. April 07, 1922, Tinnie, New México; d. March 08, 1972, Hondo, New México.

Notes for FERNANDO GUTIÉRREZ:
November 30, 1942: Enlisted in the Army. Tec 5 CN, Company 302, Infantry WW II.

        vi. SOSTENO GUTIÉRREZ[37], b. December 16, 1924, Tinnie, New México[38].

Notes for SOSTENO GUTIÉRREZ:
US Navy, Seaman First Class. World War II.

        vii. JOSEFITA GUTIÉRREZ, b. Abt. 1925[38].
        viii. DOMINGO GUTIÉRREZ, b. Abt. 1929[38].

10. JOSEFA[5] GUTIÉRREZ *(DAMIAN[4] GUTIÉRRES, JOSÉ MANUEL[3], JOSÉ ANTONIO[2], MIGUEL LORETO[1])* was born March 1892[39]. She married PROMETIVO BRADY, son of WILLIAM BRADY and BONIFACIA CHÁVES.

Notes for JOSEFA GUTIÉRREZ:
Also known as Josefita.

Children of JOSEFA GUTIÉRREZ and PROMETIVO BRADY are:
    i.   ORLANDO[6] BRADY, b. Abt. 1909[40].
    ii.   CELIA BRADY, b. Abt. 1914[41].
    iii. PROMETIVO BRADY, b. Abt. 1918[41].
    iv. ROY BRADY, b. Abt. 1920[41].
    v.   ERVIN BRADY, b. Abt. 1922[41].
    vi. BONIFACIO BRADY, b. Abt. 1925[41].

11. ISABEL[5] GUTIÉRREZ *(DAMIAN[4] GUTIÉRRES, JOSÉ MANUEL[3], JOSÉ ANTONIO[2], MIGUEL LORETO[1])*[42] was born April 02, 1893 in Hondo, Territory of New México, and died November 01, 1993 in Roswell, New México. She married MARTÍN LUCERO TORRES[43] January 05, 1911 in Hondo, Territory of New México[44], son of YGNACIO TORRES and MANUELA LUCERO.

Children of ISABEL GUTIÉRREZ and MARTÍN TORRES are:
    i.   FEDERICO[6] TORREZ[45], b. August 24, 1909, Hondo, New México; d. April 05, 2003; m. CECILIA MACKEY.
    ii.   ELOY TORREZ[46], b. February 27, 1912, Hondo, New México[47]; d. October 28, 2011, Roswell, New México; m. SAVINA SALCIDO[48].
15.   iii. IGNACIO TORREZ, b. October 02, 1913, Hondo, New México; d. September 15, 2005, San Patricio, New México.
        iv. ERMINIA TORREZ[49], b. February 04, 1916, Hondo, New México; d. May 15, 1975; m. CLOVÍS MONTES.
        v.   JULIA TORREZ[50], b. April 12, 1918, Hondo, New México[51]; d. July 17, 2003, El Paso, Téxas; m. (1) JOHN OTERO[52]; m. (2) FRED KIMBRELL[53], April 16, 1938[54].
        vi. SIL TORREZ, b. Abt. 1922, Hondo, New México[55]; m. JOSIE FLACO.
        vii. EVA TORREZ, b. Abt. 1924, Hondo, New México[55]; m. RAMÓN JIMÉNEZ.
        viii. PRESILA TORREZ, b. Abt. 1929, Hondo, New México[55]; m. ROBERT RICHARDSON.
        ix. LARRY TORREZ, b. Private, Hondo, New México; m. DOROTHY CHÁVEZ.
        x.   LIBBY TORREZ, b. Private, Hondo, New México; m. CARL AUSTIN.
        xi. PATSY TORREZ, b. Private, Hondo, New México; m. BILL TURNER.

12. ANITA[5] GUTIÉRREZ *(DAMIAN[4] GUTIÉRRES, JOSÉ MANUEL[3], JOSÉ ANTONIO[2], MIGUEL LORETO[1])* was born Abt. 1895 in Hondo, Territory of New México[56]. She married ADENAGO MARTÍNEZ Abt. 1914[56], son of MANUEL JEDAN and LUISA MARTÍNEZ.

Notes for ANITA GUTIÉRREZ:
Also known as Anne.
1910 Census: Living in Roswell, Territory of New México.

Children of ANITA GUTIÉRREZ and ADENAGO MARTÍNEZ are:

16.   i.   MACLOVIA[6] MARTÍNEZ, b. April 24, 1916; d. April 02, 1940, Hondo, New México.
        ii.   ERMILO MARTÍNEZ, b. Abt. 1919[56].
17.   iii. LOUISA MARTÍNEZ, b. December 08, 1920, San Patricio, New México; d. May 25, 1997.
        iv. FERMÍN MARTÍNEZ, b. Abt. 1925[56]; m. ELIZABETH RUE.
        v.   MARTHA MARTÍNEZ, b. January 1930[56]; m. HENRY CADENA.
        vi. ERNEST MARTÍNEZ, b. Private; m. PEGGY TITSWORTH.
        vii. THERESA MARTÍNEZ, b. Private; m. FRANK RAMÍREZ.

13. SARAFINA[5] GUTIÉRREZ *(FLORENTINO[4] GUTIÉRRES, JOSÉ MANUEL[3], JOSÉ ANTONIO[2], MIGUEL LORETO[1])* was born 1900[57]. She married ANASTACIO MARES MONTOYA[57] Abt. 1917[58], son of FELIPÉ MONTOYA and PAULA GARCÍA.

Children of SARAFINA GUTIÉRREZ and ANASTACIO MONTOYA are:

        i.   RAMÓN[6] MONTOYA, b. Abt. 1920[59].
        ii. JOVITA MONTOYA, b. Abt. 1923[60].

Generation No. 6

14. JOSÉ GONZÁLES[6] GUTIÉRREZ *(ROBERTO[5], DAMIAN[4] GUTIÉRRES, JOSÉ MANUEL[3], JOSÉ ANTONIO[2], MIGUEL LORETO[1])[61]* was born July 07, 1917 in Hondo, New México[62], and died August 13, 1997 in Hondo, New México. He married DOLÓRES SEDILLO, daughter of MARTÍN SEDILLO and PORFIRIA OTERO.

Notes for JOSÉ GONZÁLES GUTIÉRREZ:
Also known as Joe. Social Security Death index records his birthdate as July 7, 1918.
1920 Census: Living in Tinnie, New México.

Notes for DOLÓRES SEDILLO:
Also known as Lola.

Child of JOSÉ GUTIÉRREZ and DOLÓRES SEDILLO is:

        i.   PRESCILLA[7] GUTIÉRREZ, b. July 28, 1951; m. MELVIN CHÁVEZ.

15. IGNACIO[6] TORREZ *(ISABEL[5] GUTIÉRREZ, DAMIAN[4] GUTIÉRRES, JOSÉ MANUEL[3], JOSÉ ANTONIO[2], MIGUEL LORETO[1])[62]* was born October 02, 1913 in Hondo, New México, and died September 15, 2005 in San Patricio, New México. He married AMANDA MONTES December 26, 1937, daughter of JESÚS MONTES and TOMASITA ALDAZ.

16. MACLOVIA[6] MARTÍNEZ *(ANITA[5] GUTIÉRREZ, DAMIAN[4] GUTIÉRRES, JOSÉ MANUEL[3], JOSÉ ANTONIO[2], MIGUEL LORETO[1])[63]* was born April 24, 1916[64], and died April 02, 1940 in Hondo, New México. She married ERMANDO CHÁVEZ[65] December 07, 1935 in Carrizozo, New México[66], son of PABLO CHÁVEZ and AMADA SÁNCHEZ.

Children of MACLOVIA MARTÍNEZ and ERMANDO CHÁVEZ are:

        i.   PABLO MOISES[7] CHÁVEZ[67], b. July 13, 1936, San Patricio, New México; d. May 28, 2009, Amarillo, Téxas.

Notes for PABLO MOISES CHÁVEZ:
Also known as Paul.

    ii.   BOBBY MARTÍNEZ CHÁVEZ[68], b. Private, San Patricio, New México.
    iii.   LOUIS CHÁVEZ[68], b. Private.
    iv.   LILLIAN CHÁVEZ[68], b. Private; m. DANNY GARCÍA[68].
    v.   LUCY CHÁVEZ[68], b. Private.
    vi.   VIOLA CHÁVEZ, b. Private.
    vii. JEANE CHÁVEZ, b. Private.
    viii. DANNY CHÁVEZ, b. Private.

17. LOUISA[6] MARTÍNEZ *(ANITA[5] GUTIÉRREZ, DAMIAN[4] GUTIÉRRES, JOSÉ MANUEL[3], JOSÉ ANTONIO[2], MIGUEL LORETO[1])* was born December 08, 1920 in San Patricio, New México, and died May 25, 1997. She married FERMÍN SALAS October 21, 1939 in Hondo, New México[69], son of PABLO SALAS and PETRA SISNEROS.

Genealogy of Lowel Hale

Generation No. 1

1. LOWEL[1] HALE was born October 1835 in Indiana[1]. He married ANNA COWGILL Abt. 1872[1].

Notes for LOWEL HALE:
Also known as Lower Hale.
1880 Census: Living in East Las Vegas, NM.

Notes for ANNA COWGILL:
Also known as Emma.
Her mother was born in Germany, her father was born in Scotland.

Children of LOWEL HALE and ANNA COWGILL are:

2. i.   MARY REBECCA[2] HALE, b. May 1865, Missouri.
    ii.   STEFFEN ANDREW HALE, b. September 1872[1].
    iii. WILLIAM HALE[2], b. 1876[3]; d. January 29, 1936, Glencoe, New México.
3. iv.   PETER G. HALE, b. 1881; d. 1941.
    v.   RACHEL HALE, b. October 1885[4]; m. ANDREW STEFFEN, June 07, 1900[5].
    vi.   ALFRED EDGAR HALE, b. June 1888[6].

Notes for ALFRED EDGAR HALE:
Land Patent # NMLC 0029263, on the authority of the Homestead Entry-Stock Raising (39 Stat. 862), December 29, 1916. Issued 483.35 acres on July 16, 1930.

Generation No. 2

2. MARY REBECCA[2] HALE *(LOWEL[1])* was born May 1865 in Missouri[7]. She married JOEL PINKERTON SAULSBERRY[8] Abt. 1886[9], son of JAMES SAULSBERRY and HARRIET CLIFTON.

Notes for MARY REBECCA HALE:
Also known as Rebecca.

Children of MARY HALE and JOEL SAULSBERRY are:

    i.   JOSHUA[3] SAULSBERRY, b. October 1885[9].
    ii.   JAMES L. SAULSBERRY, b. April 1887[9].
    iii. HARRY SAULSBERRY, b. October 1888[9].
    iv.   JOHN FREDERICK SAULSBERRY, b. July 1891[9].
    v.   HARVEY HARTSEL SAULSBERRY[10], b. January 28, 1896, Ruidoso, Territory of New México[11]; d. August 1984, Alamagordo, New México; m. CLARA M. SAULSBERRY[12].
4. vi.   MAUDE MAY SAULSBERRY, b. May 25, 1901, Alamogordo, New México; d. October 21, 1992, Denver, Colorado.

3. PETER G.[2] HALE *(LOWEL[1])*[13] was born 1881[14], and died 1941. He married ELISIA GILL[15][16], daughter of WILLIAM GILL and ALTAGRACIA HERRERA.

Notes for ELISIA GILL:
Also known as Alice, Alicia.

Children of PETER HALE and ELISIA GILL are:

    i.   WILLIE[3] HALE[17], b. 1903; d. 1968.

    ii.   HENRY HALE[17], b. September 28, 1904; d. January 10, 1975; m. FRANCES FRITZ[17], November 1927[18].

    iii. MARY HALE, b. 1908.

    iv. SUSIE HALE[19], b. January 25, 1910, Glencoe, Territory of New México[20]; d. July 1987, Ruidoso, New México; m. JASPER W. MARABLE, November 24, 1934, Carrizozo, New México[20].

    v.   PAULIE HALE[21], b. May 07, 1913, Glencoe, New México; d. May 11, 1924, Glencoe, New México.

Notes for PAULIE HALE:
Also known as Paulito Hale.

    vi. MAGGIE HALE, b. 1916.

    vii. JAMES HALE[22], b. August 19, 1917[23]; d. 1963.

    viii. BESSIE HALE, b. 1919.

Generation No. 3

4. MAUDE MAY[3] SAULSBERRY *(MARY REBECCA[2] HALE, LOWEL[1])[24]* was born May 25, 1901 in Alamogordo, New México[25], and died October 21, 1992 in Denver, Colorado. She married FRANK HAMILTON CLIPP.

Child of MAUDE SAULSBERRY and FRANK CLIPP is:

    i.   PAUL DONALD[4] CLIPP[26], b. June 14, 1932, Cedaredge, Colorado; d. May 03, 1986, Denver, Colorado.

Genealogy of Santiago Pino Herrera

Generation No. 1

1. SANTIAGO PINO[1] HERRERA was born Abt. 1826[1]. He married MARÍA ESCALANTE[2].

Notes for SANTIAGO PINO HERRERA:
Family legend has it that he was a captive Navajo at one time.
1860 Census: Living in Pueblo de Cochití, Territory of New México.
1870 Census: Living in Las Cruces, Territory of New México.
1880 Census: Living in San Patricio, Territory of New México.
1910 Census: Living in San Patricio, Territory of New México. (Pino Herrera)

Children of SANTIAGO HERRERA and MARÍA ESCALANTE are:
      i.   SANTIAGO ESCALANTE[2] HERRERA.

Notes for SANTIAGO ESCALANTE HERRERA:
He was bitten by a rattlesnake and died young.

	ii.	MANUEL ESCALANTE HERRERA, m. NAVORA SALAZAR, August 18, 1875[2].
2.	iii.	TERESA ESCALANTE HERRERA, b. August 1856.
3.	iv.	CRUZ HERRERA, b. Abt. 1861; d. October 07, 1922, San Patricio, New México.
	v.	MARIANA HERRERA, b. Abt. 1864[3].
4.	vi.	PASQUAL HERRERA, b. May 1869, Las Cruces, Territory of New México.
	vii.	GRAVIEL HERRERA, b. Abt. 1879, San Patricio, Terrotory of New México[4].

Generation No. 2

2. TERESA ESCALANTE[2] HERRERA *(SANTIAGO PINO[1])* was born August 1856[4]. She married JUAN CHÁVEZ April 24, 1873[5].

Notes for TERESA ESCALANTE HERRERA:
Also known as Teresita.
1900 Census: Living in Ruidoso, Territory of New México.

Notes for JUAN CHÁVEZ:
Also known as Jesús Chávez.
1880 Census: Living in La Plaza de San Patricio, Territory of New México.

Children of TERESA HERRERA and JUAN CHÁVEZ are:
      i.   QUERINA[3] CHÁVEZ, b. June 1872[6]; m. MARCELINO ORTEGA[7], July 28, 1892[8].
      ii.   JOSÉ CHÁVEZ, b. Abt. 1876[9].

Notes for JOSÉ CHÁVEZ:
1900 Census: Lists his birth year as March 1878.

5.	iii.	VIVIANA CHÁVEZ, b. December 02, 1883, San Patricio, Territory of New México; d. March 11, 1936, San Patricio, New México.
6.	iv.	LUPE CHÁVEZ, b. January 1885, San Patricio, New México.
7.	v.	ANASTACIA CHÁVEZ, b. April 25, 1887, San Patricio, Territory of New México.
	vi.	ERMINIA CHÁVEZ, b. July 1892[10].

Notes for ERMINIA CHÁVEZ:
Also known as Erinea.

      vii. MANUEL CHÁVEZ, b. March 25, 1896.

3. CRUZ² HERRERA *(SANTIAGO PINO¹)* was born Abt. 1861*¹¹*, and died October 07, 1922 in San Patricio, New México. He married (1) EULOJIA MADRID*¹²*. He married (2) REDUCINDA CARDONA May 16, 1888*¹³*, daughter of TANISLADO CARDONA and RAMONA LUNA. He married (3) PETRA DOMINGUEZ March 02, 1905*¹⁴*, daughter of NICANOR DOMINGUEZ and OCTAVIANA FUENTES.

Notes for REDUCINDA CARDONA:
Also known as Domicinda.

Notes for PETRA DOMINGUEZ:
1930 Census lists her as the head of the household.

Children of CRUZ HERRERA and EULOJIA MADRID are:
8.	i.	LUÍS³ HERRERA, b. October 19, 1882, San Patricio, Territory of New México.
9.	ii.	TOMASITA HERRERA, b. December 29, 1884; d. January 16, 1965.
10.	iii.	MARTÍN HERRERA, b. March 10, 1886, San Patricio, Territory of New México; d. October 25, 1954, El Paso, Téxas.

Children of CRUZ HERRERA and REDUCINDA CARDONA are:
	iv.	BENITO³ HERRERA*¹⁵*, b. January 01, 1890, Las Chosas, Lincoln County, Territory of New México; d. November 1978, Roswell, New México; m. (1) EMMA DE HERRERA; m. (2) CRUSITA GONZÁLES.
11.	v.	FILOMENO HERRERA, b. July 05, 1894; d. September 1974, Pecos, Téxas.
12.	vi.	JUAN PABLO HERRERA, b. November 17, 1897, San Patricio, Territory of New México; d. 1969.
	vii.	SANTIAGO CARDONA HERRERA, b. August 06, 1899*¹⁶*.
13.	viii.	RITA HERRERA, b. May 22, 1900, San Patricio, Territory of New México.

Children of CRUZ HERRERA and PETRA DOMINGUEZ are:
	ix.	MARIANA³ HERRERA, b. San Patricio, New México.
14.	x.	VICENTE HERRERA, b. January 22, 1906, San Patricio, Territory of New México; d. December 31, 1993, San Patricio, New México.
15.	xi.	SANTIAGO DOMINGUEZ HERRERA, b. May 01, 1915, San Patricio, New México; d. February 18, 1995, San Patricio, New México.
	xii.	MANUEL DOMINGUEZ HERRERA, b. Abt. 1917, San Patricio, New México*¹⁷*.
	xiii.	ANTONIO HERRERA*¹⁸*, b. August 29, 1919, San Patricio, New México*¹⁹*.
	xiv.	FRANCISCO HERRERA*²⁰*, b. April 02, 1921, San Patricio, New México*²¹*; d. November 15, 1994, Tucson, Arizona; m. NATALIA CHÁVEZ*²²*.

4. PASQUAL² HERRERA *(SANTIAGO PINO¹)* was born May 1869 in Las Cruces, Territory of New México*²³*. He married NAVORA TAFOYA Abt. 1894*²⁴*.

Notes for PASQUAL HERRERA:
1910 Census: Santiago Pino Herrera was living with Pasqual.
1930 Census: Living in Carrizozo, New México.

Children of PASQUAL HERRERA and NAVORA TAFOYA are:
16.	i.	ESPIRON³ HERRERA, b. August 29, 1895, San Patricio, Territory of New México.
	ii.	MARÍA HERRERA, b. Abt. 1912*²⁵*.
	iii.	GENOVEVA HERRERA, b. Abt. 1917*²⁶*.

Generation No. 3

5. VIVIANA³ CHÁVEZ *(TERESA ESCALANTE² HERRERA, SANTIAGO PINO¹)²⁷* was born December 02, 1883 in San Patricio, Territory of New México, and died March 11, 1936 in San Patricio, New México. She married (1) YGNACIO OLGUÍN*²⁷* March 16, 1898*²⁸*, son of RAMÓN OLGUÍN and MARÍA CEDILLO. She married (2) EULOJIO GALLEGOS*²⁹* August 24, 1911*³⁰*, son of ALEJANDRO GALLEGOS and ANITA SALAS.

Notes for YGNACIO OLGUÍN:
June 18, 1904 to June 10, 1909- Was selected as the first postmaster of San Patricio.
1910 Census: Living in San Patricio, Territory of New México.

Notes for EULOJIO GALLEGOS:
Also known as Olojio.

Child of VIVIANA CHÁVEZ and YGNACIO OLGUÍN is:
17.   i.   GENOVEVA CHÁVEZ[4] OLGUÍN, b. January 22, 1904, San Patricio, Territory of New México; Adopted child.

Child of VIVIANA CHÁVEZ and EULOJIO GALLEGOS is:
       ii.   GENOVEVA[4] GALLEGOS, b. 1904[31].

6. LUPE[3] CHÁVEZ *(TERESA ESCALANTE[2] HERRERA, SANTIAGO PINO[1])* was born January 1885 in San Patricio, New México[32]. She married CHARLES PACHECO BELL[33] August 16, 1904, son of CHARLES BELL and GERONIMA PACHECO.

Notes for LUPE CHÁVEZ:
Also known as Guadalupe. She was Terecita's grand daughter.

Notes for CHARLES PACHECO BELL:
Also known as Carlos Bell.
Baptismal records indicate that he was born on Juna 09, 1886. (Microfiche# 0016754, Page 101)
1930 Census: Living in Dexter, New México.

Children of LUPE CHÁVEZ and CHARLES BELL are:
       i.   ERMINDA[4] BELL, b. Abt. 1913, Picacho, New México[34].
       ii.   ERVIN BELL, b. Abt. 1918, Picacho, New México[34].
       iii. CORA BELL, b. Abt. 1925[35].
       iv.   ELIZABETH BELL, b. Abt. 1929[35].
       v.   ROSEMARY BELL, b. Abt. 1930[35].

7. ANASTACIA[3] CHÁVEZ *(TERESA ESCALANTE[2] HERRERA, SANTIAGO PINO[1])*[36] was born April 25, 1887 in San Patricio, Territory of New México. She married ESTANISLADO OLGUÍN March 02, 1901[37], son of RAMÓN OLGUÍN and MARÍA CEDILLO.

Notes for ESTANISLADO OLGUÍN:
Also known as Estanislaus, Tanislado.

Children of ANASTACIA CHÁVEZ and ESTANISLADO OLGUÍN are:
       i.   CANDELARIA[4] OLGUÍN[38], b. February 02, 1902; d. October 03, 1934; m. PABLO CALDERON[38], June 22, 1920[39].
       ii.   JUANITA OLGUÍN, b. 1904[40]; m. OLOJIO GALLEGOS.

Notes for JUANITA OLGUÍN:
Also known as Vivianita.

       iii. AVESLÍN OLGUÍN, b. 1911[40].
18.   iv.   CECILIA OLGUÍN, b. 1914.
       v.   ROBERTO OLGUÍN[41], b. April 19, 1919, San Patricio, New México[42]; m. ELVA GALLEGOS, April 01, 1948, Carrizozo, New México[43].
       vi.   PEDRO OLGUÍN, b. 1921[44].

8. LUÍS[3] HERRERA *(CRUZ[2], SANTIAGO PINO[1])* was born October 19, 1882 in San Patricio, Territory of New México[45]. He married (1) BENJAMÍN HERNÁNDEZ November 27, 1906[46], daughter of FELIS HERNÁNDEZ and NESTORA MENDOZA. He married (2) JULIANITA SAÍZ[47] May 31, 1940 in Carrizozo, New México[48], daughter of PABLO SAÍZ and CELESTINA ARAGÓN.

Notes for LUÍS HERRERA:
1930 Census: Living in Hondo, New México.

Notes for BENJAMÍN HERNÁNDEZ:
She was not listed in the 1930 Census.

Children of LUÍS HERRERA and BENJAMÍN HERNÁNDEZ are:
19.   i.   JOSÉ[4] HERRERA, b. Abt. 1907, San Patricio, Territory of New México.
20.   ii.   MANUEL HERNÁNDEZ HERRERA, b. February 15, 1909, San Patricio, Territory of New México; d. May 15, 1971.
        iii.   ANTONIO HERRERA, b. Abt. 1912, San Patricio, New México[49]; m. FRANCISCA MIRANDA.
        iv.   AMELIA HERRERA, b. Abt. 1913, San Patricio, New México[49].
        v.   ELOJIA HERRERA, b. Abt. 1915, San Patricio, New México[49].
        vi.   ARISTEO HERRERA, b. Abt. 1919, San Patricio, New México[49]; m. MACLOFA SÁNCHEZ.
        vii.   MARÍA HERRERA, b. Abt. 1922, San Patricio, New México[49].
        viii.   FRUTOSO HERRERA, b. October 18, 1923, San Patricio, New México[50]; m. AMELIA MONTES[51], July 11, 1942, Carrizozo, New México[52].

Notes for FRUTOSO HERRERA:
Private First Class. World War II.

9. TOMASITA[3] HERRERA *(CRUZ[2], SANTIAGO PINO[1])* was born December 29, 1884[53], and died January 16, 1965. She married MARTÍN SÁNCHEZ SEDILLO March 08, 1906, son of COSMÉ SEDILLO and MASIMA SÁNCHEZ.

Notes for TOMASITA HERRERA:
Also known as Tomasita.

Children of TOMASITA HERRERA and MARTÍN SEDILLO are:
        i.   CARLOS[4] SEDILLO, b. 1908[54].
        ii.   ROSA SEDILLO, b. 1911[54].
        iii.   MARIANO SEDILLO, b. 1912[54].
        iv.   DOMACIO SEDILLO[55], b. 1913[56]; d. July 21, 1933, San Patricio, New México.
        v.   RUFINA SEDILLO, b. 1915[56].
21.   vi.   CAMILO SEDILLO, b. June 05, 1917, Roswell, New México; d. May 06, 1986, Artesia, New México.
        vii.   FRED SEDILLO, b. 1921[56].
        viii.   CRUSITA SEDILLO[57], b. April 06, 1925, Roswell, New México[58]; d. December 26, 1993, Alamogordo, New México; m. RAMÓN LUNA[59].
        ix.   CATARINA SEDILLO, b. 1928[60].
        x.   VICENTE SEDILLO, b. Private.

10. MARTÍN[3] HERRERA *(CRUZ[2], SANTIAGO PINO[1])* was born March 10, 1886 in San Patricio, Territory of New México[61], and died October 25, 1954 in El Paso, Téxas[62]. He married TEODORA MENDOSA March 08, 1906 in San Patricio, Territory of New México[63], daughter of DIONICIO MENDOSA and MARÍA MORIEL.

Notes for TEODORA MENDOSA:
Also known as Theodora.

Child of MARTÍN HERRERA and TEODORA MENDOSA is:
22.   i.   JULIAN[4] HERRERA, b. December 30, 1906, San Patricio, Territory of New México; d. May 14, 1991.

11. FILOMENO[3] HERRERA *(CRUZ[2], SANTIAGO PINO[1])[64]* was born July 05, 1894[65], and died September 1974 in Pecos, Téxas. He married BLASITA PERALES August 12, 1916 in San Patricio, New México[66], daughter of VICTORIO PERALES and SOSTENA CHÁVEZ.

Children of FILOMENO HERRERA and BLASITA PERALES are:
        i.   ROSA[4] HERRERA, b. April 19, 1918; d. October 21, 1982.
        ii.   SOSTENA HERRERA[67], b. March 06, 1920; d. October 12, 1994, Roswell, New México; m. ANDRÉS GONZÁLES[67], July 22, 1936, Roswell, New México.
        iii.   MARÍA REYES HERRERA, b. January 06, 1922, Jones County, Texas; d. October 20, 2001, Las Cruces, New México; m. HENRY GONZÁLES, May 15, 1941, Roswell, New México.

    iv.   LORENCITA HERRERA, b. Abt. 1923[68]; d. Abt. 1929, Abeline, Texas.
    v.   EMMA HERRERA, b. July 05, 1925; d. June 04, 1997, Roswell, New México.

12. JUAN PABLO[3] HERRERA *(CRUZ[2], SANTIAGO PINO[1])* was born November 17, 1897 in San Patricio, Territory of New México[69], and died 1969. He married (1) LUZ PRUDENCIO October 26, 1916 in Lincoln, New México[70], daughter of JOSÉ PRUDENCIO and VICTORIA FAJARDO. He married (2) REFUGIA SÁNCHEZ February 19, 1918 in Lincoln, New México[71], daughter of FRANCISCO SÁNCHEZ and CONCEPCIÓN TRUJILLO.

Notes for JUAN PABLO HERRERA:
Buried in Roswell.

Notes for REFUGIA SÁNCHEZ:
Died after her son Cruz was born.

Child of JUAN HERRERA and REFUGIA SÁNCHEZ is:
    i.   CRUZ[4] HERRERA, b. Abt. 1919[72].

Notes for CRUZ HERRERA:
Also known as Crusito.
1930 Census: Living in Manzano, New México. Raised by Felipe Saíz & Eloisa Sánchez de Saíz after his mother died. (Cruz Saís)
Moved from Manzano to Roswell, New México.

13. RITA[3] HERRERA *(CRUZ[2], SANTIAGO PINO[1])* was born May 22, 1900 in San Patricio, Territory of New México[73]. She married JOSÉ PEÑA November 24, 1915 in Lincoln, New México[73], son of FLORENTINO PEÑA and TOMASITA FLORES.

Notes for JOSÉ PEÑA:
1930 Census: Living in Spindle, New México.

Children of RITA HERRERA and JOSÉ PEÑA are:
    i.   ELVIDA[4] PEÑA, b. Abt. 1918[74].
    ii.   JUAN HERRERA PEÑA, b. Abt. 1920[74].
    iii.   JESÚS PEÑA, b. Abt. 1924[74].
    iv.   ALINDA PEÑA, b. Abt. 1926[74].
    v.   BENITO PEÑA, b. Abt. 1928[74].
    vi.   ESOILA PEÑA, b. Abt. 1929[74].
    vii.   LEOPOLDO PEÑA[75], b. January 27, 1919, San Patricio, New México[76]; m. MARÍA GONZÁLES[77], June 20, 1940, Lincoln, New México[78].

Notes for LEOPOLDO PEÑA:
Also known as Polo. US Navy, Seaman First Class. World War II.

14. VICENTE[3] HERRERA *(CRUZ[2], SANTIAGO PINO[1])*[79] was born January 22, 1906 in San Patricio, Territory of New México, and died December 31, 1993 in San Patricio, New México. He married CIPRIANA GONZÁLES[79] August 27, 1932 in San Patricio, New México[80], daughter of EPAMINOANDAS GONZÁLES and ELVIRA GONZÁLES.

Notes for VICENTE HERRERA:
Also known as Bisente.

Children of VICENTE HERRERA and CIPRIANA GONZÁLES are:
    i.   RUFINO[4] HERRERA[81], b. July 25, 1933, San Patricio, New México; d. January 17, 2006, San Patricio, New México; m. HELENA MONTOYA, April 04, 1957, San Patricio, New México.

Notes for RUFINO HERRERA:
Korean War Veteran

23.   ii.   BERTA HERRERA, b. Private, San Patricio, New México.

15. SANTIAGO DOMINGUEZ³ HERRERA *(CRUZ², SANTIAGO PINO¹)⁸²* was born May 01, 1915 in San Patricio, New México⁸³, and died February 18, 1995 in San Patricio, New México. He married GENOVEVA VIGIL⁸⁴ December 23, 1936 in Carrizozo, New México⁸⁵, daughter of CELESTINO VIGIL and SARA SÁNCHEZ.

Children of SANTIAGO HERRERA and GENOVEVA VIGIL are:
24.   i.   ROGER⁴ HERRERA, b. November 24, 1939.
    ii.   OLYMPIA HERRERA, b. Private.
    iii.   MINNIE HERRERA, b. Private.
    iv.   VICTORIA HERRERA, b. Private.
    v.   OLIVIA HERRERA, b. Private.
    vi.   ORALIA HERRERA⁸⁶, b. March 28, 1937; d. September 09, 1991; m. WILLIAM SÁNCHEZ BRADY⁸⁷.

16. ESPIRON³ HERRERA *(PASQUAL², SANTIAGO PINO¹)* was born August 29, 1895 in San Patricio, Territory of New México⁸⁸. He married JUANITA MAÉS March 21, 1915 in Carrizozo, New México⁸⁹.

Notes for ESPIRON HERRERA:
Also known as Ciriano, Cipriano.

Child of ESPIRON HERRERA and JUANITA MAÉS is:
    i.   ARMENIA⁴ HERRERA, b. Abt. 1924⁹⁰.

Generation No. 4

17. GENOVEVA CHÁVEZ⁴ OLGUÍN *(VIVIANA³ CHÁVEZ, TERESA ESCALANTE² HERRERA, SANTIAGO PINO¹)* was born January 22, 1904 in San Patricio, Territory of New México⁹¹. She married ANTONIO LA RIVA August 05, 1920 in San Patricio, New México⁹¹, son of AUGUSTÍN LA RIVA and ANTONIA VALENCIA.

Notes for GENOVEVA CHÁVEZ OLGUÍN:
Genoveva was an adopted daughter. Her birth parents were Anastacia Chávez and Estanislado Olguín. Baptismal records indicate that she was born on September 26, 1900. (Microfiche# 0016754, Page 80)

Children of GENOVEVA OLGUÍN and ANTONIO LA RIVA are:
    i.   JOSÉ⁵ LA RIVA, b. Abt. 1926, San Patricio, New México⁹².
    ii.   ANTONIO LA RIVA, b. Abt. 1928, San Patricio, New México⁹².
    iii.   FERNANDO LA RIVA, b. Abt. 1929, San Patricio, New México⁹².

18. CECILIA⁴ OLGUÍN *(ANASTACIA³ CHÁVEZ, TERESA ESCALANTE² HERRERA, SANTIAGO PINO¹)* was born 1914⁹³. She married RUMELIO CHÁVEZ⁹⁴ July 11, 1936⁹⁵, son of PABLO CHÁVEZ and AMADA SÁNCHEZ.

Notes for CECILIA OLGUÍN:
Also known as Yselia.

Children of CECILIA OLGUÍN and RUMELIO CHÁVEZ are:
    i.   AMADA⁵ CHÁVEZ, b. Private; m. HENRY SÁNCHEZ.

Notes for AMADA CHÁVEZ:
Also known as Amy.

    ii.   PABLO OLGUÍN CHÁVEZ, b. Private.

Notes for PABLO OLGUÍN CHÁVEZ:
Died at a young age.

    iii.   ÁBRAN OLGUÍN CHÁVEZ, b. Private.

19. JOSÉ⁴ HERRERA *(LUÍS³, CRUZ², SANTIAGO PINO¹)* was born Abt. 1907 in San Patricio, Territory of New México⁹⁶. He married EULALIA MIRANDA⁹⁷, daughter of JULIO MIRANDA and PABLITA MONTOYA.

Notes for EULALIA MIRANDA:
Also known as Ulalia.

Child of JOSÉ HERRERA and EULALIA MIRANDA is:
>   i.   PABLITA[5] HERRERA, b. Private; m. BREZEL CHÁVEZ[98].

20. MANUEL HERNÁNDEZ[4] HERRERA *(LUÍS[3], CRUZ[2], SANTIAGO PINO[1])[99]* was born February 15, 1909 in San Patricio, Territory of New México, and died May 15, 1971. He married ELISA GONZÁLES[100] November 23, 1931[101], daughter of LEOPOLDO GONZÁLES and REIMUNDA SEDILLO.

Children of MANUEL HERRERA and ELISA GONZÁLES are:
>   i.   BENITO[5] HERRERA[102], b. August 30, 1934, San Patricio, New México; d. July 23, 2002, Alburquerque, New México; m. JOSIE CHÁVEZ.

Notes for JOSIE CHÁVEZ:
Also known as Josephine.

>   ii.   FLORA HERRERA[103], b. April 30, 1936, San Patricio, New México[104]; d. April 28, 2001, Ruidoso, New México; m. PORFIRIO SÁNCHEZ, May 04, 1952, San Patricio, New México[104].

Notes for FLORA HERRERA:
Also known as Floripe.

>   iii.   JUAN HERRERA, b. May 09, 1952, Capitán, New México; d. January 22, 2011, Albuquerque, New México.

Notes for JUAN HERRERA:
Also known as Johnny Herrera.

>   iv.   LEO HERRERA, b. Private, San Patricio, New México; m. EMMA ZAMORA.
>   v.   LUÍS HERRERA, b. Private, San Patricio, New México.
>   vi.   MANUEL GONZÁLES HERRERA, b. Private, San Patricio, New México.
>   vii.   PASQUAL HERRERA, b. Private, San Patricio, New México.
>   viii.   ELENA HERRERA, b. September 10, 1939, San Patricio, New México; d. July 12, 2010, Alburquerque, New México.
>   ix.   BENJAMÍN HERRERA, b. Private.
>   x.   JOE HERRERA, b. Private.
>   xi.   JOSEPHINE HERRERA, b. Private.
>   xii.   LUCY HERRERA, b. Private.

21. CAMILO[4] SEDILLO *(TOMASITA[3] HERRERA, CRUZ[2], SANTIAGO PINO[1])[105]* was born June 05, 1917 in Roswell, New México[106], and died May 06, 1986 in Artesia, New México. He married LORENSITA MONTOYA[106] May 04, 1940 in Carrizozo, New México[107], daughter of DOROTEO MONTOYA and ALBINA SILVA.

Notes for CAMILO SEDILLO:
US Navy, Seaman Second Class. World War II.

Notes for LORENSITA MONTOYA:
Burial birthdate states she was born on August 09, 1914.

Children of CAMILO SEDILLO and LORENSITA MONTOYA are:
>   i.   CRISTINA DELFIDA[5] SEDILLO[108], b. Abt. 1941, San Patricio, New México; d. February 20, 1941, San Patricio, New México.
>   ii.   CRISTINA ROSA SEDILLO[109], b. Abt. 1942, San Patricio, New México; d. February 16, 1942, San Patricio, New México.
>   iii.   DANNY SEDILLO[110], b. November 07, 1949; d. April 14, 2003, Artesia, New México.
>   iv.   CERINIA SEDILLO, b. Private.
>   v.   DELLA SEDILLO, b. Private.
>   vi.   ELLIE SEDILLO, b. Private.

vii.   MARTÍN MONTOYA SEDILLO, b. Private.

22. JULIAN[4] HERRERA *(MARTÍN[3], CRUZ[2], SANTIAGO PINO[1])[111]* was born December 30, 1906 in San Patricio, Territory of New México[112], and died May 14, 1991. He married ANATALIA SÁNCHEZ April 28, 1934 in Carrizozo, New México[112], daughter of SALOMON SÁNCHEZ and JENNIE GILL.

Notes for ANATALIA SÁNCHEZ:
Also known as Natalia.

Children of JULIAN HERRERA and ANATALIA SÁNCHEZ are:
   i.   MARTÍN[5] HERRERA, b. Private.
   ii.   ANDREW HERRERA, b. Private.
   iii. ORLIDIA HERRERA, b. Private.
   iv.   VIRGINIA HERRERA, b. Private.

23. BERTA[4] HERRERA *(VICENTE[3], CRUZ[2], SANTIAGO PINO[1])* was born Private in San Patricio, New México. She married FRED SÁNCHEZ, son of ROMÁN SÁNCHEZ and FLORINDA SALSBERRY.

24. ROGER[4] HERRERA *(SANTIAGO DOMINGUEZ[3], CRUZ[2], SANTIAGO PINO[1])* was born November 24, 1939. He married RITA GÓMEZ, daughter of FRANK GÓMEZ and GRESELDA CHÁVEZ.

Genealogy of Miguel Lusero

Generation No. 1

1. MIGUEL[1] LUSERO. He married ROSA JARAMILLO.

Child of MIGUEL LUSERO and ROSA JARAMILLO is:
2.   i.   PEDRO ANTONIO[2] LUSERO.

Generation No. 2

2. PEDRO ANTONIO[2] LUSERO *(MIGUEL[1])*. He married MARÍA FRANCISCA MAESE September 23, 1779 in Cochití, El Reyno de Nuevo México, Nueva España[1].

Children of PEDRO LUSERO and MARÍA MAESE are:
          i.   MARÍA DESIDERIA[3] LUSERO, b. Bef. September 08, 1789, Cochití, El Reyno de Nuevo México, Nueva España[2].
3.   ii.   JOSÉ FRANCISCO LUSERO, b. Abt. 1790.
          iii.   MARÍA TOMASA LUSERO, b. Bef. December 26, 1790, Cochití, El Reyno de Nuevo México, Nueva España[2]; m. ANTONIO JOSÉ CRUZ, January 30, 1815, Abiquiu, El Reyno de Nuevo México, Nueva España[3].
          iv.   ANTONIO JOSÉ LUSERO, b. March 16, 1796, San Juan, El Reyno de Nuevo México, Nueva España[4].
          v.   JOSÉ BRUNO LUSERO, b. October 12, 1797, San Juan, El Reyno de Nuevo México, Nueva España[4].
4.   vi.   JOSÉ DE LA CONCEPCIÓN LUSERO, b. November 28, 1806, Ojo Caliente, El Reyno de Nuevo México, Nueva España.

Generation No. 3

3. JOSÉ FRANCISCO[3] LUSERO *(PEDRO ANTONIO[2], MIGUEL[1])* was born Abt. 1790[5]. He married MARÍA DE LA LUZ CHÁVES, daughter of JUAN CHÁVES and AUGUSTINA LÓPES.

Children of JOSÉ LUSERO and MARÍA CHÁVES are:
          i.   EULALIA[4] LUSERO, b. Abt. 1836[5].
          ii.   RAMONA LUCERO[6], b. Bef. February 26, 1838, Arroyo Hondo, Nuevo México, La República de México.

Notes for RAMONA LUCERO:
Also known as María Ramona Lucero.

          iii.   TOMÁS LUCERO, b. Bef. March 03, 1841, Arroyo Hondo, Nuevo México, La República de México[6].

Notes for TOMÁS LUCERO:
Also known as José Tomás Lucero.

          iv.   JOSÉ FRANCISCO LUSERO, b. Abt. 1842[7].
          v.   AUGUSTINA LUSERO, b. Abt. 1850[7].

4. JOSÉ DE LA CONCEPCIÓN[3] LUSERO *(PEDRO ANTONIO[2], MIGUEL[1])*[8] was born November 28, 1806 in Ojo Caliente, El Reyno de Nuevo México, Nueva España[9]. He married LUZ SENA[10], daughter of JUAN SENA and JOAQUINA CHÁVES.

Notes for JOSÉ DE LA CONCEPCIÓN LUSERO:
Also known as Concepción Lusero.
1860 Census: Living in Conejos, Taos County, Territory of New México.

Notes for LUZ SENA:
Also known as María de la Luz Sena.

Children of JOSÉ LUSERO and LUZ SENA are:
5.   i.   CORNELIO[4] LUCERO, b. Abt. 1830, Arroyo Hondo, Nuevo México, La República de México; d. October 19, 1911, Arabela, Territory of New México.
      ii.   FRANCISCA LUCERO, b. Abt. 1835[11].
      iii. BRIGIDA LUCERO[12], b. October 19, 1840, Abiquiu, El Reyno de Nuevo México, Nueva España[13].

Notes for BRIGIDA LUCERO:
Also known as María Brigida Lucero.

      iv.   ANTONIO LUCERO, b. Abt. 1848[13].

Generation No. 4

Cornelio Lucero

5. CORNELIO[4] LUCERO *(JOSÉ DE LA CONCEPCIÓN[3] LUSERO, PEDRO ANTONIO[2], MIGUEL[1])*[14] was born Abt. 1830 in Arroyo Hondo, Nuevo México, La República de México[15], and died October 19, 1911 in Arabela, Territory of New México[16]. He married NOBERTA ARCHULETA February 23, 1857 in Arroyo Hondo, Territory of New México[17], daughter of JOSÉ MIGUEL ARCHULETA.

Notes for CORNELIO LUCERO:
Also known as José Cornelio Lucero.
1860 Census: Living in Conejos, Taos County, Territory of New México.
1870 Census: Living in Cucharas, Huerfano County, Territory of Colorado.
1880 Census: Living in Las Animas County, Colorado.
1885 New México Territorial Census: Living in Las Palas, Territory of New México.
1900 Census: Living in Agua Azul, Territory of New México.
1910 Census: Living in Agua Azul, Territory of New México. (Born 1821)

Notes for NOBERTA ARCHULETA:
Also known as María Noberta Archuleta, Tita. Her Ute name was "Na Ho Cos" meaning the "North Star".
Noberta was an indentured servant. She was a captive Ute who was later adopted by José Miguel Archuleta and his wife María Isabel Casados.

Children of CORNELIO LUCERO and NOBERTA ARCHULETA are:
6.   i.   EPEMENIO[5] LUCERO, b. April 20, 1858, Conejos, Taos County, Territory of New México.
7.   ii.   BENINA LUCERO, b. February 13, 1865, La Sevillita de San Antonio, Colorado; d. February 19, 1921, Agua Azul, New México.
8.   iii. DOROTEO LUCERO, b. February 1866, Colorado.
9.   iv.   APOLONIO LUCERO, b. April 1868, Colorado.
10.   v.   STABRANA LUCERO, b. December 1877; d. January 07, 1941, Roswell, New México.
11.   vi.   INEZ LUCERO, b. June 21, 1880, Trinidad, Colorado; d. November 06, 1954, Hondo, New México.

Generation No. 5

6. EPEMENIO[5] LUCERO *(CORNELIO[4], JOSÉ DE LA CONCEPCIÓN[3] LUSERO, PEDRO ANTONIO[2], MIGUEL[1])*[18] was born April 20, 1858 in Conejos, Taos County, Territory of New México[19]. He married LUTENIA DE LUCERO Abt. 1880[20].

Notes for EPEMENIO LUCERO:
Also known as José Epemenio de Jesús Lucero.
1860 Census: Living in Conejos, Taos County, Territory of New México.

Children of EPEMENIO LUCERO and LUTENIA DE LUCERO are:
12.   i.   SAMUEL[6] LUCERO, b. March 1882.
      ii.   ARRAVELA LUCERO, b. Abt. 1887[21]; m. JESÚS CARRILLO, May 16, 1902.

Notes for ARRAVELA LUCERO:

Also known as Arabela.

Notes for JESÚS CARRILLO:
1900 Census: Living in Picacho, Territory of New México. (Divorced)
1910 Census: Living in Las Palas, Territory of New México.
1920 Census: Living in Roswell, New México.

> iii. EPIMENIO LUCERO[22], b. June 08, 1887, White Oaks, Territory of New México[23]; m. PRUDENCIA RAMÍREZ[24], January 30, 1916, Arabela, New México[24].
> iv. SANTIAGO LUCERO, b. July 1889[25].
> v. JULIANA LUCERO, b. October 1896[25].

7. BENINA[5] LUCERO *(CORNELIO[4], JOSÉ DE LA CONCEPCIÓN[3] LUSERO, PEDRO ANTONIO[2], MIGUEL[1])*[26] was born February 13, 1865 in La Sevillita de San Antonio, Colorado, and died February 19, 1921 in Agua Azul, New México. She married (1) ÁBRAN CANDELARIA[2728], son of PEDRO CANDELARIA and MARÍA APODACA. She married (2) ANDREW MCNEELY RICHARDSON June 15, 1893 in Lincoln, Territory of New México[29].

Notes for BENINA LUCERO:
Also known as María Benina Lucero.
1885 New México Territorial Census: Living in Las Palas, Territory of New México. (Born 1864)
1910 Census: Living in Las Palas, Territory of New México.

Notes for ÁBRAN CANDELARIA:
1850 Census: Living in Bernalillo County, Territory of New México. (Jose Abran, Born 1848)
1860 Census: Living in Barelas, Bernalillo County, Territory of New México. (Born 1849)
1870 Census: Living in Barelas, Bernalillo County, Territory of New México. (Habran, born 1848)
1880 Census: Living in Arroyo Seco, Lincoln County, Territory of New México. (Born 1851)
1885 New México Teritorial Census: Living in Las Palas, Territory of New México. (Born 1855, married to Benina Lucero)

Notes for ANDREW MCNEELY RICHARDSON:
Also known as Andrés, Andy.
His father was born in Pennsylvania and his mother was born in Ohio. Buried in Sterling, Kanas.
1885 New México Territorial Census: Living in Las Palas, Territory of New México. (Born Ohio, 1841)

Abrán Candelaria

Child of BENINA LUCERO and ÁBRAN CANDELARIA is:
13.   i. JOSÉ[6] CANDELARIA, b. November 16, 1883, Las Tablas, Territory of New México; d. February 10, 1964, Ruidoso, New México.

Andrew McNeely Richardson

Children of BENINA LUCERO and ANDREW RICHARDSON are:
14.   ii. BONIFACIA LUCERO[6] RICHARDSON, b. June 05, 1888, Las Palas, Territory of New México; d. June 21, 1923.
      iii. EDWARD HUBBEL RICHARDSON[30], b. May 19, 1890, Las Palas, Territory of New México; d. May 11, 1944, Arabela, Territory of New México.
15.   iv. TOMÁS EUBANK RICHARDSON, b. August 12, 1892, Las Palas, Territory of New México; d. April 15, 1931.
16.   v. GRANVILLE RICHARDSON, b. May 22, 1896, Las Palas, Territory of New México; d. June 16, 1963, Ruidoso, New México.
17.   vi. ELENA RICHARDSON, b. August 07, 1898, Las Palas, Territory of New México; d. September 17, 1937, Hagerman, New México.
18.   vii. MELVIN ALVINO RICHARDSON, b. March 15, 1902, Arabela, Territory of New México; d. June 1986.

8. DOROTEO[5] LUCERO *(CORNELIO[4], JOSÉ DE LA CONCEPCIÓN[3] LUSERO, PEDRO ANTONIO[2], MIGUEL[1])* was born February 1866 in Colorado[31]. He married CIMODOCEA MAÉS[32] November 09, 1885 in Lincoln County, Territory of New México[33], daughter of JOSÉ MES and JULIANA BALDEZ.

Notes for DOROTEO LUCERO:
Both his father and mother were born in New México.

Notes for CIMODOCEA MAÉS:
Also known as Simodosea Mes.

Children of DOROTEO LUCERO and CIMODOCEA MAÉS are:
19.   i.   AMARANTE[6] LUCERO, b. September 1886.
         ii.   DELFINIA LUCERO, b. February 1889[34].
       iii.   EMILIANA LUCERO, b. July 1890[35]; m. ANTONIO MAÉS SÁNCHEZ[36], December 01, 1909[37].

Notes for ANTONIO MAÉS SÁNCHEZ:
Buried on February 14, 1977, in Roswell, South Park Cemetery.

       iv.   SOLOMON LUCERO, b. December 1892[38].
        v.   ANITA LUCERO, b. March 1895[38].
20.   vi.   ELVIRA LUCERO, b. December 24, 1895; d. April 1966, Tularosa, New México.
      vii. EDUARDO LUCERO, b. October 1896[38].

9. APOLONIO[5] LUCERO *(CORNELIO[4], JOSÉ DE LA CONCEPCIÓN[3] LUSERO, PEDRO ANTONIO[2], MIGUEL[1])* was born April 1868 in Colorado[38]. He married ADELIA PACHECO February 11, 1896[39], daughter of ANSELMO PACHECO and TERESITA GALLEGOS.

Notes for APOLONIO LUCERO:
Also known as Polonio.
1910 Census: living in Las Palas, Territory of New México.

Children of APOLONIO LUCERO and ADELIA PACHECO are:
        i.   SUSANITA[6] LUCERO, b. April 1894, Las Palas, Territory of New México[40].
        ii.   ERLINDA LUCERO, b. July 1895, Las Palas, Territory of New México[40]; m. LEANDRO GONZÁLES, November 29, 1912[41].
21.   iii.   GEORGE LUCERO, b. January 25, 1899, Las Palas, Territory of New México; d. October 1970, Roswell, New México.
       iv.   BENJAMIN LUCERO, b. Abt. 1902, Las Palas, Territory of New México[42].
        v.   GUILLERMO LUCERO, b. Abt. 1906, Las Palas, Territory of New México[42].
       vi.   ROGELIO LUCERO, b. Abt. 1909, Las Palas, Territory of New México[42].

10. STABRANA[5] LUCERO *(CORNELIO[4], JOSÉ DE LA CONCEPCIÓN[3] LUSERO, PEDRO ANTONIO[2], MIGUEL[1])* was born December 1877[43], and died January 07, 1941 in Roswell, New México[44]. She married SEVERO GARCÍA GALLEGOS Abt. 1900[45], son of LUCAS GALLEGOS and FRANCISCA GARCÍA.

Notes for STABRANA LUCERO:
Also known as Habrana.

Notes for SEVERO GARCÍA GALLEGOS:
1910 Census: Living in Las Palas, Territory of New México.

Children of STABRANA LUCERO and SEVERO GALLEGOS are:
        i.   MARGARITA[6] GALLEGOS[46], b. October 26, 1901, Agua Azul, Territory of New México[47]; d. February 02, 2002, Roswell, New México.
        ii.   SMLE GALLEGOS, b. Abt. 1904[47].
       iii.   ROBERTO GALLEGOS[48], b. June 06, 1904, Agua Azul, Territory of New México[49]; d. November 28, 1989, Albuquerque, New México.
       iv.   DANIEL GALLEGOS[50], b. June 25, 1909, San Patricio, Territory of New México[51]; d. July 26, 1999, Riverside, California.

11. INEZ[5] LUCERO *(CORNELIO[4], JOSÉ DE LA CONCEPCIÓN[3] LUSERO, PEDRO ANTONIO[2], MIGUEL[1])* was born June 21, 1880 in Trinidad, Colorado[52], and died November 06, 1954 in Hondo, New México[53]. She married (1) EDWARD PATRICK MCTEIGUE May 28, 1896[54], son of PATRICK MCTIEGUE and MARGARET BELL. She married (2) AMOS HERMAN RUE April 12, 1906 in Arabela, Territory of New México[55], son of JOHN RUE and NANCY HOOD. She married (3) ANSELMO PACHECO June 26, 1920[56], son of FRANCISCO PACHECO and ROMULA SAVEDRA.

Notes for INEZ LUCERO:
1930 Census: Living in Roswell, New México.

Notes for EDWARD PATRICK MCTEIGUE:
1900 Census: Not listed.
Also known as Eduardo.

Edward Patrick McTeigue

Children of INEZ LUCERO and EDWARD MCTEIGUE are:
22.   i.   FRED[6] MCTEIGUE, b. June 27, 1897, Agua Azul, Territory of New México; d. January 30, 1968, Hondo, New México.
    ii.   MARTHA MCTEIGUE, b. July 1899, Agua Azul, Territory of New México[57].

Notes for MARTHA MCTEIGUE:
    1920 Census: Living with Anselmo Pacheco and her mother Inez Lucero de Pacheco.

Amos Herman Rue

Children of INEZ LUCERO and AMOS RUE are:
    iii.   ELIZABETH[6] RUE, b. Abt. 1907[58]; m. FERMÍN MARTÍNEZ.
23.   iv.   DUDLEY RUE, b. May 10, 1910; d. June 12, 1963, Arabela, New México.
    v.   CEDRIC RUE, b. Abt. 1911[58]; d. June 24, 1989[59]; m. ISELIA FRANCO, July 28, 1936[60].
24.   vi.   GEORGE RUE, b. October 13, 1913, Arabela, New México; d. August 16, 1987, Ruidoso Downs, New México.

Generation No. 6

12. SAMUEL[6] LUCERO *(EPEMENIO[5], CORNELIO[4], JOSÉ DE LA CONCEPCIÓN[3] LUSERO, PEDRO ANTONIO[2], MIGUEL[1])* was born March 1882[61]. He married DAMIANA BARELA Abt. 1908, daughter of ENCARNACIÓN BARELA and ANTONIA DE BARELA.

Child of SAMUEL LUCERO and DAMIANA BARELA is:
    i.   SAMUEL[7] LUCERO, b. Abt. 1909[62].

13. JOSÉ[6] CANDELARIA *(BENINA[5] LUCERO, CORNELIO[4], JOSÉ DE LA CONCEPCIÓN[3] LUSERO, PEDRO ANTONIO[2], MIGUEL[1])*[63] was born November 16, 1883 in Las Tablas, Territory of New México[64], and died February 10, 1964 in Ruidoso, New México. He married (1) DOMINGA PACHECO March 29, 1906 in Arabela, Territory of New México[65], daughter of ANSELMO PACHECO and TERESITA GALLEGOS. He married (2) REBECCA VILLESCAS[66] December 16, 1908, daughter of CASIMIRO VILLESCAS and EMILIANA TAFOYA. He married (3) ISIDRA SÁNCHEZ November 22, 1921[67], daughter of PEDRO SÁNCHEZ and RAMONA SEDILLO.

Notes for JOSÉ CANDELARIA:
Also known as José de los Ángeles Candelaria. He was raised by his step-father, Andrew McNeely Richardson.
1920 Census: Living in Las Palas, New México.
1930 Census: Living in Arabela, New México. Lists Jose's parents as both coming from Colorado.
1940 Census: Living in Arabela, New México. (Widow)

Children of JOSÉ CANDELARIA and REBECCA VILLESCAS are:
    i.   ELOY V.[7] CANDELARIA[68], b. April 01, 1909, Las Palas, Territory of New México; d. March 27, 1992, Ruidoso, New México; m. ESTEFANA LUCERO SÁNCHEZ, March 01, 1930, Carrizozo, New México[69].

Notes for ELOY V. CANDELARIA:
1940 Census: Living in Arabela, New México.

Notes for ESTEFANA LUCERO SÁNCHEZ:
Also known as Estefanita.

ii. GRACIANO CANDELARIA, b. December 11, 1910, Arabela, Territory of New México[70]; d. March 01, 1994, Irving, Texas; m. EPIFANIA FRESQUEZ, March 17, 1931, Arabela, New México.
iii. IGENIO CANDELARIA, b. Abt. 1913[70].
iv. SOILA CANDELARIA, b. Abt. 1916[70]; d. 2002.
v. VALOIS FELIX CANDELARIA, b. Abt. 1913, Las Palas, New México[71]; m. VENERANDA SÁNCHEZ.

Notes for VALOIS FELIX CANDELARIA:
1940 Census: Living in Arabela, New México.

Children of JOSÉ CANDELARIA and ISIDRA SÁNCHEZ are:
vi. BENITO[7] CANDELARIA, b. July 23, 1921, Arabela, New México[72]; m. CARMELITA GÓMEZ, December 13, 1944, Carrizozo, New México[72].
vii. CELESTINO CANDELARIA[73], b. October 16, 1922, Arabela, New México[74]; m. JOSEFITA MOYA.

Notes for CELESTINO CANDELARIA:
Tech 5. World War II.

viii. ARCENIA CANDELARIA, b. Abt. 1925[74]; m. RUBEN LUCERO.
ix. EDUARDO CANDELARIA[75], b. July 11, 1928, Arabela, New México; d. November 09, 2003; m. AMELIA GÓMEZ, October 25, 1952, San Patricio, New México[76].

Notes for EDUARDO CANDELARIA:
Also known as Edward and Lolo.
US Army Korea.

x. ASUSENA CANDELARIA, b. March 1930[77]; m. LUVÍN SÁNCHEZ[78].

Notes for ASUSENA CANDELARIA:
Also known as Susan.

14. BONIFACIA LUCERO[6] RICHARDSON *(BENINA[5] LUCERO, CORNELIO[4], JOSÉ DE LA CONCEPCIÓN[3] LUSERO, PEDRO ANTONIO[2], MIGUEL[1])*[79] was born June 05, 1888 in Las Palas, Territory of New México, and died June 21, 1923. She married ROMÁN PACHECO[80] September 29, 1904 in La Capilla de San Miguel, Arabela, Territory of New México[81], son of ANSELMO PACHECO and TERESITA GALLEGOS.

Notes for ROMÁN PACHECO:
Baptismal record indicates that he was born on May 12, 1884. Draft registration and Cemetery records indicate he was born on May 16, 1884.
1910 Census: Living in Agua Azul.
1930 Census: Living in Carrizozo.

Children of BONIFACIA RICHARDSON and ROMÁN PACHECO are:
i. FERNANDO[7] PACHECO, b. February 27, 1906.

Notes for FERNANDO PACHECO:
Died when he was young.

ii. FERMÍN PACHECO[82], b. February 27, 1906, Arabela, Territory of New México; d. August 02, 1983; m. IGNACIA GÓMEZ[82], August 29, 1932, Roswell, New México[83].

Notes for IGNACIA GÓMEZ:
Also known as Inez.

iii. CARLOS PACHECO, b. Abt. 1910.
iv. FERNANDO PACHECO[84], b. April 23, 1915, Arabela, New México[85]; d. August 14, 2006, Sahuarita, Arizona[86]; m. LUCÍA GÓMEZ, August 07, 1937[87].

Notes for FERNANDO PACHECO:
US Navy, Seaman First Class. World War II.
1940 Census: Living in San Patricio, New México.

    v.   EMMA PACHECO, b. November 27, 1918, Arabela, New México[88]; m. ALFRED MARTÍNEZ, June 25, 1937, Carrizozo, New México[89].

    vi.   UTALIA PACHECO, b. June 16, 1912; d. March 1990; m. (1) LORENZO GARCÍA; m. (2) BENJAMIN ACUNA.

    vii.   UTILIA PACHECO, b. Private; m. (1) JOE GARCÍA; m. (2) JIMMY VENDIOLA.

15. TOMÁS EUBANK[6] RICHARDSON *(BENINA[5] LUCERO, CORNELIO[4], JOSÉ DE LA CONCEPCIÓN[3] LUSERO, PEDRO ANTONIO[2], MIGUEL[1])[90]* was born August 12, 1892 in Las Palas, Territory of New México, and died April 15, 1931. He married ARABELA QUINTANA January 11, 1915 in Arabela, New México[91], daughter of JUAN QUINTANA and TRENIDAD SÁNCHEZ.

Children of TOMÁS RICHARDSON and ARABELA QUINTANA are:

    i.   GENOVEVA[7] RICHARDSON, b. November 04, 1915; d. December 11, 1990; m. JUAN PRECILIANO CANO.

    ii.   SUSANA RICHARDSON, b. Abt. 1918[92]; d. December 09, 2002, Dumas, Texas; m. DANIEL HERNÁNDEZ.

    iii.   NOBERTA RICHARDSON, b. Abt. 1919[92].

    iv.   ARCELIA RICHARDSON, b. Private; m. TEODOSO CANO.

    v.   MARGARITA RICHARDSON, b. December 25, 1923, Arabela, New México; d. August 06, 1995, Denver, Colorado; m. WILLIE WILSON.

    vi.   THOMAS RICHARDSON, b. Private; m. MARÍA CHÁVEZ.

16. GRANVILLE[6] RICHARDSON *(BENINA[5] LUCERO, CORNELIO[4], JOSÉ DE LA CONCEPCIÓN[3] LUSERO, PEDRO ANTONIO[2], MIGUEL[1])[93]* was born May 22, 1896 in Las Palas, Territory of New México, and died June 16, 1963 in Ruidoso, New México. He married AMANDA MAÉS[93] August 27, 1915 in Patos, New México[94], daughter of CORNELIO MAÉS and CONSTANCIA ZAMORA.

Notes for GRANVILLE RICHARDSON:
Also known as Guillermo. (Microfiche# 0016754, Baptismal Records, Page 263)
Land Patent # NMNMAA 010273, on the authority of the Homestead Entry-Original (12 Stat. 392), May 20, 1862. Issued 120 acres on January 23, 1901.
Land Patent # NMNMAA 010274, on the authority of the Homestead Entry-Original (12 Stat. 392), May 20, 1862. Issued 80 acres on January 23, 1901.

Children of GRANVILLE RICHARDSON and AMANDA MAÉS are:

    i.   PRESTINA[7] RICHARDSON, b. May 29, 1916, Arabela, New México[95]; d. November 09, 1995, Roswell, New México; m. FRANK JIMÉNEZ.

    ii.   EDWARD RICHARDSON, b. Abt. 1919[95].

    iii.   ANDRÉS RICHARDSON[96], b. April 30, 1920, Arabela, New México[97]; d. December 02, 1998, Capitán, New México; m. MACRINA SÁNCHEZ[98], August 08, 1949, Carrizozo, New México[98].

Notes for ANDRÉS RICHARDSON:
Private First Class, World War II Veteran.

    iv.   ALBERTO RICHARDSON, b. Abt. 1923[99]; m. EMMA MONTES.

    v.   LUCERA RICHARDSON, b. September 02, 1925, Arabela, New México[100]; d. August 07, 1982, Hondo, New México; m. ALBERTO MONTES, June 03, 1943, Capitán, New México[100].

    vi.   ALFREDO RICHARDSON, b. March 03, 1929, Roswell, New México[101]; d. January 19, 1977, El Paso, Téxas; m. MARY OLIDA SÁNCHEZ[102], January 08, 1955[102].

    vii.   ROBERTO RICHARDSON, b. August 11, 1927, Tinnie, New México[103]; m. (1) PRECILIANA TORREZ; m. (2) HELEN CHÁVEZ.

Notes for PRECILIANA TORREZ:
Also known as Pricilla.

    viii.   OLIVIA RICHARDSON, b. Private; m. JUAN JOSÉ VIGIL.

Notes for JUAN JOSÉ VIGIL:
Also known as Johnny.

    ix.   BILLY GRANVILLE RICHARDSON, b. Private; m. MARY MONTES.

Notes for BILLY GRANVILLE RICHARDSON:
Also known as Gregorio.

     x.   PHILBERT RICHARDSON, b. Private; m. (1) ALICE MONTOYA; m. (2) IRENE SALCIDO; m. (3) IRENE HERRERA.
     xi.   REBECCA DELPHINIA RICHARDSON, b. Private; m. ERVIN EUGENE TORREZ.
     xii.   JOHN SALOMON RICHARDSON, b. October 17, 1941, Hondo, New México; d. January 09, 2001, Parker, Texas; m. (1) CHERI RICHARDSON; m. (2) LYNN PEACOCK.

17. ELENA[6] RICHARDSON *(BENINA[5] LUCERO, CORNELIO[4], JOSÉ DE LA CONCEPCIÓN[3] LUSERO, PEDRO ANTONIO[2], MIGUEL[1])[104]* was born August 07, 1898 in Las Palas, Territory of New México[105], and died September 17, 1937 in Hagerman, New México. She married RAMÓN RAMÍREZ November 06, 1919 in Arabela, New México[105], son of ANTONIO RAMÍREZ and JUANITA SEDILLO.

Notes for ELENA RICHARDSON:
Also known as Lavinia.

Notes for RAMÓN RAMÍREZ:
1920 Census: Living in Las Palas, New México.

Children of ELENA RICHARDSON and RAMÓN RAMÍREZ are:
     i.   PORFIRIA[7] RAMÍREZ, b. November 30, 1920, Arabela, New México; m. (1) DAVE LUCERO; m. (2) GONZALO RAMÍREZ.
     ii.   JOSÉ RAMÍREZ, b. March 19, 1926; d. February 26, 1979, Tucson, Arizona; m. PETRA PINO.

18. MELVIN ALVINO[6] RICHARDSON *(BENINA[5] LUCERO, CORNELIO[4], JOSÉ DE LA CONCEPCIÓN[3] LUSERO, PEDRO ANTONIO[2], MIGUEL[1])[106]* was born March 15, 1902 in Arabela, Territory of New México[107], and died June 1986. He married FLORIPA LUCERO January 14, 1920 in Arabela, New México[108], daughter of PILAR LUCERO and SINFORINA GARDUÑO.

Notes for MELVIN ALVINO RICHARDSON:
Also known as Alvino.

Children of MELVIN RICHARDSON and FLORIPA LUCERO are:
     i.   MARY MARTHA[7] RICHARDSON, b. Private; m. GEORGE JOHN KAHKOSKO.
     ii.   LUCILA RICHARDSON, b. Private; m. RAMÓN GARCÍA.
     iii.   MELVIN RAÚL RICHARDSON, b. Private; m. CAROLYN BURNS.
     iv.   JOHN ARTHUR RICHARDSON, b. Private; m. HANNELIESE FRANCK.

19. AMARANTE[6] LUCERO *(DOROTEO[5], CORNELIO[4], JOSÉ DE LA CONCEPCIÓN[3] LUSERO, PEDRO ANTONIO[2], MIGUEL[1])* was born September 1886[109]. He married REBECA DE LUCERO.

Children of AMARANTE LUCERO and REBECA DE LUCERO are:
     i.   EUFRASIA[7] LUCERO, b. Abt. 1904, Arabela, Territory of New México[110]; m. PABLO FRESQUEZ[111], January 10, 1920, Arabela, New México[111].

Notes for EUFRASIA LUCERO:
Marriage records indicate that she was born on May 01, 1902. (Book of Marriages, Lincoln County. Book 5, Page 54)

Notes for PABLO FRESQUEZ:
1930 Census: Living in Arabela, New México.

     ii.   CORNELIO LUCERO, b. Abt. 1913[112]; m. ANTONIA ANALLA.

Notes for ANTONIA ANALLA:
Also known as Tonita.

     iii.   VERONICA LUCERO, b. June 28, 1918, Arabela, New México[113]; m. MELCOR CHÁVEZ, June 23, 1945, Carrizozo, New México[113].

Notes for MELCOR CHÁVEZ:
Marriage Records 1945: Living in Roswell, New México.

      iv.   LUCÍA LUCERO[114], b. April 10, 1920, Arabela, New México[115]; m. BONIFACIO FRESQUEZ, April 13, 1940, Carrizozo, New México[116].

      v.   ELENA LUCERO, b. Abt. 1922, Arabela, New México[117]; m. DANIEL TRUJILLO.

      vi.   ARISTEO LUCERO[118], b. February 12, 1925, Arabela, New México[119].

      vii.   ALONE LUCERO, b. Abt. 1926[119].

      viii.   BALSON LUCERO, b. Abt. 1929[119].

20. ELVIRA[6] LUCERO *(DOROTEO[5], CORNELIO[4], JOSÉ DE LA CONCEPCIÓN[3] LUSERO, PEDRO ANTONIO[2], MIGUEL[1])* was born December 24, 1895[120], and died April 1966 in Tularosa, New México. She married JOSÉ DE JESÚS SÁNCHEZ August 09, 1911 in Las Palas, Territory of New México[121], son of IGENIO SÁNCHEZ and NICOLÁSA MAÉS.

Notes for JOSÉ DE JESÚS SÁNCHEZ:
Also known as José de Jesús Sánchez.

Children of ELVIRA LUCERO and JOSÉ SÁNCHEZ are:
      i.   ESTEFANA LUCERO[7] SÁNCHEZ, b. December 26, 1912, Las Palas, New México[122]; m. ELOY V. CANDELARIA[123], March 01, 1930, Carrizozo, New México[124].

Notes for ESTEFANA LUCERO SÁNCHEZ:
Also known as Estefanita.

      ii.   VENERANDA SÁNCHEZ, b. August 1914, Las Palas, New México[125]; m. VALOIS FELIX CANDELARIA.

      iii.   ANATALIO SÁNCHEZ, b. August 1918, Arabela, New México[125]; m. ELVIRA MONTOYA.

Notes for ANATALIO SÁNCHEZ:
Also known as Anatalio.

      iv.   EVARISTO LUCERO SÁNCHEZ, b. June 09, 1920, Arabela, New México[126]; d. November 24, 2001, Merced, California; m. FLORA MONTOYA, December 20, 1946, Carrizozo, New México[126].

Notes for EVARISTO LUCERO SÁNCHEZ:
1930 Census: Living in Arabela, New México.

Notes for FLORA MONTOYA:
1930 Census: Living in Encinoso, New México.

      v.   DELUVINA SÁNCHEZ, b. Abt. 1922, Arabela, New México[127]; d. Tularosa, New México; m. VICTORIANO GALLEGOS.

21. GEORGE[6] LUCERO *(APOLONIO[5], CORNELIO[4], JOSÉ DE LA CONCEPCIÓN[3] LUSERO, PEDRO ANTONIO[2], MIGUEL[1])[128]* was born January 25, 1899 in Las Palas, Territory of New México[129], and died October 1970 in Roswell, New México. He married ANITA CARRILLO ANALLA[130] May 21, 1921 in Arabela, New México[131], daughter of JOSÉ CARRILLO and CRUSITA ARCHULETA.

Notes for ANITA CARRILLO ANALLA:
Anita often went by the name, Anita Analla, because she was raised with an Analla family in Arabela, New México. She was raised by the Analla family after her mother passed away when she was about four years old. She also went by Anita Torrez. Marriage records indicate that she was born on July 26, 1905.
1910 Census: Lists her parents as José Carrillo and Crusita. Her listed name was Tonita.
1920 Census: Living with her cousin, Julio Vigil in Las Palas, Territory of New México.

Child of GEORGE LUCERO and ANITA ANALLA is:
      i.   ORLANDO[7] LUCERO[132], b. July 18, 1923, Roswell, New México[133]; d. February 15, 2004; m. ERLINDA GONZÁLES, July 18, 1942, Carrizozo, New México[133].

Notes for ORLANDO LUCERO:
Private First Class. World War II.

22. FRED[6] MCTEIGUE *(INEZ[5] LUCERO, CORNELIO[4], JOSÉ DE LA CONCEPCIÓN[3] LUSERO, PEDRO ANTONIO[2], MIGUEL[1])[134]* was born June 27, 1897 in Agua Azul, Territory of New México[135], and died January 30, 1968 in Hondo, New México. He married CLEOTILDE LUCERO[136] January 10, 1920 in Arabela, New México[136], daughter of PILAR LUCERO and SINFORINA GARDUÑO.

Notes for FRED MCTEIGUE:
Also known as Fredrico.
1930 Census: Living in Roswell, New México.

Children of FRED MCTEIGUE and CLEOTILDE LUCERO are:

    i.   LINCOLN NICOLAS[7] MCTEIGUE[137], b. December 06, 1920, Arabela, New México[138]; d. July 03, 1989, Hondo, New México.

    ii.   MCKINLEY MCTEIGUE[139], b. March 09, 1923, Arabela, New México[140]; m. NAVORA SÁNCHEZ, June 22, 1951, Lincoln, New México[141].

    iii.   BILL MCTEIGUE[142], b. February 16, 1925, Clovis, New México[143].

    iv.   LUCÍA MCTEIGUE, b. December 12, 1928, Roswell, New México[144]; m. MONROY SÁNCHEZ[145], February 04, 1950, Lincoln, New México[146].

Notes for MONROY SÁNCHEZ:
Also known as Monroe. Buried in the Hondo Cemetery.
December 4, 1943: Enlisted in the Army. He was a World War Two Veteran.

    v.   ALFRED MCTEIGUE, b. May 27, 1931, Roswell, New México[147]; d. 2003; m. RAMONA SALAS[148], November 17, 1962, Hondo, New México[149].

    vi.   JIMMY MCTEIGUE, b. Private.

23. DUDLEY[6] RUE *(INEZ[5] LUCERO, CORNELIO[4], JOSÉ DE LA CONCEPCIÓN[3] LUSERO, PEDRO ANTONIO[2], MIGUEL[1])* was born May 10, 1910[150], and died June 12, 1963 in Arabela, New México[151]. He married MABEL CARABAJAL SÁNCHEZ, daughter of SIMÓN SÁNCHEZ and ANTONIA CARABAJAL.

Notes for DUDLEY RUE:
Natural father was A. H. Rue.

Children of DUDLEY RUE and MABEL SÁNCHEZ are:

    i.   FLOYD[7] RUE, b. August 30, 1930; d. December 23, 2004.

    ii.   ANDY RUE, b. August 15, 1937; d. February 12, 2003, Santa Fé, New México; m. MARION MARTINDALE.

    iii.   JOE RUE, b. October 02, 1938; d. November 01, 2004, Albuquerque, New México; m. MARY RUE.

    iv.   FELIX AMABLE RUE, b. September 03, 1941, Arabela, New México; d. September 23, 2005, Albuquerque, New México; m. EVA BENTLEY.

    v.   JIMMY RUE, b. April 03, 1946; d. November 11, 2002, Ruidoso Downs, New México.

    vi.   MELVIN RUE, b. August 16, 1949; d. June 01, 1978, Roswell, New México.

    vii.   AMOS RUE, b. Private.

    viii.   CHARMAINE RUE, b. Private.

    ix.   IRENE RUE, b. Private.

    x.   LOUIS RUE, b. Private.

    xi.   RICHARD RUE, b. Private.

    xii.   TOBY RUE, b. Private.

24. GEORGE[6] RUE *(INEZ[5] LUCERO, CORNELIO[4], JOSÉ DE LA CONCEPCIÓN[3] LUSERO, PEDRO ANTONIO[2], MIGUEL[1])* was born October 13, 1913 in Arabela, New México[152], and died August 16, 1987 in Ruidoso Downs, New México. He married LEONOR BENAVIDEZ May 29, 1934 in Arabela, New México[152], daughter of TIBURCIO BENAVIDEZ and ANTONIA ANALLA.

Notes for GEORGE RUE:
Natural father was A. H. Rue.

Notes for LEONOR BENAVIDEZ:
Raised by Elías Baca and Pablita Analla de Baca.

Children of GEORGE RUE and LEONOR BENAVIDEZ are:

  i.   INEZ[7] RUE, b. August 11, 1941, Arabela, New México[153]; m. PROSPERO F. GONZÁLES, April 25, 1959, Ruidoso Downs, New México[153].
  ii.   BARNEY RUE, b. August 21, 1939, Blue Water, New México[154]; m. LYDIA CHÁVEZ, May 23, 1959, Ruidoso, New México[154].

Genealogy of José Miguel Lucero

Generation No. 1

1. JOSÉ MIGUEL[1] LUCERO was born Abt. 1800[1]. He married LUCIANA TORRES.

Notes for JOSÉ MIGUEL LUCERO:
Also known as Miguel.
1850 Census: Living in Manzano, Territory of New México.
1860 & 1870: Census: Living in Punta de Agua, Territory of New México.
1880 Census: Living in La Junta, Territory of New México.

Children of JOSÉ LUCERO and LUCIANA TORRES are:
2.   i.   MARÍA[2] LUCERO, b. Abt. 1828, Manzano, Nuevo México, La República de México.
         ii.   SANTIAGO LUCERO, b. Abt. 1830, Manzano, Nuevo México, La República de México[2].
         iii.   MANUEL LUCERO, b. Abt. 1832, Manzano, Nuevo México, La República de México[2].
         iv.   MIGUEL LUCERO, b. Abt. 1836[2].
         v.   JOSÉ ANTONIO LUCERO, b. Abt. 1841, Manzano, Nuevo México, La República de México[3].
         vi.   DOLORES LUCERO, b. Abt. 1846, Manzano, Nuevo México, La República de México[3].
         vii.   SENOVIO LUCERO, b. Abt. 1854, Punta del Agua, Territory of New México[3].

Notes for SENOVIO LUCERO:
Died young.

         viii.   ANDREA LUCERO, b. Abt. 1855, Punta del Agua, Territory of New México[4].
         ix.   CRISTINA LUCERO, b. Abt. 1858, Punta del Agua, Territory of New México.

Generation No. 2

2. MARÍA[2] LUCERO *(JOSÉ MIGUEL[1])* was born Abt. 1828 in Manzano, Nuevo México, La República de México[5]. She married RAFAEL CASTILLO.

Notes for MARÍA LUCERO:
1850 Census: living in Manzano, Territory of New México.
1870 Census: Living in Punta de Agua, Territory of New México.
1880 Census: Living in La Junta, Territory of New México.

Notes for RAFAEL CASTILLO:
1860 Census: Living in Rio Bonito, Socorro County, Territory of New México.

Children of MARÍA LUCERO and RAFAEL CASTILLO are:
         i.   SENOVIO[3] CASTILLO, b. Abt. 1860[6].

Notes for SENOVIO CASTILLO:
Also known as Cenobio.

3.   ii.   CRISTINA CASTILLO, b. July 1866, Manzano, Territory of New México; d. July 30, 1934, San Patricio, New México.

Generation No. 3

3. CRISTINA[3] CASTILLO *(MARÍA[2] LUCERO, JOSÉ MIGUEL[1])* was born July 1866 in Manzano, Territory of New México[7], and died July 30, 1934 in San Patricio, New México[8]. She married JUAN DE DIOS ROMERO Abt. 1880[9], son of JOSÉ ROMERO and CORNELIA SISNEROS.

Notes for CRISTINA CASTILLO:
Raised by her grandparents, José Miguel Lucero & Luciana. She had an aunt, Lola Guerra.

Buried at La Capilla de San Patricio.

Children of CRISTINA CASTILLO and JUAN ROMERO are:

	i.	MANUEL[4] ROMERO, b. Abt. 1879[10].
4.	ii.	GEORGE ROMERO, b. July 14, 1880, Picacho, Territory of New México; d. February 21, 1948, Hagerman, New México.
5.	iii.	MERENCIANA ROMERO, b. August 1883, Picacho, Territory of New México.
6.	iv.	CAROLINA ROMERO, b. January 22, 1884, Picacho, Territory of New México.
7.	v.	DELFINIA ROMERO, b. December 12, 1885, Picacho, Territory of New México; d. November 13, 1926, San Patricio, New México.
8.	vi.	LUPITA ROMERO, b. December 12, 1888, San Patricio, Territory of New México; d. 1969, Picacho, New México.
9.	vii.	MARÍA ROMERO, b. January 19, 1891, San Patricio, Territory of New México; d. March 21, 1976, Roswell, New México.
10.	viii.	ANTONIO ROMERO, b. December 12, 1892, San Patricio, Territory of New México; d. February 06, 1942, San Patricio, New México.
	ix.	ARISTOTEL ROMERO[11], b. March 15, 1896, San Patricio, Territory of New México[12]; d. January 02, 1964; m. FRANCISQUITA CHÁVEZ[13], 1936[14].
11.	x.	LUCÍA ROMERO, b. December 06, 1896, San Patricio, Territory of New México.
12.	xi.	MANUEL CASTILLO ROMERO, b. October 06, 1899, San Patricio, Territory of New México; d. October 1982, Silver City, New México.

Generation No. 4

4. GEORGE[4] ROMERO *(CRISTINA[3] CASTILLO, MARÍA[2] LUCERO, JOSÉ MIGUEL[1])* was born July 14, 1880 in Picacho, Territory of New México[15], and died February 21, 1948 in Hagerman, New México[16]. He married (1) AURORA GONZÁLES[17] November 19, 1900[18], daughter of FLORENCIO GONZÁLES and RAYMUNDA SÁNCHEZ. He married (2) JOSEFITA TORRES[19] October 25, 1913 in Picacho, New México[20], daughter of EUSEVIO TORRES and EMILIA MUÑOZ.

Children of GEORGE ROMERO and AURORA GONZÁLES are:

| 13. | i. | SIGISFREDO[5] ROMERO, b. March 31, 1903; d. November 14, 1982, San Patricio, New México. |
| 14. | ii. | MELITANA ROMERO, b. February 16, 1902. |

Children of GEORGE ROMERO and JOSEFITA TORRES are:

15.	iii.	GEORGE TORRES[5] ROMERO, b. May 12, 1914, San Patricio, New México; d. July 11, 1991.
16.	iv.	JUAN ROMERO, b. September 02, 1916, San Patricio, New México; d. February 15, 1988, Hagerman, New México.
	v.	GODFREY ROMERO, b. Abt. November 1919, San Patricio, New México[21].
17.	vi.	CRISTINA ROMERO, b. November 08, 1919, San Patricio, New México; d. October 28, 1985, San Patricio, New México.
	vii.	PATRICIO ROMERO[22], b. March 18, 1929, San Patricio, New México; d. June 15, 1953, Hagerman, New México.
	viii.	BEATRICE ROMERO, b. Private, San Patricio, New México.
	ix.	EFREN ROMERO, b. Private, San Patricio, New México.
	x.	EMILIA ROMERO, b. Private, San Patricio, New México.
	xi.	LUISA ROMERO, b. Private, San Patricio, New México.

5. MERENCIANA[4] ROMERO *(CRISTINA[3] CASTILLO, MARÍA[2] LUCERO, JOSÉ MIGUEL[1])* was born August 1883 in Picacho, Territory of New México[23]. She married (1) AVESLÍN TORRES, son of JUAN TORRES and RITA DE TORRES. She married (2) ALFRED MICKS[24].

Children of MERENCIANA ROMERO and AVESLÍN TORRES are:

| | i. | RUBÉN[5] TORRES. |
| | ii. | MIGUEL ANTONIO ROMERO[25], b. March 27, 1904, San Patricio, Territory of New México; d. November 19, 1946; m. FRANCISCA TRUJILLO[25], September 16, 1928[26]. |

6. CAROLINA[4] ROMERO *(CRISTINA[3] CASTILLO, MARÍA[2] LUCERO, JOSÉ MIGUEL[1])* was born January 22, 1884 in Picacho, Territory of New México[27]. She married ANTONIO SÁNCHEZ January 09, 1901[28], son of FRANCISCO SÁNCHEZ and CONCEPCIÓN TRUJILLO.

Children of CAROLINA ROMERO and ANTONIO SÁNCHEZ are:
- i. ANEDA ROMERO[5] SÁNCHEZ, b. San Patricio, New México.
- ii. ANGELITA ROMERO SÁNCHEZ, b. San Patricio, New México.
- iii. JOSEFITA ROMERO SÁNCHEZ, b. San Patricio, New México.
- iv. CONCEPCIÓN SÁNCHEZ, b. Abt. 1902, San Patricio, Territory of New México[29].
- 18. v. MARGARITA ROMERO SÁNCHEZ, b. August 22, 1903, San Patricio, Territory of New México; d. January 31, 2004, Artesia, New México.
- vi. ISMAÉL SÁNCHEZ, b. 1916, San Patricio, New México[30].
- vii. JESÚSITA ROMERO SÁNCHEZ, b. Abt. 1926, San Patricio, New México[31].

7. DELFINIA[4] ROMERO *(CRISTINA[3] CASTILLO, MARÍA[2] LUCERO, JOSÉ MIGUEL[1])* was born December 12, 1885 in Picacho, Territory of New México[32], and died November 13, 1926 in San Patricio, New México[33]. She married MAURICIO SÁNCHEZ January 09, 1901 in San Patricio, Territory of New México[34], son of FRANCISCO SÁNCHEZ and CONCEPCIÓN TRUJILLO.

Children of DELFINIA ROMERO and MAURICIO SÁNCHEZ are:
- i. JOSÉ ROMERO[5] SÁNCHEZ, b. San Patricio, New México.
- ii. JUANITA SÁNCHEZ[35], b. February 08, 1902, San Patricio, Territory of New México[36]; d. December 06, 1975, Ruidoso, New México; m. RAMÓN TORRES, June 13, 1918, Glencoe, New Mexico[37].
- 19. iii. ROMÁN SÁNCHEZ, b. April 23, 1904, San Patricio, Territory of New México; d. February 08, 1973, Ruidoso, New México.
- 20. iv. MAXIMILIANO SÁNCHEZ, b. June 22, 1911, San Patricio, Territory of New México; d. April 15, 1972.
- v. MABEL ROMERO SÁNCHEZ[38], b. Abt. 1915, San Patricio, New México[39]; d. April 02, 1929, San Patricio, New México.
- 21. vi. MARÍA SÁNCHEZ, b. April 19, 1919, San Patricio, New México; d. July 31, 1966, Los Lunas, New México.
- 22. vii. JESÚSITA SÁNCHEZ, b. September 19, 1922, San Patricio, New México; d. July 16, 1992, Albuquerque, New México.

8. LUPITA[4] ROMERO *(CRISTINA[3] CASTILLO, MARÍA[2] LUCERO, JOSÉ MIGUEL[1])* was born December 12, 1888 in San Patricio, Territory of New México[40], and died 1969 in Picacho, New México[41]. She married GEORGE ORTEGA KIMBRELL January 03, 1920 in Carrizozo, New México[42], son of JUAN KIMBRELL and DOMISINDA ORTEGA.

Children of LUPITA ROMERO and GEORGE KIMBRELL are:
- 23. i. ELSIE ROMERO[5] KIMBRELL, b. 1922.
- ii. WILLIAM KIMBRELL[43], b. June 20, 1925, Picacho, New México[44].
- iii. ELIZABETH KIMBRELL[45], b. September 15, 1928[46]; d. January 11, 1989.
- iv. JOHN ROMERO KIMBRELL, b. Private.

9. MARÍA[4] ROMERO *(CRISTINA[3] CASTILLO, MARÍA[2] LUCERO, JOSÉ MIGUEL[1])*[47] was born January 19, 1891 in San Patricio, Territory of New México[48], and died March 21, 1976 in Roswell, New México. She married HILARIO GÓMEZ[49] June 25, 1917 in Lincoln, New México[50], son of FELIPÉ GÓMEZ and MIQUELA LUCERO.

Children of MARIA ROMERO and HILARIO GÓMEZ are:
- i. ELISEO[5] GÓMEZ[51], b. January 05, 1919, San Patricio, New México; d. October 06, 1992, Los Lunas, New México; m. ROSA CHÁVEZ.
- ii. MIQUELA GÓMEZ, b. October 28, 1924, Glencoe, New México; d. April 08, 1983, Roswell, New México; m. GEORGE MENDOZA, September 28, 1944, San Patricio, New México[52].
- iii. JOSÉ ENRÍQUEZ GÓMEZ[53], b. Abt. 1929, Glencoe, New México; d. May 05, 1929, San Patricio, New México.

10. ANTONIO[4] ROMERO *(CRISTINA[3] CASTILLO, MARÍA[2] LUCERO, JOSÉ MIGUEL[1])*[54] was born December 12, 1892 in San Patricio, Territory of New México[55], and died February 06, 1942 in San Patricio, New México. He married CAROLINA SILVA June 21, 1916 in Carrizozo, New México[55], daughter of MANUEL SILVA and LEONARDA JIRÓN.

Children of ANTONIO ROMERO and CAROLINA SILVA are:
- i. ESTER[5] ROMERO, b. Abt. 1916[56].
- ii. ARISTOTEL SILVA ROMERO, b. Abt. 1917[56].
- iii. MANUEL SILVA ROMERO, b. Abt. 1920[56].

iv. PRESILIANA ROMERO, b. January 13, 1924, Tinnie, New México[57]; m. DANIEL LUCERO, November 26, 1941, Carrizozo, New México[57].

v. PABLO SILVA ROMERO, b. Abt. 1927[58].

vi. DELFINIA SILVA ROMERO, b. Private.

vii. LEONARDA ROMERO, b. Private.

11. LUCÍA[4] ROMERO *(CRISTINA[3] CASTILLO, MARÍA[2] LUCERO, JOSÉ MIGUEL[1])* was born December 06, 1896 in San Patricio, Territory of New México[59]. She married (1) JOSÉ D. ARCHULETA[60] February 15, 1915 in Lincoln, Territory of New México[60], son of LUCIO ARCHULETA and YSABEL JIRÓN. She married (2) JUAN RUBIO July 21, 1925 in Hondo, New México[61].

Child of LUCÍA ROMERO and JOSÉ ARCHULETA is:

24.　　i.　　DOLORES ROMERO[5] ARCHULETA, b. February 03, 1916, White Oaks, New México; d. June 07, 1986, San Patricio, New México.

12. MANUEL CASTILLO[4] ROMERO *(CRISTINA[3] CASTILLO, MARÍA[2] LUCERO, JOSÉ MIGUEL[1])*[62] was born October 06, 1899 in San Patricio, Territory of New México[63], and died October 1982 in Silver City, New México. He married ESTELA GÓMEZ[64] May 30, 1930 in Carrizozo, New México[65], daughter of FELIPÉ GÓMEZ and BEATRIZ SEDILLO.

Child of MANUEL ROMERO and ESTELA GÓMEZ is:

i.　　LUCILLE[5] ROMERO, b. Private; Adopted child.

Generation No. 5

13. SIGISFREDO[5] ROMERO *(GEORGE[4], CRISTINA[3] CASTILLO, MARÍA[2] LUCERO, JOSÉ MIGUEL[1])*[66] was born March 31, 1903, and died November 14, 1982 in San Patricio, New México. He married LUCÍA YBARRA January 11, 1928 in Lincoln County, New México[67], daughter of GREGORIO YBARRA and CATARINA MONTOYA.

Notes for LUCÍA YBARRA:
Also known as Luciana, Luz.
Padrinos: Augustín Laguna born in México City, and his wife, Juana María Laguna, born in Polvadera, New México

Children of SIGISFREDO ROMERO and LUCÍA YBARRA are:

i.　　FEDELINA[6] ROMERO, b. March 28, 1932, San Patricio, New México[68]; m. ELMON RANDOLPH[69], July 01, 1950, Carrizozo, New México[70].

ii.　　CLEOFAS ROMERO[71], b. April 09, 1934, San Patricio, New México; d. March 17, 2007; m. JUAN SÁNCHEZ MONTES[71], August 25, 1951, Ruidoso, New México[72].

iii.　　SIGISFREDO YBARRA ROMERO[73], b. August 08, 1949, San Patricio, New México; d. May 24, 2010, San Patricio, New México.

iv.　　EDUVIGEN ROMERO, b. Private, San Patricio, New México.

v.　　FLORIPE ROMERO, b. Private, San Patricio, New México.

vi.　　ISABELA ROMERO, b. Private, San Patricio, New México.

vii.　　LEONIRES ROMERO, b. Private, San Patricio, New México.

viii.　　REBECCA ROMERO, b. Private, San Patricio, New México.

ix.　　RUBÉN ROMERO, b. Private, San Patricio, New México.

14. MELITANA[5] ROMERO *(GEORGE[4], CRISTINA[3] CASTILLO, MARÍA[2] LUCERO, JOSÉ MIGUEL[1])* was born February 16, 1902[74]. She married PATROCINIO ARCHULETA CHÁVEZ[75] July 13, 1921[76], son of PATROCINIO CHÁVEZ and VICENTA ARCHULETA.

Notes for MELITANA ROMERO:
Also known as Meritana.

Children of MELITANA ROMERO and PATROCINIO CHÁVEZ are:

i.　　GABRIEL[6] CHÁVEZ[77], b. 1922, Hondo, New México[78]; d. June 07, 1942, Lincoln, New México.

ii.　　AURELIA CHÁVEZ, b. Abt. 1925, Hondo, New México[78].

  iii. BRIGIDA CHÁVEZ, b. Abt. 1926, Hondo, New México[78].

  iv. ORALIA CHÁVEZ[79], b. Abt. 1927, San Patricio, New México; d. April 20, 1928, San Patricio, New México.

  v. GLORIA CHÁVEZ, b. Abt. 1929, Hondo, New México[80].

  vi. ADAN CHÁVEZ, b. Private, Hondo, New México.

  vii. MOISES CHÁVEZ, b. Private, Hondo, New México.

  viii. NORA CHÁVEZ, b. Private, Hondo, New México.

  ix. RAY CHÁVEZ, b. Private, Hondo, New México.

  x. VIRGINIA ROMERO CHÁVEZ, b. Private, Hondo, New México.

15. GEORGE TORRES[5] ROMERO *(GEORGE[4], CRISTINA[3] CASTILLO, MARÍA[2] LUCERO, JOSÉ MIGUEL[1])[81]* was born May 12, 1914 in San Patricio, New México[82], and died July 11, 1991. He married JULIANITA WARNER November 10, 1934 in San Patricio, New México[83], daughter of JUAN WARNER and EMILIA TORREZ.

16. JUAN[5] ROMERO *(GEORGE[4], CRISTINA[3] CASTILLO, MARÍA[2] LUCERO, JOSÉ MIGUEL[1])[88]* was born September 02, 1916 in San Patricio, New México, and died February 15, 1988 in Hagerman, New México. He married ENEDINA ROMERO[88].

Child of JUAN ROMERO and ENEDINA ROMERO is:

  i. JERRY DEAN[6] ROMERO[88], b. April 19, 1957, Hagerman, New México; d. April 20, 1957, Hagerman, New México.

17. CRISTINA[5] ROMERO *(GEORGE[4], CRISTINA[3] CASTILLO, MARÍA[2] LUCERO, JOSÉ MIGUEL[1])[89]* was born November 08, 1919 in San Patricio, New México[90], and died October 28, 1985 in San Patricio, New México. She married ARISTEO CHÁVEZ[91] February 10, 1936 in San Patricio, New México[92], son of TRANCITO CHÁVEZ and ANGELITA CHÁVEZ.

18. MARGARITA ROMERO[5] SÁNCHEZ *(CAROLINA[4] ROMERO, CRISTINA[3] CASTILLO, MARÍA[2] LUCERO, JOSÉ MIGUEL[1])[94]* was born August 22, 1903 in San Patricio, Territory of New México[95], and died January 31, 2004 in Artesia, New México. She married ROBERTO PÉREZ[96] Abt. 1929 in Crowley, Colorado[97].

Child of MARGARITA SÁNCHEZ and ROBERTO PÉREZ is:

  i. HELEN L.[6] PÉREZ, b. March 1930, Crowley, Colorado[97].

19. ROMÁN[5] SÁNCHEZ *(DELFINIA[4] ROMERO, CRISTINA[3] CASTILLO, MARÍA[2] LUCERO, JOSÉ MIGUEL[1])[98]* was born April 23, 1904 in San Patricio, Territory of New México[99], and died February 08, 1973 in Ruidoso, New México. He married FLORINDA SALSBERRY[100] February 20, 1927 in Mescalero, New Mexico[101], daughter of JAMES SALSBERRY and MANUELITA HERRERA.

Children of ROMÁN SÁNCHEZ and FLORINDA SALSBERRY are:

  i. ERNESTO[6] SÁNCHEZ, b. April 09, 1928, San Patricio, New México[102]; m. ORALIA CHÁVEZ, March 20, 1948, Ruidoso, New México[102].

  ii. MADELENA SÁNCHEZ[103], b. Abt. 1930, San Patricio, New México; d. December 19, 1932, San Patricio, New México.

  iii. DELFINIA OLIDIA SÁNCHEZ, b. April 18, 1934, High Rolls, New México; m. LEANDRO VEGA, December 27, 1958, Hondo, New México.

  iv. ORLANDO SÁNCHEZ, b. April 03, 1936, San Patricio, New México.

  v. FLORA MARÍA SÁNCHEZ, b. March 24, 1938, Capítan, New México; m. RICHARD VEGA.

  vi. FRED SÁNCHEZ, b. May 30, 1940, Fort Stanton, New México[104]; m. BERTA HERRERA, July 26, 1959, Ruidoso, New México[104].

  vii. BREZEL ROBERT SÁNCHEZ, b. November 04, 1941, Capítan, New México[105]; m. MINNIE ROMERO, June 15, 1963, Hondo, New México[105].

  viii. GERALDINE ELSIE SÁNCHEZ, b. January 10, 1945, San Patricio, New México; m. ROBERT MONTES.

  ix. LUVÍN SÁNCHEZ, b. October 23, 1947, San Patricio, New México; m. (1) GLORIA BACA; m. (2) FRANCES SEDILLO.

  x. CYNTHIA VIOLANDA SÁNCHEZ[106], b. September 10, 1950, Capítan, New México[107]; d. April 27, 1986, Rio Rancho, New México; m. BERRY VANDERWALL, December 22, 1972, San Patricio, New México[107].

  xi. MAURICIO SÁNCHEZ, b. Abt. 1952, San Patricio, New México.

  xii. ROMÁN SÁNCHEZ, JR., b. March 13, 1954, San Patricio, New México[108]; m. YOVANNE SALAS, May 25, 1974, Ruidoso, New México[108].

20. MAXIMILIANO[5] SÁNCHEZ *(DELFINIA[4] ROMERO, CRISTINA[3] CASTILLO, MARÍA[2] LUCERO, JOSÉ MIGUEL[1])* was born June 22, 1911 in San Patricio, Territory of New México[109], and died April 15, 1972. He married SORAIDA SÁNCHEZ February 11, 1936 in Carrizozo, New México[109], daughter of AURELIO SÁNCHEZ and ANASTACIA ARAGÓN.

Children of MAXIMILIANO SÁNCHEZ and SORAIDA SÁNCHEZ are:
    i.   BEATRICE[6] SÁNCHEZ, b. Private.
    ii.   ROSEMARY SÁNCHEZ, b. Private.

21. MARÍA[5] SÁNCHEZ *(DELFINIA[4] ROMERO, CRISTINA[3] CASTILLO, MARÍA[2] LUCERO, JOSÉ MIGUEL[1])* was born April 19, 1919 in San Patricio, New México[110], and died July 31, 1966 in Los Lunas, New México. She married MANUEL CHÁVEZ, son of PREDICANDO CHÁVEZ and REMEDIOS VIGIL.

22. JESÚSITA[5] SÁNCHEZ *(DELFINIA[4] ROMERO, CRISTINA[3] CASTILLO, MARÍA[2] LUCERO, JOSÉ MIGUEL[1])* was born September 19, 1922 in San Patricio, New México, and died July 16, 1992 in Albuquerque, New México. She married MAX SILVA November 16, 1942 in Tomé, New México[111].

23. ELSIE ROMERO[5] KIMBRELL *(LUPITA[4] ROMERO, CRISTINA[3] CASTILLO, MARÍA[2] LUCERO, JOSÉ MIGUEL[1])* was born 1922[112].

24. DOLORES ROMERO[5] ARCHULETA *(LUCÍA[4] ROMERO, CRISTINA[3] CASTILLO, MARÍA[2] LUCERO, JOSÉ MIGUEL[1])*[113] was born February 03, 1916 in White Oaks, New México, and died June 07, 1986 in San Patricio, New México. She married AMARANTE CHÁVEZ[113] September 21, 1936 in San Patricio, New México[114], son of YSIDRO CHÁVEZ and PAUBLITA SÁNCHEZ.

Genealogy of Miguel de San Juan de Luna

Generation No. 1

1. FRANCISCO[2] XAVIER *(FRANCISCO[1])* was born Abt. 1655. He married JUANA BACA, daughter of CRISTÓBAL BACA and ANA DE LARA.

Children of FRANCISCO XAVIER and JUANA BACA are:

2. i. MIGUEL DE SAN JUAN[3] DE LUNA, b. Abt. 1687, Guadalupe del Paso, El Reyno de Nuevo México, Nueva España.
    ii. JOSEFA XAVIER[1], b. Abt. 1688; d. January 20, 1735[2]; m. LUIS GARCÍA, August 08, 1704, Bernalillo, El Reyno de Nuevo México, Nueva España[3].
3. iii. JUANA BACA, b. Abt. 1698.
4. iv. MARÍA ANTONIA BACA, b. Abt. 1703; d. February 15, 1770.

Generation No. 2

2. MIGUEL DE SAN JUAN[3] DE LUNA *(FRANCISCO[2] XAVIER, FRANCISCO[1])[4]* was born Abt. 1687 in Guadalupe del Paso, El Reyno de Nuevo México, Nueva España. He married ISABEL MONTOYA[4] May 08, 1710 in Bernalillo, El Reyno de Nuevo México, Nueva España[5], daughter of DIEGO MONTOYA and JOSEFA DE HINOJOS.

Notes for MIGUEL DE SAN JUAN DE LUNA:
1716: Participated in the Moquí Campaign.

Children of MIGUEL DE LUNA and ISABEL MONTOYA are:

5. i. JOAQUÍN[4] DE LUNA.
    ii. MARGARITA DE SAN JUAN DE LUNA.

3. JUANA[3] BACA *(FRANCISCO[2] XAVIER, FRANCISCO[1])[6]* was born Abt. 1698. She married FRANCISCO DURÁN Y CHÁVES[7] May 15, 1713 in Bernalillo, El Reyno de Nuevo México, Nueva España[8], son of FERNANDO CHÁVES and LUCÍA DE SALAS.

Notes for JUANA BACA:
1750 Census: Alburquerque

Notes for FRANCISCO DURÁN Y CHÁVES:
October 4, 1693: Member of the 1693 Vargas reconquest.

Child of JUANA BACA and FRANCISCO CHÁVES is:

6. i. ANTONIA DURÁN Y[4] CHÁVES.

4. MARÍA ANTONIA[3] BACA *(FRANCISCO[2] XAVIER, FRANCISCO[1])* was born Abt. 1703[9], and died February 15, 1770[10]. She married DIEGO ANTONIO DURÁN Y CHÁVES[11] March 23, 1718 in Bernalillo, El Reyno de Nuevo México, Nueva España[12], son of FERNANDO CHÁVES and LUCÍA DE SALAS.

Children of MARÍA BACA and DIEGO CHÁVES are:

7. i. TOMÁS FRANCISCO DURÁN Y[4] CHÁVES, b. Abt. 1718, Alburquerque, El Reyno de Nuevo México, Nueva España; d. Uña de Gato, El Reyno de Nuevo México, Nueva España.
8. ii. JOSÉ ANASTACIO DURÁN Y CHÁVES, b. Abt. 1733, Alburquerque, El Reyno de Nuevo México, Nueva España; d. March 15, 1798, Los Garcia, El Reyno de Nuevo México, Nueva España.
9. iii. FELICIANA DURÁN Y CHÁVES.

Generation No. 3

Joaquín de Luna

5. JOAQUÍN[4] DE LUNA *(MIGUEL DE SAN JUAN[3], FRANCISCO[2] XAVIER, FRANCISCO[1])[13]*. He married (1) JUANA ANGELA DE SALAZAR[13]. He married (2) MARÍA TORRES July 17, 1743[14].

Children of JOAQUÍN DE LUNA and JUANA DE SALAZAR are:

i. TOMÁS[5] DE LUNA[15], m. MARGARITA ANTONIA SENA, September 16, 1773, San Felipé, El Reyno de Nuevo México, Nueva España[16].

ii. MIGUEL DE SAN JUAN DE LUNA, b. September 10, 1745, El Nacimiento, El Reyno de Nuevo México, Nueva España[17]; m. MARÍA CATALINA VALDÉS, February 18, 1772, Alburquerque, El Reyno de Nuevo México, Nueva España[18].

10. iii. BERNARDO PAULO DE LUNA, b. July 09, 1747, Los Padillas, El Reyno de Nuevo México, Nueva España.

iv. ANTONIO XAVIER DE LUNA, b. May 11, 1751[19].

v. YSIDRO DE LUNA, b. Abt. 1755.

6. ANTONIA DURÁN Y[4] CHÁVES *(JUANA[3] BACA, FRANCISCO[2] XAVIER, FRANCISCO[1])*. She married BALTASAR DE ABEYTIA March 20, 1741 in Alburquerque, El Reyno de Nuevo México, Nueva España[20].

Notes for BALTASAR DE ABEYTIA:
Also known as Baltasar de Beytia.

Child of ANTONIA CHÁVES and BALTASAR DE ABEYTIA is:

i. ROSALÍA[5] DE BEYTIA.

7. TOMÁS FRANCISCO DURÁN Y[4] CHÁVES *(MARÍA ANTONIA[3] BACA, FRANCISCO[2] XAVIER, FRANCISCO[1])[21]* was born Abt. 1718 in Alburquerque, El Reyno de Nuevo México, Nueva España[21], and died in Uña de Gato, El Reyno de Nuevo México, Nueva España. He married TOMASA PADILLA[22] December 03, 1742 in Los Padilla, El Reyno de Nuevo México, Nueva España[23].

Children of TOMÁS CHÁVES and TOMASA PADILLA are:

i. JUAN JOSÉ DURÁN Y[5] CHÁVES, b. Bef. February 04, 1745, Tomé, El Reyno de Nuevo México, Nueva España[24].

ii. ANDRÉS SEBALLOS DURÁN Y CHÁVES, b. Bef. October 28, 1746, Alburquerque, El Reyno de Nuevo México, Nueva España[25].

iii. EUGENIO FRANCISCO DURÁN Y CHÁVES, b. Bef. January 16, 1749, Alburquerque, El Reyno de Nuevo México, Nueva España[26].

iv. VICTORIANA DURÁN Y CHÁVES, b. Bef. March 27, 1751[27].

11. v. DIEGO ANTONIO DURÁN Y CHÁVES, b. Bef. December 24, 1752, Alburquerque, El Reyno de Nuevo México, Nueva España.

vi. JUAN YGNACIO DURÁN Y CHÁVES, b. Bef. February 01, 1756, Belén, El Reyno de Nuevo México, Nueva España[28].

vii. MARÍA ANTONIA DURÁN Y CHÁVES, b. Bef. November 13, 1743, Alburquerque, El Reyno de Nuevo México, Nueva España[29]; d. May 05, 1802, Tomé, El Reyno de Nuevo México, Nueva España; m. JUAN CRISTÓBAL SÁNCHES[30], November 30, 1782, Alburquerque, El Reyno de Nuevo México, Nueva España.

Notes for JUAN CRISTÓBAL SÁNCHES:
Alcálde Mayor of the Villa of Albuquerque.

8. JOSÉ ANASTACIO DURÁN Y[4] CHÁVES *(MARÍA ANTONIA[3] BACA, FRANCISCO[2] XAVIER, FRANCISCO[1])* was born Abt. 1733 in Alburquerque, El Reyno de Nuevo México, Nueva España[31], and died March 15, 1798 in Los Garcia, El Reyno de Nuevo México, Nueva España[32]. He married JUANA MARÍA BACA[33] October 15, 1758 in Isleta, El Reyno de Nuevo México, Nueva España[34], daughter of DIEGO BACA and JUANA CHÁVES.

Notes for JUANA MARÍA BACA:
1750 Census: Pajarito, El Reyno de Nuevo México, Nueva España.

Child of JOSÉ CHÁVES and JUANA BACA is:

12.   i.   MIGUEL ANTONIO BERNABÉ DURÁN Y[5] CHÁVES, b. Abt. 1768, El Reyno de Nuevo México, Nueva España.

9. FELICIANA DURÁN Y[4] CHÁVES *(MARÍA ANTONIA[3] BACA, FRANCISCO[2] XAVIER, FRANCISCO[1]).* She married DOMINGO MANUEL BACA February 22, 1746 in Albuquerque, Nuevo México, La República de México[35].

Notes for DOMINGO MANUEL BACA:
Served as Alcalde Mayor for Laguna Pueblo, El Reyno de Nuevo México, Nueva España.

Child of FELICIANA CHÁVES and DOMINGO BACA is:
13.   i.   ANTONIA NARCISA[5] BACA, b. November 29, 1750, Laguna, El Reyno de Nuevo México, Nueva España.

Generation No. 4

10. BERNARDO PAULO[5] DE LUNA *(JOAQUÍN[4], MIGUEL DE SAN JUAN[3], FRANCISCO[2] XAVIER, FRANCISCO[1])* was born July 09, 1747 in Los Padillas, El Reyno de Nuevo México, Nueva España[36]. He married MARÍA CATARINA GARCÍA[3737].

Notes for MARÍA CATARINA GARCÍA:
Also known as Catalina García de Noriega.

Children of BERNARDO DE LUNA and MARÍA GARCÍA are:
        i.   JOSÉ JOAQUÍN[6] DE LUNA, b. January 14, 1778, Alburquerque, El Reyno de Nuevo México, Nueva España[38].

Notes for JOSÉ JOAQUÍN DE LUNA:
Also known as Joseph Joaquín de Luna.

        ii.   VICENTE GERMÁN DE LUNA, b. May 27, 1780, Sandia Pueblo, El Reyno de Nuevo México, Nueva España[39].
        iii.   ISIDRO ANTONIO DE JESÚS DE LUNA, b. May 14, 1782, Sandia Pueblo, El Reyno de Nuevo México, Nueva España[39].
        iv.   MARÍA INES DE LUNA, b. Bef. January 25, 1784, Sandia Pueblo, El Reyno de Nuevo México, Nueva España[39].
        v.   MARÍA TERESA DE JESUS DE LUNA, b. Bef. July 15, 1786, Sandia Pueblo, El Reyno de Nuevo México, Nueva España[39].
        vi.   MARÍA ANTONIA DE LA ENCARNACIÓN DE LUNA, b. Bef. December 14, 1788, Sandia Pueblo, El Reyno de Nuevo México, Nueva España[39].
14.   vii.   MIGUEL SANTIAGO DE LUNA, b. Abt. 1796, Alburquerque, El Reyno de Nuevo México, Nueva España.
        viii. ANTONIA RITA DE LUNA, b. March 30, 1800, Alburquerque, El Reyno de Nuevo México, Nueva España[40].
        ix.   EUSEBIO DE LUNA, m. MARÍA DE LA LUZ LUSERO, January 10, 1797, Alburquerque, El Reyno de Nuevo México, Nueva España[41].

11. DIEGO ANTONIO DURÁN Y[5] CHÁVES *(TOMÁS FRANCISCO DURÁN Y[4], MARÍA ANTONIA[3] BACA, FRANCISCO[2] XAVIER, FRANCISCO[1])* was born Bef. December 24, 1752 in Alburquerque, El Reyno de Nuevo México, Nueva España[42]. He married MARÍA BÁRBARA SÁNCHES December 18, 1784 in Tomé, El Reyno de Nuevo México, Nueva España[43], daughter of JUAN SÁNCHES and JUANA CHÁVES.

Children of DIEGO CHÁVES and MARÍA SÁNCHES are:
        i.   FRANCISCO BERNADINO[6] CHÁVES, b. May 07, 1794[44].
        ii.   MANUEL ANTONIO CHÁVES, b. April 04, 1796[45].
        iii.   MARÍA CONCEPCIÓN MARIANA CHÁVES, b. December 05, 1798[46].
        iv.   MARÍA CANDELARIA CHÁVES, b. February 02, 1803, Los Cháves, El Reyno de Nuevo México, Nueva España[47].
        v.   MARÍA ENCARNACIÓN CHÁVES[48], b. Abt. 1810.
        vi.   FRANCISCO XAVIER CHÁVES[49], b. Abt. 1821.

Miguel Antonio Durán y Cháves

12. MIGUEL ANTONIO BERNABÉ DURÁN Y[5] CHÁVES *(JOSÉ ANASTACIO DURÁN Y[4], MARÍA ANTONIA[3] BACA, FRANCISCO[2] XAVIER, FRANCISCO[1])* was born Abt. 1768 in El Reyno de Nuevo México, Nueva España[50]. He married MARÍA GERTRUDIS VIGIL May 10, 1797 in Alburquerque, El Reyno de Nuevo México, Nueva España[51], daughter of FELIPÉ VIGIL and MARÍA ARAGÓN.

Notes for MARÍA GERTRUDIS VIGIL:
Also known as María Getrudis Bejil.

Children of MIGUEL CHÁVES and MARÍA VIGIL are:

	i.	MARÍA MICAELA[6] CHÁVES, b. Bef. May 26, 1801, Alburquerque, El Reyno de Nuevo México, Nueva España[52].
	ii.	FRANCISCO ANTONIO CHÁVES, b. March 08, 1806, Valencia, El Reyno de Nuevo México, Nueva España[53].
15.	iii.	MANUEL ANTONIO DE LOS REYES CHÁVES, b. January 02, 1812, Valencia, El Reyno de Nuevo México, Nueva España; d. Bef. 1860.
	iv.	MANUEL ANTONIO SABINO CHÁVES[54], b. December 29, 1813, Valencia, El Reyno de Nuevo México, Nueva España[55].
	v.	MARÍA TEODORA CHÁVES, b. November 05, 1815, Valencia, El Reyno de Nuevo México, Nueva España[56].
	vi.	JUANA ANDREA CHÁVES, b. February 25, 1810, Valencia, El Reyno de Nuevo México, Nueva España[57].

13. ANTONIA NARCISA[5] BACA *(FELICIANA DURÁN Yª CHÁVES, MARÍA ANTONIA[3] BACA, FRANCISCO[2] XAVIER, FRANCISCO[1])* was born November 29, 1750 in Laguna, El Reyno de Nuevo México, Nueva España[58]. She married ANTONIO FÉLIX CEDILLO[58] July 01, 1770 in Laguna, El Reyno de Nuevo México, Nueva España[58], son of ANTONIO CEDILLO and GREGORIA BAS.

Notes for ANTONIO FÉLIX CEDILLO:
1790 Mexican Colonial Census: Living in Albuquerqe. (Born 1748)

Children of ANTONIA BACA and ANTONIO CEDILLO are:

	i.	JOSÉ MANUEL[6] SEDILLO, m. MARÍA DOLÓRES PINO, October 01, 1792, Isleta, El Reyno de Nuevo México, Nueva España[59].
16.	ii.	JOSÉ BLÁS SEDILLO, b. February 20, 1777, Alburquerque, El Reyno de Nuevo México, Nueva España.
17.	iii.	JULIÁN BERNARDO SEDILLO, b. March 14, 1779, Alburquerque, El Reyno de Nuevo México, Nueva España.
	iv.	ANTONIOTORIBIO SEDILLO.

Generation No. 5

14. MIGUEL SANTIAGO[6] DE LUNA *(BERNARDO PAULO[5], JOAQUÍN[4], MIGUEL DE SAN JUAN[3], FRANCISCO[2] XAVIER, FRANCISCO[1])[60]* was born Abt. 1796 in Alburquerque, El Reyno de Nuevo México, Nueva España[61]. He married MARÍA ANASTACIA LUSERO April 22, 1821 in Albuquerque, Nuevo México, La República de México[62], daughter of JOSÉ LUSERO and GERTRUDIS PEREA.

Notes for MIGUEL SANTIAGO DE LUNA:
1845 Mexican Census: Living in Lemitar, Nuevo México, La República de México.
1850 Census: Living in Lemitar, Territory of New México.

Children of MIGUEL DE LUNA and MARÍA LUSERO are:

18.	i.	MARÍA MANUELA[7] LUNA.
19.	ii.	MARÍA YSABEL DE LUNA, b. February 20, 1822, San Fernando, Nuevo México, La República de México.
	iii.	JOSÉ GUADALUPE ANDRÉS DE LUNA, b. January 21, 1824, Tomé, Nuevo México, La República de México[63].
	iv.	MARÍA SOLEDAD DE LUNA, b. March 03, 1825, Albuquerque, Nuevo México, La República de México[64].
	v.	SOLEDAD DE ALTAGRACIA DE LUNA, b. January 06, 1827, Albuquerque, Nuevo México, La República de México[64].

Notes for SOLEDAD DE ALTAGRACIA DE LUNA:
Also known as Soledad de Altagracia de los Reyes Luna.

	vi.	MARÍA ROSALÍA DE LUNA, b. December 03, 1827, Tomé, Nuevo México, La República de México[65].

| | vii. | MARÍA DEL CARMEN DE LA CRUZ DE LUNA, b. April 30, 1829, Tomé, Nuevo México, La República de México[65]. |

vii. MARÍA DEL CARMEN DE LA CRUZ DE LUNA, b. April 30, 1829, Tomé, Nuevo México, La República de México[65].

viii. JOSÉ DE LUNA, b. June 09, 1830, Tomé, Nuevo México, La República de México[65].

ix. SERAFINA DE LUNA, b. Abt. 1832[66].

20.   x. JOSÉ MIGUEL DE LUNA, b. September 27, 1832, Tomé, Nuevo México, La República de México.

xi. MARÍA DOLÓRES DE LUNA, b. December 10, 1836, Tomé, Nuevo México, La República de México[67].

xii. PAULO DE LUNA, b. Abt. 1839[68].

xiii. JOSÉ RAMÓN BERNARDINO DE LUNA, b. October 30, 1839, Tomé, Nuevo México, La República de México[69].

xiv. MARÍA PAUBLA LIBRADA DE LUNA, b. June 17, 1844, Lemitar, Nuevo México, La República de México[70].

15. MANUEL ANTONIO DE LOS REYES[6] CHÁVES *(MIGUEL ANTONIO BERNABÉ DURÁN Y[5], JOSÉ ANASTACIO DURÁN Y[4], MARÍA ANTONIA[3] BACA, FRANCISCO[2] XAVIER, FRANCISCO[1])* was born January 02, 1812 in Valencia, El Reyno de Nuevo México, Nueva España[71], and died Bef. 1860. He married MARÍA NICOLASA RAFAELA MONTOYA.

Children of MANUEL CHÁVES and MARÍA MONTOYA are:

21.   i. JESÚS[7] CHÁVES, b. August 02, 1833, Valencia, Nuevo México, La República de México.

ii. FRANCISCO ESTEBAN CHÁVES, b. August 07, 1835, Valencia, Nuevo México, La República de México[72].

iii. JOSÉ SISTO MELITON CHÁVES, b. March 27, 1838, Valencia, Nuevo México, La República de México[73].

iv. GEORGE MONTOYA CHÁVES, b. Abt. 1840.

v. MARÍA CHÁVES, b. November 03, 1842, Tomé, Nuevo México, La República de México[74].

vi. ISABELA CHÁVES, b. Abt. 1843, Tomé, Nuevo México, La República de México.

vii. MARÍA DE JESÚS CHÁVES, b. April 30, 1845, Tajiqué, Nuevo México, La República de México[75].

viii. FRANCISCA CHÁVES, b. Abt. 1847, Tajiqué, Territory of New México.

ix. JUANA CHÁVES, b. March 30, 1848, Tajiqué, Territory of New México[76].

Notes for JUANA CHÁVES:
Also known as María Juana.

x. LUZ CHÁVES, b. Abt. 1850[77].

xi. SERILIA CHÁVES, b. Abt. 1850[77].

xii. TIRICIO CHÁVES, b. Abt. 1852[77].

José Blas Sedillo

16. JOSÉ BLÁS[6] SEDILLO *(ANTONIA NARCISA[5] BACA, FELICIANA DURÁN Y[4] CHÁVES, MARÍA ANTONIA[3] BACA, FRANCISCO[2] XAVIER, FRANCISCO[1])*[78] was born February 20, 1777 in Alburquerque, El Reyno de Nuevo México, Nueva España[79]. He married MARÍA PETRA SÁNCHES July 12, 1824 in Albuquerque, Nuevo México, La República de México[80], daughter of FELIX SÁNCHES and ANA AGUIRRE.

Children of JOSÉ SEDILLO and MARÍA SÁNCHES are:

i. MARÍA DE LOS SANTOS[7] SEDILLO, b. October 05, 1836, El Sabinal, Nuevo México, La República de México.

22.   ii. JOSÉ MIGUEL SEDILLO, b. February 24, 1842, Lemitar, Nuevo México, La República de México; d. February 25, 1899.

iii. MARÍA NESTORA SEDILLO, b. February 25, 1847, Lemitar, Territory of New México.

iv. MARÍA RITA SEDILLO, m. JOSÉ DOMINGO CANDELARIA, September 09, 1844, Socorro, Nuevo México, La República de México[81].

17. JULIÁN BERNARDO[6] SEDILLO *(ANTONIA NARCISA[5] BACA, FELICIANA DURÁN Y[4] CHÁVES, MARÍA ANTONIA[3] BACA, FRANCISCO[2] XAVIER, FRANCISCO[1])* was born March 14, 1779 in Alburquerque, El Reyno de Nuevo México, Nueva España[82]. He married CIPRIANA GARCÍA[83].

Children of JULIÁN SEDILLO and CIPRIANA GARCÍA are:

23.   i. MARÍA DOLÓRES[7] SEDILLO, b. 1824, La Cañada de Los Apaches, El Reyno de Nuevo México.

ii. MARÍA DEL ROSARIO SEDILLO, b. Bef. June 17, 1824, Albuquerque, Nuevo México, La República de México[84]; m. ANTONIO JOSÉ CARVAJAL, September 11, 1849, Albuquerque, Territory of New México[85].

      iii.   JOSEFA SEDILLO, b. Abt. 1835[86].

24.   iv.   RUFINA SEDILLO, b. Abt. 1837.

      v.   ANTONIO JOSÉ SEDILLO, b. Abt. 1839[86].

Generation No. 6

18. MARÍA MANUELA[7] LUNA *(MIGUEL SANTIAGO[6] DE LUNA, BERNARDO PAULO[5], JOAQUÍN[4], MIGUEL DE SAN JUAN[3], FRANCISCO[2] XAVIER, FRANCISCO[1]).* She married VENCESLAO LUJÁN.

Children of MARÍA LUNA and VENCESLAO LUJÁN are:
      i.   JOSEFA[8] LUJÁN.
      ii.   YGNACIO LUJÁN.
      iii.   TORIBIO LUJÁN.
      iv.   MARIANO LUJÁN.

19. MARÍA YSABEL[7] DE LUNA *(MIGUEL SANTIAGO[6], BERNARDO PAULO[5], JOAQUÍN[4], MIGUEL DE SAN JUAN[3], FRANCISCO[2] XAVIER, FRANCISCO[1])* was born February 20, 1822 in San Fernando, Nuevo México, La República de México[87]. She married JUAN JOSÉ LÓPEZ May 02, 1842 in Socorro, Nuevo México, La República de México[88].

Notes for MARÍA YSABEL DE LUNA:
1860 Census lists her birth year as 1830.

Notes for JUAN JOSÉ LÓPEZ:
1850 Census: Living in Lemitar, Territory of New México. (Born 1815)
1860 Census: Living in Lemitar, Territory of New México.

Children of MARÍA DE LUNA and JUAN LÓPEZ are:
      i.   MARÍA JOSEFA[8] LÓPEZ, b. Abt. 1842[89].
      ii.   JOSÉ LÓPEZ, b. Abt. 1847[90].
      iii.   LIBRADA LÓPEZ, b. Abt. 1856[90].
      iv.   MARÍA BARBARA LÓPEZ, b. Abt. 1862[91].

20. JOSÉ MIGUEL[7] DE LUNA *(MIGUEL SANTIAGO[6], BERNARDO PAULO[5], JOAQUÍN[4], MIGUEL DE SAN JUAN[3], FRANCISCO[2] XAVIER, FRANCISCO[1])[92]* was born September 27, 1832 in Tomé, Nuevo México, La República de México[93]. He married MARÍA JOSEFA TORRES[94].

Notes for JOSÉ MIGUEL DE LUNA:
Also known as Miguel Luna.
1850-1880 Census: living in Lemitar, Territory of New México.

Children of JOSÉ DE LUNA and MARÍA TORRES are:
      i.   EMILIA[8] LUNA, b. Abt. 1860[95].
25.   ii.   RAMÓN LUNA, b. Abt. 1865, Lemitar, Territory of New México.
      iii.   MARIANA LUNA, b. Abt. 1867[95].
      iv.   MAURICIO LUNA, b. Abt. 1873[96].
26.   v.   MIGUEL LUNA, b. November 1873.

Jesús Cháves

21. JESÚS[7] CHÁVES *(MANUEL ANTONIO DE LOS REYES[6], MIGUEL ANTONIO BERNABÉ DURÁN Y[5], JOSÉ ANASTACIO DURÁN Y[4], MARÍA ANTONIA[3] BACA, FRANCISCO[2] XAVIER, FRANCISCO[1])[97]* was born August 02, 1833 in Valencia, Nuevo México, La República de México[98]. He married (1) MARÍA PAULA ARAGÓN January 20, 1854 in Tomé, Territory of New México[99], daughter of JOSÉ ARAGÓN and DOLORES DE ARAGÓN. He married (2) NICOLASA ARAGÓN August 08, 1860 in Tomé, Territory of New México[100], daughter of JOSÉ ARAGÓN and DOLORES DE ARAGÓN.

Notes for JESÚS CHÁVES:
Also known as Ygnacio de Jesús Cháves.
1860 Census: Living in Torreón, Territory of New México. (Born 1834)

Notes for NICOLASA ARAGÓN:
Helped raise Feliciano Cháves.

Children of JESÚS CHÁVES and MARÍA ARAGÓN are:

	i.	TEOFILA[8] CHÁVES, b. Abt. 1857, Tajiqué, Territory of New México.
	ii.	FELICIANO CHÁVES, b. Abt. 1859, Tajiqué, Territory of New México[101].

Child of JESÚS CHÁVES and NICOLASA ARAGÓN is:

27.   iii.   ROBERTO[8] CHÁVEZ, b. Abt. 1863, Tajiqué, Territory of New México; d. March 23, 1947, San Patricio, New México.

22. JOSÉ MIGUEL[7] SEDILLO *(JOSÉ BLÁS[6], ANTONIA NARCISA[5] BACA, FELICIANA DURÁN Yᵃ CHÁVES, MARÍA ANTONIA[3] BACA, FRANCISCO[2] XAVIER, FRANCISCO[1])* was born February 24, 1842 in Lemitar, Nuevo México, La República de México, and died February 25, 1899. He married (1) MARÍA INEZ GARCÍA April 08, 1860 in Las Cruces, Territory of New México[102], daughter of PEDRO GARCÍA and MARÍA LUCERO. He married (2) RAMONA SÁNCHEZ January 07, 1883 in Lincoln, Territory of New México[103], daughter of REFUGIO SÁNCHEZ.

Children of JOSÉ SEDILLO and MARÍA GARCÍA are:

	i.	MARGARITA GARCÍA[8] SEDILLO, b. Abt. 1862[104]; m. ANTONIO TRUJILLO.
28.	ii.	MARTÍN GARCÍA SEDILLO, b. November 1864, San Patricio, Territory of New México; d. May 05, 1917, Brighton, Colorado.
29.	iii.	ANGELITA SEDILLO, b. Abt. 1865; d. 1940, Roswell, New México.
	iv.	RAFAEL SEDILLO, b. 1866[105]; m. REINALDA MONTOYA[106], January 28, 1893, Lincoln County, Territory of New México[107].
30.	v.	SIXTO SEDILLO, b. March 28, 1868; d. September 07, 1955.
	vi.	DANIEL SEDILLO, b. December 1873, San Patricio, Territory of New México[108]; d. February 1957, Weld County, Colorado.
	vii.	RUFINA SEDILLO, b. April 29, 1876[109].
31.	viii.	RUFINO SEDILLO, b. November 21, 1878, San Patricio, Territory of New México; d. December 09, 1955, Denver, Colorado.

23. MARÍA DOLÓRES[7] SEDILLO *(JULIÁN BERNARDO[6], ANTONIA NARCISA[5] BACA, FELICIANA DURÁN Yᵃ CHÁVES, MARÍA ANTONIA[3] BACA, FRANCISCO[2] XAVIER, FRANCISCO[1])*[110] was born 1824 in La Cañada de Los Apaches, El Reyno de Nuevo México[111]. She married (2) JOSÉ YGNACIO OLGUÍN[112] January 29, 1855 in Alburquerque, Territory of New México[113], son of JOSÉ OLGUÍN and MARÍA GARCÍA.

Child of MARÍA DOLÓRES SEDILLO is:

32.   i.   MARÍA LORENSA[8] CEDILLO, b. March 1846, Atrisco, Territory of New México.

Children of MARÍA SEDILLO and JOSÉ OLGUÍN are:

	ii.	POMISENA[8] OLGUÍN, b. Abt. 1854[114].
	iii.	JULIAN OLGUÍN[115], b. September 24, 1856, Atrisco, Territory of New México[116].
	iv.	GUADALUPE ELIZA OLGUÍN, b. Abt. 1858[116].

24. RUFINA[7] SEDILLO *(JULIÁN BERNARDO[6], ANTONIA NARCISA[5] BACA, FELICIANA DURÁN Yᵃ CHÁVES, MARÍA ANTONIA[3] BACA, FRANCISCO[2] XAVIER, FRANCISCO[1])* was born Abt. 1837[116]. She married (1) JOSÉ MARÍA CHÁVES September 08, 1850 in Albuquerque, Territory of New México[117]. She married (2) MANUEL SÁNCHEZ December 07, 1887 in Albuquerque, Territory of New México[118].

Children of RUFINA SEDILLO and JOSÉ CHÁVES are:

	i.	CANUTO[8] CHÁVES, b. Abt. 1852[119].
	ii.	OLOJIO CHÁVES, b. Abt. 1854[119].

Generation No. 7

Ramón Luna

25. RAMÓN[8] LUNA *(JOSÉ MIGUEL[7] DE LUNA, MIGUEL SANTIAGO[6], BERNARDO PAULO[5], JOAQUÍN[4], MIGUEL DE SAN JUAN[3], FRANCISCO[2] XAVIER, FRANCISCO[1])* was born Abt. 1865 in Lemitar, Territory of New México[120]. He married EMITERIA SALAZAR August 28, 1901[121], daughter of ROMULO SALAZAR and VICTORIANA BENAVIDEZ.

Notes for RAMÓN LUNA:
1870& 1880 Census: Living in Lemitar, Territory of New México.
1910-1930 Census: Living in Lincoln, Territory of New México.

Notes for EMITERIA SALAZAR:
Also known as Victoria Salazar.

Children of RAMÓN LUNA and EMITERIA SALAZAR are:
33.　　i.　SANTIAGO[9] LUNA, b. July 29, 1902, Lincoln, Territory of New México.
　　　 ii.　JUAN LUNA, b. Abt. 1908[122].
　　　iii.　RAMÓN LUNA[123], b. August 02, 1911, Lincoln, Territory of New México[124]; d. July 11, 1997, Alamogordo, New México; m. CRUSITA SEDILLO[125].
　　　iv.　JOSEFINA LUNA, b. Abt. 1919, Lincoln, New México[126]; d. 1978.

26. MIGUEL[8] LUNA *(JOSÉ MIGUEL[7] DE LUNA, MIGUEL SANTIAGO[6], BERNARDO PAULO[5], JOAQUÍN[4], MIGUEL DE SAN JUAN[3], FRANCISCO[2] XAVIER, FRANCISCO[1])* was born November 1873[127]. He married AURELIA GONZÁLES November 28, 1898 in San Patricio, Territory of New México[128], daughter of FLORENCIO GONZÁLES and RAYMUNDA SÁNCHEZ.

Child of MIGUEL LUNA and AURELIA GONZÁLES is:
　　　 i.　JOSEFA[9] LUNA, b. August 1899, Lincoln, Territory of New México[129].

27. ROBERTO[8] CHÁVEZ *(JESÚS[7] CHÁVES, MANUEL ANTONIO DE LOS REYES[6], MIGUEL ANTONIO BERNABÉ DURÁN Y[5], JOSÉ ANASTACIO DURÁN Y[4], MARÍA ANTONIA[3] BACA, FRANCISCO[2] XAVIER, FRANCISCO[1])* was born Abt. 1863 in Tajiqué, Territory of New México[130], and died March 23, 1947 in San Patricio, New México. He married LUCÍA WELDON February 11, 1888 in Ruidoso, New Mexico[131], daughter of JAMES WELDON and ANGELITA SÁNCHEZ.

Children of ROBERTO CHÁVEZ and LUCÍA WELDON are:
34.　　i.　ANGELITA[9] CHÁVEZ, b. July 25, 1889, Las Angusturas (San Ysidro), Territory of New México; d. March 04, 1973, San Patricio, New México.
35.　　ii.　YSIDRO CHÁVEZ, b. April 13, 1892, Las Angusturas (San Ysidro), Territory of New Mexico; d. June 28, 1972, San Patricio, New Mexico.
36.　　iii.　MANFOR CHÁVEZ, b. March 18, 1896, Las Angusturas (San Ysidro), Territory of New México; d. July 1971, San Patricio, New México.

28. MARTÍN GARCÍA[8] SEDILLO *(JOSÉ MIGUEL[7], JOSÉ BLÁS[6], ANTONIA NARCISA[5] BACA, FELICIANA DURÁN Y[4] CHÁVES, MARÍA ANTONIA[3] BACA, FRANCISCO[2] XAVIER, FRANCISCO[1])* was born November 1864 in San Patricio, Territory of New México[132], and died May 05, 1917 in Brighton, Colorado. He married TIMOTEA SILVA Abt. 1890[132], daughter of MANUEL SILVA and JOSEFITA ESQUIVEL.

Children of MARTÍN SEDILLO and TIMOTEA SILVA are:
37.　　i.　MARÍNEZ[9] SEDILLO, b. June 21, 1891, San Patricio, Territory of New México; d. March 25, 1940, Colorado Springs, Colorado.
　　　 ii.　FRANCISCO SEDILLO, b. December 27, 1892, San Patricio, Territory of New México[132]; d. January 29, 1938, Greeley, Colorado.
　　　iii.　JOSEFITA SEDILLO, b. December 29, 1893, San Patricio, Territory of New México[132]; d. November 12, 1991, Denver, Colorado; m. SAMUEL BECERRA, March 23, 1912.

iv.   EUFEMIA SEDILLO, b. December 1896, San Patricio, Territory of New México[132]; d. October 1930; m. JOSÉ BECERRA.

v.   ANA CECILIA SEDILLO[133], b. April 03, 1906, San Patricio, Territory of New México; d. May 1974, Greeley, Colorado; m. NOBERTO VALADEZ, March 11, 1929, Greeley, Colorado.

29. ANGELITA[8] SEDILLO *(JOSÉ MIGUEL[7], JOSÉ BLÁS[6], ANTONIA NARCISA[5] BACA, FELICIANA DURÁN Y[4] CHÁVES, MARÍA ANTONIA[3] BACA, FRANCISCO[2] XAVIER, FRANCISCO[1])* was born Abt. 1865[134], and died 1940 in Roswell, New México. She married (1) BENITO TRUJILLO. She married (2) FRANCISCO GUTIÉRRES Abt. 1890[134], son of JOSÉ GUTIÉRRES and JUANA SALAS.

Children of ANGELITA SEDILLO and FRANCISCO GUTIÉRRES are:

i.   MANUELITA[9] GUTIÉRREZ, b. Abt. 1900, San Patricio, Territory of New México[134]; m. ISIDRO ANALLA[135].

ii.   RAMÓN GUTIÉRREZ, b. Abt. 1903, San Patricio, Territory of New México[136].

30. SIXTO[8] SEDILLO *(JOSÉ MIGUEL[7], JOSÉ BLÁS[6], ANTONIA NARCISA[5] BACA, FELICIANA DURÁN Y[4] CHÁVES, MARÍA ANTONIA[3] BACA, FRANCISCO[2] XAVIER, FRANCISCO[1])[137]* was born March 28, 1868, and died September 07, 1955. He married MARGARITA CANDELARIA OLGUÍN[137] July 28, 1892 in Ruidoso, Territory of New México[138], daughter of RAMÓN OLGUÍN and MARÍA CEDILLO.

Children of SIXTO SEDILLO and MARGARITA OLGUÍN are:

38.   i.   MIGUEL[9] SEDILLO, b. November 28, 1891, San Patricio, Territory of New México; d. March 15, 1967, Carrizozo, New México.

ii.   ONESIMA SEDILLO, b. February 15, 1894, El Berendo, Territory of New México; m. AMABLE CHÁVEZ, September 23, 1914, Lincoln, New México[139].

iii. FRANCISQUITA SEDILLO, b. April 15, 1895, San Patricio, Territory of New México[140]; m. JOSÉ OROSCO, October 01, 1913, Patos, Territory of New México[140].

39.   iv.   RAMÓN SEDILLO, b. February 25, 1899, San Patricio, Territory of New México.

40.   v.   EDUARDO SEDILLO, b. October 20, 1902, Arabela, New México; d. March 08, 1991, Alamogordo, New México.

vi.   ESTELA SEDILLO[141], b. September 03, 1904, San Patricio, Territory of New México[142]; m. HILARIO SÁNCHEZ[143], July 27, 1921[144].

vii. PRESILIANA SEDILLO, b. Abt. 1906[145].

41.   viii. LEOPOLDO SEDILLO, b. March 24, 1909, San Patricio, New México; d. February 08, 1990, Roswell, New México.

ix.   DANIEL SEDILLO[146], b. February 02, 1912; d. April 18, 2006.

31. RUFINO[8] SEDILLO *(JOSÉ MIGUEL[7], JOSÉ BLÁS[6], ANTONIA NARCISA[5] BACA, FELICIANA DURÁN Y[4] CHÁVES, MARÍA ANTONIA[3] BACA, FRANCISCO[2] XAVIER, FRANCISCO[1])* was born November 21, 1878 in San Patricio, Territory of New México[147], and died December 09, 1955 in Denver, Colorado. He married FRANCISCA ESCALANTE Abt. 1900[148].

Children of RUFINO SEDILLO and FRANCISCA ESCALANTE are:

i.   EUTILIA[9] SEDILLO, b. Abt. 1900, Alamagordo, Territory of New México[149].

ii.   AVEL SEDILLO, b. Abt. 1905, San Patricio, Territory of New México[149].

iii. LYDIA SEDILLO, b. Abt. 1906, San Patricio, Territory of New México[149].

iv.   GENOVEVA SEDILLO, b. Abt. 1908, San Patricio, Territory of New México[149].

v.   ADELINA SEDILLO, b. Abt. 1909, San Patricio, Territory of New México[149].

vi.   EUGENIO SEDILLO, b. Abt. 1913[150].

vii. BEFANIO SEDILLO, b. Abt. 1916[150].

viii. RUBÉN SEDILLO, b. Abt. 1916[150].

ix.   ALBERTA SEDILLO, b. Abt. 1918[150].

xii. EDWARD SEDILLO, b. Abt. 1926[151].

xiii. MARY SEDILLO, b. Abt. 1928[151].

32. MARÍA LORENSA[8] CEDILLO *(MARÍA DOLÓRES[7] SEDILLO, JULIÁN BERNARDO[6], ANTONIA NARCISA[5] BACA, FELICIANA DURÁN Y[4] CHÁVES, MARÍA ANTONIA[3] BACA, FRANCISCO[2] XAVIER, FRANCISCO[1])* was born March 1846 in Atrisco, Territory of New México[152]. She married RAMÓN OLGUÍN October 16, 1866 in Tomé, Territory of New México[153], son of JOSÉ OLGUÍN and MARÍA GUTIÉRRES.

Children of MARÍA CEDILLO and RAMÓN OLGUÍN are:

	i.	NATIVIDAD SEDILLO⁹ OLGUÍN, b. Abt. 1864, La Plaza de San Patricio, Territory of New México[154]; m. FELIZ TRUJILLO, September 28, 1885[155].
42.	ii.	ESTANISLADO OLGUÍN, b. May 06, 1870, Ruidoso, Territory of New México.
43.	iii.	MARGARITA CANDELARIA OLGUÍN, b. January 31, 1872, San Patricio, Territory of New México; d. April 06, 1955.
	iv.	BENITO OLGUÍN, b. Abt. 1876, San Patricio, Territory of New México[156].
44.	v.	MANUELITA OLGUÍN, b. June 1887, San Patricio, Territory of New México.
45.	vi.	IGNACIO S. OLGUÍN, b. August 01, 1873, San Patricio, Territory of New México; d. October 15, 1947, El Paso, Téxas.

Generation No. 8

33. SANTIAGO⁹ LUNA *(RAMÓN⁸, JOSÉ MIGUEL⁷ DE LUNA, MIGUEL SANTIAGO⁶, BERNARDO PAULO⁵, JOAQUÍN⁴, MIGUEL DE SAN JUAN³, FRANCISCO² XAVIER, FRANCISCO¹)* was born July 29, 1902 in Lincoln, Territory of New México[157]. He married CHONITA SEDILLO March 17, 1926 in San Patricio, New México[157], daughter of GREGORIO SEDILLO and BENINA DE SEDILLO.

Notes for SANTIAGO LUNA:
Also known as Jim.
1930 Census: Living in Lincoln, New México.

Notes for CHONITA SEDILLO:
Also known as Benina.

Children of SANTIAGO LUNA and CHONITA SEDILLO are:
  i. JOSEPHINE¹⁰ LUNA, b. Abt. 1927[158].
  ii. OCTAVIA LUNA, b. Private.

34. ANGELITA⁹ CHÁVEZ *(ROBERTO⁸, JESÚS⁷ CHÁVES, MANUEL ANTONIO DE LOS REYES⁶, MIGUEL ANTONIO BERNABÉ DURÁN Y⁵, JOSÉ ANASTACIO DURÁN Y⁴, MARÍA ANTONIA³ BACA, FRANCISCO² XAVIER, FRANCISCO¹)*[159] was born July 25, 1889 in Las Angusturas (San Ysidro), Territory of New México[160], and died March 04, 1973 in San Patricio, New México. She married TRANCITO CHÁVEZ[161] April 15, 1907 in Lincoln, Territory of New México[162], son of PABLO CHÁVEZ and AMADA SÁNCHEZ.

Children of ANGELITA CHÁVEZ and TRANCITO CHÁVEZ are:
  i. ARISTEO¹⁰ CHÁVEZ[163], b. November 30, 1910, Hondo, New México[164]; d. August 21, 1993, San Patricio, New México; m. CRISTINA ROMERO[165], February 10, 1936, San Patricio, New México[166].
  ii. ISMAEL CHÁVEZ[167], b. November 12, 1912, Hondo, New México; d. July 31, 1980, San Patricio, New México; m. ELISA MENDOSA[168].
  iii. OZIEL CHÁVEZ, b. 1917, Hondo, New México[169]; d. August 19, 1942, Phillipines[170].
  iv. AVESLÍN CHÁVEZ, b. 1920, Hondo, New México[171]; d. March 20, 1945, Phillipines[172].
  v. HERALDO MODESTO CHÁVEZ[173], b. December 09, 1922, Hondo, New México; d. July 26, 1965, Hondo, New México; m. EVALINA MAE DUTCHOVER[174], February 11, 1946, Carrizozo, New México[175].
  vi. EVA CHÁVEZ, b. February 05, 1925, Hondo, New México[176]; m. (1) CARLOS CHÁVEZ; m. (2) HARRY SÁNCHEZ, February 21, 1944, Carrizozo, New México[176].

35. YSIDRO⁹ CHÁVEZ *(ROBERTO⁸, JESÚS⁷ CHÁVES, MANUEL ANTONIO DE LOS REYES⁶, MIGUEL ANTONIO BERNABÉ DURÁN Y⁵, JOSÉ ANASTACIO DURÁN Y⁴, MARÍA ANTONIA³ BACA, FRANCISCO² XAVIER, FRANCISCO¹)*[177] was born April 13, 1892 in Las Angusturas (San Ysidro), Territory of New Mexico[178], and died June 28, 1972 in San Patricio, New Mexico. He married PAUBLITA SÁNCHEZ August 04, 1913 in Lincoln, New México[178], daughter of FELIPÉ SÁNCHEZ and CANDELARIA PADILLA.

Children of YSIDRO CHÁVEZ and PAUBLITA SÁNCHEZ are:
  i. GRESELDA¹⁰ CHÁVEZ[179], b. May 03, 1914, Glencoe, New México; d. June 09, 1988, Ruidoso, New México; m. FRANK GÓMEZ[179], February 17, 1934, Carrizozo, New México[180].

ii. AMARANTE CHÁVEZ[181], b. November 09, 1915, Glencoe, New México; d. February 27, 2001, Alburquerque, New México; m. DOLORES ROMERO ARCHULETA[181], September 21, 1936, San Patricio, New México[182].

iii. SENON CHÁVEZ[183], b. March 03, 1917, San Patricio, New México; d. January 18, 2000, San Patricio, New México; m. MABEL TRUJILLO SÁNCHEZ, June 09, 1949, Carrizozo, New México[184].

iv. IGNACIA CHÁVEZ, b. January 23, 1919, San Patricio, New México[185]; m. (1) HAROLD STEELE; m. (2) VICTOR RICHARD BROOKS[186].

v. ADELA CHÁVEZ, b. July 04, 1920, San Patricio, New México; m. (1) JIMMY LARIOSA; m. (2) GUILLERMO QUIZON[186]; m. (3) MANUEL NAJERES GÓMEZ[186].

vi. EMILIANO CHÁVEZ[187], b. January 11, 1922, San Elizario, Téxas[188]; d. January 25, 1953, California; m. MÀRÍA SÁNCHEZ LUCERO[189], April 25, 1947, Carrizozo, New México[190].

vii. SIPIO CHÁVEZ[191], b. Abt. 1925, San Patricio, New México; d. June 03, 1928, San Patricio, New México.

viii. EFRAÍN CHÁVEZ, b. January 01, 1926, San Patricio, New México[192]; d. November 11, 1989, Capitán, New México[193]; m. LILLIAN ELIZABETH MILLER[193].

ix. ORALIA CHÁVEZ[194], b. Abt. 1927, San Patricio, New México; d. June 10, 1928, San Patricio, New México.

x. LUVÍN CHÁVEZ[195], b. November 15, 1929, San Patricio, New México; d. September 03, 2009, Capitán, New México; m. MARY KAMEES, July 12, 1952, Lincoln, New México[196].

xi. ORALIA CHÁVEZ, b. February 18, 1931, San Patricio, New México[197]; m. ERNESTO SÁNCHEZ, March 20, 1948, Ruidoso, New México[197].

xii. ONFRÉ CHÁVEZ, b. August 06, 1932, San Patricio, New México; m. VANGIE CHÁVEZ.

xiii. JOSIE CHÁVEZ, b. May 18, 1934, San Patricio, New México; m. (1) BENITO HERRERA[198]; m. (2) PORFIRIO SÁNCHEZ.

xiv. MELVIN CHÁVEZ, b. November 06, 1937, San Patricio, New México[199]; m. (1) PRESCILLA GUTIÉRREZ; m. (2) LORINA ROMERO, January 03, 1959, Hondo, New México[199].

xv. RAMONA CHÁVEZ, b. April 11, 1939, San Patricio, New México; m. LARRY NÚÑEZ.

xvi. DANNY CHÁVEZ, b. December 13, 1940, San Patricio, New México[200]; m. (1) CRUCITA BACA; m. (2) VANGIE MONTES, August 26, 1961, Ruidoso, New México[200].

36. MANFOR[9] CHÁVEZ *(ROBERTO[8], JESÚS[7] CHÁVES, MANUEL ANTONIO DE LOS REYES[6], MIGUEL ANTONIO BERNABÉ DURÁN Y[5], JOSÉ ANASTACIO DURÁN Y[4], MARÍA ANTONIA[3] BACA, FRANCISCO[2] XAVIER, FRANCISCO[1])*[201] was born March 18, 1896 in Las Angusturas (San Ysidro), Territory of New México[202], and died July 1971 in San Patricio, New México. He married CRUSITA GARCÍA January 24, 1916[203], daughter of SISTO GARCÍA and ANGELA TRUJILLO.

Child of MANFOR CHÁVEZ and CRUSITA GARCÍA is:

i. GABRIEL[10] CHÁVEZ[204], b. October 29, 1916, San Patricio, New México; d. April 1981, San Patricio, New México.

37. MARÍNEZ[9] SEDILLO *(MARTÍN GARCÍA[8], JOSÉ MIGUEL[7], JOSÉ BLÁS[6], ANTONIA NARCISA[5] BACA, FELICIANA DURÁN Y[4] CHÁVES, MARÍA ANTONIA[3] BACA, FRANCISCO[2] XAVIER, FRANCISCO[1])* was born June 21, 1891 in San Patricio, Territory of New México[205], and died March 25, 1940 in Colorado Springs, Colorado. She married (1) BENJAMÍN BECERRA September 01, 1910 in Roswell, Territory of New México[205], son of SUSANO BECERRA and MASIMIANA LUJÁN. She married (2) DANIEL BECERRA Abt. 1919, son of SUSANO BECERRA and MASIMIANA LUJÁN.

Child of MARÍNEZ SEDILLO and BENJAMÍN BECERRA is:

i. LEAH[10] BECERRA[206], b. August 16, 1913; d. August 03, 1934, Colorado Springs, Colorado.

Children of MARÍNEZ SEDILLO and DANIEL BECERRA are:

ii. NAOMI[10] BECERRA[207], b. October 17, 1920; d. September 09, 1988, Los Angeles, California.

iii. MAXINE BECERRA[207], b. February 08, 1925; d. February 20, 1986, Riverside, California.

38. MIGUEL[9] SEDILLO *(SIXTO[8], JOSÉ MIGUEL[7], JOSÉ BLÁS[6], ANTONIA NARCISA[5] BACA, FELICIANA DURÁN Y[4] CHÁVES, MARÍA ANTONIA[3] BACA, FRANCISCO[2] XAVIER, FRANCISCO[1])* was born November 28, 1891 in San Patricio, Territory of New México[208], and died March 15, 1967 in Carrizozo, New México[209]. He married RITA TRUJILLO October 14, 1914 in Lincoln, New México[210], daughter of BONAFICIO TRUJILLO and LORENSA SILVA.

Children of MIGUEL SEDILLO and RITA TRUJILLO are:

i. LEONEL[10] SEDILLO[211], b. November 20, 1918, San Patricio, New México[212].

    ii.   IDILIA SEDILLO, b. Abt. 1923[212].

39. RAMÓN[9] SEDILLO *(SIXTO[8], JOSÉ MIGUEL[7], JOSÉ BLÁS[6], ANTONIA NARCISA[5] BACA, FELICIANA DURÁN Y[4] CHÁVES, MARÍA ANTONIA[3] BACA, FRANCISCO[2] XAVIER, FRANCISCO[1])* was born February 25, 1899 in San Patricio, Territory of New México[213]. He married GUADALUPE URBÁN BRADY Abt. 1920[214], daughter of JUAN BRADY and MARÍLLITA URBÁN.

Children of RAMÓN SEDILLO and GUADALUPE BRADY are:
    i.   ONESIMA[10] SEDILLO, b. Abt. 1921, Roswell, New México[214].
    ii.   MARÍA DEL ROSARIO SEDILLO, b. Abt. 1922, Roswell, New México[214].
    iii.   VIOLA SEDILLO, b. Abt. 1924, Roswell, New México[214].
    iv.   OLIVIA SEDILLO, b. Abt. 1926, Roswell, New México[214].
    v.   SIXTO SEDILLO, b. Abt. 1927, Roswell, New México[214].
    vi.   JUANITA SEDILLO, b. September 23, 1940, Wilmington, California; m. FLOYD SELF, September 27, 1958, Wilmington, California.
    vii.   MICHELLE SEDILLO, b. Private, Wilmington, California.
    viii.   RAYMOND SEDILLO, b. Private.

40. EDUARDO[9] SEDILLO *(SIXTO[8], JOSÉ MIGUEL[7], JOSÉ BLÁS[6], ANTONIA NARCISA[5] BACA, FELICIANA DURÁN Y[4] CHÁVES, MARÍA ANTONIA[3] BACA, FRANCISCO[2] XAVIER, FRANCISCO[1])*[215] was born October 20, 1902 in Arabela, New México, and died March 08, 1991 in Alamogordo, New México. He married DOMINGA MAÉS[215] January 23, 1937 in San Patricio, New México[216], daughter of JESÚS MAÉS and AMANDA MOLINA.

Child of EDUARDO SEDILLO and DOMINGA MAÉS is:
    i.   EVA[10] MCKINLEY, b. Private; Adopted child; m. ALBERTO SÁNCHEZ[217].

41. LEOPOLDO[9] SEDILLO *(SIXTO[8], JOSÉ MIGUEL[7], JOSÉ BLÁS[6], ANTONIA NARCISA[5] BACA, FELICIANA DURÁN Y[4] CHÁVES, MARÍA ANTONIA[3] BACA, FRANCISCO[2] XAVIER, FRANCISCO[1])*[218] was born March 24, 1909 in San Patricio, New México, and died February 08, 1990 in Roswell, New México. He married ADELAIDA SÁNCHEZ 1936[219], daughter of DAVÍD SÁNCHEZ and FRANCISCA ARCHULETA.

42. ESTANISLADO[9] OLGUÍN *(MARÍA LORENSA[8] CEDILLO, MARÍA DOLÓRES[7] SEDILLO, JULIÁN BERNARDO[6], ANTONIA NARCISA[5] BACA, FELICIANA DURÁN Y[4] CHÁVES, MARÍA ANTONIA[3] BACA, FRANCISCO[2] XAVIER, FRANCISCO[1])* was born May 06, 1870 in Ruidoso, Territory of New México[220]. He married ANASTACIA CHÁVEZ[221] March 02, 1901[222], daughter of JUAN CHÁVEZ and TERESA HERRERA.

Children of ESTANISLADO OLGUÍN and ANASTACIA CHÁVEZ are:
    i.   CANDELARIA[10] OLGUÍN[223], b. February 02, 1902; d. October 03, 1934; m. PABLO CALDERON[223], June 22, 1920[224].
    ii.   JUANITA OLGUÍN, b. 1904[225]; m. OLOJIO GALLEGOS.
    iii.   AVESLÍN OLGUÍN, b. 1911[225].
    iv.   CECILIA OLGUÍN, b. 1914[225]; m. RUMELIO CHÁVEZ[226], July 11, 1936[227].
    v.   ROBERTO OLGUÍN[228], b. April 19, 1919, San Patricio, New México[229]; m. ELVA GALLEGOS, April 01, 1948, Carrizozo, New México[230].
    vi.   PEDRO OLGUÍN, b. 1921[231].

43. MARGARITA CANDELARIA[9] OLGUÍN *(MARÍA LORENSA[8] CEDILLO, MARÍA DOLÓRES[7] SEDILLO, JULIÁN BERNARDO[6], ANTONIA NARCISA[5] BACA, FELICIANA DURÁN Y[4] CHÁVES, MARÍA ANTONIA[3] BACA, FRANCISCO[2] XAVIER, FRANCISCO[1])*[232] was born January 31, 1872 in San Patricio, Territory of New México, and died April 06, 1955. She married SIXTO SEDILLO[232] July 28, 1892 in Ruidoso, Territory of New México[233], son of JOSÉ SEDILLO and MARÍA GARCÍA.

Children of MARGARITA OLGUÍN and SIXTO SEDILLO are:
    i.   MIGUEL[10] SEDILLO, b. November 28, 1891, San Patricio, Territory of New México[234]; d. March 15, 1967, Carrizozo, New México[235]; m. RITA TRUJILLO, October 14, 1914, Lincoln, New México[236].
    ii.   ONESIMA SEDILLO, b. February 15, 1894, El Berendo, Territory of New México; m. AMABLE CHÁVEZ, September 23, 1914, Lincoln, New México[237].

iii. FRANCISQUITA SEDILLO, b. April 15, 1895, San Patricio, Territory of New México[238]; m. JOSÉ OROSCO, October 01, 1913, Patos, Territory of New México[238].

iv. RAMÓN SEDILLO, b. February 25, 1899, San Patricio, Territory of New México[239]; m. GUADALUPE URBÁN BRADY, Abt. 1920[240].

v. EDUARDO SEDILLO[241], b. October 20, 1902, Arabela, New México; d. March 08, 1991, Alamogordo, New México; m. DOMINGA MAÉS[241], January 23, 1937, San Patricio, New México[242].

vi. ESTELA SEDILLO[243], b. September 03, 1904, San Patricio, Territory of New México[244]; m. HILARIO SÁNCHEZ[245], July 27, 1921[246].

vii. PRESILIANA SEDILLO, b. Abt. 1906[247].

viii. LEOPOLDO SEDILLO[248], b. March 24, 1909, San Patricio, New México; d. February 08, 1990, Roswell, New México; m. ADELAIDA SÁNCHEZ, 1936[249].

ix. DANIEL SEDILLO[250], b. February 02, 1912; d. April 18, 2006.

44. MANUELITA[9] OLGUÍN *(MARÍA LORENSA[8] CEDILLO, MARÍA DOLÓRES[7] SEDILLO, JULIÁN BERNARDO[6], ANTONIA NARCISA[5] BACA, FELICIANA DURÁN Yª CHÁVES, MARÍA ANTONIA[3] BACA, FRANCISCO[2] XAVIER, FRANCISCO[1])* was born June 1887 in San Patricio, Territory of New México[251]. She married (1) PROMETIVO BRADY April 03, 1899[252], son of WILLIAM BRADY and BONIFACIA CHÁVES. She married (2) HINIO LUCERO[253] February 12, 1902[254], son of ANISETO LUCERO and REFUGIA TRUJILLO.

Children of MANUELITA OLGUÍN and HINIO LUCERO are:

i. MARTÍN OLGUÍN[10] LUCERO[255], b. July 26, 1905, San Patricio, Territory of New México; d. May 15, 1953.

ii. REYES LUCERO, b. June 06, 1909, San Patricio, Territory of New México[256]; m. RITA BENAVIDEZ, December 04, 1946, Carrizozo, New México[256].

iii. EPIFANIO LUCERO, b. 1915, San Patricio, New México[257].

iv. REFUGIO LUCERO, b. 1918, San Patricio, New México[257].

v. ANISETO OLGUÍN LUCERO[258], b. November 15, 1902, San Patricio, Territory of New México[259]; d. November 18, 1965, San Patricio, New México; m. REYNALDA SÁNCHEZ[260].

45. IGNACIO S.[9] OLGUÍN *(MARÍA LORENSA[8] CEDILLO, MARÍA DOLÓRES[7] SEDILLO, JULIÁN BERNARDO[6], ANTONIA NARCISA[5] BACA, FELICIANA DURÁN Yª CHÁVES, MARÍA ANTONIA[3] BACA, FRANCISCO[2] XAVIER, FRANCISCO[1])[260]* was born August 01, 1873 in San Patricio, Territory of New México[261], and died October 15, 1947 in El Paso, Téxas. He married (1) VIVIANA CHÁVEZ[262] March 16, 1898[263], daughter of JUAN CHÁVEZ and TERESA HERRERA. He married (2) JOSEFITA RANDOLPH[264] August 19, 1911 in San Patricio, Territory of New México[265], daughter of FRANK RANDOLPH and CATARINA BRADY. He married (3) JUANITA LUCERO November 02, 1921[266], daughter of ANISETO LUCERO and REFUGIA TRUJILLO.

Child of IGNACIO OLGUÍN and VIVIANA CHÁVEZ is:

i. GENOVEVA CHÁVEZ[10] OLGUÍN, b. January 22, 1904, San Patricio, Territory of New México[267]; Adopted child; m. ANTONIO LA RIVA, August 05, 1920, San Patricio, New México[267].

Children of IGNACIO OLGUÍN and JUANITA LUCERO are:

ii. EVA H.[10] OLGUÍN, b. August 16, 1922, San Patricio, New México[268]; d. January 16, 2012, Alamogordo, New México; m. BENJAMÍN TELLES.

iii. RAMÓN OLGUÍN[269], b. February 12, 1925, San Patricio, New México[270]; d. July 07, 1983, Alamogordo, New México[271].

iv. CARLOS OLGUÍN[272], b. August 21, 1927, San Patricio, New México; d. August 23, 1958, San Patricio, New México.

Genealogy of Dionicio Mendosa

Generation No. 1

1. DIONICIO[1] MENDOSA[1] was born April 1848 in La República de México, and died November 05, 1912 in San Patricio, New México. He married (1) MARÍA DE LA LUZ MORIEL[2]. He married (2) MARÍA ROSENDA MONTOYA DE MENDOSA[3] Abt. 1895[4].

Notes for DIONICIO MENDOSA:
Also known as Dionisio. Immigrated to the U.S. in about November 1878. Buried in San Patricio.
1900 & 1910 Census: Living in San Patricio, Territory of New México.
Land Patent # NMR 0009176, on the authority of the Homestead Entry-Original (12 Stat. 392), May 20, 1862. Issued 160 acres on August 11, 1913.

Notes for MARÍA ROSENDA MONTOYA DE MENDOSA:
Buried: San Patricio.

Children of DIONICIO MENDOSA and MARÍA MORIEL are:
2.   i.   MANUEL[2] MENDOSA, b. March 1879.
      ii.   LUÍS MENDOSA, b. June 1881, Texas[5].
3.   iii. TEODORA MENDOSA, b. June 11, 1890, Isleta, Téxas.

Children of DIONICIO MENDOSA and MARÍA DE MENDOSA are:
      iv.   CARMELITA[2] MENDOSA, b. Abt. 1887[6]; Stepchild; m. ANTONIO GONZÁLES, May 11, 1922[7].

Notes for ANTONIO GONZÁLES:
1930 Census: Living in Roswell, New México.

4.   v.   LORENSO MENDOSA, b. May 21, 1896, Ruidoso, Territory of New México; d. August 1973, Roswell, New México; Stepchild.
      vi.   PEDRO MENDOSA[8], b. February 17, 1898, San Patricio, New México[9]; d. April 30, 1980; Stepchild.

Notes for PEDRO MENDOSA:
Rosenda's son.

5.   vii. ANTONIA MENDOSA, b. October 13, 1899, San Patricio, New México.
6.   viii. JUANITA MENDOSA, b. February 14, 1903, San Patricio, New México; d. December 08, 1970.
      ix.   ISABEL MENDOSA, b. Abt. 1905, San Patricio, Territory of New México[10]; m. PERFECTO CHÁVEZ, December 17, 1924[11].

Notes for ISABEL MENDOSA:
Also known as Isavel.

      x.   FERMÍN MENDOSA, b. Abt. 1907[12].

Generation No. 2

2. MANUEL[2] MENDOSA *(DIONICIO[1])* was born March 1879[13]. He married MARGARITA ROMERO March 12, 1902[14], daughter of DOROTEO ROMERO and AGAPITA GUEBARA.

Children of MANUEL MENDOSA and MARGARITA ROMERO are:
      i.   JULIANA[3] MENDOSA, b. 1903[15].
      ii.   FRANCISCA MENDOSA, b. 1905[15].
      iii. ANITA MENDOSA, b. 1907[15].

3. TEODORA[2] MENDOSA *(DIONICIO[1])* was born June 11, 1890 in Isleta, Téxas[16]. She married MARTÍN HERRERA March 08, 1906 in San Patricio, Territory of New México[16], son of CRUZ HERRERA and EULOJIA MADRID.

Notes for TEODORA MENDOSA:
Also known as Theodora.

Child of TEODORA MENDOSA and MARTÍN HERRERA is:

7.   i.   JULIAN[3] HERRERA, b. December 30, 1906, San Patricio, Territory of New México; d. May 14, 1991.

4. LORENSO[2] MENDOSA *(DIONICIO[1])*[17] was born May 21, 1896 in Ruidoso, Territory of New México[18], and died August 1973 in Roswell, New México. He married SUSANA MONTOYA[19] September 13, 1915 in Lincoln, New México[20], daughter of ESTANISLADO MONTOYA and SARAFINA ULIBARRÍ.

Notes for LORENSO MENDOSA:
Rosenda's son.

Notes for SUSANA MONTOYA:
Also known as Socorro, Susanita.

Children of LORENSO MENDOSA and SUSANA MONTOYA are:

         i.   TONITA[3] MENDOSA, b. Abt. 1917[21].
        ii.   SOCORRO MENDOSA[22], b. December 02, 1919, San Patricio, New México[23]; m. PABLO HERNÁNDEZ[24], June 19, 1940, Hondo, New México[24].
       iii.   BENJAMÍN MENDOSA[25], b. Abt. 1921, Hondo, New México[26]; d. June 25, 1942, Hondo, New México.
8.   iv.   CONSUELO MENDOSA, b. October 09, 1926; d. December 19, 2006, Roswell, New México.
         v.   ELISA MENDOSA[27], b. May 12, 1930, San Patricio, New México; d. July 02, 2000, San Patricio, New México; m. ISMAEL CHÁVEZ[28].
        vi.   DIONICIO MENDOSA, b. Private; m. ANA MAE SUTHERLAND.

Notes for DIONICIO MENDOSA:
Also known as Dennis.

       vii.   ELOY MENDOSA, b. Private.
      viii.   ERNESTO MENDOSA, b. Private.
        ix.   PORFIRIO MENDOSA, b. Private.
         x.   ROSENDA LIDIA MENDOSA[29], b. Abt. 1938, San Patricio, New México; d. January 27, 1938, San Patricio, New México.

5. ANTONIA[2] MENDOSA *(DIONICIO[1])* was born October 13, 1899 in San Patricio, New México[30]. She married RAMÓN PINEDA January 31, 1919 in Lincoln, New México[30], son of VICTOR PINEDA and CARLOTA VALENCIA.

Notes for ANTONIA MENDOSA:
Also known as Tonita

Children of ANTONIA MENDOSA and RAMÓN PINEDA are:

         i.   CARLOTA[3] PINEDA, b. April 05, 1920, Picacho, New México[31]; m. CLOVÍS SÁNCHEZ[32], December 26, 1941, Carrizozo, New México[33].

Notes for CARLOTA PINEDA:
Also known As Charlotte.

        ii.   JUANITA PINEDA, b. Abt. 1921, Picacho, New México[34].
       iii.   ELAZARIO PINEDA, b. Abt. 1923, Picacho, New México[34].
        iv.   EDUARDO PINEDA, b. Abt. 1925, Picacho, New México[34].
         v.   RAMONA PINEDA, b. Abt. 1927, Picacho, New México[34].

6. JUANITA[2] MENDOSA *(DIONICIO[1])*[35] was born February 14, 1903 in San Patricio, New México[36], and died December 08, 1970. She married JOSÉ INEZ SANDOVAL[37] April 08, 1922[38], son of PERFETO SANDOVAL and FRANCISCA ROMERO.

Notes for JOSÉ INEZ SANDOVAL:
Private US Army. Buried in Picacho, NM.

Children of JUANITA MENDOSA and JOSÉ SANDOVAL are:

    i.   MANUEL[3] SANDOVAL[39], b. June 19, 1925, Picacho, New México[40].
    ii.   POALA SANDOVAL, b. Abt. 1928[40].
    iii. RITA SANDOVAL, b. Private.

Generation No. 3

7. JULIAN[3] HERRERA *(TEODORA[2] MENDOSA, DIONICIO[1])[41]* was born December 30, 1906 in San Patricio, Territory of New México[42], and died May 14, 1991. He married ANATALIA SÁNCHEZ April 28, 1934 in Carrizozo, New México[42], daughter of SALOMON SÁNCHEZ and JENNIE GILL.

Notes for ANATALIA SÁNCHEZ:
Also known as Natalia.

Children of JULIAN HERRERA and ANATALIA SÁNCHEZ are:

    i.   MARTÍN[4] HERRERA, b. Private.
    ii.   ANDREW HERRERA, b. Private.
    iii. ORLIDIA HERRERA, b. Private.
    iv. VIRGINIA HERRERA, b. Private.

8. CONSUELO[3] MENDOSA *(LORENSO[2], DIONICIO[1])[43]* was born October 09, 1926, and died December 19, 2006 in Roswell, New México. She married ERMINIO SÁNCHEZ[43] December 07, 1944 in Roswell, New México[44], son of SIMÓN SÁNCHEZ and ANTONIA CARABAJAL.

Notes for CONSUELO MENDOSA:
Her mother died when she was 12 years old. She accepted the responibility of caring for her younger brothers and sisters.

Notes for ERMINIO SÁNCHEZ:
About 1944: Erminio and his family moved to Roswell, New México.

Children of CONSUELO MENDOSA and ERMINIO SÁNCHEZ are:

    i.   ROSE[4] SÁNCHEZ[44], b. Private.
    ii.   JOE SÁNCHEZ[44], b. Private.
    iii. LLOYD SÁNCHEZ[44], b. Private.
    iv. PRISCILLA SÁNCHEZ[44], b. Private.
    v.   BERNICE MENDOZA SÁNCHEZ[44], b. Private.
    vi. GRACE MENDOZA SÁNCHEZ[44], b. Private.
    vii. ELMO SÁNCHEZ[44], b. Private.
   viii. VELMA SÁNCHEZ[44], b. Private.
    ix. TERRY SÁNCHEZ[44], b. Private.
    x.   ELIZABETH MENDOZA SÁNCHEZ[44], b. Private.

Genealogy of José Miranda

Generation No. 1

1. BLAS ANTONIO PASCUAL[1] MIRANDA[1] was born Abt. 1755 in Ysleta, El Reyno de Nuevo México, Nueva España[2]. He married MARÍA CANDELARIA CHÁVES[3] May 31, 1778 in Ysleta, El Reyno de Nuevo México, Nueva España[4].

Children of BLAS MIRANDA and MARÍA CHÁVES are:
2. i.   PEDRO[2] MIRANDA, b. Abt. 1792.
    ii. MARÍA RAFAELA MIRANDA, m. JOSÉ MANUEL GARCÍA, May 08, 1802, Tomé, El Reyno de Nuevo México, Nueva España[5].

Generation No. 2

2. PEDRO[2] MIRANDA *(BLAS ANTONIO PASCUAL[1])* was born Abt. 1792[6]. He married ENCARNACIÓN SÁNCHES[7], daughter of JUAN SÁNCHES and MARÍA JIRÓN.

Notes for PEDRO MIRANDA:
1850 Census: Living in La Polvadera de San Lorenzo, Territory of New México.

Notes for ENCARNACIÓN SÁNCHES:
Also known as María Encarnación Sánches, Encarnación Jirón.

Children of PEDRO MIRANDA and ENCARNACIÓN SÁNCHES are:
    i.   MARCELINA[3] MIRANDA, b. Abt. 1825, La Plaza de Pulvidera, Nuevo México, La República de México[8].
3. ii.   JOSÉ MIRANDA, b. Abt. 1822, La Plaza de Pulvidera, Nuevo México, La República de México.
4. iii. FELIPÉ MIRANDA, b. Abt. 1831, La Plaza de Pulvidera, Nuevo México, La República de México.
5. iv.   SOLEDAD MIRANDA, b. March 27, 1834, La Plaza de Pulvidera, Nuevo México, La República de México.
    v.   MARÍA MIRANDA, b. Abt. 1835, La Plaza de Pulvidera, Nuevo México, La República de México[8].
    vi.   BLAS MIRANDA, b. February 11, 1836, La Plaza de Pulvidera, Nuevo México, La República de México[9].
    vii. JOSÉ EDUVIGEN MIRANDA, b. February 18, 1838, La Plaza de Pulvidera, Nuevo México, La República de México.
    viii. LUISA MIRANDA, b. February 18, 1838, La Plaza de Pulvidera, Nuevo México, La República de México[10].
    ix.   LUCÍA MIRANDA[11], b. December 15, 1840, La Plaza de Pulvidera, Nuevo México, La República de México[12].

Notes for LUCÍA MIRANDA:
Also known as María Lucía Miranda.

    x.   BENITO MIRANDA, b. Abt. 1846, San Lorenzo de Pulvidero, Nuevo México, La República de México[12].

Generation No. 3

3. JOSÉ[3] MIRANDA *(PEDRO[2], BLAS ANTONIO PASCUAL[1])* was born Abt. 1822 in La Plaza de Pulvidera, Nuevo México, La República de México[13]. He married LEONARDA FAJARDO December 12, 1847 in Socorro, Territory of New México[14], daughter of JOSÉ FAJARDO and GUADALUPE CHÁBES.

Notes for JOSÉ MIRANDA:
1850 Census: Living in La Polvadera de San Lorenzo, Territory of New México. (Born 1822)
1860 Census: Living in Rio Bonito, Socorro County, Territory of New México.
1880 Census: Living in La Junta, Territory of New México.

Children of JOSÉ MIRANDA and LEONARDA FAJARDO are:
6. i.   MARÍA INEZ[4] MIRANDA, b. Abt. 1847.
    ii. JUAN MIRANDA, b. Abt. 1851[15].

Notes for JUAN MIRANDA:
Also known as Juan Baca.

7.	iii.	MIQUELA MIRANDA, b. Abt. 1855.	
8.	iv.	PRUDENCIA MIRANDA, b. May 10, 1855, San Acasio, Territory of New México; d. November 29, 1941, Carrizozo, New México.	
9.	v.	PABLO MIRANDA, b. Abt. 1860.	
10.	vi.	PATRICIO MIRANDA, b. Abt. 1861, Río Bonito, Territory of New México.	
11.	vii.	JULIO MIRANDA, b. Abt. 1863, Rio Bonito, Territory of New México; d. Bef. March 1902.	
	viii.	CRUZ MIRANDA, b. Abt. 1865, Rio Bonito, Territory of New México[15].	
	ix.	YSABEL MIRANDA, b. Abt. 1867, Rio Bonito, Territory of New México[15]; m. LIBERTY B. WALTERS, October 09, 1886, Lincoln County, Territory of New México[16].	
	x.	ROSARIA MIRANDA, b. Abt. 1871, Río Bonito, Territory of New México[17].	
	xi.	BEATRIZ MIRANDA, b. Abt. 1874, Río Bonito, Territory of New México[17].	

4. FELIPÉ[3] MIRANDA *(PEDRO[2], BLAS ANTONIO PASCUAL[1])* was born Abt. 1831 in La Plaza de Pulvidera, Nuevo México, La República de México[18]. He married DOLÓRES DE MIRANDA.

Notes for FELIPÉ MIRANDA:
1850 Census: Living in La Polvadera de San Lorenzo, Territory of New México. (Born 1831)
1860 Census: Living in Rio Bonito, Territory of New México. (Born 1835)
1870 Census: Living in Lincoln County, Precinct 1, Territory of New México. (Born 1824)
1880 Census: Living in Lincoln, Territory of New México. (Born 1840)
1900 Census: Living in Lincoln, Territory of New México. (Born Feb 1830)

Children of FELIPÉ MIRANDA and DOLÓRES DE MIRANDA are:

	i.	JUAN[4] MIRANDA, b. Abt. 1841.
12.	ii.	JOSÉ MIRANDA, b. Abt. 1854.
	iii.	ELIZA MIRANDA, b. Abt. 1862[19].
	iv.	DIONICIA MIRANDA, b. Abt. 1865[20].
	v.	PLACIDA MIRANDA, b. Abt. 1869[20].
13.	vi.	PORFILIO MIRANDA, b. June 1872.

5. SOLEDAD[3] MIRANDA *(PEDRO[2], BLAS ANTONIO PASCUAL[1])*[21] was born March 27, 1834 in La Plaza de Pulvidera, Nuevo México, La República de México[22]. She married JOSÉ ANDRÉS SÁNCHES February 23, 1851 in Socorro, Territory of New México[23].

Notes for SOLEDAD MIRANDA:
Also known as María Soledad Miranda.

Child of SOLEDAD MIRANDA and JOSÉ SÁNCHES is:

i.	LAZARA[4] SÁNCHEZ, m. SANTIAGO JIRÓN, January 07, 1884, Las Vegas, Territory of New México[24].

Generation No. 4

6. MARÍA INEZ[4] MIRANDA *(JOSÉ[3], PEDRO[2], BLAS ANTONIO PASCUAL[1])* was born Abt. 1847[25]. She married JOSÉ LUCÍO MONTOLLA October 12, 1881 in Lincoln County, Territory of New México[26], son of PETRA MONTOLLA.

Notes for JOSÉ LUCÍO MONTOLLA:
1900 Census: Living in Lincoln, Territory of New México.

Child of MARÍA MIRANDA and JOSÉ MONTOLLA is:

i.	FLORIPA[5] MONTOYA, b. January 1885[27].

7. MIQUELA[4] MIRANDA *(JOSÉ[3], PEDRO[2], BLAS ANTONIO PASCUAL[1])* was born Abt. 1855[28]. She married CRESENCIO TORRES October 16, 1866 in Tomé, Territory of New México[29], son of JOSÉ TORRES and BARBARA GALLEGOS.

Notes for MIQUELA MIRANDA:
Also known as Miquelita.

Notes for CRESENCIO TORRES:
1880 Census: Living in La Junta, Territory of New México.
1920 Census: Living in Hondo, New México.

Children of MIQUELA MIRANDA and CRESENCIO TORRES are:
14.   i.   CARMELITA[5] TORREZ, b. March 11, 1869; d. August 07, 1934.
    ii.   EUTERNIA TORREZ, b. Abt. 1872[30].
    iii.   SEVERA TORREZ, b. Abt. 1876[30].
    iv.   JOSÉ TORREZ, b. Abt. 1878[30].
15.   v.   EMILIA TORREZ, b. April 28, 1884; d. March 10, 1975.
16.   vi.   PANTALEÓN TORRES, b. May 04, 1891, Lincoln, Territory of New México.
17.   vii.   BARBARITA TORREZ, b. July 27, 1892, Hondo, New México.

8. PRUDENCIA[4] MIRANDA *(JOSÉ[3], PEDRO[2], BLAS ANTONIO PASCUAL[1])* was born May 10, 1855 in San Acasio, Territory of New México[31], and died November 29, 1941 in Carrizozo, New México[32]. She married (1) JAQUES WOOD May 30, 1869 in Tularoso, Territory of New México[33], son of CRISTÓVAL WOOD and MARY WOOD. She married (2) CLETO LUCERO CHÁVEZ[34] Abt. 1874[35], son of MAURICIO CHÁVEZ and PAULA LUCERO.

Notes for CLETO LUCERO CHÁVEZ:
1880 Census: Living in Las Chosas (Near La Junta), Territory of New México.
1910 Census: Living in San Patricio, Territory of New México.

Children of PRUDENCIA MIRANDA and CLETO CHÁVEZ are:
    i.   BEATRIZ[5] CHÁVEZ, b. Abt. 1874[36].
    ii.   PROCOPIO CHÁVEZ, b. Abt. 1876[36].
    iii.   PORFIRIO CHÁVEZ, b. Abt. 1877[36].
18.   iv.   ELERDO CHÁVEZ, b. March 17, 1880, Las Chosas, Territory of New México; d. December 17, 1954, Carrizozo, New México.
19.   v.   ÁBRAN MIRANDA CHÁVEZ, b. March 1882, Las Chosas, Territory of New México.

9. PABLO[4] MIRANDA *(JOSÉ[3], PEDRO[2], BLAS ANTONIO PASCUAL[1])* was born Abt. 1860[37]. He married VICTORIANA GUTIÉRREZ Abt. 1877[38].

Notes for PABLO MIRANDA:
1880 Census: Living in La Junta, Territory of New México.
1900 Census: Living in Lincoln, Territory of New México.

Children of PABLO MIRANDA and VICTORIANA GUTIÉRREZ are:
    i.   AVRORA[5] MIRANDA, b. Abt. 1877[39].

Notes for AVRORA MIRANDA:
Died young.

    ii.   HELENA MIRANDA, b. July 1879[39].

Notes for HELENA MIRANDA:
Died young.

    iii.   ALBERTA MIRANDA, b. March 27, 1888, Lincoln, Territory of New México[40]; m. CANDELARIO SANDOVAL, September 16, 1907, Carrizozo, Territory of New México[40].

Notes for CANDELARIO SANDOVAL:
1910 Census: Living in Carrizozo, Territory of New México.

    iv.   ELISEO MIRANDA, b. Abt. 1889[41].
20.   v.   CAROLINA MIRANDA, b. May 14, 1893.
21.   vi.   JUANITA MIRANDA, b. 1894.

    vii.   AVRORA MIRANDA, b. Abt. 1895[41].
    viii.   RAFAEL MIRANDA, b. Abt. 1898[41].
    ix.   PETRA MIRANDA, b. Abt. 1899[41].

10. PATRICIO[4] MIRANDA *(JOSÉ[3], PEDRO[2], BLAS ANTONIO PASCUAL[1])* was born Abt. 1861 in Río Bonito, Territory of New México[42]. He married JUANITA MILLER November 01, 1880 in Lincoln County, Territory of New México[43], daughter of ALEJANDRO MILLER and MARÍA GARCÍA.

Notes for PATRICIO MIRANDA:
1900 Census: Living in Lincoln, Territory of New México.

Children of PATRICIO MIRANDA and JUANITA MILLER are:
    i.   ELISA[5] MIRANDA, b. Abt. 1891[44].
    ii.   MANUEL MIRANDA, b. Abt. 1895[44].
    iii.   MARILLITA MIRANDA[45], b. Abt. 1897[46]; d. November 23, 1919, Roswell, New México.
    iv.   HAMILTON MIRANDA, b. Abt. 1900[46].

11. JULIO[4] MIRANDA *(JOSÉ[3], PEDRO[2], BLAS ANTONIO PASCUAL[1])* was born Abt. 1863 in Rio Bonito, Territory of New México[47], and died Bef. March 1902. He married ANTONIA MOLINA January 20, 1887 in Lincoln County, Territory of New México[48], daughter of VICTOR MOLINA and ALBINA SILVA.

Child of JULIO MIRANDA and ANTONIA MOLINA is:
22.   i.   JULIO MOLINA[5] MIRANDA, b. December 18, 1887; d. March 04, 1972, San Patricio, New México.

12. JOSÉ[4] MIRANDA *(FELIPÉ[3], PEDRO[2], BLAS ANTONIO PASCUAL[1])* was born Abt. 1854[49]. He married LORENZA H DE MIRANDA.

Children of JOSÉ MIRANDA and LORENZA DE MIRANDA are:
23.   i.   EMILO H.[5] MIRANDA, b. Abt. 1891; d. 1954, Lincoln, New México.
    ii.   RAMONA MIRANDA, b. Abt. 1894[50].
    iii.   LOLA MIRANDA, b. Abt. 1905[50].

13. PORFILIO[4] MIRANDA *(FELIPÉ[3], PEDRO[2], BLAS ANTONIO PASCUAL[1])* was born June 1872[51]. He married CATARINA CHÁVEZ Abt. 1898[52], daughter of MANUEL CHÁVES.

Notes for PORFILIO MIRANDA:
1900 Census: Living in Rebentón, Territory of New México.

Child of PORFILIO MIRANDA and CATARINA CHÁVEZ is:
    i.   FRANCISCO[5] MIRANDA, b. July 1898[52].

Generation No. 5

14. CARMELITA[5] TORREZ *(MIQUELA[4] MIRANDA, JOSÉ[3], PEDRO[2], BLAS ANTONIO PASCUAL[1])[53]* was born March 11, 1869[54], and died August 07, 1934. She married FELIX GUEBARA[55], son of PLACIDO GUEBARA and MARÍA SÁNCHES.

Notes for FELIX GUEBARA:
1900 Census: Living in White Oaks, Territory of New México.

Children of CARMELITA TORREZ and FELIX GUEBARA are:
    i.   AMADO[6] GUEBARA, b. August 03, 1902.
    ii.   SAMUEL GUEBARA[55], b. May 16, 1904; d. May 10, 1947.
    iii.   SALOMON GUEBARA[55], b. Abt. 1906; d. June 12, 1944.
    iv.   BEATRIZ GUEBARA, b. Abt. 1908.

15. EMILIA[5] TORREZ *(MIQUELA[4] MIRANDA, JOSÉ[3], PEDRO[2], BLAS ANTONIO PASCUAL[1])[56]* was born April 28, 1884, and died March 10, 1975. She married JUAN JAMES SÁNCHEZ WARNER December 10, 1900[57], son of DAVID WARNER and PREDICANDA SÁNCHEZ.

Notes for JUAN JAMES SÁNCHEZ WARNER:
Also known as Juan Juana.
Baptismal Padrinos: Diego Salcido, Miquela Baca.1910 Census: Lists Juan as Juan Guana. Also known as Juan Juana.
Land Patent # NMR 0028334, on the authority of the Homestead Entry-Enlarged (35 Stat. 639), February 19, 1909. Issued 161.09 acres on October 19, 1917.
Land Patent # NMLC 0025802, on the authority of the Homestead Entry-Stock Raising (39 Stat. 862), December 29, 1916. Issued 320 acres on June 24, 1926.

Children of EMILIA TORREZ and JUAN WARNER are:
24.	i.	MANUEL[6] WARNER, b. 1903, San Patricio, Territory of New México.
25.	ii.	PREDICANDA WARNER, b. November 24, 1903, San Patricio, Territory of New México; d. August 04, 1978, Hondo, New México.
26.	iii.	APOLONIA WARNER, b. October 12, 1909, San Patricio, Territory of New México.
	iv.	STELLA WARNER[58], b. June 26, 1914, San Patricio, New México[59]; d. July 12, 2007, Ruidoso Downs, New México; m. YLARIO SALAS[60], December 01, 1951, Ruidoso, New México[61].

Notes for YLARIO SALAS:
Private US Army. World War Two.

	v.	ELOY WARNER[62], b. June 17, 1916, San Patricio, New México; d. October 20, 1968.
27.	vi.	JULIANITA WARNER, b. August 01, 1918, San Patricio, New México; d. July 07, 2006, Covington, Louisiana.
	vii.	FRANCIS WARNER[63], b. February 18, 1921, San Patricio, New México[64]; m. JOSE V. BACA, December 27, 1947, San Patricio, New México[65].
	viii.	VIOLA WARNER, b. May 19, 1923, San Patricio, New México[66]; m. TRUMAN SÁNCHEZ, January 01, 1944, Carrizozo, New México[66].
	ix.	ALICE WARNER, b. December 18, 1926, San Patricio, New México[67]; m. MANUEL C. LUCERO, October 26, 1946, Carrizozo, New México[67].

Notes for ALICE WARNER:
Also known as Alice Juana.

16. PANTALEÓN[5] TORRES *(MIQUELA[4] MIRANDA, JOSÉ[3], PEDRO[2], BLAS ANTONIO PASCUAL[1])[68]* was born May 04, 1891 in Lincoln, Territory of New México[69]. He married ANA S. DE TORRES.

Notes for PANTALEÓN TORRES:
1920 Census: Living in Hondo, New México.

Children of PANTALEÓN TORRES and ANA DE TORRES are:
	i.	MIGUEL[6] TORRES, b. Abt. 1916[70].
	ii.	DIONISIO TORRES, b. Abt. 1918[70].
	iii.	SALOMON TORRES, b. Abt. October 1919[71].
	iv.	MIQUELITA TORRES, b. Abt. 1922[72].
	v.	ALFREDO TORRES, b. Abt. 1924[72].

17. BARBARITA[5] TORREZ *(MIQUELA[4] MIRANDA, JOSÉ[3], PEDRO[2], BLAS ANTONIO PASCUAL[1])* was born July 27, 1892 in Hondo, New México[73]. She married ESTOLANO PACHECO SÁNCHEZ[74] February 28, 1910 in Lincoln, Territory of New Mexico[75], son of ESTOLANO SÁNCHEZ and CORNELIA PACHECO.

Notes for ESTOLANO PACHECO SÁNCHEZ:
Lincoln County Clerk's Book of Marriages: Born October 21, 1891.
World War One Draft Registration: Born October 16, 1892.

Children of BARBARITA TORREZ and ESTOLANO SÁNCHEZ are:
| | i. | FERMÍN[6] SÁNCHEZ, b. October 11, 1915. |
| | ii. | AMABLE SÁNCHEZ, b. Private. |

  iii. AMANDA SÁNCHEZ, b. Private.
  iv. EULALIO (LALO) SÁNCHEZ, b. Private.

18. ELERDO[5] CHÁVEZ *(PRUDENCIA[4] MIRANDA, JOSÉ[3], PEDRO[2], BLAS ANTONIO PASCUAL[1])*[76] was born March 17, 1880 in Las Chosas, Territory of New México, and died December 17, 1954 in Carrizozo, New México. He married EMELIA BENAVIDEZ[77] March 02, 1902[78], daughter of SANTIAGO BENAVIDES and ANTONIA MOYA.

Notes for ELERDO CHÁVEZ:
Served as a Lincoln County Probate Judge for eight years. Served as a Justice of the Peace for Carrizozo.
1920 Census: Living in Las Palas, New México.

Children of ELERDO CHÁVEZ and EMELIA BENAVIDEZ are:
  i. DANIEL[6] CHÁVEZ, b. Abt. 1908[79].
  ii. ANTONIO CHÁVEZ, b. Abt. 1911[79].

19. ÁBRAN MIRANDA[5] CHÁVEZ *(PRUDENCIA[4] MIRANDA, JOSÉ[3], PEDRO[2], BLAS ANTONIO PASCUAL[1])* was born March 1882 in Las Chosas, Territory of New México. He married AURELIANA HERNÁNDEZ March 05, 1908, daughter of VICTORIANO HERNÁNDEZ and ANASTACIA RUÍZ.

Notes for AURELIANA HERNÁNDEZ:
Also known as Avreliana.

Child of ÁBRAN CHÁVEZ and AURELIANA HERNÁNDEZ is:
  i. MARGARITA[6] CHÁVEZ, b. Abt. 1908, San Patricio, Territory of New México[80].

20. CAROLINA[5] MIRANDA *(PABLO[4], JOSÉ[3], PEDRO[2], BLAS ANTONIO PASCUAL[1])* was born May 14, 1893[81]. She married TELESFORO SÁNCHEZ September 11, 1912 in Lincoln, New México[82], son of DOMINGO SÁNCHEZ and JUANITA AMENDARES.

Children of CAROLINA MIRANDA and TELESFORO SÁNCHEZ are:
28. i. DOLÓRES[6] SÁNCHEZ, b. July 05, 1913, Hondo, New México; d. September 10, 2003, Artesia, New México.
  ii. ROSA SÁNCHEZ, b. 1916, San Patricio, New México[83]; m. ANTONIO ARCHULETA.
  iii. CARLOS SÁNCHEZ, b. 1920, San Patricio, New México[83].
  iv. HARRY SÁNCHEZ, b. June 22, 1922, Hondo, New México[84]; m. EVA CHÁVEZ, February 21, 1944, Carrizozo, New México[84].

Notes for HARRY SÁNCHEZ:
1930 Census: Living in San Patricio, New México.
1944 Marriage Records: Living in Artesia, New México.

  v. REYNALDA SÁNCHEZ, b. 1922, San Patricio, New México[85].
  vi. AVRORA SÁNCHEZ, b. 1927, San Patricio, New México[85].
  vii. RUBY SÁNCHEZ, b. 1928, San Patricio, New México[85].
  viii. ALBERTO SÁNCHEZ, b. Private, San Patricio, New México.
  ix. BONIFACIO SÁNCHEZ, b. Private, San Patricio, New México.
  x. RUBÉN MIRANDA SÁNCHEZ, b. Private, San Patricio, New México.

21. JUANITA[5] MIRANDA *(PABLO[4], JOSÉ[3], PEDRO[2], BLAS ANTONIO PASCUAL[1])* was born 1894[86]. She married JACOBO BACA December 06, 1909 in Hondo, Territory of New México[86], son of DAMACIO BACA and MARÍA BACA.

Notes for JACOBO BACA:
1920 Census: Living in Hondo, New México.
1930 Census: Living in Roswell, New México.

Children of JUANITA MIRANDA and JACOBO BACA are:
  i. ELISEO[6] BACA, b. 1911[87]; m. AGAPITA BENAVIDEZ, July 23, 1934[88].

Notes for ELISEO BACA:

Also known as Elijio.

  ii. FRANK BACA, b. 1915[89].
  iii. MARGARITA BACA, b. Abt. 1918[89].

22. JULIO MOLINA[5] MIRANDA *(JULIO[4], JOSÉ[3], PEDRO[2], BLAS ANTONIO PASCUAL[1])* was born December 18, 1887[90], and died March 04, 1972 in San Patricio, New México. He married PABLITA MONTOYA November 15, 1909 in San Patricio, Territory of New México[91], daughter of ESTANISLADO MONTOYA and SARAFINA ULIBARRÍ.

Notes for PABLITA MONTOYA:
Also known as Paula.

Children of JULIO MIRANDA and PABLITA MONTOYA are:
  i. CARLOS[6] MIRANDA[92], b. January 03, 1910[93]; d. January 02, 1972.
  ii. ENRÍQUE MIRANDA, b. Abt. 1913[93].
  iii. FRANCISCA MIRANDA, b. Abt. 1914[93]; m. ANTONIO HERRERA.
  iv. CANDIDO MIRANDA[94], b. September 02, 1918, San Patricio, New México[95]; d. October 17, 1990, Socorro, New México[96].

Notes for CANDIDO MIRANDA:
Private First Class. World War II.

  v. GALINA MIRANDA[97], b. January 15, 1926, San Patricio, New México; d. February 25, 1926, San Patricio, New México.
29. vi. EULALIA MIRANDA, b. December 10, 1920, San Patricio, New México; d. August 08, 1977, El Paso, Texas.
  vii. VIRGINIA MIRANDA, b. January 12, 1932, San Patricio, New México[98]; m. ANSELMO SILVA[99], November 04, 1948, Ruidoso, New México[100].

23. EMILO H.[5] MIRANDA *(JOSÉ[4], FELIPÉ[3], PEDRO[2], BLAS ANTONIO PASCUAL[1])[101]* was born Abt. 1891[102], and died 1954 in Lincoln, New México. He married FRANCISCA DE MIRANDA.

Children of EMILO MIRANDA and FRANCISCA DE MIRANDA are:
  i. NELLIE[6] MIRANDA, b. Abt. 1914, Lincoln, New México[103].
  ii. MELA MIRANDA, b. Abt. 1916, Lincoln, New México[103].
  iii. MAXIMILIANO MIRANDA, b. Abt. 1918, Lincoln, New México[103].
  iv. MABLE FRANCES MIRANDA, b. Abt. 1920, Lincoln, New México[103].
  v. LUCILA MIRANDA, b. Abt. 1921[104].
  vi. GILBERT MIRANDA, b. Abt. 1923[104].
  vii. ENRÍQUE MIRANDA, b. Abt. 1925[104].
  viii. GERALDINE MIRANDA, b. Abt. 1926[104].
  ix. BEATRICE MIRANDA, b. Abt. 1928[105].
  x. DOLÓRES MIRANDA, b. Abt. 1930[105].

Generation No. 6

24. MANUEL[6] WARNER *(EMILIA[5] TORREZ, MIQUELA[4] MIRANDA, JOSÉ[3], PEDRO[2], BLAS ANTONIO PASCUAL[1])* was born 1903 in San Patricio, Territory of New México[106]. He married TANISLADA PRUDENCIO, daughter of CATARINO PRUDENCIO and ANITA GARCÍA.

Children of MANUEL WARNER and TANISLADA PRUDENCIO are:
  i. URBANO[7] WARNER.

Notes for URBANO WARNER:
Died young.

  ii. JOE WARNER, b. Private.

25. PREDICANDA[6] WARNER *(EMILIA[5] TORREZ, MIQUELA[4] MIRANDA, JOSÉ[3], PEDRO[2], BLAS ANTONIO PASCUAL[1])[107]* was born November 24, 1903 in San Patricio, Territory of New México, and died August 04, 1978 in Hondo, New México. She married FAUSTINO CHÁVEZ SALCIDO[107] January 24, 1924[108], son of FAUSTINO SALCIDO and MARÍA CHÁVEZ.

Children of PREDICANDA WARNER and FAUSTINO SALCIDO are:
    i.   ALBERT W.[7] SALCIDO, b. October 25, 1925, Lincoln, New México[109]; m. NORA NÚÑEZ[110], November 16, 1946, Carrizozo, New México[111].
    ii.   DAVÍD SALCIDO[112], b. June 29, 1927, Hondo, New México[113]; d. October 03, 1958, Hondo, New México; m. MARTINA SILVA, December 13, 1950, Ruidoso, New México[114].
    iii.   AMELIA SALCIDO, b. Abt. 1929, Hondo, New México[115].

26. APOLONIA[6] WARNER *(EMILIA[5] TORREZ, MIQUELA[4] MIRANDA, JOSÉ[3], PEDRO[2], BLAS ANTONIO PASCUAL[1])* was born October 12, 1909 in San Patricio, Territory of New México[116]. She married MAX CORONA[117] June 04, 1932 in Carrizozo, New México[118], son of MANUEL CORONA and SUSANA TRUJILLO.

Notes for APOLONIA WARNER:
Also known as Pauline or Polonia. There are also three variations of the last name; Warner, Juana and Guana.
Land Patent # NMLC 0041178, on the authority of the Homestead Entry-Stock Raising (39 Stat. 862), December 29, 1916. Issued 640 acres on March 26, 1937.

Child of APOLONIA WARNER and MAX CORONA is:
    i.   DANIEL[7] CORONA[119], b. Abt. 1933, San Patricio, New México; d. November 03, 1933, San Patricio, New México.

27. JULIANITA[6] WARNER *(EMILIA[5] TORREZ, MIQUELA[4] MIRANDA, JOSÉ[3], PEDRO[2], BLAS ANTONIO PASCUAL[1])* was born August 01, 1918 in San Patricio, New México[120], and died July 07, 2006 in Covington, Louisiana[121]. She married GEORGE TORRES ROMERO[122] November 10, 1934 in San Patricio, New México[123], son of GEORGE ROMERO and JOSEFITA TORRES.

Children of JULIANITA WARNER and GEORGE ROMERO are:
    i.   GEORGE[7] ROMERO[124], b. February 22, 1939; d. May 03, 1976.
    ii.   SAMUEL ROMERO[125], b. September 10, 1942, San Patricio, New México; d. November 06, 1949, San Patricio, New México.
    iii.   SAMMY ROMERO[126], b. 1949; d. May 13, 2006.

28. DOLÓRES[6] SÁNCHEZ *(CAROLINA[5] MIRANDA, PABLO[4], JOSÉ[3], PEDRO[2], BLAS ANTONIO PASCUAL[1])[127]* was born July 05, 1913 in Hondo, New México[128], and died September 10, 2003 in Artesia, New México. She married ENRÍQUES SALSBERRY February 04, 1933 in Carrizozo, New México[128], son of JAMES SALSBERRY and MANUELITA HERRERA.

29. EULALIA[6] MIRANDA *(JULIO MOLINA[5], JULIO[4], JOSÉ[3], PEDRO[2], BLAS ANTONIO PASCUAL[1])[130]* was born December 10, 1920 in San Patricio, New México, and died August 08, 1977 in El Paso, Texas[131]. She married JOSÉ HERRERA, son of LUÍS HERRERA and BENJAMÍN HERNÁNDEZ.

Notes for EULALIA MIRANDA:
Also known as Ulalia.

Genealogy of Felipé Montoya

Generation No. 1

1. FRANCISCO[1] MONTOYA was born Abt. 1830[1]. He married FRANCISCA MAESTAS.

Notes for FRANCISCO MONTOYA:
1860 Census: Living in Verelis, Bernalillo County, Territory of New México.
1870 Census: Living in El Puertecito, San Miguel County, Territory of New México. Lists occupation as a Freighter.
1880 Census: Living in Las Colonias, Territory of New México.

Children of FRANCISCO MONTOYA and FRANCISCA MAESTAS are:
     i.   ERINEA[2] MONTOYA, b. Abt. 1855[1].

Notes for ERINEA MONTOYA:
Also known as Irenea.

     ii.   MARTINA MAESTAS MONTOYA, b. Abt. 1856[1]; m. FELIPÉ TORRES.
2.   iii.   FELIPÉ MAESTAS MONTOYA, b. January 07, 1857; d. January 09, 1924, Hondo, New México.
3.   iv.   ANTONIO MAESTAS MONTOYA, b. Abt. 1859, San Miguel County, New México.
4.   v.   JOSÉ BERNARDO MONTOYA, b. May 1863.
     vi.   VIDAL MONTOYA, b. Abt. 1868, El Puertecito, San Miguel County, Territory of New México[1]; m. LEANDRA SALAZAR.
     vii.   AVELINO MONTOYA, b. December 26, 1871, Las Colonias, San Miguel County, Territory of New México[2]; m. LEANDRA LUJÁN, December 01, 1906, Las Palas, Territory of New México[2].

Notes for AVELINO MONTOYA:
Also known as José Tranquelino de la Concepción Montoya(born July 12, 1871), Abelino Montoya, José Abelino Montoya.

     viii.   MARÍA MANUELA MONTOYA, b. Abt. 1877, Las Colonias, Territory of New México[3].
     ix.   MARÍA DE ATOCHA MONTOYA, b. February 20, 1878, Las Colonias, Territory of New México.

Generation No. 2

2. FELIPÉ MAESTAS[2] MONTOYA *(FRANCISCO[1])[4]* was born January 07, 1857[5], and died January 09, 1924 in Hondo, New México. He married PAULA MARES GARCÍA October 20, 1877 in Anton Chico, Territory of New México.

Notes for FELIPÉ MAESTAS MONTOYA:
1900 Census: Living in Las Tablas. Lists occupation as a freighter.
Was a Justice of the Peace.

Children of FELIPÉ MONTOYA and PAULA GARCÍA are:
     i.   MANUELITA MARES[3] MONTOYA.
     ii.   PABLO MARES MONTOYA.
5.   iii.   ANASTACIO MARES MONTOYA, b. May 16, 1880, Tres Ritos, Territory of New México.
     iv.   MANIJO MONTOYA, b. October 1881[6].
6.   v.   MAURICIO MARES MONTOYA, b. September 10, 1882, Tres Ritos, Territory of New México; d. January 25, 1925, San Patricio, New México.
7.   vi.   DOMINGO MONTOYA, b. December 20, 1884, Picacho, Territory of New México.
     vii.   SANTIAGO MARES MONTOYA, b. December 10, 1886[7].
     viii.   ROSALÍA GARCÍA MONTOYA, b. February 1890[8].
8.   ix.   FRANCISCA MONTOYA, b. February 12, 1890.
9.   x.   EUFELIA MONTOYA, b. February 1891.
     xi.   EUGENIO MONTOYA, b. August 1894[8].
     xii.   FELIPÉ MARES MONTOYA, b. October 21, 1897, Ruidoso, Territory of New México[9].
10.   xiii.   DECIDERIA MONTOYA, b. December 31, 1898, Las Angosturas (San Ysidro), Territory of New México.

3. ANTONIO MAESTAS[2] MONTOYA *(FRANCISCO[1])* was born Abt. 1859 in San Miguel County, New México[10]. He married PETRA GARDUÑO RIVERA Abt. 1880[11], daughter of JOSÉ RIBERA and FELICIANA GARDUÑO.

Notes for ANTONIO MAESTAS MONTOYA:
1900 Census: Lists occupation as a freighter.

Notes for PETRA GARDUÑO RIVERA:
Also known as Petra Cardona.
1910 Census: Living in Richardson, Territory of New México.

Children of ANTONIO MONTOYA and PETRA RIVERA are:

11.	i.	GABINO[3] MONTOYA, b. Abt. 1881.
12.	ii.	ADONIO MONTOYA, b. July 30, 1885, Picacho, Territory of New México; d. April 10, 1973, Capitán, New México.
	iii.	ÁRON MONTOYA, b. January 10, 1886, Las Tablas, Territory of New México[12]; m. ANTONIA VIGIL, April 23, 1906, Las Tablas, Territory of New México[12].
13.	iv.	LEOPOLDO MONTOYA, b. Abt. 1888.
	v.	ANDREA MONTOYA, b. December 1890[13]; m. NESTOR DIONICIO CHÁVEZ.
	vi.	GREGORIO MONTOYA, b. July 1891[13]; m. SOFIA MAÉS SÁNCHEZ.

Notes for GREGORIO MONTOYA:
1920 Census: Living in Ceder Canyon, Cháves County, New México.

	vii.	LEANDRA MONTOYA[14], b. March 13, 1892, Talles, Territory of New México; d. January 31, 1932, Capitán, New México; m. ISAAC CHÁVEZ[15], November 23, 1916, Lincoln, New México.
	viii.	TEODORA MONTOYA, b. Abt. 1894[16].
	ix.	JUAN RIVERA MONTOYA, b. June 24, 1898[17]; d. December 09, 1923, Jarales, New México; m. APOLINARIA CHÁVEZ, July 15, 1921, Richardson, New México[18].

4. JOSÉ BERNARDO[2] MONTOYA *(FRANCISCO[1])* was born May 1863[19]. He married EULALIA SÁNCHEZ Abt. 1889[19].

Notes for JOSÉ BERNARDO MONTOYA:
1900 Census: Lists occupation as a freighter.

Children of JOSÉ MONTOYA and EULALIA SÁNCHEZ are:

	i.	MANUELITA[3] MONTOYA, b. February 13, 1892, Las Tablas, Territory of New México[20]; m. GOMICINDO ROMERO, March 02, 1907[20].
	ii.	ALEJANDRO MONTOYA, b. April 1894[21].
	iii.	MARIANO MONTOYA, b. April 1897[21].

Generation No. 3

5. ANASTACIO MARES[3] MONTOYA *(FELIPÉ MAESTAS[2], FRANCISCO[1])*[22] was born May 16, 1880 in Tres Ritos, Territory of New México[23]. He married (1) PAULA GUAJACA July 09, 1900[24], daughter of FLAVIO GUAJACA and NARCISA PROVENCIO. He married (2) SARAFINA GUTIÉRREZ Abt. 1917[25], daughter of FLORENTINO GUTIÉRREZ and ANGELITA DE GUTIÉRREZ.

Notes for ANASTACIO MARES MONTOYA:
1920 Census: Living in Hondo, New México. (Juan Montoya)
1930 Census: Living in Dexter, New México. (Anastacio Montoya)

Children of ANASTACIO MONTOYA and PAULA GUAJACA are:

	i.	ELÍAS[4] MONTOYA, b. June 25, 1905, San Patricio, Territory of New México[26].
	ii.	NARCISA MONTOYA[27], b. November 05, 1907, San Patricio, Territory of New México[28]; d. January 12, 1985, Hondo, New México; m. JOSÉ SALCIDO[29].

Notes for NARCISA MONTOYA:
Cemetery records indicate that she was born on November 19, 1907.

Notes for JOSÉ SALCIDO:
Land Patent # NMLC 0038899, on the authority of the Homestead Entry-Stock Raising (39 Stat. 862), December 29, 1916. Issued 360 acres on November 21, 1934.

      iii.   ELISIA MONTOYA, b. 1912, San Patricio, New México[30].
      iv.   ANGELITA MONTOYA[31], b. May 12, 1913, San Patricio, New México[32]; d. April 22, 1980, Hondo, New México; m. SYLVESTRE SALCIDO[33].

Children of ANASTACIO MONTOYA and SARAFINA GUTIÉRREZ are:
      v.   RAMÓN[4] MONTOYA, b. Abt. 1920[34].
      vi.   JOVITA MONTOYA, b. Abt. 1923[35].

6. MAURICIO MARES[3] MONTOYA *(FELIPÉ MAESTAS[2], FRANCISCO[1])*[36] was born September 10, 1882 in Tres Ritos, Territory of New México[37], and died January 25, 1925 in San Patricio, New México. He married AVRORA SÁNCHEZ[38] December 15, 1902 in La Capilla de San Ysidro, Las Angosturas, Territory of New México[39], daughter of EUGENIO SÁNCHEZ and ROSA GRIEGO.

Notes for MAURICIO MARES MONTOYA:
1902: Living in Las Tablas.

Notes for AVRORA SÁNCHEZ:
Also known as Aurora.
1902: Living Las Angosturas (San Ysidro), near La Capilla de San Ysidro.

Children of MAURICIO MONTOYA and AVRORA SÁNCHEZ are:
14.   i.   MASIMIANA[4] MONTOYA, b. September 09, 1903, San Patricio, New México; d. June 20, 1963, Hondo, New México.
      ii.   FLAVIO MONTOYA[40], b. February 22, 1905, Lincoln, Territory of New México[41]; d. April 07, 1979, Alamagordo, New México; m. GENEVA KIMBRELL[41], December 24, 1934[41].

Notes for FLAVIO MONTOYA:
Private First Class US Army. WW II Veteran.

      iii.   JOSÉ SÁNCHEZ MONTOYA, b. 1907[42].
      iv.   SANTIAGO SÁNCHEZ MONTOYA[43], b. February 23, 1910; d. January 14, 1945.

Notes for SANTIAGO SÁNCHEZ MONTOYA:
New Mexico Private 940 Guard. Died in WW II.

15.   v.   YSIDRO MONTOYA, b. May 15, 1913, San Patricio, New México; d. December 01, 1960, Roswell, New México.
      vi.   MANUEL SÁNCHEZ MONTOYA, b. April 30, 1915, San Patricio, New México[44]; d. April 24, 1994; m. CELIA SÁNCHEZ[45].

Notes for MANUEL SÁNCHEZ MONTOYA:
WW II Veteran.

      vii.   ROSA MONTOYA[45], b. August 18, 1918, San Patricio, New México; d. July 07, 1991, San Patricio, New México; m. ELISEO GALLEGOS[45].
      viii.   EUTILIA MONTOYA[46], b. December 23, 1920, San Patricio, New México[47]; d. December 04, 2005, Mescalero, New México; m. ESTOLANO OROSCO SÁNCHEZ[48].

Notes for EUTILIA MONTOYA:
Buried in Hondo, New México.

Notes for ESTOLANO OROSCO SÁNCHEZ:
1930 Census: Living in Corona, New México. He was living with his Tia Eluticia Gavaldon.

      ix.   TAVIANA MONTOYA[49], b. December 28, 1922, San Patricio, New México[50]; d. July 26, 1968; m. ABSALÓN SÁNCHEZ[51], August 25, 1945, San Patricio, New México[52].

Notes for ABSALÓN SÁNCHEZ:

Also known as Ausolón Sánchez. World War II Veteran.

> x. JUAN SÁNCHEZ MONTOYA, b. Private, San Patricio, New México; m. EVA GONZÁLES, August 13, 1948, Carrizozo, New México[53].

Notes for JUAN SÁNCHEZ MONTOYA:
US Navy, Seaman First Class. World War II.

7. DOMINGO[3] MONTOYA *(FELIPÉ MAESTAS[2], FRANCISCO[1])* was born December 20, 1884 in Picacho, Territory of New México[54]. He married PETRA MARTÍNEZ August 04, 1906 in Ruidoso, Territory of New México[54], daughter of JOSÉ MARTÍNEZ and SALOMÉ SÁNCHEZ.

Child of DOMINGO MONTOYA and PETRA MARTÍNEZ is:
> i. ANITA[4] MONTOYA, b. Abt. 1916[55].

8. FRANCISCA[3] MONTOYA *(FELIPÉ MAESTAS[2], FRANCISCO[1])* was born February 12, 1890[56]. She married (1) MANUEL GARCÍA VIGIL[57] February 22, 1908[58], son of FRANCISCO VIGIL and DARIA GARCÍA. She married (2) JUAN MIRABAL August 16, 1933 in Carrizozo, New México[59].

Children of FRANCISCA MONTOYA and MANUEL VIGIL are:
> i. JOSÉ[4] VIGIL, b. Abt. 1915[60].
> ii. ÁBRAN VIGIL, b. Abt. 1919[60].

9. EUFELIA[3] MONTOYA *(FELIPÉ MAESTAS[2], FRANCISCO[1])* was born February 1891[61]. She married GAVINO RIVERA Abt. 1914[62], son of MAURICIO RIVERA and PETRA PADILLA.

Children of EUFELIA MONTOYA and GAVINO RIVERA are:
> i. PAULITA[4] RIVERA, b. November 10, 1915[63]; m. FELIPÉ HERRERA, August 19, 1933[63].
> ii. BEN RIVERA, b. Abt. 1920[64].

10. DECIDERIA[3] MONTOYA *(FELIPÉ MAESTAS[2], FRANCISCO[1])* was born December 31, 1898 in Las Angosturas (San Ysidro), Territory of New México[65]. She married TIVORCIO DOMINGUEZ[66] December 20, 1915 in Lincoln, New México[67], son of NICANOR DOMINGUEZ and OCTAVIANA FUENTES.

Notes for TIVORCIO DOMINGUEZ:
Death records indicate that his birth year was 1888.

Children of DECIDERIA MONTOYA and TIVORCIO DOMINGUEZ are:
> i. ESTEVAN[4] DOMINGUEZ[68], b. December 26, 1916, Hondo, New México[69].

Notes for ESTEVAN DOMINGUEZ:
Private. World War II.

> ii. MANUELITA DOMINGUEZ, b. 1918[69].

11. GABINO[3] MONTOYA *(ANTONIO MAESTAS[2], FRANCISCO[1])* was born Abt. 1881[70]. He married EUFALIA DE MONTOYA.

Notes for GABINO MONTOYA:
1920 Census, Living in Capitán, New México.

Child of GABINO MONTOYA and EUFALIA DE MONTOYA is:
> i. PAULITA[4] MONTOYA, b. Abt. 1916[71].

12. ADONIO[3] MONTOYA *(ANTONIO MAESTAS[2], FRANCISCO[1])*[72] was born July 30, 1885 in Picacho, Territory of New México, and died April 10, 1973 in Capitán, New México. He married ANTONIA VIGIL April 23, 1906 in Las Tablas, Territory of New México.

Notes for ADONIO MONTOYA:
Buried: Capítan Cemetery.

Notes for ANTONIA VIGIL:
Buried: Capítan Cemetery.

Children of ADONIO MONTOYA and ANTONIA VIGIL are:

    i.   CLAUDIO[4] MONTOYA[73], b. February 05, 1907, Encinoso, Territory of New México[74]; d. August 27, 1984, Roswell, New México; m. JUANITA C. CHÁVEZ[75], October 15, 1932[76].

Notes for CLAUDIO MONTOYA:
Buried: Capítan cemetary.

    ii.   MARÍA MONTOYA[77], b. October 22, 1908, Richardson, Territory of New México; d. June 12, 1991, Roswell, New México; m. RUBÉN ARCHULETA SÁNCHEZ[78], February 08, 1939, Roswell, New México.

Notes for MARÍA MONTOYA:
Also known as Mary.
Buried: South Park Cemetary in Roswell, New México.

    iii.   CHONITA MONTOYA[79], b. April 09, 1912, Richardson, New México; d. July 16, 1991, Capitán, New México; m. DAMACIO CHÁVEZ[79], August 16, 1936.

Notes for CHONITA MONTOYA:
Buried: Capítan cemetery.

    iv.   ELFEGO MONTOYA[79], b. April 16, 1914, Encinoso, New México[80]; d. February 02, 1993, Capitán, New México.
    v.   DELIA MONTOYA, b. Abt. 1917[80]; m. RAY LUCERO.
    vi.   CLEO MONTOYA, b. Abt. 1919[80]; m. DANIEL VARGAS.

Notes for CLEO MONTOYA:
Also known as Cleotilde.

    vii.   ELOISA MONTOYA, b. Abt. 1921[80].
    viii.   BENJAMÍN MONTOYA[81], b. September 23, 1922; d. June 16, 1957, Capitán, New México.

Notes for BENJAMÍN MONTOYA:
Buried: Capítan cemetary.

    ix.   FLORA MONTOYA, b. November 29, 1924, Richardson, New México[82]; d. March 29, 2008, Merced, California; m. EVARISTO LUCERO SÁNCHEZ, December 20, 1946, Carrizozo, New México[82].

Notes for FLORA MONTOYA:
1930 Census: Living in Encinoso, New México.

Notes for EVARISTO LUCERO SÁNCHEZ:
1930 Census: Living in Arabela, New México.

    x.   ROSA MONTOYA[83], b. May 15, 1927[84]; d. September 14, 1931.
    xi.   ANTONIO MONTOYA, b. Abt. 1929[84].
16.   xii.   ELVIRA MONTOYA, b. Private.

13. LEOPOLDO[3] MONTOYA *(ANTONIO MAESTAS[2], FRANCISCO[1])* was born Abt. 1888[84]. He married MARTINA CHÁVEZ February 22, 1909[85], daughter of NICOLÁS CHÁVEZ and PORFIRIA TRUJILLO.

Notes for LEOPOLDO MONTOYA:
1910 Census: Living in Richardson, Territory of New México.

Children of LEOPOLDO MONTOYA and MARTINA CHÁVEZ are:

    i.   PAULITA CHÁVEZ[4] MONTOYA, b. March 1911.

	ii.	EDUVIJEN MONTOYA, b. October 17, 1913.
17.	iii.	LUCÍA MONTOYA, b. January 01, 1916.
	iv.	JOSEFITA CHÁVEZ MONTOYA, b. Abt. 1918, Encinoso, Territory of New México[86]; m. YLARIO TRUJILLO[87], September 26, 1932[88].

Notes for YLARIO TRUJILLO:
Also known as Hilario and Eulalio. Nicknamed, Shorty.

v.	FERMÍN MONTOYA, b. March 11, 1922[89].
vi.	ESTELA MONTOYA, b. Abt. 1924[89].
vii.	MARÍA DEL ROSARIO MONTOYA, b. August 20, 1927[89]; m. FREDERICO NÚÑEZ.
viii.	MACARIO MONTOYA, b. March 10, 1931.

Generation No. 4

14. MASIMIANA[4] MONTOYA *(MAURICIO MARES[3], FELIPÉ MAESTAS[2], FRANCISCO[1])[90]* was born September 09, 1903 in San Patricio, New México[91], and died June 20, 1963 in Hondo, New México. She married ELFIDO SALAS[92] February 13, 1924[93], son of TEOFILO SALAS and IGENIA GALLEGOS.

Notes for MASIMIANA MONTOYA:
Also known as Maximiana.

Notes for ELFIDO SALAS:
Also known as Elfigo, Delfido.
Land Patent # NMLC 0025968, on the authority of the Homestead Entry-Stock Raising (39 Stat. 862), December 29, 1916. Issued 611 acres on August 16, 1927.

Children of MASIMIANA MONTOYA and ELFIDO SALAS are:

i.	YLARIO[5] SALAS[94], b. August 05, 1925, Hondo, New México[95]; d. October 11, 1973; m. STELLA WARNER[96], December 01, 1951, Ruidoso, New México[97].

Notes for YLARIO SALAS:
Private US Army. World War Two.

ii.	PEDRO SALAS, b. 1926[98].
iii.	REYNALDA SALAS, b. 1929[98].
iv.	TERESA SALAS[99], b. July 23, 1932; d. October 01, 2005, Roswell, New México.
v.	RAMONA SALAS[99], b. October 08, 1937, Hondo, New México; d. March 09, 1997[100].
vi.	JUAN SALAS, b. Private.
vii.	MADALENA SALAS, b. Private.
viii.	RAMÓN SALAS, b. Private.
ix.	TEOFILO MONTOYA SALAS, b. Private.

15. YSIDRO[4] MONTOYA *(MAURICIO MARES[3], FELIPÉ MAESTAS[2], FRANCISCO[1])[101]* was born May 15, 1913 in San Patricio, New México, and died December 01, 1960 in Roswell, New México. He married BLASITA PERALES, daughter of VICTORIO PERALES and SOSTENA CHÁVEZ.

Notes for YSIDRO MONTOYA:
New Mexico Private First Class 3263 Sig Service Co. Was a WW II veteran.

Child of YSIDRO MONTOYA and BLASITA PERALES is:

i.	JOSPHINE[5] MONTOYA[102], b. May 03, 1935; d. April 1991, Roswell, New México.

16. ELVIRA[4] MONTOYA *(ADONIO[3], ANTONIO MAESTAS[2], FRANCISCO[1])* was born Private. She married NATALIO SÁNCHEZ, son of JESÚS SÁNCHEZ and ELVIRA LUCERO.

Notes for NATALIO SÁNCHEZ:
Also known as Anatalio.

Child of ELVIRA MONTOYA and NATALIO SÁNCHEZ is:
    i.   MINNIE[5] SÁNCHEZ, b. Private; m. ERNEST SILVA.

17. LUCÍA[4] MONTOYA *(LEOPOLDO[3], ANTONIO MAESTAS[2], FRANCISCO[1])* was born January 01, 1916[103]. She married GUILLERMO PADILLA[104] June 10, 1933[105], son of JESÚS PADILLA and LUISA MONTOYA.

Children of LUCÍA MONTOYA and GUILLERMO PADILLA are:
    i.   MARY[5] PADILLA, b. Private; m. REYNER GONZÁLES.
    ii.   ANTONIO PADILLA, b. Private.
    iii.   EDUARDO PADILLA, b. Private.
    iv.   FRED MONTOYA PADILLA, b. Private.
    v.   WILLIE PADILLA, b. Private.
    vi.   CECILIA PADILLA[106], b. 1935; d. 1935.

Notes for CECILIA PADILLA:
Died young at the age of 9 months.

Genealogy of Tranquelino Montoya

Generation No. 1

1. TRANQUELINO[1] MONTOYA was born Abt. 1847 in Tomé, Nuevo México, La República de México[1]. He married MARÍA DE JESÚS TRUJILLO[2], daughter of ASCENCIÓN TRUJILLO.

Notes for TRANQUELINO MONTOYA:
Abt. 1860: Had migrated to Lincoln County in the 1860s with his wife.
1870 Census: Living in Lincoln County, Precinct 2 (San Patricio), Territory of New México.

Children of TRANQUELINO MONTOYA and MARÍA TRUJILLO are:

2.	i.	ISABELA[2] MONTOYA, b. October 1869, San Patricio, Territory of New México.
3.	ii.	ESTANISLADO TRUJILLO MONTOYA, b. October 29, 1869, Rio Bonito, Territory of New México; d. October 13, 1932, San Patricio, New México.
4.	iii.	ÁRON MONTOYA, b. February 23, 1873, Rio Bonito, Territory of New México.
5.	iv.	SARA MONTOYA, b. 1878, Arabela, Territory of New México.
6.	v.	LAZARO MONTOYA, b. June 29, 1879.
7.	vi.	CATARINA MONTOYA, b. 1880, San Patricio, Territory of New México; d. 1951.
8.	vii.	ELFIDA MONTOYA, b. October 23, 1883; d. March 27, 1937, San Patricio, New México.
9.	viii.	DOROTEO MONTOYA, b. February 06, 1886.
	ix.	RICARDO MONTOYA, b. April 03, 1887, San Patricio, Territory of New México[3].
	x.	GUADALUPE MONTOYA, b. 1888.
	xi.	CANDELARIO MONTOYA, b. 1890.

Notes for CANDELARIO MONTOYA:
Died at a young age.

	xii.	CANDELARIA MONTOYA, b. February 03, 1890[4].

Generation No. 2

2. ISABELA[2] MONTOYA *(TRANQUELINO[1])* was born October 1869 in San Patricio, Territory of New México[5]. She married (1) JUAN GALLEGOS ULIBARRÍ May 13, 1889[6], son of SANTIAGO ULIBARRÍ and JUANA GALLEGOS. She married (2) LUÍS CASTILLO[7] November 04, 1922[8], son of CRESENCIO CASTILLO and GERTRUDES SOTELA.

Notes for ISABELA MONTOYA:
Also known as María Isabel Montoya.

Notes for JUAN GALLEGOS ULIBARRÍ:
Also known as Juan Rivali.
1860 Census: Living in La Polvadera de San Lorenzo, Territory of New México.
1870, 1880 & 1900 Census: Living in San Patricio, Territory of New México.
One of the founding families of La Plaza de San Patricio.

Notes for LUÍS CASTILLO:
Immigrated to the U.S. in about 1908.

Child of ISABELA MONTOYA and JUAN ULIBARRÍ is:
  i.   JUANITA[3] ULIBARRÍ, b. May 1892[9].

3. ESTANISLADO TRUJILLO[2] MONTOYA *(TRANQUELINO[1])*[10] was born October 29, 1869 in Rio Bonito, Territory of New México[11], and died October 13, 1932 in San Patricio, New México. He married (1) SARAFINA SOCORRO ULIBARRÍ January 09, 1887 in San Patricio, Territory of New México[12], daughter of JUAN ULIBARRÍ and MARÍA LUCERO. He married (2) ELOISA SALAZAR August 27, 1921[13], daughter of PEDRO SALAZAR and ROSALÍA LUCERO.

Notes for ESTANISLADO TRUJILLO MONTOYA:
Also known as Tanislado, Tanislaus.
Land Patent # NMLC 0026044, on the authority of the Homestead Entry-Enlarged (35 Stat. 639), February 19, 1909. Issued 164.56 acres on April 09, 1926.

Children of ESTANISLADO MONTOYA and SARAFINA ULIBARRÍ are:
10.   i.   MANUEL ULIBARRÍ[3] MONTOYA, b. 1888, San Patricio, New México; d. Bef. 1920.
11.   ii.   PABLITA MONTOYA, b. May 21, 1890, San Patricio, Territory of New México; d. March 31, 1952, San Patricio, New México.
12.   iii.   TEODORO ULIBARRÍ MONTOYA, b. December 18, 1892, San Patricio, Territory of New México; d. March 08, 1976, Glencoe, New México.
     iv.   CANDIDO ULIBARRÍ MONTOYA, b. 1895, San Patricio, New México[14].
13.   v.   SUSANA MONTOYA, b. 1897, San Patricio, Territory of New México; d. June 17, 1938.
     vi.   ISABEL MONTOYA, b. December 29, 1899, San Patricio, New México[15]; m. (1) CONCHA DE MONTOYA, El Paso, Texas; m. (2) VICTORIA SÁNCHEZ[16], February 23, 1921[17].
     vii.   DESIDERIO MONTOYA, b. February 15, 1902, San Patricio, Territory of New México[18]; m. CATALINA SALAZAR, March 09, 1926, Capitán, New México[18].

Notes for DESIDERIO MONTOYA:
Baptismal records indicate that he was born on December 22, 1901. (Microfiche# 0016754, Page 121)

14.   viii.   SENAIDA MONTOYA, b. May 19, 1907, San Patricio, Territory of New México; d. July 10, 1944, Roswell, New México.

4. ÁRON[2] MONTOYA *(TRANQUELINO[1])* was born February 23, 1873 in Rio Bonito, Territory of New México[19]. He married (1) BEATRIZ ROMERO January 31, 1898 in San Patricio, Territory of New México[20], daughter of DOROTEO ROMERO and AGAPITA GUEBARA. He married (2) MARIA PAULITA QUINTANA May 03, 1922[21].

Notes for ÁRON MONTOYA:
Padrinos: Gregorio Trujillo and Josefa Fajardo.
1900 Census lists birthdate as: May 1874.
1910 Census: Both Crecencio Udero and Manuel Udero are listed as his brothers-in-law.
1920 Census: Living in Las Palas, New México.
1930 Census: Living in Arabela, New México.
Marriage to Paulita Quintana, church records show his birthdate as July 15, 1873.

Children of ÁRON MONTOYA and BEATRIZ ROMERO are:
     i.   PAULITA[3] MONTOYA, b. June 12, 1900[22]; m. JOSÉ AMADO CRUZ, August 22, 1918.
     ii.   DOROTEA MONTOYA, b. June 05, 1902, San Patricio, Territory of New México[23]; m. LUPE CASTILLO, November 11, 1921[24].

Notes for LUPE CASTILLO:
Also known as Guadalupe.
1900 Census: Living in Tecolocito, Territory of New México.

15.   iii.   MANUEL ROMERO MONTOYA, b. May 04, 1906, San Patricio, Territory of New México.
16.   iv.   ALTAGRACIA MONTOYA, b. May 07, 1909, San Patricio, Territory of New México; d. June 05, 2006, San Patricio, New México.

5. SARA[2] MONTOYA *(TRANQUELINO[1])* was born 1878 in Arabela, Territory of New México[25]. She married CRUZ MONTAÑO GUEBARA Abt. 1894[26], son of JUAN GUEBARA and MARÍA MONTAÑO.

Notes for CRUZ MONTAÑO GUEBARA:
Also known as Cruz Devara and Santa Cruz Montaño Guevara.
1910 & 1920 Census: Living in Las Palas, New México.
1930 Census: Living in Arabela, New México.

Children of SARA MONTOYA and CRUZ GUEBARA are:
     i.   NAVORA[3] GUEVARA, b. Abt. 1895[26].
17.   ii.   MANUELITA GUEVARA, b. Abt. 1896.

   iii. PETRA GUEVARA, b. Abt. 1900[26]; m. DAVÍD MARTÍNEZ.
   iv. GUADALUPE GUEVARA, b. Abt. 1904[27]; m. MARÍA SALAZAR.

Notes for GUADALUPE GUEVARA:
Also known as Lupe.

18. v. LAZARO GUEVARA, b. March 30, 1906, Lincoln, Territory of New México.
19. vi. CRUZ MONTOYA GUEVARA, b. Abt. 1907, Arabela, Territory of New México.
20. vii. ANTONIA GUEVARA, b. Abt. 1909.
   viii. JUAN GUEVARA, b. Abt. 1914[27].
   ix. MAGDALENA GUEVARA, b. Abt. 1917[27]; m. TRINIDAD ROMERO.

6. LAZARO[2] MONTOYA *(TRANQUELINO[1])* was born June 29, 1879[28]. He married RAMONA MÁRQUEZ July 20, 1900 in San Patricio, New México[29], daughter of PEDRO MÁRQUEZ and MARÍA PEÑA.

Notes for LAZARO MONTOYA:
1910 Census: Living in Ábo, Territory of New México.

Notes for RAMONA MÁRQUEZ:
1900 Census: Living in Lincoln, Territory of New México.

Child of LAZARO MONTOYA and RAMONA MÁRQUEZ is:
   i. MARÍA G.[3] MONTOYA, b. Abt. 1909[30].

Gregorio Ybarra

7. CATARINA[2] MONTOYA *(TRANQUELINO[1])*[31] was born 1880 in San Patricio, Territory of New México, and died 1951. She married GREGORIO YBARRA[31] January 22, 1896[32], son of MAXIMIANO YBARRA and ROBERTA RUÍZ.

Notes for CATARINA MONTOYA:
Also known as Catalina Montolla.

Notes for GREGORIO YBARRA:
Gregorio lists his parents as Margarito Ybarra and Josfa Ruíz in his marriage to Catarina Montoya.

Children of CATARINA MONTOYA and GREGORIO YBARRA are:
21. i. PABLO[3] YBARRA, b. Abt. 1898, San Patricio, Territory of New México.
22. ii. JULIANITA YBARRA, b. February 16, 1901, San Patricio, Territory of New México; d. June 04, 1986.
23. iii. GENOVEVO YBARRA, b. November 22, 1903, San Patricio, Territory of New México; d. February 13, 1975.
24. iv. CASIMIRA YBARRA, b. March 03, 1906, San Patricio, Territory of New México; d. May 30, 1977, San Patricio, New México.
25. v. LUCÍA YBARRA, b. March 17, 1908, San Patricio, Territory of New México.
26. vi. CRUSITA YBARRA, b. May 02, 1910, San Patricio, Territory of New México; d. November 1985.
   vii. TRANQUELINO YBARRA, b. 1914, San Patricio, New México; m. BESSIE APACHÉ.
   viii. WILFREDO YBARRA[33], b. April 27, 1915, San Patricio, New México; d. July 29, 1951.

Notes for WILFREDO YBARRA:
Served with NM PVT 353 Infantry. WW II veteran.

   ix. CRECENCIA YBARRA[34], b. December 06, 1918, San Patricio, New México; d. November 15, 1996; m. MIGUEL GONZÁLES[34], January 05, 1935, San Patricio, New México[35].

Notes for CRECENCIA YBARRA:
Also known as Crita.

8. ELFIDA[2] MONTOYA *(TRANQUELINO[1])*[36] was born October 23, 1883[37], and died March 27, 1937 in San Patricio, New México. She married (1) NICOLÁS SILVA May 22, 1898[38], son of MANUEL SILVA and JOSEFITA ESQUIVEL. She married (2) MACARIO CHÁVEZ December 07, 1902[39], son of NAVOR CHÁVEZ and GREGORIA TRUJILLO.

Notes for ELFIDA MONTOYA:
Also known as Delfida.
November 30, 1833: Baptized. Padrinos: Francisco Trujillo, Margarita Trujillo.

Notes for MACARIO CHÁVEZ:
1870 Census: Living in Manzano, Territory of New México.
1880 Census: Living in La Plaza de Picacho, Territory of New México.
1900 Census: Living in Las Tablas, Territory of New México.
1910 Census: Living in Richardson, Territory of New México.

Children of ELFIDA MONTOYA and MACARIO CHÁVEZ are:
| 27. | i. | PEDRO³ CHÁVEZ, b. October 23, 1903, Lincoln, Territory of New México; d. December 27, 1995, San Patricio, New México. |
| | ii. | SALVADOR MONTOYA, b. Abt. 1910⁴⁰. |

9. DOROTEO² MONTOYA *(TRANQUELINO¹)* was born February 06, 1886⁴¹. He married ALBINA SILVA⁴² November 20, 1907⁴³, daughter of HILARIO SILVA and AMBROSIA ULIBARRÍ.

Notes for DOROTEO MONTOYA:
Baptized: February 15, 1886. Padrinos: Pedro Trujillo, Andrea Miranda.
1920 Census: Living in Las Palas, New México.

Notes for ALBINA SILVA:
Also known as Alvina, Balbina.

Children of DOROTEO MONTOYA and ALBINA SILVA are:
	i.	SAMUEL³ MONTOYA⁴⁴, b. May 19, 1909; d. May 03, 1994; m. EUFRACIA MONTOYA⁴⁴, November 26, 1938⁴⁵.
	ii.	COSMÉ MONTOYA⁴⁶, b. May 1911, San Patricio, New México⁴⁷; m. AMALIA BENAVIDEZ.
28.	iii.	LORENSITA MONTOYA, b. February 12, 1912, San Patricio, New México; d. Artesia, New México.
29.	iv.	JOSEFITA MONTOYA, b. 1918; d. 2003.
30.	v.	TRANQUELINO SILVA MONTOYA, b. August 22, 1925, Arabela, New México; d. September 24, 2009, Alamagordo, New México.

Generation No. 3

10. MANUEL ULIBARRÍ³ MONTOYA *(ESTANISLADO TRUJILLO², TRANQUELINO¹)* was born 1888 in San Patricio, New México⁴⁸, and died Bef. 1920⁴⁹. He married MARTINA PRUDENCIO⁵⁰ October 01, 1911, daughter of JOSÉ PRUDENCIO and VICTORIA FAJARDO.

Children of MANUEL MONTOYA and MARTINA PRUDENCIO are:
	i.	FELIX⁴ MONTOYA.
	ii.	LUÍS MONTOYA, b. Abt. 1913⁵¹.
	iii.	JUANITA MONTOYA, b. Abt. 1914⁵¹.
	iv.	GILBERTO MONTOYA, b. Abt. 1917⁵¹.

11. PABLITA³ MONTOYA *(ESTANISLADO TRUJILLO², TRANQUELINO¹)* was born May 21, 1890 in San Patricio, Territory of New México, and died March 31, 1952 in San Patricio, New México. She married JULIO MOLINA MIRANDA November 15, 1909 in San Patricio, Territory of New México⁵², son of JULIO MIRANDA and ANTONIA MOLINA.

Notes for PABLITA MONTOYA:
Also known as Paula.

Children of PABLITA MONTOYA and JULIO MIRANDA are:
	i.	CARLOS⁴ MIRANDA⁵³, b. January 03, 1910⁵⁴; d. January 02, 1972.
	ii.	ENRÍQUE MIRANDA, b. Abt. 1913⁵⁴.
	iii.	FRANCISCA MIRANDA, b. Abt. 1914⁵⁴; m. ANTONIO HERRERA.

    iv.   CANDIDO MIRANDA[55], b. September 02, 1918, San Patricio, New México[56]; d. October 17, 1990, Socorro, New México[57].

Notes for CANDIDO MIRANDA:
Private First Class. World War II.

    v.   GALINA MIRANDA[58], b. January 15, 1926, San Patricio, New México; d. February 25, 1926, San Patricio, New México.

    vi.   EULALIA MIRANDA[59], b. December 10, 1920, San Patricio, New México; d. August 08, 1977, El Paso, Texas[60]; m. JOSÉ HERRERA.

Notes for EULALIA MIRANDA:
Also known as Ulalia.

    vii.   VIRGINIA MIRANDA, b. January 12, 1932, San Patricio, New México[61]; m. ANSELMO SILVA[62], November 04, 1948, Ruidoso, New México[63].

12. TEODORO ULIBARRÍ[3] MONTOYA *(ESTANISLADO TRUJILLO[2], TRANQUELINO[1])*[64] was born December 18, 1892 in San Patricio, Territory of New México[65], and died March 08, 1976 in Glencoe, New México. He married BERSABÉ SÁNCHEZ December 11, 1919 in San Patricio, New México[66], daughter of JUAN SÁNCHEZ and MARÍA SÁNCHEZ.

Notes for TEODORO ULIBARRÍ MONTOYA:
Also known as Theodoro.

Children of TEODORO MONTOYA and BERSABÉ SÁNCHEZ are:
    i.   AMELIA[4] MONTOYA, b. Abt. 1920, Glencoe, New México[67].
    ii.   ALVESITA MONTOYA[68], b. January 26, 1921, Glencoe, New México[69]; m. CARLOS SÁNCHEZ[70], July 22, 1940, Glencoe, New México[71].

Notes for ALVESITA MONTOYA:
Also known as Albesa.
    iii.   CANDIDO SÁNCHEZ MONTOYA[72], b. November 14, 1923, Glencoe, New México; d. June 23, 1992, Ruidoso Downs, New México; m. CRUSITA BENAVIDEZ SÁNCHEZ[73], November 09, 1946, Carrizozo, New México[74].
    iv.   ANSELMO MONTOYA, b. Abt. 1926, Glencoe, New México[75].

13. SUSANA[3] MONTOYA *(ESTANISLADO TRUJILLO[2], TRANQUELINO[1])*[76] was born 1897 in San Patricio, Territory of New México[77], and died June 17, 1938[78]. She married LORENSO MENDOSA[79] September 13, 1915 in Lincoln, New México[80], son of DIONICIO MENDOSA and MARÍA DE MENDOSA.

Notes for SUSANA MONTOYA:
Also known as Socorro, Susanita.

Notes for LORENSO MENDOSA:
Rosenda's son.

Children of SUSANA MONTOYA and LORENSO MENDOSA are:
    i.   TONITA[4] MENDOSA, b. Abt. 1917[81].
    ii.   SOCORRO MENDOSA[82], b. December 02, 1919, San Patricio, New México[83]; m. PABLO HERNÁNDEZ[84], June 19, 1940, Hondo, New México[84].
    iii.   BENJAMÍN MENDOSA[85], b. Abt. 1921, Hondo, New México[86]; d. June 25, 1942, Hondo, New México.
    iv.   CONSUELO MENDOSA[87], b. October 09, 1926; d. December 19, 2006, Roswell, New México; m. ERMINIO SÁNCHEZ[87], December 07, 1944, Roswell, New México[88].

Notes for CONSUELO MENDOSA:
Her mother died when she was 12 years old. She accepted the responsibility of caring for her younger brothers and sisters.

Notes for ERMINIO SÁNCHEZ:
About 1944: Erminio and his family moved to Roswell, New México.

v.   ELISA MENDOSA[89], b. May 12, 1930, San Patricio, New México; d. July 02, 2000, San Patricio, New México; m. ISMAEL CHÁVEZ[90].

vi. DIONICIO MENDOSA, b. Private; m. ANA MAE SUTHERLAND.

Notes for DIONICIO MENDOSA:
Also known as Dennis.

vii. ELOY MENDOSA, b. Private.
viii. ERNESTO MENDOSA, b. Private.
ix.   PORFIRIO MENDOSA, b. Private.
x.   ROSENDA LIDIA MENDOSA[91], b. Abt. 1938, San Patricio, New México; d. January 27, 1938, San Patricio, New México.

14. SENAIDA[3] MONTOYA *(ESTANISLADO TRUJILLO[2], TRANQUELINO[1])[92]* was born May 19, 1907 in San Patricio, Territory of New México, and died July 10, 1944 in Roswell, New México. She married EDUARDO BARCELON SÁNCHEZ[92] October 08, 1920 in San Patricio, New México[93], son of JUAN SÁNCHEZ and MARÍA SÁNCHEZ.

Notes for SENAIDA MONTOYA:
Also known as Maclofa Montoya.

Children of SENAIDA MONTOYA and EDUARDO SÁNCHEZ are:
i.   EDUARDO MONTOYA[4] SÁNCHEZ[94], b. May 26, 1921, San Patricio, New México; d. May 15, 1995.
ii. MACLOFA SÁNCHEZ, b. Abt. 1923, San Patricio, New México[95]; m. ARISTEO HERRERA.
iii. JUAN SÁNCHEZ[96], b. January 26, 1924, San Patricio, New México; d. January 26, 1924, San Patricio, New México.
iv. MANUEL MONTOYA SÁNCHEZ[97], b. May 20, 1925, Glencoe, New México; d. March 22, 1982, Roswell, New México; m. FLORA CARABAJAL SÁNCHEZ.

Notes for FLORA CARABAJAL SÁNCHEZ:
Also known as Florita.

v.   RAFAEL MONTOYA SÁNCHEZ, b. Abt. 1928, San Patricio, New México[98].
vi. MARGARITA MONTOYA SÁNCHEZ, b. Abt. 1929, San Patricio, New México[98].

Notes for MARGARITA MONTOYA SÁNCHEZ:
Also known as Maggie.

vii. SERAPIO SÁNCHEZ[99], b. Abt. 1937, San Patricio, New México; d. February 04, 1937, San Patricio, New México.
viii. CONFERINA MONTOYA SÁNCHEZ, b. Private, San Patricio, New México.
ix.   ELFIDES SÁNCHEZ, b. Private, San Patricio, New México.
x.   RUMELIO SÁNCHEZ, b. Private, San Patricio, New México.

15. MANUEL ROMERO[3] MONTOYA *(ÁRON[2], TRANQUELINO[1])* was born May 04, 1906 in San Patricio, Territory of New México[100]. He married JUANITA BARRERA August 26, 1931 in Arabela, New México[100], daughter of TOMÁS BARRERA and MARÍA TORRES.

Notes for JUANITA BARRERA:
Listed as Juana Barros in her marriage to Manuel Montoya.

Children of MANUEL MONTOYA and JUANITA BARRERA are:
i.   ERMILO[4] MONTOYA, b. Private[101].
ii. ELIZA MONTOYA, b. Private[101].
iii. FERNANDO MONTOYA, b. Private[101].
iv. ORALIA MONTOYA, b. Private[101].
v.   JOSÉ MONTOYA, b. Private[101].
vi. OFELIA MONTOYA, b. Private[101].

16. ALTAGRACIA[3] MONTOYA *(ÁRON[2], TRANQUELINO[1])[102]* was born May 07, 1909 in San Patricio, Territory of New México, and died June 05, 2006 in San Patricio, New México. She married (1) ALFONSO V. SOTO June 11, 1934 in Carrizozo, New México[103]. She married (2) SAMUEL MOYA SÁNCHEZ[104] September 22, 1938 in San Patricio, New México[105], son of CELESTINO SÁNCHEZ and NAVORSITA MOYA.

Notes for ALTAGRACIA MONTOYA:
Also known as Grace. She was raised by her Tios, Octaviano Gallegos and Pilar Guebara de Gallegos.

Child of ALTAGRACIA MONTOYA and SAMUEL SÁNCHEZ is:
    i.   THURMAN[4] SÁNCHEZ, b. Private.

17. MANUELITA[3] GUEVARA *(SARA[2] MONTOYA, TRANQUELINO[1])* was born Abt. 1896[106]. She married (1) ELÍAS BARELA, son of CASIMIRO BARELA and MARTINA MOLINA. She married (2) ANTONIO GARCÍA[107], son of INEZ GARCÍA and LORENCITA MOLINA.

Notes for ANTONIO GARCÍA:
1900 Census: Living in Agua Azul, Territory of New México.

Children of MANUELITA GUEVARA and ELÍAS BARELA are:
    i.   ROQUÉ[4] BARELA, b. August 16, 1912, Arabela, New México[108]; m. GEORGIA LUJÁN, August 20, 1934, Carrizozo, New México[108].
    ii.   RAQUEL BARELA, b. Abt. 1915[109].
    iii.   MARTINA BARELA, b. Abt. 1917[109]; m. FRANCISCO PACHECO.
    iv.   JOSÉ BARELA, b. Abt. 1919[109].
    v.   ORLANDO BARELA, b. Private.
    vi.   PAOLINA BARELA, b. Private.

Children of MANUELITA GUEVARA and ANTONIO GARCÍA are:
    vii.   INEZ GUEVARA[4] GARCÍA, b. November 19, 1930, Arabela, New México; d. September 15, 2006, Hondo, New México.
    viii.   ERMINIA GARCÍA, b. Private.
    ix.   FLAVIO GARCÍA, b. Private.
    x.   LORENCITA GARCÍA, b. Private.
    xi.   MANUEL GARCÍA, b. Private.
    xii.   MIGUEL GARCÍA, b. Private.
    xiii.   ONOFRÉ GARCÍA, b. Private.

18. LAZARO[3] GUEVARA *(SARA[2] MONTOYA, TRANQUELINO[1])*[110] was born March 30, 1906 in Lincoln, Territory of New México[111]. He married PERFECTA REGALADO July 30, 1930 in Carrizozo, New México[111], daughter of JOSÉ REGALADO and FRANCISCA MARRUJO.

Notes for LAZARO GUEVARA:
Name also recorded as Lazaro Gallegos.

Children of LAZARO GUEVARA and PERFECTA REGALADO are:
    i.   DORA[4] GUEVARA, b. Private.
    ii.   RUFINA GUEVARA, b. Private.
    iii.   TOMMY GUEVARA, b. Private.
    iv.   PAUL GUEVARA, b. Private.
    v.   MARY GUEVARA, b. Private.
    vi.   GLORIA GUEVARA, b. Private.
    vii.   LASARO REGALADO GUEVARA, b. Private.

19. CRUZ MONTOYA[3] GUEVARA *(SARA[2] MONTOYA, TRANQUELINO[1])* was born Abt. 1907 in Arabela, Territory of New México[112]. He married ROSA REGALADO June 05, 1922[113], daughter of JOSÉ REGALADO and FRANCISCA MARRUJO.

Children of CRUZ GUEVARA and ROSA REGALADO are:
    i.   ISMAEL[4] GUEVARA, b. Private.
    ii.   FRUTOSO GUEVARA, b. Private.

iii.   ACARIA GUEVARA, b. Private.
iv.   CLOVÍS GUEVARA, b. Private.
v.   JULIA GUEVARA, b. Private.
vi.   ISOYLA GUEVARA, b. Private.
vii.   VIOLA GUEVARA, b. Private.
viii.   GEORGE GUEVARA, b. Private.

20. ANTONIA[3] GUEVARA *(SARA[2] MONTOYA, TRANQUELINO[1])* was born Abt. 1909[114]. She married SERAFÍN PACHECO Abt. 1926[115].

Notes for SERAFÍN PACHECO:
1930 Census: Living in Cháves County, Precinct 4, New México.

Children of ANTONIA GUEVARA and SERAFÍN PACHECO are:
i.   WIILIE[4] PACHECO, b. Abt. 1926[115].
ii.   MARÍA PACHECO, b. Abt. 1928[115].

21. PABLO[3] YBARRA *(CATARINA[2] MONTOYA, TRANQUELINO[1])* was born Abt. 1898 in San Patricio, Territory of New México[116]. He married SOFIA ULIBARRÍ April 15, 1921 in San Patricio, New México[117], daughter of VICENTE ULIBARRÍ and MARÍA SEDILLO.

Child of PABLO YBARRA and SOFIA ULIBARRÍ is:
i.   TIVORCIO[4] YBARRA, b. San Patricio, New México.

Notes for TIVORCIO YBARRA:
Also known as Tive.
Raised by his grandmother, Catarina Montoya Ybarra.

22. JULIANITA[3] YBARRA *(CATARINA[2] MONTOYA, TRANQUELINO[1])[118]* was born February 16, 1901 in San Patricio, Territory of New México[119], and died June 04, 1986. She married JOSÉ PORTIO[120] January 05, 1922 in San Patricio, New México[121], son of MANUELITA HERRERA.

Children of JULIANITA YBARRA and JOSÉ PORTIO are:
i.   RICARDO[4] PORTIO, b. July 03, 1927, San Patricio, New México[122]; m. WANDA PAGE, June 30, 1948, Carrizozo, New México[122].
ii.   ARON PORTIO, b. February 14, 1932, San Patricio, New México[123]; m. ISABEL LUERAS, July 05, 1952, Carrizozo, New México[123].
iii.   MANUELITA PORTIO, b. October 28, 1933, San Patricio, New México[124]; m. RUBÉN PADILLA, October 27, 1950, Carrizozo, New México[124].

23. GENOVEVO[3] YBARRA *(CATARINA[2] MONTOYA, TRANQUELINO[1])* was born November 22, 1903 in San Patricio, Territory of New México[125], and died February 13, 1975. He married JUANITA SÁNCHEZ[126] May 10, 1932 in Glencoe, New México[127], daughter of CELESTINO SÁNCHEZ and NAVORSITA MOYA.

Notes for GENOVEVO YBARRA:
Raised Manuel Prudencio, son of Roberto Prudencio & Casimira Ybarra Prudencio.
Buried at the San Ysidro Cemetery.
Land Patent # NMLC 0034103, on the authority of the Homestead Entry-Stock Raising (39 Stat. 862), December 29, 1916. Issued 320.84 acres on August 04, 1933.

Notes for JUANITA SÁNCHEZ:
1930 Census lists Juanita as a niece.

Child of GENOVEVO YBARRA and JUANITA SÁNCHEZ is:
i.   JAIME[4] YBARRA[128], b. Abt. 1930, San Patricio, New México; d. July 10, 1930, San Patricio, New México.

24. CASIMIRA[3] YBARRA *(CATARINA[2] MONTOYA, TRANQUELINO[1])[129]* was born March 03, 1906 in San Patricio, Territory of New México[130], and died May 30, 1977 in San Patricio, New México. She married ROBERTO

PRUDENCIO[131] July 03, 1929 in San Patricio, New México[132], son of DAMACIO PRUDENCIO and CLEOFAS MUÑOZ.

Children of CASIMIRA YBARRA and ROBERTO PRUDENCIO are:
- i. FELICITA YBARRA[4] PRUDENCIO[133], b. Abt. 1930, San Patricio, New México; d. June 20, 1938, San Patricio, New México.
- ii. ONESIMO PRUDENCIO[134], b. April 18, 1934, San Patricio, New México; d. March 10, 1998, Ruidoso Downs, New México.
- iii. CLEOFAS PRUDENCIO, b. Private, San Patricio, New México.
- iv. DAMACIO PRUDENCIO, b. Private, San Patricio, New México.
- v. MANUEL PRUDENCIO, b. Private, San Patricio, New México.
- vi. RAMÓN PRUDENCIO, b. Private, San Patricio, New México.

25. LUCÍA[3] YBARRA *(CATARINA[2] MONTOYA, TRANQUELINO[1])* was born March 17, 1908 in San Patricio, Territory of New México. She married SIGISFREDO ROMERO[134] January 11, 1928[135], son of GEORGE ROMERO and AURORA GONZÁLES.

Notes for LUCÍA YBARRA:
Also known as Luciana, Luz.
Padrinos: Augustín Laguna born in México City, and his wife, Juana María Laguna, born in Polvadera, New México

Children of LUCÍA YBARRA and SIGISFREDO ROMERO are:
- i. FEDELINA[4] ROMERO, b. March 28, 1932, San Patricio, New México[136]; m. ELMON RANDOLPH[137], July 01, 1950, Carrizozo, New México[138].
- ii. CLEOFAS ROMERO[139], b. April 09, 1934, San Patricio, New México; d. March 17, 2007; m. JUAN SÁNCHEZ MONTES[139], August 25, 1951, Ruidoso, New México[140].
- iii. SIGISFREDO YBARRA ROMERO[141], b. August 08, 1949, San Patricio, New México; d. May 24, 2010, San Patricio, New México.
- iv. EDUVIGEN ROMERO, b. Private, San Patricio, New México.
- v. FLORIPE ROMERO, b. Private, San Patricio, New México.
- vi. FREDO ROMERO, b. Private, San Patricio, New México.
- vii. ISABEL ROMERO, b. Private, San Patricio, New México.
- viii. LEONIRES ROMERO, b. Private, San Patricio, New México.
- ix. REBECCA ROMERO, b. Private, San Patricio, New México.
- x. RUBÉN ROMERO, b. Private, San Patricio, New México.

26. CRUSITA[3] YBARRA *(CATARINA[2] MONTOYA, TRANQUELINO[1])*[142] was born May 02, 1910 in San Patricio, Territory of New México, and died November 1985. She married MAX CARABAJAL SÁNCHEZ[142] October 08, 1932 in San Patricio, New México[143], son of SIMÓN SÁNCHEZ and ANTONIA CARABAJAL.

Notes for CRUSITA YBARRA:
Also known as Cruz.
1930 Census: Lists as living with Elfida Montoya Chávez.

Notes for MAX CARABAJAL SÁNCHEZ:
Also known as Maximiliano. 1930 Census lists him as Marcelino.

Child of CRUSITA YBARRA and MAX SÁNCHEZ is:
- i. DOROTHY ALICE[4] SÁNCHEZ[144], b. Abt. 1940, San Patricio, New México; d. July 21, 1940, San Patricio, New México.

27. PEDRO[3] CHÁVEZ *(ELFIDA[2] MONTOYA, TRANQUELINO[1])*[145] was born October 23, 1903 in Lincoln, Territory of New México, and died December 27, 1995 in San Patricio, New México. He married LORENCITA TRUJILLO[146] July 13, 1930 in Carrizozo, New México[147], daughter of BONAFICIO TRUJILLO and LORENSA SILVA.

Notes for PEDRO CHÁVEZ:
Also known as Pedro Chávez y Montoya.

Pedro was raised by his half sister's (Elfida Chavez) daughter, Marillita and her husband Julian Romero y Torres in Manzano, NM until he was 16 years old. He was re-united with his mother in Corona, NM.
Buried in San Patricio, NM.

Notes for LORENCITA TRUJILLO:
Also known as Lorensa.

Children of PEDRO CHÁVEZ and LORENCITA TRUJILLO are:
    i.   MARÍA CIRILIA[4] CHÁVEZ[148], b. Abt. 1937, San Patricio, New México; d. March 24, 1937, San Patricio, New México.
    ii.   MACARIO TRUJILLO CHÁVEZ, b. Private; m. TERESA GÓMEZ.
    iii. RAYMOND CHÁVEZ, b. Private.
    iv. RUFINA CHÁVEZ, b. Private; m. SIGISFREDO MONTOYA.

28. LORENSITA[3] MONTOYA *(DOROTEO[2], TRANQUELINO[1])* was born February 12, 1912 in San Patricio, New México[149], and died in Artesia, New México. She married (1) FERNANDO SALSBERRY[150] June 15, 1929 in Carrizozo, New Mexico[151], son of JAMES SALSBERRY and MANUELITA HERRERA. She married (2) CAMILO SEDILLO[152] May 04, 1940 in Carrizozo, New México[153], son of MARTÍN SEDILLO and TOMASITA HERRERA.

Notes for LORENSITA MONTOYA:
Burial birthdate states she was born on August 09, 1914.

Children of LORENSITA MONTOYA and FERNANDO SALSBERRY are:
    i.   CLOVÍS[4] SALSBERRY[154], b. Abt. 1934; d. May 25, 1938, Fort Stanton, New México.
    ii.   ANATALIA SALSBERRY, b. Private; m. MANUEL SOSA.
    iii. ELOY SALSBERRY, b. Private.
    iv. FERNANDO MONTOYA SALSBERRY, b. Private.

Children of LORENSITA MONTOYA and CAMILO SEDILLO are:
    v.   CRISTINA DELFIDA[4] SEDILLO[155], b. Abt. 1941, San Patricio, New México; d. February 20, 1941, San Patricio, New México.
    vi. CRISTINA ROSA SEDILLO[156], b. Abt. 1942, San Patricio, New México; d. February 16, 1942, San Patricio, New México.
    vii. CERINIA SEDILLO, b. Private.
    viii. DANNY SEDILLO, b. Private; d. Phoenix, Arizona.
    ix. DELLA SEDILLO, b. Private.
    x.   ELLIE SEDILLO, b. Private.
    xi. MARTÍN MONTOYA SEDILLO, b. Private.

29. JOSEFITA[3] MONTOYA *(DOROTEO[2], TRANQUELINO[1])*[157] was born 1918, and died 2003. She married JUAN BACA[157], son of CRECENCIO CARRILLO and CATARINA BACA.

Notes for JOSEFITA MONTOYA:
Also known as Josephine.

Notes for JUAN BACA:
Social Security Death Index indicates that he was born on June 30, 1914. Raised with Crecencio Carrillo.

Children of JOSEFITA MONTOYA and JUAN BACA are:
    i.   CRUCITA[4] BACA, b. May 03, 1946; m. DANNY CHÁVEZ.
    ii.   PETE BACA, b. Private.

30. TRANQUELINO SILVA[3] MONTOYA *(DOROTEO[2], TRANQUELINO[1])* was born August 22, 1925 in Arabela, New México, and died September 24, 2009 in Alamagordo, New México. He married RUBY SAMORA.

Notes for TRANQUELINO SILVA MONTOYA:
Also known as Trankie.
Served in the US Army from 1944 to 1946.

Children of **TRANQUELINO MONTOYA** and **RUBY SAMORA** are:

    i.   BUDDY[4] MONTOYA, b. Private.
    ii.   CINDY MONTOYA, b. Private.
   iii. GILBERT MONTOYA, b. Private.
   iv. KATHY MONTOYA, b. Private.
    v.   PATSY MONTOYA, b. Private.
   vi. TERESA SAMORA MONTOYA, b. Private.
  vii. TRANKIE MONTOYA, b. Private.
 viii. VERLA MONTOYA, b. Private.

Genealogy of José Vicente Olguín

Generation No. 1

1. JOSÉ VICENTE[1] OLGUÍN[1] was born Abt. 1775[2]. He married DOLÓRES GARCÍA[3].

Notes for JOSÉ VICENTE OLGUÍN:
Also known as José Bicente Olguín.

Notes for DOLÓRES GARCÍA:
Also known as Dolóres Otero.

Children of JOSÉ OLGUÍN and DOLÓRES GARCÍA are:
2.   i.   JOSÉ YGNACIO[2] OLGUÍN, b. Abt. 1806, La Merced de Los Quelitos, Atrisco, El Reyno de Nuevo México.
        ii.   MANUEL OLGUÍN, b. Abt. 1817[4].

Generation No. 2

2. JOSÉ YGNACIO[2] OLGUÍN *(JOSÉ VICENTE[1])[5]* was born Abt. 1806 in La Merced de Los Quelitos, Atrisco, El Reyno de Nuevo México[6]. He married (1) MARÍA DOLÓRES SEDILLO. He married (2) MARÍA BRIGIDA GUTIÉRREZ November 01, 1827 in Alburquerque, Nuevo México, La República de México[7].

Notes for JOSÉ YGNACIO OLGUÍN:
1860 Census: Living in Atrisco, Territory of New México.
1870 Census: Living in Lincoln County, Precinct 2 (La Plaza de San Patricio), Territory of New México. Lists birth year as 1820.

Notes for MARÍA DOLÓRES SEDILLO:
1860 Census: Lists her birth year as 1833.

Children of JOSÉ OLGUÍN and MARÍA SEDILLO are:
        i.   MARÍA LORENZA[3] OLGUÍN, b. Abt. 1853[8].
        ii.   JULIAN OLGUÍN, b. Abt. 1857[8].
        iii.   GUADALUPE ELIZA OLGUÍN, b. Abt. 1858[8].

Children of JOSÉ OLGUÍN and MARÍA GUTIÉRREZ are:
        iv.   JOSÉ GORGONIO[3] OLGUÍN, b. September 08, 1840, La Polvadera de San Lorenzo, Nuevo México, La República de México[9].

Notes for JOSÉ GORGONIO OLGUÍN:
Baptized in Socorro on September 13, 1840 at 5 days of age. He was the son of José Ygnacio Olguín and María Brigida Gutiérrez. His paternal grandparents were José Biscente Olguín and Dolóres Otero. His maternal grandparents were Juan Miguel Gutiérrez and María de las Niebes Chábes. Padrinos: Patricio Peña, María Antonia Romero.

3.   v.   PETRA OLGUÍN, b. January 26, 1841, La Polvadera de San Lorenzo, Nuevo México, La República de México; d. Bef. August 1885.
4.   vi.   RAMÓN OLGUÍN, b. December 24, 1842, La Polvadera de San Lorenzo, Nuevo México, La República de México; d. Bef. 1900.

Generation No. 3

3. PETRA[3] OLGUÍN *(JOSÉ YGNACIO[2], JOSÉ VICENTE[1])* was born January 26, 1841 in La Polvadera de San Lorenzo, Nuevo México, La República de México[10], and died Bef. August 1885. She married FELIZ TRUJILLO[11].

Notes for PETRA OLGUÍN:
Also known as María Petra Olguín.

Baptized in Socorro on February 03, 1841 at 8 days of age. She was the daughter of José Ygnacio Olguín and María Brigida Gutiérrez. Her paternal grandparents were José Biscente Olguín and Dolóres García. Her maternal grandparents were Juan Miguel Gutiérrez and María de las Niebes Chábes. Padrinos: Tomás Telles, María Paula Montoya.

Notes for FELIZ TRUJILLO:
Land Patent # NMNMAA 010816, on the authority of the Homestead Entry-Original (12 Stat. 392), May 20, 1862. Issued 160 acres.

Children of PETRA OLGUÍN and FELIZ TRUJILLO are:
    i.   LORENZO⁴ TRUJILLO, b. Abt. 1866[12].
    ii.   MANUELA DE LA LUZ TRUJILLO, b. Abt. June 19, 1869[13].

4. RAMÓN³ OLGUÍN *(JOSÉ YGNACIO², JOSÉ VICENTE¹)* was born December 24, 1842 in La Polvadera de San Lorenzo, Nuevo México, La República de México[14], and died Bef. 1900. He married LORENSA SEDILLO[15].

Notes for RAMÓN OLGUÍN:
Also known as José Ramón Olguín.
Baptized in Socorro on December 31, 1842 at 7 days of age. He was the son of José Ygnacio Olguín and María Brigida Gutiérrez. His paternal grandparents were José Biscente Olguín and Dolóres Otero. His maternal grandparents were Juan Miguel Gutiérrez and María de las Niebes Chábes. Padrinos: Manuel Gutiérrez, María Petra Ortega.
1870 Census: Living in Lincoln County, Precinct 2 (La Plaza de San Patricio), Territory of New México.

Notes for LORENSA SEDILLO:
Also known as Lorencita, Lorenza Cedillo.
1900 Census: She was living with her son-in-law, Sisto Sedillo, and her daughter, Margarita Olguín de Sedillo.

Children of RAMÓN OLGUÍN and LORENSA SEDILLO are:
    i.   NATIVIDAD SEDILLO⁴ OLGUÍN, b. Abt. 1864, La Plaza de San Patricio, Territory of New México[16]; m. FELIZ TRUJILLO, September 28, 1885[17].

Notes for FELIZ TRUJILLO:
Land Patent # NMNMAA 010816, on the authority of the Homestead Entry-Original (12 Stat. 392), May 20, 1862. Issued 160 acres.

5.   ii.   ESTANISLADO OLGUÍN, b. May 06, 1870, Ruidoso, Territory of New México.
6.   iii. MARGARITA OLGUÍN, b. January 31, 1872, San Patricio, Territory of New México; d. April 06, 1955.
7.   iv. YGNACIO OLGUÍN, b. August 01, 1873, San Patricio, Territory of New México; d. October 15, 1947, San Patricio, New México.
    v.   BENITO OLGUÍN, b. Abt. 1876, San Patricio, Territory of New México[18].

Notes for BENITO OLGUÍN:
Died young.

8.   vi. MANUELITA OLGUÍN, b. June 1887, San Patricio, Territory of New México.

Generation No. 4

5. ESTANISLADO⁴ OLGUÍN *(RAMÓN³, JOSÉ YGNACIO², JOSÉ VICENTE¹)* was born May 06, 1870 in Ruidoso, Territory of New México[19]. He married ANASTACIA CHÁVEZ[20] March 02, 1901[21], daughter of JUAN CHÁVEZ and TERESA HERRERA.

Notes for ESTANISLADO OLGUÍN:
Also known as Estanislaus, Tanislado.

Children of ESTANISLADO OLGUÍN and ANASTACIA CHÁVEZ are:
    i.   CANDELARIA⁵ OLGUÍN[22], b. February 02, 1902; d. October 03, 1934; m. PABLO CALDERON[22], June 22, 1920[23].
    ii.   JUANITA OLGUÍN, b. 1904[24]; m. OLOJIO GALLEGOS.

Notes for JUANITA OLGUÍN:
Also known as Vivianita.

	iii.	AVESLÍN OLGUÍN, b. 1911[24].
9.	iv.	CECILIA OLGUÍN, b. 1914.
	v.	ROBERTO OLGUÍN[25], b. April 19, 1919, San Patricio, New México[26]; m. ELVA GALLEGOS, April 01, 1948, Carrizozo, New México[27].
	vi.	PEDRO OLGUÍN, b. 1921[28].

6. MARGARITA[4] OLGUÍN *(RAMÓN[3], JOSÉ YGNACIO[2], JOSÉ VICENTE[1])*[29] was born January 31, 1872 in San Patricio, Territory of New México, and died April 06, 1955. She married SISTO SEDILLO[29] July 28, 1892 in Ruidoso, Territory of New México[30], son of JOSÉ SEDILLO and MARÍA GARCÍA.

Notes for MARGARITA OLGUÍN:
Baptismal records indicate that she was born on January 20, 1872. (Microfiche# 0017008, Page 19)

Children of MARGARITA OLGUÍN and SISTO SEDILLO are:

10.	i.	MIGUEL[5] SEDILLO, b. November 28, 1891, San Patricio, Territory of New México; d. March 1967.
	ii.	ONESIMA SEDILLO, b. February 15, 1894, El Berendo, Territory of New México; m. AMABLE CHÁVEZ, September 23, 1914, Lincoln, New México[31].
	iii.	FRANCISQUITA SEDILLO, b. April 15, 1895, San Patricio, Territory of New México[32]; m. JOSÉ OROSCO, October 01, 1913, Patos, Territory of New México[32].

Notes for FRANCISQUITA SEDILLO:
Also known as Francisca.

11.	iv.	RAMÓN SEDILLO, b. February 25, 1899, San Patricio, Territory of New México.
12.	v.	EDUARDO SEDILLO, b. October 20, 1902, Arabela, New México; d. March 08, 1991, Alamogordo, New México.
	vi.	ESTELA SEDILLO[33], b. September 03, 1904, San Patricio, Territory of New México[34]; m. HILARIO SÁNCHEZ[35], July 27, 1921[36].
	vii.	PRESILIANA SEDILLO, b. Abt. 1906[37].
13.	viii.	LEOPOLDO SEDILLO, b. March 24, 1909, San Patricio, New México; d. February 08, 1990, Roswell, New México.
	ix.	DANIEL SEDILLO[38], b. February 02, 1912; d. April 18, 2006.

Notes for DANIEL SEDILLO:
Private First Class US Army. WWII Veteran.

7. YGNACIO[4] OLGUÍN *(RAMÓN[3], JOSÉ YGNACIO[2], JOSÉ VICENTE[1])*[39] was born August 01, 1873 in San Patricio, Territory of New México, and died October 15, 1947 in San Patricio, New México. He married (1) VIVIANA CHÁVEZ[39] March 16, 1898[40], daughter of JUAN CHÁVEZ and TERESA HERRERA. He married (2) JOSEFITA RANDOLPH[41] August 19, 1911 in San Patricio, Territory of New México[42], daughter of FRANK RANDOLPH and CATARINA BRADY.

Notes for YGNACIO OLGUÍN:
June 18, 1904 to June 10, 1909- Was selected as the first postmaster of San Patricio.
1910 Census: Living in San Patricio, Territory of New México.

Notes for JOSEFITA RANDOLPH:
Baptismal records indicate that she was born on August 27, 1895. (Microfiche# 0016754, Page 287)

Child of YGNACIO OLGUÍN and VIVIANA CHÁVEZ is:

14.	i.	GENOVEVA CHÁVEZ[5] OLGUÍN, b. January 22, 1904, San Patricio, Territory of New México; Adopted child.

8. MANUELITA[4] OLGUÍN *(RAMÓN[3], JOSÉ YGNACIO[2], JOSÉ VICENTE[1])* was born June 1887 in San Patricio, Territory of New México[43]. She married (1) PROMETIVO BRADY April 03, 1899[44], son of WILLIAM BRADY and BONIFACIA CHÁVES. She married (2) HINIO LUCERO[45] February 12, 1902[46], son of ANISETO LUCERO and REFUGIA TRUJILLO.

Notes for MANUELITA OLGUÍN:
Also known as Manuela, Manuelita Sedillo.
1900 Census: She was living with her brother-in-law, Sisto Sedillo, and her sister, Margarita Olguín de Sedillo.

Notes for HINIO LUCERO:
Also known as Iginio.

Children of MANUELITA OLGUÍN and HINIO LUCERO are:
    i.   ANISETO OLGUÍN[5] LUCERO, b. 1904, San Patricio, Territory of New México[47].
    ii.   MARTÍN OLGUÍN LUCERO[48], b. July 26, 1905, San Patricio, Territory of New México; d. May 15, 1953.
    iii. REYES LUCERO, b. June 06, 1909, San Patricio, Territory of New México[49]; m. RITA BENAVIDEZ, December 04, 1946, Carrizozo, New México[49].

Notes for REYES LUCERO:
1920 Census: Living in San Patricio, New México.

    iv.   EPIFANIO LUCERO, b. 1915, San Patricio, New México[50].
    v.   REFUGIO LUCERO, b. 1918, San Patricio, New México[50].

Generation No. 5

9. CECILIA[5] OLGUÍN *(ESTANISLADO[4], RAMÓN[3], JOSÉ YGNACIO[2], JOSÉ VICENTE[1])* was born 1914[51]. She married RUMELIO CHÁVEZ[52] July 11, 1936[53], son of PABLO CHÁVEZ and JESÚSITA SÁNCHEZ.

Notes for CECILIA OLGUÍN:
Also known as Yselia.

Children of CECILIA OLGUÍN and RUMELIO CHÁVEZ are:
    i.   AMADA[6] CHÁVEZ, b. Private; m. HENRY SÁNCHEZ.

Notes for AMADA CHÁVEZ:
Also known as Amy.

    ii.   PABLO OLGUÍN CHÁVEZ, b. Private.

Notes for PABLO OLGUÍN CHÁVEZ:
Died at a young age.

    iii. ÁBRAN OLGUÍN CHÁVEZ, b. Private.

10. MIGUEL[5] SEDILLO *(MARGARITA[4] OLGUÍN, RAMÓN[3], JOSÉ YGNACIO[2], JOSÉ VICENTE[1])* was born November 28, 1891 in San Patricio, Territory of New México[54], and died March 1967[55]. He married RITA TRUJILLO October 14, 1914 in Lincoln, New México[56], daughter of BONAFICIO TRUJILLO and LORENSA SILVA.

Notes for MIGUEL SEDILLO:
1914: Miguel was living in Reventón at the time of his marriage.
Land Patent # NMR 0042431, on the authority of the Homestead Entry-Enlarged (35 Stat. 639), February 19, 1909. Issued 320 acres on May 01, 1922.

Children of MIGUEL SEDILLO and RITA TRUJILLO are:
    i.   LEONEL[6] SEDILLO[57], b. November 20, 1918, San Patricio, New México[58].
    ii.   IDILIA SEDILLO, b. Abt. 1923[58].

11. RAMÓN[5] SEDILLO *(MARGARITA[4] OLGUÍN, RAMÓN[3], JOSÉ YGNACIO[2], JOSÉ VICENTE[1])* was born February 25, 1899 in San Patricio, Territory of New México[59]. He married GUADALUPE URBÁN BRADY Abt. 1920[60], daughter of JUAN BRADY and MARÍA URBÁN.

Notes for RAMÓN SEDILLO:
1930 Census: Living in Roswell, New México.

Children of RAMÓN SEDILLO and GUADALUPE BRADY are:
    i.   JUANITA[6] SEDILLO, b. Private, Roswell, New México.

Notes for JUANITA SEDILLO:
She was raised by her grandmother, Margarita Olguín.

      ii.   ONESIMA SEDILLO, b. Abt. 1921, Roswell, New México[60].
     iii.   MARÍA SEDILLO, b. Abt. 1922, Roswell, New México[60].
     iv.   VIOLA SEDILLO, b. Abt. 1924, Roswell, New México[60].
      v.   OLIVIA SEDILLO, b. Abt. 1926, Roswell, New México[60].
     vi.   SISTO SEDILLO, b. Abt. 1927, Roswell, New México[60].

12. EDUARDO[5] SEDILLO *(MARGARITA[4] OLGUÍN, RAMÓN[3], JOSÉ YGNACIO[2], JOSÉ VICENTE[1])*[61] was born October 20, 1902 in Arabela, New México, and died March 08, 1991 in Alamogordo, New México. He married DOMINGA MAÉS[61] January 23, 1937 in San Patricio, New México[62], daughter of JESÚS MAÉS and AMANDA MOLINA.

Notes for EDUARDO SEDILLO:
Social Security Death Index indicates that he was born on October 20, 1901.
Land Patent # NMLC 0031035, on the authority of the Homestead Entry-Stock Raising (39 Stat. 862), December 29, 1916. Issued 520 acres on May 13, 1931.

Child of EDUARDO SEDILLO and DOMINGA MAÉS is:
15.   i.   EVA[6] MCKINLEY, b. Private; Adopted child.

13. LEOPOLDO[5] SEDILLO *(MARGARITA[4] OLGUÍN, RAMÓN[3], JOSÉ YGNACIO[2], JOSÉ VICENTE[1])*[63] was born March 24, 1909 in San Patricio, New México, and died February 08, 1990 in Roswell, New México. He married ADELAIDA SÁNCHEZ 1936[64], daughter of DAVÍD SÁNCHEZ and FRANCISCA ARCHULETA.

Child of LEOPOLDO SEDILLO and ADELAIDA SÁNCHEZ is:
     i.   FRANCES[6] SEDILLO, b. Private; m. LUVÍN SÁNCHEZ.

14. GENOVEVA CHÁVEZ[5] OLGUÍN *(YGNACIO[4], RAMÓN[3], JOSÉ YGNACIO[2], JOSÉ VICENTE[1])* was born January 22, 1904 in San Patricio, Territory of New México[65]. She married ANTONIO LA RIVA August 05, 1920 in San Patricio, New México[65], son of AUGUSTÍN LA RIVA and ANTONIA VALENCIA.

Notes for GENOVEVA CHÁVEZ OLGUÍN:
Genoveva was an adopted daughter. Her birth parents were Anastacia Chávez and Estanislado Olguín.
Baptismal records indicate that she was born on September 26, 1900. (Microfiche# 0016754, Page 80)

Children of GENOVEVA OLGUÍN and ANTONIO LA RIVA are:
     i.   JOSÉ[6] LA RIVA, b. Abt. 1926, San Patricio, New México[66].
     ii.   ANTONIO LA RIVA, b. Abt. 1928, San Patricio, New México[66].
     iii. FERNANDO LA RIVA, b. Abt. 1929, San Patricio, New México[66].

Generation No. 6

15. EVA[6] MCKINLEY *(EDUARDO[5] SEDILLO, MARGARITA[4] OLGUÍN, RAMÓN[3], JOSÉ YGNACIO[2], JOSÉ VICENTE[1])* was born Private. She married ALBERTO SÁNCHEZ[67], son of SALOMON SÁNCHEZ and MANUELITA SÁNCHEZ.

Notes for EVA MCKINLEY:
Raised by Eduardo Sedillo & Dominga Maés.

Notes for ALBERTO SÁNCHEZ:
Also known as Albert.
Tec 5 US Army. WW II Veteran.

Child of EVA MCKINLEY and ALBERTO SÁNCHEZ is:

Genealogy of Francisco Pacheco

Generation No. 1

1. MANUEL ANTONIO[1] PACHECO was born Abt. 1793. He married PETRA DOMINGA DE SILVA.

Child of MANUEL PACHECO and PETRA DE SILVA is:
2.   i.   FRANCISCO[2] PACHECO, b. Abt. 1825; d. February 02, 1892, Lincoln, Territory of New México; Stepchild.

Generation No. 2

2. FRANCISCO[2] PACHECO *(MANUEL ANTONIO[1])* was born Abt. 1825[1], and died February 02, 1892 in Lincoln, Territory of New México. He married ROMULA ISABELLA SAVEDRA, daughter of JOSÉ SAAVEDRA and ANA GALLEGOS.

Notes for FRANCISCO PACHECO:
Also known as José Francisco Pacheco. His natural father's name was Silva. When his mother re-married, he took on his step-father's name.
1870 Census: Living in La Polvadera de San Lorenzo, Territory of New México.
1880 Census: Living in Lincoln, Territory of New México.

Notes for ROMULA ISABELLA SAVEDRA:
Said to be of an unknown Native American tribe, most likely an Apaché.
1900 Census: Living in Lincoln, Territory of New México. Her age is listed as 54. She is also listed as widowed.

Children of FRANCISCO PACHECO and ROMULA SAVEDRA are:
3.   i.   ANSELMO[3] PACHECO, b. March 16, 1849, San Lorenzo de Pulvidero, Territory of New México; d. February 20, 1921, Arabela, New México.
4.   ii.   NICOLASA SAVEDRA PACHECO, b. Abt. 1857.
5.   iii.   CORNELIA PACHECO, b. Abt. 1859, Socorro, Nuevo México, La República de México.
        iv.   JOSÉ ANTONIO PACHECO, b. Abt. 1861[2].
        v.   MARÍA IGNACIA PACHECO, b. Abt. 1865[2].
6.   vi.   PROCOPIO PACHECO, b. October 1870, La Polvadera de San Lorenzo, Territory of New México.

Generation No. 3

3. ANSELMO[3] PACHECO *(FRANCISCO[2], MANUEL ANTONIO[1])* was born March 16, 1849 in San Lorenzo de Pulvidero, Territory of New México[3], and died February 20, 1921 in Arabela, New México[4]. He married (1) TERESITA GALLEGOS February 13, 1874[5]. He married (2) ALICE SALAZAR June 16, 1910[6]. He married (3) ALICE TRAMPTON May 11, 1912 in Lincoln, New México. He married (4) REYES F. SISNEROS September 05, 1919 in San Patricio, New México[7]. He married (5) INEZ LUCERO June 26, 1920[8], daughter of CORNELIO LUCERO and NOBERTA ARCHULETA.

Notes for ANSELMO PACHECO:
1900 Census: Lists as living in Lincoln.
1920 Census: Lists as living in Las Palas. Anselmo's original last name was Silva, but he adopted the Pacheco name.

Notes for TERESITA GALLEGOS:
Also known as Teresa Gallegos y Chávez.

Notes for INEZ LUCERO:
1930 Census: Living in Roswell, New México.

Children of ANSELMO PACHECO and TERESITA GALLEGOS are:
7.   i.   ADELIA[4] PACHECO, b. December 1874, Lincoln, Territory of New México.

8.   ii.   LEOPOLDO PACHECO, b. November 30, 1877, Arabela, Territory of New México; d. April 1965, Arabela, New México.

           iii.   GENARO PACHECO, b. September 18, 1880[9].

9.   iv.   ROMÁN PACHECO, b. May 12, 1884, Las Palas, Territory of New México; d. January 08, 1931.

           v.   DOMINGA PACHECO, b. September 12, 1887, Tres Ritos, Territory of New México[10]; m. JOSÉ CANDELARIA[11], March 29, 1906, Arabela, Territory of New México[12].

Notes for JOSÉ CANDELARIA:
Also known as José de los Ángeles Candelaria.
1920 Census: Living in Las Palas, New México.
1930 Census: Living in Arabela, New México. Lists Jose's parents as both coming from Colorado.

4. NICOLASA SAVEDRA[3] PACHECO *(FRANCISCO[2], MANUEL ANTONIO[1])* was born Abt. 1857[13]. She married FRANCISCO SEDILLO July 21, 1871[14], son of FERNANDO SEDILLOS and PAULA CHÁVEZ.

Notes for FRANCISCO SEDILLO:
1880 Census: Living in Lincoln, Territory of New México. (Francisco Sedillos)

Children of NICOLASA PACHECO and FRANCISCO SEDILLO are:
           i.   MANUEL[4] SEDILLO, b. Abt. 1877, Lincoln, Territory of New México[15].
           ii.   JOSÉ SEDILLO, b. Abt. 1879, Lincoln, Territory of New México[16].

5. CORNELIA[3] PACHECO *(FRANCISCO[2], MANUEL ANTONIO[1])* was born Abt. 1859 in Socorro, Nuevo México, La República de México[17]. She married ESTOLANO SÁNCHEZ July 21, 1871 in La Plaza del Rio Bonito, Territory of New México[18], son of MAURICIO SÁNCHEZ and JESÚSITA GONZÁLES.

Notes for CORNELIA PACHECO:
1910 Census: Living in San Patricio, Territory of New México.

Children of CORNELIA PACHECO and ESTOLANO SÁNCHEZ are:
10.   i.   FELIPÉ E.[4] SÁNCHEZ, b. January 20, 1874, La Placita del Rio Bonito, Territory of New México; d. January 15, 1954, San Elizario, El Paso, Téxas.
11.   ii.   ELUTICIA SÁNCHEZ, b. 1875.
           iii. SIPIO SÁNCHEZ, b. Abt. 1879[19].
           iv. VALENTÍN SÁNCHEZ, b. May 14, 1881[20]; d. February 09, 1949, Carrizozo, New México.
12.   v.   PRESILIANO SÁNCHEZ, b. December 24, 1884, Rebentón, Territory of New México; d. 1918-1920.
13.   vi.   AURELIO SÁNCHEZ, b. March 12, 1886, Ruidoso, Territory of New México; d. February 23, 1975.
14.   vii. CELIA SÁNCHEZ, b. July 12, 1888, Rebentón, Territory of New México.
15.   viii. ESTOLANO PACHECO SÁNCHEZ, b. October 19, 1893, Rebentón, Territory of New México; d. September 19, 1943, Carrizozo, New México.
16.   ix.   ROSARIO SÁNCHEZ, b. August 11, 1896, Rebentón,Territory of New México; d. December 25, 1976.

6. PROCOPIO[3] PACHECO *(FRANCISCO[2], MANUEL ANTONIO[1])* was born October 1870 in La Polvadera de San Lorenzo, Territory of New México[21]. He married PIEDAD LÓPEZ Abt. 1890[21].

Notes for PROCOPIO PACHECO:
1880 Census: Living in Lincoln, Territory of New México.
1900 Census: Living in Rebentón, Territory of New México.
1930 Census: Living in Lincoln, New México.
Land Patent # NMLC 0034917, on the authority of the Homestead Entry-Stock Raising (39 Stat. 862), December 29, 1916. Issued 325.89 acres on January 09, 1935.

Children of PROCOPIO PACHECO and PIEDAD LÓPEZ are:
           i.   DOMINGO LÓPEZ[4] PACHECO, b. March 01, 1903, Lincoln, Territory of New México[22]; m. ANGELITA DURÁN, August 04, 1925, Nogal, New México[22].
           ii.   JUANITA PACHECO, b. January 1894, Rebentón, Territory of New México[23].
           iii. ISMAEL PACHECO, b. September 27, 1898, Rebentón, Territory of New México[24]; m. SANTOS SÁNCHEZ, November 13, 1916, Lincoln, New México[25].

Notes for ISMAEL PACHECO:
1900 Census: Living in Rebentón, Territory of New México.

      iv.   NICOLASA PACHECO[26], b. November 28, 1898, Rebentón, Territory of New México[27]; m. ANTONIO R. GARCÍA[28], March 06, 1915[29].

Generation No. 4

7. ADELIA[4] PACHECO *(ANSELMO[3], FRANCISCO[2], MANUEL ANTONIO[1])* was born December 1874 in Lincoln, Territory of New México[30]. She married APOLONIO LUCERO February 11, 1896[31], son of CORNELIO LUCERO and NOBERTA ARCHULETA.

Notes for APOLONIO LUCERO:
Also known as Polonio.
1910 Census: living in Las Palas, Territory of New México.

Children of ADELIA PACHECO and APOLONIO LUCERO are:
      i.   SUSANITA[5] LUCERO, b. April 1894, Las Palas, Territory of New México[32].
      ii.   ERLINDA LUCERO, b. July 1895, Las Palas, Territory of New México[32]; m. LEANDRO GONZÁLES, November 29, 1912[33].
17.   iii. GEORGE LUCERO, b. January 25, 1899, Las Palas, Territory of New México; d. October 1970, Roswell, New México.
      iv.   BENJAMIN LUCERO, b. Abt. 1902, Las Palas, Territory of New México[34].
      v.   GUILLERMO LUCERO, b. Abt. 1906, Las Palas, Territory of New México[34].
      vi.   ROGELIO LUCERO, b. Abt. 1909, Las Palas, Territory of New México[34].

8. LEOPOLDO[4] PACHECO *(ANSELMO[3], FRANCISCO[2], MANUEL ANTONIO[1])*[35] was born November 30, 1877 in Arabela, Territory of New México[36], and died April 1965 in Arabela, New México. He married (1) PAULITA FRESQUEZ[37], daughter of PABLO FRESQUEZ and EPIFANIA GARCÍA. He married (2) FELICITA LUJÁN August 15, 1900[38], daughter of TORIVIO LUJÁN and GUADALUPE GALLEGOS.

Notes for LEOPOLDO PACHECO:
Had amassed a ranch that encompassed almost 55 sections, or about 35,200 acres.

Child of LEOPOLDO PACHECO and PAULITA FRESQUEZ is:
      i.   PAUL[5] PACHECO, b. Private.

Children of LEOPOLDO PACHECO and FELICITA LUJÁN are:
      ii.   TRENIDAD[5] PACHECO, b. Abt. 1905[39].
      iii. JUAN PACHECO[40], b. February 12, 1910, Arabela, Territory of New México[41]; m. RUFINA TRUJILLO, September 21, 1939, Carrizozo, New México[42].
      iv. VITERNO PACHECO[43], b. May 1911, Lincoln, Territory of New México; d. October 26, 1923, Roswell, New México.

9. ROMÁN[4] PACHECO *(ANSELMO[3], FRANCISCO[2], MANUEL ANTONIO[1])*[44] was born May 12, 1884 in Las Palas, Territory of New México[45], and died January 08, 1931. He married (1) BONIFACIA LUCERO RICHARDSON[46] September 29, 1904 in La Capilla de San Miguel, Arabela, Territory of New México[47], daughter of ANDREW RICHARDSON and BENINA LUCERO. He married (2) EMALIA GONZÁLES November 02, 1924[48]. He married (3) MARÍA DE JESÚS ARCHULETA May 07, 1927 in Lincoln, New México[49], daughter of JUAN JESÚS ARCHULETA.

Notes for ROMÁN PACHECO:
Baptismal record indicates that he was born on May 12, 1884. Draft registration and Cemetery records indicate he was born on May 16, 1884.
1910 Census: Living in Agua Azul.
1930 Census: Living in Carrizozo.

Children of ROMÁN PACHECO and BONIFACIA RICHARDSON are:

  i. FERNANDO⁵ PACHECO, b. February 27, 1906.

Notes for FERNANDO PACHECO:
Died when he was young.

18.   ii.   FERMÍN PACHECO, b. February 27, 1906, Arabela, Territory of New México; d. August 02, 1983.
          iii. CARLOS PACHECO, b. Abt. 1910.
19.   iv.   FERNANDO PACHECO, b. April 23, 1915, Arabela, New México; d. August 14, 2006, Sahuarita, Arizona.
          v.   EMMA PACHECO, b. November 27, 1918, Arabela, New México⁵⁰; m. ALFRED MARTÍNEZ, June 25, 1937, Carrizozo, New México⁵¹.

10. FELIPÉ E.⁴ SÁNCHEZ *(CORNELIA³ PACHECO, FRANCISCO², MANUEL ANTONIO¹)* was born January 20, 1874 in La Placita del Rio Bonito, Territory of New México⁵², and died January 15, 1954 in San Elizario, El Paso, Téxas⁵³. He married CANDELARIA PADILLA⁵⁴, daughter of ANDALESIO PADILLA and PAUBLITA MARIÑO.

Children of FELIPÉ SÁNCHEZ and CANDELARIA PADILLA are:
20.   i.   ANTONIO PADILLA⁵ SÁNCHEZ, b. May 17, 1897, Tres Ritos, New México; d. February 21, 1984, San Elizario, Texas.
21.   ii.   PAUBLITA SÁNCHEZ, b. July 30, 1898, Tres Rios, Territory of New México; d. October 13, 1963, Las Vegas, New México.
          iii. SIPIO SÁNCHEZ, b. March 1900⁵⁵; m. LOLA MIRABAL.
22.   iv.   CORNELIA SÁNCHEZ, b. November 16, 1902, Lincoln County, New México.
23.   v.   EMILIANO SÁNCHEZ, b. August 11, 1904, Hondo, Territory of New México.
24.   vi.   ÁBRAN SÁNCHEZ, b. December 21, 1905, White Oaks, Territory of New México; d. November 18, 1973, El Paso, Téxas.
25.   vii. REYNALDO SÁNCHEZ, b. Abt. 1907.
          viii. CELEDONIA SÁNCHEZ, b. Abt. 1909; d. Abt. 1921.
26.   ix.   BENITO SÁNCHEZ, b. Abt. 1912.
27.   x.   ONECIMO SÁNCHEZ, b. 1915.

11. ELUTICIA⁴ SÁNCHEZ *(CORNELIA³ PACHECO, FRANCISCO², MANUEL ANTONIO¹)* was born 1875⁵⁵. She married (1) ERINEO FRANCISCO GAVALDON⁵⁶, son of ENCARNACION GAVALDON and ANTONIA DE GAVALDON. She married (2) AUGUSTÍN LUERAS CHÁVEZ April 12, 1901⁵⁷, son of MAXIMIANO CHÁVEZ and ROSITA LUERAS.

Children of ELUTICIA SÁNCHEZ and ERINEO GAVALDON are:
28.   i.   ROSA⁵ GAVALDON, b. January 1892.
          ii.   AVRORA GAVALDON⁵⁸, b. January 07, 1894⁵⁹; d. January 17, 1986, Corona, New México; m. NARCISO MONTOYA⁶⁰, October 26, 1918⁶¹.

Notes for NARCISO MONTOYA:
1920 Census: Living in White Oaks, New México.

29.   iii. LUPE GAVALDON, b. August 20, 1897, Patos, Territory of New México.

Child of ELUTICIA SÁNCHEZ and AUGUSTÍN CHÁVEZ is:
          iv.   CAROLINA SÁNCHEZ⁵ CHÁVEZ, b. Abt. 1895⁶².

12. PRESILIANO⁴ SÁNCHEZ *(CORNELIA³ PACHECO, FRANCISCO², MANUEL ANTONIO¹)* was born December 24, 1884 in Rebentón, Territory of New México⁶³, and died 1918-1920⁶⁴. He married (1) GUADALUPE MARTÍNEZ October 12, 1905 in Rebentón, Territory of New México⁶⁵, daughter of ANTONIO MARTÍNEZ and JUANA GUSTAMANTE. He married (2) LUPITA OROSCO Abt. 1906⁶⁶.

Child of PRESILIANO SÁNCHEZ and GUADALUPE MARTÍNEZ is:
          i.   CORA⁵ SÁNCHEZ.

Children of PRESILIANO SÁNCHEZ and LUPITA OROSCO are:

    ii.   FIDEL[5] SÁNCHEZ[67], b. August 04, 1913, Greeley, Colorado[68]; d. June 27, 1973; m. AMALIA TORRES[69], February 12, 1934, San Patricio, New México[70].

    iii.   ESTOLANO OROSCO SÁNCHEZ[71], b. July 07, 1915, Rebentón, Territory of New México; d. April 05, 1985, Hondo, New México; m. (1) EMMA PINO; m. (2) EUTILIA MONTOYA[71].

    iv.   FERNANDO SÁNCHEZ[72], b. June 19, 1916, Rebentón, New México[73]; m. JOSEFITA TRUJILLO[74], December 11, 1937, Carrizozo, New México[74].

13. AURELIO[4] SÁNCHEZ *(CORNELIA[3] PACHECO, FRANCISCO[2], MANUEL ANTONIO[1])*[75] was born March 12, 1886 in Ruidoso, Territory of New México, and died February 23, 1975. He married ANASTACIA ARAGÓN[76] October 13, 1907 in Rebentón, Territory of New México[77], daughter of MANUEL ARAGÓN and PORFIRIA GONZÁLES.

Children of AURELIO SÁNCHEZ and ANASTACIA ARAGÓN are:

    i.   SANTANA[5] SÁNCHEZ, b. Abt. 1910[78]; m. MAX CHÁVEZ[79], Rebentón, New México[80].

    ii.   EDUMENIO SÁNCHEZ, b. June 08, 1916, White Oaks, New México[81]; m. SEDIA SÁNCHEZ, December 11, 1946, Carrizozo, New México[81].

30.   iii.   SORAIDA SÁNCHEZ, b. August 27, 1916, Rebentón, Territory of New México.

    iv.   MACRINA SÁNCHEZ[82], b. September 09, 1920, White Oaks, New México[83]; m. ANDRÉS RICHARDSON[84], August 08, 1949, Carrizozo, New México[85].

    v.   VICENTE SÁNCHEZ, b. July 08, 1922, Ancho, New México[86]; m. LUISA SALSBERRY, July 08, 1946, Carrizozo, New México[86].

    vi.   CLOVÍS SÁNCHEZ[87], b. June 09, 1913, Rebentón, New México; d. November 06, 1995, Roswell, New México; m. CARLOTA PINEDA, December 26, 1941, Carrizozo, New México[88].

    vii.   BALDIMAR SÁNCHEZ, b. October 27, 1923, Dexter, New México[89]; m. MARGARETTE PENDLEY, June 15, 1945, Ruidoso, New México[89].

    viii. PRESILIANO SÁNCHEZ, b. 1926[90]; m. CECILIA ROMERO.

    ix.   LUCY SÁNCHEZ[91], b. February 27, 1930, Hondo, New México[92]; m. ALBERT TELLES, May 26, 1951, Carrizozo, New México[93].

    x.   EDUARDO ARAGÓN SÁNCHEZ[94], b. May 02, 1933; d. November 25, 1998; m. BONNIE SÁNCHEZ.

    xi.   IDALIA SÁNCHEZ, b. Private, Rebentón, Territory of New México[95]; m. PETRONILO OTERO SEDILLO, February 10, 1926, Picacho, Territory of New México[95].

14. CELIA[4] SÁNCHEZ *(CORNELIA[3] PACHECO, FRANCISCO[2], MANUEL ANTONIO[1])* was born July 12, 1888 in Rebentón, Territory of New México[96]. She married GEORGE TORRES November 12, 1906 in Lincoln, Territory of New México[96], son of YGNACIO TORRES and MANUELA LUCERO.

Children of CELIA SÁNCHEZ and GEORGE TORRES are:

    i.   FELIS SÁNCHEZ[5] TORRES[97], b. June 04, 1909, Lincoln, Territory of New México[98]; d. February 16, 2003, San Patricio, New México; m. PEDRO SALCIDO[99], October 24, 1928, Carrizozo, New México[100].

    ii.   ADENAGO TORRES[101], b. December 13, 1907, Hondo, New México[102]; d. August 06, 1990, Tularosa, New México; m. BEATRIZ TORREZ[103].

    iii.   GEORGE SÁNCHEZ TORRES, b. 1911[104].

    iv.   WILFIDO TORRES, b. 1913[104]; m. JULIA TORRES.

    v.   MIGUEL TORRES, b. 1917[104]; m. SOCORRO DE TORRES.

    vi.   MANUELITA TORRES, b. 1919[104]; m. JUAN BAUTISTA JUAREGUI.

    vii.   PRESCILIA TORRES, b. Abt. 1920[105]; m. ERNESTO LÓPEZ[106].

    viii. LORINA TORRES, b. Abt. 1926[107]; m. ERNESTO OTERO[108].

    ix.   JAY TORRES, b. Private; m. EDNA TORRES.

15. ESTOLANO PACHECO[4] SÁNCHEZ *(CORNELIA[3] PACHECO, FRANCISCO[2], MANUEL ANTONIO[1])*[109] was born October 19, 1893 in Rebentón, Territory of New México[110], and died September 19, 1943 in Carrizozo, New México. He married (1) BARBARITA TORREZ February 28, 1910 in Lincoln, Territory of New Mexico[110], daughter of CRESENCIO TORRES and MIQUELA MIRANDA. He married (2) ELENA CHÁVEZ[111] July 30, 1920 in Rebentón, New México[111], daughter of RAFAEL CHÁVEZ and MARTINA MAÉS.

Children of ESTOLANO SÁNCHEZ and BARBARITA TORREZ are:

    i.   FERMÍN[5] SÁNCHEZ, b. October 11, 1915.

    ii.   AMABLE SÁNCHEZ, b. Private.

    iii.   AMANDA SÁNCHEZ, b. Private.

iv.   EULALIO (LALO) SÁNCHEZ, b. Private.

16. ROSARIO⁴ SÁNCHEZ *(CORNELIA³ PACHECO, FRANCISCO², MANUEL ANTONIO¹)¹¹²* was born August 11, 1896 in Rebentón,Territory of New México¹¹³, and died December 25, 1976. She married WILLIAM LUCERO BRADY February 19, 1912 in Lincoln, New Mexico¹¹⁴, son of ROBERT BRADY and MANUELA LUCERO.

Children of ROSARIO SÁNCHEZ and WILLIAM BRADY are:

       i.   MAX⁵ BRADY, b. June 01, 1913, Hondo, New México¹¹⁵; d. July 17, 1985¹¹⁶.

      ii.   ERMILO BRADY¹¹⁷, b. March 13, 1915, Hondo, New México¹¹⁸; m. PRESCILLA PÉREZ, November 10, 1936, San Patricio, New México¹¹⁹.

31.   iii.   ELMO BRADY, b. October 30, 1917, Hondo, New México; d. December 29, 2008, Ruidoso, New México.

     iv.   ORLIDIA BRADY, b. Abt. 1920¹²⁰; m. ANDREW FRESQUEZ.

      v.   BARTOLA BRADY, b. Abt. 1922¹²⁰.

     vi.   WILLIAM SÁNCHEZ BRADY¹²¹, b. April 12, 1924, Hondo, New México¹²²; m. ORALIA HERRERA¹²³.

    vii.   PRESTINA BRADY¹²⁴, b. March 20, 1926, Hondo, New México; d. January 18, 1995, Hondo, New México.

   viii.   LEROY BENNETT BRADY, b. April 14, 1930¹²⁵.

32.   ix.   BILLY JOE BRADY, b. Private.

Generation No. 5

17. GEORGE⁵ LUCERO *(ADELIA⁴ PACHECO, ANSELMO³, FRANCISCO², MANUEL ANTONIO¹)¹²⁶* was born January 25, 1899 in Las Palas, Territory of New México¹²⁷, and died October 1970 in Roswell, New México. He married ANITA CARRILLO ANALLA¹²⁸ May 21, 1921 in Arabela, New México¹²⁹, daughter of JOSÉ CARRILLO and CRUSITA ARCHULETA.

Notes for ANITA CARRILLO ANALLA:
Anita often went by the name, Anita Analla, because she was raised with an Analla family in Arabela, New México. She was raised by the Analla family after her mother passed away when she was about four years old.
1910 Census: Lists her parents as José Carrillo and Crusita. Her listed name was Tonita.
1920 Census: Living with her cousin, Julio Vigil in Las Palas, Territory of New México.

Child of GEORGE LUCERO and ANITA ANALLA is:

       i.   ORLANDO⁶ LUCERO¹³⁰, b. July 18, 1923, Roswell, New México¹³¹; d. February 15, 2004; m. ERLINDA GONZÁLES, July 18, 1942, Carrizozo, New México¹³¹.

Notes for ORLANDO LUCERO:
Private First Class. World War II.

18. FERMÍN⁵ PACHECO *(ROMÁN⁴, ANSELMO³, FRANCISCO², MANUEL ANTONIO¹)¹³²* was born February 27, 1906 in Arabela, Territory of New México, and died August 02, 1983. He married IGNACIA GÓMEZ¹³² August 29, 1932 in Roswell, New México¹³³, daughter of FELIPÉ GÓMEZ and BEATRIZ SEDILLO.

Notes for IGNACIA GÓMEZ:
Also known as Inez.

Children of FERMÍN PACHECO and IGNACIA GÓMEZ are:

       i.   ROMÁN ALFREDO⁶ PACHECO, b. April 01, 1939, San Patricio, New México; d. April 05, 1999, Las Cruces, New México; m. LUCINA SÁNCHEZ¹³⁴.

      ii.   ORLANDO PACHECO, b. Private.

     iii.   BEATRIZ PACHECO, b. Private; m. DAVID MCKINLEY.

19. FERNANDO⁵ PACHECO *(ROMÁN⁴, ANSELMO³, FRANCISCO², MANUEL ANTONIO¹)¹³⁵* was born April 23, 1915 in Arabela, New México¹³⁶, and died August 14, 2006 in Sahuarita, Arizona¹³⁷. He married LUCÍA GÓMEZ August 07, 1937¹³⁸, daughter of FELIPÉ GÓMEZ and BEATRIZ SEDILLO.

Notes for FERNANDO PACHECO:
US Navy, Seaman First Class. World War II.

Child of FERNANDO PACHECO and LUCÍA GÓMEZ is:

 i. EMMA BEATRIZ[6] PACHECO[139], b. Abt. 1940, San Patricio, New México; d. October 06, 1940, San Patricio, New México.

20. ANTONIO PADILLA[5] SÁNCHEZ *(FELIPÉ E.[4], CORNELIA[3] PACHECO, FRANCISCO[2], MANUEL ANTONIO[1])* was born May 17, 1897 in Tres Ritos, New México[140], and died February 21, 1984 in San Elizario, Texas[141]. He met (1) MAGDALENA MARTÍNEZ. He married (2) MARTINA SALSBERRY October 13, 1915 in Lincoln, Territory of New México[142], daughter of JAMES SALSBERRY and MANUELITA HERRERA. He married (3) JUANITA CABALLERO ALVARADO Aft. December 1917.

Children of ANTONIO SÁNCHEZ and MAGDALENA MARTÍNEZ are:

 i. REYNEL[6] MARTÍNEZ, b. September 11, 1946; m. (1) SYLVIA DURFEE; m. (2) JOY BOW.
 ii. EILEEN MARTÍNEZ, b. 1947; m. NICK SERNA.

Children of ANTONIO SÁNCHEZ and JUANITA ALVARADO are:

 iii. PAUBLINA[6] SÁNCHEZ, b. Private; m. PETE MARTÍNEZ.
 iv. CECILIA ALVARADO SÁNCHEZ, b. Private; m. DANIEL ELOY ORTIZ.
 v. ELIZA SÁNCHEZ, b. Private; m. MANUEL MARTÍNEZ.
 vi. LUISA SÁNCHEZ, b. Private; m. SUSANO JIMÉNEZ MARTÍNEZ.
 vii. TONY SÁNCHEZ, b. Private; m. FRANCES ORQUIDES.
 viii. EFRIN SÁNCHEZ, b. Private; m. AMELIA LÓPEZ.
 ix. SAMUEL SÁNCHEZ, b. Private; m. MINERVA QUADRO.
 x. LUCILLA SÁNCHEZ, b. Private; m. ALBINO BENITO ALVIDREZ.
 xi. DAVÍD SÁNCHEZ, b. Private; m. ESTELLA TAUTIMER.
 xii. RUFINA SÁNCHEZ, b. Private; m. FELIZ TREVIZO.
 xiii. BENJAMÍN SÁNCHEZ, b. Private; m. GRACIELA SAUCEDO.
 xiv. MARÍA SÁNCHEZ[143], b. May 30, 1929, San Elizario, Téxas; d. June 02, 1929, El Paso, Téxas.

21. PAUBLITA[5] SÁNCHEZ *(FELIPÉ E.[4], CORNELIA[3] PACHECO, FRANCISCO[2], MANUEL ANTONIO[1])* was born July 30, 1898 in Tres Rios, Territory of New México[144], and died October 13, 1963 in Las Vegas, New México. She married YSIDRO CHÁVEZ[145] August 04, 1913 in Lincoln, New México[146], son of ROBERTO CHÁVEZ and LUCÍA WELDON.

Children of PAUBLITA SÁNCHEZ and YSIDRO CHÁVEZ are:

 i. GRESELDA[6] CHÁVEZ[147], b. May 03, 1914, Glencoe, New México; d. June 09, 1988, Ruidoso, New México; m. FRANK GÓMEZ[147], February 17, 1934, Carrizozo, New México[148].
 ii. AMARANTE CHÁVEZ[149], b. November 09, 1915, Glencoe, New México; d. February 27, 2001, Alburquerque, New México; m. DOLORES ROMERO ARCHULETA[149], September 21, 1936, San Patricio, New México[150].
 iii. SENON CHÁVEZ[151], b. March 03, 1917, San Patricio, New México; d. January 18, 2000, San Patricio, New México; m. MABEL TRUJILLO SÁNCHEZ, June 09, 1949, Carrizozo, New México[152].
 iv. IGNACIA CHÁVEZ, b. January 23, 1919, San Patricio, New México[153]; m. (1) HAROLD STEELE; m. (2) VICTOR RICHARD BROOKS[154].
 v. ADELA CHÁVEZ, b. July 04, 1920, San Patricio, New México; m. (1) JIMMY LARIOSA; m. (2) GUILLERMO QUIZON[154]; m. (3) MANUEL NAJERES GÓMEZ[154].
 vi. EMILIANO CHÁVEZ[155], b. January 11, 1922, San Elizario, Téxas[156]; d. January 25, 1953, California; m. MARÍA SÁNCHEZ LUCERO[157], April 25, 1947, Carrizozo, New México[158].
 vii. SIPIO CHÁVEZ[159], b. Abt. 1925, San Patricio, New México; d. June 03, 1928, San Patricio, New México.
 viii. EFRAÍN CHÁVEZ, b. January 01, 1926, San Patricio, New México[160]; d. November 11, 1989, Capitán, New México[161]; m. LILLIAN ELIZABETH MILLER[161].
 ix. ORALIA CHÁVEZ[162], b. Abt. 1927, San Patricio, New México; d. June 10, 1928, San Patricio, New México.
 x. LUVÍN CHÁVEZ[163], b. November 15, 1929, San Patricio, New México; d. September 03, 2009, Capitán, New México; m. MARY KAMEES, July 12, 1952, Lincoln, New México[164].
 xi. ORALIA CHÁVEZ, b. February 18, 1931, San Patricio, New México[165]; m. ERNESTO SÁNCHEZ, March 20, 1948, Ruidoso, New México[165].
 xii. ONFRÉ CHÁVEZ, b. August 06, 1932, San Patricio, New México; m. VANGIE CHÁVEZ.
 xiii. JOSIE CHÁVEZ, b. May 18, 1934, San Patricio, New México; m. (1) BENITO HERRERA[166]; m. (2) PORFIRIO SÁNCHEZ.
 xiv. MELVIN CHÁVEZ, b. November 06, 1937, San Patricio, New México; m. (1) LORENA ROMERO; m. (2) PRESCILLA GUTIÉRREZ.

xv.   RAMONA CHÁVEZ, b. April 11, 1939, San Patricio, New México; m. LARRY NÚÑEZ.
xvi.   DANNY CHÁVEZ, b. December 13, 1940, San Patricio, New México; m. (1) VANGIE MONTES; m. (2) CRUCITA BACA.

22. CORNELIA[5] SÁNCHEZ *(FELIPÉ E.[4], CORNELIA[3] PACHECO, FRANCISCO[2], MANUEL ANTONIO[1])[167]* was born November 16, 1902 in Lincoln County, New México[168]. She married ALFONSO BORREGO[169], son of ELIJIO BORREGO and FRANCISCA ARIAS.

Children of CORNELIA SÁNCHEZ and ALFONSO BORREGO are:
i.   ALFONSO[6] BORREGO, b. Private; m. (1) ALICIA LUJÁN; m. (2) ANNIE LARA.
ii.   JOSÉ BORREGO, b. Private; m. MARÍA ESTRADA.
iii.   JOSEPHINA BORREGO, b. Private; m. MANUEL LARA.
iv.   LORENZO BORREGO, b. Private; m. (1) NATALIA MONTOYA; m. (2) SYLVIA BORREGO.
v.   LUÍS FILIMON BORREGO, b. Private; m. MARÍA LARA.
vi.   MARÍA LYDIA BORREGO, b. Private; m. CLARANCE DINDINGER.
vii.   MIKE NORMAN BORREGO, b. Private; m. GLORIA DURÁN.
viii.   PEDRO BORREGO, b. Private; m. HILDA GARCÍA.
ix.   RAMÓN BORREGO, b. Private; m. MARY LOU MEDINA.
x.   RAÚL BORREGO, b. Private; m. EMALIE BAILY.
xi.   TERESA BORREGO, b. Private; m. SYLVESTER NÚÑEZ.

23. EMILIANO[5] SÁNCHEZ *(FELIPÉ E.[4], CORNELIA[3] PACHECO, FRANCISCO[2], MANUEL ANTONIO[1])* was born August 11, 1904 in Hondo, Territory of New México. He married RUBY MARTÍNEZ.

Children of EMILIANO SÁNCHEZ and RUBY MARTÍNEZ are:
i.   EMILIANO JUNIOR[6] SÁNCHEZ, b. 1927.
ii.   BERNICE MARTÍNEZ SÁNCHEZ, b. Private.
iii.   GLORIA SÁNCHEZ, b. Private.
iv.   LEROY SÁNCHEZ, b. Private.
v.   TERESA SÁNCHEZ, b. Private.
vi.   VIOLA SÁNCHEZ, b. Private.

24. ÁBRAN[5] SÁNCHEZ *(FELIPÉ E.[4], CORNELIA[3] PACHECO, FRANCISCO[2], MANUEL ANTONIO[1])* was born December 21, 1905 in White Oaks, Territory of New México, and died November 18, 1973 in El Paso, Téxas. He married (1) RAMONCITA GURULÉ. He married (2) FELIPA RODRÍQUES Abt. 1926[170].

Children of ÁBRAN SÁNCHEZ and RAMONCITA GURULÉ are:
i.   HERMAN[6] SÁNCHEZ, b. Private.
ii.   PAUBLITA GURULÉ SÁNCHEZ, b. Private.
iii.   GEORGE SÁNCHEZ, b. Private.
iv.   JOHN GURULÉ SÁNCHEZ, b. Private.
v.   RITA GURULÉ SÁNCHEZ, b. Private.
vi.   ROSYLENE SÁNCHEZ, b. Private.

Children of ÁBRAN SÁNCHEZ and FELIPA RODRÍQUES are:
vii.   FRANK RODRÍQUES[6] SÁNCHEZ, b. Abt. 1926.
viii.   MARÍA MAGDALENA SÁNCHEZ, b. Abt. 1928.
ix.   DAVÍD RODRÍQUES SÁNCHEZ, b. Private.
x.   FREDRICK SÁNCHEZ, b. Private.

25. REYNALDO[5] SÁNCHEZ *(FELIPÉ E.[4], CORNELIA[3] PACHECO, FRANCISCO[2], MANUEL ANTONIO[1])* was born Abt. 1907[171]. He married SOFIA AGUILAR[172] November 10, 1932.

Children of REYNALDO SÁNCHEZ and SOFIA AGUILAR are:
i.   MARY LILY[6] SÁNCHEZ, b. Private.
ii.   MABEL AGUILAR SÁNCHEZ, b. Private.
iii.   JO ANN SÁNCHEZ, b. Private.

26. BENITO[5] SÁNCHEZ *(FELIPÉ E.[4], CORNELIA[3] PACHECO, FRANCISCO[2], MANUEL ANTONIO[1])* was born Abt. 1912[173]. He married (1) CONCHA RAMÍREZ. He married (2) BEATRICE PINO May 09, 1932 in Tularosa, New México[174].

Children of BENITO SÁNCHEZ and CONCHA RAMÍREZ are:
  i.   HOPE[6] SÁNCHEZ, b. Private.
  ii.   ISABEL SÁNCHEZ, b. Private.
  iii. BENNY SÁNCHEZ, b. Private.

Children of BENITO SÁNCHEZ and BEATRICE PINO are:
  iv.   MARY ALICE[6] SÁNCHEZ, b. Private.
  v.   MARGIE SÁNCHEZ, b. Private.
  vi.   GRACE PINO SÁNCHEZ, b. Private.
  vii. RAY PINO SÁNCHEZ, b. Private.

27. ONECIMO[5] SÁNCHEZ *(FELIPÉ E.[4], CORNELIA[3] PACHECO, FRANCISCO[2], MANUEL ANTONIO[1])* was born 1915[175]. He married CLEOTILDE DURÁN, daughter of FRANCISCO DURÁN and HORTENCIA MONTES.

Children of ONECIMO SÁNCHEZ and CLEOTILDE DURÁN are:
  i.   YOLANDA DURÁN[6] SÁNCHEZ, b. Private.
  ii.   MAXIMO SÁNCHEZ, b. Private.
  iii.   MARY LOU SÁNCHEZ, b. Private.
  iv.   DARLENE SÁNCHEZ, b. Private.
  v.   HECTOR SÁNCHEZ, b. Private.
  vi.   LINDA SÁNCHEZ, b. Private.
  vii.   ALEX DURÁN SÁNCHEZ, b. Private.
  viii. CYNTHIA SÁNCHEZ, b. Private.

28. ROSA[5] GAVALDON *(ELUTICIA[4] SÁNCHEZ, CORNELIA[3] PACHECO, FRANCISCO[2], MANUEL ANTONIO[1])* was born January 1892[176]. She married AVRELIO MARTÍNEZ[177] December 12, 1910 in Patos, New México[178], son of ATANACIO MARTÍNEZ and RAMONA DE MARTÍNEZ.

Notes for AVRELIO MARTÍNEZ:
Also known as Aurelio. He was raised by Leandro Pacheco.
1930 Census: Lived in Corona, New México.

Children of ROSA GAVALDON and AVRELIO MARTÍNEZ are:
  i.   GUILLERMO[6] MARTÍNEZ[179], b. December 24, 1911, Ruidoso, Territory of New México[180]; m. CAROLINA SEDILLO[181], February 26, 1934, Carrizozo, New México[181].

Notes for GUILLERMO MARTÍNEZ:
Also known as Billie.
1930 Census: Living in Corona, New México.

  ii.   SENAIDA MARTÍNEZ, b. Abt. 1914[182]; m. DOLORES MÁRQUEZ, September 30, 1933[183].
  iii. MACARIO MARTÍNEZ, b. Abt. 1916[184].
  iv.   ERMINIO MARTÍNEZ[185], b. August 12, 1919, Rebentón, New México[186].
  v.   ARTURO MARTÍNEZ[187], b. March 04, 1921, Rebentón, New México[188]; d. March 27, 1987.

Notes for ARTURO MARTÍNEZ:
Private. World War II.

29. LUPE[5] GAVALDON *(ELUTICIA[4] SÁNCHEZ, CORNELIA[3] PACHECO, FRANCISCO[2], MANUEL ANTONIO[1])* was born August 20, 1897 in Patos, Territory of New México[189]. He married ELVIRA MÁRQUEZ August 13, 1921 in Rebentón, New México[190], daughter of MELCOR MÁRQUEZ and ALEJANDRA LUERAS.

Notes for LUPE GAVALDON:

Also known as Lupito, Guadalupe Gavaldon.

Patos, New México is located close to Rebentón, New México east of Sierra Capitán. Currently it is inaccesible because it is located on a private farm.

1930 Census: Living in Corona, New México.

Children of LUPE GAVALDON and ELVIRA MÁRQUEZ are:

    i.   ELIZA[6] GAVALDON, b. Abt. 1924[191].

    ii.   ERINEO GAVALDON[192], b. November 16, 1924, Rebentón, New México[193]; m. ANTONIA OLIVAS, November 15, 1947[194].

    iii. ELUTICIA GAVALDON[195], b. September 28, 1927, Carrizozo, New México[196]; m. FRANCISCO D. VEGA, July 11, 1948, Carrizozo, New México[197].

    iv. ORLANDO GAVALDON[198], b. August 09, 1929, Carrizozo, New México[199].

30. SORAIDA[5] SÁNCHEZ *(AURELIO[4], CORNELIA[3] PACHECO, FRANCISCO[2], MANUEL ANTONIO[1])* was born August 27, 1916 in Rebentón, Territory of New México[200]. She married MAXIMILIANO SÁNCHEZ February 11, 1936 in Carrizozo, New México[200], son of MAURICIO SÁNCHEZ and DELFINIA ROMERO.

Notes for MAXIMILIANO SÁNCHEZ:
Also known as Maque.
Buried in Santa Fé, New México.

Children of SORAIDA SÁNCHEZ and MAXIMILIANO SÁNCHEZ are:

    i.   BEATRICE[6] SÁNCHEZ, b. Private.

    ii.   ROSEMARY SÁNCHEZ, b. Private.

31. ELMO[5] BRADY *(ROSARIO[4] SÁNCHEZ, CORNELIA[3] PACHECO, FRANCISCO[2], MANUEL ANTONIO[1])* was born October 30, 1917 in Hondo, New México[201], and died December 29, 2008 in Ruidoso, New México[201]. He married GERALDINE KIMBRELL[202] 1946 in California[203], daughter of ALBERT KIMBRELL and CONSUELO RUBIO.

Children of ELMO BRADY and GERALDINE KIMBRELL are:

    i.   PATRICK[6] BRADY[203], b. Private.

    ii.   EMILEEN BRADY[203], b. Private.

32. BILLY JOE[5] BRADY *(ROSARIO[4] SÁNCHEZ, CORNELIA[3] PACHECO, FRANCISCO[2], MANUEL ANTONIO[1])* was born Private. He married PATSY SALCIDO.

Genealogy of José Senovio Prudencio

Generation No. 1

1. JOSÉ SENOVIO[1] PRUDENCIO was born 1845[1]. He married VICTORIA FAJARDO[2].

Notes for JOSÉ SENOVIO PRUDENCIO:
Also known as José Zenobio Provencio.
1870 Census: Living in Lincoln County, Precinct 2 (San Patricio), Territory of New México.

Notes for VICTORIA FAJARDO:
1869: Was residing in Plaza de San José, Territory of New México.
1910 & 1920 Census: Living in San Patricio, Territory of New México.
1930 Census: Living in Hondo, Territory of New México. (Victoria Prudencio)

Children of JOSÉ PRUDENCIO and VICTORIA FAJARDO are:

	i.	LUCIANA[2] PRUDENCIO, b. 1869[3]. Died young.
	ii.	MANUEL PRUDENCIO, b. October 20, 1871, Ruidoso, Territory of New México[4].
2.	iii.	MORTIMER PRUDENCIO, b. August 1879.
3.	iv.	DAMACIO PRUDENCIO, b. December 1880; d. Bef. 1903.
4.	v.	CATARINO PRUDENCIO, b. Abt. 1884, San Patricio, New México; d. April 11, 1931, San Patricio, New México.
5.	vi.	MARTINA PRUDENCIO, b. March 10, 1885.
	vii.	LUZ PRUDENCIO, b. December 25, 1890, San Patricio, Territory of New México[5]; m. JUAN PABLO HERRERA, October 26, 1916, Lincoln, New México[5].

Notes for JUAN PABLO HERRERA:
  Buried in Roswell.

Generation No. 2

2. MORTIMER[2] PRUDENCIO *(JOSÉ SENOVIO[1])* was born August 1879[6]. He married (1) CLEOFAS MUÑOZ August 31, 1903 in San Patricio, Territory of New México[7]. He married (2) LORENSA MONTOYA September 27, 1923[8], daughter of FELIPÉ MONTOYA and MARCELA CHÁVEZ.

Notes for MORTIMER PRUDENCIO:
1930 Census: Living in Dunkin, New México.

Children of MORTIMER PRUDENCIO and CLEOFAS MUÑOZ are:

6.	i.	IGNACIO[3] PRUDENCIO, b. 1904.
	ii.	NICOLÁS PRUDENCIO, b. 1907[9].
	iii.	MARTÍN PRUDENCIO, b. 1909[9].

Children of MORTIMER PRUDENCIO and LORENSA MONTOYA are:

	iv.	MORTIMER[3] PRUDENCIO, b. 1925[10].
	v.	ARCENIA PRUDENCIO, b. 1927[10].
	vi.	BETTY PRUDENCIO, b. Private.
	vii.	CLAUDIO PRUDENCIO, b. Private.
	viii.	TRENE PRUDENCIO, b. Private.
	ix.	VALENTÍN PRUDENCIO, b. Private.

3. DAMACIO[2] PRUDENCIO *(JOSÉ SENOVIO[1])* was born December 1880[11], and died Bef. 1903. He married CLEOFAS MUÑOZ[12].

Child of DAMACIO PRUDENCIO and CLEOFAS MUÑOZ is:

7.	i.	ROBERTO[3] PRUDENCIO, b. June 07, 1901, San Patricio, Territory of New México; d. March 28, 1983, San Patricio, New México.

4. CATARINO[2] PRUDENCIO *(JOSÉ SENOVIO[1])[13]* was born Abt. 1884 in San Patricio, New México[14], and died April 11, 1931 in San Patricio, New México. He married ANITA GARCÍA July 23, 1911.

Notes for CATARINO PRUDENCIO:
Buried in San Patricio, NM.

Children of CATARINO PRUDENCIO and ANITA GARCÍA are:
      i.   DOMINGA[3] PRUDENCIO, b. 1923.
      ii.   NUE PRUDENCIO, b. Private.
      iii. SALVADOR PRUDENCIO, b. November 02, 1920, Glencoe, New México[15].
8.   iv. TANISLADA PRUDENCIO, b. Private.

5. MARTINA[2] PRUDENCIO *(JOSÉ SENOVIO[1])[16]* was born March 10, 1885. She married (1) MANUEL ULIBARRÍ MONTOYA October 01, 1911, son of ESTANISLADO MONTOYA and SARAFINA ULIBARRÍ. She married (2) FRANCISCO LUNA CHÁVEZ[17] October 07, 1922[18], son of JOSÉ CHÁVEZ and MARÍA LUNA.

Notes for FRANCISCO LUNA CHÁVEZ:
Also known as Frank.

Children of MARTINA PRUDENCIO and MANUEL MONTOYA are:
      i.   FELIX[3] MONTOYA.
      ii.   LUÍS MONTOYA, b. Abt. 1913[19].
      iii. JUANITA MONTOYA, b. Abt. 1914[19].
      iv. GILBERTO MONTOYA, b. Abt. 1917[19].

Children of MARTINA PRUDENCIO and FRANCISCO CHÁVEZ are:
      v.   DOMINGO[3] CHÁVEZ, b. Abt. 1922[20].
      vi. DEMETRIA CHÁVEZ, b. Abt. 1924[21].

Generation No. 3

6. IGNACIO[3] PRUDENCIO *(MORTIMER[2], JOSÉ SENOVIO[1])* was born 1904[22].

Child of IGNACIO PRUDENCIO is:
      i.   RICHARD[4] PRUDENCIO, b. Private.

7. ROBERTO[3] PRUDENCIO *(DAMACIO[2], JOSÉ SENOVIO[1])[23]* was born June 07, 1901 in San Patricio, Territory of New México[24], and died March 28, 1983 in San Patricio, New México. He married (1) ELENA CORONA[25] August 05, 1922 in San Patricio, New México[26], daughter of MAXIMIANO CORONA and MANUELITA HERRERA. He married (2) CASIMIRA YBARRA[27] July 03, 1929 in San Patricio, New México[28], daughter of GREGORIO YBARRA and CATARINA MONTOYA.

Notes for ROBERTO PRUDENCIO:
Also known as Roberto Provencio. Private in the U.S. Army.
1920 Census: Living in Capitán, New México
1930 Census: Living in Dunkin, New México.

Notes for ELENA CORONA:
Also known as Helena.
Born at Gregorio's farm in San Juanito.

Children of ROBERTO PRUDENCIO and ELENA CORONA are:
      i.   ALBERTO[4] PRUDENCIO[29], b. Abt. 1928, San Patricio, New México; d. August 30, 1928, San Patricio, New México.
      ii.   FELICITA PRUDENCIO, b. Private; m. ADAN BARRERA[30], Artesia, New México.
      iii. MARGARITA PRUDENCIO, b. Private; m. JOSÉ TORRES.

Notes for MARGARITA PRUDENCIO:

Also known as Maggie.

Children of ROBERTO PRUDENCIO and CASIMIRA YBARRA are:

  iv.   FELICITA YBARRA⁴ PRUDENCIO³¹, b. Abt. 1930, San Patricio, New México; d. June 20, 1938, San Patricio, New México.
  v.   ONESIMO PRUDENCIO³², b. April 18, 1934, San Patricio, New México; d. March 10, 1998, Ruidoso Downs, New México.

Notes for ONESIMO PRUDENCIO:
Spec 3 US Army.

  vi.   CLEOFAS PRUDENCIO, b. Private, San Patricio, New México. Died young.
  vii. DAMACIO PRUDENCIO, b. Private, San Patricio, New México.
  viii. MANUEL PRUDENCIO, b. Private, San Patricio, New México. Died young.

Notes for MANUEL PRUDENCIO:
Raised by Genovevo Ybarra & Juanita Sanchez Ybarra.

  ix.   RAMÓN PRUDENCIO, b. Private, San Patricio, New México.

8. TANISLADA³ PRUDENCIO *(CATARINO², JOSÉ SENOVIO¹)* was born Private. She married MANUEL WARNER, son of JUAN WARNER and EMILIA TORREZ.

Children of TANISLADA PRUDENCIO and MANUEL WARNER are:

  i.   URBANO⁴ WARNER. Died young.
  ii.   JOE WARNER, b. Private.

Genealogy of Vicente Romero

Generation No. 1

1. VICENTE[1] ROMERO was born in Nambé Pueblo, El Reyno de Nuevo México, Nueva España, and died April 15, 1829 in Pojoaqué, El Reyno de Nuevo México, Nueva España[1]. He married MARÍA TOMÁSA TRUJILLO April 08, 1793 in Nambé Pueblo, El Reyno de Nuevo México, Nueva España[2], daughter of PEDRO TRUJILLO and MARÍA LUJÁN.

Notes for VICENTE ROMERO:
Also known as José Antonio Vicente Romero.

Notes for MARÍA TOMÁSA TRUJILLO:
Known names: María Antonia Trujillo, Tomása Trujillo.
1850 Census: Living in Santa Fé County, Territory of New México. (Tomasa Romero) Lists her birth year as 1790.

Children of VICENTE ROMERO and MARÍA TRUJILLO are:
	i.	MARÍA SISTA[2] ROMERO, d. April 14, 1803, Pojoaque, El Reyno de Nuevo México, Nueva España[3].
2.	ii.	YGNACIO ROMERO, b. June 30, 1795, Santa Fé, El Reyno de Nuevo México, Nueva España; d. San Patricio, Territory of New México.
	iii.	FELIPÉ ROMERO, b. March 17, 1796, Pojoaqué, El Reyno de Nuevo México, Nueva España; d. May 25, 1796.
	iv.	JOSÉ ENCARNACIÓN ROMERO[4], b. Abt. 1797, Cuyamungué, El Reyno de Nuevo México, Nueva España; d. Bef. April 1841.
	v.	MARÍA ANGELA ROMERO[5], b. April 01, 1800, Santa Cruz de la Cañada, El Reyno de Nuevo México, Nueva España; m. DIEGO ANTONIO LUCERO, October 16, 1819.
3.	vi.	JUANA MARÍA ROMERO, b. Abt. 1812, Pojoaqué, El Reyno de Nuevo México, Nueva España.
4.	vii.	VICTOR ROMERO, b. Abt. 1814, Pojoaqué, El Reyno de Nuevo México, Nueva España.

Generation No. 2

2. YGNACIO[2] ROMERO *(VICENTE[1])* was born June 30, 1795 in Santa Fé, El Reyno de Nuevo México, Nueva España[6], and died in San Patricio, Territory of New México. He married RAFAELA LUERAS March 01, 1828 in Santa Fé, Nuevo México, La República de México[7], daughter of RAMÓN LUERAS and DOLORES ARMIJO.

Notes for YGNACIO ROMERO:
Also known as José Ygnacio Romero, José Ygnacio Trifon Romero.
1845 Census: Living near La Joya, Nuevo México, La República de México.
1860 Census: Living in Manzano, Territory of New México. (Born about 1797.)
1870 Census: Living in Lincoln County, Territory of New México. (Born about 1796.)
1880 Census: Living in La Junta, Territory of New México. (Born about 1796.)

Notes for RAFAELA LUERAS:
Also known as María Rafaela Lueras, Rafaela Lueras.
1860 Census: Born about 1810.

Children of YGNACIO ROMERO and RAFAELA LUERAS are:
5.	i.	FRANCISCO ALVINO[3] ROMERO, b. January 31, 1830, Casa Colorada, Nuevo México, La República de México.
6.	ii.	JOSÉ ANTONIO ROMERO, b. Abt. 1835, Casa Colorada, Nuevo México, La República de México; d. Abt. 1877.
	iii.	MARÍA PETRA ROMERO, b. May 1838, La Joya, Nuevo México, La República de México[8].
	iv.	MARÍA ANTONIA BRIGIDA ROMERO, b. October 06, 1840, La Joya, Nuevo México, La República de México[9].
7.	v.	JUAN ROMERO, b. Abt. 1843, Casa Colorada, Nuevo México.
	vi.	BARTOLOMÉ ROMERO, b. September 19, 1844, Sevilleta, Nuevo México, La República de México[10].
8.	vii.	JOSÉ VICENTE ROMERO, b. April 20, 1846, Sevilleta, Nuevo México, La República de México; d. July 19, 1878, Lincoln, Territory of New México.
	viii.	PABLO ROMERO, b. Abt. 1851[11].

3. JUANA MARÍA[2] ROMERO *(VICENTE[1])*[12] was born Abt. 1812 in Pojoaqué, El Reyno de Nuevo México, Nueva España[13]. She married JUAN JESÚS DE HERRERA.

Notes for JUANA MARÍA ROMERO:
1860 Census: Living in Cuyamungué, Territory of New México.

Child of JUANA ROMERO and JUAN DE HERRERA is:
      i.   MANUEL ROMERO[3] HERRERA, b. Abt. 1853, Cuyamungué, Territory of New México[13].

4. VICTOR[2] ROMERO *(VICENTE[1])* was born Abt. 1814 in Pojoaqué, El Reyno de Nuevo México, Nueva España[13]. He married MARÍA ANTONINA VALDÉS.

Notes for VICTOR ROMERO:
Also known as José Victor Romero.
1850 Census: Living in Santa Fé County, Territory of New México.
1860 Census: Living in Cuyamungué, Territory of New México.

Notes for MARÍA ANTONINA VALDÉS:
Also known as Anotnia.

Children of VICTOR ROMERO and MARÍA VALDÉS are:
      i.   JUANA[3] ROMERO, b. Abt. 1852, Cuyamungué, Territory of New México[13].
      ii.   FELIX ROMERO, b. Abt. 1853, Cuyamungué, Territory of New México[13].

Generation No. 3

5. FRANCISCO ALVINO[3] ROMERO *(YGNACIO[2], VICENTE[1])*[14] was born January 31, 1830 in Casa Colorada, Nuevo México, La República de México. He married (1) ANDREA SÁNCHEZ[15]. He married (2) GENOVEVA VILLESCAS March 28, 1890[16], daughter of CASIMIRO VILLESCAS and DOLORES BALDONADO.

Notes for FRANCISCO ALVINO ROMERO:
September 06, 1869: Ran for Lincoln County Sheriff but lost to William Brady by 8 votes. Sheriff William Brady hired Francisco as his Deputy.
1870 Census: Living in Lincoln County, Precinct 1, Territory of New México.
Land patent NMNMMA 010752: 160 acres.
Land patent NMNMMA 010776: 160 acres.

Notes for ANDREA SÁNCHEZ:
Also known as María Andrea Sánchez.

Notes for GENOVEVA VILLESCAS:
Also known as Genoveva Villescas.

Children of FRANCISCO ROMERO and ANDREA SÁNCHEZ are:
9.   i.   PABLA[4] ROMERO, b. July 15, 1852, Manzano, Territory of New México; d. November 08, 1915, Picacho, New México.
       ii.   HIGINIA ROMERO, b. Abt. 1856, Manzano, Territory of New México[17].
10.   iii. JUANITA ROMERO, b. Abt. 1859, Manzano, Territory of New México.
      iv. PETRA ROMERO, b. Abt. 1864, Manzano, Territory of New México[18]; d. Bef. July 1884; m. LUCIANO TRUJILLO[19], January 09, 1882[20].

Notes for LUCIANO TRUJILLO:
1860 & 1870 Census: Living in Manzano, Territory of New México.
1880 Census: Living in La Plaza de Picacho, Territory of New México.
1910 Census: Living in Agua Azul, Territory of New México.

11.   v.   FRANCISCA SÁNCHEZ ROMERO, b. Abt. 1869; d. 1951.
      vi. PABLO SÁNCHEZ ROMERO, b. Abt. 1870[21]; m. (1) PETRA DE ROMERO; m. (2) JOSEFA SAMORA, June 22, 1897[22].

Notes for PABLO SÁNCHEZ ROMERO:
1870 Census: Living in Lincoln County, Precinct 1, Territory of New México.

6. JOSÉ ANTONIO[3] ROMERO *(YGNACIO[2], VICENTE[1])* was born Abt. 1835 in Casa Colorada, Nuevo México, La República de México, and died Abt. 1877. He married CORNELIA SISNEROS.

Child of JOSÉ ROMERO and CORNELIA SISNEROS is:
12.   i.   JUAN DE DIOS[4] ROMERO, b. March 1859, Manzano, Territory of New México; d. 1914, Picacho, New México.

7. JUAN[3] ROMERO *(YGNACIO[2], VICENTE[1])* was born Abt. 1843 in Casa Colorada, Nuevo México[23]. He married MARÍA GARCÍA[24].

Notes for MARÍA GARCÍA:
1900 Census: Living in Lincoln, Territory of New México.

Children of JUAN ROMERO and MARÍA GARCÍA are:
      i.   PABLO GARCÍA[4] ROMERO.
      ii.   JOSÉ GARCÍA ROMERO, b. October 1879[25].
      iii.   LUÍS ROMERO, b. July 07, 1887[26].

Notes for LUÍS ROMERO:
Baptismal Padrinos: Gus Peppin, Victoriano Salazar.

      iv.   ALEJANDRO ROMERO, b. February 1891[27].

8. JOSÉ VICENTE[3] ROMERO *(YGNACIO[2], VICENTE[1])* was born April 20, 1846 in Sevilleta, Nuevo México, La República de México[28], and died July 19, 1878 in Lincoln, Territory of New México. He married MARÍA MARGARITA GONZÁLES[29].

Notes for JOSÉ VICENTE ROMERO:
1860 Census: Living in Manzano, Territory of New México.
July 19, 1878: Was a regulator, killed on the forth day of the Lincoln County War.

Children of JOSÉ ROMERO and MARÍA GONZÁLES are:
13.   i.   DEMETRIA[4] ROMERO, b. December 27, 1869, San Patricio, Territory of New México.
14.   ii.   PABLO GONZÁLES ROMERO, b. March 26, 1872, Río Bonito, Territory of México.
      iii.   MARÍA DEL CARMEL ROMERO, b. June 1873[30].

Generation No. 4

George Kimbrell

9. PABLA[4] ROMERO *(FRANCISCO ALVINO[3], YGNACIO[2], VICENTE[1])*[31] was born July 15, 1852 in Manzano, Territory of New México[32], and died November 08, 1915 in Picacho, New México. She married GEORGE KIMBRELL 1863[33].

Notes for PABLA ROMERO:
Also known as Paula, Pablita, Paulita.
1870: Was living near Plaza de San José.

Children of PABLA ROMERO and GEORGE KIMBRELL are:
15.   i.   JUAN ROMERO[5] KIMBRELL, b. October 1867, Picacho, Territory of New México.
      ii.   ELEN KIMBRELL, b. 1869, Picacho, Territory of New México[34].
      iii.   BEATRIZ KIMBRELL, b. April 18, 1872, Rio Bonito, Territory of New México[35]; m. WALLACE BROCKMAN, May 15, 1889[36].
16.   iv.   BONUFANTE KIMBRELL, b. February 22, 1874, Picacho, Territory of New México.

17. v. WILLIAM E. KIMBRELL, b. June 16, 1878, Picacho, Territory of New México; d. October 13, 1960, Picacho, New México.

Martín Cháves

10. JUANITA[4] ROMERO *(FRANCISCO ALVINO[3], YGNACIO[2], VICENTE[1])* was born Abt. 1859 in Manzano, Territory of New México[37]. She married MARTÍN CHÁVEZ Abt. 1876[38].

Notes for JUANITA ROMERO:
Also known as Juana.
1860 Census: Living in Manzano.

Children of JUANITA ROMERO and MARTÍN CHÁVEZ are:
    i. DAVÍD[5] VILLESCAZ, b. October 1882[38].
18. ii. MODESTO CHÁVEZ, b. November 29, 1883, Picacho, Territory of New México; d. 1934.
19. iii. JOSEFITA CHÁVEZ, b. March 1887, Picacho, Territory of New México.
    iv. BENJAMÍN CHÁVEZ, b. June 06, 1893, Picacho, Territory of New México[39].
    v. MARILLITA ROMERO CHÁVEZ, b. Abt. 1903, Picacho, Territory of New México[40].

11. FRANCISCA SÁNCHEZ[4] ROMERO *(FRANCISCO ALVINO[3], YGNACIO[2], VICENTE[1])*[41] was born Abt. 1869[42], and died 1951. She married PERFETO A. SANDOVAL[43] May 15, 1889[44], son of ESEQUIEL SANDOVAL and MARÍA ARAGÓN.

Notes for PERFETO A. SANDOVAL:
1880 Census: Living in Santa Rosa, Territory of New México.
1910 Census: Living in Fort Sumner, Territory of New México.
1920 & 1930 Census: Living in Picacho, New México.

Children of FRANCISCA ROMERO and PERFETO SANDOVAL are:
20. i. JULIAN[5] SANDOVAL, b. September 27, 1895, Picacho, Territory of New México; d. February 05, 1976, Picacho, Territory of New México.
21. ii. ALFREDO SANDOVAL, b. February 15, 1897; d. August 16, 1946.
    iii. ARCELIA SANDOVAL, b. Abt. 1900[45].
22. iv. JOSÉ INEZ SANDOVAL, b. July 19, 1901, Puerto de Luna, New México; d. August 01, 1983, Tinnie, New México.
23. v. LUZ SANDOVAL, b. May 29, 1904, Fort Sumner, Territory of New México.
    vi. FRANCISCA SANDOVAL, b. Abt. 1909, Fort Sumner, Territory of New México[46].
    vii. PERFECTO ROMERO SANDOVAL, b. Abt. 1911, Fort Sumner, Territory of New México[46]; m. VIOLA KIMBRELL[47][48].
    viii. PABLO SANDOVAL, b. Abt. 1913, Fort Sumner, Territory of New México[49]; m. TRENIDAD ARTIAGA, August 04, 1934[50].

Juan de Dios Romero

12. JUAN DE DIOS[4] ROMERO *(JOSÉ ANTONIO[3], YGNACIO[2], VICENTE[1])* was born March 1859 in Manzano, Territory of New México[51], and died 1914 in Picacho, New México[52]. He married CRISTINA CASTILLO Abt. 1880[53], daughter of RAFAEL CASTILLO and MARÍA LUCERO.

Notes for JUAN DE DIOS ROMERO:
1860 Census: Living in Manzano, Territory of New México. Family legend has he was born in Casa Colorada, Territory of New México.
About 1870: He was raised at La Plaza de San Jose with his grandparents.
1880 Census: Living in La Junta, Territory of New México.
1900 Census: Living in San Patricio, Territory of New México.
Buried in La Capilla de San Patricio.

Notes for CRISTINA CASTILLO:
Raised by her grandparents, José Miguel Lucero & Luciana. She had an aunt, Lola Guerra.
Buried at La Capilla de San Patricio.

Children of JUAN ROMERO and CRISTINA CASTILLO are:
-     i.   MANUEL⁵ ROMERO, b. Abt. 1879⁵⁴.
- 24.   ii.   GEORGE ROMERO, b. July 14, 1880, Picacho, Territory of New México; d. February 21, 1948, Hagerman, New México.
- 25.   iii.   MERENCIANA ROMERO, b. August 1883, Picacho, Territory of New México.
- 26.   iv.   CAROLINA ROMERO, b. January 22, 1884, Picacho, Territory of New México.
- 27.   v.   DELFINIA ROMERO, b. December 12, 1885, Picacho, Territory of New México; d. November 13, 1926, San Patricio, New México.
- 28.   vi.   LUPITA ROMERO, b. December 12, 1888, San Patricio, Territory of New México; d. 1969, Picacho, New México.
- 29.   vii.   MARÍA ROMERO, b. January 19, 1891, San Patricio, Territory of New México; d. March 21, 1976, Roswell, New México.
- 30.   viii.   ANTONIO ROMERO, b. December 12, 1892, San Patricio, Territory of New México; d. February 06, 1942, San Patricio, New México.
-     ix.   ARISTOTEL ROMERO⁵⁵, b. March 15, 1896, San Patricio, Territory of New México⁵⁶; d. January 02, 1964; m. FRANCISQUITA CHÁVEZ⁵⁷, 1936⁵⁸.

Notes for ARISTOTEL ROMERO:
NM Private, Med Dept, WWI

- 31.   x.   LUCÍA ROMERO, b. December 06, 1896, San Patricio, Territory of New México.
- 32.   xi.   MANUEL CASTILLO ROMERO, b. October 06, 1899, San Patricio, Territory of New México; d. October 1982, Silver City, New México.

13. DEMETRIA⁴ ROMERO *(JOSÉ VICENTE³, YGNACIO², VICENTE¹)* was born December 27, 1869 in San Patricio, Territory of New México⁵⁹. She married JUSTO CHÁVEZ January 07, 1886 in Picacho, Territory of New México⁶⁰, son of CASIMIRO CHÁVEZ and DOLORES SERNA.

Notes for JUSTO CHÁVEZ:
1910 Census: Living in Picacho, Territory of New México.
Raised Prometiva Romero. The daughter of Pablo Romero & Lucinda Gonzales. Also raised Feliz Vigil.

Children of DEMETRIA ROMERO and JUSTO CHÁVEZ are:
- 33.   i.   FELIZ⁵ VIGIL, b. January 12, 1890, Lincoln County, Territory of New México.
-     ii.   PABLO ROMERO CHÁVEZ, b. June 29, 1895, Picacho, Territory of New México⁶¹.

Notes for PABLO ROMERO CHÁVEZ:
1900 Census: Living in Picacho, Territory of New México.

-     iii.   PERFECTO CHÁVEZ, b. Abt. 1900, Picacho, Territory of New México⁶²; m. ISABEL MENDOSA, December 17, 1924⁶³.

Notes for ISABEL MENDOSA:
Also known as Isavel.

14. PABLO GONZÁLES⁴ ROMERO *(JOSÉ VICENTE³, YGNACIO², VICENTE¹)* was born March 26, 1872 in Río Bonito, Territory of México⁶⁴. He married (1) LEONIDES CHÁVEZ Abt. 1890⁶⁵, daughter of CASIMIRO CHÁVEZ and DOLORES SERNA. He married (2) LUCINDA GONZÁLES May 17, 1900 in Picacho, Territory of New México⁶⁶, daughter of PERFECTO GONZÁLES and ANTONIA VIGIL.

Notes for PABLO GONZÁLES ROMERO:
1900 Census: Living in Picacho, Territory of New México.

Child of PABLO ROMERO and LEONIDES CHÁVEZ is:
-     i.   LOLA⁵ ROMERO, b. January 1892⁶⁷.

Child of PABLO ROMERO and LUCINDA GONZÁLES is:
- 34.   ii.   PROMETIVA⁵ ROMERO, b. February 16, 1899, Picacho, Territory of New México; d. May 28, 1975.

Generation No. 5

15. JUAN ROMERO[5] KIMBRELL *(PABLA[4] ROMERO, FRANCISCO ALVINO[3], YGNACIO[2], VICENTE[1])[68]* was born October 1867 in Picacho, Territory of New México[69]. He married DOMISINDA ORTEGA February 04, 1888[70], daughter of LEANDRO ORTEGA and ROSARIO VIGIL.

Notes for JUAN ROMERO KIMBRELL:
Also known as John.

Notes for DOMISINDA ORTEGA:
Also known as Gomicinda.

Children of JUAN KIMBRELL and DOMISINDA ORTEGA are:

	i.	MANUELITA[6] KIMBRELL, b. August 1888[71]; m. ESTEVAN GARCÍA, November 04, 1907[72].
35.	ii.	GEORGE ORTEGA KIMBRELL, b. June 01, 1892, Picacho, Territory of New México; d. 1959, Picacho, New México.
36.	iii.	JUAN ORTEGA KIMBRELL, b. December 17, 1895, Picacho, Territory of New México; d. December 17, 1971, Roswell, New México.
37.	iv.	MANUEL ORTEGA KIMBRELL, b. 1903, Picacho, Territory of New México.
38.	v.	ROSA KIMBRELL, b. September 07, 1904, Picacho, Territory of New México; d. January 07, 1980.
	vi.	DORA ORTEGA KIMBRELL, b. 1911, Picacho, Territory of New México; m. VICTORIANO ROMERO, February 10, 1930[73].
39.	vii.	BEATRICE KIMBRELL, b. August 19, 1919, Picacho, New México; d. February 16, 1988.

16. BONUFANTE[5] KIMBRELL *(PABLA[4] ROMERO, FRANCISCO ALVINO[3], YGNACIO[2], VICENTE[1])* was born February 22, 1874 in Picacho, Territory of New México[74]. He married (1) JESÚSITA BECERRA January 02, 1896[75], daughter of SUSANO BECERRA and MASIMIANA LUJÁN. He married (2) FELIZ VIGIL January 30, 1907 in Picacho, Territory of New México[76], daughter of JUSTO CHÁVEZ and DEMETRIA ROMERO.

Notes for BONUFANTE KIMBRELL:
Also known as Bonifacio, Bonie, Borie.

Notes for FELIZ VIGIL:
Raised by Justo Chávez and Demetria Romero de Chávez.
1900 Census: Listed as Felis Vigil, living with her brother Justo Chávez.

Child of BONUFANTE KIMBRELL and FELIZ VIGIL is:

| | i. | RAY[6] KIMBRELL, b. Abt. 1911[77]. |

17. WILLIAM E.[5] KIMBRELL *(PABLA[4] ROMERO, FRANCISCO ALVINO[3], YGNACIO[2], VICENTE[1])[78]* was born June 16, 1878 in Picacho, Territory of New México, and died October 13, 1960 in Picacho, New México. He married VIGINIA ROMERO[78] February 18, 1904 in Lincoln, Territory of New México[79], daughter of TRENIDAD ROMERO and EUGENIA GONZÁLES.

Children of WILLIAM KIMBRELL and VIGINIA ROMERO are:

	i.	VIOLA[6] KIMBRELL[80], b. July 05, 1905[81]; d. July 02, 1949; m. PERFECTO ROMERO SANDOVAL[82].
40.	ii.	ALBERT KIMBRELL, b. February 03, 1907, Picacho, New México; d. January 12, 1987, Roswell, New México.
	iii.	RICHARD KIMBRELL[83], b. October 27, 1910, Picacho, Territory of New México[84]; d. October 20, 1972, Picacho, New México.

Notes for RICHARD KIMBRELL:
New Mexico Corporal Med Det 378 Infantry. WW II Veteran.

| | iv. | ANITA KIMBRELL[85], b. January 20, 1912, Picacho, Territory of New México[86]; d. August 05, 1955; m. FRANK THOMAS TWITCHELL[87], April 14, 1937[88]. |

Notes for ANITA KIMBRELL:
Also known as Anna.

41.   v.   ANDREA KIMBRELL, b. February 09, 1914, Picacho, New México; d. September 04, 2007.

          vi.   JANE KIMBRELL[89], b. January 08, 1916, Picacho, New México[90]; d. May 03, 1994; m. MANUEL ORTIZ[91], December 25, 1936, Carrizozo, New México[92].

Notes for JANE KIMBRELL:
Also known as Mary Jane Kimbrell.

          vii.   JOSEPHINE KIMBRELL, b. 1918[93].

42.   viii. PAULINA KIMBRELL, b. October 05, 1920, Picacho, New México; d. September 18, 1966.

          ix.   GEORGE ROMERO KIMBRELL[94], b. September 13, 1925, Picacho, New México[95].

Notes for GEORGE ROMERO KIMBRELL:
US Navy. World War II.

          x.   WILLIE KIMBRELL[96], b. Abt. 1928[97]; d. December 04, 1930, Carrizozo, New México.

18. MODESTO[5] CHÁVEZ *(JUANITA[4] ROMERO, FRANCISCO ALVINO[3], YGNACIO[2], VICENTE[1])*[98] was born November 29, 1883 in Picacho, Territory of New México, and died 1934. He married TRENIDAD MONTOYA[98] February 26, 1906 in Lincoln, Territory of New México[99], daughter of RAFAEL MONTOYA and MAY NORMAN.

Notes for MODESTO CHÁVEZ:
Picacho Cemetary: Date of birth on tombstone given as 1882. WWI Draft registrationindicates that he was born on November 29, 1884.
1920 Census: Living in Picacho, New México.
1930 Census: Living in Santa Fé, New México.

Children of MODESTO CHÁVEZ and TRENIDAD MONTOYA are:
          i.   MARTÍN[6] CHÁVEZ, b. Abt. 1907[100].
          ii.   JUANA CHÁVEZ, b. Abt. 1910[101].

Notes for JUANA CHÁVEZ:
Also known as Juanita.

          iii.   OLA CHÁVEZ, b. Abt. 1914[101].
          iv.   FRANCISCO CHÁVEZ, b. Abt. 1915[101].
          v.   OLYMPIA CHÁVEZ, b. Abt. 1917[101].
          vi.   MARÍA CHÁVEZ, b. Abt. 1919[101].
          vii.   MODESTO CHÁVEZ[102], b. 1922[103]; d. 1953.
          viii. JOSÉ CHÁVEZ, b. Abt. 1927[103].

19. JOSEFITA[5] CHÁVEZ *(JUANITA[4] ROMERO, FRANCISCO ALVINO[3], YGNACIO[2], VICENTE[1])* was born March 1887 in Picacho, Territory of New México[104]. She married FRANCISCO SANTANA.

Notes for FRANCISCO SANTANA:
1910 Census: Living in Picacho, Territory of New México.
1920 Census: Living in Santa Fé, New México.

Children of JOSEFITA CHÁVEZ and FRANCISCO SANTANA are:
          i.   ENRÍQUE[6] SANTANA, b. Abt. 1909, Picacho, Territory of New México[105].
          ii.   FELIPÉ SANTANA, b. Abt. 1912[106].
          iii.   ANITA SANTANA, b. Abt. 1913[106].
          iv.   EUGENIA SANTANA, b. Abt. 1916[106].
          v.   FRANCISCO SANTANA, b. Abt. 1924, Téxas[107].

20. JULIAN[5] SANDOVAL *(FRANCISCA SÁNCHEZ[4] ROMERO, FRANCISCO ALVINO[3], YGNACIO[2], VICENTE[1])*[108] was born September 27, 1895 in Picacho, Territory of New México, and died February 05, 1976 in Picacho, Territory of New México. He married (1) PERFECTA MAÉS September 23, 1916 in Lincoln, New México[109], daughter of JOSÉ MAÉS and MANUELITA LUCERO. He married (2) ROSA KIMBRELL[110] October 12, 1935 in Picacho, New México[111], daughter of JUAN KIMBRELL and DOMISINDA ORTEGA.

Children of JULIAN SANDOVAL and PERFECTA MAÉS are:
    i.   JOSEFITA[6] SANDOVAL, b. Abt. 1917[112].
    ii.   DOLORES SANDOVAL, b. Abt. 1919[112].

Child of JULIAN SANDOVAL and ROSA KIMBRELL is:
    iii. JULIAN KIMBRELL[6] SANDOVAL[113], b. January 09, 1922; d. August 19, 1991, Roswell, New México.

Notes for JULIAN KIMBRELL SANDOVAL:
Corporal US Army. World War II Veteran.

21. ALFREDO[5] SANDOVAL (*FRANCISCA SÁNCHEZ*[4] *ROMERO, FRANCISCO ALVINO*[3]*, YGNACIO*[2]*, VICENTE*[1])[113] was born February 15, 1897, and died August 16, 1946. He married LUCINDA SANDOVAL January 07, 1920[114], daughter of BENINO SANDOVAL and MARGARITA CHÁVEZ.

Notes for ALFREDO SANDOVAL:
New Mexico Private First Class 19 Infantry, 18 Division. WW I Veteran.

Notes for LUCINDA SANDOVAL:
Also known as Luz, Lucy.
1930 Census: Daughter in law, living with Perfecto Sandoval and Francisca Billescas de Sandoval.

Children of ALFREDO SANDOVAL and LUCINDA SANDOVAL are:
    i.   VIOLA[6] SANDOVAL, b. September 15, 1920, Carrizozo, New México[115]; m. SALOMON PADILLA[116].
    ii.   FRED SANDOVAL, b. Abt. 1923[117].
    iii. BEN SANDOVAL, b. Abt. 1925[117].

22. JOSÉ INEZ[5] SANDOVAL (*FRANCISCA SÁNCHEZ*[4] *ROMERO, FRANCISCO ALVINO*[3]*, YGNACIO*[2]*, VICENTE*[1])[118] was born July 19, 1901 in Puerto de Luna, New México[119], and died August 01, 1983 in Tinnie, New México. He married JUANITA MENDOSA[120] April 08, 1922[121], daughter of DIONICIO MENDOSA and MARÍA DE MENDOSA.

Notes for JOSÉ INEZ SANDOVAL:
Private US Army.
Buried in Picacho, NM.

Children of JOSÉ SANDOVAL and JUANITA MENDOSA are:
    i.   MANUEL[6] SANDOVAL[122], b. June 19, 1925, Picacho, New México[123].
    ii.   POALA SANDOVAL, b. Abt. 1928[123].
    iii. RITA SANDOVAL, b. Private.

23. LUZ[5] SANDOVAL (*FRANCISCA SÁNCHEZ*[4] *ROMERO, FRANCISCO ALVINO*[3]*, YGNACIO*[2]*, VICENTE*[1])[124] was born May 29, 1904 in Fort Sumner, Territory of New México[125]. She married FELIPÉ VIGIL[126] November 24, 1919 in Carrizozo, New México[127], son of TRENIDAD VIGIL and MARÍA ROMERO.

Notes for LUZ SANDOVAL:
Also known as Lucy.

Children of LUZ SANDOVAL and FELIPÉ VIGIL are:
    i.   TRENIDAD[6] VIGIL, b. Abt. 1922[128].
    ii.   MARÍA VIGIL, b. Abt. 1924[128].
    iii. DOLORES VIGIL, b. Abt. 1927[128].

Notes for DOLORES VIGIL:
Also known as Dolorita.

24. GEORGE[5] ROMERO (*JUAN DE DIOS*[4]*, JOSÉ ANTONIO*[3]*, YGNACIO*[2]*, VICENTE*[1]) was born July 14, 1880 in Picacho, Territory of New México[129], and died February 21, 1948 in Hagerman, New México[130]. He married (1) AURORA GONZÁLES[131] November 19, 1900[132], daughter of FLORENCIO GONZÁLES and RAYMUNDA SÁNCHEZ. He married (2) JOSEFITA TORRES[133] October 25, 1913 in Picacho, New México[134], daughter of EUSEVIO TORRES and EMILIA MUÑOZ.

Notes for GEORGE ROMERO:
Also known as Jorge.
1940s: Living in Hagerman, New México.

Notes for AURORA GONZÁLES:
Also known as María Aurora Gonzáles.

Notes for JOSEFITA TORRES:
Also known as Josephine.

Children of GEORGE ROMERO and AURORA GONZÁLES are:
43.   i.   SIGISFREDO[6] ROMERO, b. March 31, 1903; d. November 14, 1982, San Patricio, New México.
44.   ii.   MELITANA ROMERO, b. February 16, 1902.

Children of GEORGE ROMERO and JOSEFITA TORRES are:
45.   iii. GEORGE TORRES[6] ROMERO, b. May 12, 1914, San Patricio, New México; d. July 11, 1991.
46.   iv.   JUAN ROMERO, b. September 02, 1916, San Patricio, New México; d. February 15, 1988, Hagerman, New México.
       v.   GODFREY ROMERO, b. Abt. November 1919, San Patricio, New México[135].
47.   vi.   CRISTINA ROMERO, b. November 08, 1919, San Patricio, New México; d. October 28, 1985, San Patricio, New México.
       vii. PATRICIO ROMERO[136], b. March 18, 1929, San Patricio, New México; d. June 15, 1953, Hagerman, New México.

Notes for PATRICIO ROMERO:
Died young.

       viii. BEATRICE ROMERO, b. Private, San Patricio, New México.
       ix.   EFREN ROMERO, b. Private, San Patricio, New México.

       x.   EMILIA ROMERO, b. Private, San Patricio, New México.

       xi.   LUISA ROMERO, b. Private, San Patricio, New México.

25. MERENCIANA[5] ROMERO *(JUAN DE DIOS[4], JOSÉ ANTONIO[3], YGNACIO[2], VICENTE[1])* was born August 1883 in Picacho, Territory of New México[137]. She married (1) AVESLÍN TORRES, son of JUAN TORRES and RITA DE TORRES. She married (2) ALFRED MICKS[138].

Notes for MERENCIANA ROMERO:
Raised by Jinio and Lola Guerra.

Notes for AVESLÍN TORRES:
Also known as Abeslín.

Children of MERENCIANA ROMERO and AVESLÍN TORRES are:
       i.   RUBÉN[6] TORRES.
       ii.   MIGUEL ANTONIO ROMERO[139], b. March 27, 1904, San Patricio, Territory of New México; d. November 19, 1946; m. FRANCISCA TRUJILLO[139], September 16, 1928[140].

Notes for MIGUEL ANTONIO ROMERO:
Raised and adopted by his grandmother Cristina Castillo de Romero.

Notes for FRANCISCA TRUJILLO:
Also known as Quica.

26. CAROLINA[5] ROMERO *(JUAN DE DIOS[4], JOSÉ ANTONIO[3], YGNACIO[2], VICENTE[1])* was born January 22, 1884 in Picacho, Territory of New México[141]. She married ANTONIO SÁNCHEZ January 09, 1901[142], son of FRANCISCO SÁNCHEZ and CONCEPCIÓN TRUJILLO.

Notes for CAROLINA ROMERO:
Other baptismal records indicate that she was born on January 22, 1886. (Microfiche# 0017008, Page 109)
Raised by Jinio and Lola Guerra.

Children of CAROLINA ROMERO and ANTONIO SÁNCHEZ are:

	i.	ANEDA ROMERO[6] SÁNCHEZ, b. San Patricio, New México.
	ii.	ANGELITA ROMERO SÁNCHEZ, b. San Patricio, New México.
	iii.	JOSEFITA ROMERO SÁNCHEZ, b. San Patricio, New México.
	iv.	CONCEPCIÓN SÁNCHEZ, b. Abt. 1902, San Patricio, Territory of New México[143].
48.	v.	MARGARITA ROMERO SÁNCHEZ, b. August 22, 1903, San Patricio, Territory of New México; d. January 31, 2004, Artesia, New México.
	vi.	ISMAÉL SÁNCHEZ, b. 1916, San Patricio, New México[144].
	vii.	JESÚSITA ROMERO SÁNCHEZ, b. Abt. 1926, San Patricio, New México[145].

27. DELFINIA[5] ROMERO *(JUAN DE DIOS[4], JOSÉ ANTONIO[3], YGNACIO[2], VICENTE[1])* was born December 12, 1885 in Picacho, Territory of New México[146], and died November 13, 1926 in San Patricio, New México[147]. She married MAURICIO SÁNCHEZ January 09, 1901 in San Patricio, Territory of New México[148], son of FRANCISCO SÁNCHEZ and CONCEPCIÓN TRUJILLO.

Notes for DELFINIA ROMERO:
December 30, 1885: Baptized in San Patricio under the name María Virginia Romero. Padrinos: Román Barragán & Andrea Torres.
Raised by her godparents, Román Barragán & Andrea Torres.
Buried: La Capilla de San Patricio.

Children of DELFINIA ROMERO and MAURICIO SÁNCHEZ are:

	i.	JOSÉ ROMERO[6] SÁNCHEZ, b. San Patricio, New México.
	ii.	JUANITA SÁNCHEZ[149], b. February 08, 1902, San Patricio, Territory of New México[150]; d. December 06, 1975, Ruidoso, New México; m. RAMÓN TORRES, June 13, 1918, Glencoe, New Mexico[151].
49.	iii.	ROMÁN SÁNCHEZ, b. April 23, 1904, San Patricio, Territory of New México; d. February 08, 1973, Ruidoso, New México.
50.	iv.	MAXIMILIANO SÁNCHEZ, b. June 22, 1911, San Patricio, Territory of New México; d. April 15, 1972.
	v.	MABEL ROMERO SÁNCHEZ[152], b. Abt. 1915, San Patricio, New México[153]; d. April 02, 1929, San Patricio, New México.
51.	vi.	MARÍA SÁNCHEZ, b. April 19, 1919, San Patricio, New México; d. July 31, 1966, Los Lunas, New México.
52.	vii.	JESÚSITA SÁNCHEZ, b. September 19, 1922, San Patricio, New México; d. July 16, 1992, Albuquerque, New México.

28. LUPITA[5] ROMERO *(JUAN DE DIOS[4], JOSÉ ANTONIO[3], YGNACIO[2], VICENTE[1])* was born December 12, 1888 in San Patricio, Territory of New México[154], and died 1969 in Picacho, New México[155]. She married GEORGE ORTEGA KIMBRELL January 03, 1920 in Carrizozo, New México[156], son of JUAN KIMBRELL and DOMISINDA ORTEGA.

Notes for LUPITA ROMERO:
Also known as Guadalupe, Lupe.
Raised by José Alvarez and Lucia de Alvarez in Socorro, New México.

Children of LUPITA ROMERO and GEORGE KIMBRELL are:

53.	i.	ELSIE ROMERO[6] KIMBRELL, b. 1922.
	ii.	WILLIAM KIMBRELL[157], b. June 20, 1925, Picacho, New México[158].

Notes for WILLIAM KIMBRELL:
US Navy, Machinist Third Class. World War II.

	iii.	ELIZABETH KIMBRELL[159], b. September 15, 1928[160]; d. January 11, 1989.
	iv.	JOHN ROMERO KIMBRELL, b. Private.

29. MARÍA[5] ROMERO *(JUAN DE DIOS[4], JOSÉ ANTONIO[3], YGNACIO[2], VICENTE[1])[161]* was born January 19, 1891 in San Patricio, Territory of New México[162], and died March 21, 1976 in Roswell, New México. She married HILARIO GÓMEZ[163] June 25, 1917 in Lincoln, New México[164], son of FELIPÉ GÓMEZ and MIQUELA LUCERO.

Notes for HILARIO GÓMEZ:
Also known as Ylario. WW I veteran. Baptismal records indicate that he was born on September 21, 1891.

Children of MARÍA ROMERO and HILARIO GÓMEZ are:
  i.   ELISEO[6] GÓMEZ[165], b. January 05, 1919, San Patricio, New México; d. October 06, 1992, Los Lunas, New México; m. ROSA CHÁVEZ.

Notes for ELISEO GÓMEZ:
WW II veteran.

  ii.   MIQUELA GÓMEZ, b. October 28, 1924, Glencoe, New México; d. April 08, 1983, Roswell, New México; m. GEORGE MENDOZA, September 28, 1944, San Patricio, New México[166].

Notes for MIQUELA GÓMEZ:
Also known as Mickey.

  iii. JOSÉ ENRÍQUEZ GÓMEZ[167], b. Abt. 1929, Glencoe, New México; d. May 05, 1929, San Patricio, New México.

30. ANTONIO[5] ROMERO *(JUAN DE DIOS[4], JOSÉ ANTONIO[3], YGNACIO[2], VICENTE[1])[168]* was born December 12, 1892 in San Patricio, Territory of New México[169], and died February 06, 1942 in San Patricio, New México. He married CAROLINA SILVA June 21, 1916 in Carrizozo, New México[169], daughter of MANUEL SILVA and LEONARDA JIRÓN.

Children of ANTONIO ROMERO and CAROLINA SILVA are:
  i.   ESTER[6] ROMERO, b. Abt. 1916[170].
  ii.   ARISTOTEL SILVA ROMERO, b. Abt. 1917[170].
  iii. MANUEL SILVA ROMERO, b. Abt. 1920[170].
  iv.   PRESILIANA ROMERO, b. January 13, 1924, Tinnie, New México[171]; m. DANIEL LUCERO, November 26, 1941, Carrizozo, New México[171].
  v.   PABLO SILVA ROMERO, b. Abt. 1927[172].
  vi.   DELFINIA SILVA ROMERO, b. Private.
  vii. LEONARDA ROMERO, b. Private.

31. LUCÍA[5] ROMERO *(JUAN DE DIOS[4], JOSÉ ANTONIO[3], YGNACIO[2], VICENTE[1])* was born December 06, 1896 in San Patricio, Territory of New México[173]. She married (1) JOSÉ D. ARCHULETA[174] February 15, 1915 in Lincoln, Territory of New México[174], son of LUCIO ARCHULETA and YSABEL JIRÓN. She married (2) JUAN RUBIO July 21, 1925 in Hondo, New México[175].

Child of LUCÍA ROMERO and JOSÉ ARCHULETA is:
54. i.   DOLORES ROMERO[6] ARCHULETA, b. February 03, 1916, White Oaks, New México; d. June 07, 1986, San Patricio, New México.

32. MANUEL CASTILLO[5] ROMERO *(JUAN DE DIOS[4], JOSÉ ANTONIO[3], YGNACIO[2], VICENTE[1])[176]* was born October 06, 1899 in San Patricio, Territory of New México[177], and died October 1982 in Silver City, New México. He married ESTELA GÓMEZ[178] May 30, 1930 in Carrizozo, New México[179], daughter of FELIPÉ GÓMEZ and BEATRIZ SEDILLO.

Child of MANUEL ROMERO and ESTELA GÓMEZ is:
  i.   LUCILLE[6] ROMERO, b. Private; Adopted child.

33. FELIZ[5] VIGIL *(DEMETRIA[4] ROMERO, JOSÉ VICENTE[3], YGNACIO[2], VICENTE[1])* was born January 12, 1890 in Lincoln County, Territory of New México[180]. She married BONUFANTE KIMBRELL January 30, 1907 in Picacho, Territory of New México[180], son of GEORGE KIMBRELL and PABLA ROMERO.

Notes for FELIZ VIGIL:
Raised by Justo Chávez and Demetria Romero de Chávez.
1900 Census: Listed as Felis Vigil, living with her brother Justo Chávez.

Notes for BONUFANTE KIMBRELL:

Also known as Bonifacio, Bonie, Borie.

Child of FELIZ VIGIL and BONUFANTE KIMBRELL is:
    i.   RAY[6] KIMBRELL, b. Abt. 1911[181].

34. PROMETIVA[5] ROMERO *(PABLO GONZÁLES[4], JOSÉ VICENTE[3], YGNACIO[2], VICENTE[1])*[182] was born February 16, 1899 in Picacho, Territory of New México, and died May 28, 1975. She married JUAN ORTEGA KIMBRELL[182] September 14, 1914[183], son of JUAN KIMBRELL and DOMISINDA ORTEGA.

Notes for PROMETIVA ROMERO:
1910 Census: Living in Picacho, Territory of New México. Lists her as an adopted daughter to Justo Chávez and Demetria Romero.

Notes for JUAN ORTEGA KIMBRELL:
Also known as John.

Children of PROMETIVA ROMERO and JUAN KIMBRELL are:
    i.   ELISA[6] KIMBRELL, b. 1920; m. ROBERT NÚÑEZ SHANK, April 24, 1940[184].
    ii.   LAURINA KIMBRELL, b. Abt. 1926[185].
    iii. CHARLIE KIMBRELL, b. Abt. 1927[185].
    iv.   MANUEL ROMERO KIMBRELL, b. Private.
    v.   MANUELA KIMBRELL, b. Private.

Notes for MANUELA KIMBRELL:
Also known as Mela.
Raised by Domisinda Kimbrell.

Generation No. 6

35. GEORGE ORTEGA[6] KIMBRELL *(JUAN ROMERO[5], PABLA[4] ROMERO, FRANCISCO ALVINO[3], YGNACIO[2], VICENTE[1])* was born June 01, 1892 in Picacho, Territory of New México[186], and died 1959 in Picacho, New México[187]. He married (1) SARA SILVA[188] December 20, 1911 in Picacho, Territory of New México[189], daughter of AUGUSTÍN SILVA and LUCÍA GARCÍA. He married (2) LUPITA ROMERO January 03, 1920 in Carrizozo, New México[190], daughter of JUAN ROMERO and CRISTINA CASTILLO.

Notes for LUPITA ROMERO:
Also known as Guadalupe, Lupe.
Raised by José Alvarez and Lucia de Alvarez in Socorro, New México.

Children of GEORGE KIMBRELL and SARA SILVA are:
    i.   GENEVA[7] KIMBRELL[191], b. September 24, 1912, Picacho, New México[192]; m. FLAVIO MONTOYA[193], December 24, 1934[194].

Notes for FLAVIO MONTOYA:
Private First Class US Army. WW II Veteran.

    ii.   FRED KIMBRELL[195], b. March 28, 1914; d. November 25, 1938, Tinnie, New México; m. JULIA TORREZ[196], April 16, 1938[197].

Notes for FRED KIMBRELL:
1930 Census: Living with his grandfather Juan Kimbrell.
Died in an accident at the age of 24. Buried in Picacho, NM.

Children of GEORGE KIMBRELL and LUPITA ROMERO are:
    iii. ELSIE ROMERO[7] KIMBRELL, b. 1922[198].
    iv.   WILLIAM KIMBRELL[199], b. June 20, 1925, Picacho, New México[200].

Notes for WILLIAM KIMBRELL:
US Navy, Machinist Third Class. World War II.

v. ELIZABETH KIMBRELL[201], b. September 15, 1928[202]; d. January 11, 1989.

vi. JOHN ROMERO KIMBRELL, b. Private.

36. JUAN ORTEGA[6] KIMBRELL *(JUAN ROMERO[5], PABLA[4] ROMERO, FRANCISCO ALVINO[3], YGNACIO[2], VICENTE[1])*[203] was born December 17, 1895 in Picacho, Territory of New México, and died December 17, 1971 in Roswell, New México. He married PROMETIVA ROMERO[203] September 14, 1914[204], daughter of PABLO ROMERO and LUCINDA GONZÁLES.

Notes for JUAN ORTEGA KIMBRELL:
Also known as John.

Notes for PROMETIVA ROMERO:
1910 Census: Living in Picacho, Territory of New México. Lists her as an adopted daughter to Justo Chávez and Demetria Romero.

Children of JUAN KIMBRELL and PROMETIVA ROMERO are:

i. ELISA[7] KIMBRELL, b. 1920; m. ROBERT NÚÑEZ SHANK, April 24, 1940[205].

ii. LAURINA KIMBRELL, b. Abt. 1926[206].

iii. CHARLIE KIMBRELL, b. Abt. 1927[206].

iv. MANUEL ROMERO KIMBRELL, b. Private.

v. MANUELA KIMBRELL, b. Private.

Notes for MANUELA KIMBRELL:
Also known as Mela.
Raised by Domisinda Kimbrell.

37. MANUEL ORTEGA[6] KIMBRELL *(JUAN ROMERO[5], PABLA[4] ROMERO, FRANCISCO ALVINO[3], YGNACIO[2], VICENTE[1])* was born 1903 in Picacho, Territory of New México. He married PETRA MAÉS July 14, 1923[207], daughter of ROMÁN MAÉS and CONCEPCIÓN MENDOZA.

Child of MANUEL KIMBRELL and PETRA MAÉS is:

i. PAULINE[7] KIMBRELL[208], b. January 1936, Picacho, New México; d. January 28, 1936, Picacho, New México.

38. ROSA[6] KIMBRELL *(JUAN ROMERO[5], PABLA[4] ROMERO, FRANCISCO ALVINO[3], YGNACIO[2], VICENTE[1])*[209] was born September 07, 1904 in Picacho, Territory of New México, and died January 07, 1980. She married (1) CARLOS FLORES November 06, 1922[210], son of VICENTE FLORES and GENOVEVA PINEDA. She married (2) JULIAN SANDOVAL[211] October 12, 1935 in Picacho, New México[212], son of PERFETO SANDOVAL and FRANCISCA ROMERO.

Notes for ROSA KIMBRELL:
Also known as Rose.

Children of ROSA KIMBRELL and CARLOS FLORES are:

i. AVESLÍN[7] FLORES[213], b. November 10, 1923, Picacho, New México[214].

ii. CECILIA FLORES, b. Abt. 1927[214].

Child of ROSA KIMBRELL and JULIAN SANDOVAL is:

iii. JULIAN KIMBRELL[7] SANDOVAL[215], b. January 09, 1922; d. August 19, 1991, Roswell, New México.

Notes for JULIAN KIMBRELL SANDOVAL:
Corporal US Army. World War II Veteran.

39. BEATRICE[6] KIMBRELL *(JUAN ROMERO[5], PABLA[4] ROMERO, FRANCISCO ALVINO[3], YGNACIO[2], VICENTE[1])*[215] was born August 19, 1919 in Picacho, New México, and died February 16, 1988. She married FRED ROMERO April 16, 1938 in Carrizozo, New México[216], son of PEDRO ROMERO and CLEOTILDE FRESQUEZ.

Child of BEATRICE KIMBRELL and FRED ROMERO is:

i. MARTHA[7] ROMERO, b. Private; m. PABLO BENITO MONTOYA.

40. ALBERT[6] KIMBRELL *(WILLIAM E.[5], PABLA[4] ROMERO, FRANCISCO ALVINO[3], YGNACIO[2], VICENTE[1])[217]* was born February 03, 1907 in Picacho, New México[218], and died January 12, 1987 in Roswell, New México. He married (1) CONSUELO RUBIO December 18, 1926[219]. He married (2) ADELINA MÁRQUEZ[220] September 03, 1934, daughter of SERAPIO MÁRQUEZ and MARGARET MACKEY.

Notes for ALBERT KIMBRELL:
Corporal US Army.

Notes for CONSUELO RUBIO:
At the Age of about 14 she immigrated from México to Laredo, Téxas on August 13, 1921.

Child of ALBERT KIMBRELL and CONSUELO RUBIO is:
       i.   GERALDINE[7] KIMBRELL[220], b. March 21, 1927, Roswell, New México; d. September 06, 2007, Hondo, New México[221]; m. ELMO BRADY, 1946, California[221].

41. ANDREA[6] KIMBRELL *(WILLIAM E.[5], PABLA[4] ROMERO, FRANCISCO ALVINO[3], YGNACIO[2], VICENTE[1])* was born February 09, 1914 in Picacho, New México[222], and died September 04, 2007. She married DANOIS SALAS[223] October 08, 1937[224], son of CRECENCIO SALAS and LUPITA VIGIL.

Notes for DANOIS SALAS:
Also known as Dan.

Children of ANDREA KIMBRELL and DANOIS SALAS are:
       i.   CEASAR RAY[7] SALAS, b. Private.
       ii.   LUPE SALAS, b. Private.
       iii.   GEORGIA SALAS, b. Private.
       iv.   DANNY SALAS[225], b. Private; m. ADRIANNE RODRÍGUEZ[225].

42. PAULINA[6] KIMBRELL *(WILLIAM E.[5], PABLA[4] ROMERO, FRANCISCO ALVINO[3], YGNACIO[2], VICENTE[1])[226]* was born October 05, 1920 in Picacho, New México[227], and died September 18, 1966. She married ROBERT S. MACKEY[228], son of LUÍS AGUILAR and MARGARET MACKEY.

Notes for PAULINA KIMBRELL:
Also known as Pablita.

Notes for ROBERT S. MACKEY:
Private First Class US Army. World War II.

Child of PAULINA KIMBRELL and ROBERT MACKEY is:
       i.   ROBERTA PAULINE[7] MACKEY[229], b. August 13, 1948, Carrizozo, New México; d. October 07, 1993, Albuquerque, New México.

43. SIGISFREDO[6] ROMERO *(GEORGE[5], JUAN DE DIOS[4], JOSÉ ANTONIO[3], YGNACIO[2], VICENTE[1])[230]* was born March 31, 1903, and died November 14, 1982 in San Patricio, New México. He married LUCÍA YBARRA January 11, 1928 in Lincoln County, New México[231], daughter of GREGORIO YBARRA and CATARINA MONTOYA.

Notes for LUCÍA YBARRA:
Also known as Luciana, Luz.
Padrinos: Augustín Laguna born in México City, and his wife, Juana María Laguna, born in Polvadera, New México

Children of SIGISFREDO ROMERO and LUCÍA YBARRA are:
       i.   FEDELINA[7] ROMERO, b. March 28, 1932, San Patricio, New México[232]; m. ELMON RANDOLPH[233], July 01, 1950, Carrizozo, New México[234].
       ii.   CLEOFAS ROMERO[235], b. April 09, 1934, San Patricio, New México; d. March 17, 2007; m. JUAN SÁNCHEZ MONTES[235], August 25, 1951, Ruidoso, New México[236].
       iii.   SIGISFREDO YBARRA ROMERO[237], b. August 08, 1949, San Patricio, New México; d. May 24, 2010, San Patricio, New México.
       iv.   EDUVIGEN ROMERO, b. Private, San Patricio, New México.

v.   FLORIPE ROMERO, b. Private, San Patricio, New México.
vi.   ISABELA ROMERO, b. Private, San Patricio, New México.
vii. LEONIRES ROMERO, b. Private, San Patricio, New México.
viii. REBECCA ROMERO, b. Private, San Patricio, New México.
ix.   RUBÉN ROMERO, b. Private, San Patricio, New México.

44. MELITANA[6] ROMERO *(GEORGE[5], JUAN DE DIOS[4], JOSÉ ANTONIO[3], YGNACIO[2], VICENTE[1])* was born February 16, 1902[238]. She married PATROCINIO ARCHULETA CHÁVEZ[239] July 13, 1921[240], son of PATROCINIO CHÁVEZ and VICENTA ARCHULETA.

Notes for MELITANA ROMERO:
Also known as Meritana.

Children of MELITANA ROMERO and PATROCINIO CHÁVEZ are:
i.   GABRIEL[7] CHÁVEZ[241], b. 1922, Hondo, New México[242]; d. June 07, 1942, Lincoln, New México.
ii.   AURELIA CHÁVEZ, b. Abt. 1925, Hondo, New México[242].
iii. BRIGIDA CHÁVEZ, b. Abt. 1926, Hondo, New México[242].
iv.   ORALIA CHÁVEZ[243], b. Abt. 1927, San Patricio, New México; d. April 20, 1928, San Patricio, New México.
v.   GLORIA CHÁVEZ, b. Abt. 1929, Hondo, New México[244].
vi.   ADAN CHÁVEZ, b. Private, Hondo, New México.
vii. MOISES CHÁVEZ, b. Private, Hondo, New México.
viii. NORA CHÁVEZ, b. Private, Hondo, New México.
ix.   RAY CHÁVEZ, b. Private, Hondo, New México.
x.   VIRGINIA ROMERO CHÁVEZ, b. Private, Hondo, New México.

45. GEORGE TORRES[6] ROMERO *(GEORGE[5], JUAN DE DIOS[4], JOSÉ ANTONIO[3], ÝGNACIO[2], VICENTE[1])*[245] was born May 12, 1914 in San Patricio, New México[246], and died July 11, 1991. He married JULIANITA WARNER November 10, 1934 in San Patricio, New México[247], daughter of JUAN WARNER and EMILIA TORREZ.

Children of GEORGE ROMERO and JULIANITA WARNER are:
i.   GEORGE[7] ROMERO[248], b. February 22, 1939, Hondo, New México[249]; d. May 03, 1976; m. DELMA SÁNCHEZ, December 30, 1960, Hondo, New México[249].
ii.   SAMUEL ROMERO[250], b. September 10, 1942, San Patricio, New México; d. November 06, 1949, San Patricio, New México.
iii. SAMMY ROMERO[251], b. 1949; d. May 13, 2006.

46. JUAN[6] ROMERO *(GEORGE[5], JUAN DE DIOS[4], JOSÉ ANTONIO[3], YGNACIO[2], VICENTE[1])*[252] was born September 02, 1916 in San Patricio, New México, and died February 15, 1988 in Hagerman, New México. He married ENEDINA ROMERO[252].

Child of JUAN ROMERO and ENEDINA ROMERO is:
i.   JERRY DEAN[7] ROMERO[252], b. April 19, 1957, Hagerman, New México; d. April 20, 1957, Hagerman, New México.

47. CRISTINA[6] ROMERO *(GEORGE[5], JUAN DE DIOS[4], JOSÉ ANTONIO[3], YGNACIO[2], VICENTE[1])*[253] was born November 08, 1919 in San Patricio, New México[254], and died October 28, 1985 in San Patricio, New México. She married ARISTEO CHÁVEZ[255] February 10, 1936 in San Patricio, New México[256], son of TRANCITO CHÁVEZ and ANGELITA CHÁVEZ.

48. MARGARITA ROMERO[6] SÁNCHEZ *(CAROLINA[5] ROMERO, JUAN DE DIOS[4], JOSÉ ANTONIO[3], YGNACIO[2], VICENTE[1])*[258] was born August 22, 1903 in San Patricio, Territory of New México[259], and died January 31, 2004 in Artesia, New México. She married ROBERTO PÉREZ[260] Abt. 1929 in Crowley, Colorado[261].

49. ROMÁN[6] SÁNCHEZ *(DELFINIA[5] ROMERO, JUAN DE DIOS[4], JOSÉ ANTONIO[3], YGNACIO[2], VICENTE[1])*[262] was born April 23, 1904 in San Patricio, Territory of New México[263], and died February 08, 1973 in Ruidoso, New México. He married FLORINDA SALSBERRY[264] February 20, 1927 in Mescalero, New Mexico[265], daughter of JAMES SALSBERRY and MANUELITA HERRERA.

Children of ROMÁN SÁNCHEZ and FLORINDA SALSBERRY are:

i. ERNESTO[7] SÁNCHEZ, b. April 09, 1928, San Patricio, New México[266]; m. ORALIA CHÁVEZ, March 20, 1948, Ruidoso, New México[266].

ii. MADELENA SÁNCHEZ[267], b. Abt. 1930, San Patricio, New México; d. December 19, 1932, San Patricio, New México.

iii. DELFINIA OLIDIA SÁNCHEZ, b. April 18, 1934, High Rolls, New México; m. LEANDRO VEGA, December 27, 1958, Hondo, New México.

iv. ORLANDO SÁNCHEZ, b. April 03, 1936, San Patricio, New México.

v. FLORA MARÍA SÁNCHEZ, b. March 24, 1938, Capítan, New México; m. RICHARD VEGA.

vi. FRED SÁNCHEZ, b. May 30, 1940, Fort Stanton, New México[268]; m. BERTA HERRERA, July 26, 1959, Ruidoso, New México[268].

vii. BREZEL ROBERT SÁNCHEZ, b. November 04, 1941, Capítan, New México[269]; m. MINNIE ROMERO, June 15, 1963, Hondo, New México[269].

viii. GERALDINE ELSIE SÁNCHEZ, b. January 10, 1945, San Patricio, New México; m. ROBERT MONTES.

ix. LUVÍN SÁNCHEZ, b. October 23, 1947, San Patricio, New México; m. (1) GLORIA BACA; m. (2) FRANCES SEDILLO.

x. CYNTHIA VIOLANDA SÁNCHEZ[270], b. September 10, 1950, Capítan, New México[271]; d. April 27, 1986, Rio Rancho, New México; m. BERRY VANDERWALL, December 22, 1972, San Patricio, New México[271].

xi. MAURICIO SÁNCHEZ, b. Abt. 1952, San Patricio, New México. Died Young.

xii. ROMÁN SÁNCHEZ, JR., b. March 13, 1954, San Patricio, New México[272]; m. YOVANNE SALAS, May 25, 1974, Ruidoso, New México[272].

50. MAXIMILIANO[6] SÁNCHEZ *(DELFINIA[5] ROMERO, JUAN DE DIOS[4], JOSÉ ANTONIO[3], YGNACIO[2], VICENTE[1])* was born June 22, 1911 in San Patricio, Territory of New México[273], and died April 15, 1972. He married SORAIDA SÁNCHEZ February 11, 1936 in Carrizozo, New México[273], daughter of AURELIO SÁNCHEZ and ANASTACIA ARAGÓN.

Children of MAXIMILIANO SÁNCHEZ and SORAIDA SÁNCHEZ are:

i. BEATRICE[7] SÁNCHEZ, b. Private.

ii. ROSEMARY SÁNCHEZ, b. Private.

51. MARÍA[6] SÁNCHEZ *(DELFINIA[5] ROMERO, JUAN DE DIOS[4], JOSÉ ANTONIO[3], YGNACIO[2], VICENTE[1])* was born April 19, 1919 in San Patricio, New México[274], and died July 31, 1966 in Los Lunas, New México. She married MANUEL CHÁVEZ, son of PREDICANDO CHÁVEZ and REMEDIOS VIGIL.

52. JESÚSITA[6] SÁNCHEZ *(DELFINIA[5] ROMERO, JUAN DE DIOS[4], JOSÉ ANTONIO[3], YGNACIO[2], VICENTE[1])* was born September 19, 1922 in San Patricio, New México, and died July 16, 1992 in Albuquerque, New México. She married MAX SILVA November 16, 1942 in Tomé, New México[275].

53. ELSIE ROMERO[6] KIMBRELL *(GEORGE ORTEGA[5], JUAN ROMERO[4], PABLA[3] ROMERO, FRANCISCO ALVINO[2], YGNACIO[1])* was born 1922[276].

54. DOLORES ROMERO[6] ARCHULETA *(LUCÍA[5] ROMERO, JUAN DE DIOS[4], JOSÉ ANTONIO[3], YGNACIO[2], VICENTE[1])[277]* was born February 03, 1916 in White Oaks, New México, and died June 07, 1986 in San Patricio, New México. She married AMARANTE CHÁVEZ[277] September 21, 1936 in San Patricio, New México[278], son of YSIDRO CHÁVEZ and PAUBLITA SÁNCHEZ.

Notes for DOLORES ROMERO ARCHULETA:
Also known as Lola.

Genealogy of José Francisco Salas

Generation No. 1

1. JOSÉ FRANCISCO[1] SALAS was born Abt. 1729[1]. He married (1) MARÍA BARBARA ARAGÓN September 13, 1746 in Alburquerque, El Reyno de Nuevo México, Nueva España[2], daughter of NICOLÁS DE ARAGÓN and MARGARITA GALLEGOS. He married (2) MARÍA PASCUALA PEREA May 28, 1784 in Isleta, El Reyno de Nuevo México, Nueva España[3].

Notes for JOSÉ FRANCISCO SALAS:
Also known as Joseph de Salas.
1784: Living in Los Chábes, El Reyno de Nuevo México, Nueva España.

Children of JOSÉ SALAS and MARÍA ARAGÓN are:
2. i. JOSÉ LORENZO[2] SALAS.
    iii. MARÍA FABIANA SALAS, b. Bef. January 02, 1757, Alburquerque, El Reyno de Nuevo México, Nueva España[4].
    iv. MARÍA BERNARDINA SALAS, b. Bef. March 25, 1763, Alburquerque, El Reyno de Nuevo México, Nueva España[4].
3. iv. PAULA GETRUDES SALAS, b. Bef. January 27, 1755, Alburquerque, El Reyno de Nuevo México, Nueva España.

Generation No. 2

2. JOSÉ LORENZO[2] SALAS *(JOSÉ FRANCISCO[1])*. He married ANTONIA TERESA GUTIÉRRES November 18, 1797 in Thomé, El Reyno de Nuevo México, Nueva España[5], daughter of JUAN GUTIÉRRES and MARÍA SALAZAR.

Children of JOSÉ SALAS and ANTONIA GUTIÉRRES are:
    i.   JOSÉ ANTONIO[3] SALAS, b. September 19, 1799, Thomé, El Reyno de Nuevo México, Nueva España[6].
    ii. MARÍA ROMANA JOSEFA SALAS, b. Bef. February 28, 1802, Thomé, El Reyno de Nuevo México, Nueva España[6].
4. iii. FRANCISCO SALAS, b. Bef. October 14, 1804, Thomé, El Reyno de Nuevo México, Nueva España.
    iv. MARÍA GUADALUPE SALAS, b. Bef. January 01, 1810, Thomé, El Reyno de Nuevo México, Nueva España[6].
    v.   JESÚS MARÍA JOSÉ SALAS, b. Bef. February 21, 1812, Belén, El Reyno de Nuevo México, Nueva España[7].

3. PAULA GETRUDES[2] SALAS *(JOSÉ FRANCISCO[1])* was born Bef. January 27, 1755 in Alburquerque, El Reyno de Nuevo México, Nueva España[8]. She married PASCUAL LUSERO November 12, 1775 in Belén, El Reyno de Nuevo México, Nueva España[9], son of BERNARDO LUSERO and BRIANDA CHÁVES.

Child of PAULA SALAS and PASCUAL LUSERO is:
5. i. PABLO DE JESÚS[3] LUSERO, b. January 25, 1778, Alburquerque, El Reyno de Nuevo México, Nueva España.

Generation No. 3

4. FRANCISCO[3] SALAS *(JOSÉ LORENZO[2], JOSÉ FRANCISCO[1])* was born Bef. October 14, 1804 in Thomé, El Reyno de Nuevo México, Nueva España. He married NICOLASA TRUJILLO May 08, 1826 in Tomé, Nuevo México, La República de México[10], daughter of MANUEL TRUJILLO and MARÍA CANDELARIA.

Notes for FRANCISCO SALAS:
Also known as Dionisio José Francisco Salas.

Children of FRANCISCO SALAS and NICOLASA TRUJILLO are:
6. i.   JUANA MARÍA[4] SALAS, b. Bef. March 25, 1827, Belén, Nuevo México, La República de México.
    ii. JOSÉ DE JESÚS SALAS, b. Bef. May 04, 1828, Belén, Nuevo México, La República de México[11].
7. iii. PABLO SALAS, b. Bef. January 24, 1830, Belén, Nuevo México, La República de México; d. 1869-1870.
    iv. JOSÉ ANICETO SALAS, b. Bef. April 10, 1831, Belén, Nuevo México, La República de México[11].
    v.   MARÍA SAVINA SALAS, b. Bef. January 04, 1836, Belén, Nuevo México, La República de México[11].
    vi. JUAN ELJEGO SALAS, b. Bef. April 19, 1838, Tomé, Nuevo México, La República de México[12].

5. PABLO DE JESÚS[3] LUSERO *(PAULA GETRUDES[2] SALAS, JOSÉ FRANCISCO[1])* was born January 25, 1778 in Alburquerque, El Reyno de Nuevo México, Nueva España[13]. He married MARÍA TOMASA SALAS.

Notes for PABLO DE JESÚS LUSERO:
Baptismal record lists his mother as Paula Zalazar.

Children of PABLO LUSERO and MARÍA SALAS are:

    i.   TRINIDAD[4] LUSERO, m. MARIANO TORRES, September 06, 1847, Tomé, Territory of New México[14].

    ii.   MARÍA MANUELA ANASTACIA LUSERO, b. Bef. May 02, 1812, Thomé, El Reyno de Nuevo México, Nueva España[15].

    iii.   ALBINO LUSERO, b. Bef. December 19, 1819, Thomé, El Reyno de Nuevo México, Nueva España[15]; m. MARÍA ALFONSA MIRABAL, December 17, 1850, Tomé, Territory of New México[16].

Notes for ALBINO LUSERO:
Also known as José Alvino Lusero.

8.   iv.   JUAN DE JESÚS LUSERO, b. Abt. 1821.

    v.   MARÍA EUGENIA LUSERO, b. Bef. November 16, 1822, Thomé, El Reyno de Nuevo México, Nueva España[17].

Generation No. 4

6. JUANA MARÍA[4] SALAS *(FRANCISCO[3], JOSÉ LORENZO[2], JOSÉ FRANCISCO[1])*[18] was born Bef. March 25, 1827 in Belén, Nuevo México, La República de México[19]. She married JOSÉ MANUEL GUTIÉRRES[20] April 23, 1848 in Socorro, Territory of New México[21], son of JOSÉ GUTIÉRRES and BARBARA LUCERO.

Notes for JUANA MARÍA SALAS:
Also known as Juana María Nepomucena Salas.

Notes for JOSÉ MANUEL GUTIÉRRES:
1860 Census: Living in Lemitar, Territory of New México. (Born about 1815)
1870 Census: Living in Lincoln County, Precinct 2 (San Patricio), Territory of New México.

Children of JUANA SALAS and JOSÉ GUTIÉRRES are:

    i.   TORNIO[5] GUTIÉRRES, b. La Luz, New México.

Notes for TORNIO GUTIÉRRES:
Also known as José Tornio.
Had a ranch in Quemado, NM.

    ii.   DOLORES GUTIÉRRES, b. 1847, Lemitar, Nuevo México, La República de México[22]; m. IRINEA MARTÍNES, April 14, 1874, Tularoso, Territory of New México[23].

Notes for DOLORES GUTIÉRRES:
Also known as José Dolores.

    iii.   JUAN JOSÉ GUTIÉRRES, b. 1849, Lemitar, Territory of New México[24]; m. LEONOR MARTÍNES, April 14, 1874, Tularoso, Territory of New México[25].

9.   iv.   RAFAEL GUTIÉRRES, b. Abt. 1850, Lemitar, Territory of New México.

10.   v.   DAMIAN GUTIÉRRES, b. 1852, Lemitar, Territory of New México.

11.   vi.   FRANCISCO GUTIÉRRES, b. 1855, Lemitar, Territory of New México.

12.   vii.   FLORENTINO GUTIÉRRES, b. March 1861, Lemitar, Territory of New México.

    viii.   JOSEFITA GUTIÉRRES, b. 1864, La Luz, New México[26].

Pablo Salas

7. PABLO[4] SALAS *(FRANCISCO[3], JOSÉ LORENZO[2], JOSÉ FRANCISCO[1])* was born Bef. January 24, 1830 in Belén, Nuevo México, La República de México[27], and died 1869-1870. He married MARGARITA TRUJILLO[28], daughter of ASCENCIÓN TRUJILLO.

Notes for PABLO SALAS:
Also known as José Pablo Salas.

Notes for MARGARITA TRUJILLO:
1900 Census: Lists her birthdate as February 1857.

Children of PABLO SALAS and MARGARITA TRUJILLO are:
13.   i.   TEOFILO TRUJILLO⁵ SALAS, b. September 15, 1862, Rio Bonito, Territory of New México; d. July 23, 1928, San Patricio, New México.
14.   ii.   ANITA SALAS, b. July 02, 1870; d. August 02, 1935, San Patricio, New México.

Juan de Jesús Lusero

8. JUAN DE JESÚS⁴ LUSERO *(PABLO DE JESÚS³, PAULA GETRUDES² SALAS, JOSÉ FRANCISCO¹)* was born Abt. 1821[29]. He married MARCELINA JARAMILLO May 08, 1843 in Tomé, Nuevo México, La República de México[30].

Notes for JUAN DE JESÚS LUSERO:
Also known as Juan Lucero.

1860 Census: Living in Arroyo Colorado, Valencia County, Territory of New México. (Born 1821)
1870 Census: Living in Lincoln County, Precinct 2 (San Patricio), Territory of New México. (Born 1828)

Land Patent # NMNMAA 010833, on the authority of the Sale cash entry (3 Stat. 566), April 24, 1820, 160 Acres.

Notes for MARCELINA JARAMILLO:
Also known as María Marcelina Jaramillo.

Children of JUAN LUSERO and MARCELINA JARAMILLO are:
15.   i.   ANISETO⁵ LUCERO, b. Bef. May 20, 1846, Tomé, Nuevo México, La República de México.
       ii.   FELIX LUCERO, b. Bef. November 20, 1848, Tomé, Territory of New México[31].

Notes for FELIX LUCERO:
Also known as José Felis Lucero.

16.   iii.   CIPRIANA LUCERO, b. Abt. 1851, Tomé, Territory of New México; d. Bef. May 1889.
17.   iv.   LEONORA LUCERO, b. Bef. April 16, 1853, Tomé, Territory of New México.
       v.   SIMÓN LUCERO, b. Abt. 1856[32].
18.   vi.   MANUELA LUCERO, b. February 19, 1859; d. December 12, 1918.

Generation No. 5

9. RAFAEL⁵ GUTIÉRRES *(JUANA MARÍA⁴ SALAS, FRANCISCO³, JOSÉ LORENZO², JOSÉ FRANCISCO¹)* was born Abt. 1850 in Lemitar, Territory of New México[33]. He married ENCARNACIÓN PATRÓN December 06, 1873[34].

Notes for RAFAEL GUTIÉRRES:
Also known as José Rafael Gutiérrez.
1880 Census: Living in La Plaza de La Junta, Territory of New México.

Land Patent # NMLC 0025956, on the authority of the Homestead Entry-Stock Raising (39 Stat. 862), December 29, 1916. Issued 646.28 acres on November 15, 1926.

Children of RAFAEL GUTIÉRRES and ENCARNACIÓN PATRÓN are:
       i.   BIRGINIA⁶ GUTIÉRREZ, b. Abt. 1876[35].
       ii.   MANUEL GUTIÉRREZ, b. Abt. 1878[35].

10. DAMIAN⁵ GUTIÉRRES *(JUANA MARÍA⁴ SALAS, FRANCISCO³, JOSÉ LORENZO², JOSÉ FRANCISCO¹)* was born 1852 in Lemitar, Territory of New México[36]. He married JUANITA SÁNCHEZ Abt. 1880[37], daughter of CRECENCIO SÁNCHEZ and MARÍA SÁNCHEZ.

Notes for DAMIAN GUTIÉRRES:
Also known as José Damian.

Children of DAMIAN GUTIÉRRES and JUANITA SÁNCHEZ are:
19.	i.	ROBERTO[6] GUTIÉRREZ, b. February 28, 1883, Hondo, Territory of New México; d. 1951, Hondo, New México.
	ii.	EPIMENIO GUTIÉRREZ, b. December 1887[38].
20.	iii.	JOSEFA GUTIÉRREZ, b. March 1892.
21.	iv.	ISABEL GUTIÉRREZ, b. April 02, 1893, Hondo, Territory of New México; d. November 01, 1993, Roswell, New México.
22.	v.	ANITA GUTIÉRREZ, b. Abt. 1895, Hondo, Territory of New México.
	vi.	CRESCENCIO GUTIÉRREZ, b. March 1900[38].
	vii.	VITERBO GUTIÉRREZ, b. March 1900[38].

11. FRANCISCO[5] GUTIÉRRES *(JUANA MARÍA[4] SALAS, FRANCISCO[3], JOSÉ LORENZO[2], JOSÉ FRANCISCO[1])* was born 1855 in Lemitar, Territory of New México[39]. He married ANGELITA SEDILLO Abt. 1890[40], daughter of JOSÉ SEDILLO and MARÍA GARCÍA.

Notes for FRANCISCO GUTIÉRRES:
Also known as José Francisco.

Children of FRANCISCO GUTIÉRRES and ANGELITA SEDILLO are:
	i.	MANUELITA[6] GUTIÉRREZ, b. Abt. 1900, San Patricio, Territory of New México[40]; m. ISIDRO ANALLA[41].
	ii.	RAMÓN GUTIÉRREZ, b. Abt. 1903, San Patricio, Territory of New México[42].

12. FLORENTINO[5] GUTIÉRRES *(JUANA MARÍA[4] SALAS, FRANCISCO[3], JOSÉ LORENZO[2], JOSÉ FRANCISCO[1])* was born March 1861 in Lemitar, Territory of New México[43]. He married ANGELITA MONTOYA November 01, 1886 in Tularoso, Territory of New México[44].

Notes for FLORENTINO GUTIÉRRES:
Also known as José Francisco.

Children of FLORENTINO GUTIÉRRES and ANGELITA MONTOYA are:
	i.	AMADO[6] GUTIÉRREZ, b. January 1893[45].
	ii.	RAFAEL GUTIÉRREZ, b. March 1895[45].
	iii.	JOSEFITA GUTIÉRREZ, b. July 1898[45].
23.	iv.	SARAFINA GUTIÉRREZ, b. 1900.

13. TEOFILO TRUJILLO[5] SALAS *(PABLO[4], FRANCISCO[3], JOSÉ LORENZO[2], JOSÉ FRANCISCO[1])*[46] was born September 15, 1862 in Rio Bonito, Territory of New México[47], and died July 23, 1928 in San Patricio, New México. He married IGENIA GALLEGOS January 09, 1887 in San Patricio, Territory of New México[48], daughter of HILARIO GALLEGOS and JOSEFITA CHÁVEZ.

Notes for IGENIA GALLEGOS:
Also known as Jinia and Higinia. Baptismal Padrinos: Juan Trujillo, Ana María Fajardo.
1920 Census: Listed as Virginia.

Land Patent # NMLC 0042337, on the authority of the Homestead Entry-Enlarged (35 Stat. 639), February 19, 1909. Issued 200 acres on October 13, 1936.

Children of TEOFILO SALAS and IGENIA GALLEGOS are:
24.	i.	PABLO GALLEGOS[6] SALAS, b. October 12, 1887, San Patricio, Territory of New México; d. June 29, 1948, San Patricio, New México.
25.	ii.	PELEGRINA SALAS, b. August 1894.
26.	iii.	ELFIDO SALAS, b. March 13, 1897, Hondo, Territory of New México; d. November 30, 1973, Hondo, New México.
	iv.	ELVIRA SALAS, b. Abt. 1898[49].
27.	v.	JACOBO SALAS, b. February 21, 1899, Hondo, Territory of New México; d. April 1973, Artesia, New Mexico.

14. ANITA[5] SALAS *(PABLO[4], FRANCISCO[3], JOSÉ LORENZO[2], JOSÉ FRANCISCO[1])* was born July 02, 1870[50], and died August 02, 1935 in San Patricio, New México[51]. She married ALEJANDRO GALLEGOS[52] December 15, 1885 in Lincoln County, Territory of New México[53], son of HILARIO GALLEGOS and JOSEFITA CHÁVEZ.

Notes for ANITA SALAS:
Also known as María Ana Trujillo, Anita Trujillo. He marriage record indicates that her father was Francisco Trujillo, who was her step-father. Her biological father was Pablo Salas.

Notes for ALEJANDRO GALLEGOS:
1870 Census: Living in Lincoln County, Precinct 2 (La Plaza de San Patricio), Territory of New México. Listed birthyear as 1863.
1900 & 1910 Census: Living in San Patricio, Territory of New México.

Children of ANITA SALAS and ALEJANDRO GALLEGOS are:
       i.   FRANCISCO[6] GALLEGOS.
       ii.   MAXIMILIANO GALLEGOS.
28.   iii. EULOJIO GALLEGOS, b. February 01, 1887; d. July 04, 1938.
       iv. ROBERTO GALLEGOS, b. July 06, 1894, Ruidoso, Territory of New México[54].
29.   v.   MANUELITA GALLEGOS, b. May 14, 1899, San Patricio, Territory of New México.
       vi. RAMONA GALLEGOS, b. Abt. 1910[55].
30.   vii. ELISEO GALLEGOS, b. May 30, 1912; d. May 16, 1995, San Patricio, New México.

15. ANISETO[5] LUCERO *(JUAN DE JESÚS[4] LUSERO, PABLO DE JESÚS[3], PAULA GETRUDES[2] SALAS, JOSÉ FRANCISCO[1])[56]* was born Bef. May 20, 1846 in Tomé, Nuevo México, La República de México[57]. He married REFUGIA TRUJILLO May 26, 1870 in Tularoso, Territory of New México[58], daughter of JOSÉ TRUJILLO and MARÍA SÁNCHEZ.

Notes for ANISETO LUCERO:
Also known as José Aniceto Lucero.

Land Patent # NMNMAA 010834, on the authority of the Sale cash entry (3 Stat. 566), April 24, 1820, 40 Acres.
Land Patent # NMR 0028238, on the authority of the Homestead Entry-Original (12 Stat. 392), May 20, 1862. Issued 160 acres on February, 12, 1921.

Notes for REFUGIA TRUJILLO:
Alos known as María del Refugio Trujillo.

Children of ANISETO LUCERO and REFUGIA TRUJILLO are:
       i.   JOSEFA[6] LUCERO, b. 1871, San Patricio, Territory of New México[59].
       ii.   VICTORIANA LUCERO, b. 1874, San Patricio, Territory of New México[59].
       iii. BESITA LUCERO, b. 1878, San Patricio, Territory of New México[59].
31.   iv. HINIO LUCERO, b. Abt. 1881, San Patricio, Territory of New México; d. March 21, 1933, San Patricio, New México.
       v.   FRANCISCO LUCERO, b. April 20, 1884, San Patricio, Territory of New México[60].
       vi. LUGARDITA LUCERO, b. March 1887, San Patricio, Territory of New México[61]; m. EULOJIO GALLEGOS[62], March 12, 1908, San Patricio, Territory of New México[63].

Notes for EULOJIO GALLEGOS:
Also known as Olojio.

32.   vii. JUANITA LUCERO, b. September 02, 1889, San Patricio, Territory of New México; d. May 11, 1958.
       viii. MARGARITA LUCERO[64], b. May 20, 1893, San Patricio, Territory of New México[65].

16. CIPRIANA[5] LUCERO *(JUAN DE JESÚS[4] LUSERO, PABLO DE JESÚS[3], PAULA GETRUDES[2] SALAS, JOSÉ FRANCISCO[1])* was born Abt. 1851 in Tomé, Territory of New México[66], and died Bef. May 1889[67]. She married JUAN GALLEGOS ULIBARRÍ January 02, 1865 in Tomé, Territory of New México[68], son of SANTIAGO ULIBARRÍ and JUANA GALLEGOS.

Notes for CIPRIANA LUCERO:
Also known as María Cipriana Lucero.

Notes for JUAN GALLEGOS ULIBARRÍ:
Also known as Juan Rivali.
1860 Census: Living in La Polvadera de San Lorenzo, Territory of New México.
1870, 1880 & 1900 Census: Living in San Patricio, Territory of New México.
One of the founding families of La Plaza de San Patricio.

Children of CIPRIANA LUCERO and JUAN ULIBARRÍ are:
33.   i.   AMBROSIA[6] ULIBARRÍ, b. Abt. 1865.
34.   ii.   SARAFINA SOCORRO ULIBARRÍ, b. Abt. 1868; d. Bef. 1921.
35.   iii.   VICENTE ULIBARRÍ, b. January 22, 1870, San Patricio, Territory of New México; d. November 08, 1949.

17. LEONORA[5] LUCERO *(JUAN DE JESÚS[4] LUSERO, PABLO DE JESÚS[3], PAULA GETRUDES[2] SALAS, JOSÉ FRANCISCO[1])*[69] was born Bef. April 16, 1853 in Tomé, Territory of New México[70]. She married (1) JOSÉ ANDELARIO RANDOLF October 17, 1866 in Tomé, Territory of New México[71], son of DOMINICO RANDOLF and SERRAGINE DE RANDOLF. She married (2) JOSÉ CHÁVEZ Y CHÁVEZ January 10, 1871 in Lincoln County, Territory of New México[72], son of JUAN CHÁVEZ and TEODORA CHÁVEZ.

Notes for LEONORA LUCERO:
Also known as María Leonora Lucero.

1860 Census: Living in Arroyo Colorado, Valencia County, Territory of New México.

Notes for JOSÉ CHÁVEZ Y CHÁVEZ:
1880 Census: Living in La Plaza de San Patricio, Territory of New México. (Born 1851)

Child of LEONORA LUCERO and JOSÉ RANDOLF is:
        i.   DOMINICO[6] LUCERO, b. Abt. 1869, San Patricio, Territory of New México[73].

Children of LEONORA LUCERO and JOSÉ CHÁVEZ are:
        ii.   JOSÉ ANASTASIO[6] CHÁVEZ, b. Bef. February 13, 1872, Lincoln County, Territory of New México[74].
        iii.   DECASIO CHÁVEZ, b. Bef. August 24, 1873, Lincoln County, Territory of New México[75].

18. MANUELA[5] LUCERO *(JUAN DE JESÚS[4] LUSERO, PABLO DE JESÚS[3], PAULA GETRUDES[2] SALAS, JOSÉ FRANCISCO[1])*[76] was born February 19, 1859[77], and died December 12, 1918. She married (1) YGNACIO TORRES February 12, 1873[78], son of MARIANO TORRES and MARÍA CHÁVES. She married (2) ROBERT BRADY[79] September 07, 1891[80], son of WILLIAM BRADY and BONIFACIA CHÁVES.

Notes for MANUELA LUCERO:
Also known as Manuelita Lucero de Torres.

Notes for YGNACIO TORRES:
Also known as José Ygnacio Torres.

1860 Census: Living in Punta de Agua, Territory of New México. (Born 1848)
1870 Census: Living in Lincoln County, Precinct 3, Territory of New México. (Born 1847)
1880 Census: living in La Plaza de San Patricio, Territory of New México. (Born 1846)

Notes for ROBERT BRADY:
Also known as Roberto.

Children of MANUELA LUCERO and YGNACIO TORRES are:
36.   i.   REFUGIO[6] TORRES, b. February 19, 1874, Tomé, Territory of New México; d. November 27, 1937, Hondo, New México.
        ii.   GAVINO TORRES, b. March 1874[81].
        iii.   MARIA PREDICANDA TORRES, b. July 16, 1884, Hondo, Territory of New México[82].
        iv.   PLACIDA TORRES, b. June 10, 1885, Hondo, Territory of New México[82].

37.   v.   GEORGE TORRES, b. July 14, 1885, San Patricio, Territory of New México.
38.   vi.   MARTÍN LUCERO TORRES, b. November 22, 1888, Hondo, Territory of New México; d. November 20, 1967, Roswell, New México.

Children of MANUELA LUCERO and ROBERT BRADY are:
39.   vii. WILLIAM LUCERO⁶ BRADY, b. March 07, 1892, Lincoln, Territory of New México; d. March 11, 1968, Hondo, New México.
      viii. FELIS BRADY, b. May 18, 1896, San Patricio, Territory of New México[83].
40.   ix.   JOHN LUCERO BRADY, b. December 03, 1899, Hondo, Territory of New México; d. December 26, 1936.

Generation No. 6

19. ROBERTO⁶ GUTIÉRREZ *(DAMIAN⁵ GUTIÉRRES, JUANA MARÍA⁴ SALAS, FRANCISCO³, JOSÉ LORENZO², JOSÉ FRANCISCO¹)[84]* was born February 28, 1883 in Hondo, Territory of New México[85], and died 1951 in Hondo, New México. He married (1) REBECCA GARCÍA May 19, 1910 in Picacho, Territory of New México[85], daughter of JOSÉ GARCÍA and CARLOTA GARCÍA. He married (2) ANITA GONZÁLES[86] September 16, 1916 in Hondo, New México[87], daughter of JOSÉ GONZÁLES and MARÍA CHÁVEZ.

Notes for ROBERTO GUTIÉRREZ:
World War One Draft Registration Card indicates that he was born on July 18, 1882.
1930 Census: Living in Hondo, New México. His name is listed as Roberto Gonzáles.

Land Patent # NMR 0026686, on the authority of the Homestead Entry-Original (12 Stat. 392), May 20, 1862. Issued 151.71 acres on August 26, 1920.

Land Patent # NMR 0029140, on the authority of the Homestead Entry-Enlarged (35 Stat. 639), February 19, 1909. Issued 168.64 acres on October 18, 1923.

Land Patent # NMR 0036537, on the authority of the Homestead Entry-Stock Raising (39 Stat. 862), December 29, 1916. Issued 320 acres on April 20, 1925.

Notes for ANITA GONZÁLES:
Also known as Anne.

Children of ROBERTO GUTIÉRREZ and REBECCA GARCÍA are:
      i.   MANUEL⁷ GUTIÉRREZ.
      ii. LUCILA GUTIÉRREZ.

Children of ROBERTO GUTIÉRREZ and ANITA GONZÁLES are:
41.   iii. JOSÉ GONZÁLES⁷ GUTIÉRREZ, b. July 07, 1917, Hondo, New México; d. August 13, 1997, Hondo, New México.
      iv. ROBERTO GONZÁLES GUTIÉRREZ[88], b. May 14, 1919, Hondo, New México[89]; d. September 1974, Hondo, New México.

Notes for ROBERTO GONZÁLES GUTIÉRREZ:
June 25, 1942: Enlisted into the Army. Corporal US Army, WW II. Wounded in Italy April 29, 1945.

      v.   FERNANDO GUTIÉRREZ[89], b. April 07, 1922, Tinnie, New México[90]; d. March 08, 1972, Hondo, New México; m. FAY RILEY, June 05, 1958, Carrizozo, New México[90].

Notes for FERNANDO GUTIÉRREZ:
November 30, 1942: Enlisted in the Army. Tec 5 CN, Company 302, Infantry WW II.

      vi. SOSTENO GUTIÉRREZ[91], b. December 16, 1924, Tinnie, New México[92].

Notes for SOSTENO GUTIÉRREZ:
US Navy, Seaman First Class. World War II.

      vii. JOSEFITA GUTIÉRREZ, b. Abt. 1925[92].
      viii. DOMINGO GUTIÉRREZ, b. Abt. 1929[92].

20. JOSEFA[6] GUTIÉRREZ *(DAMIAN[5] GUTIÉRRES, JUANA MARÍA[4] SALAS, FRANCISCO[3], JOSÉ LORENZO[2], JOSÉ FRANCISCO[1])* was born March 1892[93]. She married PROMETIVO BRADY, son of WILLIAM BRADY and BONIFACIA CHÁVES.

Notes for JOSEFA GUTIÉRREZ:
Also known as Josefita.

Notes for PROMETIVO BRADY:
1910 Census: Living in Roswell, Territory of New México. Listed as P.S. Brady.

Children of JOSEFA GUTIÉRREZ and PROMETIVO BRADY are:
  i.   ORLANDO[7] BRADY, b. Abt. 1909[94].
  ii.   CELIA BRADY, b. Abt. 1914[95].
  iii.   PROMETIVO BRADY, b. Abt. 1918[95].
  iv.   ROY BRADY, b. Abt. 1920[95].
  v.   ERVIN BRADY, b. Abt. 1922[95].
  vi.   BONIFACIO BRADY, b. Abt. 1925[95].

21. ISABEL[6] GUTIÉRREZ *(DAMIAN[5] GUTIÉRRES, JUANA MARÍA[4] SALAS, FRANCISCO[3], JOSÉ LORENZO[2], JOSÉ FRANCISCO[1])[96]* was born April 02, 1893 in Hondo, Territory of New México, and died November 01, 1993 in Roswell, New México. She married MARTÍN LUCERO TORRES[97] January 05, 1911 in Hondo, Territory of New México[98], son of YGNACIO TORRES and MANUELA LUCERO.

Children of ISABEL GUTIÉRREZ and MARTÍN TORRES are:
  i.   FEDERICO[7] TORREZ[99], b. August 24, 1909, Hondo, New México; d. April 05, 2003; m. CECILIA MACKEY.

Notes for FEDERICO TORREZ:
Also known as Fred.

  ii.   ELOY TORREZ[100], b. February 27, 1912, Hondo, New México[101]; d. October 28, 2011, Roswell, New México; m. SAVINA SALCIDO[102].

Notes for SAVINA SALCIDO:
Also known as Savina.

42.   iii.   IGNACIO TORREZ, b. October 02, 1913, Hondo, New México; d. September 15, 2005, San Patricio, New México.
       iv.   ERMINIA TORREZ[103], b. February 04, 1916, Hondo, New México; d. May 15, 1975; m. CLOVÍS MONTES.
       v.   JULIA TORREZ[104], b. April 12, 1918, Hondo, New México[105]; d. July 17, 2003, El Paso, Téxas; m. (1) JOHN OTERO[106]; m. (2) FRED KIMBRELL[107], April 16, 1938[108].

Notes for FRED KIMBRELL:
1930 Census: Living with his grandfather Juan Kimbrell.
Died in an accident at the age of 24. Buried in Picacho, NM.

       vi.   SIL TORREZ, b. Abt. 1922, Hondo, New México[109]; m. JOSIE FLACO.
       vii.   EVA TORREZ, b. Abt. 1924, Hondo, New México[109]; m. RAMÓN JIMÉNEZ.
       viii. PRESILA TORREZ, b. Abt. 1929, Hondo, New México[109]; m. ROBERT RICHARDSON.
       ix.   LARRY TORREZ, b. Private, Hondo, New México; m. DOROTHY CHÁVEZ.
       x.   LIBBY TORREZ, b. Private, Hondo, New México; m. CARL AUSTIN.
       xi.   PATSY TORREZ, b. Private, Hondo, New México; m. BILL TURNER.

22. ANITA[6] GUTIÉRREZ *(DAMIAN[5] GUTIÉRRES, JUANA MARÍA[4] SALAS, FRANCISCO[3], JOSÉ LORENZO[2], JOSÉ FRANCISCO[1])* was born Abt. 1895 in Hondo, Territory of New México[110]. She married ADENAGO MARTÍNEZ Abt. 1914[110], son of MANUEL JEDAN and LUISA MARTÍNEZ.

Notes for ANITA GUTIÉRREZ:
Also known as Anne.
1910 Census: Living in Roswell, Territory of New México.

Children of ANITA GUTIÉRREZ and ADENAGO MARTÍNEZ are:
43.   i.   MACLOVIA[7] MARTÍNEZ, b. April 24, 1916; d. April 02, 1940, Hondo, New México.
     ii.   ERMILO MARTÍNEZ, b. Abt. 1919[110].
44.   iii.   LOUISA MARTÍNEZ, b. December 08, 1920, San Patricio, New México; d. May 25, 1997.
     iv.   FERMÍN MARTÍNEZ, b. Abt. 1925[110]; m. ELIZABETH RUE.

Notes for ELIZABETH RUE:
Also known as Lizzie.
Natural father was A. H. Rue.

     v.   MARTHA MARTÍNEZ, b. January 1930[110]; m. HENRY CADENA.
     vi.   ERNEST MARTÍNEZ, b. Private; m. PEGGY TITSWORTH.
     vii.   THERESA MARTÍNEZ, b. Private; m. FRANK RAMÍREZ.

23. SARAFINA[6] GUTIÉRREZ *(FLORENTINO[5] GUTIÉRRES, JUANA MARÍA[4] SALAS, FRANCISCO[3], JOSÉ LORENZO[2], JOSÉ FRANCISCO[1])* was born 1900[111]. She married ANASTACIO MONTOYA[111] Abt. 1917[112], son of FELIPÉ MONTOYA and PAULA GARCÍA.

Notes for ANASTACIO MONTOYA:
1920 Census: Living in Hondo, New México. (Juan Montoya)
1930 Census: Living in Dexter, New México. (Anastacio Montoya)

Children of SARAFINA GUTIÉRREZ and ANASTACIO MONTOYA are:
     i.   RAMÓN[7] MONTOYA, b. Abt. 1920[113].
     ii.   JOVITA MONTOYA, b. Abt. 1923[114].

24. PABLO GALLEGOS[6] SALAS *(TEOFILO TRUJILLO[5], PABLO[4], FRANCISCO[3], JOSÉ LORENZO[2], JOSÉ FRANCISCO[1])*[115] was born October 12, 1887 in San Patricio, Territory of New México[116], and died June 29, 1948 in San Patricio, New México. He married (1) PETRA FRESQUEZ SISNEROS November 14, 1910[117], daughter of TEOFILO SISNEROS and REYES FRESQUEZ. He married (2) RUBY QUINTANA October 25, 1930 in Glencoe, New México[118], daughter of CAYETANO QUINTANA and FEDELINA SALAZAR.

Children of PABLO SALAS and PETRA SISNEROS are:
     i.   TEOFILO SINEROS[7] SALAS, b. 1912, San Patricio, New México[119].
45.   ii.   FERMÍN SALAS, b. October 23, 1915, Hondo, New México; d. March 04, 1992.
     iii.   REYES SALAS[120], b. 1919, San Patricio, New México; d. September 29, 1943, Los Angeles, California.

Notes for REYES SALAS:
Died in Los Angeles, California but was burried in San Patricio, New Mexico on October 3, 1943.

     iv.   SOFIA SALAS, b. 1925, San Patricio, New México[121].

25. PELEGRINA[6] SALAS *(TEOFILO TRUJILLO[5], PABLO[4], FRANCISCO[3], JOSÉ LORENZO[2], JOSÉ FRANCISCO[1])* was born August 1894[122]. She married (1) RAFAEL MÁRQUEZ August 08, 1909 in Hondo, Territory of New México[123], son of FELIPÉ MÁRQUEZ and CONCEPCIÓN BARELA. She married (2) REFUGIO TORRES[124] January 16, 1911[125], son of YGNACIO TORRES and MANUELA LUCERO.

Notes for REFUGIO TORRES:
1900 - 1930: Census: Living in Hondo, Territory of New México.

Land Patent # NMR 0036867, on the authority of the Homestead Entry-Enlarged (35 Stat. 639), February 19, 1909. Issued 320 acres on June 12, 1922.
Land Patent # NMLC 0041321, on the authority of the Homestead Entry-Stock Raising (39 Stat. 862), December 29, 1916. Issued 320 acres on April 27, 1936.

Children of PELEGRINA SALAS and REFUGIO TORRES are:
46.   i.   MAGGIE[7] TORRES, b. 1913.
     ii.   AMALIA TORRES[126], b. December 17, 1915, Hondo, New México; d. July 25, 1967; m. FIDEL SÁNCHEZ[126], February 12, 1934, San Patricio, New México[127].

26. ELFIDO[6] SALAS *(TEOFILO TRUJILLO[5], PABLO[4], FRANCISCO[3], JOSÉ LORENZO[2], JOSÉ FRANCISCO[1])*[128] was born March 13, 1897 in Hondo, Territory of New México[129], and died November 30, 1973 in Hondo, New México[130]. He married MASIMIANA MONTOYA[131] February 13, 1924 in Lincoln County, New México[132], daughter of MAURICIO MONTOYA and AVRORA SÁNCHEZ.

Notes for ELFIDO SALAS:
Also known as Elfigo, Delfido.

Land Patent # NMLC 0025968, on the authority of the Homestead Entry-Stock Raising (39 Stat. 862), December 29, 1916. Issued 611 acres on August 16, 1927.

Notes for MASIMIANA MONTOYA:
Also known as Maximiana.

Children of ELFIDO SALAS and MASIMIANA MONTOYA are:
  i.   YLARIO[7] SALAS[133], b. August 05, 1925, Hondo, New México[134]; d. October 11, 1973; m. STELLA WARNER[135], December 01, 1951, Ruidoso, New México[136].

Notes for YLARIO SALAS:
Private US Army. World War Two.

  ii.   PEDRO SALAS, b. December 04, 1926, Hondo, New México[137].
  iii.   REYNALDA SALAS, b. 1929[137].
  iv.   TERESA SALAS[138], b. July 23, 1932; d. October 01, 2005, Roswell, New México.
  v.   RAMONA SALAS[138], b. October 08, 1937, Hondo, New México[139]; d. March 09, 1997[140]; m. (1) GEORGE GRIEGO LUCERO, September 17, 1958[141]; m. (2) ALFRED MCTEIGUE, November 17, 1962, Hondo, New México[142].
  vi.   JUAN MONTOYA SALAS, b. Private.
  vii.   MADALENA SALAS, b. Private.
  viii.   RAMÓN SALAS, b. Private.
  ix.   TEOFILO MONTOYA SALAS, b. Private.

27. JACOBO[6] SALAS *(TEOFILO TRUJILLO[5], PABLO[4], FRANCISCO[3], JOSÉ LORENZO[2], JOSÉ FRANCISCO[1])*[143] was born February 21, 1899 in Hondo, Territory of New México, and died April 1973 in Artesia, New Mexico. He married TOMASITA SALSBERRY January 14, 1920 in San Patricio, New México[144], daughter of JAMES SALSBERRY and MANUELITA HERRERA.

Notes for JACOBO SALAS:
Also known as Jake.

Notes for TOMASITA SALSBERRY:
Also known as Tomasa.
Buried: San Patricio, NM.

Children of JACOBO SALAS and TOMASITA SALSBERRY are:
  i.   PABLITA[7] SALAS[145], b. Abt. 1924, San Patricio, New México; d. April 17, 1924, San Patricio, New México.
  ii.   MARÍA SALAS[146], b. Abt. 1932, Hondo, New México; d. February 23, 1932, Hondo, New México.
  iii.   JOSEFA SALAS, b. December 27, 1936; d. March 28, 1999, Artesia, New Mexico.

Notes for JOSEFA SALAS:
Also known as Josefita Salas Duran.

  iv.   DOMINGO SALAS, b. Private; d. Artesia, New Mexico; m. SOFIA DE SALAS.
  v.   ROSA SALAS, b. Private; d. Artesia, New Mexico.
  vi.   RUBÉN SALAS, b. Private.
  vii.   WILLIE SALAS, b. Private.
  viii.   BESSIE LUISA JULIA SALAS[147], b. Abt. 1940, Hondo, New México; d. March 05, 1940, Hondo, New México.

28. EULOJIO[6] GALLEGOS *(ANITA[5] SALAS, PABLO[4], FRANCISCO[3], JOSÉ LORENZO[2], JOSÉ FRANCISCO[1])*[148] was born February 01, 1887[149], and died July 04, 1938. He married (1) LUGARDITA LUCERO March 12, 1908 in San

Patricio, Territory of New México[150], daughter of ANISETO LUCERO and REFUGIA TRUJILLO. He married (2) VIVIANA CHÁVEZ[151] August 24, 1911[152], daughter of JUAN CHÁVEZ and TERESA HERRERA.

Notes for EULOJIO GALLEGOS:
Also known as Olojio.

Child of EULOJIO GALLEGOS and VIVIANA CHÁVEZ is:
    i.   GENOVEVA[7] GALLEGOS, b. 1904[153].

29. MANUELITA[6] GALLEGOS *(ANITA[5] SALAS, PABLO[4], FRANCISCO[3], JOSÉ LORENZO[2], JOSÉ FRANCISCO[1])* was born May 14, 1899 in San Patricio, Territory of New México[154]. She married SIMÓN SAÍZ January 10, 1920 in San Patricio, New México[155], son of BRAULIO SAÍZ and LAZARA JARAMILLO.

Child of MANUELITA GALLEGOS and SIMÓN SAÍZ is:
    i.   ELIZABETH[7] SAÍZ, b. March 22, 1928, San Patricio, New México[156].

Notes for ELIZABETH SAÍZ:
Also known as Isabel.

30. ELISEO[6] GALLEGOS *(ANITA[5] SALAS, PABLO[4], FRANCISCO[3], JOSÉ LORENZO[2], JOSÉ FRANCISCO[1])*[157] was born May 30, 1912, and died May 16, 1995 in San Patricio, New México. He married ROSA MONTOYA[157], daughter of MAURICIO MONTOYA and AVRORA SÁNCHEZ.

Children of ELISEO GALLEGOS and ROSA MONTOYA are:
    i.   CECILIA[7] GALLEGOS, b. Private.
    ii.   LUPE GALLEGOS, b. Private.
    iii.   JESÚS GALLEGOS, b. Private.
    iv.   VIRGINIA GALLEGOS, b. Private.
    v.   REBECCA GALLEGOS, b. Private.
    vi.   JOSÉ GALLEGOS, b. Private.
    vii.   PRECILLA GALLEGOS, b. Private.

31. HINIO[6] LUCERO *(ANISETO[5], JUAN DE JESÚS[4] LUSERO, PABLO DE JESÚS[3], PAULA GETRUDES[2] SALAS, JOSÉ FRANCISCO[1])*[158] was born Abt. 1881 in San Patricio, Territory of New México[159], and died March 21, 1933 in San Patricio, New México. He married MANUELITA OLGUÍN February 12, 1902[160], daughter of RAMÓN OLGUÍN and MARÍA CEDILLO.

Notes for HINIO LUCERO:
Also known as Iginio.

Notes for MANUELITA OLGUÍN:
Also known as Manuela, Manuelita Sedillo.
1900 Census: She was living with her brother-in-law, Sisto Sedillo, and her sister, Margarita Olguín de Sedillo.

Children of HINIO LUCERO and MANUELITA OLGUÍN are:
    i.   MARTÍN OLGUÍN[7] LUCERO[161], b. July 26, 1905, San Patricio, Territory of New México; d. May 15, 1953.
    ii.   REYES LUCERO, b. June 06, 1909, San Patricio, Territory of New México[162]; m. RITA BENAVIDEZ, December 04, 1946, Carrizozo, New México[162].

Notes for REYES LUCERO:
1920 Census: Living in San Patricio, New México.

    iii.   EPIFANIO LUCERO, b. 1915, San Patricio, New México[163].
    iv.   REFUGIO LUCERO, b. 1918, San Patricio, New México[163].
47.   v.   ANISETO OLGUÍN LUCERO, b. November 15, 1902, San Patricio, Territory of New México; d. November 18, 1965, San Patricio, New México.

32. JUANITA[6] LUCERO *(ANISETO[5], JUAN DE JESÚS[4] LUSERO, PABLO DE JESÚS[3], PAULA GETRUDES[2] SALAS, JOSÉ FRANCISCO[1])* was born September 02, 1889 in San Patricio, Territory of New México, and died May

11, 1958. She married IGNACIO S. OLGUÍN[164] November 02, 1921[165], son of RAMÓN OLGUÍN and MARÍA CEDILLO.

Notes for IGNACIO S. OLGUÍN:
June 18, 1904 to June 10, 1909- Was selected as the first postmaster of San Patricio.
1910 Census: Living in San Patricio, Territory of New México.

Children of JUANITA LUCERO and IGNACIO OLGUÍN are:

48.   i.   EVA H.[7] OLGUÍN, b. August 16, 1922, San Patricio, New México; d. January 16, 2012, Alamogordo, New México.
        ii.   RAMÓN OLGUÍN[166], b. February 12, 1925, San Patricio, New México[167]; d. July 07, 1983, Alamogordo, New México[168].
        iii.   CARLOS OLGUÍN[169], b. August 21, 1927, San Patricio, New México; d. August 23, 1958, San Patricio, New México.

Notes for CARLOS OLGUÍN:
WW II Veteran.

33. AMBROSIA[6] ULIBARRÍ *(CIPRIANA[5] LUCERO, JUAN DE JESÚS[4] LUSERO, PABLO DE JESÚS[3], PAULA GETRUDES[2] SALAS, JOSÉ FRANCISCO[1])* was born Abt. 1865[170]. She married HILARIO SILVA April 13, 1892[171], son of MANUEL SILVA and JOSEFITA ESQUIVEL.

Notes for HILARIO SILVA:
Also known as Ylario.

Children of AMBROSIA ULIBARRÍ and HILARIO SILVA are:

49.   i.   ALBINA[7] SILVA, b. March 19, 1884, San Patricio, Territory of New México.
50.   ii.   TELESFORO SILVA, b. April 18, 1885, Tularoso, Territory of New México; d. September 08, 1976, Ruidoso Downs, New México.

34. SARAFINA SOCORRO[6] ULIBARRÍ *(CIPRIANA[5] LUCERO, JUAN DE JESÚS[4] LUSERO, PABLO DE JESÚS[3], PAULA GETRUDES[2] SALAS, JOSÉ FRANCISCO[1])* was born Abt. 1868[172], and died Bef. 1921. She married ESTANISLADO TRUJILLO MONTOYA[173] January 09, 1887 in San Patricio, Territory of New México[174], son of TRANQUILINO MONTOYA and MARÍA TRUJILLO.

Notes for ESTANISLADO TRUJILLO MONTOYA:
Also known as Tanislado, Tanislaus.

Land Patent # NMLC 0026044, on the authority of the Homestead Entry-Enlarged (35 Stat. 639), February 19, 1909. Issued 164.56 acres on April 09, 1926.

Children of SARAFINA ULIBARRÍ and ESTANISLADO MONTOYA are:

51.   i.   MANUEL ULIBARRÍ[7] MONTOYA, b. 1888, San Patricio, New México; d. Bef. 1920.
52.   ii.   PABLITA MONTOYA, b. May 21, 1890, San Patricio, Territory of New México; d. March 31, 1952, San Patricio, New México.
53.   iii.   TEODORO ULIBARRÍ MONTOYA, b. December 18, 1892, San Patricio, Territory of New México; d. March 08, 1976, Glencoe, New México.
        iv.   CANDIDO ULIBARRÍ MONTOYA, b. 1895, San Patricio, New México[175].
54.   v.   SUSANA MONTOYA, b. 1897, San Patricio, Territory of New México; d. June 17, 1938.
        vi.   ISABEL MONTOYA, b. December 29, 1899, San Patricio, New México[176]; m. (1) CONCHA DE MONTOYA, El Paso, Texas; m. (2) VICTORIA SÁNCHEZ[177], February 23, 1921[178].
        vii.   DESIDERIO MONTOYA, b. February 15, 1902, San Patricio, Territory of New México[179]; m. CATALINA SALAZAR, March 09, 1926, Capitán, New México[179].

Notes for DESIDERIO MONTOYA:
Baptismal records indicate that he was born on December 22, 1901. (Microfiche# 0016754, Page 121)

55.   viii. SENAIDA MONTOYA, b. May 19, 1907, San Patricio, Territory of New México; d. July 10, 1944, Roswell, New México.

35. VICENTE[6] ULIBARRÍ *(CIPRIANA[5] LUCERO, JUAN DE JESÚS[4] LUSERO, PABLO DE JESÚS[3], PAULA GETRUDES[2] SALAS, JOSÉ FRANCISCO[1])* was born January 22, 1870 in San Patricio, Territory of New México[180], and died November 08, 1949. He married MARÍA SARAFINA SEDILLO November 06, 1922, daughter of JUAN SEDILLO and JOSEFA FAJARDO.

Notes for VICENTE ULIBARRÍ:
Also known as Vicente Rivali.
1920 Census: Living in Cloudcroft, New México.

Children of VICENTE ULIBARRÍ and MARÍA SEDILLO are:
56.   i.   AUGUSTINA[7] ULIBARRÍ, b. September 26, 1892, San Patricio, New México; d. April 29, 1970.
       ii.   MARÍA ULIBARRÍ[181], b. October 20, 1895, San Patricio, Territory of New México[182]; m. JOSÉ SILVA CHÁVEZ[183], November 02, 1911, Picacho, Territory of New México[183].

Notes for MARÍA ULIBARRÍ:
Also known as Marilla.

57.   iii.   EPIFANIO ULIBARRÍ, b. August 22, 1896, San Patricio, Territory of New México; d. October 17, 1928, San Patricio, New México.
58.   iv.   SOFIA ULIBARRÍ, b. 1905, San Patricio, Territory of New México; d. October 16, 1941.
59.   v.   PETRA ULIBARRÍ, b. June 27, 1907, San Patricio, Territory of New México; d. October 1977, San Patricio, New México.
60.   vi.   DOMINGA ULIBARRÍ, b. October 02, 1910, San Patricio, Territory of New México; d. June 13, 2001, Hondo, New México.

36. REFUGIO[6] TORRES *(MANUELA[5] LUCERO, JUAN DE JESÚS[4] LUSERO, PABLO DE JESÚS[3], PAULA GETRUDES[2] SALAS, JOSÉ FRANCISCO[1])[184]* was born February 19, 1874 in Tomé, Territory of New México[185], and died November 27, 1937 in Hondo, New México. He married (1) ESPERANSA SÁNCHEZ September 27, 1905 in Lincoln, Territory of New México[186], daughter of DOMINGO SÁNCHEZ and JUANITA AMENDARES. He married (2) PELEGRINA SALAS January 16, 1911[187], daughter of TEOFILO SALAS and IGENIA GALLEGOS.

Notes for REFUGIO TORRES:
1900 - 1930: Census: Living in Hondo, Territory of New México.

Land Patent # NMR 0036867, on the authority of the Homestead Entry-Enlarged (35 Stat. 639), February 19, 1909. Issued 320 acres on June 12, 1922.
Land Patent # NMLC 0041321, on the authority of the Homestead Entry-Stock Raising (39 Stat. 862), December 29, 1916. Issued 320 acres on April 27, 1936.

Children of REFUGIO TORRES and PELEGRINA SALAS are:
46.   i.   MAGGIE[7] TORRES, b. 1913.
       ii.   AMALIA TORRES[188], b. December 17, 1915, Hondo, New México; d. July 25, 1967; m. FIDEL SÁNCHEZ[188], February 12, 1934, San Patricio, New México[189].

37. GEORGE[6] TORRES *(MANUELA[5] LUCERO, JUAN DE JESÚS[4] LUSERO, PABLO DE JESÚS[3], PAULA GETRUDES[2] SALAS, JOSÉ FRANCISCO[1])* was born July 14, 1885 in San Patricio, Territory of New México[190]. He married CELIA SÁNCHEZ November 12, 1906 in Lincoln, Territory of New México[190], daughter of ESTOLANO SÁNCHEZ and CORNELIA PACHECO.

Notes for GEORGE TORRES:
Also known as Jorge.
1930 Census: Living in Rebentón, New México.

Children of GEORGE TORRES and CELIA SÁNCHEZ are:
61.   i.   FELIS SÁNCHEZ[7] TORRES, b. June 04, 1909, Lincoln, Territory of New México; d. February 16, 2003, San Patricio, New México.
       ii.   ADENAGO TORRES[191], b. December 13, 1907, Hondo, New México[192]; d. August 06, 1990, Tularosa, New México; m. BEATRIZ TORREZ[193].
       iii.   GEORGE SÁNCHEZ TORRES, b. 1911[194].

    iv.   WILFIDO TORRES, b. 1913[194]; m. JULIA TORRES.
    v.   MIGUEL TORRES, b. 1917[194]; m. SOCORRO DE TORREZ.
    vi.   MANUELITA TORRES, b. 1919[194]; m. JUAN BAUTISTA JUAREGUI.
    vii. PRESCILIA TORRES, b. Abt. 1920[195]; m. ERNESTO LÓPEZ[196].

Notes for ERNESTO LÓPEZ:
Immigrated to the U.S. in about 1908.

    viii. LORINA TORRES, b. Abt. 1926[197]; m. ERNESTO OTERO[198].
    ix.   JAY TORRES, b. Private; m. EDNA TORRES.

38. MARTÍN LUCERO[6] TORRES *(MANUELA[5] LUCERO, JUAN DE JESÚS[4] LUSERO, PABLO DE JESÚS[3], PAULA GETRUDES[2] SALAS, JOSÉ FRANCISCO[1])[199]* was born November 22, 1888 in Hondo, Territory of New México, and died November 20, 1967 in Roswell, New México. He married ISABEL GUTIÉRREZ[200] January 05, 1911 in Hondo, Territory of New México[201], daughter of DAMIAN GUTIÉRRES and JUANITA SÁNCHEZ.

Children of MARTÍN TORRES and ISABEL GUTIÉRREZ are:
    i.   FEDERICO[7] TORREZ[202], b. August 24, 1909, Hondo, New México; d. April 05, 2003; m. CECILIA MACKEY.

Notes for FEDERICO TORREZ:
Also known as Fred.

    ii.   ELOY TORREZ[203], b. February 27, 1912, Hondo, New México[204]; d. October 28, 2011, Roswell, New México; m. SAVINA SALCIDO[205].

Notes for SAVINA SALCIDO:
Also known as Savina.

42.   iii. IGNACIO TORREZ, b. October 02, 1913, Hondo, New México; d. September 15, 2005, San Patricio, New México.
         iv. ERMINIA TORREZ[206], b. February 04, 1916, Hondo, New México; d. May 15, 1975; m. CLOVÍS MONTES.
         v.   JULIA TORREZ[207], b. April 12, 1918, Hondo, New México[208]; d. July 17, 2003, El Paso, Téxas; m. (1) JOHN OTERO[209]; m. (2) FRED KIMBRELL[210], April 16, 1938[211].

Notes for FRED KIMBRELL:
1930 Census: Living with his grandfather Juan Kimbrell.
Died in an accident at the age of 24. Buried in Picacho, NM.

    vi.   SIL TORREZ, b. Abt. 1922, Hondo, New México[212]; m. JOSIE FLACO.
    vii. EVA TORREZ, b. Abt. 1924, Hondo, New México[212]; m. RAMÓN JIMÉNEZ.
    viii. PRESILA TORREZ, b. Abt. 1929, Hondo, New México[212]; m. ROBERT RICHARDSON.
    ix.   LARRY TORREZ, b. Private, Hondo, New México; m. DOROTHY CHÁVEZ.
    x.   LIBBY TORREZ, b. Private, Hondo, New México; m. CARL AUSTIN.
    xi.   PATSY TORREZ, b. Private, Hondo, New México; m. BILL TURNER.

39. WILLIAM LUCERO[6] BRADY *(MANUELA[5] LUCERO, JUAN DE JESÚS[4] LUSERO, PABLO DE JESÚS[3], PAULA GETRUDES[2] SALAS, JOSÉ FRANCISCO[1])* was born March 07, 1892 in Lincoln, Territory of New México[213], and died March 11, 1968 in Hondo, New México[214]. He married ROSARIO SÁNCHEZ[215] February 19, 1912 in Lincoln, New Mexico[216], daughter of ESTOLANO SÁNCHEZ and CORNELIA PACHECO.

Notes for WILLIAM LUCERO BRADY:
Also known as Guillermo.

Notes for ROSARIO SÁNCHEZ:
Also known as Rosarita.

Children of WILLIAM BRADY and ROSARIO SÁNCHEZ are:
    i.   MAX[7] BRADY, b. June 01, 1913, Hondo, New México[217]; d. July 17, 1985[218].

Notes for MAX BRADY:
Also known as Maximiliano.

Major in the US Army. WW II Veteran.

  ii. ERMILO BRADY²¹⁹, b. March 13, 1915, Hondo, New México²²⁰; m. PRESCILLA PÉREZ, November 10, 1936, San Patricio, New México²²¹.
62. iii. ELMO BRADY, b. October 30, 1917, Hondo, New México; d. December 29, 2008, Ruidoso, New México.
  iv. ORLIDIA BRADY, b. Abt. 1920²²²; m. ANDREW FRESQUEZ.
  v. BARTOLA BRADY, b. Abt. 1922²²².
  vi. WILLIAM SÁNCHEZ BRADY²²³, b. April 12, 1924, Hondo, New México²²⁴; m. ORALIA HERRERA²²⁵.
  vii. PRESTINA BRADY²²⁶, b. March 20, 1926, Hondo, New México; d. January 18, 1995, Hondo, New México.
  viii. LEROY BENNETT BRADY, b. April 14, 1930²²⁷.
63. ix. BILLY JOE BRADY, b. Private.

40. JOHN LUCERO⁶ BRADY *(MANUELA⁵ LUCERO, JUAN DE JESÚS⁴ LUSERO, PABLO DE JESÚS³, PAULA GETRUDES² SALAS, JOSÉ FRANCISCO¹)²²⁸* was born December 03, 1899 in Hondo, Territory of New México, and died December 26, 1936. He married AMALIA GONZÁLES July 05, 1919 in Capitán, New México²²⁹, daughter of JOSÉ GONZÁLES and MARÍA CHÁVEZ.

Notes for JOHN LUCERO BRADY:
Also known as J.E. Brady and Juan Brady.
Baptismal records indicate that he was born on October 01, 1894. (Microfiche# 0016754, Page 219)

Notes for AMALIA GONZÁLES:
Also known as Emelia, Emiliana.

Child of JOHN BRADY and AMALIA GONZÁLES is:
  i. JOHN GONZÁLES⁷ BRADY²³⁰, b. Abt. 1922, Albuquerque, New México; d. August 05, 1922, Albuquerque, New México.

Generation No. 7

41. JOSÉ GONZÁLES⁷ GUTIÉRREZ *(ROBERTO⁶, DAMIAN⁵ GUTIÉRRES, JUANA MARÍA⁴ SALAS, FRANCISCO³, JOSÉ LORENZO², JOSÉ FRANCISCO¹)²³¹* was born July 07, 1917 in Hondo, New México²³², and died August 13, 1997 in Hondo, New México. He married (1) DOLORES SEDILLO, daughter of MARTÍN SEDILLO and PORFIRIA OTERO. He married (2) EVA B. ENCINIAS August 12, 1961 in Vaughn, New México²³³.

Notes for JOSÉ GONZÁLES GUTIÉRREZ:
Also known as Joe. Social Security Death index records his birthdate as July 7, 1918.
1920 Census: Living in Tinnie, New México.

Notes for DOLORES SEDILLO:
Also known as Lola.

Child of JOSÉ GUTIÉRREZ and DOLORES SEDILLO is:
  i. PRESCILLA⁸ GUTIÉRREZ, b. July 28, 1951; m. MELVIN CHÁVEZ.

42. IGNACIO⁷ TORREZ *(MARTÍN LUCERO⁶ TORRES, MANUELA⁵ LUCERO, JUAN DE JESÚS⁴ LUSERO, PABLO DE JESÚS³, PAULA GETRUDES² SALAS, JOSÉ FRANCISCO¹)²³⁴* was born October 02, 1913 in Hondo, New México, and died September 15, 2005 in San Patricio, New México. He married AMANDA MONTES December 26, 1937, daughter of JESÚS MONTES and TOMASITA ALDAZ.

Children of IGNACIO TORREZ and AMANDA MONTES are:
  i. JOE⁸ TORREZ, b. February 18, 1947; m. PRISCILLA GÓMEZ.
  ii. ALBERT TORREZ, b. Private.
  iii. BETTY TORREZ, b. Private.
  iv. LORENA TORREZ, b. Private.
  v. LYDIA TORREZ, b. Private; m. (1) GERALD D. MAÉZ; m. (2) JOHNNY GÓMEZ.
  vi. RAY TORREZ, b. Private.

43. MACLOVIA[7] MARTÍNEZ *(ANITA[6] GUTIÉRREZ, DAMIAN[5] GUTIÉRRES, JUANA MARÍA[4] SALAS, FRANCISCO[3], JOSÉ LORENZO[2], JOSÉ FRANCISCO[1])*[235] was born April 24, 1916[236], and died April 02, 1940 in Hondo, New México. She married ERMANDO CHÁVEZ[237] December 07, 1935 in Carrizozo, New México[238], son of PABLO CHÁVEZ and AMADA SÁNCHEZ.

Notes for MACLOVIA MARTÍNEZ:
Buried: San Patricio.

Children of MACLOVIA MARTÍNEZ and ERMANDO CHÁVEZ are:

    i.   PABLO MOISES[8] CHÁVEZ[239], b. July 13, 1936, San Patricio, New México; d. May 28, 2009, Amarillo, Téxas.

Notes for PABLO MOISES CHÁVEZ:
Also known as Paul.

    ii.   BOBBY MARTÍNEZ CHÁVEZ[240], b. Private, San Patricio, New México.
    iii.   LOUIS CHÁVEZ[240], b. Private.
    iv.   LILLIAN CHÁVEZ[240], b. Private; m. DANNY GARCÍA[240].
    v.   LUCY CHÁVEZ[240], b. Private.
    vi.   VIOLA CHÁVEZ, b. Private.
    vii.   JEANE CHÁVEZ, b. Private.
    viii.   DANNY CHÁVEZ, b. Private.

44. LOUISA[7] MARTÍNEZ *(ANITA[6] GUTIÉRREZ, DAMIAN[5] GUTIÉRRES, JUANA MARÍA[4] SALAS, FRANCISCO[3], JOSÉ LORENZO[2], JOSÉ FRANCISCO[1])* was born December 08, 1920 in San Patricio, New México, and died May 25, 1997. She married FERMÍN SALAS October 21, 1939 in Hondo, New México[241], son of PABLO SALAS and PETRA SISNEROS.

Notes for LOUISA MARTÍNEZ:
Buried: The family farm in Hondo, New México.

Notes for FERMÍN SALAS:
Buried: The family farm in Hondo, New México.

Children of LOUISA MARTÍNEZ and FERMÍN SALAS are:

    i.   YOVANNE[8] SALAS, b. November 09, 1957, Roswell, New México[242]; m. ROMÁN SÁNCHEZ, JR., May 25, 1974, Ruidoso, New México[242].
    ii.   BOBBY SALAS, b. Private.
    iii.   DINA SALAS, b. Private.
    iv.   GILBERT SALAS, b. Private.
    v.   JAMES SALAS, b. Private.
    vi.   JERRY SALAS, b. Private.
    vii.   PAUL SALAS, b. Private.
    viii.   SANDRA SALAS, b. Private.
    ix.   YOLANDA SALAS, b. Private.

45. FERMÍN[7] SALAS *(PABLO GALLEGOS[6], TEOFILO TRUJILLO[5], PABLO[4], FRANCISCO[3], JOSÉ LORENZO[2], JOSÉ FRANCISCO[1])* was born October 23, 1915 in Hondo, New México[243], and died March 04, 1992. He married LOUISA MARTÍNEZ October 21, 1939 in Hondo, New México[244], daughter of ADENAGO MARTÍNEZ and ANITA GUTIÉRREZ.

Notes for FERMÍN SALAS:
Buried: The family farm in Hondo, New México.

Notes for LOUISA MARTÍNEZ:
Buried: The family farm in Hondo, New México.

Children of FERMÍN SALAS and LOUISA MARTÍNEZ are:

    i.   YOVANNE[8] SALAS, b. November 09, 1957, Roswell, New México[245]; m. ROMÁN SÁNCHEZ, JR., May 25, 1974, Ruidoso, New México[245].
    ii.   GILBERT SALAS, b. Private.

    iii.   JAMES SALAS, b. Private.
    iv.   JERRY SALAS, b. Private.
    v.   PAUL SALAS, b. Private.
    vi.   SANDRA SALAS, b. Private.
    vii.   YOLANDA SALAS, b. Private.

46. MAGGIE[7] TORRES *(REFUGIO[6], MANUELA[5] LUCERO, JUAN DE JESÚS[4] LUSERO, PABLO DE JESÚS[3], PAULA GETRUDES[2] SALAS, JOSÉ FRANCISCO[1])* was born 1913[246]. She married FRED MONTES[247,248], son of JESÚS MONTES and TOMASITA ALDAZ.

Notes for FRED MONTES:
Also known as Federico.
Social Security Death Index indicates that he was born on November 16, 1910.

Child of MAGGIE TORRES and FRED MONTES is:
    i.   HERALDA[8] MONTES[248], b. Abt. 1934, Hondo, New México; d. March 14, 1934, Hondo, New México.

47. ANISETO OLGUÍN[7] LUCERO *(HINIO[6], ANISETO[5], JUAN DE JESÚS[4] LUSERO, PABLO DE JESÚS[3], PAULA GETRUDES[2] SALAS, JOSÉ FRANCISCO[1])*[249] was born November 15, 1902 in San Patricio, Territory of New México[250], and died November 18, 1965 in San Patricio, New México. He married REYNALDA SÁNCHEZ[251], daughter of NAPOLEÓN SÁNCHEZ and MARÍA CHÁVEZ.

Notes for ANISETO OLGUÍN LUCERO:
Buried: San Patricio.

Children of ANISETO LUCERO and REYNALDA SÁNCHEZ are:
    i.   LEONIRES[8] LUCERO, b. 1926[252].
    ii.   MARÍA SÁNCHEZ LUCERO[253], b. September 23, 1931, San Patricio, New México[254]; d. September 16, 1994, Roswell, New México; m. (1) RALPH RODELA; m. (2) EMILIANO CHÁVEZ[255], April 25, 1947, Carrizozo, New México[256].

Notes for MARÍA SÁNCHEZ LUCERO:
Also known as Mary.

Notes for RALPH RODELA:
Raised by Isabel and Concha Montoya in San Patricio.

Notes for EMILIANO CHÁVEZ:
Served with N.M.2516 Base Unit AAF, and was a WW II veteran. He was murdered in California.
Buried: San Patricio.

    iii.   FELIS LUCERO[257], b. July 12, 1934, San Patricio, New México[258]; m. (1) EMILIANO VILLESCAS, March 05, 1952, Carrizozo, New México[258]; m. (2) JAMES J. LARSON, May 08, 1961, Ruidoso, New México[259].

Notes for EMILIANO VILLESCAS:
Also known as Emiliano Torres, Villescas.
NM Sgt, Comp 11, Armed Cavalry, Korea.

    iv.   ANISETO SÁNCHEZ LUCERO, b. Private.

Notes for ANISETO SÁNCHEZ LUCERO:
Living in Albuquerque, New México.

    v.   EFFIE LUCERO[260], b. Private.
    vi.   EURAQUIO LUCERO, b. Private.
    vii.   JESSIE LUCERO, b. Private.
    viii.   JOSEPH LUCERO, b. Private; m. DORIS LUCERO.

Notes for JOSEPH LUCERO:

Living in Roswell, New México.

    ix.   REYNALDA LUCERO, b. Private.

48. EVA H.[7] OLGUÍN *(JUANITA[6] LUCERO, ANISETO[5], JUAN DE JESÚS[4] LUSERO, PABLO DE JESÚS[3], PAULA GETRUDES[2] SALAS, JOSÉ FRANCISCO[1])* was born August 16, 1922 in San Patricio, New México[261], and died January 16, 2012 in Alamogordo, New México. She married BENJAMÍN TELLES.

Children of EVA OLGUÍN and BENJAMÍN TELLES are:
    i.   PATRICK[8] TELLES, b. Private.
    ii.   FREIDA TELLES, b. Private.

49. ALBINA[7] SILVA *(AMBROSIA[6] ULIBARRÍ, CIPRIANA[5] LUCERO, JUAN DE JESÚS[4] LUSERO, PABLO DE JESÚS[3], PAULA GETRUDES[2] SALAS, JOSÉ FRANCISCO[1])*[262] was born March 19, 1884 in San Patricio, Territory of New México. She married DOROTEO MONTOYA November 20, 1907 in Lincoln County, Territory of New México[263], son of TRANQUILINO MONTOYA and MARÍA TRUJILLO.

Notes for ALBINA SILVA:
Also known as Alvina, Balbina.

Notes for DOROTEO MONTOYA:
Baptized: February 15, 1886. Padrinos: Pedro Trujillo, Andrea Miranda.
1920 Census: Living in Las Palas, New México.

Children of ALBINA SILVA and DOROTEO MONTOYA are:
    i.   SAMUEL[8] MONTOYA[264], b. May 19, 1909[265]; d. May 03, 1994, Tinnie, New México; m. EUFRACIA MONTOYA[266], November 26, 1938[267].

Notes for SAMUEL MONTOYA:
Also known as Sam.

    ii.   COSMÉ MONTOYA[268], b. May 26, 1911, San Patricio, Territory of New México[269]; d. January 03, 1994, Anthony, New México[270]; m. AMALIA BENAVIDEZ.
    iii.   LORENSITA MONTOYA[270], b. February 09, 1914, San Patricio, New México[271]; d. April 21, 2000, Artesia, New México; m. (1) FERNANDO SALSBERRY[272], June 15, 1929, Carrizozo, New Mexico[273]; m. (2) CAMILO SEDILLO[274], May 04, 1940, Carrizozo, New México[275].

Notes for LORENSITA MONTOYA:
Burial birthdate states she was born on August 09, 1914.

Notes for FERNANDO SALSBERRY:
Also known as Fred.
1930 Census: Living in Fort Stanton, New México.
He died in an automobile accident in Hondo, New México. Burried: San Patricio, New México.

Notes for CAMILO SEDILLO:
US Navy, Seaman Second Class. World War II.

    iv.   JOSEFITA MONTOYA[276], b. September 06, 1918; d. May 18, 2003; m. JUAN BACA[276].

Notes for JOSEFITA MONTOYA:
Also known as Josephine.

Notes for JUAN BACA:
Social Security Death Index indicates that he was born on June 30, 1914. Raised with Crecencio Carrillo.

    v.   TRANQUELINO SILVA MONTOYA, b. August 22, 1925, Arabela, New México; d. September 24, 2009, Alamagordo, New México; m. RUBY SAMORA.

Notes for TRANQUELINO SILVA MONTOYA:

Also known as Trankie.
Served in the US Army from 1944 to 1946.
Lifelong resident of Ruidoso.

50. TELESFORO[7] SILVA *(AMBROSIA[6] ULIBARRÍ, CIPRIANA[5] LUCERO, JUAN DE JESÚS[4] LUSERO, PABLO DE JESÚS[3], PAULA GETRUDES[2] SALAS, JOSÉ FRANCISCO[1])*[277] was born April 18, 1885 in Tularoso, Territory of New México, and died September 08, 1976 in Ruidoso Downs, New México. He married (1) FRANCISCA UDERO RODELA October 27, 1905 in San Patricio, Territory of New México[278], daughter of ANDRÉS RODELA and INEZ UDERO. He married (2) ERINEA BENAVIDEZ[279] November 29, 1911, daughter of JUAN BENAVIDEZ and TEOFILA TRUJILLO.

Notes for TELESFORO SILVA:
Also known as Telesforo.
1920 Census: Living in Capitán, New México.

Notes for FRANCISCA UDERO RODELA:
Raised by Andrés Rodela.

Notes for ERINEA BENAVIDEZ:
1900 Census: Living with her grandfather, Benito Trujillo and grandmother, María Igenia Sedillo de Trujillo.

Children of TELESFORO SILVA and FRANCISCA RODELA are:
    i.   EDUARDO[8] SILVA, b. August 10, 1908[280]; d. 1998; m. CONSUELO SALAS, December 31, 1932[280].

Notes for EDUARDO SILVA:
Also known as Edward.

Notes for CONSUELO SALAS:
1930 Census: Living with Militon Sánchez and his wife Concha.

    ii.   ANGELITA SILVA, b. Abt. October 1909.

Children of TELESFORO SILVA and ERINEA BENAVIDEZ are:
    iii.   BENITO[8] SILVA[281], b. October 22, 1912, Hondo, New México[282]; d. December 1986, Ruidoso Downs, New México; m. CONSUELO SÁNCHEZ[283], February 13, 1932, Glencoe, New México[284].

Notes for BENITO SILVA:
1920 Census shows that he was living with his uncle, Manuel Benavidez.

Notes for CONSUELO SÁNCHEZ:
Also known as Consolación.
Lincoln County marriage records indicate that she was born on April 02, 1913.
Buried in Tularosa Catholic Cemetery.

    iv.   AMBROCIA SILVA, b. April 15, 1915, Hondo, New México[285]; m. PROSPERO MIRABAL GONZÁLES, January 16, 1932, Glencoe, New México[285].
    v.   ANSELMO SILVA[286], b. April 21, 1919, Hondo, New México[287]; d. December 10, 1992, Ruidoso Downs, New México; m. VIRGINIA MIRANDA, November 04, 1948, Ruidoso, New México[288].
    vi.   BONIFACIO SILVA, b. May 15, 1923, Lincoln, New México[289].
    vii.   ONESIMA SILVA, b. Private.
    viii.   RAMÓN SILVA, b. Private; m. CARMELITA SILVA.
    ix.   VICTOR SILVA, b. Private.

51. MANUEL ULIBARRÍ[7] MONTOYA *(SARAFINA SOCORRO[6] ULIBARRÍ, CIPRIANA[5] LUCERO, JUAN DE JESÚS[4] LUSERO, PABLO DE JESÚS[3], PAULA GETRUDES[2] SALAS, JOSÉ FRANCISCO[1])* was born 1888 in San Patricio, New México[290], and died Bef. 1920[291]. He married MARTINA PRUDENCIO[292] October 01, 1911, daughter of JOSÉ PRUDENCIO and VICTORIA FAJARDO.

Children of MANUEL MONTOYA and MARTINA PRUDENCIO are:
    i.   FELIX[8] MONTOYA.

    ii.   LUÍS MONTOYA, b. Abt. 1913[293].
    iii. JUANITA MONTOYA, b. Abt. 1914[293].
    iv.   GILBERTO MONTOYA, b. Abt. 1917[293].

52. PABLITA[7] MONTOYA *(SARAFINA SOCORRO[6] ULIBARRÍ, CIPRIANA[5] LUCERO, JUAN DE JESÚS[4] LUSERO, PABLO DE JESÚS[3], PAULA GETRUDES[2] SALAS, JOSÉ FRANCISCO[1])* was born May 21, 1890 in San Patricio, Territory of New México, and died March 31, 1952 in San Patricio, New México. She married JULIO MOLINA MIRANDA November 15, 1909 in San Patricio, Territory of New México[294], son of JULIO MIRANDA and ANTONIA MOLINA.

Notes for PABLITA MONTOYA:
Also known as Paula.

Children of PABLITA MONTOYA and JULIO MIRANDA are:
    i.   CARLOS[8] MIRANDA[295], b. January 03, 1910[296]; d. January 02, 1972.
    ii.   ENRÍQUE MIRANDA, b. Abt. 1913[296].
    iii. FRANCISCA MIRANDA, b. Abt. 1914[296]; m. ANTONIO HERRERA.
    iv.   CANDIDO MIRANDA[297], b. September 02, 1918, San Patricio, New México[298]; d. October 17, 1990, Socorro, New México[299].

Notes for CANDIDO MIRANDA:
Private First Class. World War II.

    v.   GALINA MIRANDA[300], b. January 15, 1926, San Patricio, New México; d. February 25, 1926, San Patricio, New México.
    vi.   EULALIA MIRANDA[301], b. December 10, 1920, San Patricio, New México; d. August 08, 1977, El Paso, Texas[302]; m. JOSÉ HERRERA.

Notes for EULALIA MIRANDA:
Also known as Ulalia.

    vii. VIRGINIA MIRANDA, b. January 12, 1932, San Patricio, New México[303]; m. ANSELMO SILVA[304], November 04, 1948, Ruidoso, New México[305].

53. TEODORO ULIBARRÍ[7] MONTOYA *(SARAFINA SOCORRO[6] ULIBARRÍ, CIPRIANA[5] LUCERO, JUAN DE JESÚS[4] LUSERO, PABLO DE JESÚS[3], PAULA GETRUDES[2] SALAS, JOSÉ FRANCISCO[1])*[306] was born December 18, 1892 in San Patricio, Territory of New México[307], and died March 08, 1976 in Glencoe, New México. He married BERSABÉ SÁNCHEZ December 11, 1919 in San Patricio, New México[308], daughter of JUAN SÁNCHEZ and VISITA SÁNCHEZ.

Notes for TEODORO ULIBARRÍ MONTOYA:
Also known as Theodoro.

Children of TEODORO MONTOYA and BERSABÉ SÁNCHEZ are:
    i.   AMELIA[8] MONTOYA, b. Abt. 1920, Glencoe, New México[309].
    ii.   ALVESITA MONTOYA[310], b. January 26, 1921, Glencoe, New México[311]; m. CARLOS SÁNCHEZ[312], July 22, 1940, Glencoe, New México[313].

Notes for ALVESITA MONTOYA:
Also known as Albesa.

Notes for CARLOS SÁNCHEZ:
Lived almost his entire life in Ruidoso, NM.

    iii. CANDIDO SÁNCHEZ MONTOYA[314], b. November 14, 1923, Glencoe, New México; d. June 23, 1992, Ruidoso Downs, New México; m. CRUSITA BENAVIDEZ SÁNCHEZ[315], November 09, 1946, Carrizozo, New México[316].
    iv.   ANSELMO MONTOYA, b. Abt. 1926, Glencoe, New México[317].

54. SUSANA[7] MONTOYA *(SARAFINA SOCORRO[6] ULIBARRÍ, CIPRIANA[5] LUCERO, JUAN DE JESÚS[4] LUSERO, PABLO DE JESÚS[3], PAULA GETRUDES[2] SALAS, JOSÉ FRANCISCO[1])[318]* was born 1897 in San Patricio, Territory of New México[319], and died June 17, 1938[320]. She married LORENSO MENDOSA[321] September 13, 1915 in Lincoln, New México[322], son of DIONICIO MENDOSA and MARÍA DE MENDOSA.

Notes for SUSANA MONTOYA:
Also known as Socorro, Susanita.

Notes for LORENSO MENDOSA:
Rosenda's son.

Children of SUSANA MONTOYA and LORENSO MENDOSA are:

    i.   TONITA[8] MENDOSA, b. Abt. 1917[323].

    ii.   SOCORRO MENDOSA[324], b. December 02, 1919, San Patricio, New México[325]; m. PABLO HERNÁNDEZ[326], June 19, 1940, Hondo, New México[326].

    iii.   BENJAMÍN MENDOSA[327], b. Abt. 1921, Hondo, New México[328]; d. June 25, 1942, Hondo, New México.

    iv.   CONSUELO MENDOSA[329], b. October 09, 1926; d. December 19, 2006, Roswell, New México; m. ERMINIO SÁNCHEZ[329], December 07, 1944, Roswell, New México[330].

Notes for CONSUELO MENDOSA:
Her mother died when she was 12 years old. She accepted the responibility of caring for her younger brothers and sisters.

Notes for ERMINIO SÁNCHEZ:
About 1944: Erminio and his family moved to Roswell, New México.

    v.   ELISA MENDOSA[331], b. May 12, 1930, San Patricio, New México; d. July 02, 2000, San Patricio, New México; m. ISMAEL CHÁVEZ[332].

    vi.   DIONICIO MENDOSA, b. Private; m. ANA MAE SUTHERLAND.

Notes for DIONICIO MENDOSA:
Also known as Dennis.

    vii.   ELOY MENDOSA, b. Private.

    viii.   ERNESTO MENDOSA, b. Private.

    ix.   PORFIRIO MENDOSA, b. Private.

    x.   ROSENDA LIDIA MENDOSA[333], b. Abt. 1938, San Patricio, New México; d. January 27, 1938, San Patricio, New México.

55. SENAIDA[7] MONTOYA *(SARAFINA SOCORRO[6] ULIBARRÍ, CIPRIANA[5] LUCERO, JUAN DE JESÚS[4] LUSERO, PABLO DE JESÚS[3], PAULA GETRUDES[2] SALAS, JOSÉ FRANCISCO[1])[334]* was born May 19, 1907 in San Patricio, Territory of New México, and died July 10, 1944 in Roswell, New México. She married EDUARDO SÁNCHEZ[334] October 08, 1920 in San Patricio, New México[335], son of JUAN SÁNCHEZ and VISITA SÁNCHEZ.

Notes for SENAIDA MONTOYA:
Also known as Maclofa Montoya.

Notes for EDUARDO SÁNCHEZ:
Raised by María de la Visitación Sánchez.
1900 Census: Indicates that he was the adopted son of José Manuel Sánchez. (Born Oct. 1893) It also indicates that he was the son of Visita Sánchez. (Born Oct 1895)
1910 Census: Indicates that he was the adopted son of José Manuel Sánchez. (Born 1895)
1920 Census: Indicates that he was the son of Visita Sánchez. (Born 1896)

Children of SENAIDA MONTOYA and EDUARDO SÁNCHEZ are:

    i.   EDUARDO MONTOYA[8] SÁNCHEZ[336], b. May 26, 1921, San Patricio, New México; d. May 15, 1995.

Notes for EDUARDO MONTOYA SÁNCHEZ:
Also known as Lalo.

    ii.   MACLOFA SÁNCHEZ, b. Abt. 1923, San Patricio, New México[337]; m. ARISTEO HERRERA.

    iii.   JUAN SÁNCHEZ[338], b. January 26, 1924, San Patricio, New México; d. January 26, 1924, San Patricio, New México.

    iv.   MANUEL MONTOYA SÁNCHEZ[339], b. May 20, 1925, Glencoe, New México; d. March 22, 1982, Roswell, New México; m. FLORA CARABAJAL SÁNCHEZ.

Notes for FLORA CARABAJAL SÁNCHEZ:
Also known as Florita, Florinda.

    v.   RAFAEL MONTOYA SÁNCHEZ, b. Abt. 1928, San Patricio, New México[340].

    vi.   MARGARITA MONTOYA SÁNCHEZ, b. Abt. 1929, San Patricio, New México[340].

Notes for MARGARITA MONTOYA SÁNCHEZ:
Also known as Maggie.

    vii.   SERAPIO SÁNCHEZ[341], b. Abt. 1937, San Patricio, New México; d. February 04, 1937, San Patricio, New México.

    viii.   CONFERINA MONTOYA SÁNCHEZ, b. Private, San Patricio, New México.

    ix.   ELFIDES SÁNCHEZ, b. Private, San Patricio, New México.

    x.   RUMELIO SÁNCHEZ, b. Private, San Patricio, New México.

56. AUGUSTINA[7] ULIBARRÍ *(VICENTE[6], CIPRIANA[5] LUCERO, JUAN DE JESÚS[4] LUSERO, PABLO DE JESÚS[3], PAULA GETRUDES[2] SALAS, JOSÉ FRANCISCO[1])*[342] was born September 26, 1892 in San Patricio, New México, and died April 29, 1970. She married RAYMUNDO SÁNCHEZ[342] December 17, 1910[343], son of JUAN SÁNCHEZ and VISITA SÁNCHEZ.

Notes for RAYMUNDO SÁNCHEZ:
1920 Census: Living in Cloudcroft, New México.

Children of AUGUSTINA ULIBARRÍ and RAYMUNDO SÁNCHEZ are:

    i.   EULALIA[8] SÁNCHEZ, b. December 15, 1912, San Patricio, New México[344]; m. PERFECTO SÁNCHEZ, June 17, 1929, Carrizozo, New México[344].

    ii.   BENNIE SÁNCHEZ, b. July 26, 1914, San Patricio, New México[345]; m. NICOLÁS TORRES, August 25, 1931, Glencoe, New México[345].

    iii.   SOFIO SÁNCHEZ[346], b. May 25, 1916, San Patricio, New México[347]; d. May 25, 1984, San Patricio, New México; m. GONSAGITA SALAS[348], May 29, 1939, Carrizozo, New México[348].

    iv.   ANEDA ULIBARRÍ SÁNCHEZ, b. July 12, 1918, San Patricio, New México[349]; m. ERMANDO CHÁVEZ[350], September 13, 1941, Carrizozo, New México[351].

    v.   OLYMPIA SÁNCHEZ[352], b. May 21, 1920, San Patricio, New México[353]; d. June 05, 2010, Ruidoso, New México; m. EPUNUCENO SÁNCHEZ[354], August 27, 1938, Carrizozo, New México[355].

    vi.   VISITA SÁNCHEZ[356], b. October 10, 1923, San Patricio, New México; d. April 10, 1924, San Patricio, New México.

    vii.   LUÍS SÁNCHEZ, b. 1928, San Patricio, New México[357].

57. EPIFANIO[7] ULIBARRÍ *(VICENTE[6], CIPRIANA[5] LUCERO, JUAN DE JESÚS[4] LUSERO, PABLO DE JESÚS[3], PAULA GETRUDES[2] SALAS, JOSÉ FRANCISCO[1])*[358] was born August 22, 1896 in San Patricio, Territory of New México[359], and died October 17, 1928 in San Patricio, New México. He married ERMINDA CHÁVEZ[360] November 04, 1915 in Lincoln, New México[361], daughter of FRANCISCO CHÁVEZ and ESLINDA GONZÁLES.

Notes for EPIFANIO ULIBARRÍ:
1900 Census: Approximate birthdate listed as May 1895.

Children of EPIFANIO ULIBARRÍ and ERMINDA CHÁVEZ are:

    i.   ANUNCIÓN[8] ULIBARRÍ[362], b. August 13, 1917, San Patricio, New México; d. September 13, 1917, San Patricio, New México.

    ii.   DIEGO ULIBARRÍ[363], b. February 20, 1920; d. April 15, 1994, Carrizozo, New México.

58. SOFIA[7] ULIBARRÍ *(VICENTE[6], CIPRIANA[5] LUCERO, JUAN DE JESÚS[4] LUSERO, PABLO DE JESÚS[3], PAULA GETRUDES[2] SALAS, JOSÉ FRANCISCO[1])* was born 1905 in San Patricio, Territory of New México[364], and died October 16, 1941. She married PABLO YBARRA April 15, 1921 in San Patricio, New México[364], son of GREGORIO YBARRA and CATARINA MONTOYA.

Child of SOFIA ULIBARRÍ and PABLO YBARRA is:

    i.   TIVORCIO[8] YBARRA, b. San Patricio, New México.

Notes for TIVORCIO YBARRA:
Also known as Tive.
Raised by his grandmother, Catarina Montoya Ybarra.

59. PETRA[7] ULIBARRÍ *(VICENTE[6], CIPRIANA[5] LUCERO, JUAN DE JESÚS[4] LUSERO, PABLO DE JESÚS[3], PAULA GETRUDES[2] SALAS, JOSÉ FRANCISCO[1])[365]* was born June 27, 1907 in San Patricio, Territory of New México[366], and died October 1977 in San Patricio, New México[367]. She married DIEGO SALCIDO[368] November 06, 1922[369], son of FAUSTINO SALCIDO and MARÍA CHÁVEZ.

Notes for PETRA ULIBARRÍ:
Buried in Roswell, New México.

Children of PETRA ULIBARRÍ and DIEGO SALCIDO are:
    i.   VICENTE[8] SALCIDO[370], b. May 05, 1924[371].
    ii.   MONICA SALCIDO[372], b. February 14, 1926, San Patricio, New México[373]; d. August 05, 1991, San Patricio, New México; m. ESTOLANO TRUJILLO SÁNCHEZ[374], January 10, 1945, Carrizozo, New México[375].
    iii. MARY SALCIDO[376], b. April 23, 1934, Hondo, New México; d. March 10, 2001, Dexter, New México; m. JERRY MARTÍNEZ[376], August 19, 1950[376].
    iv. DELLA SALCIDO[376], b. Private.
    v.   FITA SALCIDO[376], b. Private.
    vi. NORA SALCIDO[376], b. Private.

60. DOMINGA[7] ULIBARRÍ *(VICENTE[6], CIPRIANA[5] LUCERO, JUAN DE JESÚS[4] LUSERO, PABLO DE JESÚS[3], PAULA GETRUDES[2] SALAS, JOSÉ FRANCISCO[1])[377]* was born October 02, 1910 in San Patricio, Territory of New México[378], and died June 13, 2001 in Hondo, New México. She married PROCESO SALCIDO[379] December 05, 1931[380], son of FAUSTINO SALCIDO and MARÍA CHÁVEZ.

Notes for PROCESO SALCIDO:
Also known as Profeso, Proseso.

Child of DOMINGA ULIBARRÍ and PROCESO SALCIDO is:
    i.   CIRILIA OLYMPIA[8] SALCIDO[381], b. Abt. 1932, Hondo, New México; d. November 22, 1933, Hondo, New México.

61. FELIS SÁNCHEZ[7] TORRES *(GEORGE[6], MANUELA[5] LUCERO, JUAN DE JESÚS[4] LUSERO, PABLO DE JESÚS[3], PAULA GETRUDES[2] SALAS, JOSÉ FRANCISCO[1])[382]* was born June 04, 1909 in Lincoln, Territory of New México[383], and died February 16, 2003 in San Patricio, New México. She married PEDRO SALCIDO[384] October 24, 1928 in Carrizozo, New México[385], son of FAUSTINO SALCIDO and MARÍA CHÁVEZ.

Notes for PEDRO SALCIDO:
Cemetary records indicate he was born on February 23, 1905.

Land Patent # NMLC 0028752, on the authority of the Homestead Entry-Stock Raising (39 Stat. 862), December 29, 1916. Issued 629.6 acres on August 22, 1930.

Child of FELIS TORRES and PEDRO SALCIDO is:
    i.   MARÍA RELIA[8] SALCIDO[386], b. 1933, Hondo, New México; d. March 16, 1933, Tinnie, New México.

62. ELMO[7] BRADY *(WILLIAM LUCERO[6], MANUELA[5] LUCERO, JUAN DE JESÚS[4] LUSERO, PABLO DE JESÚS[3], PAULA GETRUDES[2] SALAS, JOSÉ FRANCISCO[1])* was born October 30, 1917 in Hondo, New México[387], and died December 29, 2008 in Ruidoso, New México[387]. He married GERALDINE KIMBRELL[388] 1946 in California[389], daughter of ALBERT KIMBRELL and CONSUELO RUBIO.

Notes for ELMO BRADY:
WW II Veteran.

63. BILLY JOE[7] BRADY *(WILLIAM LUCERO[6], MANUELA[5] LUCERO, JUAN DE JESÚS[4] LUSERO, PABLO DE JESÚS[3], PAULA GETRUDES[2] SALAS, JOSÉ FRANCISCO[1])* was born Private. He married PATSY SALCIDO.

Genealogy of Diego Salcido

Generation No. 1

1. DIEGO[1] SALCIDO was born 1844[1], and died Bef. December 1883. He married MIQUELA BACA October 16, 1866 in Tomé, Territory of New México[2], daughter of SANTIAGO BACA and ANA PADILLA.

Notes for DIEGO SALCIDO:
1870 Census: Living in Lincoln County, Precinct 2, Territory of New México.

Children of DIEGO SALCIDO and MIQUELA BACA are:

	i.	BARBARITA[2] SALCIDO, b. 1859[3].
	ii.	SIBRACINA SALCIDO, b. 1862[3].
	iii.	PEDRO SALCIDO, b. 1863[3].
	iv.	MANUEL SALCIDO, b. 1869[3].
	v.	SISTO SALCIDO, b. April 27, 1873.
2.	vi.	FAUSTINO BACA SALCIDO, b. January 18, 1875; d. August 22, 1935.

Generation No. 2

2. FAUSTINO BACA[2] SALCIDO *(DIEGO[1])[4]* was born January 18, 1875, and died August 22, 1935. He married MARÍA TRUJILLO CHÁVEZ January 10, 1898[5], daughter of NAVOR CHÁVEZ and GREGORIA TRUJILLO.

Notes for FAUSTINO BACA SALCIDO:
Raised by Timeo Ansul.
1898: Living in La Junta (Hondo).
Bought the Rancho de los Alamos from Alejandro Torres and Virginia Sánchez de Torres.

Notes for MARÍA TRUJILLO CHÁVEZ:
Death Records indicate that she died on November 07, 1933.

Children of FAUSTINO SALCIDO and MARÍA CHÁVEZ are:

3.	i.	DIEGO[3] SALCIDO, b. December 19, 1898, Hondo, New México ; d. March 1966, Roswell, New México.
4.	ii.	RAFAEL SALCIDO, b. May 25, 1900, Hondo, Territory of New México.
5.	iii.	FAUSTINO CHÁVEZ SALCIDO, b. November 24, 1901; d. November 05, 1959, Hondo, New México.
	iv.	PEDRO SALCIDO[6], b. February 23, 1903, Hondo, Territory of New México[7]; d. May 29, 1988, Hondo, New México; m. FELIS SÁNCHEZ TORRES[8], October 24, 1928, Carrizozo, New México[9].

Notes for PEDRO SALCIDO:
Cemetary records indicate he was born on February 23, 1905.

Land Patent # NMLC 0028752, on the authority of the Homestead Entry-Stock Raising (39 Stat. 862), December 29, 1916. Issued 629.6 acres on August 22, 1930.

	v.	JOSÉ SALCIDO[10], b. May 17, 1904[11]; d. August 24, 1974, Hondo, New México; m. NARCISA MONTOYA[12].

Notes for JOSÉ SALCIDO:
Land Patent # NMLC 0038899, on the authority of the Homestead Entry-Stock Raising (39 Stat. 862), December 29, 1916. Issued 360 acres on November 21, 1934.

Notes for NARCISA MONTOYA:
Cemetery records indicate that she was born on November 19, 1907.

	vi.	SAFINA SALCIDO, b. 1910[13]; m. ELOY TORREZ.

Notes for SAFINA SALCIDO:
Also known as Savina.

6.   vii.   PROCESO SALCIDO, b. March 23, 1911, Hondo, Territory of New México; d. April 28, 1999, Hondo, New México.

         viii.   SYLVESTRE SALCIDO[14], b. December 31, 1913[15]; d. May 08, 1975, Hondo, New México ; m. ANGELITA MONTOYA[16].

Generation No. 3

3. DIEGO[3] SALCIDO *(FAUSTINO BACA[2], DIEGO[1])*[17] was born December 19, 1898 in Hondo, New México[18], and died March 1966 in Roswell, New México. He married PETRA ULIBARRÍ[19] November 06, 1922[20], daughter of VICENTE ULIBARRÍ and MARÍA SEDILLO.

Notes for PETRA ULIBARRÍ:
Buried in Roswell, New México.

Children of DIEGO SALCIDO and PETRA ULIBARRÍ are:

        i.   VICENTE[4] SALCIDO[21], b. May 05, 1924[22].

        ii.   MONICA SALCIDO[23], b. February 14, 1926, San Patricio, New México[24]; d. August 05, 1991, San Patricio, New México; m. ESTOLANO TRUJILLO SÁNCHEZ[25], January 10, 1945, Carrizozo, New México[26].

7.   iii.   MARY SALCIDO, b. April 23, 1934, Hondo, New México; d. March 10, 2001, Dexter, New México.

        iv.   DELLA SALCIDO[27], b. Private.

        v.   FITA SALCIDO[27], b. Private.

        vi.   NORA SALCIDO[27], b. Private.

4. RAFAEL[3] SALCIDO *(FAUSTINO BACA[2], DIEGO[1])* was born May 25, 1900 in Hondo, Territory of New México[28]. He married CATARINA BACA February 08, 1923[29], daughter of DAMACIO BACA and MARÍA BACA.

Notes for RAFAEL SALCIDO:
1930 Census: Living in Hondo, New México.

Children of RAFAEL SALCIDO and CATARINA BACA are:

        i.   ARCENIA[4] SALCIDO, b. Abt. 1921[30].

        ii.   CARMELITA SALCIDO, b. Abt. 1923[30].

        iii.   FLORINDA SALCIDO, b. Abt. 1925[30].

        iv.   ISABEL SALCIDO, b. Abt. 1927[30].

5. FAUSTINO CHÁVEZ[3] SALCIDO *(FAUSTINO BACA[2], DIEGO[1])*[31] was born November 24, 1901, and died November 05, 1959 in Hondo, New México. He married PREDICANDA WARNER[31] January 24, 1924[32], daughter of JUAN WARNER and EMILIA TORREZ.

Notes for FAUSTINO CHÁVEZ SALCIDO:
Land Patent # NMLC 0028252, on the authority of the Homestead Entry-Stock Raising (39 Stat. 862), December 29, 1916. Issued 555.02 acres on October 11, 1929.

Notes for PREDICANDA WARNER:
Also known as Predicanda Juana (Warner).

Children of FAUSTINO SALCIDO and PREDICANDA WARNER are:

        i.   ALBERT W.[4] SALCIDO, b. October 25, 1925, Lincoln, New México[33]; m. NORA NÚÑEZ[34], November 16, 1946, Carrizozo, New México[35].

Notes for ALBERT W. SALCIDO:
US Navy, Seaman First Class. World War II.
1930 Census: Living in Hondo, New México.

        ii.   DAVÍD SALCIDO[36], b. June 29, 1927, Hondo, New México[37]; d. October 03, 1958, Hondo, New México; m. MARTINA SILVA, December 13, 1950, Ruidoso, New México[38].

Notes for DAVÍD SALCIDO:

Also known as Dave.

      iii.   AMELIA SALCIDO, b. Abt. 1929, Hondo, New México[39].

6. PROCESO[3] SALCIDO *(FAUSTINO BACA[2], DIEGO[1])*[40] was born March 23, 1911 in Hondo, Territory of New México[41], and died April 28, 1999 in Hondo, New México. He married DOMINGA ULIBARRÍ[42] December 05, 1931[43], daughter of VICENTE ULIBARRÍ and MARÍA SEDILLO.

Notes for PROCESO SALCIDO:
Also known as Profeso, Proseso.

Child of PROCESO SALCIDO and DOMINGA ULIBARRÍ is:
      i.   CIRILIA OLYMPIA[4] SALCIDO[44], b. Abt. 1932, Hondo, New México; d. November 22, 1933, Hondo, New México.

Generation No. 4

7. MARY[4] SALCIDO *(DIEGO[3], FAUSTINO BACA[2], DIEGO[1])*[45] was born April 23, 1934 in Hondo, New México, and died March 10, 2001 in Dexter, New México. She married JERRY MARTÍNEZ[45] August 19, 1950[45].

Children of MARY SALCIDO and JERRY MARTÍNEZ are:
      i.   CHRISTINE[5] MARTÍNEZ[45], b. Private.
      ii.   DANIEL MARTÍNEZ[45], b. Private.
      iii.   DOLÓRES MARTÍNEZ[45], b. Private.
      iv.   DONNA MARTÍNEZ[45], b. Private.
      v.   ELIZABETH MARTÍNEZ[45], b. Private.
      vi.   JERRY MARTÍNEZ[45], b. Private.
      vii.   JOANN MARTÍNEZ[45], b. Private.
      viii.   JOSEPH MARTÍNEZ[45], b. Private.
      ix.   LORETTA MARTÍNEZ[45], b. Private.
      x.   LORRAIN MARTÍNEZ[45], b. Private.
      xi.   LUCIA MARTÍNEZ[45], b. Private.
      xii.   MERCED MARTÍNEZ[45], b. Private.
      xiii.   REYNALDO MARTÍNEZ[45], b. Private.
      xiv.   RUTH MARTÍNEZ[45], b. Private.
      xv.   TERESA MARTÍNEZ[45], b. Private.

Genealogy of James R. Salsberry
See also, Jacinto Sánchez de Iñigo

Generation No. 1

1. JOHN H.[1] SAULSBURRY was born Abt. 1792 in Pennsylvania[1]. He married DELILAH HAYSLIP November 23, 1815.

Notes for JOHN H. SAULSBURRY:
Also known as John Salisbury.
1820 Census: Living in Adams County, Jefferson Township, Ohio. (John Soesberry)
1850 Census: Living in Adams County, Jefferson Township, Ohio. (John Solesbury)

Children of JOHN SAULSBURRY and DELILAH HAYSLIP are:

	i.	SAMPSON[2] SAULSBERRY, b. Abt. 1820.
	ii.	WILLIS SAULSBERRY, b. Abt. 1822.
2.	iii.	JAMES WESLEY SAULSBERRY, b. Abt. 1825, Jefferson, Adams County, Ohio; d. April 03, 1887, Ruidoso, Territory of New México.
	iv.	NANCY SAULSBERRY, b. Abt. 1828, Jefferson, Adams County, Ohio[1].
	v.	SARAH SAULSBERRY, b. Abt. 1830, Jefferson, Adams County, Ohio[1].
	vi.	SUSAN SAULSBERRY, b. Abt. 1834, Jefferson, Adams County, Ohio[1].
	vii.	RICHARD SAULSBERRY, b. Abt. 1836, Jefferson, Adams County, Ohio[1].

Notes for RICHARD SAULSBERRY:
1871: Living in Sylvania, Indiana.

	viii.	ANDREW SAULSBERRY, b. Abt. 1839, Jefferson, Adams County, Ohio[1].
	ix.	SAMUEL SAULSBERRY, b. Abt. 1844, Jefferson, Adams County, Ohio[1].
	x.	THOMAS SAULSBERRY, b. Abt. 1846, Jefferson, Adams County, Ohio[1].

Generation No. 2

2. JAMES WESLEY[2] SAULSBERRY *(JOHN H.[1] SAULSBURRY)* was born Abt. 1825 in Jefferson, Adams County, Ohio[2], and died April 03, 1887 in Ruidoso, Territory of New México. He married HARRIET CLIFTON.

Notes for JAMES WESLEY SAULSBERRY:
Listed his father as being from Pennslyvania. His mother was from Indiana.
1850 Census: Living in Adams County, Jefferson Township, Ohio. (James Solsbury)
1860 Census: Living in Adams County, Brush Creek, Ohio. (James Salesburry)
1870 Census: Living in Richland, Missouri. (James Salsbary)
1880 Census: Living in Elk Horn, Missouri. (James Salsburry)
1882: Already living in Territory of New México.
1885 Territorial Census: Living in Lincoln County, Precinct 3 (Ruidoso), Territory of New México.

Notes for HARRIET CLIFTON:
Lists both of her parents as being from Pennsylvania.

Children of JAMES SAULSBERRY and HARRIET CLIFTON are:

	i.	LAVINIA[3] SAULSBERRY, b. Abt. 1845, Jefferson, Adams County, Ohio[3]; d. San Patricio, New México; m. GEORGE TAYLOR, July 01, 1888, Lincoln, Territory of New México[4].

Notes for LAVINIA SAULSBERRY:
Also known as Vinia.
1850 Census: Living in Jefferson, Ohio. Lists her birth year as 1845.

Notes for GEORGE TAYLOR:
Civil War veteran. He also ran a stage coach out of Fort Stanton.

ii. ANDREW J. SAULSBERRY, b. Abt. 1847, Jefferson, Adams County, Ohio[5].
iii. SARAH J. SAULSBERRY, b. Abt. 1849, Jefferson, Adams County, Ohio[6].
iv. DELILAH SAULSBERRY, b. Abt. 1854, Jefferson, Adams County, Ohio[7].
3.   v. JOEL PINKERTON SAULSBERRY, b. March 14, 1863, Danville, Ohio; d. June 08, 1921, Alamagordo, New México.
vi. NANCY M. SAULSBERRY, b. Abt. 1866, Illinois[8]; m. GEORGE RUSSELL, August 10, 1884[9].

Notes for GEORGE RUSSELL:
Living in Oklahoma.

4.   vii. JAMES R. SALSBERRY, b. Abt. 1868, Iowa; d. April 18, 1947, San Patricio New Mexico.

Generation No. 3

3. JOEL PINKERTON[3] SAULSBERRY *(JAMES WESLEY[2], JOHN H.[1] SAULSBURRY)*[10] was born March 14, 1863 in Danville, Ohio[11], and died June 08, 1921 in Alamagordo, New México[12]. He married (1) MARY REBECCA HALE Abt. 1886[13], daughter of LOWEL HALE and ANNA COWGILL. He married (2) MARY LILLIAN HERMAN Abt. 1908 in Alamogordo, New México[14].

Notes for JOEL PINKERTON SAULSBERRY:
Also known as Joseph.
Death records indicate that he was born in Iowa.
Migrated to Ruidoso, Territory of New México in about 1883.
He moved from Ruidoso to Eagle Creek. From Eagle Creek he moved to Nogal. From Nogal he moved to La Luz.
Land Patent # NMNMAA 010252, on the authority of the Sale cash entry (3 Stat. 566), April 24, 1820, 160 acres.

Notes for MARY REBECCA HALE:
Also known as Rebecca.

Children of JOEL SAULSBERRY and MARY HALE are:
i. JOSHUA[4] SAULSBERRY, b. October 1885[15].
ii. JAMES L. SAULSBERRY, b. April 1887[15].
iii. HARRY SAULSBERRY, b. October 1888[15].
iv. JOHN FREDERICK SAULSBERRY, b. July 1891[15].
v. HARVEY HARTSEL SAULSBERRY[16], b. January 28, 1896, Ruidoso, Territory of New México[17]; d. August 1984, Alamagordo, New México; m. CLARA M. SAULSBERRY[18].

Notes for HARVEY HARTSEL SAULSBERRY:
Also known as Skeet.

vi. MAUDE MAY SAULSBERRY[19], b. May 25, 1901, Alamogordo, New México[20]; d. October 21, 1992, Denver, Colorado; m. FRANK HAMILTON CLIPP.

Children of JOEL SAULSBERRY and MARY HERMAN are:
vii. CHARLES W.[4] SALSBERRY, b. Abt. 1909, Alamogordo, New México[20].
viii. EDWARD F. SALSBERRY, b. Abt. December 1909[20].
ix. MARY DRAGOO, b. Abt. 1904[20]; Stepchild.

4. JAMES R.[3] SALSBERRY *(JAMES WESLEY[2] SAULSBERRY, JOHN H.[1] SAULSBURRY)* was born Abt. 1868 in Iowa[21], and died April 18, 1947 in San Patricio New Mexico. He married MANUELITA HERRERA[22,23], daughter of FERNANDO HERRERA and JULIANA MARTÍN.

Children of JAMES SALSBERRY and MANUELITA HERRERA are:
i. AUGUSTÍN[4] SALSBERRY[24], b. October 25, 1895, San Juanito (Ruidoso Downs), Territory of New México; d. May 24, 1973, Citrus Heights, California; m. (1) MARGARITA VIGIL, August 13, 1917, La Capilla de San Ysidro, New México[25]; m. (2) AGAPITA PADILLA[26], August 12, 1926, Carrizozo, New México[27].
ii. TOMASITA SALSBERRY, b. December 29, 1897, San Juanito (Ruidoso Downs), Territory of New México[28]; d. June 17, 1949, Artesia, New Mexico[29]; m. JACOBO SALAS[30], January 14, 1920, San Patricio, New México[31].
iii. MARTINA SALSBERRY, b. January 30, 1900, San Juanito (Ruidoso Downs), New México[32]; d. December 07, 1917, Glencoe, New México[33]; m. ANTONIO PADILLA SÁNCHEZ, October 13, 1915, Lincoln, Territory of New México[34].

iv. DOROTEA SALSBERRY[35], b. February 05, 1902, San Juanito (Ruidoso Downs), New México[36]; d. January 25, 1974, Artesia, New Mexico; m. RUBÉN ANDRÉS GONZÁLES, September 20, 1919, Las Angosturas (San Ysidro), New México[37].

v. FERNANDO SALSBERRY[38], b. April 13, 1904, San Juanito (Ruidoso Downs), Territory of New México[39]; d. September 11, 1937, Hondo, New Mexico; m. LORENSITA MONTOYA, June 15, 1929, Carrizozo, New Mexico[39].

vi. SANTIAGO SALSBERRY, b. June 26, 1906, San Juanito (Ruidoso Downs), Territory of New México; d. Barstow, California; m. LUCÍA ANAYA[40], March 26, 1927[41].

vii. FLORINDA SALSBERRY[42], b. March 15, 1910, Palo Verde (Ruidoso Downs), Territory of New México; d. March 27, 1978, San Patricio, New México; m. ROMÁN SÁNCHEZ[43], February 20, 1927, Mescalero, New Mexico[44].

viii. ENRÍQUES SALSBERRY, b. April 15, 1911, Palo Verde (Ruidoso Downs), Territory of New México[45]; d. January 24, 1956, Artesia, New México; m. DOLÓRES SÁNCHEZ[46], February 04, 1933, Carrizozo, New México[47].

Genealogy of Crecencio Sánchez

Generation No. 1

1. FRANCISCO[1] SÁNCHEZ was born Abt. 1820[1].

Notes for FRANCISCO SÁNCHEZ:
1880 Census: Living in Lincoln, Territory of New México.

Child of FRANCISCO SÁNCHEZ is:

2.	i.	CRECENCIO[2] SÁNCHEZ, b. Abt. 1848; d. Bef. 1903.

Generation No. 2

2. CRECENCIO[2] SÁNCHEZ *(FRANCISCO[1])* was born Abt. 1848[1], and died Bef. 1903[2]. He married MARÍA SÁNCHEZ[2].

Notes for CRECENCIO SÁNCHEZ:
1880 Census: Living in Lincoln, Territory of New México.

Children of CRECENCIO SÁNCHEZ and MARÍA SÁNCHEZ are:

	i.	LORENSO[3] SÁNCHEZ, b. Picacho, New México.
	ii.	NICOLÁS SÁNCHEZ, b. Abt. 1867[3].
3.	iii.	JUANITA SÁNCHEZ, b. June 1867, Picacho, New México.
4.	iv.	TORIVIO SÁNCHEZ, b. January 1872; d. November 01, 1921.
	v.	REFUGIO SÁNCHEZ, b. Abt. 1876[3].
5.	vi.	JOSÉ DE LOS ÁNGELES SÁNCHEZ, b. August 02, 1880.
6.	vii.	ELENA SÁNCHEZ, b. December 29, 1882, Picacho, New México.
	viii.	JOSÉ GREGORIO SÁNCHEZ, b. December 20, 1884[4].
7.	ix.	SARA SÁNCHEZ, b. June 22, 1886.

Generation No. 3

3. JUANITA[3] SÁNCHEZ *(CRECENCIO[2], FRANCISCO[1])* was born June 1867 in Picacho, New México[5]. She married DAMIAN GUTIÉRREZ Abt. 1880[6], son of JOSÉ GUTIÉRREZ and JUANA SALAS.

Notes for DAMIAN GUTIÉRREZ:
Also known as José Damian.

Children of JUANITA SÁNCHEZ and DAMIAN GUTIÉRREZ are:

8.	i.	ROBERTO[4] GUTIÉRREZ, b. February 28, 1883, Hondo, Territory of New México; d. 1951, Hondo, New México.
	ii.	EPIMENIO GUTIÉRREZ, b. December 1887[7].
9.	iii.	JOSEFA GUTIÉRREZ, b. March 1892.
10.	iv.	ISABEL GUTIÉRREZ, b. April 02, 1893, Hondo, Territory of New México; d. November 01, 1993, Roswell, New México.
11.	v.	ANITA GUTIÉRREZ, b. Abt. 1895, Hondo, Territory of New México.
	vi.	CRESCENCIO GUTIÉRREZ, b. March 1900[7].
	vii.	VITERBO GUTIÉRREZ, b. March 1900[7].

4. TORIVIO[3] SÁNCHEZ *(CRECENCIO[2], FRANCISCO[1])* was born January 1872[8], and died November 01, 1921[9]. He married AVRELIA MARTÍNEZ Abt. 1897[10].

Notes for TORIVIO SÁNCHEZ:
1910 Census: Living in Tres Ritos, Territory of New México.

Notes for AVRELIA MARTÍNEZ:
Also known as Aurelia.

Children of TORIVIO SÁNCHEZ and AVRELIA MARTÍNEZ are:
- i. NESTORA[4] SÁNCHEZ, b. September 17, 1897, Tularoso, Territory of New México[11]; d. August 19, 1921[12].
- ii. MARTÍN MARTÍNEZ SÁNCHEZ, b. November 11, 1899, Tularoso, Territory of New México[13].
- 12. iii. MANUELITA MARTÍNEZ SÁNCHEZ, b. December 07, 1900, Picacho, Territory of New México; d. February 01, 1981, Ruidoso, New México.
- iv. FIDEL SÁNCHEZ, b. April 24, 1903[14]; d. October 16, 1915[15].
- v. TOMÁS MARTÍNEZ SÁNCHEZ, b. September 18, 1905[16].
- vi. FRANCISCO MARTÍNEZ SÁNCHEZ, b. April 02, 1907[16].
- vii. MARÍA MARTÍNEZ SÁNCHEZ, b. Abt. 1909[16].
- viii. JOSÉ MARTÍNEZ SÁNCHEZ, b. November 16, 1912[17].
- ix. LORENZO SÁNCHEZ, b. August 10, 1915[18]; d. September 07, 1944[18].
- x. GRABIEL SÁNCHEZ, b. October 10, 1917[18].
- xi. EZQUIEL SÁNCHEZ, b. March 02, 1920[18].

5. JOSÉ DE LOS ÁNGELES[3] SÁNCHEZ *(CRECENCIO[2], FRANCISCO[1])*[19] was born August 02, 1880[20]. He married ADELAIDA LALONE February 12, 1903[21], daughter of TEOPHILUS LALONE and ESTANISLADA PADILLA.

Notes for JOSÉ DE LOS ÁNGELES SÁNCHEZ:
1920 Census: Living in Miami, Arizona.

Children of JOSÉ SÁNCHEZ and ADELAIDA LALONE are:
- i. SOFIA[4] SÁNCHEZ, b. Abt. 1905[22].
- ii. TERESA SÁNCHEZ, b. Abt. 1906[22].
- iii. MARY SÁNCHEZ, b. Abt. 1909[22].
- iv. ADOLPH SÁNCHEZ, b. Abt. 1912[22].

6. ELENA[3] SÁNCHEZ *(CRECENCIO[2], FRANCISCO[1])*[23] was born December 29, 1882 in Picacho, New México[24]. She married JOSÉ GARCÍA ROMERO May 15, 1899[25], son of MANUEL CHÁVEZ and LEONOR GARCÍA.

Notes for ELENA SÁNCHEZ:
Also known as Elena Sánchez. Baptismal records indicate that her mother was María Maldonado.

Notes for JOSÉ GARCÍA ROMERO:
1910 & 1920 Census: Living in Roswell, New México.

Children of ELENA SÁNCHEZ and JOSÉ ROMERO are:
- i. AVEL[4] ROMERO, b. Abt. 1900[26].
- ii. MARÍA ROMERO, b. Abt. 1902[26].
- iii. SALVADOR ROMERO, b. Abt. 1903[26].
- iv. MARGARITA ROMERO, b. Abt. 1906[26].
- v. LEONORA ROMERO, b. Abt. 1907[26].
- vi. JOHNIE ROMERO, b. Abt. 1912[27].
- vii. ANNA ROMERO, b. Abt. 1915[27].

7. SARA[3] SÁNCHEZ *(CRECENCIO[2], FRANCISCO[1])* was born June 22, 1886[28]. She married CELESTINO VIGIL[29], son of TRENIDAD VIGIL and MARÍA ROMERO.

Notes for CELESTINO VIGIL:
Also known as José Celestino Vigil.
1940s: He was a deputy sheriff for Lincoln County.

Children of SARA SÁNCHEZ and CELESTINO VIGIL are:
- i. MARÍA SÁNCHEZ[4] VIGIL, b. Picacho, New México.

Notes for MARÍA SÁNCHEZ VIGIL:
Died when she was young.

| 13. | ii. | PEDRO VIGIL, b. January 30, 1908, Picacho, Territory of New México; d. May 1971, Roswell, New México. |
| 14. | iii. | GENOVEVA VIGIL, b. September 12, 1910, Picacho, New México; d. April 12, 1989, San Patricio, New México. |

Generation No. 4

8. ROBERTO[4] GUTIÉRREZ *(JUANITA[3] SÁNCHEZ, CRECENCIO[2], FRANCISCO[1])[30]* was born February 28, 1883 in Hondo, Territory of New México[31], and died 1951 in Hondo, New México. He married (1) REBECCA GARCÍA May 19, 1910 in Picacho, Territory of New México[31], daughter of JOSÉ GARCÍA and CARLOTA GARCÍA. He married (2) ANITA GONZÁLES[32] September 16, 1916 in Hondo, New México[33], daughter of JOSÉ GONZÁLES and MARÍA CHÁVEZ.

Notes for ROBERTO GUTIÉRREZ:
World War One Draft Registration Card indicates that he was born on July 18, 1882.
1930 Census: Living in Hondo, New México. His name is listed as Roberto Gonzáles.

Land Patent # NMR 0026686, on the authority of the Homestead Entry-Original (12 Stat. 392), May 20, 1862. Issued 151.71 acres on August 26, 1920.

Land Patent # NMR 0029140, on the authority of the Homestead Entry-Enlarged (35 Stat. 639), February 19, 1909. Issued 168.64 acres on October 18, 1923.

Land Patent # NMR 0036537, on the authority of the Homestead Entry-Stock Raising (39 Stat. 862), December 29, 1916. Issued 320 acres on April 20, 1925.

Notes for ANITA GONZÁLES:
Also known as Anne.

Children of ROBERTO GUTIÉRREZ and REBECCA GARCÍA are:
| | i. | MANUEL[5] GUTIÉRREZ. |
| | ii. | LUCILA GUTIÉRREZ. |

Children of ROBERTO GUTIÉRREZ and ANITA GONZÁLES are:
| 15. | iii. | JOSÉ GONZÁLES[5] GUTIÉRREZ, b. July 07, 1917, Hondo, New México; d. August 13, 1997, Hondo, New México. |
| | iv. | ROBERTO GONZÁLES GUTIÉRREZ[34], b. May 14, 1919, Hondo, New México[35]; d. September 1974, Hondo, New México. |

Notes for ROBERTO GONZÁLES GUTIÉRREZ:
June 25, 1942: Enlisted into the Army. Corporal US Army, WW II. Wounded in Italy April 29, 1945.

| | v. | FERNANDO GUTIÉRREZ[35], b. April 07, 1922, Tinnie, New México; d. March 08, 1972, Hondo, New México. |

Notes for FERNANDO GUTIÉRREZ:
November 30, 1942: Enlisted in the Army. Tec 5 CN, Company 302, Infantry WW II.

| | vi. | SOSTENO GUTIÉRREZ[36], b. December 16, 1924, Tinnie, New México[37]. |

Notes for SOSTENO GUTIÉRREZ:
US Navy, Seaman First Class. World War II.

| | vii. | JOSEFITA GUTIÉRREZ, b. Abt. 1925[37]. |
| | viii. | DOMINGO GUTIÉRREZ, b. Abt. 1929[37]. |

9. JOSEFA[4] GUTIÉRREZ *(JUANITA[3] SÁNCHEZ, CRECENCIO[2], FRANCISCO[1])* was born March 1892[38]. She married PROMETIVO BRADY, son of WILLIAM BRADY and BONIFACIA CHÁVES.

Notes for JOSEFA GUTIÉRREZ:
Also known as Josefita.

Notes for PROMETIVO BRADY:
1910 Census: Living in Roswell, Territory of New México. Listed as P.S. Brady.

Children of JOSEFA GUTIÉRREZ and PROMETIVO BRADY are:
    i.   ORLANDO[5] BRADY, b. Abt. 1909[39].
    ii.   CELIA BRADY, b. Abt. 1914[40].
    iii. PROMETIVO BRADY, b. Abt. 1918[40].
    iv. ROY BRADY, b. Abt. 1920[40].
    v.   ERVIN BRADY, b. Abt. 1922[40].
    vi. BONIFACIO BRADY, b. Abt. 1925[40].

10. ISABEL[4] GUTIÉRREZ *(JUANITA[3] SÁNCHEZ, CRECENCIO[2], FRANCISCO[1])[41]* was born April 02, 1893 in Hondo, Territory of New México, and died November 01, 1993 in Roswell, New México. She married MARTÍN LUCERO TORRES[42] January 05, 1911 in Hondo, Territory of New México[43], son of IGNACIO TORRES and MANUELA LUCERO.

Children of ISABEL GUTIÉRREZ and MARTÍN TORRES are:
    i.   FEDERICO[5] TORREZ[44], b. August 24, 1909; d. April 05, 2003; m. CECILIA MACKEY.

Notes for FEDERICO TORREZ:
Also known as Fred.

    ii.   ELOY TORREZ, b. Abt. 1912[45]; m. SAFINA SALCIDO.

Notes for SAFINA SALCIDO:
Also known as Savina.

16.   iii. IGNACIO TORREZ, b. October 02, 1913; d. September 15, 2005, San Patricio, New México.
       iv. ERMINIA TORREZ[46], b. February 04, 1916; d. May 15, 1975; m. CLOVÍS MONTES.
       v.   JULIA TORREZ[47], b. April 12, 1918, Hondo, New México[48]; d. July 17, 2003, El Paso, Téxas; m. (1) JOHN OTERO[49]; m. (2) FRED KIMBRELL[50], April 16, 1938[51].

Notes for FRED KIMBRELL:
1930 Census: Living with his grandfather Juan Kimbrell.
Died in an accident at the age of 24. Buried in Picacho, NM.

    vi. SIL TORREZ, b. Abt. 1922[52]; m. JOSIE FLACO.
    vii. EVA TORREZ, b. Abt. 1924[52]; m. RAMÓN JIMÉNEZ.
    viii. PRESILA TORREZ, b. Abt. 1929[52]; m. ROBERT RICHARDSON.
    ix. LARRY TORREZ, b. Private; m. DOROTHY CHÁVEZ.
    x.   LIBBY TORREZ, b. Private; m. CARL AUSTIN.
    xi. PATSY TORREZ, b. Private; m. BILL TURNER.

11. ANITA[4] GUTIÉRREZ *(JUANITA[3] SÁNCHEZ, CRECENCIO[2], FRANCISCO[1])* was born Abt. 1895 in Hondo, Territory of New México[53]. She married ADENAGO MARTÍNEZ Abt. 1914[53], son of MANUEL JEDAN and LUISA MARTÍNEZ.

Notes for ANITA GUTIÉRREZ:
Also known as Anne.
1910 Census: Living in Roswell, Territory of New México.

Children of ANITA GUTIÉRREZ and ADENAGO MARTÍNEZ are:
17.   i.   MACLOVIA[5] MARTÍNEZ, b. April 24, 1916; d. April 02, 1940, Hondo, New México.
       ii.   ERMILO MARTÍNEZ, b. Abt. 1919[53].
18.   iii. LOUISA MARTÍNEZ, b. December 08, 1920, San Patricio, New México; d. May 25, 1997.
       iv. FERMÍN MARTÍNEZ, b. Abt. 1925[53]; m. ELIZABETH RUE.

Notes for ELIZABETH RUE:
Also known as Lizzie.
Natural father was A. H. Rue.

	v.	MARTHA MARTÍNEZ, b. January 1930[53]; m. HENRY CADENA.
	vi.	ERNEST MARTÍNEZ, b. Private; m. PEGGY TITSWORTH.
	vii.	THERESA MARTÍNEZ, b. Private; m. FRANK RAMÍREZ.

12. MANUELITA MARTÍNEZ[4] SÁNCHEZ *(TORIVIO[3], CRECENCIO[2], FRANCISCO[1])* was born December 07, 1900 in Picacho, Territory of New México[54], and died February 01, 1981 in Ruidoso, New México[55]. She married SALOMON SÁNCHEZ[56] February 03, 1917 in Ruidoso, New México[57], son of ANTONIO SÁNCHEZ and TELESFORA MIRABAL.

Notes for MANUELITA MARTÍNEZ SÁNCHEZ:
Also known as Emma.

Notes for SALOMON SÁNCHEZ:
November 17, 1878: Baptized. Padrinos: Florencio Luna, Pilar Gonzáles.

Worked as a rock mason until he lost his eyesight.

Children of MANUELITA SÁNCHEZ and SALOMON SÁNCHEZ are:

19.	i.	CARLOS[5] SÁNCHEZ, b. June 10, 1918, Las Cruces, New México; d. April 16, 2009, El Paso, Téxas.
20.	ii.	EUFRACIA SÁNCHEZ, b. May 27, 1920, Glencoe, New México.
	iii.	LUVÍN SÁNCHEZ[58], b. June 18, 1922, Glencoe, New México; d. February 16, 1994, Ruidoso, New México; m. SUSANA CANDELARIA.
	iv.	AMALIA SÁNCHEZ[59], b. April 03, 1924, White Tail, New México[60]; d. July 10, 1927, San Patricio, New México.
21.	v.	ALBERTO SÁNCHEZ, b. June 09, 1927, San Patricio, New México; d. February 10, 2000, San Patricio, New México.
	vi.	PORFIRIO SÁNCHEZ, b. September 13, 1933, San Patricio, New México[61]; m. FLORA HERRERA[62], May 04, 1952, San Patricio, New México[63].

Notes for FLORA HERRERA:
Also known as Floripe.

13. PEDRO[4] VIGIL *(SARA[3] SÁNCHEZ, CRECENCIO[2], FRANCISCO[1])* was born January 30, 1908 in Picacho, Territory of New México, and died May 1971 in Roswell, New México. He married ESTELA CARRILLO March 17, 1938 in Hondo, New México.

Child of PEDRO VIGIL and ESTELA CARRILLO is:

	i.	CELESTINO C.[5] VIGIL[64], b. Abt. 1939, Hondo, New México; d. March 07, 1939, Hondo, New México.

14. GENOVEVA[4] VIGIL *(SARA[3] SÁNCHEZ, CRECENCIO[2], FRANCISCO[1])*[65] was born September 12, 1910 in Picacho, New México[66], and died April 12, 1989 in San Patricio, New México. She married SANTIAGO DOMINGUEZ HERRERA[67] December 23, 1936 in Carrizozo, New México[68], son of CRUZ HERRERA and PETRA DOMINGUEZ.

Child of GENOVEVA VIGIL and SANTIAGO HERRERA is:

	i.	ROGER[5] HERRERA, b. Private.

Generation No. 5

15. JOSÉ GONZÁLES[5] GUTIÉRREZ *(ROBERTO[4], JUANITA[3] SÁNCHEZ, CRECENCIO[2], FRANCISCO[1])*[69] was born July 07, 1917 in Hondo, New México[70], and died August 13, 1997 in Hondo, New México. He married DOLÓRES SEDILLO, daughter of MARTÍN SEDILLO and PORFIRIA OTERO.

Notes for JOSÉ GONZÁLES GUTIÉRREZ:
Also known as Joe. Social Security Death index records his birthdate as July 7, 1918.
1920 Census: Living in Tinnie, New México.

Notes for DOLÓRES SEDILLO:
Also known as Lola.

Child of JOSÉ GUTIÉRREZ and DOLÓRES SEDILLO is:
22.   i.   PRESCILLA[6] GUTIÉRREZ, b. July 28, 1951.

16. IGNACIO[5] TORREZ *(ISABEL[4] GUTIÉRREZ, JUANITA[3] SÁNCHEZ, CRECENCIO[2], FRANCISCO[1])*[70] was born October 02, 1913, and died September 15, 2005 in San Patricio, New México. He married AMANDA MONTES December 26, 1937, daughter of JESÚS MONTES and TOMASITA ALDAZ.

Children of IGNACIO TORREZ and AMANDA MONTES are:
23.   i.   JOE[6] TORREZ, b. February 18, 1947.
        ii.   ALBERT TORREZ, b. Private.
        iii.   BETTY TORREZ, b. Private.
        iv.   LORENA TORREZ, b. Private.
24.   v.   LYDIA TORREZ, b. Private.
        iv.   RAY TORREZ, b. Private.

17. MACLOVIA[5] MARTÍNEZ *(ANITA[4] GUTIÉRREZ, JUANITA[3] SÁNCHEZ, CRECENCIO[2], FRANCISCO[1])*[71] was born April 24, 1916[72], and died April 02, 1940 in Hondo, New México. She married ERMANDO CHÁVEZ December 07, 1935 in Carrizozo, New México[72], son of PABLO CHÁVEZ and JESÚSITA SÁNCHEZ.

Notes for MACLOVIA MARTÍNEZ:
Buried: San Patricio.

Children of MACLOVIA MARTÍNEZ and ERMANDO CHÁVEZ are:
25.   i.   PABLO MOISES[6] CHÁVEZ, b. July 13, 1936, San Patricio, New México; d. May 28, 2009, Amarillo, Téxas.
        ii.   BOBBY MARTÍNEZ CHÁVEZ[73], b. Private, San Patricio, New México.
        iii.   OZIEL CHÁVEZ[73], b. Private.
        iv.   LOUIS CHÁVEZ[73], b. Private.
        v.   LILLIAN CHÁVEZ[73], b. Private; m. DANNY GARCÍA[73].
        vi.   LUCY CHÁVEZ[73], b. Private.
        vii.   VIOLA CHÁVEZ, b. Private.
        viii. JEANE CHÁVEZ, b. Private.
        ix.   DANNY CHÁVEZ, b. Private.

18. LOUISA[5] MARTÍNEZ *(ANITA[4] GUTIÉRREZ, JUANITA[3] SÁNCHEZ, CRECENCIO[2], FRANCISCO[1])* was born December 08, 1920 in San Patricio, New México, and died May 25, 1997. She married FERMÍN SALAS October 21, 1939 in Hondo, New México[74], son of PABLO SALAS and PETRA SISNEROS.

Notes for LOUISA MARTÍNEZ:
Buried: The family farm in Hondo, New México.

Notes for FERMÍN SALAS:
Buried: The family farm in Hondo, New México.

Children of LOUISA MARTÍNEZ and FERMÍN SALAS are:
26.   i.   YOVANNE[6] SALAS, b. November 09, 1957, Roswell, New México.
        ii.   BOBBY SALAS, b. Private.
        iii.   DINA SALAS, b. Private.
        iv.   GILBERT SALAS, b. Private.
        v.   JAMES SALAS, b. Private.
        vi.   JERRY SALAS, b. Private.
        vii.   PAUL SALAS, b. Private.
        viii. SANDRA SALAS, b. Private.
        ix.   YOLANDA SALAS, b. Private.

19. CARLOS[5] SÁNCHEZ *(MANUELITA MARTÍNEZ[4], TORIVIO[3], CRECENCIO[2], FRANCISCO[1])*[75] was born June 10, 1918 in Las Cruces, New México, and died April 16, 2009 in El Paso, Téxas. He married ALVESITA MONTOYA[76] July 22, 1940 in Glencoe, New México[77], daughter of TEODORO MONTOYA and BERSABÉ SÁNCHEZ.

Notes for CARLOS SÁNCHEZ:
Lived almost his entire life in Ruidoso, NM.

Notes for ALVESITA MONTOYA:
Also known as Albesa.

Children of CARLOS SÁNCHEZ and ALVESITA MONTOYA are:
    i.   OLA[6] SÁNCHEZ, b. Private.
    ii.   ROBERT SÁNCHEZ, b. Private.
    iii. RICHARD SÁNCHEZ, b. Private.

20. EUFRACIA[5] SÁNCHEZ *(MANUELITA MARTÍNEZ[4], TORIVIO[3], CRECENCIO[2], FRANCISCO[1])* was born May 27, 1920 in Glencoe, New México[78]. She married (1) EUGENIO ANAYA. She married (2) ESTEVAN ROMERO.

Child of EUFRACIA SÁNCHEZ and EUGENIO ANAYA is:
    i.   CRISTINIA[6] ANAYA, b. Private.

21. ALBERTO[5] SÁNCHEZ *(MANUELITA MARTÍNEZ[4], TORIVIO[3], CRECENCIO[2], FRANCISCO[1])*[79] was born June 09, 1927 in San Patricio, New México, and died February 10, 2000 in San Patricio, New México. He married EVA MCKINLEY, daughter of EDUARDO SEDILLO and DOMINGA MAÉS.

Notes for ALBERTO SÁNCHEZ:
Also known as Albert.
Tec 5 US Army. WW II Veteran.

Notes for EVA MCKINLEY:
Raised by Eduardo Sedillo & Dominga Maés.

Child of ALBERTO SÁNCHEZ and EVA MCKINLEY is:
    i.   MIKE[6] SÁNCHEZ, b. Private.

Notes for MIKE SÁNCHEZ:
Raised by Eduardo Sedillo & Dominga Maés.

Generation No. 6

22. PRESCILLA[6] GUTIÉRREZ *(JOSÉ GONZÁLES[5], ROBERTO[4], JUANITA[3] SÁNCHEZ, CRECENCIO[2], FRANCISCO[1])* was born July 28, 1951. She married MELVIN CHÁVEZ, son of YSIDRO CHÁVEZ and PAUBLITA SÁNCHEZ.

Child of PRESCILLA GUTIÉRREZ and MELVIN CHÁVEZ is:
27.   i.   JENNIFER[7] CHÁVEZ, b. September 21, 1976.

23. JOE[6] TORREZ *(IGNACIO[5], ISABEL[4] GUTIÉRREZ, JUANITA[3] SÁNCHEZ, CRECENCIO[2], FRANCISCO[1])* was born February 18, 1947. He married PRISCILLA GÓMEZ, daughter of FRANK GÓMEZ and GRESELDA CHÁVEZ.

Children of JOE TORREZ and PRISCILLA GÓMEZ are:
    i.   ANGELA[7] TORREZ, b. August 19, 1975.
    ii.   MARLINA TORREZ, b. February 05, 1977.
    iii. AMANDA TORREZ, b. April 14, 1981.

24. LYDIA[6] TORREZ *(IGNACIO[5], ISABEL[4] GUTIÉRREZ, JUANITA[3] SÁNCHEZ, CRECENCIO[2], FRANCISCO[1])* was born Private. She married (1) GERALD D. MAÉZ, son of MIGUEL MAÉZ and ETHAL CHÁVEZ. She married (2) JOHNNY GÓMEZ, son of FRANK GÓMEZ and GRESELDA CHÁVEZ.

Children of LYDIA TORREZ and GERALD MAÉZ are:
    i.   JACKIE[7] MAÉZ, b. Private.

    ii.   JERRY MAÉZ, b. Private; m. MELISSA CANDELARIA.
    iii.   STACEY MAÉZ, b. Private.
    iv.   MICHAEL MAÉZ, b. Private.

25. PABLO MOISES[6] CHÁVEZ *(MACLOVIA[5] MARTÍNEZ, ANITA[4] GUTIÉRREZ, JUANITA[3] SÁNCHEZ, CRECENCIO[2], FRANCISCO[1])[80]* was born July 13, 1936 in San Patricio, New México, and died May 28, 2009 in Amarillo, Téxas.

Notes for PABLO MOISES CHÁVEZ:
Also known as Paul.

Children of PABLO MOISES CHÁVEZ are:
    i.   ROBERTA[7] CHÁVEZ, b. Private[81].
    ii.   RACHEL CHÁVEZ, b. Private[81].
    iii. MOISES CHÁVEZ, b. Private[81].

26. YOVANNE[6] SALAS *(LOUISA[5] MARTÍNEZ, ANITA[4] GUTIÉRREZ, JUANITA[3] SÁNCHEZ, CRECENCIO[2], FRANCISCO[1])* was born November 09, 1957 in Roswell, New México[82]. She married ROMÁN SÁNCHEZ, JR. May 25, 1974 in Ruidoso, New México[82], son of ROMÁN SÁNCHEZ and FLORINDA SALSBERRY.

Children of YOVANNE SALAS and ROMÁN SÁNCHEZ are:
    i.   FELIPÉ[7] SÁNCHEZ, b. Private, Ruidoso, New México.
    ii.   FABIAN SÁNCHEZ, b. Private, Ruidoso, New México.

Generation No. 7

27. JENNIFER[7] CHÁVEZ *(PRESCILLA[6] GUTIÉRREZ, JOSÉ GONZÁLES[5], ROBERTO[4], JUANITA[3] SÁNCHEZ, CRECENCIO[2], FRANCISCO[1])* was born September 21, 1976.

Child of JENNIFER CHÁVEZ is:
    i.   RIO[8] CHÁVEZ, b. Private.

Genealogy of Domingo Sánches

Generation No. 1

1. BARTOLO[1] SÁNCHES. He married GERTRUDIS GARCÍA.

Child of BARTOLO SÁNCHES and GERTRUDIS GARCÍA is:
2.   i.   MARÍA MANUELA[2] SÁNCHES, b. Abt. 1843.

Generation No. 2

2. MARÍA MANUELA[2] SÁNCHES *(BARTOLO[1])* was born Abt. 1843[1]. She married JOSÉ CEDILLO September 15, 1861 in Tomé, Territory of New México[2].

Children of MARÍA SÁNCHES and JOSÉ CEDILLO are:
3.   i.   DOMINGO[3] SÁNCHES, b. Abt. 1858; d. January 10, 1932, Lincoln, New México.
         ii.   PEDRO SEDILLO, b. Abt. 1862, Peralta, Territory of New México[3].
         iii.   JOSEFA SEDILLO, b. Abt. 1864, Peralta, Territory of New México[3].
         iv.   LUCÍA SEDILLO[4], b. Bef. June 24, 1867, Peralta, Territory of New México[5].
         v.   YSIDORA SEDILLO, b. Bef. May 16, 1869, Peralta, Territory of New México[6].

Generation No. 3

3. DOMINGO[3] SÁNCHES *(MARÍA MANUELA[2], BARTOLO[1])*[7] was born Abt. 1858[8], and died January 10, 1932 in Lincoln, New México. He married JUANITA ALMENDARES[9] October 09, 1876 in Tomé, Territory of New México[10], daughter of TELESFORO ALMENDARES and LONGINA CHOMINA.

Notes for DOMINGO SÁNCHES:
Adopted by José Cedillo. Natural father is unknown.
1870 Census: Living in Peralta, Territory of New México. (Domingo Sedillo, Born 1858)
1880 Census: Living in Tomé, Territory of New México. (Born 1854) His occupation was a sheep herder.
1900 Census: Living in San Patricio, Territory of New México. (Born November 1853)
1910 Census: living in San Patricio, Territory of New México. (Born 1853)

Notes for JUANITA ALMENDARES:
Also known as Juana.
1870 Census: Living in Tomé, Territory of New México.

Children of DOMINGO SÁNCHES and JUANITA ALMENDARES are:
         i.   BEATRIZ[4] SÁNCHEZ.
         ii.   NICOLÁS SÁNCHEZ[11], b. Bef. September 11, 1877, Tomé, Territory of New México[12]; m. JOSEFA TURRIETA, February 13, 1899, Tomé, Territory of New México[13].
4.   iii.   MANUELA ALMENDARES SÁNCHEZ, b. November 1878, Tomé, Territory of New México.
         iv.   MARÍA SÁNCHEZ, b. Abt. 1879, Tomé, Territory of New México[14].
5.   v.   MARIANITA SÁNCHEZ, b. September 18, 1882, Tomé, Territory of New México.
6.   vi.   VIRGINIA SÁNCHEZ, b. Bef. January 31, 1884, Tomé, Territory of New México.
         vii.   ESPERANZA SÁNCHEZ, b. September 18, 1888, San Patricio, Territory of New México[15]; d. Bef. 1910, Hondo, Territory of New México[16]; m. REFUGIO TORRES[17], September 27, 1905, Lincoln, Territory of New México[18].

Notes for ESPERANZA SÁNCHEZ:
Also known as María de la Esperanza Sánchez.
July 03, 1889: Baptized in Tomé, Territory of New México.

Notes for REFUGIO TORRES:
1900 - 1930: Census: Living in Hondo, Territory of New México.
Land Patent # NMR 0036867, on the authority of the Homestead Entry-Enlarged (35 Stat. 639), February 19, 1909. Issued 320 acres on June 12, 1922.

Land Patent # NMLC 0041321, on the authority of the Homestead Entry-Stock Raising (39 Stat. 862), December 29, 1916. Issued 320 acres on April 27, 1936.

        viii.   TELESFORA SÁNCHEZ, b. July 03, 1891, Socorro, Territory of New México[19]; m. CHARLES PHILLIP FREDERICK FRITZ[20], July 24, 1926[21].

Notes for TELESFORA SÁNCHEZ:
July 04, 1891: Baptized in Socorro, Territory of New México.

7.   ix.   TELESFORO SÁNCHEZ, b. September 04, 1893, La Junta, Territory of New México; d. January 03, 1967, Artesia, New México.
        x.   PABLO ALMENDARES SÁNCHEZ[22], b. January 1896, La Junta, Territory of New México[23]; d. October 17, 1933; m. DOMINGA MAÉS[24].
8.   xi.   MARGARITA ALMENDARES SÁNCHEZ, b. February 1900, La Junta, Territory of New México.

Generation No. 4

4. MANUELA ALMENDARES[4] SÁNCHEZ *(DOMINGO[3] SÁNCHES, MARÍA MANUELA[2], BARTOLO[1])* was born November 1878 in Tomé, Territory of New México[25]. She married DOMINGO ANALLA September 08, 1895 in Lincoln County, Territory of New México[26], son of PEDRO ANALLA and MARÍA SEDILLO.

Notes for DOMINGO ANALLA:
Also known as Domingo Anaya.
1900 Census: Living in Alamogordo, Guadalupe County, Territory of New México.

Child of MANUELA SÁNCHEZ and DOMINGO ANALLA is:
        i.   OFELIA[5] ANALLA, b. July 1897[27].

5. MARIANITA[4] SÁNCHEZ *(DOMINGO[3] SÁNCHES, MARÍA MANUELA[2], BARTOLO[1])*[28] was born September 18, 1882 in Tomé, Territory of New México[29]. She married JESÚS ALMENDARES November 22, 1902[30], son of AUGUSTÍN ALMENDARES and ALVINA DE ALMENDARES.

Notes for JESÚS ALMENDARES:
1910 Census: Living in Deming, Territory of New México.

Child of MARIANITA SÁNCHEZ and JESÚS ALMENDARES is:
        i.   MARTINA[5] ALMENDARES, b. Abt. 1905[31].

6. VIRGINIA[4] SÁNCHEZ *(DOMINGO[3] SÁNCHES, MARÍA MANUELA[2], BARTOLO[1])*[32] was born Bef. January 31, 1884 in Tomé, Territory of New México[33]. She married ALISANDRO TORRES[34] April 28, 1903 in Hondo, Territory of New México[35], son of PEDRO TORRES and DARIA GARCÍA.

Notes for VIRGINIA SÁNCHEZ:
Also known as María Virginia Sánchez.

Notes for ALISANDRO TORRES:
Also known as Alejandro, Alisandro.
Owned the Rancho de los Alamos. He later sold the ranch to Faustino Salcido.
1900 Census: Living in San Patricio, Territory of New México.

Children of VIRGINIA SÁNCHEZ and ALISANDRO TORRES are:
        i.   PEDRO[5] TORRES, b. 1901[36].
        ii.   LORENSO TORRES, b. 1902[36].
        iii.   JUAN SÁNCHEZ TORRES, b. 1909[36].
        iv.   NICOLÁS TORRES, b. May 11, 1910, Hondo, Territory of New México[37]; m. BENNIE SÁNCHEZ, August 25, 1931, Glencoe, New México[37].
        v.   MANUEL SÁNCHEZ TORRES, b. 1913[38].
        vi.   ESPERANZA TORRES, b. Abt. 1915[38].
        vii.   BEATRIZ TORRES, b. Abt. 1918[38].

7. TELESFORO[4] SÁNCHEZ *(DOMINGO[3] SÁNCHES, MARÍA MANUELA[2], BARTOLO[1])* was born September 04, 1893 in La Junta, Territory of New México, and died January 03, 1967 in Artesia, New México. He married CAROLINA MIRANDA September 11, 1912 in Lincoln, New México[39], daughter of PABLO MIRANDA and VICTORIANA GUTIÉRREZ.

Children of TELESFORO SÁNCHEZ and CAROLINA MIRANDA are:

i.   DOLORES[5] SÁNCHEZ[40], b. July 05, 1913, Hondo, New México[41]; d. September 10, 2003, Artesia, New México; m. ENRÍQUES SALSBERRY, February 04, 1933, Carrizozo, New México[41].

Notes for DOLORES SÁNCHEZ:
Also known as Lola.

Notes for ENRÍQUES SALSBERRY:
Also known as Henry.
1944: Moved from San Patricio, NM to Artesia, NM.
Died in an accident.

ii.   ROSA SÁNCHEZ, b. 1916, San Patricio, New México[42]; m. ANTONIO ARCHULETA.
iii.   CARLOS SÁNCHEZ, b. 1920, San Patricio, New México[42].
iv.   HARRY SÁNCHEZ, b. June 22, 1922, Hondo, New México[43]; m. EVA CHÁVEZ, February 21, 1944, Carrizozo, New México[43].

Notes for HARRY SÁNCHEZ:
1930 Census: Living in San Patricio, New México.
1944 Marriage Records: Living in Artesia, New México.

v.   REYNALDA SÁNCHEZ, b. 1922, San Patricio, New México[44].
vi.   AVRORA MIRANDA SÁNCHEZ, b. 1927, San Patricio, New México[44].

Notes for AVRORA MIRANDA SÁNCHEZ:
Also known as Dora.

vii.   RUBY SÁNCHEZ, b. 1928, San Patricio, New México[44].
viii.   ALBERTO SÁNCHEZ, b. Private, San Patricio, New México; d. November 04, 2011, Lubbock, Texas.

Notes for ALBERTO SÁNCHEZ:
1950: living in Artesia, New México.

ix.   BONIFACIO SÁNCHEZ, b. Private, San Patricio, New México.

Notes for BONIFACIO SÁNCHEZ:
Living in Las Vegas, Nevada.

x.   RUBÉN MIRANDA SÁNCHEZ, b. Private, San Patricio, New México.

Notes for RUBÉN MIRANDA SÁNCHEZ:
Living in Tucson, Arizona.

8. MARGARITA ALMENDARES[4] SÁNCHEZ *(DOMINGO[3] SÁNCHES, MARÍA MANUELA[2], BARTOLO[1])* was born February 1900 in La Junta, Territory of New México[45]. She married CURTIS PAGE.

Notes for MARGARITA ALMENDARES SÁNCHEZ:
Also known as Maggie.

Notes for CURTIS PAGE:
Also known as Curtiso.

Children of MARGARITA SÁNCHEZ and CURTIS PAGE are:

i.   MARY CORA[5] PAGE[46], b. Abt. 1926, Hondo, New México; d. April 21, 1939, San Patricio, New México.
ii.   DORA PAGE, b. Private.
iii.   JACK PAGE, b. Private.
iv.   ORLINDA PAGE, b. Private.

Genealogy of Jacinto Sánches de Iñigo

Francisco Muños

Generation No. 1

1. FRANCISCO[1] MUÑOS[1] was born Abt. 1585 in Sevilla, Andalucia, España. He married LEONOR ORTIS[1].

Child of FRANCISCO MUÑOS and LEONOR ORTIS is:
2.   i.   JACINTO[2] MUÑOS, b. Abt. 1610, Sevilla, Andalucia, España.

Generation No. 2

2. JACINTO[2] MUÑOS *(FRANCISCO[1])[1]* was born Abt. 1610 in Sevilla, Andalucia, España. He married MADALENA SÁNCHES DE IÑIGO[1] February 09, 1627 in Puebla de los Ángeles, Nueva España[2], daughter of PEDRO DE IÑIGO and MARÍA SÁNCHES.

Children of JACINTO MUÑOS and MADALENA DE IÑIGO are:
3.   i.   FRANCISCO MUÑOS[3] SÁNCHES, b. Bef. October 22, 1629, Puebla de los Ángeles, Nueva España.
         ii.   TERESA MUÑOS SÁNCHES[3], b. Bef. June 07, 1631, Puebla de los Ángeles, Nueva España.
         iii.   BLAS MUÑOS SÁNCHES[4], b. Bef. February 09, 1635, Puebla de los Ángeles, Nueva España.

Generation No. 3

3. FRANCISCO MUÑOS[3] SÁNCHES *(JACINTO[2] MUÑOS, FRANCISCO[1])[5]* was born Bef. October 22, 1629 in Puebla de los Ángeles, Nueva España[6]. He met JUANA LÓPES DE ARAGÓN[7] Bef. 1663 in Pueblo de San Ildefonso, El Reyno de Nuevo Méjico[7], daughter of FRANCISCO DE ARAGÓN and ANA BACA.

Notes for FRANCISCO MUÑOS SÁNCHES:
Baptized: Sagrario Metropolitano, Puebla de Zaragoza, Puebla, Nueva España. A second baptism record indicates he was baptised on October 18, 1628.

Children of FRANCISCO SÁNCHES and JUANA DE ARAGÓN are:
4.   i.   JACINTO SÁNCHES[4] DE IÑIGO, b. 1663, El Reyno de Nuevo Méjico, Nueva España; d. December 14, 1734, Alburquerque, El Reyno de Nuevo Méjico, Nueva España.
5.   ii.   FRANCISCA SÁNCHES DE IÑIGO, b. Abt. 1666, Bernalillo, El Reyno de Nuevo Méjico, Nueva España; d. Guadalupe del Paso, El Reyno de Nuevo Méjico, Nueva España.
6.   iii.   PEDRO SÁNCHES DE IÑIGO, b. Abt. 1673, El Reyno de Nuevo México, Nueva España; d. Bef. 1720.

Generation No. 4

Jacinto Sánches de Iñigo

4. JACINTO SÁNCHES[4] DE IÑIGO *(FRANCISCO MUÑOS[3] SÁNCHES, JACINTO[2] MUÑOS, FRANCISCO[1])[8]* was born 1663 in El Reyno de Nuevo Méjico, Nueva España[9], and died December 14, 1734 in Alburquerque, El Reyno de Nuevo Méjico, Nueva España[9]. He married (1) ISABEL TELLES JIRÓN 1688 in El Paso del Norte, El Reyno de Nuevo Méjico, Nueva España[9]. He married (2) MARÍA RODARTE DE CASTRO XABALERA[9] March 30, 1696 in Santa Fé, El Reyno de Nuevo Méjico, Nueva España[9], daughter of MIGUEL XABALERA and JUANA DE HERRERA.

Children of JACINTO DE IÑIGO and ISABEL JIRÓN are:
         i.   ANA JUANA ISABEL SÁNCHES[5] DE IÑIGO[9], b. Abt. 1688; m. MANUEL MONTOYA, December 22, 1704, Bernalillo, El Reyno de Nuevo Méjico, Nueva España[9].
7.   ii.   JOSÉ SÁNCHES DE IÑIGO, b. Abt. 1691, Guadalupe del Paso, El Reyno de Nuevo Méjico, Nueva España; d. Aft. June 18, 1752.
         iii.   GERTRUDIS SÁNCHES DE IÑIGO[9], b. Abt. 1692.
         iv.   PEDRO SÁNCHES DE IÑIGO[9], b. Abt. 1694.

8.   v.   JOAQUÍN SÁNCHES DE IÑIGO, b. Abt. 1695.

Children of JACINTO DE IÑIGO and MARÍA XABALERA are:
             vi.   MARÍA SÁNCHES[5] DE IÑIGO[9].
9.   vii.   MIGUEL SÁNCHES.
10.   viii.   FRANCISCO SÁNCHES, b. 1705, Atrisco, El Reyno de Nuevo Méjico, Nueva España; d. Bef. 1769.
11.   ix.   MARÍA GERTRUDIS SÁNCHES, b. May 07, 1713, Santa Cruz de la Cañada, El Reyno de Nuevo Méjico, Nueva España.

5. FRANCISCA SÁNCHES[4] DE IÑIGO *(FRANCISCO MUÑOS[3] SÁNCHES, JACINTO[2] MUÑOS, FRANCISCO[1])* was born Abt. 1666 in Bernalillo, El Reyno de Nuevo Méjico, Nueva España[9], and died in Guadalupe del Paso, El Reyno de Nuevo Méjico, Nueva España. She married JUAN GARCÍA DE NORIEGA May 04, 1681 in Guadalupe del Paso, El Reyno de Nuevo Méjico, Nueva España[10], son of ALONSO GARCÍA and TERESA VARELA.

Children of FRANCISCA DE IÑIGO and JUAN DE NORIEGA are:
             i.   JUAN ANTONIO GARCÍA[5] DE NORIEGA, b. Bef. March 15, 1682, Guadalupe del Paso, El Reyno de Nuevo Méjico, Nueva España[11].
             ii.   FRANCISCO GARCÍA DE NORIEGA, b. Abt. 1684, Guadalupe del Paso, El Reyno de Nuevo Méjico, Nueva España[12]; m. MARÍA JIRÓN DE TEJADA, November 22, 1710, Guadalupe del Paso, El Reyno de Nuevo Méjico, Nueva España[13].
             iii.   JOSEPH GARCÍA DE NORIEGA, b. Abt. 1687, Guadalupe del Paso, El Reyno de Nuevo Méjico, Nueva España[14].
             iv.   MARÍA GARCÍA DE NORIEGA[15], b. Abt. 1688, Guadalupe del Paso, El Reyno de Nuevo Méjico, Nueva España[16]; m. JUAN MARTÍN NAVARRO DE QUESADA, January 07, 1705, Guadalupe del Paso, El Reyno de Nuevo Méjico, Nueva España[17].
12.   v.   MARÍA MAGDALENA GARCÍA DE NORIEGA, b. Abt. 1693, Guadalupe del Paso, El Reyno de Nuevo México, Nueva España.
             vi.   JUAN ESTEBAN GARCÍA DE NORIEGA, b. Abt. 1696, El Reyno de Nuevo Méjico, Nueva España[18].
             vii.   JUANA GARCÍA DE NORIEGA[19], b. Bef. April 03, 1703, Bernalillo, El Reyno de Nuevo Méjico, Nueva España[20].

Pedro Sánches de Iñigo

6. PEDRO SÁNCHES[4] DE IÑIGO *(FRANCISCO MUÑOS[3] SÁNCHES, JACINTO[2] MUÑOS, FRANCISCO[1])[21]* was born Abt. 1673 in El Reyno de Nuevo México, Nueva España[22], and died Bef. 1720[22]. He married (1) LEONORA BACA[22] January 07, 1692 in Reál de San Lorenzo, El Reyno de Nuevo Méjico, Nueva España[22], daughter of IGNACIO BACA and JUANA ALMAZAN. He married (2) MARÍA JUANA LUJÁN[22] Abt. January 1698 in Bernalillo, El Reyno de Nuevo México, Nueva España[23], daughter of MATÍAS LUJÁN and FRANCISCA ROMERO.

Child of PEDRO DE IÑIGO and LEONORA BACA is:
13.   i.   PEDRO[5] SÁNCHES, b. Abt. 1696, El Reyno de Nuevo México, Nueva España.

Children of PEDRO DE IÑIGO and MARÍA LUJÁN are:
             ii.   ANTONIO SÁNCHES[5] DE IÑIGO[24].
             iii.   CRISTÓBAL SÁNCHES DE IÑIGO[24].
14.   iv.   EFIGENIA SÁNCHES DE IÑIGO, b. Atrisco, El Reyno de Nuevo Méjico, Nueva España.
             v.   JOSEPH SÁNCHES DE IÑIGO[24].
15.   vi.   JUANA SÁNCHES DE IÑIGO.
             vii.   LUGARDA SÁNCHES DE IÑIGO[24].
             viii.   MARÍA SÁNCHES DE IÑIGO[24].
16.   ix.   MANUELA SÁNCHES DE IÑIGO, b. Bef. January 13, 1701, Bernalillo, El Reyno de Nuevo Méjico, Nueva España.
17.   x.   ANTONIA SÁNCHES DE IÑIGO, b. Abt. 1703, El Reyno de Nuevo Méjico, Nueva España.
18.   xi.   OLAYA SÁNCHES DE IÑIGO, b. Abt. 1707, El Reyno de Nuevo Méjico, Nueva España; d. February 16, 1764, Villa de Santa Fé, El Reyno de Nuevo Méjico, Nueva España.
19.   xii.   FRANCISCA XAVIERA SÁNCHES DE IÑIGO, b. Bef. December 13, 1715, San Yldefonso, El Reyno de Nuevo Méjico, Nueva España.

Generation No. 5

7. JOSÉ SÁNCHES[5] DE IÑIGO *(JACINTO SÁNCHES[4], FRANCISCO MUÑOS[3] SÁNCHES, JACINTO[2] MUÑOS, FRANCISCO[1])* was born Abt. 1691 in Guadalupe del Paso, El Reyno de Nuevo Méjico, Nueva España[25], and died Aft. June 18, 1752[26]. He married (1) TERESA JARAMILLO[27]. He married (2) APOLONIA BERNAL[28] February 18, 1734 in Santa Cruz de la Cañada, El Reyno de Nuevo Méjico, Nueva España[29].

Children of JOSÉ DE IÑIGO and TERESA JARAMILLO are:

20.	i.	JACINTO[6] SÁNCHES, b. 1704, Atrisco, Nuevo México; d. February 04, 1763.
	ii.	ANTONIA SÁNCHES[30], b. Abt. 1727; d. April 27, 1794, Los Cháves, El Reyno de Nuevo Méjico.
21.	iii.	JUAN SÁNCHES, b. Abt. 1730.
	iv.	MARÍA GERTRUDIS SÁNCHES[30], b. July 20, 1731.

8. JOAQUÍN SÁNCHES[5] DE IÑIGO *(JACINTO SÁNCHES[4], FRANCISCO MUÑOS[3] SÁNCHES, JACINTO[2] MUÑOS, FRANCISCO[1])*[31] was born Abt. 1695. He married (1) MANUELA MONTOYA[32] December 10, 1719 in Santa Fé, El Reyno de Nuevo Méjico, Nueva España[33], daughter of ANDRES MONTOYA and ANTONIA DE GODOY. He married (2) MANUELA FRANCISCA GUERRERO DE LA MORA[34] August 20, 1725 in Albuquerque, El Reyno de Nuevo Méjico, Nueva España[35], daughter of FRANCISCO DE LA MORA and HARIA DE SELORGA.

Child of JOAQUÍN DE IÑIGO and MANUELA DE LA MORA is:

| | i. | MARÍA PAULA[6] SÁNCHES, m. JUAN BAUTISTA QUINTANA, April 17, 1746, Santa Cruz de la Cañada, El Reyno de Nuevo Méjico, Nueva España[36]. |

9. MIGUEL[5] SÁNCHES *(JACINTO SÁNCHES[4] DE IÑIGO, FRANCISCO MUÑOS[3] SÁNCHES, JACINTO[2] MUÑOS, FRANCISCO[1])*[37]. He married JUANA ROSALÍA BERNAL.

Child of MIGUEL SÁNCHES and JUANA BERNAL is:

| 22. | i. | BARBARA[6] BERNAL. |

10. FRANCISCO[5] SÁNCHES *(JACINTO SÁNCHES[4] DE IÑIGO, FRANCISCO MUÑOS[3] SÁNCHES, JACINTO[2] MUÑOS, FRANCISCO[1])*[38] was born 1705 in Atrisco, El Reyno de Nuevo Méjico, Nueva España, and died Bef. 1769. He married JOSEFA DURÁN Y CHÁVES[39] 1725 in Alburquerque, El Reyno de Nuevo Méjico, Nueva España[40], daughter of PEDRO CHÁVES and JUANA HINOJOS.

Children of FRANCISCO SÁNCHES and JOSEFA CHÁVES are:

23.	i.	JUAN CRISTÓBAL[6] SÁNCHES, b. Bef. September 21, 1726, Atrisco, El Reyno de Nuevo Méjico, Nueva España; d. February 27, 1798, Tomé, El Reyno de Nuevo Méjico, Nueva España.
24.	ii.	MARÍA BARBARA SÁNCHES, b. November 26, 1730, Alburquerque, El Reyno de Nuevo México, Nueva España.
25.	iii.	TERESA SÁNCHES, b. 1732; d. November 28, 1761, Alburquerque, El Reyno de Nuevo México, Nueva España.
26.	iv.	DIEGO ANTONIO SÁNCHES, b. Abt. 1736, El Reyno de Nuevo Méjico, Nueva España.
	v.	MARCOS SÁNCHES[41], b. Abt. 1742, Tomé, El Reyno de Nuevo Méjico, Nueva España; m. MARGARITA VALDÉS[41], February 22, 1763, Alburquerque, El Reyno de Nuevo Méjico, Nueva España[41].
27.	vi.	JOAQUÍN SÁNCHES, b. 1746, Tomé, El Reyno de Neuvo México, Nueva España.

Pedro Durán y Cháves

11. MARÍA GERTRUDIS[5] SÁNCHES *(JACINTO SÁNCHES[4] DE IÑIGO, FRANCISCO MUÑOS[3] SÁNCHES, JACINTO[2] MUÑOS, FRANCISCO[1])*[42] was born May 07, 1713 in Santa Cruz de la Cañada, El Reyno de Nuevo Méjico, Nueva España. She married PEDRO DURÁN Y CHÁVES[43] January 12, 1728 in Alburquerque, El Reyno de Nuevo Méjico, Nueva España[44], son of FERNANDO CHÁVES and LUCÍA DE SALAS.

Notes for PEDRO DURÁN Y CHÁVES:

Feb 17, 1706: Was a soldier in the military, he was one of the founders of San Francisco de Alburquerque.

1713-1716: Was promoted to squadron leader of his militia.

1714-1715: Was appointed as the Alcalde Mayor of Los Padillas.

Aug 20, 1716: Was involved in a Hopi campaign.

1706: One member of the twelve founding families of San Francisco de Alburquerque.

1713: Was listed as a squadron leader of the militia. He escorted ex-Gobernador Felix Martínez back to Ciudad de México.

1716: Took part in the Moqui Campaign.

Children of MARÍA SÁNCHES and PEDRO CHÁVES are:
    i.   ANTONIO DURÁN Y[6] CHÁVES[45], b. Abt. 1729.
    ii.   MARÍA DURÁN Y CHÁVES[46], b. Abt. 1730.
    iii. SALVADOR MANUEL DURÁN Y CHÁVES[47], b. June 09, 1731, Alburquerque, El Reyno de Nuevo Méjico.
    iv. JOSÉ DURÁN Y CHÁVES[48], b. June 01, 1733, Alburquerque, El Reyno de Nuevo Méjico; d. December 09, 1772.

Notes for JOSÉ DURÁN Y CHÁVES:
December 9, 1772: Known as José Cháves de Nuevo Méjico. He was killed by Apaches near El Paso.

    v.   PEDRO DURÁN Y CHÁVES[49], b. Abt. 1734, Atrisco, El Reyno de Nuevo Méjico; d. January 1846.

12. MARÍA MAGDALENA GARCÍA[5] DE NORIEGA *(FRANCISCA SÁNCHES[4] DE IÑIGO, FRANCISCO MUÑOS[3] SÁNCHES, JACINTO[2] MUÑOS, FRANCISCO[1])* was born Abt. 1693 in Guadalupe del Paso, El Reyno de Nuevo México, Nueva España[50]. She married JOSÉ TELLES JIRÓN January 20, 1712 in Guadalupe del Paso, El Reyno de Nuevo México, Nueva España[51].

Children of MARÍA DE NORIEGA and JOSÉ JIRÓN are:
    i.   JUANA TELLES[6] JIRÓN.
    ii. MARÍA CANDELARIA TELLES JIRÓN, b. Abt. 1720; m. ALEJADRO PADILLA.

13. PEDRO[5] SÁNCHES *(PEDRO SÁNCHES[4] DE IÑIGO, FRANCISCO MUÑOS[3] SÁNCHES, JACINTO[2] MUÑOS, FRANCISCO[1])* was born Abt. 1696 in El Reyno de Nuevo México, Nueva España[52]. He married MICAELA QUINTANA January 20, 1720 in Santa Cruz de la Cañada, El Reyno de Nuevo Méjico, Nueva España[52], daughter of MIGUEL DE QUINTANA and GERTRUDIS TRUJILLO.

Children of PEDRO SÁNCHES and MICAELA QUINTANA are:
28.   i.   PEDRO YGNACIO[6] SÁNCHES.
29.   ii. FRANCISCO XAVIER SÁNCHES, b. Abt. 1728.
30.   iii. MARÍA ANTONIA TERESA SÁNCHES, b. December 11, 1731, Santa Cruz de la Cañada, El Reyno de Nuevo Méjico.
31.   iv. BERNARDO ANTONIO SÁNCHES, b. Bef. April 09, 1733.

14. EFIGENIA SÁNCHES[5] DE IÑIGO *(PEDRO SÁNCHES[4], FRANCISCO MUÑOS[3] SÁNCHES, JACINTO[2] MUÑOS, FRANCISCO[1])*[53] was born in Atrisco, El Reyno de Nuevo Méjico, Nueva España.

Child of EFIGENIA SÁNCHES DE IÑIGO is:
32.   i.   PEDRO YGNACIO[6] SÁNCHES, b. Abt. 1741.

15. JUANA SÁNCHES[5] DE IÑIGO *(PEDRO SÁNCHES[4], FRANCISCO MUÑOS[3] SÁNCHES, JACINTO[2] MUÑOS, FRANCISCO[1])*[53]. She married FRANCISCO GONZÁLES August 30, 1731 in Santa Cruz de la Cañada, El Reyno de Nuevo México, Nueva España[54].

Children of JUANA DE IÑIGO and FRANCISCO GONZÁLES are:
    i.   MARÍA ANTONIA[6] GONZÁLES[55], b. Bef. February 12, 1733, Santa Cruz de la Cañada, El Reyno de Nuevo México, Nueva España.
    ii. JUANA DE LA CRUZ GONZÁLES[55], b. Bef. May 10, 1744, Santa Cruz de la Cañada, El Reyno de Nuevo México, Nueva España.
    iii. MARÍA MANUELA GONZÁLES[55], b. Bef. December 24, 1745, Santa Cruz de la Cañada, El Reyno de Nuevo México, Nueva España.
    iv. MARÍA GONZÁLES[55], b. Bef. September 08, 1747, Santa Cruz de la Cañada, El Reyno de Nuevo México, Nueva España.
    v. JUAN BAPTISTA GONZÁLES[55], b. Bef. December 17, 1749, Santa Cruz de la Cañada, El Reyno de Nuevo México, Nueva España.
    vi. MARÍA CLARA GONZÁLES[56], b. February 20, 1766, Santa Cruz de la Cañada, El Reyno de Nuevo México, Nueva España.

16. MANUELA SÁNCHES[5] DE IÑIGO *(PEDRO SÁNCHES[4], FRANCISCO MUÑOS[3] SÁNCHES, JACINTO[2] MUÑOS, FRANCISCO[1])*[57] was born Bef. January 13, 1701 in Bernalillo, El Reyno de Nuevo Méjico, Nueva España. She married MANUEL MONTES VIGIL 1720.

Children of MANUELA DE IÑIGO and MANUEL VIGIL are:
    i.   JUAN LUÍS⁶ VIGIL.
    ii. MARÍA ANTONIA VIGIL.
    iii. JOSEFA VIGIL.
    iv. ISABEL VIGIL.
    v. MANUEL ANTONIO VIGIL.

17. ANTONIA SÁNCHES⁵ DE IÑIGO *(PEDRO SÁNCHES⁴, FRANCISCO MUÑOS³ SÁNCHES, JACINTO² MUÑOS, FRANCISCO¹)* was born Abt. 1703 in El Reyno de Nuevo Méjico, Nueva España[58]. She married JUAN JOSÉ DE LA CERDA January 10, 1721 in Santa Cruz de la Cañada, El Reyno de Nuevo Méjico, Nueva España[59], son of JUAN DE LA CERDA and MARÍA DE CHAVARRIA.

Children of ANTONIA DE IÑIGO and JUAN DE LA CERDA are:
    i.   FRANCISCO⁶ DE LA CERDA, b. Abt. 1721.
    ii. JUAN DE LA CERDA, b. September 07, 1723, San Yldefonso, El Reyno de Nuevo Méjico, Nueva España.

18. OLAYA SÁNCHES⁵ DE IÑIGO *(PEDRO SÁNCHES⁴, FRANCISCO MUÑOS³ SÁNCHES, JACINTO² MUÑOS, FRANCISCO¹)*[60] was born Abt. 1707 in El Reyno de Nuevo Méjico, Nueva España[61], and died February 16, 1764 in Villa de Santa Fé, El Reyno de Nuevo Méjico, Nueva España. She married DIEGO GONZÁLES April 04, 1720 in Santa Cruz de la Cañada, El Reyno de Nuevo Méjico, Nueva España[61], son of ANDRÉS GONZÁLES and FRANCISCA DE GAMBOA.

Children of OLAYA DE IÑIGO and DIEGO GONZÁLES are:
33.   i.   CRISTÓBAL⁶ GONZÁLES, b. Abt. 1720.
       ii. JOSÉ GONZÁLES, b. Abt. 1745.

19. FRANCISCA XAVIERA SÁNCHES⁵ DE IÑIGO *(PEDRO SÁNCHES⁴, FRANCISCO MUÑOS³ SÁNCHES, JACINTO² MUÑOS, FRANCISCO¹)*[62] was born Bef. December 13, 1715 in San Yldefonso, El Reyno de Nuevo Méjico, Nueva España[63]. She married JUAN TADEO DE QUINTANA[64] September 06, 1734 in Santa Cruz de la Cañada, El Reyno de Nuevo México, Nueva España[65].

Children of FRANCISCA DE IÑIGO and JUAN DE QUINTANA are:
    i.   JOSÉ JULIÁN⁶ QUINTANA.
    ii. MARÍA PETRONILA QUINTANA, b. Bef. May 31, 1735.
    iii. MANUELA QUINTANA, b. Bef. April 10, 1739.
    iv. CLAUDIA QUINTANA, b. Bef. January 23, 1745.
    v. ANTONIA JULIANA QUINTANA, b. Bef. February 23, 1749.
    vi. ANTONIA QUINTANA, b. Bef. September 27, 1750.
    vii. XAVIERA QUINTANA, b. Bef. April 04, 1753.
    viii. GREGORIO QUINTANA, b. Bef. November 18, 1755.
    ix. SEBASTIANA QUINTANA, b. Bef. January 24, 1756.

Generation No. 6

20. JACINTO⁶ SÁNCHES *(JOSÉ SÁNCHES⁵ DE IÑIGO, JACINTO SÁNCHES⁴, FRANCISCO MUÑOS³ SÁNCHES, JACINTO² MUÑOS, FRANCISCO¹)*[66] was born 1704 in Atrisco, Nuevo México[67], and died February 04, 1763[67]. He married EFIGENIA DURÁN Y CHÁVES[68] September 28, 1732 in Alburquerque, El Reyno de Nuevo Méjico, Nueva España[69], daughter of PEDRO CHÁVES and JUANA HINOJOS.

Children of JACINTO SÁNCHES and EFIGENIA CHÁVES are:
    i.   MARÍA GERTRUDIS⁷ SÁNCHES[70], b. Atrisco, El Reyno de Nuevo Méjico.
34.   ii. PEDRO SÁNCHES, b. Abt. 1734, Atrisco, El Reyno de Nuevo Méjico.
      iii. JUAN DOMINGO SÁNCHES, b. Abt. 1741[71]; d. Bef. March 10, 1780, Alburquerque, El Reyno de Nuevo Méjico.
      iv. URSULA BERNADINA SÁNCHES, b. Abt. 1743[71].
      v. FELICIANA (FELICIDAD) SÁNCHES, b. Abt. 1744[71].
      vi. DOROTEA SÁNCHES, b. Abt. 1747[71].
      vii. MARÍA JOSEFA SÁNCHES, b. Abt. 1750[71].
      viii. JUAN MANUEL SÁNCHES, b. Abt. 1755[72].

21. JUAN[6] SÁNCHES *(JOSÉ SÁNCHES[5] DE IÑIGO, JACINTO SÁNCHES[4], FRANCISCO MUÑOS[3] SÁNCHES, JACINTO[2] MUÑOS, FRANCISCO[1])[73]* was born Abt. 1730. He married BARBARA GALLEGOS October 02, 1752 in Alburquerque, El Reino de Nuevo Méjico, Nueva España[74].

Children of JUAN SÁNCHES and BARBARA GALLEGOS are:
35.	i.	TERESA[7] SÁNCHES.
	ii.	ANTONIA GERTRUDIS SÁNCHES, b. Bef. June 12, 1753, Albuquerque, Nuevo México, La República de México[75].
	iii.	FRANCISCA MARTINA SÁNCHES, b. Bef. February 04, 1755, Alburquerque, El Reino de Nuevo Méjico, Nueva España[75].

22. BARBARA[6] BERNAL *(MIGUEL[5] SÁNCHES, JACINTO SÁNCHES[4] DE IÑIGO, FRANCISCO MUÑOS[3] SÁNCHES, JACINTO[2] MUÑOS, FRANCISCO[1]).* She married JOSÉ MIGUEL LÓPEZ January 20, 1764 in Santa Cruz de la Cañada, El Reino de Nuevo Méjico, Nueva España.

Child of BARBARA BERNAL and JOSÉ LÓPEZ is:
	i.	MARÍA LORENZA[7] LÓPEZ, b. August 10, 1785, Santa Cruz de la Cañada, El Reino de Nuevo Méjico, Nueva España[76].

Juan Cristóbal Sánches

23. JUAN CRISTÓBAL[6] SÁNCHES *(FRANCISCO[5], JACINTO SÁNCHES[4] DE IÑIGO, FRANCISCO MUÑOS[3] SÁNCHES, JACINTO[2] MUÑOS, FRANCISCO[1])[77]* was born Bef. September 21, 1726 in Atrisco, El Reyno de Nuevo Méjico, Nueva España, and died February 27, 1798 in Tomé, El Reyno de Nuevo Méjico, Nueva España. He married (1) ELENA JARAMILLO Abt. 1746[78]. He married (2) JUANA TOMÁSA DURÁN Y CHÁVES[79] September 24, 1758 in Alburquerque, El Reyno de Nuevo Méjico, Nueva España[80]. He married (3) MARÍA ANTONIA DURÁN Y CHÁVES November 30, 1782 in Alburquerque, El Reyno de Nuevo Méjico, Nueva España, daughter of TOMÁS CHÁVES and TOMASA PADILLA.

Notes for JUAN CRISTÓBAL SÁNCHES:
Alcálde Mayor of the Villa of Albuquerque.

Child of JUAN SÁNCHES and ELENA JARAMILLO is:
	i.	ANTONIO ROMÁN[7] SÁNCHES, b. 1754[81]; d. April 03, 1826.

Children of JUAN SÁNCHES and JUANA CHÁVES are:
	ii.	MANUELA DE JESÚS[7] SÁNCHES[82], d. December 12, 1772, Alburquerque, El Reyno de Nuevo Méjico, Nueva España[83].
36.	iii.	MARIANO SÁNCHES, b. Abt. 1750.
	iv.	LUGARDA SÁNCHES, b. Abt. 1760[84]; d. October 30, 1761, Alburquerque, El Reyno de Nuevo Méjico, Nueva España[85].
37.	v.	MARÍA BÁRBARA SÁNCHES, b. Abt. 1762, Los Cháves, El Reyno de Nuevo Méjico, Nueva España.
38.	vi.	PEDRO JUAN BAUTISTA SÁNCHES, b. Abt. 1762; d. October 27, 1798, Valencia, El Reyno de Nuevo Méjico, Nueva España.
39.	vii.	JOSÉ SÁNCHES, b. Abt. 1765, Los Cháves, El Reyno de Nuevo Méjico, Nueva España; d. Abt. February 1803.
	viii.	JUAN CRISTÓBAL SÁNCHES, b. Abt. 1769[85]; d. February 12, 1812[86].
40.	ix.	DOMINGO DE JESÚS SÁNCHES, b. Abt. 1773, Los Cháves, El Reyno de Nuevo Méjico, Nueva España.
	x.	MARÍA YSABEL DE LA LUZ SÁNCHES, b. Bef. January 30, 1776[87].
41.	xi.	JOSÉ GREGORIO DE LA TRINIDAD SÁNCHES, b. November 19, 1777, Los Cháves, El Reyno de Nuevo Méjico, Nueva España; d. Bef. 1856.
	vii.	MANUEL SÁNCHES, b. 1779[88].
42.	xiii.	DIEGO ANTONIO SÁNCHES, b. Abt. 1769, Pueblo de Ysleta, El Reyno de Nuevo Méjico, Nueva España.

24. MARÍA BARBARA[6] SÁNCHES *(FRANCISCO[5], JACINTO SÁNCHES[4] DE IÑIGO, FRANCISCO MUÑOS[3] SÁNCHES, JACINTO[2] MUÑOS, FRANCISCO[1])[89]* was born November 26, 1730 in Alburquerque, El Reyno de Nuevo México, Nueva España. She married JOAQUÍN JOSÉ PINO August 28, 1764 in Tomé, El Reyno de Nuevo México, Nueva España[90].

Children of MARÍA SÁNCHES and JOAQUÍN PINO are:
    i.   JOAQUÍN MARIANO[7] PINO, b. Abt. 1765[91].
    ii.   ANA MARÍA CATALINA PINO, b. Abt. 1766[91].

25. TERESA[6] SÁNCHES *(FRANCISCO[5], JACINTO SÁNCHES[4] DE IÑIGO, FRANCISCO MUÑOS[3] SÁNCHES, JACINTO[2] MUÑOS, FRANCISCO[1])*[92] was born 1732, and died November 28, 1761 in Alburquerque, El Reyno de Nuevo México, Nueva España. She married MATEO JOSÉ PINO Abt. 1751[93].

Notes for MATEO JOSÉ PINO:
Also known as Juan Mateo Pino.

Children of TERESA SÁNCHES and MATEO PINO are:
    i.   PEDRO BAUTISTA[7] PINO[94], b. Abt. 1752, Tomé, El Reyno de Nuevo Méjico, Nueva España.
    ii.   MARIANO ANTONIO PINO[95], b. February 06, 1752.
    iii.   JUAN FRANCISCO PINO[96], b. March 19, 1753.
    iv.   ALEJANDRO RICARDO PINO[97], b. April 07, 1756[98].
    v.   CARLOS CASMIRO PINO[99], b. November 28, 1761[100].

26. DIEGO ANTONIO[6] SÁNCHES *(FRANCISCO[5], JACINTO SÁNCHES[4] DE IÑIGO, FRANCISCO MUÑOS[3] SÁNCHES, JACINTO[2] MUÑOS, FRANCISCO[1])*[101] was born Abt. 1736 in El Reyno de Nuevo Méjico, Nueva España[101]. He married ANA MARÍA OLAYA ALVAREZ DEL CASTILLO[101] April 06, 1756 in Los Padillas, El Reyno de Nuevo México, Nueva España.

Children of DIEGO SÁNCHES and ANA DEL CASTILLO are:
    i.   ANTONIO JOSÉ[7] SÁNCHES[102], m. MARÍA CONCEPCIÓN PADILLA, March 24, 1790, Isleta, El Reino de Nuevo Méjico, Nueva España[103].
    ii.   DIEGO SÁNCHES[104].
    iii.   MARÍA MANUELA SÁNCHES, b. Abt. 1758[104].
    iv.   MARÍA JOSEFA SILVERIA SÁNCHES[104], b. Abt. 1760[105].
    v.   MARÍA MICHAELA SÁNCHES, b. Abt. 1765[106]; m. JOAQUÍN LAIN, November 07, 1787, Isleta, El Reino de Nuevo Méjico, Nueva España[107].
    vi.   TERESA DE JESÚS SÁNCHES, b. Abt. 1766[108].
    vii.   MANUELA ANTONIA SÁNCHES[108], b. Abt. 1767[109]; m. (1) JUAN FRANCISCO BACA, December 05, 1781, Isleta, El Reino de Nuevo Méjico, Nueva España[110]; m. (2) MARIANO ARAGÓN, May 05, 1789, Isleta, El Reino de Nuevo Méjico, Nueva España[110].
    viii. ANA MARÍA SÁNCHES[111], b. Abt. 1769[112].
    ix.   BARBARA SÁNCHES[113], b. June 07, 1774, Isleta, El Reino de Nuevo Méjico, Nueva España[114].
43.   x.   MARIANA ANTONIA SÁNCHES, b. Abt. 1773; d. May 1834, Valencia, El Reyno de Nuevo Méjico, Nueva España.

27. JOAQUÍN[6] SÁNCHES *(FRANCISCO[5], JACINTO SÁNCHES[4] DE IÑIGO, FRANCISCO MUÑOS[3] SÁNCHES, JACINTO[2] MUÑOS, FRANCISCO[1])*[115] was born 1746 in Tomé, El Reyno de Neuvo México, Nueva España. He married ANA MARÍA PADILLA[115] April 16, 1769 in Los Padillas, El Reyno de Nuevo Mexico, Nueva España[116].

Children of JOAQUÍN SÁNCHES and ANA PADILLA are:
    i.   JULIAN[7] SÁNCHES[117], b. Abt. 1772.
44.   ii.   DIEGO ANTONIO SÁNCHES.

28. PEDRO YGNACIO[6] SÁNCHES *(PEDRO[5], PEDRO SÁNCHES[4] DE IÑIGO, FRANCISCO MUÑOS[3] SÁNCHES, JACINTO[2] MUÑOS, FRANCISCO[1])*. He married MARÍA DE LA LUZ MESTAS October 28, 1755 in Santa Cruz de la Cañada, El Reyno de Nuevo México, Nueva España[118].

Children of PEDRO SÁNCHES and MARÍA MESTAS are:
    i.   ANA JOSEFA[7] SÁNCHES[119], b. Bef. May 29, 1757, Ranchitos de Ojo Caliente, El Reyno de Nuevo Méjico, Nueva España.
    ii.   JOAQUÍN MARIANO SÁNCHES[119], b. Bef. October 06, 1759, Ranchitos de Ojo Caliente, El Reyno de Nuevo Méjico, Nueva España.
    iii.   MARÍA GREGORIA DE LA CONSOLACIÓN SÁNCHES[119], b. Bef. November 19, 1761, Ranchitos de Ojo Caliente, El Reyno de Nuevo Méjico, Nueva España.

    iv.   MARÍA LUISA SÁNCHES[119], b. Bef. July 09, 1768, Ranchitos de Ojo Caliente, El Reyno de Nuevo Méjico, Nueva España.

    v.   JOSÉ YGNACIO SÁNCHES[119], b. August 08, 1776, Ranchitos de Ojo Caliente, El Reyno de Nuevo Méjico, Nueva España.

29. FRANCISCO XAVIER[6] SÁNCHES *(PEDRO[5], PEDRO SÁNCHES[4] DE IÑIGO, FRANCISCO MUÑOS[3] SÁNCHES, JACINTO[2] MUÑOS, FRANCISCO[1])*[120] was born Abt. 1728. He married ISABEL PACHECO[120] August 20, 1743 in San Juan de los Caballeros, El Reyno de Nuevo Méjico, Nueva España[120].

Children of FRANCISCO SÁNCHES and ISABEL PACHECO are:

    i.   DIEGO RAFAEL[7] SÁNCHES.
    ii.   ELENA SÁNCHES, Adopted child.
    iii.   FRANCISCO XAVIER SÁNCHES, Adopted child.
    iv.   FRANSICSO JOSÉ SÁNCHES.
    v.   GERTRUDIS SÁNCHES.
    vi.   MARÍA DE LA CONCEPCIÓN SÁNCHES, Adopted child.
    vii.   JUAN ANTONIO SÁNCHES, b. Bef. January 09, 1748, San Juan de los Caballeros, El Reyno de Nuevo Méjico, Nueva España.
    viii.   JOAQUÍN JOSÉ SÁNCHES, b. Bef. March 18, 1757, San Juan de los Caballeros, El Reyno de Nuevo Méjico, Nueva España.
    ix.   JOSÉ ANTONIO SÁNCHES, b. Bef. March 02, 1760.
    x.   YGNACIO MARIANO SÁNCHES, b. March 02, 1762, San Juan de los Caballeros, El Reyno de Nuevo Méjico, Nueva España.
    xi.   ANA MARÍA SÁNCHES, b. Bef. March 20, 1764, San Juan de los Caballeros, El Reyno de Nuevo Méjico, Nueva España.

30. MARÍA ANTONIA TERESA[6] SÁNCHES *(PEDRO[5], PEDRO SÁNCHES[4] DE IÑIGO, FRANCISCO MUÑOS[3] SÁNCHES, JACINTO[2] MUÑOS, FRANCISCO[1])* was born December 11, 1731 in Santa Cruz de la Cañada, El Reyno de Nuevo Méjico[121]. She married JUAN JOSÉ BUSTOS May 24, 1746 in Santa Cruz de la Cañada, El Reyno de Nuevo Méjico[122], son of JOSÉ DE VALDES and JOSEFA ONTIVEROS.

Notes for JUAN JOSÉ BUSTOS:
Also known as Juan Ontiveros.

Children of MARÍA SÁNCHES and JUAN BUSTOS are:

    i.   MARÍA[7] BUSTOS, b. Bef. June 01, 1747.
    ii.   JOSÉ ANTONIO BUSTOS, b. Bef. October 22, 1749.
    iii.   MARÍA GERTRUDIS BUSTOS, b. Bef. September 30, 1750.
    iv.   JOSÉ ANTONIO BUSTOS, b. Bef. April 07, 1753.
    v.   FRANCISCO BUSTOS, b. Bef. January 19, 1756.
    vi.   MARÍA MIQUELA BUSTOS, b. Bef. January 29, 1759.
    vii.   JUAN JOSÉ DOMINGO BUSTOS, b. July 15, 1763, Santa Cruz de la Cañada, El Reyno de Nuevo Méjico[123]; m. ANA MARIA ARCHULETA, September 04, 1788, Santa Cruz de la Cañada, El Reyno de Nuevo Méjico[124].
    viii.   MARÍA DE LA TRINIDAD BUSTOS, b. Abt. 1767.
    ix.   JOSÉ RAFAEL BUSTOS, b. Bef. November 29, 1770.
45.   x.   MARÍA JOSEFA BUSTOS, b. Abt. 1775, Santa Cruz de la Cañada, El Reyno de Nuevo Méjico, Nueva España.

31. BERNARDO ANTONIO[6] SÁNCHES *(PEDRO[5], PEDRO SÁNCHES[4] DE IÑIGO, FRANCISCO MUÑOS[3] SÁNCHES, JACINTO[2] MUÑOS, FRANCISCO[1])* was born Bef. April 09, 1733[125]. He married (1) BARBARA GALLEGOS. He married (2) NICOLASA VALDÉS December 22, 1783 in Abiquiu, El Reyno de Nuevo Méjico, Nueva España.

Children of BERNARDO SÁNCHES and BARBARA GALLEGOS are:

    i.   GERTRUDIS YLDEFONSA[7] SÁNCHES, b. Bef. April 25, 1767.
    ii.   JUANA PAULA SÁNCHES, b. Bef. November 17, 1769.
    iii.   MANUEL ANTONIO SÁNCHES, b. Abt. 1778.

Child of BERNARDO SÁNCHES and NICOLASA VALDÉS is:

    iv.   JOSÉ MANUEL[7] SÁNCHES.

32. PEDRO YGNACIO⁶ SÁNCHES *(EFIGENIA SÁNCHES⁵ DE IÑIGO, PEDRO SÁNCHES⁴, FRANCISCO MUÑOS³ SÁNCHES, JACINTO² MUÑOS, FRANCISCO¹)* was born Abt. 1741[126]. He married (1) MARÍA MANUELA MONTES VIGIL November 22, 1761 in Santa Fé, El Reyno de Nuevo México, Nueva España[127]. He married (2) MARÍA DOLÓRES QUINTANA July 06, 1781 in Santa Cruz de la Cañada, El Reyno de Nuevo México, Nueva España[128].

Children of PEDRO SÁNCHES and MARÍA QUINTANA are:

    i.   MARCOS RAFAÉL⁷ SÁNCHES[129], b. April 25, 1782, Santa Cruz de la Cañada, El Reyno de Nuevo México, Nueva España.

    ii.   JUAN YGNACIO SÁNCHES[129], b. April 02, 1785, Santa Cruz de la Cañada, El Reyno de Nuevo México, Nueva España.

    iii.   MARÍA FELICIANA SÁNCHES[129], b. November 21, 1786, Santa Cruz de la Cañada, El Reyno de Nuevo México, Nueva España.

    iv.   JUAN MANUEL SÁNCHES[130], b. September 22, 1788, Santa Cruz de la Cañada, El Reyno de Nuevo México, Nueva España.

    v.   MARÍA FIGENIA SÁNCHES[130], b. December 30, 1791, Santa Cruz de la Cañada, El Reyno de Nuevo México, Nueva España.

33. CRISTÓBAL⁶ GONZÁLES *(OLAYA SÁNCHES⁵ DE IÑIGO, PEDRO SÁNCHES⁴, FRANCISCO MUÑOS³ SÁNCHES, JACINTO² MUÑOS, FRANCISCO¹)* was born Abt. 1720[131]. He married (1) ANA ARMIJO September 29, 1757 in Alburquerque, El Reyno de Nuevo México, Nueva España[132]. He married (2) ANDREA RITA GARCÍA JURADO February 22, 1765 in Alburquerque, El Reyno de Nuevo México, Nueva España[133].

Notes for CRISTÓBAL GONZÁLES:
Also known as Cristóbal Cruz Gonzáles y Gamboa.

Children of CRISTÓBAL GONZÁLES and ANDREA JURADO are:

    i.   FELIPÉ⁷ GONZÁLES.

    ii.   JOSÉ ANTONIO DE LA CANDELARIA GONZÁLES.

    iii.   MARÍA GERTRUDIS GONZÁLES.

    iv.   MARÍA ORALIA GONZÁLES.

    v.   MARÍA ROSALÍA GONZÁLES.

    vi.   ANA MARÍA DE JESÚS GONZÁLES, b. Bef. April 15, 1766, Alburquerque, El Reyno de Nuevo México, Nueva España[134].

    vii.   MARÍA CANDELARIA GONZÁLES, b. Bef. February 04, 1773, Alburquerque, El Reyno de Nuevo México, Nueva España[134].

    viii.   MARÍA JULIANA DE LOS DOLÓRES GONZÁLES, b. Bef. February 22, 1782, Alburquerque, El Reyno de Nuevo México, Nueva España[134]; m. FRANCISCO ROMÁN LUCERO, February 02, 1797, San Felipé, El Reyno de Nuevo México, Nueva España[135].

    ix.   JOSEPH ANTONIO LUCRECIO DE LOS DOLÓRES GONZÁLES, b. April 19, 1784, Alburquerque, El Reyno de Nuevo México, Nueva España[136].

Generation No. 7

34. PEDRO⁷ SÁNCHES *(JACINTO⁶, JOSÉ SÁNCHES⁵ DE IÑIGO, JACINTO SÁNCHES⁴, FRANCISCO MUÑOS³ SÁNCHES, JACINTO² MUÑOS, FRANCISCO¹)*[137] was born Abt. 1734 in Atrisco, El Reyno de Nuevo Méjico[138]. He married MARÍA DE LA LUZ BACA October 25, 1761 in Pueblo de Laguna, El Reyno de Nuevo Méjico, Nueva España[139], daughter of DOMINGO BACA and FELICIANA CHÁVES.

Children of PEDRO SÁNCHES and MARÍA BACA are:

46.   i.   JUANA⁸ SÁNCHES, b. Atrisco, El Reyno de Nuevo Méjico, Nueva España.

47.   ii.   MANUEL RAFAEL SÁNCHES, b. Atrisco, El Reyno de Nuevo Méjico.

    iii.   JACINTO BACA SÁNCHES[140], b. Abt. 1765[141]; m. GERTRUDIS ALVAREZ DEL CASTILLO, April 28, 1795, Tomé, El Reyno de Nuevo Méjico.

    iv.   MARÍA ANTONIA SÁNCHES, b. Abt. 1770[142]; m. BARTOLOME PADIA, April 13, 1784, Alburquerque, El Reyno de Nuevo Méjico, Nueva España[143].

48.   v.   ANA ROSALÍA SÁNCHES, b. Abt. 1774.

35. TERESA⁷ SÁNCHES *(JUAN⁶, JOSÉ SÁNCHES⁵ DE IÑIGO, JACINTO SÁNCHES⁴, FRANCISCO MUÑOS³ SÁNCHES, JACINTO² MUÑOS, FRANCISCO¹)*. She married JULIAN RAÉL DE AGUILAR.

Ernest S. Sanchez & Paul R. Sanchez

Children of TERESA SÁNCHES and JULIAN DE AGUILAR are:
    i.   ANTONIO JOSEPH[8] RAÉL, b. July 14, 1779, Sandia Pueblo, El Reyno de Nuevo Méjico, Nueva España[144]; m. MARÍA FRANCISCA PADILLA, June 29, 1801, Isleta, El Reino de Nuevo Méjico, Nueva España[145].
    ii. ANTONIO ILDEFONSO DE LOS DOLORES RAÉL, b. December 21, 1782, Sandia Pueblo, El Reyno de Nuevo Méjico, Nueva España[146].

36. MARIANO[7] SÁNCHES *(JUAN CRISTÓBAL[6], FRANCISCO[5], JACINTO SÁNCHES[4] DE IÑIGO, FRANCISCO MUÑOS[3] SÁNCHES, JACINTO[2] MUÑOS, FRANCISCO[1])[147]* was born Abt. 1750[148]. He married (1) JUANA MARÍA DE LA CONCEPCIÓN CHÁVES[149] September 30, 1781 in Los Padillas, El Reyno de Nuevo Méjico, Nueva España[150]. He married (2) MARÍA DEL CARMEN PADILLA February 29, 1808 in Pueblo de Ysleta, El Reyno de Nuevo Méjico.

Child of MARIANO SÁNCHES and JUANA CHÁVES is:
    i.   MARÍA ENCARNACIÓN RAFAELA[8] SÁNCHES, b. Abt. 1784[151]; m. FRANCISCO RAMÓN DURÁN Y CHÁVES, April 20, 1799, Tomé, El Reyno de Nuevo Méjico, Nueva España[151].

Children of MARIANO SÁNCHES and MARÍA PADILLA are:
    ii. GERTRUDIS[8] SÁNCHES, b. Bef. November 21, 1808, Tomé, El Reyno de Nuevo Méjico, Nueva España[152].
    iii. FRANCISCO JAVIER SÁNCHES, b. Bef. December 02, 1810[153].
    iv. MARÍA ESTEFANA SÁNCHES, b. Bef. January 03, 1813[154].
    v. MARÍA CATALINA SÁNCHES, b. Bef. December 03, 1814[155].
    vi. BIBIANA SÁNCHES[156], b. November 30, 1817, Sausal, El Reyno de Nuevo México, Nueva España; d. January 19, 1876; m. JOSÉ MARÍA SÁNCHES, January 24, 1843, Belén, Nuevo México, La República de México.
    vii. JUAN MANUEL SÁNCHES, b. Bef. January 09, 1820[157].

37. MARÍA BÁRBARA[7] SÁNCHES *(JUAN CRISTÓBAL[6], FRANCISCO[5], JACINTO SÁNCHES[4] DE IÑIGO, FRANCISCO MUÑOS[3] SÁNCHES, JACINTO[2] MUÑOS, FRANCISCO[1])* was born Abt. 1762 in Los Cháves, El Reyno de Nuevo Méjico, Nueva España[158]. She married DIEGO ANTONIO DURÁN Y CHÁVES December 18, 1784 in Tomé, El Reyno de Nuevo Méjico, Nueva España[159], son of TOMÁS CHÁVES and TOMASA PADILLA.

Children of MARÍA SÁNCHES and DIEGO CHÁVES are:
    i.   FRANCISCO BERNADINO[8] CHÁVES, b. May 07, 1794[160].
    ii. MANUEL ANTONIO CHÁVES, b. April 04, 1796[161].
    iii. MARÍA CONCEPCIÓN MARIANA CHÁVES, b. December 05, 1798[162].
    iv. MARÍA CANDELARIA CHÁVES, b. February 02, 1803, Los Cháves, El Reyno de Nuevo Méjico, Nueva España[163].
    v. MARÍA ENCARNACIÓN CHÁVES[164], b. Abt. 1810.
    vi. FRANCISCO XAVIER CHÁVES[165], b. Abt. 1821.

38. PEDRO JUAN BAUTISTA[7] SÁNCHES *(JUAN CRISTÓBAL[6], FRANCISCO[5], JACINTO SÁNCHES[4] DE IÑIGO, FRANCISCO MUÑOS[3] SÁNCHES, JACINTO[2] MUÑOS, FRANCISCO[1])* was born Abt. 1762[166], and died October 27, 1798 in Valencia, El Reyno de Nuevo Méjico, Nueva España[167]. He married MARÍA MANUELA SÁNCHES December 18, 1784 in Los Padillas, El Reyno de Nuevo Méjico, Nueva España[168].

Children of PEDRO SÁNCHES and MARÍA SÁNCHES are:
    i.   RAFAELA DE LA LUZ[8] SÁNCHES, b. June 14, 1795, Thomé, El Reino de Nuevo Méjico, Nueva España[169].
    ii. MARÍA ESTEFANA SÁNCHES, b. August 03, 1798, Thomé, El Reino de Nuevo Méjico, Nueva España[169].

39. JOSÉ[7] SÁNCHES *(JUAN CRISTÓBAL[6], FRANCISCO[5], JACINTO SÁNCHES[4] DE IÑIGO, FRANCISCO MUÑOS[3] SÁNCHES, JACINTO[2] MUÑOS, FRANCISCO[1])[170]* was born Abt. 1765 in Los Cháves, El Reyno de Nuevo Méjico, Nueva España[171], and died Abt. February 1803[172]. He married MARÍA GUADALUPE DE LOS REYES PADILLA July 31, 1783 in Belén, El Reyno de Nuevo Méjico, Nueva España[173].

Children of JOSÉ SÁNCHES and MARÍA PADILLA are:
    i.   JOSÉ ANTONIO[8] SÁNCHES, b. April 15, 1795, Los Cháves, El Reyno de Nuevo Méjico, Nueva España[174].
    ii. MARÍA BIBIANA SÁNCHES, b. March 30, 1796, Los Cháves, El Reyno de Nuevo Méjico, Nueva España[175].
    iii. JOSEFA APOLONIA SÁNCHES, b. April 07, 1798, Los Cháves, El Reyno de Nuevo Méjico, Nueva España[176].
    iv. MARÍA MANUELA SÁNCHES, b. April 02, 1799, Los Cháves, El Reyno de Nuevo Méjico, Nueva España[177].
    v. MARÍA ASCENCIÓN SÁNCHES, b. May 19, 1800, Los Cháves, El Reyno de Nuevo Méjico, Nueva España[178].
    vi. JOSÉ SANTIAGO GUADALUPE SÁNCHES, b. December 10, 1801, Los Cháves, El Reyno de Nuevo Méjico, Nueva España[179].

vii. JOSÉ MARIANO BENITO SÁNCHES, b. March 21, 1803, Los Cháves, El Reyno de Nuevo Méjico, Nueva España[180].

40. DOMINGO DE JESÚS[7] SÁNCHES *(JUAN CRISTÓBAL[6], FRANCISCO[5], JACINTO SÁNCHES[4] DE IÑIGO, FRANCISCO MUÑOS[3] SÁNCHES, JACINTO[2] MUÑOS, FRANCISCO[1])* was born Abt. 1773 in Los Cháves, El Reyno de Nuevo Méjico, Nueva España[181]. He married MARÍA GUADALUPE BACA November 1796 in Belén, El Reyno de Nuevo Méjico, Nueva España[181], daughter of JOSÉ BACA and JUANA CHÁVEZ.

Children of DOMINGO SÁNCHES and MARÍA BACA are:

    i. MANCISEA ANTONIA JUANA[8] SÁNCHES[182], b. Belén, El Reyno de Nuevo Méjico, Nueva España.

49.   ii. JOSÉ RAFAEL MARIANO SÁNCHES, b. Bef. September 13, 1801, Belén, Nuevo México, La República de México.

50.   iii. MANUEL DE JESÚS JOSÉ SÁNCHES, b. January 03, 1804, Belén, El Reyno de Nuevo Méjico, Nueva España.

    iv. MARÍA DE ALTAGRACIA DOROTEA SÁNCHES, b. February 06, 1810[183].

51.   v. JUAN JOSÉ SÁNCHES, b. Abt. 1820.

41. JOSÉ GREGORIO DE LA TRINIDAD[7] SÁNCHES *(JUAN CRISTÓBAL[6], FRANCISCO[5], JACINTO SÁNCHES[4] DE IÑIGO, FRANCISCO MUÑOS[3] SÁNCHES, JACINTO[2] MUÑOS, FRANCISCO[1])[184]* was born November 19, 1777 in Los Cháves, El Reyno de Nuevo Méjico, Nueva España[185], and died Bef. 1856. He married MARÍA RITA BACA[186] June 05, 1805 in Belén, El Reyno de Nuevo Méjico, Nueva España[187], daughter of BARTOLOMÉ BACA and MARÍA CHÁVES.

Children of JOSÉ SÁNCHES and MARÍA BACA are:

    i. JUAN CRISTÓVAL GUILLERMO[8] SÁNCHES[188], b. February 12, 1810, San Fernandes, El Reyno de Nuevo Méjico, Nueva España[189].

52.   ii. JOSÉ MANUEL SÁNCHES, b. January 31, 1812, Santo Tomás de la Mesilla, El Reyno de Nuevo Méjico, Nueva España; d. Tomé, Territory of New México.

    iii. DIEGO ANTONIO ALVINO SÁNCHES[190], b. December 17, 1813, San Fernandes, El Reyno de Nuevo Méjico, Nueva España[191].

53.   iv. SANTIAGO SÁNCHES, b. July 24, 1816, San Fernandes, El Reyno de Nuevo Méjico, Nueva España.

    v. JOSÉ MARÍA SÁNCHES, b. Bef. July 22, 1818, San Fernandes, El Reyno de Nuevo Méjico, Nueva España[191].

54.   vi. MAURICIO DE LA TRINIDAD SÁNCHES, b. September 22, 1820, San Fernandes, El Reyno de Nuevo Méjico, Nueva España; d. November 1892, San Patricio, Territory of New México.

    vii. MARÍA FRANCISCA DE PAULA BENIGNA ROMULA SÁNCHES[191], b. February 15, 1822, San Fernando, Nuevo Mexico, La República de México[192].

    viii. JULIAN DE JESÚS SÁNCHES[193], b. Bef. January 09, 1827, San Fernandes, Nuevo México, La República de México[194]; m. MARÍA TERESA DE JESÚS SÁNCHES, September 20, 1847, Tomé, Territory of New México[195].

42. DIEGO ANTONIO[7] SÁNCHES *(JUAN CRISTÓBAL[6], FRANCISCO[5], JACINTO SÁNCHES[4] DE IÑIGO, FRANCISCO MUÑOS[3] SÁNCHES, JACINTO[2] MUÑOS, FRANCISCO[1])* was born Abt. 1769 in Pueblo de Ysleta, El Reyno de Nuevo Méjico, Nueva España[196].[197] He married MARÍA MANUELA GALLEGOS September 09, 1793 in Santa Fé, El Reyno de Nuevo Méjico, Nueva España[198].

Children of DIEGO SÁNCHES and MARÍA GALLEGOS are:

    i. MARÍA CONCEPCIÓN[8] SÁNCHES, b. Bef. August 16, 1795, Thomé, El Reyno de Nuevo Méjico, Nueva España[199].

    ii. RAFAEL SÁNCHES, b. Bef. January 16, 1810, Thomé, El Reyno de Nuevo Méjico, Nueva España[199].

55.   iii. FRANCISCO ANTONIO SÁNCHES, b. Bef. March 07, 1812, Belén, El Reyno de Nuevo Méjico, Nueva España.

56.   iv. DESIDERIO SÁNCHES, b. Bef. February 15, 1815, Thomé, El Reyno de Nuevo Méjico, Nueva España.

    v. MARÍA DE LA LUZ SÁNCHES, m. MANUEL ANDRES TRUJILLO, May 02, 1815, Thomé, El Reyno de Nuevo Méjico, Nueva España[200].

57.   vi. MARÍA ENCARNACIÓN SÁNCHES.

43. MARIANA ANTONIA[7] SÁNCHES *(DIEGO ANTONIO[6], FRANCISCO[5], JACINTO SÁNCHES[4] DE IÑIGO, FRANCISCO MUÑOS[3] SÁNCHES, JACINTO[2] MUÑOS, FRANCISCO[1])[201]* was born Abt. 1773[202], and died May 1834 in Valencia, El Reyno de Nuevo Méjico, Nueva España. She married MANUEL ANTONIO ARAGÓN September 06, 1789 in Tomé, El Reyno de Nuevo Méjico, Nueva España[203], son of MANUEL ARAGÓN and MARÍA VALLEJOS.

Child of MARIANA SÁNCHES and MANUEL ARAGÓN is:

58.   i.   MARÍA MANUELA[8] ARAGÓN, b. Abt. 1808.

44. DIEGO ANTONIO[7] SÁNCHES *(JOAQUÍN[6], FRANCISCO[5], JACINTO SÁNCHES[4] DE IÑIGO, FRANCISCO MUÑOS[3] SÁNCHES, JACINTO[2] MUÑOS, FRANCISCO[1])*. He married MARÍA JOSEFA BARELA September 02, 1810 in Thomé, El Reino de Nuevo Méjico, Nueva España[204].

Children of DIEGO SÁNCHES and MARÍA BARELA are:
       i.   MARÍA ROSALÍA[8] SÁNCHES, b. Bef. July 04, 1811, Tomé, El Reino de Nuevo Méjico, Nueva España[205].
       ii.   JUAN JOSÉ ALVINO SÁNCHES, b. Bef. March 07, 1813, Tomé, El Reino de Nuevo Méjico, Nueva España[205].
       iii.   JUAN CRISTÓVAL SÁNCHES, b. Bef. October 20, 1817, Tomé, El Reyno de Nuevo Méjico, Nueva España[206].
       iv.   MARÍA SOLEDAD SÁNCHES, b. Bef. December 26, 1819, Tomé, El Reino de Nuevo Méjico, Nueva España[206].
       v.   JOSÉ MAURICIO SÁNCHES, b. Bef. December 18, 1821, Tomé, Nuevo México, La República de México[206].
       vi.   MARÍA DE LA LUZ SÁNCHES, b. Bef. October 25, 1824, Tomé, Nuevo México, La República de México[206].
       vii.   MARÍA ANTONIA SÁNCHES, b. Bef. May 14, 1830, Tomé, Nuevo México, La República de México[206].

José Joaquín de Herrera

45. MARÍA JOSEFA[7] BUSTOS *(MARÍA ANTONIA TERESA[6] SÁNCHES, PEDRO[5], PEDRO SÁNCHES[4] DE IÑIGO, FRANCISCO MUÑOS[3] SÁNCHES, JACINTO[2] MUÑOS, FRANCISCO[1])[207]* was born Abt. 1775 in Santa Cruz de la Cañada, El Reyno de Nuevo Méjico, Nueva España. She married JOSÉ JOAQUÍN DE HERRERA[208] October 02, 1791 in Santa Cruz de la Cañada, El Reyno de Nuevo Méjico, Nueva España[209], son of TOMÁS DE HERRERA and ANTONIA DE ARCHULETA.

Children of MARÍA BUSTOS and JOSÉ DE HERRERA are:
       i.   MARÍA DE LA ASCENCIÓN[8] HERRERA, b. Santa Cruz de la Cañada, El Reyno de Nuevo Méjico, Nueva España; m. JOSÉ YGNACIO OLIVAS.
       ii.   TERESA DE JESÚS HERRERA[210], b. October 28, 1797, Santa Cruz de la Cañada, El Reyno de Nuevo Méjico, Nueva España[211].
59.   iii.   PEDRO ALCANTARA DE HERRERA, b. October 18, 1800, Santa Cruz de la Cañada, El Reyno de Nuevo Méjico, Nueva España.
       iv.   JUAN JOSÉ HERRERA, b. March 16, 1804, Santa Cruz de la Cañada, El Reyno de Nuevo Méjico, Nueva España[211].
       v.   MARÍA NICOLASA HERRERA[212], b. December 22, 1807, Santa Cruz de la Cañada, El Reyno de Nuevo Méjico, Nueva España[213].
       vi.   JUAN ANTONIO HERRERA, b. April 13, 1811, Santa Cruz de la Cañada, El Reyno de Nuevo Méjico, Nueva España[213]; m. MARÍA DEL REFUGIO VIGIL.
       vii.   MARÍA JOSEFA MANUELA HERRERA[214], b. Bef. June 14, 1816, Santa Cruz de la Cañada, El Reyno de Nuevo Méjico, Nueva España[215].

Generation No. 8

46. JUANA[8] SÁNCHES *(PEDRO[7], JACINTO[6], JOSÉ SÁNCHES[5] DE IÑIGO, JACINTO SÁNCHES[4], FRANCISCO MUÑOS[3] SÁNCHES, JACINTO[2] MUÑOS, FRANCISCO[1])[216]* was born in Atrisco, El Reyno de Nuevo Méjico, Nueva España. She married AUGUSTÍN DURÁN Y CHÁVES, son of TOMÁS CHÁVES and MARÍA PADILLA.

Child of JUANA SÁNCHES and AUGUSTÍN CHÁVES is:
60.   i.   ROSALÍA[9] CHÁVEZ, b. Abt. 1820, Atrisco, El Reyno de Nuevo Méjico, Nueva España.

47. MANUEL RAFAEL[8] SÁNCHES *(PEDRO[7], JACINTO[6], JOSÉ SÁNCHES[5] DE IÑIGO, JACINTO SÁNCHES[4], FRANCISCO MUÑOS[3] SÁNCHES, JACINTO[2] MUÑOS, FRANCISCO[1])[217]* was born in Atrisco, El Reyno de Nuevo Méjico. He married MARÍA GERTRUDIS DURÁN Y CHÁVES[218] March 12, 1801 in Alburquerque, El Reyno de Nuevo Méjico[219].

Children of MANUEL SÁNCHES and MARÍA CHÁVES are:
61.   i.   JUAN RAFAEL FERNANDO[9] SÁNCHES, b. Abt. 1790, Valencia, El Reyno de Nuevo México, Nueva España.
62.   ii.   MATÍAS SÁNCHES, b. Abt. 1800.

48. ANA ROSALÍA[8] SÁNCHES *(PEDRO[7], JACINTO[6], JOSÉ SÁNCHES[5] DE IÑIGO, JACINTO SÁNCHES[4], FRANCISCO MUÑOS[3] SÁNCHES, JACINTO[2] MUÑOS, FRANCISCO[1])* was born Abt. 1774[220]. She married RAFAÉL DE JESÚS APODACA January 12, 1792 in Alburquerque, El Reyno de Nuevo Méjico, Nueva España[221].

Child of ANA SÁNCHES and RAFAÉL APODACA is:
63.   i.   MARÍA SOLEDAD[9] APODACA, b. Abt. 1794.

49. JOSÉ RAFAEL MARIANO[8] SÁNCHES *(DOMINGO DE JESÚS[7], JUAN CRISTÓBAL[6], FRANCISCO[5], JACINTO SÁNCHES[4] DE IÑIGO, FRANCISCO MUÑOS[3] SÁNCHES, JACINTO[2] MUÑOS, FRANCISCO[1])[222]* was born Bef. September 13, 1801 in Belén, Nuevo México, La República de México[223]. He married MARÍA DOLÓRES CHÁVES February 10, 1823 in Isleta, Nuevo México, La República de México[224], daughter of FRANCISCO CHÁVES and MARÍA PADILLA.

Children of JOSÉ SÁNCHES and MARÍA CHÁVES are:
       i.   MARÍA CLARA JUAQUÍNA DE JESÚS[9] SÁNCHES, b. August 21, 1825, Belén, Nuevo México, La República de México[225].
       ii.   JOSÉ LUCIO SÁNCHES, b. Bef. March 09, 1829, Belén, Nuevo México, La República de México[226].
       iii.   JUAN BAUTISTA SÁNCHES, b. Abt. 1831.
       iv.   MARÍA LAZARA SÁNCHES, b. Abt. 1833.
       v.   MARÍA DE LOS ÁNGELES SÁNCHES, b. Abt. 1836.
       vi.   JOSÉ ANASTACIO SÁNCHES, b. Bef. May 18, 1840, Belén, Nuevo México, La República de México[227].
       vii.   MARÍA IGNACIA DE JESÚS SÁNCHES, b. Bef. August 06, 1842, Belén, Nuevo México, La República de México[227].
       viii.   RAMÓN SÁNCHES, b. Abt. 1848.

50. MANUEL DE JESÚS JOSÉ[8] SÁNCHES *(DOMINGO DE JESÚS[7], JUAN CRISTÓBAL[6], FRANCISCO[5], JACINTO SÁNCHES[4] DE IÑIGO, FRANCISCO MUÑOS[3] SÁNCHES, JACINTO[2] MUÑOS, FRANCISCO[1])[228]* was born January 03, 1804 in Belén, El Reyno de Nuevo Méjico, Nueva España[229]. He married MARÍA JOSEFA LUNA[230] December 14, 1827 in Belén, Nuevo México, La República de México[231].

Child of MANUEL SÁNCHES and MARÍA LUNA is:
64.   i.   MANUEL[9] SÁNCHES, b. Abt. 1823.

51. JUAN JOSÉ[8] SÁNCHES *(DOMINGO DE JESÚS[7], JUAN CRISTÓBAL[6], FRANCISCO[5], JACINTO SÁNCHES[4] DE IÑIGO, FRANCISCO MUÑOS[3] SÁNCHES, JACINTO[2] MUÑOS, FRANCISCO[1])* was born Abt. 1820[232]. He married CLARA PADILLA.

Children of JUAN SÁNCHES and CLARA PADILLA are:
       i.   MARIJILDO[9] SÁNCHES[233], b. Bef. April 15, 1835, Belén, Nuevo México, La República de México[234].
       ii.   RUMALDO SÁNCHES[235], b. Bef. February 12, 1837, Belén, Nuevo México, La República de México[236].
       iii.   JOSÉ APOLONIO SÁNCHES[237], b. Bef. February 21, 1841, Belén, Nuevo México, La República de México[238].
       iv.   VICENTE SÁNCHES[239], b. Bef. June 17, 1841, Belén, Nuevo México, La República de México[240].
       v.   SEBASTIANA EUSEBIA SÁNCHES[241], b. March 06, 1843, Belén, Nuevo México, La República de México[242].
       vi.   JOSÉ NICOLÁS SÁNCHES[243], b. Bef. December 07, 1846, Belén, Nuevo México, La República de México[244].
       vii.   JOSÉ BENIGNO SÁNCHES[245], b. Bef. August 26, 1849, Belén, Territory of New México[246].
       viii.   MARÍA PAULA DE JESÚS SÁNCHES, b. Bef. January 17, 1852, Belén, Territory of New México[247].
       ix.   APOLINARIO SÁNCHES, b. Bef. July 22, 1854, Belén, Territory of New México[248].

52. JOSÉ MANUEL[8] SÁNCHES *(JOSÉ GREGORIO DE LA TRINIDAD[7], JUAN CRISTÓBAL[6], FRANCISCO[5], JACINTO SÁNCHES[4] DE IÑIGO, FRANCISCO MUÑOS[3] SÁNCHES, JACINTO[2] MUÑOS, FRANCISCO[1])[249]* was born January 31, 1812 in Santo Tomás de la Mesilla, El Reyno de Nuevo Méjico, Nueva España, and died in Tomé, Territory of New México. He married JUANA BAZÁN.

Child of JOSÉ SÁNCHES and JUANA BAZÁN is:
       i.   NICANOR[9] SÁNCHES, m. LORENZA PADILLA, April 21, 1873, Socorro, Territory of New México.

53. SANTIAGO[8] SÁNCHES *(JOSÉ GREGORIO DE LA TRINIDAD[7], JUAN CRISTÓBAL[6], FRANCISCO[5], JACINTO SÁNCHES[4] DE IÑIGO, FRANCISCO MUÑOS[3] SÁNCHES, JACINTO[2] MUÑOS, FRANCISCO[1])[249]* was born July 24, 1816 in San Fernandes, El Reyno de Nuevo Méjico, Nueva España[250]. He married (1) CATARINA

LUNA March 28, 1837 in Ysleta, Nuevo México, La República de México[251], daughter of JOSÉ LUNA and JUANA GAVALDON. He married (2) MARIANA PEREA March 26, 1870 in Tularoso, Territory of New México[252].

Notes for CATARINA LUNA:
Also known as María Catarina Luna, Conferina.

Child of SANTIAGO SÁNCHES and CATARINA LUNA is:
    i.   JOSÉ DE LA PAZ[9] SÁNCHES, b. January 30, 1838, Tomé, Nuevo México, La República de México[253].

Children of SANTIAGO SÁNCHES and MARIANA PEREA are:
65.   ii.   IGNACIO[9] SÁNCHES, b. Abt. 1846.
66.   iii.   SAMUEL SÁNCHES, b. Abt. 1852; d. August 14, 1924, Glencoe, New México.
    iv.   AMANCIO SÁNCHES[254], b. Bef. April 09, 1853, La Mesilla, Territory of New México[255].

Notes for AMANCIO SÁNCHES:
Also known as José Dionicio Amado Sánches.

67.   v.   MARÍA DOLORES SÁNCHES, b. Abt. 1856, La Mesilla, Territory of New México.
68.   vi.   ANGELITA PEREA SÁNCHES, b. Abt. 1857, La Mesilla, Territory of New México; d. Abt. 1962, San Patricio, New México.
    vii.   RITA SÁNCHES, b. 1862.

Mauricio de la Trinidad Sánches

54. MAURICIO DE LA TRINIDAD[8] SÁNCHES *(JOSÉ GREGORIO DE LA TRINIDAD[7], JUAN CRISTÓBAL[6], FRANCISCO[5], JACINTO SÁNCHES[4] DE IÑIGO, FRANCISCO MUÑOS[3] SÁNCHES, JACINTO[2] MUÑOS, FRANCISCO[1])* was born September 22, 1820 in San Fernandes, El Reyno de Nuevo Méjico, Nueva España[256], and died November 1892 in San Patricio, Territory of New México[257]. He married JESÚSITA GONZÁLES June 02, 1843 in Tomé, Nuevo México, La República de México[258], daughter of RAMÓN GONZÁLES and MARÍA MONTOYA.

Children of MAURICIO SÁNCHES and JESÚSITA GONZÁLES are:
69.   i.   ANTONIO[9] SÁNCHEZ, b. December 12, 1844, San Fernando, Nuevo México, La República de México; d. August 22, 1894, San Patricio, Territory of New México.
70.   ii.   ESTOLANO SÁNCHEZ, b. Abt. 1847, Torreón, Nuevo México, La República de México; d. June 20, 1907, San Patricio, Territory of New México.
    iii.   JOSÉ TORIBIO SÁNCHEZ, b. April 12, 1847, Torreón, Territory of New México[259].
71.   iv.   RAYMUNDA SEGUNDA SÁNCHEZ, b. June 24, 1851, Torreón, Territory of New México; d. San Patricio, New México.
72.   v.   FRANCISCO SÁNCHEZ, b. 1852, Torreón, Territory of New México; d. El Berendo, New México.
73.   vi.   JUAN RAFAEL GONZÁLES SÁNCHEZ, b. 1855, Torreón, New México.
    vii.   JOSÉ MANUEL SÁNCHEZ, b. March 1860, Torreón, Territory of New México[260]; m. (1) MARÍA SÁNCHEZ, July 20, 1883, Lincoln, Territory of New México[261]; m. (2) MARÍA ANTONIA HERRERA, Abt. 1884[262].

Notes for JOSÉ MANUEL SÁNCHEZ:
Land Patent # NMNMAA 010638, on the authority of the Homestead Entry-Original (12 Stat. 392), May 20, 1862. Issued 160 acres.

Notes for MARÍA ANTONIA HERRERA:
Also known as Toñita.

74.   viii.   BESITA SÁNCHEZ, b. 1863, Manzano, Territory of New México.
75.   ix.   DONACIANO SÁNCHEZ, b. 1866, El Berendo, Territory of New México; d. March 01, 1929, Tularosa, New México.
76.   x.   AMADA SÁNCHEZ, b. December 22, 1870, La Plaza de San José, Lincoln County, Territory of New México.

55. FRANCISCO ANTONIO[8] SÁNCHES *(DIEGO ANTONIO[7], JUAN CRISTÓBAL[6], FRANCISCO[5], JACINTO SÁNCHES[4] DE IÑIGO, FRANCISCO MUÑOS[3] SÁNCHES, JACINTO[2] MUÑOS, FRANCISCO[1])* was born Bef. March 07, 1812 in Belén, El Reyno de Nuevo Méjico, Nueva España[263]. He married MARÍA GREGORIA BACA March 10, 1847 in Tomé, Territory of New México[264].

Children of FRANCISCO SÁNCHES and MARÍA BACA are:
    i.   JULIAN[9] SÁNCHES[265], b. Bef. January 12, 1848, Tomé, Territory of New México[266].

Notes for JULIAN SÁNCHES:
Also known as Julian de Jesús María Sánches.

    ii.   REMEDIOS SÁNCHES, b. Bef. July 02, 1850, Tomé, Territory of New México[266].

Notes for REMEDIOS SÁNCHES:
Also known as María Petra De Los Remedios Sánches.

    iii.   SOLEDAD SÁNCHES[267], b. Bef. January 23, 1854, Tomé, Territory of New México[268].
    iv.   MAXIMO SÁNCHES[269], b. Bef. June 09, 1856, Torréon, Territory of New México[270].

56. DESIDERIO[8] SÁNCHES *(DIEGO ANTONIO[7], JUAN CRISTÓBAL[6], FRANCISCO[5], JACINTO SÁNCHES[4] DE IÑIGO, FRANCISCO MUÑOS[3] SÁNCHES, JACINTO[2] MUÑOS, FRANCISCO[1])* was born Bef. February 15, 1815 in Thomé, El Reyno de Nuevo Méjico, Nueva España[271]. He married YSIDORA CHÁVES February 09, 1836 in Tomé, Nuevo México, La República de México[272], daughter of JOSÉ CHÁVES and MICHAELA BACA.

Children of DESIDERIO SÁNCHES and YSIDORA CHÁVES are:
    i.   MARÍA PAULA DE JESÚS[9] SÁNCHES, b. Bef. January 17, 1836, Tomé, Nuevo México, La República de México[273].
77.   ii.   YSABEL SÁNCHES, b. Bef. July 11, 1838, Tomé, Nuevo México, La República de México.
    iii.   SUSANA SÁNCHES, b. Bef. May 30, 1841, Tomé, Territory of New México[273].
    iv.   MANUEL SÁNCHES, b. Abt. 1842[274].
    v.   MARCELINA SÁNCHES, b. Bef. January 25, 1846, Tomé, Nuevo México, La República de México[275].
    vi.   MARÍA CONCEPCIÓN SÁNCHES, b. Bef. December 19, 1850, Tomé, Territory of New México[276].
    vii.   PEDRO ANTONIO SÁNCHES, b. Bef. May 07, 1853, Tomé, Territory of New México[277].
    viii.   LORENZO SÁNCHES, b. Bef. September 16, 1857, Tomé, Territory of New México[278].

57. MARÍA ENCARNACIÓN[8] SÁNCHES *(DIEGO ANTONIO[7], JUAN CRISTÓBAL[6], FRANCISCO[5], JACINTO SÁNCHES[4] DE IÑIGO, FRANCISCO MUÑOS[3] SÁNCHES, JACINTO[2] MUÑOS, FRANCISCO[1])*. She married JUAN MIGUEL CANDELARIA SALAS November 30, 1817 in Thomé, El Reyno de Nuevo Méjico, Nueva España[279].

Children of MARÍA SÁNCHES and JUAN SALAS are:
    i.   JOSÉ GREGORIO[9] SALAS, b. Bef. March 28, 1819, Thomé, El Reyno de Nuevo Méjico, Nueva España[280].
    ii.   MARÍA FELICIANA SALAS, b. Bef. October 21, 1821, Tomé, Nuevo México, La República de México[280].

58. MARÍA MANUELA[8] ARAGÓN *(MARIANA ANTONIA[7] SÁNCHES, DIEGO ANTONIO[6], FRANCISCO[5], JACINTO SÁNCHES[4] DE IÑIGO, FRANCISCO MUÑOS[3] SÁNCHES, JACINTO[2] MUÑOS, FRANCISCO[1])* was born Abt. 1808[281]. She married SANTIAGO DE JESÚS GONZÁLES[281] August 25, 1828[282], son of JUAN GONZÁLES and MARÍA ARMIJO.

Children of MARÍA ARAGÓN and SANTIAGO GONZÁLES are:
    i.   JOSÉ[9] GONZÁLES[283], b. Abt. 1830.
    ii.   ANTONIO MANUEL GONZÁLES[283], b. Bef. May 02, 1832[284].
78.   iii.   MARÍA ALTAGRACIA GONZÁLES, b. Bef. December 17, 1833, Los Corrales, Nuevo México, República de México.
    iv.   MARÍA CISTA DE LOS DELORES GONZÁLES[285], b. Bef. March 30, 1836[286].
    v.   JOSÉ IGNACIO GONZÁLES[287], b. Bef. August 04, 1838[288].
79.   vi.   FLORENCIO GONZÁLES, b. November 07, 1843, Los Corrales, Nuevo México, La República de México; d. December 18, 1897, San Patricio, Territory of New México.

59. PEDRO ALCANTARA[8] DE HERRERA *(MARÍA JOSEFA[7] BUSTOS, MARÍA ANTONIA TERESA[6] SÁNCHES, PEDRO[5], PEDRO SÁNCHES[4] DE IÑIGO, FRANCISCO MUÑOS[3] SÁNCHES, JACINTO[2] MUÑOS, FRANCISCO[1])*[289] was born October 18, 1800 in Santa Cruz de la Cañada, El Reyno de Nuevo Méjico, Nueva España[290]. He married (1) MARÍA MANUELA CASIAS[291]. He married (2) MARÍA MANUELA ESQUIBEL May 11, 1825 in Santa Cruz de la Cañada, El Reyno de Nuevo Méjico, Nueva España[292], daughter of JUAN ESQUIBEL and GERTRUDIS TRUXILLO.

He married (3) MARÍA CELEDONIA ARCHULETA May 17, 1827 in Santa Cruz de la Cañada, Nuevo México, La República de México[293], daughter of LUÍS ARCHULETA and MARÍA MONTOYA.

Child of PEDRO DE HERRERA and MARÍA CASIAS is:

    i.   MARÍA ESTEFANA[9] HERRERA, b. February 05, 1839, San Antonio de Servilleta, Nuevo Mexico, La República de México.

Child of PEDRO DE HERRERA and MARÍA ESQUIBEL is:

    ii.   JUAN MANUEL[9] HERRERA, b. January 08, 1826, Santa Cruz de la Cañada, El Reyno de Nuevo Méjico, Nueva España[294].

Children of PEDRO DE HERRERA and MARÍA ARCHULETA are:

80.   iii.   FERNANDO[9] HERRERA, b. July 02, 1836, Santa Cruz de la Cañada, Nuevo México, La República de México; d. December 14, 1915, Alamogordo, New México.

    iv.   MARÍA ANTONIA NICOLASA HERRERA, b. May 24, 1840, San Francisco del Rancho (Ranchos de Taos), Nuevo México, La República de México[295].

    v.   JOSÉ HERRERA, b. February 21, 1842, Santa Cruz de la Cañada, Nuevo México, La República de México[296].

Generation No. 9

Juan Ricardo Padilla

60. ROSALÍA[9] CHÁVEZ *(JUANA[8] SÁNCHES, PEDRO[7], JACINTO[6], JOSÉ SÁNCHES[5] DE IÑIGO, JACINTO SÁNCHES[4], FRANCISCO MUÑOS[3] SÁNCHES, JACINTO[2] MUÑOS, FRANCISCO[1])* was born Abt. 1820 in Atrisco, El Reyno de Nuevo Méjico, Nueva España[297]. She married JUAN RICARDO PADILLA[298] June 01, 1833 in Ysleta Pueblo, Nuevo México, La República de México, son of PABLO PADILLA and FELIPA GONZÁLES.

Children of ROSALÍA CHÁVEZ and JUAN PADILLA are:

    i.   PEDRO[10] PADILLA, b. Abt. 1837[299].

    ii.   JOSÉ ANTONIO PADILLA[300], b. August 08, 1842.

    iii.   MARÍA YSABEL PADILLA, b. Abt. 1843[300]; d. November 15, 1853.

    iv.   TOMÁS PADILLA, b. Abt. 1847[300].

    v.   MARÍA DE LA LUZ PADILLA, b. March 11, 1848.

    vi.   MERCED PADILLA, b. Abt. 1852[301].

    vii.   MANUELITA PADILLA, b. Abt. 1855[301].

81.   viii.   ANDALESIO PADILLA, b. Abt. 1856, Los Padilla, Territory of New México; d. March 16, 1913, Tres Rios, Territory of New México.

    ix.   REYNA PADILLA, b. Abt. 1856[302].

61. JUAN RAFAEL FERNANDO[9] SÁNCHES *(MANUEL RAFAEL[8], PEDRO[7], JACINTO[6], JOSÉ SÁNCHES[5] DE IÑIGO, JACINTO SÁNCHES[4], FRANCISCO MUÑOS[3] SÁNCHES, JACINTO[2] MUÑOS, FRANCISCO[1])[303]* was born Abt. 1790 in Valencia, El Reyno de Nuevo México, Nueva España. He married MARÍA DE LA LUZ BARCELÓ[304] November 03, 1822 in Tomé, Nuevo México, La República de México[305], daughter of JUAN BARCELÓ and MARÍA HERRERA.

Notes for MARÍA DE LA LUZ BARCELÓ:
Also known as María de la Luz Barcelón.

Children of JUAN SÁNCHES and MARÍA BARCELÓ are:

82.   i.   MARÍA ALTAGRACIA DEL REFUGIO[10] SÁNCHES, b. Bef. January 31, 1824, Tomé, Nuevo México, La República de México.

    ii.   MARÍA LUISA SÁNCHES, b. Bef. March 05, 1826[306].

83.   iii.   ROMUALDO SÁNCHES, b. Bef. February 16, 1828, Valencia, Nuevo México, La República de México.

84.   iv.   VICTORIA SÁNCHES, b. Bef. March 05, 1830.

    v.   MARÍA TERESA DE JESÚS SÁNCHES, b. October 18, 1833[306]; m. JULIAN DE JESÚS SÁNCHES[307], September 20, 1847, Tomé, Territory of New México[308].

85.   vi.   PABLO SÁNCHES, b. Abt. 1838.

86.   vii.   VICENTE SÁNCHES, b. Bef. April 05, 1840.

    viii.   JESÚS SÁNCHES[309], b. Bef. January 04, 1843[310].

Notes for JESÚS SÁNCHES:
Also known as José de Jesús Martiniano Sánches.

87.	ix.	FERNANDES SÁNCHES, b. Bef. May 04, 1845.
88.	x.	JUAN RAFAEL BERCELÓ SÁNCHES, b. Bef. November 21, 1847, Tomé, Territory of New México.

62. MATÍAS[9] SÁNCHES *(MANUEL RAFAEL[8], PEDRO[7], JACINTO[6], JOSÉ SÁNCHES[5] DE IÑIGO, JACINTO SÁNCHES[4], FRANCISCO MUÑOS[3] SÁNCHES, JACINTO[2] MUÑOS, FRANCISCO[1])* was born Abt. 1800[311]. He married ANA MARÍA VALLEJOS September 13, 1828 in Tomé, Nuevo México, La República de México[312].

Children of MATÍAS SÁNCHES and ANA VALLEJOS are:

	i.	VICENTE[10] SÁNCHES, b. Abt. 1830[313].
	ii.	MANUEL SÁNCHES, b. Abt. 1834[313].
89.	iii.	JOSEFA SÁNCHES, b. Abt. 1835; d. Bef. 1880.
90.	iv.	CATALINA SÁNCHES, b. Abt. 1838.
	v.	LUCÍA SÁNCHES, b. Abt. 1842[313].
	vi.	QUETERIA SÁNCHES, b. Abt. 1843[313].
	vii.	JESÚS SÁNCHES, b. Abt. 1852[314].

63. MARÍA SOLEDAD[9] APODACA *(ANA ROSALÍA[8] SÁNCHES, PEDRO[7], JACINTO[6], JOSÉ SÁNCHES[5] DE IÑIGO, JACINTO SÁNCHES[4], FRANCISCO MUÑOS[3] SÁNCHES, JACINTO[2] MUÑOS, FRANCISCO[1])[315]* was born Abt. 1794[316]. She married MANUEL ANTONIO VIGIL[317], son of FELIPÉ VIGIL and MARÍA ARAGÓN.

Children of MARÍA APODACA and MANUEL VIGIL are:

	i.	JOSÉ ANTONIO[10] VIGIL.
	ii.	MARÍA GERTRUDIS VIGIL[318], b. September 05, 1808, Alburquerque, El Reyno de Nuevo Méjico, Nueva España.
	iii.	MARÍA TEODORA VIGIL, b. November 01, 1810, Valencia, El Reyno de Nuevo Méjico, Nueva España[319].
91.	iv.	JUAN FRANCISCO PABLO VIGIL, b. March 08, 1821, Tomé, Nuevo México, La República de México.
92.	v.	FRANCISCO ANTONIO VIGIL, b. Bef. April 12, 1823, Tomé, Nuevo México, La República de México; d. February 07, 1890.
	vi.	JUANA MARÍA VIGIL, b. February 04, 1825[320]; m. JOSÉ ANDRÉS LUJÁN, December 08, 1837, Tomé, Nuevo México, La República de México[320].
	vii.	MARÍA ROSALÍA VIGIL[321], b. May 04, 1829, Valencia, Nuevo México, La República de México.
	viii.	JUAN RAMÓN VIGIL[321], b. January 10, 1835, Valencia, Nuevo México, La República de México.
	ix.	JESÚS MARÍA VIGIL[321], b. May 02, 1837, Valencia, Nuevo México, La República de México.

64. MANUEL[9] SÁNCHES *(MANUEL DE JESÚS JOSÉ[8], DOMINGO DE JESÚS[7], JUAN CRISTÓBAL[6], FRANCISCO[5], JACINTO SÁNCHES[4] DE IÑIGO, FRANCISCO MUÑOS[3] SÁNCHES, JACINTO[2] MUÑOS, FRANCISCO[1])* was born Abt. 1823[322]. He married ADELAIDA JARAMILLO February 04, 1859 in Tomé, Territory of New México[323], daughter of ROMÁN JARAMILLO and MARÍA TORRES.

Children of MANUEL SÁNCHES and ADELAIDA JARAMILLO are:

	i.	SEFERINA[10] SÁNCHEZ, b. Abt. 1852[324]; m. RUPERTO BOJÓRQUE, September 04, 1874, Tularoso, Territory of New México[325].
93.	ii.	MASIMA JARAMILLO SÁNCHEZ, b. Abt. 1856.
94.	iii.	PEDRO JARAMILLO SÁNCHEZ, b. Abt. 1860.

65. IGNACIO[9] SÁNCHES *(SANTIAGO[8], JOSÉ GREGORIO DE LA TRINIDAD[7], JUAN CRISTÓBAL[6], FRANCISCO[5], JACINTO SÁNCHES[4] DE IÑIGO, FRANCISCO MUÑOS[3] SÁNCHES, JACINTO[2] MUÑOS, FRANCISCO[1])* was born Abt. 1846[326]. He married JULIANA DE SÁNCHEZ.

Child of IGNACIO SÁNCHES and JULIANA DE SÁNCHEZ is:

	i.	ANGELITA[10] SÁNCHEZ, b. Abt. 1867[327].

66. SAMUEL[9] SÁNCHES *(SANTIAGO[8], JOSÉ GREGORIO DE LA TRINIDAD[7], JUAN CRISTÓBAL[6], FRANCISCO[5], JACINTO SÁNCHES[4] DE IÑIGO, FRANCISCO MUÑOS[3] SÁNCHES, JACINTO[2] MUÑOS, FRANCISCO[1])[328]* was born Abt. 1852[329], and died August 14, 1924 in Glencoe, New México. He married ANTONIA MAESTAS[330].

Children of SAMUEL SÁNCHES and ANTONIA MAESTAS are:
95.   i.   CELESTINO[10] SÁNCHEZ, b. June 25, 1870, La Plaza de San José, Territory of New México.
      ii.   CRISTÓVAL SÁNCHEZ, b. August 1875[331].
      iii.   MARÍA JESÚS SÁNCHEZ, b. June 15, 1878, La Mesilla, Doña Ana County, Territory of New México[332].
96.   iv.   MARIANA CALMARIA SÁNCHEZ, b. May 27, 1885.
97.   v.   SANTIAGO MAESTAS SÁNCHEZ, b. April 15, 1892, Ruidoso, Territory of New México.

67. MARÍA DOLORES[9] SÁNCHES *(SANTIAGO[8], JOSÉ GREGORIO DE LA TRINIDAD[7], JUAN CRISTÓBAL[6], FRANCISCO[5], JACINTO SÁNCHES[4] DE IÑIGO, FRANCISCO MUÑOS[3] SÁNCHES, JACINTO[2] MUÑOS, FRANCISCO[1])* was born Abt. 1856 in La Mesilla, Territory of New México[333]. She married AGAPITO GALLEGOS March 25, 1869[334], son of ANTONIO GALLEGOS and MARÍA SÁNCHEZ.

Notes for MARÍA DOLORES SÁNCHES:
Also known as Lola, Dolores.

Notes for AGAPITO GALLEGOS:
Land Patent # NMNMAA 010244, on the authority of the Homestead Entry-Original (12 Stat. 392), May 20, 1862. Issued 80 acres.

Children of MARÍA SÁNCHES and AGAPITO GALLEGOS are:
      i.   LUCÍA[10] GALLEGOS, b. Abt. 1872[335].
      ii.   EULALIO GALLEGOS, b. Abt. 1875[335].
98.   iii.   JESUSITA GALLEGOS, b. Abt. 1883.
      iv.   ESQUIPULO GALLEGOS, b. December 1885[336]; m. LEONOR DE GALLEGOS.
99.   v.   MANUELITA GALLEGOS, b. March 12, 1887; d. 1972.
      vi.   EVARISTA GALLEGOS, b. October 1892[336].

Alejo Montes

68. ANGELITA PEREA[9] SÁNCHES *(SANTIAGO[8], JOSÉ GREGORIO DE LA TRINIDAD[7], JUAN CRISTÓBAL[6], FRANCISCO[5], JACINTO SÁNCHES[4] DE IÑIGO, FRANCISCO MUÑOS[3] SÁNCHES, JACINTO[2] MUÑOS, FRANCISCO[1])* was born Abt. 1857 in La Mesilla, Territory of New México[337], and died Abt. 1962 in San Patricio, New México. She married (1) JAMES WELDON[338]. She married (2) ALEJO MONTES[339] May 15, 1881 in Lincoln County, Territory of New México[340], son of BACILIO MONTES and JESÚSITA RONQUILLO.

Notes for ALEJO MONTES:
Land Patent # NMR 0027779, on the authority of the Homestead Entry-Enlarged (35 Stat. 639), February 19, 1909. Issued 334.50 acres on January 29, 1920.
Land Patent # NMLC 0025706, on the authority of the Homestead Entry-Stock Raising (39 Stat. 862), December 29, 1916. Issued 320 acres on April 19, 1926.

James Weldon

Child of ANGELITA SÁNCHES and JAMES WELDON is:
100.   i.   LUCÍA[10] WELDON, b. Abt. 1871, Lincoln County, Territory of New México; d. San Patricio, New México.

Children of ANGELITA SÁNCHES and ALEJO MONTES are:
101.   ii.   JESÚS MARÍA[10] MONTES, b. 1883, La Junta, Territory of New México; d. 1954, Hondo, New México.
      iii.   ALEJO SÁNCHEZ MONTES, b. August 27, 1883[341].

Notes for ALEJO SÁNCHEZ MONTES:
Baptized: September 27, 1883. Died when he was young.

102.   iv.   IGNACIA MONTES, b. December 1885.
      v.   AMANDA MONTES, b. August 16, 1886[342].

Notes for AMANDA MONTES:
Died when she was young.

vi. EULALIO MONTES, b. November 1889[343].

vii. REINALDO MONTES, b. June 1891[343].

103. viii. JUAN SÁNCHEZ MONTES, b. February 18, 1893, Ruidoso, New México; d. August 1978, Glencoe, New México.

ix. JUANITA MONTES, b. March 1896[343].

x. RAMÓN MONTES, b. August 15, 1897.

Notes for RAMÓN MONTES:
Died when he was young.

69. ANTONIO[9] SÁNCHEZ *(MAURICIO DE LA TRINIDAD[8] SÁNCHES, JOSÉ GREGORIO DE LA TRINIDAD[7], JUAN CRISTÓBAL[6], FRANCISCO[5], JACINTO SÁNCHES[4] DE IÑIGO, FRANCISCO MUÑOS[3] SÁNCHES, JACINTO[2] MUÑOS, FRANCISCO[1])* was born December 12, 1844 in San Fernando, Nuevo México, La República de México[344], and died August 22, 1894 in San Patricio, Territory of New México. He married TELESFORA MIRABAL[345] March 09, 1877 in Tularoso, Territory of New México[346], daughter of JUAN MIRABAL and GUADALUPE TRUJILLO.

Notes for ANTONIO SÁNCHEZ:
Also known as Antonio José Sánches.
Had a homestead in Glencoe, NM. Died when the horse he was riding fell while attempting to jump an arroyo.

Notes for TELESFORA MIRABAL:
December 29, 1939: Died in an auto accident. Buried in La Capilla de San Ysidro.
Land Patent # NMNMAA 010633, on the authority of the Homestead Entry-Original (12 Stat. 392), May 20, 1862. Issued 160 acres.

Children of ANTONIO SÁNCHEZ and TELESFORA MIRABAL are:

104. i. SALOMON[10] SÁNCHEZ, b. Abt. November 17, 1878, Tularoso, Territory of New México; d. May 31, 1952, Ruidoso, New México.

105. ii. MARÍA DE JESÚS SÁNCHEZ, b. July 26, 1881, Tularoso, Territory of New México; d. December 29, 1954, Glencoe, New Mexico.

106. iii. MANUEL MIRABAL SÁNCHEZ, b. November 18, 1884, Glencoe, Territory of New México; d. December 28, 1945, Lake Arther, New México.

107. iv. DANOIS SÁNCHEZ, b. October 24, 1890, Ruidoso, Territory of New México; d. May 05, 1955, Tularosa, New México.

108. v. LUPITA SÁNCHEZ, b. March 13, 1892; d. September 1973, Glencoe, New México.

109. vi. SENAIDA SÁNCHEZ, b. August 06, 1894, Glencoe, Territory of New México; d. November 12, 1981.

70. ESTOLANO[9] SÁNCHEZ *(MAURICIO DE LA TRINIDAD[8] SÁNCHES, JOSÉ GREGORIO DE LA TRINIDAD[7], JUAN CRISTÓBAL[6], FRANCISCO[5], JACINTO SÁNCHES[4] DE IÑIGO, FRANCISCO MUÑOS[3] SÁNCHES, JACINTO[2] MUÑOS, FRANCISCO[1])* was born Abt. 1847 in Torreón, Nuevo México, La República de México[347], and died June 20, 1907 in San Patricio, Territory of New México[348]. He married CORNELIA PACHECO July 21, 1871 in La Plaza del Rio Bonito, Territory of New México[349], daughter of FRANCISCO PACHECO and ROMULA SAVEDRA.

Notes for ESTOLANO SÁNCHEZ:
Land Patent # NMNMAA 010411, on the authority of the Homestead Act, May 20, 1862, 158.91 Acres.

Children of ESTOLANO SÁNCHEZ and CORNELIA PACHECO are:

110. i. FELIPÉ E.[10] SÁNCHEZ, b. January 21, 1874, La Placita del Rio Bonito, Territory of New México; d. January 15, 1954, San Elizario, El Paso, Téxas.

111. ii. ELUTICIA SÁNCHEZ, b. 1875.

iii. SIPIO SÁNCHEZ, b. Abt. 1879[350].

iv. VALENTÍN SÁNCHEZ, b. May 14, 1881[351]; d. February 09, 1949, Carrizozo, New México.

112. v. PRECILIANO SÁNCHEZ, b. December 24, 1884, Rebentón, Territory of New México; d. 1918-1920.

113. vi. AURELIO SÁNCHEZ, b. March 12, 1886, Ruidoso, Territory of New México; d. February 23, 1975.

114. vii. CELIA SÁNCHEZ, b. July 12, 1888, Rebentón, Territory of New México.

115. viii. ESTOLANO PACHECO SÁNCHEZ, b. October 19, 1893, Rebentón, Territory of New México; d. September 19, 1943, Carrizozo, New México.

116. ix. ROSARITA SÁNCHEZ, b. August 11, 1896, Rebentón,Territory of New México; d. December 25, 1976, Hondo, New México.

71. RAYMUNDA SEGUNDA[9] SÁNCHEZ *(MAURICIO DE LA TRINIDAD[8] SÁNCHES, JOSÉ GREGORIO DE LA TRINIDAD[7], JUAN CRISTÓBAL[6], FRANCISCO[5], JACINTO SÁNCHES[4] DE IÑIGO, FRANCISCO MUÑOS[3]*

SÁNCHES, JACINTO[2] MUÑOS, FRANCISCO[1]) was born June 24, 1851 in Torreón, Territory of New México[352], and died in San Patricio, New México. She married (1) FLORENCIO GONZÁLES[353] in Manzano, Territory of New México[354], son of SANTIAGO GONZÁLES and MARÍA ARAGÓN. She married (2) AMBROCIO AVEITA CHÁVEZ October 24, 1898 in San Patricio, Territory of New México[355], son of CRUZ CHÁVEZ and JOSEFA AVEITA.

Notes for RAYMUNDA SEGUNDA SÁNCHEZ:
Also known as Reimunda, Cigismunda, Sigismunda Chávez y Sánchez, Reimunda Gonzáles.

Notes for AMBROCIO AVEITA CHÁVEZ:
Raised Florencio Gonzales & Esoila Gonzales.

Children of RAYMUNDA SÁNCHEZ and FLORENCIO GONZÁLES are:
    i.   ARISTOTEL[10] GONZÁLES.

Notes for ARISTOTEL GONZÁLES:
Died young.

    ii.   FILOTEA GONZÁLES.

Notes for FILOTEA GONZÁLES:
Died young.

117.	iii.	ESLINDA GONZÁLES, b. 1867, La Placita del Rio Bonito, Territory of New México; d. Bef. October 1922.
	iv.	JUAN GONZÁLES, b. 1869, La Placita del Rio Bonito, Territory of New México.
118.	v.	PROSPERO GONZÁLES, b. July 20, 1871, Lincoln, Territory of New México; d. August 20, 1937, Glencoe, New México.
119.	vi.	LEOPOLDO SÁNCHEZ GONZÁLES, b. April 08, 1875, Lincoln, Territory of New México; d. June 10, 1937, San Patricio, New México.
120.	vii.	ALFREDO GONZÁLES, b. 1876, Lincoln, Territory of New México; d. 1927, San Patricio, New México.
121.	viii.	EPAMINOANDAS GONZÁLES, b. April 04, 1876, Lincoln, Territory of New México; d. February 20, 1970, San Patricio, New México.
122.	ix.	AVRORA GONZÁLES, b. May 23, 1880, San Patricio, Territory of New México; d. August 15, 1971, San Patricio, New México.
123.	x.	AROPAJITA GONZÁLES, b. October 12, 1882, San Patricio, Territory of New México; d. San Patricio, New México.
124.	xi.	AURELIA GONZÁLES, b. May 15, 1883, San Patricio, Territory of New México.
125.	xii.	FLORENCIO SÁNCHEZ GONZÁLES, b. November 09, 1892, San Patricio, Territory of New México; d. July 09, 1979.
126.	xiii.	ESOILA GONZÁLES, b. August 08, 1894, San Patricio, Territory of New México.

72. FRANCISCO[9] SÁNCHEZ *(MAURICIO DE LA TRINIDAD[8] SÁNCHES, JOSÉ GREGORIO DE LA TRINIDAD[7], JUAN CRISTÓBAL[6], FRANCISCO[5], JACINTO SÁNCHES[4] DE IÑIGO, FRANCISCO MUÑOS[3] SÁNCHES, JACINTO[2] MUÑOS, FRANCISCO[1])* was born 1852 in Torreón, Territory of New México[356], and died in El Berendo, New México. He married (1) CONCEPCIÓN TRUJILLO May 19, 1873 in Tularoso, Territory of New México[357], daughter of ASCENCIÓN TRUJILLO. He married (2) VIRGINIA PADILLA[358] November 14, 1910 in Lincoln, Territory of New México[359], daughter of JOSÉ PADILLA and NESTORA SAMORA.

Notes for FRANCISCO SÁNCHEZ:
Also known as José Panfilo Francisco Sánchez, Pancho Sánchez, Francisco Sánchez y Gonzáles.
Land Patent # NMNMAA 011156, on the authority of the Sale cash entry, April 24, 1820, 41.76 Acres.

Notes for CONCEPCIÓN TRUJILLO:
Also known as María Concepción Trujillo. The 1860 Census of La Polvadera de San Lorenzo lists her name as Manuela. It is possible that her Christian name may have been María Manuela de la Concepción Trujillo.
1900 Census: Lists her birthdate as January 1860.

Children of FRANCISCO SÁNCHEZ and CONCEPCIÓN TRUJILLO are:
127.	i.	NAPOLEÓN[10] SÁNCHEZ, b. January 04, 1874, San Patricio, Territory of New México.
128.	ii.	DAVÍD SÁNCHEZ, b. November 06, 1876, San Patricio, Territory of New México; d. Roswell, New México.

129.	iii.	ANTONIO SÁNCHEZ, b. February 08, 1878, San Patricio, Territory of New México.
130.	iv.	MAURICIO SÁNCHEZ, b. October 04, 1880, San Patricio, Territory of New México; d. September 17, 1961, San Fernandez, New México.
131.	v.	PATRICIO SÁNCHEZ, b. January 30, 1882, San Patricio, Territory of New México; d. April 1955, San Patricio, New México.
132.	vi.	JACOBO SÁNCHEZ, b. April 22, 1886, San Patricio, Territory of New México; d. July 06, 1968, San Patricio, New México.
133.	vii.	ELOISA SÁNCHEZ, b. February 10, 1891, San Patricio, Territory of New México; d. Manzano, New México.
134.	viii.	CONRADO SÁNCHEZ, b. July 15, 1894, San Patricio, Territory of New México; d. August 1977, Casa Grande, Arizona.
135.	ix.	REFUGIA SÁNCHEZ, b. July 04, 1899, San Patricio, Territory of New México.

Children of FRANCISCO SÁNCHEZ and VIRGINIA PADILLA are:
	x.	LEANDRA[10] SÁNCHEZ, b. Abt. 1913[360]; m. PEDRO LOSOYA[361].
	xi.	MANUEL SÁNCHEZ[361], b. April 27, 1914[362]; d. March 1985, Roswell, New México; m. JOSEFITA SAÍZ.
	xii.	MAXIMILIANO SÁNCHEZ, b. July 28, 1916[362]; m. LOLA DE SÁNCHEZ.

73. JUAN RAFAEL GONZÁLES[9] SÁNCHEZ *(MAURICIO DE LA TRINIDAD[8] SÁNCHES, JOSÉ GREGORIO DE LA TRINIDAD[7], JUAN CRISTÓBAL[6], FRANCISCO[5], JACINTO SÁNCHES[4] DE IÑIGO, FRANCISCO MUÑOS[3] SÁNCHES, JACINTO[2] MUÑOS, FRANCISCO[1])* was born 1855 in Torreón, New México[363]. He married EVARISTA GONZÁLES May 09, 1877 in Tularoso, New México[364], daughter of AGAPITO GONZÁLES and MARÍA PRUDENCIO.

Child of JUAN SÁNCHEZ and EVARISTA GONZÁLES is:
	i.	EVARISTA GONZÁLES[10] SÁNCHEZ, b. February 28, 1878, Tularoso, Territory of New México[365].

74. BESITA[9] SÁNCHEZ *(MAURICIO DE LA TRINIDAD[8] SÁNCHES, JOSÉ GREGORIO DE LA TRINIDAD[7], JUAN CRISTÓBAL[6], FRANCISCO[5], JACINTO SÁNCHES[4] DE IÑIGO, FRANCISCO MUÑOS[3] SÁNCHES, JACINTO[2] MUÑOS, FRANCISCO[1])* was born 1863 in Manzano, Territory of New México[366]. She married JUAN RAFAEL BERCELÓ SÁNCHES[367] August 29, 1875 in Manzano, Territory of New México[368], son of JUAN SÁNCHES and MARÍA BARCELÓ.

Notes for BESITA SÁNCHEZ:
Also known as María de la Visitación Sánchez, Visita, Vesita.

Notes for JUAN RAFAEL BERCELÓ SÁNCHES:
Also known as Rafael.

Children of BESITA SÁNCHEZ and JUAN SÁNCHES are:
	i.	BEATRIZ[10] SÁNCHEZ.
136.	ii.	RAYMUNDO SÁNCHEZ, b. March 15, 1879, Tajiqué, Territory of New México; d. November 26, 1958.
137.	iii.	AMADITA SÁNCHEZ, b. August 21, 1883, Glencoe, Territory of New México; d. June 12, 1934.
	iv.	LUZ SÁNCHEZ, b. June 28, 1887, Glencoe, Territory of New México[369].
138.	v.	RITA SÁNCHEZ, b. July 12, 1889, Ruidoso, Territory of New México; d. January 1984, Artesia, New México.
	vi.	CONFERINA ORISITACIÓN SÁNCHEZ[370], b. November 16, 1890, Glencoe, Territory of New México[371]; d. November 17, 1938[372]; m. (1) MARCELO HERRERA[373], July 10, 1911, Ruidoso, Territory of New México[374]; m. (2) WILLIAM HERRERA GILL, January 13, 1916, Glencoe, New Mexico[375].

Notes for CONFERINA ORISITACIÓN SÁNCHEZ:
Also known as Conferencia Herrera de Sánchez. Conferina Visitación Herrera de Sánchez.
February 04, 1892: Baptized. Padrinos: Julian Silva and Jesusita Sánchez.

139.	vii.	EDUARDO SÁNCHEZ, b. October 13, 1893, Glencoe, Territory of New México; d. May 28, 1954, San Patricio, New México.
140.	viii.	BERSABÉ SÁNCHEZ, b. June 10, 1897, Glencoe, Territory of New México.
	ix.	SOFIA SÁNCHEZ[376], b. January 01, 1898, Ruidoso, Territory of New México[377]; m. JOSÉ OROSCO, August 09, 1919, La Capilla de San Ysidro, Territory of New México[378].
141.	x.	VICTORIA SÁNCHEZ, b. February 28, 1899, Chililí, Territory of New México; d. February 14, 1983, Albuquerque, New México.
	xi.	MANUEL SÁNCHEZ[379], b. January 20, 1901[380]; d. February 19, 1990.

Notes for MANUEL SÁNCHEZ:
Private US Army. WW II.

142.   xii.   MACLOFA SÁNCHEZ, b. August 21, 1903; d. Abt. February 1922.

75. DONACIANO[9] SÁNCHEZ *(MAURICIO DE LA TRINIDAD[8] SÁNCHES, JOSÉ GREGORIO DE LA TRINIDAD[7], JUAN CRISTÓBAL[6], FRANCISCO[5], JACINTO SÁNCHES[4] DE IÑIGO, FRANCISCO MUÑOS[3] SÁNCHES, JACINTO[2] MUÑOS, FRANCISCO[1])[381]* was born 1866 in El Berendo, Territory of New México[382], and died March 01, 1929 in Tularosa, New México[383]. He married (1) FELICITA SERRANO, daughter of MIGUEL SERRANO and JUANA LUCERO. He married (2) BIDAL ANALLA May 11, 1884 in Tularoso, Territory of New México[384], daughter of PEDRO ANALLA and MARÍA CHÁVES. He married (3) ADELA VIGIL Abt. 1898[385], daughter of LUÍS VIGIL.

Child of DONACIANO SÁNCHEZ and FELICITA SERRANO is:
      i.   MARGARITA SERRANO[10] SÁNCHEZ, b. November 07, 1883, Picacho, Territory of New México[386].
Children of DONACIANO SÁNCHEZ and BIDAL ANALLA are:
      ii.   JUAN BAUTISTA[10] SÁNCHEZ, b. December 05, 1885[387].
      iii.   DANIEL SÁNCHEZ, b. January 03, 1896, Analla, Territory of New México[388]; m. REBECCA ANALLA[389], December 18, 1919, Lincoln, New México[389].

Children of DONACIANO SÁNCHEZ and ADELA VIGIL are:
      iv.   MARÍA VIGIL[10] SÁNCHEZ, b. October 31, 1898, Tularoso, Territory of New México[390]; d. March 25, 1929[391].
      v.   DONANCIANO SÁNCHEZ, b. Abt. 1902, Tularoso, Territory of New México[392].
      vi.   CHANO SÁNCHEZ, b. July 10, 1904, Tularoso, Territory of New México.

Notes for CHANO SÁNCHEZ:
Also known as Francisco Sánchez.

      vii.   FRANCISCA SÁNCHEZ, b. Abt. 1905, Tularoso, Territory of New México[392].
      viii.   JOSÉ VIGIL SÁNCHEZ, b. February 01, 1913, Tularosa, New México[393].

76. AMADA[9] SÁNCHEZ *(MAURICIO DE LA TRINIDAD[8] SÁNCHES, JOSÉ GREGORIO DE LA TRINIDAD[7], JUAN CRISTÓBAL[6], FRANCISCO[5], JACINTO SÁNCHES[4] DE IÑIGO, FRANCISCO MUÑOS[3] SÁNCHES, JACINTO[2] MUÑOS, FRANCISCO[1])* was born December 22, 1870 in La Plaza de San José, Lincoln County, Territory of New México[394]. She married (1) ABEL MIRABAL. She married (2) PABLO CHÁVEZ[395] July 20, 1883 in Las Angusturas (San Ysidro), Territory of New México[396], son of JOSÉ CHÁVES and MARÍA LUNA.

Notes for AMADA SÁNCHEZ:
Also known as Jesúsita Amada Sánchez.

Children of AMADA SÁNCHEZ and PABLO CHÁVEZ are:
      i.   AMADA[10] SÁNCHEZ[397], b. August 1886, La Junta, Territory of New México.
143.   ii.   TRANSITO CHÁVEZ, b. July 20, 1887, La Junta, Territory of New México; d. April 07, 1975, San Patricio, New México.
144.   iii.   CANDIDO CHÁVEZ, b. April 12, 1889, La Junta, Territory of New México; d. May 20, 1979.
      iv.   FLORINDA CHÁVEZ, b. July 08, 1891, La Junta, Territory of New México[398]; m. JUAN BLEA, July 03, 1908, Lincoln, Territory of New México[399].
145.   v.   OLYMPIA CHÁVEZ, b. 1894, La Junta, Territory of New México; d. Abt. 1911, Hondo, Territory of New México.
      vi.   ADELAIDO CHÁVEZ[400], b. December 16, 1903, Hondo, Territory of New México; d. November 1984, San Patricio, New México; m. LUPE VALENSUELA[400], August 21, 1935, Picacho, New México[401].

Notes for ADELAIDO CHÁVEZ:
Land Patent # NMLC 0029127, on the authority of the Homestead Entry-Stock Raising (39 Stat. 862), December 29, 1916. Issued 610.88 acres on January 30, 1931.

146.   vii.   LEOPOLDO CHÁVEZ, b. April 25, 1907, Hondo, Territory of New México.
147.   viii.   RUMELIO CHÁVEZ, b. 1909, Hondo, Territory of New México; d. 1963.
148.   ix.   ERMANDO CHÁVEZ, b. February 24, 1914, Hondo, New México; d. June 05, 2010, Ruidoso, New México.
      x.   PABLO CHÁVEZ, b. June 24, 1900; d. November 23, 1916.

Notes for PABLO CHÁVEZ:
Pablo had fallen ill with appendicitus. His parents were enroute to the doctor in Roswell when he had passed on. They were traveling in a wagon at the time.

77. YSABEL[9] SÁNCHES *(DESIDERIO[8], DIEGO ANTONIO[7], JUAN CRISTÓBAL[6], FRANCISCO[5], JACINTO SÁNCHES[4] DE IÑIGO, FRANCISCO MUÑOS[3] SÁNCHES, JACINTO[2] MUÑOS, FRANCISCO[1])[402]* was born Bef. July 11, 1838 in Tomé, Nuevo México, La República de México[403]. She married REYES SALAS[404] January 07, 1861 in Tomé, Territory of New México[405], son of MANUEL SALAS and NICOLÁSA ROMERO.

Notes for YSABEL SÁNCHES:
Also known as María Ysabel De Jesús Sánches.

Notes for REYES SALAS:
Also known as José de los Reyes Salas.

Children of YSABEL SÁNCHES and REYES SALAS are:
149.   i.   ANDRÉS[10] SALAS, b. November 1863, Manzano, Territory of New México.
150.   ii.   RAYMUNDO SALAS, b. February 1863, Manzano, Territory of New México.
        iii.   MARTÍN SALAS, b. Abt. 1867, Manzano, Territory of New México[406].
        iv.   PEDRO SALAS, b. Bef. September 04, 1869, Manzano, Territory of New México[407].
        v.   JOSÉ DE JESÚS SALAS, b. Abt. 1872, Manzano, Territory of New México[408].
        vi.   PABLO SALAS, b. Abt. 1875, Manzano, Territory of New México[408].

Serafín Polaco

78. MARÍA ALTAGRACIA[9] GONZÁLES *(MARÍA MANUELA[8] ARAGÓN, MARIANA ANTONIA[7] SÁNCHES, DIEGO ANTONIO[6], FRANCISCO[5], JACINTO SÁNCHES[4] DE IÑIGO, FRANCISCO MUÑOS[3] SÁNCHES, JACINTO[2] MUÑOS, FRANCISCO[1])[409]* was born Bef. December 17, 1833 in Los Corrales, Nuevo México, República de México[410]. She married SERAFÍN POLACO September 16, 1853 in Albuquerque, Territory of New México[411], son of JUAN POLACO and CATARINA CHAPAME.

Children of MARÍA GONZÁLES and SERAFÍN POLACO are:
        i.   MARÍA JUANA[10] POLACO, b. December 31, 1853, Los Corrales, Territory of New México[412].
151.   ii.   CRECENSIA POLACO, b. Abt. 1854, Los Corrales, Territory of New México; d. April 17, 1937, Las Vegas, New México.
152.   iii.   ANASTACIA POLACO, b. Abt. 1855, Los Corrales, Territory of New México; d. April 25, 1927, Albuquerque, New México.
153.   iv.   TRANCITO POLACO, b. July 26, 1858, Los Corrales, Territory of New México; d. San Patricio, New México.
154.   v.   CANDIDO POLACO, b. Bef. July 30, 1860, Los Corrales, Territory of New México; d. October 18, 1932, Cordillera, New México.
155.   vi.   ELFIGO POLACO, b. Bef. March 11, 1862, Los Corrales, Territory of New México; d. August 23, 1926, Tiptonville, New México.
156.   vii.   RUDOLFO POLACO, b. Bef. October 11, 1864, Los Corrales, Territory of New México.
        viii.   ALTAGRACIA POLACO, b. Abt. November 1866, La Plaza de San Patricio, Territory of New México[413]; m. MARIANO GONZÁLES, December 17, 1883, Bernalillo, Territory of New México[414].
        ix.   CONSOLACION POLACO, b. Abt. 1873, Las Vegas, Territory of New México[415]; m. JOSÉ LEONARDO ABEYTA, February 06, 1894, Las Vegas, Territory of New México[416].
        x.   SANTIAGO POLACO, b. July 26, 1874, Las Vegas, Territory of New México[417].

Florencio Gonzáles

79. FLORENCIO[9] GONZÁLES *(MARÍA MANUELA[8] ARAGÓN, MARIANA ANTONIA[7] SÁNCHES, DIEGO ANTONIO[6], FRANCISCO[5], JACINTO SÁNCHES[4] DE IÑIGO, FRANCISCO MUÑOS[3] SÁNCHES, JACINTO[2] MUÑOS, FRANCISCO[1])[418]* was born November 07, 1843 in Los Corrales, Nuevo México, La República de México, and died December 18, 1897 in San Patricio, Territory of New México. He married RAYMUNDA SEGUNDA SÁNCHEZ in Manzano, Territory of New México[419], daughter of MAURICIO SÁNCHES and JESÚSITA GONZÁLES.

Notes for FLORENCIO GONZÁLES:

Also known as José Florencio Gonzáles. In 1867 he also went by Florencio Gonzáles y Aragón.
Land Patent # NMNMAA 010635, on the authority of the Sale cash entry, April 24, 1820, 120 Acres.

Children of FLORENCIO GONZÁLES and RAYMUNDA SÁNCHEZ are:
    i.   ARISTOTEL[10] GONZÁLES.

Notes for ARISTOTEL GONZÁLES:
Died young.

    ii.   FILOTEA GONZÁLES.

Notes for FILOTEA GONZÁLES:
Died young.

117.   iii.   ESLINDA GONZÁLES, b. 1867, La Placita del Rio Bonito, Territory of New México; d. Bef. October 1922.
    iv.   JUAN GONZÁLES, b. 1869, La Placita del Rio Bonito, Territory of New México.
118.   v.   PROSPERO GONZÁLES, b. July 20, 1871, Lincoln, Territory of New México; d. August 20, 1937, Glencoe, New México.
119.   vi.   LEOPOLDO SÁNCHEZ GONZÁLES, b. April 08, 1875, Lincoln, Territory of New México; d. June 10, 1937, San Patricio, New México.
120.   vii.   ALFREDO GONZÁLES, b. 1876, Lincoln, Territory of New México; d. 1927, San Patricio, New México.
121.   viii.   EPAMINOANDAS GONZÁLES, b. April 04, 1876, Lincoln, Territory of New México; d. February 20, 1970, San Patricio, New México.
122.   ix.   AVRORA GONZÁLES, b. May 23, 1880, San Patricio, Territory of New México; d. August 15, 1971, San Patricio, New México.
123.   x.   AROPAJITA GONZÁLES, b. October 12, 1882, San Patricio, Territory of New México; d. San Patricio, New México.
124.   xi.   AURELIA GONZÁLES, b. May 15, 1883, San Patricio, Territory of New México.
125.   xii.   FLORENCIO SÁNCHEZ GONZÁLES, b. November 09, 1892, San Patricio, Territory of New México; d. July 09, 1979.
126.   xiii.   ESOILA GONZÁLES, b. August 08, 1894, San Patricio, Territory of New México.

Fernando Herrera

80. FERNANDO[9] HERRERA *(PEDRO ALCANTARA[8] DE HERRERA, MARÍA JOSEFA[7] BUSTOS, MARÍA ANTONIA TERESA[6] SÁNCHES, PEDRO[5], PEDRO SÁNCHES[4] DE IÑIGO, FRANCISCO MUÑOS[3] SÁNCHES, JACINTO[2] MUÑOS, FRANCISCO[1])[420]* was born July 02, 1836 in Santa Cruz de la Cañada, Nuevo México, La República de México[421], and died December 14, 1915 in Alamogordo, New México. He married (1) JULIANA MARTÍN October 13, 1856 in Santa Cruz de la Cañada, Territory of New México[422], daughter of JOSÉ MARTÍN and MARÍA GÓMES. He married (2) MARTA RODRÍGUEZ Abt. 1874[423].

Notes for FERNANDO HERRERA:
Also known as José Fernando de Herrera and Fernandes de Herrera. Fernando Herrera is buried in an unmarked gravesite in Alamogordo, New México.
Land Patent # NMNMAA 010251, on the authority of the Homestead Act, May 20, 1862, 160 Acres.

Notes for JULIANA MARTÍN:
Also known as María Juliana Martín, Julianita.

Children of FERNANDO HERRERA and JULIANA MARTÍN are:
157.   i.   ALTAGRACIA[10] HERRERA, b. April 15, 1857, Santa Cruz de la Cañada, Territory of New México; d. June 26, 1893, San Juanito (Ruidoso Downs), Territory of New México.
158.   ii.   ANDRÉS HERRERA, b. November 27, 1858, Santa Cruz de la Cañada, New México; d. 1911, Carrizozo, New México.
159.   iii.   ANTONIA MIGUELA HERRERA, b. June 13, 1860, Santa Cruz de la Cañada, Territory of New México; d. November 27, 1912, Acton, Texas.
    iv.   MARÍA ANTONIA HERRERA, b. December 08, 1862, Santa Cruz de la Cañada, Territory of New México[424]; d. December 11, 1862, Santa Cruz de la Cañada, Territory of New México.
    v.   NICOLÁSA HERRERA, b. December 08, 1862, Santa Cruz de la Cañada, New México[424]; m. ANTONIO VALENZUELA, October 17, 1902, San Patricio, New México[425].

160.   vi.   MARTA HERRERA, b. April 24, 1865, Santa Cruz de la Cañada, New México.
161.   vii.   MANUELITA HERRERA, b. April 20, 1866, Santa Cruz de la Cañada, Territory of New México; d. February 12, 1939, San Patricio, New México.
          viii.   MACEDONIO HERRERA, b. September 05, 1868, Rio Colorado, Territory of New México[426].
          ix.   SELEDONIA HERRERA, b. April 20, 1870, Rio Colorado, Territory of New México[426]; d. San Juanito (Ruidoso Downs), Territory of New México.
          x.   AUGUSTÍN HERRERA, b. April 04, 1872, Santa Cruz de la Cañada, Territory of New México.

Notes for AUGUSTÍN HERRERA:
Land Patent # NMNMAA 010262, on the authority of the Homestead Act, May 20, 1862, 160 Acres.

162.   xi.   TEODORO HERRERA, b. April 1873, San Juanito (Ruidoso Downs), Territory of New México; d. Alamogordo, New México.

Generation No. 10

Andalesio Padilla

81. ANDALESIO[10] PADILLA *(ROSALÍA[9] CHÁVEZ, JUANA[8] SÁNCHES, PEDRO[7], JACINTO[6], JOSÉ SÁNCHES[5] DE IÑIGO, JACINTO SÁNCHES[4], FRANCISCO MUÑOS[3] SÁNCHES, JACINTO[2] MUÑOS, FRANCISCO[1])[427]* was born Abt. 1856 in Los Padilla, Territory of New México, and died March 16, 1913 in Tres Rios, Territory of New México[428]. He married PAUBLITA MARIÑO[429] Abt. 1875[430], daughter of JOSÉ MARIÑO and MARÍA CHÁVES.

Children of ANDALESIO PADILLA and PAUBLITA MARIÑO are:
163.   i.   CANDELARIA[11] PADILLA, b. February 1879, Tres Ritos, Territory of New México; d. March 13, 1956, San Elizario, Téxas.
164.   ii.   BENITO PADILLA, b. April 16, 1883; d. June 26, 1906.
          iii.   FLORA PADILLA, b. Abt. 1884[431].
          iv.   MANUELITA PADILLA[432], b. March 22, 1884, Tres Ritos, Territory of New México[433].
          v.   EVANGELISTA PADILLA[434], b. September 20, 1885, Tres Ritos, Territory of New México[435].
          vi.   ROSARIO PADILLA, b. March 12, 1887, Tularoso, Territory of New México[436].
165.   vii.   ANDALESIO MARIÑO PADILLA, b. May 31, 1892.
166.   viii.   NESTOR PADILLA, b. February 27, 1896, Tres Ritos, Territory of New México.
          ix.   JUAN PADILLA, b. September 1897[437].
          x.   JOSÉ JESÚS PADILLA[438], b. February 09, 1900, Tres Ritos, Territory of New México[439].
          xi.   PABLO PADILLA, b. Abt. 1902, Tres Ritos, Territory of New México[440].
          xii.   SOFIA PADILLA, b. September 22, 1903, Tres Ritos, Territory of New México[441].

Notes for SOFIA PADILLA:
Died young.

          xiii.   FRANCISCO PADILLA, b. Abt. 1907, Tres Ritos, Territory of New México[442].
          xiv.   MANUEL PADILLA, b. Abt. 1908, Tres Ritos, Territory of New México[443].

82. MARÍA ALTAGRACIA DEL REFUGIO[10] SÁNCHES *(JUAN RAFAEL FERNANDO[9], MANUEL RAFAEL[8], PEDRO[7], JACINTO[6], JOSÉ SÁNCHES[5] DE IÑIGO, JACINTO SÁNCHES[4], FRANCISCO MUÑOS[3] SÁNCHES, JACINTO[2] MUÑOS, FRANCISCO[1])[444]* was born Bef. January 31, 1824 in Tomé, Nuevo México, La República de México[445]. She married JUAN FRANCISCO PABLO VIGIL, son of MANUEL VIGIL and MARÍA APODACA.

Notes for MARÍA ALTAGRACIA DEL REFUGIO SÁNCHES:
Also known as Refugio. 1860 Census lists her birth year as 1829.

Children of MARÍA SÁNCHES and JUAN VIGIL are:
          i.   MARÍA CATARINA DE LA LUZ[11] VIGIL[445], b. May 16, 1841, Valencia, Nuevo México, La República de México.
167.   ii.   JUANA MARÍA VIGIL, b. June 15, 1844, Tomé, Nuevo México, La República de México; d. 1878-1880.
168.   iii.   JOSÉ MANUEL VIGIL, b. June 10, 1846, Valencia, Nuevo México, La República de México; d. 1931.
          iv.   JESÚS VIGIL, b. Abt. 1848, Tajiqué, Territory of New México[446].
          v.   BARSABÉ VIGIL, b. Abt. 1850, Tajiqué, Territory of New México[446]; m. AGAPITO SÁNCHEZ.
          vi.   ÁBRAN VIGIL, b. March 16, 1851, Tajíque, Territory of New México.
          vii.   VITERBO VIGIL, b. Abt. 1853, Tajiqué, Territory of New México[446].

viii.   BEATRIZ VIGIL, b. Abt. 1855, Tajiqué, Territory of New México[446].

83. ROMAULDO[10] SÁNCHES *(JUAN RAFAEL FERNANDO[9], MANUEL RAFAEL[8], PEDRO[7], JACINTO[6], JOSÉ SÁNCHES[5] DE IÑIGO, JACINTO SÁNCHES[4], FRANCISCO MUÑOS[3] SÁNCHES, JACINTO[2] MUÑOS, FRANCISCO[1])* was born Bef. February 16, 1828 in Valencia, Nuevo México, La República de México[447]. He married (1) MARÍA RITA LUNA April 29, 1848 in Tomé, Territory of New México[448], daughter of VICENTE LUNA and GREGORIA GABALDON. He married (2) JULIANA VARELA August 19, 1873 in Tomé, Territory of New México[449].

Children of ROMAULDO SÁNCHES and MARÍA LUNA are:
    i.   MARÍA LINA LEONOR[11] SÁNCHES, b. Bef. October 01, 1854[450].
    ii.   JOSÉ FRANCISCO SÁNCHES, b. Bef. April 03, 1861[451]; m. VIRGINIA OTERO, January 07, 1881, Manzano, Territory of New México[452].
    iii. ANTONIO SÁNCHES, b. Bef. November 26, 1863[453]; m. DOMITILIA OTERO, December 14, 1887, Manzano, Territory of New México[454].
    iv.   NESTORA SÁNCHES, b. Bef. March 11, 1866[455]; m. MANUEL OTERO, November 14, 1883, Tomé, Territory of New México[456].
    v.   JESÚS SÁNCHES, b. Abt. 1868[457]; m. CAROLINA BARELA, December 12, 1889, Manzano, Territory of New México[458].

Child of ROMAULDO SÁNCHES and JULIANA VARELA is:
    vi.   VENCESLAO[11] SÁNCHEZ, b. Bef. November 08, 1873[459].

84. VICTORIA[10] SÁNCHES *(JUAN RAFAEL FERNANDO[9], MANUEL RAFAEL[8], PEDRO[7], JACINTO[6], JOSÉ SÁNCHES[5] DE IÑIGO, JACINTO SÁNCHES[4], FRANCISCO MUÑOS[3] SÁNCHES, JACINTO[2] MUÑOS, FRANCISCO[1])[460]* was born Bef. March 05, 1830[461]. She married FILOMENO SÁNCHES[462] Abt. 1845[463], son of TOMÁS SÁNCHES and MARÍA LUSERO.

Notes for FILOMENO SÁNCHES:
Also known as José Filomeno de Jesús Sánches.

Children of VICTORIA SÁNCHES and FILOMENO SÁNCHES are:
    i.   BARTOLA[11] SÁNCHEZ, Adopted child.
    ii.   CRUZ SÁNCHEZ, Adopted child.
    iii. RAFAEL SÁNCHEZ, Adopted child; m. MAXIMILIANA DE SÁNCHEZ, May 18, 1893, Manzano, Territory of New México[464].
    iv.   JULIAN SÁNCHEZ, b. Abt. 1853[465]; Adopted child.
    v.   MARÍA SÁNCHEZ, b. Abt. 1856[466].
169.   vi.   EUGENIO SÁNCHEZ, b. September 1856, Manzano, Territory of New México; d. September 17, 1935, Manzano, New México.
    vii. TOMASITA SÁNCHEZ, b. Abt. 1858[467]; Adopted child.
170.   viii. MANUEL SÁNCHEZ, b. Abt. 1859; Adopted child.
    ix.   GUADALUPE SÁNCHEZ, b. Abt. 1861[468].
    x.   JUAN SÁNCHEZ, b. Abt. 1867[469]; Adopted child.
    xi.   JESÚS SÁNCHEZ, b. Abt. 1868[470].

85. PABLO[10] SÁNCHES *(JUAN RAFAEL FERNANDO[9], MANUEL RAFAEL[8], PEDRO[7], JACINTO[6], JOSÉ SÁNCHES[5] DE IÑIGO, JACINTO SÁNCHES[4], FRANCISCO MUÑOS[3] SÁNCHES, JACINTO[2] MUÑOS, FRANCISCO[1])[471]* was born Abt. 1838[472]. He married JOSEFA SÁNCHES November 28, 1854 in Tomé, Territory of New México[473], daughter of MATÍAS SÁNCHES and ANA VALLEJOS.

Children of PABLO SÁNCHES and JOSEFA SÁNCHES are:
    i.   CANDIDO[11] SÁNCHEZ, b. Abt. 1856, Tajiqué, Territory of New México[474].
    ii.   RAFAEL SÁNCHEZ, b. Abt. 1859, Tajiqué, Territory of New México[474].

86. VICENTE[10] SÁNCHES *(JUAN RAFAEL FERNANDO[9], MANUEL RAFAEL[8], PEDRO[7], JACINTO[6], JOSÉ SÁNCHES[5] DE IÑIGO, JACINTO SÁNCHES[4], FRANCISCO MUÑOS[3] SÁNCHES, JACINTO[2] MUÑOS, FRANCISCO[1])[475]* was born Bef. April 05, 1840[476]. He married RAMONA SÁNCHES January 11, 1860 in Tomé, Territory of New México[477], daughter of DOMINGO SÁNCHES and JUANA ARAGÓN.

Children of VICENTE SÁNCHES and RAMONA SÁNCHES are:

    i.   JOSÉ CECILIO¹¹ SÁNCHES, b. Bef. November 27, 1860⁴⁷⁸.
    ii.   DELFINIA SÁNCHES, b. Abt. 1863⁴⁷⁹.
    iii. PEDRO SÁNCHES, b. Bef. July 04, 1866.
    iv. SOCORRO SÁNCHES, b. Abt. September 1868, Manzano, Territory of New México⁴⁸⁰.
    v.   MANUELA SÁNCHES, b. Bef. January 12, 1871, Lincoln County, Territory of New México⁴⁸¹.

87. FERNANDES¹⁰ SÁNCHES *(JUAN RAFAEL FERNANDO⁹, MANUEL RAFAEL⁸, PEDRO⁷, JACINTO⁶, JOSÉ SÁNCHES⁵ DE IÑIGO, JACINTO SÁNCHES⁴, FRANCISCO MUÑOS³ SÁNCHES, JACINTO² MUÑOS, FRANCISCO¹)*⁴⁸² was born Bef. May 04, 1845⁴⁸³. He married FRANCISQUITA BENAVIDES⁴⁸⁴.

Notes for FERNANDES SÁNCHES:
Also known as: Pedro José Fernando de Jesús Sánches.

Children of FERNANDES SÁNCHES and FRANCISQUITA BENAVIDES are:

171.   i.   PEDRO¹¹ SÁNCHEZ, b. Abt. 1867.
    ii.   JOSÉ AMBROCIO SÁNCHEZ, b. Bef. December 13, 1869⁴⁸⁵.
    iii. SEVERO SÁNCHEZ, b. Abt. 1870⁴⁸⁶.
    iv. PABLO SÁNCHEZ, b. Abt. 1872⁴⁸⁶; m. CELESTE SÁNCHEZ, June 27, 1895, Manzano, Territory of New México⁴⁸⁷.
    v.   REYMUNDO SÁNCHEZ, b. Bef. February 25, 1874⁴⁸⁸.
    vi. MARÍA LEANDRA SÁNCHEZ, b. August 12, 1877⁴⁸⁹.
    vii. ANDELESIO SÁNCHEZ, b. May 22, 1879⁴⁸⁹.
    viii. TRANQUILINO ABEL SÁNCHEZ, b. May 21, 1881⁴⁸⁹.
    ix. MARÍA DEL REFUGIO SÁNCHEZ, b. May 23, 1885⁴⁸⁹.

Juan Rafael Berceló Sánches

88. JUAN RAFAEL BERCELÓ¹⁰ SÁNCHES *(JUAN RAFAEL FERNANDO⁹, MANUEL RAFAEL⁸, PEDRO⁷, JACINTO⁶, JOSÉ SÁNCHES⁵ DE IÑIGO, JACINTO SÁNCHES⁴, FRANCISCO MUÑOS³ SÁNCHES, JACINTO² MUÑOS, FRANCISCO¹)*⁴⁹⁰ was born Bef. November 21, 1847 in Tomé, Territory of New México⁴⁹¹. He married BESITA SÁNCHEZ August 29, 1875 in Manzano, Territory of New México⁴⁹¹, daughter of MAURICIO SÁNCHES and JESÚSITA GONZÁLES.

Children of JUAN SÁNCHES and BESITA SÁNCHEZ are:

    i.   BEATRIZ¹¹ SÁNCHEZ.
    ii.   RAYMUNDO SÁNCHEZ⁴⁹², b. March 15, 1879, Tajiqué, Territory of New México; d. November 26, 1958; m. AUGUSTINA ULIBARRÍ⁴⁹², December 17, 1910⁴⁹³.
    iii. AMADITA SÁNCHEZ⁴⁹⁴, b. August 21, 1883, Glencoe, Territory of New México; d. June 12, 1934; m. (1) FEDERICO PEÑA; m. (2) LUÍS LÓPEZ PEÑA, January 12, 1903⁴⁹⁵.
    iv. LUZ SÁNCHEZ, b. June 28, 1887, Glencoe, Territory of New México⁴⁹⁶.
    v.   RITA SÁNCHEZ⁴⁹⁷, b. July 12, 1889, Ruidoso, Territory of New México⁴⁹⁸; d. January 1984, Artesia, New México⁴⁹⁹; m. NEWMAN GILL, July 03, 1915, La Capilla de San Ysidro, New México⁵⁰⁰.
    vi. CONFERINA ORISITACIÓN SÁNCHEZ⁵⁰¹, b. November 16, 1890, Glencoe, Territory of New México⁵⁰²; d. November 17, 1938⁵⁰³; m. (1) MARCELO HERRERA⁵⁰⁴, July 10, 1911, Ruidoso, Territory of New México⁵⁰⁵; m. (2) WILLIAM HERRERA GILL, January 13, 1916, Glencoe, New Mexico⁵⁰⁶.
    vii. EDUARDO SÁNCHEZ⁵⁰⁷, b. October 13, 1893, Glencoe, Territory of New México⁵⁰⁸; d. May 28, 1954, San Patricio, New México; m. SENAIDA MONTOYA⁵⁰⁹, October 08, 1920, San Patricio, New México⁵¹⁰.

Notes for SENAIDA MONTOYA:
Also known as Maclofa Montoya.

    viii. BERSABÉ SÁNCHEZ, b. June 10, 1897, Glencoe, Territory of New México⁵¹¹; m. TEODORO ULIBARRÍ MONTOYA⁵¹², December 11, 1919, San Patricio, New México⁵¹³.
    ix. SOFIA SÁNCHEZ⁵¹⁴, b. January 01, 1898, Ruidoso, Territory of New México⁵¹⁵; m. JOSÉ OROSCO, August 09, 1919, La Capilla de San Ysidro, Territory of New México⁵¹⁶.
    x.   VICTORIA SÁNCHEZ⁵¹⁷, b. February 28, 1899, Chililí, Territory of New México⁵¹⁸; d. February 14, 1983, Albuquerque, New México; m. (1) CELSO TRUJILLO⁵¹⁹; m. (2) ISABEL MONTOYA, February 23, 1921⁵²⁰.
    xi. MANUEL SÁNCHEZ⁵²¹, b. January 20, 1901⁵²²; d. February 19, 1990.
    xii. MACLOFA SÁNCHEZ, b. August 21, 1903; d. Abt. February 1922; m. DOMINGO PACHECO.

89. JOSEFA[10] SÁNCHES *(MATÍAS[9], MANUEL RAFAEL[8], PEDRO[7], JACINTO[6], JOSÉ SÁNCHES[5] DE IÑIGO, JACINTO SÁNCHES[4], FRANCISCO MUÑOS[3] SÁNCHES, JACINTO[2] MUÑOS, FRANCISCO[1])* was born Abt. 1835[523], and died Bef. 1880. She married PABLO SÁNCHES[524] November 28, 1854 in Tomé, Territory of New México[525], son of JUAN SÁNCHES and MARÍA BARCELÓ.

Children of JOSEFA SÁNCHES and PABLO SÁNCHES are:
    i.   CANDIDO[11] SÁNCHEZ, b. Abt. 1856, Tajiqué, Territory of New México[526].
    ii.   RAFAEL SÁNCHEZ, b. Abt. 1859, Tajiqué, Territory of New México[526].

90. CATALINA[10] SÁNCHES *(MATÍAS[9], MANUEL RAFAEL[8], PEDRO[7], JACINTO[6], JOSÉ SÁNCHES[5] DE IÑIGO, JACINTO SÁNCHES[4], FRANCISCO MUÑOS[3] SÁNCHES, JACINTO[2] MUÑOS, FRANCISCO[1])* was born Abt. 1838[527]. She married JESÚS LÓPEZ.

Notes for CATALINA SÁNCHES:
Also known as Catarina.

Children of CATALINA SÁNCHES and JESÚS LÓPEZ are:
    i.   JOSÉ URBÁN[11] LÓPEZ, b. Abt. 1858[528].
    ii.   MANUEL SÁNCHEZ LÓPEZ, b. Abt. 1866[528].
    iii.   GREGORIO LÓPEZ, b. Abt. 1868[528].

91. JUAN FRANCISCO PABLO[10] VIGIL *(MARÍA SOLEDAD[9] APODACA, ANA ROSALÍA[8] SÁNCHES, PEDRO[7], JACINTO[6], JOSÉ SÁNCHES[5] DE IÑIGO, JACINTO SÁNCHES[4], FRANCISCO MUÑOS[3] SÁNCHES, JACINTO[2] MUÑOS, FRANCISCO[1])* was born March 08, 1821 in Tomé, Nuevo México, La República de México[529]. He married MARÍA ALTAGRACIA DEL REFUGIO SÁNCHES[530], daughter of JUAN SÁNCHES and MARÍA BARCELÓ.

Notes for MARÍA ALTAGRACIA DEL REFUGIO SÁNCHES:
Also known as Refugio. 1860 Census lists her birth year as 1829.

Children of JUAN VIGIL and MARÍA SÁNCHES are:
    i.   MARÍA CATARINA DE LA LUZ[11] VIGIL[531], b. May 16, 1841, Valencia, Nuevo México, La República de México.
167. ii.   JUANA MARÍA VIGIL, b. June 15, 1844, Tomé, Nuevo México, La República de México; d. 1878-1880.
168. iii.   JOSÉ MANUEL VIGIL, b. June 10, 1846, Valencia, Nuevo México, La República de México; d. 1931.
    iv.   JESÚS VIGIL, b. Abt. 1848, Tajiqué, Territory of New México[532].
    v.   BARSABÉ VIGIL, b. Abt. 1850, Tajiqué, Territory of New México[532]; m. AGAPITO SÁNCHEZ.

Notes for AGAPITO SÁNCHEZ:
1880 Census: Living in La Plaza de Picacho, Territory of New México.

    vi.   ÁBRAN VIGIL, b. March 16, 1851, Tajíque, Territory of New México.
    vii.   VITERBO VIGIL, b. Abt. 1853, Tajiqué, Territory of New México[532].
    viii.   BEATRIZ VIGIL, b. Abt. 1855, Tajiqué, Territory of New México[532].

92. FRANCISCO ANTONIO[10] VIGIL *(MARÍA SOLEDAD[9] APODACA, ANA ROSALÍA[8] SÁNCHES, PEDRO[7], JACINTO[6], JOSÉ SÁNCHES[5] DE IÑIGO, JACINTO SÁNCHES[4], FRANCISCO MUÑOS[3] SÁNCHES, JACINTO[2] MUÑOS, FRANCISCO[1])[533]* was born Bef. April 12, 1823 in Tomé, Nuevo México, La República de México[534], and died February 07, 1890. He married MARÍA DEL REFUGIO MADARIAGA[535] February 16, 1844 in Tomé, Nuevo México, La República de México[536], daughter of JUAN MADARIAGA and MARÍA SEDILLO.

Children of FRANCISCO VIGIL and MARÍA MADARIAGA are:
    i.   MANUEL[11] VIGIL, b. Abt. 1851[537].
172. ii.   ESCOLASTICO VIGIL, b. February 1853.
    iii.   PEDRO VIGIL, b. Abt. 1855[537].
    iv.   JUAN VIGIL, b. Abt. 1858[537].
    v.   RAMÓN VIGIL, b. Abt. 1863[537].
    vi.   DOLÓRES VIGIL, b. Abt. 1866[537].
    vii.   VIRGINIA VIGIL, b. Abt. 1869[537].

93. MASIMA JARAMILLO[10] SÁNCHEZ *(MANUEL[9] SÁNCHES, MANUEL DE JESÚS JOSÉ[8], DOMINGO DE JESÚS[7], JUAN CRISTÓBAL[6], FRANCISCO[5], JACINTO SÁNCHES[4] DE IÑIGO, FRANCISCO MUÑOS[3] SÁNCHES, JACINTO[2] MUÑOS, FRANCISCO[1])* was born Abt. 1856[538]. She married COSMÉ SEDILLO November 05, 1873 in Tularoso, Territory of New México[539], son of JUAN SEDILLO and ANA CHÁVES.

Notes for MASIMA JARAMILLO SÁNCHEZ:
Also known as Maxima and Masimiana.

Children of MASIMA SÁNCHEZ and COSMÉ SEDILLO are:

173.	i.	MARTÍN SÁNCHEZ[11] SEDILLO, b. April 30, 1875, El Berendo, Territory of New México.
174.	ii.	FEDERICO SEDILLO, b. February 10, 1880, El Berendo, Territory of New México.
175.	iii.	JUANITA SEDILLO, b. Abt. 1884, El Berendo, Territory of New México.
	iv.	DEMETRIO SEDILLO, b. April 07, 1885, El Berendo, Territory of New México[540].
	v.	CATARINA SEDILLO, b. Abt. 1894, El Berendo, Territory of New México; m. MANUEL FRESQUEZ.
	vi.	TELESFORA SEDILLO, b. December 24, 1895, El Berendo, New México[541].
	vii.	FILOMENO SEDILLO, b. August 16, 1900[542].
	viii.	SOFIA SEDILLO, b. June 11, 1901[543].

94. PEDRO JARAMILLO[10] SÁNCHEZ *(MANUEL[9] SÁNCHES, MANUEL DE JESÚS JOSÉ[8], DOMINGO DE JESÚS[7], JUAN CRISTÓBAL[6], FRANCISCO[5], JACINTO SÁNCHES[4] DE IÑIGO, FRANCISCO MUÑOS[3] SÁNCHES, JACINTO[2] MUÑOS, FRANCISCO[1])* was born Abt. 1860[544]. He married RAMONA SEDILLO November 29, 1885 in Lincoln County, Territory of New México[545], daughter of JUAN SEDILLO and JOSEFA FAJARDO.

Children of PEDRO SÁNCHEZ and RAMONA SEDILLO are:

176.	i.	YSABEL[11] SÁNCHEZ, b. July 07, 1888, San Patricio, Territory of New México.
177.	ii.	ISIDRA SÁNCHEZ, b. May 15, 1889, Roswell, Territory of New México; d. July 16, 1992.
	iii.	PROCOPIO SÁNCHEZ, b. Abt. 1892[546].
	iv.	DOROTEA SÁNCHEZ, b. Abt. 1894[546].
	v.	RUFINA SÁNCHEZ, b. February 06, 1896, El Berendo, Territory of New México[547]; m. SANTIAGO GALLEGOS, June 01, 1913, Lincoln, New México[547].
	vi.	BENITO SÁNCHEZ, b. Abt. 1899[548].
	vii.	ISIDRO SÁNCHEZ, b. Abt. 1902[548].
	viii.	PEDRO SEDILLO SÁNCHEZ, b. May 15, 1902[549].

95. CELESTINO[10] SÁNCHEZ *(SAMUEL[9] SÁNCHES, SANTIAGO[8], JOSÉ GREGORIO DE LA TRINIDAD[7], JUAN CRISTÓBAL[6], FRANCISCO[5], JACINTO SÁNCHES[4] DE IÑIGO, FRANCISCO MUÑOS[3] SÁNCHES, JACINTO[2] MUÑOS, FRANCISCO[1])* was born June 25, 1870 in La Plaza de San José, Territory of New México[550]. He married NAVORSITA MOYA 1896[551].

Children of CELESTINO SÁNCHEZ and NAVORSITA MOYA are:

178.	i.	MAURO[11] SÁNCHEZ, b. July 27, 1897, Ruidoso, Territory of New México; d. March 23, 1982, Hondo, New México.
179.	ii.	JOSÉ MOYA SÁNCHEZ, b. September 25, 1899, Ruidoso, Territory of New México; d. September 1952.
180.	iii.	SAMUEL MOYA SÁNCHEZ, b. April 16, 1900, Ruidoso, Territory of New México; d. May 29, 1966, San Patricio, New México.
181.	iv.	MILITÓN SÁNCHEZ, b. March 10, 1905, Ruidoso, Territory of New México; d. October 08, 1991, Ruidoso Downs, New México.
182.	v.	JUANITA SÁNCHEZ, b. March 31, 1907, Rebentón, Territory of New México; d. March 17, 1998.
183.	vi.	SYLVANO MOYA SÁNCHEZ, b. May 09, 1909, Ruidoso, Territory of New México; d. March 08, 1976, Ruidoso Downs, New México.

96. MARIANA CALMARIA[10] SÁNCHEZ *(SAMUEL[9] SÁNCHES, SANTIAGO[8], JOSÉ GREGORIO DE LA TRINIDAD[7], JUAN CRISTÓBAL[6], FRANCISCO[5], JACINTO SÁNCHES[4] DE IÑIGO, FRANCISCO MUÑOS[3] SÁNCHES, JACINTO[2] MUÑOS, FRANCISCO[1])* was born May 27, 1885[552]. She married JUAN MAESTAS CHÁVEZ September 11, 1903[553], son of PERFECTO CHÁVEZ and AGAPITA MAESTAS.

Children of MARIANA SÁNCHEZ and JUAN CHÁVEZ are:

	i.	RUMALDO[11] CHÁVEZ, b. Abt. 1908, Ruidoso, Territory of New México[554].

    ii.   ALBERTO CHÁVEZ, b. April 16, 1911, Glencoe, Territory of New México[555]; m. NELLIE CANDELARIA, January 18, 1935, Carrizozo, New México[555].

    iii.   ELVIRA CHÁVEZ, b. Abt. 1911, Ruidoso, Territory of New México[556].

    iv.   LUGARDITA SÁNCHEZ CHÁVEZ, b. Abt. 1913, Ruidoso, Territory of New México[556].

97. SANTIAGO MAESTAS[10] SÁNCHEZ *(SAMUEL[9] SÁNCHES, SANTIAGO[8], JOSÉ GREGORIO DE LA TRINIDAD[7], JUAN CRISTÓBAL[6], FRANCISCO[5], JACINTO SÁNCHES[4] DE IÑIGO, FRANCISCO MUÑOS[3] SÁNCHES, JACINTO[2] MUÑOS, FRANCISCO[1])* was born April 15, 1892 in Ruidoso, Territory of New México[557]. He married CARLOTA TRUJILLO[558] January 15, 1913, daughter of JUAN TRUJILLO and CRUSITA ARCHIBEQUE.

Child of SANTIAGO SÁNCHEZ and CARLOTA TRUJILLO is:

    i.   BERNERANDA[11] SÁNCHEZ[558], b. February 06, 1914, Glencoe, New México; d. October 16, 1982; m. NASARIO MONTOYA[558], October 06, 1930, Carrizozo, New México[559].

Notes for BERNERANDA SÁNCHEZ:
Also known as Bennie.

Notes for NASARIO MONTOYA:
Also known as Ted.
Nasario and his wife Bennie raised Erineo Benavidez Sánchez and Frank Trujillo.

98. JESUSITA[10] GALLEGOS *(MARÍA DOLORES[9] SÁNCHES, SANTIAGO[8], JOSÉ GREGORIO DE LA TRINIDAD[7], JUAN CRISTÓBAL[6], FRANCISCO[5], JACINTO SÁNCHES[4] DE IÑIGO, FRANCISCO MUÑOS[3] SÁNCHES, JACINTO[2] MUÑOS, FRANCISCO[1])* was born Abt. 1883[560]. She married REYES MIRABAL February 07, 1898[561], son of JUAN MIRABAL and GUADALUPE TRUJILLO.

Children of JESUSITA GALLEGOS and REYES MIRABAL are:

184.   i.   NERES[11] MIRABAL, b. Abt. 1899, Glencoe, Territory of New México.

    ii.   ERINEA MIRABAL, b. Abt. 1901[562]; m. ISA CHÁVEZ.

Notes for ERINEA MIRABAL:
Also known as Irene.

    iii.   LOLA MIRABAL, b. Abt. 1903[562]; m. SIPIO SÁNCHEZ.

    iv.   LUPE MIRABAL, b. Abt. 1906[562].

    v.   RUFINA MIRABAL, b. Abt. 1907[563]; m. JULIO MESTAS.

    vi.   DAVÍD MIRABAL, b. Abt. 1908[564]; m. ROSA RAMÍREZ.

    vii.   MARTA MIRABAL, b. Abt. 1911; m. (1) ROBERTO SÁNCHEZ; m. (2) MANUEL MONTOYA.

    viii. JUAN MIRABAL, b. Abt. 1914[565]; m. SUSIE SANDOVAL.

    ix.   FRANKIE MIRABAL, b. Abt. 1917[566]; m. BESSIE MONTOYA.

    x.   MAX MIRABAL, b. Abt. 1919[566]; m. MAGGIE ROBLE.

    xi.   SOFIA MIRABAL, b. Abt. 1920[567]; m. JACK WEST.

    xii.   DAN MIRABAL, b. Abt. 1923[568]; m. LUPE DE MIRABAL.

    xiii. GENOVEVA MIRABAL, b. Abt. 1928[568]; m. ARTURO LUCERO.

99. MANUELITA[10] GALLEGOS *(MARÍA DOLORES[9] SÁNCHES, SANTIAGO[8], JOSÉ GREGORIO DE LA TRINIDAD[7], JUAN CRISTÓBAL[6], FRANCISCO[5], JACINTO SÁNCHES[4] DE IÑIGO, FRANCISCO MUÑOS[3] SÁNCHES, JACINTO[2] MUÑOS, FRANCISCO[1])* was born March 12, 1887[569], and died 1972. She married JOSÉ ÁNGEL DURÁN[570], son of TIBORCIO DURÁN and MONICA MARTÍNEZ.

Notes for JOSÉ ÁNGEL DURÁN:
Land Patent # NMR 0041662, on the authority of the Homestead Entry-Stock Raising (39 Stat. 862), December 29, 1916. Issued 640 acres on October 8, 1923.

Children of MANUELITA GALLEGOS and JOSÉ DURÁN are:

    i.   TIBORCIO[11] DURÁN, b. 1905, Glencoe, New México[571].

    ii.   MIGUEL DURÁN, b. 1907, Glencoe, New México[571].

    iii.   DEMETRIO DURÁN, b. 1909, Glencoe, New México[571].

    iv.   ALIFONZO DURÁN, b. 1911, Glencoe, New México[571].

    v.   BELSON DURÁN, b. 1913, Glencoe, New México[571].

    vi.   ESIQUIEL DURÁN[572], b. December 02, 1918, Glencoe, New México[573].

100. LUCÍA[10] WELDON *(ANGELITA PEREA[9] SÁNCHES, SANTIAGO[8], JOSÉ GREGORIO DE LA TRINIDAD[7], JUAN CRISTÓBAL[6], FRANCISCO[5], JACINTO SÁNCHES[4] DE IÑIGO, FRANCISCO MUÑOS[3] SÁNCHES, JACINTO[2] MUÑOS, FRANCISCO[1])* was born Abt. 1871 in Lincoln County, Territory of New México[574], and died in San Patricio, New México. She married ROBERTO CHÁVES February 11, 1888 in Ruidoso, New Mexico[575], son of JESÚS CHÁVES and NICOLÁSA ARAGÓN.

Notes for LUCÍA WELDON:
1880 Census: Living in Tularoso, Territory of New México. (Lucía Waldo)

Children of LUCÍA WELDON and ROBERTO CHÁVES are:
185.   i.   ANGELITA[11] CHÁVEZ, b. July 25, 1889, Las Angusturas (San Ysidro), Territory of New México; d. March 04, 1973, San Patricio, New México.
186.   ii.   YSIDRO CHÁVEZ, b. April 20, 1892, Ruidoso, Territory of New México; d. June 28, 1972, San Patricio, New Mexico.
187.   iii. MANFOR CHÁVEZ, b. March 18, 1896, Las Angusturas (San Ysidro), Territory of New México; d. July 1971, San Patricio, New México.

101. JESÚS MARÍA[10] MONTES *(ANGELITA PEREA[9] SÁNCHES, SANTIAGO[8], JOSÉ GREGORIO DE LA TRINIDAD[7], JUAN CRISTÓBAL[6], FRANCISCO[5], JACINTO SÁNCHES[4] DE IÑIGO, FRANCISCO MUÑOS[3] SÁNCHES, JACINTO[2] MUÑOS, FRANCISCO[1])*[576] was born 1883 in La Junta, Territory of New México, and died 1954 in Hondo, New México. He married TOMASITA ALDAZ[576] February 22, 1908[577], daughter of MARIANO ALDAZ and FRANCISCA TORRES.

Notes for JESÚS MARÍA MONTES:
Land Patent # NMR 0021235, on the authority of the Homestead Entry-Original (12 Stat. 392), May 20, 1862. Issued 160 acres on May 29, 1915.
Land Patent # NMR 0036195, on the authority of the Homestead Entry-Original (12 Stat. 392), May 20, 1862. Issued 160 acres on June 23, 1922.
Land Patent # NMLC 0025987, on the authority of the Homestead Entry-Stock Raising (39 Stat. 862), December 29, 1916. Issued 320 acres on January 30, 1931.

Children of JESÚS MONTES and TOMASITA ALDAZ are:
188.   i.   LUCÍA[11] MONTES, b. January 24, 1909, Rancho Torres, New México; d. July 11, 2005, Roswell, New México.
189.   ii.   FRED MONTES, b. November 26, 1910, Capitán, New México; d. December 17, 1994, Hondo, New México.
190.   iii. JOSÉ DOLÓRES MONTES, b. November 14, 1912, San Patricio, New México; d. May 12, 2010, Roswell, New México.
        iv.   SERAPIO MONTES[578], b. November 14, 1912, Capitán, New México; d. April 30, 1985, Capitán, New México; m. LUCINDA SALAZAR, April 11, 1937[579].

Notes for SERAPIO MONTES:
US Navy, Seaman Second Class, World War II.

191.   v.   AMANDA MONTES, b. 1914, Hondo, New México.
        vi.   CLOVÍS MONTES, b. 1916, Hondo, New México[580]; d. 1956, Hondo, New México; m. ERMINIA TORREZ[581].
192.   vii. OLYMPIA MONTES, b. October 06, 1919, Hondo, New México; d. December 20, 2009, Santa Fé, New México.
193.   viii. EMMA MONTES, b. 1921, Hondo, New México.
194.   ix.   ALBERTO MONTES, b. September 25, 1923, Hondo, New México; d. November 03, 2004, Lincoln, New México.
        x.   ELOY MONTES, b. 1925, Hondo, New México[582].

Notes for ELOY MONTES:
Died during WW II.

        xi.   JESÚS ALDAZ MONTES, b. 1928, Hondo, New México[582]; m. LUCY HERNÁNDEZ.

102. IGNACIA[10] MONTES *(ANGELITA PEREA[9] SÁNCHES, SANTIAGO[8], JOSÉ GREGORIO DE LA TRINIDAD[7], JUAN CRISTÓBAL[6], FRANCISCO[5], JACINTO SÁNCHES[4] DE IÑIGO, FRANCISCO MUÑOS[3] SÁNCHES, JACINTO[2] MUÑOS, FRANCISCO[1])* was born December 1885[583]. She married FRANCISCO ULIBARRÍ ARMERA August 28, 1901 in San Patricio, Territory of New México[584], son of FRANCISCO ARMERA and MARGARITA ULIBARRÍ.

Children of IGNACIA MONTES and FRANCISCO ARMERA are:
195.   i.   ERMINIA[11] ARMERA, b. Abt. 1909.
        ii.   ROMATILDA ARMERA, b. Abt. 1910[585]; m. JUAN CHÁVEZ.

Notes for ROMATILDA ARMERA:
Raised by Alejo Montes and Angelita Sánchez de Montes.

103. JUAN SÁNCHEZ[10] MONTES *(ANGELITA PEREA[9] SÁNCHES, SANTIAGO[8], JOSÉ GREGORIO DE LA TRINIDAD[7], JUAN CRISTÓBAL[6], FRANCISCO[5], JACINTO SÁNCHES[4] DE IÑIGO, FRANCISCO MUÑOS[3] SÁNCHES, JACINTO[2] MUÑOS, FRANCISCO[1])* was born February 18, 1893 in Ruidoso, New México[586], and died August 1978 in Glencoe, New México[587]. He married LUPITA SÁNCHEZ May 01, 1912 in Ruidoso, New México[588], daughter of ANTONIO SÁNCHEZ and TELESFORA MIRABAL.

Notes for JUAN SÁNCHEZ MONTES:
Land Patent # NMR 0036194, on the authority of the Homestead Entry-Enlarged (35 Stat. 639), February 19, 1909. Issued 320 acres on July 21, 1922.
Land Patent # NMR 0037648, on the authority of the Homestead Entry-Stock Raising (39 Stat. 862), December 29, 1916. Issued 320 acres on October 03, 1924.

Notes for LUPITA SÁNCHEZ:
Also known as Guadalupe.
Social Security Death Index indicates that her birthdate was on May 17, 1892.

Children of JUAN MONTES and LUPITA SÁNCHEZ are:
196.   i.   FERMÍN[11] MONTES, b. February 20, 1914; d. May 10, 1984, Roswell, New México.
197.   ii.   ORLANDO MONTES, b. February 14, 1922, Glencoe, New México; d. November 15, 1994.
        iii. AMELIA MONTES[589], b. October 1925, Glencoe, New México; d. February 15, 1981; m. FRUTOSO HERRERA, July 11, 1942, Carrizozo, New México[590].

Notes for FRUTOSO HERRERA:
Private First Class. World War II.

198.   iv.   JUAN SÁNCHEZ MONTES, b. December 27, 1932, Glencoe, New México; d. February 16, 1987.

104. SALOMON[10] SÁNCHEZ *(ANTONIO[9], MAURICIO DE LA TRINIDAD[8] SÁNCHES, JOSÉ GREGORIO DE LA TRINIDAD[7], JUAN CRISTÓBAL[6], FRANCISCO[5], JACINTO SÁNCHES[4] DE IÑIGO, FRANCISCO MUÑOS[3] SÁNCHES, JACINTO[2] MUÑOS, FRANCISCO[1])[591]* was born Abt. November 17, 1878 in Tularoso, Territory of New México[592], and died May 31, 1952 in Ruidoso, New México[593]. He married (1) JENNIE GILL December 06, 1900 in Ruidoso, Territory of New México[594], daughter of WILLIAM GILL and ALTAGRACIA HERRERA. He married (2) MANUELITA MARTÍNEZ SÁNCHEZ February 03, 1917 in Ruidoso, New México[595], daughter of TORIVIO SÁNCHEZ and AVRELIA MARTÍNEZ.

Notes for MANUELITA MARTÍNEZ SÁNCHEZ:
Also known as Emma.

Children of SALOMON SÁNCHEZ and JENNIE GILL are:
199.   i.   VIRGINIA[11] SÁNCHEZ, b. April 13, 1902, Glencoe, Territory of New México; d. December 14, 1980, Ruidoso, New México.
200.   ii.   ENRÍQUE GILL SÁNCHEZ, b. September 25, 1904, Glencoe, Territory of New México.
201.   iii. SALOMON GILL SÁNCHEZ, b. March 17, 1905, Glencoe, Territory of New México; d. August 11, 1995, Carrizozo, New México.
202.   iv.   TELESFORA SÁNCHEZ, b. July 15, 1906, Glencoe, Territory of New México; d. November 18, 1993, Alamagordo, New México.
203.   v.   EDUVIJEN SÁNCHEZ, b. April 23, 1908, Glencoe, Territory of New México; d. March 07, 1999, Roswell, New México.
204.   vi.   ANATALIA SÁNCHEZ, b. September 10, 1911, Glencoe, Territory of New México; d. February 23, 1969.
205.   vii. CONSUELO SÁNCHEZ, b. April 24, 1914, Glencoe, New México; d. April 28, 1996, Tularosa, New México.

Children of SALOMON SÁNCHEZ and MANUELITA SÁNCHEZ are:

206.	viii.	CARLOS[11] SÁNCHEZ, b. June 10, 1918, Las Cruces, New México; d. April 16, 2009, El Paso, Téxas.
207.	ix.	EUFRACIA SÁNCHEZ, b. May 27, 1920, Glencoe, New México.
208.	x.	LUVÍN SÁNCHEZ, b. June 18, 1922, Glencoe, New México; d. February 16, 1994, Ruidoso, New México.
	vi.	AMALIA SÁNCHEZ[596], b. April 03, 1924, White Tail, New México[597]; d. July 10, 1927, San Patricio, New México.
209.	xii.	ALBERTO SÁNCHEZ, b. June 09, 1927, San Patricio, New México; d. February 10, 2000, San Patricio, New México.
210.	xiii.	PORFIRIO SÁNCHEZ, b. September 13, 1933, San Patricio, New México.

105. MARÍA DE JESÚS[10] SÁNCHEZ *(ANTONIO[9], MAURICIO DE LA TRINIDAD[8] SÁNCHES, JOSÉ GREGORIO DE LA TRINIDAD[7], JUAN CRISTÓBAL[6], FRANCISCO[5], JACINTO SÁNCHES[4] DE IÑIGO, FRANCISCO MUÑOS[3] SÁNCHES, JACINTO[2] MUÑOS, FRANCISCO[1])[598]* was born July 26, 1881 in Tularoso, Territory of New México, and died December 29, 1954 in Glencoe, New Mexico. She married JULIAN SILVA November 23, 1906 in Las Angusturas (San Ysidro), Territory of New México[599], son of MANUEL SILVA and LEONARDA JIRÓN.

Notes for MARÍA DE JESÚS SÁNCHEZ:
Also known as Jesusita.

Children of MARÍA SÁNCHEZ and JULIAN SILVA are:

	i.	CARMELITA[11] SILVA, b. 1910[600]; m. RAMÓN SILVA.
211.	ii.	ERNESTO SILVA, b. June 27, 1912, Glencoe, New México; d. July 1981, Glencoe, New México.

106. MANUEL MIRABAL[10] SÁNCHEZ *(ANTONIO[9], MAURICIO DE LA TRINIDAD[8] SÁNCHES, JOSÉ GREGORIO DE LA TRINIDAD[7], JUAN CRISTÓBAL[6], FRANCISCO[5], JACINTO SÁNCHES[4] DE IÑIGO, FRANCISCO MUÑOS[3] SÁNCHES, JACINTO[2] MUÑOS, FRANCISCO[1])[601]* was born November 18, 1884 in Glencoe, Territory of New México[602], and died December 28, 1945 in Lake Arther, New México. He married ESTELA GILL[603] June 14, 1909 in San Patricio, Territory of New México[604], daughter of WILLIAM GILL and ALTAGRACIA HERRERA.

Children of MANUEL SÁNCHEZ and ESTELA GILL are:

212.	i.	AMANDA[11] SÁNCHEZ, b. July 15, 1910, Glencoe, Territory of New México; d. March 19, 1982, Roswell, New México.
	ii.	ESTOLANO SÁNCHEZ, b. Abt. 1910, Glencoe, Territory of New México; d. Abt. 1910, Glencoe, Territory of New México.

Notes for ESTOLANO SÁNCHEZ:
Died young.

107. DANOIS[10] SÁNCHEZ *(ANTONIO[9], MAURICIO DE LA TRINIDAD[8] SÁNCHES, JOSÉ GREGORIO DE LA TRINIDAD[7], JUAN CRISTÓBAL[6], FRANCISCO[5], JACINTO SÁNCHES[4] DE IÑIGO, FRANCISCO MUÑOS[3] SÁNCHES, JACINTO[2] MUÑOS, FRANCISCO[1])* was born October 24, 1890 in Ruidoso, Territory of New México[605], and died May 05, 1955 in Tularosa, New México[606]. He married GUADALUPE VALLES May 1909[607].

Children of DANOIS SÁNCHEZ and GUADALUPE VALLES are:

	i.	TELESFORA[11] SÁNCHEZ, b. 1912.
	ii.	DANOIS VALLES SÁNCHEZ[608], b. January 28, 1913, Tularosa, New México; d. September 23, 1996, Tularosa, New México.
	iii.	ANTONIO VALLES SÁNCHEZ, b. 1915.
	iv.	SERAFÍN SÁNCHEZ, b. 1916.
	v.	MABEL VALLES SÁNCHEZ, b. 1917.
	vi.	GODFREY SÁNCHEZ, b. Abt. 1920.
213.	vii.	ISMAÉL SÁNCHEZ, b. July 16, 1921, Glencoe, New México; d. March 16, 2009, Alamogordo, New México.
	viii.	ADELINA SÁNCHEZ[609], b. May 15, 1923, Tularosa, New México[610]; d. September 18, 1924, Tularosa, New México.
	ix.	NARCISO SÁNCHEZ, b. October 29, 1926[611].
	x.	FLORA SÁNCHEZ, b. Private.
	xi.	MARÍA AMABLE SÁNCHEZ, b. Private.
	xii.	RUBÉN VALLES SÁNCHEZ, b. Private.

108. LUPITA[10] SÁNCHEZ *(ANTONIO[9], MAURICIO DE LA TRINIDAD[8] SÁNCHES, JOSÉ GREGORIO DE LA TRINIDAD[7], JUAN CRISTÓBAL[6], FRANCISCO[5], JACINTO SÁNCHES[4] DE IÑIGO, FRANCISCO MUÑOS[3] SÁNCHES, JACINTO[2] MUÑOS, FRANCISCO[1])* was born March 13, 1892[612], and died September 1973 in Glencoe,

New México[613]. She married JUAN SÁNCHEZ MONTES May 01, 1912 in Ruidoso, New México[614], son of ALEJO MONTES and ANGELITA SÁNCHES.

Children of LUPITA SÁNCHEZ and JUAN MONTES are:

196.   i.   FERMÍN[11] MONTES, b. February 20, 1914; d. May 10, 1984, Roswell, New México.
197.   ii.   ORLANDO MONTES, b. February 14, 1922, Glencoe, New México; d. November 15, 1994.
       iii.   AMELIA MONTES[615], b. October 1925, Glencoe, New México; d. February 15, 1981; m. FRUTOSO HERRERA, July 11, 1942, Carrizozo, New México[616].
198.   iv.   JUAN SÁNCHEZ MONTES, b. December 27, 1932, Glencoe, New México; d. February 16, 1987.

John Mackey

109. SENAIDA[10] SÁNCHEZ *(ANTONIO[9], MAURICIO DE LA TRINIDAD[8] SÁNCHES, JOSÉ GREGORIO DE LA TRINIDAD[7], JUAN CRISTÓBAL[6], FRANCISCO[5], JACINTO SÁNCHES[4] DE IÑIGO, FRANCISCO MUÑOS[3] SÁNCHES, JACINTO[2] MUÑOS, FRANCISCO[1])[617]* was born August 06, 1894 in Glencoe, Territory of New México[618], and died November 12, 1981. She married (1) YSIDRO CHÁVEZ[619] April 29, 1909 in Ruidoso, Territory of New México[620], son of ROBERTO CHÁVES and LUCÍA WELDON. She married (2) JOHN MACKEY February 01, 1912[621], son of PATRICK MACKEY and GUADALUPE SAMORA.

Notes for JOHN MACKEY:
Was Justice of the Peace in San Patricio.
Land Patent # NMR 0035308, on the authority of the Homestead Entry-Enlarged (35 Stat. 639), February 19, 1909. Issued 320 acres on May 01, 1922.

Children of SENAIDA SÁNCHEZ and JOHN MACKEY are:

214.   i.   CECILIA[11] MACKEY, b. June 22, 1913, San Patricio, New México; d. April 09, 2010, Glen Burnie, Maryland.
       ii.   DILIA MACKEY, b. August 30, 1916, San Patricio, New México; d. Bef. 1920.
       iii.   MONROE MACKEY[622], b. March 18, 1919, San Patricio, New México[623]; d. April 19, 1973, Raton, New México.
       iv.   EULALIA MACKEY, b. April 25, 1920, San Patricio, New México[623]; d. May 12, 2002, Clinton, Indiana.

Notes for EULALIA MACKEY:
Died young.

       v.   JAMES MACKEY[624], b. April 10, 1922, San Patricio, New México[625]; d. March 19, 1983, Ruidoso, New México; m. ELIZABETH CHÁVEZ[626].

Notes for JAMES MACKEY:
Also known as Jaime Mackey.

Notes for ELIZABETH CHÁVEZ:
Also known as Libby.

       vi.   NORA MACKEY, b. February 26, 1928, San Patricio, New México[627]; m. TRANQUELINO SILVA[628].

Notes for NORA MACKEY:
Also known as María Leonor Mackey.

Felipé E. Sánchez

110. FELIPÉ E.[10] SÁNCHEZ *(ESTOLANO[9], MAURICIO DE LA TRINIDAD[8] SÁNCHES, JOSÉ GREGORIO DE LA TRINIDAD[7], JUAN CRISTÓBAL[6], FRANCISCO[5], JACINTO SÁNCHES[4] DE IÑIGO, FRANCISCO MUÑOS[3] SÁNCHES, JACINTO[2] MUÑOS, FRANCISCO[1])* was born January 21, 1874 in La Placita del Rio Bonito, Territory of New México[629], and died January 15, 1954 in San Elizario, El Paso, Téxas[630]. He married CANDELARIA PADILLA Abt. 1897[631], daughter of ANDALESIO PADILLA and PAUBLITA MARIÑO.

Notes for FELIPÉ E. SÁNCHEZ:
Land Patent # NMNMAA 010654, on the authority of the Homestead Entry-Original (12 Stat. 392), May 20, 1862. Issued 160 acres on September 24, 1908.

Land Patent # NMLC 0046530, on the authority of the Homestead Entry-Stock Raising (39 Stat. 862), December 29, 1916. Issued 480 acres on June 27, 1936.

Children of FELIPÉ SÁNCHEZ and CANDELARIA PADILLA are:

215.	i.	ANTONIO PADILLA[11] SÁNCHEZ, b. May 17, 1897, Tres Ritos, New México; d. February 21, 1984, San Elizario, Texas.
216.	ii.	PAUBLITA SÁNCHEZ, b. July 30, 1898, Tres Rios, Territory of New México; d. October 13, 1963, Las Vegas, New México.
	iii.	SIPIO SÁNCHEZ, b. March 1900[632]; m. LOLA MIRABAL.
217.	iv.	CORNELIA SÁNCHEZ, b. November 16, 1902, Lincoln County, New México.
218.	v.	EMILIANO SÁNCHEZ, b. August 11, 1904, Hondo, Territory of New México.
219.	vi.	ABRÁN SÁNCHEZ, b. December 24, 1905, White Oaks, Territory of New México; d. November 18, 1973, El Paso, Téxas.
220.	vii.	RENALDO SÁNCHEZ, b. March 22, 1907, Patos, New México; d. May 1981, Tularosa, New México.
	viii.	CELEDONIA SÁNCHEZ, b. Abt. 1909; d. Abt. 1921.
221.	ix.	BENITO SÁNCHEZ, b. Abt. 1912.
222.	x.	ONECIMO SÁNCHEZ, b. 1915.

Erineo Gavaldon

111. ELUTICIA[10] SÁNCHEZ *(ESTOLANO[9], MAURICIO DE LA TRINIDAD[8] SÁNCHES, JOSÉ GREGORIO DE LA TRINIDAD[7], JUAN CRISTÓBAL[6], FRANCISCO[5], JACINTO SÁNCHES[4] DE IÑIGO, FRANCISCO MUÑOS[3] SÁNCHES, JACINTO[2] MUÑOS, FRANCISCO[1])* was born 1875[632]. She married (1) ERINEO FRANCISCO GAVALDON[633], son of ENCARNACION GAVALDON and ANTONIA DE GAVALDON. She married (2) AUGUSTÍN LUERAS CHÁVEZ April 12, 1901[634], son of MAXIMIANO CHÁVEZ and ROSITA LUERAS.

Notes for ELUTICIA SÁNCHEZ:
Also known as Luticia.

Notes for AUGUSTÍN LUERAS CHÁVEZ:
Had a brother, Rafael Chávez, the son of Maximiano Chávez.
June 28, 1910 to December 19, 1914 and March 2, 1921 to December 7, 1922: Was the Post Master for the Reventón Post Office.

Children of ELUTICIA SÁNCHEZ and ERINEO GAVALDON are:

223.	i.	ROSA[11] GAVALDON, b. January 1892.
	ii.	AVRORA GAVALDON[635], b. January 07, 1894[636]; d. January 17, 1986, Corona, New México; m. NARCISO MONTOYA[637], October 26, 1918[638].
224.	iii.	LUPE GAVALDON, b. August 20, 1897, Patos, Territory of New México.

Child of ELUTICIA SÁNCHEZ and AUGUSTÍN CHÁVEZ is:
      CAROLINA SÁNCHEZ[11] CHÁVEZ, b. Abt. 1895[639].

112. PRECILIANO[10] SÁNCHEZ *(ESTOLANO[9], MAURICIO DE LA TRINIDAD[8] SÁNCHES, JOSÉ GREGORIO DE LA TRINIDAD[7], JUAN CRISTÓBAL[6], FRANCISCO[5], JACINTO SÁNCHES[4] DE IÑIGO, FRANCISCO MUÑOS[3] SÁNCHES, JACINTO[2] MUÑOS, FRANCISCO[1])* was born December 24, 1884 in Rebentón, Territory of New México[640], and died 1918-1920[641]. He married (1) GUADALUPE MARTÍNEZ October 12, 1905 in Rebentón, Territory of New México[642], daughter of ANTONIO MARTÍNEZ and JUANA GUSTAMANTE. He married (2) LUPITA OROSCO Abt. 1906[643].

Child of PRECILIANO SÁNCHEZ and GUADALUPE MARTÍNEZ is:
      i.   CORA[11] SÁNCHEZ.

Children of PRECILIANO SÁNCHEZ and LUPITA OROSCO are:

	ii.	FIDEL[11] SÁNCHEZ[644], b. August 04, 1913, Greeley, Colorado[645]; d. June 27, 1973; m. AMALIA TORRES[646], February 12, 1934, San Patricio, New México[647].
225.	iii.	ESTOLANO OROSCO SÁNCHEZ, b. July 07, 1915, Rebentón, Territory of New México; d. April 05, 1985, Hondo, New México.
	iv.	FERNANDO SÁNCHEZ[648], b. June 19, 1916, Rebentón, New México[649]; m. JOSEFITA TRUJILLO[650], December 11, 1937, Carrizozo, New México[650].

113. AURELIO[10] SÁNCHEZ *(ESTOLANO[9], MAURICIO DE LA TRINIDAD[8] SÁNCHES, JOSÉ GREGORIO DE LA TRINIDAD[7], JUAN CRISTÓBAL[6], FRANCISCO[5], JACINTO SÁNCHES[4] DE IÑIGO, FRANCISCO MUÑOS[3] SÁNCHES, JACINTO[2] MUÑOS, FRANCISCO[1])[651]* was born March 12, 1886 in Ruidoso, Territory of New México, and died February 23, 1975. He married ANASTACIA ARAGÓN[652] October 13, 1907 in Rebentón, Territory of New México[653], daughter of MANUEL ARAGÓN and PORFIRIA GONZÁLES.

Children of AURELIO SÁNCHEZ and ANASTACIA ARAGÓN are:

	i.	SANTANA[11] SÁNCHEZ, b. Abt. 1910[654]; m. MAX CHÁVEZ[655], Rebentón, New México[656].
	ii.	EDUMENIO SÁNCHEZ, b. June 08, 1916, White Oaks, New México[657]; m. SEDIA SÁNCHEZ[658], December 11, 1946, Carrizozo, New México[659].
226.	iii.	SORAIDA SÁNCHEZ, b. August 27, 1916, Rebentón, Territory of New México.
227.	iv.	MACRINA SÁNCHEZ, b. September 09, 1920, White Oaks, New México; d. October 13, 2010, Ruidoso Downs, New México.
228.	v.	VICENTE SÁNCHEZ, b. July 08, 1922, Ancho, New México.
	vi.	CLOVÍS SÁNCHEZ[660], b. June 09, 1913, Rebentón, New México; d. November 06, 1995, Roswell, New México; m. CARLOTA PINEDA, December 26, 1941, Carrizozo, New México[661].

Notes for CARLOTA PINEDA:
Also known As Charlotte.

	vii.	BALDIMAR SÁNCHEZ, b. October 27, 1923, Dexter, New México[662]; m. MARGARETTE PENDLEY, June 15, 1945, Ruidoso, New México[662].
	viii.	PRESILIANO SÁNCHEZ, b. 1926[663]; m. CECILIA ROMERO.
	ix.	LUCY SÁNCHEZ[664], b. February 27, 1930, Hondo, New México[665]; m. ALBERT TELLES, May 26, 1951, Carrizozo, New México[666].
	x.	EDUARDO ARAGÓN SÁNCHEZ[667], b. May 02, 1933; d. November 25, 1998, Ruidoso, New México; m. BONNIE SÁNCHEZ.

Notes for EDUARDO ARAGÓN SÁNCHEZ:
Also known as Edward. PFC US Army, Korea.
Social Security Death index indicates that he was born on May 02, 1932.

229.	xi.	IDALIA SÁNCHEZ, b. Private, Rebentón, Territory of New México.

114. CELIA[10] SÁNCHEZ *(ESTOLANO[9], MAURICIO DE LA TRINIDAD[8] SÁNCHES, JOSÉ GREGORIO DE LA TRINIDAD[7], JUAN CRISTÓBAL[6], FRANCISCO[5], JACINTO SÁNCHES[4] DE IÑIGO, FRANCISCO MUÑOS[3] SÁNCHES, JACINTO[2] MUÑOS, FRANCISCO[1])* was born July 12, 1888 in Rebentón, Territory of New México[668]. She married GEORGE TORRES November 12, 1906 in Lincoln, Territory of New México[668], son of YGNACIO TORRES and MANUELA LUCERO.

Children of CELIA SÁNCHEZ and GEORGE TORRES are:

230.	i.	FELIS SÁNCHEZ[11] TORRES, b. June 04, 1909, Lincoln, Territory of New México; d. February 16, 2003, San Patricio, New México.
	ii.	ADENAGO TORRES[669], b. December 13, 1907, Hondo, New México[670]; d. August 06, 1990, Tularosa, New México; m. BEATRIZ TORREZ[671].
	iii.	GEORGE SÁNCHEZ TORRES, b. 1911[672].
	iv.	WILFIDO TORRES, b. 1913[672]; m. JULIA TORRES.
	v.	MIGUEL TORRES, b. 1917[672]; m. SOCORRO DE TORREZ.
	vi.	MANUELITA TORRES, b. 1919[672]; m. JUAN BAUTISTA JUAREGUI.
	vii.	PRESCILIA TORRES, b. Abt. 1920[673]; m. ERNESTO LÓPEZ[674].

Notes for ERNESTO LÓPEZ:
Immigrated to the U.S. in about 1908.

	viii.	LORINA TORRES, b. Abt. 1926[675]; m. ERNESTO OTERO[676].
	ix.	JAY TORRES, b. Private; m. EDNA TORRES.

115. ESTOLANO PACHECO[10] SÁNCHEZ *(ESTOLANO[9], MAURICIO DE LA TRINIDAD[8] SÁNCHES, JOSÉ GREGORIO DE LA TRINIDAD[7], JUAN CRISTÓBAL[6], FRANCISCO[5], JACINTO SÁNCHES[4] DE IÑIGO, FRANCISCO MUÑOS[3] SÁNCHES, JACINTO[2] MUÑOS, FRANCISCO[1])[677]* was born October 19, 1893 in Rebentón, Territory of New México[678], and died September 19, 1943 in Carrizozo, New México. He married (1) BARBARITA

TORREZ February 28, 1910 in Lincoln, Territory of New Mexico[678], daughter of CRESENCIO TORRES and MIQUELA MIRANDA. He married (2) ELENA CHÁVEZ[679] July 30, 1920 in Rebentón, New México[679], daughter of RAFAEL CHÁVEZ and MARTINA MAÉS.

Notes for ESTOLANO PACHECO SÁNCHEZ:
Lincoln County Clerk's Book of Marriages: Born October 21, 1891.
World War One Draft Registration: Born October 16, 1892.

Children of ESTOLANO SÁNCHEZ and BARBARITA TORREZ are:
  i.   FERMÍN[11] SÁNCHEZ, b. October 11, 1915.
  ii.   AMABLE SÁNCHEZ, b. Private.
  iii. AMANDA SÁNCHEZ, b. Private.
  iv.   EULALIO (LALO) SÁNCHEZ, b. Private.

116. ROSARITA[10] SÁNCHEZ *(ESTOLANO[9], MAURICIO DE LA TRINIDAD[8] SÁNCHES, JOSÉ GREGORIO DE LA TRINIDAD[7], JUAN CRISTÓBAL[6], FRANCISCO[5], JACINTO SÁNCHES[4] DE IÑIGO, FRANCISCO MUÑOS[3] SÁNCHES, JACINTO[2] MUÑOS, FRANCISCO[1])*[680] was born August 11, 1896 in Rebentón, Territory of New México[681], and died December 25, 1976 in Hondo, New México. She married WILLIAM LUCERO BRADY February 19, 1912 in Lincoln, New Mexico[682], son of ROBERT BRADY and MANUELA LUCERO.

Notes for ROSARITA SÁNCHEZ:
Also known as Rosario.

Notes for WILLIAM LUCERO BRADY:
Also known as Guillermo.

Children of ROSARITA SÁNCHEZ and WILLIAM BRADY are:
  i.   MAX[11] BRADY, b. June 01, 1913, Hondo, New México[683]; d. July 17, 1985[684].

Notes for MAX BRADY:
Also known as Maximiliano.
Major in the US Army. WW II Veteran.

       ii.   ERMILO BRADY[685], b. March 13, 1915, Hondo, New México[686]; m. PRESCILLA PÉREZ, November 10, 1936, San Patricio, New México[687].
231.   iii.   ELMO BRADY, b. October 30, 1917, Hondo, New México; d. December 29, 2008, Ruidoso, New México.
232.   iv.   ORLIDIA BRADY, b. January 06, 1920, Hondo, New México; d. March 09, 2011, Roswell, New México.
       v.   BARTOLA JEAN BRADY, b. August 24, 1922[688]; d. November 11, 1994, Roswell, New México.
       vi.   WILLIAM SÁNCHEZ BRADY[689], b. April 11, 1924, Hondo, New México[690]; d. December 28, 2005; m. ORALIA HERRERA[691].
233.   vii.   PRESTINA BRADY, b. March 20, 1926, Hondo, New México; d. January 18, 1995, Hondo, New México.
       viii. LEROY BENNETT BRADY, b. April 14, 1930[692].
234.   ix.   BILLY JOE BRADY, b. Private.

117. ESLINDA[10] GONZÁLES *(FLORENCIO[9], MARÍA MANUELA[8] ARAGÓN, MARIANA ANTONIA[7] SÁNCHES, DIEGO ANTONIO[6], FRANCISCO[5], JACINTO SÁNCHES[4] DE IÑIGO, FRANCISCO MUÑOS[3] SÁNCHES, JACINTO[2] MUÑOS, FRANCISCO[1])* was born 1867 in La Placita del Rio Bonito, Territory of New México[693], and died Bef. October 1922[694]. She married FRANCISCO LUNA CHÁVEZ[695] March 29, 1891 in Lincoln County, Territory of New México[696], son of JOSÉ CHÁVES and MARÍA LUNA.

Notes for FRANCISCO LUNA CHÁVEZ:
Also known as Frank.

Children of ESLINDA GONZÁLES and FRANCISCO CHÁVEZ are:
  i.   FIDEL[11] CHÁVEZ[697], b. June 30, 1893, San Patricio, Territory of New México[698]; d. August 29, 1937, San Patricio, New México; m. DELFINIA PADILLA Y WEST, June 28, 1915, Lincoln, New México[698].

Notes for FIDEL CHÁVEZ:
Lists his mother as Francisquita Luna.

Notes for DELFINIA PADILLA Y WEST:
Also known as Delfinia Sánchez, Delfinia Sánchez y West.
Raised and adopted by John C. West.

235.   ii.   ERMINDA CHÁVEZ, b. July 12, 1894, San Patricio, Territory of New México; d. November 01, 1956.

       iii.   PALMIRA CHÁVEZ, b. 1896[699]; m. IGNACIO MAÉS[700].

       iv.   RAMÓN CHÁVEZ[701], b. February 12, 1897, San Patricio, Territory of New México[702]; d. October 17, 1985, San Patricio, New México.

       v.   ENCARNACION CHÁVEZ, b. November 15, 1899[703].

Notes for ENCARNACION CHÁVEZ:
Died young.

118. PROSPERO[10] GONZÁLES *(FLORENCIO[9], MARÍA MANUELA[8] ARAGÓN, MARIANA ANTONIA[7] SÁNCHES, DIEGO ANTONIO[6], FRANCISCO[5], JACINTO SÁNCHES[4] DE IÑIGO, FRANCISCO MUÑOS[3] SÁNCHES, JACINTO[2] MUÑOS, FRANCISCO[1])[704]* was born July 20, 1871 in Lincoln, Territory of New México, and died August 20, 1937 in Glencoe, New México. He married TELESFORA MIRABAL[705] March 28, 1900 in Las Angusturas (San Ysidro), Territory of New México[706], daughter of JUAN MIRABAL and GUADALUPE TRUJILLO.

Notes for PROSPERO GONZÁLES:
Land Patent # NMNMAA 010632, on the authority of the Homestead Entry-Original (12 Stat. 392), May 20, 1862. Issued 120 acres.

Children of PROSPERO GONZÁLES and TELESFORA MIRABAL are:

236.   i.   ARCENIA[11] GONZÁLES, b. February 20, 1898, Glencoe, Territory of New México.

237.   ii.   RUBÉN ANDRÉS GONZÁLES, b. November 02, 1900, Glencoe, Territory of New México; d. Artesia, New Mexico.

       iii.   PORFIRIO GONZÁLES[707], b. August 10, 1903, Glencoe, Territory of New México; d. June 13, 1947, San Patricio, New México; m. ANGELINA RUÍZ, October 15, 1936[708].

238.   iv.   PROSPERO MIRABAL GONZÁLES, b. January 20, 1909, Glencoe, Territory of New México; d. January 17, 1960.

119. LEOPOLDO SÁNCHEZ[10] GONZÁLES *(FLORENCIO[9], MARÍA MANUELA[8] ARAGÓN, MARIANA ANTONIA[7] SÁNCHES, DIEGO ANTONIO[6], FRANCISCO[5], JACINTO SÁNCHES[4] DE IÑIGO, FRANCISCO MUÑOS[3] SÁNCHES, JACINTO[2] MUÑOS, FRANCISCO[1])[709]* was born April 08, 1875 in Lincoln, Territory of New México, and died June 10, 1937 in San Patricio, New México. He married REIMUNDA SEDILLO November 28, 1895[710], daughter of JUAN SEDILLO and JOSEFA FAJARDO.

Notes for LEOPOLDO SÁNCHEZ GONZÁLES:
Land Patent # NMR 0009110, on the authority of the Homestead Entry-Original (12 Stat. 392), May 20, 1862. Issued 160 acres on January 13, 1912.
Land Patent # NMR 0033933, on the authority of the Homestead Entry-Original (12 Stat. 392), May 20, 1862. Issued 160 acres on July 21, 1922.

Children of LEOPOLDO GONZÁLES and REIMUNDA SEDILLO are:

       i.   JUAN SEDILLO[11] GONZÁLES, b. November 10, 1896, San Patricio, Territory of New México[711].

Notes for JUAN SEDILLO GONZÁLES:
Died young.

       ii.   AROPAJITA SEDILLO GONZÁLES, b. 1900, San Patricio, Territory of New México[712]; d. December 05, 1918, San Patricio, New México[713].

Notes for AROPAJITA SEDILLO GONZÁLES:
Died from the influenza.

239.   iii.   CRUSITA GONZÁLES, b. May 02, 1904, San Patricio, Territory of New México.

240.   iv.   ELISA GONZÁLES, b. February 27, 1912, San Patricio, New México; d. April 01, 2001, San Patricio, New México.

120. ALFREDO[10] GONZÁLES *(FLORENCIO[9], MARÍA MANUELA[8] ARAGÓN, MARIANA ANTONIA[7] SÁNCHES, DIEGO ANTONIO[6], FRANCISCO[5], JACINTO SÁNCHES[4] DE IÑIGO, FRANCISCO MUÑOS[3] SÁNCHES, JACINTO[2] MUÑOS, FRANCISCO[1])[714]* was born 1876 in Lincoln, Territory of New México, and died 1927 in San Patricio, New México. He married REBECCA SALAZAR February 07, 1904 in Lincoln, Territory of New México[715], daughter of SIPIO SALAZAR and MARTINA ROMERO.

Notes for ALFREDO GONZÁLES:
1901-1902: Was elected as Lincoln County Sheriff.

Notes for REBECCA SALAZAR:
Also known as Rebecca Salazar de Sisneros, Rebecca Curry.

Child of ALFREDO GONZÁLES and REBECCA SALAZAR is:
     i.   GODFREY[11] GONZÁLES, b. 1904, San Patricio, Territory of New México[716].

121. EPAMINOANDAS[10] GONZÁLES *(FLORENCIO[9], MARÍA MANUELA[8] ARAGÓN, MARIANA ANTONIA[7] SÁNCHES, DIEGO ANTONIO[6], FRANCISCO[5], JACINTO SÁNCHES[4] DE IÑIGO, FRANCISCO MUÑOS[3] SÁNCHES, JACINTO[2] MUÑOS, FRANCISCO[1])[717]* was born April 04, 1876 in Lincoln, Territory of New México, and died February 20, 1970 in San Patricio, New México. He married ELVIRA GONZÁLES[717] February 14, 1900[718], daughter of JOSÉ GONZÁLES and MARÍA CHÁVEZ.

Notes for EPAMINOANDAS GONZÁLES:
Also known as Domingo Epaminoandaz Gonzáles.
Land Patent # NMR 0016475, on the authority of the Homestead Entry-Original (12 Stat. 392), May 20, 1862. Issued 160 acres on March 10, 1914.
Land Patent # NMR 0032987, on the authority of the Homestead Entry-Original (12 Stat. 392), May 20, 1862. Issued 160 acres on August 30, 1920.
Land Patent # NMLC 0028881, on the authority of the Homestead Entry-Stock Raising (39 Stat. 862), December 29, 1916. Issued 327.99 acres on July 23, 1931.

Children of EPAMINOANDAS GONZÁLES and ELVIRA GONZÁLES are:
241.   i.   AGIDA[11] GONZÁLES, b. December 05, 1900, San Patricio, Territory of New México; d. October 28, 1941.
242.   ii.   EPAMINOANDAS GONZÁLES GONZÁLES, b. October 21, 1901, San Patricio, Territory of New México; d. January 05, 1945.
243.   iii.   CIPRIANA GONZÁLES, b. August 21, 1903, San Patricio, Territory of New México; d. November 11, 2006, San Patricio, New México.
    iv.   CRECENSIANA GONZÁLES, b. Abt. 1906, San Patricio, Territory of New México[719]; m. TITO MAÉS.
244.   v.   FLORENCIO GONZÁLES GONZÁLES, b. September 17, 1907, San Patricio, Territory of New México; d. October 11, 1973, San Patricio, New México.
    vi.   BRESELIA GONZÁLES, b. October 10, 1910, San Patricio, Territory of New México; d. January 09, 1973, Morenci, Arizona; m. (1) JUAN TRUJILLO SÁNCHEZ[720721]; m. (2) MAX CORONA[722].
245.   vii.   RAFAEL GONZÁLES, b. March 23, 1914, San Patricio, New México.
    viii.   MARÍA GONZÁLES[723], b. May 20, 1917, San Patricio, New México[724]; m. LEOPOLDO PEÑA[724], June 20, 1940, Lincoln, New México[724].

Notes for LEOPOLDO PEÑA:
Also known as Polo. US Navy, Seaman First Class. World War II.

246.   ix.   SIGISMUNDA GONZÁLES, b. February 07, 1920, San Patricio, New México.
247.   x.   EVA GONZÁLES, b. Private, San Patricio, New México.

122. AVRORA[10] GONZÁLES *(FLORENCIO[9], MARÍA MANUELA[8] ARAGÓN, MARIANA ANTONIA[7] SÁNCHES, DIEGO ANTONIO[6], FRANCISCO[5], JACINTO SÁNCHES[4] DE IÑIGO, FRANCISCO MUÑOS[3] SÁNCHES, JACINTO[2] MUÑOS, FRANCISCO[1])[725]* was born May 23, 1880 in San Patricio, Territory of New México[726], and died August 15, 1971 in San Patricio, New México[727]. She married (2) GEORGE ROMERO November 19, 1900[728], son of JUAN ROMERO and CRISTINA CASTILLO.

Notes for AVRORA GONZÁLES:
Also known as María Aurora Gonzáles.

Children of AVRORA GONZÁLES are:
    i.   EMMA[11] GONZÁLES[729], b. July 04, 1915, San Patricio, New México[730]; m. RUBÉN PINEDA, August 10, 1936[731].

248. ii. TRENIDAD GONZÁLES, b. September 21, 1918, San Patricio, New México; d. July 01, 2010, San Patricio, New México.

249. iii. ERLINDA GONZÁLES, b. November 05, 1921, San Patricio, New México.

Children of AVRORA GONZÁLES and GEORGE ROMERO are:

250. iv. SIGISFREDO[11] ROMERO, b. March 31, 1903; d. November 14, 1982, San Patricio, New México.

251. v. MELITANA ROMERO, b. February 16, 1902.

123. AROPAJITA[10] GONZÁLES *(FLORENCIO[9], MARÍA MANUELA[8] ARAGÓN, MARIANA ANTONIA[7] SÁNCHES, DIEGO ANTONIO[6], FRANCISCO[5], JACINTO SÁNCHES[4] DE IÑIGO, FRANCISCO MUÑOS[3] SÁNCHES, JACINTO[2] MUÑOS, FRANCISCO[1])* was born October 12, 1882 in San Patricio, Territory of New México[732], and died in San Patricio, New México. She married (1) TRANCITO POLACO[733] November 08, 1900 in San Patricio, Territory of New México[734], son of SERAFÍN POLACO and MARÍA GONZÁLES. She married (2) FRANK LUCERO RANDOLPH September 03, 1941 in Carrizozo, New México[735], son of JOSEPH RANDOLPH and ELENOR LUCERO.

Children of AROPAJITA GONZÁLES and TRANCITO POLACO are:

252. i. DULCINEA[11] POLACO, b. October 28, 1902, San Patricio, New México; d. March 25, 1990, Ruidoso, New México.

253. ii. TRANCITO POLACO, b. September 16, 1907, San Patricio, New México; d. December 14, 1998, Ruidoso Downs, New México.

254. iii. ALTAGRACIA POLACO, b. August 24, 1910, San Patricio, Territory of New México.

255. iv. ELFIGO POLACO, b. April 23, 1913, San Patricio, New México; d. August 31, 1991, Tularosa, New México.

124. AURELIA[10] GONZÁLES *(FLORENCIO[9], MARÍA MANUELA[8] ARAGÓN, MARIANA ANTONIA[7] SÁNCHES, DIEGO ANTONIO[6], FRANCISCO[5], JACINTO SÁNCHES[4] DE IÑIGO, FRANCISCO MUÑOS[3] SÁNCHES, JACINTO[2] MUÑOS, FRANCISCO[1])* was born May 15, 1883 in San Patricio, Territory of New México. She married MIGUEL LUNA November 28, 1898 in San Patricio, Territory of New México[736], son of JOSÉ DE LUNA and MARÍA TORRES.

Child of AURELIA GONZÁLES and MIGUEL LUNA is:

i. JOSEFA[11] LUNA, b. August 1899, Lincoln, Territory of New México[737].

125. FLORENCIO SÁNCHEZ[10] GONZÁLES *(FLORENCIO[9], MARÍA MANUELA[8] ARAGÓN, MARIANA ANTONIA[7] SÁNCHES, DIEGO ANTONIO[6], FRANCISCO[5], JACINTO SÁNCHES[4] DE IÑIGO, FRANCISCO MUÑOS[3] SÁNCHES, JACINTO[2] MUÑOS, FRANCISCO[1])[738]* was born November 09, 1892 in San Patricio, Territory of New México, and died July 09, 1979. He married AVELINA CHÁVEZ[738] November 09, 1911 in Lincoln, Territory of New Mexico[739], daughter of PATROCINIO CHÁVEZ and VICENTA ARCHULETA.

Children of FLORENCIO GONZÁLES and AVELINA CHÁVEZ are:

256. i. GENOVEVA[11] GONZÁLES, b. April 11, 1915, San Patricio, New México; d. June 09, 1998, Glencoe, New México.

ii. MIGUEL GONZÁLES[740], b. July 21, 1913, San Patricio, New México; d. April 08, 1999, San Patricio, New México; m. CRECENCIA YBARRA[740], January 05, 1935, San Patricio, New México[741].

Notes for CRECENCIA YBARRA:
Also known as Crita.

iii. JUANITA GONZÁLES, b. Abt. 1919, San Patricio, New México[742]; m. CHARLIE REYNOLDS, September 28, 1940, San Patricio, New México[743].

iv. DULCINEA GONZÁLES[744], b. September 11, 1921, San Patricio, New México[745]; m. GEORGE D. REYNOLDS, August 10, 1940, Carrizozo, New México[746].

v. ALFREDO GONZÁLES[747], b. March 14, 1928, San Patricio, New México; d. May 22, 2008, Ruidoso, New México; m. CIDELIA CANDELARIA[747], June 22, 1952, Ruidoso, New México[748].

vi. VIRGINIA DOROTEA GONZÁLES, b. Abt. March 1930, San Patricio, New México[749].

257. vii. ELOY CHÁVEZ GONZÁLES, b. May 28, 1933, San Patricio, New México.

126. ESOILA[10] GONZÁLES *(FLORENCIO[9], MARÍA MANUELA[8] ARAGÓN, MARIANA ANTONIA[7] SÁNCHES, DIEGO ANTONIO[6], FRANCISCO[5], JACINTO SÁNCHES[4] DE IÑIGO, FRANCISCO MUÑOS[3] SÁNCHES, JACINTO[2] MUÑOS, FRANCISCO[1])* was born August 08, 1894 in San Patricio, Territory of New México[750]. She married

FRANCISCO MAÉS VIGIL December 05, 1909 in San Patricio, Territory of New México[750], son of RAMÓN VIGIL and VICTORIA MAÉS.

Children of ESOILA GONZÁLES and FRANCISCO VIGIL are:
- i. FRANCISCO GONZÁLES[11] VIGIL, b. Abt. 1912, Picacho, New México[751].
- ii. RAMÓN VIGIL, b. Abt. 1915, Picacho, New México[751].
- iii. REBECCA VIGIL, b. Abt. 1918, Picacho, New México[751].
- iv. PRESCILLA VIGIL, b. Abt. 1923, Picacho, New México[751].
- v. ROSALVA VIGIL, b. Abt. 1925, Picacho, New México[751].
- vi. ERNESTINA VIGIL, b. Abt. 1928, Picacho, New México[751].

127. NAPOLEÓN[10] SÁNCHEZ *(FRANCISCO[9], MAURICIO DE LA TRINIDAD[8] SÁNCHES, JOSÉ GREGORIO DE LA TRINIDAD[7], JUAN CRISTÓBAL[6], FRANCISCO[5], JACINTO SÁNCHES[4] DE IÑIGO, FRANCISCO MUÑOS[3] SÁNCHES, JACINTO[2] MUÑOS, FRANCISCO[1])* was born January 04, 1874 in San Patricio, Territory of New México[752]. He married MARÍA CHÁVEZ[753] February 10, 1902 in San Patricio, Territory of New México[754], daughter of MERIJILDO CHÁVEZ and DOLORES SILVA.

Children of NAPOLEÓN SÁNCHEZ and MARÍA CHÁVEZ are:
- i. LUPE[11] SÁNCHEZ, b. December 12, 1902, San Patricio, Territory of New México[755].
- 258. ii. REYNALDA SÁNCHEZ, b. February 21, 1905, San Patricio, Territory of New México; d. May 12, 1970, San Patricio, New México.
- iii. FRANK SÁNCHEZ, b. 1908, San Patricio, Territory of New México[756].
- iv. CECILIA SÁNCHEZ, b. 1910, San Patricio, Territory of New México[756].
- v. MERIJILDO SÁNCHEZ, b. 1914, San Patricio, New México[756].
- vi. JUAN CHÁVEZ SÁNCHEZ, b. 1916, San Patricio, New México[756].
- vii. LOLA SÁNCHEZ, b. 1920, San Patricio, New México[756].

128. DAVÍD[10] SÁNCHEZ *(FRANCISCO[9], MAURICIO DE LA TRINIDAD[8] SÁNCHES, JOSÉ GREGORIO DE LA TRINIDAD[7], JUAN CRISTÓBAL[6], FRANCISCO[5], JACINTO SÁNCHES[4] DE IÑIGO, FRANCISCO MUÑOS[3] SÁNCHES, JACINTO[2] MUÑOS, FRANCISCO[1])* was born November 06, 1876 in San Patricio, Territory of New México[757], and died in Roswell, New México. He married FRANCISCA ARCHULETA May 05, 1902 in San Patricio, Territory of New México[758], daughter of ANTONIO ARCHULETA and SIMONA PACHECO.

Notes for FRANCISCA ARCHULETA:
Also known as Panchita.

Children of DAVÍD SÁNCHEZ and FRANCISCA ARCHULETA are:
- i. AVRELIA[11] SÁNCHEZ, b. San Patricio, New México.

Notes for AVRELIA SÁNCHEZ:
Died at 4 years of age.

- 259. ii. JOSEFITA ARCHULETA SÁNCHEZ, b. Abt. 1905, San Patricio, Territory of New México.
- iii. ANTONIO ARCHULETA SÁNCHEZ, b. Abt. 1907, San Patricio, Territory of New México[759].
- iv. SANTIAGO ARCHULETA SÁNCHEZ, b. Abt. 1910, San Patricio, Territory of New México[759].
- v. EDUARDO SÁNCHEZ, b. 1912, San Patricio, New México[760].
- 260. vi. ADELAIDA SÁNCHEZ, b. July 06, 1915, San Patricio, New México.
- vii. ANEDA ARCHULETA SÁNCHEZ, b. 1917, San Patricio, New México[760].
- viii. RUBÉN ARCHULETA SÁNCHEZ[761], b. September 16, 1920, San Patricio, New México; d. August 05, 2001, Roswell, New México; m. MARÍA MONTOYA[762], February 08, 1939, Roswell, New México.

Notes for MARÍA MONTOYA:
Also known as Mary.

129. ANTONIO[10] SÁNCHEZ *(FRANCISCO[9], MAURICIO DE LA TRINIDAD[8] SÁNCHES, JOSÉ GREGORIO DE LA TRINIDAD[7], JUAN CRISTÓBAL[6], FRANCISCO[5], JACINTO SÁNCHES[4] DE IÑIGO, FRANCISCO MUÑOS[3] SÁNCHES, JACINTO[2] MUÑOS, FRANCISCO[1])* was born February 08, 1878 in San Patricio, Territory of New México[763]. He married CAROLINA ROMERO January 09, 1901[764], daughter of JUAN ROMERO and CRISTINA CASTILLO.

Notes for ANTONIO SÁNCHEZ:

Antonio and his family migrated to Colorado for a brief time to work in the agricultural industry. He and his family returned to New México and opted to settle in Roswell.

Notes for CAROLINA ROMERO:
Other baptismal records indicate that she was born on January 22, 1886. (Microfiche# 0017008, Page 109)
Raised by Jinio and Lola Guerra.

Children of ANTONIO SÁNCHEZ and CAROLINA ROMERO are:
	i.	ANEDA ROMERO[11] SÁNCHEZ, b. San Patricio, New México.
	ii.	ANGELITA ROMERO SÁNCHEZ, b. San Patricio, New México.
	iii.	JOSEFITA ROMERO SÁNCHEZ, b. San Patricio, New México.
	iv.	CONCEPCIÓN SÁNCHEZ, b. Abt. 1902, San Patricio, Territory of New México[765].
261.	v.	MARGARITA ROMERO SÁNCHEZ, b. August 22, 1903, San Patricio, Territory of New México; d. January 31, 2004, Artesia, New México.
	vi.	ISMAÉL SÁNCHEZ, b. 1916, San Patricio, New México[766].
	vii.	JESÚSITA ROMERO SÁNCHEZ, b. Abt. 1926, San Patricio, New México[767].

130. MAURICIO[10] SÁNCHEZ *(FRANCISCO[9], MAURICIO DE LA TRINIDAD[8] SÁNCHES, JOSÉ GREGORIO DE LA TRINIDAD[7], JUAN CRISTÓBAL[6], FRANCISCO[5], JACINTO SÁNCHES[4] DE IÑIGO, FRANCISCO MUÑOS[3] SÁNCHES, JACINTO[2] MUÑOS, FRANCISCO[1])[768]* was born October 04, 1880 in San Patricio, Territory of New México[769], and died September 17, 1961 in San Fernandez, New México. He married (1) DELFINIA ROMERO January 09, 1901 in San Patricio, Territory of New México[770], daughter of JUAN ROMERO and CRISTINA CASTILLO. He married (2) CLARA BARTLETT July 28, 1927 in Hondo, Territory of New México[771], daughter of CHARLES BARTLETT and ADELA GALINDRO.

Notes for MAURICIO SÁNCHEZ:
Land Patent # NMR 0021586, on the authority of the Homestead Entry-Enlarged (35 Stat. 639), February 19, 1909. Issued 320 acres on April 05, 1916.
Land Patent # NMLC 0025687, on the authority of the Homestead Entry-Stock Raising (39 Stat. 862), December 29, 1916. Issued 320 acres on April 12, 1927.

Notes for DELFINIA ROMERO:
December 30, 1885: Baptized in San Patricio under the name María Virginia Romero, birthdate December 18, 1885. Padrinos: Román Barragán & Andrea Torres. Raised by her godparents, Román Barragán & Andrea Torres.

Notes for CLARA BARTLETT:
Land Patent # NMLC 0035363, on the authority of the Homestead Entry-Stock Raising (39 Stat. 862), December 29, 1916. Issued 640 acres on September 1, 1933.

Children of MAURICIO SÁNCHEZ and DELFINIA ROMERO are:
	i.	JUANITA[11] SÁNCHEZ[772], b. February 08, 1902, San Patricio, Territory of New México[773]; d. December 06, 1975, Ruidoso, New México; m. RAMÓN TORRES, June 13, 1918, Glencoe, New Mexico[774].
262.	ii.	ROMÁN SÁNCHEZ, b. April 23, 1904, San Patricio, Territory of New México; d. February 08, 1973, Ruidoso, New México.
263.	iii.	MAXIMILIANO SÁNCHEZ, b. June 22, 1911, San Patricio, Territory of New México; d. April 15, 1972.
	iv.	MABEL ROMERO SÁNCHEZ[775], b. Abt. 1915, San Patricio, New México[776]; d. April 02, 1929, San Patricio, New México.
264.	v.	MARÍA SÁNCHEZ, b. April 19, 1919, San Patricio, New México; d. July 31, 1966, Los Lunas, New México.
265.	vi.	JESÚSITA SÁNCHEZ, b. September 19, 1922, San Patricio, New México; d. July 16, 1992, Albuquerque, New México.

131. PATRICIO[10] SÁNCHEZ *(FRANCISCO[9], MAURICIO DE LA TRINIDAD[8] SÁNCHES, JOSÉ GREGORIO DE LA TRINIDAD[7], JUAN CRISTÓBAL[6], FRANCISCO[5], JACINTO SÁNCHES[4] DE IÑIGO, FRANCISCO MUÑOS[3] SÁNCHES, JACINTO[2] MUÑOS, FRANCISCO[1])[777]* was born January 30, 1882 in San Patricio, Territory of New México[778], and died April 1955 in San Patricio, New México[779]. He married CELIA TRUJILLO[780] March 17, 1915 in San Patricio, Territory of New México[781], daughter of JUAN TRUJILLO and VICENTA GUEBARA.

Notes for PATRICIO SÁNCHEZ:
Marriage records list his birthdate as January 30, 1883. Raised by his Padrinos, Francisco Trujillo & Margarita Trujillo. Farm located on land originally patented to Feliz Trujillo.

Land Patent # NMR 0009248, on the authority of the Homestead Entry-Original (12 Stat. 392), May 20, 1862. Issued 40 acres on July 26, 1910.

Children of PATRICIO SÁNCHEZ and CELIA TRUJILLO are:
266.   i.   ABSALÓN[11] SÁNCHEZ, b. February 04, 1916, San Patricio, New México; d. January 10, 1996, Alamogordo, New México.
    ii.   ADONIS SÁNCHEZ[782], b. September 16, 1918, San Patricio, New México; d. July 01, 1992, San Patricio, New México.

Notes for ADONIS SÁNCHEZ:
US Army. WW II Veteran.

    iii.   ARCILIA SÁNCHEZ, b. Abt. 1920, San Patricio, New México[783]; d. December 21, 1944, San Patricio, New México.
267.   iv.   ERMINIA SÁNCHEZ, b. September 29, 1922, San Patricio, New México.
    v.   LOYOLA SÁNCHEZ, b. July 26, 1926, Roswell, New México[784]; m. TOMÁS SÁNCHEZ, March 26, 1947, Carrizozo, New México[784].

Notes for TOMÁS SÁNCHEZ:
Also known as Tom, Tomasito.

268.   vi.   CELIA SÁNCHEZ, b. July 19, 1929, San Patricio, New México; d. October 05, 2003.
    vii.   ORALIA SÁNCHEZ[785], b. February 26, 1932, San Patricio, New México; d. September 11, 1982, Wilmington, California; m. PANFILO B. APRODA, January 07, 1949[786].

Notes for PANFILO B. APRODA:
1949: Was living in Wilmington, California.

    viii.   PATRICIO TRUJILLO SÁNCHEZ, b. Abt. 1935, San Patricio, New México[787].
    ix.   EVA SÁNCHEZ, b. Abt. 1937, San Patricio, New México[787].
    x.   DANNY SÁNCHEZ, b. Private, San Patricio, New México; m. NORA RUE.
    xi.   MADALENA SÁNCHEZ, b. Private, San Patricio, New México; m. RAMÓN MONTAÑO.

132. JACOBO[10] SÁNCHEZ *(FRANCISCO[9], MAURICIO DE LA TRINIDAD[8] SÁNCHES, JOSÉ GREGORIO DE LA TRINIDAD[7], JUAN CRISTÓBAL[6], FRANCISCO[5], JACINTO SÁNCHES[4] DE IÑIGO, FRANCISCO MUÑOS[3] SÁNCHES, JACINTO[2] MUÑOS, FRANCISCO[1])[788]* was born April 22, 1886 in San Patricio, Territory of New México, and died July 06, 1968 in San Patricio, New México. He married MARÍA TRUJILLO[788] December 07, 1906[789], daughter of JUAN TRUJILLO and VICENTA GUEBARA.

Notes for JACOBO SÁNCHEZ:
Baptismal records state that he was born on June 26, 1886. (Microfiche# 0016754, Baptismal Records) Social Security Death Index indicates he was born on April 22, 1886.
Owned land that was originally patented to Feliz Trujillo.
Land Patent # NMR 0035104, on the authority of the Homestead Entry-Enlarged (35 Stat. 639), February 19, 1909. Issued 320 acres on January 04, 1923.

Children of JACOBO SÁNCHEZ and MARÍA TRUJILLO are:
    i.   JUAN TRUJILLO[11] SÁNCHEZ[790], b. 1909, San Patricio, Territory of New México[791]; d. 1940; m. BRESELIA GONZÁLES[792].
269.   ii.   ALBESITA SÁNCHEZ, b. March 10, 1914, San Patricio, New México.
270.   iii.   PILAR TRUJILLO SÁNCHEZ, b. July 16, 1917, San Patricio, New México; d. September 20, 1999, Ruidoso Downs, New México.
271.   iv.   ESTER SÁNCHEZ, b. September 30, 1920, San Patricio, New México; d. 1966.
    v.   CLOVÍS SÁNCHEZ, b. May 17, 1923, San Patricio, New México[793]; d. 1995[794]; m. EMMA GUERRERO, September 23, 1948, Ruidoso, New México[795].
    vi.   ESTOLANO TRUJILLO SÁNCHEZ[796], b. September 12, 1925, San Patricio, New México; d. August 27, 1970, San Patricio, New México; m. MONICA SALCIDO[796], January 10, 1945, Carrizozo, New México[797].
    vii.   MABEL TRUJILLO SÁNCHEZ, b. August 06, 1930, San Patricio, New México; d. December 06, 1996, Roswell, New México; m. (1) SENON CHÁVEZ[798], June 09, 1949, Carrizozo, New México[799]; m. (2) DON CLEMENT, January 15, 1964, Alamagordo, New México.

133. ELOISA[10] SÁNCHEZ *(FRANCISCO[9], MAURICIO DE LA TRINIDAD[8] SÁNCHES, JOSÉ GREGORIO DE LA TRINIDAD[7], JUAN CRISTÓBAL[6], FRANCISCO[5], JACINTO SÁNCHES[4] DE IÑIGO, FRANCISCO MUÑOS[3] SÁNCHES, JACINTO[2] MUÑOS, FRANCISCO[1])* was born February 10, 1891 in San Patricio, Territory of New México[800], and died in Manzano, New México. She married FELIPÉ SAÍZ January 12, 1908 in San Patricio, Territory of New México[801], son of PABLO SAÍZ and CELESTINA ARAGÓN.

Notes for FELIPÉ SAÍZ:
Raised Cruz Herrera after his mother, Refujia Sánchez died.
Land Patent # NMR 0025724, on the authority of the Homestead Entry-Original (12 Stat. 392), May 20, 1862. Issued 120 acres on March 30, 1915.

Children of ELOISA SÁNCHEZ and FELIPÉ SAÍZ are:
   i.   CONCHA[11] SAÍZ, b. Abt. 1920, San Patricio, Territory of New México[802].

Notes for CONCHA SAÍZ:
Also known as Concepción.

   ii.   FLORA SAÍZ, b. Abt. 1925, San Patricio, Territory of New México[802].
   iii. ELOISA SAÍZ, b. Abt. 1927[802].

134. CONRADO[10] SÁNCHEZ *(FRANCISCO[9], MAURICIO DE LA TRINIDAD[8] SÁNCHES, JOSÉ GREGORIO DE LA TRINIDAD[7], JUAN CRISTÓBAL[6], FRANCISCO[5], JACINTO SÁNCHES[4] DE IÑIGO, FRANCISCO MUÑOS[3] SÁNCHES, JACINTO[2] MUÑOS, FRANCISCO[1])[803]* was born July 15, 1894 in San Patricio, Territory of New México[804], and died August 1977 in Casa Grande, Arizona. He married JOSEFITA PADILLA January 20, 1912 in Lincoln, New México[805], daughter of JOSÉ PADILLA and NESTORA SAMORA.

Notes for CONRADO SÁNCHEZ:
Was a WW I war veteran.

Children of CONRADO SÁNCHEZ and JOSEFITA PADILLA are:
   i.   CHANITO PADILLA[11] SÁNCHEZ, b. Private.
   ii.   MARY SÁNCHEZ, b. Private; Adopted child.

135. REFUGIA[10] SÁNCHEZ *(FRANCISCO[9], MAURICIO DE LA TRINIDAD[8] SÁNCHES, JOSÉ GREGORIO DE LA TRINIDAD[7], JUAN CRISTÓBAL[6], FRANCISCO[5], JACINTO SÁNCHES[4] DE IÑIGO, FRANCISCO MUÑOS[3] SÁNCHES, JACINTO[2] MUÑOS, FRANCISCO[1])* was born July 04, 1899 in San Patricio, Territory of New México[806]. She married JUAN PABLO HERRERA February 19, 1918 in Lincoln, New México[807], son of CRUZ HERRERA and REDUCINDA CARDONA.

Notes for REFUGIA SÁNCHEZ:
Died after her son Cruz was born.

Child of REFUGIA SÁNCHEZ and JUAN HERRERA is:
   i.   CRUZ[11] HERRERA, b. Abt. 1919[808].

Notes for CRUZ HERRERA:
Also known as Crusito.
1930 Census: Living in Manzano, New México. Raised by Felipe Saíz & Eloisa Sánchez de Saíz after his mother died. (Cruz Saís)
Moved from Manzano to Roswell, New México.

136. RAYMUNDO[10] SÁNCHEZ *(JUAN RAFAEL BERCELÓ[9] SÁNCHES, JUAN RAFAEL FERNANDO[8], MANUEL RAFAEL[7], PEDRO[6], JACINTO[5], JOSÉ SÁNCHES[4] DE IÑIGO, JACINTO SÁNCHES[3], FRANCISCO MUÑOS[2] SÁNCHES, JACINTO[1] MUÑOS)[809]* was born March 15, 1879 in Tajiqué, Territory of New México, and died November 26, 1958. He married AUGUSTINA ULIBARRÍ[809] December 17, 1910[810], daughter of VICENTE ULIBARRÍ and MARÍA SEDILLO.

Children of RAYMUNDO SÁNCHEZ and AUGUSTINA ULIBARRÍ are:
   i.   EULALIA[11] SÁNCHEZ, b. December 15, 1912, San Patricio, New México[811]; m. PERFECTO SÁNCHEZ, June 17, 1929, Carrizozo, New México[811].

      ii.   BENNIE SÁNCHEZ, b. July 26, 1914, San Patricio, New México[812]; m. NICOLÁS TORRES, August 25, 1931, Glencoe, New México[812].

272.   iii.   SOFIO SÁNCHEZ, b. May 25, 1916, San Patricio, New México; d. May 25, 1984, San Patricio, New México.

273.   iv.   ANEDA ULIBARRÍ SÁNCHEZ, b. July 12, 1918, San Patricio, New México; d. September 24, 1999.

      v.   OLYMPIA SÁNCHEZ[813], b. May 21, 1920, San Patricio, New México[814]; d. June 05, 2010, Ruidoso, New México; m. EPUNUCENO SÁNCHEZ[815], August 27, 1938, Carrizozo, New México[816].

      vi.   VISITA SÁNCHEZ[817], b. October 10, 1923, San Patricio, New México; d. April 10, 1924, San Patricio, New México.

      vii.   LUÍS SÁNCHEZ, b. 1928, San Patricio, New México[818].

137. AMADITA[10] SÁNCHEZ *(JUAN RAFAEL BERCELÓ[9] SÁNCHES, JUAN RAFAEL FERNANDO[8], MANUEL RAFAEL[7], PEDRO[6], JACINTO[5], JOSÉ SÁNCHES[4] DE IÑIGO, JACINTO SÁNCHES[3], FRANCISCO MUÑOS[2] SÁNCHES, JACINTO[1] MUÑOS)[819]* was born August 21, 1883 in Glencoe, Territory of New México, and died June 12, 1934. She married (1) FEDERICO PEÑA, son of TEODORO PEÑA and MARGARITA LÓPEZ. She married (2) LUÍS LÓPEZ PEÑA January 12, 1903[820], son of TEODORO PEÑA and MARGARITA LÓPEZ.

Child of AMADITA SÁNCHEZ and LUÍS PEÑA is:

274.   i.   TEODORO SÁNCHEZ[11] PEÑA, b. December 19, 1903, Glencoe, Territory of New México; d. April 13, 1968, Tularosa, New México.

138. RITA[10] SÁNCHEZ *(JUAN RAFAEL BERCELÓ[9] SÁNCHES, JUAN RAFAEL FERNANDO[8], MANUEL RAFAEL[7], PEDRO[6], JACINTO[5], JOSÉ SÁNCHES[4] DE IÑIGO, JACINTO SÁNCHES[3], FRANCISCO MUÑOS[2] SÁNCHES, JACINTO[1] MUÑOS)[821]* was born July 12, 1889 in Ruidoso, Territory of New México[822], and died January 1984 in Artesia, New México[823]. She married NEWMAN GILL July 03, 1915 in La Capilla de San Ysidro, New México[824], son of WILLIAM GILL and ALTAGRACIA HERRERA.

Children of RITA SÁNCHEZ and NEWMAN GILL are:

      i.   OLIVIA[11] GILL, b. 1919[825]; m. PORFIRIO VALENZUELA.

      ii.   ESTOLANO GILL[826], b. July 06, 1921, Glencoe, New México[827]; d. January 24, 1990.

      iii.   PRESILIANO GILL[828], b. December 27, 1923, Glencoe, New México[829]; d. September 1979, Sacramento, California.

      iv.   PABLITA GILL, b. 1925[829]; m. TORIVIO PADILLA.

      v.   RITA GILL, b. 1928[829].

139. EDUARDO[10] SÁNCHEZ *(JUAN RAFAEL BERCELÓ[9] SÁNCHES, JUAN RAFAEL FERNANDO[8], MANUEL RAFAEL[7], PEDRO[6], JACINTO[5], JOSÉ SÁNCHES[4] DE IÑIGO, JACINTO SÁNCHES[3], FRANCISCO MUÑOS[2] SÁNCHES, JACINTO[1] MUÑOS)[830]* was born October 13, 1893 in Glencoe, Territory of New México[831], and died May 28, 1954 in San Patricio, New México. He married SENAIDA MONTOYA[832] October 08, 1920 in San Patricio, New México[833], daughter of ESTANISLADO MONTOYA and SARAFINA ULIBARRÍ.

Children of EDUARDO SÁNCHEZ and SENAIDA MONTOYA are:

      i.   EDUARDO MONTOYA[11] SÁNCHEZ[834], b. May 26, 1921, San Patricio, New México; d. May 15, 1995.

      ii.   MACLOFA SÁNCHEZ, b. Abt. 1923, San Patricio, New México[835]; m. ARISTEO HERRERA.

      iii.   JUAN SÁNCHEZ[836], b. January 26, 1924, San Patricio, New México; d. January 26, 1924, San Patricio, New México.

      iv.   MANUEL MONTOYA SÁNCHEZ[837], b. May 20, 1925, Glencoe, New México; d. March 22, 1982, Roswell, New México; m. FLORINDA SÁNCHEZ.

      v.   RAFAEL MONTOYA SÁNCHEZ, b. Abt. 1928, San Patricio, New México[838].

      vi.   MARGARITA MONTOYA SÁNCHEZ, b. Abt. 1929, San Patricio, New México[838].

      vii.   SERAPIO SÁNCHEZ[839], b. Abt. 1937, San Patricio, New México; d. February 04, 1937, San Patricio, New México.

      viii.   CONFERINA MONTOYA SÁNCHEZ, b. Private, San Patricio, New México.

      ix.   ELFIDES SÁNCHEZ, b. Private, San Patricio, New México.

      x.   RUMELIO SÁNCHEZ, b. Private, San Patricio, New México.

140. BERSABÉ[10] SÁNCHEZ *(JUAN RAFAEL BERCELÓ[9] SÁNCHES, JUAN RAFAEL FERNANDO[8], MANUEL RAFAEL[7], PEDRO[6], JACINTO[5], JOSÉ SÁNCHES[4] DE IÑIGO, JACINTO SÁNCHES[3], FRANCISCO MUÑOS[2] SÁNCHES, JACINTO[1] MUÑOS)* was born June 10, 1897 in Glencoe, Territory of New México[840]. She married TEODORO ULIBARRÍ MONTOYA[841] December 11, 1919 in San Patricio, New México[842], son of ESTANISLADO MONTOYA and SARAFINA ULIBARRÍ.

Children of BERSABÉ SÁNCHEZ and TEODORO MONTOYA are:

      i.   AMELIA[11] MONTOYA, b. Abt. 1920, Glencoe, New México[843].

275.   ii.   ALVESITA MONTOYA, b. January 26, 1921, Glencoe, New México.

      iii.   CANDIDO SÁNCHEZ MONTOYA[844], b. November 14, 1923, Glencoe, New México; d. June 23, 1992, Ruidoso Downs, New México; m. CRUSITA BENAVIDEZ SÁNCHEZ[845], November 09, 1946, Carrizozo, New México[846].

      iv.   ANSELMO MONTOYA, b. Abt. 1926, Glencoe, New México[847].

141. VICTORIA[10] SÁNCHEZ *(JUAN RAFAEL BERCELÓ[9] SÁNCHES, JUAN RAFAEL FERNANDO[8], MANUEL RAFAEL[7], PEDRO[6], JACINTO[5], JOSÉ SÁNCHES[4] DE IÑIGO, JACINTO SÁNCHES[3], FRANCISCO MUÑOS[2] SÁNCHES, JACINTO[1] MUÑOS)[848]* was born February 28, 1899 in Chililí, Territory of New México[849], and died February 14, 1983 in Albuquerque, New México. She married (1) CELSO TRUJILLO[850], son of JUAN TRUJILLO and VICENTA GUEBARA. She married (2) ISABEL MONTOYA February 23, 1921[851], son of ESTANISLADO MONTOYA and SARAFINA ULIBARRÍ.

Children of VICTORIA SÁNCHEZ and CELSO TRUJILLO are:

      i.   MELVIN[11] TRUJILLO[852], b. April 06, 1930, Glencoe, New México; d. April 13, 2007, Davis, California.

      ii.   JOSÉ NICODEMAS TRUJILLO[852], b. May 07, 1932, Glencoe, New México; d. September 24, 2007, Albuquerque, New México.

142. MACLOFA[10] SÁNCHEZ *(JUAN RAFAEL BERCELÓ[9] SÁNCHES, JUAN RAFAEL FERNANDO[8], MANUEL RAFAEL[7], PEDRO[6], JACINTO[5], JOSÉ SÁNCHES[4] DE IÑIGO, JACINTO SÁNCHES[3], FRANCISCO MUÑOS[2] SÁNCHES, JACINTO[1] MUÑOS)* was born August 21, 1903, and died Abt. February 1922. She married DOMINGO PACHECO.

Child of MACLOFA SÁNCHEZ and DOMINGO PACHECO is:

      i.   SUSIE[11] PACHECO[852], b. February 24, 1922; d. January 1986, Artesia, New México; m. TORIBIO BARRERA[852].

143. TRANSITO[10] CHÁVEZ *(AMADA[9] SÁNCHEZ, MAURICIO DE LA TRINIDAD[8] SÁNCHES, JOSÉ GREGORIO DE LA TRINIDAD[7], JUAN CRISTÓBAL[6], FRANCISCO[5], JACINTO SÁNCHES[4] DE IÑIGO, FRANCISCO MUÑOS[3] SÁNCHES, JACINTO[2] MUÑOS, FRANCISCO[1])[853]* was born July 20, 1887 in La Junta, Territory of New México, and died April 07, 1975 in San Patricio, New México. He married ANGELITA CHÁVEZ[854] April 15, 1907 in Lincoln, Territory of New México[855], daughter of ROBERTO CHÁVES and LUCÍA WELDON.

Notes for TRANSITO CHÁVEZ:
Land Patent # NMR 0025917, on the authority of the Homestead Entry-Enlarged (35 Stat. 639), February 19, 1909. Issued 320 acres on November 15, 1917.
Land Patent # NMR 003740, on the authority of the Homestead Entry-Stock Raising (39 Stat. 862), December 29, 1916. Issued 320 acres on July 17, 1924.

Children of TRANSITO CHÁVEZ and ANGELITA CHÁVEZ are:

276.   i.   ARISTEO[11] CHÁVEZ, b. November 30, 1910, Hondo, New México; d. August 21, 1993, San Patricio, New México.

      ii.   ISMAEL CHÁVEZ[856], b. November 12, 1912, Hondo, New México; d. July 31, 1980, San Patricio, New México; m. ELISA MENDOSA[857].

      iii.   OZIEL CHÁVEZ, b. 1917, Hondo, New México[858]; d. August 19, 1942, Phillipines[859].

Notes for OZIEL CHÁVEZ:
Also known as Ouciel.
March 15, 1941: Enlisted into the Army, 200th Cavalry Regiment. Fought in the Southwest Pacific Theatre, Philippines. Died as a Prisoner of War during World War Two.

      iv.   AVESLÍN CHÁVEZ, b. 1920, Hondo, New México[860]; d. March 20, 1945, Phillipines[861].

Notes for AVESLÍN CHÁVEZ:
January 24, 1941: Enlisted into the Army. 158th Infantry Regiment. He was awarded a Purple Heart Medal and a Bronze Star Medal. He was killed on March 20, 1945.

277.   v.   HERALDO MODESTO CHÁVEZ, b. December 09, 1922, Hondo, New México; d. July 26, 1965, Hondo, New México.

      vi.   EVA CHÁVEZ, b. February 05, 1925, Hondo, New México[862]; m. (1) CARLOS CHÁVEZ; m. (2) HARRY SÁNCHEZ, February 21, 1944, Carrizozo, New México[862].

144. CANDIDO[10] CHÁVEZ *(AMADA[9] SÁNCHEZ, MAURICIO DE LA TRINIDAD[8] SÁNCHES, JOSÉ GREGORIO DE LA TRINIDAD[7], JUAN CRISTÓBAL[6], FRANCISCO[5], JACINTO SÁNCHES[4] DE IÑIGO, FRANCISCO MUÑOS[3] SÁNCHES, JACINTO[2] MUÑOS, FRANCISCO[1])[863]* was born April 12, 1889 in La Junta, Territory of New México, and died May 20, 1979. He married ESTELA LUCY WEST[864] October 31, 1910[865], daughter of JOHN WEST and MARÍA MONNET.

Notes for CANDIDO CHÁVEZ:
Land Patent # NMR 0029544, on the authority of the Homestead Entry-Enlarged (35 Stat. 639), February 19, 1909. Issued 240 acres on October 28, 1921.
Land Patent # NMLC 0037460, on the authority of the Homestead Entry-Stock Raising (39 Stat. 862), December 29, 1916. Issued 400 acres on August 7, 1925.

Children of CANDIDO CHÁVEZ and ESTELA WEST are:
    i.   CECILIA[11] CHÁVEZ, b. Abt. 1912[866]; m. REFUGIO ROMERO.
278. ii. ETHAL CHÁVEZ, b. September 14, 1913; d. January 18, 1970.
    iii. CANDIDO CHÁVEZ[867], b. December 25, 1915, San Patricio, New México[868]; d. June 14, 1995; m. NORA S. RANDOLPH, February 15, 1947, Carrizozo, New México[868].

Notes for CANDIDO CHÁVEZ:
Private First Class. World War II.

    iv. VIOLA CHÁVEZ, b. Abt. 1918[869].
    v. ELIZABETH CHÁVEZ[870], b. March 15, 1922, San Patricio, New México[871]; d. November 03, 2007, Ruidoso, New México; m. JAMES MACKEY[872].
    vi. CLIFFORD WEST CHÁVEZ, b. Private.
    vii. DOROTHY CHÁVEZ, b. Private; m. LARRY TORREZ.
    viii. JOHNNY CHÁVEZ, b. Private.
    ix. WILLIE DEAN CHÁVEZ, b. Private.

145. OLYMPIA[10] CHÁVEZ *(AMADA[9] SÁNCHEZ, MAURICIO DE LA TRINIDAD[8] SÁNCHES, JOSÉ GREGORIO DE LA TRINIDAD[7], JUAN CRISTÓBAL[6], FRANCISCO[5], JACINTO SÁNCHES[4] DE IÑIGO, FRANCISCO MUÑOS[3] SÁNCHES, JACINTO[2] MUÑOS, FRANCISCO[1])[873]* was born 1894 in La Junta, Territory of New México[874], and died Abt. 1911 in Hondo, Territory of New México. She married JOHN MACKEY April 26, 1909[875], son of PATRICK MACKEY and GUADALUPE SAMORA.

Child of OLYMPIA CHÁVEZ and JOHN MACKEY is:
    i. OLYMPIA[11] MACKEY, b. June 05, 1910; d. Abt. 1912.

Notes for OLYMPIA MACKEY:
Died young.

146. LEOPOLDO[10] CHÁVEZ *(AMADA[9] SÁNCHEZ, MAURICIO DE LA TRINIDAD[8] SÁNCHES, JOSÉ GREGORIO DE LA TRINIDAD[7], JUAN CRISTÓBAL[6], FRANCISCO[5], JACINTO SÁNCHES[4] DE IÑIGO, FRANCISCO MUÑOS[3] SÁNCHES, JACINTO[2] MUÑOS, FRANCISCO[1])* was born April 25, 1907 in Hondo, Territory of New México[876]. He married ALTAGRACIA POLACO May 24, 1930 in Carrizozo, New México[876], daughter of TRANCITO POLACO and AROPAJITA GONZÁLES.

Notes for ALTAGRACIA POLACO:
Also known as Grace.

Children of LEOPOLDO CHÁVEZ and ALTAGRACIA POLACO are:
    i. BREZEL[11] CHÁVEZ[877], b. June 01, 1934; d. March 29, 1992; m. PABLITA HERRERA.
    ii. RICHARD CHÁVEZ[877], b. October 07, 1938; d. March 24, 2003.
279. iii. LYDIA CHÁVEZ, b. Private.
280. iv. ROY CHÁVEZ, b. January 08, 1931, Glencoe, New México; d. February 27, 2001, Tularosa, New México.

147. RUMELIO[10] CHÁVEZ *(AMADA[9] SÁNCHEZ, MAURICIO DE LA TRINIDAD[8] SÁNCHES, JOSÉ GREGORIO DE LA TRINIDAD[7], JUAN CRISTÓBAL[6], FRANCISCO[5], JACINTO SÁNCHES[4] DE IÑIGO, FRANCISCO MUÑOS[3]*

SÁNCHES, JACINTO[2] MUÑOS, FRANCISCO[1])[878] was born 1909 in Hondo, Territory of New México, and died 1963. He married CECILIA OLGUÍN July 11, 1936[879], daughter of ESTANISLADO OLGUÍN and ANASTACIA CHÁVEZ.

Notes for CECILIA OLGUÍN:
Also known as Yselia.

Children of RUMELIO CHÁVEZ and CECILIA OLGUÍN are:
  i. AMADA[11] CHÁVEZ, b. Private; m. HENRY SÁNCHEZ.

Notes for AMADA CHÁVEZ:
Also known as Amy.

  ii. PABLO OLGUÍN CHÁVEZ, b. Private.

Notes for PABLO OLGUÍN CHÁVEZ:
Died at a young age.

  iii. ÁBRAN OLGUÍN CHÁVEZ, b. Private.

148. ERMANDO[10] CHÁVEZ *(AMADA[9] SÁNCHEZ, MAURICIO DE LA TRINIDAD[8] SÁNCHES, JOSÉ GREGORIO DE LA TRINIDAD[7], JUAN CRISTÓBAL[6], FRANCISCO[5], JACINTO SÁNCHES[4] DE IÑIGO, FRANCISCO MUÑOS[3] SÁNCHES, JACINTO[2] MUÑOS, FRANCISCO[1])[880]* was born February 24, 1914 in Hondo, New México[881], and died June 05, 2010 in Ruidoso, New México. He married (1) MACLOVIA MARTÍNEZ[882] December 07, 1935 in Carrizozo, New México[883], daughter of ADENAGO MARTÍNEZ and ANITA GUTIÉRREZ. He married (2) ANEDA ULIBARRÍ SÁNCHEZ September 13, 1941 in Carrizozo, New México[884], daughter of RAYMUNDO SÁNCHEZ and AUGUSTINA ULIBARRÍ.

Children of ERMANDO CHÁVEZ and MACLOVIA MARTÍNEZ are:
281. i. PABLO MOISES[11] CHÁVEZ, b. July 13, 1936, San Patricio, New México; d. May 28, 2009, Amarillo, Téxas.
  ii. BOBBY MARTÍNEZ CHÁVEZ[885], b. Private, San Patricio, New México.
  iii. LUÍS CHÁVEZ[885], b. Private.
  iv. LILLIAN CHÁVEZ[885], b. Private; m. DANNY GARCÍA[885].
  v. LUCY CHÁVEZ[885], b. Private.
  vi. VIOLA CHÁVEZ, b. Private.
  vii. JEANE CHÁVEZ, b. Private.
  viii. DANNY CHÁVEZ, b. Private.

Children of ERMANDO CHÁVEZ and ANEDA SÁNCHEZ are:
  ix. ABRAHAM[11] CHÁVEZ[886], b. November 28, 1946, San Patricio, New México; d. October 30, 1998, San Patricio, New México.
  x. OZIEL CHÁVEZ[887], b. Private.

149. ANDRÉS[10] SALAS *(YSABEL[9] SÁNCHES, DESIDERIO[8], DIEGO ANTONIO[7], JUAN CRISTÓBAL[6], FRANCISCO[5], JACINTO SÁNCHES[4] DE IÑIGO, FRANCISCO MUÑOS[3] SÁNCHES, JACINTO[2] MUÑOS, FRANCISCO[1])* was born November 1863 in Manzano, Territory of New México[888]. He married DOLORITAS PEREA November 18, 1883 in Lincoln County, Territory of New México[889], daughter of JUAN PEREA and MARTA BALLEJOS.

Children of ANDRÉS SALAS and DOLORITAS PEREA are:
  i. GUADALUPE[11] SALAS, b. January 1890[890].
  ii. SARA SALAS, b. February 1892[890].
  iii. FRANCISCO SALAS, b. May 1894[890].
  iv. AURORA SALAS, b. March 1896[890].
  v. ABELINA SALAS, b. September 1898[890].

150. RAYMUNDO[10] SALAS *(YSABEL[9] SÁNCHES, DESIDERIO[8], DIEGO ANTONIO[7], JUAN CRISTÓBAL[6], FRANCISCO[5], JACINTO SÁNCHES[4] DE IÑIGO, FRANCISCO MUÑOS[3] SÁNCHES, JACINTO[2] MUÑOS,*

FRANCISCO¹) was born February 1863 in Manzano, Territory of New México[891]. He married ANTONIA CHÁVEZ February 18, 1889 in Manzano, Territory of New México[892].

Children of RAYMUNDO SALAS and ANTONIA CHÁVEZ are:
   i.   ISABEL¹¹ SALAS, b. February 1893[893].
   ii. JOSÉ MARÍA SALAS, b. April 1898[893].
   iii. DOLÓRES SALAS, b. March 1900[893].

151. CRECENSIA¹⁰ POLACO *(MARÍA ALTAGRACIA⁹ GONZÁLES, MARÍA MANUELA⁸ ARAGÓN, MARIANA ANTONIA⁷ SÁNCHES, DIEGO ANTONIO⁶, FRANCISCO⁵, JACINTO SÁNCHES⁴ DE IÑIGO, FRANCISCO MUÑOS³ SÁNCHES, JACINTO² MUÑOS, FRANCISCO¹)* was born Abt. 1854 in Los Corrales, Territory of New México[894], and died April 17, 1937 in Las Vegas, New México[895]. She married CHRISTIAN PHILLIPPI JACOBI June 19, 1877 in Las Vegas, Territory of New México[896].

Notes for CHRISTIAN PHILLIPPI JACOBI:
Parents were from Prussia.

Child of CRECENSIA POLACO and CHRISTIAN JACOBI is:
   i.   LUCINDA¹¹ JACOBI, b. Abt. 1879[897].

152. ANASTACIA¹⁰ POLACO *(MARÍA ALTAGRACIA⁹ GONZÁLES, MARÍA MANUELA⁸ ARAGÓN, MARIANA ANTONIA⁷ SÁNCHES, DIEGO ANTONIO⁶, FRANCISCO⁵, JACINTO SÁNCHES⁴ DE IÑIGO, FRANCISCO MUÑOS³ SÁNCHES, JACINTO² MUÑOS, FRANCISCO¹)* was born Abt. 1855 in Los Corrales, Territory of New México[898], and died April 25, 1927 in Albuquerque, New México[899]. She married TORRIBIO ARMIJO July 12, 1877 in Bernalillo, Territory of New México[900].

Children of ANASTACIA POLACO and TORRIBIO ARMIJO are:
   i.   MAURICA¹¹ ARMIJO, b. Abt. 1878[901].
   ii. ANTONIO ARMIJO, b. Abt. 1882[901].
282. iii. PETRA ARMIJO, b. May 29, 1894, Corrales, Territory of New México.
   iv. MACLOVIA ARMIJO, b. January 10, 1897; m. ALFONSO JOSE TRUJILLO.

153. TRANCITO¹⁰ POLACO *(MARÍA ALTAGRACIA⁹ GONZÁLES, MARÍA MANUELA⁸ ARAGÓN, MARIANA ANTONIA⁷ SÁNCHES, DIEGO ANTONIO⁶, FRANCISCO⁵, JACINTO SÁNCHES⁴ DE IÑIGO, FRANCISCO MUÑOS³ SÁNCHES, JACINTO² MUÑOS, FRANCISCO¹)*[902] was born July 26, 1858 in Los Corrales, Territory of New México[903], and died in San Patricio, New México. He married AROPAJITA GONZÁLES November 08, 1900 in San Patricio, Territory of New México[904], daughter of FLORENCIO GONZÁLES and RAYMUNDA SÁNCHEZ.

Children of TRANCITO POLACO and AROPAJITA GONZÁLES are:
252. i.   DULCINEA¹¹ POLACO, b. October 28, 1902, San Patricio, New México; d. March 25, 1990, Ruidoso, New México.
253. ii. TRANCITO POLACO, b. September 16, 1907, San Patricio, New México; d. December 14, 1998, Ruidoso Downs, New México.
254. iii. ALTAGRACIA POLACO, b. August 24, 1910, San Patricio, Territory of New México.
255. iv. ELFIGO POLACO, b. April 23, 1913, San Patricio, New México; d. August 31, 1991, Tularosa, New México.

154. CANDIDO¹⁰ POLACO *(MARÍA ALTAGRACIA⁹ GONZÁLES, MARÍA MANUELA⁸ ARAGÓN, MARIANA ANTONIA⁷ SÁNCHES, DIEGO ANTONIO⁶, FRANCISCO⁵, JACINTO SÁNCHES⁴ DE IÑIGO, FRANCISCO MUÑOS³ SÁNCHES, JACINTO² MUÑOS, FRANCISCO¹)*[905] was born Bef. July 30, 1860 in Los Corrales, Territory of New México[906], and died October 18, 1932 in Cordillera, New México[907]. He married FILOMENA OTERO Abt. 1895[908].

Child of CANDIDO POLACO and FILOMENA OTERO is:
283. i.   LUÍS¹¹ POLACO, b. June 1895.

155. ELFIGO¹⁰ POLACO *(MARÍA ALTAGRACIA⁹ GONZÁLES, MARÍA MANUELA⁸ ARAGÓN, MARIANA ANTONIA⁷ SÁNCHES, DIEGO ANTONIO⁶, FRANCISCO⁵, JACINTO SÁNCHES⁴ DE IÑIGO, FRANCISCO MUÑOS³ SÁNCHES, JACINTO² MUÑOS, FRANCISCO¹)*[909] was born Bef. March 11, 1862 in Los Corrales, Territory of New México[910], and died August 23, 1926 in Tiptonville, New México. He married SABINITA LUCERO[911], daughter of LIBRADA LUCERO.

Notes for ELFIGO POLACO:
Also known as Delfido Polaco.
His mother-in-law, Librada Lucero de Abeyta was living and helping raise the family.

Notes for SABINITA LUCERO:
Also known as Sabina Lucero.

Children of ELFIGO POLACO and SABINITA LUCERO are:
	i.	SERAFÍN LUCERO[11] POLACO, b. February 1892[912]; d. October 22, 1928, Dulce, New México[913].
284.	ii.	PEDRO POLACO, b. February 1894, Las Vegas, Territory of New México.
	iii.	TEODORO POLACO[914], b. November 07, 1897, Las Vegas, Territory of New México[915].
	iv.	JULIAN POLACO, b. February 1899[915].

156. RUDOLFO[10] POLACO *(MARÍA ALTAGRACIA[9] GONZÁLES, MARÍA MANUELA[8] ARAGÓN, MARIANA ANTONIA[7] SÁNCHES, DIEGO ANTONIO[6], FRANCISCO[5], JACINTO SÁNCHES[4] DE IÑIGO, FRANCISCO MUÑOS[3] SÁNCHES, JACINTO[2] MUÑOS, FRANCISCO[1])[916]* was born Bef. October 11, 1864 in Los Corrales, Territory of New México[917]. He married ROSA BAIROL LEDOUX January 05, 1891 in Las Vegas, Territory of New México[918], daughter of FELIPÉ LEDOUX and YSABEL LEDOUX.

Notes for RUDOLFO POLACO:
Also known as Bruno Redolfo Polaco.

Child of RUDOLFO POLACO and ROSA LEDOUX is:
	i.	MARTÍN[11] POLACO, b. January 28, 1891, Las Vegas, Territory of New México[919].

157. ALTAGRACIA[10] HERRERA *(FERNANDO[9], PEDRO ALCANTARA[8] DE HERRERA, MARÍA JOSEFA[7] BUSTOS, MARÍA ANTONIA TERESA[6] SÁNCHES, PEDRO[5], PEDRO SÁNCHES[4] DE IÑIGO, FRANCISCO MUÑOS[3] SÁNCHES, JACINTO[2] MUÑOS, FRANCISCO[1])* was born April 15, 1857 in Santa Cruz de la Cañada, Territory of New México[920], and died June 26, 1893 in San Juanito (Ruidoso Downs), Territory of New México. She married (1) WILLIAM JAMES GILL November 15, 1880 in Nogal, Territory of New México. She married (2) ANTONIO VALENZUELA July 27, 1892 in Ruidoso, Territory of New México[921], son of JESÚS VALENZUELA and RITA MUÑOZ.

Notes for ALTAGRACIA HERRERA:
Buried: Herrera Family cemetary in San Juanito (Ruidoso Downs.)

William Gill

Children of ALTAGRACIA HERRERA and WILLIAM GILL are:
285.	i.	JENNIE[11] GILL, b. March 19, 1881, Nogal, Territory of New México; d. December 13, 1913, Glencoe, Territory of New México.
	ii.	MACEDONIO GILL[922], b. February 02, 1882, Nogal, Territory of New México; d. July 24, 1938.
286.	iii.	ELISIA GILL, b. 1881, Nogal, Territory of New México; d. 1949.
	iv.	WILLIAM HERRERA GILL, b. September 05, 1884, Nogal, Territory of New México[923]; m. CONFERINA ORISITACIÓN SÁNCHEZ[924], January 13, 1916, Glencoe, New Mexico[925].

Notes for WILLIAM HERRERA GILL:
Also known as Julian.

287.	v.	NEWMAN GILL, b. November 30, 1885, Nogal, Territory of New México; d. Artesia, New México.
288.	vi.	ESTELA GILL, b. August 12, 1887, Nogal, Territory of New México; d. March 29, 1938, Glencoe, New México.

Children of ALTAGRACIA HERRERA and ANTONIO VALENZUELA are:
	vii.	ROSALÍA[11] VALENZUELA, b. June 23, 1891, Ruidoso, Territory of New México[926].
	viii.	BENANCIO VALENZUELA, b. Abt. March 16, 1893, San Juanito (Ruidoso Downs), Territory of New México[927]; m. RUMALTILDA FLORES, August 01, 1920[928].

Notes for BENANCIO VALENZUELA:
Also known as Venancio, Venceslado Valenzuela.
He was raised by his father and his step mother Nicolasa Herrera.

158. ANDRÉS[10] HERRERA *(FERNANDO[9], PEDRO ALCANTARA[8] DE HERRERA, MARÍA JOSEFA[7] BUSTOS, MARÍA ANTONIA TERESA[6] SÁNCHES, PEDRO[5], PEDRO SÁNCHES[4] DE IÑIGO, FRANCISCO MUÑOS[3] SÁNCHES, JACINTO[2] MUÑOS, FRANCISCO[1])* was born November 27, 1858 in Santa Cruz de la Cañada, New México[929], and died 1911 in Carrizozo, New México. He married ROSARIO RODRÍGUEZ[930], daughter of JESÚS RODRÍGUEZ and FRANCISCA SÁNCHEZ.

Notes for ANDRÉS HERRERA:
Also known as José Andrés de Herrera.
Land Patent # NMNMAA 010260, on the authority of the Homestead Act, May 20, 1862, 160 Acres.

Children of ANDRÉS HERRERA and ROSARIO RODRÍGUEZ are:
    i.   FERNANDO ANTONIO[11] HERRERA, b. May 13, 1885, Rebentón, Territory of New México[931]; m. PAULA WARNER, January 16, 1916, Carrizozo, New México[931].

Notes for FERNANDO ANTONIO HERRERA:
Alson known as Antonio Herrera.

Notes for PAULA WARNER:
Also known as Pabla, Paula Juana.

    ii.   LINO HERRERA[932], b. September 23, 1888, San Juanito (Ruidoso), Territory of New México; d. September 29, 1944, Carrizozo, New México.
    iii.   TEODORA HERRERA, b. November 09, 1889, San Juanito (Ruidoso), Territory of New México[933]; m. JOSÉ SAÍZ, October 18, 1914, Carrizozo, New México[933].
    iv.   MARCELO HERRERA[934], b. January 16, 1892, San Juanito (Ruidoso Downs), Territory of New México[935]; d. October 1970, Roswell, New México; m. CONFERINA ORISITACIÓN SÁNCHEZ[936], July 10, 1911, Ruidoso, Territory of New México[937].
    v.   JUAN HERRERA, b. March 08, 1894, San Juanito (Ruidoso), Territory of New México[938]; d. February 12, 1954, Carrizozo, New México[939]; m. DELFINIA MEDINA, February 02, 1935[940].

Notes for JUAN HERRERA:
Also known as Juan de Santismo Sacramento Herrera.
Mid 1930s: Juan was the constable of in Carrizozo, New México.

Notes for DELFINIA MEDINA:
Also known as Delfinia Durán y Sedillo.

    vi.   MARÍA PERFECTA HERRERA, b. April 28, 1896, San Juanito (Ruidoso Downs), Territory of New México[941].
    vii.   PETRA HERRERA, b. May 13, 1898, San Juanito (Ruidoso Downs), Territory of New México[942]; m. BENJAMÍN SÁNCHEZ, February 20, 1914, Carrizozo, New México[942].
    viii.   MARCELINO HERRERA[943], b. June 02, 1901, Glencoe, Territory of New México; d. May 07, 1980, Alamagordo, New México.
    ix.   DONACIANO HERRERA, b. July 17, 1905, Ruidoso, Territory of New México[944]; m. FEDELINA JARAMILLO, November 12, 1950, Carrizozo, New México[944].
    x.   ANDRÉS RODRÍGUEZ HERRERA[945], b. August 07, 1909, Glencoe, Territory of New México[946]; d. December 18, 1998, Alamagordo, New México; m. SARAFINA APODACA, April 21, 1930, Carrizozo, New México[947].

Josiah G. Scurlock

159. ANTONIA MIGUELA[10] HERRERA *(FERNANDO[9], PEDRO ALCANTARA[8] DE HERRERA, MARÍA JOSEFA[7] BUSTOS, MARÍA ANTONIA TERESA[6] SÁNCHES, PEDRO[5], PEDRO SÁNCHES[4] DE IÑIGO, FRANCISCO MUÑOS[3] SÁNCHES, JACINTO[2] MUÑOS, FRANCISCO[1])[948]* was born June 13, 1860 in Santa Cruz de la Cañada, Territory of New México[949], and died November 27, 1912 in Acton, Texas. She married JOSIAH G. SCURLOCK[950] October 19, 1876 in Lincoln, Territory of New México.

Notes for ANTONIA MIGUELA HERRERA:
Also known as María Antonia Miguela Herrera.

Buried: Initially in Acton, Téxas. Her remains were then relocted next to her husband in Eastland, Téxas.
Another birthdate: May 07, 1860.

Notes for JOSIAH G. SCURLOCK:
Also known as Doc Scurlock.
1879: Migrated to Ft Sumner, New México.
1879: In the winter, the family migrated to Tascosa, Téxas.

Children of ANTONIA HERRERA and JOSIAH SCURLOCK are:
      i.   MARÍA ELENA HERRERA[11] SCURLOCK[951], b. August 19, 1877, San Juanito (Ruidoso), New México; d. August 17, 1879, San Juanito (Ruidoso), New México.
      ii.   VIOLA INEZ HERRERA SCURLOCK[951], b. August 13, 1878, San Juanito (Ruidoso), New México; d. June 07, 1894.
      iii.   JOSIAH GORDEN HERRERA SCURLOCK[951], b. October 11, 1879, San Miguel County, New México.
      iv.   JOHN JOSHUA HERRERA SCURLOCK[951], b. May 21, 1881, Rica Ranch, Oldham County, Téxas.
      v.   AMY ANTONIA HERRERA SCURLOCK[951], b. July 14, 1884, Wilbarger County, Téxas.
      vi.   MARTHA ETHLINDA HERRERA SCURLOCK[951], b. May 10, 1886, Wilbarger County, Téxas.
      vii. PRESLEY FERNANDO HERRERA SCURLOCK[951], b. August 27, 1888, Wilbarger County, Téxas.
      viii. DELORES HERRERA SCURLOCK[951], b. March 10, 1891, Wilbarger County, Téxas.
      ix.   WILLIAM ANDREW HERRERA SCURLOCK[951], b. April 14, 1893, Wilbarger County, Téxas.
      x.   JOSEPHINE GLADYS HERRERA SCURLOCK[951], b. August 02, 1895, Johnson County, Téxas.

Adrian Muñoz

160. MARTA[10] HERRERA *(FERNANDO[9], PEDRO ALCANTARA[8] DE HERRERA, MARÍA JOSEFA[7] BUSTOS, MARÍA ANTONIA TERESA[6] SÁNCHES, PEDRO[5], PEDRO SÁNCHES[4] DE IÑIGO, FRANCISCO MUÑOS[3] SÁNCHES, JACINTO[2] MUÑOS, FRANCISCO[1])* was born April 24, 1865 in Santa Cruz de la Cañada, New México[952]. She married ADRIAN MUÑOZ November 12, 1880[953].

Notes for ADRIAN MUÑOZ:
Land Patent # NMNMAA 010259, on the authority of the Homestead Act, May 20, 1862, 160 Acres.

Children of MARTA HERRERA and ADRIAN MUÑOZ are:
289.	i.	JULIANA[11] MUÑOZ, b. April 1881, San Juanito (Ruidoso Downs), Territory of New México.
290.	ii.	EPIFANIA MUÑOZ, b. April 07, 1884, San Juanito (Ruidoso Downs), Territory of New México.
	iii.	ESTANISLAUS MUÑOZ, b. November 15, 1885, San Juanito (Ruidoso Downs), Territory of New México.
291.	iv.	MARGARITA MUÑOZ, b. September 09, 1889, San Juanito (Ruidoso Downs), Territory of New México.
292.	v.	BEATRIZ MUÑOZ, b. September 30, 1892, San Juanito (Ruidoso Downs), Territory of New México; d. December 29, 1989, El Paso, Téxas.
293.	vi.	GENOVEVA MUÑOZ, b. September 1894, San Juanito (Ruidoso Downs), Territory of New México.
	vii.	JUANA MUÑOZ, b. July 1896, San Juanito (Ruidoso Downs), Territory of New México[954].
294.	viii.	JOSÉ MUÑOZ, b. November 22, 1897, San Juanito (Ruidoso Downs), Territory of New México.
295.	ix.	ROSALÍA MUÑOZ, b. April 29, 1899, San Juanito (Ruidoso Downs), Territory of New México.
296.	x.	ANDRÉS MUÑOZ, b. February 04, 1901.
297.	xi.	ANTONIA MUÑOZ, b. Abt. 1904.

161. MANUELITA[10] HERRERA *(FERNANDO[9], PEDRO ALCANTARA[8] DE HERRERA, MARÍA JOSEFA[7] BUSTOS, MARÍA ANTONIA TERESA[6] SÁNCHES, PEDRO[5], PEDRO SÁNCHES[4] DE IÑIGO, FRANCISCO MUÑOS[3] SÁNCHES, JACINTO[2] MUÑOS, FRANCISCO[1])[955]* was born April 20, 1866 in Santa Cruz de la Cañada, Territory of New México[956], and died February 12, 1939 in San Patricio, New México[957]. She married (1) JAMES R. SALSBERRY[958], son of JAMES SAULSBERRY and HARRIET CLIFTON. She married (3) CHARLES BOWDRE Abt. 1879[959]. She married (4) MAXIMIANO CORONA[960] February 25, 1884 in Tularoso, Territory of New Mexico[961], son of DIONISIO CORONA and SEFERINA CHÁBES.

Notes for MANUELITA HERRERA:
Also known as María Manuelita Herrera
Land Patent # NMLC 0042211, on the authority of the Homestead Entry-Stock Raising (39 Stat. 862), December 29, 1916. Issued 640 acres on February 13, 1935.

Notes for JAMES R. SALSBERRY:
Also known as James Salsberete, Santiago, Jim and Jimmy.
Land Patent # NMR 0024875, on the authority of the Homestead Entry-Original (12 Stat. 392), May 20, 1862. Issued 20 acres on February 18, 1916.

Notes for MAXIMIANO CORONA:
Also known as José Masimiano Calistro Corona y Chábes.
He immigrated to the United States in about 1865.

James Salsberry

Children of MANUELITA HERRERA and JAMES SALSBERRY are:

298.   i.   AUGUSTÍN[11] SALSBERRY, b. October 25, 1895, San Juanito (Ruidoso Downs), Territory of New México; d. May 24, 1973, Citrus Heights, California.

299.   ii. TOMASITA SALSBERRY, b. December 29, 1897, San Juanito (Ruidoso Downs), Territory of New México; d. June 17, 1949, Artesia, New Mexico.

    iii. MARTINA SALSBERRY, b. January 30, 1900, San Juanito (Ruidoso Downs), New México[962]; d. September 07, 1917, Glencoe, New México[963]; m. ANTONIO PADILLA SÁNCHEZ, October 13, 1915, Lincoln, Territory of New México[964].

Notes for MARTINA SALSBERRY:
She died 8 days after giving birth to a child. Her child also died during birth.
Ruidoso, New Mexico: Today the 7th of September 1917, was the funeral for Martina Salsberry Sanchez in the chapel of San Isidro de Ruidoso where she was laid to rest. Martina Salsberry Sanchez wife of Antonio Sanchez died as a result of (parto) leaving an 8 day old baby girl and her husband Antonio Sanchez. Signed Fr. J.H.J Girma
Buried: La Capilla de San Ysidro.

300.   iv. DOROTEA SALSBERRY, b. February 05, 1902, San Juanito (Ruidoso Downs), New México; d. January 25, 1974, Artesia, New Mexico.

301.   v.   FERNANDO SALSBERRY, b. April 13, 1904, San Juanito (Ruidoso Downs), Territory of New México; d. September 11, 1937, Hondo, New Mexico.

302.   vi. JAMES SALSBERRY, b. June 26, 1906, San Juanito (Ruidoso Downs), Territory of New México; d. January 14, 1986, Barstow, California.

303.   vii. FLORINDA SALSBERRY, b. March 15, 1910, Palo Verde (Ruidoso Downs), Territory of New México; d. March 27, 1978, San Patricio, New México.

304.   viii. ENRÍQUES SALSBERRY, b. August 11, 1912, Palo Verde (Ruidoso Downs), Territory of New México; d. January 24, 1956, Artesia, New México.

Child of MANUELITA HERRERA is:

305.   ix. JOSÉ[11] PORTIO, b. December 03, 1893, San Juanito (Ruidoso Downs), Territory of New México; d. September 18, 1959, San Patricio, New México.

Maximiano Corona

Children of MANUELITA HERRERA and MAXIMIANO CORONA are:

306.   x.   MANUEL HERRERA[11] CORONA, b. January 01, 1885, San Juanito (Ruidoso Downs), Territory of New México; d. July 12, 1966, San Patricio, New México.

    xi. DOROTEA CORONA, b. February 06, 1887, Ruidoso, Territory of New México[965]; d. Ruidoso, New México.

307.   xii. ELENA CORONA, b. February 17, 1890, San Juanito (Ruidoso Downs), Territory of New México; d. March 14, 1928, San Patricio, New México.

162. TEODORO[10] HERRERA *(FERNANDO[9], PEDRO ALCANTARA[8] DE HERRERA, MARÍA JOSEFA[7] BUSTOS, MARÍA ANTONIA TERESA[6] SÁNCHES, PEDRO[5], PEDRO SÁNCHES[4] DE IÑIGO, FRANCISCO MUÑOS[3] SÁNCHES, JACINTO[2] MUÑOS, FRANCISCO[1])* was born April 1873 in San Juanito (Ruidoso Downs), Territory of New México[966], and died in Alamogordo, New México. He married TOMASITA MONTOYA September 16, 1896[967], daughter of FELIPÉ MONTOYA and MARCELA CHÁVEZ.

Notes for TEODORO HERRERA:
After both parents died, the children lived with their Tia Manuela.
Eldest brother came back and moved his siblings to El Paso, Texas.

Children of TEODORO HERRERA and TOMASITA MONTOYA are:
    i.   LIBORIO[11] HERRERA.

Notes for LIBORIO HERRERA:
Also known as Livorio, Lalo.
Killed in Action during World War I.

    ii.   MANUEL MONTOYA HERRERA, b. June 19, 1899[968].

Notes for MANUEL MONTOYA HERRERA:
He may have died young.

    iii.   FELIPÉ HERRERA, b. April 28, 1905[969]; m. PAULITA RIVERA, August 19, 1933[969].
    iv.   JULIAN HERRERA, b. 1910, San Patricio, Territory of New México[970].

Notes for JULIAN HERRERA:
Julian had migrated to El Paso, Téxas. After his parents died, he came back to San Juanito and took his younger siblings back to El Paso. Carmen, the youngest sister remained with her Tía Manuelita.

    v.   FERNANDO MONTOYA HERRERA, b. May 18, 1914, San Patricio, New México.

Notes for FERNANDO MONTOYA HERRERA:
July 05, 1914: Baptized in San Patricio. Padrinos: Marcial Sambrano and Refugia Padilla.

    vi.   GREGORIO MONTOYA HERRERA, b. 1917, San Patricio, New México[970].

Notes for GREGORIO MONTOYA HERRERA:
Killed in action during WW II.

    vii.   CARMEN HERRERA, b. May 29, 1920, San Patricio, New México.

Generation No. 11

163. CANDELARIA[11] PADILLA *(ANDALESIO[10], ROSALÍA[9] CHÁVEZ, JUANA[8] SÁNCHES, PEDRO[7], JACINTO[6], JOSÉ SÁNCHES[5] DE IÑIGO, JACINTO SÁNCHES[4], FRANCISCO MUÑOS[3] SÁNCHES, JACINTO[2] MUÑOS, FRANCISCO[1])* was born February 1879 in Tres Ritos, Territory of New México[971], and died March 13, 1956 in San Elizario, Téxas[972]. She married FELIPÉ E. SÁNCHEZ Abt. 1897[973], son of ESTOLANO SÁNCHEZ and CORNELIA PACHECO.

Children of CANDELARIA PADILLA and FELIPÉ SÁNCHEZ are:
    i.   ANTONIO PADILLA[12] SÁNCHEZ, b. May 17, 1897, Tres Ritos, New México[974]; d. February 21, 1984, San Elizario, Texas[975]; m. (1) MAGDALENA MARTÍNEZ; m. (2) MARTINA SALSBERRY, October 13, 1915, Lincoln, Territory of New México[976]; m. (3) JUANITA CABALLERO ALVARADO, Aft. December 1917.
    ii.   PAUBLITA SÁNCHEZ, b. July 30, 1898, Tres Rios, Territory of New México[977]; d. October 13, 1963, Las Vegas, New México; m. YSIDRO CHÁVEZ[978], August 04, 1913, Lincoln, New México[979].
    iii.   SIPIO SÁNCHEZ, b. March 1900[980]; m. LOLA MIRABAL.
    iv.   CORNELIA SÁNCHEZ[981], b. November 16, 1902, Lincoln County, New México[982]; m. ALFONSO BORREGO[983].
    v.   EMILIANO SÁNCHEZ, b. August 11, 1904, Hondo, Territory of New México; m. RUBY MARTÍNEZ.
    vi.   ÁBRAN SÁNCHEZ[984], b. December 24, 1905, White Oaks, Territory of New México; d. November 18, 1973, El Paso, Téxas; m. (1) RAMONCITA GURULÉ; m. (2) ANTONIA JUAREGUI[985]; m. (3) FELIPA RODRÍQUES, Abt. 1926[986].
    vii.   RENALDO SÁNCHEZ, b. March 22, 1907, Patos, New México[987]; d. May 1981, Tularosa, New México; m. SOFIA AGUILAR[988], November 10, 1932.
    viii.   CELEDONIA SÁNCHEZ, b. Abt. 1909; d. Abt. 1921.
    ix.   BENITO SÁNCHEZ, b. Abt. 1912[989]; m. (1) CONCHA RAMÍREZ; m. (2) BEATRICE PINO, May 09, 1932, Tularosa, New México[990].
    x.   ONECIMO SÁNCHEZ, b. 1915[991]; m. CLEOTILDE DURÁN.

164. BENITO[11] PADILLA *(ANDALESIO[10], ROSALÍA[9] CHÁVEZ, JUANA[8] SÁNCHES, PEDRO[7], JACINTO[6], JOSÉ SÁNCHES[5] DE IÑIGO, JACINTO SÁNCHES[4], FRANCISCO MUÑOS[3] SÁNCHES, JACINTO[2] MUÑOS, FRANCISCO[1])[992]* was born April 16, 1883, and died June 26, 1906. He married MARIANA MARTÍNEZ.

Child of BENITO PADILLA and MARIANA MARTÍNEZ is:
    i.   PRESCILIANO[12] PADILLA, b. Abt. 1902[993].

165. ANDALESIO MARIÑO[11] PADILLA *(ANDALESIO[10], ROSALÍA[9] CHÁVEZ, JUANA[8] SÁNCHES, PEDRO[7], JACINTO[6], JOSÉ SÁNCHES[5] DE IÑIGO, JACINTO SÁNCHES[4], FRANCISCO MUÑOS[3] SÁNCHES, JACINTO[2] MUÑOS, FRANCISCO[1])[994]* was born May 31, 1892. He married EUFELIA MARTÍNEZ July 16, 1912[995], daughter of RUMALDO MARTÍNEZ and ISABEL MONTOYA.

Notes for EUFELIA MARTÍNEZ:
Also known as Rafalia.

Children of ANDALESIO PADILLA and EUFELIA MARTÍNEZ are:
    i.   JUAN[12] PADILLA, b. Abt. 1916[996].
    ii.   MANUEL PADILLA[997], b. January 01, 1918[998].

Notes for MANUEL PADILLA:
Corporal. World War II Veteran.

166. NESTOR[11] PADILLA *(ANDALESIO[10], ROSALÍA[9] CHÁVEZ, JUANA[8] SÁNCHES, PEDRO[7], JACINTO[6], JOSÉ SÁNCHES[5] DE IÑIGO, JACINTO SÁNCHES[4], FRANCISCO MUÑOS[3] SÁNCHES, JACINTO[2] MUÑOS, FRANCISCO[1])[999]* was born February 27, 1896 in Tres Ritos, Territory of New México. He married GERTRUDES LUNA September 28, 1916[1000], daughter of AUGUSTÍN LUNA and MANUELA FAJARDO.

Children of NESTOR PADILLA and GERTRUDES LUNA are:
    i.   FRANK[12] PADILLA, b. Abt. 1920[1001].
    ii.   CANDELARIA LUNA PADILLA, b. Abt. 1923[1001].
    iii. ESTELA PADILLA, b. Abt. 1925[1001].
    iv. AUGUSTÍN PADILLA, b. Abt. 1928[1001].

167. JUANA MARÍA[11] VIGIL *(JUAN FRANCISCO PABLO[10], MARÍA SOLEDAD[9] APODACA, ANA ROSALÍA[8] SÁNCHES, PEDRO[7], JACINTO[6], JOSÉ SÁNCHES[5] DE IÑIGO, JACINTO SÁNCHES[4], FRANCISCO MUÑOS[3] SÁNCHES, JACINTO[2] MUÑOS, FRANCISCO[1])[1002]* was born June 15, 1844 in Tomé, Nuevo México, La República de México[1003], and died 1878-1880[1004]. She married LUCIANO TRUJILLO[1005], son of JOSÉ TRUJILLO and SOLEDAD DE TRUJILLO.

Children of JUANA VIGIL and LUCIANO TRUJILLO are:
    i.   MARCLOFA[12] TRUJILLO, b. Abt. 1864, Tajiqué, Territory of New México[1006]; m. MANUEL TORRES, Abt. 1884[1007].
    ii.   PORFIRIA TRUJILLO[1008], b. December 18, 1866, Tajiqué, Territory of New México[1009]; d. April 21, 1960; m. NICOLÁS CHÁVEZ[1010], November 10, 1880[1011].
    iii. JOSÉ TRUJILLO, b. Abt. 1869, Manzano, Territory of New México[1012]; m. PILAR CHÁVEZ, March 15, 1899[1013].
    iv. JESÚS TRUJILLO[1014], b. Abt. 1872[1015]; d. November 04, 1959.
    v.   REFUGIA TRUJILLO, b. Abt. 1873[1015].
    vi. FELICITAS TRUJILLO, b. Abt. 1876[1015].
    vii. MASIMIANO TRUJILLO, b. Abt. 1878[1015].

168. JOSÉ MANUEL[11] VIGIL *(JUAN FRANCISCO PABLO[10], MARÍA SOLEDAD[9] APODACA, ANA ROSALÍA[8] SÁNCHES, PEDRO[7], JACINTO[6], JOSÉ SÁNCHES[5] DE IÑIGO, JACINTO SÁNCHES[4], FRANCISCO MUÑOS[3] SÁNCHES, JACINTO[2] MUÑOS, FRANCISCO[1])* was born June 10, 1846 in Valencia, Nuevo México, La República de México, and died 1931[1016]. He married MARÍA POLINARIA TRUJILLO[1017][1018].

Notes for MARÍA POLINARIA TRUJILLO:
Also known as María Polinaria Trujillo de Sánchez.

Child of JOSÉ VIGIL and MARÍA TRUJILLO is:

    i.   DANIEL TRUJILLO[12] VIGIL[1019], b. November 01, 1864[1020]; d. 1951; m. ELFIDA CHÁVEZ[1021], May 08, 1888, Manzano, Territory of New México[1022].

Notes for DANIEL TRUJILLO VIGIL:
1900 Census: Living with his parents in Las Tablas.

Eugenio Sánchez

169. EUGENIO[11] SÁNCHEZ *(VICTORIA[10] SÁNCHES, JUAN RAFAEL FERNANDO[9], MANUEL RAFAEL[8], PEDRO[7], JACINTO[6], JOSÉ SÁNCHES[5] DE IÑIGO, JACINTO SÁNCHES[4], FRANCISCO MUÑOS[3] SÁNCHES, JACINTO[2] MUÑOS, FRANCISCO[1])[1023]* was born September 1856 in Manzano, Territory of New México[1024], and died September 17, 1935 in Manzano, New México[1025]. He married ROSA GRIEGO 1882 in Manzano, New México[1026].

Notes for EUGENIO SÁNCHEZ:
Also known as Eusevio.
Captured Navajo, who took the Sánchez surname. Adopted by Filomeno "El Patron" Sánchez & his wife, Victoria.
Death records indicate that his parents were Filomeno Sánchez, Victoria G. Varseton .
Migrated to Lincoln County and settled in an area known as Las Angusturas.
Land Patent # NMR 0001454, on the authority of the Homestead Entry-Original (12 Stat. 392), May 20, 1862. Issued 80 acres on June 09, 1910.

Children of EUGENIO SÁNCHEZ and ROSA GRIEGO are:
    i.   JOSÉ GRIEGO[12] SÁNCHEZ, b. Abt. 1906; m. PABLITA DE SÁNCHEZ[1027].
    ii.   AVRORA GRIEGO SÁNCHEZ[1028], b. March 14, 1884, Manzano, Territory of New México; d. September 30, 1955, San Patricio, New México; m. MAURICIO MONTOYA[1029], December 15, 1902, La Capilla de San Ysidro, Las Angusturas, Territory of New México[1030].
    iii.   TEODORO GRIEGO SÁNCHEZ, b. April 01, 1886[1031]; m. JUANITA VIGIL[1032].
    iv.   FILOMENO GRIEGO SÁNCHEZ, b. December 1887, Manzano, Territory of New México[1033]; d. February 11, 1937, Manzano,New México[1034]; m. REFUGIA VIGIL, 1915.
    v.   JUAN GRIEGO SÁNCHEZ, b. December 1890[1035]; m. FLORA AMELIA DE SÁNCHEZ[1036].
    vi.   RITA GRIEGO SÁNCHEZ, b. July 1892[1037]; m. PEDRO NUÑEZ.
    vii.   GERTRUDES GRIEGO SÁNCHEZ, b. December 1894[1037].

Notes for GERTRUDES GRIEGO SÁNCHEZ:
Died young.

    viii.   MANUEL GRIEGO SÁNCHEZ, b. November 1896[1037].

Notes for MANUEL GRIEGO SÁNCHEZ:
Died young.
    ix.   ENRÍQUES GRIEGO SÁNCHEZ, b. May 1898[1037]; m. PEREGRINA SÁNCHEZ[1038].
    x.   MARÍA AGIDA GRIEGO SÁNCHEZ, b. March 10, 1900[1039]; m. FRANCISCO SÁNCHEZ.
    xi.   TELESFORO GRIEGO SÁNCHEZ, b. February 21, 1902, Ruidoso, Territory of New México[1040]; m. IGINIA DE SÁNCHEZ[1041].
    xii.   REYES GRIEGO SÁNCHEZ.

Notes for REYES GRIEGO SÁNCHEZ:
Died young.

170. MANUEL[11] SÁNCHEZ *(VICTORIA[10] SÁNCHES, JUAN RAFAEL FERNANDO[9], MANUEL RAFAEL[8], PEDRO[7], JACINTO[6], JOSÉ SÁNCHES[5] DE IÑIGO, JACINTO SÁNCHES[4], FRANCISCO MUÑOS[3] SÁNCHES, JACINTO[2] MUÑOS, FRANCISCO[1])* was born Abt. 1859[1042]. He married GUADALUPE PADILLA April 23, 1876 in Manzano, Territory of New México[1043], daughter of ANTONIO PADILLA and FRANCISCA LÓPEZ.

Notes for MANUEL SÁNCHEZ:
Captured Navajo, who took the Sánchez surname. Adopted by Filomeno "El Patron" Sánchez & his wife, Victoria.

Children of MANUEL SÁNCHEZ and GUADALUPE PADILLA are:
    i.   EUGENIO[12] SÁNCHEZ.
    ii.   JOSEFA SÁNCHEZ, b. March 15, 1877, Manzano, Territory of New México[1044].
    iii.   MARÍA HILARIA SÁNCHEZ, b. January 14, 1879, Manzano, Territory of New México[1044].
    iv.   MARÍA EPIFANIA SÁNCHEZ, b. April 05, 1881, Manzano, Territory of New México[1044].

    v.   NATIVIDAD SÁNCHEZ, b. December 25, 1882, Manzano, Territory of New México[1044].

171. PEDRO[11] SÁNCHEZ *(FERNANDES[10] SÁNCHES, JUAN RAFAEL FERNANDO[9], MANUEL RAFAEL[8], PEDRO[7], JACINTO[6], JOSÉ SÁNCHES[5] DE IÑIGO, JACINTO SÁNCHES[4], FRANCISCO MUÑOS[3] SÁNCHES, JACINTO[2] MUÑOS, FRANCISCO[1])* was born Abt. 1867[1045]. He married CONFERINA SÁNCHEZ December 01, 1892 in Manzano, Territory of New México[1046], daughter of MANUEL SÁNCHES and EPIFANIA BENAVIDES.

Children of PEDRO SÁNCHEZ and CONFERINA SÁNCHEZ are:
    i.   GREGORIO[12] SÁNCHEZ, b. Abt. 1894[1047]; Adopted child.
    ii.   JOSÉ MARÍA SÁNCHEZ, b. Abt. May 1896[1048].
    iii.   RAFAELA SÁNCHEZ, b. Abt. April 1900[1048].
    iv.   FRANCISCO SÁNCHEZ, b. Abt. 1904[1049].
    v.   JUAN SÁNCHEZ, b. Abt. 1910[1049].
    vi.   SOFIA SÁNCHEZ, b. Abt. 1911[1050].
    vii.   GRISELDA SÁNCHEZ[1050], b. June 23, 1916; d. December 05, 1998, Santa Fé, New México; m. TONY BENTA.

Escolastico Vigil

172. ESCOLASTICO[11] VIGIL *(FRANCISCO ANTONIO[10], MARÍA SOLEDAD[9] APODACA, ANA ROSALÍA[8] SÁNCHES, PEDRO[7], JACINTO[6], JOSÉ SÁNCHES[5] DE IÑIGO, JACINTO SÁNCHES[4], FRANCISCO MUÑOS[3] SÁNCHES, JACINTO[2] MUÑOS, FRANCISCO[1])* was born February 1853. He married ANTONIA CAMPOS February 04, 1880 in Tomé, Territory of New México[1051], daughter of FRANCISCO CAMPOS and RAMONA CEDILLO.

Child of ESCOLASTICO VIGIL and ANTONIA CAMPOS is:
    i.   REMEDIOS CAMPOS[12] VIGIL, b. 1886; d. 1971; m. PREDICANDO CHÁVEZ, June 26, 1902, Tomé, Territory of New México[1052].

173. MARTÍN SÁNCHEZ[11] SEDILLO *(MASIMA JARAMILLO[10] SÁNCHEZ, MANUEL[9] SÁNCHES, MANUEL DE JESÚS JOSÉ[8], DOMINGO DE JESÚS[7], JUAN CRISTÓBAL[6], FRANCISCO[5], JACINTO SÁNCHES[4] DE IÑIGO, FRANCISCO MUÑOS[3] SÁNCHES, JACINTO[2] MUÑOS, FRANCISCO[1])* was born April 30, 1875 in El Berendo, Territory of New México[1053]. He married TOMASITA HERRERA March 08, 1906, daughter of CRUZ HERRERA and EULOJIA MADRID.

Children of MARTÍN SEDILLO and TOMASITA HERRERA are:
    i.   CARLOS[12] SEDILLO, b. 1908[1054].
    ii.   ROSA SEDILLO, b. 1911[1054].
    iii.   MARIANO SEDILLO, b. 1912[1054].
    iv.   DOMACIO SEDILLO[1055], b. 1913[1056]; d. July 21, 1933, San Patricio, New México.
    v.   RUFINA HERRERA SEDILLO, b. 1915[1056].
    vi.   CAMILO SEDILLO[1057], b. June 05, 1917, Roswell, New México[1058]; d. May 06, 1986, Artesia, New México; m. LORENSITA MONTOYA[1058], May 04, 1940, Carrizozo, New México[1059].

Notes for CAMILO SEDILLO:
US Navy, Seaman Second Class. World War I.
1948: Moved to Artesia, New México.

    vii.   FRED SEDILLO, b. 1921[1060].
    viii.   CRUSITA SEDILLO[1061], b. April 06, 1925, Roswell, New México[1062]; d. December 26, 1993, Alamogordo, New México; m. RAMÓN LUNA[1063].
    ix.   CATARINA SEDILLO, b. 1928[1064].
    x.   VICENTE SEDILLO, b. Private.

174. FEDERICO[11] SEDILLO *(MASIMA JARAMILLO[10] SÁNCHEZ, MANUEL[9] SÁNCHES, MANUEL DE JESÚS JOSÉ[8], DOMINGO DE JESÚS[7], JUAN CRISTÓBAL[6], FRANCISCO[5], JACINTO SÁNCHES[4] DE IÑIGO, FRANCISCO MUÑOS[3] SÁNCHES, JACINTO[2] MUÑOS, FRANCISCO[1])* was born February 10, 1880 in El Berendo, Territory of New México. He married MARÍA LOVE January 19, 1903[1065], daughter of ANNA RICE.

Children of FEDERICO SEDILLO and MARÍA LOVE are:
    i.   ADELIDA[12] SEDILLO, b. 1904[1066].

    ii.   ELLEN SEDILLO, b. March 1908[1066].

175. JUANITA[11] SEDILLO *(MASIMA JARAMILLO[10] SÁNCHEZ, MANUEL[9] SÁNCHES, MANUEL DE JESÚS JOSÉ[8], DOMINGO DE JESÚS[7], JUAN CRISTÓBAL[6], FRANCISCO[5], JACINTO SÁNCHES[4] DE IÑIGO, FRANCISCO MUÑOS[3] SÁNCHES, JACINTO[2] MUÑOS, FRANCISCO[1])* was born Abt. 1884 in El Berendo, Territory of New México[1067]. She married CANDELARIO CHÁVEZ February 19, 1898[1068], son of JESÚS CHÁVEZ and RAFAELA ROMERO.

Children of JUANITA SEDILLO and CANDELARIO CHÁVEZ are:
    i.   LUPE[12] CHÁVEZ, b. Abt. 1913, San Patricio, New México[1069].
    ii.   DULCINEA CHÁVEZ, b. Abt. 1914, San Patricio, New México[1069].
    iii.   JULIA CHÁVEZ, b. Abt. 1921, San Patricio, New México[1069].

176. YSABEL[11] SÁNCHEZ *(PEDRO JARAMILLO[10], MANUEL[9] SÁNCHES, MANUEL DE JESÚS JOSÉ[8], DOMINGO DE JESÚS[7], JUAN CRISTÓBAL.[6], FRANCISCO[5], JACINTO SÁNCHES[4] DE IÑIGO, FRANCISCO MUÑOS[3] SÁNCHES, JACINTO[2] MUÑOS, FRANCISCO[1])* was born July 07, 1888 in San Patricio, Territory of New México[1070]. She married JUAN VALDÉZ November 13, 1913 in Lincoln, New México[1070], son of JULIO VALDÉS and SINFORIANA SERRANO.

Child of YSABEL SÁNCHEZ and JUAN VALDÉZ is:
    i.   JULIO SÁNCHEZ[12] VALDÉZ, b. Abt. 1919[1071].

José Candelaria

177. ISIDRA[11] SÁNCHEZ *(PEDRO JARAMILLO[10], MANUEL[9] SÁNCHES, MANUEL DE JESÚS JOSÉ[8], DOMINGO DE JESÚS[7], JUAN CRISTÓBAL[6], FRANCISCO[5], JACINTO SÁNCHES[4] DE IÑIGO, FRANCISCO MUÑOS[3] SÁNCHES, JACINTO[2] MUÑOS, FRANCISCO[1])* was born May 15, 1889 in Roswell, Territory of New México[1072], and died July 16, 1992. She married JOSÉ CANDELARIA[1073] November 22, 1921[1074], son of ÁBRAN CANDELARIA and BENINA LUCERO.

Notes for JOSÉ CANDELARIA:
Also known as José de los Ángeles Candelaria. He was raised by his step-father, Andrew McNeely Richardson.

Children of ISIDRA SÁNCHEZ and JOSÉ CANDELARIA are:
    i.   BENITO[12] CANDELARIA, b. July 23, 1921, Arabela, New México[1075]; m. CARMELITA GÓMEZ, December 13, 1944, Carrizozo, New México[1075].
    ii.   CELESTINO CANDELARIA[1076], b. October 16, 1922, Arabela, New México[1077]; m. JOSEFITA MOYA.

Notes for CELESTINO CANDELARIA:
Tech 5. World War II.

    iii.   ARCENIA CANDELARIA, b. Abt. 1925[1077]; m. RUBEN LUCERO.
    iv.   EDUARDO CANDELARIA[1078], b. July 11, 1928, Arabela, New México; d. November 09, 2003; m. AMELIA GÓMEZ, October 25, 1952, San Patricio, New México[1079].

Notes for EDUARDO CANDELARIA:
Also known as Edward and Lolo.
US Army Korea.

    v.   ASUSENA CANDELARIA, b. March 1930[1080]; m. LUVÍN SÁNCHEZ[1081].

Notes for ASUSENA CANDELARIA:
Also known as Susan.

178. MAURO[11] SÁNCHEZ *(CELESTINO[10], SAMUEL[9] SÁNCHES, SANTIAGO[8], JOSÉ GREGORIO DE LA TRINIDAD[7], JUAN CRISTÓBAL[6], FRANCISCO[5], JACINTO SÁNCHES[4] DE IÑIGO, FRANCISCO MUÑOS[3] SÁNCHES, JACINTO[2] MUÑOS, FRANCISCO[1])[1082]* was born July 27, 1897 in Ruidoso, Territory of New México, and died March 23, 1982 in Hondo, New México. He married TONITA ALDAZ February 19, 1919 in Lincoln, New México[1083], daughter of MARIANO ALDAZ and FRANCISCA TORRES.

Notes for MAURO SÁNCHEZ:
Also known as Mauricio. Private in the US Army. WWI Veteran.
Land Patent # NMLC 0026078, on the authority of the Homestead Entry-Enlarged (35 Stat. 639), February 19, 1909. Issued 322.02 acres on June 08, 1926.
Land Patent # NMLC 0028312, on the authority of the Homestead Entry-Stock Raising (39 Stat. 862), December 29, 1916, Issued 320.76 acres on August 22, 1930.

Notes for TONITA ALDAZ:
Also known as Antonia.

Children of MAURO SÁNCHEZ and TONITA ALDAZ are:
  i.   ANGELITA ALDAZ[12] SÁNCHEZ, b. December 01, 1919, Hondo, New México[1084]; m. ESIQUIEL CHÁVEZ[1084], June 25, 1939, Carrizozo, New México[1084].

Notes for ESIQUIEL CHÁVEZ:
US Navy, Seaman Second Class. World War II.

  ii.   MARIANA ALDAZ SÁNCHEZ[1085], b. April 21, 1921, Lincoln, New México; d. October 12, 2009, Roswell, New México; m. ERNESTO TORRES[1085].

Notes for MARIANA ALDAZ SÁNCHEZ:
Also known as Mary.

  iii. NAVORA SÁNCHEZ, b. June 18, 1924, Hondo, New México[1086]; m. MCKINLEY MCTEIGUE[1087], June 22, 1951, Lincoln, New México[1088].
  iv.   MONROY SÁNCHEZ[1089], b. September 14, 1925, Hondo, New México[1090]; d. December 19, 1998, Albuquerque, New México; m. LUCÍA MCTEIGUE, February 04, 1950, Lincoln, New México[1090].

Notes for MONROY SÁNCHEZ:
Also known as Monroe. Buried in the Hondo Cemetery.
December 4, 1943: Enlisted in the Army. He was a World War Two Veteran.

  v.   ERNESTO ALDAZ SÁNCHEZ, b. December 29, 1927, Hondo, New México[1091]; m. GENOVA OTERO.
  vi.   CELIA ALDAZ SÁNCHEZ, b. December 01, 1929, Hondo, New México[1092]; m. ERNEST JAMES BOOKY, February 26, 1949, Carrizozo, New México[1092].

179. JOSÉ MOYA[11] SÁNCHEZ *(CELESTINO[10], SAMUEL[9] SÁNCHES, SANTIAGO[8], JOSÉ GREGORIO DE LA TRINIDAD[7], JUAN CRISTÓBAL[6], FRANCISCO[5], JACINTO SÁNCHES[4] DE IÑIGO, FRANCISCO MUÑOS[3] SÁNCHES, JACINTO[2] MUÑOS, FRANCISCO[1])[1093]* was born September 25, 1899 in Ruidoso, Territory of New México, and died September 1952. He married ESTEFANA BENAVIDEZ[1093] September 04, 1927 in Mescalero, New México[1094], daughter of GUILLERMO BENAVIDES and ALCARIA TRUJILLO.

Notes for JOSÉ MOYA SÁNCHEZ:
This birthdate may be incorrect.

Notes for ESTEFANA BENAVIDEZ:
Also known as Estefanita.

Children of JOSÉ SÁNCHEZ and ESTEFANA BENAVIDEZ are:
  i.   WILLIE[12] SÁNCHEZ[1095], b. March 19, 1935; d. October 02, 2000.
  ii.   LYDIA SÁNCHEZ, b. August 31, 1938, Ruidoso Downs, New México; d. December 24, 2011; m. BILLY LIGON[1096].
  iii. ALFRED SÁNCHEZ[1097], b. September 10, 1940; d. June 05, 1968.
  iv.   CELESTINO BENAVIDEZ SÁNCHEZ, b. Private.
  v.   DULCINEA SÁNCHEZ, b. Private.
  vi.   ELISEO BENAVIDEZ SÁNCHEZ, b. Private.
  vii. ELIZABETH BENAVIDEZ SÁNCHEZ, b. Private.
  viii. FLORA BENAVIDEZ SÁNCHEZ, b. Private.
  ix.   VIOLA BENAVIDEZ SÁNCHEZ, b. Private.

180. SAMUEL MOYA[11] SÁNCHEZ *(CELESTINO*[10]*, SAMUEL*[9] *SÁNCHES, SANTIAGO*[8]*, JOSÉ GREGORIO DE LA TRINIDAD*[7]*, JUAN CRISTÓBAL*[6]*, FRANCISCO*[5]*, JACINTO SÁNCHES*[4] *DE IÑIGO, FRANCISCO MUÑOS*[3] *SÁNCHES, JACINTO*[2] *MUÑOS, FRANCISCO*[1]*)*[1097] was born April 16, 1900 in Ruidoso, Territory of New México, and died May 29, 1966 in San Patricio, New México. He married ALTAGRACIA MONTOYA[1097] September 22, 1938 in San Patricio, New México[1098], daughter of ÁRON MONTOYA and BEATRIZ ROMERO.

Notes for ALTAGRACIA MONTOYA:
Also known as Grace. She was raised by her Tios, Octaviano Gallegos and Pilar Guebara de Gallegos.

Child of SAMUEL SÁNCHEZ and ALTAGRACIA MONTOYA is:
    i.   THURMAN[12] SÁNCHEZ, b. Private.

181. MILITÓN[11] SÁNCHEZ *(CELESTINO*[10]*, SAMUEL*[9] *SÁNCHES, SANTIAGO*[8]*, JOSÉ GREGORIO DE LA TRINIDAD*[7]*, JUAN CRISTÓBAL*[6]*, FRANCISCO*[5]*, JACINTO SÁNCHES*[4] *DE IÑIGO, FRANCISCO MUÑOS*[3] *SÁNCHES, JACINTO*[2] *MUÑOS, FRANCISCO*[1]*)*[1099] was born March 10, 1905 in Ruidoso, Territory of New México, and died October 08, 1991 in Ruidoso Downs, New México. He married CONCEPCIÓN TRUJILLO BENAVIDEZ[1099] October 27, 1927 in Carrizozo, New México[1100], daughter of GUILLERMO BENAVIDES and ALCARIA TRUJILLO.

Notes for CONCEPCIÓN TRUJILLO BENAVIDEZ:
Also known as Concha.

Children of MILITÓN SÁNCHEZ and CONCEPCIÓN BENAVIDEZ are:
    i.   CRUSITA BENAVIDEZ[12] SÁNCHEZ[1101], b. May 18, 1929, Hollywood (Ruidoso Downs), New México[1102]; d. October 03, 2006, Albuquerque, New México; m. CANDIDO SÁNCHEZ MONTOYA[1103], November 09, 1946, Carrizozo, New México[1104].
    ii.   MILITÓN BENAVIDEZ SÁNCHEZ, b. Private.
    iii. VIRGINIA BENAVIDEZ SÁNCHEZ, b. Private.
    iv.   ALICE SÁNCHEZ, b. Private.
    v.   MARY BENAVIDEZ SÁNCHEZ, b. Private.
    vi.   HENRY BENAVIDEZ SÁNCHEZ, b. Private.
    vii. YVONNE SÁNCHEZ, b. Private.
    viii. MAUROSA SÁNCHEZ[1105], b. Abt. 1931, Glencoe, New México; d. August 23, 1931, Glencoe, New México.

182. JUANITA[11] SÁNCHEZ *(CELESTINO*[10]*, SAMUEL*[9] *SÁNCHES, SANTIAGO*[8]*, JOSÉ GREGORIO DE LA TRINIDAD*[7]*, JUAN CRISTÓBAL*[6]*, FRANCISCO*[5]*, JACINTO SÁNCHES*[4] *DE IÑIGO, FRANCISCO MUÑOS*[3] *SÁNCHES, JACINTO*[2] *MUÑOS, FRANCISCO*[1]*)*[1106] was born March 31, 1907 in Rebentón, Territory of New México, and died March 17, 1998. She married GENOVEVO YBARRA May 10, 1932 in Glencoe, New México[1107], son of GREGORIO YBARRA and CATARINA MONTOYA.

Notes for GENOVEVO YBARRA:
Raised Manuel Prudencio, son of Roberto Prudencio & Casimira Ybarra Prudencio.
Buried at the San Ysidro Cemetery.
Land Patent # NMLC 0034103, on the authority of the Homestead Entry-Stock Raising (39 Stat. 862), December 29, 1916. Issued 320.84 acres on August 04, 1933.

Child of JUANITA SÁNCHEZ and GENOVEVO YBARRA is:
    i.   JAIME[12] YBARRA[1108], b. Abt. 1930, San Patricio, New México; d. July 10, 1930, San Patricio, New México.

183. SYLVANO MOYA[11] SÁNCHEZ *(CELESTINO*[10]*, SAMUEL*[9] *SÁNCHES, SANTIAGO*[8]*, JOSÉ GREGORIO DE LA TRINIDAD*[7]*, JUAN CRISTÓBAL*[6]*, FRANCISCO*[5]*, JACINTO SÁNCHES*[4] *DE IÑIGO, FRANCISCO MUÑOS*[3] *SÁNCHES, JACINTO*[2] *MUÑOS, FRANCISCO*[1]*)*[1109] was born May 09, 1909 in Ruidoso, Territory of New México, and died March 08, 1976 in Ruidoso Downs, New México. He married PILAR TRUJILLO SÁNCHEZ[1109] August 23, 1934 in San Patricio, New México[1110], daughter of JACOBO SÁNCHEZ and MARÍA TRUJILLO.

Children of SYLVANO SÁNCHEZ and PILAR SÁNCHEZ are:
    i.   SANTIAGO SÁNCHEZ[12] SÁNCHEZ, b. Private.
    ii.   REYNALDO SÁNCHEZ SÁNCHEZ, b. Private.
    iii. JUAN SÁNCHEZ SÁNCHEZ, b. Private.
    iv.   MARY SÁNCHEZ SÁNCHEZ, b. Private.
    v.   ELOISA SÁNCHEZ SÁNCHEZ, b. Private.

vi. TONI SÁNCHEZ, b. Private.
vii. AMIE SÁNCHEZ, b. Private.
viii. LELA SÁNCHEZ, b. Private.
ix. EMMA SÁNCHEZ, b. Private.
x. CHRIS SÁNCHEZ, b. Private.
xi. RAMÓN SÁNCHEZ SÁNCHEZ, b. Private.
xii. LEO SÁNCHEZ, b. Private.

184. NERES[11] MIRABAL *(JESUSITA[10] GALLEGOS, MARÍA DOLORES[9] SÁNCHES, SANTIAGO[8], JOSÉ GREGORIO DE LA TRINIDAD[7], JUAN CRISTÓBAL[6], FRANCISCO[5], JACINTO SÁNCHES[4] DE IÑIGO, FRANCISCO MUÑOS[3] SÁNCHES, JACINTO[2] MUÑOS, FRANCISCO[1])* was born Abt. 1899 in Glencoe, Territory of New México[1111]. He married LOLA VERDUGO.

Notes for NERES MIRABAL:
Also known as Nerio.

Notes for LOLA VERDUGO:
Also known as Dolóres.

Children of NERES MIRABAL and LOLA VERDUGO are:
i. NERES[12] MIRABAL, b. Abt. 1920[1112].
ii. GUADALUPE MIRABAL, b. Abt. 1924[1112].
iii. ELISA MIRABAL[1113], b. Abt. 1926, Las Cruces, New México; d. June 25, 1926, Las Cruces, New México.
iv. CARLOS MIRABAL, b. Abt. 1927, Las Cruces, New México[1114].
v. ENRIQUE MIRABAL, b. Abt. 1928[1114].

185. ANGELITA[11] CHÁVEZ *(LUCÍA[10] WELDON, ANGELITA PEREA[9] SÁNCHES, SANTIAGO[8], JOSÉ GREGORIO DE LA TRINIDAD[7], JUAN CRISTÓBAL[6], FRANCISCO[5], JACINTO SÁNCHES[4] DE IÑIGO, FRANCISCO MUÑOS[3] SÁNCHES, JACINTO[2] MUÑOS, FRANCISCO[1])[1115]* was born July 25, 1889 in Las Angusturas (San Ysidro), Territory of New México[1116], and died March 04, 1973 in San Patricio, New México. She married TRANSITO CHÁVEZ[1117] April 15, 1907 in Lincoln, Territory of New México[1118], son of PABLO CHÁVEZ and AMADA SÁNCHEZ.

Notes for ANGELITA CHÁVEZ:
Also known as Angela.

Children of ANGELITA CHÁVEZ and TRANSITO CHÁVEZ are:
i. ARISTEO[12] CHÁVEZ[1119], b. November 30, 1910, Hondo, New México[1120]; d. August 21, 1993, San Patricio, New México; m. CRISTINA ROMERO[1121], February 10, 1936, San Patricio, New México[1122].
ii. ISMAEL CHÁVEZ[1123], b. November 12, 1912, Hondo, New México; d. July 31, 1980, San Patricio, New México; m. ELISA MENDOSA[1124].
iii. OZIEL CHÁVEZ, b. 1917, Hondo, New México[1125]; d. August 19, 1942, Phillipines[1126].
iv. AVESLÍN CHÁVEZ, b. 1920, Hondo, New México[1127]; d. March 20, 1945, Phillipines[1128].
v. HERALDO MODESTO CHÁVEZ[1129], b. December 09, 1922, Hondo, New México; d. July 26, 1965, Hondo, New México; m. EVALINA MAE DUTCHOVER[1130], February 11, 1946, Carrizozo, New México[1131].
vi. EVA CHÁVEZ, b. February 05, 1925, Hondo, New México[1132]; m. (1) CARLOS CHÁVEZ; m. (2) HARRY SÁNCHEZ, February 21, 1944, Carrizozo, New México[1132].

186. YSIDRO[11] CHÁVEZ *(LUCÍA[10] WELDON, ANGELITA PEREA[9] SÁNCHES, SANTIAGO[8], JOSÉ GREGORIO DE LA TRINIDAD[7], JUAN CRISTÓBAL[6], FRANCISCO[5], JACINTO SÁNCHES[4] DE IÑIGO, FRANCISCO MUÑOS[3] SÁNCHES, JACINTO[2] MUÑOS, FRANCISCO[1])[1133]* was born April 20, 1892 in Ruidoso, Territory of New México[1134], and died June 28, 1972 in San Patricio, New Mexico. He married (1) SENAIDA SÁNCHEZ[1135] April 29, 1909 in Ruidoso, Territory of New México[1136], daughter of ANTONIO SÁNCHEZ and TELESFORA MIRABAL. He married (2) PAUBLITA SÁNCHEZ August 04, 1913 in Lincoln, New México[1137], daughter of FELIPÉ SÁNCHEZ and CANDELARIA PADILLA.

Notes for YSIDRO CHÁVEZ:
Buried: La Capilla de San Patricio.
Land Patent # NMR 0033095, on the authority of the Homestead Entry-Enlarged (Stat. 639), February 19, 1909. Issued 320 acres on July 29, 1920. (Patentee name: Ysidro Chábes)

Land Patent # NMLC 0028870, on the authority of the Homestead Entry-Stock Raising (39 Stat. 862), December 29, 1916. Issued 320 acres on October 23, 1931.

Children of YSIDRO CHÁVEZ and PAUBLITA SÁNCHEZ are:

   i.   GRESELDA[12] CHÁVEZ[1138], b. May 03, 1914, Glencoe, New México; d. June 09, 1988, Ruidoso, New México; m. FRANK GÓMEZ[1138], February 17, 1934, Carrizozo, New México[1139].

Notes for GRESELDA CHÁVEZ:
Also known as Grace.
Buried: San Patricio, New México.

   ii. AMARANTE CHÁVEZ[1140], b. November 09, 1915, Glencoe, New México; d. February 27, 2001, Alburquerque, New México; m. DOLORES ROMERO ARCHULETA[1140], September 21, 1936, San Patricio, New México[1141].

Notes for AMARANTE CHÁVEZ:
Also known as Jack.
Land Patent # NMNM 0558535, on the authority of the Sale Public Lands-RS 2455 (RS 245), August 3, 1846. 40 acres on May 16, 1967.

Notes for DOLORES ROMERO ARCHULETA:
Also known as Lola.

   iii. SENON CHÁVEZ[1142], b. March 03, 1917, San Patricio, New México; d. January 18, 2000, San Patricio, New México; m. MABEL TRUJILLO SÁNCHEZ, June 09, 1949, Carrizozo, New México[1143].

Notes for SENON CHÁVEZ:
WW II veteran, Darby's Rangers, Third battalion. The Battle of Anzio-Cisterna. He was a POW.
Cremated, Ashes spread on the mountain behind the old Chávez house in San Patricio.

   iv. IGNACIA CHÁVEZ, b. January 23, 1919, San Patricio, New México[1144]; m. (1) HAROLD STEELE; m. (2) VICTOR RICHARD BROOKS[1145].

Notes for IGNACIA CHÁVEZ:
Also known as Inez.

Notes for VICTOR RICHARD BROOKS:
Corporal US Marine Corps. US Navy WWII, Korea.

   v.   ADELA CHÁVEZ, b. July 04, 1920, San Patricio, New México; m. (1) JIMMY LARIOSA; m. (2) GUILLERMO QUIZON[1145]; m. (3) MANUEL NAJERES GÓMEZ[1145].

Notes for ADELA CHÁVEZ:
Also known as Della.

Notes for JIMMY LARIOSA:
Also known as Santiago.

Notes for GUILLERMO QUIZON:
Also known as William, Bill.

Notes for MANUEL NAJERES GÓMEZ:
Private First Class US Army. Korean War Veteran.

   vi. EMILIANO CHÁVEZ[1146], b. January 11, 1922, San Elizario, Téxas[1147]; d. January 25, 1953, California; m. MARÍA SÁNCHEZ LUCERO[1148], April 25, 1947, Carrizozo, New México[1149].

Notes for EMILIANO CHÁVEZ:
Served with N.M.2516 Base Unit AAF, and was a WW II veteran. He was murdered in California.
Buried: San Patricio.

Notes for MARÍA SÁNCHEZ LUCERO:
Also known as Mary.

    vii.   SIPIO CHÁVEZ[1150], b. Abt. 1925, San Patricio, New México; d. June 03, 1928, San Patricio, New México.

Notes for SIPIO CHÁVEZ:
Died young.

    viii.   EFRAÍN CHÁVEZ, b. January 01, 1926, San Patricio, New México[1151]; d. November 11, 1989, Capitán, New México[1152]; m. LILLIAN ELIZABETH MILLER[1152].

Notes for EFRAÍN CHÁVEZ:
Social Security Death Index indicates that he was born on January 1, 1924.
WW II veteran.

    ix.   ORALIA CHÁVEZ[1153], b. Abt. 1927, San Patricio, New México; d. June 10, 1928, San Patricio, New México.

Notes for ORALIA CHÁVEZ:
Died young from Dytheria.

    x.   LUVÍN CHÁVEZ[1154], b. November 15, 1929, San Patricio, New México; d. September 03, 2009, Capitán, New México; m. MARY KAMEES, July 12, 1952, Lincoln, New México[1155].

Notes for LUVÍN CHÁVEZ:
WW II veteran, US Marines.

    xi.   ORALIA CHÁVEZ, b. February 18, 1931, San Patricio, New México[1156]; m. ERNESTO SÁNCHEZ, March 20, 1948, Ruidoso, New México[1156].
    xii.   ONFRÉ CHÁVEZ, b. August 06, 1932, San Patricio, New México; m. VANGIE CHÁVEZ.

Notes for ONFRÉ CHÁVEZ:
Also known as Humphrey.
Navy veteran.

    xiii.   JOSIE CHÁVEZ, b. May 18, 1934, San Patricio, New México; m. (1) BENITO HERRERA[1157]; m. (2) PORFIRIO SÁNCHEZ.

Notes for JOSIE CHÁVEZ:
Also known as Josephine.

    xiv.   MELVIN CHÁVEZ, b. November 06, 1937, San Patricio, New México[1158]; m. (1) PRESCILLA GUTIÉRREZ; m. (2) LORENA ROMERO, January 03, 1959, Hondo, New México[1158].
    xv.   RAMONA CHÁVEZ, b. April 11, 1939, San Patricio, New México; m. LARRY NUÑEZ.
    xvi.   DANNY CHÁVEZ, b. December 13, 1940, San Patricio, New México[1159]; m. (1) CRUCITA BACA; m. (2) VANGIE MONTES, August 26, 1961, Ruidoso, New México[1159].

Notes for DANNY CHÁVEZ:
Also known as Daniel Chávez. Marriage records indicate that he was born in Fort Stanton.

187. MANFOR[11] CHÁVEZ *(LUCÍA[10] WELDON, ANGELITA PEREA[9] SÁNCHES, SANTIAGO[8], JOSÉ GREGORIO DE LA TRINIDAD[7], JUAN CRISTÓBAL[6], FRANCISCO[5], JACINTO SÁNCHES[4] DE IÑIGO, FRANCISCO MUÑOS[3] SÁNCHES, JACINTO[2] MUÑOS, FRANCISCO[1])[1160]* was born March 18, 1896 in Las Angusturas (San Ysidro), Territory of New México[1161], and died July 1971 in San Patricio, New México. He married CRUSITA GARCÍA January 24, 1916[1162], daughter of SISTO GARCÍA and ANGELA TRUJILLO.

Notes for MANFOR CHÁVEZ:
Also known as Gabriel Manfor Chávez.
Land Patent # NMR 0041360, on the authority of the Homestead Entry-Stock Raising (39 Stat. 862), December 29, 1916. Issued 640 acres on August 15, 1924.

Child of MANFOR CHÁVEZ and CRUSITA GARCÍA is:
    i.   GABRIEL[12] CHÁVEZ[1163], b. October 29, 1916, San Patricio, New México; d. April 1981, San Patricio, New México.

188. LUCÍA[11] MONTES *(JESÚS MARÍA[10], ANGELITA PEREA[9] SÁNCHES, SANTIAGO[8], JOSÉ GREGORIO DE LA TRINIDAD[7], JUAN CRISTÓBAL[6], FRANCISCO[5], JACINTO SÁNCHES[4] DE IÑIGO, FRANCISCO MUÑOS[3] SÁNCHES, JACINTO[2] MUÑOS, FRANCISCO[1])[1163]* was born January 24, 1909 in Rancho Torres, New México, and died July 11, 2005 in Roswell, New México. She married FERNANDO GONZÁLES[1163] April 04, 1937 in Carrizozo, New México[1164], son of CIPRIANO GONZÁLES and PABLITA CÓRDOVA.

Children of LUCÍA MONTES and FERNANDO GONZÁLES are:
    i.   BEATRICE[12] GONZÁLES, b. Private.
    ii.   FERNANDO GONZÁLES, b. Private.
    iii. ROSELLA GONZÁLES, b. Private.
    iv.   DOLORES GONZÁLES, b. Private.

189. FRED[11] MONTES *(JESÚS MARÍA[10], ANGELITA PEREA[9] SÁNCHES, SANTIAGO[8], JOSÉ GREGORIO DE LA TRINIDAD[7], JUAN CRISTÓBAL[6], FRANCISCO[5], JACINTO SÁNCHES[4] DE IÑIGO, FRANCISCO MUÑOS[3] SÁNCHES, JACINTO[2] MUÑOS, FRANCISCO[1])[1165]* was born November 26, 1910 in Capitán, New México, and died December 17, 1994 in Hondo, New México. He married (1) MAGGIE TORRES[1166], daughter of REFUGIO TORRES and PELEGRINA SALAS. He married (2) CONCEPCIÓN HERNÁNDEZ May 12, 1959 in Carrizozo, New México, daughter of ESTEVAN HERNÁNDEZ and MIQUELA HERNÁNDEZ.

Notes for FRED MONTES:
Social Security Death Index indicates that he was born on November 16, 1910.

Child of FRED MONTES and MAGGIE TORRES is:
    i.   HERALDA[12] MONTES[1166], b. Abt. 1934, Hondo, New México; d. March 14, 1934, Hondo, New México.

Children of FRED MONTES and CONCEPCIÓN HERNÁNDEZ are:
    ii.   LEROY[12] MONTES, b. Private.
    iii. REYNALDO MONTES, b. Private.
    iv.   DOLORES MONTES, b. Private.
    v.   MARY MONTES, b. March 24, 1937; d. July 03, 2003, Roswell, New México; m. BILLY GRANVILLE RICHARDSON.

190. JOSÉ DOLÓRES[11] MONTES *(JESÚS MARÍA[10], ANGELITA PEREA[9] SÁNCHES, SANTIAGO[8], JOSÉ GREGORIO DE LA TRINIDAD[7], JUAN CRISTÓBAL[6], FRANCISCO[5], JACINTO SÁNCHES[4] DE IÑIGO, FRANCISCO MUÑOS[3] SÁNCHES, JACINTO[2] MUÑOS, FRANCISCO[1])* was born November 14, 1912 in San Patricio, New México[1167], and died May 12, 2010 in Roswell, New México. He married EMILIA MONTOYA July 25, 1940 in Picacho, New México[1167].

Children of JOSÉ MONTES and EMILIA MONTOYA are:
    i.   ALFRED[12] MONTES, b. Private.
    ii.   ELOY MONTES, b. Private.

191. AMANDA[11] MONTES *(JESÚS MARÍA[10], ANGELITA PEREA[9] SÁNCHES, SANTIAGO[8], JOSÉ GREGORIO DE LA TRINIDAD[7], JUAN CRISTÓBAL[6], FRANCISCO[5], JACINTO SÁNCHES[4] DE IÑIGO, FRANCISCO MUÑOS[3] SÁNCHES, JACINTO[2] MUÑOS, FRANCISCO[1])* was born 1914 in Hondo, New México[1168]. She married IGNACIO TORREZ[1169] December 26, 1937, son of MARTÍN TORRES and ISABEL GUTIÉRREZ.

Children of AMANDA MONTES and IGNACIO TORREZ are:
    i.   JOE[12] TORREZ, b. February 18, 1947; m. PRISCILLA GÓMEZ.
    ii.   ALBERT TORREZ, b. Private; d. Albuquerque, New México.
    iii. BETTY TORREZ, b. Private.
    iv.   LORENA TORREZ, b. Private.
    v.   LYDIA TORREZ, b. Private; m. (1) GERALD D. MAÉZ; m. (2) JOHNNY GÓMEZ.
    vi.   RAY TORREZ, b. Private.

192. OLYMPIA[11] MONTES *(JESÚS MARÍA[10], ANGELITA PEREA[9] SÁNCHES, SANTIAGO[8], JOSÉ GREGORIO DE LA TRINIDAD[7], JUAN CRISTÓBAL[6], FRANCISCO[5], JACINTO SÁNCHES[4] DE IÑIGO, FRANCISCO MUÑOS[3] SÁNCHES, JACINTO[2] MUÑOS, FRANCISCO[1])* was born October 06, 1919 in Hondo, New México[1170], and died December 20, 2009 in Santa Fé, New México. She married FERNANDO GARCÍA.

Notes for OLYMPIA MONTES:
Also known as Ola.

Children of OLYMPIA MONTES and FERNANDO GARCÍA are:
- i. ELOY[12] GARCÍA[1171], b. Abt. 1944, Hondo, New México; d. July 05, 1944, Hondo, New México.
- ii. DAVID GARCÍA, b. February 15, 1950, Mescalero, New México; d. August 05, 2012.
- iii. RICHARD GARCÍA, b. Private.

Notes for RICHARD GARCÍA:
Also known as Rick.

- iv. FERNANDO GARCÍA, b. Private; m. EVELYN GARCÍA.
- v. LINDA GARCÍA, b. Private.

193. EMMA[11] MONTES *(JESÚS MARÍA[10], ANGELITA PEREA[9] SÁNCHES, SANTIAGO[8], JOSÉ GREGORIO DE LA TRINIDAD[7], JUAN CRISTÓBAL[6], FRANCISCO[5], JACINTO SÁNCHES[4] DE IÑIGO, FRANCISCO MUÑOS[3] SÁNCHES, JACINTO[2] MUÑOS, FRANCISCO[1])* was born 1921 in Hondo, New México[1172]. She married ALBERTO RICHARDSON, son of GRANVILLE RICHARDSON and AMANDA MAÉS.

Children of EMMA MONTES and ALBERTO RICHARDSON are:
- i. IRENE[12] RICHARDSON, b. Private.
- ii. IDA JO RICHARDSON, b. Private.
- iii. ALBERT CARL RICHARDSON, b. Private; m. (1) ADELINA LARAY CHÁVEZ; m. (2) KATHY MCCOLLUM.
- iv. BARBARA JEAN RICHARDSON, b. Private.
- v. LYNETTE RENEE RICHARDSON, b. Private.

194. ALBERTO[11] MONTES *(JESÚS MARÍA[10], ANGELITA PEREA[9] SÁNCHES, SANTIAGO[8], JOSÉ GREGORIO DE LA TRINIDAD[7], JUAN CRISTÓBAL[6], FRANCISCO[5], JACINTO SÁNCHES[4] DE IÑIGO, FRANCISCO MUÑOS[3] SÁNCHES, JACINTO[2] MUÑOS, FRANCISCO[1])* was born September 25, 1923 in Hondo, New México[1172], and died November 03, 2004 in Lincoln, New México. He married LUCERA RICHARDSON June 03, 1943 in Capitán, New México[1173], daughter of GRANVILLE RICHARDSON and AMANDA MAÉS.

Notes for ALBERTO MONTES:
PFC US Army, WWII.

Children of ALBERTO MONTES and LUCERA RICHARDSON are:
- i. ALBERTA[12] MONTES, b. Private.
- ii. EDWARD PATRICK MONTES, b. Private.
- iii. GERALD MONTES, b. Private.
- iv. LLOYD CARL MONTES, b. Private.
- v. RALPH MONTES, b. Private.
- vi. THOMAS MONTES, b. Private.
- vii. MARCELLA MONTES, b. Private.
- viii. PATRICIA MONTES, b. Private.
- ix. DANNY MONTES, b. Private.

195. ERMINIA[11] ARMERA *(IGNACIA[10] MONTES, ANGELITA PEREA[9] SÁNCHES, SANTIAGO[8], JOSÉ GREGORIO DE LA TRINIDAD[7], JUAN CRISTÓBAL[6], FRANCISCO[5], JACINTO SÁNCHES[4] DE IÑIGO, FRANCISCO MUÑOS[3] SÁNCHES, JACINTO[2] MUÑOS, FRANCISCO[1])* was born Abt. 1909[1174]. She married SERAPIO NUÑEZ[1175], son of SERAPIO NUÑEZ and LEONOR CHÁVEZ.

Notes for ERMINIA ARMERA:
Raised by Alejo Montes and Angelita Sánchez de Montes.

Child of ERMINIA ARMERA and SERAPIO NUÑEZ is:
- i. SERAPIO[12] NUÑEZ[1176], b. Abt. 1929; d. November 13, 1929, Roswell, New México.

196. FERMÍN[11] MONTES *(JUAN SÁNCHEZ[10], ANGELITA PEREA[9] SÁNCHES, SANTIAGO[8], JOSÉ GREGORIO DE LA TRINIDAD[7], JUAN CRISTÓBAL[6], FRANCISCO[5], JACINTO SÁNCHES[4] DE IÑIGO, FRANCISCO MUÑOS[3] SÁNCHES, JACINTO[2] MUÑOS, FRANCISCO[1])[1177]* was born February 20, 1914, and died May 10, 1984 in Roswell, New México. He married CERENIA CONTRERAS[1177] August 22, 1938 in Alburquerque, New México, daughter of GUADALUPE CONTRERAS and ADELA ARMIJO.

Notes for FERMÍN MONTES:
Hondo Valley School Superintendant.
Founded the Hondo Valley Fiesta Dancers.
1983: Published a book: Dreams Can Become a Reality

Notes for CERENIA CONTRERAS:
Founded the Hondo Valley Fiesta Dancers.

Children of FERMÍN MONTES and CERENIA CONTRERAS are:
- i. BECKY[12] MONTES, b. Private; m. RICHARD NALLEY.
- ii. DIANA MONTES, b. August 02, 1939; d. May 04, 2006, Dexter, New México; m. RUFINO SÁNCHEZ.
- iii. GILBERT MONTES, b. Private.
- iv. ROBERT MONTES, b. Private; m. GERALDINE ELSIE SÁNCHEZ.
- v. VANGIE MONTES, b. March 20, 1942[1178]; m. (1) TONY GARCÍA; m. (2) DANNY CHÁVEZ, August 26, 1961, Ruidoso, New México[1178].

197. ORLANDO[11] MONTES *(JUAN SÁNCHEZ[10], ANGELITA PEREA[9] SÁNCHES, SANTIAGO[8], JOSÉ GREGORIO DE LA TRINIDAD[7], JUAN CRISTÓBAL[6], FRANCISCO[5], JACINTO SÁNCHES[4] DE IÑIGO, FRANCISCO MUÑOS[3] SÁNCHES, JACINTO[2] MUÑOS, FRANCISCO[1])* was born February 14, 1922 in Glencoe, New México[1179], and died November 15, 1994. He married (1) GLORIA CHÁVEZ. He married (2) CECILIA CHÁVEZ[1180] January 28, 1942 in Fort Stanton, New México[1181].

Notes for ORLANDO MONTES:
Private First Class, World War II. Wounded in Italy on January 07, 1944.

Child of ORLANDO MONTES and CECILIA CHÁVEZ is:
- i. RICHARD N.[12] MONTES, b. April 03, 1944, Carrizozo, New México; d. August 30, 2012, Alamogordo, New México; m. JANE MONTES.

198. JUAN SÁNCHEZ[11] MONTES *(JUAN SÁNCHEZ[10], ANGELITA PEREA[9] SÁNCHES, SANTIAGO[8], JOSÉ GREGORIO DE LA TRINIDAD[7], JUAN CRISTÓBAL[6], FRANCISCO[5], JACINTO SÁNCHES[4] DE IÑIGO, FRANCISCO MUÑOS[3] SÁNCHES, JACINTO[2] MUÑOS, FRANCISCO[1])[1182]* was born December 27, 1932 in Glencoe, New México, and died February 16, 1987. He married CLEOFAS ROMERO[1182] August 25, 1951 in Ruidoso, New México[1183], daughter of SIGISFREDO ROMERO and LUCÍA YBARRA.

Notes for JUAN SÁNCHEZ MONTES:
Also known as Johnny.

Children of JUAN MONTES and CLEOFAS ROMERO are:
- i. MONROY[12] MONTES, b. Private.
- ii. GARY MONTES, b. Private.
- iii. LUCY MONTES, b. Private.
- iv. JOHNNY MONTES, b. Private.
- v. CARLOS MONTES, b. Private.

199. VIRGINIA[11] SÁNCHEZ *(SALOMON[10], ANTONIO[9], MAURICIO DE LA TRINIDAD[8] SÁNCHES, JOSÉ GREGORIO DE LA TRINIDAD[7], JUAN CRISTÓBAL[6], FRANCISCO[5], JACINTO SÁNCHES[4] DE IÑIGO, FRANCISCO MUÑOS[3] SÁNCHES, JACINTO[2] MUÑOS, FRANCISCO[1])[1184]* was born April 13, 1902 in Glencoe, Territory of New México[1185], and died December 14, 1980 in Ruidoso, New México[1186]. She married ANDELARIO RANDOLPH[1187] September 14, 1918 in Lincoln, New México[1188], son of FRANK RANDOLPH and CATARINA BRADY.

Children of VIRGINIA SÁNCHEZ and ANDELARIO RANDOLPH are:

    i.   JOSEPHINE[12] RANDOLPH[1189], b. March 04, 1920, San Patricio, New México[1190]; m. EDDIE SÁNCHEZ, November 04, 1939, Carrizozo, New México[1191].

    ii.   AROPAJITA RANDOLPH, b. May 05, 1922, San Patricio, New México; d. September 12, 2007, Tularosa, New México.

    iii.   ELMON RANDOLPH[1192], b. March 14, 1926, San Patricio, New México; d. March 1986, Ruidoso Downs, New México; m. FEDELINA ROMERO, July 01, 1950, Carrizozo, New México[1193].

Notes for ELMON RANDOLPH:
Also known as Elmer.

    iv.   CATHERINE RANDOLPH, b. July 10, 1928[1194].

    v.   NORA S. RANDOLPH, b. December 05, 1930, San Patricio, New México[1195]; m. CANDIDO CHÁVEZ[1196], February 15, 1947, Carrizozo, New México[1197].

200. ENRÍQUE GILL[11] SÁNCHEZ *(SALOMON[10], ANTONIO[9], MAURICIO DE LA TRINIDAD[8] SÁNCHES, JOSÉ GREGORIO DE LA TRINIDAD[7], JUAN CRISTÓBAL[6], FRANCISCO[5], JACINTO SÁNCHES[4] DE IÑIGO, FRANCISCO MUÑOS[3] SÁNCHES, JACINTO[2] MUÑOS, FRANCISCO[1])* was born September 25, 1904 in Glencoe, Territory of New México[1198]. He married CAROLINA GAMBOA[1199] August 04, 1925 in Nogal, New México[1200], daughter of TEODORO GAMBOA and MARCELINA LÓPEZ.

Notes for ENRÍQUE GILL SÁNCHEZ:
He was also known as Henry Gill Sánchez, José Enríque Gill Sánchez. Family records indicate that he was born on September 03, 1904.

Children of ENRÍQUE SÁNCHEZ and CAROLINA GAMBOA are:
    i.   ERNEST R.[12] SÁNCHEZ, b. Abt. 1927[1201].
    ii.   HENRY SÁNCHEZ, b. Abt. 1928[1201].

201. SALOMON GILL[11] SÁNCHEZ *(SALOMON[10], ANTONIO[9], MAURICIO DE LA TRINIDAD[8] SÁNCHES, JOSÉ GREGORIO DE LA TRINIDAD[7], JUAN CRISTÓBAL[6], FRANCISCO[5], JACINTO SÁNCHES[4] DE IÑIGO, FRANCISCO MUÑOS[3] SÁNCHES, JACINTO[2] MUÑOS, FRANCISCO[1])[1202]* was born March 17, 1905 in Glencoe, Territory of New México[1203], and died August 11, 1995 in Carrizozo, New México. He married (1) TERESITA SALAS October 11, 1928 in Carrizozo, New México[1204]. He married (2) RAMONA OTERO[1205] November 20, 1932 in Carrizozo, New México[1206], daughter of ANTONIO OTERO and EMILIANA ZAMORA.

Children of SALOMON SÁNCHEZ and TERESITA SALAS are:
    i.   FABIOLA[12] SÁNCHEZ, b. Abt. September 1929[1207].
    ii.   ORLANDO SALAS SÁNCHEZ, b. Private.

Children of SALOMON SÁNCHEZ and RAMONA OTERO are:
    iii.   MARY OLIDA[12] SÁNCHEZ[1208], b. September 27, 1934, Roswell, New México; d. January 27, 2011, Tularosa, New México; m. (1) ALFREDO RICHARDSON, January 08, 1955[1208]; m. (2) RALPH VULLO, 1982.
    iv.   LORRINE SÁNCHEZ[1208], b. Private.
    v.   ELMON SÁNCHEZ[1208], b. Private.
    vi.   ERNEST OTERO SÁNCHEZ[1208], b. Private.
    vii.   ORLANDO SÁNCHEZ[1208], b. Private.
    viii. FAVOLIA SÁNCHEZ[1208], b. Private.

202. TELESFORA[11] SÁNCHEZ *(SALOMON[10], ANTONIO[9], MAURICIO DE LA TRINIDAD[8] SÁNCHES, JOSÉ GREGORIO DE LA TRINIDAD[7], JUAN CRISTÓBAL[6], FRANCISCO[5], JACINTO SÁNCHES[4] DE IÑIGO, FRANCISCO MUÑOS[3] SÁNCHES, JACINTO[2] MUÑOS, FRANCISCO[1])[1209]* was born July 15, 1906 in Glencoe, Territory of New México, and died November 18, 1993 in Alamagordo, New México. She married TEODORO SÁNCHEZ PEÑA[1209] March 01, 1926 in Carrizozo, New México[1210], son of LUÍS PEÑA and AMADITA SÁNCHEZ.

Children of TELESFORA SÁNCHEZ and TEODORO PEÑA are:
    i.   JOSEPHINE[12] PEÑA, b. Abt. 1927[1211].
    ii.   LUÍS SÁNCHEZ PEÑA[1212], b. May 30, 1933; d. November 14, 1984.

Notes for LUÍS SÁNCHEZ PEÑA:
Corporal in the US Army, Korea.

iii.   REYES PEÑA[1213], b. October 05, 1940, Glencoe, New México; d. March 06, 1997, Roswell, New México.
iv.   IDALIA PEÑA, b. Private.
v.   RAFAEL PEÑA, b. Private.
vi.   TEODORO SÁNCHEZ PEÑA, b. Private.

203. EDUVIJEN[11] SÁNCHEZ *(SALOMON[10], ANTONIO[9], MAURICIO DE LA TRINIDAD[8] SÁNCHES, JOSÉ GREGORIO DE LA TRINIDAD[7], JUAN CRISTÓBAL[6], FRANCISCO[5], JACINTO SÁNCHES[4] DE IÑIGO, FRANCISCO MUÑOS[3] SÁNCHES, JACINTO[2] MUÑOS, FRANCISCO[1])[1214]* was born April 23, 1908 in Glencoe, Territory of New México[1215], and died March 07, 1999 in Roswell, New México. She married JOSÉ ANTONIO SILVA[1216] April 09, 1928[1217], son of AUGUSTÍN SILVA and LUCÍA GARCÍA.

Notes for EDUVIJEN SÁNCHEZ:
Family records indicate that she was born on August 06, 1909.

Notes for JOSÉ ANTONIO SILVA:
Also known as Joe.

Children of EDUVIJEN SÁNCHEZ and JOSÉ SILVA are:
i.   TONY[12] SILVA[1218], b. January 09, 1929[1219]; d. November 27, 2000, Roswell, New México.

Notes for TONY SILVA:
Also known as José Antonio Silva.

ii.   LUCIA SILVA, b. Private.
iii. DICK SILVA, b. Private.
iv.   ROGER SILVA, b. Private.
v.   BETTY SILVA, b. Private.
vi.   ERNIE SILVA, b. Private.

204. ANATALIA[11] SÁNCHEZ *(SALOMON[10], ANTONIO[9], MAURICIO DE LA TRINIDAD[8] SÁNCHES, JOSÉ GREGORIO DE LA TRINIDAD[7], JUAN CRISTÓBAL[6], FRANCISCO[5], JACINTO SÁNCHES[4] DE IÑIGO, FRANCISCO MUÑOS[3] SÁNCHES, JACINTO[2] MUÑOS, FRANCISCO[1])* was born September 10, 1911 in Glencoe, Territory of New México[1220], and died February 23, 1969. She married JULIAN HERRERA[1221] April 28, 1934 in Carrizozo, New México[1222], son of MARTÍN HERRERA and TEODORA MENDOSA.

Notes for ANATALIA SÁNCHEZ:
Also known as Natalia.

Children of ANATALIA SÁNCHEZ and JULIAN HERRERA are:
i.   MARTÍN[12] HERRERA, b. Private.
ii.   ANDREW HERRERA, b. Private.
iii. ORLIDIA HERRERA, b. Private.
iv.   VIRGINIA HERRERA, b. Private.

205. CONSUELO[11] SÁNCHEZ *(SALOMON[10], ANTONIO[9], MAURICIO DE LA TRINIDAD[8] SÁNCHES, JOSÉ GREGORIO DE LA TRINIDAD[7], JUAN CRISTÓBAL[6], FRANCISCO[5], JACINTO SÁNCHES[4] DE IÑIGO, FRANCISCO MUÑOS[3] SÁNCHES, JACINTO[2] MUÑOS, FRANCISCO[1])[1223]* was born April 24, 1914 in Glencoe, New México, and died April 28, 1996 in Tularosa, New México. She married BENITO SILVA[1223] February 13, 1932 in Glencoe, New México[1224], son of TELESFORO SILVA and ERINEA BENAVIDEZ.

Notes for CONSUELO SÁNCHEZ:
Also known as Consolación. Lincoln County marriage records indicate that she was born on April 02, 1913.

Children of CONSUELO SÁNCHEZ and BENITO SILVA are:
i.   MARY L.[12] SILVA, b. Abt. 1937, San Patricio, New México[1225].
ii.   BEN SILVA, b. Abt. 1939, San Patricio, New México[1225].

206. CARLOS[11] SÁNCHEZ *(SALOMON[10], ANTONIO[9], MAURICIO DE LA TRINIDAD[8] SÁNCHES, JOSÉ GREGORIO DE LA TRINIDAD[7], JUAN CRISTÓBAL[6], FRANCISCO[5], JACINTO SÁNCHES[4] DE IÑIGO, FRANCISCO MUÑOS[3] SÁNCHES, JACINTO[2] MUÑOS, FRANCISCO[1])[1226]* was born June 10, 1918 in Las Cruces, New

México, and died April 16, 2009 in El Paso, Téxas. He married ALVESITA MONTOYA[1227] July 22, 1940 in Glencoe, New México[1228], daughter of TEODORO MONTOYA and BERSABÉ SÁNCHEZ.

Children of CARLOS SÁNCHEZ and ALVESITA MONTOYA are:
  i.   OLA[12] SÁNCHEZ, b. Private.
  ii. ROBERT SÁNCHEZ, b. Private.
  iii. RICHARD SÁNCHEZ, b. Private.

207. EUFRACIA[11] SÁNCHEZ *(SALOMON[10], ANTONIO[9], MAURICIO DE LA TRINIDAD[8] SÁNCHES, JOSÉ GREGORIO DE LA TRINIDAD[7], JUAN CRISTÓBAL[6], FRANCISCO[5], JACINTO SÁNCHES[4] DE IÑIGO, FRANCISCO MUÑOS[3] SÁNCHES, JACINTO[2] MUÑOS, FRANCISCO[1])* was born May 27, 1920 in Glencoe, New México[1229]. She married (1) EUGENIO ANAYA. She married (2) ESTEVAN ROMERO January 15, 1949 in Carrizozo, New México[1230].

Notes for ESTEVAN ROMERO:
Also known as Steve M. Romero.

Child of EUFRACIA SÁNCHEZ and EUGENIO ANAYA is:
  i.   CRISTINIA[12] ANAYA, b. Private.

208. LUVÍN[11] SÁNCHEZ *(SALOMON[10], ANTONIO[9], MAURICIO DE LA TRINIDAD[8] SÁNCHES, JOSÉ GREGORIO DE LA TRINIDAD[7], JUAN CRISTÓBAL[6], FRANCISCO[5], JACINTO SÁNCHES[4] DE IÑIGO, FRANCISCO MUÑOS[3] SÁNCHES, JACINTO[2] MUÑOS, FRANCISCO[1])[1231]* was born June 18, 1922 in Glencoe, New México, and died February 16, 1994 in Ruidoso, New México. He married ASUSENA CANDELARIA, daughter of JOSÉ CANDELARIA and ISIDRA SÁNCHEZ.

Notes for ASUSENA CANDELARIA:
Also known as Susan.

Children of LUVÍN SÁNCHEZ and ASUSENA CANDELARIA are:
  i.   RAYMOND[12] SÁNCHEZ, b. Private.
  ii. DAVID SÁNCHEZ, b. Private.
  iii. VERONICA SÁNCHEZ, b. Private.
  iv. SANDRA SÁNCHEZ, b. Private.
  v.   WANDA SÁNCHEZ, b. Private.
  vi. DANNY SÁNCHEZ, b. Private.

209. ALBERTO[11] SÁNCHEZ *(SALOMON[10], ANTONIO[9], MAURICIO DE LA TRINIDAD[8] SÁNCHES, JOSÉ GREGORIO DE LA TRINIDAD[7], JUAN CRISTÓBAL[6], FRANCISCO[5], JACINTO SÁNCHES[4] DE IÑIGO, FRANCISCO MUÑOS[3] SÁNCHES, JACINTO[2] MUÑOS, FRANCISCO[1])[1232]* was born June 09, 1927 in San Patricio, New México, and died February 10, 2000 in San Patricio, New México. He married EVA MCKINLEY, daughter of EDUARDO SEDILLOS and DOMINGA MAÉS.

Notes for ALBERTO SÁNCHEZ:
Also known as Albert.
Tec 5 US Army. WW II Veteran.

210. PORFIRIO[11] SÁNCHEZ *(SALOMON[10], ANTONIO[9], MAURICIO DE LA TRINIDAD[8] SÁNCHES, JOSÉ GREGORIO DE LA TRINIDAD[7], JUAN CRISTÓBAL[6], FRANCISCO[5], JACINTO SÁNCHES[4] DE IÑIGO, FRANCISCO MUÑOS[3] SÁNCHES, JACINTO[2] MUÑOS, FRANCISCO[1])* was born September 13, 1933 in San Patricio, New México[1233]. He married (1) JOSIE CHÁVEZ, daughter of YSIDRO CHÁVEZ and PAUBLITA SÁNCHEZ. He married (2) FLORA HERRERA[1234] May 04, 1952 in San Patricio, New México[1235], daughter of MANUEL HERRERA and ELISA GONZÁLES.

211. ERNESTO[11] SILVA *(MARÍA DE JESÚS[10] SÁNCHEZ, ANTONIO[9], MAURICIO DE LA TRINIDAD[8] SÁNCHES, JOSÉ GREGORIO DE LA TRINIDAD[7], JUAN CRISTÓBAL[6], FRANCISCO[5], JACINTO SÁNCHES[4] DE IÑIGO, FRANCISCO MUÑOS[3] SÁNCHES, JACINTO[2] MUÑOS, FRANCISCO[1])[1236]* was born June 27, 1912 in Glencoe, New

México[1237], and died July 1981 in Glencoe, New México. He married GENOVEVA GONZÁLES[1238] February 02, 1933 in San Patricio, New México[1239], daughter of FLORENCIO GONZÁLES and AVELINA CHÁVEZ.

Notes for ERNESTO SILVA:
US Navy, Seaman Second Class. World War II.

Notes for GENOVEVA GONZÁLES:
Also known as Geneva.

Children of ERNESTO SILVA and GENOVEVA GONZÁLES are:
  i.   JOSEPHINE[12] SILVA, b. November 30, 1934, Glencoe, New México; m. WILLIAM GÓMEZ.
  ii.   ERNEST SILVA, b. February 15, 1939, Glencoe, New México[1240]; m. MINNIE SÁNCHEZ, January 22, 1961, San Patricio, New México[1240].
  iii. JESUSITA SILVA, b. Private, Glencoe, New México.

212. AMANDA[11] SÁNCHEZ *(MANUEL MIRABAL[10], ANTONIO[9], MAURICIO DE LA TRINIDAD[8] SÁNCHES, JOSÉ GREGORIO DE LA TRINIDAD[7], JUAN CRISTÓBAL[6], FRANCISCO[5], JACINTO SÁNCHES[4] DE IÑIGO, FRANCISCO MUÑOS[3] SÁNCHES, JACINTO[2] MUÑOS, FRANCISCO[1])* was born July 15, 1910 in Glencoe, Territory of New México[1241], and died March 19, 1982 in Roswell, New México[1241]. She married LUÍS BACA TORRES November 30, 1927 in Tularosa, New México[1242], son of PRECILIANO TORRES and DELFINIA BACA.

Notes for LUÍS BACA TORRES:
After selling the farm, he and his wife migrated to Roswell, New México.
August 26, 1918: Discharged WW I Veteran.

Children of AMANDA SÁNCHEZ and LUÍS TORRES are:
  i.   MAX[12] TORRES[1243], b. October 12, 1928, Glencoe, New México; d. August 24, 2008, Willcox, Arizona; m. ESTER MENDOZA, October 25, 1952, Roswell, New México[1244].

Notes for MAX TORRES:
Also known as Luís Maximiliano Torres.

  ii.   TERESITA TORRES[1245], b. December 04, 1929, Glencoe, New México; d. December 28, 1997, Alburquerque, New México; m. JOHNNY MATA[1245], December 28, 1950, Roswell, New México[1246].

Notes for TERESITA TORRES:
Also known as Marie Barbara Torres.

  iii. EPIFANIA TORRES, b. January 11, 1931, Glencoe, New México[1247]; d. October 31, 1986, Roswell, New México[1247]; m. JOSEPH THOMAS ATKINSON[1247], November 25, 1952, Pecos, Texas[1247].

Notes for EPIFANIA TORRES:
Also known as Fannie.

  iv.   CLARITA TORRES, b. June 04, 1932, Glencoe, New México[1247]; m. BUDDY BAKER[1247].

Notes for CLARITA TORRES:
Also known as Francisca Clarita Torres.

  v.   PRECILIANO SÁNCHEZ TORRES, b. April 27, 1935, Glencoe, New México[1247]; m. MARY LOU MARRUJO[1247], May 05, 1957, Roswell, New México[1247].
  vi.   ESTELLA JUANITA TORRES, b. May 04, 1936[1247]; m. ROY BASCOM[1247].
  vii. BILLY SÁNCHEZ TORRES, b. March 13, 1938, Glencoe, New México[1247]; m. MARTHA MOYERS.
  viii. ANTONIO TORRES, b. November 18, 1944, Lake Arthur, New México[1247]; m. PATRICIA GRZELACHOWSKI[1247].
  ix.   JOSÉ JESÚS TORRES, b. December 15, 1946, Glencoe, New México[1247]; d. March 04, 2006, Edgewood, New México[1247]; m. IRENE MARGARETE GRZELACHOWSKI.

213. ISMAÉL[11] SÁNCHEZ *(DANOIS[10], ANTONIO[9], MAURICIO DE LA TRINIDAD[8] SÁNCHES, JOSÉ GREGORIO DE LA TRINIDAD[7], JUAN CRISTÓBAL[6], FRANCISCO[5], JACINTO SÁNCHES[4] DE IÑIGO, FRANCISCO MUÑOS[3] SÁNCHES, JACINTO[2] MUÑOS, FRANCISCO[1])* was born July 16, 1921 in Glencoe, New México[1248], and died March 16, 2009 in Alamogordo, New México. He married BESSIE GARCÍA BACA.

214. CECILIA[11] MACKEY *(SENAIDA[10] SÁNCHEZ, ANTONIO[9], MAURICIO DE LA TRINIDAD[8] SÁNCHES, JOSÉ GREGORIO DE LA TRINIDAD[7], JUAN CRISTÓBAL[6], FRANCISCO[5], JACINTO SÁNCHES[4] DE IÑIGO, FRANCISCO MUÑOS[3] SÁNCHES, JACINTO[2] MUÑOS, FRANCISCO[1])[1249]* was born June 22, 1913 in San Patricio, New México[1250], and died April 09, 2010 in Glen Burnie, Maryland. She married FEDERICO TORREZ[1251], son of MARTÍN TORRES and ISABEL GUTIÉRREZ.

Notes for FEDERICO TORREZ:
Also known as Fred.

Children of CECILIA MACKEY and FEDERICO TORREZ are:
    i.   MARÍA IRENE[12] TORREZ[1252], b. September 01, 1931, San Patricio, New México; d. April 26, 2005, Placentia, California.
    ii. ERVIN EUGENE TORREZ, b. Private; m. REBECCA DELPHINIA RICHARDSON.

215. ANTONIO PADILLA[11] SÁNCHEZ *(FELIPÉ E.[10], ESTOLANO[9], MAURICIO DE LA TRINIDAD[8] SÁNCHES, JOSÉ GREGORIO DE LA TRINIDAD[7], JUAN CRISTÓBAL[6], FRANCISCO[5], JACINTO SÁNCHES[4] DE IÑIGO, FRANCISCO MUÑOS[3] SÁNCHES, JACINTO[2] MUÑOS, FRANCISCO[1])* was born May 17, 1897 in Tres Ritos, New México[1253], and died February 21, 1984 in San Elizario, Texas[1254]. He met (1) MAGDALENA MARTÍNEZ. He married (2) MARTINA SALSBERRY October 13, 1915 in Lincoln, Territory of New México[1255], daughter of JAMES SALSBERRY and MANUELITA HERRERA. He married (3) JUANITA CABALLERO ALVARADO Aft. December 1917.

Notes for ANTONIO PADILLA SÁNCHEZ:
Land Patent # NMR 0027417, on the authority of the Homestead Act, February 19, 1909, 320 Acres. (Enlarged property) Issued: October 28, 1921
Land Patent # NMLC 0026012, on the authority of the Homestead Act, December 29, 1926, 320 Acres. (Cattle Grazing) Issued: January 12, 1926
Land Patent # NMLC 0054541, on the authority of Sale cash entry, April 24, 1820, 84.92 Acres. Issued: December 13, 1941

Children of ANTONIO SÁNCHEZ and MAGDALENA MARTÍNEZ are:
    i.   REYNEL[12] MARTÍNEZ, b. September 11, 1946; m. (1) SYLVIA DURFEE; m. (2) JOY BOW.
    ii. EILEEN MARTÍNEZ, b. 1947; m. NICK SERNA.

Children of ANTONIO SÁNCHEZ and JUANITA ALVARADO are:
    iii. PAUBLINA[12] SÁNCHEZ, b. Private; m. PETE MARTÍNEZ.
    iv. CECILIA ALVARADO SÁNCHEZ, b. Private; m. DANIEL ELOY ORTIZ.
    v.   ELIZA SÁNCHEZ, b. Private; m. MANUEL MARTÍNEZ.
    vi. LUISA SÁNCHEZ, b. Private; m. SUSANO JIMÉNEZ MARTÍNEZ.
    vii. TONY SÁNCHEZ, b. Private; m. FRANCES ORQUIDES.
    viii. EFRIN SÁNCHEZ, b. Private; m. AMELIA LÓPEZ.
    ix. SAMUEL SÁNCHEZ, b. Private; m. MINERVA QUADRO.
    x.   LUCILLA SÁNCHEZ, b. Private; m. ALBINO BENITO ALVIDREZ.
    xi. DAVÍD SÁNCHEZ, b. Private; m. ESTELLA TAUTIMER.
    xii. RUFINA SÁNCHEZ, b. Private; m. FELIZ TREVIZO.
    xiii. BENJAMÍN SÁNCHEZ, b. Private; m. GRACIELA SAUCEDO.
    xiv. MARÍA SÁNCHEZ[1256], b. May 30, 1929, San Elizario, Téxas; d. June 02, 1929, El Paso, Téxas.

216. PAUBLITA[11] SÁNCHEZ *(FELIPÉ E.[10], ESTOLANO[9], MAURICIO DE LA TRINIDAD[8] SÁNCHES, JOSÉ GREGORIO DE LA TRINIDAD[7], JUAN CRISTÓBAL[6], FRANCISCO[5], JACINTO SÁNCHES[4] DE IÑIGO, FRANCISCO MUÑOS[3] SÁNCHES, JACINTO[2] MUÑOS, FRANCISCO[1])* was born July 30, 1898 in Tres Rios, Territory of New México[1257], and died October 13, 1963 in Las Vegas, New México. She married YSIDRO CHÁVEZ[1258] August 04, 1913 in Lincoln, New México[1259], son of ROBERTO CHÁVES and LUCÍA WELDON.

Notes for PAUBLITA SÁNCHEZ:
Also known as Pablita, Pabla.

Children of PAUBLITA SÁNCHEZ and YSIDRO CHÁVEZ are:
    i.   GRESELDA[12] CHÁVEZ[1260], b. May 03, 1914, Glencoe, New México; d. June 09, 1988, Ruidoso, New México; m. FRANK GÓMEZ[1260], February 17, 1934, Carrizozo, New México[1261].

    ii.   AMARANTE CHÁVEZ[1262], b. November 09, 1915, Glencoe, New México; d. February 27, 2001, Alburquerque, New México; m. DOLORES ROMERO ARCHULETA[1262], September 21, 1936, San Patricio, New México[1263].

    iii. SENON CHÁVEZ[1264], b. March 03, 1917, San Patricio, New México; d. January 18, 2000, San Patricio, New México; m. MABEL TRUJILLO SÁNCHEZ, June 09, 1949, Carrizozo, New México[1265].

    iv. IGNACIA CHÁVEZ, b. January 23, 1919, San Patricio, New México[1266]; m. (1) HAROLD STEELE; m. (2) VICTOR RICHARD BROOKS[1267].

    v.   ADELA CHÁVEZ, b. July 04, 1920, San Patricio, New México; m. (1) JIMMY LARIOSA; m. (2) GUILLERMO QUIZON[1267]; m. (3) MANUEL NAJERES GÓMEZ[1267].

    vi. EMILIANO CHÁVEZ[1268], b. January 11, 1922, San Elizario, Téxas[1269]; d. January 25, 1953, California; m. MARÍA SÁNCHEZ LUCERO[1270], April 25, 1947, Carrizozo, New México[1271].

    vii. SIPIO CHÁVEZ[1272], b. Abt. 1925, San Patricio, New México; d. June 03, 1928, San Patricio, New México.

    viii. EFRAÍN CHÁVEZ, b. January 01, 1926, San Patricio, New México[1273]; d. November 11, 1989, Capitán, New México[1274]; m. LILLIAN ELIZABETH MILLER[1274].

    ix. ORALIA CHÁVEZ[1275], b. Abt. 1927, San Patricio, New México; d. June 10, 1928, San Patricio, New México.

    x.   LUVÍN CHÁVEZ[1276], b. November 15, 1929, San Patricio, New México; d. September 03, 2009, Capitán, New México; m. MARY KAMEES, July 12, 1952, Lincoln, New México[1277].

    xi. ORALIA CHÁVEZ, b. February 18, 1931, San Patricio, New México[1278]; m. ERNESTO SÁNCHEZ, March 20, 1948, Ruidoso, New México[1278].

    xii. ONFRÉ CHÁVEZ, b. August 06, 1932, San Patricio, New México; m. VANGIE CHÁVEZ.

    xiii. JOSIE CHÁVEZ, b. May 18, 1934, San Patricio, New México; m. (1) BENITO HERRERA[1279]; m. (2) PORFIRIO SÁNCHEZ.

    xiv. MELVIN CHÁVEZ, b. November 06, 1937, San Patricio, New México[1280]; m. (1) PRESCILLA GUTIÉRREZ; m. (2) LORENA ROMERO, January 03, 1959, Hondo, New México[1280].

    xv. RAMONA CHÁVEZ, b. April 11, 1939, San Patricio, New México; m. LARRY NUÑEZ.

    xvi. DANNY CHÁVEZ, b. December 13, 1940, San Patricio, New México[1281]; m. (1) CRUCITA BACA; m. (2) VANGIE MONTES, August 26, 1961, Ruidoso, New México[1281].

Alfonzo Borrego

217. CORNELIA[11] SÁNCHEZ *(FELIPÉ E.[10], ESTOLANO[9], MAURICIO DE LA TRINIDAD[8] SÁNCHES, JOSÉ GREGORIO DE LA TRINIDAD[7], JUAN CRISTÓBAL[6], FRANCISCO[5], JACINTO SÁNCHES[4] DE IÑIGO, FRANCISCO MUÑOS[3] SÁNCHES, JACINTO[2] MUÑOS, FRANCISCO[1])[1282]* was born November 16, 1902 in Lincoln County, New México[1283]. She married ALFONSO BORREGO[1284], son of ELIJIO BORREGO and FRANCISCA ARIAS.

Notes for ALFONSO BORREGO:
World War I veteran.
September 01, 2001: Commemorated the naming of Alfonso Borrego Elementary School in San Elizario, Téxas. This was in honor of his dedication to promote better schools within the community.

Children of CORNELIA SÁNCHEZ and ALFONSO BORREGO are:
    i.   ALFONSO[12] BORREGO, b. Private; m. (1) ALICIA LUJÁN; m. (2) ANNIE LARA.
    ii. JOSÉ BORREGO, b. Private; m. MARÍA ESTRADA.
    iii. JOSEPHINA BORREGO, b. Private; m. MANUEL LARA.
    iv. LORENZO BORREGO, b. Private; m. (1) NATALIA MONTOYA; m. (2) SYLVIA BORREGO.
    v.   LUÍS FILIMON BORREGO, b. Private; m. MARÍA LARA.
    vi. MARÍA LYDIA BORREGO, b. Private; m. CLARANCE DINDINGER.
    vii. MIKE NORMAN BORREGO, b. Private; m. GLORIA DURÁN.
    viii. PEDRO BORREGO, b. Private; m. HILDA GARCÍA.
    ix. RAMÓN BORREGO, b. Private; m. MARY LOU MEDINA.
    x.   RAÚL BORREGO, b. Private; m. EMALIE BAILY.
    xi. TERESA BORREGO, b. Private; m. SYLVESTER NUÑEZ.

218. EMILIANO[11] SÁNCHEZ *(FELIPÉ E.[10], ESTOLANO[9], MAURICIO DE LA TRINIDAD[8] SÁNCHES, JOSÉ GREGORIO DE LA TRINIDAD[7], JUAN CRISTÓBAL[6], FRANCISCO[5], JACINTO SÁNCHES[4] DE IÑIGO, FRANCISCO MUÑOS[3] SÁNCHES, JACINTO[2] MUÑOS, FRANCISCO[1])* was born August 11, 1904 in Hondo, Territory of New México. He married RUBY MARTÍNEZ.

Children of EMILIANO SÁNCHEZ and RUBY MARTÍNEZ are:
    i.   EMILIANO JUNIOR[12] SÁNCHEZ, b. 1927.
    ii. BERNICE MARTÍNEZ SÁNCHEZ, b. Private.
    iii. GLORIA SÁNCHEZ, b. Private.

iv.   LEROY SÁNCHEZ, b. Private.
v.   TERESA SÁNCHEZ, b. Private.
vi.   VIOLA MARTÍNEZ SÁNCHEZ, b. Private.

219. ÁBRAN[11] SÁNCHEZ *(FELIPÉ E.[10], ESTOLANO[9], MAURICIO DE LA TRINIDAD[8] SÁNCHES, JOSÉ GREGORIO DE LA TRINIDAD[7], JUAN CRISTÓBAL[6], FRANCISCO[5], JACINTO SÁNCHES[4] DE IÑIGO, FRANCISCO MUÑOS[3] SÁNCHES, JACINTO[2] MUÑOS, FRANCISCO[1])[1285]* was born December 24, 1905 in White Oaks, Territory of New México, and died November 18, 1973 in El Paso, Téxas. He married (1) RAMONCITA GURULÉ, daughter of JUAN GURULÉ and LUISA ARAGÓN. He married (2) ANTONIA JUAREGUI[1286]. He married (3) FELIPA RODRÍQUES Abt. 1926[1287].

Notes for ÁBRAN SÁNCHEZ:
Also known as Abraham and Abe. Buried: Carrizozo, New México.
1930 Census: Living in Carrizozo, New México. (Abe)
Land Patent # NMLC 0042738, on the authority of the Homestead Act, December 29, 1916, 640 Acres. (Stock raising) Issued: June 27, 1936

Children of ABRÁN SÁNCHEZ and RAMONCITA GURULÉ are:
i.   PAUBLITA ELIZA[12] SÁNCHEZ[1288], b. August 24, 1940, Trujillo, New México; m. NATIVIDAD JOSEPH CHÁVEZ[1288].
ii.   GEORGE ABE SÁNCHEZ[1289], b. July 11, 1942, Las Vegas, New México; m. JUANA JESÚS EVARO[1289].

Notes for JUANA JESÚS EVARO:
Also known as Kila.

iii. RAYNELL XAVIER SÁNCHEZ[1289], b. February 09, 1945, Carrizozo, New México; m. LUCY TERESA LUJÁN[1289].
iv.   HERMAN LEWIS SÁNCHEZ[1289], b. January 30, 1947, Carrizozo, New México; m. LEE ANN BROSNAHAN[1289].
v.   RITA LINDA SÁNCHEZ[1289], b. March 14, 1949, Carrizozo, New México; m. PEDRO DANIEL NARVAEZ[1289].
vi.   ROSYLENE BELÉN SÁNCHEZ[1289], b. July 17, 1950, Carrizozo, New México; m. TIOFILO MARTÍNEZ[1289].
vii. JOHN PATRICK SÁNCHEZ, b. September 13, 1959.

Child of ABRÁN SÁNCHEZ and ANTONIA JUAREGUI is:
viii. ARTHUR[12] SÁNCHEZ[1290], b. Private; d. California.

Children of ABRÁN SÁNCHEZ and FELIPA RODRÍQUES are:
ix.   FRANK F.[12] SÁNCHEZ[1291], b. April 16, 1927, San Elizario, Téxas; m. (1) ANA MARGIE JIRÓN; m. (2) BEATRICE MONTAÑO[1291], May 05, 1949, Long Beach, California[1291].
x.   MARÍA MAGDALENA SÁNCHEZ[1292], b. November 03, 1928, San Elizario, Téxas; m. JOE L. ORTIZ[1292].
xi.   DAVÍD A. SÁNCHEZ[1292], b. October 05, 1930, Ancho, New México; m. CARMÉN GONZÁLES[1292].
xii. FREDRICK SÁNCHEZ, b. May 31, 1932, Ancho, New México; m. (1) JOSEPHINE TRUJILLO[1292]; m. (2) FRANCES MORENO[1292].

Notes for FREDRICK SÁNCHEZ:
Also known as Chavalo.

220. RENALDO[11] SÁNCHEZ *(FELIPÉ E.[10], ESTOLANO[9], MAURICIO DE LA TRINIDAD[8] SÁNCHES, JOSÉ GREGORIO DE LA TRINIDAD[7], JUAN CRISTÓBAL[6], FRANCISCO[5], JACINTO SÁNCHES[4] DE IÑIGO, FRANCISCO MUÑOS[3] SÁNCHES, JACINTO[2] MUÑOS, FRANCISCO[1])* was born March 22, 1907 in Patos, New México[1293], and died May 1981 in Tularosa, New México. He married SOFIA AGUILAR[1294] November 10, 1932.

Notes for RENALDO SÁNCHEZ:
Also known as José Renaldo Sánchez.

Children of RENALDO SÁNCHEZ and SOFIA AGUILAR are:
i.   MARY LILY[12] SÁNCHEZ, b. Private.
ii.   MABEL AGUILAR SÁNCHEZ, b. Private.
iii. JO ANN SÁNCHEZ, b. Private.

221. BENITO[11] SÁNCHEZ *(FELIPÉ E.[10], ESTOLANO[9], MAURICIO DE LA TRINIDAD[8] SÁNCHES, JOSÉ GREGORIO DE LA TRINIDAD[7], JUAN CRISTÓBAL[6], FRANCISCO[5], JACINTO SÁNCHES[4] DE IÑIGO, FRANCISCO MUÑOS[3] SÁNCHES, JACINTO[2] MUÑOS, FRANCISCO[1])* was born Abt. 1912[1295]. He married (1) CONCHA RAMÍREZ. He married (2) BEATRICE PINO May 09, 1932 in Tularosa, New México[1296].

Children of BENITO SÁNCHEZ and CONCHA RAMÍREZ are:
 i. HOPE[12] SÁNCHEZ, b. Private.
 ii. ISABEL SÁNCHEZ, b. Private.
 iii. BENNY SÁNCHEZ, b. Private.

Children of BENITO SÁNCHEZ and BEATRICE PINO are:
 iv. MARY ALICE[12] SÁNCHEZ, b. Private.
 v. MARGIE SÁNCHEZ, b. Private.
 vi. GRACE PINO SÁNCHEZ, b. Private.
 vii. RAY PINO SÁNCHEZ, b. Private.

222. ONECIMO[11] SÁNCHEZ *(FELIPÉ E.[10], ESTOLANO[9], MAURICIO DE LA TRINIDAD[8] SÁNCHES, JOSÉ GREGORIO DE LA TRINIDAD[7], JUAN CRISTÓBAL[6], FRANCISCO[5], JACINTO SÁNCHES[4] DE IÑIGO, FRANCISCO MUÑOS[3] SÁNCHES, JACINTO[2] MUÑOS, FRANCISCO[1])* was born 1915[1297]. He married CLEOTILDE DURÁN, daughter of FRANCISCO DURÁN and HORTENCIA MONTES.

Children of ONECIMO SÁNCHEZ and CLEOTILDE DURÁN are:
 i. YOLANDA DURÁN[12] SÁNCHEZ, b. Private.
 ii. MAXIMO SÁNCHEZ, b. Private.
 iii. MARY LOU SÁNCHEZ, b. Private.
 iv. DARLENE SÁNCHEZ, b. Private.
 v. HECTOR SÁNCHEZ, b. Private.
 vi. LINDA SÁNCHEZ, b. Private.
 vii. ALEX DURÁN SÁNCHEZ, b. Private.
 viii. CYNTHIA SÁNCHEZ, b. Private.

223. ROSA[11] GAVALDON *(ELUTICIA[10] SÁNCHEZ, ESTOLANO[9], MAURICIO DE LA TRINIDAD[8] SÁNCHES, JOSÉ GREGORIO DE LA TRINIDAD[7], JUAN CRISTÓBAL[6], FRANCISCO[5], JACINTO SÁNCHES[4] DE IÑIGO, FRANCISCO MUÑOS[3] SÁNCHES, JACINTO[2] MUÑOS, FRANCISCO[1])* was born January 1892[1298]. She married AVRELIO MARTÍNEZ[1299] December 12, 1910 in Patos, New México[1300], son of ATANACIO MARTÍNEZ and RAMONA DE MARTÍNEZ.

Notes for AVRELIO MARTÍNEZ:
Also known as Aurelio. He was raised by Leandro Pacheco.

Children of ROSA GAVALDON and AVRELIO MARTÍNEZ are:
 i. GUILLERMO[12] MARTÍNEZ[1301], b. December 24, 1911, Ruidoso, Territory of New México[1302]; m. CAROLINA SEDILLO[1303], February 26, 1934, Carrizozo, New México[1303].

Notes for GUILLERMO MARTÍNEZ:
Also known as Billie.

 ii. SENAIDA MARTÍNEZ, b. Abt. 1914[1304]; m. DOLORES MÁRQUEZ, September 30, 1933[1305].
 iii. MACARIO MARTÍNEZ, b. Abt. 1916[1306].
 iv. ERMINIO MARTÍNEZ[1307], b. August 12, 1919, Rebentón, New México[1308].
 v. ARTURO MARTÍNEZ[1309], b. March 04, 1921, Rebentón, New México[1310]; d. March 27, 1987.

Notes for ARTURO MARTÍNEZ:
Private. World War II.

224. LUPE[11] GAVALDON *(ELUTICIA[10] SÁNCHEZ, ESTOLANO[9], MAURICIO DE LA TRINIDAD[8] SÁNCHES, JOSÉ GREGORIO DE LA TRINIDAD[7], JUAN CRISTÓBAL[6], FRANCISCO[5], JACINTO SÁNCHES[4] DE IÑIGO, FRANCISCO MUÑOS[3] SÁNCHES, JACINTO[2] MUÑOS, FRANCISCO[1])* was born August 20, 1897 in Patos, Territory of New México[1311]. He married ELVIRA MÁRQUEZ August 13, 1921 in Rebentón, New México[1312], daughter of MELCOR MÁRQUEZ and ALEJANDRA LUERAS.

Notes for LUPE GAVALDON:
Also known as Lupito, Guadalupe Gavaldon.

Children of LUPE GAVALDON and ELVIRA MÁRQUEZ are:
    i.   ELIZA[12] GAVALDON, b. Abt. 1924[1313].
    ii.   ERINEO GAVALDON[1314], b. November 16, 1924, Rebentón, New México[1315]; m. ANTONIA OLIVAS, November 15, 1947, Carrizozo, New México[1316].
    iii. ELUTICIA GAVALDON[1317], b. September 28, 1927, Carrizozo, New México[1318]; m. FRANCISCO D. VEGA, July 11, 1948, Carrizozo, New México[1319].
    iv. ORLANDO GAVALDON[1320], b. August 09, 1929, Carrizozo, New México[1321]; m. JOSEPHINE BAROZ, January 03, 1953, Carrizozo, New México[1322].

225. ESTOLANO OROSCO[11] SÁNCHEZ *(PRECILIANO[10], ESTOLANO[9], MAURICIO DE LA TRINIDAD[8] SÁNCHES, JOSÉ GREGORIO DE LA TRINIDAD[7], JUAN CRISTÓBAL[6], FRANCISCO[5], JACINTO SÁNCHES[4] DE IÑIGO, FRANCISCO MUÑOS[3] SÁNCHES, JACINTO[2] MUÑOS, FRANCISCO[1])*[1323] was born July 07, 1915 in Rebentón, Territory of New México, and died April 05, 1985 in Hondo, New México. He married (1) EMMA PINO. He married (2) EUTILIA MONTOYA[1323], daughter of MAURICIO MONTOYA and AVRORA SÁNCHEZ.

Child of ESTOLANO SÁNCHEZ and EUTILIA MONTOYA is:
    i.   MANUEL[12] SÁNCHEZ, b. Private.

226. SORAIDA[11] SÁNCHEZ *(AURELIO[10], ESTOLANO[9], MAURICIO DE LA TRINIDAD[8] SÁNCHES, JOSÉ GREGORIO DE LA TRINIDAD[7], JUAN CRISTÓBAL[6], FRANCISCO[5], JACINTO SÁNCHES[4] DE IÑIGO, FRANCISCO MUÑOS[3] SÁNCHES, JACINTO[2] MUÑOS, FRANCISCO[1])* was born August 27, 1916 in Rebentón, Territory of New México[1324]. She married MAXIMILIANO SÁNCHEZ February 11, 1936 in Carrizozo, New México[1324], son of MAURICIO SÁNCHEZ and DELFINIA ROMERO.

Notes for MAXIMILIANO SÁNCHEZ:
Also known as Maque.

Children of SORAIDA SÁNCHEZ and MAXIMILIANO SÁNCHEZ are:
    i.   BEATRICE[12] SÁNCHEZ, b. Private; m. ANTHONY RICK SALAZAR.
    ii.   ROSE MARIE SÁNCHEZ, b. Private.

227. MACRINA[11] SÁNCHEZ *(AURELIO[10], ESTOLANO[9], MAURICIO DE LA TRINIDAD[8] SÁNCHES, JOSÉ GREGORIO DE LA TRINIDAD[7], JUAN CRISTÓBAL[6], FRANCISCO[5], JACINTO SÁNCHES[4] DE IÑIGO, FRANCISCO MUÑOS[3] SÁNCHES, JACINTO[2] MUÑOS, FRANCISCO[1])*[1325] was born September 09, 1920 in White Oaks, New México[1326], and died October 13, 2010 in Ruidoso Downs, New México[1327]. She married ANDRÉS RICHARDSON[1328] August 08, 1949 in Carrizozo, New México[1329], son of GRANVILLE RICHARDSON and AMANDA MAÉS.

Notes for ANDRÉS RICHARDSON:
Private First Class, World War II Veteran.

228. VICENTE[11] SÁNCHEZ *(AURELIO[10], ESTOLANO[9], MAURICIO DE LA TRINIDAD[8] SÁNCHES, JOSÉ GREGORIO DE LA TRINIDAD[7], JUAN CRISTÓBAL[6], FRANCISCO[5], JACINTO SÁNCHES[4] DE IÑIGO, FRANCISCO MUÑOS[3] SÁNCHES, JACINTO[2] MUÑOS, FRANCISCO[1])* was born July 08, 1922 in Ancho, New México[1330]. He married LUISA SALSBERRY July 08, 1946 in Carrizozo, New México[1330], daughter of AUGUSTÍN SALSBERRY and AGAPITA PADILLA.

Notes for VICENTE SÁNCHEZ:
1930 Census: Living in Rebentón, New México.

Notes for LUISA SALSBERRY:
Also known as Louise.

Children of VICENTE SÁNCHEZ and LUISA SALSBERRY are:
    i.   LYDIA[12] SÁNCHEZ, b. Private; m. MIKE AMARAL.
    ii.   PATRICIA SÁNCHEZ, b. Private.
    iii. LOREENA SÁNCHEZ, b. Private.
    iv. ERNIE SÁNCHEZ, b. Private.

229. IDALIA[11] SÁNCHEZ *(AURELIO[10], ESTOLANO[9], MAURICIO DE LA TRINIDAD[8] SÁNCHES, JOSÉ GREGORIO DE LA TRINIDAD[7], JUAN CRISTÓBAL[6], FRANCISCO[5], JACINTO SÁNCHES[4] DE IÑIGO, FRANCISCO MUÑOS[3] SÁNCHES, JACINTO[2] MUÑOS, FRANCISCO[1])* was born Private in Rebentón, Territory of New México[1331]. She married PETRONILO OTERO SEDILLO February 10, 1926 in Picacho, Territory of New México[1331], son of MARTÍN SEDILLO and ELENA OTERO.

Notes for PETRONILO OTERO SEDILLO:
Also known as Petro.

Children of IDALIA SÁNCHEZ and PETRONILO SEDILLO are:
    i.   JAMES[12] SEDILLO, b. Private.
    ii.   ELMO SEDILLO, b. Private.
    iii. RUBEN SEDILLO, b. Private.
    iv. DALL SEDILLO, b. Private.
    v.   GILBERT SEDILLO, b. Private.
    vi. NENA SEDILLO, b. Private.
    vii. DELLA SEDILLO, b. Private.

230. FELIS SÁNCHEZ[11] TORRES *(CELIA[10] SÁNCHEZ, ESTOLANO[9], MAURICIO DE LA TRINIDAD[8] SÁNCHES, JOSÉ GREGORIO DE LA TRINIDAD[7], JUAN CRISTÓBAL[6], FRANCISCO[5], JACINTO SÁNCHES[4] DE IÑIGO, FRANCISCO MUÑOS[3] SÁNCHES, JACINTO[2] MUÑOS, FRANCISCO[1])[1332]* was born June 04, 1909 in Lincoln, Territory of New México[1333], and died February 16, 2003 in San Patricio, New México. She married PEDRO SALCIDO[1334] October 24, 1928 in Carrizozo, New México[1335], son of FAUSTINO SALCIDO and MARÍA CHÁVES.

Notes for PEDRO SALCIDO:
Cemetary records indicate he was born on February 23, 1905.

Land Patent # NMLC 0028752, on the authority of the Homestead Entry-Stock Raising (39 Stat. 862), December 29, 1916. Issued 629.6 acres on August 22, 1930.

Child of FELIS TORRES and PEDRO SALCIDO is:
    i.   MARÍA RELIA[12] SALCIDO[1336], b. 1933, Hondo, New México; d. March 16, 1933, Tinnie, New México.

231. ELMO[11] BRADY *(ROSARITA[10] SÁNCHEZ, ESTOLANO[9], MAURICIO DE LA TRINIDAD[8] SÁNCHES, JOSÉ GREGORIO DE LA TRINIDAD[7], JUAN CRISTÓBAL[6], FRANCISCO[5], JACINTO SÁNCHES[4] DE IÑIGO, FRANCISCO MUÑOS[3] SÁNCHES, JACINTO[2] MUÑOS, FRANCISCO[1])* was born October 30, 1917 in Hondo, New México[1337], and died December 29, 2008 in Ruidoso, New México[1337]. He married GERALDINE KIMBRELL[1338] 1946 in California[1339], daughter of ALBERT KIMBRELL and CONSUELO RUBIO.

Notes for ELMO BRADY:
WW II Veteran.

Children of ELMO BRADY and GERALDINE KIMBRELL are:
    i.   PATRICK[12] BRADY[1339], b. Private.
    ii.   EMILEEN BRADY[1339], b. Private.

232. ORLIDIA[11] BRADY *(ROSARITA[10] SÁNCHEZ, ESTOLANO[9], MAURICIO DE LA TRINIDAD[8] SÁNCHES, JOSÉ GREGORIO DE LA TRINIDAD[7], JUAN CRISTÓBAL[6], FRANCISCO[5], JACINTO SÁNCHES[4] DE IÑIGO, FRANCISCO MUÑOS[3] SÁNCHES, JACINTO[2] MUÑOS, FRANCISCO[1])[1340]* was born January 06, 1920 in Hondo, New México[1341], and died March 09, 2011 in Roswell, New México. She married ANDREW FRESQUEZ[1342] March 19, 1942 in Carrizozo, New México, son of LUTARIO FRESQUEZ and TERESITA PINEDA.

Notes for ANDREW FRESQUEZ:
Also known as Andrés

Children of ORLIDIA BRADY and ANDREW FRESQUEZ are:
    i.   DELLA[12] FRESQUEZ, b. Private.
    ii.   JOYCE FRESQUEZ, b. Private.
    iii. ROBERTA FRESQUEZ, b. Private.
    iv. ANDY FRESQUEZ, b. Private.

233. PRESTINA[11] BRADY *(ROSARITA[10] SÁNCHEZ, ESTOLANO[9], MAURICIO DE LA TRINIDAD[8] SÁNCHES, JOSÉ GREGORIO DE LA TRINIDAD[7], JUAN CRISTÓBAL[6], FRANCISCO[5], JACINTO SÁNCHES[4] DE IÑIGO, FRANCISCO MUÑOS[3] SÁNCHES, JACINTO[2] MUÑOS, FRANCISCO[1])[1343]* was born March 20, 1926 in Hondo, New México, and died January 18, 1995 in Hondo, New México.

Child of PRESTINA BRADY is:
    i.   WALTER RUDY[12] BRADY, b. January 31, 1946; d. November 05, 1985.

234. BILLY JOE[11] BRADY *(ROSARITA[10] SÁNCHEZ, ESTOLANO[9], MAURICIO DE LA TRINIDAD[8] SÁNCHES, JOSÉ GREGORIO DE LA TRINIDAD[7], JUAN CRISTÓBAL[6], FRANCISCO[5], JACINTO SÁNCHES[4] DE IÑIGO, FRANCISCO MUÑOS[3] SÁNCHES, JACINTO[2] MUÑOS, FRANCISCO[1])* was born Private. He married PATSY SALCIDO.

Child of BILLY BRADY and PATSY SALCIDO is:
    i.   ROSEY[12] BRADY, b. September 14, 1978; m. PHILBERT CANDELARIA.

235. ERMINDA[11] CHÁVEZ *(ESLINDA[10] GONZÁLES, FLORENCIO[9], MARÍA MANUELA[8] ARAGÓN, MARIANA ANTONIA[7] SÁNCHES, DIEGO ANTONIO[6], FRANCISCO[5], JACINTO SÁNCHES[4] DE IÑIGO, FRANCISCO MUÑOS[3] SÁNCHES, JACINTO[2] MUÑOS, FRANCISCO[1])[1344]* was born July 12, 1894 in San Patricio, Territory of New México, and died November 01, 1956. She married (1) EPIFANIO ULIBARRÍ[1345] November 04, 1915 in Lincoln, New México[1346], son of VICENTE ULIBARRÍ and MARÍA SEDILLO. She married (2) JOSÉ JÁQUEZ[1347] May 17, 1950[1348].

Notes for EPIFANIO ULIBARRÍ:
1900 Census: Approximate birthdate listed as May 1895.

Children of ERMINDA CHÁVEZ and EPIFANIO ULIBARRÍ are:
    i.   ANUNCIÓN[12] ULIBARRÍ[1349], b. August 13, 1917, San Patricio, New México; d. September 13, 1917, San Patricio, New México.
    ii.   DIEGO ULIBARRÍ[1350], b. February 20, 1920; d. April 15, 1994, Carrizozo, New México.

236. ARCENIA[11] GONZÁLES *(PROSPERO[10], FLORENCIO[9], MARÍA MANUELA[8] ARAGÓN, MARIANA ANTONIA[7] SÁNCHES, DIEGO ANTONIO[6], FRANCISCO[5], JACINTO SÁNCHES[4] DE IÑIGO, FRANCISCO MUÑOS[3] SÁNCHES, JACINTO[2] MUÑOS, FRANCISCO[1])* was born February 20, 1898 in Glencoe, Territory of New México[1351]. She married CHARLIE CURRY[1352] December 20, 1915 in Lincoln, New México[1353], son of GEORGE CURRY and REBECCA SALAZAR.

Notes for ARCENIA GONZÁLES:
Also known as María Arcenia Gonzáles.

Notes for CHARLIE CURRY:
Also known as Charles and Chaz.
1930 Census: Living in Las Cruces, New México.

Children of ARCENIA GONZÁLES and CHARLIE CURRY are:
    i.   GEORGE[12] CURRY[1354], b. September 16, 1916, Glencoe, New México[1355]; d. March 19, 1922.
    ii.   REBECCA CURRY, b. Abt. 1921[1355].

237. RUBÉN ANDRÉS[11] GONZÁLES *(PROSPERO[10], FLORENCIO[9], MARÍA MANUELA[8] ARAGÓN, MARIANA ANTONIA[7] SÁNCHES, DIEGO ANTONIO[6], FRANCISCO[5], JACINTO SÁNCHES[4] DE IÑIGO, FRANCISCO MUÑOS[3] SÁNCHES, JACINTO[2] MUÑOS, FRANCISCO[1])* was born November 02, 1900 in Glencoe, Territory of New México[1356], and died in Artesia, New Mexico. He married DOROTEA SALSBERRY[1357] September 20, 1919 in Las Angusturas (San Ysidro), New México[1358], daughter of JAMES SALSBERRY and MANUELITA HERRERA.

Notes for RUBÉN ANDRÉS GONZÁLES:
Also known as Rubé.

Notes for DOROTEA SALSBERRY:
Church marriage records indicate that they were married on February 22, 1919. (LDS Center, Alamogordo, Microfiche # 001674, Page 130)

Children of RUBÉN GONZÁLES and DOROTEA SALSBERRY are:

    i.   OLIVIA[12] GONZÁLES, b. August 25, 1920, Glencoe, New México[1359]; d. May 27, 2005, Carlsbad, New México; m. JUAN RODRÍGUEZ, September 02, 1943.

    ii.   ADELINA GONZÁLES, b. Abt. 1922, Glencoe, New México[1359]; m. LOLO RODRÍGUEZ.

    iii.   ORALIA GONZÁLES[1360], b. Abt. 1923, Glencoe, New México[1361]; d. June 17, 1941, San Patricio, New México; m. CRISTÓVAL PEREA.

    iv.   VIOLA GONZÁLES[1362], b. April 14, 1925, San Patricio, New México; d. October 09, 2009, Alamogordo, New México; m. MANUEL P. REYES[13621363].

    v.   RUFINA GONZÁLES, b. Abt. 1928, Glencoe, New México[1364]; m. JOSÉ RODRÍGUEZ.

Notes for RUFINA GONZÁLES:
Living in San Bernadino, California.

    vi.   EMILIO GONZÁLES, b. April 05, 1927, Glencoe, New México; d. July 28, 2011, Artesia, New México; m. RACHEL ALANIZ, September 16, 1948.

    vii.   FEDELINA GONZÁLES, b. November 10, 1930, Glencoe, New México; d. May 27, 2011, Lubbock, Texas; m. COSMÉ GÓMEZ, June 29, 1960, Las Vegas, Nevada.

Notes for FEDELINA GONZÁLES:
Also known as Fela, Faye.

    viii.   HELEN GONZÁLES, b. Private, Glencoe, New México; m. MACARIO CHÁVEZ.

    ix.   REYNER GONZÁLES, b. Private, Glencoe, New México; m. MARY PADILLA.

Notes for REYNER GONZÁLES:
Living in Artesia.

    x.   RUBÉN GONZÁLES, b. August 27, 1932, Glencoe, New México; m. MANUELA PAS.

Notes for RUBÉN GONZÁLES:
Living in Carlsbad.

    xi.   TELESFORA GONZÁLES, b. Private, Glencoe, New México; m. TEMO GARCÍA.

Notes for TELESFORA GONZÁLES:
Also known as Tillie.

238. PROSPERO MIRABAL[11] GONZÁLES *(PROSPERO[10], FLORENCIO[9], MARÍA MANUELA[8] ARAGÓN, MARIANA ANTONIA[7] SÁNCHES, DIEGO ANTONIO[6], FRANCISCO[5], JACINTO SÁNCHES[4] DE IÑIGO, FRANCISCO MUÑOS[3] SÁNCHES, JACINTO[2] MUÑOS, FRANCISCO[1])* was born January 20, 1909 in Glencoe, Territory of New México[1365], and died January 17, 1960[1366]. He married AMBROCIA SILVA January 16, 1932 in Glencoe, New México[1367], daughter of TELESFORO SILVA and ERINEA BENAVIDEZ.

Children of PROSPERO GONZÁLES and AMBROCIA SILVA are:

    i.   LILIA[12] GONZÁLES, b. Private.

    ii.   FELIX GONZÁLES, b. Private.

    iii.   DORTHY GONZÁLES, b. Private.

    iv.   FLOYD GONZÁLES, b. Private.

239. CRUSITA[11] GONZÁLES *(LEOPOLDO SÁNCHEZ[10], FLORENCIO[9], MARÍA MANUELA[8] ARAGÓN, MARIANA ANTONIA[7] SÁNCHES, DIEGO ANTONIO[6], FRANCISCO[5], JACINTO SÁNCHES[4] DE IÑIGO, FRANCISCO MUÑOS[3] SÁNCHES, JACINTO[2] MUÑOS, FRANCISCO[1])* was born May 02, 1904 in San Patricio, Territory of New México[1368]. She married (1) BENITO HERRERA[1369], son of CRUZ HERRERA and REDUCINDA CARDONA. She married (2) CASIMIRO TAFOYA VILLESCAS February 14, 1925 in San Patricio, New México[1370], son of CASIMIRO VILLESCAS and EMILIANA TAFOYA.

Child of CRUSITA GONZÁLES and CASIMIRO VILLESCAS is:
    i.   ERNESTINA[12] VILLESCAS, b. Abt. 1933, San Patricio, New México[1371].

240. ELISA[11] GONZÁLES *(LEOPOLDO SÁNCHEZ[10], FLORENCIO[9], MARÍA MANUELA[8] ARAGÓN, MARIANA ANTONIA[7] SÁNCHES, DIEGO ANTONIO[6], FRANCISCO[5], JACINTO SÁNCHES[4] DE IÑIGO, FRANCISCO MUÑOS[3] SÁNCHES, JACINTO[2] MUÑOS, FRANCISCO[1])[1372]* was born February 27, 1912 in San Patricio, New México, and died April 01, 2001 in San Patricio, New México. She married MANUEL HERNÁNDEZ HERRERA[1373] November 23, 1931[1374], son of LUÍS HERRERA and BENJAMÍNA HERNÁNDEZ.

Notes for MANUEL HERNÁNDEZ HERRERA:
1940 Census: Living in San Patricio, New México.

Children of ELISA GONZÁLES and MANUEL HERRERA are:
    i.   BENJAMÍN[12] HERRERA[1375], b. August 27, 1932, San Patricio, New México; d. October 27, 1998, Ruidoso Downs, New México; m. BRIJIDA CHÁVEZ[1375], November 16, 1953, Ruidoso Downs, New México.
    ii.   BENITO HERRERA[1376], b. August 30, 1934, San Patricio, New México; d. July 23, 2002, Alburquerque, New México; m. JOSIE CHÁVEZ.

Notes for JOSIE CHÁVEZ:
Also known as Josephine.

    iii.   FLORA HERRERA[1377], b. April 30, 1936, San Patricio, New México[1378]; d. April 28, 2001, Ruidoso, New México; m. PORFIRIO SÁNCHEZ, May 04, 1952, San Patricio, New México[1378].

Notes for FLORA HERRERA:
Also known as Floripe.

Notes for PORFIRIO SÁNCHEZ:
1940 Census: Living in San Patricio, New México.

    iv.   ELENA HERRERA, b. September 10, 1939, San Patricio, New México; d. July 12, 2010, Alburquerque, New México.
    v.   LUÍS HERRERA, b. September 19, 1941, San Patricio, New México; d. January 23, 2003, Alamogordo, New México; m. CELIA O. TELLES.
    vi.   LEOPOLDO HERRERA, b. December 29, 1945, San Patricio, New México; d. June 20, 2012, San Patricio, New México; m. EMMA ZAMORA.

Notes for LEOPOLDO HERRERA:
Also known as Leo.

    vii.   JUAN HERRERA, b. May 09, 1952, Capitán, New México; d. January 22, 2011, Albuquerque, New México.

Notes for JUAN HERRERA:
Also known as Johnny Herrera.

    viii.   JOE HERRERA, b. Private.
    ix.   JOSEPHINE HERRERA, b. Private.
    x.   LUCY HERRERA, b. Private.
    xi.   MANUEL GONZÁLES HERRERA, b. Private, San Patricio, New México.
    xii.   PASQUAL HERRERA, b. Private, San Patricio, New México.

241. AGIDA[11] GONZÁLES *(EPAMINOANDAS[10], FLORENCIO[9], MARÍA MANUELA[8] ARAGÓN, MARIANA ANTONIA[7] SÁNCHES, DIEGO ANTONIO[6], FRANCISCO[5], JACINTO SÁNCHES[4] DE IÑIGO, FRANCISCO MUÑOS[3] SÁNCHES, JACINTO[2] MUÑOS, FRANCISCO[1])* was born December 05, 1900 in San Patricio, Territory of New México[1379], and died October 28, 1941[1380]. She married BENITO SALAS December 16, 1921[1381], son of CRECENCIO SALAS and LUPITA VIGIL.

Children of AGIDA GONZÁLES and BENITO SALAS are:
  i.   LUZ[12] SALAS, b. Abt. 1923[1382].
  ii.   FLORENCIO SALAS, b. Abt. 1925[1382].
  iii. LULIO SALAS, b. Abt. 1927[1383].
  iv.   ROGER SALAS, b. Abt. November 1928[1384].

242. EPAMINOANDAS GONZÁLES[11] GONZÁLES *(EPAMINOANDAS[10], FLORENCIO[9], MARÍA MANUELA[8] ARAGÓN, MARIANA ANTONIA[7] SÁNCHES, DIEGO ANTONIO[6], FRANCISCO[5], JACINTO SÁNCHES[4] DE IÑIGO, FRANCISCO MUÑOS[3] SÁNCHES, JACINTO[2] MUÑOS, FRANCISCO[1])[1385]* was born October 21, 1901 in San Patricio, Territory of New México, and died January 05, 1945. He married IGNACIA PRUDENCIO[1386] September 11, 1928 in Mescalero, New México[1387], daughter of MORTIMER PROVENCIO and CLEOFAS MUÑOZ.

Notes for EPAMINOANDAS GONZÁLES GONZÁLES:
Also known as Epaminio.

Child of EPAMINOANDAS GONZÁLES and IGNACIA PRUDENCIO is:
  i.   JOHN WILLIAM[12] GONZÁLES[1388], b. Abt. 1937, San Patricio, New México; d. July 17, 1937, San Patricio, New México.

243. CIPRIANA[11] GONZÁLES *(EPAMINOANDAS[10], FLORENCIO[9], MARÍA MANUELA[8] ARAGÓN, MARIANA ANTONIA[7] SÁNCHES, DIEGO ANTONIO[6], FRANCISCO[5], JACINTO SÁNCHES[4] DE IÑIGO, FRANCISCO MUÑOS[3] SÁNCHES, JACINTO[2] MUÑOS, FRANCISCO[1])[1389]* was born August 21, 1903 in San Patricio, Territory of New México[1390], and died November 11, 2006 in San Patricio, New México[1391]. She married VICENTE HERRERA[1392] August 27, 1932 in San Patricio, New México[1393], son of CRUZ HERRERA and PETRA DOMINGUEZ.

Notes for VICENTE HERRERA:
Also known as Bisente.

Children of CIPRIANA GONZÁLES and VICENTE HERRERA are:
  i.   RUFINO[12] HERRERA[1394], b. July 25, 1933, San Patricio, New México; d. January 17, 2006, San Patricio, New México; m. HELENA MONTOYA, April 04, 1957, San Patricio, New México.

Notes for RUFINO HERRERA:
Korean War Veteran

  ii.   BERTA HERRERA, b. January 30, 1942, San Patricio, New México[1395]; m. FRED SÁNCHEZ, July 26, 1959, Ruidoso, New México[1395].

244. FLORENCIO GONZÁLES[11] GONZÁLES *(EPAMINOANDAS[10], FLORENCIO[9], MARÍA MANUELA[8] ARAGÓN, MARIANA ANTONIA[7] SÁNCHES, DIEGO ANTONIO[6], FRANCISCO[5], JACINTO SÁNCHES[4] DE IÑIGO, FRANCISCO MUÑOS[3] SÁNCHES, JACINTO[2] MUÑOS, FRANCISCO[1])[1396]* was born September 17, 1907 in San Patricio, Territory of New México, and died October 11, 1973 in San Patricio, New México. He married ALBESITA SÁNCHEZ December 19, 1932 in San Patricio, New México[1397], daughter of JACOBO SÁNCHEZ and MARÍA TRUJILLO.

Notes for FLORENCIO GONZÁLES GONZÁLES:
Land Patent # NMLC 0041758, on the authority of the Homestead Entry-Stock Raising (39 Stat. 862), December 29, 1916. Issued 646.78 acres on January 12, 1940.

Notes for ALBESITA SÁNCHEZ:
Also known as Albesa, Alvesa.

Children of FLORENCIO GONZÁLES and ALBESITA SÁNCHEZ are:
- i.   JOSÉ[12] GONZÁLES, b. November 10, 1934, San Patricio, New México; d. August 24, 1991.
- ii.   FRANK GONZÁLES[1398], b. May 30, 1942, San Patricio, New México[1399]; d. August 05, 2006, Ruidoso Downs, New México; m. MILDRED RANDOLPH, July 09, 1961, Ruidoso, New México[1399].

Notes for FRANK GONZÁLES:
Marriage records indicate that he was born on May 30, 1941.

- iii. ELVIRA SÁNCHEZ GONZÁLES, b. Private, San Patricio, New México.
- iv.   ISAQUIO GONZÁLES, b. Private, San Patricio, New México.

245. RAFAEL[11] GONZÁLES *(EPAMINOANDAS[10], FLORENCIO[9], MARÍA MANUELA[8] ARAGÓN, MARIANA ANTONIA[7] SÁNCHES, DIEGO ANTONIO[6], FRANCISCO[5], JACINTO SÁNCHES[4] DE IÑIGO, FRANCISCO MUÑOS[3] SÁNCHES, JACINTO[2] MUÑOS, FRANCISCO[1])[1400]* was born March 23, 1914 in San Patricio, New México[1401]. He married AVRORA BACA[1402] June 05, 1936 in San Patricio, New México[1403], daughter of ELÍAS BACA and PAUBLITA ANALLA.

Children of RAFAEL GONZÁLES and AVRORA BACA are:
- i.   DOMINGO[12] GONZÁLES[1404], b. Abt. 1937, San Patricio, New México; d. October 28, 1937, San Patricio, New México.
- ii.   ARMANDO GONZÁLES[1405], b. Abt. 1940, San Patricio, New México; d. October 08, 1940, San Patricio, New México.

246. SIGISMUNDA[11] GONZÁLES *(EPAMINOANDAS[10], FLORENCIO[9], MARÍA MANUELA[8] ARAGÓN, MARIANA ANTONIA[7] SÁNCHES, DIEGO ANTONIO[6], FRANCISCO[5], JACINTO SÁNCHES[4] DE IÑIGO, FRANCISCO MUÑOS[3] SÁNCHES, JACINTO[2] MUÑOS, FRANCISCO[1])[1406]* was born February 07, 1920 in San Patricio, New México[1407]. She married ADAN SÁNCHEZ[1407] August 18, 1948 in Carrizozo, New México[1407], son of SIMÓN SÁNCHEZ and ANTONIA CARABAJAL.

Notes for ADAN SÁNCHEZ:
Lived in Arizona.

Child of SIGISMUNDA GONZÁLES and ADAN SÁNCHEZ is:
- i.   YOLANDA GONZÁLES[12] SÁNCHEZ, b. Private.

247. EVA[11] GONZÁLES *(EPAMINOANDAS[10], FLORENCIO[9], MARÍA MANUELA[8] ARAGÓN, MARIANA ANTONIA[7] SÁNCHES, DIEGO ANTONIO[6], FRANCISCO[5], JACINTO SÁNCHES[4] DE IÑIGO, FRANCISCO MUÑOS[3] SÁNCHES, JACINTO[2] MUÑOS, FRANCISCO[1])* was born Private in San Patricio, New México. She married JUAN SÁNCHEZ MONTOYA August 13, 1948 in Carrizozo, New México[1408], son of MAURICIO MONTOYA and AVRORA SÁNCHEZ.

Notes for JUAN SÁNCHEZ MONTOYA:
US Navy, Seaman First Class. World War II.

Children of EVA GONZÁLES and JUAN MONTOYA are:
- i.   RAQUEL[12] MONTOYA, b. Private.
- ii.   PORFIRIA MONTOYA, b. Private.
- iii. RICHARD MONTOYA, b. Private.

248. TRENIDAD[11] GONZÁLES *(AVRORA[10], FLORENCIO[9], MARÍA MANUELA[8] ARAGÓN, MARIANA ANTONIA[7] SÁNCHES, DIEGO ANTONIO[6], FRANCISCO[5], JACINTO SÁNCHES[4] DE IÑIGO, FRANCISCO MUÑOS[3] SÁNCHES, JACINTO[2] MUÑOS, FRANCISCO[1])[1409]* was born September 21, 1918 in San Patricio, New México[1410], and died July 01, 2010 in San Patricio, New México. She married BENINO SÁNCHEZ[1411] June 01, 1934 in Carrizozo, New México[1412], son of SIMÓN SÁNCHEZ and ANTONIA CARABAJAL.

Notes for BENINO SÁNCHEZ:
Also known as Ben.

Child of TRENIDAD GONZÁLES and BENINO SÁNCHEZ is:
  i.   SONNY[12] SÁNCHEZ, b. Private.

249. ERLINDA[11] GONZÁLES *(AVRORA[10], FLORENCIO[9], MARÍA MANUELA[8] ARAGÓN, MARIANA ANTONIA[7] SÁNCHES, DIEGO ANTONIO[6], FRANCISCO[5], JACINTO SÁNCHES[4] DE IÑIGO, FRANCISCO MUÑOS[3] SÁNCHES, JACINTO[2] MUÑOS, FRANCISCO[1])* was born November 05, 1921 in San Patricio, New México[1413]. She married ORLANDO LUCERO[1414] July 18, 1942 in Carrizozo, New México[1415], son of GEORGE LUCERO and ANITA ANALLA.

Notes for ORLANDO LUCERO:
Private First Class. World War II.

Child of ERLINDA GONZÁLES and ORLANDO LUCERO is:
  i.   ORLANDO[12] LUCERO, b. April 17, 1943, Roswell, New México; d. April 26, 2012, El Paso, Texas; m. MARGARITA PEÑA, October 10, 1970, Alamogordo, New México.

250. SIGISFREDO[11] ROMERO *(AVRORA[10] GONZÁLES, FLORENCIO[9], MARÍA MANUELA[8] ARAGÓN, MARIANA ANTONIA[7] SÁNCHES, DIEGO ANTONIO[6], FRANCISCO[5], JACINTO SÁNCHES[4] DE IÑIGO, FRANCISCO MUÑOS[3] SÁNCHES, JACINTO[2] MUÑOS, FRANCISCO[1])[1416]* was born March 31, 1903, and died November 14, 1982 in San Patricio, New México. He married LUCÍA YBARRA January 11, 1928 in Lincoln County, New México[1417], daughter of GREGORIO YBARRA and CATARINA MONTOYA.

Notes for LUCÍA YBARRA:
Also known as Luciana, Luz.
Padrinos: Augustín Laguna born in México City, and his wife, Juana María Laguna, born in Polvadera, New México

Children of SIGISFREDO ROMERO and LUCÍA YBARRA are:
  i.   FEDELINA[12] ROMERO, b. March 28, 1932, San Patricio, New México[1418]; m. ELMON RANDOLPH[1419], July 01, 1950, Carrizozo, New México[1420].

Notes for ELMON RANDOLPH:
Also known as Elmer.

  ii.   CLEOFAS ROMERO[1421], b. April 09, 1934, San Patricio, New México; d. March 17, 2007; m. JUAN SÁNCHEZ MONTES[1421], August 25, 1951, Ruidoso, New México[1422].

Notes for JUAN SÁNCHEZ MONTES:
Also known as Johnny.

  iii. SIGISFREDO YBARRA ROMERO[1423], b. August 08, 1949, San Patricio, New México; d. May 24, 2010, San Patricio, New México.
  iv.   EDUVIGEN ROMERO, b. Private, San Patricio, New México.
  v.   FLORIPE ROMERO, b. Private, San Patricio, New México.
  vi.   ISABELA ROMERO, b. Private, San Patricio, New México.
  vii. LEONIRES ROMERO, b. Private, San Patricio, New México.
  viii. REBECCA ROMERO, b. Private, San Patricio, New México.
  ix.   RUBÉN ROMERO, b. Private, San Patricio, New México.

251. MELITANA[11] ROMERO *(AVRORA[10] GONZÁLES, FLORENCIO[9], MARÍA MANUELA[8] ARAGÓN, MARIANA ANTONIA[7] SÁNCHES, DIEGO ANTONIO[6], FRANCISCO[5], JACINTO SÁNCHES[4] DE IÑIGO, FRANCISCO MUÑOS[3] SÁNCHES, JACINTO[2] MUÑOS, FRANCISCO[1])* was born February 16, 1902[1424]. She married PATROCINIO ARCHULETA CHÁVEZ[1425] July 13, 1921[1426], son of PATROCINIO CHÁVEZ and VICENTA ARCHULETA.

Notes for MELITANA ROMERO:
Also known as Meritana.

Children of MELITANA ROMERO and PATROCINIO CHÁVEZ are:
  i.   GABRIEL[12] CHÁVEZ[1427], b. 1922, Hondo, New México[1428]; d. June 07, 1942, Lincoln, New México.
  ii.   AURELIA CHÁVEZ, b. Abt. 1925, Hondo, New México[1428].

    iii.   ORALIA CHÁVEZ[1429], b. Abt. 1927, San Patricio, New México; d. April 20, 1928, San Patricio, New México.
    iv.   GLORIA CHÁVEZ, b. Abt. 1929, Hondo, New México[1430].
    v.   ADAN CHÁVEZ, b. Private, Hondo, New México.
    vi.   MOISES CHÁVEZ, b. Private, Hondo, New México.
    vii.   NORA CHÁVEZ, b. Private, Hondo, New México.
    viii.   RAY CHÁVEZ, b. Private, Hondo, New México.
    ix.   VIRGINIA ROMERO CHÁVEZ, b. Private, Hondo, New México.
    x.   BRIJIDA CHÁVEZ[1431], b. April 05, 1925, Hondo, New México[1432]; d. April 18, 2011, Ruidoso Downs, New México; m. BENJAMÍN HERRERA[1433], November 16, 1953, Ruidoso Downs, New México.

252. DULCINEA[11] POLACO *(TRANCITO[10], MARÍA ALTAGRACIA[9] GONZÁLES, MARÍA MANUELA[8] ARAGÓN, MARIANA ANTONIA[7] SÁNCHES, DIEGO ANTONIO[6], FRANCISCO[5], JACINTO SÁNCHES[4] DE IÑIGO, FRANCISCO MUÑOS[3] SÁNCHES, JACINTO[2] MUÑOS, FRANCISCO[1])* was born October 28, 1902 in San Patricio, New México[1434], and died March 25, 1990 in Ruidoso, New México[1435]. She married WILLIAM RANDOLPH[1436] July 09, 1920 in San Patricio, New México[1437], son of FRANK RANDOLPH and CATARINA BRADY.

Notes for WILLIAM RANDOLPH:
Also known as: Willie, Guillermo and Billy.

Children of DULCINEA POLACO and WILLIAM RANDOLPH are:
    i.   FRANK POLACO[12] RANDOLPH, b. Abt. 1921[1438].
    ii.   VIOLA RANDOLPH, b. Abt. 1923[1438].
    iii.   WILLIE POLACO RANDOLPH[1439], b. 1926[1440]; d. 1954.
    iv.   KYSTER RANDOLPH, b. Abt. 1929[1440].

253. TRANCITO[11] POLACO *(TRANCITO[10], MARÍA ALTAGRACIA[9] GONZÁLES, MARÍA MANUELA[8] ARAGÓN, MARIANA ANTONIA[7] SÁNCHES, DIEGO ANTONIO[6], FRANCISCO[5], JACINTO SÁNCHES[4] DE IÑIGO, FRANCISCO MUÑOS[3] SÁNCHES, JACINTO[2] MUÑOS, FRANCISCO[1])[1441]* was born September 16, 1907 in San Patricio, New México, and died December 14, 1998 in Ruidoso Downs, New México. He married MARÍA L. POLACO.

Notes for TRANCITO POLACO:
1940 Census: Living in San Patricio, New México.

Children of TRANCITO POLACO and MARÍA POLACO are:
    i.   TRANCITO[12] POLACO, b. Abt. 1934[1442]; m. RAMONA SALCIDO.
    ii.   RODOLFO POLACO, b. Abt. 1937[1442].
    iii.   VIRGINIA POLACO, b. Abt. December 1939[1442].
    iv.   LUÍS POLACO, b. July 23, 1940, San Patricio, New México[1443]; m. ERNESTINA LÓPEZ[1444], December 17, 1960, Carrizozo, New México[1445].

254. ALTAGRACIA[11] POLACO *(TRANCITO[10], MARÍA ALTAGRACIA[9] GONZÁLES, MARIA MANUELA[8] ARAGÓN, MARIANA ANTONIA[7] SÁNCHES, DIEGO ANTONIO[6], FRANCISCO[5], JACINTO SÁNCHES[4] DE IÑIGO, FRANCISCO MUÑOS[3] SÁNCHES, JACINTO[2] MUÑOS, FRANCISCO[1])* was born August 24, 1910 in San Patricio, Territory of New México[1446]. She married LEOPOLDO CHÁVEZ May 24, 1930 in Carrizozo, New México[1446], son of PABLO CHÁVEZ and AMADA SÁNCHEZ.

Notes for ALTAGRACIA POLACO:
Also known as Grace.

Children of ALTAGRACIA POLACO and LEOPOLDO CHÁVEZ are:
    i.   BREZEL[12] CHÁVEZ[1447], b. June 01, 1934; d. March 29, 1992; m. PABLITA HERRERA.
    ii.   RICHARD CHÁVEZ[1447], b. October 07, 1938; d. March 24, 2003.
    iii.   LYDIA CHÁVEZ, b. Private; m. BOBBY CHÁVEZ[1448].

Notes for BOBBY CHÁVEZ:
Died suddenly of a heart attack. He was mowing the lawn on a very hot day. He drank some very cold ice tea and went into cardiac arrest.

    iv.   ROY CHÁVEZ[1449], b. January 08, 1931, Glencoe, New México; d. February 27, 2001, Tularosa, New México; m. CRUSITA SILVA[1449].

255. ELFIGO[11] POLACO *(TRANCITO[10], MARÍA ALTAGRACIA[9] GONZÁLES, MARÍA MANUELA[8] ARAGÓN, MARIANA ANTONIA[7] SÁNCHES, DIEGO ANTONIO[6], FRANCISCO[5], JACINTO SÁNCHES[4] DE IÑIGO, FRANCISCO MUÑOS[3] SÁNCHES, JACINTO[2] MUÑOS, FRANCISCO[1])[1450]* was born April 23, 1913 in San Patricio, New México, and died August 31, 1991 in Tularosa, New México. He married CAROLINA SÁNCHEZ[1451] September 13, 1939 in Carrizozo, New México[1452], daughter of SIMÓN SÁNCHEZ and ANTONIA CARABAJAL.

Notes for ELFIGO POLACO:
Social Security Death index indicates that he was born on April 22, 1913.

Child of ELFIGO POLACO and CAROLINA SÁNCHEZ is:
  i.   LORENCITA[12] POLACO, b. August 10, 1944, San Patricio, New México; d. August 30, 1944, San Patricio, New México.

256. GENOVEVA[11] GONZÁLES *(FLORENCIO SÁNCHEZ[10], FLORENCIO[9], MARÍA MANUELA[8] ARAGÓN, MARIANA ANTONIA[7] SÁNCHES, DIEGO ANTONIO[6], FRANCISCO[5], JACINTO SÁNCHES[4] DE IÑIGO, FRANCISCO MUÑOS[3] SÁNCHES, JACINTO[2] MUÑOS, FRANCISCO[1])[1453]* was born April 11, 1915 in San Patricio, New México, and died June 09, 1998 in Glencoe, New México. She married ERNESTO SILVA[1453] February 02, 1933 in San Patricio, New México[1454], son of JULIAN SILVA and MARÍA SÁNCHEZ.

Notes for GENOVEVA GONZÁLES:
Also known as Geneva.

Notes for ERNESTO SILVA:
US Navy, Seaman Second Class. World War II.

Children of GENOVEVA GONZÁLES and ERNESTO SILVA are:
  i.   JOSEPHINE[12] SILVA, b. November 30, 1934, Glencoe, New México; m. WILLIAM GÓMEZ.

Notes for JOSEPHINE SILVA:
Also known as Josie.

  ii. ERNEST SILVA, b. February 15, 1939, Glencoe, New México[1455]; m. MINNIE SÁNCHEZ, January 22, 1961, San Patricio, New México[1455].

Notes for MINNIE SÁNCHEZ:
Also known as Erminda Gloria Sánchez.

  iii. JESUSITA SILVA, b. Private, Glencoe, New México.

257. ELOY CHÁVEZ[11] GONZÁLES *(FLORENCIO SÁNCHEZ[10], FLORENCIO[9], MARÍA MANUELA[8] ARAGÓN, MARIANA ANTONIA[7] SÁNCHES, DIEGO ANTONIO[6], FRANCISCO[5], JACINTO SÁNCHES[4] DE IÑIGO, FRANCISCO MUÑOS[3] SÁNCHES, JACINTO[2] MUÑOS, FRANCISCO[1])* was born May 28, 1933 in San Patricio, New México[1456]. He married ANDREA DELOVINA ROMERO February 08, 1958 in Carrizozo, New México[1456].

Children of ELOY GONZÁLES and ANDREA ROMERO are:
  i.   FRANK[12] GONZÁLES, b. Private.
  ii. IRVIN GONZÁLES, b. Private.

Notes for IRVIN GONZÁLES:
2005: Living in Tularosa, New México.

258. REYNALDA[11] SÁNCHEZ *(NAPOLEÓN[10], FRANCISCO[9], MAURICIO DE LA TRINIDAD[8] SÁNCHES, JOSÉ GREGORIO DE LA TRINIDAD[7], JUAN CRISTÓBAL[6], FRANCISCO[5], JACINTO SÁNCHES[4] DE IÑIGO, FRANCISCO MUÑOS[3] SÁNCHES, JACINTO[2] MUÑOS, FRANCISCO[1])[1457]* was born February 21, 1905 in San Patricio, Territory of New México, and died May 12, 1970 in San Patricio, New México. She married ANISETO OLGUÍN LUCERO[1457], son of HINIO LUCERO and MANUELITA OLGUÍN.

Notes for ANISETO OLGUÍN LUCERO:

Buried: San Patricio.

Children of REYNALDA SÁNCHEZ and ANISETO LUCERO are:

    i.   LEONIRES[12] LUCERO, b. 1926, San Patricio, New México[1458].

    ii.   MARÍA SÁNCHEZ LUCERO[1459], b. September 23, 1931, San Patricio, New México[1460]; d. September 16, 1994, Roswell, New México; m. (1) RALPH RODELA; m. (2) EMILIANO CHÁVEZ[1461], April 25, 1947, Carrizozo, New México[1462].

Notes for MARÍA SÁNCHEZ LUCERO:
Also known as Mary.

Notes for RALPH RODELA:
Also known as Rafael Rodela. Raised by Isabel and Concha Montoya in San Patricio.

Notes for EMILIANO CHÁVEZ:
Served with N.M.2516 Base Unit AAF, and was a WW II veteran. He was murdered in California.
Buried: San Patricio.

    iii.   FELIS LUCERO[1463], b. July 12, 1934, San Patricio, New México[1464]; m. (1) EMILIANO VILLESCAS, March 05, 1952, Carrizozo, New México[1464]; m. (2) JAMES J. LARSON, May 08, 1961, Ruidoso, New México[1465].

Notes for EMILIANO VILLESCAS:
Also known as Emiliano Torres, Villescas.
NM Sgt, Comp 11, Armed Cavalry, Korea.

    iv.   EFFIE LUCERO[1466], b. Abt. 1939, San Patricio, New México[1467].
    v.   JOSEPH LUCERO, b. Abt. 1940, San Patricio, New México[1467]; m. DORIS LUCERO.

Notes for JOSEPH LUCERO:
Living in Roswell, New México.

    vi.   ANISETO SÁNCHEZ LUCERO, b. Private, San Patricio, New México.

Notes for ANISETO SÁNCHEZ LUCERO:
Living in Albuquerque, New México.

    vii.   EURAQUIO LUCERO, b. Private, San Patricio, New México.
    viii.   JESSIE LUCERO, b. Private, San Patricio, New México.
    ix.   REYNALDA LUCERO, b. Private, San Patricio, New México.

259. JOSEFITA ARCHULETA[11] SÁNCHEZ *(DAVÍD[10], FRANCISCO[9], MAURICIO DE LA TRINIDAD[8] SÁNCHES, JOSÉ GREGORIO DE LA TRINIDAD[7], JUAN CRISTÓBAL[6], FRANCISCO[5], JACINTO SÁNCHES[4] DE IÑIGO, FRANCISCO MUÑOS[3] SÁNCHES, JACINTO[2] MUÑOS, FRANCISCO[1])* was born Abt. 1905 in San Patricio, Territory of New México[1468]. She married PEDRO GARCÍA Abt. 1927[1469].

Notes for JOSEFITA ARCHULETA SÁNCHEZ:
Also known as Josephine.

Child of JOSEFITA SÁNCHEZ and PEDRO GARCÍA is:
    i.   ELENOR[12] GARCÍA, b. Abt. 1929[1469].

260. ADELAIDA[11] SÁNCHEZ *(DAVÍD[10], FRANCISCO[9], MAURICIO DE LA TRINIDAD[8] SÁNCHES, JOSÉ GREGORIO DE LA TRINIDAD[7], JUAN CRISTÓBAL[6], FRANCISCO[5], JACINTO SÁNCHES[4] DE IÑIGO, FRANCISCO MUÑOS[3] SÁNCHES, JACINTO[2] MUÑOS, FRANCISCO[1])* was born July 06, 1915 in San Patricio, New México[1470]. She married LEOPOLDO SEDILLOS[1470] April 14, 1946[1471], son of SIXTO SEDILLOS and MARGARITA OLGUÍN.

Children of ADELAIDA SÁNCHEZ and LEOPOLDO SEDILLOS are:

    ii.   FRANCIS[12] SEDILLOS, b. Private; m. LUVÍN SÁNCHEZ.

    iii.   TITO SEDILLOS, b. Private.

261. MARGARITA ROMERO[11] SÁNCHEZ *(ANTONIO[10], FRANCISCO[9], MAURICIO DE LA TRINIDAD[8] SÁNCHES, JOSÉ GREGORIO DE LA TRINIDAD[7], JUAN CRISTÓBAL[6], FRANCISCO[5], JACINTO SÁNCHES[4] DE IÑIGO, FRANCISCO MUÑOS[3] SÁNCHES, JACINTO[2] MUÑOS, FRANCISCO[1])[1472]* was born August 22, 1903 in San Patricio, Territory of New México[1473], and died January 31, 2004 in Artesia, New México. She married ROBERTO PÉREZ[1474] Abt. 1929 in Crowley, Colorado[1475].

Notes for MARGARITA ROMERO SÁNCHEZ:
Also known as Margaret or Marge.

Notes for ROBERTO PÉREZ:
1930 Census: Living in Crowley, Colorado.
1940 Census: Living in San Patricio, New México.

Children of MARGARITA SÁNCHEZ and ROBERTO PÉREZ are:

    i.   HELEN L.[12] PÉREZ, b. March 1930, Crowley, Colorado[1475].

    ii.   FRANCIS PÉREZ, b. Abt. 1930[1476].

    iii. ANATALIA PÉREZ, b. Abt. 1933[1476].

    iv. MARTHA PÉREZ, b. Abt. 1937[1476].

262. ROMÁN[11] SÁNCHEZ *(MAURICIO[10], FRANCISCO[9], MAURICIO DE LA TRINIDAD[8] SÁNCHES, JOSÉ GREGORIO DE LA TRINIDAD[7], JUAN CRISTÓBAL[6], FRANCISCO[5], JACINTO SÁNCHES[4] DE IÑIGO, FRANCISCO MUÑOS[3] SÁNCHES, JACINTO[2] MUÑOS, FRANCISCO[1])[1477]* was born April 23, 1904 in San Patricio, Territory of New México[1478], and died February 08, 1973 in Ruidoso, New México. He married FLORINDA SALSBERRY[1479] February 20, 1927 in Mescalero, New Mexico[1480], daughter of JAMES SALSBERRY and MANUELITA HERRERA.

Notes for ROMÁN SÁNCHEZ:
May 29, 1904: Baptized by Román Barragán and his wife Andrea Torres de Barragán in San Patricio. Baptismal records state that he was born on April 23, 1904.
Lived most of his childhood with Román Barragán and his wife Andrea Torres de Barragán
Farm was located on land originally patented to Esiquio Sánchez.
Died in an automobile accident in Ruidoso Downs.
Buried: La Capilla de San Patricio

Notes for FLORINDA SALSBERRY:
Florinda was born on the Rancho Salsberry by Cañon de Salsberry. The house is no longer standing but a grove of trees is all that remains.

1910 Census: Listed as Manuelita Salsberry born March 1910.

Children of ROMÁN SÁNCHEZ and FLORINDA SALSBERRY are:

    i.   ERNESTO[12] SÁNCHEZ, b. April 09, 1928, San Patricio, New México[1481]; m. ORALIA CHÁVEZ, March 20, 1948, Ruidoso, New México[1481].

Notes for ERNESTO SÁNCHEZ:
Also known as José Ernesto Sánchez, Ernest S. Sánchez.

    ii.   MADELENA SÁNCHEZ[1482], b. Abt. 1930, San Patricio, New México; d. December 19, 1932, San Patricio, New México.

Notes for MADELENA SÁNCHEZ:
Died young after she contracted an illness. She was born as the second child.

    iii. DELFINIA OLIDIA SÁNCHEZ, b. April 18, 1934, San Patricio, New México; m. LEANDRO VEGA, December 27, 1958, Hondo, New México.

Notes for LEANDRO VEGA:
Korean War Veteran.
Served as a Lincoln County Deputy Sheriff from 1960-1964, and from 1968-1972. He served as Lincoln County Sheriff from 1964-1968, and from 1972-1976. He served as a criminal investigator for 18 years for the 12ᵗʰ Judicial District.

    iv.   ORLANDO SÁNCHEZ, b. April 03, 1936, San Patricio, New México; m. CHRISTINA SÁNCHEZ.
    v.   FLORA MARÍA SÁNCHEZ, b. March 24, 1938, Capitán, New México; m. RICHARD VEGA.
    vi.   FRED SÁNCHEZ, b. May 30, 1940, Fort Stanton, New México[1483]; m. BERTA HERRERA, July 26, 1959, Ruidoso, New México[1483].
    vii.   BREZEL ROBERT SÁNCHEZ, b. November 04, 1941, Capitán, New México[1484]; m. MINNIE ROMERO, June 15, 1963, Hondo, New México[1484].

Notes for BREZEL ROBERT SÁNCHEZ:
Moved to Roswell, New México.

Notes for MINNIE ROMERO:
Also known as Erminia Romero.

    viii.   GERALDINE ELSIE SÁNCHEZ, b. January 10, 1945, Artesia, New México; m. ROBERT MONTES.

Notes for GERALDINE ELSIE SÁNCHEZ:
Also known as Geralda.

Notes for ROBERT MONTES:
Also known as Bobby.

    ix.   LUVÍN SÁNCHEZ, b. October 23, 1947, San Patricio, New México; m. (1) GLORIA BACA; m. (2) FRANCIS SEDILLOS.
    x.   CYNTHIA VIOLANDA SÁNCHEZ[1485], b. September 10, 1950, Capitán, New México[1486]; d. April 27, 1986, Rio Rancho, New México; m. BERRY VANDERWALL, December 22, 1972, San Patricio, New México[1486].

Notes for CYNTHIA VIOLANDA SÁNCHEZ:
Also known as Cynthia.

    xi.   MAURICIO SÁNCHEZ, b. Abt. 1952, San Patricio, New México.

Notes for MAURICIO SÁNCHEZ:
Died Young.

    xii.   ROMÁN SÁNCHEZ, JR., b. March 13, 1954, Ruidoso, New México[1487]; m. YOVANNE SALAS, May 25, 1974, Ruidoso, New México[1487].

263. MAXIMILIANO[11] SÁNCHEZ *(MAURICIO[10], FRANCISCO[9], MAURICIO DE LA TRINIDAD[8] SÁNCHES, JOSÉ GREGORIO DE LA TRINIDAD[7], JUAN CRISTÓBAL[6], FRANCISCO[5], JACINTO SÁNCHES[4] DE IÑIGO, FRANCISCO MUÑOS[3] SÁNCHES, JACINTO[2] MUÑOS, FRANCISCO[1])* was born June 22, 1911 in San Patricio, Territory of New México[1488], and died April 15, 1972. He married SORAIDA SÁNCHEZ February 11, 1936 in Carrizozo, New México[1488], daughter of AURELIO SÁNCHEZ and ANASTACIA ARAGÓN.

Notes for MAXIMILIANO SÁNCHEZ:
Also known as Maque.
Buried in Santa Fé, New México.

Children of MAXIMILIANO SÁNCHEZ and SORAIDA SÁNCHEZ are:
    i.   BEATRICE[12] SÁNCHEZ, b. Private; m. ANTHONY RICK SALAZAR.
    ii.   ROSE MARIE SÁNCHEZ, b. Private.

264. MARÍA[11] SÁNCHEZ *(MAURICIO[10], FRANCISCO[9], MAURICIO DE LA TRINIDAD[8] SÁNCHES, JOSÉ GREGORIO DE LA TRINIDAD[7], JUAN CRISTÓBAL[6], FRANCISCO[5], JACINTO SÁNCHES[4] DE IÑIGO, FRANCISCO MUÑOS[3] SÁNCHES, JACINTO[2] MUÑOS, FRANCISCO[1])* was born April 19, 1919 in San Patricio, New México[1489], and died July 31, 1966 in Los Lunas, New México. She married MANUEL CHÁVEZ, son of PREDICANDO CHÁVEZ and REMEDIOS VIGIL.

Notes for MARÍA SÁNCHEZ:
Also known as Marillita and Mary.

Children of MARÍA SÁNCHEZ and MANUEL CHÁVEZ are:
    i.   WILLIE M.[12] CHÁVEZ, b. December 07, 1941; d. February 22, 1982.
    ii.   VIRGINIA CHÁVEZ, b. January 16, 1943; d. August 31, 1994.
    iii.   ANDY P. CHÁVEZ, b. 1946; d. 1971.
    iv.   DENNIS CHÁVEZ, b. October 23, 1952; m. BELINDA CHÁVEZ.
    v.   CLIFFORD CHÁVEZ, b. Private.
    vi.   LUISA CHÁVEZ, b. Private.

265. JESÚSITA[11] SÁNCHEZ *(MAURICIO[10], FRANCISCO[9], MAURICIO DE LA TRINIDAD[8] SÁNCHES, JOSÉ GREGORIO DE LA TRINIDAD[7], JUAN CRISTÓBAL[6], FRANCISCO[5], JACINTO SÁNCHES[4] DE IÑIGO, FRANCISCO MUÑOS[3] SÁNCHES, JACINTO[2] MUÑOS, FRANCISCO[1])* was born September 19, 1922 in San Patricio, New México, and died July 16, 1992 in Albuquerque, New México. She married MAX SILVA November 16, 1942 in Tomé, New México[1490].

Notes for JESÚSITA SÁNCHEZ:
Also known as Susie.

Notes for MAX SILVA:
Also known as Maqué José Silva, Marc.
Was a WW II veteran.

Children of JESÚSITA SÁNCHEZ and MAX SILVA are:
    i.   PATRICK[12] SILVA, b. February 23, 1949; m. MARGARET SILVA.
    ii.   ANTHONY SILVA, b. Private.
    iii.   FRANK SILVA, b. Private.
    iv.   JIMMIE SILVA, b. Private.
    v.   RENÉ SILVA, b. Private; Adopted child.
    vi.   RICHARD SILVA, b. Private.

266. ABSALÓN[11] SÁNCHEZ *(PATRICIO[10], FRANCISCO[9], MAURICIO DE LA TRINIDAD[8] SÁNCHES, JOSÉ GREGORIO DE LA TRINIDAD[7], JUAN CRISTÓBAL[6], FRANCISCO[5], JACINTO SÁNCHES[4] DE IÑIGO, FRANCISCO MUÑOS[3] SÁNCHES, JACINTO[2] MUÑOS, FRANCISCO[1])[1491]* was born February 04, 1916 in San Patricio, New México[1492], and died January 10, 1996 in Alamogordo, New México. He married TAVIANA MONTOYA[1493] August 25, 1945 in San Patricio, New México[1494], daughter of MAURICIO MONTOYA and AVRORA SÁNCHEZ.

Notes for ABSALÓN SÁNCHEZ:
Also known as Ausolón Sánchez. World War II Veteran.

Children of ABSALÓN SÁNCHEZ and TAVIANA MONTOYA are:
    i.   JERRY[12] SÁNCHEZ, b. Private.
    ii.   RUDY SÁNCHEZ, b. Private.
    iii.   BEATRICE SÁNCHEZ, b. Private.

267. ERMINIA[11] SÁNCHEZ *(PATRICIO[10], FRANCISCO[9], MAURICIO DE LA TRINIDAD[8] SÁNCHES, JOSÉ GREGORIO DE LA TRINIDAD[7], JUAN CRISTÓBAL[6], FRANCISCO[5], JACINTO SÁNCHES[4] DE IÑIGO, FRANCISCO MUÑOS[3] SÁNCHES, JACINTO[2] MUÑOS, FRANCISCO[1])[1495]* was born September 29, 1922 in San Patricio, New México[1496]. She married SEVERO M. GALLEGOS September 09, 1939 in Carrizozo, New México[1497].

Children of ERMINIA SÁNCHEZ and SEVERO GALLEGOS are:
    i.   ESMILO[12] GALLEGOS[1498], b. February 16, 1951, San Patricio, New México; d. July 07, 2009, Las Cruces, New México.

Notes for ESMILO GALLEGOS:
Also known as Milo.

    ii.   OLIVIA GALLEGOS[1498], b. Private.

    iii.   GLORIA GALLEGOS*1498*, b. Private.
    iv.   MARY LOU GALLEGOS*1498*, b. Private.
    v.   LUCY GALLEGOS*1498*, b. Private.
    vi.   VICTOR WILLIAM GALLEGOS*1498*, b. Private.

Notes for VICTOR WILLIAM GALLEGOS:
Also known as Billy.

    vii.   PATRICIA GALLEGOS*1498*, b. Private.
    viii.   MONROE GALLEGOS*1498*, b. Private.

268. CELIA[11] SÁNCHEZ *(PATRICIO[10], FRANCISCO[9], MAURICIO DE LA TRINIDAD[8] SÁNCHES, JOSÉ GREGORIO DE LA TRINIDAD[7], JUAN CRISTÓBAL[6], FRANCISCO[5], JACINTO SÁNCHES[4] DE IÑIGO, FRANCISCO MUÑOS[3] SÁNCHES, JACINTO[2] MUÑOS, FRANCISCO[1])[1499]* was born July 19, 1929 in San Patricio, New México*1500*, and died October 05, 2003. She married MANUEL SÁNCHEZ MONTOYA, son of MAURICIO MONTOYA and AVRORA SÁNCHEZ.

Notes for MANUEL SÁNCHEZ MONTOYA:
WW II Veteran.

Children of CELIA SÁNCHEZ and MANUEL MONTOYA are:
    i.   JERRY[12] MONTOYA, b. Private; m. CHARLOTTE MONTOYA.
    ii.   JIMMY MONTOYA, b. Private.
    iii.   MANUEL MONTOYA, b. Private.
    iv.   HENRY MONTOYA, b. Private.
    v.   RUEBEN MONTOYA, b. Private.
    vi.   JOSEFINA MONTOYA.

Notes for JOSEFINA MONTOYA:
Died young.

    vii.   HELEN MONTOYA.

Notes for HELEN MONTOYA:
Died young.

269. ALBESITA[11] SÁNCHEZ *(JACOBO[10], FRANCISCO[9], MAURICIO DE LA TRINIDAD[8] SÁNCHES, JOSÉ GREGORIO DE LA TRINIDAD[7], JUAN CRISTÓBAL[6], FRANCISCO[5], JACINTO SÁNCHES[4] DE IÑIGO, FRANCISCO MUÑOS[3] SÁNCHES, JACINTO[2] MUÑOS, FRANCISCO[1])* was born March 10, 1914 in San Patricio, New México*1501*. She married FLORENCIO GONZÁLES GONZÁLES*1502* December 19, 1932 in San Patricio, New México*1503*, son of EPAMINOANDAS GONZÁLES and ELVIRA GONZÁLES.

Notes for ALBESITA SÁNCHEZ:
Also known as Albesa, Alvesa.

Notes for FLORENCIO GONZÁLES GONZÁLES:
Land Patent # NMLC 0041758, on the authority of the Homestead Entry-Stock Raising (39 Stat. 862), December 29, 1916. Issued 646.78 acres on January 12, 1940.

Children of ALBESITA SÁNCHEZ and FLORENCIO GONZÁLES are:
    i.   JOSÉ[12] GONZÁLES, b. November 10, 1934, San Patricio, New México; d. August 24, 1991.
    ii.   FRANK GONZÁLES*1504*, b. May 30, 1942, San Patricio, New México*1505*; d. August 05, 2006, Ruidoso Downs, New México; m. MILDRED RANDOLPH, July 09, 1961, Ruidoso, New México*1505*.

Notes for FRANK GONZÁLES:
Marriage records indicate that he was born on May 30, 1941.

    iii.   ELVIRA SÁNCHEZ GONZÁLES, b. Private, San Patricio, New México.
    iv.   ISAQUIO GONZÁLES, b. Private, San Patricio, New México.

270. PILAR TRUJILLO[11] SÁNCHEZ *(JACOBO[10], FRANCISCO[9], MAURICIO DE LA TRINIDAD[8] SÁNCHES, JOSÉ GREGORIO DE LA TRINIDAD[7], JUAN CRISTÓBAL[6], FRANCISCO[5], JACINTO SÁNCHES[4] DE IÑIGO, FRANCISCO MUÑOS[3] SÁNCHES, JACINTO[2] MUÑOS, FRANCISCO[1])[1506]* was born July 16, 1917 in San Patricio, New México[1507], and died September 20, 1999 in Ruidoso Downs, New México. She married SYLVANO MOYA SÁNCHEZ[1508] August 23, 1934 in San Patricio, New México[1509], son of CELESTINO SÁNCHEZ and NAVORSITA MOYA.

Notes for SYLVANO MOYA SÁNCHEZ:
Also known as Silvano.

Children of PILAR SÁNCHEZ and SYLVANO SÁNCHEZ are:
    i.   SANTIAGO SÁNCHEZ[12] SÁNCHEZ, b. Private.
    ii.   REYNALDO SÁNCHEZ SÁNCHEZ, b. Private.
    iii.   JUAN SÁNCHEZ SÁNCHEZ, b. Private.
    iv.   MARY SÁNCHEZ SÁNCHEZ, b. Private.
    v.   ELOISA SÁNCHEZ SÁNCHEZ, b. Private.
    vi.   TONI SÁNCHEZ, b. Private.
    vii.   AMIE SÁNCHEZ, b. Private.
    viii.   LELA SÁNCHEZ, b. Private.
    ix.   EMMA SÁNCHEZ, b. Private.
    x.   CHRIS SÁNCHEZ, b. Private.
    xi.   RAMÓN SÁNCHEZ SÁNCHEZ, b. Private.
    xii.   LEO SÁNCHEZ, b. Private.

271. ESTER[11] SÁNCHEZ *(JACOBO[10], FRANCISCO[9], MAURICIO DE LA TRINIDAD[8] SÁNCHES, JOSÉ GREGORIO DE LA TRINIDAD[7], JUAN CRISTÓBAL[6], FRANCISCO[5], JACINTO SÁNCHES[4] DE IÑIGO, FRANCISCO MUÑOS[3] SÁNCHES, JACINTO[2] MUÑOS, FRANCISCO[1])[1510]* was born September 30, 1920 in San Patricio, New México[1511], and died 1966. She married PATROCINIO ARCHULETA CHÁVEZ[1512] January 16, 1954 in Palo Verde, New México[1513], son of PATROCINIO CHÁVEZ and VICENTA ARCHULETA.

Children of ESTER SÁNCHEZ and PATROCINIO CHÁVEZ are:
    i.   VICENTA[12] CHÁVEZ, b. Private.
    ii.   PATSY CHÁVEZ, b. Private.
    iii.   MARGARET CHÁVEZ, b. Private.
    iv.   ROGER CHÁVEZ, b. Private.

272. SOFIO[11] SÁNCHEZ *(RAYMUNDO[10], JUAN RAFAEL BERCELÓ[9] SÁNCHES, JUAN RAFAEL FERNANDO[8], MANUEL RAFAEL[7], PEDRO[6], JACINTO[5], JOSÉ SÁNCHES[4] DE IÑIGO, JACINTO SÁNCHES[3], FRANCISCO MUÑOS[2] SÁNCHES, JACINTO[1] MUÑOS)[1514]* was born May 25, 1916 in San Patricio, New México[1515], and died May 25, 1984 in San Patricio, New México. He married GONSAGITA SALAS[1516] May 29, 1939 in Carrizozo, New México[1516], daughter of PEDRO SALAS and TEOFILA BENAVIDES.

Children of SOFIO SÁNCHEZ and GONSAGITA SALAS are:
    i.   ELMON[12] SÁNCHEZ, b. Private; m. CECILIA GÓMEZ.

Notes for ELMON SÁNCHEZ:
Also known as Elmo.

    ii.   RAY SÁNCHEZ, b. Private.
    iii.   RICHARD SÁNCHEZ, b. Private.
    iv.   ADELINA SÁNCHEZ, b. Private.
    v.   PRISCILLA SÁNCHEZ, b. Private.
    vi.   ELENOR SÁNCHEZ, b. Private.
    vii.   FRANCES SÁNCHEZ, b. Private; m. (1) JAMES SALAS; m. (2) TITO SALCIDO.
    viii.   FILBERT SÁNCHEZ, b. Private.
    ix.   IDA SÁNCHEZ, b. Private.
    x.   JERRY SÁNCHEZ, b. Private.

273. ANEDA ULIBARRÍ[11] SÁNCHEZ *(RAYMUNDO[10], JUAN RAFAEL BERCELÓ[9] SÁNCHES, JUAN RAFAEL FERNANDO[8], MANUEL RAFAEL[7], PEDRO[6], JACINTO[5], JOSÉ SÁNCHES[4] DE IÑIGO, JACINTO SÁNCHES[3],*

FRANCISCO MUÑOS² SÁNCHES, JACINTO¹ MUÑOS) was born July 12, 1918 in San Patricio, New México[1517], and died September 24, 1999. She married ERMANDO CHÁVEZ[1518] September 13, 1941 in Carrizozo, New México[1519], son of PABLO CHÁVEZ and AMADA SÁNCHEZ.

Children of ANEDA SÁNCHEZ and ERMANDO CHÁVEZ are:
- i.   ABRAHAM¹² CHÁVEZ[1520], b. November 28, 1946, San Patricio, New México; d. October 30, 1998, San Patricio, New México.
- ii. OZIEL CHÁVEZ[1521], b. Private.

274. TEODORO SÁNCHEZ¹¹ PEÑA *(AMADITA¹⁰ SÁNCHEZ, JUAN RAFAEL BERCELÓ⁹ SÁNCHES, JUAN RAFAEL FERNANDO⁸, MANUEL RAFAEL⁷, PEDRO⁶, JACINTO⁵, JOSÉ SÁNCHES⁴ DE IÑIGO, JACINTO SÁNCHES³, FRANCISCO MUÑOS² SÁNCHES, JACINTO¹ MUÑOS)*[1522] was born December 19, 1903 in Glencoe, Territory of New México, and died April 13, 1968 in Tularosa, New México. He married TELESFORA SÁNCHEZ[1522] March 01, 1926 in Carrizozo, New México[1523], daughter of SALOMON SÁNCHEZ and JENNIE GILL.

Notes for TEODORO SÁNCHEZ PEÑA:
1930 Census: Living in Tularosa, New México.

Children of TEODORO PEÑA and TELESFORA SÁNCHEZ are:
- i.   JOSEPHINE¹² PEÑA, b. Abt. 1927[1524].
- ii. LUÍS SÁNCHEZ PEÑA[1525], b. May 30, 1933; d. November 14, 1984.

Notes for LUÍS SÁNCHEZ PEÑA:
Corporal in the US Army, Korea.

- iii. REYES PEÑA[1526], b. October 05, 1940, Glencoe, New México; d. March 06, 1997, Roswell, New México.
- iv.   IDALIA PEÑA, b. Private.
- v.   RAFAEL PEÑA, b. Private.
- vi.   TEODORO SÁNCHEZ PEÑA, b. Private.

275. ALVESITA¹¹ MONTOYA *(BERSABÉ¹⁰ SÁNCHEZ, JUAN RAFAEL BERCELÓ⁹ SÁNCHES, JUAN RAFAEL FERNANDO⁸, MANUEL RAFAEL⁷, PEDRO⁶, JACINTO⁵, JOSÉ SÁNCHES⁴ DE IÑIGO, JACINTO SÁNCHES³, FRANCISCO MUÑOS² SÁNCHES, JACINTO¹ MUÑOS)*[1527] was born January 26, 1921 in Glencoe, New México[1528]. She married CARLOS SÁNCHEZ[1529] July 22, 1940 in Glencoe, New México[1530], son of SALOMON SÁNCHEZ and MANUELITA SÁNCHEZ.

Notes for ALVESITA MONTOYA:
Also known as Albesa.

Notes for CARLOS SÁNCHEZ:
Lived almost his entire life in Ruidoso, NM.

Children of ALVESITA MONTOYA and CARLOS SÁNCHEZ are:
- i.   OLA¹² SÁNCHEZ, b. Private.
- ii. ROBERT SÁNCHEZ, b. Private.
- iii. RICHARD SÁNCHEZ, b. Private.

276. ARISTEO¹¹ CHÁVEZ *(TRANSITO¹⁰, AMADA⁹ SÁNCHEZ, MAURICIO DE LA TRINIDAD⁸ SÁNCHES, JOSÉ GREGORIO DE LA TRINIDAD⁷, JUAN CRISTÓBAL⁶, FRANCISCO⁵, JACINTO SÁNCHES⁴ DE IÑIGO, FRANCISCO MUÑOS³ SÁNCHES, JACINTO² MUÑOS, FRANCISCO¹)*[1531] was born November 30, 1910 in Hondo, New México[1532], and died August 21, 1993 in San Patricio, New México. He married CRISTINA ROMERO[1533] February 10, 1936 in San Patricio, New México[1534], daughter of GEORGE ROMERO and JOSEFITA TORRES.

Children of ARISTEO CHÁVEZ and CRISTINA ROMERO are:
- i.   LYDIA¹² CHÁVEZ, b. June 22, 1940, San Patricio, New México[1535]; m. BARNEY RUE, May 23, 1959, Ruidoso, New México[1535].
- ii. RAYNER CHÁVEZ, b. December 17, 1941, San Patricio, New México; d. December 05, 2011, Ruidoso, New México; m. BONNIE ZAMORA, December 27, 1972, Las Vegas, Nevada.
- iii. HELEN CHÁVEZ, b. April 05, 1949; m. GILBERT CHÁVEZ.

    iv.   LILLIAN CHÁVEZ, b. March 08, 1956.
    v.   ADELINA CHÁVEZ, b. Private.
    vi.   ARTURO CHÁVEZ, b. Private.
    vii.   BENJAMIN CHÁVEZ, b. Private.
    viii.   CHARLIE CHÁVEZ, b. Private.
    ix.   DOLORES CHÁVEZ, b. Private.
    x.   ESPERANZA CHÁVEZ, b. Private.
    xi.   FELIX CHÁVEZ, b. Private; m. AMY JANE CONTRERAS.
    xii.   ISRAEL CHÁVEZ, b. Private.
    xiii.   MARÍA CHÁVEZ, b. Private.
    xiv.   MODESTO CHÁVEZ, b. Private.
    xv.   MONROY CHÁVEZ, b. Private.
    xvi.   RUEBEN CHÁVEZ, b. Private.
    xvii.   THERESA CHÁVEZ, b. Private.

277. HERALDO MODESTO[11] CHÁVEZ *(TRANSITO[10], AMADA[9] SÁNCHEZ, MAURICIO DE LA TRINIDAD[8] SÁNCHES, JOSÉ GREGORIO DE LA TRINIDAD[7], JUAN CRISTÓBAL[6], FRANCISCO[5], JACINTO SÁNCHES[4] DE IÑIGO, FRANCISCO MUÑOS[3] SÁNCHES, JACINTO[2] MUÑOS, FRANCISCO[1])[1536]* was born December 09, 1922 in Hondo, New México, and died July 26, 1965 in Hondo, New México. He married EVALINA MAE DUTCHOVER[1537] February 11, 1946 in Carrizozo, New México[1538], daughter of JOSÉ DUTCHOVER and ANITA NIETO.

Notes for EVALINA MAE DUTCHOVER:
Also known as Eva Mae.
Lived in Lincoln County since 1946.

Children of HERALDO CHÁVEZ and EVALINA DUTCHOVER are:
    i.   ALICE[12] CHÁVEZ, b. Private; m. PORFIRIO ROMERO[1539].
    ii.   BETTY CHÁVEZ, b. Private.
    iii.   DICKIE CHÁVEZ, b. Private.
    iv.   HAROLD CHÁVEZ, b. Private.
    v.   JIMMY CHÁVEZ, b. Private.
    vi.   LUCY CHÁVEZ, b. Private.
    vii.   MAE CHÁVEZ, b. Private.
    viii.   ROSEMARY CHÁVEZ, b. Private; m. JOSÉ MONTOYA.

278. ETHAL[11] CHÁVEZ *(CANDIDO[10], AMADA[9] SÁNCHEZ, MAURICIO DE LA TRINIDAD[8] SÁNCHES, JOSÉ GREGORIO DE LA TRINIDAD[7], JUAN CRISTÓBAL[6], FRANCISCO[5], JACINTO SÁNCHES[4] DE IÑIGO, FRANCISCO MUÑOS[3] SÁNCHES, JACINTO[2] MUÑOS, FRANCISCO[1])[1539]* was born September 14, 1913[1540], and died January 18, 1970. She married MIGUEL MAÉZ[1541].

Notes for MIGUEL MAÉZ:
Buried in Hondo, New México.

Child of ETHAL CHÁVEZ and MIGUEL MAÉZ is:
    i.   GERALD D.[12] MAÉZ, b. August 23, 1940; d. September 12, 1998, Roswell, New México; m. LYDIA TORREZ.

279. LYDIA[11] CHÁVEZ *(LEOPOLDO[10], AMADA[9] SÁNCHEZ, MAURICIO DE LA TRINIDAD[8] SÁNCHES, JOSÉ GREGORIO DE LA TRINIDAD[7], JUAN CRISTÓBAL[6], FRANCISCO[5], JACINTO SÁNCHES[4] DE IÑIGO, FRANCISCO MUÑOS[3] SÁNCHES, JACINTO[2] MUÑOS, FRANCISCO[1])* was born Private. She married BOBBY CHÁVEZ[1542], son of EMILIANO CHÁVEZ and MARÍA LUCERO.

Notes for BOBBY CHÁVEZ:
Died suddenly of a heart attack. He was mowing the lawn on a very hot day. He drank some very cold ice tea and went into cardiac arrest.

Children of LYDIA CHÁVEZ and BOBBY CHÁVEZ are:
    i.   APRIL[12] CHÁVEZ, b. Private; m. (1) MICHAEL CHÁVEZ; m. (2) DAVID CHÁVEZ.
    ii.   DWAIN CHÁVEZ, b. Private.

280. ROY[11] CHÁVEZ *(LEOPOLDO[10], AMADA[9] SÁNCHEZ, MAURICIO DE LA TRINIDAD[8] SÁNCHES, JOSÉ GREGORIO DE LA TRINIDAD[7], JUAN CRISTÓBAL[6], FRANCISCO[5], JACINTO SÁNCHES[4] DE IÑIGO, FRANCISCO MUÑOS[3] SÁNCHES, JACINTO[2] MUÑOS, FRANCISCO[1])[1543]* was born January 08, 1931 in Glencoe, New México, and died February 27, 2001 in Tularosa, New México. He married CRUSITA SILVA[1543], daughter of EDUARDO SILVA and CONSUELO SALAS.

Children of ROY CHÁVEZ and CRUSITA SILVA are:
  i.   PRESTINA[12] CHÁVEZ[1543], b. Private.
  ii.   SYLVIA CHÁVEZ[1543], b. Private; m. EDDIE TELLES[1543].
  iii. BILLY CHÁVEZ[1543], b. Private.
  iv.   MICHAEL CHÁVEZ[1543], b. Private.

281. PABLO MOISES[11] CHÁVEZ *(ERMANDO[10], AMADA[9] SÁNCHEZ, MAURICIO DE LA TRINIDAD[8] SÁNCHES, JOSÉ GREGORIO DE LA TRINIDAD[7], JUAN CRISTÓBAL[6], FRANCISCO[5], JACINTO SÁNCHES[4] DE IÑIGO, FRANCISCO MUÑOS[3] SÁNCHES, JACINTO[2] MUÑOS, FRANCISCO[1])[1544]* was born July 13, 1936 in San Patricio, New México, and died May 28, 2009 in Amarillo, Téxas.

Notes for PABLO MOISES CHÁVEZ:
Also known as Paul.

Children of PABLO MOISES CHÁVEZ are:
  i.   ROBERTA[12] CHÁVEZ, b. Private[1545].
  ii.   RACHEL CHÁVEZ, b. Private[1545].
  iii. MOISES CHÁVEZ, b. Private[1545].

282. PETRA[11] ARMIJO *(ANASTACIA[10] POLACO, MARÍA ALTAGRACIA[9] GONZÁLES, MARÍA MANUELA[8] ARAGÓN, MARIANA ANTONIA[7] SÁNCHES, DIEGO ANTONIO[6], FRANCISCO[5], JACINTO SÁNCHES[4] DE IÑIGO, FRANCISCO MUÑOS[3] SÁNCHES, JACINTO[2] MUÑOS, FRANCISCO[1])* was born May 29, 1894 in Corrales, Territory of New México. She married AMBROCIO C. CHÁVEZ October 14, 1924[1546], son of EDUARDO CHÁVEZ and EXCELSA ARMIJO.

Child of PETRA ARMIJO and AMBROCIO CHÁVEZ is:
  i.   RUDOLPH[12] CHÁVEZ, b. Private.

283. LUÍS[11] POLACO *(CANDIDO[10], MARÍA ALTAGRACIA[9] GONZÁLES, MARÍA MANUELA[8] ARAGÓN, MARIANA ANTONIA[7] SÁNCHES, DIEGO ANTONIO[6], FRANCISCO[5], JACINTO SÁNCHES[4] DE IÑIGO, FRANCISCO MUÑOS[3] SÁNCHES, JACINTO[2] MUÑOS, FRANCISCO[1])* was born June 1895[1547]. He married SARAH ARCHULETA.

Child of LUÍS POLACO and SARAH ARCHULETA is:
  i.   PETROLMO[12] POLACO[1548], b. Abt. 1929; d. September 05, 1929, Mora, New México.

284. PEDRO[11] POLACO *(ELFIGO[10], MARÍA ALTAGRACIA[9] GONZÁLES, MARÍA MANUELA[8] ARAGÓN, MARIANA ANTONIA[7] SÁNCHES, DIEGO ANTONIO[6], FRANCISCO[5], JACINTO SÁNCHES[4] DE IÑIGO, FRANCISCO MUÑOS[3] SÁNCHES, JACINTO[2] MUÑOS, FRANCISCO[1])* was born February 1894 in Las Vegas, Territory of New México[1549]. He married BERNADITA MEDINA.

Notes for PEDRO POLACO:
1920 Census: Living in Monero, Rio Arriba County, Territory of New México.

Children of PEDRO POLACO and BERNADITA MEDINA are:
  i.   LUÍS[12] POLACO[1550], b. Abt. 1920; d. December 09, 1942.
  ii.   VIATRIAS POLACO[1551], b. December 30, 1925, Chama, New México; d. December 14, 1926, Rio Arriba, New México.

285. JENNIE[11] GILL *(ALTAGRACIA[10] HERRERA, FERNANDO[9], PEDRO ALCANTARA[8] DE HERRERA, MARÍA JOSEFA[7] BUSTOS, MARÍA ANTONIA TERESA[6] SÁNCHES, PEDRO[5], PEDRO SÁNCHES[4] DE IÑIGO,*

FRANCISCO MUÑOS³ SÁNCHES, JACINTO² MUÑOS, FRANCISCO¹) was born March 19, 1881 in Nogal, Territory of New México[1552], and died December 13, 1913 in Glencoe, Territory of New México. She married SALOMON SÁNCHEZ[1553] December 06, 1900 in Ruidoso, Territory of New México[1554], son of ANTONIO SÁNCHEZ and TELESFORA MIRABAL.

Notes for JENNIE GILL:
Also known as Josefa.
Buried at Campo Santo de San Ysidro.

Notes for SALOMON SÁNCHEZ:
November 17, 1878: Baptized. Padrinos: Florencio Luna, Pilar Gonzáles.

Worked as a rock mason until he lost his eyesight.
1940 Census: Living in San Patricio, New México.

Children of JENNIE GILL and SALOMON SÁNCHEZ are:

  i.   VIRGINIA¹² SÁNCHEZ[1555], b. April 13, 1902, Glencoe, Territory of New México[1556]; d. December 14, 1980, Ruidoso, New México[1557]; m. ANDELARIO RANDOLPH[1558], September 14, 1918, Lincoln, New México[1559].

Notes for ANDELARIO RANDOLPH:
Also known as, José Candelario Randolph, Candelario, Andy.

  ii. ENRÍQUE GILL SÁNCHEZ, b. September 25, 1904, Glencoe, Territory of New México[1560]; m. CAROLINA GAMBOA[1561], August 04, 1925, Nogal, New México[1562].

Notes for ENRÍQUE GILL SÁNCHEZ:
He was also known as Henry Gill Sánchez, José Enríque Gill Sánchez. Family records indicate that he was born on September 03, 1904.
1930 Census: Living in Fort Stanton, New México.

  iii. SALOMON GILL SÁNCHEZ[1563], b. March 17, 1905, Glencoe, Territory of New México[1564]; d. August 11, 1995, Carrizozo, New México; m. (1) TERESITA SALAS, October 11, 1928, Carrizozo, New México[1565]; m. (2) RAMONA OTERO[1566], November 20, 1932, Carrizozo, New México[1567].

Notes for SALOMON GILL SÁNCHEZ:
1942: Living in Carrizozo, New México.

Notes for RAMONA OTERO:
Also known as Ramoncita.

  iv. TELESFORA SÁNCHEZ[1568], b. July 15, 1906, Glencoe, Territory of New México; d. November 18, 1993, Alamagordo, New México; m. TEODORO SÁNCHEZ PEÑA[1568], March 01, 1926, Carrizozo, New México[1569].

Notes for TEODORO SÁNCHEZ PEÑA:
1930 Census: Living in Tularosa, New México.

  v.   EDUVIJEN SÁNCHEZ[1570], b. April 23, 1908, Glencoe, Territory of New México[1571]; d. March 07, 1999, Roswell, New México; m. JOSÉ ANTONIO SILVA[1572], April 09, 1928[1573].

Notes for EDUVIJEN SÁNCHEZ:
Family records indicate that she was born on August 06, 1909.

Notes for JOSÉ ANTONIO SILVA:
Also known as Joe.

  vi. ANATALIA SÁNCHEZ, b. September 10, 1911, Glencoe, Territory of New México[1574]; d. February 23, 1969; m. JULIAN HERRERA[1575], April 28, 1934, Carrizozo, New México[1576].

Notes for ANATALIA SÁNCHEZ:
Also known as Natalia.

  vii. CONSUELO SÁNCHEZ[1577], b. April 24, 1914, Glencoe, New México; d. April 28, 1996, Tularosa, New México; m. BENITO SILVA[1577], February 13, 1932, Glencoe, New México[1578].

Notes for CONSUELO SÁNCHEZ:
Also known as Consolación.
Lincoln County marriage records indicate that she was born on April 02, 1913.
Buried in Tularosa Catholic Cemetery.

Notes for BENITO SILVA:
1920 Census shows that he was living with his uncle, Manuel Benavidez.

286. ELISIA[11] GILL *(ALTAGRACIA[10] HERRERA, FERNANDO[9], PEDRO ALCANTARA[8] DE HERRERA, MARÍA JOSEFA[7] BUSTOS, MARÍA ANTONIA TERESA[6] SÁNCHES, PEDRO[5], PEDRO SÁNCHES[4] DE IÑIGO, FRANCISCO MUÑOS[3] SÁNCHES, JACINTO[2] MUÑOS, FRANCISCO[1])[1579]* was born 1881 in Nogal, Territory of New México, and died 1949. She married PETER G. HALE[1579][1580], son of LOWEL HALE and ANNA COWGILL.

Notes for ELISIA GILL:
Also known as Alice, Alicia.

Children of ELISIA GILL and PETER HALE are:
  i.   WILLIE[12] HALE[1581], b. 1903; d. 1968.
  ii.   HENRY HALE[1581], b. September 28, 1904; d. January 10, 1975; m. FRANCES FRITZ[1581], November 1927[1582].
  iii. MARY HALE, b. 1908.
  iv.   SUSIE HALE[1583], b. January 25, 1910, Glencoe, Territory of New México[1584]; d. July 1987, Ruidoso, New México; m. JASPER W. MARABLE, November 24, 1934, Carrizozo, New México[1584].
  v.   PAULIE HALE[1585], b. May 07, 1913, Glencoe, New México; d. May 11, 1924, Glencoe, New México.

Notes for PAULIE HALE:
Also known as Paulito Hale.

  vi.   MAGGIE HALE, b. 1916.
  vii. JAMES HALE[1586], b. August 19, 1917[1587]; d. 1963.
  viii. BESSIE HALE, b. 1919.

287. NEWMAN[11] GILL *(ALTAGRACIA[10] HERRERA, FERNANDO[9], PEDRO ALCANTARA[8] DE HERRERA, MARÍA JOSEFA[7] BUSTOS, MARÍA ANTONIA TERESA[6] SÁNCHES, PEDRO[5], PEDRO SÁNCHES[4] DE IÑIGO, FRANCISCO MUÑOS[3] SÁNCHES, JACINTO[2] MUÑOS, FRANCISCO[1])* was born November 30, 1885 in Nogal, Territory of New México[1588], and died in Artesia, New México. He married RITA SÁNCHEZ[1589] July 03, 1915 in La Capilla de San Ysidro, New México[1590], daughter of JUAN SÁNCHES and BESITA SÁNCHEZ.

Notes for NEWMAN GILL:
Land Patent # NMR, on the authority of the Homestead Entry-Original (12 Stat. 392), May 20, 1862. Issued 100 acres on May 19, 1924.

Notes for RITA SÁNCHEZ:
Marriage records indicate she was born on July 12, 1891. Was living in Visilia, California.

Children of NEWMAN GILL and RITA SÁNCHEZ are:
  i.   OLIVIA[12] GILL, b. 1919[1591]; m. PORFIRIO VALENZUELA.
  ii.   ESTOLANO GILL[1592], b. July 06, 1921, Glencoe, New México[1593]; d. January 24, 1990.
  iii. PRESILIANO GILL[1594], b. December 27, 1923, Glencoe, New México[1595]; d. September 1979, Sacramento, California.
  iv.   PABLITA GILL, b. 1925[1595]; m. TORIVIO PADILLA.
  v.   RITA GILL, b. 1928[1595].

288. ESTELA[11] GILL *(ALTAGRACIA[10] HERRERA, FERNANDO[9], PEDRO ALCANTARA[8] DE HERRERA, MARÍA JOSEFA[7] BUSTOS, MARÍA ANTONIA TERESA[6] SÁNCHES, PEDRO[5], PEDRO SÁNCHES[4] DE IÑIGO, FRANCISCO MUÑOS[3] SÁNCHES, JACINTO[2] MUÑOS, FRANCISCO[1])[1596]* was born August 12, 1887 in Nogal, Territory of New México[1597], and died March 29, 1938 in Glencoe, New México. She married MANUEL MIRABAL SÁNCHEZ[1598] June 14, 1909 in San Patricio, Territory of New México[1599], son of ANTONIO SÁNCHEZ and TELESFORA MIRABAL.

Notes for ESTELA GILL:
Given name was María Estela Gill. Also known as Stella.

Buried: La Capilla de San Ysidro, Glencoe.

Children of ESTELA GILL and MANUEL SÁNCHEZ are:
  i.   AMANDA[12] SÁNCHEZ, b. July 15, 1910, Glencoe, Territory of New México[1600]; d. March 19, 1982, Roswell, New México[1600]; m. LUÍS BACA TORRES, November 30, 1927, Tularosa, New México[1601].

Notes for AMANDA SÁNCHEZ:
Baptized: Capilla de San Ysidro, Glencoe NM

Notes for LUÍS BACA TORRES:
After selling the farm, he and his wife migrated to Roswell, New México.
August 26, 1918: Discharged WW I Veteran.

  ii. ESTOLANO SÁNCHEZ, b. Abt. 1910, Glencoe, Territory of New México; d. Abt. 1910, Glencoe, Territory of New México.

Notes for ESTOLANO SÁNCHEZ:
Died young.

289. JULIANA[11] MUÑOZ *(MARTA[10] HERRERA, FERNANDO[9], PEDRO ALCANTARA[8] DE HERRERA, MARÍA JOSEFA[7] BUSTOS, MARÍA ANTONIA TERESA[6] SÁNCHES, PEDRO[5], PEDRO SÁNCHES[4] DE IÑIGO, FRANCISCO MUÑOS[3] SÁNCHES, JACINTO[2] MUÑOS, FRANCISCO[1])* was born April 1881 in San Juanito (Ruidoso Downs), Territory of New México[1602]. She married ANDRÉS GONZÁLES March 30, 1903 in San Patricio, Territory of New México[1603].

Notes for JULIANA MUÑOZ:
Also known as Julianita.

Child of JULIANA MUÑOZ and ANDRÉS GONZÁLES is:
  i.   GUADALUPE[12] GONZÁLES[1604], b. February 26, 1905; d. March 15, 1955, El Paso, Téxas.

Notes for GUADALUPE GONZÁLES:
1920 Census: Living in El Paso, Téxas with her Tío Tomás Ruíz and her Tía Rosa Muños de Ruíz.

290. EPIFANIA[11] MUÑOZ *(MARTA[10] HERRERA, FERNANDO[9], PEDRO ALCANTARA[8] DE HERRERA, MARÍA JOSEFA[7] BUSTOS, MARÍA ANTONIA TERESA[6] SÁNCHES, PEDRO[5], PEDRO SÁNCHES[4] DE IÑIGO, FRANCISCO MUÑOS[3] SÁNCHES, JACINTO[2] MUÑOS, FRANCISCO[1])* was born April 07, 1884 in San Juanito (Ruidoso Downs), Territory of New México[1605]. She married SISTO RICO.

Notes for EPIFANIA MUÑOZ:
Also known as María Epifania Muños.
1920 Census: Living in El Paso, Téxas.

Child of EPIFANIA MUÑOZ and SISTO RICO is:
  i.   REFUGIA[12] MUÑOZ, b. July 20, 1899, San Juanito (Ruidoso Downs), Territory of New México[1606].

Notes for REFUGIA MUÑOZ:
Baptized on January 05, 1900. Padrinos: Andrés Apodaca, Juliana Muñoz.
1900 Census: Living in Ruidoso, Territory of New México. (Born July 1899)
1910 Census: Living in Alamogordo, Territory of New México. (Born about 1902)

291. MARGARITA[11] MUÑOZ *(MARTA[10] HERRERA, FERNANDO[9], PEDRO ALCANTARA[8] DE HERRERA, MARÍA JOSEFA[7] BUSTOS, MARÍA ANTONIA TERESA[6] SÁNCHES, PEDRO[5], PEDRO SÁNCHES[4] DE IÑIGO, FRANCISCO MUÑOS[3] SÁNCHES, JACINTO[2] MUÑOS, FRANCISCO[1])* was born September 09, 1889 in San Juanito (Ruidoso Downs), Territory of New México[1607]. She married HIPOLITO FLORES Abt. 1910[1608], son of JOSÉ FLORES and REGINA BARELA.

Notes for HIPOLITO FLORES:

1900 Census: Living in La Luz, Territory of New México. he was living with his grandparents, José and Loreta Varela. His name was recorded as Claro.
1910 Census: Living in Alamogordo, Territory of New México. He was listed as the Head of household. His other siblings were also living with him.
1920 & 1930 Census: Living in High Rolls Village, New México.

Children of MARGARITA MUÑOZ and HIPOLITO FLORES are:
    i.   ANNA[12] FLORES, b. Abt. 1912[1608].

Notes for ANNA FLORES:
Also known as Fannie.

    ii.   HIPOLITO FLORES, b. Abt. 1915[1608].
    iii.   JOE FLORES, b. Abt. 1916[1608].
    iv.   MARGARET FLORES, b. Abt. 1918[1608].
    v.   ERNEST FLORES, b. Abt. 1921[1608].
    vi.   FRED FLORES, b. Abt. 1928[1608].
    vii.   BEATRICE FLORES, b. Private.
    viii.   PATRICIO FLORES, b. Private.

292. BEATRIZ[11] MUÑOZ *(MARTA[10] HERRERA, FERNANDO[9], PEDRO ALCANTARA[8] DE HERRERA, MARÍA JOSEFA[7] BUSTOS, MARÍA ANTONIA TERESA[6] SÁNCHES, PEDRO[5], PEDRO SÁNCHES[4] DE IÑIGO, FRANCISCO MUÑOS[3] SÁNCHES, JACINTO[2] MUÑOS, FRANCISCO[1])*[1609] was born September 30, 1892 in San Juanito (Ruidoso Downs), Territory of New México[1610], and died December 29, 1989 in El Paso, Téxas. She married TRANQUELINO LAFAYETTE.

Notes for TRANQUELINO LAFAYETTE:
Also known as Frank.
1930 Census: Living in El Paso, Téxas.

Children of BEATRIZ MUÑOZ and TRANQUELINO LAFAYETTE are:
    i.   LEONOR[12] LAFAYETTE, b. Abt. 1922[1611].
    ii.   FRANKIE LAFAYETTE, b. Abt. 1925[1611].
    iii.   MARGARET LAFAYETTE, b. Abt. 1927[1611].
    iv.   MARÍA LAFAYETTE, b. Abt. 1929[1611].
    v.   ALBERT LAFAYETTE, b. Private.

293. GENOVEVA[11] MUÑOZ *(MARTA[10] HERRERA, FERNANDO[9], PEDRO ALCANTARA[8] DE HERRERA, MARÍA JOSEFA[7] BUSTOS, MARÍA ANTONIA TERESA[6] SÁNCHES, PEDRO[5], PEDRO SÁNCHES[4] DE IÑIGO, FRANCISCO MUÑOS[3] SÁNCHES, JACINTO[2] MUÑOS, FRANCISCO[1])* was born September 1894 in San Juanito (Ruidoso Downs), Territory of New México[1612]. She married ARTURO ACUNA Abt. 1913[1613], son of FAUSTINO ACUNA and ANTONIA VILLAREAL.

Children of GENOVEVA MUÑOZ and ARTURO ACUNA are:
    i.   BENJAMÍN[12] ACUNA[1614], b. July 04, 1914, Alamogordo, New México[1615]; d. March 05, 2003, Duncan, Arizona.
    ii.   ARTURO ACUNA[1616], b. June 09, 1916, Alamogordo, New México[1617]; d. April 1987, Safford, Arizona.
    iii.   FEDERICO ACUNA[1618], b. April 06, 1919, Alamogordo, New México[1619]; d. August 19, 2004, Alamogordo, New México.
    iv.   ERNESTO ACUNA[1620], b. April 03, 1927, Alamogordo, New México[1621]; d. February 19, 1991, Albuquerque, New México.
    v.   EDUARDO ACUNA[1622], b. September 04, 1926, Alamogordo, New México[1623]; d. July 1981, Alamogordo, New México.

Notes for EDUARDO ACUNA:
Was living in Safford, Arizona.

    vi.   ROBERTO ACUNA, b. September 20, 1930, Alamogordo, New México[1624]; d. October 06, 1978, Safford, Arizona[1624].
    vii.   BRUNO ACUNA, b. Private, Alamogordo, New México.

294. JOSÉ[11] MUÑOZ *(MARTA[10] HERRERA, FERNANDO[9], PEDRO ALCANTARA[8] DE HERRERA, MARÍA JOSEFA[7] BUSTOS, MARÍA ANTONIA TERESA[6] SÁNCHES, PEDRO[5], PEDRO SÁNCHES[4] DE IÑIGO, FRANCISCO MUÑOS[3] SÁNCHES, JACINTO[2] MUÑOS, FRANCISCO[1])* was born November 22, 1897 in San Juanito (Ruidoso Downs), Territory of New México[1625]. He married CARMEN AUBEL January 25, 1922, daughter of JUAN AUBEL and TERESA DE AUBEL.

Notes for JOSÉ MUÑOZ:
1930 Census: Living in El Paso, Téxas.

Children of JOSÉ MUÑOZ and CARMEN AUBEL are:
    i.   JUANITA[12] MUÑOZ, b. Abt. 1923[1626].
    ii.   MARTA MUÑOZ, b. Abt. 1926[1626].
    iii. ADRIAN MUÑOZ, b. Private.
    iv. JOSÉ MUÑOZ, b. Private.
    v.   CARMEN MUÑOZ, b. Private.

295. ROSALÍA[11] MUÑOZ *(MARTA[10] HERRERA, FERNANDO[9], PEDRO ALCANTARA[8] DE HERRERA, MARÍA JOSEFA[7] BUSTOS, MARÍA ANTONIA TERESA[6] SÁNCHES, PEDRO[5], PEDRO SÁNCHES[4] DE IÑIGO, FRANCISCO MUÑOS[3] SÁNCHES, JACINTO[2] MUÑOS, FRANCISCO[1])* was born April 29, 1899 in San Juanito (Ruidoso Downs), Territory of New México[1627]. She married TOMÁS RUÍZ.

Notes for ROSALÍA MUÑOZ:
Also known as Rosa.

Notes for TOMÁS RUÍZ:
Immigrated to the U.S. in about 1917.

Children of ROSALÍA MUÑOZ and TOMÁS RUÍZ are:
    i.   TOMÁS[12] RUÍZ, b. Abt. 1917, Alamogordo, New México[1628]; m. SARAH KAMEES.
    ii.   EVA RUÍZ, b. Abt. 1921, El Paso, Téxas[1629].
    iii. ROSA RUÍZ, b. Abt. 1926, El Paso, Téxas[1629].
    iv. MARTA RUÍZ, b. Abt. 1928, El Paso, Téxas[1629].
    v.   RAÚL RUÍZ, b. Abt. 1930, El Paso, Téxas[1629].
    vi. ELSIE RUÍZ, b. Private.
    vii. ESTELA RUÍZ, b. Private.
    viii. FREDDY RUÍZ, b. Private.
    ix. MARGARET RUÍZ, b. Private.

296. ANDRÉS[11] MUÑOZ *(MARTA[10] HERRERA, FERNANDO[9], PEDRO ALCANTARA[8] DE HERRERA, MARÍA JOSEFA[7] BUSTOS, MARÍA ANTONIA TERESA[6] SÁNCHES, PEDRO[5], PEDRO SÁNCHES[4] DE IÑIGO, FRANCISCO MUÑOS[3] SÁNCHES, JACINTO[2] MUÑOS, FRANCISCO[1])[1630]* was born February 04, 1901[1631]. He married ROSALÍA JARAMILLO[1632].

Notes for ANDRÉS MUÑOZ:
1900 Census lists him as a boarder.

Children of ANDRÉS MUÑOZ and ROSALÍA JARAMILLO are:
    i.   ANDY[12] MUÑOZ, b. Private.
    ii.   RAMÓN MUÑOZ, b. Private.
    iii. JOHNNY MUÑOZ, b. Private.
    iv. BEATRICE MUÑOZ, b. Private.
    v.   REBECCA MUÑOZ, b. Private.
    vi. RUBÉN MUÑOZ, b. Private.
    vii. MAGDALENA MUÑOZ, b. Private.

297. ANTONIA[11] MUÑOZ *(MARTA[10] HERRERA, FERNANDO[9], PEDRO ALCANTARA[8] DE HERRERA, MARÍA JOSEFA[7] BUSTOS, MARÍA ANTONIA TERESA[6] SÁNCHES, PEDRO[5], PEDRO SÁNCHES[4] DE IÑIGO, FRANCISCO MUÑOS[3] SÁNCHES, JACINTO[2] MUÑOS, FRANCISCO[1])* was born Abt. 1904[1633]. She married CIPRIANO MILLIGAN Abt. 1920[1634], son of GRANT MILLIGAN and VIRGINIA MILLIGAN.

Notes for ANTONIA MUÑOZ:
1900 Census lists her as a boarder.

Notes for CIPRIANO MILLIGAN:
1900 Census: Living in Frisco, Territory of New México.
1930 Census: Living in El Paso, Territory of New México.

Children of ANTONIA MUÑOZ and CIPRIANO MILLIGAN are:
    i.   SAM[12] MILLIGAN, b. Abt. 1922[1634].
    ii.   JIMMY MILLIGAN, b. Abt. 1924[1634].
    iii. VIRGINIA MILLIGAN, b. Abt. 1925[1634].
    iv. JOE MILLIGAN, b. Abt. 1926[1634].

298. AUGUSTÍN[11] SALSBERRY *(MANUELITA[10] HERRERA, FERNANDO[9], PEDRO ALCANTARA[8] DE HERRERA, MARÍA JOSEFA[7] BUSTOS, MARÍA ANTONIA TERESA[6] SÁNCHES, PEDRO[5], PEDRO SÁNCHES[4] DE IÑIGO, FRANCISCO MUÑOS[3] SÁNCHES, JACINTO[2] MUÑOS, FRANCISCO[1])[1635]* was born October 25, 1895 in San Juanito (Ruidoso Downs), Territory of New México, and died May 24, 1973 in Citrus Heights, California. He married (1) MARGARITA VIGIL August 13, 1917 in La Capilla de San Ysidro, New México[1636], daughter of EDUARDO VIGIL and TOMASA ZAMORA. He married (2) AGAPITA PADILLA[1637] August 12, 1926 in Carrizozo, New México[1638], daughter of JESÚS PADILLA and LUISA MONTOYA.

Notes for AUGUSTÍN SALSBERRY:
1930 Census: Living in Fort Stanton, New México.
1947: Migrated to Roseville, California.
Land Patent # NMR 0044297, on the authority of the Homestead Entry-Original (12 Stat. 392), May 20, 1862. Issued 160 acres on February 05, 1924.

Children of AUGUSTÍN SALSBERRY and AGAPITA PADILLA are:
    i.   LUISA[12] SALSBERRY, b. October 01, 1927, Capitán, New México[1639]; d. Citrus Heights, California; m. VICENTE SÁNCHEZ, July 08, 1946, Carrizozo, New México[1639].

Notes for LUISA SALSBERRY:
Also known as Louise.

Notes for VICENTE SÁNCHEZ:
1930 Census: Living in Rebentón, New México.

    ii.   AUGUSTÍN SALSBERRY[1640], b. September 01, 1928, Fort Stanton, New México; d. August 25, 2005, Carmichael, California; m. AVRORA CALDERON.
    iii. EMMA SALSBERRY[1641], b. October 05, 1929, Fort Stanton, New México; d. August 01, 1995, Citrus Heights, California; m. ALFONSO CALDERON.
    iv. WILLIAM RICHARD SALSBERRY[1642], b. December 17, 1940, Fort Stanton, New México; d. October 08, 2009, Roseville, California; m. MITZI SALSBERRY.

Notes for WILLIAM RICHARD SALSBERRY:
Also known as Dick.

    v.   ANEDA MARÍA SALSBERRY, b. July 05, 1931, Fort Stanton, New México; m. RAY GARCÍA.

Notes for ANEDA MARÍA SALSBERRY:
Also known as Anita.

    vi. HELEN PAULA SALSBERRY, b. Private, Fort Stanton, New México; m. JOE HURTADO.

299. TOMASITA[11] SALSBERRY *(MANUELITA[10] HERRERA, FERNANDO[9], PEDRO ALCANTARA[8] DE HERRERA, MARÍA JOSEFA[7] BUSTOS, MARÍA ANTONIA TERESA[6] SÁNCHES, PEDRO[5], PEDRO SÁNCHES[4] DE IÑIGO, FRANCISCO MUÑOS[3] SÁNCHES, JACINTO[2] MUÑOS, FRANCISCO[1])* was born December 29, 1897 in San Juanito (Ruidoso Downs), Territory of New México[1643], and died June 17, 1949 in Artesia, New Mexico[1644]. She married JACOBO SALAS[1645] January 14, 1920 in San Patricio, New México[1646], son of TEOFILO SALAS and IGENIA GALLEGOS.

Notes for TOMASITA SALSBERRY:
Also known as Tomasa.
Buried: San Patricio, NM.

Notes for JACOBO SALAS:
Also known as Jake.

Children of TOMASITA SALSBERRY and JACOBO SALAS are:
    i.   PABLITA[12] SALAS[1647], b. Abt. 1924, San Patricio, New México; d. April 17, 1924, San Patricio, New México.
    ii.   MARÍA SALAS[1648], b. Abt. 1932, Hondo, New México; d. February 23, 1932, Hondo, New México.
    iii.   JOSEFA SALAS, b. December 27, 1936; d. March 28, 1999, Artesia, New Mexico.

Notes for JOSEFA SALAS:
Also known as Josefita Salas Duran.

    iv.   BESSIE LUISA JULIA SALAS[1649], b. Abt. 1940, Hondo, New México; d. March 05, 1940, Hondo, New México.
    v.   DOMINGO SALAS, b. Private; d. Artesia, New Mexico; m. SOFIA DE SALAS.
    vi.   ROSA SALAS, b. Private; d. Artesia, New Mexico.
    vii.   RUBÉN SALAS, b. Private.
    viii.   WILLIE SALAS, b. Private.

300. DOROTEA[11] SALSBERRY *(MANUELITA[10] HERRERA, FERNANDO[9], PEDRO ALCANTARA[8] DE HERRERA, MARÍA JOSEFA[7] BUSTOS, MARÍA ANTONIA TERESA[6] SÁNCHES, PEDRO[5], PEDRO SÁNCHES[4] DE IÑIGO, FRANCISCO MUÑOS[3] SÁNCHES, JACINTO[2] MUÑOS, FRANCISCO[1])[1650]* was born February 05, 1902 in San Juanito (Ruidoso Downs), New México[1651], and died January 25, 1974 in Artesia, New Mexico. She married RUBÉN ANDRÉS GONZÁLES September 20, 1919 in Las Angusturas (San Ysidro), New México[1652], son of PROSPERO GONZÁLES and TELESFORA MIRABAL.

Notes for DOROTEA SALSBERRY:
Church marriage records indicate that they were married on February 22, 1919. (LDS Center, Alamogordo, Microfiche # 001674, Page 130)

Notes for RUBÉN ANDRÉS GONZÁLES:
Also known as Rubé.

Children of DOROTEA SALSBERRY and RUBÉN GONZÁLES are:
    i.   OLIVIA[12] GONZÁLES, b. August 25, 1920, Glencoe, New México[1653]; d. May 27, 2005, Carlsbad, New México; m. JUAN RODRÍGUEZ, September 02, 1943.
    ii.   ADELINA GONZÁLES, b. Abt. 1922, Glencoe, New México[1653]; m. LOLO RODRÍGUEZ.
    iii.   ORALIA GONZÁLES[1654], b. Abt. 1923, Glencoe, New México[1655]; d. June 17, 1941, San Patricio, New México; m. CRISTÓVAL PEREA.
    iv.   VIOLA GONZÁLES[1656], b. April 14, 1925, San Patricio, New México; d. October 09, 2009, Alamogordo, New México; m. MANUEL P. REYES[16561657].
    v.   RUFINA GONZÁLES, b. Abt. 1928, Glencoe, New México[1658]; m. JOSÉ RODRÍGUEZ.

Notes for RUFINA GONZÁLES:
Living in San Bernadino, California.

    vi.   EMILIO GONZÁLES, b. April 05, 1927, Glencoe, New México; d. July 28, 2011, Artesia, New México; m. RACHEL ALANIZ, September 16, 1948.
    vii.   FEDELINA GONZÁLES, b. November 10, 1930, Glencoe, New México; d. May 27, 2011, Lubbock, Texas; m. COSMÉ GÓMEZ, June 29, 1960, Las Vegas, Nevada.

Notes for FEDELINA GONZÁLES:
Also known as Fela, Faye.

    viii.   HELEN GONZÁLES, b. Private, Glencoe, New México; m. MACARIO CHÁVEZ.
    ix.   REYNER GONZÁLES, b. Private, Glencoe, New México; m. MARY PADILLA.

Notes for REYNER GONZÁLES:
Living in Artesia.

      x.   RUBÉN GONZÁLES, b. August 27, 1932, Glencoe, New México; m. MANUELA PAS.

Notes for RUBÉN GONZÁLES:
Living in Carlsbad.

      xi.   TELESFORA GONZÁLES, b. Private, Glencoe, New México; m. TEMO GARCÍA.

Notes for TELESFORA GONZÁLES:
Also known as Tillie.

301. FERNANDO[11] SALSBERRY *(MANUELITA[10] HERRERA, FERNANDO[9], PEDRO ALCANTARA[8] DE HERRERA, MARÍA JOSEFA[7] BUSTOS, MARÍA ANTONIA TERESA[6] SÁNCHES, PEDRO[5], PEDRO SÁNCHES[4] DE IÑIGO, FRANCISCO MUÑOS[3] SÁNCHES, JACINTO[2] MUÑOS, FRANCISCO[1])*[1659] was born April 13, 1904 in San Juanito (Ruidoso Downs), Territory of New México[1660], and died September 11, 1937 in Hondo, New Mexico. He married LORENSITA MONTOYA[1661] June 15, 1929 in Carrizozo, New Mexico[1662], daughter of DOROTEO MONTOYA and ALBINA SILVA.

Notes for FERNANDO SALSBERRY:
Also known as Fred.
1930 Census: Living in Fort Stanton, New México.
He died in an automobile accident in Hondo, New México. He was run over by a vehicle. Burried: San Patricio, New México.

Notes for LORENSITA MONTOYA:
Burial birthdate states she was born on August 09, 1914.

Children of FERNANDO SALSBERRY and LORENSITA MONTOYA are:
      i.   ANATALIA[12] SALSBERRY, b. December 16, 1930; m. MANUEL SOSA, September 27, 1950, Artesia, New México.
      ii.   CLOVÍS SALSBERRY[1663], b. April 04, 1934, Fort Stanton, New México; d. May 25, 1938, Fort Stanton, New México.
      iii.   ELOY SALSBERRY, b. January 21, 1938, San Patricio, New México; m. RICARDA BRISENO, 1961, Artesia, New México.
      iv.   FREDDIE SALSBERRY, b. March 03, 1936, Fort Stanton, New México; d. July 23, 1999, Roswell, New México; m. (1) FRANCIS GARZA; m. (2) FRANCES HUERTA.

Notes for FREDDIE SALSBERRY:
Also known as Fernando Salsberry.

302. JAMES[11] SALSBERRY *(MANUELITA[10] HERRERA, FERNANDO[9], PEDRO ALCANTARA[8] DE HERRERA, MARÍA JOSEFA[7] BUSTOS, MARÍA ANTONIA TERESA[6] SÁNCHES, PEDRO[5], PEDRO SÁNCHES[4] DE IÑIGO, FRANCISCO MUÑOS[3] SÁNCHES, JACINTO[2] MUÑOS, FRANCISCO[1])* was born June 26, 1906 in San Juanito (Ruidoso Downs), Territory of New México, and died January 14, 1986 in Barstow, California. He married LUCÍA ANAYA[1664] March 26, 1927[1665], daughter of PEDRO ANALLA and SOFIA TORRES.

Notes for JAMES SALSBERRY:
Also known as Santiago Salsberry.
1930 Census: Living in Fort Stanton, New México.

Children of JAMES SALSBERRY and LUCÍA ANAYA are:
      i.   BERTHA GRACE[12] SALSBERRY[1666], b. October 13, 1928, Capitán, New México[1667]; m. JOE M. BARELA, February 05, 1948, Carrizozo, New México[1668].

Notes for BERTHA GRACE SALSBERRY:
Living in Alamogordo, New México.

    ii.   JAMES ANAYA SALSBERRY[1669], b. March 16, 1930, Ruidoso, New México; d. November 26, 2009, Dulzura, California; m. (1) GLORIA SALSBERRY; m. (2) ALICIA ESPERANSA CARABAJAL, March 16, 1951.

    iii.   BETTY SALSBERRY, b. May 28, 1932, Capítan, New México; m. PATROCINIO GARCÍA, April 12, 1951.

Notes for BETTY SALSBERRY:
Also known as Virginia Salsberry.
July 17, 1932: Baptized in Carrizozo, New México. Padrinos: Román Sánchez and Florinda Salsberry-Sánchez.

    iv.   MARY ROSE SALSBERRY[1670], b. March 02, 1934, Fort Stanton, New México; d. November 11, 1985, San Bernadino, California; m. MAX CÓRDOVA, September 30, 1956, Barstow, California.

Notes for MARY ROSE SALSBERRY:
Also known as María Rosa Salsberry.

    v.   PEDRO JOSÉ SALSBERRY, b. January 29, 1937, Capítan, New México; m. MARLENE MARTÍNEZ, September 30, 1957, San Bernadino, California.

Notes for PEDRO JOSÉ SALSBERRY:
Also known as Joe Salsberry.
Lives in San Bernadino, California.

    vi.   ANTHONY SALSBERRY, b. June 10, 1939, Capítan, New México; m. (1) PATRICIA SANDOVAL, San Bernadino, California; m. (2) WANDA SALSBERRY.

Notes for ANTHONY SALSBERRY:
Also known as Anthony Luís Arthur Salsberry.

    vii.   LUCY SOCORRO SALSBERRY[1670], b. January 02, 1941, Capítan, New México; d. July 13, 1992, San Bernadino, California; m. (1) SULLIVAN COOK; m. (2) HENRY HESTER ANGLIN, July 19, 1960, San Bernadino, California[1671].

    viii.   MANUEL SALOMON SALSBERRY, b. April 05, 1943, Fort Stockton, New México; m. LYDIA RAMOS, June 03, 1963, San Bernadino, California.

Notes for MANUEL SALOMON SALSBERRY:
May 23, 1943: Basptized. Padrinos: José Portio and Julianita Ybarra-Portio.

    ix.   CARMEN DORA SALSBERRY, b. November 15, 1945, Fort Stockton, New México; m. (1) ARNOLD CARLOS; m. (2) RONNIE C. LARA, October 02, 1965, San Bernadino, California.

    x.   DAVÍD JESÚS SALSBERRY, b. April 23, 1949, Roswell, New México; d. March 03, 1995, San Bernadino, California; m. (1) ANA LEE GUTIÉRREZ; m. (2) ELIZABETH MARTÍNEZ.

Notes for DAVÍD JESÚS SALSBERRY:
Also known as David Richard Jesús Salsberry.

    xi.   LUPE SALSBERRY, b. June 15, 1951, Alamogordo, New México; m. RUBÉN JOE CHÁVEZ, April 07, 1975, San Bernadino, California.

    xii.   MARÍA BONITA SALSBERRY, b. September 1953, San Bernadino, California.

    xiii.   ELIZABETH SALSBERRY, b. February 02, 1956, San Bernadino, California; m. (1) ROBERT VITO COMITO; m. (2) DANNY ENRÍQUEZ, February 02, 1975, Las Vegas, Nevada.

303. FLORINDA[11] SALSBERRY *(MANUELITA[10] HERRERA, FERNANDO[9], PEDRO ALCANTARA[8] DE HERRERA, MARÍA JOSEFA[7] BUSTOS, MARÍA ANTONIA TERESA[6] SÁNCHES, PEDRO[5], PEDRO SÁNCHES[4] DE IÑIGO, FRANCISCO MUÑOS[3] SÁNCHES, JACINTO[2] MUÑOS, FRANCISCO[1])[1672]* was born March 15, 1910 in Palo Verde (Ruidoso Downs), Territory of New México, and died March 27, 1978 in San Patricio, New México. She married ROMÁN SÁNCHEZ[1673] February 20, 1927 in Mescalero, New Mexico[1674], son of MAURICIO SÁNCHEZ and DELFINIA ROMERO.

Notes for FLORINDA SALSBERRY:
Florinda was born on the Rancho Salsberry by Cañon de Salsberry. The house is no longer standing but a grove of trees is all that remains.

1910 Census: Listed as Manuelita Salsberry born March 1910.

Notes for ROMÁN SÁNCHEZ:
May 29, 1904: Baptized by Román Barragán and his wife Andrea Torres de Barragán in San Patricio. Baptismal records state that he was born on April 23, 1904.
Lived most of his childhood with Román Barragán and his wife Andrea Torres de Barragán
Farm was located on land originally patented to Esiquio Sánchez.
Died in an automobile accident in Ruidoso Downs.
Buried: La Capilla de San Patricio

Children of FLORINDA SALSBERRY and ROMÁN SÁNCHEZ are:
  i.   ERNESTO[12] SÁNCHEZ, b. April 09, 1928, San Patricio, New México[1675]; m. ORALIA CHÁVEZ, March 20, 1948, Ruidoso, New México[1675].

Notes for ERNESTO SÁNCHEZ:
Also known as José Ernesto Sánchez, Ernest S. Sánchez.

  ii. MADELENA SÁNCHEZ[1676], b. Abt. 1930, San Patricio, New México; d. December 19, 1932, San Patricio, New México.

Notes for MADELENA SÁNCHEZ:
Died young after she contracted an illness. She was born as the second child.

  iii. DELFINIA OLIDIA SÁNCHEZ, b. April 18, 1934, San Patricio, New México; m. LEANDRO VEGA, December 27, 1958, Hondo, New México.

Notes for LEANDRO VEGA:
Korean War Veteran.
Served as a Lincoln County Deputy Sheriff from 1960-1964, and from 1968-1972. He served as Lincoln County Sheriff from 1964-1968, and from 1972-1976. He served as a criminal investigator for 18 years for the 12th Judicial District.

  iv. ORLANDO SÁNCHEZ, b. April 03, 1936, San Patricio, New México; m. CHRISTINA SÁNCHEZ.
  v.   FLORA MARÍA SÁNCHEZ, b. March 24, 1938, Capitán, New México; m. RICHARD VEGA.
  vi. FRED SÁNCHEZ, b. May 30, 1940, Fort Stanton, New México[1677]; m. BERTA HERRERA, July 26, 1959, Ruidoso, New México[1677].
  vii. BREZEL ROBERT SÁNCHEZ, b. November 04, 1941, Capitán, New México[1678]; m. MINNIE ROMERO, June 15, 1963, Hondo, New México[1678].

Notes for BREZEL ROBERT SÁNCHEZ:
Moved to Roswell, New México.

Notes for MINNIE ROMERO:
Also known as Erminia Romero.

  viii. GERALDINE ELSIE SÁNCHEZ, b. January 10, 1945, Artesia, New México; m. ROBERT MONTES.

Notes for GERALDINE ELSIE SÁNCHEZ:
Also known as Geralda.

Notes for ROBERT MONTES:
Also known as Bobby.

  ix. LUVÍN SÁNCHEZ, b. October 23, 1947, San Patricio, New México; m. (1) GLORIA BACA; m. (2) FRANCIS SEDILLOS.
  x.   CYNTHIA VIOLANDA SÁNCHEZ[1679], b. September 10, 1950, Capitán, New México[1680]; d. April 27, 1986, Rio Rancho, New México; m. BERRY VANDERWALL, December 22, 1972, San Patricio, New México[1680].

Notes for CYNTHIA VIOLANDA SÁNCHEZ:
Also known as Cynthia.

  xi. MAURICIO SÁNCHEZ, b. Abt. 1952, San Patricio, New México.

Notes for MAURICIO SÁNCHEZ:
Died Young.

xii.   ROMÁN SÁNCHEZ, JR., b. March 13, 1954, Ruidoso, New México[1681]; m. YOVANNE SALAS, May 25, 1974, Ruidoso, New México[1681].

304. ENRÍQUES[11] SALSBERRY *(MANUELITA[10] HERRERA, FERNANDO[9], PEDRO ALCANTARA[8] DE HERRERA, MARÍA JOSEFA[7] BUSTOS, MARÍA ANTONIA TERESA[6] SÁNCHES, PEDRO[5], PEDRO SÁNCHES[4] DE IÑIGO, FRANCISCO MUÑOS[3] SÁNCHES, JACINTO[2] MUÑOS, FRANCISCO[1])* was born August 11, 1912 in Palo Verde (Ruidoso Downs), Territory of New México[1682], and died January 24, 1956 in Artesia, New México. He married DOLORES SÁNCHEZ[1683] February 05, 1933 in Carrizozo, New México[1684], daughter of TELESFORO SÁNCHEZ and CAROLINA MIRANDA.

Notes for ENRÍQUES SALSBERRY:
Also known as Henry.
1940 Census: Living in San Patricio, New México.
1944: Moved from San Patricio, NM to Artesia, NM.
Enriquez died in a construction accident. He was hit in the head by the ball of a big crane. Operator error. The story goes that he always kissed Lola every morning before he left for work. The night before they had an argument. In the morning Enriquez left for work without kissing Lola goodbye. He died later that morning.

Notes for DOLORES SÁNCHEZ:
Also known as Lola.

Children of ENRÍQUES SALSBERRY and DOLORES SÁNCHEZ are:
i.   HENRY[12] SALSBERRY, b. November 27, 1933, San Patricio, New México; m. LEONILLA GANDARA.
ii.   PABLO SALSBERRY, b. April 24, 1934, San Patricio, New México; m. REFUGIA SÁNCHEZ, December 21, 1951, Ojinaga, México.

Notes for PABLO SALSBERRY:
Also known as Pablo Luís Salsberry.

Notes for REFUGIA SÁNCHEZ:
Also known as Cuca Salsberry.

iii.   WILLIAM SALSBERRY[1685], b. November 28, 1936; d. December 05, 1967, Los Angeles, California; m. AMY RAMÍREZ.
iv.   WOODROW SALSBERRY, b. July 27, 1940, San Patricio, New México; m. VERA SOSA.

Notes for WOODROW SALSBERRY:
Also known as Woody.

v.   TRINA CAROLINA SALSBERRY, b. August 31, 1942; m. MANUEL CHÁVEZ.

Notes for TRINA CAROLINA SALSBERRY:
Also known as Trinidad Carolina Salsberry.

vi.   JANE SALSBERRY, b. Private; m. MAXWELL CONTRERAS.

305. JOSÉ[11] PORTIO *(MANUELITA[10] HERRERA, FERNANDO[9], PEDRO ALCANTARA[8] DE HERRERA, MARÍA JOSEFA[7] BUSTOS, MARÍA ANTONIA TERESA[6] SÁNCHES, PEDRO[5], PEDRO SÁNCHES[4] DE IÑIGO, FRANCISCO MUÑOS[3] SÁNCHES, JACINTO[2] MUÑOS, FRANCISCO[1])[1686]* was born December 03, 1893 in San Juanito (Ruidoso Downs), Territory of New México, and died September 18, 1959 in San Patricio, New México. He married JULIANITA YBARRA[1686] January 05, 1922 in San Patricio, New México[1687], daughter of GREGORIO YBARRA and CATARINA MONTOYA.

Notes for JOSÉ PORTIO:
New Mexico Private Company C.
Born at Gregorio Ybarra's farm.

Land Patent # NMR 0032399, on the authority of the Homestead Entry-Enlarged (35 Stat. 639), February 19, 1909. Issued 320 acres on February 23, 1922.

Children of JOSÉ PORTIO and JULIANITA YBARRA are:
    i.   RICARDO[12] PORTIO, b. July 03, 1927, San Patricio, New México[1688]; m. WANDA PAGE, June 30, 1948, Carrizozo, New México[1688].

Notes for RICARDO PORTIO:
He was a WW II veteran.

    ii.   ARON PORTIO, b. February 14, 1932, San Patricio, New México[1689]; m. ISABEL LUERAS, July 05, 1952, Carrizozo, New México[1689].

Notes for ARON PORTIO:
He was a WW II veteran.

    iii.   MANUELITA PORTIO, b. October 28, 1933, San Patricio, New México[1690]; m. RUBÉN PADILLA, October 27, 1950, Carrizozo, New México[1690].

Notes for RUBÉN PADILLA:
He was a WW II veteran.

306. MANUEL HERRERA[11] CORONA *(MANUELITA[10] HERRERA, FERNANDO[9], PEDRO ALCANTARA[8] DE HERRERA, MARÍA JOSEFA[7] BUSTOS, MARÍA ANTONIA TERESA[6] SÁNCHES, PEDRO[5], PEDRO SÁNCHES[4] DE IÑIGO, FRANCISCO MUÑOS[3] SÁNCHES, JACINTO[2] MUÑOS, FRANCISCO[1])[1691]* was born January 01, 1885 in San Juanito (Ruidoso Downs), Territory of New México[1692], and died July 12, 1966 in San Patricio, New México. He married (1) JESÚSITA DOMINGUEZ January 26, 1905 in Lincoln, Territory of New México[1693], daughter of NICANOR DOMINGUEZ and OCTAVIANA FUENTES. He married (2) SUSANA TRUJILLO[1694] February 24, 1909 in Lincoln, Territory of New México[1695], daughter of BONAFICIO TRUJILLO and LORENSA SILVA.

Notes for MANUEL HERRERA CORONA:
Born at Gregorio Ybarra's farm in San Juanito (Ruidoso Downs).
The 1920 Census shows that his daughter, Sara was living with him and Susana.
1933-1936: Served as probate judge.
Served as a Constable and as a Lincoln County Commisioner.
Killed in an accident while crossing the road.

Land Patent # NMR 0027296, on the authority of the Homestead Entry-Enlarged (35 Stat. 639), February 19, 1909. Issued 161.36 acres on November 15, 1917.
Land Patent # NMLC 0041525, on the authority of the Homestead Entry-Stock Raising (39 Stat. 862), December 29, 1916. Issued 480 acres on February 6, 1936.

Notes for JESÚSITA DOMINGUEZ:
She divorced Manuel Corona.

Child of MANUEL CORONA and JESÚSITA DOMINGUEZ is:
    i.   SARA[12] CORONA, b. December 17, 1905, Arabela, Territory of New México[1696]; m. JOSÉ MIGUEL ARCHULETA[1697], March 01, 1924, Arabela, New México[1698].

Notes for JOSÉ MIGUEL ARCHULETA:
He was the adopted son of Antonio José Archuleta.

Children of MANUEL CORONA and SUSANA TRUJILLO are:
    ii.   MAX[12] CORONA[1699], b. September 05, 1912, San Patricio, New México[1700]; d. January 09, 1973, Morenci, Arizona; m. (1) BRESELIA GONZÁLES; m. (2) APOLONIA WARNER, June 04, 1932, Carrizozo, New México[1701].

Notes for APOLONIA WARNER:
Also known as Pauline or Polonia. There are also three variations of the last name; Warner, Juana and Guana.

Land Patent # NMLC 0041178, on the authority of the Homestead Entry-Stock Raising (39 Stat. 862), December 29, 1916. Issued 640 acres on March 26, 1937.

iii. ANASTACIO CORONA[1702], b. October 23, 1916, San Patricio, New México[1703]; d. July 11, 2000, Ruidoso, New México; m. ESPERANZA MAÉS, August 28, 1939, Arabela, New México[1703].

iv. MANUEL TRUJILLO CORONA[1704], b. March 27, 1921, San Patricio, New México; d. August 25, 2007, San Patricio, New México; m. (1) ONESIMA SILVA; m. (2) CRUZ CORONA.

Notes for MANUEL TRUJILLO CORONA:
Private First Class US Army. WW II Veteran. Worked at Holloman Air Force base for 30 years.

307. ELENA[11] CORONA *(MANUELITA[10] HERRERA, FERNANDO[9], PEDRO ALCANTARA[8] DE HERRERA, MARÍA JOSEFA[7] BUSTOS, MARÍA ANTONIA TERESA[6] SÁNCHES, PEDRO[5], PEDRO SÁNCHES[4] DE IÑIGO, FRANCISCO MUÑOS[3] SÁNCHES, JACINTO[2] MUÑOS, FRANCISCO[1])*[1705] was born February 17, 1890 in San Juanito (Ruidoso Downs), Territory of New México, and died March 14, 1928 in San Patricio, New México[1706]. She married ROBERTO PRUDENCIO[1707] August 05, 1922 in San Patricio, New México[1708], son of DAMACIO PROVENCIO and CLEOFAS MUÑOZ.

Notes for ELENA CORONA:
Also known as Helena.
Born at Gregorio's farm in San Juanito.

Notes for ROBERTO PRUDENCIO:
Also known as Roberto Provencio. Private in the U.S. Army.
1920 Census: Living in Capitán, New México
1930 Census: Living in Dunkin, New México.

Children of ELENA CORONA and ROBERTO PRUDENCIO are:
i. ALBERTO[12] PRUDENCIO[1709], b. Abt. 1928, San Patricio, New México; d. August 30, 1928, San Patricio, New México.

ii. FELICITA PRUDENCIO, b. Private; m. ADAN BARRERA[1710], Artesia, New México.

iii. MARGARITA PRUDENCIO, b. Private; m. JOSÉ TORRES.

Notes for MARGARITA PRUDENCIO:
Also known as Maggie.

Genealogy of José Sánchez

Generation No. 1

1. JOSÉ[1] SÁNCHEZ was born Abt. 1820 in El Reyno de Nuevo México, Nueva España[1]. He married MARÍA DOLÓRES CHÁVEZ.

Notes for JOSÉ SÁNCHEZ:
1860 Census: Living in Manzano, Territory of New México. (José Sánchez y Lerma. Born in about 1820)
1870 Census: Living in Lincoln County, Precinct 1, Territory of New México. Lists his occupation as a musician. (Born in about 1809)
1880 Census: Living in Lincoln, Territory of New México. (Born in about 1820)

Notes for MARÍA DOLÓRES CHÁVEZ:
1860 Census: Living in Manzano, Territory of New México (Born about 1831).
1870 Census: Living in Lincoln County, Territory of New México (Born about About 1830).
1880 Census: Living in Lincoln, Territory of New México (Born about About 1830).
1930 Census: list her age as 110 years.

Children of JOSÉ SÁNCHEZ and MARÍA CHÁVEZ are:
2.   i.   ROSALÍA CHÁVEZ[2] SÁNCHEZ, b. Abt. 1845, Manzano, Territory of New México; d. December 09, 1932, Arabela, New México.
3.   ii.   FRANCISCA SÁNCHEZ, b. Abt. 1852, Manzano, Territory of New México.
        iii.   PERFECTA SÁNCHEZ, b. Abt. 1855[2].
        iv.   MARIA SÁNCHEZ, b. Abt. 1858[3].
        v.   LUISA SÁNCHEZ, b. Abt. 1859[4]; m. GEORGE WASHINGTON, December 1874[5].
        vi.   CIFROSA SÁNCHEZ, b. Abt. 1863[6].
        vii.   JOSEFA SÁNCHEZ[7], b. Abt. 1865[8]; d. December 16, 1933, Arabela, New México.
        viii.   ÁBRAN SÁNCHEZ, b. Abt. 1872, Lincoln County, Territory of New México[9].
4.   ix.   SIMÓN WILSON SÁNCHEZ, b. March 22, 1874, Fort Stanton, Territory of New México; d. January 30, 1953, Roswell, New México.
        x.   CAMILA SÁNCHEZ, b. Abt. 1876[9].

Generation No. 2

Juan Regalado

2. ROSALÍA CHÁVEZ[2] SÁNCHEZ (*JOSÉ*[1])[10] was born Abt. 1845 in Manzano, Territory of New México[11], and died December 09, 1932 in Arabela, New México. She married (1) JUAN REGALADO[12] October 15, 1889 in Manzano, Territory of New México[13], son of MARTÍN REGALADO and MARTINA CHACON. She married (2) FRANCISCO SAÍZ Abt. 1890[14].

Notes for ROSALÍA CHÁVEZ SÁNCHEZ:
1860 Census: Living in Manzano, Territory of New México. (Born about 1844)
1910 Census: Living in Las Palas, Territory of New México.

Notes for JUAN REGALADO:
Also known as Juan Regalao.
1875: Emigrated from México.
1900 Census: Living in Rebentón, New
Buried: Rebentón, New México.

Children of ROSALÍA SÁNCHEZ and JUAN REGALADO are:
        i.   JOSEFITA[3] REGALADO.
5.   ii.   MARTINA REGALADO, b. April 12, 1884, Rio Bonito, Territory of New México.
6.   iii.   JOSÉ REGALADO, b. February 25, 1887, Lincoln, Territory of New México; d. June 1972, Roswell, New México.

3. FRANCISCA[2] SÁNCHEZ *(JOSÉ[1])* was born Abt. 1852 in Manzano, Territory of New México[15]. She married (1) RAMÓN VIGIL. She married (2) JESÚS RODRÍGUEZ Abt. 1866 in Lincoln, Territory of New México[16], son of MARTA RODRÍGUEZ.

Notes for JESÚS RODRÍGUEZ:
Was a Private in Company A, First Regiment Cavalry in Fort Stanton.
He Was a member of the Lincoln County Riflemen.
He was killed in Lincoln, New México by Constable Amado Chávez.
1870 Census: Living in Lincoln County, Precinct 3, Territory of New México.

Children of FRANCISCA SÁNCHEZ and RAMÓN VIGIL are:
	i.	PEDRO[3] VIGIL.
7.	ii.	LUISA VIGIL, b. August 1882; d. 1936, Clovis, New México.

Children of FRANCISCA SÁNCHEZ and JESÚS RODRÍGUEZ are:
8.	iii.	ROSARIO[3] RODRÍGUEZ, b. Abt. January 1869; d. January 24, 1940, Carrizozo, New México.
	iv.	ABRAN RODRÍGUEZ, b. May 15, 1871.

Notes for ABRAN RODRÍGUEZ:
Also known as Abraham.

	v.	JUAN RODRÍGUEZ, b. Abt. 1876[17].
	vi.	PEDRO RODRÍGUEZ, b. September 01, 1874, Tres Ritos, Territory of New México[18]; d. January 04, 1941, Carrizozo, New México; m. EUFELIA GARCÍA, November 27, 1897, San Patricio, Territory of New México[19].

Notes for PEDRO RODRÍGUEZ:
He was raised by Fernando Herrera after his father was killed in Lincoln, New México by Constable Amado Chávez.
1930 Census: Living with his sister in Carrizozo.

4. SIMÓN WILSON[2] SÁNCHEZ *(JOSÉ[1])* was born March 22, 1874 in Fort Stanton, Territory of New México[20], and died January 30, 1953 in Roswell, New México. He married (1) GREGORIA MARRUJO Abt. 1895[21], daughter of VICTOR MARRUJO and TOMASA RIOS. He married (2) ANTONIA CARABAJAL July 01, 1909 in Arabela, Territory of New México[22], daughter of POMUCIANO CARABAJAL and PILAR DE GUEBARA.

Notes for SIMÓN WILSON SÁNCHEZ:
Both Simón and Antonia are buried at South Park Cemetary in Roswell, New México.
1900 Census: Living in Rebentón, Territory of New México

Notes for ANTONIA CARABAJAL:
Also known as Toñita.

Children of SIMÓN SÁNCHEZ and GREGORIA MARRUJO are:
	i.	MARÍA MARRUJO[3] SÁNCHEZ, b. May 1896, Rebentón, Territory of New México[23].
	ii.	SARA MARRUJO SÁNCHEZ, b. June 1897, Rebentón, Territory of New México[23].
9.	iii.	PAULITA SÁNCHEZ, b. September 01, 1900, Rebentón, Territory of New México; d. 1928-1930.

Children of SIMÓN SÁNCHEZ and ANTONIA CARABAJAL are:
	iv.	HILARIO[3] SÁNCHEZ[24], b. October 17, 1904, Rebentón, Territory of New México[25]; d. June 1979, Roswell, New México; m. ESTELA SEDILLO[26], July 27, 1921[26].
	v.	PERFECTO SÁNCHEZ, b. May 21, 1910, Arabela, Territory of New México[27]; m. EULALIA SÁNCHEZ, June 17, 1929, Carrizozo, New México[27].
10.	vi.	MAX CARABAJAL SÁNCHEZ, b. November 25, 1911, Arabela, Territory of New México; d. October 11, 1988, San Patricio, New México.
11.	vii.	BENINO SÁNCHEZ, b. January 25, 1914, Arabela, New México; d. September 15, 1983, San Patricio, New México.
12.	viii.	ADAN SÁNCHEZ, b. September 02, 1915, Arabela, New México.
13.	ix.	ERMINIO SÁNCHEZ, b. March 29, 1917, Arabela, New México; d. March 04, 1998, Roswell, New México.
	x.	EPUNUCENO SÁNCHEZ[28], b. January 17, 1919, Arabela, New México; d. August 01, 1987, Tinnie, New México; m. OLYMPIA SÁNCHEZ[29], August 27, 1938, Carrizozo, New México[30].
	xi.	MABEL CARABAJAL SÁNCHEZ, b. 1920, Arabela, New México[31].

xii.   CAROLINA SÁNCHEZ[32], b. August 05, 1922, Arabela, New México[33]; d. November 05, 1980; m. ELFIGO POLACO[34], September 13, 1939, Carrizozo, New México[35].

xiii.   PILAR SÁNCHEZ, b. November 25, 1924, Arabela, New México; d. January 15, 2005, San Leandro, California; m. HENRY DUTCHOVER.

Notes for PILAR SÁNCHEZ:
Also known as Pearl S. Dutchover.

Notes for HENRY DUTCHOVER:
WW II Veteran. Served 12/02/1943 to 01/19/1946.
Buried in San Joaquin Valley National Cemetary.

xiv.   EVA SÁNCHEZ, b. 1926, Arabela, New México[36].

xv.   FLORA CARABAJAL SÁNCHEZ, b. 1928, Arabela, New México[36]; m. MANUEL MONTOYA SÁNCHEZ[37].

Notes for FLORA CARABAJAL SÁNCHEZ:
Also known as Florita.

Generation No. 3

5. MARTINA[3] REGALADO *(ROSALÍA CHÁVEZ[2] SÁNCHEZ, JOSÉ[1])[38]* was born April 12, 1884 in Rio Bonito, Territory of New México[39]. She married JOSÉ PEREA July 24, 1899 in Rebentón, Territory of New México[40], son of DELFINIA SÁNCHEZ.

Notes for JOSÉ PEREA:
1900 Census: Living in Rebentón, Territory of New México.
1910 Census: Living in Las Palas, Territory of New México.
1920 Census: Living in Carizozo, New México.

Children of MARTINA REGALADO and JOSÉ PEREA are:

i.   ELISEO[4] PEREA[41], b. June 15, 1900, Rebentón, Territory of New México[42]; d. November 10, 1984, Carrizozo, New México; m. JOSEFITA LUERAS, September 07, 1939, Ancho, New México[43].

ii.   CATALINA PEREA[44], b. Abt. 1903, Rebentón, Territory of New México[45]; d. May 12, 1923, Carrizozo, New México.

iii.   JOSÉ PEREA[46], b. May 13, 1910, Las Palas, Territory of New México[47]; d. January 1982, Carrizozo, New México.

iv.   ANTONIO PEREA[48], b. October 08, 1913, Carrizozo, New México[49]; d. October 02, 1994.

v.   SEFERINA PEREA, b. Abt. 1916, Carrizozo, New México[49].

vi.   MARÍA PEREA, b. Abt. 1919, Carrizozo, New México[49].

6. JOSÉ[3] REGALADO *(ROSALÍA CHÁVEZ[2] SÁNCHEZ, JOSÉ[1])[50]* was born February 25, 1887 in Lincoln, Territory of New México[51], and died June 1972 in Roswell, New México. He married FRANCISCA MARRUJO September 04, 1905 in Rebentón, Territory of New México[51], daughter of VICTOR MARRUJO and TOMASA RIOS.

Notes for JOSÉ REGALADO:
Also known as José Regalao.
1900 Census: José has been listed twice in the Census. He is shown to be living with his father Juan Regalado and he is also shown to be living with his sister Martina Regalado de Perea.

Notes for FRANCISCA MARRUJO:
Also known as Francisca Marrufo.

Children of JOSÉ REGALADO and FRANCISCA MARRUJO are:

    i.   MARGARITA[4] REGALADO.

14.   ii.   ROSA REGALADO, b. May 25, 1907.

    iii.   LUCIA REGALADO, b. May 17, 1909.

    iv.   LUCIO REGALADO, b. May 11, 1911.

15.   v.   SARA REGALADO, b. July 25, 1913, Arabela, New México.

16.   vi.   PERFECTA REGALADO, b. May 13, 1914, Arabela, New México.

17.   vii.   INEZ REGALADO, b. September 20, 1919, Arabela, New México.

    viii.   JUAN MARRUJO REGALADO, b. August 09, 1923.

> ix. ISIDRO REGALADO, b. March 14, 1925.
> x. DAMACIO REGALADO, b. July 23, 1927.
> xi. EROPAJITA REGALADO, b. October 18, 1930.
> xii. JULIAN REGALADO, b. July 10, 1933.

7. LUISA[3] VIGIL *(FRANCISCA[2] SÁNCHEZ, JOSÉ[1])* was born August 1882[52], and died 1936 in Clovis, New México. She married J.T. ALLEN Abt. 1901[53].

Notes for LUISA VIGIL:
The 1900 Census listed her as a neice of Andrés and Rosario. She was living with them at the time that the census was taken.

Children of LUISA VIGIL and J.T. ALLEN are:
> i. JOE[4] ALLEN, b. Abt. 1902, Ruidoso, New México[53].
> ii. GEORGE ALLEN, b. Abt. 1903, Ruidoso, New México[53].
> iii. JOHN ALLEN, b. Abt. 1905, Ruidoso, New México[53].
> iv. WILLIE ALLEN, b. Abt. 1906, Ruidoso, New México[53].
> v. ROBERT ALLEN, b. Abt. 1910, Ruidoso, New México[53].

8. ROSARIO[3] RODRÍGUEZ *(FRANCISCA[2] SÁNCHEZ, JOSÉ[1])* was born Abt. January 1869[54], and died January 24, 1940 in Carrizozo, New México[55]. She married ANDRÉS HERRERA[56], son of FERNANDO HERRERA and JULIANA MARTÍN.

Children of ROSARIO RODRÍGUEZ and ANDRÉS HERRERA are:
> i. FERNANDO ANTONIO[4] HERRERA, b. May 13, 1885, Rebentón, Territory of New México[57]; m. PAULA WARNER, January 16, 1916, Carrizozo, New México[57].
> ii. LINO HERRERA[58], b. September 23, 1888, San Juanito (Ruidoso), Territory of New México; d. September 29, 1944, Carrizozo, New México.
> iii. TEODORA HERRERA, b. November 09, 1889, San Juanito (Ruidoso), Territory of New México[59]; m. JOSÉ SAÍZ, October 18, 1914, Carrizozo, New México[59].
> iv. MARCELO HERRERA[60], b. January 16, 1892, San Juanito (Ruidoso Downs), Territory of New México[61]; d. October 1970, Roswell, New México; m. CONFERINA ORISITACIÓN SÁNCHEZ[62], July 10, 1911, Ruidoso, Territory of New México[63].
> v. JUAN HERRERA, b. March 08, 1894, San Juanito (Ruidoso), Territory of New México[64]; d. February 12, 1954, Carrizozo, New México[65]; m. DELFINIA MEDINA, February 02, 1935[66].
> vi. MARÍA PERFECTA HERRERA, b. April 28, 1896, San Juanito (Ruidoso Downs), Territory of New México[67].
> vii. PETRA HERRERA, b. May 13, 1898, San Juanito (Ruidoso Downs), Territory of New México[68]; m. BENJAMÍN SÁNCHEZ, February 20, 1914, Carrizozo, New México[68].
> viii. MARCELINO HERRERA[69], b. June 02, 1901, Glencoe, Territory of New México; d. May 07, 1980, Alamagordo, New México.
> ix. DONACIANO HERRERA, b. July 17, 1905, Ruidoso, Territory of New México[70]; m. FEDELINA JARAMILLO, November 12, 1950, Carrizozo, New México[70].
> x. ANDRÉS RODRÍGUEZ HERRERA[71], b. August 07, 1909, Glencoe, Territory of New México[72]; d. December 18, 1998, Alamagordo, New México; m. SARAFINA APODACA, April 21, 1930, Carrizozo, New México[73].

9. PAULITA[3] SÁNCHEZ *(SIMÓN WILSON[2], JOSÉ[1])* was born September 01, 1900 in Rebentón, Territory of New México[74], and died 1928-1930[75]. She married CRESENCIO UDERO[76] December 02, 1916 in Arabela, New México[77], son of MACEDONIO UDERO and AGAPITA GUEBARA.

Notes for CRESENCIO UDERO:
1910 Census: Living in San Patricio, Territory of New México.
1920 Census: Living in Las Palas, New México.
1930 Census: Living in Lake Arthur, New México.

Children of PAULITA SÁNCHEZ and CRESENCIO UDERO are:
> i. AGAPITA[4] UDERO, b. Abt. 1914[78].
> ii. GOMICINDA UDERO, b. Abt. 1917[79].
> iii. FELICITA UDERO, b. Abt. 1920[79].
> iv. MACEDONIO UDERO, b. Abt. 1922[79].
> v. MANUEL UDERO, b. Abt. 1925[79].
> vi. ABIRA UDERO, b. Abt. 1928[79].

10. MAX CARABAJAL[3] SÁNCHEZ *(SIMÓN WILSON[2], JOSÉ[1])*[80] was born November 25, 1911 in Arabela, Territory of New México, and died October 11, 1988 in San Patricio, New México. He married CRUSITA YBARRA[80] October 08, 1932 in San Patricio, New México[81], daughter of GREGORIO YBARRA and CATARINA MONTOYA.

Notes for MAX CARABAJAL SÁNCHEZ:
Also known as Maximiliano. 1930 Census lists him as Marcelino.

Notes for CRUSITA YBARRA:
Also known as Cruz.
1930 Census: Lists as living with Elfida Montoya Chávez.

Child of MAX SÁNCHEZ and CRUSITA YBARRA is:
    i.   DOROTHY ALICE[4] SÁNCHEZ[82], b. Abt. 1940, San Patricio, New México; d. July 21, 1940, San Patricio, New México.

11. BENINO[3] SÁNCHEZ *(SIMÓN WILSON[2], JOSÉ[1])*[83] was born January 25, 1914 in Arabela, New México, and died September 15, 1983 in San Patricio, New México. He married TRENIDAD GONZÁLES[84] June 01, 1934 in Carrizozo, New México[85], daughter of AURORA GONZÁLES.

Notes for BENINO SÁNCHEZ:
Also known as Ben.

Child of BENINO SÁNCHEZ and TRENIDAD GONZÁLES is:
    i.   SONNY[4] SÁNCHEZ, b. Private.

12. ADAN[3] SÁNCHEZ *(SIMÓN WILSON[2], JOSÉ[1])*[86] was born September 02, 1915 in Arabela, New México[87]. He married SIGISMUNDA GONZÁLES[88] August 18, 1948 in Carrizozo, New México[89], daughter of EPAMINOANDAS GONZÁLES and ELVIRA GONZÁLES.

Notes for ADAN SÁNCHEZ:
Lived in Arizona.

Child of ADAN SÁNCHEZ and SIGISMUNDA GONZÁLES is:
    i.   YOLANDA GONZÁLES[4] SÁNCHEZ, b. Private.

13. ERMINIO[3] SÁNCHEZ *(SIMÓN WILSON[2], JOSÉ[1])*[90] was born March 29, 1917 in Arabela, New México, and died March 04, 1998 in Roswell, New México. He married (1) DELICIA GUSTAMONTE January 29, 1940 in Carrizozo, New México[91]. He married (2) CONSUELO MENDOSA[92] December 07, 1944 in Roswell, New México[93], daughter of LORENSO MENDOSA and SUSANA MONTOYA.

Notes for ERMINIO SÁNCHEZ:
About 1944: Erminio and his family moved to Roswell, New México.

Notes for CONSUELO MENDOSA:
Her mother died when she was 12 years old. She accepted the responibility of caring for her younger brothers and sisters.

Children of ERMINIO SÁNCHEZ and DELICIA GUSTAMONTE are:
    i.   CHRISTINE[4] SÁNCHEZ, b. January 12, 1942, Arabela, New México; d. June 13, 1942, Arabela, New México.
    ii.   ANTONIA CELESTINA SÁNCHEZ, b. January 13, 1943.

Children of ERMINIO SÁNCHEZ and CONSUELO MENDOSA are:
    iii.   ROSE[4] SÁNCHEZ[93], b. Private.
    iv.   JOE SÁNCHEZ[93], b. Private.
    v.   LLOYD SÁNCHEZ[93], b. Private.
    vi.   PRISCILLA SÁNCHEZ[93], b. Private.
    vii.   BERNICE MENDOZA SÁNCHEZ[93], b. Private.
    viii.   GRACE MENDOZA SÁNCHEZ[93], b. Private.
    ix.   ELMO SÁNCHEZ[93], b. Private.

    x.   VELMA SÁNCHEZ[93], b. Private.
    xi.   TERRY SÁNCHEZ[93], b. Private.
    xii. ELIZABETH MENDOZA SÁNCHEZ[93], b. Private.

Generation No. 4

14. ROSA[4] REGALADO *(JOSÉ[3], ROSALÍA CHÁVEZ[2] SÁNCHEZ, JOSÉ[1])* was born May 25, 1907[94]. She married CRUZ MONTOYA GUEVARA June 05, 1922[94], son of CRUZ GUEBARA and SARA MONTOYA.

Children of ROSA REGALADO and CRUZ GUEVARA are:
    i.   ISMAEL[5] GUEVARA, b. Private.
    ii.   FRUTOSO GUEVARA, b. Private.
    iii. ACARIA GUEVARA, b. Private.
    iv. CLOVÍS GUEVARA, b. Private.
    v.   JULIA GUEVARA, b. Private.
    vi. ISOYLA GUEVARA, b. Private.
    vii. VIOLA GUEVARA, b. Private.
    viii. GEORGE GUEVARA, b. Private.

15. SARA[4] REGALADO *(JOSÉ[3], ROSALÍA CHÁVEZ[2] SÁNCHEZ, JOSÉ[1])* was born July 25, 1913 in Arabela, New México[95]. She married MIGUEL ROMERO December 18, 1934 in Arabela, New México[96], son of PORFIRIO ROMERO and AVRORA GONZÁLES.

Children of SARA REGALADO and MIGUEL ROMERO are:
    i.   PORFIRIO[5] ROMERO[97], b. January 26, 1944, Arabela, New México; d. January 12, 2000; m. ALICE CHÁVEZ.
    ii.   AVRORA ROMERO, b. Private.
    iii. FRANK ROMERO, b. Private.
    iv. IRENE ROMERO, b. Private.
    v.   JOYCE ROMERO, b. Private.
    vi. ROSA ROMERO, b. Private.
    vii. RUDOLFO ROMERO, b. Private.

16. PERFECTA[4] REGALADO *(JOSÉ[3], ROSALÍA CHÁVEZ[2] SÁNCHEZ, JOSÉ[1])* was born May 13, 1914 in Arabela, New México[98]. She married LAZARO GUEVARA[99] July 30, 1930 in Carrizozo, New México[100], son of CRUZ GUEBARA and SARA MONTOYA.

Notes for LAZARO GUEVARA:
Name also recorded as Lazaro Gallegos.

Children of PERFECTA REGALADO and LAZARO GUEVARA are:
    i.   DORA[5] GUEVARA, b. Private.
    ii.   RUFINA GUEVARA, b. Private.
    iii. TOMMY GUEVARA, b. Private.
    iv. PAUL GUEVARA, b. Private.
    v.   MARY GUEVARA, b. Private.
    vi. GLORIA GUEVARA, b. Private.
    vii. LASARO REGALADO GUEVARA, b. Private.

17. INEZ[4] REGALADO *(JOSÉ[3], ROSALÍA CHÁVEZ[2] SÁNCHEZ, JOSÉ[1])* was born September 20, 1919 in Arabela, New México[101]. She married CLAUDIO ROMERO July 24, 1935 in Carrizozo, New México[101], son of PEDRO ROMERO and CLEOTILDE FRESQUEZ.

Children of INEZ REGALADO and CLAUDIO ROMERO are:
    i.   MINNIE[5] ROMERO, b. Private, Arabela, New México; m. BREZEL ROBERT SÁNCHEZ.
    ii.   ALBERT ROMERO, b. Private, Arabela, New México.
    iii. RALPH ROMERO, b. Private, Arabela, New México.
    iv. LORENA ROMERO, b. Private, Arabela, New México.

Genealogy of Juan José Bitello Sánches

Generation No. 1

1. JUAN JOSÉ BITELLO[1] SÁNCHES was born Abt. 1800[1]. He married MARÍA MANUELA CHÁVES.

Notes for JUAN JOSÉ BITELLO SÁNCHES:
1850 Census: Living in Valencia, Territory of New México.

Notes for MARÍA MANUELA CHÁVES:
Also known as María Manuela Cháves de Sánches.

Children of JUAN SÁNCHES and MARÍA CHÁVES are:
2.   i.   JUAN JOSÉ[2] SÁNCHES, b. Abt. 1827.
       ii.   FRANCISCO SÁNCHES, b. Abt. 1830[1].
       iii.   MANUEL SÁNCHES, b. Abt. 1836[1].
       iv.   TRINIDAD SÁNCHES, b. Abt. 1838[1].
       v.   CONCEPCIÓN SÁNCHES, b. Abt. 1841[1].
       vi.   CANDELARIA SÁNCHES, b. Abt. 1843[1].
       vii.   JESÚS SÁNCHES, b. Abt. 1844[1].
       viii. JUANA SÁNCHES, b. Abt. 1849[1].

Generation No. 2

2. JUAN JOSÉ[2] SÁNCHES *(JUAN JOSÉ BITELLO[1])* was born Abt. 1827[2]. He married MARÍA ANDREA ANALLA, daughter of YSIDORO ANALLA and DOLÓRES GALLEGOS.

Notes for JUAN JOSÉ SÁNCHES:
Also known as José Chávez y Sánchez.
1850 Census: Living in Valencia, Territory of New México
1860 Census: Living in Punta de Agua, Territory of New México.

Notes for MARÍA ANDREA ANALLA:
Also known as María Antonia Anaya, María Andrea Analla, Andrea.

Child of JUAN SÁNCHES and MARÍA ANALLA is:
3.   i.   ESIQUIO[3] SÁNCHEZ, b. November 1854, Punta de Agua, Territory of New México; d. Bef. 1904.

Generation No. 3

3. ESIQUIO[3] SÁNCHEZ *(JUAN JOSÉ[2] SÁNCHES, JUAN JOSÉ BITELLO[1])* was born November 1854 in Punta de Agua, Territory of New México[3], and died Bef. 1904[4]. He married MARÍA ISABEL ANALLA April 24, 1873 in Lincoln County, Territory of New México[5], daughter of JOSÉ ANALLA and MARÍA SEDILLO.

Notes for ESIQUIO SÁNCHEZ:
Also known as Isaquio.
1860 Census: Living in Punta de Agua, Territory of New México.
1880 Census: Living in La Plaza de San Patricio, Territory of New México.
Land Patent # NMNMAA 010830, on the authority of the Homestead Entry-Original (12 Stat. 392), May 20, 1862. Issued 160 acres.
Land Patent # NMNMAA 010832, on the authority of the Sale cash entry (3 Stat. 566), April 24, 1820, 240.17 acres.
Esiquio Sánchez owned all the farm land from the Coe Ranch on the west to Florencio Gonzáles farm near San Patricio on the east. His land holdings were about 2 1/2 miles long and 1/5 mile wide, and fronted both banks of the Río Ruidoso.

Children of ESIQUIO SÁNCHEZ and MARÍA ANALLA are:
       i.   JOSÉ ANALLA[4] SÁNCHEZ, b. Abt. 1874[6]; m. NESTORA FLORES, February 01, 1893, Lincoln County, Territory of New México[7].
       ii.   MIGUEL ANALLA SÁNCHEZ, b. Abt. 1876[8].

    iii.   NICOLASA ANALLA SÁNCHEZ, b. Abt. 1878[8].
    iv.   LYDIA SÁNCHEZ, b. Abt. 1879[8]; m. PEDRO VILLESCAS, December 04, 1895, Lincoln County, Territory of New México[9].

    Notes for PEDRO VILLESCAS:
    1900 Census: Living in Ruidoso, Territory of New México.

4.   v.   JOSEFA ANALLA SÁNCHEZ, b. August 27, 1881, Picacho, Territory of New México.
    vi.   ROSENDA SÁNCHEZ, b. March 1883, San Patricio, Territory of New México[10]; m. CELESTINO VIGIL, July 15, 1901[11].

    Notes for CELESTINO VIGIL:
    Also known as José Celestino Vigil.
    1940s: He was a deputy sheriff for Lincoln County.

    vii.   GERONIMO SÁNCHEZ, b. September 30, 1885, San Patricio, Territory of New México[12].
    viii.   ESIQUIO SÁNCHEZ[13], b. April 15, 1887, San Patricio, Territory of New México[14]; m. CARMEN A. WILSON, September 26, 1938, San Patricio, New México[15].

    Notes for ESIQUIO SÁNCHEZ:
    September 26, 1938 Marriage record: Living in Alamogordo, New México.

    ix.   MALCLOVIA SÁNCHEZ, b. November 1892, San Patricio, Territory of New México[16].
    x.   VICTORIANA SÁNCHEZ, b. May 1900, San Patricio, Territory of New México[16].

Generation No. 4

4. JOSEFA ANALLA[4] SÁNCHEZ *(ESIQUIO[3], JUAN JOSÉ[2] SÁNCHES, JUAN JOSÉ BITELLO[1])* was born August 27, 1881 in Picacho, Territory of New México[17]. She married SEVERO PADILLA March 04, 1899[18], son of CENOBIO PADILLA and SATURNINA TORRES.

Child of JOSEFA SÁNCHEZ and SEVERO PADILLA is:
    i.   DELFINIA PADILLA Y[5] WEST, b. November 21, 1900, San Patricio, Territory of New México[19]; m. FIDEL CHÁVEZ[20], June 28, 1915, Lincoln, New México[21].

    Notes for DELFINIA PADILLA Y WEST:
    Also known as Delfinia Sánchez, Delfinia Sánchez y West.
    Raised and adopted by John C. West.

    Notes for FIDEL CHÁVEZ:
    Lists his mother as Francisquita Luna.

Genealogy of Tomás Sánches

Generation No. 1

1. TOMÁS[1] SÁNCHES was born Abt. 1770[1]. He married MARÍA RITA JULIANA LUSERO.

Notes for TOMÁS SÁNCHES:
One of the original petitioners for the Manzano Land Grant.
1850 Census: Living in Manzano, Territory of New México. (Born 1870)

Children of TOMÁS SÁNCHES and MARÍA LUSERO are:
2.   i.   FILOMENO[2] SÁNCHES, b. July 05, 1819, San Rafael del Guique, El Reyno de Nuevo México, Nueva España.
        ii.   ANTONIO JOSEF SÁNCHES, b. April 12, 1816, Taos, El Reyno de Nuevo México, Nueva España[2].

Generation No. 2

2. FILOMENO[2] SÁNCHES *(TOMÁS[1])[3]* was born July 05, 1819 in San Rafael del Guique, El Reyno de Nuevo México, Nueva España[4]. He married VICTORIA SÁNCHES[5] Abt. 1845[6], daughter of LUZ BARCELO SÁNCHES.

Notes for FILOMENO SÁNCHES:
Also known as José Filomeno de Jesús Sánches.
July 08, 1819: Baptized in San Juan de los Caballeros, El Reyno de Nuevo México, Nueva España.
1850, 1860, 1880 & 1900 Census: Living in Manzano, Territory of New México.
March 02, 1867: A bill was passed abolishing peonage, and Filomeno released his servants. He immediately adopted them as his children.

Notes for VICTORIA SÁNCHES:
Also known as Victorita, Victoriana.

Children of FILOMENO SÁNCHES and VICTORIA SÁNCHES are:
        i.   BARTOLA[3] SÁNCHEZ, Adopted child.

               Notes for BARTOLA SÁNCHEZ:
               Captured Navajo, who took the Sánchez surname. Adopted by Filomeno "El Patron" Sánchez & his wife, Victoria.

       ii.   CRUZ SÁNCHEZ, Adopted child.

               Notes for CRUZ SÁNCHEZ:
               Captured Navajo, who took the Sánchez surname. Adopted by Filomeno "El Patron" Sánchez & his wife, Victoria.
               Baptismal records indicate she may have had a daughter, Emilia Sánchez in Lincoln County, Territory of New México.

      iii.   RAFAEL SÁNCHEZ, Adopted child; m. MAXIMILIANA DE SÁNCHEZ, May 18, 1893, Manzano, Territory of New México[7].

               Notes for RAFAEL SÁNCHEZ:
               Captured Navajo, who took the Sánchez surname. Adopted by Filomeno "El Patron" Sánchez & his wife, Victoria.

      iv.   JULIAN SÁNCHEZ, b. Abt. 1853[8]; Adopted child.

               Notes for JULIAN SÁNCHEZ:
               Captured Navajo, who took the Sánchez surname. Adopted by Filomeno "El Patron" Sánchez & his wife, Victoria.

       v.   MARÍA SÁNCHEZ, b. Abt. 1856[9].

               Notes for MARÍA SÁNCHEZ:
               Captured Navajo, who took the Sánchez surname. Adopted by Filomeno "El Patron" Sánchez & his wife, Victoria.
               1870 Census: Lists her name as Atamaria.

3.   vi.   EUGENIO SÁNCHEZ, b. September 1856, Manzano, Territory of New México; d. September 17, 1935, Manzano, New México.

vii.   TOMASITA SÁNCHEZ, b. Abt. 1858[10]; Adopted child.

Notes for TOMASITA SÁNCHEZ:
Captured Navajo, who took the Sánchez surname.

4.   viii.   MANUEL SÁNCHEZ, b. Abt. 1859; Adopted child.
         ix.   GUADALUPE SÁNCHEZ, b. Abt. 1861[11].

Notes for GUADALUPE SÁNCHEZ:
Captured Navajo, who took the Sánchez surname. Adopted by Filomeno "El Patron" Sánchez & his wife, Victoria.

         x.   JUAN SÁNCHEZ, b. Abt. 1867[12]; Adopted child.
         xi.   JESÚS SÁNCHEZ, b. Abt. 1868[13].

Generation No. 3

Eugenio Sánchez

3. EUGENIO[3] SÁNCHEZ *(FILOMENO[2] SÁNCHES, TOMÁS[1])*[14] was born September 1856 in Manzano, Territory of New México[15], and died September 17, 1935 in Manzano, New México[16]. He married ROSA GRIEGO 1882 in Manzano, New México[17].

Notes for EUGENIO SÁNCHEZ:
Also known as Eusevio.
Captured Navajo, who took the Sánchez surname. Adopted by Filomeno "El Patron" Sánchez & his wife, Victoria.
Death records indicate that his parents were Filomeno Sánchez, Victoria G. Varseton .
Migrated to Lincoln County and settled in an area known as Las Angusturas.
1870 Census: Lists his birthyear as 1861.
Land Patent # NMR 0001454, on the authority of the Homestead Entry-Original (12 Stat. 392), May 20, 1862. Issued 80 acres on June 09, 1910.

Children of EUGENIO SÁNCHEZ and ROSA GRIEGO are:
5.   i.   JOSÉ GRIEGO[4] SÁNCHEZ, b. Abt. 1906.
6.   ii.   AVRORA GRIEGO SÁNCHEZ, b. March 14, 1884, Manzano, Territory of New México; d. September 30, 1955, San Patricio, New México.
7.   iii.   TEODORO GRIEGO SÁNCHEZ, b. March 1886.
8.   iv.   FILOMENO GRIEGO SÁNCHEZ, b. December 1887, Manzano, Territory of New México; d. February 11, 1937, Manzano,New México.
9.   v.   JUAN GRIEGO SÁNCHEZ, b. December 1890.
10.   vi.   RITA GRIEGO SÁNCHEZ, b. July 1892.
         vii.   GERTRUDES GRIEGO SÁNCHEZ, b. December 1894[18]. Died young.
         viii.   MANUEL GRIEGO SÁNCHEZ, b. November 1896[18]. Died young.
11.   ix.   ENRÍQUES GRIEGO SÁNCHEZ, b. May 1898.
12.   x.   MARÍA AGIDA GRIEGO SÁNCHEZ, b. March 10, 1900.
13.   xi.   TELESFORO GRIEGO SÁNCHEZ, b. February 21, 1902, Ruidoso, Territory of New México.
         xii.   REYES GRIEGO SÁNCHEZ. Died young.

4. MANUEL[3] SÁNCHEZ *(FILOMENO[2] SÁNCHES, TOMÁS[1])* was born Abt. 1859[19]. He married GUADALUPE PADILLA April 23, 1876 in Manzano, Territory of New México[20], daughter of ANTONIO PADILLA and FRANCISCA LÓPEZ.

Notes for MANUEL SÁNCHEZ:
Captured Navajo, who took the Sánchez surname. Adopted by Filomeno "El Patron" Sánchez & his wife, Victoria.

Children of MANUEL SÁNCHEZ and GUADALUPE PADILLA are:
         i.   EUGENIO[4] SÁNCHEZ.
         ii.   JOSEFA SÁNCHEZ, b. March 15, 1877, Manzano, Territory of New México[21].
         iii.   MARÍA HILARIA SÁNCHEZ, b. January 14, 1879, Manzano, Territory of New México[21].

iv.   MARÍA EPIFANIA SÁNCHEZ, b. April 05, 1881, Manzano, Territory of New México[21].
v.   NATIVIDAD SÁNCHEZ, b. December 25, 1882, Manzano, Territory of New México[21].

Generation No. 4

5. JOSÉ GRIEGO[4] SÁNCHEZ *(EUGENIO[3], FILOMENO[2] SÁNCHES, TOMÁS[1])* was born Abt. 1906. He married PABLITA DE SÁNCHEZ[22].

Children of JOSÉ SÁNCHEZ and PABLITA DE SÁNCHEZ are:
  i.   MARCELINA[5] SÁNCHEZ[22], b. Private.
  ii.   FILOMENO SÁNCHEZ[22], b. Private.
  iii. PAULINE SÁNCHEZ[22], b. Private.
  iv.   FERNANDA SÁNCHEZ[22], b. Private.
  v.   ISABEL SÁNCHEZ[22], b. Private.
  vi.   CARMELA SÁNCHEZ[22], b. Private.

6. AVRORA GRIEGO[4] SÁNCHEZ *(EUGENIO[3], FILOMENO[2] SÁNCHES, TOMÁS[1])[23]* was born March 14, 1884 in Manzano, Territory of New México, and died September 30, 1955 in San Patricio, New México. She married MAURICIO MONTOYA[24] December 15, 1902 in La Capilla de San Ysidro, Las Angusturas, Territory of New México[25], son of FELIPÉ MONTOYA and PAULA GARCÍA.

Notes for AVRORA GRIEGO SÁNCHEZ:
Also known as Aurora.
1902: Living Las Angusturas (San Ysidro), near La Capilla de San Ysidro.

Children of AVRORA SÁNCHEZ and MAURICIO MONTOYA are:
  i.   MASIMIANA[5] MONTOYA[26], b. September 09, 1903, San Patricio, New México[27]; d. June 20, 1963, Hondo, New México; m. ELFIDO SALAS[28], February 13, 1924, Lincoln County, New México[29].

        Notes for MASIMIANA MONTOYA:
        Also known as Maximiana.

        Notes for ELFIDO SALAS:
        Also known as Elfigo, Delfido.
        Land Patent # NMLC 0025968, on the authority of the Homestead Entry-Stock Raising (39 Stat. 862), December 29, 1916. Issued 611 acres on August 16, 1927.

  ii.   FLAVIO MONTOYA[30], b. February 22, 1905, Lincoln, Territory of New México[31]; d. April 07, 1979, Alamagordo, New México; m. GENEVA KIMBRELL[31], December 24, 1934[31].

        Notes for FLAVIO MONTOYA:
        Private First Class US Army. WW II Veteran.

  iii. JOSÉ SÁNCHEZ MONTOYA, b. 1907[32].
  iv.   SANTIAGO SÁNCHEZ MONTOYA[33], b. February 23, 1910; d. January 14, 1945.

        Notes for SANTIAGO SÁNCHEZ MONTOYA:
        New Mexico Private 940 Guard. Died in WW II.

  v.   YSIDRO MONTOYA[33], b. May 15, 1913, San Patricio, New México; d. December 01, 1960, Roswell, New México; m. BLASITA PERALES.

        Notes for YSIDRO MONTOYA:
        New Mexico Private First Class 3263 Sig Service Co. Was a WW II veteran.

  vi.   MANUEL SÁNCHEZ MONTOYA, b. April 30, 1915, San Patricio, New México[34]; d. April 24, 1994; m. CELIA SÁNCHEZ[35].

        Notes for MANUEL SÁNCHEZ MONTOYA:
        WW II Veteran.

  vii. ROSA MONTOYA[35], b. August 18, 1918, San Patricio, New México; d. July 07, 1991, San Patricio, New México; m. ELISEO GALLEGOS[35].

  viii. EUTILIA MONTOYA[36], b. December 23, 1920, San Patricio, New México[37]; d. December 04, 2005, Mescalero, New México; m. ESTOLANO OROSCO SÁNCHEZ[38].

  ix. TAVIANA MONTOYA[39], b. December 28, 1922, San Patricio, New México[40]; d. July 26, 1968; m. ABSALÓN SÁNCHEZ[41], August 25, 1945, San Patricio, New México[42].

  x. JUAN SÁNCHEZ MONTOYA, b. Private, San Patricio, New México; m. EVA GONZÁLES, August 13, 1948, Carrizozo, New México[43].

  Notes for JUAN SÁNCHEZ MONTOYA:
  US Navy, Seaman First Class. World War II.

7. TEODORO GRIEGO[4] SÁNCHEZ *(EUGENIO[3], FILOMENO[2] SÁNCHES, TOMÁS[1])* was born March 1886[44]. He married JUANITA VIGIL[45].

Children of TEODORO SÁNCHEZ and JUANITA VIGIL are:
  i. ERNESTO[5] SÁNCHEZ[45], b. Private; m. CONCHA DE SÁNCHEZ[45].
  ii. MANUEL SÁNCHEZ[45], b. Private; m. LUCY DE SÁNCHEZ[45].
  iii. MARGARITA SÁNCHEZ[45], b. Private.

8. FILOMENO GRIEGO[4] SÁNCHEZ *(EUGENIO[3], FILOMENO[2] SÁNCHES, TOMÁS[1])* was born December 1887 in Manzano, Territory of New México[46], and died February 11, 1937 in Manzano, New México[47]. He married REFUGIA VIGIL 1915, daughter of BITERBO VIGIL and ROMANSITA ROMERO.

Notes for FILOMENO GRIEGO SÁNCHEZ:
1900 Census: Living in Ruidoso, Territory of New México.
1920 Census: Living in Manzano, New México.

Children of FILOMENO SÁNCHEZ and REFUGIA VIGIL are:
  i. SAMUEL[5] SÁNCHEZ, b. Abt. 1919, Manzano, New México[48].
  ii. MARÍA SÁNCHEZ[49], b. Private.
  iii. JACOBO SÁNCHEZ[49], b. Private.
  iv. FLORENCIO SÁNCHEZ[49], b. Private.

9. JUAN GRIEGO[4] SÁNCHEZ *(EUGENIO[3], FILOMENO[2] SÁNCHES, TOMÁS[1])* was born December 1890[50]. He married FLORA AMELIA DE SÁNCHEZ[51].

Children of JUAN SÁNCHEZ and FLORA DE SÁNCHEZ are:
  i. VICTORIA[5] SÁNCHEZ[51], b. Private; m. PROCOPIO LÓPEZ[51].
  ii. TERESA SÁNCHEZ[51], b. Private.
  iii. ELARIO SÁNCHEZ[51], b. Private; m. PETRA MOLINA[51].
  iv. CARMEL SÁNCHEZ[51], b. Private.

10. RITA GRIEGO[4] SÁNCHEZ *(EUGENIO[3], FILOMENO[2] SÁNCHES, TOMÁS[1])* was born July 1892[52]. She married PEDRO NÚÑEZ.

Children of RITA SÁNCHEZ and PEDRO NÚÑEZ are:
  i. RAY[5] NÚÑEZ, b. Private.
  ii. SALOMÓN NÚÑEZ, b. Private.
  iii. ELÍAS NÚÑEZ, b. Private.
  iv. GERTRUDES NÚÑEZ, b. Private.

11. ENRÍQUES GRIEGO[4] SÁNCHEZ *(EUGENIO[3], FILOMENO[2] SÁNCHES, TOMÁS[1])* was born May 1898[52]. He married PEREGRINA SÁNCHEZ[53].

Children of ENRÍQUES SÁNCHEZ and PEREGRINA SÁNCHEZ are:
  i. GREGORITA[5] SÁNCHEZ[53], b. Private.
  ii. MARCELA SÁNCHEZ[53], b. Private; m. RAMÓN SISNEROS[53].
  iii. HELEN SÁNCHEZ[53], b. Private.
  iv. ISMENIA SÁNCHEZ[53], b. Private; m. FELIX GUTIERREZ[53].

v.   JOSEFITA SÁNCHEZ[53], b. Private.
vi.   FRANCES SÁNCHEZ[53], b. Private; m. HERMAN GALLEGOS[53].

12. MARÍA AGIDA GRIEGO[4] SÁNCHEZ *(EUGENIO[3], FILOMENO[2] SÁNCHES, TOMÁS[1])* was born March 10, 1900[54]. She married FRANCISCO SÁNCHEZ.

Children of MARÍA SÁNCHEZ and FRANCISCO SÁNCHEZ are:
i.   FLORA[5] SÁNCHEZ, b. Private; m. DAVÍD LÓPEZ.
ii.   FLORENCIO SÁNCHEZ, b. Private; m. JUANITA SEDILLO.
iii.   REGINA SÁNCHEZ, b. Private; m. ALVINO SILVA.
iv.   EUGENIO SÁNCHEZ, b. Private.

13. TELESFORO GRIEGO[4] SÁNCHEZ *(EUGENIO[3], FILOMENO[2] SÁNCHES, TOMÁS[1])* was born February 21, 1902 in Ruidoso, Territory of New México[55]. He married IGINIA DE SÁNCHEZ[56].

Children of TELESFORO SÁNCHEZ and IGINIA DE SÁNCHEZ are:
i.   ANTONIO[5] SÁNCHEZ[56], b. Private.
ii.   WILLIE SÁNCHEZ[56], b. Private.
iii.   ROSA SÁNCHEZ[56], b. Private; m. LEO APODACA[56].
iv.   CORRINA SÁNCHEZ[56], b. Private.
v.   JESÚS SÁNCHEZ[56], b. Private.
vi.   ROBERTO SÁNCHEZ[56], b. Private.
vii.   ANGELINA SÁNCHEZ[56], b. Private.

Genealogy of Pedro de Cedillo Rico de Rojas

Generation No. 1

1. PEDRO DE CEDILLO RICO[1] DE ROJAS[1]. He married ISABEL LÓPES DE GRACIA[1].

Children of PEDRO DE ROJAS and ISABEL DE GRACIA are:
- i.   CASILDA CEDILLO RICO[2] DE ROJAS[1], m. CRISTÓBAL VARELA JARAMILLO[1].
- ii.   FELIPA CEDILLO RICO DE ROJAS[2], m. FRANCISCO ANALLA ALMAZÁN[3].
- iii. ISABEL CEDILLO RICO DE ROJAS[3], m. JUAN VARELA JARAMILLO[3], February 11, 1692, San Lorenzo del Paso, El Reino de Nuevo Méjico, Nueva España[3].
- iv.   PEDRO CEDILLO RICO DE ROJAS[3].
- 2. v.   JUAN CEDILLO RICO DE ROJAS, b. Abt. 1669; d. Bef. 1736.
- 3. vi.   JOAQUÍN CEDILLO RICO DE ROJAS, b. Abt. 1674.

Generation No. 2

2. JUAN CEDILLO RICO[2] DE ROJAS *(PEDRO DE CEDILLO RICO[1])*[3] was born Abt. 1669[4], and died Bef. 1736[5]. He married MARÍA DE LA CONCEPCIÓN GUTIÉRRES April 21, 1698 in La Villa de Santa Fé, El Reino de Nuevo Méjico, Nueva España[6].

Child of JUAN DE ROJAS and MARÍA GUTIÉRRES is:
- i.   JUANA CEDILLO RICO[3] DE ROJAS, b. Abt. 1700[7]; m. GREGORIO GARDUÑO, Abt. December 12, 1720, La Villa de Santa Fé, El Reino de Nuevo Méjico, Nueva España[7].

3. JOAQUÍN CEDILLO RICO[2] DE ROJAS *(PEDRO DE CEDILLO RICO[1])*[8] was born Abt. 1674[9]. He married MARÍA VARELA October 30, 1695 in La Villa de Santa Fé, El Reino de Nuevo Méjico, Nueva España[9], daughter of PEDRO JARAMILLO and LUCÍA MADRID.

Notes for JOAQUÍN CEDILLO RICO DE ROJAS:
Migrated to the Río Abajo shortly after his marriage in 1695.
Was one of the founding families of Albuquerque.

Children of JOAQUÍN DE ROJAS and MARÍA VARELA are:
- i.   JUANA[3] CEDILLO[10], m. (1) FRANCISCO GARCÍA[10]; m. (2) CARLOS LÓPEZ[10], December 10, 1715.
- ii.   MAGDALENA CEDILLO[10], m. (1) JUAN DE DIOS MARTÍN[10]; m. (2) ANTONIO MARTÍN[10], May 03, 1734, San Juan, El Reino de Nuevo Méjico, Nueva España[11].
- 4. iii.   MIGUEL DE SAN JUAN CEDILLO RICO DE ROJAS, b. San Juan, El Reino de Nuevo Méjico, Nueva España.
- iv.   YSABEL CEDILLO, b. Bef. January 13, 1700, Bernalillo, El Reino de Nuevo Méjico, Nueva España[12].
- v.   ANA CEDILLO, b. Bef. August 01, 1702, Bernalillo, El Reino de Nuevo Méjico, Nueva España[13].
- 5. vi.   ANTONIO CEDILLO, b. Bef. October 09, 1704, Bernalillo, El Reino de Nuevo Méjico, Nueva España.
- vii.   ISABEL CEDILLO, b. April 13, 1707[14].
- 6. viii. DOMINGO FRANCISCO CEDILLO, b. August 16, 1709.

Generation No. 3

4. MIGUEL DE SAN JUAN CEDILLO RICO[3] DE ROJAS *(JOAQUÍN CEDILLO RICO[2], PEDRO DE CEDILLO RICO[1])* was born in San Juan, El Reino de Nuevo Méjico, Nueva España. He married RITA SAMORA October 06, 1754 in Alburquerque, El Reyno de Nuevo Méjico, Nueva España[15].

Notes for MIGUEL DE SAN JUAN CEDILLO RICO DE ROJAS:
Also known as Miguel De San Juan Zedillo, Juan Cedillo.

Children of MIGUEL DE ROJAS and RITA SAMORA are:
- i.   DOMINGO[4] CEDILLO, m. BARBARA LUNA, January 15, 1797, Ysleta, El Reino de Nuevo Méjico, Nueva España[16].
- ii.   JOSÉ RAMOS CEDILLO, m. MARGARITA PEÑA, December 16, 1792, Isleta, El Reino de Nuevo Méjico, Nueva España[16].

     iii.   JUANA CEDILLO, m. JUAN TOMÁS DE LOS ÁNGELES GUERRERO, May 06, 1790, Isleta, El Reino de Nuevo Méjico, Nueva España[17].

     iv.   MARÍA ANTONIA CEDILLO, m. MARCELO TAFOLLA, September 21, 1799, Isleta, El Reino de Nuevo Méjico, Nueva España[18].

7.   v.   BLAS ANTONIO CEDILLO, d. Bef. 1839.

8.   vi.   SIMÓN CEDILLO, b. Abt. 1765, Los Lentes, El Reino de Nuevo Méjico, Nueva España.

     vii.   MARÍA JOSEFA CEDILLO, b. Abt. 1775; m. JOSÉ YGNACIO GALINDO, January 01, 1791, Isleta, El Reino de Nuevo Méjico, Nueva España[18].

5. ANTONIO[3] CEDILLO *(JOAQUÍN CEDILLO RICO[2] DE ROJAS, PEDRO DE CEDILLO RICO[1])* was born Bef. October 09, 1704 in Bernalillo, El Reino de Nuevo Méjico, Nueva España[19]. He married GREGORIA GONZÁLES BAS[20], daughter of JUAN BAS and MARÍA DEL CASTILLO.

Children of ANTONIO CEDILLO and GREGORIA BAS are:

     i.   JOANA MARÍA[4] CEDILLO, b. Bef. November 01, 1733, Alburquerque, El Reino de Nuevo Méjico, Nueva España[21].

     ii.   LAZARO CEDILLO[22], b. Abt. 1736.

     iii.   ALFONZA CEDILLO, b. Bef. January 29, 1736, Albuquerque, Nuevo México, La República de México[23].

     iv.   JUANA MARÍA CEDILLO, b. Bef. January 13, 1737, Albuquerque, Nuevo México, La República de México[23]; m. PEDRO ROMERO, December 18, 1768, Alburquerque, El Reino de Nuevo Méjico, Nueva España[24].

9.   v.   ANTONIO FÉLIX CEDILLO, b. Abt. 1740.

     vi.   FRANCISCA DE LA LUZ CEDILLO, b. Bef. March 17, 1744, Alburquerque, El Reino de Nuevo Méjico, Nueva España[25].

     vii.   JOSEFA CEDILLO[26], b. Abt. 1749.

     viii.   ANDRÉS CEDILLO[26], b. Abt. 1750.

     ix.   ANA FRANCISCA DE LOS DOLORES CEDILLO, b. Bef. October 14, 1751, Alburquerque, El Reino de Nuevo Méjico, Nueva España[27].

6. DOMINGO FRANCISCO[3] CEDILLO *(JOAQUÍN CEDILLO RICO[2] DE ROJAS, PEDRO DE CEDILLO RICO[1])* was born August 16, 1709[28]. He married MARÍA MICHAELA GONZÁLES BAS.

Children of DOMINGO CEDILLO and MARÍA BAS are:

     i.   GREGORIO[4] CEDILLO.

     ii.   BLÁS CEDILLO.

     iii.   MARÍA CEDILLO[29].

     iv.   JOSEFA CEDILLO[29].

     v.   BERNARDO CEDILLO[29].

     vi.   MARÍA DOLORES CEDILLO[29].

Generation No. 4

7. BLAS ANTONIO[4] CEDILLO *(MIGUEL DE SAN JUAN CEDILLO RICO[3] DE ROJAS, JOAQUÍN CEDILLO RICO[2], PEDRO DE CEDILLO RICO[1])* died Bef. 1839[30]. He married MARÍA GUADALUPE QUINTANA September 19, 1795 in Tomé, El Reyno de Nuevo México, Nueva España[31], daughter of GREGORIO QUINTANA and MARÍA SILVA.

Children of BLAS CEDILLO and MARÍA QUINTANA are:

     i.   JESÚS[5] SEDILLO, b. La Polvadera; m. JUANA MARÍA GALLEGOS, April 21, 1839, Socorro, Nuevo México, La República de México[32].

10.   ii.   JOSÉ ÁNGEL SEDILLO, b. Bef. October 07, 1796, Tomé, El Reyno de Nuevo Méjico, Nueva España.

     ii.   MARÍA FELIPA SEDILLO, b. Bef. May 11, 1798, Tomé, El Reyno de Nuevo Méjico, Nueva España[33].

     iii.   MARIA JULIANA NEPOMUCENA SEDILLO, b. Bef. February 16, 1802, Tomé, El Reyno de Nuevo Méjico, Nueva España[33].

     iv.   JOSÉ MANUEL ANTONIO SEDILLO, b. Bef. January 08, 1805, Tomé, El Reyno de Nuevo Méjico, Nueva España[33].

     v.   MARÍA MANUELA SEDILLO, b. Bef. March 01, 1806, Tomé, El Reyno de Nuevo Méjico, Nueva España[33].

8. SIMÓN[4] CEDILLO *(MIGUEL DE SAN JUAN CEDILLO RICO[3] DE ROJAS, JOAQUÍN CEDILLO RICO[2], PEDRO DE CEDILLO RICO[1])* was born Abt. 1765 in Los Lentes, El Reino de Nuevo Méjico, Nueva España[34]. He married GERTRUDIS MORA May 14, 1789 in Alburquerque, El Reino de Nuevo Méjico, Nueva España[34].

Child of SIMÓN CEDILLO and GERTRUDIS MORA is:
11.   i.   PABLO⁵ SEDILLO.

9. ANTONIO FÉLIX⁴ CEDILLO *(ANTONIO³, JOAQUÍN CEDILLO RICO² DE ROJAS, PEDRO DE CEDILLO RICO¹)³⁵* was born Abt. 1740³⁶. He married ANTONIA NARCISA BACA July 01, 1770 in Laguna, El Reino de Nuevo Méjico, Nueva España³⁷, daughter of DOMINGO BACA and FELICIANA CHÁVES.

Children of ANTONIO CEDILLO and ANTONIA BACA are:
    i.   JOSÉ MANUEL⁵ SEDILLO, m. MARÍA DOLÓRES PINO, October 01, 1792, Isleta, El Reino de Nuevo Méjico, Nueva España³⁸.
12.   ii.   JOSÉ BLÁS SEDILLO, b. February 20, 1777, Alburquerque, El Reino de Nuevo Méjico, Nueva España.
13.   iii.   JULIÁN BERNARDO SEDILLO, b. March 14, 1779, Alburquerque, El Reino de Nuevo Méjico, Nueva España.
    iv.   ANTONIOTORIBIO SEDILLO.

Generation No. 5

10. JOSÉ ÁNGEL⁵ SEDILLO *(BLAS ANTONIO⁴ CEDILLO, MIGUEL DE SAN JUAN CEDILLO RICO³ DE ROJAS, JOAQUÍN CEDILLO RICO², PEDRO DE CEDILLO RICO¹)* was born Bef. October 07, 1796 in Tomé, El Reyno de Nuevo Méjico, Nueva España³⁹. He married ANA MARÍA CHÁVES February 04, 1817 in Tomé, El Reyno de Nuevo Méjico, Nueva España⁴⁰, daughter of PABLO CHÁVES and MARÍA GARCÍA.

Children of JOSÉ SEDILLO and ANA CHÁVES are:
    i.   MARÍA GUMERCINDA⁶ SEDILLO, b. Bef. January 21, 1818, Tomé, El Reyno de Nuevo Méjico, Nueva España⁴¹.
    ii.   JOSÉ GUMERCINDO SEDILLO, b. Bef. January 17, 1819, Tomé, El Reyno de Nuevo Méjico, Nueva España⁴¹.
14.   iii.   MARÍA GUADALUPE SEDILLO, b. Bef. January 17, 1820, Tomé, El Reyno de Nuevo Méjico, Nueva España.
    iv.   BISENTE SEDILLO, b. Bef. April 13, 1828, Tomé, El Reyno de Nuevo Méjico, Nueva España⁴¹.
15.   v.   JUAN NEPOMUCENO SEDILLO, b. April 08, 1834, La Joya, Nuevo México, La República de México; d. San Patricio, New México.
    vi.   JUANA MARÍA POMUSENA SEDILLO, b. Bef. May 28, 1836, La Plaza de Pulvidera, Nuevo México, La República de México⁴².

11. PABLO⁵ SEDILLO *(SIMÓN⁴ CEDILLO, MIGUEL DE SAN JUAN CEDILLO RICO³ DE ROJAS, JOAQUÍN CEDILLO RICO², PEDRO DE CEDILLO RICO¹)*. He married ROSALÍA SÁNCHES March 15, 1812 in Thomé, El Reino de Nuevo Méjico, Nueva España⁴³, daughter of JACINTO SÁNCHES and YSABEL MOLINA.

Children of PABLO SEDILLO and ROSALÍA SÁNCHES are:
    i.   JUANA MARÍA⁶ SEDILLO, b. Bef. June 22, 1814, Thomé, El Reino de Nuevo Méjico, Nueva España⁴⁴.
    ii.   JOSÉ BENITO CEDILLO, b. Bef. January 17, 1817, Thomé, El Reino de Nuevo Méjico, Nueva España⁴⁴.
    iii.   MARÍA CANDELARIA CEDILLO, b. Bef. February 13, 1818, Thomé, El Reino de Nuevo Méjico, Nueva España⁴⁴.
16.   iv.   JOSÉ ALBERTO SEDILLO, b. Bef. March 28, 1820, Thomé, El Reino de Nuevo Méjico, Nueva España.
    v.   GREGORIO SEDILLO, b. Bef. January 17, 1822, Tomé, Nuevo México, La República de México⁴⁴.
    vi.   PEDRO NOLASCO SEDILLO, b. Bef. January 31, 1824, Tomé, Nuevo México, La República de México⁴⁴.
    vii.   MARÍA FRANCISCA SEDILLO, b. Bef. December 11, 1826, Tomé, Nuevo México, La República de México⁴⁴.
    viii.   JOSÉ DESIDERIO SEDILLO, b. Bef. February 13, 1828, Tomé, Nuevo México, La República de México⁴⁴.

12. JOSÉ BLÁS⁵ SEDILLO *(ANTONIO FÉLIX⁴ CEDILLO, ANTONIO³, JOAQUÍN CEDILLO RICO² DE ROJAS, PEDRO DE CEDILLO RICO¹)⁴⁵* was born February 20, 1777 in Alburquerque, El Reino de Nuevo Méjico, Nueva España⁴⁶. He married MARÍA PETRA SÁNCHES July 12, 1824 in Albuquerque, Nuevo México, La República de México⁴⁷, daughter of FELIX SÁNCHES and ANA AGUIRRE.

Notes for JOSÉ BLÁS SEDILLO:
Also known as Juan Blas Sedillo.

Notes for MARÍA PETRA SÁNCHES:
Also known as María Petra de Altagracia Sánches.

Children of JOSÉ SEDILLO and MARÍA SÁNCHES are:
    i.   MARÍA DE LOS SANTOS⁶ SEDILLO, b. October 05, 1836, El Sabinal, Nuevo México, La República de México.

17.   ii.   JOSÉ MIGUEL SEDILLO, b. February 24, 1842, Lemitar, Nuevo México, La República de México; d. February 25, 1899.

        iii.   MARÍA NESTORA SEDILLO, b. February 25, 1847, Lemitar, Territory of New México.

        iv.   MARÍA RITA SEDILLO, m. JOSÉ DOMINGO CANDELARIA, September 09, 1844, Socorro, Nuevo México, La República de México[48].

13. JULIÁN BERNARDO[5] SEDILLO *(ANTONIO FÉLIX[4] CEDILLO, ANTONIO[3], JOAQUÍN CEDILLO RICO[2] DE ROJAS, PEDRO DE CEDILLO RICO[1])* was born March 14, 1779 in Alburquerque, El Reino de Nuevo Méjico, Nueva España[49]. He married CIPRIANA GARCÍA[50].

Children of JULIÁN SEDILLO and CIPRIANA GARCÍA are:

18.   i.   MARÍA DOLÓRES[6] SEDILLO, b. 1824, La Cañada de Los Apaches, El Reyno de Nuevo Méjico.

        ii.   MARÍA DEL ROSARIO SEDILLO, b. Bef. June 17, 1824, Albuquerque, Nuevo México, La República de México[51]; m. ANTONIO JOSÉ CARVAJAL, September 11, 1849, Albuquerque, Territory of New México[52].

        iii.   JOSEFA SEDILLO, b. Abt. 1835[53].

19.   iv.   RUFINA SEDILLO, b. Abt. 1837.

        v.   ANTONIO JOSÉ SEDILLO, b. Abt. 1839[53].

Generation No. 6

14. MARÍA GUADALUPE[6] SEDILLO *(JOSÉ ÁNGEL[5], BLAS ANTONIO[4] CEDILLO, MIGUEL DE SAN JUAN CEDILLO RICO[3] DE ROJAS, JOAQUÍN CEDILLO RICO[2], PEDRO DE CEDILLO RICO[1])*[54] was born Bef. January 17, 1820 in Tomé, El Reyno de Nuevo Méjico, Nueva España[55]. She married JOSÉ DOLÓRES ALDERETE November 11, 1844 in Socorro, Nuevo México, La República de México[56].

Children of MARÍA SEDILLO and JOSÉ ALDERETE are:

        i.   SILVESTRE[7] ALDERETE, b. Abt. 1845[57].

        ii.   ANA MARÍA ALDERETE, b. Abt. 1847[57].

        iii.   VICTORIA ALDERETE, b. Abt. 1849[57].

        iv.   JOSEFA ALDERETE, b. Abt. 1852[57].

        v.   JOSÉ MARÍA ALDERETE, b. Abt. 1857[57].

15. JUAN NEPOMUCENO[6] SEDILLO *(JOSÉ ÁNGEL[5], BLAS ANTONIO[4] CEDILLO, MIGUEL DE SAN JUAN CEDILLO RICO[3] DE ROJAS, JOAQUÍN CEDILLO RICO[2], PEDRO DE CEDILLO RICO[1])*[58] was born April 08, 1834 in La Joya, Nuevo México, La República de México[59], and died in San Patricio, New México. He married (1) ANA MARÍA CHÁVES August 25, 1850 in Socorro, Territory of New México[60], daughter of JOSÉ CHÁVES and MARÍA ARMIJO. He married (2) JOSEFA FAJARDO Abt. 1870[61].

Children of JUAN SEDILLO and ANA MARÍA CHÁVES are:

20.   i.   COSMÉ[7] SEDILLO, b. Abt. 1850, Socorro County, Territory of New México; d. March 05, 1935, San Patricio, New México.

        ii.   FRANCISCA SEDILLO, b. Abt. 1852, la Polvadera de San Lorenzo, Territory of New México[62].

        iii.   GENOVEVA SEDILLO, b. Abt. 1854, La Polvadera de San Lorenzo, Territory of New México[62].

Children of JUAN SEDILLO and JOSEFA FAJARDO are:

21.   iv.   JUANITA[7] SEDILLO, b. July 13, 1871, San Patricio, Territory of New México.

22.   v.   RAMONA SEDILLO, b. Abt. 1873; d. Bef. December 1913.

23.   vi.   MARÍA SARAFINA SEDILLO, b. January 11, 1875, San Patricio, Territory of New México.

24.   vii.   REIMUNDA SEDILLO, b. April 1881.

José Alberto Sedillo

16. JOSÉ ALBERTO[6] SEDILLO *(PABLO[5], SIMÓN[4] CEDILLO, MIGUEL DE SAN JUAN CEDILLO RICO[3] DE ROJAS, JOAQUÍN CEDILLO RICO[2], PEDRO DE CEDILLO RICO[1])*[63] was born Bef. March 28, 1820 in Thomé, El Reino de Nuevo Méjico, Nueva España[64]. He married MARÍA FILIPA SAMORA[65].

Children of JOSÉ SEDILLO and MARÍA SAMORA are:

        i.   NICOLÁSA[7] SEDILLO[66], b. Bef. December 10, 1844[67].

      ii.   JUAN PEDRO SEDILLO[68], b. Bef. October 24, 1846, Tomé, Nuevo México, La República de México[69]; m. MARÍA RAMONA MÁRQUEZ[7070].

      iii.   MARÍA RITA EPITACIA SEDILLO, b. Bef. May 23, 1849, Tomé, Territory of New México[71].

      iv.   MARÍA LODUBINA ESTEFANA SEDILLO[71], b. Bef. December 27, 1850[72].

      v.   RAMONA SEDILLO[73], b. Bef. March 01, 1853, Tomé, Territory of New México[74].

      vi.   ANTONIA SEDILLO[75], b. Bef. May 13, 1855, Tomé, Territory of New México[76].

25.   vii. CALIXTRO SEDILLO, b. October 20, 1859, Manzano, Territory of New México; d. May 15, 1941, Palo Verde (Ruidoso Downs), New México.

      viii. JOSÉ DE LOS NIEVES SEDILLO[77], b. Bef. August 07, 1860, Manzano, Territory of New México[78].

      ix.   CASTULO SEDILLO[79], b. Bef. May 01, 1866, Manzano, Territory of New México[80].

José Miguel Sedillo

17. JOSÉ MIGUEL[6] SEDILLO *(JOSÉ BLÁS[5], ANTONIO FÉLIX[4] CEDILLO, ANTONIO[3], JOAQUÍN CEDILLO RICO[2] DE ROJAS, PEDRO DE CEDILLO RICO[1])* was born February 24, 1842 in Lemitar, Nuevo México, La República de México, and died February 25, 1899. He married (1) MARÍA INEZ GARCÍA April 08, 1860 in Las Cruces, Territory of New México[81], daughter of PEDRO GARCÍA and MARÍA LUCERO. He married (2) RAMONA SÁNCHEZ January 07, 1883 in Lincoln, Territory of New México[82], daughter of REFUGIO SÁNCHEZ.

Children of JOSÉ SEDILLO and MARÍA GARCÍA are:

      i.   MARGARITA GARCÍA[7] SEDILLO, b. Abt. 1862[83]; m. ANTONIO TRUJILLO.

26.   ii.   MARTÍN GARCÍA SEDILLO, b. November 1864, San Patricio, Territory of New México; d. May 05, 1917, Brighton, Colorado.

27.   iii.   ANGELITA SEDILLO, b. Abt. 1865; d. 1940, Roswell, New México.

      iv.   RAFAEL SEDILLO, b. 1866[84]; m. REINALDA MONTOYA[85], January 28, 1893, Lincoln County, Territory of New México[86].

28.   v.   SIXTO SEDILLOS, b. March 28, 1868; d. September 07, 1955.

      vi.   DANIEL SEDILLO, b. December 1873, San Patricio, Territory of New México[87]; d. February 1957, Weld County, Colorado.

      vii.   RUFINA SEDILLO, b. April 29, 1876[88].

29.   viii. RUFINO SEDILLO, b. November 21, 1878, San Patricio, Territory of New México; d. December 09, 1955, Denver, Colorado.

18. MARÍA DOLÓRES[6] SEDILLO *(JULIÁN BERNARDO[5], ANTONIO FÉLIX[4] CEDILLO, ANTONIO[3], JOAQUÍN CEDILLO RICO[2] DE ROJAS, PEDRO DE CEDILLO RICO[1])[89]* was born 1824 in La Cañada de Los Apaches, El Reyno de Nuevo Méjico[90]. She married (2) JOSÉ YGNACIO OLGUÍN[91] January 29, 1855 in Alburquerque, Territory of New México[92], son of JOSÉ OLGUÍN and MARÍA GARCÍA.

Child of MARÍA DOLÓRES SEDILLO is:

30.   i.   MARÍA LORENSA[7] CEDILLO, b. March 1846, Atrisco, Territory of New México.

Children of MARÍA SEDILLO and JOSÉ OLGUÍN are:

      ii.   POMISENA[7] OLGUÍN, b. Abt. 1854[93].

      iii.   JULIAN OLGUÍN[94], b. September 24, 1856, Atrisco, Territory of New México[95].

      iv.   GUADALUPE ELIZA OLGUÍN, b. Abt. 1858[95].

19. RUFINA[6] SEDILLO *(JULIÁN BERNARDO[5], ANTONIO FÉLIX[4] CEDILLO, ANTONIO[3], JOAQUÍN CEDILLO RICO[2] DE ROJAS, PEDRO DE CEDILLO RICO[1])* was born Abt. 1837[95]. She married (1) JOSÉ MARÍA CHÁVES September 08, 1850 in Albuquerque, Territory of New México[96]. She married (2) MANUEL SÁNCHEZ December 07, 1887 in Albuquerque, Territory of New México[97].

Children of RUFINA SEDILLO and JOSÉ CHÁVES are:

      i.   CANUTO[7] CHÁVES, b. Abt. 1852[98].

      ii.   OLOJIO CHÁVES, b. Abt. 1854[98].

Generation No. 7

Cosmé Sedillo

20. COSMÉ[7] SEDILLO *(JUAN NEPOMUCENO[6], JOSÉ ÁNGEL[5], BLAS ANTONIO[4] CEDILLO, MIGUEL DE SAN JUAN CEDILLO RICO[3] DE ROJAS, JOAQUÍN CEDILLO RICO[2], PEDRO DE CEDILLO RICO[1])* was born Abt. 1850 in Socorro County, Territory of New México[99], and died March 05, 1935 in San Patricio, New México[100]. He married MASIMA JARAMILLO SÁNCHEZ November 05, 1873 in Tularoso, Territory of New México[101], daughter of MANUEL SÁNCHES and ADELAIDA JARAMILLO.

Children of COSMÉ SEDILLO and MASIMA SÁNCHEZ are:
31.   i.   MARTÍN SÁNCHEZ[8] SEDILLO, b. April 30, 1875, El Berendo, Territory of New México.
32.   ii.   FEDERICO SEDILLO, b. February 10, 1880, El Berendo, Territory of New México.
33.   iii.   JUANITA SEDILLO, b. Abt. 1884, El Berendo, Territory of New México.
     iv.   DEMETRIO SEDILLO, b. April 07, 1885, El Berendo, Territory of New México[102].
     v.   CATARINA SEDILLO, b. Abt. 1894, El Berendo, Territory of New México; m. MANUEL FRESQUEZ.
     vi.   TELESFORA SEDILLO, b. December 24, 1895, El Berendo, New México[103].
     vii.   FILOMENO SEDILLO, b. August 16, 1900[104].
     viii.   SOFIA SEDILLO, b. June 11, 1901[105].

21. JUANITA[7] SEDILLO *(JUAN NEPOMUCENO[6], JOSÉ ÁNGEL[5], BLAS ANTONIO[4], SAN JUAN CEDILLO RICO[3] DE ROJAS, JOAQUÍN CEDILLO RICO[2], PEDRO DE CEDILLO RICO[1])[106]* was born July 13, 1871 in San Patricio, Territory of New México[107]. She married ANTONIO RAMÍREZ February 23, 1885 in Lincoln County, Territory of New México[108].

Children of JUANITA SEDILLO and ANTONIO RAMÍREZ are:
34.   i.   FLORIPA[8] RAMÍREZ, b. May 1886, Agua Azul, Territory of New México.
     ii.   MARÍA RAMÍREZ, b. June 1891, Agua Azul, Territory of New México[109].
     iii.   VICTORIA RAMÍREZ, b. March 06, 1896, San Patricio, Territory of New México[110]; m. ANTONIO MAÉS SÁNCHEZ[111], November 07, 1922, Arabela, New México[112].
     iv.   PRUDENCIA RAMÍREZ[113], b. June 16, 1896, San Patricio, Territory of New México[114]; m. EPIMENIO LUCERO[115], January 30, 1916, Arabela, New México[115].
35.   v.   RAMÓN RAMÍREZ, b. April 08, 1899, Agua Azul, Territory of New México.
     vi.   LUÍS RAMÍREZ, b. Abt. 1905[116].

22. RAMONA[7] SEDILLO *(JUAN NEPOMUCENO[6], JOSÉ ÁNGEL[5], BLAS ANTONIO[4] CEDILLO, MIGUEL DE SAN JUAN CEDILLO RICO[3] DE ROJAS, JOAQUÍN CEDILLO RICO[2], PEDRO DE CEDILLO RICO[1])* was born Abt. 1873[117], and died Bef. December 1913. She married PEDRO JARAMILLO SÁNCHEZ November 29, 1885 in Lincoln County, Territory of New México[118], son of MANUEL SÁNCHES and ADELAIDA JARAMILLO.

Children of RAMONA SEDILLO and PEDRO SÁNCHEZ are:
36.   i.   YSABEL[8] SÁNCHEZ, b. July 07, 1888, San Patricio, Territory of New México.
37.   ii.   ISIDRA SÁNCHEZ, b. May 15, 1889, Roswell, Territory of New México; d. July 16, 1992.
     iii.   PROCOPIO SÁNCHEZ, b. Abt. 1892[119].
     iv.   DOROTEA SÁNCHEZ, b. Abt. 1894[119].
     v.   RUFINA SÁNCHEZ, b. February 06, 1896, El Berendo, Territory of New México[120]; m. SANTIAGO GALLEGOS, June 01, 1913, Lincoln, New México[120].
     vi.   BENITO SÁNCHEZ, b. Abt. 1899[121].
     vii.   ISIDRO SÁNCHEZ, b. Abt. 1902[121].
     viii.   PEDRO SEDILLO SÁNCHEZ, b. May 15, 1902[122].

23. MARÍA SARAFINA[7] SEDILLO *(JUAN NEPOMUCENO[6], JOSÉ ÁNGEL[5], BLAS ANTONIO[4] CEDILLO, MIGUEL DE SAN JUAN CEDILLO RICO[3] DE ROJAS, JOAQUÍN CEDILLO RICO[2], PEDRO DE CEDILLO RICO[1])* was born January 11, 1875 in San Patricio, Territory of New México[123]. She married VICENTE ULIBARRÍ November 06, 1922, son of JUAN ULIBARRÍ and CIPRIANA LUCERO.

Children of MARÍA SEDILLO and VICENTE ULIBARRÍ are:
38.   i.   AUGUSTINA[8] ULIBARRÍ, b. September 26, 1892, San Patricio, New México; d. April 29, 1970.
     ii.   MARÍA ULIBARRÍ[124], b. October 20, 1895, San Patricio, Territory of New México[125]; m. JOSÉ SILVA CHÁVEZ[126], November 02, 1911, Picacho, Territory of New México[126].
39.   iii.   EPIFANIO ULIBARRÍ, b. August 22, 1896, San Patricio, Territory of New México; d. October 17, 1928, San Patricio, New México.
40.   iv.   SOFIA ULIBARRÍ, b. 1905, San Patricio, Territory of New México; d. October 16, 1941.

41.   v.   PETRA ULIBARRÍ, b. June 27, 1907, San Patricio, Territory of New México; d. October 1977, San Patricio, New México.

42.   vi.   DOMINGA ULIBARRÍ, b. October 02, 1910, San Patricio, Territory of New México; d. June 13, 2001, Hondo, New México.

24. REIMUNDA[7] SEDILLO *(JUAN NEPOMUCENO[6], JOSÉ ÁNGEL[5], BLAS ANTONIO[4] CEDILLO, MIGUEL DE SAN JUAN CEDILLO RICO[3] DE ROJAS, JOAQUÍN CEDILLO RICO[2], PEDRO DE CEDILLO RICO[1])* was born April 1881[127]. She married LEOPOLDO SÁNCHEZ GONZÁLES[128] November 28, 1895[129], son of FLORENCIO GONZÁLES and RAYMUNDA SÁNCHEZ.

Children of REIMUNDA SEDILLO and LEOPOLDO GONZÁLES are:
        i.   JUAN SEDILLO[8] GONZÁLES, b. November 10, 1896, San Patricio, Territory of New México[130].
        ii.   AROPAJITA SEDILLO GONZÁLES, b. 1900, San Patricio, Territory of New México[131]; d. December 05, 1918, San Patricio, New México[132].
43.   iii.   CRUSITA GONZÁLES, b. May 02, 1904, San Patricio, Territory of New México.
44.   iv.   ELISA GONZÁLES, b. February 27, 1912, San Patricio, New México; d. April 01, 2001, San Patricio, New México.

25. CALIXTRO[7] SEDILLO *(JOSÉ ALBERTO[6], PABLO[5], SIMÓN[4] CEDILLO, MIGUEL DE SAN JUAN CEDILLO RICO[3] DE ROJAS, JOAQUÍN CEDILLO RICO[2], PEDRO DE CEDILLO RICO[1])* was born October 20, 1859 in Manzano, Territory of New México[133], and died May 15, 1941 in Palo Verde (Ruidoso Downs), New México. He married CARMELITA GALLEGOS[134] November 07, 1880 in Rancho Torres, Territory of New México[135], daughter of ANTONIO GALLEGOS and MARÍA MÁRQUEZ.

Children of CALIXTRO SEDILLO and CARMELITA GALLEGOS are:
45.   i.   BEATRIZ[8] SEDILLO, b. March 16, 1884, Picacho, Territory of New México; d. September 14, 1940.
        ii.   PEDRO ALEJANDRO SEDILLO, b. November 27, 1885[136].
46.   iii.   SALVADOR SEDILLO, b. May 29, 1887; d. May 18, 1951, Los Ángeles, California.
        iv.   ADOLFO SEDILLO, b. March 1889.

26. MARTÍN GARCÍA[7] SEDILLO *(JOSÉ MIGUEL[6], JOSÉ BLÁS[5], ANTONIO FÉLIX[4] CEDILLO, ANTONIO[3], JOAQUÍN CEDILLO RICO[2] DE ROJAS, PEDRO DE CEDILLO RICO[1])* was born November 1864 in San Patricio, Territory of New México[137], and died May 05, 1917 in Brighton, Colorado. He married TIMOTEA SILVA Abt. 1890[137], daughter of MANUEL SILVA and JOSEFITA ESQUIVEL.

Children of MARTÍN SEDILLO and TIMOTEA SILVA are:
47.   i.   MARÍNEZ[8] SEDILLO, b. June 21, 1891, San Patricio, Territory of New México; d. March 25, 1940, Colorado Springs, Colorado.
        ii.   FRANCISCO SEDILLO, b. December 27, 1892, San Patricio, Territory of New México[137]; d. January 29, 1938, Greeley, Colorado.
        iii.   JOSEFITA SEDILLO, b. December 29, 1893, San Patricio, Territory of New México[137]; d. November 12, 1991, Denver, Colorado; m. SAMUEL BECERRA, March 23, 1912.
        iv.   EUFEMIA SEDILLO, b. December 1896, San Patricio, Territory of New México[137]; d. October 1930; m. JOSÉ BECERRA.
        v.   ANA CECILIA SEDILLO[138], b. April 03, 1906, San Patricio, Territory of New México; d. May 1974, Greeley, Colorado; m. NOBERTO VALADEZ, March 11, 1929, Greeley, Colorado.

27. ANGELITA[7] SEDILLO *(JOSÉ MIGUEL[6], JOSÉ BLÁS[5], ANTONIO FÉLIX[4] CEDILLO, ANTONIO[3], JOAQUÍN CEDILLO RICO[2] DE ROJAS, PEDRO DE CEDILLO RICO[1])* was born Abt. 1865[139], and died 1940 in Roswell, New México. She married (1) BENITO TRUJILLO. She married (2) FRANCISCO GUTIÉRRES Abt. 1890[139], son of JOSÉ GUTIÉRRES and JUANA SALAS.

Children of ANGELITA SEDILLO and FRANCISCO GUTIÉRRES are:
        i.   MANUELITA[8] GUTIÉRREZ, b. Abt. 1900, San Patricio, Territory of New México[139]; m. ISIDRO ANALLA[140].
        ii.   RAMÓN GUTIÉRREZ, b. Abt. 1903, San Patricio, Territory of New México[141].

28. SIXTO[7] SEDILLOS *(JOSÉ MIGUEL[6] SEDILLO, JOSÉ BLÁS[5], ANTONIO FÉLIX[4] CEDILLO, ANTONIO[3], JOAQUÍN CEDILLO RICO[2] DE ROJAS, PEDRO DE CEDILLO RICO[1])[142]* was born March 28, 1868, and died

September 07, 1955. He married MARGARITA CANDELARIA OLGUÍN[142] July 28, 1892 in Ruidoso, Territory of New México[143], daughter of RAMÓN OLGUÍN and MARÍA CEDILLO.

Notes for MARGARITA CANDELARIA OLGUÍN:
Baptismal records indicate that she was born on January 20, 1872. (Microfiche# 0017008, Page 19)

Children of SIXTO SEDILLOS and MARGARITA OLGUÍN are:

48.	i.	MIGUEL[8] SEDILLOS, b. November 28, 1891, San Patricio, Territory of New México; d. March 15, 1967, Carrizozo, New México.
	ii.	ONESIMA SEDILLOS, b. February 15, 1894, El Berendo, Territory of New México; m. AMABLE CHÁVEZ, September 23, 1914, Lincoln, New México[144].
	iii.	FRANCISQUITA SEDILLOS, b. April 15, 1895, San Patricio, Territory of New México[145]; m. JOSÉ OROSCO, October 01, 1913, Patos, Territory of New México[145].
49.	iv.	RAMÓN SEDILLOS, b. February 25, 1899, San Patricio, Territory of New México.
50.	v.	EDUARDO SEDILLOS, b. October 20, 1902, Arabela, New México; d. March 08, 1991, Alamogordo, New México.
	vi.	ESTELA SEDILLOS[146], b. September 03, 1904, San Patricio, Territory of New México[147]; m. HILARIO SÁNCHEZ[148], July 27, 1921[149].
	vii.	PRESILIANA SEDILLOS, b. Abt. 1906[150].
51.	viii.	LEOPOLDO SEDILLOS, b. March 24, 1909, San Patricio, New México; d. February 08, 1990, Roswell, New México.
52.	ix.	DANIEL SEDILLOS, b. February 02, 1912, Patos, New México; d. April 18, 2006, Alamogordo, New México.

29. RUFINO[7] SEDILLO *(JOSÉ MIGUEL[6], JOSÉ BLÁS[5], ANTONIO FÉLIX[4] CEDILLO, ANTONIO[3], JOAQUÍN CEDILLO RICO[2] DE ROJAS, PEDRO DE CEDILLO RICO[1])* was born November 21, 1878 in San Patricio, Territory of New México[151], and died December 09, 1955 in Denver, Colorado. He married FRANCISCA ESCALANTE Abt. 1900[152].

Children of RUFINO SEDILLO and FRANCISCA ESCALANTE are:

	i.	EUTILIA[8] SEDILLO, b. Abt. 1900, Alamagordo, Territory of New México[153].
	ii.	AVEL SEDILLO, b. Abt. 1905, San Patricio, Territory of New México[153].
	iii.	LYDIA SEDILLO, b. Abt. 1906, San Patricio, Territory of New México[153]; m. JOE APODACA, August 25, 1923, Denver, Colorado.
	iv.	GENOVEVA SEDILLO, b. January 03, 1908, San Patricio, Territory of New México[153]; d. January 23, 1968, Denver, Colorado; m. MIGUEL ALBERT FRANCO.
	v.	ADELINA SEDILLO[154], b. November 01, 1909, San Patricio, Territory of New México[155]; d. October 23, 1981, San Francisco, California.
	vi.	EUGENIO SEDILLO, b. March 13, 1912, San Patricio, New México[156]; d. October 18, 1996, Riverside, California.
	vii.	ROBERT RUBÉN SEDILLOS[157], b. March 13, 1916, Roswell, New México[158]; d. July 10, 2010, Westminster, Colorado; m. MARIE CORA SEDILLOS.
	viii.	ALBERTA SEDILLO, b. Abt. 1918[158].
53.	ix.	ALFRED EPIFANIO SEDILLOS, b. February 08, 1918, El Paso, Texas; d. October 05, 1997.
	x.	DELPHI SEDILLO, b. Abt. 1921, Brighton, Colorado[159].
	xi.	EDWARD SEDILLO, b. Abt. 1926[159].
	xii.	MARY SEDILLO, b. Abt. 1928[159].

30. MARÍA LORENSA[7] CEDILLO *(MARÍA DOLÓRES[6] SEDILLO, JULIÁN BERNARDO[5], ANTONIO FÉLIX[4] CEDILLO, ANTONIO[3], JOAQUÍN CEDILLO RICO[2] DE ROJAS, PEDRO DE CEDILLO RICO[1])* was born March 1846 in Atrisco, Territory of New México[160]. She married RAMÓN OLGUÍN October 16, 1866 in Tomé, Territory of New México[161], son of JOSÉ OLGUÍN and MARÍA GUTIÉRRES.

Children of MARÍA CEDILLO and RAMÓN OLGUÍN are:

	i.	NATIVIDAD SEDILLO[8] OLGUÍN, b. Abt. 1864, La Plaza de San Patricio, Territory of New México[162]; m. FELIZ TRUJILLO, September 28, 1885[163].
54.	ii.	ESTANISLADO OLGUÍN, b. May 06, 1870, Ruidoso, Territory of New México.
55.	iii.	MARGARITA CANDELARIA OLGUÍN, b. January 31, 1872, San Patricio, Territory of New México; d. April 06, 1955.
	iv.	BENITO OLGUÍN, b. Abt. 1876, San Patricio, Territory of New México[164].
56.	v.	MANUELITA OLGUÍN, b. June 1887, San Patricio, Territory of New México.

57.   vi.   IGNACIO S. OLGUÍN, b. August 01, 1873, San Patricio, Territory of New México; d. October 15, 1947, El Paso, Téxas.

Generation No. 8

31. MARTÍN SÁNCHEZ[8] SEDILLO *(COSMÉ[7], JUAN NEPOMUCENO[6], JOSÉ ÁNGEL[5], BLAS ANTONIO[4] CEDILLO, MIGUEL DE SAN JUAN CEDILLO RICO[3] DE ROJAS, JOAQUÍN CEDILLO RICO[2], PEDRO DE CEDILLO RICO[1])* was born April 30, 1875 in El Berendo, Territory of New México[165]. He married TOMASITA HERRERA March 08, 1906, daughter of CRUZ HERRERA and EULOJIA MADRID.

Children of MARTÍN SEDILLO and TOMASITA HERRERA are:
>   i.   CARLOS[9] SEDILLO, b. 1908[166].
>   ii.   ROSA SEDILLO, b. 1911[166].
>   iii.   MARIANO SEDILLO, b. 1912[166].
>   iv.   DOMACIO SEDILLO[167], b. 1913[168]; d. July 21, 1933, San Patricio, New México.
>   v.   RUFINA HERRERA SEDILLO, b. 1915[168].
58.   vi.   CAMILO SEDILLO, b. June 05, 1917, Roswell, New México; d. May 06, 1986, Artesia, New México.
>   vii.   FRED SEDILLO, b. 1921[168].
59.   viii.   CRUSITA SEDILLO, b. April 06, 1925, Roswell, New México; d. December 26, 1993, Alamogordo, New México.
>   ix.   CATARINA SEDILLO, b. 1928[168].
>   x.   VICENTE SEDILLO, b. Private.

32. FEDERICO[8] SEDILLO *(COSMÉ[7], JUAN NEPOMUCENO[6], JOSÉ ÁNGEL[5], BLAS ANTONIO[4] CEDILLO, MIGUEL DE SAN JUAN CEDILLO RICO[3] DE ROJAS, JOAQUÍN CEDILLO RICO[2], PEDRO DE CEDILLO RICO[1])* was born February 10, 1880 in El Berendo, Territory of New México. He married MARÍA LOVE January 19, 1903[169], daughter of ANNA RICE.

Children of FEDERICO SEDILLO and MARÍA LOVE are:
>   i.   ADELIDA[9] SEDILLO, b. 1904[170].
>   ii.   ELLEN SEDILLO, b. March 1908[170].

33. JUANITA[8] SEDILLO *(COSMÉ[7], JUAN NEPOMUCENO[6], JOSÉ ÁNGEL[5], BLAS ANTONIO[4] CEDILLO, MIGUEL DE SAN JUAN CEDILLO RICO[3] DE ROJAS, JOAQUÍN CEDILLO RICO[2], PEDRO DE CEDILLO RICO[1])* was born Abt. 1884 in El Berendo, Territory of New México[171]. She married CANDELARIO CHÁVEZ February 19, 1898[172], son of JESÚS CHÁVEZ and RAFAELA ROMERO.

Children of JUANITA SEDILLO and CANDELARIO CHÁVEZ are:
>   i.   LUPE[9] CHÁVEZ, b. Abt. 1913, San Patricio, New México[173].
>   ii.   DULCINEA CHÁVEZ, b. Abt. 1914, San Patricio, New México[173].
>   iii.   JULIA CHÁVEZ, b. Abt. 1921, San Patricio, New México[173].

34. FLORIPA[8] RAMÍREZ *(JUANITA[7] SEDILLO, JUAN NEPOMUCENO[6], JOSÉ ÁNGEL[5], BLAS ANTONIO[4] CEDILLO, MIGUEL DE SAN JUAN CEDILLO RICO[3] DE ROJAS, JOAQUÍN CEDILLO RICO[2], PEDRO DE CEDILLO RICO[1])* was born May 1886 in Agua Azul, Territory of New México[174]. She married PLACIDO ARCHULETA[175] Abt. 1899[176].

Children of FLORIPA RAMÍREZ and PLACIDO ARCHULETA are:
>   i.   PLACIDO[9] ARCHULETA, b. Abt. 1901, Las Palas, Territory of New México[176].
>   ii.   FEDELIA ARCHULETA, b. Abt. 1905, Las Palas, Territory of New México[176]; m. ADOLFO MAÉS.
>   iii.   SEBERATO ARCHULETA, b. Abt. 1906, Las Palas, Territory of New México[176].
>   iv.   MANUEL ARCHULETA, b. Abt. 1913, Las Palas, New México[177].
>   v.   ANTONIO ARCHULETA, b. Abt. 1916, Las Palas, New México[177].

35. RAMÓN[8] RAMÍREZ *(JUANITA[7] SEDILLO, JUAN NEPOMUCENO[6], JOSÉ ÁNGEL[5], BLAS ANTONIO[4] CEDILLO, MIGUEL DE SAN JUAN CEDILLO RICO[3] DE ROJAS, JOAQUÍN CEDILLO RICO[2], PEDRO DE CEDILLO RICO[1])* was born April 08, 1899 in Agua Azul, Territory of New México[178]. He married ELENA

RICHARDSON[179] November 06, 1919 in Arabela, New México[180], daughter of ANDREW RICHARDSON and BENINA LUCERO.

Children of RAMÓN RAMÍREZ and ELENA RICHARDSON are:
60.   i.   PORFIRIA[9] RAMÍREZ, b. November 30, 1920, Arabela, New México.
61.   ii.   JOSÉ RAMÍREZ, b. March 19, 1926; d. February 26, 1979, Tucson, Arizona.

36. YSABEL[8] SÁNCHEZ *(RAMONA[7] SEDILLO, JUAN NEPOMUCENO[6], JOSÉ ÁNGEL[5], BLAS ANTONIO[4] CEDILLO, MIGUEL DE SAN JUAN CEDILLO RICO[3] DE ROJAS, JOAQUÍN CEDILLO RICO[2], PEDRO DE CEDILLO RICO[1])* was born July 07, 1888 in San Patricio, Territory of New México[181]. She married JUAN VALDÉZ November 13, 1913 in Lincoln, New México[181], son of JULIO VALDÉS and SINFORIANA SERRANO.

Child of YSABEL SÁNCHEZ and JUAN VALDÉZ is:
      i.   JULIO SÁNCHEZ[9] VALDÉZ, b. Abt. 1919[182].

37. ISIDRA[8] SÁNCHEZ *(RAMONA[7] SEDILLO, JUAN NEPOMUCENO[6], JOSÉ ÁNGEL[5], BLAS ANTONIO[4] CEDILLO, MIGUEL DE SAN JUAN CEDILLO RICO[3] DE ROJAS, JOAQUÍN CEDILLO RICO[2], PEDRO DE CEDILLO RICO[1])* was born May 15, 1889 in Roswell, Territory of New México[183], and died July 16, 1992. She married JOSÉ CANDELARIA[184] November 22, 1921[185], son of ÁBRAN CANDELARIA and BENINA LUCERO.

Children of ISIDRA SÁNCHEZ and JOSÉ CANDELARIA are:
62.   i.   BENITO[9] CANDELARIA, b. July 23, 1921, Arabela, New México.
63.   ii.   CELESTINO CANDELARIA, b. October 16, 1922, Arabela, New México.
64.   iii. ARCENIA CANDELARIA, b. Abt. 1925.
65.   iv.   EDUARDO CANDELARIA, b. July 11, 1928, Arabela, New México; d. November 09, 2003.
66.   v.   ASUSENA CANDELARIA, b. March 1930.

38. AUGUSTINA[8] ULIBARRÍ *(MARÍA SARAFINA[7] SEDILLO, JUAN NEPOMUCENO[6], JOSÉ ÁNGEL[5], BLAS ANTONIO[4] CEDILLO, MIGUEL DE SAN JUAN CEDILLO RICO[3] DE ROJAS, JOAQUÍN CEDILLO RICO[2], PEDRO DE CEDILLO RICO[1])[186]* was born September 26, 1892 in San Patricio, New México, and died April 29, 1970. She married RAYMUNDO SÁNCHEZ[186] December 17, 1910[187], son of JUAN SÁNCHES and BESITA SÁNCHEZ.

Children of AUGUSTINA ULIBARRÍ and RAYMUNDO SÁNCHEZ are:
      i.   EULALIA[9] SÁNCHEZ, b. December 15, 1912, San Patricio, New México[188]; m. PERFECTO SÁNCHEZ, June 17, 1929, Carrizozo, New México[188].
      ii.   BENNIE SÁNCHEZ, b. July 26, 1914, San Patricio, New México[189]; m. NICOLÁS TORRES, August 25, 1931, Glencoe, New México[189].
67.   iii. SOFIO SÁNCHEZ, b. May 25, 1916, San Patricio, New México; d. May 25, 1984, San Patricio, New México.
68.   iv.   ANEDA ULIBARRÍ SÁNCHEZ, b. July 12, 1918, San Patricio, New México; d. September 24, 1999.
      v.   OLYMPIA SÁNCHEZ[190], b. May 21, 1920, San Patricio, New México[191]; d. June 05, 2010, Ruidoso, New México; m. EPUNUCENO SÁNCHEZ[192], August 27, 1938, Carrizozo, New México[193].
      vi.   VISITA SÁNCHEZ[194], b. October 10, 1923, San Patricio, New México; d. April 10, 1924, San Patricio, New México.
      vii. LUÍS SÁNCHEZ, b. 1928, San Patricio, New México[195].

39. EPIFANIO[8] ULIBARRÍ *(MARÍA SARAFINA[7] SEDILLO, JUAN NEPOMUCENO[6], JOSÉ ÁNGEL[5], BLAS ANTONIO[4] CEDILLO, MIGUEL DE SAN JUAN CEDILLO RICO[3] DE ROJAS, JOAQUÍN CEDILLO RICO[2], PEDRO DE CEDILLO RICO[1])[196]* was born August 22, 1896 in San Patricio, Territory of New México[197], and died October 17, 1928 in San Patricio, New México. He married ERMINDA CHÁVEZ[198] November 04, 1915 in Lincoln, New México[199], daughter of FRANCISCO CHÁVEZ and ESLINDA GONZÁLES.

Children of EPIFANIO ULIBARRÍ and ERMINDA CHÁVEZ are:
      i.   ANUNCIÓN[9] ULIBARRÍ[200], b. August 13, 1917, San Patricio, New México; d. September 13, 1917, San Patricio, New México.
      ii.   DIEGO ULIBARRÍ[201], b. February 20, 1920; d. April 15, 1994, Carrizozo, New México.

40. SOFIA[8] ULIBARRÍ *(MARÍA SARAFINA[7] SEDILLO, JUAN NEPOMUCENO[6], JOSÉ ÁNGEL[5], BLAS ANTONIO[4] CEDILLO, MIGUEL DE SAN JUAN CEDILLO RICO[3] DE ROJAS, JOAQUÍN CEDILLO RICO[2], PEDRO DE CEDILLO RICO[1])* was born 1905 in San Patricio, Territory of New México[202], and died October 16, 1941. She married

PABLO YBARRA April 15, 1921 in San Patricio, New México[202], son of GREGORIO YBARRA and CATARINA MONTOYA.

Child of SOFIA ULIBARRÍ and PABLO YBARRA is:
    i.   TIVORCIO[9] YBARRA, b. San Patricio, New México.

41. PETRA[8] **ULIBARRÍ** *(MARÍA SARAFINA*[7] *SEDILLO, JUAN NEPOMUCENO*[6]*, JOSÉ ÁNGEL*[5]*, BLAS ANTONIO*[4] *CEDILLO, MIGUEL DE SAN JUAN CEDILLO RICO*[3] *DE ROJAS, JOAQUÍN CEDILLO RICO*[2]*, PEDRO DE CEDILLO RICO*[1]*)*[203] was born June 27, 1907 in San Patricio, Territory of New México[204], and died October 1977 in San Patricio, New México[205]. She married DIEGO SALCIDO[206] November 06, 1922[207], son of FAUSTINO SALCIDO and MARÍA CHÁVES.

Children of PETRA ULIBARRÍ and DIEGO SALCIDO are:
    i.   VICENTE[9] SALCIDO[208], b. May 05, 1924[209].
    ii.   MONICA SALCIDO[210], b. February 14, 1926, San Patricio, New México[211]; d. August 05, 1991, San Patricio, New México; m. ESTOLANO TRUJILLO SÁNCHEZ[212], January 10, 1945, Carrizozo, New México[213].
69.   iii.   MARY SALCIDO, b. April 23, 1934, Hondo, New México; d. March 10, 2001, Dexter, New México.
    iv.   DELLA SALCIDO[214], b. Private.
    v.   FITA SALCIDO[214], b. Private.
    vi.   NORA SALCIDO[214], b. Private.

42. DOMINGA[8] **ULIBARRÍ** *(MARÍA SARAFINA*[7] *SEDILLO, JUAN NEPOMUCENO*[6]*, JOSÉ ÁNGEL*[5]*, BLAS ANTONIO*[4] *CEDILLO, MIGUEL DE SAN JUAN CEDILLO RICO*[3] *DE ROJAS, JOAQUÍN CEDILLO RICO*[2]*, PEDRO DE CEDILLO RICO*[1]*)*[215] was born October 02, 1910 in San Patricio, Territory of New México[216], and died June 13, 2001 in Hondo, New México. She married PROCESO SALCIDO[217] December 05, 1931[218], son of FAUSTINO SALCIDO and MARÍA CHÁVES.

Child of DOMINGA ULIBARRÍ and PROCESO SALCIDO is:
    i.   CIRILIA OLYMPIA[9] SALCIDO[219], b. Abt. 1932, Hondo, New México; d. November 22, 1933, Hondo, New México.

43. CRUSITA[8] **GONZÁLES** *(REIMUNDA*[7] *SEDILLO, JUAN NEPOMUCENO*[6]*, JOSÉ ÁNGEL*[5]*, BLAS ANTONIO*[4] *CEDILLO, MIGUEL DE SAN JUAN CEDILLO RICO*[3] *DE ROJAS, JOAQUÍN CEDILLO RICO*[2]*, PEDRO DE CEDILLO RICO*[1]*)* was born May 02, 1904 in San Patricio, Territory of New México[220]. She married (1) BENITO HERRERA[221], son of CRUZ HERRERA and REDUCINDA CARDONA. She married (2) CASIMIRO TAFOYA VILLESCAS February 14, 1925 in San Patricio, New México[222], son of CASIMIRO VILLESCAS and EMILIANA TAFOYA.

Child of CRUSITA GONZÁLES and CASIMIRO VILLESCAS is:
    i.   ERNESTINA[9] VILLESCAS, b. Abt. 1933, San Patricio, New México[223].

44. ELISA[8] **GONZÁLES** *(REIMUNDA*[7] *SEDILLO, JUAN NEPOMUCENO*[6]*, JOSÉ ÁNGEL*[5]*, BLAS ANTONIO*[4] *CEDILLO, MIGUEL DE SAN JUAN CEDILLO RICO*[3] *DE ROJAS, JOAQUÍN CEDILLO RICO*[2]*, PEDRO DE CEDILLO RICO*[1]*)*[224] was born February 27, 1912 in San Patricio, New México, and died April 01, 2001 in San Patricio, New México. She married MANUEL HERNÁNDEZ HERRERA[225] November 23, 1931[226], son of LUÍS HERRERA and BENJAMÍNA HERNÁNDEZ.

Children of ELISA GONZÁLES and MANUEL HERRERA are:
70.   i.   BENJAMÍN[9] HERRERA, b. August 27, 1932, San Patricio, New México; d. October 27, 1998, Ruidoso Downs, New México.
71.   ii.   BENITO HERRERA, b. August 30, 1934, San Patricio, New México; d. July 23, 2002, Alburquerque, New México.
72.   iii.   FLORA HERRERA, b. April 30, 1936, San Patricio, New México; d. April 28, 2001, Ruidoso, New México.
73.   iv.   ELENA HERRERA, b. September 10, 1939, San Patricio, New México; d. July 12, 2010, Alburquerque, New México.
    v.   LUÍS HERRERA, b. September 19, 1941, San Patricio, New México; d. January 23, 2003, Alamogordo, New México; m. CELIA O. TELLES.
74.   vi.   LEOPOLDO HERRERA, b. December 29, 1945, San Patricio, New México; d. June 20, 2012, San Patricio, New México.

75.	vii.	JUAN HERRERA, b. May 09, 1952, Capitán, New México; d. January 22, 2011, Albuquerque, New México.
	viii.	JOE HERRERA, b. Private.
	ix.	JOSEPHINE HERRERA, b. Private.
	x.	LUCY HERRERA, b. Private.
	xi.	MANUEL GONZÁLES HERRERA, b. Private, San Patricio, New México.
	xii.	PASQUAL HERRERA, b. Private, San Patricio, New México.

Felipé Gómez

45. BEATRIZ[8] SEDILLO *(CALIXTRO[7], JOSÉ ALBERTO[6], PABLO[5], SIMÓN[4] CEDILLO, MIGUEL DE SAN JUAN CEDILLO RICO[3] DE ROJAS, JOAQUÍN CEDILLO RICO[2], PEDRO DE CEDILLO RICO[1])*[227] was born March 16, 1884 in Picacho, Territory of New México, and died September 14, 1940. She married FELIPÉ GÓMEZ[227] Abt. 1897[228], son of FRANCISCO GÓMEZ and IGNACIA RODRÍGUES.

Children of BEATRIZ SEDILLO and FELIPÉ GÓMEZ are:

76.	i.	FLORENCIO[9] GÓMEZ, b. October 16, 1898; d. December 06, 1975.
77.	ii.	DOMINIA GÓMEZ, b. April 06, 1901; d. October 28, 1982.
78.	iii.	ESTELA GÓMEZ, b. August 15, 1903; d. December 26, 2001, Fort Bayard, New México.
79.	iv.	DANIEL GÓMEZ, b. February 07, 1906, Ruidoso, New México; d. May 02, 1986, Lincoln, New México.
80.	v.	IGNACIA GÓMEZ, b. May 09, 1909, San Patricio, Territory of New México; d. July 29, 2005, Ruidoso, New México.
81.	vi.	FRANK GÓMEZ, b. December 13, 1911, Ruidoso, Territory of New México; d. April 27, 1999, Glencoe, New México.
82.	vii.	LUCÍA GÓMEZ, b. December 13, 1913, San Patricio, New México; d. January 22, 1980, Tucson, Arizona.
	viii.	SOSTENO GÓMEZ[229], b. July 01, 1915, San Patricio, New México[230]; d. March 07, 1987, Las Cruces, New México; m. EDWINA MARIE MONTOYA.
	ix.	VICENTE GÓMEZ[231], b. February 11, 1918, San Patricio, New México[232]; d. April 29, 1979, Mescalero, New México; m. MATILDE VALDÉZ.
83.	x.	CARMELITA GÓMEZ, b. June 30, 1920, San Patricio, New México.
	xi.	ROBERTO GÓMEZ, b. June 05, 1925, San Patricio, New México[232]; d. February 21, 2007, Alburquerque, New México; m. DOLORES DE GÓMEZ.
	xii.	ALBERTO GÓMEZ[233], b. June 05, 1925, San Patricio, New México[234]; d. February 22, 2001, Santa Fé, New México; m. DORA ARELLANO[235], January 20, 1946, Silver City, New México[236].

46. SALVADOR[8] SEDILLO *(CALIXTRO[7], JOSÉ ALBERTO[6], PABLO[5], SIMÓN[4] CEDILLO, MIGUEL DE SAN JUAN CEDILLO RICO[3] DE ROJAS, JOAQUÍN CEDILLO RICO[2], PEDRO DE CEDILLO RICO[1])* was born May 29, 1887[237], and died May 18, 1951 in Los Ángeles, California[238]. He married CLEOTILDE GALLEGOS December 19, 1911[239], daughter of JOSÉ MIRABAL and ELVIRA DE MIRABAL.

Children of SALVADOR SEDILLO and CLEOTILDE GALLEGOS are:

	i.	ENRÍQUES[9] SEDILLO, b. Abt. 1915[240].
	ii.	BONIFACIA SEDILLO, b. Abt. 1918[241].
	iii.	URBANITA SEDILLO, b. Abt. 1919[242].
	iv.	JUAN SEDILLO, b. Abt. 1921[243].
	v.	ERMINIO SEDILLO, b. Abt. 1923[243].
	vi.	FRANCISCO SEDILLO, b. June 03, 1926[243].
	vii.	EVANGELINA SEDILLO, b. Abt. 1928[243].
	viii.	GILBERT SEDILLO, b. Private.

47. MARÍNEZ[8] SEDILLO *(MARTÍN GARCÍA[7], JOSÉ MIGUEL[6], JOSÉ BLÁS[5], ANTONIO FÉLIX[4] CEDILLO, ANTONIO[3], JOAQUÍN CEDILLO RICO[2] DE ROJAS, PEDRO DE CEDILLO RICO[1])* was born June 21, 1891 in San Patricio, Territory of New México[244], and died March 25, 1940 in Colorado Springs, Colorado. She married (1) BENJAMÍN BECERRA September 01, 1910 in Roswell, Territory of New México[244], son of SUSANO BECERRA and MASIMIANA LUJÁN. She married (2) DANIEL BECERRA Abt. 1919, son of SUSANO BECERRA and MASIMIANA LUJÁN.

Child of MARÍNEZ SEDILLO and BENJAMÍN BECERRA is:

| | i. | LEAH[9] BECERRA[245], b. August 16, 1913; d. August 03, 1934, Colorado Springs, Colorado. |

Children of MARÍNEZ SEDILLO and DANIEL BECERRA are:

  ii. NAOMI[9] BECERRA[246], b. October 17, 1920; d. September 09, 1988, Los Angeles, California.

  iii. MAXINE BECERRA[246], b. February 08, 1925; d. February 20, 1986, Riverside, California.

48. MIGUEL[8] SEDILLOS *(SIXTO[7], JOSÉ MIGUEL[6] SEDILLO, JOSÉ BLÁS[5], ANTONIO FÉLIX[4] CEDILLO, ANTONIO[3], JOAQUÍN CEDILLO RICO[2] DE ROJAS, PEDRO DE CEDILLO RICO[1])* was born November 28, 1891 in San Patricio, Territory of New México[247], and died March 15, 1967 in Carrizozo, New México[248]. He married RITA TRUJILLO October 14, 1914 in Lincoln, New México[249], daughter of BONAFICIO TRUJILLO and LORENSA SILVA.

Children of MIGUEL SEDILLOS and RITA TRUJILLO are:

  i. LEONEL[9] SEDILLO[250], b. November 20, 1918, San Patricio, New México[251].

  ii. IDILIA SEDILLO, b. Abt. 1923[251].

49. RAMÓN[8] SEDILLOS *(SIXTO[7], JOSÉ MIGUEL[6] SEDILLO, JOSÉ BLÁS[5], ANTONIO FÉLIX[4] CEDILLO, ANTONIO[3], JOAQUÍN CEDILLO RICO[2] DE ROJAS, PEDRO DE CEDILLO RICO[1])* was born February 25, 1899 in San Patricio, Territory of New México[252]. He married GUADALUPE URBÁN BRADY Abt. 1920[253], daughter of JUAN BRADY and MARÍLLITA URBÁN.

Children of RAMÓN SEDILLOS and GUADALUPE BRADY are:

  i. ONESIMA[9] SEDILLO, b. Abt. 1921, Roswell, New México[253].

  ii. MARÍA DEL ROSARIO SEDILLO, b. Abt. 1922, Roswell, New México[253].

  iii. VIOLA SEDILLO, b. Abt. 1924, Roswell, New México[253].

  iv. OLIVIA SEDILLO, b. Abt. 1926, Roswell, New México[253].

  v. SIXTO SEDILLO, b. Abt. 1927, Roswell, New México[253].

84. vi. JUANITA SEDILLO, b. September 23, 1940, Wilmington, California.

  vii. MICHELLE SEDILLO, b. Private, Wilmington, California.

  viii. RAYMOND SEDILLO, b. Private.

50. EDUARDO[8] SEDILLOS *(SIXTO[7], JOSÉ MIGUEL[6] SEDILLO, JOSÉ BLÁS[5], ANTONIO FÉLIX[4] CEDILLO, ANTONIO[3], JOAQUÍN CEDILLO RICO[2] DE ROJAS, PEDRO DE CEDILLO RICO[1])[254]* was born October 20, 1902 in Arabela, New México, and died March 08, 1991 in Alamogordo, New México. He married DOMINGA MAÉS[254] January 23, 1937 in San Patricio, New México[255], daughter of JOSÉ MAÉS and AMADA MOLINA.

Child of EDUARDO SEDILLOS and DOMINGA MAÉS is:

85. i. EVA[9] MCKINLEY, b. Private; Adopted child.

51. LEOPOLDO[8] SEDILLOS *(SIXTO[7], JOSÉ MIGUEL[6] SEDILLO, JOSÉ BLÁS[5], ANTONIO FÉLIX[4] CEDILLO, ANTONIO[3], JOAQUÍN CEDILLO RICO[2] DE ROJAS, PEDRO DE CEDILLO RICO[1])[256]* was born March 24, 1909 in San Patricio, New México, and died February 08, 1990 in Roswell, New México. He married ADELAIDA SÁNCHEZ April 14, 1946[257], daughter of DAVÍD SÁNCHEZ and FRANCISCA ARCHULETA.

Children of LEOPOLDO SEDILLOS and ADELAIDA SÁNCHEZ are:

  i. FRANCIS[9] SEDILLOS, b. Private; m. LUVÍN SÁNCHEZ.

86. ii. TITO SEDILLOS, b. Private.

52. DANIEL[8] SEDILLOS *(SIXTO[7], JOSÉ MIGUEL[6] SEDILLO, JOSÉ BLÁS[5], ANTONIO FÉLIX[4] CEDILLO, ANTONIO[3], JOAQUÍN CEDILLO RICO[2] DE ROJAS, PEDRO DE CEDILLO RICO[1])[258]* was born February 02, 1912 in Patos, New México, and died April 18, 2006 in Alamogordo, New México[259]. He married FLORA MONTAÑO, daughter of ABEL MONTAÑO and MOLLIE STEWART.

Child of DANIEL SEDILLOS and FLORA MONTAÑO is:

  i. DANIEL YSIDRO[9] SEDILLOS.

53. ALFRED EPIFANIO[8] SEDILLOS *(RUFINO[7] SEDILLO, JOSÉ MIGUEL[6], JOSÉ BLÁS[5], ANTONIO FÉLIX[4] CEDILLO, ANTONIO[3], JOAQUÍN CEDILLO RICO[2] DE ROJAS, PEDRO DE CEDILLO RICO[1])* was born February 08, 1918 in El Paso, Texas[260], and died October 05, 1997. He married RITA MARIE GONZÁLES December 1939 in Denver, Colorado.

Children of ALFRED SEDILLOS and RITA GONZÁLES are:
  i. ALFRED E.[9] SEDILLOS, b. October 14, 1940, Denver, Colorado; d. November 07, 2008, Denver, Colorado.
  ii. DOLORES SEDILLOS, b. February 17, 1943; d. December 20, 2000, Denver, Colorado.

54. ESTANISLADO[8] OLGUÍN *(MARÍA LORENSA[7] CEDILLO, MARÍA DOLÓRES[6] SEDILLO, JULIÁN BERNARDO[5], ANTONIO FÉLIX[4] CEDILLO, ANTONIO[3], JOAQUÍN CEDILLO RICO[2] DE ROJAS, PEDRO DE CEDILLO RICO[1])* was born May 06, 1870 in Ruidoso, Territory of New México[261]. He married ANASTACIA CHÁVEZ[262] March 02, 1901[263], daughter of JUAN CHÁVEZ and TERESA HERRERA.

Children of ESTANISLADO OLGUÍN and ANASTACIA CHÁVEZ are:
  i. CANDELARIA[9] OLGUÍN[264], b. February 02, 1902; d. October 03, 1934; m. PABLO CALDERON[264], June 22, 1920[265].
  ii. JUANITA OLGUÍN, b. Abt. 1904[266]; m. OLOJIO GALLEGOS.
  iii. AVESLÍN OLGUÍN, b. Abt. 1911[266].
87. iv. CECILIA OLGUÍN, b. Abt. 1914.
  v. ROBERTO OLGUÍN[267], b. April 19, 1919, San Patricio, New México[268]; m. ELVA GALLEGOS, April 01, 1948, Carrizozo, New México[269].
  vi. PEDRO OLGUÍN, b. Abt. 1921[270].
  vii. PETRA OLGUÍN, b. Abt. 1923[271].

55. MARGARITA CANDELARIA[8] OLGUÍN *(MARÍA LORENSA[7] CEDILLO, MARÍA DOLÓRES[6] SEDILLO, JULIÁN BERNARDO[5], ANTONIO FÉLIX[4] CEDILLO, ANTONIO[3], JOAQUÍN CEDILLO RICO[2] DE ROJAS, PEDRO DE CEDILLO RICO[1])[272]* was born January 31, 1872 in San Patricio, Territory of New México, and died April 06, 1955. She married SIXTO SEDILLOS[272] July 28, 1892 in Ruidoso, Territory of New México[273], son of JOSÉ SEDILLO and MARÍA GARCÍA.

Children of MARGARITA OLGUÍN and SIXTO SEDILLOS are:
  i. MIGUEL[9] SEDILLOS, b. November 28, 1891, San Patricio, Territory of New México[274]; d. March 15, 1967, Carrizozo, New México[275]; m. RITA TRUJILLO, October 14, 1914, Lincoln, New México[276].
  ii. ONESIMA SEDILLOS, b. February 15, 1894, El Berendo, Territory of New México; m. AMABLE CHÁVEZ, September 23, 1914, Lincoln, New México[277].
  iii. FRANCISQUITA SEDILLOS, b. April 15, 1895, San Patricio, Territory of New México[278]; m. JOSÉ OROSCO, October 01, 1913, Patos, Territory of New México[278].
  iv. RAMÓN SEDILLOS, b. February 25, 1899, San Patricio, Territory of New México[279]; m. GUADALUPE URBÁN BRADY, Abt. 1920[280].
  v. EDUARDO SEDILLOS[281], b. October 20, 1902, Arabela, New México; d. March 08, 1991, Alamogordo, New México; m. DOMINGA MAÉS[281], January 23, 1937, San Patricio, New México[282].
  vi. ESTELA SEDILLOS[283], b. September 03, 1904, San Patricio, Territory of New México[284]; m. HILARIO SÁNCHEZ[285], July 27, 1921[286].
  vii. PRESILIANA SEDILLOS, b. Abt. 1906[287].
  viii. LEOPOLDO SEDILLOS[288], b. March 24, 1909, San Patricio, New México; d. February 08, 1990, Roswell, New México; m. ADELAIDA SÁNCHEZ, April 14, 1946[289].
  ix. DANIEL SEDILLOS[290], b. February 02, 1912, Patos, New México; d. April 18, 2006, Alamogordo, New México[291]; m. FLORA MONTAÑO.

56. MANUELITA[8] OLGUÍN *(MARÍA LORENSA[7] CEDILLO, MARÍA DOLÓRES[6] SEDILLO, JULIÁN BERNARDO[5], ANTONIO FÉLIX[4] CEDILLO, ANTONIO[3], JOAQUÍN CEDILLO RICO[2] DE ROJAS, PEDRO DE CEDILLO RICO[1])* was born June 1887 in San Patricio, Territory of New México[292]. She married (1) PROMETIVO BRADY April 03, 1899[293], son of WILLIAM BRADY and BONIFACIA CHÁVES. She married (2) HINIO LUCERO[294] February 12, 1902[295], son of ANISETO LUCERO and REFUGIA TRUJILLO.

Children of MANUELITA OLGUÍN and HINIO LUCERO are:
  i. MARTÍN OLGUÍN[9] LUCERO[296], b. July 26, 1905, San Patricio, Territory of New México; d. May 15, 1953.
  ii. REYES LUCERO, b. June 06, 1909, San Patricio, Territory of New México[297]; m. RITA BENAVIDEZ, December 04, 1946, Carrizozo, New México[297].
  iii. EPIFANIO LUCERO, b. 1915, San Patricio, New México[298].
  iv. REFUGIO LUCERO, b. 1918, San Patricio, New México[298].
88. v. ANISETO OLGUÍN LUCERO, b. November 15, 1902, San Patricio, Territory of New México; d. November 18, 1965, San Patricio, New México.

57. IGNACIO S.[8] OLGUÍN *(MARÍA LORENSA[7] CEDILLO, MARÍA DOLÓRES[6] SEDILLO, JULIÁN BERNARDO[5], ANTONIO FÉLIX[4] CEDILLO, ANTONIO[3], JOAQUÍN CEDILLO RICO[2] DE ROJAS, PEDRO DE CEDILLO RICO[1])[299]* was born August 01, 1873 in San Patricio, Territory of New México[300], and died October 15, 1947 in El Paso, Téxas. He married (1) VIVIANA CHÁVEZ[301] March 16, 1898[302], daughter of JUAN CHÁVEZ and TERESA HERRERA. He married (2) JOSEFITA RANDOLPH[303] August 19, 1911 in San Patricio, Territory of New México[304], daughter of FRANK RANDOLPH and CATARINA BRADY. He married (3) JUANITA LUCERO November 02, 1921[305], daughter of ANISETO LUCERO and REFUGIA TRUJILLO.

Child of IGNACIO OLGUÍN and VIVIANA CHÁVEZ is:

89.   i.   GENOVEVA CHÁVEZ[9] OLGUÍN, b. January 22, 1904, San Patricio, Territory of New México; Adopted child.

Children of IGNACIO OLGUÍN and JUANITA LUCERO are:

90.   ii.   EVA H.[9] OLGUÍN, b. August 16, 1922, San Patricio, New México; d. January 16, 2012, Alamogordo, New México.
          iii.   RAMÓN OLGUÍN[306], b. February 12, 1925, San Patricio, New México[307]; d. July 07, 1983, Alamogordo, New México[308].
          iv.   CARLOS OLGUÍN[309], b. August 21, 1927, San Patricio, New México; d. August 23, 1958, San Patricio, New México.

Generation No. 9

58. CAMILO[9] SEDILLO *(MARTÍN SÁNCHEZ[8], COSMÉ[7], JUAN NEPOMUCENO[6], JOSÉ ÁNGEL[5], BLAS ANTONIO[4] CEDILLO, MIGUEL DE SAN JUAN CEDILLO RICO[3] DE ROJAS, JOAQUÍN CEDILLO RICO[2], PEDRO DE CEDILLO RICO[1])[310]* was born June 05, 1917 in Roswell, New México[311], and died May 06, 1986 in Artesia, New México. He married LORENSITA MONTOYA[311] May 04, 1940 in Carrizozo, New México[312], daughter of DOROTEO MONTOYA and ALBINA SILVA.

59. CRUSITA[9] SEDILLO *(MARTÍN SÁNCHEZ[8], COSMÉ[7], JUAN NEPOMUCENO[6], JOSÉ ÁNGEL[5], BLAS ANTONIO[4] CEDILLO, MIGUEL DE SAN JUAN CEDILLO RICO[3] DE ROJAS, JOAQUÍN CEDILLO RICO[2], PEDRO DE CEDILLO RICO[1])[315]* was born April 06, 1925 in Roswell, New México[316], and died December 26, 1993 in Alamogordo, New México. She married RAMÓN LUNA[317], son of RAMÓN LUNA and EMITERIA SALAZAR.

60. PORFIRIA[9] RAMÍREZ *(RAMÓN[8], JUANITA[7] SEDILLO, JUAN NEPOMUCENO[6], JOSÉ ÁNGEL[5], BLAS ANTONIO[4] CEDILLO, MIGUEL DE SAN JUAN CEDILLO RICO[3] DE ROJAS, JOAQUÍN CEDILLO RICO[2], PEDRO DE CEDILLO RICO[1])* was born November 30, 1920 in Arabela, New México. She married (1) DAVE LUCERO. She married (2) GONZALO RAMÍREZ.

61. JOSÉ[9] RAMÍREZ *(RAMÓN[8], JUANITA[7] SEDILLO, JUAN NEPOMUCENO[6], JOSÉ ÁNGEL[5], BLAS ANTONIO[4] CEDILLO, MIGUEL DE SAN JUAN CEDILLO RICO[3] DE ROJAS, JOAQUÍN CEDILLO RICO[2], PEDRO DE CEDILLO RICO[1])* was born March 19, 1926, and died February 26, 1979 in Tucson, Arizona. He married PETRA PINO.

62. BENITO[9] CANDELARIA *(ISIDRA[8] SÁNCHEZ, RAMONA[7] SEDILLO, JUAN NEPOMUCENO[6], JOSÉ ÁNGEL[5], BLAS ANTONIO[4] CEDILLO, MIGUEL DE SAN JUAN CEDILLO RICO[3] DE ROJAS, JOAQUÍN CEDILLO RICO[2], PEDRO DE CEDILLO RICO[1])* was born July 23, 1921 in Arabela, New México[318]. He married CARMELITA GÓMEZ December 13, 1944 in Carrizozo, New México[318], daughter of FELIPÉ GÓMEZ and BEATRIZ SEDILLO.

63. CELESTINO[9] CANDELARIA *(ISIDRA[8] SÁNCHEZ, RAMONA[7] SEDILLO, JUAN NEPOMUCENO[6], JOSÉ ÁNGEL[5], BLAS ANTONIO[4] CEDILLO, MIGUEL DE SAN JUAN CEDILLO RICO[3] DE ROJAS, JOAQUÍN CEDILLO RICO[2], PEDRO DE CEDILLO RICO[1])[319]* was born October 16, 1922 in Arabela, New México[320]. He married JOSEFITA MOYA.

64. ARCENIA[9] CANDELARIA *(ISIDRA[8] SÁNCHEZ, RAMONA[7] SEDILLO, JUAN NEPOMUCENO[6], JOSÉ ÁNGEL[5], BLAS ANTONIO[4] CEDILLO, MIGUEL DE SAN JUAN CEDILLO RICO[3] DE ROJAS, JOAQUÍN CEDILLO RICO[2], PEDRO DE CEDILLO RICO[1])* was born Abt. 1925[320]. She married RUBEN LUCERO.

65. EDUARDO[9] CANDELARIA *(ISIDRA[8] SÁNCHEZ, RAMONA[7] SEDILLO, JUAN NEPOMUCENO[6], JOSÉ ÁNGEL[5], BLAS ANTONIO[4] CEDILLO, MIGUEL DE SAN JUAN CEDILLO RICO[3] DE ROJAS, JOAQUÍN CEDILLO RICO[2], PEDRO DE CEDILLO RICO[1])[321]* was born July 11, 1928 in Arabela, New México, and died November 09, 2003. He married AMELIA GÓMEZ October 25, 1952 in San Patricio, New México[322], daughter of FRANK GÓMEZ and GRESELDA CHÁVEZ.

Notes for EDUARDO CANDELARIA:
Also known as Edward and Lolo. US Army Korea.

66. ASUSENA[9] CANDELARIA *(ISIDRA[8] SÁNCHEZ, RAMONA[7] SEDILLO, JUAN NEPOMUCENO[6], JOSÉ ÁNGEL[5], BLAS ANTONIO[4] CEDILLO, MIGUEL DE SAN JUAN CEDILLO RICO[3] DE ROJAS, JOAQUÍN CEDILLO RICO[2], PEDRO DE CEDILLO RICO[1])* was born March 1930[324]. She married LUVÍN SÁNCHEZ[325], son of SALOMON SÁNCHEZ and MANUELITA SÁNCHEZ.

Notes for ASUSENA CANDELARIA:
Also known as Susan.

67. SOFIO[9] SÁNCHEZ *(AUGUSTINA[8] ULIBARRÍ, MARÍA SARAFINA[7] SEDILLO, JUAN NEPOMUCENO[6], JOSÉ ÁNGEL[5], BLAS ANTONIO[4] CEDILLO, MIGUEL DE SAN JUAN CEDILLO RICO[3] DE ROJAS, JOAQUÍN CEDILLO RICO[2], PEDRO DE CEDILLO RICO[1])[325]* was born May 25, 1916 in San Patricio, New México[326], and died May 25, 1984 in San Patricio, New México. He married GONSAGITA SALAS[327] May 29, 1939 in Carrizozo, New México[327], daughter of PEDRO SALAS and TEOFILA BENAVIDES.

68. ANEDA ULIBARRÍ[9] SÁNCHEZ *(AUGUSTINA[8] ULIBARRÍ, MARÍA SARAFINA[7] SEDILLO, JUAN NEPOMUCENO[6], JOSÉ ÁNGEL[5], BLAS ANTONIO[4] CEDILLO, MIGUEL DE SAN JUAN CEDILLO RICO[3] DE ROJAS, JOAQUÍN CEDILLO RICO[2], PEDRO DE CEDILLO RICO[1])* was born July 12, 1918 in San Patricio, New México[328], and died September 24, 1999. She married ERMANDO CHÁVEZ[329] September 13, 1941 in Carrizozo, New México[330], son of PABLO CHÁVEZ and AMADA SÁNCHEZ.

69. MARY[9] SALCIDO *(PETRA[8] ULIBARRÍ, MARÍA SARAFINA[7] SEDILLO, JUAN NEPOMUCENO[6], JOSÉ ÁNGEL[5], BLAS ANTONIO[4] CEDILLO, MIGUEL DE SAN JUAN CEDILLO RICO[3] DE ROJAS, JOAQUÍN CEDILLO RICO[2], PEDRO DE CEDILLO RICO[1])[333]* was born April 23, 1934 in Hondo, New México, and died March 10, 2001 in Dexter, New México. She married JERRY MARTÍNEZ[333] August 19, 1950[333].

70. BENJAMÍN[9] HERRERA *(ELISA[8] GONZÁLES, REIMUNDA[7] SEDILLO, JUAN NEPOMUCENO[6], JOSÉ ÁNGEL[5], BLAS ANTONIO[4] CEDILLO, MIGUEL DE SAN JUAN CEDILLO RICO[3] DE ROJAS, JOAQUÍN CEDILLO RICO[2], PEDRO DE CEDILLO RICO[1])[334]* was born August 27, 1932 in San Patricio, New México, and died October 27, 1998 in Ruidoso Downs, New México. He married BRIJIDA CHÁVEZ[334] November 16, 1953 in Ruidoso Downs, New México, daughter of PATROCINIO CHÁVEZ and MELITANA ROMERO.

71. BENITO[9] HERRERA *(ELISA[8] GONZÁLES, REIMUNDA[7] SEDILLO, JUAN NEPOMUCENO[6], JOSÉ ÁNGEL[5], BLAS ANTONIO[4] CEDILLO, MIGUEL DE SAN JUAN CEDILLO RICO[3] DE ROJAS, JOAQUÍN CEDILLO RICO[2], PEDRO DE CEDILLO RICO[1])[335]* was born August 30, 1934 in San Patricio, New México, and died July 23, 2002 in Alburquerque, New México. He married JOSIE CHÁVEZ, daughter of YSIDRO CHÁVEZ and PAUBLITA SÁNCHEZ.

72. FLORA[9] HERRERA *(ELISA[8] GONZÁLES, REIMUNDA[7] SEDILLO, JUAN NEPOMUCENO[6], JOSÉ ÁNGEL[5], BLAS ANTONIO[4] CEDILLO, MIGUEL DE SAN JUAN CEDILLO RICO[3] DE ROJAS, JOAQUÍN CEDILLO RICO[2], PEDRO DE CEDILLO RICO[1])[336]* was born April 30, 1936 in San Patricio, New México[337], and died April 28, 2001 in Ruidoso, New México. She married PORFIRIO SÁNCHEZ May 04, 1952 in San Patricio, New México[337], son of SALOMON SÁNCHEZ and MANUELITA SÁNCHEZ.

73. ELENA[9] HERRERA *(ELISA[8] GONZÁLES, REIMUNDA[7] SEDILLO, JUAN NEPOMUCENO[6], JOSÉ ÁNGEL[5], BLAS ANTONIO[4] CEDILLO, MIGUEL DE SAN JUAN CEDILLO RICO[3] DE ROJAS, JOAQUÍN CEDILLO RICO[2], PEDRO DE CEDILLO RICO[1])* was born September 10, 1939 in San Patricio, New México, and died July 12, 2010 in Alburquerque, New México.

74. LEOPOLDO[9] HERRERA *(ELISA[8] GONZÁLES, REIMUNDA[7] SEDILLO, JUAN NEPOMUCENO[6], JOSÉ ÁNGEL[5], BLAS ANTONIO[4] CEDILLO, MIGUEL DE SAN JUAN CEDILLO RICO[3] DE ROJAS, JOAQUÍN CEDILLO RICO[2], PEDRO DE CEDILLO RICO[1])* was born December 29, 1945 in San Patricio, New México, and died June 20, 2012 in San Patricio, New México. He married EMMA ZAMORA, daughter of PABLO ZAMORA and EMMA ZAMORA.

75. JUAN[9] HERRERA *(ELISA[8] GONZÁLES, REIMUNDA[7] SEDILLO, JUAN NEPOMUCENO[6], JOSÉ ÁNGEL[5], BLAS ANTONIO[4] CEDILLO, MIGUEL DE SAN JUAN CEDILLO RICO[3] DE ROJAS, JOAQUÍN CEDILLO RICO[2], PEDRO DE CEDILLO RICO[1])* was born May 09, 1952 in Capitán, New México, and died January 22, 2011 in Albuquerque, New México.

76. FLORENCIO[9] GÓMEZ *(BEATRIZ[8] SEDILLO, CALIXTRO[7], JOSÉ ALBERTO[6], PABLO[5], SIMÓN[4] CEDILLO, MIGUEL DE SAN JUAN CEDILLO RICO[3] DE ROJAS, JOAQUÍN CEDILLO RICO[2], PEDRO DE CEDILLO RICO[1])[338]* was born October 16, 1898, and died December 06, 1975. He married JUAQUINITA NAJERES[339] August 26, 1926 in Roswell, New México[340], daughter of ANDRÉS NEJERES and ANTONIA MAÉS.

Children of FLORENCIO GÓMEZ and JUAQUINITA NAJERES are:
    i.   MANUEL NAJERES[10] GÓMEZ[341], b. April 01, 1928; d. August 03, 1993, San Patricio, New México; m. ADELA CHÁVEZ.

77. DOMINIA[9] GÓMEZ *(BEATRIZ[8] SEDILLO, CALIXTRO[7], JOSÉ ALBERTO[6], PABLO[5], SIMÓN[4] CEDILLO, MIGUEL DE SAN JUAN CEDILLO RICO[3] DE ROJAS, JOAQUÍN CEDILLO RICO[2], PEDRO DE CEDILLO RICO[1])[347]* was born April 06, 1901[348], and died October 28, 1982. She married PABLO MONTOYA[349] November 09, 1918 in San Patricio, New México[350], son of MAURICIO MONTOYA and CLEOFAS HERRERA.

Children of DOMINIA GÓMEZ and PABLO MONTOYA are:
    i.   JULIA[10] MONTOYA, b. Abt. 1918[351].
    ii.   OLIVIA MONTOYA[352], b. December 17, 1922, Glencoe, New México[353]; d. December 02, 2002, San Patricio, New México; m. RALPH MIRANDA[354], June 28, 1948, Carrizozo, New México[355].
    iii.   PABLO BENITO MONTOYA, b. Abt. 1938[356]; m. MARTHA ROMERO.
    iv.   ERMELINDA MONTOYA, b. Private.
    v.   ROSALÍA GÓMEZ MONTOYA, b. Private.

78. ESTELA[9] GÓMEZ *(BEATRIZ[8] SEDILLO, CALIXTRO[7], JOSÉ ALBERTO[6], PABLO[5], SIMÓN[4] CEDILLO, MIGUEL DE SAN JUAN CEDILLO RICO[3] DE ROJAS, JOAQUÍN CEDILLO RICO[2], PEDRO DE CEDILLO RICO[1])[357]* was born August 15, 1903[358], and died December 26, 2001 in Fort Bayard, New México[359]. She married MANUEL CASTILLO ROMERO[359] May 30, 1930 in Carrizozo, New México[360], son of JUAN ROMERO and CRISTINA CASTILLO.

79. DANIEL[9] GÓMEZ *(BEATRIZ[8] SEDILLO, CALIXTRO[7], JOSÉ ALBERTO[6], PABLO[5], SIMÓN[4] CEDILLO, MIGUEL DE SAN JUAN CEDILLO RICO[3] DE ROJAS, JOAQUÍN CEDILLO RICO[2], PEDRO DE CEDILLO RICO[1])[361]* was born February 07, 1906 in Ruidoso, New México[362], and died May 02, 1986 in Lincoln, New México. He married JUANITA SALAS[363] June 02, 1928 in Carrizozo, New México[364], daughter of TANISLAO SALAS and FILOMENA ROMERO.

Children of DANIEL GÓMEZ and JUANITA SALAS are:
    i.   DORA[10] GÓMEZ, b. Abt. 1929.
    ii.   VIRGINIA GÓMEZ, b. January 09, 1932; d. March 16, 1990.
    iii.   ERNESTO DANIEL GÓMEZ[365], b. May 21, 1933[366]; d. July 26, 2000, Alburquerque, New México.
    iv.   JOE GÓMEZ, b. Private.
    v.   JERRY GÓMEZ, b. October 05, 1949, Lincoln, New México; m. YVONNE GÓMEZ.

80. IGNACIA[9] GÓMEZ *(BEATRIZ[8] SEDILLO, CALIXTRO[7], JOSÉ ALBERTO[6], PABLO[5], SIMÓN[4] CEDILLO, MIGUEL DE SAN JUAN CEDILLO RICO[3] DE ROJAS, JOAQUÍN CEDILLO RICO[2], PEDRO DE CEDILLO RICO[1])[367]* was born May 09, 1909 in San Patricio, Territory of New México[368], and died July 29, 2005 in Ruidoso, New México. She married FERMÍN PACHECO[369] August 29, 1932 in Roswell, New México[370], son of ROMÁN PACHECO and BONIFACIA RICHARDSON.

Children of IGNACIA GÓMEZ and FERMÍN PACHECO are:
  i.   ROMÁN ALFREDO[10] PACHECO, b. April 01, 1939, San Patricio, New México; d. April 05, 1999, Las Cruces, New México; m. LUCINA SÁNCHEZ[371].
  ii. ORLANDO PACHECO, b. Private.
  iii. BEATRIZ PACHECO, b. Private; m. DAVID MCKINLEY.

81. FRANK[9] GÓMEZ *(BEATRIZ[8] SEDILLO, CALIXTRO[7], JOSÉ ALBERTO[6], PABLO[5], SIMÓN[4] CEDILLO, MIGUEL DE SAN JUAN CEDILLO RICO[3] DE ROJAS, JOAQUÍN CEDILLO RICO[2], PEDRO DE CEDILLO RICO[1])[372]* was born December 13, 1911 in Ruidoso, Territory of New México, and died April 27, 1999 in Glencoe, New México. He married GRESELDA CHÁVEZ[372] February 17, 1934 in Carrizozo, New México[373], daughter of YSIDRO CHÁVEZ and PAUBLITA SÁNCHEZ.

Children of FRANK GÓMEZ and GRESELDA CHÁVEZ are:
  i.   WILLIAM[10] GÓMEZ, b. November 10, 1934, Glencoe, New México; m. JOSEPHINE SILVA.
  ii.   AMELIA GÓMEZ, b. April 10, 1936, San Patricio, New México[374]; m. EDUARDO CANDELARIA[375], October 25, 1952, San Patricio, New México[376].
  iii. BEATRICE GÓMEZ, b. February 21, 1938, Glencoe, New México[377]; m. HENRY SILVA, June 01, 1957, San Patricio, New México[377].
  iv.   JOHNNY GÓMEZ, b. February 20, 1941, Glencoe, New México; m. (1) OLIVIA GÓMEZ; m. (2) LYDIA TORREZ.
  v.   RITA GÓMEZ, b. July 01, 1942, Glencoe, New México[378]; m. ROGER HERRERA, August 03, 1958, Ruidoso, New México[378].
  vi.   LEROY GÓMEZ, b. December 30, 1943, Glencoe, New México; m. LOUELLA RAÉL.
  vii. PRISCILLA GÓMEZ, b. June 12, 1946, Glencoe, New México; m. JOE TORREZ.
  viii. LYDIA GÓMEZ, b. July 24, 1950, Glencoe, New México; m. GEORGE MORENO.

82. LUCÍA[9] GÓMEZ *(BEATRIZ[8] SEDILLO, CALIXTRO[7], JOSÉ ALBERTO[6], PABLO[5], SIMÓN[4] CEDILLO, MIGUEL DE SAN JUAN CEDILLO RICO[3] DE ROJAS, JOAQUÍN CEDILLO RICO[2], PEDRO DE CEDILLO RICO[1])* was born December 13, 1913 in San Patricio, New México[379], and died January 22, 1980 in Tucson, Arizona. She married FERNANDO PACHECO[380] August 07, 1937[381], son of ROMÁN PACHECO and BONIFACIA RICHARDSON.

Children of LUCÍA GÓMEZ and FERNANDO PACHECO are:
  i.   ARTURO[10] PACHECO, b. Abt. 1937, San Patricio, New México[382].
  ii.   ENRÍQUE PACHECO, b. Abt. 1938, San Patricio, New México[382].
  iii. RAMONA PACHECO, b. Abt. 1939, San Patricio, New México[382].
  iv.   EMMA BEATRIZ PACHECO[383], b. Abt. 1940, San Patricio, New México; d. October 06, 1940, San Patricio, New México.
  v.   ALFREDO FERNANDO PACHECO, b. Private.
  vi.   DAVID PACHECO, b. Private.
  vii. HELEN PACHECO, b. Private.
  viii. BONNIE PACHECO, b. Private.

83. CARMELITA[9] GÓMEZ *(BEATRIZ[8] SEDILLO, CALIXTRO[7], JOSÉ ALBERTO[6], PABLO[5], SIMÓN[4] CEDILLO, MIGUEL DE SAN JUAN CEDILLO RICO[3] DE ROJAS, JOAQUÍN CEDILLO RICO[2], PEDRO DE CEDILLO RICO[1])* was born June 30, 1920 in San Patricio, New México[384]. She married BENITO CANDELARIA December 13, 1944 in Carrizozo, New México[384], son of JOSÉ CANDELARIA and ISIDRA SÁNCHEZ.

Children of CARMELITA GÓMEZ and BENITO CANDELARIA are:
  i.   GILBERT[10] CANDELARIA, b. Private.
  ii.   JAMES CANDELARIA, b. Private.
  iii. SYLVIA CANDELARIA, b. Private.
  iv.   TONY CANDELARIA, b. Private.

84. JUANITA[9] SEDILLO *(RAMÓN[8] SEDILLOS, SIXTO[7], JOSÉ MIGUEL[6] SEDILLO, JOSÉ BLÁS[5], ANTONIO FÉLIX[4] CEDILLO, ANTONIO[3], JOAQUÍN CEDILLO RICO[2] DE ROJAS, PEDRO DE CEDILLO RICO[1])* was born September 23, 1940 in Wilmington, California. She married FLOYD SELF September 27, 1958 in Wilmington, California.

Children of JUANITA SEDILLO and FLOYD SELF are:
  i.   MICHAEL[10] SELF, b. December 29, 1961.

ii.   BERNADETTE SELF, b. August 21, 1963.
iii. ANNA SELF, b. November 24, 1965.

85. EVA[9] MCKINLEY *(EDUARDO[8] SEDILLOS, SIXTO[7], JOSÉ MIGUEL[6] SEDILLO, JOSÉ BLÁS[5], ANTONIO FÉLIX[4] CEDILLO, ANTONIO[3], JOAQUÍN CEDILLO RICO[2] DE ROJAS, PEDRO DE CEDILLO RICO[1])* was born Private. She married ALBERTO SÁNCHEZ[385], son of SALOMON SÁNCHEZ and MANUELITA SÁNCHEZ.

86. TITO[9] SEDILLOS *(LEOPOLDO[8], SIXTO[7], JOSÉ MIGUEL[6] SEDILLO, JOSÉ BLÁS[5], ANTONIO FÉLIX[4] CEDILLO, ANTONIO[3], JOAQUÍN CEDILLO RICO[2] DE ROJAS, PEDRO DE CEDILLO RICO[1])* was born Private.

87. CECILIA[9] OLGUÍN *(ESTANISLADO[8], MARÍA LORENSA[7] CEDILLO, MARÍA DOLÓRES[6] SEDILLO, JULIÁN BERNARDO[5], ANTONIO FÉLIX[4] CEDILLO, ANTONIO[3], JOAQUÍN CEDILLO RICO[2] DE ROJAS, PEDRO DE CEDILLO RICO[1])* was born Abt. 1914[386]. She married RUMELIO CHÁVEZ[387] July 11, 1936[388], son of PABLO CHÁVEZ and AMADA SÁNCHEZ.

88. ANISETO OLGUÍN[9] LUCERO *(MANUELITA[8] OLGUÍN, MARÍA LORENSA[7] CEDILLO, MARÍA DOLÓRES[6] SEDILLO, JULIÁN BERNARDO[5], ANTONIO FÉLIX[4] CEDILLO, ANTONIO[3], JOAQUÍN CEDILLO RICO[2] DE ROJAS, PEDRO DE CEDILLO RICO[1])[389]* was born November 15, 1902 in San Patricio, Territory of New México[390], and died November 18, 1965 in San Patricio, New México. He married REYNALDA SÁNCHEZ[391], daughter of NAPOLEÓN SÁNCHEZ and MARÍA CHÁVEZ.

Notes for ANISETO OLGUÍN LUCERO:
Buried: San Patricio.

Children of ANISETO LUCERO and REYNALDA SÁNCHEZ are:
i.   LEONIRES[10] LUCERO, b. 1926, San Patricio, New México[392].
ii.   MARÍA SÁNCHEZ LUCERO[393], b. September 23, 1931, San Patricio, New México[394]; d. September 16, 1994, Roswell, New México; m. (1) RALPH RODELA; m. (2) EMILIANO CHÁVEZ[395], April 25, 1947, Carrizozo, New México[396].
iii. FELIS LUCERO[397], b. July 12, 1934, San Patricio, New México[398]; m. (1) EMILIANO VILLESCAS, March 05, 1952, Carrizozo, New México[398]; m. (2) JAMES J. LARSON, May 08, 1961, Ruidoso, New México[399].
iv.   EFFIE LUCERO[400], b. Abt. 1939, San Patricio, New México[401].
v.   JOSEPH LUCERO, b. Abt. 1940, San Patricio, New México[401]; m. DORIS LUCERO.
vi.   ANISETO SÁNCHEZ LUCERO, b. Private, San Patricio, New México.
vii. EURAQUIO LUCERO, b. Private, San Patricio, New México.
viii. JESSIE LUCERO, b. Private, San Patricio, New México.
ix.   REYNALDA LUCERO, b. Private, San Patricio, New México.

89. GENOVEVA CHÁVEZ[9] OLGUÍN *(IGNACIO S.[8], MARÍA LORENSA[7] CEDILLO, MARÍA DOLÓRES[6] SEDILLO, JULIÁN BERNARDO[5], ANTONIO FÉLIX[4] CEDILLO, ANTONIO[3], JOAQUÍN CEDILLO RICO[2] DE ROJAS, PEDRO DE CEDILLO RICO[1])* was born January 22, 1904 in San Patricio, Territory of New México[402]. She married ANTONIO LA RIVA August 05, 1920 in San Patricio, New México[402], son of AUGUSTÍN LA RIVA and ANTONIA VALENCIA.

Children of GENOVEVA OLGUÍN and ANTONIO LA RIVA are:
i.   JOSÉ[10] LA RIVA, b. Abt. 1926, San Patricio, New México[403].
ii.   ANTONIO LA RIVA, b. Abt. 1928, San Patricio, New México[403].
iii. FERNANDO LA RIVA, b. Abt. 1929, San Patricio, New México[403].

90. EVA H.[9] OLGUÍN *(IGNACIO S.[8], MARÍA LORENSA[7] CEDILLO, MARÍA DOLÓRES[6] SEDILLO, JULIÁN BERNARDO[5], ANTONIO FÉLIX[4] CEDILLO, ANTONIO[3], JOAQUÍN CEDILLO RICO[2] DE ROJAS, PEDRO DE CEDILLO RICO[1])* was born August 16, 1922 in San Patricio, New México[404], and died January 16, 2012 in Alamogordo, New México. She married BENJAMÍN TELLES.

Children of EVA OLGUÍN and BENJAMÍN TELLES are:
i.   PATRICK[10] TELLES, b. Private.
ii.   FREIDA TELLES, b. Private.

Genealogy of Manuel Silva

Generation No. 1

1. MANUEL[1] SILVA was born Abt. 1830[1]. He married JOSEFITA ESQUIVEL[2].

Notes for JOSEFITA ESQUIVEL:
Three different names are used from various documents. Those three names are Josefita Esquivel, Josefa Alarid, and Josefa Lueras

Children of MANUEL SILVA and JOSEFITA ESQUIVEL are:

2.   i.   DOLÓRES[2] SILVA, b. Abt. 1847.
         ii.   CECILIO SILVA, b. Abt. 1850[3].
         iii.   JOSEFA SILVA, b. Abt. 1853[4].
         iv.   MARÍA SILVA, b. Abt. 1853[5].
         v.   MAURICIO SILVA, b. Abt. 1855[5].
3.   vi.   HILARIO SILVA, b. Abt. 1857.
4.   vii.   NICOLÁS SILVA, b. September 15, 1857, Sabinal, Territory of New México; d. May 06, 1933.
         viii.   JOSÉ SILVA, b. Abt. 1858[5].
5.   ix.   LORENSA SILVA, b. Abt. 1863; d. June 14, 1944, San Patricio, New México.
6.   x.   TIMOTEA SILVA, b. August 22, 1866, El Sabinal, Territory of New México; d. February 14, 1928, Brighton, Colorado.
         xi.   FRANCISCA SILVA, b. Abt. 1868[6].

Generation No. 2

2. DOLÓRES[2] SILVA *(MANUEL[1])* was born Abt. 1847[7]. She married MERIJILDO CHÁVEZ[8].

Children of DOLÓRES SILVA and MERIJILDO CHÁVEZ are:

         i.   PABLA[3] CHÁVEZ, b. 1866[9].
         ii.   PREMIA CHÁVEZ, b. 1867[9].
         iii.   LAZARO CHÁVEZ, b. 1869[9].
7.   iv.   GREGORIO CHÁVEZ, b. December 1870, San Patricio, Territory of New México; d. April 06, 1943, San Patricio, New México.
         v.   RUMELIO CHÁVEZ, b. 1877, San Patricio, Territory of New México.
         vi.   JOSÉ SILVA CHÁVEZ[10], b. November 29, 1883, San Patricio, Territory of New México; m. MARÍA ULIBARRÍ[10], November 02, 1911, Picacho, Territory of New México[10].
8.   vii.   MARÍA CHÁVEZ, b. 1881, San Patricio, Territory of New México.
         viii.   FEDERICO CHÁVEZ[11], b. February 1882, San Patricio, Territory of New México; d. September 20, 1943, San Patricio, New México.
         ix.   BEATRIZ CHÁVEZ, b. June 02, 1885, San Patricio, Territory of New México.
         x.   ROMALDO CHÁVEZ[11], b. January 01, 1887, San Patricio, Territory of New México; d. June 27, 1970, San Patricio, New México.

3. HILARIO[2] SILVA *(MANUEL[1])* was born Abt. 1857[12]. He married AMBROSIA ULIBARRÍ April 13, 1892[13], daughter of JUAN ULIBARRÍ and MARÍA LUCERO.

Children of HILARIO SILVA and AMBROSIA ULIBARRÍ are:

9.   i.   ALBINA[3] SILVA, b. March 19, 1884, San Patricio, Territory of New México.
10.   ii.   TELESFORO SILVA, b. April 18, 1885, Tularoso, Territory of New México; d. September 08, 1976, Ruidoso Downs, New México.

4. NICOLÁS[2] SILVA *(MANUEL[1])* was born September 15, 1857 in Sabinal, Territory of New México[14], and died May 06, 1933. He married (1) ELFIDA MONTOYA[15] May 22, 1898[16], daughter of TRANQUELINO MONTOYA and MARÍA TRUJILLO. He married (2) MANUELITA RODELA Y UDERO February 16, 1903 in San Patricio, New México[17], daughter of ANDRÉS RODELA and INEZ UDERO.

Child of NICOLÁS SILVA and MANUELITA UDERO is:
         i.   ESTER UDERO[3] SILVA.

5. LORENSA[2] SILVA *(MANUEL[1])* was born Abt. 1863[18], and died June 14, 1944 in San Patricio, New México[19]. She married BONAFICIO TRUJILLO[20] Abt. 1882[21], son of JOSÉ TRUJILLO and MARÍA SÁNCHEZ.

Children of LORENSA SILVA and BONAFICIO TRUJILLO are:

	i.	ANASTACIO[3] TRUJILLO, b. December 10, 1883, San Patricio, Territory of New México[22].
11.	ii.	SUSANA TRUJILLO, b. May 15, 1886, Ruidoso, Territory of New México; d. January 20, 1974.
12.	iii.	REYMUNDA TRUJILLO, b. January 17, 1888, San Patricio, Territory of New México.
	iv.	ALEJANDRO SILVA TRUJILLO, b. January 04, 1891, San Patricio, Territory of New México[23].
	v.	CARMELITA TRUJILLO, b. April 15, 1893, San Patricio, Territory of New México[24]; m. LORENZO MONTOYA, June 03, 1933[25].
13.	vi.	RITA TRUJILLO, b. January 04, 1894, San Patricio, Territory of New México.
14.	vii.	ROSA TRUJILLO, b. July 16, 1895, San Patricio, Territory of New México; d. February 21, 1988, Los Ángeles, California.
15.	viii.	VICTORIANO TRUJILLO, b. November 20, 1897, San Patricio, Territory of New México; d. February 1976, San Patricio, New México.
	ix.	PEDRO TRUJILLO, b. May 1899, San Patricio, Territory of New México[26].
16.	x.	LORENCITA TRUJILLO, b. August 10, 1905, San Patricio, Territory of New México; d. August 25, 1960.

6. TIMOTEA[2] SILVA *(MANUEL[1])* was born August 22, 1866 in El Sabinal, Territory of New México[27], and died February 14, 1928 in Brighton, Colorado. She married MARTÍN GARCÍA SEDILLO Abt. 1890[28], son of JOSÉ SEDILLO and MARÍA GARCÍA.

Children of TIMOTEA SILVA and MARTÍN SEDILLO are:

17.	i.	MARÍNEZ[3] SEDILLO, b. June 21, 1891, San Patricio, Territory of New México; d. March 25, 1940, Colorado Springs, Colorado.
	ii.	FRANCISCO SEDILLO, b. December 27, 1892, San Patricio, Territory of New México[28]; d. January 29, 1938, Greeley, Colorado.
	iii.	JOSEFITA SEDILLO, b. December 29, 1893, San Patricio, Territory of New México[28]; d. November 12, 1991, Denver, Colorado; m. SAMUEL BECERRA, March 23, 1912.
	iv.	EUFEMIA SEDILLO, b. December 1896, San Patricio, Territory of New México[28]; d. October 1930; m. JOSÉ BECERRA.
	v.	ANA CECILIA SEDILLO[29], b. April 03, 1906, San Patricio, Territory of New México; d. May 1974, Greeley, Colorado; m. NOBERTO VALADEZ, March 11, 1929, Greeley, Colorado.

Generation No. 3

7. GREGORIO[3] CHÁVEZ *(DOLÓRES[2] SILVA, MANUEL[1])*[30] was born December 1870 in San Patricio, Territory of New México[31], and died April 06, 1943 in San Patricio, New México. He married JULIANITA SAÍZ[32] December 21, 1907 in San Patricio, Territory of New México[33], daughter of PABLO SAÍZ and CELESTINA ARAGÓN.

Child of GREGORIO CHÁVEZ and JULIANITA SAÍZ is:

| | i. | FERNANDO[4] CHÁVEZ, b. Abt. 1909. |

8. MARÍA[3] CHÁVEZ *(DOLÓRES[2] SILVA, MANUEL[1])*[34] was born 1881 in San Patricio, Territory of New México[35]. She married NAPOLEÓN SÁNCHEZ February 10, 1902 in San Patricio, Territory of New México[36], son of FRANCISCO SÁNCHEZ and CONCEPCIÓN TRUJILLO.

Children of MARÍA CHÁVEZ and NAPOLEÓN SÁNCHEZ are:

	i.	LUPE[4] SÁNCHEZ, b. December 12, 1902, San Patricio, Territory of New México[37].
18.	ii.	REYNALDA SÁNCHEZ, b. February 21, 1905, San Patricio, Territory of New México; d. May 12, 1970, San Patricio, New México.
	iii.	FRANK SÁNCHEZ, b. 1908, San Patricio, Territory of New México[38].
	iv.	CECILIA SÁNCHEZ, b. 1910, San Patricio, Territory of New México[38].
	v.	MERIJILDO SÁNCHEZ, b. 1914, San Patricio, New México[38].
	vi.	JUAN CHÁVEZ SÁNCHEZ, b. 1916, San Patricio, New México[38].
	vii.	LOLA SÁNCHEZ, b. 1920, San Patricio, New México[38].

9. ALBINA[3] SILVA *(HILARIO[2], MANUEL[1])[39]* was born March 19, 1884 in San Patricio, Territory of New México. She married DOROTEO MONTOYA November 20, 1907[40], son of TRANQUELINO MONTOYA and MARÍA TRUJILLO.

Children of ALBINA SILVA and DOROTEO MONTOYA are:

	i.	SAMUEL[4] MONTOYA[41], b. May 19, 1909; d. May 03, 1994; m. EUFRACIA MONTOYA[41], November 26, 1938[42].
	ii.	COSMÉ MONTOYA[43], b. May 1911, San Patricio, New México[44]; m. AMALIA BENAVIDEZ.
19.	iii.	LORENSITA MONTOYA, b. February 12, 1912, San Patricio, New México; d. Artesia, New México.
20.	iv.	JOSEFITA MONTOYA, b. 1918; d. 2003.
21.	v.	TRANQUELINO SILVA MONTOYA, b. August 22, 1925, Arabela, New México; d. September 24, 2009, Alamagordo, New México.

10. TELESFORO[3] SILVA *(HILARIO[2], MANUEL[1])[45]* was born April 18, 1885 in Tularoso, Territory of New México, and died September 08, 1976 in Ruidoso Downs, New México. He married (1) FRANCISCA UDERO RODELA October 27, 1905 in San Patricio, Territory of New México[46], daughter of ANDRÉS RODELA and INEZ UDERO. He married (2) ERINEA BENAVIDEZ[47] November 29, 1911, daughter of JUAN BENAVIDEZ and TEOFILA TRUJILLO.

Children of TELESFORO SILVA and FRANCISCA RODELA are:

22.	i.	EDUARDO[4] SILVA, b. August 10, 1908; d. 1998.
	ii.	ANGELITA SILVA, b. Abt. October 1909.

Children of TELESFORO SILVA and ERINEA BENAVIDEZ are:

	iii.	BENITO[4] SILVA[48], b. October 22, 1912, Hondo, New México[49]; d. December 1986, Ruidoso Downs, New México; m. CONSUELO SÁNCHEZ[50], February 13, 1932, Glencoe, New México[51].
23.	iv.	AMBROCIA SILVA, b. April 15, 1915, Hondo, New México.
	v.	ANSELMO SILVA[52], b. April 21, 1919, Hondo, New México[53]; d. December 10, 1992, Ruidoso Downs, New México; m. VIRGINIA MIRANDA, November 04, 1948, Ruidoso, New México[54].
	vi.	BONIFACIO SILVA, b. May 15, 1923, Lincoln, New México[55].
	vii.	ONESIMA SILVA, b. Private.
	viii.	RAMÓN SILVA, b. Private; m. CARMELITA SILVA.
	ix.	VICTOR SILVA, b. Private.

11. SUSANA[3] TRUJILLO *(LORENSA[2] SILVA, MANUEL[1])[56]* was born May 15, 1886 in Ruidoso, Territory of New México, and died January 20, 1974. She married MANUEL CORONA[56] February 24, 1909 in Lincoln, Territory of New México[57], son of MAXIMIANO CORONA and MANUELITA HERRERA.

Children of SUSANA TRUJILLO and MANUEL CORONA are:

24.	i.	MAX[4] CORONA, b. September 05, 1912, San Patricio, New México; d. January 09, 1973, Morenci, Arizona.
	ii.	ANASTACIO CORONA, b. October 23, 1916, San Patricio, New México[58]; d. July 11, 2000, Ruidoso, New México; m. ESPERANZA MAÉS, August 28, 1939, Arabela, New México[58].
	iii.	MANUEL TRUJILLO CORONA[59], b. March 27, 1921, San Patricio, New México; d. August 25, 2007, San Patricio, New México.

12. REYMUNDA[3] TRUJILLO *(LORENSA[2] SILVA, MANUEL[1])* was born January 17, 1888 in San Patricio, Territory of New México[60]. She married FRUGENCIO FLORES February 05, 1906 in Lincoln, Territory of New México[60], son of JOSÉ FLORES and VICTORIA MAÉS.

Children of REYMUNDA TRUJILLO and FRUGENCIO FLORES are:

i.	JOSÉ[4] FLORES, b. 1910[61].
ii.	CORINA FLORES, b. 1912[61].
iii.	RAFAEL FLORES, b. 1914[61].
iv.	ISMAEL FLORES, b. 1917[61].
v.	ALBERTO FLORES, b. 1919[61].
vi.	ADELAIDA FLORES[62], b. December 01, 1922, San Patricio, New México; d. April 17, 1924, San Patricio, New México.

13. RITA[3] TRUJILLO *(LORENSA[2] SILVA, MANUEL[1])* was born January 04, 1894 in San Patricio, Territory of New México[63]. She married MIGUEL SEDILLO October 14, 1914 in Lincoln, New México[63], son of SISTO SEDILLO and MARGARITA OLGUÍN.

Children of RITA TRUJILLO and MIGUEL SEDILLO are:
  i.   LEONEL[4] SEDILLO[64], b. November 20, 1918, San Patricio, New México[65].
  ii. IDILIA SEDILLO, b. Abt. 1923[65].

14. ROSA[3] TRUJILLO *(LORENSA[2] SILVA, MANUEL[1])*[66] was born July 16, 1895 in San Patricio, Territory of New México[67], and died February 21, 1988 in Los Ángeles, California. She married ALFREDO ZAMORA September 25, 1925 in San Patricio, New México[68], son of JUAN SAMORA and EVARISTA GAMBOA.

Children of ROSA TRUJILLO and ALFREDO ZAMORA are:
  i.   EVA[4] ZAMORA, b. Abt. 1928, Lincoln, New México[69].
  ii. VICTORIANO ZAMORA, b. Private, Lincoln, New México.

15. VICTORIANO[3] TRUJILLO *(LORENSA[2] SILVA, MANUEL[1])*[70] was born November 20, 1897 in San Patricio, Territory of New México[71], and died February 1976 in San Patricio, New México. He married ENEDINA GUTIÉRREZ May 17, 1933[72], daughter of JULIAN GUTIÉRREZ and JULIANITA ROSILLOS.

Children of VICTORIANO TRUJILLO and ENEDINA GUTIÉRREZ are:
  i.   MARÍA[4] TRUJILLO[73], b. Abt. 1941, San Patricio, New México; d. January 27, 1941, San Patricio, New México.
  ii.   ARTURO TRUJILLO, b. Private; m. CORINA CRUZ.
  iii. VICTOR TRUJILLO, b. Private; m. AMELIA CRUZ.

16. LORENCITA[3] TRUJILLO *(LORENSA[2] SILVA, MANUEL[1])*[74] was born August 10, 1905 in San Patricio, Territory of New México[75], and died August 25, 1960. She married PEDRO CHÁVEZ[76] July 13, 1930 in Carrizozo, New México[77], son of MACARIO CHÁVEZ and ELFIDA MONTOYA.

Children of LORENCITA TRUJILLO and PEDRO CHÁVEZ are:
       i.   MARÍA CIRILIA[4] CHÁVEZ[78], b. Abt. 1937, San Patricio, New México; d. March 24, 1937, San Patricio, New México.
  25. ii. MACARIO TRUJILLO CHÁVEZ, b. Private.
       iii. RAYMOND CHÁVEZ, b. Private.
       iv. RUFINA CHÁVEZ, b. Private; m. SIGISFREDO MONTOYA.

17. MARÍNEZ[3] SEDILLO *(TIMOTEA[2] SILVA, MANUEL[1])* was born June 21, 1891 in San Patricio, Territory of New México[79], and died March 25, 1940 in Colorado Springs, Colorado. She married (1) BENJAMÍN BECERRA September 01, 1910 in Roswell, Territory of New México[79], son of SUSANO BECERRA and MASIMIANA LUJÁN. She married (2) DANIEL BECERRA Abt. 1919, son of SUSANO BECERRA and MASIMIANA LUJÁN.

Child of MARÍNEZ SEDILLO and BENJAMÍN BECERRA is:
  i.   LEAH[4] BECERRA[80], b. August 16, 1913; d. August 03, 1934, Colorado Springs, Colorado.

Children of MARÍNEZ SEDILLO and DANIEL BECERRA are:
  ii.   NAOMI[4] BECERRA[81], b. October 17, 1920; d. September 09, 1988, Los Angeles, California.
  iii. MAXINE BECERRA[81], b. February 08, 1925; d. February 20, 1986, Riverside, California.

Generation No. 4

18. REYNALDA[4] SÁNCHEZ *(MARÍA[3] CHÁVEZ, DOLÓRES[2] SILVA, MANUEL[1])*[82] was born February 21, 1905 in San Patricio, Territory of New México, and died May 12, 1970 in San Patricio, New México. She married ANISETO LUCERO[82].

Children of REYNALDA SÁNCHEZ and ANISETO LUCERO are:
  i.   LEONIRES[5] LUCERO, b. 1926[83].

ii.   MARÍA SÁNCHEZ LUCERO[84], b. September 23, 1931, San Patricio, New México[85]; d. September 16, 1994, Roswell, New México; m. (1) RALPH RODELA; m. (2) EMILIANO CHÁVEZ[86], April 25, 1947, Carrizozo, New México[87].

iii. FELIS LUCERO, b. July 12, 1934, San Patricio, New México[88]; m. EMILIANO VILLESCAS, March 05, 1952, Carrizozo, New México[88].

iv.   ANISETO SÁNCHEZ LUCERO, b. Private.

v.   EFFIE LUCERO, b. Private.

vi.   EURAQUIO LUCERO, b. Private.

vii. JESSIE LUCERO, b. Private.

viii. JOSEPH LUCERO, b. Private.

ix.   REYNALDA LUCERO, b. Private.

19. LORENSITA[4] MONTOYA *(ALBINA[3] SILVA, HILARIO[2], MANUEL[1])* was born February 12, 1912 in San Patricio, New México[89], and died in Artesia, New México. She married (1) FERNANDO SALSBERRY[90] June 15, 1929 in Carrizozo, New Mexico[91], son of JAMES SALSBERRY and MANUELITA HERRERA. She married (2) CAMILO SEDILLO[92] May 04, 1940 in Carrizozo, New México[93], son of MARTÍN SEDILLO and TOMASITA HERRERA.

Children of LORENSITA MONTOYA and FERNANDO SALSBERRY are:

i.   CLOVÍS[5] SALSBERRY[94], b. Abt. 1934; d. May 25, 1938, Fort Stanton, New México.

ii.   ANATALIA SALSBERRY, b. Private; m. MANUEL SOSA.

iii. ELOY SALSBERRY, b. Private.

iv.   FERNANDO MONTOYA SALSBERRY, b. Private.

Children of LORENSITA MONTOYA and CAMILO SEDILLO are:

v.   CRISTINA DELFIDA[5] SEDILLO[95], b. Abt. 1941, San Patricio, New México; d. February 20, 1941, San Patricio, New México.

vi.   CRISTINA ROSA SEDILLO[96], b. Abt. 1942, San Patricio, New México; d. February 16, 1942, San Patricio, New México.

vii. CERINIA SEDILLO, b. Private.

viii. DANNY SEDILLO, b. Private; d. Phoenix, Arizona.

ix.   DELLA SEDILLO, b. Private.

x.   ELLIE SEDILLO, b. Private.

xi.   MARTÍN MONTOYA SEDILLO, b. Private.

20. JOSEFITA[4] MONTOYA *(ALBINA[3] SILVA, HILARIO[2], MANUEL[1])*[97] was born 1918, and died 2003. She married JUAN BACA[97], son of CRECENCIO CARRILLO and CATARINA BACA.

Children of JOSEFITA MONTOYA and JUAN BACA are:

i.   CRUCITA[5] BACA, b. May 03, 1946; m. DANNY CHÁVEZ.

ii.   PETE BACA, b. Private.

21. TRANQUELINO SILVA[4] MONTOYA *(ALBINA[3] SILVA, HILARIO[2], MANUEL[1])* was born August 22, 1925 in Arabela, New México, and died September 24, 2009 in Alamagordo, New México. He married RUBY SAMORA.

Children of TRANQUELINO MONTOYA and RUBY SAMORA are:

i.   BUDDY[5] MONTOYA, b. Private.

ii.   CINDY MONTOYA, b. Private.

iii. GILBERT MONTOYA, b. Private.

iv.   KATHY MONTOYA, b. Private.

v.   PATSY MONTOYA, b. Private.

vi.   TERESA SAMORA MONTOYA, b. Private.

vii. TRANKIE MONTOYA, b. Private.

viii. VERLA MONTOYA, b. Private.

22. EDUARDO[4] SILVA *(TELESFORO[3], HILARIO[2], MANUEL[1])* was born August 10, 1908[98], and died 1998. He married CONSUELO SALAS December 31, 1932[98], daughter of PEDRO SALAS and TEOFILA BENAVIDES.

Children of EDUARDO SILVA and CONSUELO SALAS are:

i.   CRUSITA[5] SILVA, b. Private; m. ROY CHÁVEZ.

ii.   HENRY SILVA, b. February 04, 1937; m. BEATRIZ GÓMEZ.

23. AMBROCIA[4] SILVA *(TELESFORO[3], HILARIO[2], MANUEL[1])* was born April 15, 1915 in Hondo, New México[99]. She married PROSPERO MIRABAL GONZÁLES January 16, 1932 in Glencoe, New México[99], son of PROSPERO GONZÁLES and TELESFORA MIRABAL.

Children of AMBROCIA SILVA and PROSPERO GONZÁLES are:
    i.   LILIA[5] GONZÁLES, b. Private.
    ii.   FELIX GONZÁLES, b. Private.
    iii. DORTHY GONZÁLES, b. Private.
    iv. FLOYD GONZÁLES, b. Private.

24. MAX[4] CORONA *(SUSANA[3] TRUJILLO, LORENSA[2] SILVA, MANUEL[1])*[100] was born September 05, 1912 in San Patricio, New México[101], and died January 09, 1973 in Morenci, Arizona. He married (1) BRESELIA GONZÁLES, daughter of EPAMINOANDAS GONZÁLES and ELVIRA GONZÁLES. He married (2) APOLONIA WARNER June 04, 1932 in Carrizozo, New México[102], daughter of JUAN WARNER and EMILIA TORREZ.

Child of MAX CORONA and APOLONIA WARNER is:
    i.   DANIEL[5] CORONA[103], b. Abt. 1933, San Patricio, New México; d. November 03, 1933, San Patricio, New México.

25. MACARIO TRUJILLO[4] CHÁVEZ *(LORENCITA[3] TRUJILLO, LORENSA[2] SILVA, MANUEL[1])* was born Private. He married TERESA GÓMEZ.

Genealogy of Sipio Salazar

Generation No. 1

1. SIPIO[1] SALAZAR was born December 17, 1846 in La Fragua, San Miguel County, Territory of New Mexico[1]. He married (1) MARTINA ROMERO November 28, 1880[2]. He married (2) ANITA BARTLETT March 06, 1906 in Lincoln, Territory of New México[3], daughter of CHARLES BARTLETT and ADELA GALINDRO.

Notes for SIPIO SALAZAR:
Also known as Serafino Salazar.
1880 Census: Living in Las Tablas, Territory of New México.

Notes for ANITA BARTLETT:
Also known as Annie.

Children of SIPIO SALAZAR and MARTINA ROMERO are:
2. i.   REBECCA[2] SALAZAR, b. January 1874.
    ii. BENIGA SALAZAR, b. Abt. 1885[4].
    iii. LUISA SALAZAR, b. Abt. 1886[4].

Generation No. 2

2. REBECCA[2] SALAZAR *(SIPIO[1])* was born January 1874[5]. She married (1) GEORGE CURRY[6]. She married (2) MANUEL A. SISNEROS[7] May 22, 1890[8]. She married (3) SYLVANO HENDERSON October 19, 1902[9], son of DAVID HENDERSON and EMMA GRAHAM. She married (4) ALFREDO GONZÁLES[10] February 07, 1904 in Lincoln, Territory of New México[11], son of FLORENCIO GONZÁLES and RAYMUNDA SÁNCHEZ.

Notes for REBECCA SALAZAR:
Also known as Rebecca Salazar de Sisneros, Rebecca Curry.
1900 Census: Living with her parents in Lincoln, New México. She is also listed as living in another household in Lincoln. Her given name is Rebecca Curry.
1930 Census: Living with her son Clifford in Las Cruces, New México.

Notes for ALFREDO GONZÁLES:
1901-1902: Was elected as Lincoln County Sheriff.
Buried: La Capilla de San Patricio.

Children of REBECCA SALAZAR and GEORGE CURRY are:
    i.   FRANK[3] CURRY, b. August 1889[12].
3. ii. CHARLIE CURRY, b. January 15, 1891.
4. iii. CLIFFORD CURRY, b. July 1894.

Children of REBECCA SALAZAR and MANUEL SISNEROS are:
5. iv. GEORGE[3] SISNEROS, b. February 12, 1891, Lincoln, Territory of New México; d. 1918.
    v.   MARTINITA SISNEROS, b. Abt. 1894[13].

         Notes for MARTINITA SISNEROS:
         Also known as Martina.
         1900 Census: Living with her grandfather, Sipio Salazar, in Lincoln, Territory of New México.

    vi. MANUEL SALAZAR SISNEROS, b. Abt. 1898[13].

         Notes for MANUEL SALAZAR SISNEROS:
         1900 Census: Living with his grandfather, Sipio Salazar, in Lincoln, Territory of New México.

    vii. ANTONIO SISNEROS, b. July 04, 1895[14].

Child of REBECCA SALAZAR and ALFREDO GONZÁLES is:
    viii.   GODFREY[3] GONZÁLES, b. 1904, San Patricio, Territory of New México[15].

Generation No. 3

3. CHARLIE[3] CURRY *(REBECCA[2] SALAZAR, SIPIO[1])[16]* was born January 15, 1891[17]. He married ARCENIA GONZÁLES December 20, 1915 in Lincoln, New México[18], daughter of PROSPERO GONZÁLES and TELESFORA MIRABAL.

Notes for CHARLIE CURRY:
Also known as Charles and Chaz.
1930 Census: Living in Las Cruces, New México.

Notes for ARCENIA GONZÁLES:
Also known as María Arcenia Gonzáles.

Children of CHARLIE CURRY and ARCENIA GONZÁLES are:
    i.   GEORGE[4] CURRY[19], b. September 16, 1916, Glencoe, New México[20]; d. March 19, 1922.
    ii.   REBECCA CURRY, b. Abt. 1921[20].

4. CLIFFORD[3] CURRY *(REBECCA[2] SALAZAR, SIPIO[1])* was born July 1894[21]. He married ANGELA GARCÍA February 26, 1916[22], daughter of LORENZO GARCÍA and JOAQUINA MOYA.

Children of CLIFFORD CURRY and ANGELA GARCÍA are:
    i.   JOHN[4] CURRY, b. Abt. 1921[23].
    ii.   EVA CURRY, b. Abt. 1922[23].
    iii.   CLIFFORD G. CURRY, b. Abt. 1924[23].
    iv.   HAZEL CURRY, b. Abt. 1926[23].
    v.   ALFRED CURRY, b. Abt. 1927[23].

5. GEORGE[3] SISNEROS *(REBECCA[2] SALAZAR, SIPIO[1])[24]* was born February 12, 1891 in Lincoln, Territory of New México[25], and died 1918. He married PAULITA FRESQUEZ[25] December 01, 1912 in Lincoln, New México[25], daughter of PABLO FRESQUEZ and EPIFANIA GARCÍA.

Notes for GEORGE SISNEROS:
1900 Census: Living with his grandfather, Sipio Salazar, in Lincoln, Territory of New México.

Children of GEORGE SISNEROS and PAULITA FRESQUEZ are:
    i.   GEORGE[4] SISNEROS, b. May 21, 1918; d. October 13, 2010; m. ROSE MARY SISNEROS.
    ii.   CLOFAS SISNEROS, b. Private; m. TOM MONTOYA.

Genealogy of José Marcial Torres

Generation No. 1

1. JUAN JOSÉ[1] TOLEDO was born Abt. 1741 in San Fernando, El Reyno de Nuevo México, Nueva España. He married MARÍA ENCARNACIÓN TORRES[1].

Notes for JUAN JOSÉ TOLEDO:
He was a priest.

Child of JUAN TOLEDO and MARÍA TORRES is:
2.   i.   JOSÉ MARCIAL[2] TORRES, b. 1779.

Generation No. 2

2. JOSÉ MARCIAL[2] TORRES (*JUAN JOSÉ[1] TOLEDO*)[2] was born 1779[3]. He married MARÍA GERTRUDIS VENAVIDES[4] July 29, 1796 in Tomé, El Reyno de Nuevo México, Nueva España[5], daughter of MIGUEL VENAVIDES and CATARINA TOLEDO.

Notes for JOSÉ MARCIAL TORRES:
Also known as José Marcial Manuel Toledo Torres.

Children of JOSÉ TORRES and MARÍA VENAVIDES are:
3.   i.   MARIANO[3] TORRES, b. Abt. 1808.
        ii.   JUAN MIGUEL TORRES, b. December 14, 1794.
       iii.   JUANA DOMINGA TORRES, b. December 15, 1800.
       iv.   JOSÉ ANTONIO TORRES, b. Abt. 1802.
        v.   MARÍA ANTONIA TORRES, b. Abt. 1804.
4.   vi.   NICOLÁS TORRES, b. November 30, 1814, San Fernando, El Reyno de Nuevo México, Nueva España.

Generation No. 3

3. MARIANO[3] TORRES (*JOSÉ MARCIAL[2], JUAN JOSÉ[1] TOLEDO*) was born Abt. 1808[6]. He married (1) MARÍA GUADALUPE CHÁVES December 25, 1825 in Tomé, Nuevo México, La República de México[7], daughter of BERNARDINO CHÁVES and JOSEFA SÁNCHES. He married (2) MARÍA DE LA TRINIDAD LUCERO Y SALAS September 06, 1847 in Tomé, Nuevo México, La República de México[8].

Notes for MARIANO TORRES:
1860 Census: Living in Punta del Agua, Territory of New México. (Born 1819)
1870 Census: Living in Lincoln County, Precinct 3, Territory of New México.

Children of MARIANO TORRES and MARÍA CHÁVES are:
5.   i.   CIPRIANO[4] TORRES, b. Abt. 1827, San Fernando, Nuevo México, La República de México; d. July 17, 1906, Punta de Agua, Territory of New México.
       ii.   RICARDO TORRES, b. Abt. 1829, Punta de Agua, Nuevo México, La República de México.

Notes for RICARDO TORRES:
Also known as José Ricardo Torres.
Died Young.

      iii.   JUANA MARÍA TORRES, b. Abt. 1830.

Notes for JUANA MARÍA TORRES:
Died Young.

iv.   JUANA ANDREA TORRES, b. Abt. 1832, Punta de Agua, Nuevo México, La República de México.

6.   v.   MARÍA CESARIA TORRES, b. Abt. 1835, Punta de Agua, Nuevo México, La República de México.

vi.   JOSÉ ANASTACIO TORRES, b. Abt. 1838, Punta de Agua, Nuevo México, La República de México.

Notes for JOSÉ ANASTACIO TORRES:
Died Young.

vii.   PABLO TORRES, b. Abt. 1840, Punta de Agua, Nuevo México, La República de México[9]; m. MARÍA NIEVES CONTRERAS, April 08, 1861, Tomé, Territory of New México[10].

7.   viii. MARÍA DE LOS SANTOS TORRES, b. Abt. 1842, Punta de Agua, Nuevo México, La República de México.

8.   ix.   YGNACIO TORRES, b. Abt. 1846, Punta de Agua, Nuevo México, La República de México.

Children of MARIANO TORRES and MARÍA SALAS are:

x.   LEONIDES[4] TORRES, b. Abt. 1854[11].

xi.   PABLITO TORRES, b. Abt. 1863[11].

4. NICOLÁS[3] TORRES *(JOSÉ MARCIAL[2], JUAN JOSÉ[1] TOLEDO)* was born November 30, 1814 in San Fernando, El Reyno de Nuevo México, Nueva España[12]. He married JUANITA CHÁVEZ May 26, 1843[13].

Notes for NICOLÁS TORRES:
Also known as Antonio José Nicolás Benavidez Torres.
1860 Census: Living in Punta de Agua, Territory of New México.
1870 Census: Living in Lincoln County, Precinct 3, Territory of New México.
1880 Census: Living in Lincoln, Territory of New México.

Notes for JUANITA CHÁVEZ:
Also known as María Juana Chávez.
1900 Census: Living with her son in Lincoln, Territory of New México. She was already a widow.
1910 Census: Living with her son in White Oaks, Territory of New México.

Child of NICOLÁS TORRES and JUANITA CHÁVEZ is:

9.   i.   JUAN PEDRO[4] TORRES, b. November 28, 1844, Punta de Agua, Territory of New México.

Generation No. 4

5. CIPRIANO[4] TORRES *(MARIANO[3], JOSÉ MARCIAL[2], JUAN JOSÉ[1] TOLEDO)* was born Abt. 1827 in San Fernando, Nuevo México, La República de México[14], and died July 17, 1906 in Punta de Agua, Territory of New México. He married MARÍA MIQUELA LUCERO.

Notes for CIPRIANO TORRES:
Also known as José Cipriano Torres.
1860 - 1880 Census: Living in Punta de Agua.

Children of CIPRIANO TORRES and MARÍA LUCERO are:

i.   NIEVES[5] TORRES, b. Abt. 1847, Punta de Agua, Territory of New México[15].

10. ii.   ADELAIDO TORRES, b. Abt. 1850, Punta de Agua, Territory of New México.

iii. VICENTA TORRES, b. Abt. 1863, Punta de Agua, Territory of New México[16].

6. MARÍA CESARIA[4] TORRES *(MARIANO[3], JOSÉ MARCIAL[2], JUAN JOSÉ[1] TOLEDO)* was born Abt. 1835 in Punta de Agua, Nuevo México, La República de México[17]. She married JOSÉ CÓRDOVA[18].

Notes for MARÍA CESARIA TORRES:
Also known as Ana María Cesaria Torres.

Notes for JOSÉ CÓRDOVA:
1860 Census: Living in Punta de Agua, Territory of New México.
1870 Census: Living in Lincoln County, Precinct 3, Territory of New México.
1880 Census: Living in Las Tablas, Territory of New México.

Children of MARÍA TORRES and JOSÉ CÓRDOVA are:
- i. URBANA[5] CÓRDOVA, b. Abt. 1854[19].
- ii. PATRICIA CÓRDOVA, b. Abt. 1857[19].
- 11. iii. CESARIA CÓRDOVA, b. August 1859.
- iv. PAZ CÓRDOVA, b. Abt. 1862[20].
- v. NARCISA CÓRDOVA, b. Abt. 1863[21].
- 12. vi. FRANCISCO CÓRDOVA, b. June 1865.
- vii. MARÍA ANTONIA CÓRDOVA, b. Abt. 1867[21].
- viii. FRANCISCA CÓRDOVA, b. Abt. 1869[21].
- ix. ANTONIO CÓRDOVA, b. Abt. 1871, Las Tablas, Territory of New México[22].
- x. VICTORIANA CÓRDOVA, b. Abt. 1875, Las Tablas, Territory of New México[22].

7. MARÍA DE LOS SANTOS[4] TORRES *(MARIANO[3], JOSÉ MARCIAL[2], JUAN JOSÉ[1] TOLEDO)* was born Abt. 1842 in Punta de Agua, Nuevo México, La República de México[23]. She married JESÚS BELDARING March 26, 1870 in Tularoso, Territory of New México[24].

Child of MARÍA TORRES and JESÚS BELDARING is:
- 13. i. MAXIMILIANA[5] BELDARING, b. Abt. 1875.

Ygnacio Torres

8. YGNACIO[4] TORRES *(MARIANO[3], JOSÉ MARCIAL[2], JUAN JOSÉ[1] TOLEDO)* was born Abt. 1846 in Punta de Agua, Nuevo México, La República de México[25]. He married MANUELA LUCERO[26] February 12, 1873[27], daughter of JUAN LUSERO and MARCELINA JARAMILLO.

Notes for YGNACIO TORRES:
Also known as José Ygnacio Torres.
1860 Census: Living in Punta de Agua, Territory of New México. (Born 1848)
1870 Census: Living in Lincoln County, Precinct 3, Territory of New México. (Born 1847)
1880 Census: living in La Plaza de San Patricio, Territory of New México. (Born 1846)

Notes for MANUELA LUCERO:
Also known as Manuelita Lucero de Torres.

Children of YGNACIO TORRES and MANUELA LUCERO are:
- 14. i. REFUGIO[5] TORRES, b. February 19, 1874, Tomé, Territory of New México; d. November 27, 1937, Hondo, New México.
- ii. GAVINO TORRES, b. March 1874[28].
- iii. MARIA PREDICANDA TORRES, b. July 16, 1884, Hondo, Territory of New México[29].
- iv. PLACIDA TORRES, b. June 10, 1885, Hondo, Territory of New México[29].
- 15. v. GEORGE TORRES, b. July 14, 1885, San Patricio, Territory of New México.
- 16. vi. MARTÍN LUCERO TORRES, b. November 22, 1888, Hondo, Territory of New México; d. November 20, 1967, Roswell, New México.

Juan Pedro Torres

9. JUAN PEDRO[4] TORRES *(NICOLÁS[3], JOSÉ MARCIAL[2], JUAN JOSÉ[1] TOLEDO)* was born November 28, 1844 in Punta de Agua, Territory of New México[30]. He married (1) LUGUARDITA CEDILLO October 24, 1866 in Tomé, Territory of New México[31], daughter of VENTURA CEDILLO and PAULA CHÁVES. He married (2) GREGORIA ARAGÓN June 11, 1881 in Manzano, Territory of New México[32].

Notes for JUAN PEDRO TORRES:
1860 Census: Lived in Punta de Agua, Territory of New México.
1870 Census: Lived in Fort Stanton, Pct 3, Territory of New México.
1880 Census: Living in Lincoln, Territory of New México. Listed as a Widower.
1900 Census: Living in Lincoln, Territory of New México.
1910 Census: Living in White Oaks, Territory of New México.

Children of JUAN TORRES and LUGUARDITA CEDILLO are:
17. i.   PRECILIANO[5] TORRES, b. Abt. 1866, Manzano, Territory of New México; d. October 21, 1931, Glencoe, New México.
     ii. JOSÉ ÁNGEL TORRES, b. Abt. 1871[33].
18. iii. MARÍA MAURICIA TORRES, b. Abt. 1873.
     iv. NICOLÁS TORRES, b. Abt. 1875[33].
19. v.   JOSÉ TORRES, b. September 1865; d. February 25, 1928, Capitán, New México.

Generation No. 5

10. ADELAIDO[5] TORRES *(CIPRIANO[4], MARIANO[3], JOSÉ MARCIAL[2], JUAN JOSÉ[1] TOLEDO)* was born Abt. 1850 in Punta de Agua, Territory of New México[34]. He married MARÍA ANDREA TORRES.

Notes for ADELAIDO TORRES:
Also known as José Adelaido Torres.
1860 Census: Living in Punta del Agua, Territory of New México.
1880 Census: Living in La Cienega, Territory of New México.

Children of ADELAIDO TORRES and MARÍA TORRES are:
20. i.   DANIEL[6] TORRES, b. March 31, 1875, Punta de Agua, Territory of New México.
     ii. FRANCISCO TORRES, b. Abt. 1879[35].

11. CESARIA[5] CÓRDOVA *(MARÍA CESARIA[4] TORRES, MARIANO[3], JOSÉ MARCIAL[2], JUAN JOSÉ[1] TOLEDO)* was born August 1859[36]. She married (1) PETRONILO SEDILLO August 25, 1873[37], son of YGNACIO SEDILLO and FELIPA DE SEDILLO. She married (2) LEANDRO GUTIÉRREZ February 11, 1896 in Lincoln, Territory of New México[38].

Notes for CESARIA CÓRDOVA:
Also known as María Cesaria Córdova, Sesaria.

Notes for PETRONILO SEDILLO:
1870 Census: Living in Lincoln County, Precinct 3, Territory of New México.
1880 Census: Living in Las Tablas, Territory of New México.
1900 Census: Living in Rebentón, Territory of New México.

Children of CESARIA CÓRDOVA and PETRONILO SEDILLO are:
     i.   TIBORCIO[6] SEDILLO, b. Abt. 1877[39].
21. ii.   MARTÍN CÓRDOVA SEDILLO, b. January 30, 1877, Cháves County, Territory of New México.
     iii. BALBINO SEDILLO, b. March 1882[40].
22. iv.   MARTÍN SEDILLO, b. February 1884.
23. v.   SABINO SEDILLO, b. December 30, 1887, Las Palas, Territory of New México.
24. vi.   ANITA SEDILLO, b. August 1889.
     vii. ROSENDO SEDILLO[41], b. February 1891[42]; d. 1972; m. DOLORES ROMERO[43], August 26, 1910, Lincoln, Territory of New México[44].

Notes for ROSENDO SEDILLO:
1900 Census: Living in Agua Azul, Territory of New México.

Child of CESARIA CÓRDOVA and LEANDRO GUTIÉRREZ is:
     viii. EVANGELISTA CÓRDOVA[6] GUTIÉRREZ, b. October 1899[45].

12. FRANCISCO[5] CÓRDOVA *(MARÍA CESARIA[4] TORRES, MARIANO[3], JOSÉ MARCIAL[2], JUAN JOSÉ[1] TOLEDO)* was born June 1865[46]. He married MARIANA ROMERO August 24, 1885[47], daughter of FRANCISCO ROMERO and LUCÍA MIRANDA.

Notes for FRANCISCO CÓRDOVA:
1900-1910 Census: Living in Agua Azul, Territory of New México.
1920 Census: Living in Roswell, New México.

Children of FRANCISCO CÓRDOVA and MARIANA ROMERO are:

25.   i.   AURELIA[6] CÓRDOVA, b. Abt. 1888.
       ii.   ELISEO CÓRDOVA, b. March 1889[48].
      iii.   MAURICIA CÓRDOVA, b. December 1890[48].
      iv.   FRANCISCA CÓRDOVA, b. July 1893[48].
       v.   MANUEL CÓRDOVA, b. January 1895[48].
      vi.   MERENCIANO CÓRDOVA, b. November 1896[48].
     vii.   AMADA CÓRDOVA, b. October 1899[48].

13. MAXIMILIANA[5] BELDARING *(MARÍA DE LOS SANTOS[4] TORRES, MARIANO[3], JOSÉ MARCIAL[2], JUAN JOSÉ[1] TOLEDO)* was born Abt. 1875[49]. She married LORENZO GUEBARA Abt. 1891[50], son of PLACIDO GUEBARA and MARÍA SÁNCHES.

Notes for LORENZO GUEBARA:
1880 Census: Living in Lincoln, Territory of New México. (Born 1873)
1910 Census: Living in White Oaks, Territory of New México.
1920 Census: Living in Carrizozo, New México.
1930 Census: Living in Jicarilla, New México. (Born 1874)

Children of MAXIMILIANA BELDARING and LORENZO GUEBARA are:
       i.   LOLA B.[6] GUEBARA, b. Abt. 1894[51].
      ii.   CRUZ B. GUEBARA, b. Abt. 1897[51].
     iii.   ALVINO GUEBARA[52], b. October 02, 1901[53]; d. March 04, 1946; m. MANUELA GALLEGOS, May 25, 1935.

Notes for MANUELA GALLEGOS:
Also known as Nellie.

      iv.   ADELE GUEBARA, b. Abt. 1902[53].
       v.   FLORA GUEBARA, b. Abt. 1904[53].
      vi.   LORENZO GUEBARA, b. Abt. 1906[53].
     vii.   ADELIA GUEBARA, b. Abt. 1907[53].
    viii.   SANDINE GUEBARA, b. Abt. 1910[53].

14. REFUGIO[5] TORRES *(YGNACIO[4], MARIANO[3], JOSÉ MARCIAL[2], JUAN JOSÉ[1] TOLEDO)*[54] was born February 19, 1874 in Tomé, Territory of New México[55], and died November 27, 1937 in Hondo, New México. He married (1) ESPERANSA SÁNCHEZ September 27, 1905 in Lincoln, Territory of New México[56], daughter of DOMINGO SÁNCHEZ and JUANITA AMENDARES. He married (2) PELEGRINA SALAS January 16, 1911[57], daughter of TEOFILO SALAS and IGENIA GALLEGOS.

Notes for REFUGIO TORRES:
1900 - 1930: Census: Living in Hondo, Territory of New México.
Land Patent # NMR 0036867, on the authority of the Homestead Entry-Enlarged (35 Stat. 639), February 19, 1909. Issued 320 acres on June 12, 1922.
Land Patent # NMLC 0041321, on the authority of the Homestead Entry-Stock Raising (39 Stat. 862), December 29, 1916. Issued 320 acres on April 27, 1936.

Children of REFUGIO TORRES and PELEGRINA SALAS are:
26.   i.   MAGGIE[6] TORRES, b. 1913.
      ii.   AMALIA TORRES[58], b. December 17, 1915, Hondo, New México; d. July 25, 1967; m. FIDEL SÁNCHEZ[58], February 12, 1934, San Patricio, New México[59].

15. GEORGE[5] TORRES *(YGNACIO[4], MARIANO[3], JOSÉ MARCIAL[2], JUAN JOSÉ[1] TOLEDO)* was born July 14, 1885 in San Patricio, Territory of New México[60]. He married CELIA SÁNCHEZ November 12, 1906 in Lincoln, Territory of New México[60], daughter of ESTOLANO SÁNCHEZ and CORNELIA PACHECO.

Notes for GEORGE TORRES:
Also known as Jorge.
1930 Census: Living in Rebentón, New México.

Children of GEORGE TORRES and CELIA SÁNCHEZ are:

27.   i.   FELIS SÁNCHEZ[6] TORRES, b. June 04, 1909, Lincoln, Territory of New México; d. February 16, 2003, San Patricio, New México.
        ii.   ADENAGO TORRES[61], b. December 13, 1907, Hondo, New México[62]; d. August 06, 1990, Tularosa, New México; m. BEATRIZ TORREZ[63].
        iii. GEORGE SÁNCHEZ TORRES, b. 1911[64].
        iv.   WILFIDO TORRES, b. 1913[64]; m. JULIA TORRES.
        v.   MIGUEL TORRES, b. 1917[64]; m. SOCORRO DE TORRES.
        vi.   MANUELITA TORRES, b. 1919[64]; m. JUAN BAUTISTA JUAREGUI.
        vii. PRESCILIA TORRES, b. Abt. 1920[65]; m. ERNESTO LÓPEZ[66].

Notes for ERNESTO LÓPEZ:
Immigrated to the U.S. in about 1908.

        viii. LORINA TORRES, b. Abt. 1926[67]; m. ERNESTO OTERO[68].
        ix.   JAY TORRES, b. Private; m. EDNA TORRES.

16. MARTÍN LUCERO[5] TORRES *(YGNACIO[4], MARIANO[3], JOSÉ MARCIAL[2], JUAN JOSÉ[1] TOLEDO)[69]* was born November 22, 1888 in Hondo, Territory of New México, and died November 20, 1967 in Roswell, New México. He married ISABEL GUTIÉRREZ[70] January 05, 1911 in Hondo, Territory of New México[71], daughter of DAMIAN GUTIÉRRES and JUANITA SÁNCHEZ.

Children of MARTÍN TORRES and ISABEL GUTIÉRREZ are:
        i.   FEDERICO[6] TORREZ[72], b. August 24, 1909, Hondo, New México; d. April 05, 2003; m. CECILIA MACKEY.

Notes for FEDERICO TORREZ:
Also known as Fred.

        ii.   ELOY TORREZ[73], b. February 27, 1912, Hondo, New México[74]; d. October 28, 2011, Roswell, New México; m. SAVINA SALCIDO[75].
28.   iii. IGNACIO TORREZ, b. October 02, 1913, Hondo, New México; d. September 15, 2005, San Patricio, New México.
        iv.   ERMINIA TORREZ[76], b. February 04, 1916, Hondo, New México; d. May 15, 1975; m. CLOVÍS MONTES.
        v.   JULIA TORREZ[77], b. April 12, 1918, Hondo, New México[78]; d. July 17, 2003, El Paso, Téxas; m. (1) JOHN OTERO[79]; m. (2) FRED KIMBRELL[80], April 16, 1938[81].

Notes for FRED KIMBRELL:
1930 Census: Living with his grandfather Juan Kimbrell.
Died in an accident at the age of 24. Buried in Picacho, NM.

        vi.   SIL TORREZ, b. Abt. 1922, Hondo, New México[82]; m. JOSIE FLACO.
        vii. EVA TORREZ, b. Abt. 1924, Hondo, New México[82]; m. RAMÓN JIMÉNEZ.
        viii. PRESILA TORREZ, b. Abt. 1929, Hondo, New México[82]; m. ROBERT RICHARDSON.
        ix.   LARRY TORREZ, b. Private, Hondo, New México; m. DOROTHY CHÁVEZ.
        x.   LIBBY TORREZ, b. Private, Hondo, New México; m. CARL AUSTIN.
        xi.   PATSY TORREZ, b. Private, Hondo, New México; m. BILL TURNER.

17. PRECILIANO[5] TORRES *(JUAN PEDRO[4], NICOLÁS[3], JOSÉ MARCIAL[2], JUAN JOSÉ[1] TOLEDO)[83]* was born Abt. 1866 in Manzano, Territory of New México[84], and died October 21, 1931 in Glencoe, New México. He married DELFINIA LUNA BACA Abt. 1893[84], daughter of DAMACIO BACA and MARÍA BACA.

Children of PRECILIANO TORRES and DELFINIA BACA are:
29.   i.   MARTÍN BACA[6] TORRES, b. January 13, 1895, Rebentón, Territory of New México.
30.   ii.   LUÍS BACA TORRES, b. October 11, 1897, Patos, Territory of New México; d. November 03, 1970, Roswell, New México.
31.   iii. JOSÉ BACA TORRES, b. August 15, 1898, Hondo, Territory of New México; d. April 25, 1970, Roswell, New México.

18. MARÍA MAURICIA[5] TORRES *(JUAN PEDRO[4], NICOLÁS[3], JOSÉ MARCIAL[2], JUAN JOSÉ[1] TOLEDO)* was born Abt. 1873[85].

Children of MARÍA MAURICIA TORRES are:

     i.   PORFIRIO[6] TORRES.
    ii.   PORFIRIA TORRES.

19. JOSÉ[5] TORRES *(JUAN PEDRO[4], NICOLÁS[3], JOSÉ MARCIAL[2], JUAN JOSÉ[1] TOLEDO)* was born September 1865[86], and died February 25, 1928 in Capitán, New México[87]. He married ROSA CHÁVEZ[88] February 12, 1888[89], daughter of JOSÉ CHÁVES and APOLINARIA LÓPEZ.

Notes for JOSÉ TORRES:
1910 Census: Living in Capitán, Territory of New México.

Notes for ROSA CHÁVEZ:
Also known as Rosalita Cháves, Rosaria Cháves, and Rosaura Cháves.

Children of JOSÉ TORRES and ROSA CHÁVEZ are:
32.   i.   SOFIA[6] TORRES, b. November 20, 1892, Lincoln, Territory of New México.
       ii.   JAIME TORRES, b. April 1896[90].
      iii. ALEJANDRO TORRES, b. January 1900[90].

Generation No. 6

20. DANIEL[6] TORRES *(ADELAIDO[5], CIPRIANO[4], MARIANO[3], JOSÉ MARCIAL[2], JUAN JOSÉ[1] TOLEDO)*[91] was born March 31, 1875 in Punta de Agua, Territory of New México[92]. He married MARÍA RITA GALLEGOS November 30, 1895 in Manzano, Territory of New México[93], daughter of JOSÉ GALLEGOS and MARÍA ALDERETE.

Children of DANIEL TORRES and MARÍA GALLEGOS are:
       i.   SOSTENO[7] TORRES, b. Abt. 1898, Punta de Agua, Territory of New México[94].
      ii.   JOSÉ ANTONIO TORRES, b. Abt. 1901, Punta de Agua, Territory of New México[94].
    iii. JESÚSITA TORRES, b. Abt. 1905, Punta de Agua, Territory of New México[94].
    iv. ADELAIDA TORRES, b. Abt. 1908, Punta de Agua, Territory of New México[94].
     v. MARÍA TORRES, b. Abt. 1907, Punta de Agua, Territory of New México[94].

21. MARTÍN CÓRDOVA[6] SEDILLO *(CESARIA[5] CÓRDOVA, MARÍA CESARIA[4] TORRES, MARIANO[3], JOSÉ MARCIAL[2], JUAN JOSÉ[1] TOLEDO)* was born January 30, 1877 in Cháves County, Territory of New México[95]. He married PORFIRIA OTERO August 25, 1916 in Arabela, Territory of New México[95], daughter of ANTONIO OTERO and MARÍA ARCHIBEQUE.

Notes for MARTÍN CÓRDOVA SEDILLO:
1920 & 1930 Census: Living in Arabela, New México.

Children of MARTÍN SEDILLO and PORFIRIA OTERO are:
       i.   ANDRÉS[7] SEDILLO, b. Abt. 1908[96].
      ii.   EVA SEDILLO, b. Abt. 1912[96].
    iii. CAROLINA SEDILLO[97], b. March 15, 1915, White Oaks, New México[98]; m. GUILLERMO MARTÍNEZ[99], February 26, 1934, Carrizozo, New México[99].

Notes for GUILLERMO MARTÍNEZ:
Also known as Billie.
1930 Census: Living in Corona, New México.

    iv. JACOBO SEDILLO, b. Abt. 1919, Arabela, New México[100].
     v. DOLORES SEDILLO, b. Abt. 1922[101]; m. JOSÉ GONZÁLES GUTIÉRREZ[102].

Notes for DOLORES SEDILLO:
Also known as Lola.

Notes for JOSÉ GONZÁLES GUTIÉRREZ:
Also known as Joe. Social Security Death index records his birthdate as July 7, 1918.

1920 Census: Living in Tinnie, New México.

      vi.   PORFIRIA SEDILLO, b. Abt. 1924[103].

22. MARTÍN[6] SEDILLO *(CESARIA[5] CÓRDOVA, MARÍA CESARIA[4] TORRES, MARIANO[3], JOSÉ MARCIAL[2], JUAN JOSÉ[1] TOLEDO)* was born February 1884[104]. He married ELENA OTERO July 07, 1902[105], daughter of ANTONIO OTERO and MARÍA ARCHIBEQUE.

Notes for ELENA OTERO:
Also known as Elena Sedillo de Vigil.

Children of MARTÍN SEDILLO and ELENA OTERO are:
      i.   PETRONILO OTERO[7] SEDILLO, b. 1905[106]; m. IDALIA SÁNCHEZ, February 10, 1926, Picacho, Territory of New México[107].

Notes for PETRONILO OTERO SEDILLO:
Also known as Petro.

      ii.   MARGARITA SEDILLOS, b. September 1908[108].
      iii.   SEVERO SEDILLO, b. Abt. 1911[109].

Notes for SEVERO SEDILLO:
1930 Census: living in Picacho with his mother and stepfather, Celestino Vigil.

23. SABINO[6] SEDILLO *(CESARIA[5] CÓRDOVA, MARÍA CESARIA[4] TORRES, MARIANO[3], JOSÉ MARCIAL[2], JUAN JOSÉ[1] TOLEDO)* was born December 30, 1887 in Las Palas, Territory of New México[110]. He married MARGARITA CANDELARIA SÁNCHEZ[111] January 14, 1909[112], daughter of FELIPÉ SÁNCHEZ and ANTONIA CANDELARIA.

Child of SABINO SEDILLO and MARGARITA SÁNCHEZ is:
      i.   MARGARITA[7] SEDILLO, b. July 1909[113].

24. ANITA[6] SEDILLO *(CESARIA[5] CÓRDOVA, MARÍA CESARIA[4] TORRES, MARIANO[3], JOSÉ MARCIAL[2], JUAN JOSÉ[1] TOLEDO)* was born August 1889[114]. She married SEFARINO ARCHULETA Abt. 1904[115], son of MARCELINO ARCHULETA and ANTONIA CÓRDOVA.

Notes for SEFARINO ARCHULETA:
1910 & 1920 Census: Living in Las Palas, Territory of New México.

Children of ANITA SEDILLO and SEFARINO ARCHULETA are:
      i.   GENOVEVA[7] ARCHULETA, b. Abt. 1906, Las Palas, Territory of New México[115]; m. PAZ NAJERES, June 04, 1921[116].
      ii.   JUANITA ARCHULETA, b. Abt. 1908, Las Palas, Territory of New México[117].
      iii.   SESARIA ARCHULETA[118], b. July 27, 1912; d. June 29, 1991, Tinnie, New México; m. JACOBO FRESQUEZ[119], July 09, 1935[120].

Notes for SESARIA ARCHULETA:
Also known as Suzie.

Notes for JACOBO FRESQUEZ:
Also known as Jake.

      iv.   ERMINDA ARCHULETA[121], b. October 07, 1914; d. December 27, 2001, Roswell, New México; m. JUAN SILVA[121].

Notes for JUAN SILVA:
1920 Census: Living in Picacho, New México.

25. AURELIA[6] CÓRDOVA *(FRANCISCO[5], MARÍA CESARIA[4] TORRES, MARIANO[3], JOSÉ MARCIAL[2], JUAN JOSÉ[1] TOLEDO)* was born Abt. 1888[122]. She married MANUEL ROMERO.

Notes for MANUEL ROMERO:
1920 Census: Living in Roswell, New México. (Born 1884)
1930 Census: Living in Scotsdale, Arizona. (Born 1887)

Children of AURELIA CÓRDOVA and MANUEL ROMERO are:
  i.   MANUEL[7] ROMERO, b. Abt. 1906[122].
  ii.   CAROLINA ROMERO, b. Abt. 1908[122].
  iii. VIOLA ROMERO, b. Abt. 1913[122].
  iv.   PORFINA ROMERO, b. Abt. 1917[122].
  v.   MARTHA ROMERO, b. Abt. 1920[122].
  vi.   ELMA ROMERO, b. Abt. 1922[123].

26. MAGGIE[6] TORRES *(REFUGIO[5], YGNACIO[4], MARIANO[3], JOSÉ MARCIAL[2], JUAN JOSÉ[1] TOLEDO)* was born 1913[124]. She married FRED MONTES[125126], son of JESÚS MONTES and TOMASITA ALDAZ.

Notes for FRED MONTES:
Also known as Federico.
Social Security Death Index indicates that he was born on November 16, 1910.

Child of MAGGIE TORRES and FRED MONTES is:
  i.   HERALDA[7] MONTES[126], b. Abt. 1934, Hondo, New México; d. March 14, 1934, Hondo, New México.

27. FELIS SÁNCHEZ[6] TORRES *(GEORGE[5], YGNACIO[4], MARIANO[3], JOSÉ MARCIAL[2], JUAN JOSÉ[1] TOLEDO)[127]* was born June 04, 1909 in Lincoln, Territory of New México[128], and died February 16, 2003 in San Patricio, New México. She married PEDRO SALCIDO[129] October 24, 1928 in Carrizozo, New México[130], son of FAUSTINO SALCIDO and MARÍA CHÁVEZ.

Child of FELIS TORRES and PEDRO SALCIDO is:
  i.   MARÍA RELIA[7] SALCIDO[131], b. 1933, Hondo, New México; d. March 16, 1933, Tinnie, New México.

28. IGNACIO[6] TORREZ *(MARTÍN LUCERO[5] TORRES, YGNACIO[4], MARIANO[3], JOSÉ MARCIAL[2], JUAN JOSÉ[1] TOLEDO)[132]* was born October 02, 1913 in Hondo, New México, and died September 15, 2005 in San Patricio, New México. He married AMANDA MONTES December 26, 1937, daughter of JESÚS MONTES and TOMASITA ALDAZ.

29. MARTÍN BACA[6] TORRES *(PRECILIANO[5], JUAN PEDRO[4], NICOLÁS[3], JOSÉ MARCIAL[2], JUAN JOSÉ[1] TOLEDO)* was born January 13, 1895 in Rebentón, Territory of New México[133]. He married (1) RITA VALLES February 05, 1915 in San Patricio, New México[134], daughter of FELIPA ORONA. He married (2) JUANITA CHÁVEZ[135] March 16, 1933[136], daughter of PLACIDO CHÁVEZ and TRENIDAD LUNA.

Children of MARTÍN TORRES and RITA VALLES are:
  i.   MANUEL VALLES[7] TORRES, b. Abt. November 1919[137].
  ii.   ERNESTO TORRES[138], b. February 14, 1922, Hondo, New México; d. April 21, 2010, Roswell, New México; m. MARIANA ALDAZ SÁNCHEZ[138].

Notes for MARIANA ALDAZ SÁNCHEZ:
Also known as Mary.

30. LUÍS BACA[6] TORRES *(PRECILIANO[5], JUAN PEDRO[4], NICOLÁS[3], JOSÉ MARCIAL[2], JUAN JOSÉ[1] TOLEDO)* was born October 11, 1897 in Patos, Territory of New México[139], and died November 03, 1970 in Roswell, New México[139]. He married AMANDA SÁNCHEZ November 30, 1927 in Tularosa, New México[140], daughter of MANUEL SÁNCHEZ and ESTELA GILL.

Notes for LUÍS BACA TORRES:
After selling the farm, he and his wife migrated to Roswell, New México.
August 26, 1918: Discharged WW I Veteran.

Notes for AMANDA SÁNCHEZ:
Baptized: La Capilla de San Ysidro, Glencoe NM

Children of LUÍS TORRES and AMANDA SÁNCHEZ are:
    i.   MAX[7] TORRES[141], b. October 12, 1928, Glencoe, New México; d. August 24, 2008, Willcox, Arizona; m. ESTER MENDOZA, October 25, 1952, Roswell, New México[142].

Notes for MAX TORRES:
Also known as Luís Maximiliano Torres.

    ii.   TERESITA TORRES[143], b. December 04, 1929, Glencoe, New México; d. December 28, 1997, Alburquerque, New México; m. JOHNNY MATA[143], December 28, 1950, Roswell, New México[144].

Notes for TERESITA TORRES:
Also known as Marie Barbara Torres.

    iii. EPIFANIA TORRES, b. January 11, 1931, Glencoe, New México[145]; d. October 31, 1986, Roswell, New México[145]; m. JOSEPH THOMAS ATKINSON[145], November 25, 1952, Pecos, Texas[145].

Notes for EPIFANIA TORRES:
Also known as Fannie.

    iv.   CLARITA TORRES, b. June 04, 1932, Glencoe, New México[145]; m. BUDDY BAKER[145].

Notes for CLARITA TORRES:
Also known as Francisca Clarita Torres.

    v.   PRECILIANO SÁNCHEZ TORRES, b. April 27, 1935, Glencoe, New México[145]; m. MARY LOU MARRUJO[145], May 05, 1957, Roswell, New México[145].
    vi.   ESTELLA JUANITA TORRES, b. May 04, 1936[145]; m. ROY BASCOM[145].
    vii. BILLY SÁNCHEZ TORRES, b. March 13, 1938, Glencoe, New México[145]; m. MARTHA MOYERS.
    viii. ANTONIO TORRES, b. November 18, 1944, Lake Arthur, New México[145]; m. PATRICIA GRZELACHOWSKI[145].
    ix.   JOSÉ JESÚS TORRES, b. December 15, 1946, Glencoe, New México[145]; d. March 04, 2006, Edgewood, New México[145]; m. IRENE MARGARETE GRZELACHOWSKI.

31. JOSÉ BACA[6] TORRES *(PRECILIANO[5], JUAN PEDRO[4], NICOLÁS[3], JOSÉ MARCIAL[2], JUAN JOSÉ[1] TOLEDO)[146]* was born August 15, 1898 in Hondo, Territory of New México, and died April 25, 1970 in Roswell, New México. He married EMILIA CHÁVEZ[146] December 30, 1918 in Lincoln, New México[147], daughter of ANTONIO CHÁVEZ and JUANA CARRILLO.

Notes for JOSÉ BACA TORRES:
About 1928: Moved to Roswell.

Children of JOSÉ TORRES and EMILIA CHÁVEZ are:
    i.   HILARIO CHÁVEZ[7] TORRES, b. Abt. 1922[148].
    ii.   TOM CHÁVEZ TORRES, b. Abt. 1924[148].
    iii. MANUEL CHÁVEZ TORRES, b. Abt. 1926[148].
    iv.   AMABLE J CHÁVEZ TORRES[149], b. June 19, 1928[150]; d. October 12, 1999, Roswell, New México.
    v.   JOE CHÁVEZ TORRES, b. Private.
    vi.   MARY CHÁVEZ TORRES, b. Private.

32. SOFIA[6] TORRES *(JOSÉ[5], JUAN PEDRO[4], NICOLÁS[3], JOSÉ MARCIAL[2], JUAN JOSÉ[1] TOLEDO)* was born November 20, 1892 in Lincoln, Territory of New México[151]. She married PEDRO ANALLA December 25, 1911[152], son of JOSÉ ANALLA and DULCESNOMBRES MONTOYA.

Children of SOFIA TORRES and PEDRO ANALLA are:
    i.   LUCÍA[7] ANAYA[153], b. September 20, 1912; d. August 02, 1967, Barstow, California; m. JAMES SALSBERRY, March 26, 1927[154].
    ii.   AVRORA ANAYA, b. Abt. 1914[155].
    iii. CARMEN ANAYA, b. Abt. 1918, Capitán, New México[155].
    iv.   PABLA ANAYA, b. Abt. 1919, Capitán, New México[155].

  v. DORA T. CHÁVEZ, b. July 12, 1927, Capitán, New México[156]; m. LUCIANO ARAGÓN OTERO, January 31, 1946, Carrizozo, New México[156].

Notes for LUCIANO ARAGÓN OTERO:
1930 Census: Living in Encinoso, New México.

  vi. MANUEL FREEMAN, b. Private.
  vii. RICHARD TORRES, b. Private.

Genealogy of Pablo Torres

Generation No. 1

1. PABLO[1] TORRES was born Abt. 1810[1]. He married PETRA ARMIJO[2], daughter of JOSE ARMIJO and JUANA SILVA.

Notes for PABLO TORRES:
1850 Census: Living in Belén, Territory of New México.
1860 Census: Living in Torreón, Territory of New México. (Born about 1810)
1870 Census: Living in Lincoln County, Precinct 3, Territory of New México.

Children of PABLO TORRES and PETRA ARMIJO are:

  i.   JOSÉ LORENSO[2] TORRES[2], b. Bef. August 11, 1833, Belén, Nuevo México, La República de México[3].
  ii. DIEGO TORRES[4], b. Bef. September 13, 1835, Belén, Nuevo México, La República de México[5].

      Notes for DIEGO TORRES:
      Also known as Diego Antonio Gorgonio Francisco de Paula Torres.

  iii. ISADORA TORRES[6], b. Bef. September 15, 1839, Belén, Nuevo México, La República de México[7]; m. TOMÁS CHÁVES, August 29, 1864, Isleta, Territory of New México[8].

      Notes for ISADORA TORRES:
      Also known as María Ysidora de los Reyes Torres.

  iv. VICTORIA TORRES[9], b. Bef. March 31, 1841, Belén, Nuevo México, La República de México[10].
2. v.   TONITA TORRES, b. Abt. 1842, Belén, Nuevo México, La República de México.
  vi. GERONIMO TORRES[11], b. Bef. September 30, 1845, Belén, Nuevo México, La República de México[12].
  vii. GUADALUPE TORRES, b. Abt. 1848, Belén, Territory of New México[12].
  viii. PEDRO JOSÉ TORRES[13], b. Bef. April 25, 1848, Belén, Nuevo México, La República de México[14]; m. YGNACIA LUJÁN, October 30, 1873, Tomé, Territory of New México[15].
  ix. MANUELA TORRES, b. Abt. 1850, Belén, Territory of New México[16].
  x.   MARÍA TORRES, b. Abt. 1854[17].
  xi. BIVIANA TORRES[18], b. Bef. March 09, 1854, Belén, Territory of New México[19].
  xii. DOLÓRES TORRES, b. Abt. 1857, Torreón, Territory of New México[20]; m. JUAN VIGIL, September 25, 1874, Tomé, Territory of New México[21].

Generation No. 2

2. TONITA[2] TORRES *(PABLO[1])* was born Abt. 1842 in Belén, Nuevo México, La República de México[22]. She married SANTIAGO GONZÁLES February 21, 1857 in Tomé, Territory of New México[23], son of MANUEL GONZÁLES and JUANA MONTOYA.

Notes for TONITA TORRES:
1860 Census: Living in Torreón, Territory of New México. (Born About 1842)
1870 Census: Living in Lincoln County, Precinct 3, Territory of New México. (María Antonia, b. About 1849)
1900 Census: Living in Picacho, Territory of New México. (Antonia Cleny)

Notes for SANTIAGO GONZÁLES:
1860 Census: Living in Torreón, Territory of New México.
1870: Living in La Plaza de San José, Territory of New México.
1880 Census: Living in La Plaza de La Junta, Territory of New México. (Avery Cleny)

Children of TONITA TORRES and SANTIAGO GONZÁLES are:
3. i.   JOSÉ TORRES[3] GONZÁLES, b. December 1860; d. January 28, 1928, San Patricio, New México.
4. ii. SANTIAGO TORREZ GONZÁLES, b. Abt. 1868; d. June 21, 1935, Hondo, New México.
  iii. PRESILIANA GONZÁLES, b. Abt. 1869[24].

Generation No. 3

3. JOSÉ TORRES³ GONZÁLES *(TONITA² TORRES, PABLO¹)²⁵* was born December 1860²⁶, and died January 28, 1928 in San Patricio, New México. He married MARÍA CHÁVEZ²⁷²⁸.

Notes for JOSÉ TORRES GONZÁLES:
1880 Census: Living in La Plaza de Picacho, Territory of New México.
1900 Census: Living in Picacho, Territory of New México.

Notes for MARÍA CHÁVEZ:
Also known as Marillita.

Children of JOSÉ GONZÁLES and MARÍA CHÁVEZ are:
5.   i.   ELVIRA⁴ GONZÁLES, b. October 28, 1879, Picacho, Territory of New México; d. March 22, 1945, San Patricio, New México.
       ii.   RAMÓN GONZÁLES, b. September 23, 1886.
6.   iii.   ANITA GONZÁLES, b. June 29, 1888, San Patricio, Territory of New México; d. September 1962, Hondo, New México.
7.   iv.   SANTIAGO CHÁVEZ GONZÁLES, b. December 26, 1884.
       v.   RAFAEL CHÁVEZ GONZÁLES²⁹, b. November 27, 1892³⁰; d. August 18, 1918, San Patricio, New México.
8.   vi.   LOYOLA GONZÁLES, b. July 1893.
9.   vii.   AMALIA GONZÁLES, b. January 1897.

4. SANTIAGO TORREZ³ GONZÁLES *(TONITA² TORRES, PABLO¹)³¹* was born Abt. 1868, and died June 21, 1935 in Hondo, New México. He married JESÚSITA DE GONZÁLES Abt. 1893³².

Notes for SANTIAGO TORREZ GONZÁLES:
Also known as Jim, James.
1870 Census: Living in Lincoln County, Precinct 3, Territory of New México.
1900 & 1910 Census: Living in San Patricio, Territory of New México.
1930 Census: Living in Las Cruces, New México.

Children of SANTIAGO GONZÁLES and JESÚSITA DE GONZÁLES are:
       i.   ESQUIPULA⁴ GONZÁLES, b. Abt. 1894³².
       ii.   PEDRO GONZÁLES, b. Abt. 1896³².
       iii.   DARIA GONZÁLES, b. Abt. 1898³².
       iv.   PRECILIANA GONZÁLES, b. Abt. 1900³².
       v.   SARA GONZÁLES, b. Abt. 1902³².
       vi.   JOSÉ GONZÁLES, b. Abt. 1910, San Patricio, Territory of New México³².
       vii.   ALBERTO GONZÁLES, b. Abt. 1913³³.
       viii.   EDUARDO GONZÁLES, b. Abt. 1919³³.
       ix.   DAVÍD GONZÁLES, b. Abt. 1920³⁴.

Generation No. 4

5. ELVIRA⁴ GONZÁLES *(JOSÉ TORRES³, TONITA² TORRES, PABLO¹)³⁵* was born October 28, 1879 in Picacho, Territory of New México, and died March 22, 1945 in San Patricio, New México. She married EPAMINOANDAS GONZÁLES³⁵ February 14, 1900³⁶, son of FLORENCIO GONZÁLES and RAYMUNDA SÁNCHEZ.

Children of ELVIRA GONZÁLES and EPAMINOANDAS GONZÁLES are:
10.   i.   AGIDA⁵ GONZÁLES, b. December 05, 1900, San Patricio, Territory of New México; d. October 28, 1941.
11.   ii.   EPAMINOANDAS GONZÁLES GONZÁLES, b. October 21, 1901, San Patricio, Territory of New México; d. January 05, 1945.
12.   iii.   CIPRIANA GONZÁLES, b. August 21, 1903, San Patricio, Territory of New México; d. November 11, 2006, San Patricio, New México.
       iv.   CRECENSIANA GONZÁLES, b. Abt. 1906, San Patricio, Territory of New México³⁷; m. TITO MAÉS.
13.   v.   FLORENCIO GONZÁLES GONZÁLES, b. September 17, 1907, San Patricio, Territory of New México; d. October 11, 1973, San Patricio, New México.
       vi.   BRESELIA GONZÁLES, b. October 10, 1910, San Patricio, Territory of New México; d. January 09, 1973, Morenci, Arizona; m. (1) JUAN TRUJILLO SÁNCHEZ³⁸³⁹; m. (2) MAX CORONA⁴⁰.
14.   vii.   RAFAEL GONZÁLES, b. March 23, 1914, San Patricio, New México.

viii.   MARÍA GONZÁLES[41], b. May 20, 1917, San Patricio, New México[42]; m. LEOPOLDO PEÑA[42], June 20, 1940, Lincoln, New México[42].

15.   ix.   SIGISMUNDA GONZÁLES, b. February 07, 1920, San Patricio, New México.

16.   x.   EVA GONZÁLES, b. Private, San Patricio, New México.

6. ANITA[4] GONZÁLES *(JOSÉ TORRES[3], TONITA[2] TORRES, PABLO[1])[43]* was born June 29, 1888 in San Patricio, Territory of New México[44], and died September 1962 in Hondo, New México[45]. She married (1) IGNACIO MAÉS[46] April 05, 1914 in Lincoln, New México[46], son of JOSÉ MAÉS and MANUELITA LUCERO. She married (2) ROBERTO GUTIÉRREZ[47] September 16, 1916 in Hondo, New México[48], son of DAMIAN GUTIÉRRES and JUANITA SÁNCHEZ.

Notes for ANITA GONZÁLES:
Also known as Anne.

Notes for IGNACIO MAÉS:
1900-1920 Census: Living in Picacho, New México.

Notes for ROBERTO GUTIÉRREZ:
World War One Draft Registration Card indicates that he was born on July 18, 1882.
1930 Census: Living in Hondo, New México. His name is listed as Roberto Gonzáles.
Land Patent # NMR 0026686, on the authority of the Homestead Entry-Original (12 Stat. 392), May 20, 1862. Issued 151.71 acres on August 26, 1920.
Land Patent # NMR 0029140, on the authority of the Homestead Entry-Enlarged (35 Stat. 639), February 19, 1909. Issued 168.64 acres on October 18, 1923.
Land Patent # NMR 0036537, on the authority of the Homestead Entry-Stock Raising (39 Stat. 862), December 29, 1916. Issued 320 acres on April 20, 1925.

Children of ANITA GONZÁLES and ROBERTO GUTIÉRREZ are:

17.   i.   JOSÉ GONZÁLES[5] GUTIÉRREZ, b. July 07, 1917, Hondo, New México; d. August 13, 1997, Hondo, New México.

       ii.   ROBERTO GONZÁLES GUTIÉRREZ[49], b. May 14, 1919, Hondo, New México[50]; d. September 1974, Hondo, New México.

             Notes for ROBERTO GONZÁLES GUTIÉRREZ:
             June 25, 1942: Enlisted into the Army. Corporal US Army, WW II. Wounded in Italy April 29, 1945.

       iii.   FERNANDO GUTIÉRREZ[50], b. April 07, 1922, Tinnie, New México[51]; d. March 08, 1972, Hondo, New México; m. FAY RILEY, June 05, 1958, Carrizozo, New México[51].

             Notes for FERNANDO GUTIÉRREZ:
             November 30, 1942: Enlisted in the Army. Tec 5 CN, Company 302, Infantry WW II.

       iv.   SOSTENO GUTIÉRREZ[52], b. December 16, 1924, Tinnie, New México[53].

             Notes for SOSTENO GUTIÉRREZ:
             US Navy, Seaman First Class. World War II.

       v.   JOSEFITA GUTIÉRREZ, b. Abt. 1925[53].
       vi.   DOMINGO GUTIÉRREZ, b. Abt. 1929[53].

7. SANTIAGO CHÁVEZ[4] GONZÁLES *(JOSÉ TORRES[3], TONITA[2] TORRES, PABLO[1])* was born December 26, 1884[54]. He married (1) JESÚSITA CHÁVEZ. He married (2) ADELINA MONTOYA November 22, 1918 in Lincoln, New México[54], daughter of FREDERICO MONTOYA and AMADA PACHECO.

Notes for SANTIAGO CHÁVEZ GONZÁLES:
Also known as Jim.
1930 Census: Living in Roswell, New México.

Children of SANTIAGO GONZÁLES and ADELINA MONTOYA are:
       i.   RAFAEL MONTOYA[5] GONZÁLES, b. Abt. April 1919[55].
       ii.   JOE GONZÁLES, b. Abt. 1921[56].

 iii. JULIO GONZÁLES, b. Abt. 1922[56].
 iv. FRED GONZÁLES, b. Abt. 1926[56].

   Notes for FRED GONZÁLES:
   Also known as Fredrick.

 v. RAMONA GONZÁLES, b. Abt. 1928[56].
 vi. FRANCIS GONZÁLES, b. Private.
 vii. SONYA GONZÁLES, b. Private.

8. LOYOLA[4] GONZÁLES *(JOSÉ TORRES[3], TONITA[2] TORRES, PABLO[1])* was born July 1893[57]. She married LASARO GALLEGOS June 20, 1917 in Lincoln, New México[58], son of LAZARO GALLEGOS and ANTONIA MOLINA.

Notes for LOYOLA GONZÁLES:
Also known as María Loyola Gonzáles.

Children of LOYOLA GONZÁLES and LASARO GALLEGOS are:
 i. FEDERICO[5] GALLEGOS, b. Abt. 1918[59].
 ii. MARÍA GALLEGOS, b. Abt. 1920[59].
 iii. ROSA GALLEGOS, b. Abt. 1923[59].
 iv. CRUZ GALLEGOS, b. Abt. 1924[59].
 v. JOSÉ GALLEGOS, b. Abt. 1927[59].
 vi. MANUEL GALLEGOS, b. Abt. 1927[59].

9. AMALIA[4] GONZÁLES *(JOSÉ TORRES[3], TONITA[2] TORRES, PABLO[1])* was born January 1897[60]. She married JOHN LUCERO BRADY[61] July 05, 1919 in Capitán, New México[62], son of ROBERT BRADY and MANUELA LUCERO.

Notes for AMALIA GONZÁLES:
Also known as Emelia, Emiliana.

Notes for JOHN LUCERO BRADY:
Also known as J.E. Brady and Juan Brady.
Baptismal records indicate that he was born on October 01, 1894. (Microfiche# 0016754, Page 219)

Child of AMALIA GONZÁLES and JOHN BRADY is:
 i. JOHN GONZÁLES[5] BRADY[63], b. Abt. 1922, Albuquerque, New México; d. August 05, 1922, Albuquerque, New México.

Generation No. 5

10. AGIDA[5] GONZÁLES *(ELVIRA[4], JOSÉ TORRES[3], TONITA[2] TORRES, PABLO[1])* was born December 05, 1900 in San Patricio, Territory of New México[64], and died October 28, 1941[65]. She married BENITO SALAS December 16, 1921[66], son of CRECENCIO SALAS and LUPITA VIGIL.

Children of AGIDA GONZÁLES and BENITO SALAS are:
 i. LUZ[6] SALAS, b. Abt. 1923[67].
 ii. FLORENCIO SALAS, b. Abt. 1925[67].
 iii. LULIO SALAS, b. Abt. 1927[68].
 iv. ROGER SALAS, b. Abt. November 1928[69].

11. EPAMINOANDAS GONZÁLES[5] GONZÁLES *(ELVIRA[4], JOSÉ TORRES[3], TONITA[2] TORRES, PABLO[1])*[70] was born October 21, 1901 in San Patricio, Territory of New México, and died January 05, 1945. He married IGNACIA PRUDENCIO[71] September 11, 1928 in Mescalero, New México[72], daughter of MORTIMER PROVENCIO and CLEOFAS MUÑOZ.

Notes for EPAMINOANDAS GONZÁLES GONZÁLES:
Also known as Epaminio.

Child of EPAMINOANDAS GONZÁLES and IGNACIA PRUDENCIO is:
  i.   JOHN WILLIAM[6] GONZÁLES[73], b. Abt. 1937, San Patricio, New México; d. July 17, 1937, San Patricio, New México.

12. CIPRIANA[5] GONZÁLES *(ELVIRA[4], JOSÉ TORRES[3], TONITA[2] TORRES, PABLO[1])[74]* was born August 21, 1903 in San Patricio, Territory of New México[75], and died November 11, 2006 in San Patricio, New México[76]. She married VICENTE HERRERA[77] August 27, 1932 in San Patricio, New México[78], son of CRUZ HERRERA and PETRA DOMINGUEZ.

Children of CIPRIANA GONZÁLES and VICENTE HERRERA are:
  i.   RUFINO[6] HERRERA[79], b. July 25, 1933, San Patricio, New México; d. January 17, 2006, San Patricio, New México; m. HELENA MONTOYA, April 04, 1957, San Patricio, New México.
  ii. BERTA HERRERA, b. January 30, 1942, San Patricio, New México[80]; m. FRED SÁNCHEZ, July 26, 1959, Ruidoso, New México[80].

13. FLORENCIO GONZÁLES[5] GONZÁLES *(ELVIRA[4], JOSÉ TORRES[3], TONITA[2] TORRES, PABLO[1])[81]* was born September 17, 1907 in San Patricio, Territory of New México, and died October 11, 1973 in San Patricio, New México. He married ALBESITA SÁNCHEZ December 19, 1932 in San Patricio, New México[82], daughter of JACOBO SÁNCHEZ and MARÍA TRUJILLO.

Children of FLORENCIO GONZÁLES and ALBESITA SÁNCHEZ are:
  i.   JOSÉ[6] GONZÁLES, b. November 10, 1934, San Patricio, New México; d. August 24, 1991.
  ii. FRANK GONZÁLES[83], b. May 30, 1942, San Patricio, New México[84]; d. August 05, 2006, Ruidoso Downs, New México; m. MILDRED RANDOLPH, July 09, 1961, Ruidoso, New México[84].
  iii. ELVIRA SÁNCHEZ GONZÁLES, b. Private, San Patricio, New México.
  iv. ISAQUIO GONZÁLES, b. Private, San Patricio, New México.

14. RAFAEL[5] GONZÁLES *(ELVIRA[4], JOSÉ TORRES[3], TONITA[2] TORRES, PABLO[1])[85]* was born March 23, 1914 in San Patricio, New México[86]. He married AVRORA BACA June 05, 1936 in San Patricio, New México[86], daughter of ELÍAS BACA and PABLA ANALLA.

Children of RAFAEL GONZÁLES and AVRORA BACA are:
  i.   DOMINGO[6] GONZÁLES[87], b. Abt. 1937, San Patricio, New México; d. October 28, 1937, San Patricio, New México.
  ii. ARMANDO GONZÁLES[88], b. Abt. 1940, San Patricio, New México; d. October 08, 1940, San Patricio, New México.

15. SIGISMUNDA[5] GONZÁLES *(ELVIRA[4], JOSÉ TORRES[3], TONITA[2] TORRES, PABLO[1])[89]* was born February 07, 1920 in San Patricio, New México[90]. She married ADAN SÁNCHEZ[90] August 18, 1948 in Carrizozo, New México[90], son of SIMÓN SÁNCHEZ and ANTONIA CARABAJAL.

Child of SIGISMUNDA GONZÁLES and ADAN SÁNCHEZ is:
  i.   YOLANDA GONZÁLES[6] SÁNCHEZ, b. Private.

16. EVA[5] GONZÁLES *(ELVIRA[4], JOSÉ TORRES[3], TONITA[2] TORRES, PABLO[1])* was born Private in San Patricio, New México. She married JUAN SÁNCHEZ MONTOYA August 13, 1948 in Carrizozo, New México[91], son of MAURICIO MONTOYA and AVRORA SÁNCHEZ.

17. JOSÉ GONZÁLES[5] GUTIÉRREZ *(ANITA[4] GONZÁLES, JOSÉ TORRES[3], TONITA[2] TORRES, PABLO[1])[92]* was born July 07, 1917 in Hondo, New México[93], and died August 13, 1997 in Hondo, New México. He married (1) DOLORES SEDILLO, daughter of MARTÍN SEDILLO and PORFIRIA OTERO. He married (2) EVA B. ENCINIAS August 12, 1961 in Vaughn, New México[94].

Child of JOSÉ GUTIÉRREZ and DOLORES SEDILLO is:
  i.   PRESCILLA[6] GUTIÉRREZ, b. July 28, 1951; m. MELVIN CHÁVEZ.

Genealogy of José Manuel Trujillo

Generation No. 1

1. JOSÉ MANUEL[1] TRUJILLO. He married MARÍA DOLÓRES SÁNCHEZ[1].

Notes for MARÍA DOLÓRES SÁNCHEZ:
Also known as Dolorita.

Children of JOSÉ TRUJILLO and MARÍA SÁNCHEZ are:
2.   i.   REFUGIA[2] TRUJILLO, b. Abt. 1853.
3.   ii.   BENITO SÁNCHEZ TRUJILLO, b. October 1854.
       iii.   PATRICIO TRUJILLO, b. April 1860[2].
4.   iv.   BONAFICIO TRUJILLO, b. May 1864; d. March 09, 1928, San Patricio, New México.

Generation No. 2

2. REFUGIA[2] TRUJILLO *(JOSÉ MANUEL[1])* was born Abt. 1853[3]. She married ANISETO LUCERO May 26, 1870 in Tularoso, Territory of New México[4], son of JUAN LUCERO and MARCELINA JARAMILLO.

Notes for REFUGIA TRUJILLO:
Alos known as María del Refugio Trujillo.

Notes for ANISETO LUCERO:
Land Patent # NMNMAA 010834, on the authority of the Sale cash entry (3 Stat. 566), April 24, 1820, 40 Acres.
Land Patent # NMR 0028238, on the authority of the Homestead Entry-Original (12 Stat. 392), May 20, 1862. Issued 160 acres on February, 12, 1921.

Children of REFUGIA TRUJILLO and ANISETO LUCERO are:
       i.   JOSEFA[3] LUCERO, b. 1871, San Patricio, Territory of New México[5].
       ii.   VICTORIANA LUCERO, b. 1874, San Patricio, Territory of New México[5].
       iii.   BESITA LUCERO, b. 1878, San Patricio, Territory of New México[5].
       iv.   FRANCISCO LUCERO, b. April 20, 1884, San Patricio, Territory of New México[6].
       v.   LUGARDITA LUCERO, b. March 1887, San Patricio, Territory of New México[7]; m. EULOJIO GALLEGOS[8], March 12, 1908, San Patricio, Territory of New México[9].

Notes for EULOJIO GALLEGOS:
Also known as Olojio.

5.   vi.   JUANITA LUCERO, b. September 02, 1889, San Patricio, Territory of New México.
6.   vii.   HINIO LUCERO, b. Abt. 1881, San Patricio, Territory of New México; d. March 21, 1933, San Patricio, New México.
       viii.   MARGARITA LUCERO[10], b. May 20, 1893, San Patricio, Territory of New México[11].

3. BENITO SÁNCHEZ[2] TRUJILLO *(JOSÉ MANUEL[1])* was born October 1854[12]. He married MARÍA IGENIA SEDILLO[13].

Notes for BENITO SÁNCHEZ TRUJILLO:
1870 Census: Living in Precinct 3, Lincoln County.
1900 & 1910 Census: Living in San Patricio, Territory of New México.

Notes for MARÍA IGENIA SEDILLO:
1870 Census: Living in Lincoln County, Precinct 3, Territory of New México.1920 Census shows that she was living with her grandson, Manuel Benavidez.

Children of BENITO TRUJILLO and MARÍA SEDILLO are:
       i.   JOSÉ MARÍA[3] TRUJILLO, b. Abt. 1866[14].
7.   ii.   TEOFILA TRUJILLO, b. Abt. 1869.

4. BONAFICIO[2] TRUJILLO *(JOSÉ MANUEL[1])*[15] was born May 1864[16], and died March 09, 1928 in San Patricio, New México. He married LORENSA SILVA Abt. 1882[17], daughter of MANUEL SILVA and JOSEFITA ESQUIVEL.

Notes for LORENSA SILVA:
Also known as Lorencita.
Death records indicate that her birth year was about 1869. Buried in San Patricio.

Children of BONAFICIO TRUJILLO and LORENSA SILVA are:

      i.   ANASTACIO[3] TRUJILLO, b. December 10, 1883, San Patricio, Territory of New México[18].

Notes for ANASTACIO TRUJILLO:
Died young.

8.	ii.	SUSANA TRUJILLO, b. May 15, 1886, Ruidoso, Territory of New México; d. January 20, 1974.
9.	iii.	REYMUNDA TRUJILLO, b. January 17, 1888, San Patricio, Territory of New México.
	iv.	ALEJANDRO SILVA TRUJILLO, b. January 04, 1891, San Patricio, Territory of New México[19].
	v.	CARMELITA TRUJILLO, b. April 15, 1893, San Patricio, Territory of New México[20]; m. LORENZO MONTOYA, June 03, 1933[21].

Notes for CARMELITA TRUJILLO:
Also known as Carmen.

10.	vi.	RITA TRUJILLO, b. January 04, 1894, San Patricio, Territory of New México.
11.	vii.	ROSA TRUJILLO, b. July 16, 1895, San Patricio, Territory of New México; d. February 21, 1988, Los Ángeles, California.
12.	viii.	VICTORIANO TRUJILLO, b. November 20, 1897, San Patricio, Territory of New México; d. February 1976, San Patricio, New México.
	ix.	PEDRO TRUJILLO, b. May 1899, San Patricio, Territory of New México[22].
13.	x.	LORENCITA TRUJILLO, b. August 10, 1905, San Patricio, Territory of New México; d. August 25, 1960.

Generation No. 3

5. JUANITA[3] LUCERO *(REFUGIA[2] TRUJILLO, JOSÉ MANUEL[1])* was born September 02, 1889 in San Patricio, Territory of New México. She married ANASTACIO OLGUÍN November 02, 1921[23].

Children of JUANITA LUCERO and ANASTACIO OLGUÍN are:

      i.   CARLOS[4] OLGUÍN[24], b. August 21, 1927; d. August 23, 1958.

Notes for CARLOS OLGUÍN:
WW II Veteran.

      ii.   AVA OLGUÍN, b. Abt. 1922[25].
      iii. RAMÓN OLGUÍN[26], b. February 12, 1925[27]; d. July 07, 1983.

6. HINIO[3] LUCERO *(REFUGIA[2] TRUJILLO, JOSÉ MANUEL[1])*[28] was born Abt. 1881 in San Patricio, Territory of New México[29], and died March 21, 1933 in San Patricio, New México. He married MANUELITA OLGUÍN February 12, 1902[30], daughter of RAMÓN OLGUÍN and LORENSA SEDILLO.

Notes for HINIO LUCERO:
Also known as Iginio.

Notes for MANUELITA OLGUÍN:
Also known as Manuela, Manuelita Sedillo.
1900 Census: She was living with her brother-in-law, Sisto Sedillo, and her sister, Margarita Olguín de Sedillo.

Children of HINIO LUCERO and MANUELITA OLGUÍN are:

      i.   ANISETO OLGUÍN[4] LUCERO, b. 1904, San Patricio, Territory of New México[31].
      ii.   MARTÍN OLGUÍN LUCERO[32], b. July 26, 1905, San Patricio, Territory of New México; d. May 15, 1953.
      iii. REYES LUCERO, b. June 06, 1909, San Patricio, Territory of New México[33]; m. RITA BENAVIDEZ, December 04, 1946, Carrizozo, New México[33].

Notes for REYES LUCERO:
1920 Census: Living in San Patricio, New México.

      iv.   EPIFANIO LUCERO, b. 1915, San Patricio, New México[34].
      v.   REFUGIO LUCERO, b. 1918, San Patricio, New México[34].

7. TEOFILA[3] TRUJILLO *(BENITO SÁNCHEZ[2], JOSÉ MANUEL[1])*[35] was born Abt. 1869[36]. She married JUAN ZENON BENAVIDEZ January 31, 1885[37], son of JOSÉ BENAVIDEZ and PETRA ARCHULETA.

Notes for TEOFILA TRUJILLO:
Also known as María Teofila Trujillo.

Children of TEOFILA TRUJILLO and JUAN BENAVIDEZ are:
14.   i.   ERINEA[4] BENAVIDEZ, b. October 22, 1887; d. 1953.
15.   ii.   MANUEL BENAVIDEZ, b. November 06, 1891, Ruidoso, Territory of New México; d. May 11, 1972.
16.   iii.   CANDELARIO BENAVIDEZ, b. February 02, 1885, Hondo, Territory of New México; d. 1962.

8. SUSANA[3] TRUJILLO *(BONAFICIO[2], JOSÉ MANUEL[1])*[38] was born May 15, 1886 in Ruidoso, Territory of New México, and died January 20, 1974. She married MANUEL CORONA[38] February 24, 1909 in Lincoln, Territory of New México[39], son of MAXIMIANO CORONA and MANUELITA HERRERA.

Children of SUSANA TRUJILLO and MANUEL CORONA are:
17.   i.   MAX[4] CORONA, b. September 05, 1912, San Patricio, New México; d. January 09, 1973, Morenci, Arizona.
      ii.   ANASTACIO CORONA, b. October 23, 1916, San Patricio, New México[40]; d. July 11, 2000, Ruidoso, New México; m. ESPERANZA MAÉS, August 28, 1939, Arabela, New México[40].
      iii.   MANUEL TRUJILLO CORONA[41], b. March 27, 1921, San Patricio, New México; d. August 25, 2007, San Patricio, New México.

Notes for MANUEL TRUJILLO CORONA:
Private First Class US Army. WW II Veteran.

9. REYMUNDA[3] TRUJILLO *(BONAFICIO[2], JOSÉ MANUEL[1])* was born January 17, 1888 in San Patricio, Territory of New México[42]. She married FRUGENCIO FLORES February 05, 1906 in Lincoln, Territory of New México[42], son of JOSÉ FLORES and VICTORIA MAÉS.

Notes for FRUGENCIO FLORES:
Also known as Fulgencio.
Born at El Rancho del Padre.
His daughter, Adelaida's death record indicates he was born in Tierra Amarilla, Territory of New México.
1900 Census: Living with his stepfather, Ramón Vigil and his mother Victoria Maés de Vigil.

Children of REYMUNDA TRUJILLO and FRUGENCIO FLORES are:
      i.   JOSÉ[4] FLORES, b. 1910[43].
      ii.   CORINA FLORES, b. 1912[43].
      iii.   RAFAEL FLORES, b. 1914[43].
      iv.   ISMAEL FLORES, b. 1917[43].
      v.   ALBERTO FLORES, b. 1919[43].
      vi.   ADELAIDA FLORES[44], b. December 01, 1922, San Patricio, New México; d. April 17, 1924, San Patricio, New México.

10. RITA[3] TRUJILLO *(BONAFICIO[2], JOSÉ MANUEL[1])* was born January 04, 1894 in San Patricio, Territory of New México[45]. She married MIGUEL SEDILLO October 14, 1914 in Lincoln, New México[45], son of SISTO SEDILLO and MARGARITA OLGUÍN.

Notes for MIGUEL SEDILLO:
1914: Miguel was living in Reventón at the time of his marriage.
Land Patent # NMR 0042431, on the authority of the Homestead Entry-Enlarged (35 Stat. 639), February 19, 1909. Issued 320 acres on May 01, 1922.

Children of RITA TRUJILLO and MIGUEL SEDILLO are:

     i.   LEONEL[4] SEDILLO[46], b. November 20, 1918, San Patricio, New México[47].
     ii.   IDILIA SEDILLO, b. Abt. 1923[47].

11. ROSA[3] TRUJILLO *(BONAFICIO[2], JOSÉ MANUEL[1])[48]* was born July 16, 1895 in San Patricio, Territory of New México[49], and died February 21, 1988 in Los Ángeles, California. She married ALFREDO ZAMORA September 25, 1925 in San Patricio, New México[50], son of JUAN SAMORA and EVARISTA GAMBOA.

Notes for ROSA TRUJILLO:
Also known as Rosa Trujillo Montaño.

Notes for ALFREDO ZAMORA:
1910 Census: Living in San Patricio, Territory of New México.
1930 Census: Living in Lincoln, Territory of New México.

Children of ROSA TRUJILLO and ALFREDO ZAMORA are:
     i.   EVA[4] ZAMORA, b. Abt. 1928, Lincoln, New México[51].
     ii.   VICTORIANO ZAMORA, b. Private, Lincoln, New México.

12. VICTORIANO[3] TRUJILLO *(BONAFICIO[2], JOSÉ MANUEL[1])[52]* was born November 20, 1897 in San Patricio, Territory of New México[53], and died February 1976 in San Patricio, New México. He married ENEDINA GUTIÉRREZ May 17, 1933[54], daughter of JULIAN GUTIÉRREZ and JULIANITA ROSILLOS.

Notes for VICTORIANO TRUJILLO:
The patent on Victoriano's farm goes back to Jose Ulibarrí.
1900 Census: Living in San Patricio, Territory of New México.
Land Patent # NMLC 0041659, on the authority of the Homestead Entry-Stock Raising (39 Stat. 862), December 29, 1916. Issued 360 acres on March 14, 1939.

Children of VICTORIANO TRUJILLO and ENEDINA GUTIÉRREZ are:
     i.   MARÍA[4] TRUJILLO[55], b. Abt. 1941, San Patricio, New México; d. January 27, 1941, San Patricio, New México.
     ii.   ARTURO TRUJILLO, b. Private; m. CORINA CRUZ.
     iii. VICTOR TRUJILLO, b. Private; m. AMELIA CRUZ.

13. LORENCITA[3] TRUJILLO *(BONAFICIO[2], JOSÉ MANUEL[1])[56]* was born August 10, 1905 in San Patricio, Territory of New México[57], and died August 25, 1960. She married PEDRO CHÁVEZ[58] July 13, 1930 in Carrizozo, New México[59], son of MACARIO CHÁVEZ and ELFIDA MONTOYA.

Notes for LORENCITA TRUJILLO:
Also known as Lorensa.

Notes for PEDRO CHÁVEZ:
Also known as Pedro Chávez y Montoya.
Pedro was raised by his half sister's (Elfida Chavez) daughter, Marillita and her husband Julian Romero y Torres in Manzano, NM until he was 16 years old. He was re-united with his mother in Corona, NM.
Buried in San Patricio, NM.

Children of LORENCITA TRUJILLO and PEDRO CHÁVEZ are:
     i.   MARÍA CIRILIA[4] CHÁVEZ[60], b. Abt. 1937, San Patricio, New México; d. March 24, 1937, San Patricio, New México.
18.   ii.   MACARIO TRUJILLO CHÁVEZ, b. Private.
     iii. RAYMOND CHÁVEZ, b. Private.
     iv. RUFINA CHÁVEZ, b. Private; m. SIGISFREDO MONTOYA.

Generation No. 4

14. ERINEA[4] BENAVIDEZ *(TEOFILA[3] TRUJILLO, BENITO SÁNCHEZ[2], JOSÉ MANUEL[1])[61]* was born October 22, 1887[62], and died 1953. She married TELESFORO SILVA[63] November 29, 1911, son of HILARIO SILVA and AMBROSIA ULIBARRÍ.

Notes for ERINEA BENAVIDEZ:
1900 Census: Living with her grandfather, Benito Trujillo and grandmother, María Igenia Sedillo de Trujillo.

Notes for TELESFORO SILVA:
Also known as Telesforo.
1920 Census: Living in Capitán, New México.

Children of ERINEA BENAVIDEZ and TELESFORO SILVA are:
      i.   BENITO⁵ SILVA[64], b. October 22, 1912, Hondo, New México[65]; d. December 1986, Ruidoso Downs, New México; m. CONSUELO SÁNCHEZ[66], February 13, 1932, Glencoe, New México[67].

Notes for BENITO SILVA:
1920 Census shows that he was living with his uncle, Manuel Benavidez.

Notes for CONSUELO SÁNCHEZ:
Also known as Consolación.
Lincoln County marriage records indicate that she was born on April 2, 1913.
Buried in Tularosa Catholic Cemetery.

19.   ii.   AMBROCIA SILVA, b. April 15, 1915, Hondo, New México.
      iii.   ANSELMO SILVA[68], b. April 21, 1919, Hondo, New México[69]; d. December 10, 1992, Ruidoso Downs, New México; m. VIRGINIA MIRANDA, November 04, 1948, Ruidoso, New México[70].
      iv.   BONIFACIO SILVA, b. May 15, 1923, Lincoln, New México[71].
      v.   ONESIMA SILVA, b. Private.
      vi.   RAMÓN SILVA, b. Private; m. CARMELITA SILVA.
      vii.   VICTOR SILVA, b. Private.

15. MANUEL⁴ BENAVIDEZ *(TEOFILA³ TRUJILLO, BENITO SÁNCHEZ², JOSÉ MANUEL¹)[72]* was born November 06, 1891 in Ruidoso, Territory of New México[73], and died May 11, 1972. He married MARGARITA TORRES[74] February 28, 1921[75], daughter of EUSEVIO TORRES and EMILIA MUÑOZ.

Notes for MANUEL BENAVIDEZ:
Lincoln cemetery records indicate that he was born on July 21, 1891.
NM Private, Company H, 305 Infantry, WWI.
1900 Census: Living with hir grandfather, Benito Trujillo and grandmother, María Igenia Sedillo de Trujillo.
1920 Census shows that Manuel's grandmother, María Igenia Sedillo and his nephew, Benito Silva lived with him.

Child of MANUEL BENAVIDEZ and MARGARITA TORRES is:
      i.   JUANITA TORRES⁵ BENAVIDEZ, b. March 08, 1926, Alamogordo, New México[76]; m. HENRY CALDERON, November 03, 1946, Carrizozo, New México[76].

16. CANDELARIO⁴ BENAVIDEZ *(TEOFILA³ TRUJILLO, BENITO SÁNCHEZ², JOSÉ MANUEL¹)* was born February 02, 1885 in Hondo, Territory of New México[77], and died 1962[78]. He married PETRA BACA March 10, 1907 in Lincoln, Territory of New México[79].

Notes for CANDELARIO BENAVIDEZ:
WWI Draft Registration indicates that he was born on February 2, 1886.
1900 Census: Living with his grandfather, Benito Trujillo and grandmother, María Igenia Sedillo de Trujillo.
1910 Census: Living in San Patricio, Territory of New México.
1920 Census: Living in Capitán, New México.

Children of CANDELARIO BENAVIDEZ and PETRA BACA are:
      i.   JIMMY⁵ BENAVIDEZ.
      ii.   EULOJIA BENAVIDEZ, b. Abt. 1907[80].
20.   iii.   DOLORITA BENAVIDEZ, b. Abt. 1911.
      iv.   ANTONIO BENAVIDEZ[81], b. July 05, 1912, Hondo, Territory of New México[82]; d. May 11, 1957, Hondo, New México; m. CONCEPCIÓN HERNÁNDEZ, July 29, 1935, Carrizozo, New México[82].

Notes for ANTONIO BENAVIDEZ:
NM Private 1614 SVC Command Unit, World War II.

Notes for CONCEPCIÓN HERNÁNDEZ:
Also known as Concha.

   v.   AGAPITA BENAVIDEZ, b. Abt. 1914[83]; m. ELISEO BACA, July 23, 1934[84].

Notes for ELISEO BACA:
Also known as Elijio.

   vi.   SERAFÍN BENAVIDEZ, b. Abt. 1915[85].
   vii. ISIDORA BENAVIDEZ, b. December 31, 1919, Hondo, New México[86]; m. DAVÍD LUCERO SÁNCHEZ[86], November 24, 1936, Arabela, New México[86].
   viii. TEOFILA BACA BENAVIDEZ, b. February 17, 1922, Lincoln, New México[87]; m. LUPE GARCÍA, March 23, 1940, Carrizozo, New México[87].
   ix.   MANUELITA BENAVIDEZ[88], b. March 16, 1924, Lincoln, New México; d. May 14, 1924, Lincoln, New México.

17. MAX[4] CORONA *(SUSANA[3] TRUJILLO, BONAFICIO[2], JOSÉ MANUEL[1])*[89] was born September 05, 1912 in San Patricio, New México[90], and died January 09, 1973 in Morenci, Arizona. He married (1) BRESELIA GONZÁLES, daughter of EPAMINOANDAS GONZÁLES and ELVIRA GONZÁLES. He married (2) APOLONIA WARNER June 04, 1932 in Carrizozo, New México[91], daughter of JUAN WARNER and EMILIA TORREZ.

Child of MAX CORONA and APOLONIA WARNER is:
   i.   DANIEL[5] CORONA[92], b. Abt. 1933, San Patricio, New México; d. November 03, 1933, San Patricio, New México.

18. MACARIO TRUJILLO[4] CHÁVEZ *(LORENCITA[3] TRUJILLO, BONAFICIO[2], JOSÉ MANUEL[1])* was born Private. He married TERESA GÓMEZ.

Child of MACARIO CHÁVEZ and TERESA GÓMEZ is:
   i.   PATRICIA[5] CHÁVEZ, b. Private.

Generation No. 5

19. AMBROCIA[5] SILVA *(ERINEA[4] BENAVIDEZ, TEOFILA[3] TRUJILLO, BENITO SÁNCHEZ[2], JOSÉ MANUEL[1])* was born April 15, 1915 in Hondo, New México[93]. She married PROSPERO MIRABAL GONZÁLES January 16, 1932 in Glencoe, New México[93], son of PROSPERO GONZÁLES and TELESFORA MIRABAL.

Children of AMBROCIA SILVA and PROSPERO GONZÁLES are:
   i.   LILIA[6] GONZÁLES, b. Private.
   ii.   FELIX GONZÁLES, b. Private.
   iii. DORTHY GONZÁLES, b. Private.
   iv.   FLOYD GONZÁLES, b. Private.

20. DOLORITA[5] BENAVIDEZ *(CANDELARIO[4], TEOFILA[3] TRUJILLO, BENITO SÁNCHEZ[2], JOSÉ MANUEL[1])* was born Abt. 1911[94]. She married RAMÓN PÉREZ[95], son of VICTORIANO PÉREZ and FRANCISCA TORRES.

Child of DOLORITA BENAVIDEZ and RAMÓN PÉREZ is:
   i.   RUJERIO[6] PÉREZ[95], b. Abt. 1940, Hondo, New México; d. December 17, 1940, Hondo, New México.

Genealogy of Juan de Ulibarrí

Generation No. 1

1. JOSÉ ENRÍQUES[1] DE LOS REYES[1] was born in San Luís Potosi, Nueva España. He married MARÍA DE YNOJOS.

Children of JOSÉ DE LOS REYES and MARÍA DE YNOJOS are:

2.   i.   JUAN[2] DE ULIBARRÍ, b. 1670, San Luís Potosi, Nueva España; d. Bef. 1718.

       ii.   ANTONIO DE ULIBARRÍ[2], b. Abt. 1680, San Juan de la Paz, Ciudad de México, Nueva España; d. November 02, 1762, Santa Fé, El Reyno de Nuevo México; m. MARÍA DURÁN Y CHÁVEZ, Abt. 1711.

          Notes for ANTONIO DE ULIBARRÍ:
          1714: Was appointed as the Alcalde of the Pueblos of Acoma, Zuñi, and Laguna.
          1731: Was appointed as the Alcalde and the Capitán de Guerra of La Villa de Santa Fé.

Generation No. 2

2. JUAN[2] DE ULIBARRÍ *(JOSÉ ENRÍQUES[1] DE LOS REYES)*[3] was born 1670 in San Luís Potosi, Nueva España, and died Bef. 1718. He married (1) JUANA HURTADO[4]. He married (2) FRANCISCA DE MIZQUIA Y LUCERO.

Notes for JUAN DE ULIBARRÍ:
1693: Was a member of the 1693 Vargas reconquest.
1701: Inscribed his name on "Inscription Rock".
1704: Stationed at the Presidio de Santa Fé. He was appointed as the second in command.
1706: Appointed as Procurator of his garrison in the Presidio de Santa Fé.
1706-1707: Liberated the Picurís from their Apache captors.

Children of JUAN DE ULIBARRÍ and JUANA HURTADO are:

3.   i.   JUAN HURTADO[3] DE ULIBARRÍ, b. 1690, San Luís Potosi, Nueva España.

       ii.   ANTONIO HURTADO DE ULIBARRÍ[4].

Generation No. 3

3. JUAN HURTADO[3] DE ULIBARRÍ *(JUAN[2], JOSÉ ENRÍQUES[1] DE LOS REYES)*[5] was born 1690 in San Luís Potosi, Nueva España. He married ROSALIA DE ARMIJO[6] July 01, 1732 in Alburquerque, El Reyno de Nuevo México[6], daughter of JOSÉ DE ARMIJO and MANUELA VELASQUES.

Children of JUAN DE ULIBARRÍ and ROSALIA DE ARMIJO are:

4.   i.   JOAQUÍN SANTA ANA[4] ULIBARRÍ, b. Abt. 1730, Belén, El Reyno de Nuevo México.

       ii.   JUAN PEDRO CRISOSTOMO ULIBARRÍ[6], b. Abt. 1733; d. July 24, 1799, San Juan de los Caballeros, El Reyno de Nuevo México.

      iii.   JUANA GETRUDES ULIBARRÍ[6], b. November 20, 1735, Alburquerque, El Reyno de Nuevo México[7].

      iv.   ANDRES ULIBARRÍ[8], b. Abt. 1743[9].

       v.   BERNARDA ULIBARRÍ[10], b. Abt. 1744[11].

Generation No. 4

4. JOAQUÍN SANTA ANA[4] ULIBARRÍ *(JUAN HURTADO[3] DE ULIBARRÍ, JUAN[2], JOSÉ ENRÍQUES[1] DE LOS REYES)*[12] was born Abt. 1730 in Belén, El Reyno de Nuevo México[13]. He married JUANA MARÍA DURÁN[14].

Notes for JOAQUÍN SANTA ANA ULIBARRÍ:
1790: Lists his his birth year in about 1730.

Notes for JUANA MARÍA DURÁN:
1790 Census: Lists her birth year in about 1740.

Children of JOAQUÍN ULIBARRÍ and JUANA DURÁN are:
  i.   JOSÉ ANTONIO DE JESÚS[5] ULIBARRÍ[15], b. Abt. 1767[16].
  ii. URSULA DE JESÚS ULIBARRÍ[17], b. Abt. 1770[18].
  iii. JUAN MIGUEL ANTONIO ULIBARRÍ[19], b. September 12, 1773[20].
5. iv. SANTIAGO JOSÉ ULIBARRÍ, b. 1775, Belén, El Reyno de Nuevo México.
  v.   FRANCISCO JOAQUÍN ULIBARRÍ[21], b. Abt. 1778, Los Bacas, El Reyno de Nuevo México, Nueva España; d. January 15, 1817, Sabinal, El Reyno de Nuevo México, Nueva España.
  vi. JUAN CRISTÓBAL ULIBARRÍ[22], b. Abt. 1780[23].
  vii. SALVADOR ULIBARRÍ[24], b. Abt. 1782[25].
  viii. MARÍA DOLORES ULIBARRÍ[26], b. Abt. 1785[27].
  ix. MARÍA GERTRUDES ULIBARRÍ[28], b. Abt. 1787[29].

Generation No. 5

5. SANTIAGO JOSÉ[5] ULIBARRÍ *(JOAQUÍN SANTA ANA[4], JUAN HURTADO[3] DE ULIBARRÍ, JUAN[2], JOSÉ ENRÍQUES[1] DE LOS REYES)*[30] was born 1775 in Belén, El Reyno de Nuevo México[31]. He married MARÍA ENCARNACIÓN LUCERO[32].

Child of SANTIAGO ULIBARRÍ and MARÍA LUCERO is:
6. i.   SANTIAGO LUCERO[6] ULIBARRÍ, b. Abt. 1818, Belén, El Reyno de Nuevo México, Nueva España.

Generation No. 6

6. SANTIAGO LUCERO[6] ULIBARRÍ *(SANTIAGO JOSÉ[5], JOAQUÍN SANTA ANA[4], JUAN HURTADO[3] DE ULIBARRÍ, JUAN[2], JOSÉ ENRÍQUES[1] DE LOS REYES)*[33] was born Abt. 1818 in Belén, El Reyno de Nuevo México, Nueva España[34]. He married (1) JUANA BERNARDINA ROMERO GALLEGOS[35,36], daughter of JOSÉ GALLEGOS and JUANA ROMERO.

Notes for SANTIAGO LUCERO ULIBARRÍ:
Also known as Santiago Rivali.
1850 & 1860 Census: Living in La Polvadera de San Lorenzo, Territory of New México.
1870 Census: Living in San Patricio, Territory of New México.

Children of SANTIAGO ULIBARRÍ and JUANA GALLEGOS are:
  i.   CARMELIA[7] ULIBARRÍ, b. Abt. 1842, La Plaza de Pulvidera, Nuevo México, La República de México[37].

        Notes for CARMELIA ULIBARRÍ:
        Also known as María del Carmel Ulibarrí.

  ii. JUANA ULIBARRÍ, b. Abt. 1844, La Plaza de Pulvidera, Nuevo México, La República de México[37].
7. iii. JUAN GALLEGOS ULIBARRÍ, b. Abt. 1846, San Lorenzo de Pulvidero, Territory of New México.
8. iv. BENITO ULIBARRÍ, b. Abt. 1849, San Lorenzo de Pulvidero, Territory of New México.
  v.   MARÍA ULIBARRÍ, b. Abt. 1853, La Polvadera de San Lorenzo, Territory of New México[38].

Child of SANTIAGO LUCERO ULIBARRÍ is:
9. vi. JOSÉ ANTONIO[7] ULIBARRÍ, b. Abt. 1832, Belén, Nuevo México, La República de México.

Generation No. 7

7. JUAN GALLEGOS[7] ULIBARRÍ *(SANTIAGO LUCERO[6], SANTIAGO JOSÉ[5], JOAQUÍN SANTA ANA[4], JUAN HURTADO[3] DE ULIBARRÍ, JUAN[2], JOSÉ ENRÍQUES[1] DE LOS REYES)* was born Abt. 1846 in San Lorenzo de Pulvidero, Territory of New México[39]. He married (1) CIPRIANA LUCERO January 02, 1865 in Tomé, Territory of New México[40], daughter of JUAN LUSERO and MARCELINA JARAMILLO. He married (2) ISABELA MONTOYA May 13, 1889 in Lincoln County, Territory of New México[41], daughter of TRANQUILINO MONTOYA and MARÍA TRUJILLO.

Notes for JUAN GALLEGOS ULIBARRÍ:
Also known as Juan Rivali.

1860 Census: Living in La Polvadera de San Lorenzo, Territory of New México.
1870, 1880 & 1900 Census: Living in San Patricio, Territory of New México.
One of the founding families of La Plaza de San Patricio.

Notes for CIPRIANA LUCERO:
Also known as María Cipriana Lucero.

Notes for ISABELA MONTOYA:
Also known as María Isabel Montoya.

Children of JUAN ULIBARRÍ and CIPRIANA LUCERO are:
10.   i.   AMBROSIA[8] ULIBARRÍ, b. Abt. 1865.
11.   ii.   SARAFINA SOCORRO ULIBARRÍ, b. Abt. 1868; d. Bef. 1921.
12.   iii. VICENTE ULIBARRÍ, b. January 22, 1870, San Patricio, Territory of New México; d. November 08, 1949.

Child of JUAN ULIBARRÍ and ISABELA MONTOYA is:
       iv.   JUANITA[8] ULIBARRÍ, b. May 1892[42].

8. BENITO[7] ULIBARRÍ *(SANTIAGO LUCERO[6], SANTIAGO JOSÉ[5], JOAQUÍN SANTA ANA[4], JUAN HURTADO[3] DE ULIBARRÍ, JUAN[2], JOSÉ ENRÍQUES[1] DE LOS REYES)* was born Abt. 1849 in San Lorenzo de Pulvidero, Territory of New México[43]. He married JUANITA SÁNCHEZ.

Notes for BENITO ULIBARRÍ:
1870: Living in La Plaza de San José, Territory of New México.

Children of BENITO ULIBARRÍ and JUANITA SÁNCHEZ are:
       i.   MARÍA[8] ULIBARRÍ.
       ii.   TIBORCIA ULIBARRÍ, b. Abt. 1866[44].

9. JOSÉ ANTONIO[7] ULIBARRÍ *(SANTIAGO LUCERO[6], SANTIAGO JOSÉ[5], JOAQUÍN SANTA ANA[4], JUAN HURTADO[3] DE ULIBARRÍ, JUAN[2], JOSÉ ENRÍQUES[1] DE LOS REYES)* was born Abt. 1832 in Belén, Nuevo México, La República de México[45]. He married MANUELA DE ULIBARRÍ.

Notes for JOSÉ ANTONIO ULIBARRÍ:
1860 Census: Living in La Polvadera de San Lorenzo, Territory of New México.
1870 Census: Living in Lincoln County, Precinct 2, Territory of New México.
Land Patent # NMNMAA 010817, on the authority of the Homestead Entry-Original (12 Stat. 392), May 20, 1862. Issued 160 acres.

Children of JOSÉ ULIBARRÍ and MANUELA DE ULIBARRÍ are:
       i.   LORENSA[8] ULIBARRÍ, b. 1857[46].
       ii.   JUANA ULIBARRÍ, b. 1862[46].
       iii. FELIS ULIBARRÍ, b. 1864[46].
       iv.   JUAN ULIBARRÍ, b. 1866[46].

       Notes for JUAN ULIBARRÍ:
       Land Patent # NMNMAA 010823, on the authority of the Homestead Entry-Original (12 Stat. 392), May 20, 1862. Issued 160 acres.

Generation No. 8

10. AMBROSIA[8] ULIBARRÍ *(JUAN GALLEGOS[7], SANTIAGO LUCERO[6], SANTIAGO JOSÉ[5], JOAQUÍN SANTA ANA[4], JUAN HURTADO[3] DE ULIBARRÍ, JUAN[2], JOSÉ ENRÍQUES[1] DE LOS REYES)* was born Abt. 1865[47]. She married HILARIO SILVA April 13, 1892[48], son of MANUEL SILVA and JOSEFITA ESQUIVEL.

Notes for HILARIO SILVA:
Also known as Ylario.

Children of AMBROSIA ULIBARRÍ and HILARIO SILVA are:
13.   i.   ALBINA[9] SILVA, b. March 19, 1884, San Patricio, Territory of New México.

14.   ii.   TELESFORO SILVA, b. April 18, 1885, Tularoso, Territory of New México; d. September 08, 1976, Ruidoso Downs, New México.

11. SARAFINA SOCORRO[8] ULIBARRÍ *(JUAN GALLEGOS[7], SANTIAGO LUCERO[6], SANTIAGO JOSÉ[5], JOAQUÍN SANTA ANA[4], JUAN HURTADO[3] DE ULIBARRÍ, JUAN[2], JOSÉ ENRÍQUES[1] DE LOS REYES)* was born Abt. 1868[49], and died Bef. 1921. She married ESTANISLADO TRUJILLO MONTOYA[50] January 09, 1887 in San Patricio, Territory of New México[51], son of TRANQUILINO MONTOYA and MARÍA TRUJILLO.

Notes for ESTANISLADO TRUJILLO MONTOYA:
Also known as Tanislado, Tanislaus.
Land Patent # NMLC 0026044, on the authority of the Homestead Entry-Enlarged (35 Stat. 639), February 19, 1909. Issued 164.56 acres on April 09, 1926.

Children of SARAFINA ULIBARRÍ and ESTANISLADO MONTOYA are:
15.   i.   MANUEL ULIBARRÍ[9] MONTOYA, b. 1888, San Patricio, New México; d. Bef. 1920.
16.   ii.   PABLITA MONTOYA, b. May 21, 1890, San Patricio, Territory of New México; d. March 31, 1952, San Patricio, New México.
17.   iii.   TEODORO ULIBARRÍ MONTOYA, b. December 18, 1892, San Patricio, Territory of New México; d. March 08, 1976, Glencoe, New México.
        iv.   CANDIDO ULIBARRÍ MONTOYA, b. 1895, San Patricio, New México[52].
18.   v.   SUSANA MONTOYA, b. 1897, San Patricio, Territory of New México; d. June 17, 1938.
        vi.   ISABEL MONTOYA, b. December 29, 1899, San Patricio, New México[53]; m. (1) CONCHA DE MONTOYA, El Paso, Texas; m. (2) VICTORIA SÁNCHEZ[54], February 23, 1921[55].
        vii.   DESIDERIO MONTOYA, b. February 15, 1902, San Patricio, Territory of New México[56]; m. CATALINA SALAZAR, March 09, 1926, Capitán, New México[56].

            Notes for DESIDERIO MONTOYA:
            Baptismal records indicate that he was born on December 22, 1901. (Microfiche# 0016754, Page 121)

19.   viii.   SENAIDA MONTOYA, b. May 19, 1907, San Patricio, Territory of New México; d. July 10, 1944, Roswell, New México.

12. VICENTE[8] ULIBARRÍ *(JUAN GALLEGOS[7], SANTIAGO LUCERO[6], SANTIAGO JOSÉ[5], JOAQUÍN SANTA ANA[4], JUAN HURTADO[3] DE ULIBARRÍ, JUAN[2], JOSÉ ENRÍQUES[1] DE LOS REYES)* was born January 22, 1870 in San Patricio, Territory of New México[57], and died November 08, 1949. He married MARÍA SARAFINA SEDILLO November 06, 1922, daughter of JUAN SEDILLO and JOSEFA FAJARDO.

Notes for VICENTE ULIBARRÍ:
Also known as Vicente Rivali.
1920 Census: Living in Cloudcroft, New México.

Children of VICENTE ULIBARRÍ and MARÍA SEDILLO are:
20.   i.   AUGUSTINA[9] ULIBARRÍ, b. September 26, 1892, San Patricio, New México; d. April 29, 1970.
        ii.   MARÍA ULIBARRÍ[58], b. October 20, 1895, San Patricio, Territory of New México[59]; m. JOSÉ SILVA CHÁVEZ[60], November 02, 1911, Picacho, Territory of New México[60].

            Notes for MARÍA ULIBARRÍ:
            Also known as Marilla.

21.   iii.   EPIFANIO ULIBARRÍ, b. August 22, 1896, San Patricio, Territory of New México; d. October 17, 1928, San Patricio, New México.
22.   iv.   SOFIA ULIBARRÍ, b. 1905, San Patricio, Territory of New México; d. October 16, 1941.
23.   v.   PETRA ULIBARRÍ, b. June 27, 1907, San Patricio, Territory of New México; d. October 1977, San Patricio, New México.
24.   vi.   DOMINGA ULIBARRÍ, b. October 02, 1910, San Patricio, Territory of New México; d. June 13, 2001, Hondo, New México.

Generation No. 9

13. ALBINA[9] SILVA *(AMBROSIA[8] ULIBARRÍ, JUAN GALLEGOS[7], SANTIAGO LUCERO[6], SANTIAGO JOSÉ[5], JOAQUÍN SANTA ANA[4], JUAN HURTADO[3] DE ULIBARRÍ, JUAN[2], JOSÉ ENRÍQUES[1] DE LOS REYES)[61]* was born March 19, 1884 in San Patricio, Territory of New México. She married DOROTEO MONTOYA November 20, 1907 in Lincoln County, Territory of New México[62], son of TRANQUILINO MONTOYA and MARÍA TRUJILLO.

Notes for ALBINA SILVA:
Also known as Alvina, Balbina.

Notes for DOROTEO MONTOYA:
Baptized: February 15, 1886. Padrinos: Pedro Trujillo, Andrea Miranda.
1920 Census: Living in Las Palas, New México.

Children of ALBINA SILVA and DOROTEO MONTOYA are:

	i.	SAMUEL[10] MONTOYA[63], b. May 19, 1909[64]; d. May 03, 1994, Tinnie, New México; m. EUFRACIA MONTOYA[65], November 26, 1938[66].

         Notes for SAMUEL MONTOYA:
         Also known as Sam.

	ii.	COSMÉ MONTOYA[67], b. May 26, 1911, San Patricio, Territory of New México[68]; d. January 03, 1994, Anthony, New México[69]; m. AMALIA BENAVIDEZ.
25.	iii.	LORENSITA MONTOYA, b. February 09, 1914, San Patricio, New México; d. April 21, 2000, Artesia, New México.
26.	iv.	JOSEFITA MONTOYA, b. September 06, 1918; d. May 18, 2003.
27.	v.	TRANQUELINO SILVA MONTOYA, b. August 22, 1925, Arabela, New México; d. September 24, 2009, Alamagordo, New México.

14. TELESFORO[9] SILVA *(AMBROSIA[8] ULIBARRÍ, JUAN GALLEGOS[7], SANTIAGO LUCERO[6], SANTIAGO JOSÉ[5], JOAQUÍN SANTA ANA[4], JUAN HURTADO[3] DE ULIBARRÍ, JUAN[2], JOSÉ ENRÍQUES[1] DE LOS REYES)[70]* was born April 18, 1885 in Tularoso, Territory of New México, and died September 08, 1976 in Ruidoso Downs, New México. He married (1) FRANCISCA UDERO RODELA October 27, 1905 in San Patricio, Territory of New México[71], daughter of ANDRÉS RODELA and INEZ UDERO. He married (2) ERINEA BENAVIDEZ[72] November 29, 1911, daughter of JUAN BENAVIDEZ and TEOFILA TRUJILLO.

Notes for TELESFORO SILVA:
Also known as Telesforo.
1920 Census: Living in Capitán, New México.

Notes for FRANCISCA UDERO RODELA:
Raised by Andrés Rodela.

Notes for ERINEA BENAVIDEZ:
1900 Census: Living with her grandfather, Benito Trujillo and grandmother, María Igenia Sedillo de Trujillo.

Children of TELESFORO SILVA and FRANCISCA RODELA are:

28.	i.	EDUARDO[10] SILVA, b. August 10, 1908; d. 1998.
	ii.	ANGELITA SILVA, b. Abt. October 1909.

Children of TELESFORO SILVA and ERINEA BENAVIDEZ are:

         BENITO[10] SILVA[73], b. October 22, 1912, Hondo, New México[74]; d. December 1986, Ruidoso Downs, New México; m. CONSUELO SÁNCHEZ[75], February 13, 1932, Glencoe, New México[76].

         Notes for BENITO SILVA:
         1920 Census shows that he was living with his uncle, Manuel Benavidez.

         Notes for CONSUELO SÁNCHEZ:
         Also known as Consolación.
         Lincoln County marriage records indicate that she was born on April 02, 1913.

Buried in Tularosa Catholic Cemetery.

29.   iv.   AMBROCIA SILVA, b. April 15, 1915, Hondo, New México.
             v.   ANSELMO SILVA[77], b. April 21, 1919, Hondo, New México[78]; d. December 10, 1992, Ruidoso Downs, New México; m. VIRGINIA MIRANDA, November 04, 1948, Ruidoso, New México[79].
             vi.   BONIFACIO SILVA, b. May 15, 1923, Lincoln, New México[80].
             vii.   ONESIMA SILVA, b. Private.
             viii.   RAMÓN SILVA, b. Private; m. CARMELITA SILVA.
             ix.   VICTOR SILVA, b. Private.

15. MANUEL ULIBARRÍ[9] MONTOYA *(SARAFINA SOCORRO[8] ULIBARRÍ, JUAN GALLEGOS[7], SANTIAGO LUCERO[6], SANTIAGO JOSÉ[5], JOAQUÍN SANTA ANA[4], JUAN HURTADO[3] DE ULIBARRÍ, JUAN[2], JOSÉ ENRÍQUES[1] DE LOS REYES)* was born 1888 in San Patricio, New México[81], and died Bef. 1920[82]. He married MARTINA PROVENCIO[83] October 01, 1911, daughter of JOSÉ PROVENCIO and VICTORIA FAJARDO.

Children of MANUEL MONTOYA and MARTINA PROVENCIO are:
             i.   FELIX[10] MONTOYA.
             ii.   LUÍS MONTOYA, b. Abt. 1913[84].
             iii.   JUANITA MONTOYA, b. Abt. 1914[84].
             iv.   GILBERTO MONTOYA, b. Abt. 1917[84].

16. PABLITA[9] MONTOYA *(SARAFINA SOCORRO[8] ULIBARRÍ, JUAN GALLEGOS[7], SANTIAGO LUCERO[6], SANTIAGO JOSÉ[5], JOAQUÍN SANTA ANA[4], JUAN HURTADO[3] DE ULIBARRÍ, JUAN[2], JOSÉ ENRÍQUES[1] DE LOS REYES)* was born May 21, 1890 in San Patricio, Territory of New México, and died March 31, 1952 in San Patricio, New México. She married JULIO MOLINA MIRANDA November 15, 1909 in San Patricio, Territory of New México[85], son of JULIO MIRANDA and ANTONIA MOLINA.

Notes for PABLITA MONTOYA:
Also known as Paula.

Children of PABLITA MONTOYA and JULIO MIRANDA are:
             i.   CARLOS[10] MIRANDA[86], b. January 03, 1910[87]; d. January 02, 1972.
             ii.   ENRÍQUE MIRANDA, b. Abt. 1913[87].
             iii.   FRANCISCA MIRANDA, b. Abt. 1914[87]; m. ANTONIO HERRERA.
             iv.   CANDIDO MIRANDA[88], b. September 02, 1918, San Patricio, New México[89]; d. October 17, 1990, Socorro, New México[90].

                     Notes for CANDIDO MIRANDA:
                     Private First Class. World War II.

             v.   GALINA MIRANDA[91], b. January 15, 1926, San Patricio, New México; d. February 25, 1926, San Patricio, New México.
30.   vi.   EULALIA MIRANDA, b. December 10, 1920, San Patricio, New México; d. August 08, 1977, El Paso, Texas.
             vii.   VIRGINIA MIRANDA, b. January 12, 1932, San Patricio, New México[92]; m. ANSELMO SILVA[93], November 04, 1948, Ruidoso, New México[94].

17. TEODORO ULIBARRÍ[9] MONTOYA *(SARAFINA SOCORRO[8] ULIBARRÍ, JUAN GALLEGOS[7], SANTIAGO LUCERO[6], SANTIAGO JOSÉ[5], JOAQUÍN SANTA ANA[4], JUAN HURTADO[3] DE ULIBARRÍ, JUAN[2], JOSÉ ENRÍQUES[1] DE LOS REYES)[95]* was born December 18, 1892 in San Patricio, Territory of New México[96], and died March 08, 1976 in Glencoe, New México. He married BERSABÉ SÁNCHEZ December 11, 1919 in San Patricio, New México[97], daughter of JUAN SÁNCHES and VISITA SÁNCHEZ.

Notes for TEODORO ULIBARRÍ MONTOYA:
Also known as Theodoro.

Children of TEODORO MONTOYA and BERSABÉ SÁNCHEZ are:
             i.   AMELIA[10] MONTOYA, b. Abt. 1920, Glencoe, New México[98].
31.   ii.   ALVESITA MONTOYA, b. January 26, 1921, Glencoe, New México.
             iii.   CANDIDO SÁNCHEZ MONTOYA[99], b. November 14, 1923, Glencoe, New México; d. June 23, 1992, Ruidoso Downs, New México; m. CRUSITA BENAVIDEZ SÁNCHEZ[100], November 09, 1946, Carrizozo, New México[101].

    iv.   ANSELMO MONTOYA, b. Abt. 1926, Glencoe, New México[102].

18. SUSANA[9] MONTOYA *(SARAFINA SOCORRO[8] ULIBARRÍ, JUAN GALLEGOS[7], SANTIAGO LUCERO[6], SANTIAGO JOSÉ[5], JOAQUÍN SANTA ANA[4], JUAN HURTADO[3] DE ULIBARRÍ, JUAN[2], JOSÉ ENRÍQUES[1] DE LOS REYES)[103]* was born 1897 in San Patricio, Territory of New México[104], and died June 17, 1938[105]. She married LORENSO MENDOSA[106] September 13, 1915 in Lincoln, New México[107], son of DIONICIO MENDOSA and MARÍA DE MENDOSA.

Notes for SUSANA MONTOYA:
Also known as Socorro, Susanita.

Notes for LORENSO MENDOSA:
Rosenda's son.

Children of SUSANA MONTOYA and LORENSO MENDOSA are:
    i.   TONITA[10] MENDOSA, b. Abt. 1917[108].
    ii.   SOCORRO MENDOSA[109], b. December 02, 1919, San Patricio, New México[110]; m. PABLO HERNÁNDEZ[111], June 19, 1940, Hondo, New México[111].
    iii.   BENJAMÍN MENDOSA[112], b. Abt. 1921, Hondo, New México[113]; d. June 25, 1942, Hondo, New México.
32.   iv.   CONSUELO MENDOSA, b. October 09, 1926; d. December 19, 2006, Roswell, New México.
    v.   ELISA MENDOSA[114], b. May 12, 1930, San Patricio, New México; d. July 02, 2000, San Patricio, New México; m. ISMAEL CHÁVEZ[115].
    vi.   DIONICIO MENDOSA, b. Private; m. ANA MAE SUTHERLAND.

        Notes for DIONICIO MENDOSA:
        Also known as Dennis.

    vii.   ELOY MENDOSA, b. Private.
    viii.   ERNESTO MENDOSA, b. Private.
    ix.   PORFIRIO MENDOSA, b. Private.
    x.   ROSENDA LIDIA MENDOSA[116], b. Abt. 1938, San Patricio, New México; d. January 27, 1938, San Patricio, New México.

19. SENAIDA[9] MONTOYA *(SARAFINA SOCORRO[8] ULIBARRÍ, JUAN GALLEGOS[7], SANTIAGO LUCERO[6], SANTIAGO JOSÉ[5], JOAQUÍN SANTA ANA[4], JUAN HURTADO[3] DE ULIBARRÍ, JUAN[2], JOSÉ ENRÍQUES[1] DE LOS REYES)[117]* was born May 19, 1907 in San Patricio, Territory of New México, and died July 10, 1944 in Roswell, New México. She married EDUARDO SÁNCHEZ[117] October 08, 1920 in San Patricio, New México[118], son of JUAN SÁNCHES and VISITA SÁNCHEZ.

Notes for SENAIDA MONTOYA:
Also known as Maclofa Montoya.

Notes for EDUARDO SÁNCHEZ:
Raised by María de la Visitación Sánchez.
1900 Census: Indicates that he was the adopted son of José Manuel Sánchez. (Born Oct. 1893) It also indicates that he was the son of Visita Sánchez. (Born Oct 1895)
1910 Census: Indicates that he was the adopted son of José Manuel Sánchez. (Born 1895)
1920 Census: Indicates that he was the son of Visita Sánchez. (Born 1896)

Children of SENAIDA MONTOYA and EDUARDO SÁNCHEZ are:
    i.   EDUARDO MONTOYA[10] SÁNCHEZ[119], b. May 26, 1921, San Patricio, New México; d. May 15, 1995.

        Notes for EDUARDO MONTOYA SÁNCHEZ:
        Also known as Lalo.

    ii.   MACLOFA SÁNCHEZ, b. Abt. 1923, San Patricio, New México[120]; m. ARISTEO HERRERA.
    iii.   JUAN SÁNCHEZ[121], b. January 26, 1924, San Patricio, New México; d. January 26, 1924, San Patricio, New México.
    iv.   MANUEL MONTOYA SÁNCHEZ[122], b. May 20, 1925, Glencoe, New México; d. March 22, 1982, Roswell, New México; m. FLORA CARABAJAL SÁNCHEZ.

        Notes for FLORA CARABAJAL SÁNCHEZ:

Also known as Florita, Florinda.

    v.   RAFAEL MONTOYA SÁNCHEZ, b. Abt. 1928, San Patricio, New México[123].
    vi. MARGARITA MONTOYA SÁNCHEZ, b. Abt. 1929, San Patricio, New México[123].

         Notes for MARGARITA MONTOYA SÁNCHEZ:
         Also known as Maggie.

    vii. SERAPIO SÁNCHEZ[124], b. Abt. 1937, San Patricio, New México; d. February 04, 1937, San Patricio, New México.
    viii. CONFERINA MONTOYA SÁNCHEZ, b. Private, San Patricio, New México.
    ix. ELFIDES SÁNCHEZ, b. Private, San Patricio, New México.
    x.   RUMELIO SÁNCHEZ, b. Private, San Patricio, New México.

20. AUGUSTINA[9] ULIBARRÍ *(VICENTE[8], JUAN GALLEGOS[7], SANTIAGO LUCERO[6], SANTIAGO JOSÉ[5], JOAQUÍN SANTA ANA[4], JUAN HURTADO[3] DE ULIBARRÍ, JUAN[2], JOSÉ ENRÍQUES[1] DE LOS REYES)[125]* was born September 26, 1892 in San Patricio, New México, and died April 29, 1970. She married RAYMUNDO SÁNCHEZ[125] December 17, 1910[126], son of JUAN SÁNCHES and VISITA SÁNCHEZ.

Notes for RAYMUNDO SÁNCHEZ:
1920 Census: Living in Cloudcroft, New México.

Children of AUGUSTINA ULIBARRÍ and RAYMUNDO SÁNCHEZ are:
    i.   EULALIA[10] SÁNCHEZ, b. December 15, 1912, San Patricio, New México[127]; m. PERFECTO SÁNCHEZ, June 17, 1929, Carrizozo, New México[127].
    ii. BENNIE SÁNCHEZ, b. July 26, 1914, San Patricio, New México[128]; m. NICOLÁS TORRES, August 25, 1931, Glencoe, New México[128].
33. iii. SOFIO SÁNCHEZ, b. May 25, 1916, San Patricio, New México; d. May 25, 1984, San Patricio, New México.
34. iv.   ANEDA ULIBARRÍ SÁNCHEZ, b. July 12, 1918, San Patricio, New México.
    v.   OLYMPIA SÁNCHEZ[129], b. May 21, 1920, San Patricio, New México[130]; d. June 05, 2010, Ruidoso, New México; m. EPUNUCENO SÁNCHEZ[131], August 27, 1938, Carrizozo, New México[132].
    vi. VISITA SÁNCHEZ[133], b. October 10, 1923, San Patricio, New México; d. April 10, 1924, San Patricio, New México.
    vii. LUÍS SÁNCHEZ, b. 1928, San Patricio, New México[134].

21. EPIFANIO[9] ULIBARRÍ *(VICENTE[8], JUAN GALLEGOS[7], SANTIAGO LUCERO[6], SANTIAGO JOSÉ[5], JOAQUÍN SANTA ANA[4], JUAN HURTADO[3] DE ULIBARRÍ, JUAN[2], JOSÉ ENRÍQUES[1] DE LOS REYES)[135]* was born August 22, 1896 in San Patricio, Territory of New México[136], and died October 17, 1928 in San Patricio, New México. He married ERMINDA CHÁVEZ[137] November 04, 1915 in Lincoln, New México[138], daughter of FRANCISCO CHÁVEZ and ESLINDA GONZÁLES.

Notes for EPIFANIO ULIBARRÍ:
1900 Census: Approximate birthdate listed as May 1895.

Children of EPIFANIO ULIBARRÍ and ERMINDA CHÁVEZ are:
    i.   ANUNCIÓN[10] ULIBARRÍ[139], b. August 13, 1917, San Patricio, New México; d. September 13, 1917, San Patricio, New México.
    ii. DIEGO ULIBARRÍ[140], b. February 20, 1920; d. April 15, 1994, Carrizozo, New México.

22. SOFIA[9] ULIBARRÍ *(VICENTE[8], JUAN GALLEGOS[7], SANTIAGO LUCERO[6], SANTIAGO JOSÉ[5], JOAQUÍN SANTA ANA[4], JUAN HURTADO[3] DE ULIBARRÍ, JUAN[2], JOSÉ ENRÍQUES[1] DE LOS REYES)* was born 1905 in San Patricio, Territory of New México[141], and died October 16, 1941. She married PABLO YBARRA April 15, 1921 in San Patricio, New México[141], son of GREGORIO YBARRA and CATARINA MONTOYA.

Child of SOFIA ULIBARRÍ and PABLO YBARRA is:
    i.   TIVORCIO[10] YBARRA, b. San Patricio, New México.

         Notes for TIVORCIO YBARRA:
         Also known as Tive.
         Raised by his grandmother, Catarina Montoya Ybarra.

23. PETRA[9] ULIBARRÍ *(VICENTE[8], JUAN GALLEGOS[7], SANTIAGO LUCERO[6], SANTIAGO JOSÉ[5], JOAQUÍN SANTA ANA[4], JUAN HURTADO[3] DE ULIBARRÍ, JUAN[2], JOSÉ ENRÍQUES[1] DE LOS REYES)[142]* was born June 27, 1907 in San Patricio, Territory of New México[143], and died October 1977 in San Patricio, New México[144]. She married DIEGO SALCIDO[145] November 06, 1922[146], son of FAUSTINO SALCIDO and MARÍA CHÁVEZ.

Notes for PETRA ULIBARRÍ:
Buried in Roswell, New México.

Children of PETRA ULIBARRÍ and DIEGO SALCIDO are:
- i.   VICENTE[10] SALCIDO[147], b. May 05, 1924[148].
- ii.   MONICA SALCIDO[149], b. February 14, 1926, San Patricio, New México[150]; d. August 05, 1991, San Patricio, New México; m. ESTOLANO TRUJILLO SÁNCHEZ[151], January 10, 1945, Carrizozo, New México[152].
- 35.   iii.   MARY SALCIDO, b. April 23, 1934, Hondo, New México; d. March 10, 2001, Dexter, New México.
- iv.   DELLA SALCIDO[153], b. Private.
- v.   FITA SALCIDO[153], b. Private.
- vi.   NORA SALCIDO[153], b. Private.

24. DOMINGA[9] ULIBARRÍ *(VICENTE[8], JUAN GALLEGOS[7], SANTIAGO LUCERO[6], SANTIAGO JOSÉ[5], JOAQUÍN SANTA ANA[4], JUAN HURTADO[3] DE ULIBARRÍ, JUAN[2], JOSÉ ENRÍQUES[1] DE LOS REYES)[154]* was born October 02, 1910 in San Patricio, Territory of New México[155], and died June 13, 2001 in Hondo, New México. She married PROCESO SALCIDO[156] December 05, 1931[157], son of FAUSTINO SALCIDO and MARÍA CHÁVEZ.

Notes for PROCESO SALCIDO:
Also known as Profeso, Proseso.

Child of DOMINGA ULIBARRÍ and PROCESO SALCIDO is:
- i.   CIRILIA OLYMPIA[10] SALCIDO[158], b. Abt. 1932, Hondo, New México; d. November 22, 1933, Hondo, New México.

Generation No. 10

25. LORENSITA[10] MONTOYA *(ALBINA[9] SILVA, AMBROSIA[8] ULIBARRÍ, JUAN GALLEGOS[7], SANTIAGO LUCERO[6], SANTIAGO JOSÉ[5], JOAQUÍN SANTA ANA[4], JUAN HURTADO[3] DE ULIBARRÍ, JUAN[2], JOSÉ ENRÍQUES[1] DE LOS REYES)[159]* was born February 09, 1914 in San Patricio, New México[160], and died April 21, 2000 in Artesia, New México. She married (1) FERNANDO SALSBERRY[161] June 15, 1929 in Carrizozo, New Mexico[162], son of JAMES SALSBERRY and MANUELITA HERRERA. She married (2) CAMILO SEDILLO[163] May 04, 1940 in Carrizozo, New México[164], son of MARTÍN SEDILLO and TOMASITA HERRERA.

Children of LORENSITA MONTOYA and FERNANDO SALSBERRY are:
- i.   CLOVÍS[11] SALSBERRY[165], b. Abt. 1934; d. May 25, 1938, Fort Stanton, New México.
- ii.   ANATALIA SALSBERRY, b. Private; m. MANUEL SOSA.
- iii.   ELOY SALSBERRY, b. Private.
- iv.   FERNANDO SALSBERRY, b. Private.

Children of LORENSITA MONTOYA and CAMILO SEDILLO are:
- v.   CRISTINA DELFIDA[11] SEDILLO[166], b. Abt. 1941, San Patricio, New México; d. February 20, 1941, San Patricio, New México.
- vi.   CRISTINA ROSA SEDILLO[167], b. Abt. 1942, San Patricio, New México; d. February 16, 1942, San Patricio, New México.
- vii.   DANNY SEDILLO[168], b. November 07, 1949; d. April 14, 2003, Artesia, New México.
- viii.   CERINIA SEDILLO, b. Private.
- ix.   DELLA SEDILLO, b. Private.
- x.   ELLIE SEDILLO, b. Private.
- xi.   MARTÍN MONTOYA SEDILLO, b. Private.

26. JOSEFITA[10] MONTOYA *(ALBINA[9] SILVA, AMBROSIA[8] ULIBARRÍ, JUAN GALLEGOS[7], SANTIAGO LUCERO[6], SANTIAGO JOSÉ[5], JOAQUÍN SANTA ANA[4], JUAN HURTADO[3] DE ULIBARRÍ, JUAN[2], JOSÉ*

ENRÍQUES[1] DE LOS REYES)[169] was born September 06, 1918, and died May 18, 2003. She married JUAN BACA[169], son of CRECENCIO CARRILLO and CATARINA BACA.

Children of JOSEFITA MONTOYA and JUAN BACA are:
    i.   CRUCITA[11] BACA, b. May 03, 1946; m. (1) DANNY CHÁVEZ.
    ii.   PETE BACA, b. Private.

27. TRANQUELINO SILVA[10] MONTOYA *(ALBINA[9] SILVA, AMBROSIA[8] ULIBARRÍ, JUAN GALLEGOS[7], SANTIAGO LUCERO[6], SANTIAGO JOSÉ[5], JOAQUÍN SANTA ANA[4], JUAN HURTADO[3] DE ULIBARRÍ, JUAN[2], JOSÉ ENRÍQUES[1] DE LOS REYES)* was born August 22, 1925 in Arabela, New México, and died September 24, 2009 in Alamagordo, New México. He married RUBY SAMORA.

Notes for TRANQUELINO SILVA MONTOYA:
Also known as Trankie.
Served in the US Army from 1944 to 1946.
Lifelong resident of Ruidoso.

Children of TRANQUELINO MONTOYA and RUBY SAMORA are:
    i.   BUDDY[11] MONTOYA, b. Private.
    ii.   CINDY MONTOYA, b. Private.
    iii.   GILBERT MONTOYA, b. Private.
    iv.   KATHY MONTOYA, b. Private.
    v.   PATSY MONTOYA, b. Private.
    vi.   TERESA SAMORA MONTOYA, b. Private.
    vii. TRANKIE MONTOYA, b. Private.
    viii. VERLA MONTOYA, b. Private.

28. EDUARDO[10] SILVA *(TELESFORO[9], AMBROSIA[8] ULIBARRÍ, JUAN GALLEGOS[7], SANTIAGO LUCERO[6], SANTIAGO JOSÉ[5], JOAQUÍN SANTA ANA[4], JUAN HURTADO[3] DE ULIBARRÍ, JUAN[2], JOSÉ ENRÍQUES[1] DE LOS REYES)* was born August 10, 1908[170], and died 1998. He married CONSUELO SALAS December 31, 1932[170], daughter of PEDRO SALAS and TEOFILA BENAVIDES.

Notes for EDUARDO SILVA:
Also known as Edward.

Notes for CONSUELO SALAS:
1930 Census: Living with Militon Sánchez and his wife Concha.

Children of EDUARDO SILVA and CONSUELO SALAS are:
    i.   CRUSITA[11] SILVA[171], b. May 03, 1935, Ruidoso, New México; d. February 13, 2012, Tularosa, New México; m. ROY CHÁVEZ[171].
    ii.   HENRY SILVA, b. February 04, 1937, Hollywood, New México[172]; m. BEATRICE GÓMEZ, June 01, 1957, San Patricio, New México[172].

29. AMBROCIA[10] SILVA *(TELESFORO[9], AMBROSIA[8] ULIBARRÍ, JUAN GALLEGOS[7], SANTIAGO LUCERO[6], SANTIAGO JOSÉ[5], JOAQUÍN SANTA ANA[4], JUAN HURTADO[3] DE ULIBARRÍ, JUAN[2], JOSÉ ENRÍQUES[1] DE LOS REYES)* was born April 15, 1915 in Hondo, New México[173]. She married PROSPERO MIRABAL GONZÁLES January 16, 1932 in Glencoe, New México[173], son of PROSPERO GONZÁLES and TELESFORA MIRABAL.

Children of AMBROCIA SILVA and PROSPERO GONZÁLES are:
    i.   LILIA[11] GONZÁLES, b. Private.
    ii.   FELIX GONZÁLES, b. Private.
    iii. DORTHY GONZÁLES, b. Private.
    iv. FLOYD GONZÁLES, b. Private.

30. EULALIA[10] MIRANDA *(PABLITA[9] MONTOYA, SARAFINA SOCORRO[8] ULIBARRÍ, JUAN GALLEGOS[7], SANTIAGO LUCERO[6], SANTIAGO JOSÉ[5], JOAQUÍN SANTA ANA[4], JUAN HURTADO[3] DE ULIBARRÍ, JUAN[2], JOSÉ ENRÍQUES[1] DE LOS REYES)[174]* was born December 10, 1920 in San Patricio, New México, and died August 08, 1977 in El Paso, Texas[175]. She married JOSÉ HERRERA, son of LUÍS HERRERA and BENJAMÍN HERNÁNDEZ.

Notes for EULALIA MIRANDA:
Also known as Ulalia.

Child of EULALIA MIRANDA and JOSÉ HERRERA is:
    i.   PABLITA[11] HERRERA, b. Private; m. BREZEL CHÁVEZ[176].

31. ALVESITA[10] MONTOYA *(TEODORO ULIBARRÍ[9], SARAFINA SOCORRO[8] ULIBARRÍ, JUAN GALLEGOS[7], SANTIAGO LUCERO[6], SANTIAGO JOSÉ[5], JOAQUÍN SANTA ANA[4], JUAN HURTADO[3] DE ULIBARRÍ, JUAN[2], JOSÉ ENRÍQUES[1] DE LOS REYES)[177]* was born January 26, 1921 in Glencoe, New México[178]. She married CARLOS SÁNCHEZ[179] July 22, 1940 in Glencoe, New México[180], son of SALOMON SÁNCHEZ and MANUELITA SÁNCHEZ.

Notes for ALVESITA MONTOYA:
Also known as Albesa.

32. CONSUELO[10] MENDOSA *(SUSANA[9] MONTOYA, SARAFINA SOCORRO[8] ULIBARRÍ, JUAN GALLEGOS[7], SANTIAGO LUCERO[6], SANTIAGO JOSÉ[5], JOAQUÍN SANTA ANA[4], JUAN HURTADO[3] DE ULIBARRÍ, JUAN[2], JOSÉ ENRÍQUES[1] DE LOS REYES)[181]* was born October 09, 1926, and died December 19, 2006 in Roswell, New México. She married ERMINIO SÁNCHEZ[181] December 07, 1944 in Roswell, New México[182], son of SIMÓN SÁNCHEZ and ANTONIA CARABAJAL.

Notes for CONSUELO MENDOSA:
Her mother died when she was 12 years old. She accepted the responibility of caring for her younger brothers and sisters.

Notes for ERMINIO SÁNCHEZ:
About 1944: Erminio and his family moved to Roswell, New México.

33. SOFIO[10] SÁNCHEZ *(AUGUSTINA[9] ULIBARRÍ, VICENTE[8], JUAN GALLEGOS[7], SANTIAGO LUCERO[6], SANTIAGO JOSÉ[5], JOAQUÍN SANTA ANA[4], JUAN HURTADO[3] DE ULIBARRÍ, JUAN[2], JOSÉ ENRÍQUES[1] DE LOS REYES)[183]* was born May 25, 1916 in San Patricio, New México[184], and died May 25, 1984 in San Patricio, New México. He married GONSAGITA SALAS[185] May 29, 1939 in Carrizozo, New México[185], daughter of PEDRO SALAS and TEOFILA BENAVIDES.

34. ANEDA ULIBARRÍ[10] SÁNCHEZ *(AUGUSTINA[9] ULIBARRÍ, VICENTE[8], JUAN GALLEGOS[7], SANTIAGO LUCERO[6], SANTIAGO JOSÉ[5], JOAQUÍN SANTA ANA[4], JUAN HURTADO[3] DE ULIBARRÍ, JUAN[2], JOSÉ ENRÍQUES[1] DE LOS REYES)* was born July 12, 1918 in San Patricio, New México[186]. She married ERMANDO CHÁVEZ[187] September 13, 1941 in Carrizozo, New México[188], son of PABLO CHÁVEZ and AMADA SÁNCHEZ.

35. MARY[10] SALCIDO *(PETRA[9] ULIBARRÍ, VICENTE[8], JUAN GALLEGOS[7], SANTIAGO LUCERO[6], SANTIAGO JOSÉ[5], JOAQUÍN SANTA ANA[4], JUAN HURTADO[3] DE ULIBARRÍ, JUAN[2], JOSÉ ENRÍQUES[1] DE LOS REYES)[191]* was born April 23, 1934 in Hondo, New México, and died March 10, 2001 in Dexter, New México. She married JERRY MARTÍNEZ[191] August 19, 1950[191].

Genealogy of José María de Vega

Generation No. 1

1. JOSÉ MARÍA[1] DE LA VEGA was born August 1845 in Morelia, Michiocán, La República de México[1], and died 1918[2]. He married (1) ESIQUIA TORRES[3]. He married (2) JOSEFA SANDOVAL[4] Abt. 1890[5], daughter of JESÚS SANDOVAL and MARÍA TORRES.

Notes for JOSÉ MARÍA DE LA VEGA:
1880 Census: Was listed as a stone mason.

Notes for ESIQUIA TORRES:
Also known as Isaquia.
José María and Esiquia had three children who died at a very young age. Antonio died at age three. Elvira died at age three. Alejandra died at age two.

Children of JOSÉ DE LA VEGA and ESIQUIA TORRES are:
- i. ANTONIO[2] VEGA, b. March 1881, Nogal, Territory of New México[6].
- ii. FLORENCIO VEGA, b. June 29, 1883, Nogal, Territory of New México[7]; d. May 15, 1966, Carrizozo, New México[8]; m. JUANA UDERO, November 02, 1909[9].
- 2. iii. MARGARITA VEGA, b. July 21, 1884, Nogal, Territory of New México.

Children of JOSÉ DE LA VEGA and JOSEFA SANDOVAL are:
- iv. PETRA[2] VEGA, b. Nogal, Territory of New México.
- v. ANTONIA VEGA, b. September 30, 1891, Nogal, Territory of New México[10].
- vi. ROSA VEGA, b. August 22, 1893, Nogal, Territory of New México[11].
- vii. PETRA VEGA, b. June 1896, Nogal, Territory of New México[12]; d. Abt. 1910.
- viii. SUSANA VEGA, b. May 24, 1899, Nogal, Territory of New México[13].
- 3. ix. JOSÉ SANDOVAL VEGA, b. June 19, 1901, Nogal, Territory of New México; d. May 26, 1945.
- 4. x. LEANDRO SANDOVAL VEGA, b. March 13, 1903, Tularoso, Territory of New México; d. April 15, 1995.
- vi. TRANQUELINO VEGA, b. July 06, 1905.
- vii. NICOLÁS VEGA, b. September 07, 1907, Nogal, Territory of New México[14]; d. 1953[15]; m. NATALIA MONTOYA, February 09, 1931, Carrizozo, New México[16].
- viii. MARTÍN VEGA, b. Abt. 1910[17].

Generation No. 2

2. MARGARITA[2] VEGA *(JOSÉ MARÍA[1] DE LA VEGA)* was born July 21, 1884 in Nogal, Territory of New México[18]. She married (1) FREDERICO LALONE November 23, 1903[19], son of TEOPHILUS LALONE and ESTANISLADA PADILLA. She married (2) MARCELINO RAMÍREZ April 17, 1921[20], son of MARGARITO RAMÍREZ and NARCISA GARCÍA.

Notes for FREDERICO LALONE:
Also known as Fred.

Notes for MARCELINO RAMÍREZ:
Also known as Max.

Children of MARGARITA VEGA and FREDERICO LALONE are:
- i. JOSEPHINE[3] LALONE, b. Abt. 1905[21].
- ii. ALBERT LALONE, b. Abt. 1906[21].
- iii. JULIAN LALONE, b. Abt. 1907[21].
- iv. FREDRICK LALONE, b. Abt. 1909[21].

3. JOSÉ SANDOVAL[2] VEGA *(JOSÉ MARÍA[1] DE LA VEGA)*[22] was born June 19, 1901 in Nogal, Territory of New México[23], and died May 26, 1945. He married AMADA VEGA.

Children of JOSÉ VEGA and AMADA VEGA are:
5.   i.   JOE S.[3] VEGA, b. December 06, 1926, Carrizozo, New México; d. September 21, 2001, Carrizozo, New México.
      ii.   MARY VEGA, b. April 05, 1928, Carrizozo, New México[24]; m. GORGONIO MCKINLEY, June 01, 1946, Lincoln, New México[24].

            Notes for GORGONIO MCKINLEY:
            US Navy. World War II.

4. LEANDRO SANDOVAL[2] VEGA *(JOSÉ MARÍA[1] DE LA VEGA)*[25] was born March 13, 1903 in Tularoso, Territory of New México, and died April 15, 1995. He married NARCISA RAMÍREZ[25] August 08, 1922 in Carrizozo, New México[26], daughter of MARGARITO RAMÍREZ and NARCISA GARCÍA.

Notes for NARCISA RAMÍREZ:
Buried: Rebentón

Children of LEANDRO VEGA and NARCISA RAMÍREZ are:
      i.   SOFIA[3] VEGA, b. March 29, 1923, Nogal, New México; d. March 23, 1992.
      ii.   IDA VEGA, b. October 30, 1924[27]; m. JOE HERRERA, October 25, 1941, Carrizozo, New México[27].
      iii. BETTY VEGA, b. July 31, 1927, Nogal, New México[28]; m. DANIEL LUERAS, June 08, 1946, Carrizozo, New México[28].
6.   iv.   LEANDRO VEGA, b. October 13, 1931, Nogal, New México; d. September 02, 2002, Ruidoso, New México.
      v.   ROBERT F. VEGA, b. October 10, 1935, Nogal, New México[29]; m. VIVIAN SANDOVAL, April 21, 1958, Carrizozo, New México[29].
      vi.   HELEN VEGA, b. July 06, 1941, Carrizozo, New México[30]; m. GORDON E. KING, January 15, 1960, Carrizozo, New México[30].
      vii. FRANCES VEGA, b. Private.
      viii. HENRY VEGA, b. Private.
7.   ix.   RICHARD VEGA, b. Private.

Generation No. 3

5. JOE S.[3] VEGA *(JOSÉ SANDOVAL[2], JOSÉ MARÍA[1] DE LA VEGA)*[31] was born December 06, 1926 in Carrizozo, New México, and died September 21, 2001 in Carrizozo, New México. He married ISABELA SANDOVAL[32].

6. LEANDRO[3] VEGA *(LEANDRO SANDOVAL[2], JOSÉ MARÍA[1] DE LA VEGA)* was born October 13, 1931 in Nogal, New México, and died September 02, 2002 in Ruidoso, New México. He married DELFINIA OLIDIA SÁNCHEZ December 27, 1958 in Hondo, New México, daughter of ROMÁN SÁNCHEZ and FLORINDA SALSBERRY.

Notes for LEANDRO VEGA:
Korean War Veteran.
Served as a Lincoln County Deputy Sheriff from 1960-1964, and from 1968-1972. He served as Lincoln County Sheriff from 1964-1968, and from 1972-1976. He served as a criminal investigator for 18 years for the 12th Judicial District.

7. RICHARD[3] VEGA *(LEANDRO SANDOVAL[2], JOSÉ MARÍA[1] DE LA VEGA)* was born Private. He married FLORA MARÍA SÁNCHEZ, daughter of ROMÁN SÁNCHEZ and FLORINDA SALSBERRY.

Genealogy of David Warner

Generation No. 1

1. DAVID[2] WARNER *(J.B.[1])* was born Abt. 1839[1]. He married PREDICANDA SÁNCHEZ[2] June 06, 1869[3], daughter of JOSÉ CHÁVEZ and MARÍA APODACA.

Notes for DAVID WARNER:
1870: Was residing in La Plaza de San José.

Notes for PREDICANDA SÁNCHEZ:
1860 Census: Living in Los Lunas, Territory of New México.
1870 Census: Living in Fort Stanton, Precinct 1, Territory of New México.
1880 Census: Living in La Plaza de San Patricio, Territory of New México.

Children of DAVID WARNER and PREDICANDA SÁNCHEZ are:
| | i. | CANDELARIA[3] WARNER, m. MANUEL CHÁVEZ SÁNCHEZ, November 29, 1883[4]. |

        Notes for MANUEL CHÁVEZ SÁNCHEZ:
        1880 Census: Living in La Plaza de San Patricio, Territory of New México. He is listed as a boarder.

	ii.	DAVÍD SÁNCHEZ WARNER.
	iii.	MANUEL SÁNCHEZ WARNER.
	iv.	EMILIA WARNER, b. Abt. 1866[5].
2.	v.	EULOJIO WARNER, b. Abt. 1869.
	v.	PRESILIANA WARNER, b. January 12, 1870, La Plaza de San José, Territory of New México[6].
	vi.	FLORENCIO WARNER, b. November 02, 1871, La Junta, Territory of New México[7].
3.	viii.	JUAN JAMES SÁNCHEZ WARNER, b. October 10, 1873, San Patricio, Territory of New México; d. April 03, 1945, San Patricio, New México.
	ix.	JACOBO WARNER, b. Abt. 1878, San Patricio, Territory of New México.

Generation No. 2

2. EULOJIO[3] WARNER *(DAVID[2], J.B.[1])* was born Abt. 1869. He married DELFINIA MEDINA in White Oaks, Territory of New México[8], daughter of JOSÉ MEDINA and MACARINA SEDILLO.

Notes for EULOJIO WARNER:
Also known as Eulojio Juana, Ologio Warner y Sánchez.

Children of EULOJIO WARNER and DELFINIA MEDINA are:
	i.	JUANA[4] WARNER, b. Abt. 1892[9].
	ii.	FELIPA WARNER, b. Abt. 1894[9].
	iii.	PABLO WARNER, b. Abt. 1895[9].
	iv.	LEONOR WARNER, b. Abt. 1899[9].
	v.	REYES WARNER, b. Abt. 1900[9].
	vi.	PAULA WARNER, b. July 04, 1900[10]; m. FERNANDO ANTONIO HERRERA, January 16, 1916, Carrizozo, New México[10].

        Notes for PAULA WARNER:
        Also known as Pabla, Paula Juana.
        About 1916: Living in Carrizozo.

        Notes for FERNANDO ANTONIO HERRERA:
        Also known as Antonio Herrera.
        About 1916: Living in White Oaks.

| | vii. | EUGENIO WARNER, b. Abt. 1907[11]. |
| 4. | viii. | ROSA WARNER, b. February 25, 1911, White Oaks, Territory of New México. |

3. JUAN JAMES SÁNCHEZ³ WARNER *(DAVID², J.B.¹)* was born October 10, 1873 in San Patricio, Territory of New México[12], and died April 03, 1945 in San Patricio, New México[13]. He married EMILIA TORREZ[14] December 10, 1900[15], daughter of CRESENCIO TORRES and MIQUELA MIRANDA.

Notes for JUAN JAMES SÁNCHEZ WARNER:
Also known as Juan Juana, Juan Guana.
Baptismal Padrinos: Diego Salcido, Miquela Baca.
Land Patent # NMR 0028334, on the authority of the Homestead Entry-Enlarged (35 Stat. 639), February 19, 1909. Issued 161.09 acres on October 19, 1917.
Land Patent # NMLC 0025802, on the authority of the Homestead Entry-Stock Raising (39 Stat. 862), December 29, 1916. Issued 320 acres on June 24, 1926.

Children of JUAN WARNER and EMILIA TORREZ are:
5.   i.   MANUEL⁴ WARNER, b. 1903, San Patricio, Territory of New México.
6.   ii.   PREDICANDA WARNER, b. November 24, 1903, San Patricio, Territory of New México; d. August 04, 1978, Hondo, New México.
7.   iii.   APOLONIA WARNER, b. October 12, 1909, San Patricio, Territory of New México.
    iv.   STELLA WARNER[16], b. June 26, 1914, San Patricio, New México[17]; d. July 12, 2007, Ruidoso Downs, New México; m. YLARIO SALAS[18], December 01, 1951, Ruidoso, New México[19].

         Notes for YLARIO SALAS:
         Private US Army. World War Two.

    v.   ELOY WARNER[20], b. June 17, 1916, San Patricio, New México; d. October 20, 1968.
8.   vi.   JULIANITA WARNER, b. August 01, 1918, San Patricio, New México; d. July 07, 2006, Covington, Louisiana.
9.   vii.   FRANCIS WARNER, b. February 18, 1921, San Patricio, New México.
    viii.   VIOLA WARNER, b. May 19, 1923, San Patricio, New México[21]; m. TRUMAN SÁNCHEZ, January 01, 1944, Carrizozo, New México[21].
    ix.   ALICE WARNER, b. December 18, 1926, San Patricio, New México[22]; m. MANUEL C. LUCERO, October 26, 1946, Carrizozo, New México[22].

Generation No. 3

4. ROSA⁴ WARNER *(EULOJIO³, DAVID², J.B.¹)* was born February 25, 1911 in White Oaks, Territory of New México[23]. She married (1) JOSÉ SANDOVAL CHÁVEZ September 19, 1926 in Carrizozo, New México[24], son of JOSÉ CHÁVEZ and DOLORES SANDOVAL. She married (2) MANUEL CHÁVEZ[25] June 13, 1934 in Carrizozo, New México[26], son of SATURNINO CHÁVEZ and MAGGIE VAN SYCKLE.

Notes for JOSÉ SANDOVAL CHÁVEZ:
Also known as Joe.
1930 Census: Living in Carrizozo, New México.

Children of ROSA WARNER and JOSÉ CHÁVEZ are:
    i.   JOE⁵ CHÁVEZ, b. Abt. 1928, Carrizozo, New México[27].
    ii.   FELIPA CHÁVEZ, b. Abt. 1930, Carrizozo, New México[27].

5. MANUEL⁴ WARNER *(JUAN JAMES SÁNCHEZ³, DAVID², J.B.¹)* was born 1903 in San Patricio, Territory of New México[28]. He married TANISLADA PRUDENCIO, daughter of CATARINO PROVENCIO and ANITA GARCÍA.

Children of MANUEL WARNER and TANISLADA PRUDENCIO are:
    i.   URBANO⁵ WARNER. Died young.
    ii.   JOE WARNER, b. Private.

6. PREDICANDA⁴ WARNER *(JUAN JAMES SÁNCHEZ³, DAVID², J.B.¹)*[29] was born November 24, 1903 in San Patricio, Territory of New México, and died August 04, 1978 in Hondo, New México. She married FAUSTINO CHÁVEZ SALCIDO[29] January 24, 1924[30], son of FAUSTINO SALCIDO and MARÍA CHÁVEZ.

Notes for PREDICANDA WARNER:
Also known as Predicanda Juana (Warner).

Notes for FAUSTINO CHÁVEZ SALCIDO:
Land Patent # NMLC 0028252, on the authority of the Homestead Entry-Stock Raising (39 Stat. 862), December 29, 1916. Issued 555.02 acres on October 11, 1929.

Children of PREDICANDA WARNER and FAUSTINO SALCIDO are:
    i.   ALBERT W.⁵ SALCIDO, b. October 25, 1925, Lincoln, New México³¹; m. NORA NÚÑEZ³², November 16, 1946, Carrizozo, New México³³.
    ii.   DAVÍD SALCIDO³⁴, b. June 29, 1927, Hondo, New México³⁵; d. October 03, 1958, Hondo, New México; m. MARTINA SILVA, December 13, 1950, Ruidoso, New México³⁶.
    iii. AMELIA SALCIDO, b. Abt. 1929, Hondo, New México³⁷.

7. APOLONIA⁴ WARNER *(JUAN JAMES SÁNCHEZ³, DAVID², J.B.¹)* was born October 12, 1909 in San Patricio, Territory of New México³⁸. She married MAX CORONA³⁹ June 04, 1932 in Carrizozo, New México⁴⁰, son of MANUEL CORONA and SUSANA TRUJILLO.

Notes for APOLONIA WARNER:
Also known as Pauline or Polonia.
Land Patent # NMLC 0041178, on the authority of the Homestead Entry-Stock Raising (39 Stat. 862), December 29, 1916. Issued 640 acres on March 26, 1937.

Child of APOLONIA WARNER and MAX CORONA is:
    i.   DANIEL⁵ CORONA⁴¹, b. Abt. 1933, San Patricio, New México; d. November 03, 1933, San Patricio, New México.

8. JULIANITA⁴ WARNER *(JUAN JAMES SÁNCHEZ³, DAVID², J.B.¹)* was born August 01, 1918 in San Patricio, New México⁴², and died July 07, 2006 in Covington, Louisiana⁴³. She married GEORGE TORRES ROMERO⁴⁴ November 10, 1934 in San Patricio, New México⁴⁵, son of GEORGE ROMERO and JOSEFITA TORRES.

Children of JULIANITA WARNER and GEORGE ROMERO are:
    i.   GEORGE⁵ ROMERO⁴⁶, b. February 22, 1939, Hondo, New México⁴⁷; d. May 03, 1976; m. DELMA SÁNCHEZ, December 30, 1960, Hondo, New México⁴⁷.
    ii.   SAMUEL ROMERO⁴⁸, b. September 10, 1942, San Patricio, New México; d. November 06, 1949, San Patricio, New México.
    iii. SAMMY ROMERO⁴⁹, b. 1949; d. May 13, 2006.

9. FRANCIS⁴ WARNER *(JUAN JAMES SÁNCHEZ³, DAVID², J.B.¹)⁵⁰* was born February 18, 1921 in San Patricio, New México⁵¹. She married JOSE V. BACA⁵² December 27, 1947 in San Patricio, New México⁵³, son of JOSÉ BACA and FRANCISQUITA VIGIL.

Bibliography

Athearn Frederic J. A Forgotten Kingdom: The Spanish Frontier in Colorado and New Mexico, 1540-1821 [Online] = A Forgotten Kingdom: The Spanish Frontier in Colorado and New Mexico, 1540-1821. - 1989. - September 8, 2012. - http://www.nps.gov/history/history/online_books/blm/ut/29/chap2.htm.

Blazer Almer N. Santana: War Chief of the Mescalero Apaché [Book]. - [s.l.] : Dog Soldier Press, 1999.

Bustamante Adrian H. Santa Fe: History of an Ancient City [Book] = Santa Fé Society in the Eighteenth Century: Españoles, Castas y Labradores / ed. Noble David Grant. - [s.l.] : School of American Research Press, 1989.

Carnegie Institution of Washington Historical Documents Relating to New México, Nueva Vizcaya, and Approaches Thereto, to 1773 [Book] / ed. Hackett Charles Wilson. - [s.l.] : Carnegie Institution of Washington, 1937. - Vol. 3.

Chávez Angélico Orgins of New México Families [Book]. - [s.l.] : Museum of New México Press, 1992. - Revised.

Clements Arthur A History of Lincoln County Post Offices [Book]. - [s.l.] : Lincoln County Postmasters, 1994.

Colligan John B. The Juan Paéz Hurtado Expedition of 1695: Fraud in Recruiting Colonists for New México [Book].

Crawford Edith L. Pedro M. Rodríguez Pioneer Story [Online] // Rootsweb. - Library of Congress, Manuscript Division: WPA Federal Writers' Project Collection, August 29, 1938. - http://ftp.rootsweb.com/pub/usgenweb/nm/lincoln/bios/pedrorodriguez.txt.

Cummings Billy Charles Patrick Frontier Parish: Recovered Catholic History of Lincoln County, 1860-1884 [Book]. - [s.l.] : Lincoln County Society Publications, 1995.

Esquibel José Antonio The Sánchez de Iñigo Puzzle: New Genealogical Considerations [Article] // El Farolito. - Winter 2003. - 4 : Vol. 6.

Fulton Maurice G. History of the Lincoln county War: A Classic Account of Billy the Kid [Book]. - [s.l.] : The University of Arizona Press, 1968.

Garate Donald T. [Online]. - http://www.anzasociety.org/Garate.html.

Greenleaf Richard E. The Founding of Albuquerque, 1706: An Historical Legal Problem [Journal]. - [s.l.] : New Mexico Historical Review, January 1964.

Hackett Charles Wilson [Journal] = The Retreat of the Spaniards from New México in 1680, and the Beginnings of El Paso I // Southwestern Historical Quarterly . - [s.l.] : Carnegie Institution of Washington.

Hackett Charles Wilson The Retreat of the Spainiards from New México in 1680 and the Beginnings of El Paso II [Journal] // Southwestern Historical Quarterly. - Vol. 16. - pp. 259-276. - 3.

Hardin Paul Polvadera y Chamisal: Two of Socorro County's Historic Villages and the San Lorenzo Land Grant [Article]. - Socorro : El Defensor Chieftain, September 04, 2010.

Harmon Roy A History of Lincoln County Post Offices [Book]. - [s.l.] : New México Chapter of the National Association of Postmasters of the United States, 1994.

Herrera Vicente [Interview]. - October 1967.

Hispanic Genealogical Research Center of New México [Online] // Hispanic Genealogical Research Center of New Mexico. - www.hgrc-nm.org.

Hughes Anne E. Studies in American History: The Beginnings of Spanish Settlement in the El Paso District [Book]. - Berkeley : University of California Press, 1914.

Hurt Wesley R. Manzano: A Study of Community Disorganization [Book]. - [s.l.] : AMS Press, Inc, 1989.

Ivey James E. "In the Midst of Lonliness": The Architectural History of the Salinas Missions [Online]. - 1988. - http://www.nps.gov/archive/sapu/hsr/hsrt.htm.

James George Wharton Indian Blankets and their Makers [Book]. - Chicago : M.A. Donahue & Co., Printers and Binders, 1914.

Keleher William A. Violence in Lincoln County: 1869-1881 [Book]. - [s.l.] : New México University Press, 1957.

Larson Carole Forgotten Frontier: The Story of Southeastern New Mexico [Book]. - Albuquerque : University of New Mexico Press, 1993.

Lincoln County Clerks Office Performance bonds June 1869 [Book]. - Carrizozo : Lincoln County Clerks Office, 1869.

memory.loc.gov [Online] // American Notes: Travels in America, 1750-1920. - http://memory.loc.gov/cgi-bin/query/r?ammem/lhbtn:@field.

Navajo History [Online] // Navajo History. - January 22, 2007. - http://www.lapahie.com/Timeline_Spanish_1751_1820.cfm.

New México Genealogical Society Aquí Se Comienza: A Genealogical History of the Founding Families of La Villa de San Felipé de Alburquerque [Book] / ed. Gloria M. Valencia y Valdez José Antonio Esquíbel, Robert D. Martínez, Francisco Sisneros. - Albuquerque : New México Genealogical Society, 2007.

New Mexico Genealogical Study New Mexico Genealogical Study [Journal]. - 1981. - 1.

Pacheco Fermín [Interview].

Reeve Frank D. History of New Mexico: Volume 2 [Book]. - [s.l.] : Lewis Historical Publishing Company, 1961.

Salsberry Augustín [Interview].

Sánchez Joseph P. Santa Fe: History of an Ancient City [Book] = Santa Fé Society in the Eighteenth Century, Twelve Days in August: The Pueblo Revolt in Santa Fé:. - [s.l.] : School of American Research Press, 1989.

Sánchez Román [Interview]. - June 1972.

Shinkle James D. Robert Casey and the Ranch on the Río Hondo [Book]. - [s.l.] : Hall-Poorbaugh Press, Inc., 1970.

Simmons Marc Ranchers Ramblers & Renegades, Shootout at Estancia Spring [Book]. - Santa Fé : Ancient City Press, 1984.

Stewart George Names of the Land: A Hiostorical Account of Place-Naming in the United States [Book]. - New York : NYRB Classics, 2008. - pp. 23-24.

The Center for Land Grant Studies [Online] // Land Grant Database Project. - http://www.southwestbooks.org/.

The University of New México Press American Guide Series, New México: A Guide to the Colorful State [Book]. - Albuquerque : The University ofr New México Press, 1940. - p. 63.

The University of New México Press To the Royal Crown Restored: The Journals of Don Diego de Vargas, New México, 1692-1694 [Book] / ed. Kessell John L., Hendricks Rick and Dodge Meredith D.. - [s.l.] : The University of New México Press, 1995.

Twitchell Ralph Emerson The Spanish Archives of New México [Book]. - [s.l.] : The Torch Press, 1914. - Vol. 1.

United States Census Bureau 1850 Population Census.

United States Census Bureau 1860 Population Census.

United States Census Bureau 1870 Population Census.

United States Census Bureau 1880 Population Census.

United States Census Bureau 1885 New México Territorial Population Census.

United States Census Bureau 1910 Population Census.

United States Census Bureau 1920 Population Census.

United States Census Bureau 1930 Population Census.

United States Census Bureau 1940 Population Census.

Web de Anza Web de Anza [Online]. - http://anza.uoregon.edu/.

Weigle Marta The Penitentes of the Southwest [Book]. - [s.l.] : Ancient City Press, 1970.

Wilson John P. Merchants Guns & Money: The Story of Lincoln County and its Wars [Book]. - [s.l.] : Museum of New Mexico Press, 1987.

wyomcases.courts.state.wy.us U.S. Supreme Court Case, Bergere vs. U.S., 168 U.S. 66 [Online]. - http://wyomcases. courts.state.wy.us/applications/oscn/DeliverDocument.asp?CiteID=414633.

Endnotes

Chapter One: Los Sánchez: Colonia, La Reconquista y el Río Abajo 1663-1777

1. George Stewart, Names of the Land: A Historical Account of Place-Naming in the United States, Page 23-24, (New York: NYRB Classics, 2008)

2. American Guide Series, New México: A Guide to the Colorful State, p.63 (The University of New México Press, 1940)

3. Fray Angélico Chávez, Origins of New México Families: Revised Edition, Introduction p. 15 (Museum of New México Press,1992)

4. Caste systems were based on purity of Spanish blood. Adrian H. Bustamante, Españoles, Castas, y Labradores: Santa Fe Society in the Eighteenth Century, p.70-74. Santa Fe: History of an Ancient City. Edited by David Grant Noble. (School of American Research Press, 1989)

5. Trades and education. Adrian H. Bustamante, Españoles, Castas, y Labradores: Santa Fe Society in the Eighteenth Century, p.68. Santa Fe: History of an Ancient City. Edited by David Grant Noble. (School of American Research Press, 1989)

6. James E Ivey, *"In the Midst of Loneliness": The Architectural History of the Salinas Missions.*. The US National Park Service. Internet website: **http://www.nps.gov/archive/sapu/hsr/hsrt.htm**, 1988, Chapter 2

7. *"In the Midst of Loneliness": The Architectural History of the Salinas Missions.* James E Ivey. The US National Park Service. Internet website: **http://www.nps.gov/archive/sapu/hsr/hsrt.htm**, 1988, Chapter 2, Sub-heading: The Administration of the Colony.

8. *"In the Midst of Loneliness": The Architectural History of the Salinas Missions.* James E Ivey. The US National Park Service. Internet website: **http://www.nps.gov/archive/sapu/hsr/hsrt.htm**, 1988, Chapter 2, Sub-heading: The Administration of the Colony.

9. *"In the Midst of Loneliness": The Architectural History of the Salinas Missions.* James E Ivey. The US National Park Service. Internet website: **http://www.nps.gov/archive/sapu/hsr/hsrt.htm**, 1988, Chapter 2, Sub-heading: The Administration of the Colony.

10. *"In the Midst of Loneliness": The Architectural History of the Salinas Missions.* James E Ivey. The US National Park Service. Internet website: **http://www.nps.gov/archive/sapu/hsr/hsrt.htm**, 1988, Chapter 2, Sub-heading: The Private Sector: Estancias and Ecomiendas.

11. *"In the Midst of Loneliness": The Architectural History of the Salinas Missions.* James E Ivey. The US National Park Service. Internet website: **http://www.nps.gov/archive/sapu/hsr/hsrt.htm**, 1988, Chapter 2, Sub-heading: The Private Sector: Estancias and Ecomiendas.

12. *"In the Midst of Loneliness": The Architectural History of the Salinas Missions.* James E Ivey. The US National Park Service. Internet website: **http://www.nps.gov/archive/sapu/hsr/hsrt.htm**, 1988, Chapter 2, Sub-heading: The Private Sector: Estancias and Ecomiendas.

13. *"In the Midst of Loneliness": The Architectural History of the Salinas Missions.* James E Ivey. The US National Park Service. Internet website: **http://www.nps.gov/archive/sapu/hsr/hsrt.htm**, 1988, Chapter 2, Sub-heading: The Private Sector: Estancias and Ecomiendas.

14. *"In the Midst of Loneliness": The Architectural History of the Salinas Missions.* James E Ivey. The US National Park Service. Internet website: **http://www.nps.gov/archive/sapu/hsr/hsrt.htm**, 1988, Chapter 2, Sub-heading: The Private Sector: Estancias and Ecomiendas.

15. *"In the Midst of Loneliness": The Architectural History of the Salinas Missions.* James E Ivey. The US National Park Service. Internet website: **http://www.nps.gov/archive/sapu/hsr/hsrt.htm**, 1988, Chapter 2, Sub-heading: The Private Sector: Estancias and Ecomiendas.

16. *"In the Midst of Loneliness": The Architectural History of the Salinas Missions.* James E Ivey. The US National Park Service. Internet website: **http://www.nps.gov/archive/sapu/hsr/hsrt.htm**, 1988, Chapter 2, Sub-heading: Ecclesiastical Administration.

17. *"In the Midst of Loneliness": The Architectural History of the Salinas Missions.* James E Ivey. The US National Park Service. Internet website: **http://www.nps.gov/archive/sapu/hsr/hsrt.htm**, 1988, Chapter 2, Sub-heading: Ecclesiastical Administration

18. *"In the Midst of Loneliness": The Architectural History of the Salinas Missions.* James E Ivey. The US National Park Service. Internet website: **http://www.nps.gov/archive/sapu/hsr/hsrt.htm,** 1988, Chapter 2

19. *"In the Midst of Loneliness": The Architectural History of the Salinas Missions.* James E Ivey. The US National Park Service. Internet website: **http://www.nps.gov/archive/sapu/hsr/hsrt.htm,** 1988, Chapter 2, Sub-heading: The Administration of the Colony.

20. American Guide Series, New México: A Guide to the Colorful State, p.67 (The University of New México Press, 1940)

21. American Guide Series, New México: A Guide to the Colorful State, p.67 (The University of New México Press, 1940)

22. American Guide Series, New México: A Guide to the Colorful State, p.67 (The University of New México Press, 1940)

23. *"In the Midst of Loneliness": The Architectural History of the Salinas Missions.* James E Ivey. The US National Park Service. Internet website: **http://www.nps.gov/archive/sapu/hsr/hsrt.htm,** 1988, Chapter 2, Sub-heading: Ecclesiastical Administration

24. *"In the Midst of Loneliness": The Architectural History of the Salinas Missions.* James E Ivey. The US National Park Service. Internet website: **http://www.nps.gov/archive/sapu/hsr/hsrt.htm,** 1988, Chapter 2, Sub-heading: Ecclesiastical Administration

25. Fray Angélico Chávez, Origins of New México Families: Revised Edition, p.280 (Museum of New México Press,1992)

26. José Antonio Esquibel, *The Sánches de Iñigo Puzzle: New Genealogical Considerations*, El Farolito Winter 2003 Vol. 6, No. 4 of the Olibama Lopez Tushar Hispanic Legacy Research Center.

27. José Antonio Esquibel, *The Sánches de Iñigo Puzzle: New Genealogical Considerations*, El Farolito Winter 2003 Vol. 6, No. 4 of the Olibama Lopez Tushar Hispanic Legacy Research Center.

28. The witch hunt of 1675 was a precursor to the Pueblo Revolt of 1680. Joseph P. Sánchez, Twelve Days in August: The Pueblo Revolt in Santa Fé: Santa Fe Society in the Eighteenth Century, p.41-42. Santa Fe: History of an Ancient City. Edited by David Grant Noble. (School of American Research Press, 1989)

29. All of the events that took place while Lt. General Alonzo García took refuge in Pueblo de Ysleta. Charles Wilson Hackett, The Retreat of the Spaniards from New México in 1680, and the Beginnings of El Paso I, p. 137-168 (Southwestern Historical Quarterly Online, Volume 016, Number 2, http://www.tsha.utexas.edu/publications/ journals/shq/online/v016/n2/article_2.html [Accessed Sun Jan 21 12:58:55 CST 2007]

30. All of the events that took place in Villa de Santa Fé as described in a letter written by Gobernador Don Antonio de Otermín on September 08, 1680. Charles Wilson Hackett, ed., Historical Documents Relating to New México, Nueva Vizcaya, and Approaches Thereto, to 1773, p.327-335 (Washington: Carnegie Institution of Washington, Volume 3, 1937)

31. Hackett, Charles Wilson, "The Retreat Of The Spaniards From New México In 1680, And The Beginnings Of El Paso I ", Volume 016, Number 2, Southwestern Historical Quarterly Online, Page 137 - 168. **http://www.tsha. utexas.edu/publications/journals/shq/online/v016/n2/article_2.html** [Accessed Sun Jan 2, 2007]

32. Hackett, Charles Wilson, "THE RETREAT OF THE SPANIARDS FROM NEW MEXICO IN 1680, AND THE BEGINNINGS OF EL PASO II ", Volume 016, Number 3, Southwestern Historical Quarterly Online, Page 259-276. http://www.tsha.utexas.edu/publications/journals/shq/online/v016/n3/article_2.html [Accessed Tue Jan 30 19:59:19 CST 2007]

33. France V. Scholes, Marc Simmons, José Antonio Esquíbel, Translated by Eleanor B. Adams, Juan Domínguez de Mendoza: Soldier and Frontiersman of the Spanish Southwest, 1627-1693, p. 33 (University of New México Press, 2012)

34. Anne E. Huges, Studies in American History, The Beginnings of Spanish Settlement in the El Paso District, p.370 (University of California Publications in History, University of California Press, Volume 1, 1914)

35. Edited by France V. Scholes, Marc Simmons, José Antonio Esquíbel, Translated by Eleanor B. Adams, Juan Domínguez de Mendoza: Soldier and Frontiersman of the Spanish Southwest, 1627-1693, p. 34 (University of New México Press, 2012)

36. France V. Scholes, Marc Simmons, José Antonio Esquíbel, Translated by Eleanor B. Adams, Juan Domínguez de Mendoza: Soldier and Frontiersman of the Spanish Southwest, 1627-1693, p. 34-36 (University of New México Press, 2012)

37. John L. Kessell, Rick Hendricks, Meredith D. Dodge (editors), To the Royal Crown Restored: The Journals of Don Diego de Vargas, New México, 1692-1694, p. 82-83 (University of New México Press, 1995)

38. Ralph Emerson Twitchell, The Spanish Archives of New México, Volume One, p. 333 (The Torch Press, 1914)

39. Edited by: France V. Scholes, Marc Simmons, José Anotnio Esquíbel, Translated by Elenor B. Adams, Juan Dimínguez de Mendoza: Soldiwer and Frontiersman of the Spanish Southwest, 1627-1693, Document 51 p. 235-237 (The University of New México Press, 2012)

40. Anne E. Huges, Studies in American History, The Beginnings of Spanish Settlement in the El Paso District, p.371-381 (University of California Publications in History, University of California Press, Volume 1, 1914)

41. American Guide Series, New México: A Guide to the Colorful State, p.68 (The University of New México Press, 1940)

42. American Guide Series, New México: A Guide to the Colorful State, p.68 (The University of New México Press, 1940)

43. Frederic J. Athearn, A Forgotten Kingdom: The Spanish Frontier in Colorado and New México, 1540-1821, p.Chapter 2 The Reconquest of New México, 1692-1704 (Bureau of Land Management- Colorado, 1989, Number 29)

44. Fray Angélico Chávez, Origins of New México Families: Revised Edition, p.280 (Museum of New México Press,1992)

45. John B. Colligan, The Juan Paéz Hurtado Expedition of 1695: Fraud in Recruiting Colonists for New México, Page 98-99 ()

46. Fray Angélico Chávez, Origins of New México Families: Revised Edition, p.280 (Museum of New México Press,1992)

47. Ralph Emerson Twitchell, The Spanish Archives of New México, Volume One, p. 230 (The Torch Press, 1914)

48. Fray Angélico Chávez, Origins of New México Families: Revised Edition, p.161 (Museum of New México Press,1992)

49. On April 27, 1713 he was listed as Alcalde for Santa Cruz de la Cañada. Ralph Emerson Twitchell, The Spanish Archives of New México, Volume One, p. 133 (The Torch Press, 1914)

50. Ralph Emerson Twitchell, The Spanish Archives of New México, Volume One, p. 99 (The Torch Press, 1914)

51. Ralph Emerson Twitchell, The Spanish Archives of New México, Volume One, p. 100 (The Torch Press, 1914)

52. HGRC Website: Hispanic Genealogical Research Center of New Mexico, www.hgrc-nm.org., Jacinto Sánches de Iñigo.

53. Fray Angélico Chávez, Origins of New México Families: Revised Edition, p.280 (Museum of New México Press,1992)

54. Fray Angélico Chávez, Origins of New México Families: Revised Edition, p.279-280 (Museum of New México Press,1992)

55. Frederic J. Athearn, A Forgotten Kingdom: The Spanish Frontier in Colorado and New México, 1540-1821, p.Chapter 2 The Reconquest of New México, 1692-1704 (Bureau of Land Management- Colorado, 1989, Number 29)

56. Fray Angélico Chávez, Origins of New México Families: Revised Edition, p.281 (Museum of New México Press,1992)

57. Juan de Candelaria provided a list of the founding families, which indicate that there were originally 12 families. Richard E. Greenleaf. The Founding of Albuquerque, 1706: An Historical Legal Problem, p. 10, (New Mexico Historical Review, January 1964)

58. American Guide Series, New México: A Guide to the Colorful State, p.68 (The University of New México Press, 1940)

59. American Guide Series, New México: A Guide to the Colorful State, p.68 (The University of New México Press, 1940)

60. Fray Angélico Chávez, Origins of New México Families: Revised Edition, p.161 (Museum of New México Press,1992)

61. American Guide Series, New México: A Guide to the Colorful State, p.69 (The University of New México Press, 1940)

Chapter Two: Migration to the Salinas Basin 1777- 1820

1. The name Juan Bautista de Anza is more commonly used today. In colonial New México, his surname was more commonly spelled with an "s" as in "Ansa", rather than a "z". Of note, Juan Bautista did spell it as "Anza". Donald T. Garate. Internet web article. http://www.anzasociety.org/Garate.html

2. The English translation of Juan Bautista de Anza's diary gives a detailed account of Juan Bautista de Anza's Comanche Campaign. Place names were given to various geologic features such as streams and mountains. Web de Anza, Internet website: http://anza.uoregon.edu/

3. The English translation of Juan Bautista de Anza's diary gives a detailed account of Juan Bautista de Anza's Comanche Campaign. Web de Anza, Internet website: http://anza.uoregon.edu/

4. American Guide Series, New México: A Guide to the Colorful State, p.69 (The University of New México Press, 1940)

5.   American Guide Series, New México: A Guide to the Colorful State, p.70 (The University of New México Press, 1940)
6.   American Guide Series, New México: A Guide to the Colorful State, p.70 (The University of New México Press, 1940)
7.   American Guide Series, New México: A Guide to the Colorful State, p.70 (The University of New México Press, 1940)
8.   American Guide Series, New México: A Guide to the Colorful State, p.71 (The University of New México Press, 1940)
9.   Marta Weigle, The Penitentes of the Southwest, p.5 (Ancient City Press, 1970)
10. All elected officers. Marta Weigle, The Penitentes of the Southwest, p.20 (Ancient City Press, 1970)
11. Marta Weigle, The Penitentes of the Southwest, *La Cuaresma*, p.28; *La Semana Santa*, *El Ejercicio*, p.31; *Descansos*, p. 28 (Ancient City Press, 1970)
12. Navajo History, Website: http://www.lapahie.com/Timeline_Spanish_1751_1820.cfm, accessed January 22, 2007.
13. Navajo History, Website: http://www.lapahie.com/Timeline_Spanish_1751_1820.cfm, accessed January 22, 2007.
14. *"In the Midst of Loneliness": The Architectural History of the Salinas Missions*. James E Ivey. The US National Park Service. Internet website: **http://www.nps.gov/archive/sapu/hsr/hsrt.htm**, 1988, Chapter 8, Sub-heading: The Manzano Grant.
15. U.S. Supreme Court Case, Bergere vs. U.S., 168 U.S. 66 (1897). Case can be found on the following website: http://wyomcases.courts.state.wy.us/applications/oscn/DeliverDocument.asp?CiteID=414633
16. *"In the Midst of Loneliness": The Architectural History of the Salinas Missions*. James E Ivey. The US National Park Service. Internet website: **http://www.nps.gov/archive/sapu/hsr/hsrt.htm**, 1988, Chapter 8, Sub-heading: Land Grants in the Salinas Basin.
17. George Wharton James, Indian Blankets and their Makers, p. 13 (M.A. Donahue & Co., Printers and Binders, Chicago, 1914) Website: http://southwest.library.arizona.edu/inbl/index.html
18. Marc Simmons, Ranchers Ramblers & Renegades, Shootout at Estancia Spring, p.45-47 (Ancient City Press, Santa Fé, New México, 1984)
19. The documentation that was provided by Bergere was written in San Fernando and was dated February 4, 1819. U.S. Supreme Court Case, Bergere vs. U.S., 168 U.S. 66 (1897). Case can be found on the following website: http://wyomcases.courts.state.wy.us/applications/oscn/DeliverDocument.asp?CiteID=414633
20. The documentation that was provided by Bergere was written in San Fernando and was dated September 12, 1819. U.S. Supreme Court Case, Bergere vs. U.S., 168 U.S. 66 (1897). Case can be found on the following website: http://wyomcases.courts.state.wy.us/applications/oscn/DeliverDocument.asp?CiteID=414633
21. Navajo History, Website: http://www.lapahie.com/Timeline_Spanish_1751_1820.cfm, accessed January 22, 2007.
22. McNitt, Tratados de paz, Jemez, Jan. 20, 1824, p.66, (1972)
23. Land Grant Database Project, Updated March 21, 2005. The Center for Land Grant Studies. Website: http://www.southwestbooks.org/.
24. *American Notes: Travels in America, 1750-1920, Part II of Greg's Commerce of the Praries*, 1831-1839, Page 23. Internet website: http://memory.loc.gov/cgi-bin/query/r?ammem/lhbtn:@field(DOCID+@lit(lhbtnth020_0023))
25. David J. Weber, The Taos Trappers: The Fur Trade in the Far Southwest, 1540-1846, pg.87 (University of Oklahoma Press, 1971)
26. *"In the Midst of Loneliness": The Architectural History of the Salinas Missions*. James E Ivey. The US National Park Service. Internet website: **http://www.nps.gov/archive/sapu/hsr/hsrt.htm**, 1988, Chapter 8, Sub-heading: The Manzano Grant.
27. Wesley R. Hurt, Manzano: A Study of Community Disorganization, p.22 (AMS Press, Inc., 1989)
28. Wesley R. Hurt, Manzano: A Study of Community Disorganization, p.173 (AMS Press, Inc., 1989)
29. The Center for Land Grant Studies, Southwest. Accessed on January 2007. Books.org, Internet website: http://www.southwestbooks.org/grants_guadalupe_torrance.htm
30. The Author visited Manzano and had discovered that the torreón is in severe disrepair. There are only remnants of the walls of the existing building, in which a grove of trees has grown amongst the ruins.
31. Wesley R. Hurt, Manzano: A Study of Community Disorganization, p.24 (AMS Press, Inc., 1989)
32. Wesley R. Hurt, Manzano: A Study of Community Disorganization, p.27-28 (AMS Press, Inc., 1989)
33. It was a village legend that the missionary friars planted the first apple orchards during the mid 1600's. A later study of the tree ring growth place the date closer to the early 1800's. Wesley R. Hurt, Manzano: A Study of Community Disorganization, p.19 (AMS Press, Inc., 1989)
34. Wesley R. Hurt, Manzano: A Study of Community Disorganization, p.25-32 (AMS Press, Inc., 1989)
35. New Mexico Genealogical Study, p.5 (No. 1, March 1981)
36. Wesley R. Hurt, Manzano: A Study of Community Disorganization, p.60 (AMS Press, Inc., 1989)
37. Wesley R. Hurt, Manzano: A Study of Community Disorganization, p.31 (AMS Press, Inc., 1989)

Chapter Three: Los Sánchez Migrate to Lincoln County, 1820-1892

1. American Guide Series, New México: A Guide to the Colorful State, p.71 (The University of New México Press, 1940)
2. American Guide Series, New México: A Guide to the Colorful State, p.71 (The University of New México Press, 1940)
3. American Guide Series, New México: A Guide to the Colorful State, p.71-72 (The University of New México Press, 1940)
4. American Guide Series, New México: A Guide to the Colorful State, p.72 (The University of New México Press, 1940)
5. American Guide Series, New México: A Guide to the Colorful State, p.72 (The University of New México Press, 1940)
6. American Guide Series, New México: A Guide to the Colorful State, p.72 (The University of New México Press, 1940)
7. American Guide Series, New México: A Guide to the Colorful State, p.73 (The University of New México Press, 1940)
8. American Guide Series, New México: A Guide to the Colorful State, p.73 (The University of New México Press, 1940)
9. American Guide Series, New México: A Guide to the Colorful State, p.73 (The University of New México Press, 1940)
10. American Guide Series, New México: A Guide to the Colorful State, p.73 (The University of New México Press, 1940)
11. American Guide Series, New México: A Guide to the Colorful State, p.73 (The University of New México Press, 1940)
12. American Guide Series, New México: A Guide to the Colorful State, p.74 (The University of New México Press, 1940)
13. American Guide Series, New México: A Guide to the Colorful State, p.74 (The University of New México Press, 1940)
14. Frank D. Reeve PhD, History of New Mexico: Volume 2, p.167-176 (Lewis Historical Publishing Company, 1961)
15. It is believed that Santana had faked his own death and had gone into seclusion. Santana resurfaced many years later after his death. Almer N. Blazer, Santana: War Chief of the Mescalero Apaché p.9-12 (Dog Soldier Press, 1999)
16. William A. Keleher, Violence in Lincoln County: 1869-1881, p. (New México University Press, 1957)
17. The settlement didn't have any official name but was referred to as Chihuahuita because many of the settlers were from Chihuahua, México. Carole Larson, Forgotten Frontier: The Story of Southeastern New Mexico, p.69 (University of New Mexico Press: Albuquerque, 1993)
18. As told by Amelia Bolton Church who had lived in Lincoln (La Placita del Río Bonito) in 1873 The local New Mexicans had claimed that El Torreón was built between 1840 and 1850. There was no record of when it was actually built. Carole Larson, Forgotten Frontier: The Story of Southeastern New Mexico, p. 69 (University of New Mexico Press: Albuquerque, 1993)
19. Billy Charles Patrick Cummings, Frontier Parish: Recovered Catholic History of Lincoln County, 1860-1884, p.11 (Lincoln County Society Publications, 1995)
20. John P. Wilson, Merchants Guns & Money: The Story of Lincoln County and its Wars, p.3 (Museum of New Mexico Press, 1987)
21. American Guide Series, New México: A Guide to the Colorful State, p.75 (The University of New México Press, 1940)
22. James D. Shinkle, Robert Casey and the Ranch on the Río Hondo, p.58 (Hall-Poorbaugh Press, Inc., 1970)
23. La Plaza de San José was Missouri Bottom's original name. Carole Larson, Forgotten Frontier: The Story of Southeastern New Mexico, p. 59 (University of New Mexico Press: Albuquerque, 1993)
24. James D. Shinkle, Robert Casey and the Ranch on the Río Hondo, p.58 (Hall-Poorbaugh Press, Inc., 1970)
25. Los Sánchez as traveling merchants as told in an interview with Román Sánchez in June of 1972 concerning the family history while they lived in La Plaza de San José/ La Plaza de Misúri.
26. Baptism records show that the Oratorio de San José, in La Plaza de San José, was in use from 1869 to 1872. A few families may have remained behind after 1872, but they surely had left soon thereafter. These baptism records can be found at the LDS Family Library in Alamogordo, New México.
27. Carole Larson, Forgotten Frontier: The Story of Southeastern New Mexico, p.104 (University of New Mexico Press: Albuquerque, 1993)
28. John P. Wilson, Merchants Guns & Money: The Story of Lincoln County and Its Wars, p.24 (Museum of New México Press, 1987)
29. Lincoln County Book of Records, Performance bonds June 1869, p. 2
30. Sometime in the 1950's this crevasse became known as Fox Cave. It is said that ? Villescaz had constructed a rock wall facing to enclose the crevasse. Eventually Fox Cave became a curio shop.
31. Derechos de Fabrica del Cemetario de San Patricio, Libro Fabrica, Enero de 1899. Accepted on behalf of the Church by Feliz Trujillo. LDS Family Library, Tularosa Church Records.

Chapter Four: Comunidades del Valle (Communities of the Valley)

1. Both Rebentón and Patos were founded at the same time. Both communities were within 1½ miles of each other. John P. Wilson, Merchants Guns & Money: The Story of Lincoln County and its Wars, p.4 (Museum of New Mexico Press, 1987)

2. A book containing a compilation of Post Offices within Lincoln County. Several different people authored the book. Roy Harmon, A History of Lincoln County Post Offices, p.23 (New México Chapter of the National Association of Postmasters of the United States, Revised July 04, 1994)

3. The U.S. Census often lists Los Maés as "Mez" or "Mace". Maurice G. Fulton, History of the Lincoln county War: A Classic Account of Billy the Kid, pg.65 (The University of Arizona Press, 1968)

4. Billy Charles Patrick Cummings, Frontier Parish: Recovered Catholic History of Lincoln County, 1860-1884, p.14 (Lincoln County Society Publications, 1995)

5. Interview with Vicente Herrera who was a lifelong resident of the community. Interview was conducted in October 1967. Peter Hurd, the world reknowed artist bought some land adjacent to La Sentinela and had appropriately named his property Rancho de la Sentinela.

6. Arthur Clements, A History of Lincoln County Post Offices, p. 27 (Lincoln County Postmasters, Revised July 04, 1994)

7. Information provided by Fermín Pacheco. Interview was conducted by Inez Gómez-Pacheco.

8. La Polvadera de San Lorenzo was known by many different names since its founding. During the early 1800's the community was refered to as La Plaza de Pulvidera. The 1845 Mexican Census referred to the community as San Lorenzo de Pulvidero. The 1850 U.S. Census referred to the community as Pulvidera. The 1860 U.S. Census refers to the community as La Polvadera de San Lorenzo. Linguistically, the correct pronunciation is Polvareda. Paul Hardin, Polvadera y Chamisal: Two of Socorro County's Historic Villages and the San Lorenzo Land Grant, p. 1 (El Defensor Chieftain, September 04, 2010) Website: http://www.caminorealheritage.org

9. The 1910 US Census still referred to the community as Las Palas. The 1920 US Census referred to the community as Los Palos. Several of the older residents of the community still refer to the area by its original name of Las Palas. Mary Louise Joiner, A History of Lincoln County Post Offices, p. 27 (Lincoln County Postmasters, Revised July 04, 1994)

10. The 1900 US Census still refered to the community as Las Tablas. Ann Earling & Oleta V. Cloud (original authors), Updated by Maxine Wright and Mike Currin, A History of Lincoln County Post Offices, p. 25 (Lincoln County Postmasters, Revised July 04, 1994)

11. Information provided by Augustín Salsberry during an interview.

12. James D. Shinkle, Robert Casey and the Ranch on the Río Hondo, p.54 (Hall-Poorbaugh Press, Inc., 1970)

13. Marciál Rodríguez had a brother named Jesús Rodríguez. This was the story of Marciál's death at the hands of the Mescalero per an account by Pedro M. Rodriguez in an interview conducted by Edith L. Crawford. Edith L Crawford, Pedro M. Rodríguez Pioneer Story, Aug 29, 1938. Library of Congress, Manuscript Division, WPA Federal Writers' Project Collection. Web site:
http://ftp.rootsweb.com/pub/usgenweb/nm/lincoln/bios/pedrorodriguez.txt

Chapter Five: Los Hijos de Sánchez

1. Francisco Sánchez provided this information during a hearing conducted in Lincoln County, in the Court of Claims in the December session of 1893. James D. Shinkle, Robert Casey and the Ranch on the Río Hondo, p.71-75 (Hall-Poorbaugh Press, Inc., 1970)

2. Maurice G. Fulton, history of the Lincoln county War: A Classic Account of Billy the Kid, pg.22 (The University of Arizona Press, 1968)

3. There were several differing accounts of the events that took place that night. Frederick Nolan, The Lincoln County War: A Documentary History, p.50-51 (University of Oklahoma Press, 1992)

4. Frederick Nolan, The Lincoln County War: A Documentary History, p.52 (University of Oklahoma Press, 1992)

5. Lily Casey Klasner, My Girlhood Among Outlaws, p.162 (University of Arizona Press, 1972)

6. Information gathered in an interview with Francisco Trujillo and conducted by Edith L. Crawford in 1937. Robert F. Kadlec, They "Knew" Billy the Kid: Interviews with Old-Time New Mexicans, p.67-71 (Ancient City Press, 1987)

7. Interview with Candido Chávez, who was Mauricio de la Trinidad Sanchez's grandson. The interview was conducted in 1975. Candido had first heard about the story from his mother, Amada Sánchez de Chávez, who was an eyewitness to the event. The names of the two brothers were Antonio Sánchez, and Juanguerro Sánchez. It had been noted that

the Sánchez brothers were responsible for the death of James "Jim" B. Reese on August 02, 1878. Frederick Nolan, The West of Billy the Kid, p.170 (University of Oklahoma Press, 1998)

8. Interview with Candido Chávez, who was an eyewitness to the events that took place. The interview was conducted in 1975.

9. Interview with Candido Chávez who was Pablo Chávez's son. The interview was conducted in 1975.

10. Family legend was that Avrora Sánchez de Chávez had died in Torreón. José and his children were not living in Lincoln County by the time Pablo Chávez was born. Thus it is presumed that Pablo was the son of Avrora, rather than María Francisca Luna. Interview with Candido Chávez who was Pablo Chávez's son. The interview was conducted in 1975.

11. The events that lead to Pablo and Amada losing their land. Interview with Hermando Chávez who was Pablo Chávez's youngest son.

Chapter Six: La Vida Díaria (Daily Life)

1. Phil Lovato, Las Acequias del Norte, p.13 (Four Corners Regional Commission and Kit Carson Memorial Foundation, 1974)
2. Phil Lovato, Las Acequias del Norte, p.25 (Four Corners Regional Commission and Kit Carson Memorial Foundation, 1974)
3. State of New México: State Engineer Office, State vs. Lewis No. 20294 and 22600, Río Hondo Stream System Adjudicated Water Rights, p.1-2 (April, 01, 1987)
4. State of New México: State Engineer Office, State vs. Lewis No. 20294 and 22600, Río Hondo Stream System Adjudicated Water Rights, p.4 (April, 01, 1987)
5. Alejandro Polaco's real name was Alexander Jan Grzelachowski. Billy Charles Patrick Cummings, Frontier Parish: Recovered Catholic History of Lincoln County, 1860-1884, p.1-2 (Lincoln County Society Publications, 1995)
6. Jean Baptiste Lamy was actually returning from a trip from Colorado. The Archbishop and his entourage came through the Capitán Gap to Fort Stanton. The entire trip was estimated to be about 900 miles. Paul Horgan, Lamy of Santa Fé: His Life and Times, p.327 (Farrar, Straus and Giroux, 1975)
7. The chapel on the Río Bonito was listed as a mission church in the Manzano parish. Sadlier, Sadlier's Catholic Directory, p. 160 (Sadlier & Co., 1867). The chapel was also known as *La Bonita capilla del Río Bonito*. Billy Charles Patrick Cummings, Frontier Parish: Recovered Catholic History of Lincoln County, 1860-1884, p.9-13 (Lincoln County Society Publications, 1995)
8. Padre Sambrano was born in Arroyo Seco, which is located in northern New México. Billy Charles Patrick Cummings, Frontier Parish: Recovered Catholic History of Lincoln County, 1860-1884, p.39 (Lincoln County Society Publications, 1995)
9. Billy Charles Patrick Cummings, Frontier Parish: Recovered Catholic History of Lincoln County, 1860-1884, p.47 (Lincoln County Society Publications, 1995)
10. Billy Charles Patrick Cummings, Frontier Parish: Recovered Catholic History of Lincoln County, 1860-1884, p.54-63 (Lincoln County Society Publications, 1995)
11. Aniceto Lucero land patent, BLM Serial # NMNMAA 010834. Lucas Gallegos land patent, BLM Serial # NMNMAA 010820. The land patents show that Aniseto Lucero did in fact own the land that La Capilla de San Francisco was situated on and that the campo santo would have fallen on Lucas Gallegos' land. Local legend was that the capilla was known as La Capilla de San Francisco, rather than La Capilla de San Patricio. Also, according to local legend, Lucas Gallegos had claimed that La Capilla de San Francisco was actually on his property. After rebuking the Church's desire for the deed to the land, Gallegos had turned the capilla into a livestock barn. Aniceto Lucero thus claimed the site of the campo santo. Only Gallegos had actually been excommunicated. Eventually, in a drunken stupor, Gallegos proceeded to demolish most of the capilla. As was often the case, landmarks had distinguished land boundaries and therefore property lines were not always so concise. This could have lead Lucas Gallegos to believe that the capilla was on his property without any further question from Aniceto Lucero.
12. The events that lead to the controversy concerning La Capilla de San Francisco. Billy Charles Patrick Cummings, Frontier Parish: Recovered Catholic History of Lincoln County, 1860-1884, p.73 (Lincoln County Society Publications, 1995)
13. Billy Charles Patrick Cummings, Frontier Parish: Recovered Catholic History of Lincoln County, 1860-1884, p.75-78 (Lincoln County Society Publications, 1995)
14. Billy Charles Patrick Cummings, Frontier Parish: Recovered Catholic History of Lincoln County, 1860-1884, p.73 (Lincoln County Society Publications, 1995)
15. The story of who donated the bell to La Capilla de San Patricio as told by Román Sánchez, Román Barragán's godson, during an interview with the author.
16. Father Juan María (JM) Garnier on behalf of the Archbishop Juan Bautista (Jean Batiste) Salpointe had signed the deed. The deed is dated May 19, 1886 and outlines the dimensions of the land. A copy of the deed can be found at the LDS Family Library in Alamogordo, New México.
17. Interview with Fermín Pacheco. Interview was conducted by Inez Gómez-Pacheco.
18. Adivinanzas numbered 1-7. Joe Hayes, ¡Adivinanzas! Hispanic Folk Riddles of New México, p.22-24 (New México Magazine, May 1984)

Chapter Seven: Florencio Gonzáles

1. Nancy Hanks PhD, Lamy's Legion: From 1850 to 1912, p.118 (HRM Books, 2000)

2. 1860 U.S. Census lists Florencio Gonzáles as being a student. 1860 U.S. Census, Santa Fé, p.113
3. Ancestry.com. U.S., Union Soldiers Compiled Service Records, 1861-1865 [database on-line]. Provo, UT, USA: Ancestry.com Operations, Inc., 2011. U.S., Union Soldiers Compiled Service Records, 1861-1865 provided by Fold3
4. Book of Land Claims, June 12, 1869. Recorded in Socorro County.
5. Donald R. Lavash, Sheriff William Brady: Tragic hero of the Lincoln County War, p.34 (Sunstone Press, 1986)
6. Donald R. Lavash, Sheriff William Brady: Tragic hero of the Lincoln County War, p.35 (Sunstone Press, 1986)
7. Joel Jacobsen, Such Men as Billy the Kid, p.6 (University of Nebraska Press, 1994)
8. William A. Keleher, Violence in Lincoln County: 1869-1881, p.33 (University of New México Press, 1957)
9. Frederick Nolan, The Lincoln County War: A Documentary History, p.32 (University of Oklahoma Press, 1992)
10. Joel Jacobsen, Such Men as Billy the Kid, p.7 (University of Nebraska Press, 1994)
11. Concerning the events that lead to Alexander McSween's business trip to New York. Joel Jacobsen, Such Men as Billy the Kid, p.12-13 (University of Nebraska Press, 1994)
12. Joel Jacobsen, Such Men as Billy the Kid, p.20-21 (University of Nebraska Press, 1994)
13. Carole Larson, Forgotten Frontier: The Story of Southeastern New Mexico, p.73 (University of New Mexico Press: Albuquerque, 1993)
14. Frederick Nolan, The Lincoln County War: A Documentary History, p.108 (University of Oklahoma Press, 1992)
15. Joel Jacobsen, Such Men as Billy the Kid, p.22 (University of Nebraska Press, 1994)
16. John P. Wilson, Merchants, Guns, and Money: The Story of Lincoln County and its Wars, p.50 (Museum of New México Press, 1987)
17. Robert M. Utley, High Noon in Lincoln Violence on the Western Frontier, p.39 (University of New Mexico Press, 1987)
18. As described by the duties of Probate judge Lawrence Murphy. Joel Jacobsen, Such Men as Billy the Kid, p.10 (University of Nebraska Press, 1994)
19. Donald R. Lavash, Sheriff William Brady: Tragic hero of the Lincoln County War, p.52 (Sunstone Press, 1986)
20. Joel Jacobsen, Such Men as Billy the Kid, p.24 (University of Nebraska Press, 1994) Carrizo was a ranching community that spanned several thousand acres. In 1899 the El Paso & Northeastern Railroad laid their tracks and placed a station at what became known as Carrizo Springs. Later, James Allcook renamed the small community Carrizozo indicating an abundance of reed grass.
21. Frederick Nolan, The Lincoln County War: A Documentary History, p.147 (University of Oklahoma Press, 1992)
22. Joel Jacobsen, Such Men as Billy the Kid, p.25 (University of Nebraska Press, 1994)
23. Joel Jacobsen, Such Men as Billy the Kid, p.47 (University of Nebraska Press, 1994)
24. Frederick Nolan, The Lincoln County War: A Documentary History, p.177 (University of Oklahoma Press, 1992)
25. Robert M. Utley, High Noon in Lincoln: Violence on the Western Frontier, p.39 (University of New México Press, 1987)
26. William A. Keleher, Violence in Lincoln County: 1869-1881, p.41, (University of New México Press, 1957)
27. Joel Jacobsen, Such Men as Billy the Kid, p.54-55 (University of Nebraska Press, 1994)
28. José María Gutiérrez was the original owner of the land that Reimunda Sánchez de Gonzáles had eventually had bought. He sold his land to his son, Rafael Gutiérrez on April 20, 1877. Rafael sold his stake on January 11, 1878. Lincoln County Clerks Office, Bill of Sales, p. 55
29. Frederick Nolan, The Lincoln County War: A Documentary History, p.183-186 (University of Oklahoma Press, 1992)
30. Joel Jacobsen, Such Men as Billy the Kid, p.65 (University of Nebraska Press, 1994)
31. Turkey Springs was located a few miles away from Tunstall's ranch. Frederick Nolan, The Lincoln County War: A Documentary History, p.194 (University of Oklahoma Press, 1992)
32. Joel Jacobsen, Such Men as Billy the Kid, p.79-80 (University of Nebraska Press, 1994)
33. Joel Jacobsen, Such Men as Billy the Kid, p.80-81 (University of Nebraska Press, 1994)
34. Maurice G. Fulton, History of the Lincoln County War, p.116 (The University of Arizona Press, 1968)
35. Maurice G. Fulton, History of the Lincoln County War, p.123 (The University of Arizona Press, 1968)
36. Frederick Nolan, The Lincoln County War: A Documentary History, p.201 (University of Oklahoma Press, 1992)
37. This account was told to Special Agent Angel by Pantelón Gallegos who was in the employment of Jimmy Dolan. Gallegos was in William Morton's posse the day Tunstall was murdered. Morton had recounted the events of the shooting to Gallegos. John Hurley collaborated the story with the other members of the posse, according to Gallegos. Joel Jacobsen, Such Men as Billy the Kid, p.88 (University of Nebraska Press, 1994)
38. Joel Jacobsen, Such Men as Billy the Kid, p.88-90 (University of Nebraska Press, 1994)
39. Frederick Nolan, The Lincoln County War: A Documentary History, p.213 (University of Oklahoma Press, 1992)

40. The House did not recognize John Wilson as the Justice of the Peace because he was appointed by the county commissioners rather than being elected by a common vote. This was a point of contention when Constable Martínez attempted to arrest Sheriff Brady. Maurice G. Fulton, History of the Lincoln County War, p.131, (The University of Arizona Press, 1968)

41. Joel Jacobsen, Such Men as Billy the Kid, p.97 (University of Nebraska Press, 1994)

42. Angel Report, p. 352

43. Frederick Nolan, The Lincoln County War: A Documentary History, p.203 (University of Oklahoma Press, 1992)

44. Joel Jacobsen, Such Men as Billy the Kid, p.102-103 (University of Nebraska Press, 1994)

45. Maurice G. Fulton, History of the Lincoln County War, p.131, (The University of Arizona Press, 1968)

46. John P. Wilson, Merchants, Guns, and Money: The Story of Lincoln County and its Wars, p.84 (Museum of New México Press, 1987)

47. Donald R. Lavash, Sheriff William Brady: Tragic hero of the Lincoln County War, p.99 (Sunstone Press, 1986)

48. Joel Jacobsen, Such Men as Billy the Kid, p.114 (University of Nebraska Press, 1994)

49. Frederick Nolan, The West of Billy the Kid, p.117, (University of Oklahoma Press, 1998)

50. Joel Jacobsen, Such Men as Billy the Kid, p.125 (University of Nebraska Press, 1994)

51. Joel Jacobsen, Such Men as Billy the Kid, p.132 (University of Nebraska Press, 1994)

52. Frederick Nolan, The Lincoln County War: A Documentary History, p.249 (University of Oklahoma Press, 1992)

53. Concerning the grand jury and their opinion. Joel Jacobsen, Such Men as Billy the Kid, p.150-152 (University of Nebraska Press, 1994)

54. Joel Jacobsen, Such Men as Billy the Kid, p.153 (University of Nebraska Press, 1994)

55. Frederick Nolan, The West of Billy the Kid, p.144 (University of Oklahoma Press, 1998)

56. Robert M. Utley, High Noon in Lincoln, Violence on the Western Frontier, p.81 (University of New México Press, 1987)

57. Joel Jacobsen, Such Men as Billy the Kid, p.165 (University of Nebraska Press, 1994)

58. Maurice G. Fulton, Lincoln County War, p. 245 (University of Arizona Press, 1968)

59. Frederick Nolan, The Lincoln County War: A Documentary History, p.382 (University of Oklahoma Press, 1992)

60. Lincoln County, Record of Bill of Sales 1881-1887 p.45

Chapter Eight: Fernando Herrera

1. The 1860 and 1870 Census both show that Fernando and his family were living in the Río Arriba, and Taos regions respectfully. However during this time, in 1867, Fernando had applied for water rights on his ditch from the north and south. The place name, El San Juanito was reference when Fernando's son-in-law, Adrian Muñoz had petitioned for the right to use the water from El Ojo de San Juanito dated November 10, 1900. 1860 Census, Rio Arriba p.40. 1870 census, Rio Colorado: Taos County, p.13. **El Ojo de San Juanito** Lincoln County Appropriation of Water Rights, Book A, p.68. **Fernando Herrera north ditch and south ditch (later also known as the Gómez ditch),** State of New México: State Engineer Office, State vs. Lewis No. 20294 and 22600, Río Hondo Stream System Adjudicated Water Rights, p.61 (April, 01, 1987)

2. Interview with Florinda Salsberry de Sánchez, who was Manuelita's daughter. The interview was conducted on March 22, 1974.

3. José Ernesto Sánchez (Ernest S. Sánchez) collected a sample of the rock façade, which was taken to the New Mexico Bureau of Geology and Mineral Resources at the New México School of Mines in Socorro, New México. The tests revealed that the material submitted was made of Travertine. After further investigation, it was determined that the rock wall was actually a natural formation rather than man-made.

4. A building contractor named Jack DiPaulo excavated the land that comprised the campo santo about 90 years later. His company was building a housing subdivision, and as they were prepping the land for construction they had unearthed several human remains. Initially, it was assumed that the gravesites were an ancient Native American burial ground. Agustín Salsberry, Fernando Herrera's grandson told that those human remains were of Julianita, Macedonio, Seledonia, Basilio Saís, and a few others.

5. Scurlock was living with Fernando Herrera when his two youngest children were born. Charles Bowdre was also living on Fernando's farm while in San Juanito.

6. An account by Ábran Miller in an interview conducted by Edith L. Crawford. Edith L Crawford, Pedro M. Rodriguez Pioneer Story, Sept 30, 1938. Library of Congress, Manuscript Division, WPA Federal Writers' Project Web site:http://ftp.rootsweb.com/pub/usgenweb/nm/lincoln/bios/pedrorodriguez.txt

7. The story of how Fernando Herrera handled the Mescalero raids against his cattle as told in an account by Pedro M. Rodriguez in an interview conducted by Edith L. Crawford. Edith L Crawford, Pedro M. Rodriguez Pioneer Story, Aug 29, 1938. Library of Congress, Manuscript Division, WPA Federal Writers' Project Collection. Web site:http://ftp.rootsweb.com/pub/usgenweb/nm/lincoln/bios/pedrorodriguez.txt

8. Robert M. Utley, High Noon in Lincoln: Violence on the Western Frontier, p.84 (University of New Mexico Press, 1984)

9. Per the events that transpired during the first incursion into San Patricio. Fernando Herrera and Martín Chávez were not listed as some of the members in the party however they were two of the three Hispanics that Utley was referring to. Robert M. Utley, High Noon in Lincoln: Violence on the Western Frontier, p.83 (University of New Mexico Press, 1984)

10. Joel Jacobsen, Such Men as Billy the Kid, p.170 (University of Nebraska Press, 1994)

11. Robert M. Utley, High Noon in Lincoln: Violence on the Western Frontier, p.85 (University of New Mexico Press, 1984)

12. Maurice G. Fulton, History of the Lincoln county War: A Classic Account of Billy the Kid, p.244 (The University of Arizona Press, 1968)

13. Frederick Nolan, The Lincoln County War: A Documentary History, p.308, family names p.558 (University of Oklahoma Press, 1992)

14. Joel Jacobsen, Such Men as Billy the Kid, p.174 (University of Nebraska Press, 1994)

15. Joel Jacobsen, Such Men as Billy the Kid, p.174-175 (University of Nebraska Press, 1994)

16. Frederick Nolan, The West of Billy the Kid, p.158 (University of Oklahoma Press, 1998)

17. Padre Sambrano had given the crucifix to Martín Chávez as a young boy. Billy Charles Patrick Cummings, Frontier Parish: Recovered Catholic History of Lincoln County, 1860-1884, p.35 (Lincoln County Society Publications, 1995)

18. The events that led to Fernando Herrera killing Charles Crawford. Robert M. Utley, High Noon in Lincoln: Violence on the Western Frontier, p.94 (University of New México Press, 1987)

19. Frederick Nolan, The West of Billy the Kid, p. 158 (University of Oklahoma Press, 1998)

20. Frederick Nolan, The Lincoln County War: A Documentary History, p.324-325 (University of Oklahoma Press, 1992)

21. Many of the New Mexicans were never mentioned concerning La Batalla de Lincoln although they constituted the bulk of the Regulators that descended upon Lincoln. I have noted the most prominent New Mexicans that periodically rode with the "core" Regulators as mentioned in many history texts. Joel Jacobsen, Such Men as Billy the Kid, p.180 (University of Nebraska Press, 1994)

22. Frederick Nolan, The Lincoln County War: A Documentary History, p.312 (University of Oklahoma Press, 1992)

23. Joel Jacobsen, Such Men as Billy the Kid, p.181 (University of Nebraska Press, 1994)

24. Frederick Nolan, The West of Billy the Kid, p.167 (University of Oklahoma Press, 1998)

25. Joel Jacobsen, Such Men as Billy the Kid, p.186 (University of Nebraska Press, 1994)

26. Frederick Nolan, The West of Billy the Kid, p.165 (University of Oklahoma Press, 1998)

27. Joel Jacobsen, Such Men as Billy the Kid, p.190 (University of Nebraska Press, 1994)

28. Bill Kelley, The Lincoln County War (1878-79): Competition Wasn't Welcome. Article can be found on website: http://www.southernnewmexico.com/Articles/Southeast/Lincoln/TheLincolnCountyWar.html

29. Joel Jacobsen, Such Men as Billy the Kid, p.192-193 (University of Nebraska Press, 1994)

30. Frederick Nolan, The Lincoln County War: A Documentary History, p.352 (University of Oklahoma Press, 1992)

31. Frederick Nolan, The Lincoln County War: A Documentary History, p.346 (University of Oklahoma Press, 1992)

32. Frederick Nolan, The Lincoln County War: A Documentary History, p.348 (University of Oklahoma Press, 1992)

33. Maurice G. Fulton, History of the Lincoln county War: A Classic Account of Billy the Kid, p.292, (The University of Arizona Press, 1968)

34. Shinkle, Fifty Years of Roswell History, p.74

35. Joel Jacobsen, Such Men as Billy the Kid, p.207-208 (University of Nebraska Press, 1994)

36. Maurice G. Fulton, History of the Lincoln County War, p.326-327 (The University of Arizona Press, 1968)

37. Joel Jacobsen, Such Men as Billy the Kid, p.209 (University of Nebraska Press, 1994)

38. Nolan, The Lincoln County War: A Documentary History, p.381 (University of Oklahoma Press, 1992)

39. William A. Keleher, Violence in Lincoln County: 1869-1881, p.218-219 (University of New México Press, 1957)

40. Frederick Nolan, The Lincoln County War: A Documentary History, p.384 (University of Oklahoma Press, 1992)

41. Joel Jacobsen, Such Men as Billy the Kid, p.212-213 (University of Nebraska Press, 1994)

42. The story of how Pedro Rodríguez's father had died in an account by Pedro M. Rodriguez in an interview conducted by Edith L. Crawford. Edith L Crawford, Pedro M. Rodriguez Pioneer Story, Aug 29, 1938. Library of Congress, Manuscript Division, WPA Federal Writers' Project Collection. Web site: http://ftp.rootsweb.com/pub/usgenweb/nm/lincoln/bios/pedrorodriguez.txt

43. Information concerning the sharecropper was obtained by the author during an interview with Florinda Salsberry de Sánchez. She was Fernando Herrera's granddaughter. Interview conducted in 1975. The judgment recorded on the Lincoln County Judgment Docket Book C, pg.3, Case number 1443, filed on July 31, 1905.

44. Enumerator district 34, Surviving Soldiers p.1

45. The one-room log cabin as shown to the author by Henry Hale.

46. Lincoln County, Record of Sales p.94

47. Lincoln County, Record of Sales p.94

48. Lincoln County, Book of Deeds, Book G p.299

49. Lincoln County, Probate Records, May 1889

50. Gill family history. Website Rootsweb:http://wc.rootsweb.com/cgi-bin/igm.cgi?op=GET&db=:3249973&id=I0109 Accessed on January 2007.

Chapter Nine: Manuelita Herrera

1. Frederick Nolan, The Lincoln County War: A Documentary History, p.484 (University of Oklahoma Press, 1992)

2. Frederick Nolan, The Lincoln County War: A Documentary History, p.514 (University of Oklahoma Press, 1992)

3. Bill Kelly, The Lincoln County War (1878-79): Competition Wasn't Welcome, July 17, 2003. San Miguel County Probate Court. Website: http://www.southernnewmexico.com/Articles/Southeast/Lincoln/TheLincolnCountyWar.html

4. Robert M. Utley, Billy the Kid: A Short and Violent Life, p.107, (University of Nebraska Press, 1989)

5. Interview with Florinda Salsberry de Sánchez, the daughter of Manuelita Herrera.

6. Alejandro Polaco was also known as Padre Polaco, whose real name was Alexander Jan Grzelachowski. Frederick Nolan, Pat F. Garrett's The Authentic Life of Billy, The Kid, p.96-97 (University of Oklahoma Press, 2000)

7. Frederick Nolan, The West of Billy the Kid, p.182 (University of Oklahoma Press, 1998)

8. The events that occurred while Lt. French sought out Bonney and his men in Lincoln. Frederick Nolan, The Lincoln County War: A Documentary History, p.362-363 (University of Oklahoma Press, 1992)

9. Frederick Nolan, The West of Billy the Kid, p.215 (University of Oklahoma Press, 1998)

10. Frederick Nolan, The Lincoln County War: A Documentary History, p.397 (University of Oklahoma Press, 1992)

11. Frederick Nolan, Pat F. Garrett's The Authentic Life of Billy, The Kid, p.125 (University of Oklahoma Press, 2000)

12. Frederick Nolan, Pat F. Garrett's The Authentic Life of Billy, The Kid, p.131-132 (University of Oklahoma Press, 2000)

13. Frederick Nolan, The West of Billy the Kid, p.239 (University of Oklahoma Press, 1998)

14. Frederick Nolan, The Lincoln County War: A Documentary History, p.405-406 (University of Oklahoma Press, 1992)

15. Frederick Nolan, The Lincoln County War: A Documentary History, p.406-407 (University of Oklahoma Press, 1992)

16. Cal Polk and Jim East had dismounted their horses and crawled to the house to scout for structural weaknesses; as told by Cal Polk who was one of the members of Garrett's posse. Frederick Nolan, The Lincoln County War: A Documentary History, p.407 (University of Oklahoma Press, 1992) New Mexicans in the area knew Stinking Springs as Ojo Hediendo. This reference is sited in a book written by Paco Anaya, I buried Billy, p.102 (Creative Publishing Company, 1991)

17. There have been different accounts pertaining to Charlie Bowdre's last moments before death. In Cal Polk's account, as stated in Frederick Nolan's previous book, The Lincoln County War: A Documentary History, p.407, Sheriff Pat Garrett had called out to Bowdre to raise his hands in the air. Bowdre responded, "in a minute" during which he had grabbed his pistols and commenced firing upon Garrett and his men. Garrett and his men returned fire, hitting Bowdre three times. Bowdre then stumbled towards the posse and fell over with Lee Smith catching him and turning him over. Frederick Nolan, Pat F. Garrett's The Authentic Life of Billy, The Kid, p.153 (University of Oklahoma Press, 2000)

18. Accounts of the standoff after Bowdre's death, as told by Cal Polk. Frederick Nolan, The Lincoln County War: A Documentary History, p.408 (University of Oklahoma Press, 1992)

19. Frederick Nolan, The West of Billy the Kid, p. 248 (University of Oklahoma Press, 1998)

20. Interview with Florinda Salsberry de Sánchez who was Manuel Corona's sister.
21. Richard Saulsberry, letter written by his brother dated January 29, 1871.
22. Harvey Harstel Saulsberry, letter written on February 28, 1970.
23. Joel P. Salisbury land patent, BLM Serial number NMNMAA 010252
24. Lincoln County Clerks Office, The District Court of the 6ᵗʰ Judicial District of the Territory of New México, Order of Confirmation. Dated January 19, 1910.

Chapter Ten: Other Pioneering Families

1. 1880 U.S. Census, Plaza de San Patricio, Page 24.
2. 1885 New México Territorial Census, Precinct 4, Page 32-15.
3. Transcribed by C. Anthony, Santa Fe New Mexican, April 18, 1899.
4. Transcribed by C. Anthony, Santa Fe New Mexican, April 18, 1899.
5. Donald R. Lavish, Sheriff William Brady, Tragic Hero of The Lincoln County War, p.32-41 (Sunstone Press, 1986)
6. Donald R. Lavish, Sheriff William Brady, Tragic Hero of The Lincoln County War, p.51-52 (Sunstone Press, 1986)
7. Robert M. Utley, High Noon in Lincoln: Violence on the Western Frontier, p.85 (University of New México Press, 1987)
8. Robert M. Utley, High Noon in Lincoln: Violence on the Western Frontier, p.113 (University of New México Press, 1987)
9. In an interview with Román Sánchez on June of 1972
10. Crawford. Edith L Crawford, Elerdo Chávez Pioneer Story. Library of Congress, Manuscript Division, WPA Federal Writers' Project Collection. Web site: http://ftp.rootsweb.com/pub/usgenweb/nm/lincoln/bios/pedrorodriguez.txt
11. Crawford. Edith L Crawford, Ambrocio Chávez Pioneer Story. Library of Congress, Manuscript Division, WPA Federal Writers' Project Collection. Web site: http://ftp.rootsweb.com/pub/usgenweb/nm/lincoln/bios/pedrorodriguez.txt
12. Presidio Courthouse, District Court Records. Record for a petition of citizenship. Diedrick Dutchover states that he had entered the United States at the Port of Galveston in 1845.
13. Allan O. Kownslar, The European Texans, pages 56-57 (University of Texas at Institute of Texan Cultures at San Antonio, 2004)
14. The events that lead to the controversy concerning La Capilla de San Francisco. Billy Charles Patrick Cummings, Frontier Parish: Recovered Catholic History of Lincoln County, 1860-1884, p.73 (Lincoln County Society Publications, 1995)
15. Crawford. Edith L Crawford, Francisco Trujillo Pioneer Story. Library of Congress, Manuscript Division, WPA Federal Writers' Project Collection. May 10, 1937. Web site: http://ftp.rootsweb.com/pub/usgenweb/nm/lincoln/bios/pedrorodriguez.txt
16. John P. Wilson, Merchants Guns & Money: The Story of Lincoln County and Its Wars, p.124, (Museum of New México Press, 1987)
17. Information concerning Felipé Gómez and the family, as told by Francisco "Frank" Gómez, his son, on December 08, 1998.
18. The Gutiérrez house is a state-registered historical building.
19. Crawford. Edith L Crawford, Ábran Miller Pioneer Story. Library of Congress, Manuscript Division, WPA Federal Writers' Project Collection. Web site: http://ftp.rootsweb.com/pub/usgenweb/nm/lincoln/bios/pedrorodriguez.txt
20. Interview with Juanita Barrera Montoya. Interview conducted on April 02, 2011.
21. Interview with Orlando Pacheco. Interview was conducted on June 15, 2007.
22. Interview with Orlando Pacheco. Interview was conducted on June 15, 2007.
23. Interview with George Sisneros. Interview was conducted on April 23, 2009.
24. Interview with Orlando Pacheco. Interview was conducted on June 15, 2007.
25. Interview with George Sisneros. Interview was conducted on April 23, 2009.
26. Many of the local Spanish-speaking people refered to the ranch as **Rancho Bloqué**. Interview with George Sisneros. Interview was conducted on April 23, 2009.
27. Mary Louise Joiner, A History of Lincoln County Post Offices, p. 27 (Lincoln County Postmasters, Revised July 04, 1994)
28. Interview with Orlando Pacheco who was Ignacia Gómez de Pacheco's son. Interview was conducted on June 15, 2007.

29. 1860 Census, Los Corrales, Page 111
30. 1900 Census, Las Vegas
31. Hoy día 21 de Noviembre 1866, bautisé a Altagracia Polaco, hija de Serafín Polaco y Altagracia Gonzáles. Padrinos son; Trancito Polaco y Crecensia Polaca de La Plaza de San Patricio. Por Padre Y. Frilon. From the Archives of the Santa Fé Archdiocese, 1852-1955. Roll #81-A, p. 150
32. 1900 Census, Ruidoso, p.16A
33. Padre Girand, Tularosa Church Records, Book of Marriages, November 08, 1900, Entry # 33
34. Interview with Trancito Polaco y Gonzáles, the son of Trancito Polaco. Interview conducted in 1993.
35. Wesley R. Hurt, Manzano: A Study of Community Disorganization, p.30 (AMS Press, Inc., 1989)
36. Wesley R. Hurt, Manzano: A Study of Community Disorganization, p.60 (AMS Press, Inc., 1989)
37. Wesley R. Hurt, Manzano: A Study of Community Disorganization, p.31 (AMS Press, Inc., 1989)
38. 1860 Census, Valencia County, Tajique, Page 45
39. LDS Family Genealogy Center, Alamogordo, Microfiche# 0016754, Baptismal Records, Page 131.
40. Fray Angélico Chávez, Origins of New México Families: Revised Edition, p.285 (Museum of New México Press,1992)
41. New Mexico Genealogist p. 67 (Vol. XIX, No. 3, September 1980).
42. Juanita Sedillos Self, Sedillos and Brady Families of Lincoln County, N.M. p. 18-19, (Southwest Heritage Magazine)
43. Board of Commissioners minutes, March 01, 1876 to July 08, 1879, p.10
44. Fray Angélico Chávez, Origins of New México Families: Revised Edition, p.299 (Museum of New México Press,1992)
45. Fray Angélico Chávez, Origins of New México Families: Revised Edition, p.300 (Museum of New México Press,1992)
46. 1870 Lincoln County Census,
47. The following historical account of Los Vega in Lincoln County was forwarded to the author. The family history was documented and researched by Leandro (Lee) Vega III. Vega III, Leandro, The Life of José María Vega As Told By Family, Friends, and Documents. (Personal family history document, May 29, 2008)

Chapter Eleven: Los Romero

1. The Romero migration to Picacho as told in an interview with María Romero de Gómez, the daughter of Juan de Dios Romero, and Elsie Kimbrell his granddaughter. June 1972.
2. 1860 U.S. Census, Valencia County, Manzano p. 51-52.
3. 1870 U.S. Census, Lincoln County, Precinct 1, p. 11-15.
4. 1860 U.S. Census, Valencia County, Manzano, p. 52.
5. As told in an interview with María Romero de Gómez, the daughter of Juan de Dios Romero, June 1972
6. Juan de Dios Romero provided this information during a hearing conducted in Lincoln County, in the Court of Claims in the December session of 1893. James D. Shinkle, Robert Casey and the Ranch on the Río Hondo, p.71-75 (Hall-Poorbaugh Press, Inc., 1970)
7. 1860 U.S. Census, Socorro County, Río Bonito, p. 146.
8. Frederick Nolan, The West of Billy the Kid, p.155 (University of Oklahoma Press, 1998)
9. William A. Keleher, Violence in Lincoln County 1869-1881, p.144 (University of New México Press, 1957)
10. Frederick Nolan, The Lincoln County War: A Documentary history, p.332 (University of Oklahoma Press, 1992)
11. Billy Charles Patrick Cummings, Frontier Parish: Recovered Catholic History of Lincoln County, 1860-1884, p.35 (Lincoln County Society Publications, 1995)
12. Father Robert Kirsch, Saint Jude Thaddeus Catholic Church, p.4 (Souvenir Brochure, 1967)
13. As told in an interview with María Romero de Gómez, the daughter of Juan de Dios Romero, June 1972
14. Billy Charles Patrick Cummings, Frontier Parish: Recovered Catholic History of Lincoln County, 1860-1884, p.69 (Lincoln County Society Publications, 1995)
15. Fredrick Nolan, The Lincoln County War: A Documentary History, p.307 (University of Oklahoma Press, 1992)
16. Crawford. Edith L Crawford, Ambrocio Chávez Pioneer Story. Library of Congress, Manuscript Division, WPA Federal Writers' Project Collection. Web site: http://ftp.rootsweb.com/pub/usgenweb/nm/lincoln/bios/pedrorodriguez.txt
17. Fredrick Nolan, The Lincoln County War: A Documentary History, p.469 (University of Oklahoma Press, 1992)
18. Fredrick Nolan, The Lincoln County War: A Documentary History, p.371-372 (University of Oklahoma Press, 1992)
19. Maurice G. Fulton, History of the Lincoln County War, p.327 (The University of Arizona Press, 1968)

Chapter Twelve: Los Sánchez, 1880-2008

1. Interview with Delfinia Sánchez-Vega in July 2009.
2. All CCC information. CCC Alumni, A Brief History of the Civilian Conservation Corps, Website: http://www.cccalumni.org/history1.html Accessed on April 26, 2007.
3. Lincoln County Commissioners Records, Book 4.
4. Hugh Stiles, Nepotism reason for action: Officer ordered dismissed, p. 8, (Roswell Daily Record, Sunday, March 16, 1975)
5. Letter from Jeff Bingaman to Ernesto Sánchez dated December 01, 1980.
6. The account of Thomas Bedford's murder as given by the Co-Author, former Lincoln County Sheriff Ernesto Sánchez.
7. Dianne Stallings, "Killer of a Lincoln County Deputy up for parole again, p.1A, cont. 8A (Ruidoso News, Friday, December 12, 1997. Issue #59)

Chapter Thirteen: Los Chávez

1. Interview with Oralia Chávez-Sánchez on April 05, 2007.
2. Lincoln County Clerk, Book of Marriages, Book 4, p.43
3. Interview with Oralia Chávez-Sánchez on April 05, 2007.

Chapter Fourteen: The Patriots

1. Terry Wooten, The Battle of Valverde, (CivilWar.Com, February 22, 2006) Website: http://www.civilwar.com/content/view/1796/39/ Accessed on October 18, 2007
2. Terry Wooten, The Battle of Glorieta Pass, (CivilWar.Com, February 22, 2006) Website: http://www.civilwar.com/content/view/1796/39/ Accessed on October 18, 2007
3. Carole Gomey, Roots in Lincoln County: A History of Fort Stanton Hospital, p.11-13 (State Planning Office, 1969)
4. These statistics are derived from the U.S. Department of Defense. These statistics are for the period ending December 31, 1918.
5. List of World War One veterans can be found throughout the book. Most of the names gathered are residents of the Río Bonito, Río Hondo, and Río Ruidoso regions. Lincoln County Clerk, Book of Discharges, Book 1. Those WWI Veterans who were reported to have died during the war. Howard W. Henry, World War I Deaths: New México-1918, p. 235-238 (New México Genealogist: Military Issue, December 2003)
6. The author Reynel "Rey" Martínez had conducted an interview with Senon in December of 1993. Staying true to the words of the original author, Rey Martínez is the only source for this story. Rey is also a War veteran who served two tours of duty with the 101st Airborne Division Rangers from 1966-1968 in Vietnam. The story of Senon's campaign in Anzio, Italy. Rey Martínez, I Died at Anzio, Senon Chávez: A Ranger's Story, p.6 (Behind the Lines, The Journal of U.S. Military Special Operations, Jan/Feb 1995

Chapter Fifteen: Changing Times 1900-2007

1. Fermín S. Montes, Dreams Can Become a Reality, p.1, (Hall-Poorbaugh Press, Inc, 1983)
2. Fermín S. Montes, Dreams Can Become a Reality, p.2, Forward (Hall-Poorbaugh Press, Inc, 1983)
3. Fermín S. Montes, Dreams Can Become a Reality, p. vii, Autobiographical Sketch (Hall-Poorbaugh Press, Inc, 1983)
4. Fermín S. Montes, Dreams Can Become a Reality, p.8, Forward (Hall-Poorbaugh Press, Inc, 1983)
5. Fermín S. Montes, Dreams Can Become a Reality, Corona, El Paso, Ruidoso, Santa Fé p.15; Tucson 1951 p.25 Forward (Hall-Poorbaugh Press, Inc, 1983)
6. How the community of San Juanito was re-named to Palo Verde. Lincoln County Clerks Office, Certificate of Dedication of the Streets and Alleys in the Town site of Palo Verde, Lincoln County, New México, Approved by Jane LaRue on December 28, 1944.
7. How the community of Palo Verde was re-named to Ruidoso Downs. James W. White, The History of Lincoln County Post Offices, pg.139-140 (First Edition April 03,2007)

GENEALOGY

Note:

The following appendix is representative of some of the ancestors and their descendants of some of those Nuevo Mexicanos that had originally settled in Lincoln County. The following information is not a complete genealogy nor should it be viewed as such. The following information also does not list all Nuevo Mexicano families that had settled in Lincoln County. Although most of the information is correct to the best of the author's knowledge there may be some inaccuracies. Not all information has been validated with sourced documentation. Some family's descendants may be duplicated in more than one family due to marriage. The software package, The Family Tree MakerÓ 1993-1998 Version 4.0 from Broderbund Software Inc., was used to construct all family trees.

Descendants of Jacinto Sánchez de Iñigo

Generation No. 1

1. FRANCISCO[1] MUÑOZ. He married LEONOR ORTIZ.

Child of FRANCISCO MUÑOZ and LEONOR ORTIZ is:
2.   i.   JACINTO[2] MUÑOZ.

Generation No. 2

2. JACINTO[2] MUÑOZ *(FRANCISCO[1])*. He married MADALENA SÁNCHEZ DE IÑIGO, daughter of PEDRO DE IÑIGO and MARÍA SÁNCHEZ.

Child of JACINTO MUÑOZ and MADALENA DE IÑIGO is:
3.   i.   FRANCISCO[3] MUÑOZ, b. Abt. 1629, Puebla de los Ángeles, Nueva España.

Generation No. 3

3. FRANCISCO[3] MUÑOZ *(JACINTO[2], FRANCISCO[1])* was born Abt. 1629 in Puebla de los Ángeles, Nueva España. He met JUANA LÓPEZ DE ARAGÓN Bef. 1663 in Pueblo de San Ildefonso, El Reyno de Nuevo Méjico, daughter of FRANCISCO DE ARAGÓN and ANA BACA.

Children of FRANCISCO MUÑOZ and JUANA DE ARAGÓN are:
4.   i.   JACINTO SÁNCHEZ[4] DE IÑIGO, b. 1663, El Reyno de Nuevo Méjico; d. December 14, 1734, Alburquerque, El Reyno de Nuevo Méjico.
       ii.   FRANCISCA SÁNCHEZ DE IÑIGO, b. 1666, Bernalillo, El Reyno de Nuevo Méjico; m. JUAN GARCIA DE NORIEGA, May 04, 1681, Guadalupe del Paso, Nueva Vizcaya.

              More About FRANCISCA SÁNCHEZ DE IÑIGO:
              Fact 1: Member of the Vargas 1693 reconquest

       iii.   PEDRO SÁNCHEZ DE IÑIGO, b. 1673, El Reyno de Nuevo Méjico; d. 1720; m. (1) MONA LEONORA BACA, January 07, 1691/92, San Lorenzo, Nuevo Mexico; m. (2) MARÍA JUANA LUJÁN, 1698, Bernalillo, El Reyno de Nuevo Méjico.

Generation No. 4

4. JACINTO SÁNCHEZ[4] DE IÑIGO *(FRANCISCO[3] MUÑOZ, JACINTO[2], FRANCISCO[1])*[1] was born 1663 in El Reyno de Nuevo Méjico, and died December 14, 1734 in Alburquerque, El Reyno de Nuevo Méjico. He married (1) ISABEL TELLES JIRÓN 1688 in El Paso del Norte, Nueva Vizcaya. He married (2) MARÍA RODARTE DE CASTRO XABALERA March 30, 1696 in Santa Fé, El Reyno de Nuevo Méjico, daughter of MIGUEL XABALERA and JUANA DE HERRERA.

Notes for JACINTO SÁNCHEZ DE IÑIGO:
1680- He escaped the Pueblo Revolt.
1685- He tried to desert El Paso del Norte with Juan Domingo de Mendoza.
October 04, 1693- He was a member of the Vargas 1693 reconquest.
1703- He had received a grant of land on the Río del Norte (Río Grande), east of Cochití Pueblo.
1713- He was named the Alcalde Mayor of Santa Cruz de la Cañada. He was not considered to be competent by the Governor.
1715- He had asked for a permit to visit outside of El Reyno de Nuevo Méjico with his son, Francisco. Upon his return he settled in the Río Abajo district.
1728- Led an unauthorized, small expedition into the Moquí country.
Dec 14, 1734: Believed to have died in Alameda, Bernalillo, El Reyno de Nuevo Méjico.

Children of JACINTO DE IÑIGO and ISABEL JIRÓN are:

    i.   ANA JUANA ISABEL SÁNCHEZ[5] DE IÑIGO.

    ii.   GERTRUDIS SÁNCHEZ DE IÑIGO.

5.   iii. JOSÉ SÁNCHEZ, b. 1690, Gudalupe del Paso, Nueva Vizcaya.

    iv. PEDRO SÁNCHEZ.

    v.   JUAQUÍN SÁNCHEZ DE IÑIGO[2], m. (1) MANUELA MONTOYA; m. (2) FRANCISCA GUERRERO DE LA MORA.

Children of JACINTO DE IÑIGO and MARÍA XABALERA are:

    vi. MARÍA SÁNCHEZ[5] DE IÑIGO.

    vii. MIGUEL SÁNCHEZ.

6.   viii. FRANCISCO SÁNCHEZ, b. 1705, Atrisco, El Reyno de Nuevo Méjico; d. Bef. 1769.

7.   ix. MARÍA GERTRUDIS SÁNCHEZ, b. May 07, 1713, Santa Cruz de la Cañada, El Reyno de Nuevo Méjico.

Generation No. 5

5. JOSÉ[5] SÁNCHEZ *(JACINTO SÁNCHEZ[4] DE IÑIGO, FRANCISCO[3] MUÑOZ, JACINTO[2], FRANCISCO[1])[3]* was born 1690 in Gudalupe del Paso, Nueva Vizcaya. He married TERESA JARAMILLO[4].

Notes for JOSÉ SÁNCHEZ:

Oct 04, 1693: Was a member of the Vargas Reconquest.

Children of JOSÉ SÁNCHEZ and TERESA JARAMILLO are:

8.   i.   JACINTO[6] SÁNCHEZ, b. 1704, Atrisco, Nuevo México.

    ii.   ANTONIA SÁNCHEZ, b. Abt. 1727; d. April 27, 1794, Los Cháves, El Reyno de Nuevo Méjico.

    iii. JUAN SÁNCHEZ[4], b. Abt. 1730; m. BARBARA GALLEGOS.

    iv. MARÍA GERTRUDIS SÁNCHEZ[4], b. July 20, 1731.

6. FRANCISCO[5] SÁNCHEZ *(JACINTO SÁNCHEZ[4] DE IÑIGO, FRANCISCO[3] MUÑOZ, JACINTO[2], FRANCISCO[1])[4]* was born 1705 in Atrisco, El Reyno de Nuevo Méjico, and died Bef. 1769. He married JOSEFA (DE CHÁVEZ) DURÁN Y CHÁVEZ[4] 1725 in Alburquerque, El Reyno de Nuevo Méjico, daughter of PEDRO CHÁVEZ and JUANA HINOJOS.

Children of FRANCISCO SÁNCHEZ and JOSEFA CHÁVEZ are:

9.   i.   JUAN CRISTÓBAL[6] SÁNCHEZ, b. September 21, 1726, Atrisco Bernalillo, El Reyno de Nuevo Méjico; d. February 27, 1798, Tomé, El Reyno de Nuevo Méjico.

10.   ii.   MARÍA BARBARA SÁNCHEZ, b. November 26, 1730, Alburquerque, Nuevo México.

11.   iii. TERESA SÁNCHEZ, b. 1732; d. November 28, 1761, Alburquerque, Nuevo México.

12.   iv. DIEGO ANTONIO SÁNCHEZ, b. 1736.

    v.   MARCOS SÁNCHEZ, b. Abt. 1742, Tomé, El Reyno de Nuevo Méjico; m. MARGARITA VALDÉS, February 22, 1763, Alburquerque, El Reyno de Nuevo Méjico.

13.   vi. JUAQUÍN SÁNCHEZ, b. 1746, Tomé, Neuvo México.

7. MARÍA GERTRUDIS[5] SÁNCHEZ *(JACINTO SÁNCHEZ[4] DE IÑIGO, FRANCISCO[3] MUÑOZ, JACINTO[2], FRANCISCO[1])* was born May 07, 1713 in Santa Cruz de la Cañada, El Reyno de Nuevo Méjico. She married PEDRO DURÁN Y CHÁVEZ[5] January 12, 1727/28 in Alburquerque, El Reyno de Nuevo Méjico, son of FERNANDO CHÁVEZ and LUCÍA DE SALAS.

Notes for PEDRO DURÁN Y CHÁVEZ:

Feb 17, 1706: Was a soldier in the military, he was one of the founders of San Francisco de Alburquerque.

1713-1716: Was promoted to squadron leader of his militia.

1714-1715: Was appointed as the Alcalde Mayor of Los Padillas.

Aug 20, 1716: Was involved in a Hopi campaign.

1706: One member of the twelve founding families of San Francisco de Alburquerque.

1713: Was listed as a squadron leader of the militia. He escorted ex-Gobernador Felix Martínez back to Ciudad de México.

1716: Took part in the Moqui Campaign.

Children of MARÍA SÁNCHEZ and PEDRO CHÁVEZ are:

    i.   ANTONIO DURÁN Y[6] CHÁVEZ, b. Abt. 1729.

    ii.   MARÍA DURÁN Y CHÁVEZ, b. Abt. 1730.

iii.   SALVADOR MANUEL DURÁN Y CHÁVEZ, b. June 09, 1731, Alburquerque, El Reyno de Nuevo Méjico.

iv.   JOSÉ DURÁN Y CHÁVEZ⁶, b. June 01, 1733, Alburquerque, El Reyno de Nuevo Méjico; d. December 09, 1772.

Notes for JOSÉ DURÁN Y CHÁVEZ:
December 9, 1772: Known as José Cháves de Nuevo Méjico. He was killed by Apaches near El Paso.

v.   PEDRO DURÁN Y CHÁVEZ, b. Abt. 1734, Atrisco, El Reyno de Nuevo Méjico; d. January 1846.

Generation No. 6

8. JACINTO⁶ SÁNCHEZ *(JOSÉ⁵, JACINTO SÁNCHEZ⁴ DE IÑIGO, FRANCISCO³ MUÑOZ, JACINTO², FRANCISCO¹)⁷* was born 1704 in Atrisco, Nuevo México. He married EFIGENIA DURÁN Y CHÁVEZ 1732, daughter of PEDRO CHÁVEZ and JUANA HINOJOS.

Children of JACINTO SÁNCHEZ and EFIGENIA CHÁVEZ are:

	i.	MARÍA GERTRUDIS⁷ SÁNCHEZ, b. Atrisco, El Reyno de Nuevo Méjico.
14.	ii.	JOSÉ PEDRO SÁNCHEZ, b. Abt. 1734, Atrisco, El Reyno de Nuevo Méjico.
	iii.	JOSEPH SÁNCHEZ, b. Abt. 1736.
	iv.	JUAN DOMINGO SÁNCHEZ, b. Abt. 1741; d. Bef. March 10, 1780, Alburquerque, El Reyno de Nuevo Méjico.
	v.	URSULA BERNADINA SÁNCHEZ, b. Abt. 1743.
	vi.	FELICIANA (FELICIDAD) SÁNCHEZ, b. 1744.
	vii.	DOROTEA SÁNCHEZ, b. Abt. 1747.
	viii.	MARÍA JOSEFA SÁNCHEZ, b. Abt. 1750.
	ix.	JUAN MANUEL SÁNCHEZ, b. 1755.
	x.	JOSEPHE SÁNCHEZ, b. Abt. 1760; d. January 11, 1765.

9. JUAN CRISTÓBAL⁶ SÁNCHEZ *(FRANCISCO⁵, JACINTO SÁNCHEZ⁴ DE IÑIGO, FRANCISCO³ MUÑOZ, JACINTO², FRANCISCO¹)* was born September 21, 1726 in Atrisco Bernalillo, El Reyno de Nuevo Méjico, and died February 27, 1798 in Tomé, El Reyno de Nuevo Méjico. He married (1) ELENA JARAMILLO. He married (2) JUANA TOMÁSA DURÁN Y CHÁVEZ September 24, 1758 in Alburquerque, El Reyno de Nuevo Méjico⁸. He married (3) MARÍA ANTONIA CHÁVEZ November 30, 1782 in Alburquerque, El Reyno de Nuevo Méjico.

Notes for JUAN CRISTÓBAL SÁNCHEZ:
Alcálde Mayor of the Villa of Albuquerque.

Child of JUAN SÁNCHEZ and ELENA JARAMILLO is:

	i.	ANTONIO ROMÁN⁷ SÁNCHEZ, b. 1754.

Children of JUAN SÁNCHEZ and JUANA CHÁVEZ are:

	ii.	LUGARDA⁷ SÁNCHEZ, d. October 30, 1761, Alburquerque, El Reyno de Nuevo Méjico.
	iii.	MANUELA DE JESÚS SÁNCHEZ, d. December 12, 1772, Alburquerque, El Reyno de Nuevo Méjico.
15.	iv.	MARIANO SÁNCHEZ.
16.	v.	JOSÉ SÁNCHEZ, b. Abt. 1760, Los Cháves, El Reyno de Nuevo Méjico; d. Abt. February 1803.
	vi.	PEDRO JUAN BAUTISTA SÁNCHEZ, b. Abt. 1761; m. MARÍA MANUELA SÁNCHEZ, December 18, 1784, Los Padillas, El Reyno de Nuevo Méjico.
17.	vii.	MARÍA BÁRBARA SÁNCHEZ, b. 1762, Los Cháves, El Reyno de Nuevo Méjico.
	viii.	JUAN CRISTÓBAL CHÁVEZ SÁNCHEZ, b. 1769; d. February 12, 1812.
	ix.	DIEGO ANTONIO SÁNCHEZ, b. Abt. 1770, Pueblo de Ysleta, El Reyno de Nuevo Méjico; d. February 25, 1812.

Notes for DIEGO ANTONIO SÁNCHEZ:
Aug 21, 1789: Listed as a soldier, 5'1" tall, 20 years of age.

	x.	MARÍA YSABEL DE LA LUZ SÁNCHEZ, b. January 30, 1776.
18.	xi.	JOSÉ GREGORIO DE LA TRINIDAD SÁNCHEZ, b. November 19, 1777, Los Cháves, El Reyno de Nuevo Méjico; d. Bef. 1856.
19.	xii.	DOMINGO SÁNCHEZ, b. Abt. 1778, El Reyno de Nuevo Méjico.
	xiii.	MANUEL SÁNCHEZ, b. 1779.

10. MARÍA BARBARA⁶ SÁNCHEZ *(FRANCISCO⁵, JACINTO SÁNCHEZ⁴ DE IÑIGO, FRANCISCO³ MUÑOZ, JACINTO², FRANCISCO¹)* was born November 26, 1730 in Alburquerque, Nuevo México. She married JUAQUÍN JOSÉ PINO August 28, 1764 in Tomé, Nuevo México.

Children of MARÍA SÁNCHEZ and JUAQUÍN PINO are:
  i. JUAQUÍN MARIANO⁷ PINO.
  ii. ANA MARÍA CATALINA PINO.

11. TERESA⁶ SÁNCHEZ *(FRANCISCO⁵, JACINTO SÁNCHEZ⁴ DE IÑIGO, FRANCISCO³ MUÑOZ, JACINTO², FRANCISCO¹)* was born 1732, and died November 28, 1761 in Alburquerque, Nuevo México. She married MATEO JOSE PINO 1751.

Children of TERESA SÁNCHEZ and MATEO PINO are:
  i. MARIANO ANTONIO⁷ PINO.
  ii. JUAN FRANCISCO PINO.
  iii. ALEJANDRO RICARDO PINO.
  iv. CARLOS CASMIRO PINO.

12. DIEGO ANTONIO⁶ SÁNCHEZ *(FRANCISCO⁵, JACINTO SÁNCHEZ⁴ DE IÑIGO, FRANCISCO³ MUÑOZ, JACINTO², FRANCISCO¹)* was born 1736. He married ANA MARÍA OLAYA ALVAREZ DEL CASTILLO April 06, 1756 in Los Padillas, Nuevo México.

Children of DIEGO SÁNCHEZ and ANA DEL CASTILLO are:
  i. MARÍA JOSEPHA SILVERIA⁷ SÁNCHEZ.
  ii. MARÍA MANUELA SÁNCHES.
  iii. MARÍA MICHAELA SÁNCHEZ.
  iv. MANUELA ANTONIA SÁNCHEZ.
  v. ANA MARIA SÁNCHEZ.
  vi. TERESA DE JESUS SÁNCHEZ.
  vii. MARIANA ANTONIA SÁNCHEZ.
  viii. ANTONIO JOSÉ SÁNCHEZ.
  ix. BARBARA SÁNCHEZ.

13. JUAQUÍN⁶ SÁNCHEZ *(FRANCISCO⁵, JACINTO SÁNCHEZ⁴ DE IÑIGO, FRANCISCO³ MUÑOZ, JACINTO², FRANCISCO¹)* was born 1746 in Tomé, Neuvo México. He married ANA MARÍA PADILLA April 16, 1769 in Los Padillas, Nuevo Mexico.

Child of JUAQUÍN SÁNCHEZ and ANA PADILLA is:
  i. JULIAN⁷ SÁNCHEZ.

Generation No. 7

14. JOSÉ PEDRO⁷ SÁNCHEZ *(JACINTO⁶, JOSÉ⁵, JACINTO SÁNCHEZ⁴ DE IÑIGO, FRANCISCO³ MUÑOZ, JACINTO², FRANCISCO¹)* was born Abt. 1734 in Atrisco, El Reyno de Nuevo Méjico. He married MARÍA DE LA LUZ BACA October 25, 1761.

Children of JOSÉ SÁNCHEZ and MARÍA BACA are:
  i. JACINTO BACA⁸ SÁNCHEZ, m. GERTRUDIS ALVAREZ DEL CASTILLO, April 28, 1795, Tomé, El Reyno de Nuevo Méjico.
  ii. JUANA SÁNCHEZ.
20. iii. MANUEL RAFAEL SÁNCHEZ, b. Atrisco, El Reyno de Nuevo Méjico.
  iv. MARÍA ANTONIA SÁNCHEZ.
  v. ROSALIA SÁNCHEZ, b. Abt. 1774.

15. MARIANO⁷ SÁNCHEZ *(JUAN CRISTÓBAL⁶, FRANCISCO⁵, JACINTO SÁNCHEZ⁴ DE IÑIGO, FRANCISCO³ MUÑOZ, JACINTO², FRANCISCO¹)*. He married (1) JUANA MARÍA DE LA CONCEPCIÓN CHÁVES September 30, 1781 in Los Padillas, El Reyno de Nuevo Méjico. He married (2) MARÍA DEL CARMEN PADILLA February 29, 1808 in Pueblo de Ysleta, El Reyno de Nuevo Méjico.

Child of MARIANO SÁNCHEZ and MARÍA PADILLA is:
  i.   VIVIANA⁸ SÁNCHEZ, b. November 30, 1817; d. January 19, 1876; m. JOSÉ MARÍA SÁNCHEZ, January 24, 1843, Belén, Nuevo México, La República de México.

16. JOSÉ⁷ SÁNCHEZ *(JUAN CRISTÓBAL⁶, FRANCISCO⁵, JACINTO SÁNCHEZ⁴ DE IÑIGO, FRANCISCO³ MUÑOZ, JACINTO², FRANCISCO¹)* was born Abt. 1760 in Los Cháves, El Reyno de Nuevo Méjico, and died Abt. February 1803. He married MARÍA GUADALUPE DE LOS REYES PADILLA July 31, 1783 in Belén, El Reyno de Nuevo Méjico.

Child of JOSÉ SÁNCHEZ and MARÍA PADILLA is:
  i.   JOSÉ ANTONIO⁸ SÁNCHEZ, b. April 15, 1795.

17. MARÍA BÁRBARA⁷ SÁNCHEZ *(JUAN CRISTÓBAL⁶, FRANCISCO⁵, JACINTO SÁNCHEZ⁴ DE IÑIGO, FRANCISCO³ MUÑOZ, JACINTO², FRANCISCO¹)* was born 1762 in Los Cháves, El Reyno de Nuevo Méjico. She married DIEGO ANTONIO DURAN Y CHÁVES December 18, 1784 in Tomé, El Reyno de Nuevo Méjico.

Children of MARÍA SÁNCHEZ and DIEGO CHÁVES are:
  i.   MARÍA CANDELARIA⁸ CHÁVES.
  ii. FRANCISCO XAVIER CHÁVES, b. Abt. 1821.

18. JOSÉ GREGORIO DE LA TRINIDAD⁷ SÁNCHEZ *(JUAN CRISTÓBAL⁶, FRANCISCO⁵, JACINTO SÁNCHEZ⁴ DE IÑIGO, FRANCISCO³ MUÑOZ, JACINTO², FRANCISCO¹)* was born November 19, 1777 in Los Cháves, El Reyno de Nuevo Méjico, and died Bef. 1856. He married MARÍA RITA BACA June 05, 1805 in Belén, El Reyno de Nuevo Méjico, daughter of BARTOLOMÉ BACA and MARÍA CHÁVES.

Children of JOSÉ SÁNCHEZ and MARÍA BACA are:
  i.   JUAN CRISTÓVAL GUILLERMO⁸ SÁNCHEZ, b. February 12, 1810.
  ii. JOSÉ MANUEL SÁNCHEZ, b. January 31, 1812, Santo Tomás de la Mesilla, El Reyno de Nuevo Méjico; d. Tomé, Territory of New México.
  iii. DIEGO ANTONIO ALVINO SÁNCHEZ, b. December 17, 1813.
  iv. SANTIAGO SÁNCHEZ, b. July 24, 1816, San Fernando, Nuevo México.

      More About SANTIAGO SÁNCHEZ:
      Fact 1: July 25, 1816, Baptized in Tomé.

21.   v.   MAURICIO DE LA TRINIDAD SÁNCHEZ, b. September 22, 1820, San Fernando, El Reyno de Nuevo México; d. November 1892, San Patricio, Territory of New México.
      vi. MARÍA FRANCISCA DE PAULA BENIGNA ROMULA SÁNCHEZ, b. February 15, 1822, San Fernando, Nuevo Mexico.
      vii. JULIAN SÁNCHEZ, b. 1824.

19. DOMINGO⁷ SÁNCHEZ *(JUAN CRISTÓBAL⁶, FRANCISCO⁵, JACINTO SÁNCHEZ⁴ DE IÑIGO, FRANCISCO³ MUÑOZ, JACINTO², FRANCISCO¹)* was born Abt. 1778 in El Reyno de Nuevo Méjico. He married MARÍA GUADALUPE BACA.

Children of DOMINGO SÁNCHEZ and MARÍA BACA are:
  i.   MANUEL⁸ SÁNCHEZ, b. January 03, 1804, Belén, El Reyno de Nuevo Méjico; m. MARÍA JOSEFA DE LUNA, December 14, 1827, Belén, Nuevo Méjico, La República de México.
  ii. MANCISEA ANTONIA JUANA SÁNCHEZ.
  iii. JUAN JOSÉ SÁNCHEZ, m. MARÍA ANDREA ANALLA, April 24, 1873.
  iv. JOSÉ RAFAEL SÁNCHEZ.

Generation No. 8

20. MANUEL RAFAEL⁸ SÁNCHEZ *(JOSÉ PEDRO⁷, JACINTO⁶, JOSÉ⁵, JACINTO SÁNCHEZ⁴ DE IÑIGO, FRANCISCO³ MUÑOZ, JACINTO², FRANCISCO¹)* was born in Atrisco, El Reyno de Nuevo Méjico. He married MARÍA GERTRUDIS DURÁN Y CHÁVEZ March 12, 1801 in Alburquerque, El Reyno de Nuevo Méjico.

Children of MANUEL SÁNCHEZ and MARÍA CHÁVEZ are:
22.   i.   JUAN RAFAEL CHÁVEZ⁹ SÁNCHEZ, b. Abt. 1790, Valencia, El Reyno de Nuevo Méjico.
23.   ii.   MATÍAS SÁNCHEZ.

21. MAURICIO DE LA TRINIDAD⁸ SÁNCHEZ *(JOSÉ GREGORIO DE LA TRINIDAD⁷, JUAN CRISTÓBAL⁶, FRANCISCO⁵, JACINTO SÁNCHEZ⁴ DE IÑIGO, FRANCISCO³ MUÑOZ, JACINTO², FRANCISCO¹)* was born September 22, 1820 in San Fernando, El Reyno de Nuevo México, and died November 1892 in San Patricio, Territory of New México⁹. He married MARÍA CANDIDA DE JESÚS GONZÁLES June 02, 1843 in Tomé, Nuevo México, La República de México¹⁰, daughter of RAMON GONZÁLES and MARÍA MONTOYA.

Notes for MAURICIO DE LA TRINIDAD SÁNCHEZ:
September 24, 1820: Baptized in Tomé, Nuevo México.
1844: Migrated from Tomé to Manzano.
1862: Migrated from Manzano to El Berendo, New México.
1869: Appointed as the first Lincoln County sheriff.
Before 1870: Church records show that he was residing in Plaza de San José.

Notes for MARÍA CANDIDA DE JESÚS GONZÁLES:
1870: Church records show that she was residing in Plaza de San José.
1900 Census: Shows that she was living with her daughter Jesusita Amada and her husband Pablo Chávez.

More About MARÍA CANDIDA DE JESÚS GONZÁLES:
Fact 1: October 15, 1826, Baptized in Tomé, Nuevo México.

Children of MAURICIO SÁNCHEZ and MARÍA GONZÁLES are:
24.   i.   JOSÉ ANTONIO⁹ SÁNCHEZ, b. December 12, 1844, San Fernando, Nuevo México, La República de México; d. August 22, 1894, San Patricio, Territory of New México.
25.   ii.   ESTOLANO SÁNCHEZ, b. 1847, Torreón, Nuevo México, La República de México; d. June 20, 1907, San Patricio, Territory of New México.
        iii.   JOSÉ TORIBIO SÁNCHEZ, b. April 12, 1847, Torreón, Territory of New México.
26.   iv.   RAYMUNDA (REIMUNDA) SEGUNDA (CIGISMUNDA) SÁNCHEZ, b. June 24, 1851, Torreón, Territory of New México; d. San Patricio, New México.
27.   v.   FRANCISCO SÁNCHEZ, b. 1852, Torreón, New México; d. El Berendo, New México.
28.   vi.   JUAN RAFAEL GONZÁLES SÁNCHEZ, b. 1855, Torreón, New México.
29.   vii.   JOSÉ MANUEL SÁNCHEZ, b. 1859, Torreón, New México.
30.   viii.   MARÍA DE LA VISITACIÓN (VISITA) (BESITA) SÁNCHEZ, b. 1863, Manzano, Territory of New México.
31.   ix.   DONACIANO SÁNCHEZ, b. 1866, Lincoln County, New México; d. January 03, 1929, Tularosa, New México.
32.   x.   JESÚSITA AMADA SÁNCHEZ, b. December 02, 1870, La Plaza de San José, Territory of New México.

Generation No. 9

22. JUAN RAFAEL CHÁVEZ⁹ SÁNCHEZ *(MANUEL RAFAEL⁸, JOSÉ PEDRO⁷, JACINTO⁶, JOSÉ⁵, JACINTO SÁNCHEZ⁴ DE IÑIGO, FRANCISCO³ MUÑOZ, JACINTO², FRANCISCO¹)* was born Abt. 1790 in Valencia, El Reyno de Nuevo Méjico. He married MARÍA DE LA LUZ BERCELÓ November 03, 1822 in Tomé, Nuevo México, La República de México, daughter of JUAN BERCELÓ and MARÍA HERRERA.

Children of JUAN SÁNCHEZ and MARÍA BERCELÓ are:
        i.   PABLO¹⁰ SÁNCHEZ, m. JOSEFA SÁNCHEZ, November 28, 1854, Tomé, Territory of New México.
        ii.   LOUISA SÁNCHEZ, b. Abt. 1815.
33.   iii.   MARÍA DE REFUGIO SÁNCHEZ, b. 1826, Tomé, Nuevo México.
34.   iv.   JUAN RAFAEL BERCELÓ SÁNCHEZ, b. November 21, 1847, Tomé, Nuevo México, La República de México.

23. MATÍAS⁹ SÁNCHEZ *(MANUEL RAFAEL⁸, JOSÉ PEDRO⁷, JACINTO⁶, JOSÉ⁵, JACINTO SÁNCHEZ⁴ DE IÑIGO, FRANCISCO³ MUÑOZ, JACINTO², FRANCISCO¹)*. He married ANA MARÍA VALLEJOS September 13, 1828 in Tomé, Nuevo México, La República de México.

Children of MATÍAS SÁNCHEZ and ANA VALLEJOS are:
        i.   JOSEFA¹⁰ SÁNCHEZ, m. PABLO SÁNCHEZ, November 28, 1854, Tomé, Territory of New México.
        ii.   JUANA MARÍA SÁNCHEZ.

iii.   CATALINA SÁNCHEZ, b. Abt. 1835.

24. JOSÉ ANTONIO[9] SÁNCHEZ *(MAURICIO DE LA TRINIDAD[8], JOSÉ GREGORIO DE LA TRINIDAD[7], JUAN CRISTÓBAL[6], FRANCISCO[5], JACINTO SÁNCHEZ[4] DE IÑIGO, FRANCISCO[3] MUÑOZ, JACINTO[2], FRANCISCO[1])[11]* was born December 12, 1844 in San Fernando, Nuevo México, La República de México[12], and died August 22, 1894 in San Patricio, Territory of New México. He married TELESFORA MIRABAL[13] March 09, 1877 in Tularosa, New México[14], daughter of JUAN MIRABAL and GUADALUPE TRUJILLO.

Notes for JOSÉ ANTONIO SÁNCHEZ:
Had a homestead in Glencoe, NM.
Died when the horse he was riding fell while attempting to jump an arroyo.

More About JOSÉ ANTONIO SÁNCHEZ:
Fact 1: December 27, 1844, Baptized in Tomé, Nuevo México.

Notes for TELESFORA MIRABAL:
December 29, 1939: Died in an accident.
Buried in La Capilla de San Ysidro.

More About TELESFORA MIRABAL:
Fact 1: January 28, 1862, Baptized.

Children of JOSÉ SÁNCHEZ and TELESFORA MIRABAL are:
35.   i.   SALOMON[10] SÁNCHEZ, b. July 17, 1881, Tularosa, Territory of New México; d. 1952, Ruidoso, New México.
36.   ii.   MARÍA DE JESÚS (JESUSITA) SÁNCHEZ, b. June 25, 1882, San Patricio, Territory of New México; d. December 29, 1954, Glencoe, New Mexico.
37.   iii.   MANUEL SÁNCHEZ, b. December 17, 1884.
38.   iv.   DANOIS SÁNCHEZ, b. October 24, 1890, Ruidoso, Territory of New México; d. May 05, 1955, Tularosa, New México.
39.   v.   LUPITA (GUADALUPE) SÁNCHEZ, b. March 13, 1892.
40.   vi.   SENAIDA SÁNCHEZ, b. August 06, 1895.

25. ESTOLANO[9] SÁNCHEZ *(MAURICIO DE LA TRINIDAD[8], JOSÉ GREGORIO DE LA TRINIDAD[7], JUAN CRISTÓBAL[6], FRANCISCO[5], JACINTO SÁNCHEZ[4] DE IÑIGO, FRANCISCO[3] MUÑOZ, JACINTO[2], FRANCISCO[1])[15]* was born 1847 in Torreón, Nuevo México, La República de México[16], and died June 20, 1907 in San Patricio, Territory of New México[17]. He married CORNELIA PACHECO July 21, 1871 in La Plaza del Rio Bonito, Territory of New México[18], daughter of JOSÉ PACHECO and ROMULA SAVEDRA.

Notes for ESTOLANO SÁNCHEZ:
1900 US Census lists Estolano and family as living in Reventon, New México.

Children of ESTOLANO SÁNCHEZ and CORNELIA PACHECO are:
41.   i.   FELIPÉ E.[10] SÁNCHEZ, b. January 20, 1874, Placita del Rio Bonito, (Lincoln) New México; d. January 15, 1959, El Paso, Téxas.
42.   ii.   ELUTICIA GAVALDON (LUTISIA) SÁNCHEZ, b. 1875.
        iii.   VALENTÍN (BALENTÍN) SÁNCHEZ, b. April 14, 1881.
43.   iv.   PRESILIANO SÁNCHEZ, b. December 02, 1883, Lincoln, Territory of New México.
44.   v.   AURELIO (AVRELIO) SÁNCHEZ, b. March 12, 1885, Ruidoso, Territory of New México.
45.   vi.   CELIA SÁNCHEZ, b. July 12, 1888, Reventón, Territory of New México.
46.   vii.   ESTOLANO PACHECO SÁNCHEZ, b. 1891.
47.   viii.   ROSARIO SÁNCHEZ, b. August 11, 1896, Reventón, Territory of New México.

26. RAYMUNDA (REIMUNDA) SEGUNDA (CIGISMUNDA)[9] SÁNCHEZ *(MAURICIO DE LA TRINIDAD[8], JOSÉ GREGORIO DE LA TRINIDAD[7], JUAN CRISTÓBAL[6], FRANCISCO[5], JACINTO SÁNCHEZ[4] DE IÑIGO, FRANCISCO[3] MUÑOZ, JACINTO[2], FRANCISCO[1])* was born June 24, 1851 in Torreón, Territory of New México[19], and died in San Patricio, New México. She married (1) FLORENCIO GONZÁLES in Manzano, Territory of New México, son of SANTIAGO GONZÁLES and MARÍA ARAGÓN. She married (2) AMBROCIO CHÁVEZ October 24, 1898, son of CRUZ CHÁVEZ and JOSEFA AVEITA.

Notes for RAYMUNDA (REIMUNDA) SEGUNDA (CIGISMUNDA) SÁNCHEZ:
Buried: La Capilla de San Patricio.

Notes for FLORENCIO GONZÁLES:
Corrales is near present day Albuquerque.
1860 Census: Resided in Corrales.
In 1867: he also went by Florencio Gonzáles y Aragón.
1870 Census: Resided in Precinct 1, Fort Stanton
Buried: La Capilla de San Patricio.

Notes for AMBROCIO CHÁVEZ:
Raised FlorencioGonzales 2nd & Esoila Gonzales.

Children of RAYMUNDA SÁNCHEZ and FLORENCIO GONZÁLES are:
        i.   ARISTOTEL[10] GONZÁLES.

               Notes for ARISTOTEL GONZÁLES:
               Died young.

        ii.   ESOILA GONZÁLES, m. FRANK VIGIL, December 05, 1909.
        iii. FILOTEA GONZÁLES.

               Notes for FILOTEA GONZÁLES:
               Died young.

48.   iv.   ESLINDA GONZÁLES, b. 1867, San Patricio, Territory of New México; d. Bef. September 1923.
        v.   JUAN GONZÁLES, b. 1869.
49.   vi.   PROSPERO GONZÁLES, b. July 20, 1871; d. August 20, 1937, San Patricio, New México.
50.   vii. ALFREDO GONZÁLES, b. 1872; d. 1927, San Patricio, New México.
51.   viii. LEOPOLDO GONZÁLES, b. April 08, 1875; d. June 10, 1937.
52.   ix.   DOMINGO EPAMINOANDAZ GONZÁLES, b. April 04, 1876; d. February 20, 1970.
53.   x.   MARÍA AURORA (AVRORA) GONZÁLES, b. May 23, 1880; d. 1971.
54.   xi.   AROPAJITA (EROPAJITA) GONZÁLES, b. 1882.
        vii. AURELIA GONZÁLES, b. May 15, 1883; m. MIGUEL (2ND) LUNA, November 28, 1898, San Patricio, Territory of New México.
55.   xiii. FLORENCIO SÁNCHEZ GONZÁLES, b. November 24, 1893.

27. FRANCISCO[9] SÁNCHEZ *(MAURICIO DE LA TRINIDAD[8], JOSÉ GREGORIO DE LA TRINIDAD[7], JUAN CRISTÓBAL[6], FRANCISCO[5], JACINTO SÁNCHEZ[4] DE IÑIGO, FRANCISCO[3] MUÑOZ, JACINTO[2], FRANCISCO[1])* was born 1852 in Torreón, New México, and died in El Berendo, New México. He married (1) CONCEPCIÓN TRUJILLO March 19, 1873 in San Patricio, Territory of New México, daughter of ASENCION (CHINITA) TRUJILLO. He married (2) VIRGINIA PADILLA November 16, 1910[20], daughter of JOSÉ PADILLA and NESTORA SAMORA.

Notes for FRANCISCO SÁNCHEZ:
Was a member of the Lincoln County Mounted Riflemen.
Buried: Campo Santo Familiar en El Berendo (Near Roswell)

Notes for CONCEPCIÓN TRUJILLO:
She was blind. At age 50 lived with Francisco & Margarita Trujillo Salas.

Marriage Notes for FRANCISCO SÁNCHEZ and CONCEPCIÓN TRUJILLO:
Padrinos: Feliz Trujillo and Petra Olguín.

More About VIRGINIA PADILLA:
Fact 1: April 14, 1890, Baptized.

Children of FRANCISCO SÁNCHEZ and CONCEPCIÓN TRUJILLO are:
56.   i.   NAPOLEÓN[10] SÁNCHEZ, b. December 1873, San Patricio, Territory of New México.

57.	ii.	DAVÍD SÁNCHEZ, b. November 06, 1876, Libertad (San Patricio), Territory of New México; d. Roswell, New México.
58.	iii.	ANTONIO SÁNCHEZ, b. February 08, 1878.
59.	iv.	MAURICIO SÁNCHEZ, b. October 31, 1880, San Patricio, Territory of New México; d. San Patricio, New México.
60.	v.	PATRICIO SÁNCHEZ, b. January 30, 1883, San Patricio, Territory of New México; d. 1955, San Patricio, New México.
61.	vi.	JACOBO SÁNCHEZ, b. April 22, 1881; d. July 06, 1968.
62.	vii.	ELOISA SÁNCHEZ, b. February 10, 1891, Manzano, New México; d. Manzano, New México.
63.	viii.	CONRADO SÁNCHEZ, b. July 15, 1894; d. Casa Grande, Arizona.
64.	ix.	REFUGIA SÁNCHEZ, b. July 02, 1899, San Patricio, Territory of New México.

Children of FRANCISCO SÁNCHEZ and VIRGINIA PADILLA are:
     x.   MANUEL[10] SÁNCHEZ, b. 1914; m. JOSEFITA SAÍZ.
     xi.   MAXIMILIANO SÁNCHEZ, b. July 28, 1916; m. LOLA -----.
     xii.   LEANDRA SÁNCHEZ, m. PEDRO LOSOYA.

28. JUAN RAFAEL GONZÁLES[9] SÁNCHEZ *(MAURICIO DE LA TRINIDAD[8], JOSÉ GREGORIO DE LA TRINIDAD[7], JUAN CRISTÓBAL[6], FRANCISCO[5], JACINTO SÁNCHEZ[4] DE IÑIGO, FRANCISCO[3] MUÑOZ, JACINTO[2], FRANCISCO[1])* was born 1855 in Torreón, New México[21]. He married EVARISTA GONZÁLES May 09, 1877 in Tularosa, New México.

Child of JUAN SÁNCHEZ and EVARISTA GONZÁLES is:
     i.   EVARISTA GONZÁLES[10] SÁNCHEZ, b. February 28, 1878.

         More About EVARISTA GONZÁLES SÁNCHEZ:
         Fact 1: March 13, 1878, Baptized.

29. JOSÉ MANUEL[9] SÁNCHEZ *(MAURICIO DE LA TRINIDAD[8], JOSÉ GREGORIO DE LA TRINIDAD[7], JUAN CRISTÓBAL[6], FRANCISCO[5], JACINTO SÁNCHEZ[4] DE IÑIGO, FRANCISCO[3] MUÑOZ, JACINTO[2], FRANCISCO[1])* was born 1859 in Torreón, New México. He married (1) MARÍA ANTONIA HERRERA. He married (2) MARÍA SÁNCHEZ July 20, 1883 in Lincoln, New México, daughter of LEANDRO SÁNCHEZ and MARÍA SÁNCHEZ.

Notes for JOSÉ MANUEL SÁNCHEZ:
1920s: Lived with his sister, María de la Visitacion Sánchez.

Child of JOSÉ SÁNCHEZ and MARÍA HERRERA is:
     i.   EDUARDO[10] SÁNCHEZ, b. 1894.

30. MARÍA DE LA VISITACIÓN (VISITA) (BESITA)[9] SÁNCHEZ *(MAURICIO DE LA TRINIDAD[8], JOSÉ GREGORIO DE LA TRINIDAD[7], JUAN CRISTÓBAL[6], FRANCISCO[5], JACINTO SÁNCHEZ[4] DE IÑIGO, FRANCISCO[3] MUÑOZ, JACINTO[2], FRANCISCO[1])* was born 1863 in Manzano, Territory of New México. She married JUAN RAFAEL BERCELÓ SÁNCHEZ[22] August 29, 1875 in Manzano, Territory of New México[23], son of JUAN SÁNCHEZ and MARÍA BERCELÓ.

Notes for JUAN RAFAEL BERCELÓ SÁNCHEZ:
1860 Census: Living in Tajique.
1870 Census: Living in Tajique.

Marriage Notes for MARÍA SÁNCHEZ and JUAN SÁNCHEZ:
Padrinos:

Children of MARÍA SÁNCHEZ and JUAN SÁNCHEZ are:
	i.	BEATRIZ[10] SÁNCHEZ.
	ii.	SOFIA SÁNCHEZ, b. Glencoe, Territory of New México; m. JOSÉ OROSCO[24].
	iii.	SOFIO SÁNCHEZ, m. GONSAGITA SALAS, May 29, 1939[25].
65.	iv.	RAYMUNDO SÁNCHEZ, b. March 15, 1879, Glencoe, Territory of New México; d. November 26, 1958.
66.	v.	AMADITA SÁNCHEZ, b. 1887, Glencoe, Territory of New México; d. July 22, 1936.
	vi.	LUZ SÁNCHEZ, b. June 28, 1887, Glencoe, Territory of New México[26].

67.	vii.	RITA SÁNCHEZ, b. July 12, 1891, Ruidoso, Territory of New México; d. Artesia, New México.
	viii.	CONFERINA ORISITACIÓN SÁNCHEZ, b. November 16, 1891, Glencoe, Territory of New México; d. November 17, 1938[27]; m. (1) WILLIAM (JULIAN) HERRERA GILL[28], January 13, 1916, Glencoe, New Mexico; m. (2) MARCELO HERRERA[29], July 10, 1917[30].

Notes for CONFERINA ORISITACIÓN SÁNCHEZ:
February 04, 1892: Baptized. Padrinos: Julian Silva and Jesusita Sánchez.

More About CONFERINA ORISITACIÓN SÁNCHEZ:
Fact 1: Baptized at 2 months old.

More About WILLIAM (JULIAN) HERRERA GILL:
Fact 1: September 24, 1884, Baptized.

Marriage Notes for CONFERINA SÁNCHEZ and WILLIAM GILL:
Married in La Capilla de San Ysidro. Padrinos: Manuel Sánchez and Estela Gill Sánchez.

68.	ix.	EDUARDO BARCELON SÁNCHEZ, b. October 13, 1893, Glencoe, Territory of New México; d. May 28, 1954.
69.	x.	BERSABE SÁNCHEZ, b. June 10, 1897, Glencoe, Territory of New México.
	xi.	VICTORIA SÁNCHEZ, b. February 27, 1899[31]; m. (1) CELSO TRUJILLO; m. (2) ISABEL MONTOYA, February 23, 1921.

More About VICTORIA SÁNCHEZ:
Fact 1: August 03, 1899, Baptized.

	xii.	MANUEL SÁNCHEZ, b. January 20, 1901[32].

More About MANUEL SÁNCHEZ:
Fact 1: May 25, 1901, Baptized.

70.	xiii.	MACLOFA SÁNCHEZ, b. 1904.

31. DONACIANO[9] SÁNCHEZ *(MAURICIO DE LA TRINIDAD[8], JOSÉ GREGORIO DE LA TRINIDAD[7], JUAN CRISTÓBAL[6], FRANCISCO[5], JACINTO SÁNCHEZ[4] DE IÑIGO, FRANCISCO[3] MUÑOZ, JACINTO[2], FRANCISCO[1])* was born 1866 in Lincoln County, New México, and died January 03, 1929 in Tularosa, New México. He married (1) FELECITA SERRANO. He married (2) ADELA VIGIL. He married (3) BIDAL (VIDAL) ANALLA May 11, 1884, daughter of PEDRO ANALLA and MARÍA CHÁVEZ.

Notes for DONACIANO SÁNCHEZ:
Buried: Tularosa, New México.

Notes for ADELA VIGIL:
Buried: Tularosa, New México.

Children of DONACIANO SÁNCHEZ and FELECITA SERRANO are:
    i.   FRANCIS[10] SÁNCHEZ.
    ii.   MARÍA SERRANO SÁNCHEZ.
    iii. DANIEL SÁNCHEZ.
    iv. CHANO SÁNCHEZ.
    v.   MARGARITA SÁNCHEZ, b. November 07, 1883, Picacho, Territory of New México[33].

Notes for MARGARITA SÁNCHEZ:
Buried: Tularosa, New México.

Children of DONACIANO SÁNCHEZ and ADELA VIGIL are:
    vi. FRANCISCO[10] SÁNCHEZ, b. July 10, 1904.
    vii. JOSÉ SÁNCHEZ, b. February 01, 1913.
    viii. MARÍA SÁNCHEZ, d. March 25, 1929.

Notes for MARÍA SÁNCHEZ:
Buried: El Paso, Téxas.

Children of DONACIANO SÁNCHEZ and BIDAL ANALLA are:
  ix.   JUAN BAUTISTA[10] SÁNCHEZ, b. December 05, 1885.

           More About JUAN BAUTISTA SÁNCHEZ:
           Fact 1: January 03, 1886, Baptized.

  x.   MARÍA ANAYA SÁNCHEZ, b. March 15, 1900; d. Tularosa, New México.

           Notes for MARÍA ANAYA SÁNCHEZ:
           Buried: Tularosa, New México.

32. JESÚSITA AMADA[9] SÁNCHEZ *(MAURICIO DE LA TRINIDAD[8], JOSÉ GREGORIO DE LA TRINIDAD[7], JUAN CRISTÓBAL[6], FRANCISCO[5], JACINTO SÁNCHEZ[4] DE IÑIGO, FRANCISCO[3] MUÑOZ, JACINTO[2], FRANCISCO[1])* was born December 02, 1870 in La Plaza de San José, Territory of New México[34]. She married (1) ABEL MIRABAL. She married (2) PABLO CHÁVEZ July 20, 1883 in Las Angusturas, Territory of New México[35], son of JOSÉ CHÁVEZ and MARÍA LUNA.

Notes for JESÚSITA AMADA SÁNCHEZ:
Padrinos: Juan Torres, Trinidad Chávez.

Children of JESÚSITA SÁNCHEZ and PABLO CHÁVEZ are:
        i.   AMADA[10] SÁNCHEZ[36], b. August 1886.
71.   ii.   TRANCITO CHÁVEZ, b. July 20, 1887, Glencoe, Territory of New México; d. April 07, 1975, San Patricio, New México.
72.   iii.   CANDIDO CHÁVEZ, b. 1889; d. 1979.
       iv.   FLORINDA CHÁVEZ, b. September 08, 1891[37]; m. JUAN BLEA, July 03, 1908.

           More About FLORINDA CHÁVEZ:
           Fact 1: October 08, 1891, Baptized.

        v.   OLYMPIA CHÁVEZ[38], b. 1894[39]; m. JOHN MACKEY[40], April 26, 1909[41].

           Notes for JOHN MACKEY:
  Was Justice of the Peace in San Patricio.

       vi.   ADELAIDO CHÁVEZ[42], b. December 17, 1903; m. LUPE VALENSUELA, July 05, 1934, Picacho, New México.

           Marriage Notes for ADELAIDO CHÁVEZ and LUPE VALENSUELA:
           Married by: Justice of the Peace, Ramon Salas.

73.   vii.   LEOPOLDO CHÁVEZ, b. April 25, 1907.
74.   viii.   RUMELIO CHÁVEZ, b. 1910.
75.   ix.   HERMANDO (ERMANDO) CHÁVEZ, b. February 22, 1914.

Generation No. 10

33. MARÍA DE REFUGIO[10] SÁNCHEZ *(JUAN RAFAEL CHÁVEZ[9], MANUEL RAFAEL[8], JOSÉ PEDRO[7], JACINTO[6], JOSÉ[5], JACINTO SÁNCHEZ[4] DE IÑIGO, FRANCISCO[3] MUÑOZ, JACINTO[2], FRANCISCO[1])* was born 1826 in Tomé, Nuevo México. She married JUAN FRANCISCO PABLO VIGIL, son of MANUEL VIGIL and SOLEDAD APODACA.

Children of MARÍA SÁNCHEZ and JUAN VIGIL are:
        i.   BEATRIZ[11] VIGIL, m. ADENAGO TORREZ.
       ii.   BERSABE VIGIL, m. AGAPITO SÁNCHEZ.
       iii.   JESÚS VIGIL.

    iv.   JUANA VIGIL, m. LUCIANO TRUJILLO.
    v.   MANUEL VIGIL, m. MARÍA POLINARIA TRUJILLO.
    vi.   VITERBO VIGIL.
    vii. MARÍA CATARINA DE LA LUZ VIGIL, b. May 16, 1841, Valencia, Nuevo México, La República de México.
    viii. JUANA (MARÍA) VIGIL, b. June 15, 1844, Tomé, Nuevo México, La República de México; m. ANDRÉS LUJÁN.
    ix.   JOSÉ MANUEL VIGIL, b. June 10, 1846, Valencia, Nuevo México, La República de México.
    x.   ABRAN VIGIL, b. March 16, 1851, Tajíque, Territory of New México.

34. JUAN RAFAEL BERCELÓ[10] SÁNCHEZ *(JUAN RAFAEL CHÁVEZ*[9]*, MANUEL RAFAEL*[8]*, JOSÉ PEDRO*[7]*, JACINTO*[6]*, JOSÉ*[5]*, JACINTO SÁNCHEZ*[4] *DE IÑIGO, FRANCISCO*[3] *MUÑOZ, JACINTO*[2]*, FRANCISCO*[1]*)*[43] was born November 21, 1847 in Tomé, Nuevo México, La República de México. He married MARÍA DE LA VISITACIÓN (VISITA) (BESITA) SÁNCHEZ August 29, 1875 in Manzano, Territory of New México[44], daughter of MAURICIO SÁNCHEZ and MARÍA GONZÁLES.

Notes for JUAN RAFAEL BERCELÓ SÁNCHEZ:
1860 Census: Living in Tajique.
1870 Census: Living in Tajique.

Marriage Notes for JUAN SÁNCHEZ and MARÍA SÁNCHEZ:
Padrinos:

Children of JUAN SÁNCHEZ and MARÍA SÁNCHEZ are:
    i.   BEATRIZ[11] SÁNCHEZ.
    ii.   SOFIA SÁNCHEZ, b. Glencoe, Territory of New México; m. JOSÉ OROSCO[45].
    iii. SOFIO SÁNCHEZ, m. GONSAGITA SALAS, May 29, 1939[46].
    iv.   RAYMUNDO SÁNCHEZ[47], b. March 15, 1879, Glencoe, Territory of New México[48]; d. November 26, 1958[49]; m. AUGUSTINA ULIBARRÍ, December 17, 1910[50].

        Marriage Notes for RAYMUNDO SÁNCHEZ and AUGUSTINA ULIBARRÍ:
        Padrinos: Cosme Sedillos and daughter.

    v.   AMADITA SÁNCHEZ, b. 1887, Glencoe, Territory of New México; d. July 22, 1936[51]; m. (1) FEDERICO PEÑA; m. (2) LUÍS PEÑA, January 12, 1903[52].
    vi.   LUZ SÁNCHEZ, b. June 28, 1887, Glencoe, Territory of New México[53].
    vii. RITA SÁNCHEZ, b. July 12, 1891, Ruidoso, Territory of New México; d. Artesia, New México[54]; m. NEWMAN GILL[55], July 03, 1915[56].
    viii. CONFERINA ORISITACIÓN SÁNCHEZ, b. November 16, 1891, Glencoe, Territory of New México; d. November 17, 1938[57]; m. (1) WILLIAM (JULIAN) HERRERA GILL[58], January 13, 1916, Glencoe, New Mexico; m. (2) MARCELO HERRERA[59], July 10, 1917[60].

        Notes for CONFERINA ORISITACIÓN SÁNCHEZ:
        February 04, 1892: Baptized. Padrinos: Julian Silva and Jesusita Sánchez.

        More About CONFERINA ORISITACIÓN SÁNCHEZ:
        Fact 1: Baptized at 2 months old.

        More About WILLIAM (JULIAN) HERRERA GILL:
        Fact 1: September 24, 1884, Baptized.

        Marriage Notes for CONFERINA SÁNCHEZ and WILLIAM GILL:
        Married in La Capilla de San Ysidro. Padrinos: Manuel Sánchez and Estela Gill Sánchez.

    ix.   EDUARDO BARCELON SÁNCHEZ, b. October 13, 1893, Glencoe, Territory of New México[61]; d. May 28, 1954[62]; m. SENAIDA MONTOYA, October 08, 1920, Carrizozo, New México.
    x.   BERSABE SÁNCHEZ, b. June 10, 1897, Glencoe, Territory of New México[63]; m. TEODORO (THEODORO) MONTOYA, December 11, 1919[64].

        More About BERSABE SÁNCHEZ:
        Fact 1: October 28, 1897, Baptized.

        More About TEODORO (THEODORO) MONTOYA:
        Fact 1: June 18, 1893, Baptized.

Fact 2: April 18, 1919, WW I veteran. Discharged from Camp Owen Bierne, Texas.[65]

xi. VICTORIA SÁNCHEZ, b. February 27, 1899[66]; m. (1) CELSO TRUJILLO; m. (2) ISABEL MONTOYA, February 23, 1921.

More About VICTORIA SÁNCHEZ:
Fact 1: August 03, 1899, Baptized.

xii. MANUEL SÁNCHEZ, b. January 20, 1901[67].

More About MANUEL SÁNCHEZ:
Fact 1: May 25, 1901, Baptized.

xiii. MACLOFA SÁNCHEZ, b. 1904; m. DOMINGO PACHECO.

35. SALOMON[10] SÁNCHEZ *(JOSÉ ANTONIO[9], MAURICIO DE LA TRINIDAD[8], JOSÉ GREGORIO DE LA TRINIDAD[7], JUAN CRISTÓBAL[6], FRANCISCO[5], JACINTO SÁNCHEZ[4] DE IÑIGO, FRANCISCO[3] MUÑOZ, JACINTO[2], FRANCISCO[1])* was born July 17, 1881 in Tularosa, Territory of New México, and died 1952 in Ruidoso, New México[68]. He married (1) JENNIE (JOSEFA) GILL December 06, 1900[69], daughter of WILLIAM GILL and MARÍA HERRERA. He married (2) MANUELITA SÁNCHEZ[70] February 03, 1917 in Ruidoso, New México[71], daughter of TORIVIO SÁNCHEZ and AVRELIA MARTÍNEZ.

More About SALOMON SÁNCHEZ:
Fact 1: November 17, 1878, Baptized in Tularosa, Territory of New México

Marriage Notes for SALOMON SÁNCHEZ and JENNIE GILL:
Married by: Father Girand.
Padrinos: Abel Mirabal and Jesúsita Sánchez.

Marriage Notes for SALOMON SÁNCHEZ and MANUELITA SÁNCHEZ:
Married by: Father Girma.

Children of SALOMON SÁNCHEZ and JENNIE GILL are:
76. i. VIRGINIA[11] SÁNCHEZ, b. April 13, 1902, Ruidoso, Territory of New México; d. Ruidoso, New México.
77. ii. TELESFORA SÁNCHEZ, b. November 19, 1903, Glencoe, Territory of New México.
iii. ENRÍQUES GILL SÁNCHEZ, b. September 25, 1904, Glencoe, New México[72]; m. CAROLINA GAMBOA[73].

Notes for ENRÍQUES GILL SÁNCHEZ:
He was also known as Henry Gill.

78. iv. SALOMON GILL SÁNCHEZ, b. March 17, 1905, Glencoe, Territory of New México.
v. EDUVIJEN SÁNCHEZ, b. 1910; m. JOSÉ ANTONIO SILVA, April 09, 1928[74].
79. vi. ANATALIA (NATALIA) SÁNCHEZ, b. 1912.
vii. CONSOLACION (CONSUELO) SÁNCHEZ, b. September 10, 1914; d. April 28, 1996, Tularosa, New México; m. BENITO SILVA, February 13, 1932[75].

Children of SALOMON SÁNCHEZ and MANUELITA SÁNCHEZ are:
viii. PORFIRIO[11] SÁNCHEZ, m. FLORIPE HERRERA.
ix. CARLOS SÁNCHEZ, b. 1917; m. ALVESITA MONTOYA.
x. EUFRACIA SÁNCHEZ, b. 1920; m. (1) EUGENIO ANAYA; m. (2) ESTEVAN ROMERO.
xi. LUVIN SÁNCHEZ, b. 1922; m. SUSANA CANDELARIA.
xii. AMALIA SÁNCHEZ, b. April 03, 1924[76].

Notes for AMALIA SÁNCHEZ:
Died young.

xiii. ALBERTO SÁNCHEZ, b. 1927; m. EVA MCKINLEY.

Notes for EVA MCKINLEY:
Raised by Eduardo Sedillo & Dominga Maés.

36. MARÍA DE JESÚS (JESUSITA)[10] SÁNCHEZ *(JOSÉ ANTONIO[9], MAURICIO DE LA TRINIDAD[8], JOSÉ GREGORIO DE LA TRINIDAD[7], JUAN CRISTÓBAL[6], FRANCISCO[5], JACINTO SÁNCHEZ[4] DE IÑIGO, FRANCISCO[3] MUÑOZ, JACINTO[2], FRANCISCO[1])* was born June 25, 1882 in San Patricio, Territory of New México[77], and died December 29, 1954 in Glencoe, New Mexico. She married JULIAN SILVA November 23, 1906 in San Patricio, Territory of New México[78], son of MANUEL GUTIÉRREZ and LEONARDA JIRÓN.

More About MARÍA DE JESÚS (JESUSITA) SÁNCHEZ:
Fact 1: July 30, 1882, Baptized.

Marriage Notes for MARÍA SÁNCHEZ and JULIAN SILVA:
Married by Father Girma.

Children of MARÍA SÁNCHEZ and JULIAN SILVA are:
    i.   CARMELITA[11] SILVA, b. 1910[79]; m. RAMON SILVA.
80.   ii.   ERNESTO SILVA, b. June 27, 1912; d. 1981.

37. MANUEL[10] SÁNCHEZ *(JOSÉ ANTONIO[9], MAURICIO DE LA TRINIDAD[8], JOSÉ GREGORIO DE LA TRINIDAD[7], JUAN CRISTÓBAL[6], FRANCISCO[5], JACINTO SÁNCHEZ[4] DE IÑIGO, FRANCISCO[3] MUÑOZ, JACINTO[2], FRANCISCO[1])* was born December 17, 1884[80]. He married STELLA (ESTELA) GILL June 14, 1909[81], daughter of WILLIAM GILL and MARÍA HERRERA.

Notes for STELLA (ESTELA) GILL:
Buried: La Capilla de San Ysidro, Glencoe.

Child of MANUEL SÁNCHEZ and STELLA GILL is:
    i.   AMANDA[11] SÁNCHEZ, m. LUÍS TORREZ, November 30, 1927[82].

        Notes for LUÍS TORREZ:
        After selling the farm, he and his wife migrated to Roswell, New México.
        WW I Veteran.

        More About LUÍS TORREZ:
        Fact 1: August 26, 1918, Discharged, WW I veteran.

38. DANOIS[10] SÁNCHEZ *(JOSÉ ANTONIO[9], MAURICIO DE LA TRINIDAD[8], JOSÉ GREGORIO DE LA TRINIDAD[7], JUAN CRISTÓBAL[6], FRANCISCO[5], JACINTO SÁNCHEZ[4] DE IÑIGO, FRANCISCO[3] MUÑOZ, JACINTO[2], FRANCISCO[1])* was born October 24, 1890 in Ruidoso, Territory of New México[83], and died May 05, 1955 in Tularosa, New México[84]. He married GUADALUPE VALLES May 1909.

Notes for DANOIS SÁNCHEZ:
Moved family to Tularosa, New México.

More About DANOIS SÁNCHEZ:
Fact 1: November 05, 1890, Baptized.[85]

Children of DANOIS SÁNCHEZ and GUADALUPE VALLES are:
    i.   ADELINA[11] SÁNCHEZ[86].
    ii.   FLORA SÁNCHEZ.
    iii.   MARÍA AMABLE SÁNCHEZ.
    iv.   RUBÉN VALLES SÁNCHEZ.
    v.   TELESFORA SÁNCHEZ, b. 1912.
    vi.   DANOIS VALLES SÁNCHEZ, b. 1914.
    vii.   ANTONIO SÁNCHEZ, b. 1915.
    viii.   SARAFIN SÁNCHEZ, b. 1916.
    ix.   MABEL SÁNCHEZ, b. 1917.
    x.   GODFREY SÁNCHEZ, b. Abt. 1920.
    xi.   ISMAEL SÁNCHEZ, b. July 16, 1921[87].

        More About ISMAEL SÁNCHEZ:
        Fact 1: August 09, 1921, Baptized.

xii.　NARCISO SÁNCHEZ, b. October 29, 1926[88].

　　　More About NARCISO SÁNCHEZ:
　　　Fact 1: November 01, 1926, Baptized.

39. LUPITA (GUADALUPE)[10] SÁNCHEZ *(JOSÉ ANTONIO[9], MAURICIO DE LA TRINIDAD[8], JOSÉ GREGORIO DE LA TRINIDAD[7], JUAN CRISTÓBAL[6], FRANCISCO[5], JACINTO SÁNCHEZ[4] DE IÑIGO, FRANCISCO[3] MUÑOZ, JACINTO[2], FRANCISCO[1])* was born March 13, 1892[89]. She married JUAN MONTES May 01, 1912[90], son of ALEJO MONTES and ANGELA SÁNCHEZ.

More About LUPITA (GUADALUPE) SÁNCHEZ:
Fact 1: June 18, 1892, Baptized.[91]

Children of LUPITA SÁNCHEZ and JUAN MONTES are:
　　i.　ALEJO SÁNCHEZ[11] MONTES.

　　　　　More About ALEJO SÁNCHEZ MONTES:
　　　　　Fact 1: September 27, 1883, Baptized.
　　　　　Fact 2: Died young.

　　ii.　FERMÍN MONTES, m. CERINIA CONTRERAS, August 22, 1938, Alburquerque, New México.
　　iii.　JUAN SÁNCHEZ MONTES, m. CLEOFAS ROMERO.
　　iv.　ORLANDO MONTES, m. (1) CECILIA CHÁVEZ; m. (2) GLORIA CHÁVEZ.
　　v.　AMELIA MONTES, b. October 1925; d. February 15, 1981[92]; m. FRUTOSO HERRERA.

40. SENAIDA[10] SÁNCHEZ *(JOSÉ ANTONIO[9], MAURICIO DE LA TRINIDAD[8], JOSÉ GREGORIO DE LA TRINIDAD[7], JUAN CRISTÓBAL[6], FRANCISCO[5], JACINTO SÁNCHEZ[4] DE IÑIGO, FRANCISCO[3] MUÑOZ, JACINTO[2], FRANCISCO[1])* was born August 06, 1895[93]. She married JOHN MACKEY[94] February 01, 1912[95], son of PATRICK MACKEY and GUADALUPE SAMORA.

More About SENAIDA SÁNCHEZ:
Fact 1: August 22, 1895, Baptized.[96]

Notes for JOHN MACKEY:
　　Was Justice of the Peace in San Patricio.

Children of SENAIDA SÁNCHEZ and JOHN MACKEY are:
　　i.　CECILIA[11] MACKEY, b. 1913; m. FRED TORREZ.
　　ii.　RUBE MACKEY, b. 1919.

　　　　　Notes for RUBE MACKEY:
　　　　　Died young.

　　iii.　NORA MACKEY, m. TRANQUELINO SILVA.
　　iv.　JAMES MACKEY, m. (1) LIBBY CHÁVEZ; m. (2) ELIZABETH CHÁVEZ.

41. FELIPÉ E.[10] SÁNCHEZ *(ESTOLANO[9], MAURICIO DE LA TRINIDAD[8], JOSÉ GREGORIO DE LA TRINIDAD[7], JUAN CRISTÓBAL[6], FRANCISCO[5], JACINTO SÁNCHEZ[4] DE IÑIGO, FRANCISCO[3] MUÑOZ, JACINTO[2], FRANCISCO[1])* was born January 20, 1874 in Placita del Rio Bonito, (Lincoln) New México[97], and died January 15, 1959 in El Paso, Téxas[98]. He married CANDELARIA PADILLA, daughter of ANDALESIO PADILLA and PAUBLITA MARIÑO.

Notes for FELIPÉ E. SÁNCHEZ:
Ranched on the Río Ruidoso and Reventón.
Migrated to San Elizario, Téxas
Migrated back to Tularosa, New México.

More About FELIPÉ E. SÁNCHEZ:
Fact 1: January 21, 1874, Baptized.[99]

Children of FELIPÉ SÁNCHEZ and CANDELARIA PADILLA are:

81.   i.   ANTONIO[11] SÁNCHEZ, b. May 13, 1897, Tres Ritos, New México; d. February 21, 1984, San Elizario, Texas.
82.   ii.   PAUBLITA (PABLITA) SÁNCHEZ, b. July 30, 1898, Tres Rios, Territory of New México; d. October 13, 1963, Las Vegas, New México.
       iii. SIPIO SÁNCHEZ, b. 1899; m. LOLA MIRABAL.
83.   iv.   CORNELIA SÁNCHEZ, b. November 16, 1902, Lincoln County, New México.
84.   v.   EMILIANO SÁNCHEZ, b. August 11, 1904, Hondo, Territory of New México.
85.   vi.   ABRAHAM (ABRAN) SÁNCHEZ, b. December 21, 1905, White Oaks, Territory of New México; d. November 18, 1973, El Paso, Téxas.
86.   vii. REYNALDO SÁNCHEZ, b. Abt. 1906.
       viii. CELEDONIA SÁNCHEZ, b. Abt. 1909; d. Abt. 1921.

              Notes for CELEDONIA SÁNCHEZ:
              Died when she was 12 years old.

87.   ix.   ONECIMO SÁNCHEZ, b. 1915.
88.   x.   BENITO SÁNCHEZ, b. Private.

42. ELUTICIA GAVALDON (LUTISIA)[10] SÁNCHEZ *(ESTOLANO[9], MAURICIO DE LA TRINIDAD[8], JOSÉ GREGORIO DE LA TRINIDAD[7], JUAN CRISTÓBAL[6], FRANCISCO[5], JACINTO SÁNCHEZ[4] DE IÑIGO, FRANCISCO[3] MUÑOZ, JACINTO[2], FRANCISCO[1])[100]* was born 1875. She married (1) ERINELLO FRANCISCO (ERINEO) GAVALDON[101], son of ENCARNACION GAVALDON and ANTONIA DE GAVALDON. She married (2) AUGUSTÍN MIRANDA CHÁVEZ April 12, 1901[102], son of DIONICIA MIRANDA.

Notes for ELUTICIA GAVALDON (LUTISIA) SÁNCHEZ:
1900 Census: Eluticia and her children were living with her parents.

Notes for ERINELLO FRANCISCO (ERINEO) GAVALDON:
1880 Census lists that he lived in Torreón, Valencia County, New México.

Notes for AUGUSTÍN MIRANDA CHÁVEZ:
Had a brother, Rafael Chávez, the son of Maximiano Chávez.

June 28, 1910 to December 19, 1914 and March 2, 1921 to December 7, 1922: Was the Post Master for the Reventón Post Office.

Children of ELUTICIA SÁNCHEZ and ERINELLO GAVALDON are:
       i.   ROSA[11] GAVALDON, b. 1891; m. AVRELIO MARTÍNEZ, December 12, 1910, Patos, New México[103].

              Notes for AVRELIO MARTÍNEZ:
              Raised by Leandro Pacheco.

              Marriage Notes for ROSA GAVALDON and AVRELIO MARTÍNEZ:
              Married at Nuestra Señora de Guadalupe Church in Patos, New México.
              Married by: Father Girma.

       ii.   AVRORA GAVALDON, b. 1895[104]; m. NARCISO MONTOYA[105106].
       iii. LUPE GAVALDON, b. August 20, 1897, Patos, Territory of New México[107]; m. ELVIRA MÁRQUES, August 13, 1921[108].

              Notes for LUPE GAVALDON:
              Patos, New México is located close to Reventón, New México east of Sierra Capitán. Currently it is inaccesible because it is located on a private farm.

              More About LUPE GAVALDON:
              Fact 1: December 12, 1897, Baptized.

43. PRESILIANO[10] SÁNCHEZ *(ESTOLANO[9], MAURICIO DE LA TRINIDAD[8], JOSÉ GREGORIO DE LA TRINIDAD[7], JUAN CRISTÓBAL[6], FRANCISCO[5], JACINTO SÁNCHEZ[4] DE IÑIGO, FRANCISCO[3] MUÑOZ,*

JACINTO², FRANCISCO¹)¹⁰⁹ was born December 02, 1883 in Lincoln, Territory of New México. He married (1) LUPITA OROSCO. He married (2) GUADALUPE (LUPITA) MARTÍNEZ October 12, 1905 in Reventón, Territory of New México¹¹⁰, daughter of ANTONIO MARTÍNEZ and JUANA GUSTAMANTE.

More About PRESILIANO SÁNCHEZ:
Fact 1: September 12, 1896, Church records show that he was in Reventon at the time.

Children of PRESILIANO SÁNCHEZ and LUPITA OROSCO are:
  i.   FIDEL¹¹ SÁNCHEZ, m. AMALIA TORRES.
  ii.   FERNANDO SÁNCHEZ, m. JOSEFITA TRUJILLO, December 11, 1937¹¹¹.
  iii.   ESTOLANO OROSCO SÁNCHEZ, m. (1) EMMA PINO; m. (2) UTILIA (EUTILIA) MONTOYA.

Child of PRESILIANO SÁNCHEZ and GUADALUPE MARTÍNEZ is:
       CORA¹¹ SÁNCHEZ.

44. AURELIO (AVRELIO)¹⁰ SÁNCHEZ *(ESTOLANO⁹, MAURICIO DE LA TRINIDAD⁸, JOSÉ GREGORIO DE LA TRINIDAD⁷, JUAN CRISTÓBAL⁶, FRANCISCO⁵, JACINTO SÁNCHEZ⁴ DE IÑIGO, FRANCISCO³ MUÑOZ, JACINTO², FRANCISCO¹)¹¹²* was born March 12, 1885 in Ruidoso, Territory of New México. He married ANASTACIA ARAGÓN¹¹³ October 11, 1907 in Reventón, Territory of New México, daughter of MANUEL ARAGÓN and PORFIRIA GONZÁLES.

More About AURELIO (AVRELIO) SÁNCHEZ:
Fact 1: September 12, 1896, Chgurch records show that he was in Reventon at the time.

Children of AURELIO SÁNCHEZ and ANASTACIA ARAGÓN are:
  i.   EDUARDO (EDWARD)¹¹ SÁNCHEZ, m. BONNIE -----.
  ii.   IDALIA SÁNCHEZ, m. PETROLINO SEDILLOS¹¹⁴, February 22, 1926.
  iii.   SANTANA SÁNCHEZ, m. MAX CHÁVEZ¹¹⁵, Reventón, New México.
         EDUMENIO SÁNCHEZ, b. 1916; m. SERIA SÁNCHEZ.
89.   v.   SORAIDA SÁNCHEZ, b. August 27, 1916.
  vi.   MACRINA SÁNCHEZ, b. 1920; m. ANDRÉS RICHARDSON.
  vii.   VICENTE SÁNCHEZ, b. 1922; m. LUISA SALSBERRY.
  viii. CLOVIS SÁNCHEZ, b. May 17, 1923, San Patricio, New México; m. CARLOTA PIÑEDA.

         More About CLOVIS SÁNCHEZ:
         Fact 1: September 07, 1943, WW II veteran. Navy, Discharged from San Diego, California.¹¹⁶

  ix.   BALDAMAR SÁNCHEZ, b. 1924; m. MARGARETTE PENDLEY.
  x.   PRESILIANO SÁNCHEZ, b. 1926; m. CECILIA ROMERO.
  xi.   LUCY SÁNCHEZ, b. 1930; m. ALBERT TELLES.

45. CELIA¹⁰ SÁNCHEZ *(ESTOLANO⁹, MAURICIO DE LA TRINIDAD⁸, JOSÉ GREGORIO DE LA TRINIDAD⁷, JUAN CRISTÓBAL⁶, FRANCISCO⁵, JACINTO SÁNCHEZ⁴ DE IÑIGO, FRANCISCO³ MUÑOZ, JACINTO², FRANCISCO¹)¹¹⁷* was born July 12, 1888 in Reventón, Territory of New México. She married JORGE (GEORGE) TORREZ¹¹⁸ November 12, 1906, son of IGNACIO TORRES and MANUELA LUCERO.

Children of CELIA SÁNCHEZ and JORGE TORREZ are:
  i.   ADENAGO¹¹ TORREZ, b. 1908, Hondo, New México; m. (1) BEATRIZ VIGIL; m. (2) BEATRIZ TORREZ.
  ii.   FELIS TORREZ, b. 1909; m. PEDRO SALCIDO, October 24, 1928¹¹⁹.
  iii.   GEORGE SÁNCHEZ TORREZ, b. 1911.
  iv.   WILFIDO TORREZ, b. 1913; m. JULIA -----.
  v.   MIGUEL TORREZ, b. 1917; m. SOCORRO -----.
  vi.   MANUELITA TORREZ, b. 1919; m. JUAN JAURIQUE.
  vii.   JAY TORREZ, b. Aft. 1920; m. EDNA -----.
  viii. LORINA TORREZ, b. Aft. 1920; m. ERNESTO OTERO.
  ix.   PRESCILIA TORREZ, b. Aft. 1920; m. ERNESTO LÓPEZ.

46. ESTOLANO PACHECO¹⁰ SÁNCHEZ *(ESTOLANO⁹, MAURICIO DE LA TRINIDAD⁸, JOSÉ GREGORIO DE LA TRINIDAD⁷, JUAN CRISTÓBAL⁶, FRANCISCO⁵, JACINTO SÁNCHEZ⁴ DE IÑIGO, FRANCISCO³ MUÑOZ, JACINTO², FRANCISCO¹)* was born 1891. He married (1) ELENA CHÁVEZ, daughter of RAFAEL CHÁVEZ and

MARTINA MAÉS. He married (2) BARBARITA TORREZ February 28, 1910, daughter of CRECENCIO TORREZ and MIQUELA MIRANDA.

Children of ESTOLANO SÁNCHEZ and BARBARITA TORREZ are:
  i.   AMANDA[11] SÁNCHEZ.
  ii.   AMABLE SÁNCHEZ.
  iii. FERMÍN SÁNCHEZ, b. October 11, 1915.
  iv.   EULALIO (LALO) SÁNCHEZ.

47. ROSARIO[10] SÁNCHEZ *(ESTOLANO[9], MAURICIO DE LA TRINIDAD[8], JOSÉ GREGORIO DE LA TRINIDAD[7], JUAN CRISTÓBAL[6], FRANCISCO[5], JACINTO SÁNCHEZ[4] DE IÑIGO, FRANCISCO[3] MUÑOZ, JACINTO[2], FRANCISCO[1])* was born August 11, 1896 in Reventón, Territory of New México[120]. She married WILLIAM LUCERO BRADY[121] February 19, 1912[122], son of ROBERT BRADY and MANUELA LUCERO.

More About ROSARIO SÁNCHEZ:
Fact 1: September 12, 1896, Baptized.

More About WILLIAM LUCERO BRADY:
Fact 1: March 22, 1892

Marriage Notes for ROSARIO SÁNCHEZ and WILLIAM BRADY:
Rosario's mother, Cornelia gave consent for this marriage.

Children of ROSARIO SÁNCHEZ and WILLIAM BRADY are:
  i.   MAX[11] BRADY.
  ii.   ORLINDA BRADY, m. ANDREW FRESQUEZ.
  iii. BARTOLA BRADY.
  iv.   WILLIAM SÁNCHEZ BRADY, m. ORALIA HERRERA.
  v.   PRESTINA BRADY.
  vi.   LEROY BENNETT BRADY.
  vii. BILLY JOE BRADY, b. Private; m. PATSY SALCIDO.
  viii. ERMILO BRADY.
  ix.   ELMO BRADY, m. JERRY KIMBRELL.

48. ESLINDA[10] GONZÁLES *(RAYMUNDA (REIMUNDA) SEGUNDA (CIGISMUNDA)[9] SÁNCHEZ, MAURICIO DE LA TRINIDAD[8], JOSÉ GREGORIO DE LA TRINIDAD[7], JUAN CRISTÓBAL[6], FRANCISCO[5], JACINTO SÁNCHEZ[4] DE IÑIGO, FRANCISCO[3] MUÑOZ, JACINTO[2], FRANCISCO[1])* was born 1867 in San Patricio, Territory of New México[123], and died Bef. September 1923. She married RICARDO FRANCISCO (FRANK) CHÁVEZ May 23, 1890[124], son of JOSÉ CHÁVEZ and MARÍA LUNA.

Children of ESLINDA GONZÁLES and RICARDO CHÁVEZ are:
  i.   FIDEL[11] CHÁVEZ, b. June 30, 1893, San Patricio, Territory of New México; m. DELFINIA PADILLA Y WEST, June 28, 1915, Lincoln, New México[125].

        Notes for DELFINIA PADILLA Y WEST:
        Criada y adoptiva de John C. West (Raised and adopted by John C. West). Also known as Delfinia Sánchez y West.

        Marriage Notes for FIDEL CHÁVEZ and DELFINIA WEST:
        Married by: Father Girma.
        Padrinos: Candido Chávez and Estela West.

90.   ii.   ERMINDA CHÁVEZ, b. June 22, 1895, San Patricio, Territory of New México; d. November 01, 1956.
      iii. PALMIRA CHÁVEZ, b. 1896.
      iv.   RAMON CHÁVEZ, b. 1898.
      v.   ENCARNACION CHÁVEZ, b. November 15, 1899.

            Notes for ENCARNACION CHÁVEZ:
            Died young.

49. PROSPERO[10] GONZÁLES *(RAYMUNDA (REIMUNDA) SEGUNDA (CIGISMUNDA)[9] SÁNCHEZ, MAURICIO DE LA TRINIDAD[8], JOSÉ GREGORIO DE LA TRINIDAD[7], JUAN CRISTÓBAL[6], FRANCISCO[5],*

JACINTO SÁNCHEZ[4] DE IÑIGO, FRANCISCO[3] MUÑOZ, JACINTO[2], FRANCISCO[1]) was born July 20, 1871[126], and died August 20, 1937 in San Patricio, New México. He married TELESFORA MIRABAL[127] March 28, 1900 in Glencoe, Territory of New México[128], daughter of JUAN MIRABAL and GUADALUPE TRUJILLO.

Notes for PROSPERO GONZÁLES:
Buried: La Capilla de San Patricio.

Notes for TELESFORA MIRABAL:
December 29, 1939: Died in an accident.
Buried in La Capilla de San Ysidro.

More About TELESFORA MIRABAL:
Fact 1: January 28, 1862, Baptized.

Marriage Notes for PROSPERO GONZÁLES and TELESFORA MIRABAL:
Married in La Capilla de San Ysidro.

Children of PROSPERO GONZÁLES and TELESFORA MIRABAL are:
91.   i.   RUBÉN ANDRES[11] GONZÁLES, b. November 02, 1900, Glencoe, Territory of New México; d. Artesia, New Mexico.
92.   ii.   PROSPERO MIRABAL GONZÁLES, b. January 1909; d. January 17, 1960.
       iii. MARÍA RESENIA (ARCENIA) GONZÁLES, b. February 20, 1898[129]; m. CHARLIE (CHARLES) CURRY, December 20, 1915[130].

             More About MARÍA RESENIA (ARCENIA) GONZÁLES:
             Fact 1: May 03, 1898, Baptized.[131]

       iv.   PORFIRIO GONZÁLES, b. August 10, 1903[132]; d. June 13, 1947, San Patricio, New México; m. ANGELINA RUIZ, October 15, 1936.

50. ALFREDO[10] GONZÁLES *(RAYMUNDA (REIMUNDA) SEGUNDA (CIGISMUNDA)[9] SÁNCHEZ, MAURICIO DE LA TRINIDAD[8], JOSÉ GREGORIO DE LA TRINIDAD[7], JUAN CRISTÓBAL[6], FRANCISCO[5], JACINTO SÁNCHEZ[4] DE IÑIGO, FRANCISCO[3] MUÑOZ, JACINTO[2], FRANCISCO[1])[133]* was born 1872, and died 1927 in San Patricio, New México. He married REBECCA SISNEROS SALAZAR February 07, 1904.

Notes for ALFREDO GONZÁLES:
1901-1902: Was elected as Lincoln County Sheriff.
Buried: San Patricio.

Child of ALFREDO GONZÁLES and REBECCA SALAZAR is:
       i.   GODFREY[11] GONZÁLES, b. 1904.

51. LEOPOLDO[10] GONZÁLES *(RAYMUNDA (REIMUNDA) SEGUNDA (CIGISMUNDA)[9] SÁNCHEZ, MAURICIO DE LA TRINIDAD[8], JOSÉ GREGORIO DE LA TRINIDAD[7], JUAN CRISTÓBAL[6], FRANCISCO[5], JACINTO SÁNCHEZ[4] DE IÑIGO, FRANCISCO[3] MUÑOZ, JACINTO[2], FRANCISCO[1])[134]* was born April 08, 1875, and died June 10, 1937. He married REIMUNDA (RAYMUNDA) SEDILLO[135] November 28, 1895, daughter of JUAN SEDILLO and JOSEFA FAJARDO.

Children of LEOPOLDO GONZÁLES and REIMUNDA SEDILLO are:
       i.   JUAN[11] GONZÁLES, b. November 10, 1896[136].

             Notes for JUAN GONZÁLES:
             Died young.

       ii.   AROPAJITA GONZÁLES, b. 1900[137]; d. December 05, 1918.
93.   iii. CRUSITA GONZÁLES, b. May 02, 1904.
94.   iv.   ELISA GONZÁLES, b. February 23, 1912.

52. DOMINGO EPAMINOANDAZ[10] GONZÁLES *(RAYMUNDA (REIMUNDA) SEGUNDA (CIGISMUNDA)[9] SÁNCHEZ, MAURICIO DE LA TRINIDAD[8], JOSÉ GREGORIO DE LA TRINIDAD[7], JUAN CRISTÓBAL[6],*

FRANCISCO[5], JACINTO SÁNCHEZ[4] DE IÑIGO, FRANCISCO[3] MUÑOZ, JACINTO[2], FRANCISCO[1]) was born April 04, 1876[138], and died February 20, 1970[139]. He married ELVIRA GONZÁLES February 12, 1900[140], daughter of JOSÉ GONZÁLES and MARÍA CHÁVEZ.

More About DOMINGO EPAMINOANDAZ GONZÁLES:
Fact 1: August 04, 1876, Baptized.

Children of DOMINGO GONZÁLES and ELVIRA GONZÁLES are:

	i.	CRECENSIANA[11] GONZÁLES, m. TITO MAÉS.
	ii.	MARÍA GONZÁLES, m. POLO PEÑA.
	iii.	RAFAEL GONZÁLES, m. AVRORA BACA.
	iv.	SIGISMUNDA GONZÁLES, m. ABRAN SÁNCHEZ.
	v.	AGIDA GONZÁLES, b. December 05, 1900[141]; d. October 28, 1941[142]; m. BEN SALAS, December 16, 1921[143].
	vi.	EPAMINOANDAS GONZÁLES GONZÁLES, b. October 21, 1902[144]; m. IGNACIA PRUDENCIO, September 14, 1928, Mescalero, New México[145].
95.	vii.	CIPRIANA GONZÁLES, b. August 21, 1903; d. August 2006, San Patricio, New México.
96.	viii.	FLORENCIO GONZÁLES GONZÁLES, b. September 17, 1907; d. October 11, 1973.
	ix.	BRESELIA GONZÁLES, b. October 10, 1910; d. January 09, 1973, Morenci, Arizona; m. (1) JUAN SÁNCHEZ; m. (2) MAX CORONA.

More About BRESELIA GONZÁLES:
Fact 1: January 09, 1973, Died in an automobile accident.

More About MAX CORONA:
Fact 1: January 09, 1973, Died in an automobile accident.

	x.	EVA GONZÁLES, b. Private; m. JUAN MONTOYA.

Notes for JUAN MONTOYA:
WW II war veteran, Navy.

53. MARÍA AURORA (AVRORA)[10] GONZÁLES *(RAYMUNDA (REIMUNDA) SEGUNDA (CIGISMUNDA)[9] SÁNCHEZ, MAURICIO DE LA TRINIDAD[8], JOSÉ GREGORIO DE LA TRINIDAD[7], JUAN CRISTÓBAL[6], FRANCISCO[5], JACINTO SÁNCHEZ[4] DE IÑIGO, FRANCISCO[3] MUÑOZ, JACINTO[2], FRANCISCO[1])* was born May 23, 1880[146], and died 1971[147]. She married (2) JORGE (GEORGE) ROMERO November 17, 1900[148], son of JUAN ROMERO and CRISTINA CASTILLO.

More About MARÍA AURORA (AVRORA) GONZÁLES:
Fact 1: August 04, 1880, Baptized.
Fact 2: 1920 Census notes that she was divorced.[149]

More About JORGE (GEORGE) ROMERO:
Fact 1: August 03, 1880, Baptized.

Children of MARÍA AURORA (AVRORA) GONZÁLES are:

	i.	ERLINDA[11] GONZÁLES.
	ii.	EMMA GONZÁLES, b. 1915.
	iii.	TRENIDAD GONZÁLES, b. 1919; m. BENINO SÁNCHEZ, April 01, 1934[150].

Children of MARÍA GONZÁLES and JORGE ROMERO are:

97.	iv.	SIGISFREDO[11] ROMERO, b. March 31, 1903.
98.	v.	MELITANA ROMERO, b. February 16, 1902.

54. AROPAJITA (EROPAJITA)[10] GONZÁLES *(RAYMUNDA (REIMUNDA) SEGUNDA (CIGISMUNDA)[9] SÁNCHEZ, MAURICIO DE LA TRINIDAD[8], JOSÉ GREGORIO DE LA TRINIDAD[7], JUAN CRISTÓBAL[6], FRANCISCO[5], JACINTO SÁNCHEZ[4] DE IÑIGO, FRANCISCO[3] MUÑOZ, JACINTO[2], FRANCISCO[1])* was born 1882. She married TRANCITO (FRANCISCO) POLACO November 08, 1900[151], son of SERAFÍN POLACO and ALTAGRACIA GONZÁLES.

More About TRANCITO (FRANCISCO) POLACO:

Fact 1: 1920 Census shows that Francisco was later known as Transito.[152]

Children of AROPAJITA GONZÁLES and TRANCITO POLACO are:
99. i.   DULCINEA[11] POLACO, b. 1903.
     ii. TRANSITO GONZÁLES POLACO[153], b. September 01, 1907; d. December 14, 1998.
100. iii. ALTAGRACIA POLACO, b. August 24, 1910.
     iv. ELFIGO GONZÁLES POLACO, b. 1913.

55. FLORENCIO SÁNCHEZ[10] GONZÁLES *(RAYMUNDA (REIMUNDA) SEGUNDA (CIGISMUNDA)[9] SÁNCHEZ, MAURICIO DE LA TRINIDAD[8], JOSÉ GREGORIO DE LA TRINIDAD[7], JUAN CRISTÓBAL[6], FRANCISCO[5], JACINTO SÁNCHEZ[4] DE IÑIGO, FRANCISCO[3] MUÑOZ, JACINTO[2], FRANCISCO[1])* was born November 24, 1893[154]. He married MARÍA AVELINA CHÁVEZ November 09, 1911, daughter of PATROCINIO CHÁVEZ and MARÍA ARCHULETA.

More About FLORENCIO SÁNCHEZ GONZÁLES:
Fact 1: February 10, 1894, Baptized.

More About MARÍA AVELINA CHÁVEZ:
Fact 1: May 07, 1890, Baptized.[155]

Children of FLORENCIO GONZÁLES and MARÍA CHÁVEZ are:
     i.   MIGUEL[11] GONZÁLES, b. July 21, 1918, San Patricio, New México[156]; d. April 08, 1999, San Patricio, New México; m. CRECENCIA YBARRA, May 24, 1935[157].

          Marriage Notes for MIGUEL GONZÁLES and CRECENCIA YBARRA:
          Married by: Justice of the Peace, John Mackey.

101. ii. GENEVA GONZÁLES, b. April 11, 1915.
     iii. JUANITA GONZÁLES, b. Private; m. CHARLIE REYNOLD.
     iv. DULCINEA GONZÁLES, m. GEORGE REYNOLD.
     v.   ALFEDO GONZÁLES, b. Private.
     vi. ELOY GONZÁLES.

56. NAPOLEÓN[10] SÁNCHEZ *(FRANCISCO[9], MAURICIO DE LA TRINIDAD[8], JOSÉ GREGORIO DE LA TRINIDAD[7], JUAN CRISTÓBAL[6], FRANCISCO[5], JACINTO SÁNCHEZ[4] DE IÑIGO, FRANCISCO[3] MUÑOZ, JACINTO[2], FRANCISCO[1])[158]* was born December 1873 in San Patricio, Territory of New México[159]. He married MARÍA CHÁVEZ February 10, 1902[160], daughter of MERIJILDO CHÁVEZ and DOLORES SILVA.

Notes for NAPOLEÓN SÁNCHEZ:
Migrated to Arizona.

More About NAPOLEÓN SÁNCHEZ:
Fact 1: June 19, 1874, Baptized.

Children of NAPOLEÓN SÁNCHEZ and MARÍA CHÁVEZ are:
     i.   LUPE (GUADALUPE)[11] SÁNCHEZ, b. December 12, 1902[161].
102. ii. REYNALDA SÁNCHEZ, b. February 21, 1905, San Patricio, Territory of New México; d. May 12, 1970, San Patricio, New México.
     iii. FRANK SÁNCHEZ, b. 1908.
     iv. CECILIA SÁNCHEZ, b. 1910.
     v.   MERIJILDO SÁNCHEZ, b. 1914.
     vi. JUAN SÁNCHEZ, b. 1916.
     vii. LOLA SÁNCHEZ, b. 1920.

57. DAVÍD[10] SÁNCHEZ *(FRANCISCO[9], MAURICIO DE LA TRINIDAD[8], JOSÉ GREGORIO DE LA TRINIDAD[7], JUAN CRISTÓBAL[6], FRANCISCO[5], JACINTO SÁNCHEZ[4] DE IÑIGO, FRANCISCO[3] MUÑOZ, JACINTO[2], FRANCISCO[1])[162]* was born November 06, 1876 in Libertad (San Patricio), Territory of New México[163], and died in Roswell, New México. He married FRANCISCA (PANCHITA) ARCHULETA May 05, 1902[164], daughter of ANTONIO ARCHULETA and SIMONA PACHECO.

Notes for DAVÍD SÁNCHEZ:
Davíd and his family eventually moved to Roswell, New México.

More About DAVÍD SÁNCHEZ:
Fact 1: December 10, 1876, Baptized.

Notes for FRANCISCA (PANCHITA) ARCHULETA:
1881: Raised by her grandparents, Leandro Pacheco and Vicenta Herrera, when her mother died.

Children of DAVÍD SÁNCHEZ and FRANCISCA ARCHULETA are:
    i.   AVRELIA[11] SÁNCHEZ.

            Notes for AVRELIA SÁNCHEZ:
            Died at 4 years of age.

    ii.   JOSEFITA ARCHULETA SÁNCHEZ, b. 1906; m. PEDRO GARCÍA.
    iii. SANTIAGO SÁNCHEZ, b. 1911.
    iv. EDUARDO SÁNCHEZ, b. 1912.
    v.   ADELAIDA SÁNCHEZ, b. July 04, 1915, San Patricio, New México; m. LEOPOLDO SEDILLOS, April 14, 1940[165].
    vi. ANEDA ARCHULETA SÁNCHEZ, b. 1917.
    vii. RUBÉN ARCHULETA SÁNCHEZ, b. September 16, 1920; d. August 05, 2001, Roswell, New México.

58. ANTONIO[10] SÁNCHEZ *(FRANCISCO[9], MAURICIO DE LA TRINIDAD[8], JOSÉ GREGORIO DE LA TRINIDAD[7], JUAN CRISTÓBAL[6], FRANCISCO[5], JACINTO SÁNCHEZ[4] DE IÑIGO, FRANCISCO[3] MUÑOZ, JACINTO[2], FRANCISCO[1])* was born February 08, 1878[166]. He married CAROLINA ROMERO January 09, 1901[167], daughter of JUAN ROMERO and CRISTINA CASTILLO.

Notes for CAROLINA ROMERO:
Raised by Jinio and Lola Guerra.

More About CAROLINA ROMERO:
Fact 1: March 23, 1884, Baptized.[168]

Children of ANTONIO SÁNCHEZ and CAROLINA ROMERO are:
    i.   ANEDA ROMERO[11] SÁNCHEZ.
    ii.   ANGELITA ROMERO SÁNCHEZ.
    iii. JESUSITA SÁNCHEZ.
    iv. JOSEFITA ROMERO SÁNCHEZ.
    v.   MARGARITA (MARGARET) SÁNCHEZ, b. August 22, 1903[169]; m. ROBERTO PÉREZ.
    vi. ISMAEL SÁNCHEZ, b. 1916[170].

59. MAURICIO[10] SÁNCHEZ *(FRANCISCO[9], MAURICIO DE LA TRINIDAD[8], JOSÉ GREGORIO DE LA TRINIDAD[7], JUAN CRISTÓBAL[6], FRANCISCO[5], JACINTO SÁNCHEZ[4] DE IÑIGO, FRANCISCO[3] MUÑOZ, JACINTO[2], FRANCISCO[1])* was born October 31, 1880 in San Patricio, Territory of New México[171], and died in San Patricio, New México. He married (1) DELFINIA ROMERO January 09, 1901[172], daughter of JUAN ROMERO and CRISTINA CASTILLO. He married (2) CLARA BARTLETT July 28, 1927 in Hondo, Territory of New México[173], daughter of CHARLES BARTLETT and ADELA GALINDRE.

Notes for DELFINIA ROMERO:
December 18, 1885: Baptized in San Patricio under the name María Virginia Romero. Padrinos: Román Barragán & Andrea Torres.
Raised by her godparents, Román Barragán & Andrea Torres.
Buried: La Capilla de San Patricio.

Marriage Notes for MAURICIO SÁNCHEZ and CLARA BARTLETT:
Sponsors: Hilario Gómez and María Romero de Gómez.

Children of MAURICIO SÁNCHEZ and DELFINIA ROMERO are:
103.   i.   JESUSITA ROMERO[11] SÁNCHEZ, b. San Patricio, New México.
       ii.   JOSÉ SÁNCHEZ, b. San Patricio, New México.

     iii.   JUANITA SÁNCHEZ, b. February 08, 1902, San Patricio, New México; d. December 06, 1975, Ruidoso, New México; m. RAMÓN TORRES, June 13, 1918, Glencoe, New Mexico[174].

         More About JUANITA SÁNCHEZ:
         Fact 1: March 17, 1902, Baptized.
         Fact 2: December 06, 1975, Died in an automobile accident.

         Marriage Notes for JUANITA SÁNCHEZ and RAMÓN TORRES:
         Married by: Justice of the Peace, Wilber Coe. Mauricio Sánchez gave consent to the marriage.

104.   iv.   ROMÁN SÁNCHEZ, b. April 23, 1904, San Patricio, New México; d. February 08, 1973, San Patricio, New México.
105.   v.   MAXIMILIANO SÁNCHEZ, b. August 21, 1911, San Patricio, New México.
      vi.   MABEL SÁNCHEZ, b. Abt. 1914, San Patricio, New México.
106.   vii.   MARÍA (MARÍLLITA) SÁNCHEZ, b. May 1919, San Patricio, New México.

60. PATRICIO[10] SÁNCHEZ *(FRANCISCO[9], MAURICIO DE LA TRINIDAD[8], JOSÉ GREGORIO DE LA TRINIDAD[7], JUAN CRISTÓBAL[6], FRANCISCO[5], JACINTO SÁNCHEZ[4] DE IÑIGO, FRANCISCO[3] MUÑOZ, JACINTO[2], FRANCISCO[1])[175]* was born January 30, 1883 in San Patricio, Territory of New México, and died 1955 in San Patricio, New México[176]. He married ISELIA (CELIA) TRUJILLO March 17, 1915 in San Patricio, Territory of New México[177], daughter of JUAN TRUJILLO and VICENTA DEVARA.

Notes for PATRICIO SÁNCHEZ:
Raised by his Padrinos, Francisco & Margarita Trujillo.

More About PATRICIO SÁNCHEZ:
Fact 1: March 17, 1884, Baptized.

More About ISELIA (CELIA) TRUJILLO:
Fact 1: August 03, 1899, Baptized.[178]

Marriage Notes for PATRICIO SÁNCHEZ and ISELIA TRUJILLO:
Married in La Capilla de San Patricio.

Children of PATRICIO SÁNCHEZ and ISELIA TRUJILLO are:
     i.   ARCILIA[11] SÁNCHEZ, b. Private.
     ii.   DANNY SÁNCHEZ, b. Private.
     iii.   EVA SÁNCHEZ, b. Private.
     iv.   MADALENA SÁNCHEZ, b. Private.
     v.   PATRICIO TRUJILLO SÁNCHEZ, b. Private.
     vi.   AUSALON SÁNCHEZ, b. February 04, 1916; d. January 10, 1996, Alamogordo, New México.
     vii.   ADONIS SÁNCHEZ, b. 1918.
     viii.   ERMINIA SÁNCHEZ, b. 1922.
     ix.   LOYOLA SÁNCHEZ, b. 1925; m. TOMASITO SÁNCHEZ.
     x.   CELIA SÁNCHEZ, b. 1929.
     xi.   ORALIA SÁNCHEZ[179], b. February 26, 1932; d. September 11, 1982, Wilmington, California.

61. JACOBO[10] SÁNCHEZ *(FRANCISCO[9], MAURICIO DE LA TRINIDAD[8], JOSÉ GREGORIO DE LA TRINIDAD[7], JUAN CRISTÓBAL[6], FRANCISCO[5], JACINTO SÁNCHEZ[4] DE IÑIGO, FRANCISCO[3] MUÑOZ, JACINTO[2], FRANCISCO[1])[180]* was born April 22, 1881[181], and died July 06, 1968. He married MARÍA TRUJILLO December 07, 1906[182], daughter of JUAN TRUJILLO and VICENTA DEVARA.

Children of JACOBO SÁNCHEZ and MARÍA TRUJILLO are:
     i.   MABEL TRUJILLO[11] SÁNCHEZ, m. DON CLEMENT.
     ii.   JUAN SÁNCHEZ, b. 1909[183]; d. 1940; m. BRESELIA GONZÁLES.

         More About BRESELIA GONZÁLES:
         Fact 1: January 09, 1973, Died in an automobile accident.

107.   iii.   ALBESITA (ALBESA) SÁNCHEZ, b. March 10, 1914.

108.	iv.	PILAR TRUJILLO SÁNCHEZ, b. May 02, 1917.
109.	v.	ESTER SÁNCHEZ, b. 1922.
	vi.	CLOVIS SÁNCHEZ, b. 1924[184]; d. 1995; m. EMMA GUERERO.
	vii.	ESTOLANO TRUJILLO SÁNCHEZ, b. September 12, 1925, San Patricio, New México[185]; d. August 27, 1970; m. MONICA SALCIDO.

More About ESTOLANO TRUJILLO SÁNCHEZ:
Fact 1: December 21, 1943, WW II veteran. Navy, Discharged from San Diego, California.[186]

62. ELOISA[10] SÁNCHEZ *(FRANCISCO[9], MAURICIO DE LA TRINIDAD[8], JOSÉ GREGORIO DE LA TRINIDAD[7], JUAN CRISTÓBAL[6], FRANCISCO[5], JACINTO SÁNCHEZ[4] DE IÑIGO, FRANCISCO[3] MUÑOZ, JACINTO[2], FRANCISCO[1])* was born February 10, 1891 in Manzano, New México[187], and died in Manzano, New México. She married FELIPÉ (SAÍS) SAÍZ January 12, 1908[188], son of PABLO SAÍZ and CELESTINA ARAGÓN.

More About ELOISA SÁNCHEZ:
Fact 1: July 21, 1891

Notes for FELIPÉ (SAÍS) SAÍZ:
Raised Cruz Herrera after his mother, Refujia Sánchez died.
Moved from San Patricio, New México to Manzano, New México.

Children of ELOISA SÁNCHEZ and FELIPÉ SAÍZ are:
  i.   CONCHA[11] SAÍZ.

       Notes for CONCHA SAÍZ:
       Moved from Manzano to Albuquerque.

  ii. FLORA SAÍZ.

       Notes for FLORA SAÍZ:
       Moved from Manzano to Roswell.

63. CONRADO[10] SÁNCHEZ *(FRANCISCO[9], MAURICIO DE LA TRINIDAD[8], JOSÉ GREGORIO DE LA TRINIDAD[7], JUAN CRISTÓBAL[6], FRANCISCO[5], JACINTO SÁNCHEZ[4] DE IÑIGO, FRANCISCO[3] MUÑOZ, JACINTO[2], FRANCISCO[1])* was born July 15, 1894[189], and died in Casa Grande, Arizona. He married JOSEFITA (JOSEFA) PADILLA January 20, 1912[190], daughter of JOSÉ PADILLA and NESTORA SAMORA.

Notes for CONRADO SÁNCHEZ:
1940s: Moved from Roswell, New México to Manzano, New México.
1940s: Moved from Manzano, New México to Las Cruces, New México.
1940s: Moved from Las Cruces, New México to Casa Grande, Arizona.
Was a WW I war veteran.

Children of CONRADO SÁNCHEZ and JOSEFITA PADILLA are:
  i.   CHANITO PADILLA[11] SÁNCHEZ.
  ii. MARY SÁNCHEZ, Adopted child.

64. REFUGIA[10] SÁNCHEZ *(FRANCISCO[9], MAURICIO DE LA TRINIDAD[8], JOSÉ GREGORIO DE LA TRINIDAD[7], JUAN CRISTÓBAL[6], FRANCISCO[5], JACINTO SÁNCHEZ[4] DE IÑIGO, FRANCISCO[3] MUÑOZ, JACINTO[2], FRANCISCO[1])* was born July 02, 1899 in San Patricio, Territory of New México. She married JUAN PABLO HERRERA[191] February 19, 1919 in Lincoln, New México, son of CRUZ HERRERA and REDUCINDA CARDONA.

Notes for REFUGIA SÁNCHEZ:
Died after her son Cruz was born.

More About REFUGIA SÁNCHEZ:
Fact 1: August 03, 1899, Baptized.

More About JUAN PABLO HERRERA:
Fact 1: January 21, 1894, Baptized.

Marriage Notes for REFUGIA SÁNCHEZ and JUAN HERRERA:
Married by: Father Girma. Married in La Capilla de San Juan Bautista.

Children of REFUGIA SÁNCHEZ and JUAN HERRERA are:
    i.   CRUZ (CRUSITO)¹¹ HERRERA.

        Notes for CRUZ (CRUSITO) HERRERA:
        Raised by Felipe Saíz & Eloisa Sanchez after his mother died.
        Moved to Roswell from Manzano.

    ii.   MARÍA GUADALUPE SÁNCHEZ HERRERA, b. December 11, 1873[192].

        More About MARÍA GUADALUPE SÁNCHEZ HERRERA:
        Fact 1: December 21, 1873, Baptized.

65. RAYMUNDO¹⁰ SÁNCHEZ *(JUAN RAFAEL BERCELÓ⁹, JUAN RAFAEL CHÁVEZ⁸, MANUEL RAFAEL⁷, JOSÉ PEDRO⁶, JACINTO⁵, JOSÉ⁴, JACINTO SÁNCHEZ³ DE IÑIGO, FRANCISCO² MUÑOZ, JACINTO¹)*[193] was born March 15, 1879 in Glencoe, Territory of New México[194], and died November 26, 1958[195]. He married AUGUSTINA ULIBARRÍ December 17, 1910[196], daughter of VICENTE ULIBARRÍ and MARÍA SEDILLO.

Marriage Notes for RAYMUNDO SÁNCHEZ and AUGUSTINA ULIBARRÍ:
Padrinos: Cosme Sedillos and daughter.

Children of RAYMUNDO SÁNCHEZ and AUGUSTINA ULIBARRÍ are:
    i.   EULALIA¹¹ SÁNCHEZ, b. 1913; m. PERFECTO SÁNCHEZ.
    ii.   BENNIE SÁNCHEZ, b. July 26, 1914; m. NICOLÁS TORRES.
    iii.   SOFIA SÁNCHEZ, b. 1917.
    iv.   ANEDA ULIBARRÍ SÁNCHEZ, b. 1919; m. HERMANDO (ERMANDO) CHÁVEZ[197].
    v.   OLYMPIA SÁNCHEZ, b. 1920; m. EPUNUCENO SÁNCHEZ.
    vi.   LUÍS SÁNCHEZ, b. 1928.

66. AMADITA¹⁰ SÁNCHEZ *(JUAN RAFAEL BERCELÓ⁹, JUAN RAFAEL CHÁVEZ⁸, MANUEL RAFAEL⁷, JOSÉ PEDRO⁶, JACINTO⁵, JOSÉ⁴, JACINTO SÁNCHEZ³ DE IÑIGO, FRANCISCO² MUÑOZ, JACINTO¹)* was born 1887 in Glencoe, Territory of New México, and died July 22, 1936[198]. She married (1) FEDERICO PEÑA, son of TEODORO PEÑA and MARGARITA LÓPEZ. She married (2) LUÍS PEÑA January 12, 1903[199], son of TEODORO PEÑA and MARGARITA LÓPEZ.

Child of AMADITA SÁNCHEZ and LUÍS PEÑA is:
110.   i.   TEODORO SÁNCHEZ¹¹ PEÑA, b. July 15, 1907, Glencoe, Territory of New México.

67. RITA¹⁰ SÁNCHEZ *(JUAN RAFAEL BERCELÓ⁹, JUAN RAFAEL CHÁVEZ⁸, MANUEL RAFAEL⁷, JOSÉ PEDRO⁶, JACINTO⁵, JOSÉ⁴, JACINTO SÁNCHEZ³ DE IÑIGO, FRANCISCO² MUÑOZ, JACINTO¹)* was born July 12, 1891 in Ruidoso, Territory of New México, and died in Artesia, New México[200]. She married NEWMAN GILL[201] July 03, 1915[202], son of WILLIAM GILL and MARÍA HERRERA.

Children of RITA SÁNCHEZ and NEWMAN GILL are:
    i.   OLIVIA¹¹ GILL, b. 1919; m. PORFIRIO VALENZUELA.
    ii.   ESTOLANO GILL, b. 1921.
    iii.   PRESILIANO GILL, b. 1923.
    iv.   PABLITA GILL, b. 1925; m. TORIVIO PADILLA.
    v.   RITA GILL, b. 1928.

68. EDUARDO BARCELON¹⁰ SÁNCHEZ *(JUAN RAFAEL BERCELÓ⁹, JUAN RAFAEL CHÁVEZ⁸, MANUEL RAFAEL⁷, JOSÉ PEDRO⁶, JACINTO⁵, JOSÉ⁴, JACINTO SÁNCHEZ³ DE IÑIGO, FRANCISCO² MUÑOZ, JACINTO¹)* was born October 13, 1893 in Glencoe, Territory of New México[203], and died May 28, 1954[204]. He married SENAIDA MONTOYA October 08, 1920 in Carrizozo, New México, daughter of ESTANISLADO MONTOYA and SARAFINA ULIBARRÍ.

Children of EDUARDO SÁNCHEZ and SENAIDA MONTOYA are:

    i.   EDUARDO MONTOYA[11] SÁNCHEZ, b. Abt. August 1921.

        More About EDUARDO MONTOYA SÁNCHEZ:
        Fact 1: July 03, 1943, WW II veteran. Discharged from Camp White, Oregon.[205]

    ii.   CONFERINA MONTOYA SÁNCHEZ, b. Private.
    iii. ELFIDES SÁNCHEZ, b. Private.
    iv. MACLOFA SÁNCHEZ, b. Private; m. ARISTEO HERRERA.
    v.   MAGGIE SÁNCHEZ, b. Private.
    vi. MANUEL MONTOYA SÁNCHEZ, b. Private; m. FLORINDA CARABAJAL Y SÁNCHEZ.
    vii. RAFAEL MONTOYA SÁNCHEZ, b. Private.
    viii. RUMELIO SÁNCHEZ, b. Private.

69. BERSABE[10] SÁNCHEZ *(JUAN RAFAEL BERCELÓ[9], JUAN RAFAEL CHÁVEZ[8], MANUEL RAFAEL[7], JOSÉ PEDRO[6], JACINTO[5], JOSÉ[4], JACINTO SÁNCHEZ[3] DE IÑIGO, FRANCISCO[2] MUÑOZ, JACINTO[1])* was born June 10, 1897 in Glencoe, Territory of New México[206]. She married TEODORO (THEODORO) MONTOYA December 11, 1919[207], son of ESTANISLADO MONTOYA and SARAFINA ULIBARRÍ.

More About BERSABE SÁNCHEZ:
Fact 1: October 28, 1897, Baptized.

More About TEODORO (THEODORO) MONTOYA:
Fact 1: June 18, 1893, Baptized.
Fact 2: April 18, 1919, WW I veteran. Discharged from Camp Owen Bierne, Texas.[208]

Child of BERSABE SÁNCHEZ and TEODORO MONTOYA is:
    i.   ALVESITA[11] MONTOYA, m. CARLOS SÁNCHEZ.

70. MACLOFA[10] SÁNCHEZ *(JUAN RAFAEL BERCELÓ[9], JUAN RAFAEL CHÁVEZ[8], MANUEL RAFAEL[7], JOSÉ PEDRO[6], JACINTO[5], JOSÉ[4], JACINTO SÁNCHEZ[3] DE IÑIGO, FRANCISCO[2] MUÑOZ, JACINTO[1])* was born 1904. She married DOMINGO PACHECO.

Child of MACLOFA SÁNCHEZ and DOMINGO PACHECO is:
    i.   SUSIE[11] PACHECO.

71. TRANCITO[10] CHÁVEZ *(JESÚSITA AMADA[9] SÁNCHEZ, MAURICIO DE LA TRINIDAD[8], JOSÉ GREGORIO DE LA TRINIDAD[7], JUAN CRISTÓBAL[6], FRANCISCO[5], JACINTO SÁNCHEZ[4] DE IÑIGO, FRANCISCO[3] MUÑOZ, JACINTO[2], FRANCISCO[1])*[209] was born July 20, 1887 in Glencoe, Territory of New México[210], and died April 07, 1975 in San Patricio, New México[211]. He married ANGELITA (ANGELA) CHÁVEZ April 15, 1906 in San Patricio, Territory of New México[212], daughter of ROBERTO CHÁVEZ and LUCIA WELDON.

Notes for TRANCITO CHÁVEZ:
Buried: Hondo cemetary.

More About TRANCITO CHÁVEZ:
Fact 1: October 17, 1887, Baptized.

Marriage Notes for TRANCITO CHÁVEZ and ANGELITA CHÁVEZ:
Married by: Fahter Girma.

Children of TRANCITO CHÁVEZ and ANGELITA CHÁVEZ are:
    i.   AVESLÍN[11] CHÁVEZ.

        Notes for AVESLÍN CHÁVEZ:
        Was killed during WW II.
    ii.   EVA CHÁVEZ, m. (1) HARRY SÁNCHEZ; m. (2) CARLOS CHÁVEZ.
    iii. HAROLD CHÁVEZ, m. EVA DUTCHOVER.
    iv. ARISTEO CHÁVEZ, b. 1910; m. CRISTINA ROMERO.
    v.   ISMAEL CHÁVEZ, b. 1912; m. ELISA MENDOSA.
    vi. OUCIEL CHÁVEZ, b. 1917.

Notes for OUCIEL CHÁVEZ:
Was killed during WW II.

72. CANDIDO[10] CHÁVEZ *(JESÚSITA AMADA[9] SÁNCHEZ, MAURICIO DE LA TRINIDAD[8], JOSÉ GREGORIO DE LA TRINIDAD[7], JUAN CRISTÓBAL[6], FRANCISCO[5], JACINTO SÁNCHEZ[4] DE IÑIGO, FRANCISCO[3] MUÑOZ, JACINTO[2], FRANCISCO[1])[213]* was born 1889, and died 1979. He married ESTELA (ESTELLE) LUCY WEST October 31, 1910, daughter of JOHN WEST and MARÍA MONNET.

Notes for CANDIDO CHÁVEZ:
Buried: Hondo cemetary.

Notes for ESTELA (ESTELLE) LUCY WEST:
Baptismal Witnesses: Estelle Kaestler and George Ulricks.

More About ESTELA (ESTELLE) LUCY WEST:
Fact 1: July 22, 1895, Baptized in Lincoln, Territory of New México.

Children of CANDIDO CHÁVEZ and ESTELA WEST are:
    i.   CECILIA[11] CHÁVEZ, m. REFUGIO ROMERO.
    ii.   ETHAL CHÁVEZ, m. MIGUEL MAÉS.
    iii. CANDIDO WEST CHÁVEZ.
    iv.   VIOLA CHÁVEZ.
    v.   ELIZABETH CHÁVEZ, m. JAMES MACKEY.
    vi.   WILLIE DEAN CHÁVEZ.
    vii. JOHNNY CHÁVEZ.
    viii. DOROTHY CHÁVEZ, m. LARRY TORREZ.
    ix.   CLIFFORD WEST CHÁVEZ.

73. LEOPOLDO[10] CHÁVEZ *(JESÚSITA AMADA[9] SÁNCHEZ, MAURICIO DE LA TRINIDAD[8], JOSÉ GREGORIO DE LA TRINIDAD[7], JUAN CRISTÓBAL[6], FRANCISCO[5], JACINTO SÁNCHEZ[4] DE IÑIGO, FRANCISCO[3] MUÑOZ, JACINTO[2], FRANCISCO[1])[214]* was born April 25, 1907. He married ALTAGRACIA POLACO, daughter of TRANCITO POLACO and AROPAJITA GONZÁLES.

Marriage Notes for LEOPOLDO CHÁVEZ and ALTAGRACIA POLACO:
Married by: Justice of the Peace, B.H. Harvey.
Married May 24. The date is unclear but it was sometime in the 1930s.

Children of LEOPOLDO CHÁVEZ and ALTAGRACIA POLACO are:
    i.   ROY[11] CHÁVEZ, m. CRUSITA SILVA.
    ii.   BREZEL CHÁVEZ, m. PABLITA HERRERA.
    iii. RICHARD CHÁVEZ.
    iv.   LYDIA CHÁVEZ, b. Private; m. BOBBY CHÁVEZ.

74. RUMELIO[10] CHÁVEZ *(JESÚSITA AMADA[9] SÁNCHEZ, MAURICIO DE LA TRINIDAD[8], JOSÉ GREGORIO DE LA TRINIDAD[7], JUAN CRISTÓBAL[6], FRANCISCO[5], JACINTO SÁNCHEZ[4] DE IÑIGO, FRANCISCO[3] MUÑOZ, JACINTO[2], FRANCISCO[1])* was born 1910. He married CECILIA (YSELIA) OLGUÍN July 11, 1936[215], daughter of ESTANISLADO OLGUÍN and ANASTACIA CHÁVEZ.

Children of RUMELIO CHÁVEZ and CECILIA OLGUÍN are:
    i.   AMADA (AMY)[11] CHÁVEZ, m. HENRY SÁNCHEZ.
    ii.   PABLO OLGUÍN CHÁVEZ.

          Notes for PABLO OLGUÍN CHÁVEZ:
          Died at a young age.

    iii. ABRAN CHÁVEZ.

75. HERMANDO (ERMANDO)[10] CHÁVEZ *(JESÚSITA AMADA[9] SÁNCHEZ, MAURICIO DE LA TRINIDAD[8], JOSÉ GREGORIO DE LA TRINIDAD[7], JUAN CRISTÓBAL[6], FRANCISCO[5], JACINTO SÁNCHEZ[4] DE IÑIGO, FRANCISCO[3] MUÑOZ, JACINTO[2], FRANCISCO[1])[216]* was born February 22, 1914. He married (1) ANEDA

ULIBARRÍ SÁNCHEZ, daughter of RAYMUNDO SÁNCHEZ and AUGUSTINA ULIBARRÍ. He married (2) MACLOVIA MARTÍNEZ December 07, 1935, daughter of ADENAGO MARTÍNEZ and ANNE GONZÁLES.

Notes for MACLOVIA MARTÍNEZ:
Buried: San Patricio.

Marriage Notes for HERMANDO CHÁVEZ and MACLOVIA MARTÍNEZ:
Married by: Justice of the Peace, Elerdo Chávez.

Children of HERMANDO CHÁVEZ and MACLOVIA MARTÍNEZ are:
 i. PAUL[11] CHÁVEZ.
 ii. BOBBY MARTÍNEZ CHÁVEZ.

Generation No. 11

76. VIRGINIA[11] SÁNCHEZ *(SALOMON[10], JOSÉ ANTONIO[9], MAURICIO DE LA TRINIDAD[8], JOSÉ GREGORIO DE LA TRINIDAD[7], JUAN CRISTÓBAL[6], FRANCISCO[5], JACINTO SÁNCHEZ[4] DE IÑIGO, FRANCISCO[3] MUÑOZ, JACINTO[2], FRANCISCO[1])* was born April 13, 1902 in Ruidoso, Territory of New México, and died in Ruidoso, New México. She married JOSÉ CANDELARIO (ANDELARIO) RANDOLPH[217] September 14, 1918 in Lincoln, New México[218], son of JOSÉ RANDOLPH and CATARINA BRADY.

Children of VIRGINIA SÁNCHEZ and JOSÉ RANDOLPH are:
 i. JOSEPHINE[12] RANDOLPH, b. Abt. 1920.
 ii. AROPAJITA RANDOLPH, b. Abt. 1922.
 iii. ELMER RANDOLPH, b. Abt. 1926.
 iv. CATHERINE RANDOLPH, b. Abt. 1928.

77. TELESFORA[11] SÁNCHEZ *(SALOMON[10], JOSÉ ANTONIO[9], MAURICIO DE LA TRINIDAD[8], JOSÉ GREGORIO DE LA TRINIDAD[7], JUAN CRISTÓBAL[6], FRANCISCO[5], JACINTO SÁNCHEZ[4] DE IÑIGO, FRANCISCO[3] MUÑOZ, JACINTO[2], FRANCISCO[1])* was born November 19, 1903 in Glencoe, Territory of New México. She married TEODORO SÁNCHEZ PEÑA March 01, 1926 in Carrizozo, New México[219], son of LUÍS PEÑA and AMADITA SÁNCHEZ.

Children of TELESFORA SÁNCHEZ and TEODORO PEÑA are:
 i. JOSEPHINE[12] PEÑA, b. Private.
 ii. IDALIA PEÑA.
 iii. LUÍS PEÑA.
 iv. THEODORO (TEODORO) (3) PEÑA.
 v. RAFAEL PEÑA.
 vi. REYES PEÑA.

78. SALOMON GILL[11] SÁNCHEZ *(SALOMON[10], JOSÉ ANTONIO[9], MAURICIO DE LA TRINIDAD[8], JOSÉ GREGORIO DE LA TRINIDAD[7], JUAN CRISTÓBAL[6], FRANCISCO[5], JACINTO SÁNCHEZ[4] DE IÑIGO, FRANCISCO[3] MUÑOZ, JACINTO[2], FRANCISCO[1])* was born March 17, 1905 in Glencoe, Territory of New México[220]. He married (1) TERESITA SALAS[221] October 11, 1928 in Lincoln, New México. He married (2) RAMONA OTERO November 20, 1932.

Marriage Notes for SALOMON SÁNCHEZ and TERESITA SALAS:
Married by: Padre Reyes.

Children of SALOMON SÁNCHEZ and TERESITA SALAS are:
 i. ORLANDO[12] SÁNCHEZ, b. Private.
 ii. FABIOLA SÁNCHEZ, b. Abt. September 1929.

Children of SALOMON SÁNCHEZ and RAMONA OTERO are:
 iii. MARY OLINDA[12] SÁNCHEZ, b. Private.
 iv. LORENA SÁNCHEZ, b. Private.
 v. ELMON SÁNCHEZ, b. Private.

vi.   ERNEST OTERO SÁNCHEZ, b. Private.

79. ANATALIA (NATALIA)[11] SÁNCHEZ *(SALOMON[10], JOSÉ ANTONIO[9], MAURICIO DE LA TRINIDAD[8], JOSÉ GREGORIO DE LA TRINIDAD[7], JUAN CRISTÓBAL[6], FRANCISCO[5], JACINTO SÁNCHEZ[4] DE IÑIGO, FRANCISCO[3] MUÑOZ, JACINTO[2], FRANCISCO[1])* was born 1912. She married JULIAN HERRERA April 28, 1934, son of MARTÍN HERRERA and TEODORA MENDOSA.

Children of ANATALIA SÁNCHEZ and JULIAN HERRERA are:
    i.   MARTÍN[12] HERRERA, d. October 25, 1954, El Paso, Téxas.
    ii.   ANDREW HERRERA.
    iii.   ORLIDIA HERRERA.
    iv.   VIRGINIA HERRERA.

80. ERNESTO[11] SILVA *(MARÍA DE JESÚS (JESUSITA)[10] SÁNCHEZ, JOSÉ ANTONIO[9], MAURICIO DE LA TRINIDAD[8], JOSÉ GREGORIO DE LA TRINIDAD[7], JUAN CRISTÓBAL[6], FRANCISCO[5], JACINTO SÁNCHEZ[4] DE IÑIGO, FRANCISCO[3] MUÑOZ, JACINTO[2], FRANCISCO[1])* was born June 27, 1912[222], and died 1981. He married GENEVA GONZÁLES February 02, 1933, daughter of FLORENCIO GONZÁLES and MARÍA CHÁVEZ.

Notes for ERNESTO SILVA:
Served with S2 US Navy during WW 2

Children of ERNESTO SILVA and GENEVA GONZÁLES are:
    i.   ERNEST[12] SILVA, b. Private; m. MINNIE SÁNCHEZ.
    ii.   JOSEPHINE SILVA, b. Private; m. WILLIAM GÓMEZ.
    iii.   JESUSITA SILVA, b. Private.

81. ANTONIO[11] SÁNCHEZ *(FELIPÉ E.[10], ESTOLANO[9], MAURICIO DE LA TRINIDAD[8], JOSÉ GREGORIO DE LA TRINIDAD[7], JUAN CRISTÓBAL[6], FRANCISCO[5], JACINTO SÁNCHEZ[4] DE IÑIGO, FRANCISCO[3] MUÑOZ, JACINTO[2], FRANCISCO[1])* was born May 13, 1897 in Tres Ritos, New México, and died February 21, 1984 in San Elizario, Texas[223]. He married (1) MARTINA SALSBERRY October 30, 1915 in Lincoln, Territory of New México[224], daughter of JAMES SALSBERRY and MANUELITA HERRERA. He married (2) JUANITA CABALLERO ALVARADO Aft. December 1917.

Notes for MARTINA SALSBERRY:
She died 8 days after giving birth to a child. Her child also died during birth.
Buried: San Ysidro church cemetary.

Marriage Notes for ANTONIO SÁNCHEZ and MARTINA SALSBERRY:
Married in La Capilla de San Ysidro. James Salsberry, Manuelita Herrera de Salsberry, Felipe Sánchez and Candelaria Padilla de Sánchez gave consent to the marriage.

Children of ANTONIO SÁNCHEZ and JUANITA ALVARADO are:
    i.   PAUBLINA[12] SÁNCHEZ.
    ii.   CECILIA ALVARADO SÁNCHEZ.
    iii.   ELISA SÁNCHEZ.
    iv.   LUISA SÁNCHEZ.
    v.   TONY SÁNCHEZ, b. Private.
    vi.   EFRIN SÁNCHEZ.
    vii.   SAMUEL SÁNCHEZ, b. Private.
    viii. LUCILA SÁNCHEZ.
    ix.   DAVÍD SÁNCHEZ.
    x.   RUFINA SÁNCHEZ.
    xi.   BENJAMIN SÁNCHEZ, b. Private.
    xii.   EILEEN MARTÍNEZ SÁNCHEZ, b. Private.
    xiii. RAY MARTÍNEZ SÁNCHEZ, b. Private.

82. PAUBLITA (PABLITA)[11] SÁNCHEZ *(FELIPÉ E.[10], ESTOLANO[9], MAURICIO DE LA TRINIDAD[8], JOSÉ GREGORIO DE LA TRINIDAD[7], JUAN CRISTÓBAL[6], FRANCISCO[5], JACINTO SÁNCHEZ[4] DE IÑIGO, FRANCISCO[3] MUÑOZ, JACINTO[2], FRANCISCO[1])* was born July 30, 1898 in Tres Rios, Territory of New México, and died October 13, 1963 in Las Vegas, New México. She married YSIDRO CHÁVEZ[225] August 04, 1913 in Lincoln, New México, son of ROBERTO CHÁVEZ and LUCIA WELDON.

Notes for PAUBLITA (PABLITA) SÁNCHEZ:
Buried: San Patricio, New México.

More About PAUBLITA (PABLITA) SÁNCHEZ:
Fact 1: October 15, 1898, Baptized in Patos Territory of New México.

Notes for YSIDRO CHÁVEZ:
Buried: La Capilla de San Patricio.

More About YSIDRO CHÁVEZ:
Fact 1: May 06, 1892, Baptized.

Marriage Notes for PAUBLITA SÁNCHEZ and YSIDRO CHÁVEZ:
Married by: Father J.H. Girma in La Capilla de San Juan Bautista. Felipe E. Sánchez gave consent to the marriage. Padrinos: Avrora Gavaldon and Antonio Sánchez.

Children of PAUBLITA SÁNCHEZ and YSIDRO CHÁVEZ are:

    i.   ORALIA[12] CHÁVEZ, b. San Patricio, New México; d. San Patricio, New México.

        Notes for ORALIA CHÁVEZ:
        Died young.

    ii.   SIPIO CHÁVEZ, b. San Patricio, New México; d. San Patricio, New México.

        Notes for SIPIO CHÁVEZ:
        Died young.

    iii.   GRESELDA CHÁVEZ, b. May 13, 1914, San Patricio, New México; d. June 09, 1988, Ruidoso, New México; m. FRANCISCO (FRANK) GÓMEZ, February 17, 1934.

        Notes for GRESELDA CHÁVEZ:
        Buried: San Patricio, New México.

    iv.   AMARANTE (JACK) CHÁVEZ, b. November 09, 1915, San Patricio, New México; d. Alburquerque, New México; m. DOLORES (LOLA) ROMERO ARCHULETA, September 21, 1936, San Patricio, New México.

        Notes for DOLORES (LOLA) ROMERO ARCHULETA:
        Buried: San Patricio, New México.

    v.   SENON CHÁVEZ, b. March 03, 1917, San Patricio, New México; d. San Patricio, New México.

        Notes for SENON CHÁVEZ:
        WW II veteran, Darby's Rangers, Third battalion. The Battle of Anzio-Cisterna. He was a POW.
        Cremated, Ashes spread on the mountain behind the old Chávez house in San Patricio.

111.   vi.   IGNACIA (INES) CHÁVEZ, b. January 23, 1919, San Patricio, New México.
        viii.   ADELITA (DELLA) CHÁVEZ, b. July 04, 1920, San Patricio, New México; m. (1) SANTIAGO (JIMMY) LARIOSA; m. (2) GUILLERMO QUIZON; m. (3) MANUEL GÓMEZ.
112.   viii.   EMILIANO CHÁVEZ, b. January 11, 1922, San Patricio, New México; d. January 23, 1953, California.
        ix.   EFRAÍN CHÁVEZ, b. January 01, 1926, San Patricio, New México; m. LILLIAN MILLER.

        Notes for EFRAÍN CHÁVEZ:
        WW II veteran.
        Died, date unknown.

        More About EFRAÍN CHÁVEZ:
        Fact 1: February 09, 1926, Baptized.

    x.   LUVÍN CHÁVEZ, b. November 15, 1929, San Patricio, New México; m. MARY KAMEES.

Notes for LUVÍN CHÁVEZ:
WW II veteran, US Marines.

113. xi.   ORALIA CHÁVEZ, b. February 18, 1931, San Patricio, New México.
      xii. ONOFRÉ (HUMPHREY) CHÁVEZ, b. August 06, 1932, San Patricio, New México; m. VANGIE -----.

            Notes for ONOFRÉ (HUMPHREY) CHÁVEZ:
            Navy veteran.

      xiii. JOSIE (JOSEPHINE) CHÁVEZ, b. May 18, 1934, San Patricio, New México; m. BENITO HERRERA.
      xiv. MELVIN CHÁVEZ, b. November 06, 1937, San Patricio, New México; m. (1) LORENA ROMERO; m. (2) PRESCILLA GUTIERREZ.
      xv.   RAMONA CHÁVEZ, b. April 11, 1939, San Patricio, New México; m. LARRY NUNEZ.
      xvi. DANNY CHÁVEZ, b. December 13, 1940, San Patricio, New México; m. (1) VANGIE MONTES; m. (2) CRUCITA BACA.
      xvii. RAY MARTÍNEZ, b. September 11, 1946.

            Notes for RAY MARTÍNEZ:
            Was raised by Ysidro and Pablita.

      xviii. EILEEN MARTÍNEZ, b. September 25, 1947.

            Notes for EILEEN MARTÍNEZ:
            Was raised by Ysidro and Pablita.

83. CORNELIA[11] SÁNCHEZ *(FELIPÉ E.[10], ESTOLANO[9], MAURICIO DE LA TRINIDAD[8], JOSÉ GREGORIO DE LA TRINIDAD[7], JUAN CRISTÓBAL[6], FRANCISCO[5], JACINTO SÁNCHEZ[4] DE IÑIGO, FRANCISCO[3] MUÑOZ, JACINTO[2], FRANCISCO[1])* was born November 16, 1902 in Lincoln County, New México. She married ALFONSO BORREGO, son of ELIJIO BORREGO and FRANCISCA ARIAS.

More About ALFONSO BORREGO:
Fact 1: WW I veteran.

Children of CORNELIA SÁNCHEZ and ALFONSO BORREGO are:
      i.   MARIA LYDIA[12] BORREGO, b. Private.
      ii.   LORENZO BORREGO.
      iii. LUIS FILIMON BORREGO.
      iv.   RAÚL BORREGO, b. Private.
      v.   JOSEPHINA BORREGO, b. Private.
      vi.   PEDRO BORREGO.
      vii. ALFONSO (2ND) BORREGO.
      viii. JOE BORREGO.
      ix.   MIKE NOMAN BORREGO, b. Private.
      x.   TERESA BORREGO, b. Private.
      xi.   RAMÓN BORREGO, b. Private.

84. EMILIANO[11] SÁNCHEZ *(FELIPÉ E.[10], ESTOLANO[9], MAURICIO DE LA TRINIDAD[8], JOSÉ GREGORIO DE LA TRINIDAD[7], JUAN CRISTÓBAL[6], FRANCISCO[5], JACINTO SÁNCHEZ[4] DE IÑIGO, FRANCISCO[3] MUÑOZ, JACINTO[2], FRANCISCO[1])* was born August 11, 1904 in Hondo, Territory of New México. He married RUBY MARTÍNEZ.

Children of EMILIANO SÁNCHEZ and RUBY MARTÍNEZ are:
      i.   EMILIANO JUNIOR[12] SÁNCHEZ, b. 1927.
      ii.   BERNICE SÁNCHEZ, b. Private.
      iii. GLORIA SÁNCHEZ, b. Private.
      iv.   LEROY SÁNCHEZ, b. Private.
      v.   TERESA SÁNCHEZ, b. Private.
      vi.   VIOLA SÁNCHEZ, b. Private.

85. ABRAHAM (ABRAN)[11] SÁNCHEZ *(FELIPÉ E.[10], ESTOLANO[9], MAURICIO DE LA TRINIDAD[8], JOSÉ GREGORIO DE LA TRINIDAD[7], JUAN CRISTÓBAL[6], FRANCISCO[5], JACINTO SÁNCHEZ[4] DE IÑIGO, FRANCISCO[3] MUÑOZ, JACINTO[2], FRANCISCO[1])* was born December 21, 1905 in White Oaks, Territory of New México, and died November 18, 1973 in El Paso, Téxas. He married (1) FELIPA RODRÍQUES. He married (2) RAMONSITA GURULÉ.

Notes for ABRAHAM (ABRAN) SÁNCHEZ:
Buried: Carrizozo, New México.

Children of ABRAHAM SÁNCHEZ and FELIPA RODRÍQUES are:
  i.   FRANK RODRÍQUES[12] SÁNCHEZ.
  ii.   MARÍA MAGDALENA SÁNCHEZ.
  iii. DAVÍD RODRÍQUES SÁNCHEZ.
  iv.   FREDRICK SÁNCHEZ.

Children of ABRAHAM SÁNCHEZ and RAMONSITA GURULÉ are:
  v.   PAUBLITA GURULÉ[12] SÁNCHEZ.
  vi.   GEORGE SÁNCHEZ, b. Private.
  vii. RAYNEL SÁNCHEZ, b. Private.
  viii. HERMAN SÁNCHEZ.
  ix.   RITA GURULÉ SÁNCHEZ, b. Private.
  x.   ROSYLENE SÁNCHEZ, b. Private.
  xi.   JOHN GURULÉ SÁNCHEZ, b. Private.

86. REYNALDO[11] SÁNCHEZ *(FELIPÉ E.[10], ESTOLANO[9], MAURICIO DE LA TRINIDAD[8], JOSÉ GREGORIO DE LA TRINIDAD[7], JUAN CRISTÓBAL[6], FRANCISCO[5], JACINTO SÁNCHEZ[4] DE IÑIGO, FRANCISCO[3] MUÑOZ, JACINTO[2], FRANCISCO[1])* was born Abt. 1906. He married SOFIA AGUILAR November 10, 1932.

Children of REYNALDO SÁNCHEZ and SOFIA AGUILAR are:
  i.   MARY LILY[12] SÁNCHEZ.
  ii.   MABEL SÁNCHEZ.
  iii. JO ANN SÁNCHEZ.

87. ONECIMO[11] SÁNCHEZ *(FELIPÉ E.[10], ESTOLANO[9], MAURICIO DE LA TRINIDAD[8], JOSÉ GREGORIO DE LA TRINIDAD[7], JUAN CRISTÓBAL[6], FRANCISCO[5], JACINTO SÁNCHEZ[4] DE IÑIGO, FRANCISCO[3] MUÑOZ, JACINTO[2], FRANCISCO[1])* was born 1915. He married CLEOTILDE DURÁN, daughter of FRANCISCO DURÁN and HORTENCIA MONTES.

Children of ONECIMO SÁNCHEZ and CLEOTILDE DURÁN are:
  i.   YOLANDA[12] SÁNCHEZ, b. Private.
  ii.   MAXIMO SÁNCHEZ, b. Private.
  iii. MARY LOU SÁNCHEZ, b. Private.
  iv.   DARLENE SÁNCHEZ, b. Private.
  v.   HECTOR SÁNCHEZ, b. Private.
  vi.   LINDA SÁNCHEZ, b. Private.
  vii. ALEX SÁNCHEZ, b. Private.
  viii. CYNTHIA SÁNCHEZ, b. Private.

88. BENITO[11] SÁNCHEZ *(FELIPÉ E.[10], ESTOLANO[9], MAURICIO DE LA TRINIDAD[8], JOSÉ GREGORIO DE LA TRINIDAD[7], JUAN CRISTÓBAL[6], FRANCISCO[5], JACINTO SÁNCHEZ[4] DE IÑIGO, FRANCISCO[3] MUÑOZ, JACINTO[2], FRANCISCO[1])* was born Private. He married (1) CONCHA RAMÍREZ. He married (2) BEATRICE PINO May 09, 1932 in Tularosa, New México[226].

Children of BENITO SÁNCHEZ and CONCHA RAMÍREZ are:
  i.   HOPE[12] SÁNCHEZ.
  ii.   ISABEL SÁNCHEZ.
  iii. BENNY SÁNCHEZ.

Children of BENITO SÁNCHEZ and BEATRICE PINO are:

iv.   MARY ALICE[12] SÁNCHEZ.
v.   MARGIE SÁNCHEZ.
vi.   GRACE SÁNCHEZ.
vii. RAY SÁNCHEZ.

89. SORAIDA[11] SÁNCHEZ *(AURELIO (AVRELIO)[10], ESTOLANO[9], MAURICIO DE LA TRINIDAD[8], JOSÉ GREGORIO DE LA TRINIDAD[7], JUAN CRISTÓBAL[6], FRANCISCO[5], JACINTO SÁNCHEZ[4] DE IÑIGO, FRANCISCO[3] MUÑOZ, JACINTO[2], FRANCISCO[1])* was born August 27, 1916. She married MAXIMILIANO SÁNCHEZ February 11, 1936[227], son of MAURICIO SÁNCHEZ and DELFINIA ROMERO.

More About MAXIMILIANO SÁNCHEZ:
Fact 1: January 05, 1945, WW II veteran. Discharged from Indiana Town Gap, Pennsylvania.[228]

Marriage Notes for SORAIDA SÁNCHEZ and MAXIMILIANO SÁNCHEZ:
Married by: Justice of the Peace, Elerdo Cháves.

Children of SORAIDA SÁNCHEZ and MAXIMILIANO SÁNCHEZ are:
i.   BEATRICE[12] SÁNCHEZ.
ii.   ROSEMARY SÁNCHEZ.

90. ERMINDA[11] CHÁVEZ *(ESLINDA[10] GONZÁLES, RAYMUNDA (REIMUNDA) SEGUNDA (CIGISMUNDA)[9] SÁNCHEZ, MAURICIO DE LA TRINIDAD[8], JOSÉ GREGORIO DE LA TRINIDAD[7], JUAN CRISTÓBAL[6], FRANCISCO[5], JACINTO SÁNCHEZ[4] DE IÑIGO, FRANCISCO[3] MUÑOZ, JACINTO[2], FRANCISCO[1])* was born June 22, 1895 in San Patricio, Territory of New México, and died November 01, 1956[229]. She married (1) EPIFANIO ULIBARRÍ November 04, 1915 in Lincoln, New México[230], son of VICENTE ULIBARRÍ and MARÍA SEDILLO. She married (2) JOSÉ JÁQUEZ May 17, 1950[231].

More About ERMINDA CHÁVEZ:
Fact 1: July 20, 1894, Baptized.

Marriage Notes for ERMINDA CHÁVEZ and EPIFANIO ULIBARRÍ:
Padrinos: Florencio Gonzáles, Raymundo Sánchez, Augustín Ulibarrí.

Child of ERMINDA CHÁVEZ and EPIFANIO ULIBARRÍ is:
i.   DIEGO[12] ULIBARRÍ.

91. RUBÉN ANDRES[11] GONZÁLES *(PROSPERO[10], RAYMUNDA (REIMUNDA) SEGUNDA (CIGISMUNDA)[9] SÁNCHEZ, MAURICIO DE LA TRINIDAD[8], JOSÉ GREGORIO DE LA TRINIDAD[7], JUAN CRISTÓBAL[6], FRANCISCO[5], JACINTO SÁNCHEZ[4] DE IÑIGO, FRANCISCO[3] MUÑOZ, JACINTO[2], FRANCISCO[1])* was born November 02, 1900 in Glencoe, Territory of New México[232], and died in Artesia, New Mexico. He married DOROTEA SALSBERRY February 22, 1918, daughter of JAMES SALSBERRY and MANUELITA HERRERA.

More About RUBÉN ANDRES GONZÁLES:
Fact 1: January 16, 1900, Baptized.

More About DOROTEA SALSBERRY:
Fact 1: July 26, 1902, Baptized.[233]

Children of RUBÉN GONZÁLES and DOROTEA SALSBERRY are:
i.   OLIVIA[12] GONZÁLES, m. JUAN RODRÍGUEZ.
ii.   ADELINA GONZÁLES, m. LOLO RODRÍGUEZ.
iii.   ORALIA GONZÁLES, m. CRISTÓVAL PEREA.
iv.   VIOLA GONZÁLES, b. Private; m. MANUEL REYES.
v.   EMILIO GONZÁLES, b. Private; m. RACHEL ALANIS.
vi.   RUFINA GONZÁLES, b. Private; m. JOSÉ RODRÍGUEZ.
vii.   FEDELINA GONZÁLES, b. Private; m. COSMÉ GÓMES.
viii. RUBÉN GONZÁLES, b. Private; m. MANUELA PAS.
ix.   REYNER GONZÁLES, b. Private; m. MARY PADILLA.
x.   TELESFORA (TILLIE) GONZÁLES, m. UNKOWN -----.
xi.   HELEN GONZÁLES, m. UNKNOWN -----.

92. PROSPERO MIRABAL[11] GONZÁLES *(PROSPERO[10], RAYMUNDA (REIMUNDA) SEGUNDA (CIGISMUNDA)[9] SÁNCHEZ, MAURICIO DE LA TRINIDAD[8], JOSÉ GREGORIO DE LA TRINIDAD[7], JUAN CRISTÓBAL[6], FRANCISCO[5], JACINTO SÁNCHEZ[4] DE IÑIGO, FRANCISCO[3] MUÑOZ, JACINTO[2], FRANCISCO[1])* was born January 1909, and died January 17, 1960[234]. He married AMBROCIA SILVA May 15, 1936[235], daughter of TELESFOR SILVA and ERINEA BENAVIDEZ.

Children of **PROSPERO GONZÁLES** and **AMBROCIA SILVA** are:
  i.   LILIA[12] GONZÁLES.
  ii. FELIX GONZÁLES.
  iii. DORTHY GONZÁLES.
  iv. FLOYD GONZÁLES.

93. CRUSITA[11] GONZÁLES *(LEOPOLDO[10], RAYMUNDA (REIMUNDA) SEGUNDA (CIGISMUNDA)[9] SÁNCHEZ, MAURICIO DE LA TRINIDAD[8], JOSÉ GREGORIO DE LA TRINIDAD[7], JUAN CRISTÓBAL[6], FRANCISCO[5], JACINTO SÁNCHEZ[4] DE IÑIGO, FRANCISCO[3] MUÑOZ, JACINTO[2], FRANCISCO[1])* was born May 02, 1904[236]. She married (1) BENITO HERRERA, son of CRUZ HERRERA and REDUCINDA CARDONA. She married (2) CASIMIRO TAFOYA VILLESCAZ 1925 in Lincoln, New México[237], son of CASIMIRO VILLESCAZ and EMILIANA TAFOYA.

Notes for BENITO HERRERA:
Padrinos (baptismal): Ramon Olguín and Lorensa Sedillo.

More About BENITO HERRERA:
Fact 1: April 02, 1890, Baptized.

More About CASIMIRO TAFOYA VILLESCAZ:
Fact 1: January 12, 1895, Baptized.

Marriage Notes for CRUSITA GONZÁLES and CASIMIRO VILLESCAZ:
Another record has them married on February 19, 1928.

Child of **CRUSITA GONZÁLES** and **CASIMIRO VILLESCAZ** is:
  i.   ERNESTINA[12] VILLESCAZ.

94. ELISA[11] GONZÁLES *(LEOPOLDO[10], RAYMUNDA (REIMUNDA) SEGUNDA (CIGISMUNDA)[9] SÁNCHEZ, MAURICIO DE LA TRINIDAD[8], JOSÉ GREGORIO DE LA TRINIDAD[7], JUAN CRISTÓBAL[6], FRANCISCO[5], JACINTO SÁNCHEZ[4] DE IÑIGO, FRANCISCO[3] MUÑOZ, JACINTO[2], FRANCISCO[1])* was born February 23, 1912. She married MANUEL HERRERA November 23, 1931[238], son of LUÍS HERRERA and BENJAMIN HERNÁNDEZ.

Children of **ELISA GONZÁLES** and **MANUEL HERRERA** are:
  i.   LEO[12] HERRERA, m. EMMA ZAMORA.
  ii. FLORIPE HERRERA, m. PORFIRIO SÁNCHEZ.

95. CIPRIANA[11] GONZÁLES *(DOMINGO EPAMINOANDAZ[10], RAYMUNDA (REIMUNDA) SEGUNDA (CIGISMUNDA)[9] SÁNCHEZ, MAURICIO DE LA TRINIDAD[8], JOSÉ GREGORIO DE LA TRINIDAD[7], JUAN CRISTÓBAL[6], FRANCISCO[5], JACINTO SÁNCHEZ[4] DE IÑIGO, FRANCISCO[3] MUÑOZ, JACINTO[2], FRANCISCO[1])* was born August 21, 1903[239], and died August 2006 in San Patricio, New México. She married VICENTE HERRERA August 27, 1932[240], son of CRUZ HERRERA and PETRA DOMINGUEZ.

More About CIPRIANA GONZÁLES:
Fact 1: August 21, 2006, 103 years of age.

Children of **CIPRIANA GONZÁLES** and **VICENTE HERRERA** are:
  i.   RUFINO[12] HERRERA, b. July 25, 1933, San Patricio, New México; d. January 17, 2006, San Patricio, New México; m. HELENA MONTOYA, April 04, 1957, San Patricio, New México.

Notes for RUFINO HERRERA:
Korean War Veteran

114.   ii.   BERTA HERRERA, b. Private, San Patricio, New México.

96. FLORENCIO GONZÁLES[11] GONZÁLES *(DOMINGO EPAMINOANDAZ[10], RAYMUNDA (REIMUNDA) SEGUNDA (CIGISMUNDA)[9] SÁNCHEZ, MAURICIO DE LA TRINIDAD[8], JOSÉ GREGORIO DE LA TRINIDAD[7], JUAN CRISTÓBAL[6], FRANCISCO[5], JACINTO SÁNCHEZ[4] DE IÑIGO, FRANCISCO[3] MUÑOZ, JACINTO[2], FRANCISCO[1])* was born September 17, 1907[241], and died October 11, 1973. He married ALBESITA (ALBESA) SÁNCHEZ, daughter of JACOBO SÁNCHEZ and MARÍA TRUJILLO.

Children of FLORENCIO GONZÁLES and ALBESITA SÁNCHEZ are:
    i.   JOSÉ[12] GONZÁLES.
    ii.   ISAQUIO GONZÁLES, b. Private.
    iii.   FRANK GONZÁLES.
    iv.   ELVIRA SÁNCHEZ GONZÁLES, b. Private.

97. SIGISFREDO[11] ROMERO *(MARÍA AURORA (AVRORA)[10] GONZÁLES, RAYMUNDA (REIMUNDA) SEGUNDA (CIGISMUNDA)[9] SÁNCHEZ, MAURICIO DE LA TRINIDAD[8], JOSÉ GREGORIO DE LA TRINIDAD[7], JUAN CRISTÓBAL[6], FRANCISCO[5], JACINTO SÁNCHEZ[4] DE IÑIGO, FRANCISCO[3] MUÑOZ, JACINTO[2], FRANCISCO[1])* was born March 31, 1903. He married LUCIA (LUCIANA) YBARRA January 11, 1928, daughter of GREGORIO YBARRA and CATARINA MONTOYA.

Notes for LUCIA (LUCIANA) YBARRA:
Padrinos: Augustín Laguna born in México City, and his wife, Juana María Laguna, born in Polvadera, New México

Children of SIGISFREDO ROMERO and LUCIA YBARRA are:
    i.   FLORIPE[12] ROMERO, b. Private.
    ii.   FEDELINA ROMERO, b. Private.
    iii.   CLEOFAS ROMERO, b. Private; m. JUAN SÁNCHEZ MONTES.
    iv.   ISABEL ROMERO, b. Private.
    v.   RUBÉN ROMERO, b. Private.
    vi.   EDUVIGEN ROMERO, b. Private.
    vii.   LEONIRES ROMERO, b. Private.
    viii.   FREDO ROMERO, b. Private.
    ix.   REBECCA ROMERO, b. Private.

98. MELITANA[11] ROMERO *(MARÍA AURORA (AVRORA)[10] GONZÁLES, RAYMUNDA (REIMUNDA) SEGUNDA (CIGISMUNDA)[9] SÁNCHEZ, MAURICIO DE LA TRINIDAD[8], JOSÉ GREGORIO DE LA TRINIDAD[7], JUAN CRISTÓBAL[6], FRANCISCO[5], JACINTO SÁNCHEZ[4] DE IÑIGO, FRANCISCO[3] MUÑOZ, JACINTO[2], FRANCISCO[1])* was born February 16, 1902. She married PATROCINIO ARCHULETA CHÁVEZ[242] July 13, 1921, son of PATROCINIO CHÁVEZ and MARÍA ARCHULETA.

Children of MELITANA ROMERO and PATROCINIO CHÁVEZ are:
    i.   GABRIEL[12] CHÁVEZ.
    ii.   AURELIA CHÁVEZ.
    iii.   BRIGIDA CHÁVEZ.
    iv.   GLORIA CHÁVEZ.
    v.   MOISES CHÁVEZ.
    vi.   ADAN CHÁVEZ.
    vii.   RAY CHÁVEZ.
    viii.   VIRGINIA ROMERO CHÁVEZ.
    ix.   NORA CHÁVEZ.

99. DULCINEA[11] POLACO *(AROPAJITA (EROPAJITA)[10] GONZÁLES, RAYMUNDA (REIMUNDA) SEGUNDA (CIGISMUNDA)[9] SÁNCHEZ, MAURICIO DE LA TRINIDAD[8], JOSÉ GREGORIO DE LA TRINIDAD[7], JUAN CRISTÓBAL[6], FRANCISCO[5], JACINTO SÁNCHEZ[4] DE IÑIGO, FRANCISCO[3] MUÑOZ, JACINTO[2], FRANCISCO[1])[243]* was born 1903. She married GUILLERMO (WILLIAM) (WILLIE) RANDOLPH[244] July 09, 1920 in San Patricio, New México, son of JOSÉ RANDOLPH and CATARINA BRADY.

Marriage Notes for DULCINEA POLACO and GUILLERMO RANDOLPH:
Married by: Reverand Girma.

Children of DULCINEA POLACO and GUILLERMO RANDOLPH are:
    i.   FRANK[12] RANDOLPH, b. Abt. 1921.
    ii.   VIOLA RANDOLPH, b. Abt. 1923.
    iii.   WILLIE POLACO RANDOLPH, b. Abt. 1926.

100. ALTAGRACIA[11] POLACO *(AROPAJITA (EROPAJITA)[10] GONZÁLES, RAYMUNDA (REIMUNDA) SEGUNDA (CIGISMUNDA)[9] SÁNCHEZ, MAURICIO DE LA TRINIDAD[8], JOSÉ GREGORIO DE LA TRINIDAD[7], JUAN CRISTÓBAL[6], FRANCISCO[5], JACINTO SÁNCHEZ[4] DE IÑIGO, FRANCISCO[3] MUÑOZ, JACINTO[2], FRANCISCO[1])* was born August 24, 1910. She married LEOPOLDO CHÁVEZ[245], son of PABLO CHÁVEZ and JESÚSITA SÁNCHEZ.

Marriage Notes for ALTAGRACIA POLACO and LEOPOLDO CHÁVEZ:
Married by: Justice of the Peace, B.H. Harvey.
Married May 24. The date is unclear but it was sometime in the 1930s.

Children of ALTAGRACIA POLACO and LEOPOLDO CHÁVEZ are:
    i.   ROY[12] CHÁVEZ, m. CRUSITA SILVA.
    ii.   BREZEL CHÁVEZ, m. PABLITA HERRERA.
    iii.   RICHARD CHÁVEZ.
    iv.   LYDIA CHÁVEZ, b. Private; m. BOBBY CHÁVEZ.

101. GENEVA[11] GONZÁLES *(FLORENCIO SÁNCHEZ[10], RAYMUNDA (REIMUNDA) SEGUNDA (CIGISMUNDA)[9] SÁNCHEZ, MAURICIO DE LA TRINIDAD[8], JOSÉ GREGORIO DE LA TRINIDAD[7], JUAN CRISTÓBAL[6], FRANCISCO[5], JACINTO SÁNCHEZ[4] DE IÑIGO, FRANCISCO[3] MUÑOZ, JACINTO[2], FRANCISCO[1])* was born April 11, 1915. She married ERNESTO SILVA February 02, 1933, son of JULIAN SILVA and MARÍA SÁNCHEZ.

Notes for ERNESTO SILVA:
Served with S2 US Navy during WW 2

Children of GENEVA GONZÁLES and ERNESTO SILVA are:
    i.   ERNEST[12] SILVA, b. Private; m. MINNIE SÁNCHEZ.
    ii.   JOSEPHINE SILVA, b. Private; m. WILLIAM GÓMEZ.
    iii.   JESUSITA SILVA, b. Private.

102. REYNALDA[11] SÁNCHEZ *(NAPOLEÓN[10], FRANCISCO[9], MAURICIO DE LA TRINIDAD[8], JOSÉ GREGORIO DE LA TRINIDAD[7], JUAN CRISTÓBAL[6], FRANCISCO[5], JACINTO SÁNCHEZ[4] DE IÑIGO, FRANCISCO[3] MUÑOZ, JACINTO[2], FRANCISCO[1])* was born February 21, 1905 in San Patricio, Territory of New México[246], and died May 12, 1970 in San Patricio, New México. She married ANISETO LUCERO[247].

Notes for ANISETO LUCERO:
Buried: San Patricio.

Children of REYNALDA SÁNCHEZ and ANISETO LUCERO are:
            i.   LEONIRES[12] LUCERO.
115.   ii.   MARÍA (MARY) LUCERO.
            iii.   EFFIE LUCERO.
            iv.   FELIS LUCERO.
            v.   REYNALDA LUCERO, b. Private.
            vi.   EURAQUIO LUCERO.
            vii.   ANISETO SÁNCHEZ LUCERO.
            viii.   JOSEPH LUCERO.
            ix.   JESSIE LUCERO.

103. JESUSITA ROMERO¹¹ SÁNCHEZ *(MAURICIO¹⁰, FRANCISCO⁹, MAURICIO DE LA TRINIDAD⁸, JOSÉ GREGORIO DE LA TRINIDAD⁷, JUAN CRISTÓBAL⁶, FRANCISCO⁵, JACINTO SÁNCHEZ⁴ DE IÑIGO, FRANCISCO³ MUÑOZ, JACINTO², FRANCISCO¹)* was born in San Patricio, New México. She married MAX SILVA.

Notes for MAX SILVA:
Was a WW II veteran.

Children of JESUSITA SÁNCHEZ and MAX SILVA are:
 i. FRANK¹² SILVA, b. Private.
 ii. PAT SILVA, b. Private.
 iii. ANTHONY SILVA, b. Private.
 iv. RICHARD SILVA.
 v. JIMMIE SILVA, b. Private.

104. ROMÁN¹¹ SÁNCHEZ *(MAURICIO¹⁰, FRANCISCO⁹, MAURICIO DE LA TRINIDAD⁸, JOSÉ GREGORIO DE LA TRINIDAD⁷, JUAN CRISTÓBAL⁶, FRANCISCO⁵, JACINTO SÁNCHEZ⁴ DE IÑIGO, FRANCISCO³ MUÑOZ, JACINTO², FRANCISCO¹)* was born April 23, 1904 in San Patricio, New México[248], and died February 08, 1973 in San Patricio, New México. He married FLORINDA SALSBERRY February 20, 1927 in Mescalero, New Mexico[249], daughter of JAMES SALSBERRY and MANUELITA HERRERA.

Notes for ROMÁN SÁNCHEZ:
May 29, 1904: Baptized by Román Barragán and his wife Andrea Torres de Barragán in San Patricio.

Died in an automobile accident in Ruidoso Downs.
Buried: La Capilla de San Patricio

Notes for FLORINDA SALSBERRY:
Florinda was born on the Rancho Salsberry by Cañon de Salsberry. The house is no longer standing but a grove of trees is all that remains of their house.

More About FLORINDA SALSBERRY:
Fact 1: June 15, 1910, Baptized. Padrinos: Manuel Corona and Susana Trujillo.[250]

Children of ROMÁN SÁNCHEZ and FLORINDA SALSBERRY are:
 i. MADELENA¹² SÁNCHEZ, b. San Patricio, New México.

   More About MADELENA SÁNCHEZ:
   Fact 1: Died Young

 ii. MAURICIO SALSBERRY SÁNCHEZ, b. San Patricio, New México.

   More About MAURICIO SALSBERRY SÁNCHEZ:
   Fact 1: Died Young

116. iii. JOSÉ ERNESTO SÁNCHEZ, b. April 09, 1928, San Patricio, New México.
117. iv. DELFINIA OLIDIA SÁNCHEZ, b. April 18, 1934, San Patricio, New México.
  v. ORLANDO SÁNCHEZ, b. April 03, 1936, San Patricio, New México.
118. vi. FLORA MARÍA SÁNCHEZ, b. March 24, 1938, Capítan, New México.
119. vii. FRED SÁNCHEZ, b. May 30, 1940, Fort Stanton, New México.
120. viii. BREZEL ROBERT SÁNCHEZ, b. November 04, 1941, San Patricio, New México.
  ix. GERALDINE (GERALDA) ELSIE SÁNCHEZ, b. January 10, 1945, San Patricio, New México; m. ROBERT MONTES.
  x. LUVIN SÁNCHEZ, b. October 23, 1947, San Patricio, New México; m. GLORIA BACA.

   More About LUVIN SÁNCHEZ:
   Fact 1: Moved to Roswell, New México.

121. xi. CINTHIA (CYNTHIA) YOLANDA SÁNCHEZ, b. September 10, 1950, Capítan, New México; d. April 27, 1986, Rio Rancho, New México.

122.   xii. ROMÁN SÁNCHEZ, JR., b. March 13, 1954, San Patricio, New México.

105. MAXIMILIANO[11] SÁNCHEZ *(MAURICIO[10], FRANCISCO[9], MAURICIO DE LA TRINIDAD[8], JOSÉ GREGORIO DE LA TRINIDAD[7], JUAN CRISTÓBAL[6], FRANCISCO[5], JACINTO SÁNCHEZ[4] DE IÑIGO, FRANCISCO[3] MUÑOZ, JACINTO[2], FRANCISCO[1])* was born August 21, 1911 in San Patricio, New México. He married SORAIDA SÁNCHEZ February 11, 1936[251], daughter of AURELIO SÁNCHEZ and ANASTACIA ARAGÓN.

More About MAXIMILIANO SÁNCHEZ:
Fact 1: January 05, 1945, WW II veteran. Discharged from Indiana Town Gap, Pennsylvania.[252]

Marriage Notes for MAXIMILIANO SÁNCHEZ and SORAIDA SÁNCHEZ:
Married by: Justice of the Peace, Elerdo Cháves.

Children of MAXIMILIANO SÁNCHEZ and SORAIDA SÁNCHEZ are:
    i.   BEATRICE[12] SÁNCHEZ.
    ii.   ROSEMARY SÁNCHEZ.

106. MARÍA (MARÍLLITA)[11] SÁNCHEZ *(MAURICIO[10], FRANCISCO[9], MAURICIO DE LA TRINIDAD[8], JOSÉ GREGORIO DE LA TRINIDAD[7], JUAN CRISTÓBAL[6], FRANCISCO[5], JACINTO SÁNCHEZ[4] DE IÑIGO, FRANCISCO[3] MUÑOZ, JACINTO[2], FRANCISCO[1])* was born May 1919 in San Patricio, New México. She married MANUEL CHÁVEZ.

Children of MARÍA SÁNCHEZ and MANUEL CHÁVEZ are:
    i.   WILLIE[12] CHÁVEZ.
    ii.   VIRGINIA SÁNCHEZ CHÁVEZ.
    iii. ANDY CHÁVEZ.
    iv. LUISA CHÁVEZ, b. Private.
    v.   DENNIS CHÁVEZ, b. Private.
    vi. CLIFFORD CHÁVEZ, b. Private.

107. ALBESITA (ALBESA)[11] SÁNCHEZ *(JACOBO[10], FRANCISCO[9], MAURICIO DE LA TRINIDAD[8], JOSÉ GREGORIO DE LA TRINIDAD[7], JUAN CRISTÓBAL[6], FRANCISCO[5], JACINTO SÁNCHEZ[4] DE IÑIGO, FRANCISCO[3] MUÑOZ, JACINTO[2], FRANCISCO[1])* was born March 10, 1914. She married FLORENCIO GONZÁLES GONZÁLES, son of DOMINGO GONZÁLES and ELVIRA GONZÁLES.

Children of ALBESITA SÁNCHEZ and FLORENCIO GONZÁLES are:
    i.   JOSÉ[12] GONZÁLES.
    ii.   ISAQUIO GONZÁLES, b. Private.
    iii. FRANK GONZÁLES.
    iv. ELVIRA SÁNCHEZ GONZÁLES, b. Private.

108. PILAR TRUJILLO[11] SÁNCHEZ *(JACOBO[10], FRANCISCO[9], MAURICIO DE LA TRINIDAD[8], JOSÉ GREGORIO DE LA TRINIDAD[7], JUAN CRISTÓBAL[6], FRANCISCO[5], JACINTO SÁNCHEZ[4] DE IÑIGO, FRANCISCO[3] MUÑOZ, JACINTO[2], FRANCISCO[1])* was born May 02, 1917. She married SYLVANO (SILVANO) SÁNCHEZ, son of CELESTINO SÁNCHEZ and NAVORSITA MOYA.

Notes for SYLVANO (SILVANO) SÁNCHEZ:
Buried: La Capilla de San Ysidro.

Children of PILAR SÁNCHEZ and SYLVANO SÁNCHEZ are:
    i.   SANTIAGO SÁNCHEZ Y[12] SÁNCHEZ, b. Private.
    ii.   REYNALDO SÁNCHEZ Y SÁNCHEZ, b. Private.
    iii. JUAN SÁNCHEZ Y SÁNCHEZ, b. Private.
    iv. MARY SÁNCHEZ Y SÁNCHEZ, b. Private.
    v.   ELOISA SÁNCHEZ Y SÁNCHEZ, b. Private.
    vi. TONI SÁNCHEZ, b. Private.
    vii. AMIE SÁNCHEZ, b. Private.
    viii. LELA SÁNCHEZ, b. Private.
    ix. EMMA SÁNCHEZ, b. Private.
    x.   CHRIS SÁNCHEZ, b. Private.

xi. RAMÓN SÁNCHEZ, b. Private.
xii. LEO SÁNCHEZ, b. Private.

109. ESTER[11] SÁNCHEZ *(JACOBO[10], FRANCISCO[9], MAURICIO DE LA TRINIDAD[8], JOSÉ GREGORIO DE LA TRINIDAD[7], JUAN CRISTÓBAL[6], FRANCISCO[5], JACINTO SÁNCHEZ[4] DE IÑIGO, FRANCISCO[3] MUÑOZ, JACINTO[2], FRANCISCO[1])* was born 1922. She married PATROCINIO ARCHULETA CHÁVEZ[253], son of PATROCINIO CHÁVEZ and MARÍA ARCHULETA.

Children of ESTER SÁNCHEZ and PATROCINIO CHÁVEZ are:
i. VICENTA[12] CHÁVEZ, b. Private.
ii. PATSY CHÁVEZ, b. Private.
iii. MARGARET CHÁVEZ, b. Private.
iv. ROGER CHÁVEZ, b. Private.

110. TEODORO SÁNCHEZ[11] PEÑA *(AMADITA[10] SÁNCHEZ, JUAN RAFAEL BERCELÓ[9], JUAN RAFAEL CHÁVEZ[8], MANUEL RAFAEL[7], JOSÉ PEDRO[6], JACINTO[5], JOSÉ[4], JACINTO SÁNCHEZ[3] DE IÑIGO, FRANCISCO[2] MUÑOZ, JACINTO[1])* was born July 15, 1907 in Glencoe, Territory of New México. He married TELESFORA SÁNCHEZ March 01, 1926 in Carrizozo, New México[254], daughter of SALOMON SÁNCHEZ and JENNIE GILL.

Children of TEODORO PEÑA and TELESFORA SÁNCHEZ are:
i. JOSEPHINE[12] PEÑA, b. Private.
ii. IDALIA PEÑA.
iii. LUÍS PEÑA.
iv. THEODORO (TEODORO) (3) PEÑA.
v. RAFAEL PEÑA.
vi. REYES PEÑA.

Generation No. 12

111. IGNACIA (INES)[12] CHÁVEZ *(PAUBLITA (PABLITA)[11] SÁNCHEZ, FELIPÉ E.[10], ESTOLANO[9], MAURICIO DE LA TRINIDAD[8], JOSÉ GREGORIO DE LA TRINIDAD[7], JUAN CRISTÓBAL[6], FRANCISCO[5], JACINTO SÁNCHEZ[4] DE IÑIGO, FRANCISCO[3] MUÑOZ, JACINTO[2], FRANCISCO[1])* was born January 23, 1919 in San Patricio, New México. She married (1) HAROLD STEELE. She married (2) VICTOR BROOKS.

Notes for VICTOR BROOKS:
WW II veteran.

Child of IGNACIA CHÁVEZ and HAROLD STEELE is:
i. HAROLD (2ND)[13] STEELE.

112. EMILIANO[12] CHÁVEZ *(PAUBLITA (PABLITA)[11] SÁNCHEZ, FELIPÉ E.[10], ESTOLANO[9], MAURICIO DE LA TRINIDAD[8], JOSÉ GREGORIO DE LA TRINIDAD[7], JUAN CRISTÓBAL[6], FRANCISCO[5], JACINTO SÁNCHEZ[4] DE IÑIGO, FRANCISCO[3] MUÑOZ, JACINTO[2], FRANCISCO[1])* was born January 11, 1922 in San Patricio, New México, and died January 23, 1953 in California. He married MARÍA (MARY) LUCERO, daughter of ANISETO LUCERO and REYNALDA SÁNCHEZ.

Notes for EMILIANO CHÁVEZ:
Served with N.M.2516 Base Unit AAF, and was a WW II veteran.
Buried: San Patricio.

Children of EMILIANO CHÁVEZ and MARÍA LUCERO are:
i. BOBBY[13] CHÁVEZ, m. LYDIA CHÁVEZ.
ii. ALEX CHÁVEZ.

   Notes for ALEX CHÁVEZ:
   Vietnam War Veteran. Died in Vietnam War.

iii. JERRY CHÁVEZ.

Notes for JERRY CHÁVEZ:
Died in an accident.

iv. LAURENCE CHÁVEZ, b. Private.

113. ORALIA[12] CHÁVEZ *(PAUBLITA (PABLITA)[11] SÁNCHEZ, FELIPÉ E.[10], ESTOLANO[9], MAURICIO DE LA TRINIDAD[8], JOSÉ GREGORIO DE LA TRINIDAD[7], JUAN CRISTÓBAL[6], FRANCISCO[5], JACINTO SÁNCHEZ[4] DE IÑIGO, FRANCISCO[3] MUÑOZ, JACINTO[2], FRANCISCO[1])* was born February 18, 1931 in San Patricio, New México. She married JOSÉ ERNESTO SÁNCHEZ March 20, 1948 in Ruidoso, New Mexico, son of ROMÁN SÁNCHEZ and FLORINDA SALSBERRY.

Children of ORALIA CHÁVEZ and JOSÉ SÁNCHEZ are:
123. i. ERNEST JOSEPH[13] SÁNCHEZ, b. July 08, 1951, Long Beach, California.
124. ii. JAMES CHARLES SÁNCHEZ, b. October 29, 1953, Long Beach, California.
      iii. STEVE ANTHONY SÁNCHEZ, b. December 24, 1959, Ruidoso, New México; d. January 08, 1978, San Patricio, New México.
125. iv. JANICE MARIE SÁNCHEZ, b. August 23, 1968, Ruidoso, New Mexico.

114. BERTA[12] HERRERA *(CIPRIANA[11] GONZÁLES, DOMINGO EPAMINOANDAZ[10], RAYMUNDA (REIMUNDA) SEGUNDA (CIGISMUNDA)[9] SÁNCHEZ, MAURICIO DE LA TRINIDAD[8], JOSÉ GREGORIO DE LA TRINIDAD[7], JUAN CRISTÓBAL[6], FRANCISCO[5], JACINTO SÁNCHEZ[4] DE IÑIGO, FRANCISCO[3] MUÑOZ, JACINTO[2], FRANCISCO[1])* was born Private in San Patricio, New México. She married FRED SÁNCHEZ, son of ROMÁN SÁNCHEZ and FLORINDA SALSBERRY.

Children of BERTA HERRERA and FRED SÁNCHEZ are:
i. DAVÍD[13] SÁNCHEZ, b. Private.
ii. ELIZABETH SÁNCHEZ, b. Private.
iii. PATRICK SÁNCHEZ, b. Private.
iv. JESSICA SÁNCHEZ, b. Private.

115. MARÍA (MARY)[12] LUCERO *(REYNALDA[11] SÁNCHEZ, NAPOLEÓN[10], FRANCISCO[9], MAURICIO DE LA TRINIDAD[8], JOSÉ GREGORIO DE LA TRINIDAD[7], JUAN CRISTÓBAL[6], FRANCISCO[5], JACINTO SÁNCHEZ[4] DE IÑIGO, FRANCISCO[3] MUÑOZ, JACINTO[2], FRANCISCO[1])*. She married (1) EMILIANO CHÁVEZ, son of YSIDRO CHÁVEZ and PAUBLITA SÁNCHEZ. She married (2) RALPH RODELA, son of ELIJIO RODELA and MARTINA SALAZAR.

Notes for EMILIANO CHÁVEZ:
Served with N.M.2516 Base Unit AAF, and was a WW II veteran.
Buried: San Patricio.

Notes for RALPH RODELA:
Raised by Isabel and Concha Montoya in San Patricio.

Children of MARÍA LUCERO and EMILIANO CHÁVEZ are:
i. BOBBY[13] CHÁVEZ, m. LYDIA CHÁVEZ.
ii. ALEX CHÁVEZ.

Notes for ALEX CHÁVEZ:
Vietnam War Veteran. Died in Vietnam War.

iii. JERRY CHÁVEZ.

Notes for JERRY CHÁVEZ:
Died in an accident.

iv. LAURENCE CHÁVEZ, b. Private.

Children of MARÍA LUCERO and RALPH RODELA are:
v. RALPH LUCERO[13] RODELA.
vi. FRANK RODELA.

116. JOSÉ ERNESTO¹² SÁNCHEZ *(ROMÁN¹¹, MAURICIO¹⁰, FRANCISCO⁹, MAURICIO DE LA TRINIDAD⁸, JOSÉ GREGORIO DE LA TRINIDAD⁷, JUAN CRISTÓBAL⁶, FRANCISCO⁵, JACINTO SÁNCHEZ⁴ DE IÑIGO, FRANCISCO³ MUÑOZ, JACINTO², FRANCISCO¹)* was born April 09, 1928 in San Patricio, New México. He married ORALIA CHÁVEZ March 20, 1948 in Ruidoso, New Mexico, daughter of YSIDRO CHÁVEZ and PAUBLITA SÁNCHEZ.

Children of JOSÉ SÁNCHEZ and ORALIA CHÁVEZ are:
123.	i.	ERNEST JOSEPH¹³ SÁNCHEZ, b. July 08, 1951, Long Beach, California.
124.	ii.	JAMES CHARLES SÁNCHEZ, b. October 29, 1953, Long Beach, California.
	iii.	STEVE ANTHONY SÁNCHEZ, b. December 24, 1959, Ruidoso, New México; d. January 08, 1978, San Patricio, New México.
125.	iv.	JANICE MARIE SÁNCHEZ, b. August 23, 1968, Ruidoso, New Mexico.

117. DELFINIA OLIDIA¹² SÁNCHEZ *(ROMÁN¹¹, MAURICIO¹⁰, FRANCISCO⁹, MAURICIO DE LA TRINIDAD⁸, JOSÉ GREGORIO DE LA TRINIDAD⁷, JUAN CRISTÓBAL⁶, FRANCISCO⁵, JACINTO SÁNCHEZ⁴ DE IÑIGO, FRANCISCO³ MUÑOZ, JACINTO², FRANCISCO¹)* was born April 18, 1934 in San Patricio, New México. She married LEANDRO VEGA, son of LEANDRO VEGA and NARCISA RAMIREZ.

Children of DELFINIA SÁNCHEZ and LEANDRO VEGA are:
	i.	LEE (LEANDRO)¹³ VEGA, b. July 14, 1960, Carrizozo, New México; m. CATHERINE MARIE GARCÍA.
126.	ii.	GARY ANTHONY VEGA, b. June 17, 1961, Carrizozo, New México.

118. FLORA MARÍA¹² SÁNCHEZ *(ROMÁN¹¹, MAURICIO¹⁰, FRANCISCO⁹, MAURICIO DE LA TRINIDAD⁸, JOSÉ GREGORIO DE LA TRINIDAD⁷, JUAN CRISTÓBAL⁶, FRANCISCO⁵, JACINTO SÁNCHEZ⁴ DE IÑIGO, FRANCISCO³ MUÑOZ, JACINTO², FRANCISCO¹)* was born March 24, 1938 in Capítan, New México. She married RICHARD VEGA.

Children of FLORA SÁNCHEZ and RICHARD VEGA are:
	i.	DEBBI¹³ VEGA, b. Private.
	ii.	JAYLYN VEGA, b. Private.
	iii.	RICHARD SÁNCHEZ VEGA, b. Private.
	iv.	KENNETH VEGA, b. Private.

119. FRED¹² SÁNCHEZ *(ROMÁN¹¹, MAURICIO¹⁰, FRANCISCO⁹, MAURICIO DE LA TRINIDAD⁸, JOSÉ GREGORIO DE LA TRINIDAD⁷, JUAN CRISTÓBAL⁶, FRANCISCO⁵, JACINTO SÁNCHEZ⁴ DE IÑIGO, FRANCISCO³ MUÑOZ, JACINTO², FRANCISCO¹)* was born May 30, 1940 in Fort Stanton, New México. He married BERTA HERRERA, daughter of VICENTE HERRERA and CIPRIANA GONZÁLES.

Children of FRED SÁNCHEZ and BERTA HERRERA are:
	i.	DAVÍD¹³ SÁNCHEZ, b. Private.
	ii.	ELIZABETH SÁNCHEZ, b. Private.
	iii.	PATRICK SÁNCHEZ, b. Private.
	iv.	JESSICA SÁNCHEZ, b. Private.

120. BREZEL ROBERT¹² SÁNCHEZ *(ROMÁN¹¹, MAURICIO¹⁰, FRANCISCO⁹, MAURICIO DE LA TRINIDAD⁸, JOSÉ GREGORIO DE LA TRINIDAD⁷, JUAN CRISTÓBAL⁶, FRANCISCO⁵, JACINTO SÁNCHEZ⁴ DE IÑIGO, FRANCISCO³ MUÑOZ, JACINTO², FRANCISCO¹)* was born November 04, 1941 in San Patricio, New México. He married MINNIE ROMERO.

More About BREZEL ROBERT SÁNCHEZ:
Fact 1: Moved to Roswell, New México.

Children of BREZEL SÁNCHEZ and MINNIE ROMERO are:
	i.	RAY¹³ SÁNCHEZ, b. Private.
	ii.	ANTHONY SÁNCHEZ, b. Private.
	iii.	ROSANA SÁNCHEZ, b. Private.
	iv.	VERONICA SÁNCHEZ, b. Private.

121. CINTHIA (CYNTHIA) YOLANDA[12] SÁNCHEZ *(ROMÁN[11], MAURICIO[10], FRANCISCO[9], MAURICIO DE LA TRINIDAD[8], JOSÉ GREGORIO DE LA TRINIDAD[7], JUAN CRISTÓBAL[6], FRANCISCO[5], JACINTO SÁNCHEZ[4] DE IÑIGO, FRANCISCO[3] MUÑOZ, JACINTO[2], FRANCISCO[1])* was born September 10, 1950 in Capítan, New México, and died April 27, 1986 in Rio Rancho, New México. She married BERRY VANDERWALL.

Children of CINTHIA SÁNCHEZ and BERRY VANDERWALL are:
    i.   NEIL SIMON[13] VANDERWALL, b. Private.
    ii.   MELISSA STEPHANIE VANDERWALL, b. Private.
    iii. AMANDA DESIREE VANDERWALL, b. Private.
    iv. AMBER DAWN VANDERWALL, b. Private.

122. ROMÁN[12] SÁNCHEZ, JR. *(ROMÁN[11], MAURICIO[10], FRANCISCO[9], MAURICIO DE LA TRINIDAD[8], JOSÉ GREGORIO DE LA TRINIDAD[7], JUAN CRISTÓBAL[6], FRANCISCO[5], JACINTO SÁNCHEZ[4] DE IÑIGO, FRANCISCO[3] MUÑOZ, JACINTO[2], FRANCISCO[1])* was born March 13, 1954 in San Patricio, New México. He married YOVONNE SALAS.

Children of ROMÁN SÁNCHEZ and YOVONNE SALAS are:
    i.   FELIPÉ[13] SÁNCHEZ, b. Private, Ruidoso, New México.
    ii.   FABIAN SÁNCHEZ, b. Private, Ruidoso, New México.

Generation No. 13

123. ERNEST JOSEPH[13] SÁNCHEZ *(JOSÉ ERNESTO[12], ROMÁN[11], MAURICIO[10], FRANCISCO[9], MAURICIO DE LA TRINIDAD[8], JOSÉ GREGORIO DE LA TRINIDAD[7], JUAN CRISTÓBAL[6], FRANCISCO[5], JACINTO SÁNCHEZ[4] DE IÑIGO, FRANCISCO[3] MUÑOZ, JACINTO[2], FRANCISCO[1])* was born July 08, 1951 in Long Beach, California. He married EUGENIE JOYCE HOFF in Carrizozo, New México, daughter of ALFRIED HOFF and PAULINA KUSCHEL.

Children of ERNEST SÁNCHEZ and EUGENIE HOFF are:
         i.   PAUL RAY[14] SÁNCHEZ, b. October 22, 1970, Tularosa, New Mexico.
127.   ii.   ERIK JOSEPH SÁNCHEZ, b. February 19, 1977, Denver, Colorado.

124. JAMES CHARLES[13] SÁNCHEZ *(JOSÉ ERNESTO[12], ROMÁN[11], MAURICIO[10], FRANCISCO[9], MAURICIO DE LA TRINIDAD[8], JOSÉ GREGORIO DE LA TRINIDAD[7], JUAN CRISTÓBAL[6], FRANCISCO[5], JACINTO SÁNCHEZ[4] DE IÑIGO, FRANCISCO[3] MUÑOZ, JACINTO[2], FRANCISCO[1])* was born October 29, 1953 in Long Beach, California. He married RUBY ROMO, daughter of PLACIDO ROMO and GENOVEVA CHÁVEZ.

Children of JAMES SÁNCHEZ and RUBY ROMO are:
128.   i.   JAMES MICHAEL[14] SÁNCHEZ.
        ii.   STEPHANIE RAE SÁNCHEZ, b. Socorro, New México.

125. JANICE MARIE[13] SÁNCHEZ *(JOSÉ ERNESTO[12], ROMÁN[11], MAURICIO[10], FRANCISCO[9], MAURICIO DE LA TRINIDAD[8], JOSÉ GREGORIO DE LA TRINIDAD[7], JUAN CRISTÓBAL[6], FRANCISCO[5], JACINTO SÁNCHEZ[4] DE IÑIGO, FRANCISCO[3] MUÑOZ, JACINTO[2], FRANCISCO[1])* was born August 23, 1968 in Ruidoso, New Mexico. She married EDDIE BERNAL.

Children of JANICE SÁNCHEZ and EDDIE BERNAL are:
    i.   MONICA[14] BERNAL.
    ii.   EDDIE BERNAL.

126. GARY ANTHONY[13] VEGA *(DELFINIA OLIDIA[12] SÁNCHEZ, ROMÁN[11], MAURICIO[10], FRANCISCO[9], MAURICIO DE LA TRINIDAD[8], JOSÉ GREGORIO DE LA TRINIDAD[7], JUAN CRISTÓBAL[6], FRANCISCO[5], JACINTO SÁNCHEZ[4] DE IÑIGO, FRANCISCO[3] MUÑOZ, JACINTO[2], FRANCISCO[1])* was born June 17, 1961 in Carrizozo, New México. He married LISA GAIL CRENSHAW.

Child of GARY VEGA and LISA CRENSHAW is:
    i.   KAITLYN[14] VEGA

Generation No. 14

127. ERIK JOSEPH[14] SÁNCHEZ *(ERNEST JOSEPH[13], JOSÉ ERNESTO[12], ROMÁN[11], MAURICIO[10], FRANCISCO[9], MAURICIO DE LA TRINIDAD[8], JOSÉ GREGORIO DE LA TRINIDAD[7], JUAN CRISTÓBAL[6], FRANCISCO[5], JACINTO SÁNCHEZ[4] DE IÑIGO, FRANCISCO[3] MUÑOZ, JACINTO[2], FRANCISCO[1])* was born February 19, 1977 in Denver, Colorado. He married (1) VANESSA -----. He married (2) BRITNEY VIGIL December 01, 2002 in Loveland, Colorado.

Child of ERIK SÁNCHEZ and BRITNEY VIGIL is:
    i.   ALEXA[15] SÁNCHEZ, b. Denver, Colorado.

128. JAMES MICHAEL[14] SÁNCHEZ *(JAMES CHARLES[13], JOSÉ ERNESTO[12], ROMÁN[11], MAURICIO[10], FRANCISCO[9], MAURICIO DE LA TRINIDAD[8], JOSÉ GREGORIO DE LA TRINIDAD[7], JUAN CRISTÓBAL[6], FRANCISCO[5], JACINTO SÁNCHEZ[4] DE IÑIGO, FRANCISCO[3] MUÑOZ, JACINTO[2], FRANCISCO[1]).* He married ANGIE.

Children of JAMES SÁNCHEZ and ANGIE are:
    i.   CHAYANNE JADEN[15] SÁNCHEZ, b. Albuquerque, New México.
    ii.   JAMES GEORGE SÁNCHEZ, b. Albuquerque, New México.

Endnotes

1. *Fray Angélico Chávez,, Origins of New Mexico Families: Revised Edition*, Page 280, (Museum of New México Press, 1992). Lists birth date, both his marriages and their respective dates, and all of his children. All of the significant events of his life are also listed.
2. *Fray Angélico Chávez,, Origins of New Mexico Families: Revised Edition*, Page 280-281, (Museum of New México Press, 1992).
3. *Fray Angélico Chávez,, Origins of New Mexico Families: Revised Edition*, Page 281, (Museum of New México Press, 1992). Lists birth date, marriage date, and children.
4. *Fray Angélico Chávez,, Origins of New Mexico Families: Revised Edition*, Page 281, (Museum of New México Press, 1992).
5. *Fray Angélico Chávez, Origins of New Mexico Families: Revised Edition*, Page 161, (Museum of New México Press, 1992). Lists both of his marriages, death and significant events in his life. His children were listed in his will.
6. *Fray Angélico Chávez,, Origins of New Mexico Families: Revised Edition*, Page 162, (Museum of New México Press, 1992).
7. *Fray Angélico Chávez,, Origins of New Mexico Families: Revised Edition*, Page 281, (Museum of New México Press, 1992). Lists marriage.
8. *Fray Angélico Chávez,, Origins of New Mexico Families: Revised Edition*, Page 281, (Museum of New México Press, 1992).
9. *Lincoln County Clerk, Probate Records.*
10. *1870 Census of Ft. Stanton*, Microfiche# 0552393, Page 1.
11. *LDS Historical Library, Alamogordo*, Fiche # 754, Birth date and death.
12. *LDS Historical Library, Alamogordo*, Reel # 754.
13. *1870 Census of Ft. Stanton*, Page 4, Fiche # 0552393.
14. *LDS Historical Library, Alamogordo*, Reel # 756, Page 12.
15. *1900 Census Lincoln County*, Fiche # 1241001-2b, Lincoln County.
16. *LDS Historical Library, Alamogordo*, Fiche # 754.
17. *Lincoln County Clerk, Probate Records.*
18. *LDS Historical Library, Alamogordo*, Page 6, Fiche # 756.
19. *1870 Census of Ft. Stanton*, Fiche # 0552393.
20. *LDS Historical Library, Alamogordo*, Microfiche # 756, Page 159..
21. *LDS Historical Library, Alamogordo*, Page 167, Fiche # 756.
22. *1920 Census Lincoln County*, Fiche # 1821077, 5B, Lists his wife and children and their ages.
23. *LDS Historical Library, Alamogordo*, Page 167, Fiche # 167.
24. *Lincoln County Clerk, Book of Marriages*, Page 561, Book 4.
25. *LDS Historical Library, Alamogordo*, Page 27, Fiche # 756.
26. *LDS Historical Library, Alamogordo*, Page 131, Fiche # 754.
27. *LDS Historical Library, Alamogordo*, Fiche # 0017009-1.
28. *Lincoln County Clerk, Book of Marriages*, Page 254, Book 4, Lists birth date and marriage dates for the bride and groom.
29. *Lincoln County Clerk, Book of Marriages*, Page 4, Book 1 Applications, Lists birth dates for the bride and groom.
30. *LDS Historical Library, Alamogordo*, Fiche # 0017009-3.
31. *LDS Historical Library, Alamogordo*, Page 48, Fiche # 754.
32. *LDS Historical Library, Alamogordo*, Page 99, Fiche # 754.
33. *LDS Historical Library, Alamogordo*, Page 64, Fiche # 0017008.

34. *LDS Historical Library, Alamogordo*, Page 61, Fiche # 0017008.
35. *LDS Historical Library, Alamogordo*, Page 167, Fiche # 756.
36. *1900 Census Lincoln County*, Page 5A, Picacho.
37. *LDS Historical Library, Alamogordo*, Page 178, Fiche # 754.
38. *1900 Census Lincoln County*, Page 5A, Picacho.
39. *LDS Historical Library, Alamogordo*, Page 186, Fiche # 754.
40. *LDS Historical Library, Alamogordo*, Page 67, Microfiche # 1821077, Sheet 3B, Lists all family members.
41. *LDS Historical Library, Alamogordo*, Page 186, Fiche # 754.
42. *Lincoln County Clerk, Book of Marriages*, Page 384, Lists birthdate and marriage date for the bride and groom.
43. *1920 Census Lincoln County*, Fiche # 1821077, 5B, Lists his wife and children and their ages.
44. *LDS Historical Library, Alamogordo*, Page 167, Fiche # 167.
45. *Lincoln County Clerk, Book of Marriages*, Page 561, Book 4.
46. *LDS Historical Library, Alamogordo*, Page 27, Fiche # 756.
47. *Lincoln County Clerk, Book of Marriages*, Page 352, Book 3, List birthdate and marriage date for the bride and groom.
48. 1930 Census Lincoln County, Page 2B, Hondo, Lists all children born before 1930.
49. 1930 Census Lincoln County.
50. *LDS Historical Library, Alamogordo*, Reel # 756, Page 16.
51. *LDS Historical Library, Alamogordo*, Fiche # 0017009-1.
52. *LDS Historical Library, Alamogordo*, Page 167, Fiche # 756.
53. *LDS Historical Library, Alamogordo*, Page 131, Fiche # 754.
54. *LDS Historical Library, Alamogordo*, Page 156, Fiche # 754.
55. *Lincoln County Clerk, Book of Marriages*, Page 162, Book 1 Applications, Lists birth dates for the bride and groom.
56. *LDS Historical Library, Alamogordo*, Page 156, Fiche # 754.
57. *LDS Historical Library, Alamogordo*, Fiche # 0017009-1.
58. *Lincoln County Clerk, Book of Marriages*, Page 254, Book 4, Lists birth date and marriage dates for the bride and groom.
59. *Lincoln County Clerk, Book of Marriages*, Page 4, Book 1 Applications, Lists birth dates for the bride and groom.
60. *LDS Historical Library, Alamogordo*, Fiche # 0017009-3.
61. *Lincoln County Clerk, Book of Marriages*, Page 100, Book 5, Lists birthdate and marriage date for the bride and groom.
62. 1930 Census Lincoln County.
63. *LDS Historical Library, Alamogordo*, Page 3, Fiche # 754.
64. *Lincoln County Clerk, Book of Marriages*, Page 41, Book 5.
65. Lincoln County Clerk, Soldiers Discharge Book, Page 166, Book 1, Lists date of birth.
66. *LDS Historical Library, Alamogordo*, Page 48, Fiche # 754.
67. *LDS Historical Library, Alamogordo*, Page 99, Fiche # 754.
68. 1930 Census Lincoln County.
69. *LDS Historical Library, Alamogordo*, Page 140, Fiche # 756.
70. 1930 Census Lincoln County, Page 9A, Hondo, Lists all children born before 1930.
71. *Lincoln County Clerk, Book of Marriages*, Page 347, Book 4, Lists birth dates and marriage date for the bride and groom.
72. *LDS Historical Library, Alamogordo*, Page 11, Fiche # 754.
73. *Lincoln County Clerk, Book of Marriages*, Page 427, Book 5.
74. *LDS Historical Library, Alamogordo*, Page 6, Fiche # 0017006.
75. *LDS Historical Library, Alamogordo*, Page 17, Fiche # 756.
76. *LDS Historical Library, Alamogordo*, Page 24, Fiche # 0017008.
77. *LDS Historical Library, Alamogordo*, Page 61, Fiche # 0017008.
78. *Lincoln County Clerk, Book of Marriages*, Page 81, Book 3.
79. 1930 Census Lincoln County, Page 4A, Hollywood.
80. *LDS Historical Library, Alamogordo*, Page 71, Fiche # 754.
81. *LDS Historical Library, Alamogordo*, Page 5, Fiche # 756.
82. *LDS Historical Library, Alamogordo*, Page 5, Fiche # 0017009.
83. *LDS Historical Library, Alamogordo*, Page 166, Fiche # 754.
84. *LDS Historical Library, Alamogordo*, Page 13, Fiche # 0017009.
85. *LDS Historical Library, Alamogordo*, Page 166, Fiche # 754.
86. *LDS Historical Library, Alamogordo*, Page 24, Fiche # 0017008.
87. *LDS Historical Library, Alamogordo*, Page 10, Fiche # 0017008.
88. *LDS Historical Library, Alamogordo*, Page 105, Fiche # 0017008.
89. *LDS Historical Library, Alamogordo*, Page 186, Fiche # 754.
90. *LDS Historical Library, Alamogordo*, Page 28, Fiche # 756.
91. *LDS Historical Library, Alamogordo*, Page 186, Fiche # 754.
92. 1930 Census Lincoln County.
93. *LDS Historical Library, Alamogordo*, Page 235, Fiche # 754.
94. *LDS Historical Library, Alamogordo*, Page 67, Microfiche # 1821077, Sheet 3B, Lists all family members.
95. *LDS Historical Library, Alamogordo*, Page 25, Fiche # 756.

96. *LDS Historical Library, Alamogordo*, Page 235, Fiche # 754.
97. *LDS Historical Library, Alamogordo*, Page 54, Fiche # 0017008.
98. *LDS Historical Library, Alamogordo*, Page 12, Fiche # 0017009.
99. *LDS Historical Library, Alamogordo*, Page 22, Fiche # 754, Personal information provided by a descendant of his family.
100. *1900 Census Lincoln County*, Page 2B, Reventón, Lists all the children born before 1900.
101. *1880 Census Lincoln County*, Fiche # 8206107, Census # 77, Lists Erinello, his wife and their children and all of their ages.
102. *Lincoln County Clerk, Book of Marriages*, Page 141, Book B.
103. *Lincoln County Clerk, Book of Marriages*, Page 353, Book 3.
104. *LDS Historical Library, Alamogordo*, Page 206, Fiche # 754.
105. *1920 Census Lincoln County*, Page 3B, White Oaks.
106. *LDS Historical Library, Alamogordo*, Page 207, Fiche # 754.
107. *LDS Historical Library, Alamogordo*, Page 10, Fiche # 754.
108. *LDS Historical Library, Alamogordo*, Page 109, Fiche # 756.
109. *Lincoln County Clerk, Book of Marriages*, Page 25, Book 3, Lists birth date and marriage date for bride and groom.
110. *LDS Historical Library, Alamogordo*, Page 188, Fiche # 188, Marriage location.
111. *LDS Historical Library, Alamogordo*, Page 22 # 5, Fiche # 756.
112. *Lincoln County Clerk, Book of Marriages*, Page 133, Book 3, Lists birthdate and marriage date for bride and groom.
113. 1930 Census Lincoln County, Page 2A, Reventon, Lists all children born before 1930.
114. *Lincoln County Clerk, Book of Marriages*, Page 449, Book 5.
115. *Lincoln County Clerk, Book of Marriages*, Page 547, Book 5.
116. Lincoln County Clerk, Soldiers Discharge Book, Page 129, Book 3, Lists date of birth.
117. *1920 Census Lincoln County*, Fiche # 144157, 5B-Ln 31, Lists husband and children and their respective ages.
118. *Lincoln County Clerk, Book of Marriages*, Page 76, Book 3, Lists birth date and marriage date for bride and groom.
119. *LDS Historical Library, Alamogordo*, Page 160, Fiche # 756.
120. *LDS Historical Library, Alamogordo*, Page 252, Fiche # 754.
121. *1900 Census Lincoln County*, Page 2B, San Patricio.
122. *LDS Historical Library, Alamogordo*, Page 26, Fiche # 756.
123. *LDS Historical Library, Alamogordo*, Page 11, Fiche # 0017008.
124. *LDS Historical Library, Alamogordo*, Page 63, Fiche # 756.
125. *Lincoln County Clerk, Book of Marriages*, Page 190, Book 4, Lists birth dates and marriage date for the bride and groom.
126. 1930 Census Lincoln County, Both his birth and death records.
127. *1870 Census of Ft. Stanton*, Page 4, Fiche # 0552393.
128. *LDS Historical Library, Alamogordo*, Page 130, Fiche # 756.
129. *LDS Historical Library, Alamogordo*, Page 17, Fiche # 756.
130. *LDS Historical Library, Alamogordo*, Page 60, Fiche # 756.
131. *LDS Historical Library, Alamogordo*, Page 17, Fiche # 754.
132. *LDS Historical Library, Alamogordo*, Page 170, Fiche # 754.
133. *Lincoln County Clerk, Book of Marriages*, Page 277, Book A, Lists birth date and marriage date for bride and groom.
134. 1930 Census Lincoln County, Birth and death records.
135. *1920 Census Lincoln County*, Fiche # 1821077.
136. *LDS Historical Library, Alamogordo*, Page 258, Fiche # 754.
137. *LDS Historical Library, Alamogordo*, Page 28, Fiche # 754.
138. *LDS Historical Library, Alamogordo*, Page 14, Fiche # 754.
139. 1930 Census Lincoln County.
140. *LDS Historical Library, Alamogordo*, Page 127, Fiche # 756.
141. *LDS Historical Library, Alamogordo*, Page 92, Fiche # 754.
142. 1930 Census Lincoln County.
143. *LDS Historical Library, Alamogordo*, Page 112, Fiche # 756.
144. *LDS Historical Library, Alamogordo*, Page 116, Fiche # 754.
145. *LDS Historical Library, Alamogordo*, Page 158, Fiche # 756.
146. *LDS Historical Library, Alamogordo*, Page 13, Fiche 754.
147. 1930 Census Lincoln County.
148. *LDS Historical Library, Alamogordo*, Page 138, Fiche 756.
149. *1920 Census Lincoln County*, Fiche # 21077-1A.
150. *LDS Historical Library, Alamogordo*, Page 8, Fiche # 756.
151. *LDS Historical Library, Alamogordo*, Page 138, Fiche # 756.
152. *1920 Census Lincoln County*, Fiche # 1821077-1A.
153. 1930 Census Lincoln County, Birth and death records.
154. *LDS Historical Library, Alamogordo*, Page 190, Fiche # 754, Lists birth and marriage dates.
155. *LDS Historical Library, Alamogordo*, Page 160, Fiche # 754.
156. 1930 Census Lincoln County.
157. *Lincoln County Clerk, Book of Marriages*.

158. *1920 Census Lincoln County*, Page 3B, Fiche # 1821077, Lists his wife, their children and their ages.
159. *LDS Historical Library, Alamogordo*, Page 27, Fiche # 754.
160. *LDS Historical Library, Alamogordo*, Page 152, Fiche # 756.
161. *LDS Historical Library, Alamogordo*, Page 144, Fiche # 754.
162. *1920 Census Lincoln County*, Fiche # 1821077-2A, Lists his wife, children and their ages.
163. *LDS Historical Library, Alamogordo*, Page 8, Fiche # 754.
164. *LDS Historical Library, Alamogordo*, Page 156, Fiche # 756.
165. *LDS Historical Library, Alamogordo*, Page 30, Fiche # 756.
166. *LDS Historical Library, Alamogordo*, Page 7, Fiche # 754.
167. *LDS Historical Library, Alamogordo*, Page 142, Fiche # 756.
168. *LDS Historical Library, Alamogordo*, Fiche # 0017008-1.
169. *LDS Historical Library, Alamogordo*, Page 161, Fiche # 754.
170. 1920 Census for Lincoln County, Page 1B, San patricio.
171. *LDS Historical Library, Alamogordo*, Page 34, Fiche # 754.
172. *LDS Historical Library, Alamogordo*, Page 142, Fiche # 756.
173. *Lincoln County Clerk, Book of Marriages*, Page 536, Book 5, Lists birth dates and marriage date for the bride and groom.
174. *Lincoln County Clerk, Book of Marriages*, Page 471, Book 4, Lists birth dates and marriage date for the bride and groom.
175. 1930 Census Lincoln County, Page 2A, Lists all of the children born before 1930.
176. 1930 Census Lincoln County.
177. *Lincoln County Clerk, Book of Marriages*, Page 179, Book 4, Lists birth dates and marriage date for the bride and groom.
178. *LDS Historical Library, Alamogordo*, Page 42, Fiche 754.
179. Family Member.
180. *1920 Census Lincoln County*, Fiche # 1821077.
181. *LDS Historical Library, Alamogordo*, Page 40, Fiche # 754.
182. *LDS Historical Library, Alamogordo*, Page 191, Fiche # 756.
183. 1930 Census Lincoln County, Birth and death records.
184. Ballard Funeral Home, Birth and death.
185. 1930 Census Lincoln County, Birth and death records.
186. Lincoln County Clerk, Soldiers Discharge Book, Page 158, Book 3, Lists date of birth.
187. *LDS Historical Library, Alamogordo*, Page 175, Fiche # 754.
188. *LDS Historical Library, Alamogordo*, Page 199, Fiche # 756.
189. *LDS Historical Library, Alamogordo*, Page 215, Fiche # 754.
190. *Lincoln County Clerk, Book of Marriages*, Page 442, Book 3.
191. *Lincoln County Clerk, Book of Marriages*, Page 516, Book 4, Lists birth date and marriage date for bride and groom.
192. *LDS Historical Library, Alamogordo*, Page 26, Fiche # 754.
193. *Lincoln County Clerk, Book of Marriages*, Page 352, Book 3, List birthdate and marriage date for the bride and groom.
194. 1930 Census Lincoln County, Page 2B, Hondo, Lists all children born before 1930.
195. 1930 Census Lincoln County.
196. *LDS Historical Library, Alamogordo*, Reel # 756, Page 16.
197. *Lincoln County Clerk, Book of Marriages*, Page 615, Lists birthdate and marriage date for both the bride and groom.
198. *LDS Historical Library, Alamogordo*, Fiche # 0017009-1.
199. *LDS Historical Library, Alamogordo*, Page 167, Fiche # 756.
200. *LDS Historical Library, Alamogordo*, Page 156, Fiche # 754.
201. *Lincoln County Clerk, Book of Marriages*, Page 162, Book 1 Applications, Lists birth dates for the bride and groom.
202. *LDS Historical Library, Alamogordo*, Page 156, Fiche # 754.
203. *Lincoln County Clerk, Book of Marriages*, Page 100, Book 5, Lists birthdate and marriage date for the bride and groom.
204. 1930 Census Lincoln County.
205. Lincoln County Clerk, Soldiers Discharge Book, Page 109, Book 3, Lists date of birth.
206. *LDS Historical Library, Alamogordo*, Page 3, Fiche # 754.
207. *Lincoln County Clerk, Book of Marriages*, Page 41, Book 5.
208. Lincoln County Clerk, Soldiers Discharge Book, Page 166, Book 1, Lists date of birth.
209. *1920 Census Lincoln County*, 1821077 Sheet 4A, Line 1, Lists family members.
210. *LDS Historical Library, Alamogordo*, Page 131, Fiche # 754.
211. Hondo Cemetary.
212. *LDS Historical Library, Alamogordo*, Page 192, Fiche # 756.
213. *Lincoln County Clerk, Book of Marriages*, Page 346, Book 3, Lists birthdate and marriage date for the bride and groom.
214. *Lincoln County Clerk, Book of Marriages*, Page 133, Lists birthdate and marriage date for the bride and groom.
215. *LDS Historical Library, Alamogordo*, Page 14, Fiche # 756.
216. *Lincoln County Clerk, Book of Marriages*, Page 615, Lists birthdate and marriage date for both the bride and groom.
217. 1930 Census Lincoln County, Page 3A, Lists all children as of 1930.
218. *Lincoln County Clerk, Book of Marriages*, Page 489, Book 4, Lists birth dates and marriage date for the bride and groom.
219. *Lincoln County Clerk, Book of Marriages*, Book 5, Lists birth dates and marriage date for the bride and groom.

220. *LDS Historical Library, Alamogordo*, Page 48, Fiche # 0017008.
221. 1930 Census Lincoln County, Page 3B, Lincoln, Lists all children born before 1930.
222. 1930 Census Lincoln County, Birth and death records.
223. Martin Funeral Home, El Paso, Téxas.
224. *Lincoln County Clerk, Book of Marriages*, Page 227, Book 4, Lists birth dates and marriage date for the bride and groom.
225. *Lincoln County Clerk, Book of Marriages*, Page 43, Book 4, Lists birth date and marriage dates for the bride and groom.
226. *LDS Historical Library, Alamogordo*, Page 12, Fiche # 0017009.
227. *LDS Historical Library, Alamogordo*, Page 39, Fiche # 756.
228. Lincoln County Clerk, Soldiers Discharge Book, Page 226, Book 3.
229. 1930 Census Lincoln County.
230. *Lincoln County Clerk, Book of Marriages*, Page 229, Book 4, Lists birth dates and marriage date for the bride and groom.
231. *LDS Historical Library, Alamogordo*, Fiche # 754.
232. *LDS Historical Library, Alamogordo*, Page 86, Fiche # 754, Birth and marriage dates.
233. *LDS Historical Library, Alamogordo*, Page 130, Fiche # 754.
234. 1930 Census Lincoln County.
235. *LDS Historical Library, Alamogordo*, Page 14, Fiche # 756.
236. *LDS Historical Library, Alamogordo*, Page 172, Fiche # 754.
237. *LDS Historical Library, Alamogordo*, Page 224, Fiche # 754.
238. *LDS Historical Library, Alamogordo*, Page 3, Fiche # 756.
239. *LDS Historical Library, Alamogordo*, Page 167, Fiche # 754.
240. *Lincoln County Clerk, Book of Marriages*, Page 22, Book 1.
241. 1930 Census Lincoln County.
242. *Lincoln County Clerk, Book of Marriages*, Page 153, Book 5, Lists birth date and marriage date for bride and groom.
243. 1930 Census Lincoln County, 3A, Lists all children as of 1930.
244. *Lincoln County Clerk, Book of Marriages*, Page 74, Book 5, Lists birth date and marriage date for bride and groom.
245. *Lincoln County Clerk, Book of Marriages*, Page 133, Lists birthdate and marriage date for the bride and groom.
246. 1930 Census Lincoln County, Birth and death records.
247. *1920 Census Lincoln County*, Fiche # 1821077-2B.
248. *LDS Historical Library, Alamogordo*, Page 11, Fiche # 754.
249. *LDS Historical Library, Alamogordo*, Page 150, 756.
250. *LDS Historical Library, Alamogordo*, Page 119, Fiche # 754.
251. *LDS Historical Library, Alamogordo*, Page 39, Fiche # 756.
252. Lincoln County Clerk, Soldiers Discharge Book, Page 226, Book 3.
253. *Lincoln County Clerk, Book of Marriages*, Page 153, Book 5, Lists birth date and marriage date for the bride and groom.
254. *Lincoln County Clerk, Book of Marriages*, Book 5, Lists birth dates and marriage date for the bride and groom.

Descendants of Fernando de Herrera

Generation No. 1

1. JOSÉ JOAQUÍN[1] DE HERRERA was born Abt. 1773 in Santa Cruz de la Cañada, El Reyno de Nuevo Méjico. He married MARÍA JOSEFA BUSTOS October 02, 1791 in Santa Cruz de la Cañada, El Reyno de Nuevo Méjico.

Children of JOSÉ DE HERRERA and MARÍA BUSTOS are:

	i.	MARÍA DE LA ASCENCION[2] HERRERA, b. Santa Cruz de la Cañada, El Reyno de Nuevo Méjico.
	ii.	TERESA DE JESUS HERRERA, b. October 28, 1797, Santa Cruz de la Cañada, Reyno de Nuevo Méjico.
2.	iii.	PEDRO ALCANTAR DE HERRERA, b. October 18, 1800, Santa Cruz de la Cañada, El Reyno de Nuevo Méjico.
	iv.	JUAN JOSÉ HERRERA, b. March 16, 1804, Santa Cruz de la Cañada, Nuevo México.

> More About JUAN JOSÉ HERRERA:
> Fact 1: March 18, 1804, Baptized in Santa Cruz de la Cañada.

     v.   MARÍA NICOLASA HERRERA, b. December 22, 1807, Santa Cruz de la Cañada, Nuevo México.

> More About MARÍA NICOLASA HERRERA:
> Fact 1: December 23, 1807, Baptized in Santa Cruz de la Cañada.

     vi.   JUAN ANTONIO HERRERA, b. April 13, 1811; m. MARÍA DEL REFUGIO VIGIL.

> More About MARÍA DEL REFUGIO VIGIL:
> Fact 1: August 20, 1816, Baptized in Taos, El Reyno de Nuevo Méjico

     vii.   MARÍA JOSEFA MANUELA HERRERA, b. June 1816, Santa Cruz de la Cañada, El Reyno de Nuevo Méjico.

> More About MARÍA JOSEFA MANUELA HERRERA:
> Fact 1: June 14, 1816, Baptized in Santa Cruz de la Cañada.

Generation No. 2

2. PEDRO ALCANTAR[2] DE HERRERA *(JOSÉ JOAQUÍN[1])[1]* was born October 18, 1800 in Santa Cruz de la Cañada, El Reyno de Nuevo Méjico. He married (1) MARÍA MANUELA CASIAS[2]. He married (2) MARÍA MANUELA ESQUIBEL May 11, 1825. He married (3) MARÍA CELEDONIA ARCHULETA May 27, 1827 in Santa Cruz de la Cañada, Nuevo México, La República de México, daughter of LUÍS ARCHULETA and FRANCISCA MONTOYA.

Notes for PEDRO ALCANTAR DE HERRERA:
1860 Census: Born in 1810

More About PEDRO ALCANTAR DE HERRERA:
Fact 1: October 19, 1800, Baptized in Santa Cruz de la Cañada.

More About MARÍA MANUELA ESQUIBEL:
Fact 1: June 05, 1807, Baptized in Santa Cruz de la Cañada.

Child of PEDRO DE HERRERA and MARÍA CASIAS is:

     i.   MARÍA ESTEFANA[3] HERRERA, b. February 05, 1839, San Antonio de Servilleta, Nuevo Mexico.

Child of PEDRO DE HERRERA and MARÍA ESQUIBEL is:

     ii.   JUAN MANUEL[3] HERRERA, b. January 08, 1826, Santa Cruz de la Cañada, El Reyno de Nuevo Méjico.

> More About JUAN MANUEL HERRERA:
> Fact 1: January 10, 1826, Baptized in Santa Cruz de la Cañada.

Children of PEDRO DE HERRERA and MARÍA ARCHULETA are:

3.   iii.   FERNANDO³ HERRERA, b. July 02, 1836, Santa Cruz de la Cañada, Nuevo México, La República de México; d. December 14, 1915, Alamogordo, New México.
      iv.   MARÍA ANTONIA NICOLASA HERRERA, b. May 24, 1840, San Francisco del Rancho (Ranchos de Taos), Nuevo México, República de México.
      v.   JOSÉ HERRERA, b. February 21, 1842, Santa Cruz de la Cañada, Nuevo México, República de México.

Generation No. 3

3. FERNANDO³ HERRERA *(PEDRO ALCANTAR² DE HERRERA, JOSÉ JOAQUÍN¹)* was born July 02, 1836 in Santa Cruz de la Cañada, Nuevo México, La República de México, and died December 14, 1915 in Alamogordo, New México. He married (1) MARÍA JULIANA MARTÍNEZ September 24, 1856 in Santa Cruz de la Cañada, Territory of New México, daughter of JOSÉ MARTÍNEZ and MARÍA GÓMEZ. He married (2) MARTA RODRÍGUEZ Aft. 1867.

Notes for FERNANDO HERRERA:
July 17, 1836: Baptized in Santa Cruz de la Cañada, La República de México. Padrinos: Celedon Herrera y María de la Cruz Lopez.
Before 1867: Fernando migrated from Santa Cruz de la Cañada to the Rio Ruidoso valley. He settled at the southern end of the valley, and called it San Juanito. This settlement later became known as Palo Verde, then Green Tree, and most recently Ruidoso Downs.
1870 Census: Listed as living in Río Colorado
Fernando Herrera is buried in an unmarked gravesite in Alamogordo, New México.

Notes for MARÍA JULIANA MARTÍNEZ:
February 18, 1832: Baptized In Santa Cruz de la Cañada, República de México.

Children of FERNANDO HERRERA and MARÍA MARTÍNEZ are:
4.   i.   MARÍA ALTAGRACIA⁴ HERRERA, b. April 15, 1857, Santa Cruz de la Cañada, Territory of New México; d. June 26, 1893, San Juanito (Ruidoso), Territory of New México.
5.   ii.   JOSÉ ANDRÉS HERRERA, b. November 27, 1858, Santa Cruz de la Cañada, New México; d. 1911, Carrizozo, New México.
6.   iii. MARÍA ANTONIA MIGUELA HERRERA, b. June 13, 1860, Santa Cruz de la Cañada, Territory of New México; d. 1912, Acton, Texas.
      iv.   MARÍA ANTONIA HERRERA, b. December 08, 1862, Santa Cruz de la Cañada, Territory of New México; d. December 11, 1862, Santa Cruz de la Cañada, Territory of New México.

        Notes for MARÍA ANTONIA HERRERA:
        December 11, 1862: Baptized in Santa Cruz de la Cañada, Territory of New México.

      v.   MARÍA NICOLÁSA (NICOLASITA) HERRERA, b. December 08, 1862, Santa Cruz de la Cañada, New México; m. ANTONIO VALENZUELA, October 17, 1902.
7.   vi.   MARÍA MARTA (MARTITA) HERRERA, b. April 24, 1865, Santa Cruz de la Cañada, New México.
8.   vii. MANUELITA HERRERA, b. April 20, 1866, Santa Cruz de la Cañada, Territory of New México; d. February 13, 1939, San Patricio, New México.
      viii. MACEDONIO HERRERA, b. Abt. 1869, San Juanito, Territory of New México.

        Notes for MACEDONIO HERRERA:
        Was killed by a lightning strike.

      ix.   SELEDONIA HERRERA, b. Abt. June 1870, San Juanito, Territory of New México; d. San Juanito, Territory of New México.

        Notes for SELEDONIA HERRERA:
        Was killed by a lightning strike.

      x.   AUGUSTÍN HERRERA, b. April 04, 1872, San Juanito, Territory of New México.
9.   xi.   TEODORO HERRERA, b. April 1873, San Juanito, Territory of New México.

Generation No. 4

4. MARÍA ALTAGRACIA⁴ HERRERA *(FERNANDO³, PEDRO ALCANTAR² DE HERRERA, JOSÉ JOAQUÍN¹)* was born April 15, 1857 in Santa Cruz de la Cañada, Territory of New México, and died June 26, 1893 in San Juanito

(Ruidoso), Territory of New México. She married (1) WILLIAM JAMES GILL November 15, 1880 in Nogal, Territory of New México. She married (2) ANTONIO VALENZUELA July 27, 1892, son of JESÚS VALENZUELA and RITA MUÑOZ.

Notes for MARÍA ALTAGRACIA HERRERA:
Buried: Herrera Family cemetery in San Juanito.

Notes for WILLIAM JAMES GILL:
He was a soldier stationed out of Fort Stanton.

Children of MARÍA HERRERA and WILLIAM GILL are:
10. i.   JENNIE (JOSEFA)[5] GILL, b. March 19, 1881, Nogal, Territory of New México; d. Bef. February 1917.
     ii. MACEDONIO GILL, b. February 09, 1882, Nogal, Territory of New México; d. July 24, 1938.
11. iii. ELISIA (ALICIA) (ALICE) GILL, b. 1883, Nogal, Territory of New México.
     iv. WILLIAM (JULIAN) HERRERA GILL[3], b. September 10, 1884, Nogal, Territory of New México; m. CONFERINA ORISITACIÓN SÁNCHEZ, January 13, 1916, Glencoe, New Mexico.

         More About WILLIAM (JULIAN) HERRERA GILL:
         Fact 1: September 24, 1884, Baptized.

         Notes for CONFERINA ORISITACIÓN SÁNCHEZ:
         February 04, 1892: Baptized. Padrinos: Julian Silva and Jesusita Sánchez.

         More About CONFERINA ORISITACIÓN SÁNCHEZ:
         Fact 1: Baptized at 2 months old.

         Marriage Notes for WILLIAM GILL and CONFERINA SÁNCHEZ:
         Married in La Capilla de San Ysidro. Padrinos: Manuel Sánchez and Estela Gill Sánchez.

12. v.   NEWMAN GILL, b. November 30, 1885, Nogal, Territory of New México; d. Artesia, New México.
13. vi. STELLA (ESTELA) GILL, b. August 12, 1887, Nogal, Territory of New México; d. March 29, 1938.

Children of MARÍA HERRERA and ANTONIO VALENZUELA are:
     vii. ROSALIA[5] VALENZUELA, b. June 23, 1891.

         More About ROSALIA VALENZUELA:
         Fact 1: July 15, 1891, Baptized.

     viii. BENANCIO VALENZUELA, b. March 1893; m. RUMALTILDA FLORES, August 01, 1920.

         Notes for BENANCIO VALENZUELA:
         He was raised by his father and his step mother Nicolasa Herrera.

         More About BENANCIO VALENZUELA:
         Fact 1: June 16, 1893, Baptized.

5. JOSÉ ANDRÉS[4] HERRERA *(FERNANDO[3], PEDRO ALCANTAR[2] DE HERRERA, JOSÉ JOAQUÍN[1])* was born November 27, 1858 in Santa Cruz de la Cañada, New México, and died 1911 in Carrizozo, New México. He married ROSARIO RODRÍGUEZ, daughter of JESÚS RODRÍGUEZ and FRANCISCA SÁNCHEZ.

Notes for JOSÉ ANDRÉS HERRERA:
November 28, 1858: Baptized in Santa Cruz de la Cañada.
Moved to Carrizozo, New México.

Children of JOSÉ HERRERA and ROSARIO RODRÍGUEZ are:
     i.   FERNANDO ANTONIO[5] HERRERA, b. May 13, 1885, San Juanito (Ruidoso), New México; m. PAULA JUANA, January 16, 1916.

         Notes for PAULA JUANA:
         Juana was the Spanish equivalent for Warner.

    ii.   LINO HERRERA, b. September 1887, San Juanito (Ruidoso), Territory of New México; d. September 29, 1944, Carrizozo, New México.

           More About LINO HERRERA:
           Fact 1: January 21, 1919, Discharged WW II veteran.

    iii.   TEODORA HERRERA, b. November 09, 1889, San Juanito (Ruidoso), Territory of New México; m. JOSÉ SAÍZ, October 18, 1914, Carrizozo, New México*.*

           Marriage Notes for TEODORA HERRERA and JOSÉ SAÍZ:
           Padrinos: Ben Sánchez and Petra Herrera.

    iv.   MARCELO HERRERA[5], b. January 16, 1890, San Juanito (Ruidoso), Territory of New México; m. CONFERINA ORISITACIÓN SÁNCHEZ, July 10, 1917[6].

           Notes for CONFERINA ORISITACIÓN SÁNCHEZ:
           February 04, 1892: Baptized. Padrinos: Julian Silva and Jesusita Sánchez.

           More About CONFERINA ORISITACIÓN SÁNCHEZ:
           Fact 1: Baptized at 2 months old.

    v.   JUAN HERRERA, b. March 08, 1894, San Juanito (Ruidoso), Territory of New México; m. DELFINIA MEDINA, February 02, 1935.

           Notes for JUAN HERRERA:
           Mid 1930s: Juan was the constable of in Carrizozo, New México.

    vi.   MARÍA PERFECTA HERRERA, b. April 28, 1896, San Juanito (Ruidoso), Territory of New México.

           More About MARÍA PERFECTA HERRERA:
           Fact 1: May have died young.

    vii. PETRA HERRERA, b. May 13, 1898, San Juanito (Ruidoso), Territory of New México; m. BENJAMIN SÁNCHEZ[7], February 20, 1914, Carrizozo, New México.

           Marriage Notes for PETRA HERRERA and BENJAMIN SÁNCHEZ:
           Married by: Father Girma.
           Padrinos: Andrés Herrera and Rosa Lueras
           Both Benjamin and Petra were living in Carrizozo at the time of their marriage.

    viii. DONACIANO HERRERA, b. July 17, 1905, Glencoe, Territory of New México; m. FEDELINA JARAMILLO, November 11, 1950.
    ix.   ANDRÉS RODRIQUEZ HERRERA, b. August 07, 1909, Glencoe, Territory of New México; m. SARAFINA APODACA, April 21, 1939.
    x.   MARCELINO HERRERA, b. June 05, 1901; d. May 07, 1980, Alamogordo, New México.

           Notes for MARCELINO HERRERA:
           Buried: Carrizozo, New México.

6. MARÍA ANTONIA MIGUELA[4] HERRERA *(FERNANDO[3], PEDRO ALCANTAR[2] DE HERRERA, JOSÉ JOAQUÍN[1])* was born June 13, 1860 in Santa Cruz de la Cañada, Territory of New México, and died 1912 in Acton, Texas. She married JOSIAH G. (DOC) SCURLOCK October 19, 1876 in Lincoln, Territory of New México.

Notes for MARÍA ANTONIA MIGUELA HERRERA:
Buried: Initially in Acton, Téxas. Her remains were then relocated next to her husband in Eastland, Téxas.
Another birth date: May 07, 1860.

Notes for JOSIAH G. (DOC) SCURLOCK:
1879: Migrated to Ft Sumner, New México.
1879: In the winter, the family migrated to Tascosa, Téxas.

Marriage Notes for MARÍA HERRERA and JOSIAH SCURLOCK:
Married in Iglesia de San Juan.
Married by: Padre Sambrano.

Children of MARÍA HERRERA and JOSIAH SCURLOCK are:
  i.   MARÍA ELENA HERRERA[5] SCURLOCK, b. August 19, 1877, San Juanito (Ruidoso), New México; d. August 17, 1879, San Juanito (Ruidoso), New México.
  ii.   VIOLA INEZ HERRERA SCURLOCK, b. August 13, 1878, San Juanito (Ruidoso), New México.
  iii. JOSIAH GORDEN HERRERA SCURLOCK, b. October 11, 1879, San Miguel County, New México.
  iv.   JOHN JOSHUA HERRERA SCURLOCK, b. May 21, 1881, Oldham County, Téxas.
  v.   AMY ANTONIA HERRERA SCURLOCK, b. July 14, 1884, Wilbarger County, Téxas.
  vi.   MARTHA ETHLINDA HERRERA SCURLOCK, b. May 10, 1886, Wilbarger County, Téxas.
  vii. PRESLEY FERNANDO HERRERA SCURLOCK, b. August 27, 1888, Wilbarger County, Téxas.
  viii. DELORES HERRERA SCURLOCK, b. March 10, 1891, Wilbarger County, Téxas.
  ix.   WILLIAM ANDREW HERRERA SCURLOCK, b. April 14, 1893, Wilbarger County, Téxas.
  x.   JOSEPHINE GLADYS HERRERA SCURLOCK, b. August 02, 1895, Johnson County, Téxas.

7. MARÍA MARTA (MARTITA)[4] HERRERA *(FERNANDO[3], PEDRO ALCANTAR[2] DE HERRERA, JOSÉ JOAQUÍN[1])* was born April 24, 1865 in Santa Cruz de la Cañada, New México. She married ADRIAN MUÑOZ[8] November 12, 1880, son of CIGISFREDO MUÑOZ and JOSEFITA DE MUÑOZ.

Children of MARÍA HERRERA and ADRIAN MUÑOZ are:
  i.   ANTONIA[5] APODACA, m. CIPRIANO MILLIGAN.

        Notes for ANTONIA APODACA:
        1900 Census lists her as a boarder.

  ii.   JULIANA (JULIANITA) MUÑOZ, b. April 1882; m. ANDRÉS GONZÁLES, March 30, 1903, San Patricio, Territory of New México.

        More About JULIANA (JULIANITA) MUÑOZ:
        Fact 1: June 07, 1882, Baptized.

        Marriage Notes for JULIANA MUÑOZ and ANDRÉS GONZÁLES:
        Married by: Justice of the Peace, Teofilo Salas.

  iii. EPIFANIA MUÑOZ, b. April 07, 1884; m. SISTO RICO.

        More About EPIFANIA MUÑOZ:
        Fact 1: June 20, 1884, Baptized.

  iv.   ESTANISLAUS MUÑOZ, b. November 15, 1885, San Juanito (Ruidoso), New México.
  v.   MARGARITA MUÑOZ, b. 1886; m. HIPOLITO (EPOLOLITO) FLORES, May 15, 1900.

        More About MARGARITA MUÑOZ:
        Fact 1: September 09, 1886, Baptized.

        More About HIPOLITO (EPOLOLITO) FLORES:
        Fact 1: August 13, 1884, Baptized.

  vi.   BEATRICE MUÑOZ, b. 1893; m. TRANQUELINO LAFAYETTE.
  vii. REFUGIA MUÑOZ, b. 1893.
  viii. GENOVEVA MUÑOZ, b. 1895; m. ARTURO ACUNA.
  ix.   JUANA (JUANITA) MUÑOZ, b. 1897.
  x.   JOSÉ MUÑOZ, b. November 22, 1897; m. CARMEN AUBEL, January 25, 1922.

        More About JOSÉ MUÑOZ:
        Fact 1: January 25, 1898, Baptized.

  xi.   ROSALIA MUÑOZ, b. April 29, 1899; m. TOMÁS RUIZ.

        More About ROSALIA MUÑOZ:

Fact 1: November 02, 1899, Baptized.

xii.   ANDRÉS APODACA, b. 1902; m. ROSALIA JARAMILLO.

Notes for ANDRÉS APODACA:
1900 Census lists him as a boarder.

More About ANDRÉS APODACA:
Fact 1: February 04, 1902, Baptized.

8. MANUELITA[4] HERRERA *(FERNANDO[3], PEDRO ALCANTAR[2] DE HERRERA, JOSÉ JOAQUÍN[1])* was born April 20, 1866 in Santa Cruz de la Cañada, Territory of New México, and died February 13, 1939 in San Patricio, New México. She married (1) JAMES SALSBERRY, son of JAMES SALSBERRY and HARRIET CLIFTON. She married (2) CHARLES BOWDRE. She married (4) MAXIMIANO CORONA February 25, 1884 in Tularosa, Territory of New Mexico, son of DIONISIO CORONA and SERAFINA LUCERO.

Notes for MANUELITA HERRERA:
Was too young to initially make the move from Santa Cruz to San Juanito.
Lived with Juanita Bojorque in Santa Cruz, moved to San Juanito with Juanita.

More About JAMES SALSBERRY:
Fact 1: 1882, Migrated to New Mexico

Marriage Notes for MANUELITA HERRERA and MAXIMIANO CORONA:
Married at Iglesia San Francisco de Paula in Tularosa, Territory of New México.

Children of MANUELITA HERRERA and JAMES SALSBERRY are:
14.   i.   AUGUSTÍN[5] SALSBERRY, b. October 25, 1895, San Juanito (Ruidoso), Territory of New México.
15.   ii.   TOMASITA SALSBERRY, b. December 29, 1897, San Juanito (Ruidoso), New México; d. Artesia, New Mexico.
         iii.   MARTINA SALSBERRY, b. January 30, 1900, San Juanito (Ruidoso), New México; d. December 07, 1917, Glencoe, New México; m. ANTONIO SÁNCHEZ, October 30, 1915, Lincoln, Territory of New México[9].

                 Notes for MARTINA SALSBERRY:
                 She died 8 days after giving birth to a child. Her child also died during birth.
                 Buried: San Ysidro church cemetary.

                 Marriage Notes for MARTINA SALSBERRY and ANTONIO SÁNCHEZ:
                 Married in La Capilla de San Ysidro. James Salsberry, Manuelita Herrera de Salsberry, Felipe Sánchez and Candelaria Padilla de Sánchez gave consent to the marriage.

16.   iv.   DOROTEA SALSBERRY, b. February 05, 1902, San Juanito (Ruidoso), New México; d. Artesia, New Mexico.
17.   v.   FERNANDO (FRED) SALSBERRY, b. April 13, 1904, San Juanito (Ruidoso), Territory of New México; d. September 11, 1937, Hondo, New Mexico.
18.   vi.   SANTIAGO (JAMES) SALSBERRY, b. June 26, 1906, San Juanito (Ruidoso), Territory of New México; d. Barstow, California.
19.   vii.   FLORINDA SALSBERRY, b. March 15, 1910, Palo Verde (Ruidoso), New México; d. March 27, 1978, San Patricio, New México.
20.   viii.   ENRÍQUES (HENRY) SALSBERRY, b. April 15, 1911, Palo Verde (Ruidoso), Territory of New México; d. Artesia, New México.

Child of MANUELITA HERRERA is:
21.   ix.   JOSÉ[5] PORTIO, b. December 03, 1893; d. September 18, 1959, San Patricio New Mexico.

Children of MANUELITA HERRERA and MAXIMIANO CORONA are:
22.   x.   MANUEL[5] CORONA, b. January 01, 1885, San Juanito (Ruidoso), Territory of New México; d. July 17, 1966, San Patricio, New México.
         xi.   DOROTEA CORONA, b. February 06, 1887, Ruidoso, New México; d. Ruidoso, New México.

                 Notes for DOROTEA CORONA:
                 Born at Gregorio's farm in San Juanito.
                 Died while he was young.

23.   xii.   HELENA (ELENA) CORONA, b. February 11, 1889, San Juanito (Ruidoso), Territory of New México; d. March 14, 1928, San Patricio, New México.

9. TEODORO[4] HERRERA *(FERNANDO[3], PEDRO ALCANTAR[2] DE HERRERA, JOSÉ JOAQUÍN[1])* was born April 1873 in San Juanito, Territory of New México. He married TOMASITA (TOMASA) MONTOYA September 16, 1896, daughter of FELIPÉ MONTOYA and MARCIALA CHÁVEZ.

Notes for TEODORO HERRERA:
After both parents died, the children lived with their Tia Manuela.
Eldest brother came back and moved his siblings to El Paso, Texas.

Children of TEODORO HERRERA and TOMASITA MONTOYA are:
        i.   MANUEL[5] HERRERA, b. June 19, 1899.

                Notes for MANUEL HERRERA:
                He may have died young.

        ii.   FELIPÉ HERRERA, b. 1907.
        iii.   JULIAN HERRERA, b. 1910.

                Notes for JULIAN HERRERA:
                Julian had migrated to El Paso, Téxas. After his parents died, he came back to San Juanito and took his younger siblings back to El Paso. Carmen, the youngest sister remained with her Aunt Manuelita.

        iv.   FERNANDO MONTOYA HERRERA, b. May 18, 1914, San Patricio, New México.

                Notes for FERNANDO MONTOYA HERRERA:
                July 05, 1914: Baptized in San Patricio. Padrinos: Marcial Sambrano and Refugia Padilla.

        v.   GREGORIO HERRERA, b. 1917.

                Notes for GREGORIO HERRERA:
                Killed in action during WW II.

        vi.   CARMEN HERRERA, b. May 29, 1920, San Patricio, New México.

Generation No. 5

10. JENNIE (JOSEFA)[5] GILL *(MARÍA ALTAGRACIA[4] HERRERA, FERNANDO[3], PEDRO ALCANTAR[2] DE HERRERA, JOSÉ JOAQUÍN[1])* was born March 19, 1881 in Nogal, Territory of New México, and died Bef. February 1917. She married SALOMON SÁNCHEZ December 06, 1900[10], son of JOSÉ SÁNCHEZ and TELESFORA MIRABAL.

More About SALOMON SÁNCHEZ:
Fact 1: November 17, 1878, Baptized in Tularosa, Territory of New México

Marriage Notes for JENNIE GILL and SALOMON SÁNCHEZ:
Married by: Father Girand.
Padrinos: Abel Mirabal and Jesúsita Sánchez.

Children of JENNIE GILL and SALOMON SÁNCHEZ are:
24.   i.   VIRGINIA[6] SÁNCHEZ, b. April 13, 1902, Ruidoso, Territory of New México; d. Ruidoso, New México.
25.   ii.   TELESFORA SÁNCHEZ, b. November 19, 1903, Glencoe, Territory of New México.
        iii.   ENRÍQUES GILL SÁNCHEZ, b. September 25, 1904, Glencoe, New México[11]; m. CAROLINA GAMBOA[12].

                Notes for ENRÍQUES GILL SÁNCHEZ:
                He was also known as Henry Gill.

26.	iv.	SALOMON GILL SÁNCHEZ, b. March 17, 1905, Glencoe, Territory of New México.
	v.	EDUVIJEN SÁNCHEZ, b. 1910; m. JOSÉ ANTONIO SILVA, April 09, 1928[13].
27.	vi.	ANATALIA (NATALIA) SÁNCHEZ, b. 1912.
	vii.	CONSOLACION (CONSUELO) SÁNCHEZ, b. September 10, 1914; d. April 28, 1996, Tularosa, New México; m. BENITO SILVA, February 13, 1932[14].

11. ELISIA (ALICIA) (ALICE)[5] GILL *(MARÍA ALTAGRACIA[4] HERRERA, FERNANDO[3], PEDRO ALCANTAR[2] DE HERRERA, JOSÉ JOAQUÍN[1])* was born 1883 in Nogal, Territory of New México. She married PETER G. HALE, son of LOWEL HALE and EMMA HALE.

Children of ELISIA GILL and PETER HALE are:
	i.	WILLIE[6] HALE, b. 1904.
	ii.	HENRY HALE, b. 1906.
	iii.	MARY HALE, b. 1908.
	iv.	SUSIE HALE, b. 1912.
	v.	PAULIE HALE, b. 1914.
	vi.	MAGGIE HALE, b. 1916.
	vii.	JAMES HALE, b. 1918.
	viii.	BESSIE HALE, b. 1919.

12. NEWMAN[5] GILL *(MARÍA ALTAGRACIA[4] HERRERA, FERNANDO[3], PEDRO ALCANTAR[2] DE HERRERA, JOSÉ JOAQUÍN[1])*[15] was born November 30, 1885 in Nogal, Territory of New México[16], and died in Artesia, New México. He married RITA SÁNCHEZ July 03, 1915[17], daughter of JUAN SÁNCHEZ and MARÍA SÁNCHEZ.

Children of NEWMAN GILL and RITA SÁNCHEZ are:
	i.	OLIVIA[6] GILL, b. 1919; m. PORFIRIO VALENZUELA.
	ii.	ESTOLANO GILL, b. 1921.
	iii.	PRESILIANO GILL, b. 1923.
	iv.	PABLITA GILL, b. 1925; m. TORIVIO PADILLA.
	v.	RITA GILL, b. 1928.

13. STELLA (ESTELA)[5] GILL *(MARÍA ALTAGRACIA[4] HERRERA, FERNANDO[3], PEDRO ALCANTAR[2] DE HERRERA, JOSÉ JOAQUÍN[1])* was born August 12, 1887 in Nogal, Territory of New México[18], and died March 29, 1938. She married MANUEL SÁNCHEZ June 14, 1909[19], son of JOSÉ SÁNCHEZ and TELESFORA MIRABAL.

Notes for STELLA (ESTELA) GILL:
Buried: La Capilla de San Ysidro, Glencoe.

Child of STELLA GILL and MANUEL SÁNCHEZ is:
| | i. | AMANDA[6] SÁNCHEZ, m. LUÍS TORREZ, November 30, 1927[20]. |

Notes for LUÍS TORREZ:
After selling the farm, he and his wife migrated to Roswell, New México.
WW I Veteran.

More About LUÍS TORREZ:
Fact 1: August 26, 1918, Discharged, WW I veteran.

14. AUGUSTÍN[5] SALSBERRY *(MANUELITA[4] HERRERA, FERNANDO[3], PEDRO ALCANTAR[2] DE HERRERA, JOSÉ JOAQUÍN[1])* was born October 25, 1895 in San Juanito (Ruidoso), Territory of New México. He married (1) MARGARITA VIGIL August 13, 1917 in Ruidoso, New México, daughter of EDUARDO VIGIL and TOMASA ZAMORA. He married (2) AGAPITA PADILLA August 04, 1926 in Carrizozo, New México[21], daughter of JESÚS PADILLA and LUISA MONTOYA.

More About AUGUSTÍN SALSBERRY:
Fact 1: January 12, 1896, Baptized in Lincoln, Territory of New México.

Marriage Notes for AUGUSTÍN SALSBERRY and MARGARITA VIGIL:
Married by: Father Girma. Married at La Capilla de San Ysidro.
Padrinos: José Portio and Elena Corona.

Children of AUGUSTÍN SALSBERRY and AGAPITA PADILLA are:
  i.   ANEDA[6] SALSBERRY, b. Private; m. RAY GARCÍA.
  ii.   HELEN SALSBERRY, b. Private; m. JOE HORTADO.
  iii. RICHARD SALSBERRY, b. Private.
  iv.   LUISA SALSBERRY, b. 1927; m. VICENTE SÁNCHEZ.
  v.   AUGUSTÍN PADILLA SALSBERRY, b. 1929; d. Roseville, California; m. AVRORA CALDERON.
  vi.   EMMA SALSBERRY, b. 1930; m. ALFONSO CALDERON.

15. TOMASITA[5] SALSBERRY *(MANUELITA[4] HERRERA, FERNANDO[3], PEDRO ALCANTAR[2] DE HERRERA, JOSÉ JOAQUÍN[1])* was born December 29, 1897 in San Juanito (Ruidoso), New México, and died in Artesia, New Mexico. She married JACOBO SALAS January 12, 1920, son of TEOFILO SALAS and IGENIA GALLEGOS.

Notes for TOMASITA SALSBERRY:
Buried: San Patricio, NM.

More About TOMASITA SALSBERRY:
Fact 1: July 24, 1898, Baptized.

More About JACOBO SALAS:
Fact 1: May 01, 1899, Baptized.

Children of TOMASITA SALSBERRY and JACOBO SALAS are:
  i.   DOMINGO[6] SALAS, d. Artesia, New Mexico.
  ii.   ROSA SALAS, d. Artesia, New Mexico.
  iii. RUBÉN SALAS.
  iv.   WILLIE SALAS.
  v.   JOSEFA SALAS, d. Artesia, New Mexico.

16. DOROTEA[5] SALSBERRY *(MANUELITA[4] HERRERA, FERNANDO[3], PEDRO ALCANTAR[2] DE HERRERA, JOSÉ JOAQUÍN[1])* was born February 05, 1902 in San Juanito (Ruidoso), New México, and died in Artesia, New Mexico. She married RUBÉN ANDRES GONZÁLES February 22, 1918, son of PROSPERO GONZÁLES and TELESFORA MIRABAL.

More About DOROTEA SALSBERRY:
Fact 1: July 26, 1902, Baptized.[22]

More About RUBÉN ANDRES GONZÁLES:
Fact 1: January 16, 1900, Baptized.

Children of DOROTEA SALSBERRY and RUBÉN GONZÁLES are:
  i.   OLIVIA[6] GONZÁLES, m. JUAN RODRÍGUEZ.
  ii.   ADELINA GONZÁLES, m. LOLO RODRÍGUEZ.
  iii. ORALIA GONZÁLES, m. CRISTÓVAL PEREA.
  iv.   VIOLA GONZÁLES, b. Private; m. MANUEL REYES.
  v.   EMILIO GONZÁLES, b. Private; m. RACHEL ALANIS.
  vi.   RUFINA GONZÁLES, b. Private; m. JOSÉ RODRÍGUEZ.
  vii. FEDELINA GONZÁLES, b. Private; m. COSMÉ GÓMES.
  viii. RUBÉN GONZÁLES, b. Private; m. MANUELA PAS.
  ix.   REYNER GONZÁLES, b. Private; m. MARY PADILLA.
  x.   TELESFORA (TILLIE) GONZÁLES, m. UNKOWN -----.
  xi.   HELEN GONZÁLES, m. UNKNOWN -----.

17. FERNANDO (FRED)[5] SALSBERRY *(MANUELITA[4] HERRERA, FERNANDO[3], PEDRO ALCANTAR[2] DE HERRERA, JOSÉ JOAQUÍN[1])* was born April 13, 1904 in San Juanito (Ruidoso), Territory of New México, and died September 11, 1937 in Hondo, New Mexico. He married LORENSITA MONTOYA June 15, 1929 in Carrizozo, New Mexico, daughter of DOROTEO MONTOYA and ALBINA SILVA.

Notes for FERNANDO (FRED) SALSBERRY:
He died in an automobile accident in Hondo, New México.
Burried: San Patricio, New México.

Notes for LORENSITA MONTOYA:
Burial birthdate states she was born on August 09, 1914.

Children of FERNANDO SALSBERRY and LORENSITA MONTOYA are:
    i.   ANATALIA[6] SALSBERRY, b. Private; m. MANUEL SOSA.
    ii.   FERNANDO MONTOYA SALSBERRY, b. Private.
    iii. ELOY SALSBERRY, b. Private.

18. SANTIAGO (JAMES)[5] SALSBERRY *(MANUELITA[4] HERRERA, FERNANDO[3], PEDRO ALCANTAR[2] DE HERRERA, JOSÉ JOAQUÍN[1])[23]* was born June 26, 1906 in San Juanito (Ruidoso), Territory of New México, and died in Barstow, California. He married LUCIA ANAYA March 26, 1927, daughter of PEDRO ANAYA and SOFIA TORRES.

Children of SANTIAGO SALSBERRY and LUCIA ANAYA are:
    i.   BERTHA[6] SALSBERRY, b. Abt. 1929; m. JOE BARELA.
    ii.   JAMES ANAYA SALSBERRY, b. Abt. 1930; m. (1) ESPERANSA CARABAJAL; m. (2) GLORIA -----.
    iii. BETTY SALSBERRY, b. Private; m. PATROCINIO GARCÍA.
    iv. JOE SALSBERRY, b. Private; m. MARLYNE MARTÍNEZ.
    v.   LUCY SALSBERRY, b. Private; m. HENRY ANGELAN.
    vi. MARY SALSBERRY, b. Private; m. MAX CORDOVA.
    vii. TONY SALSBERRY, b. Private; m. PATRICIA SANDOVAL.

19. FLORINDA[5] SALSBERRY *(MANUELITA[4] HERRERA, FERNANDO[3], PEDRO ALCANTAR[2] DE HERRERA, JOSÉ JOAQUÍN[1])* was born March 15, 1910 in Palo Verde (Ruidoso), New México, and died March 27, 1978 in San Patricio, New México. She married ROMÁN SÁNCHEZ February 20, 1927 in Mescalero, New Mexico[24], son of MAURICIO SÁNCHEZ and DELFINIA ROMERO.

Notes for FLORINDA SALSBERRY:
Florinda was born on the Rancho Salsberry by Cañon de Salsberry. The house is no longer standing but a grove of trees is all that remains of their house.

More About FLORINDA SALSBERRY:
Fact 1: June 15, 1910, Baptized. Padrinos: Manuel Corona and Susana Trujillo.[25]

Notes for ROMÁN SÁNCHEZ:
May 29, 1904: Baptized by Román Barragán and his wife Andrea Torres de Barragán in San Patricio.

Died in an automobile accident in Ruidoso Downs.
Buried: La Capilla de San Patricio

Children of FLORINDA SALSBERRY and ROMÁN SÁNCHEZ are:
    i.   MADELENA[6] SÁNCHEZ, b. San Patricio, New México.

         More About MADELENA SÁNCHEZ:
         Fact 1: Died Young

    ii.   MAURICIO SALSBERRY SÁNCHEZ, b. San Patricio, New México.

         More About MAURICIO SALSBERRY SÁNCHEZ:
         Fact 1: Died Young

28.   iii. JOSÉ ERNESTO SÁNCHEZ, b. April 09, 1928, San Patricio, New México.
29.   iv. DELFINIA OLIDIA SÁNCHEZ, b. April 18, 1934, San Patricio, New México.
       v.   ORLANDO SÁNCHEZ, b. April 03, 1936, San Patricio, New México.
30.   vi. FLORA MARÍA SÁNCHEZ, b. March 24, 1938, Capítan, New México.
31.   vii. FRED SÁNCHEZ, b. May 30, 1940, Fort Stanton, New México.
32.   viii. BREZEL ROBERT SÁNCHEZ, b. November 04, 1941, San Patricio, New México.
       ix. GERALDINE (GERALDA) ELSIE SÁNCHEZ, b. January 10, 1945, San Patricio, New México; m. ROBERT MONTES.
       x.   LUVIN SÁNCHEZ, b. October 23, 1947, San Patricio, New México; m. GLORIA BACA.

More About LUVIN SÁNCHEZ:
Fact 1: Moved to Roswell, New México.

33.   xi.   CINTHIA (CYNTHIA) YOLANDA SÁNCHEZ, b. September 10, 1950, Capítan, New México; d. April 27, 1986, Rio Rancho, New México.

34.   xii.   ROMÁN SÁNCHEZ, JR., b. March 13, 1954, San Patricio, New México.

20. ENRÍQUES (HENRY)[5] SALSBERRY *(MANUELITA[4] HERRERA, FERNANDO[3], PEDRO ALCANTAR[2] DE HERRERA, JOSÉ JOAQUÍN[1])* was born April 15, 1911 in Palo Verde (Ruidoso), Territory of New México, and died in Artesia, New México. He married DOLORES (LOLA) SÁNCHEZ February 04, 1933 in Carrizozo, New México, daughter of TELESFORO SÁNCHEZ and CAROLINA MIRANDA.

More About ENRÍQUES (HENRY) SALSBERRY:
Fact 1: Died in a freak accident

Marriage Notes for ENRÍQUES SALSBERRY and DOLORES SÁNCHEZ:
Married by: Reverand James A. Brady.

Children of ENRÍQUES SALSBERRY and DOLORES SÁNCHEZ are:
    i.   HENRY[6] SALSBERRY, b. Private.
    ii.   PAUL SALSBERRY, b. Private.
    iii.   JANE SALSBERRY, b. Private.
    iv.   WOODROW (WOODY) SALSBERRY, b. Private.
    v.   WILLIAM SALSBERRY, b. Private.
    vi.   TRINA SALSBERRY, b. Private.

21. JOSÉ[5] PORTIO *(MANUELITA[4] HERRERA, FERNANDO[3], PEDRO ALCANTAR[2] DE HERRERA, JOSÉ JOAQUÍN[1])* was born December 03, 1893, and died September 18, 1959 in San Patricio New Mexico. He married JULIANITA YBARRA January 05, 1922, daughter of GREGORIO YBARRA and CATARINA MONTOYA.

Notes for JOSÉ PORTIO:
Born at Gregorio Ybarra's farm.

More About JOSÉ PORTIO:
Fact 1: May 10, 1918, WW I veteran. Discharged from Camp Fremont, California.[26]

More About JULIANITA YBARRA:
Fact 1: March 17, 1901, Baptized.

Children of JOSÉ PORTIO and JULIANITA YBARRA are:
    i.   RICARDO[6] PORTIO, m. WANDA PAGE.

        Notes for RICARDO PORTIO:
        He was a WW II veteran.

    ii.   ARON PORTIO, m. ISABEL LUERAS.

        Notes for ARON PORTIO:
        He was a WW II veteran.

    iii.   MANUELITA PORTIO, m. RUBÉN PADILLA.

        Notes for RUBÉN PADILLA:
        He was a WW II veteran.

22. MANUEL[5] CORONA *(MANUELITA[4] HERRERA, FERNANDO[3], PEDRO ALCANTAR[2] DE HERRERA, JOSÉ JOAQUÍN[1])* was born January 01, 1885 in San Juanito (Ruidoso), Territory of New México, and died July 17, 1966 in San Patricio, New México. He married (1) JESÚSITA DOMINGUEZ January 26, 1905, daughter of NICANOR

DOMINGUEZ and OCTAVIANA FUENTES. He married (2) SUSANA TRUJILLO February 21, 1909, daughter of BONAFICIO TRUJILLO and LORENSA SILVA.

Notes for MANUEL CORONA:
Born at Gregorio's farm in San Juanito.
The 1920 Census shows that his daughter, Sara was living with him and Susana.
1933-1936: Served as probate judge.
He also serves as a Constable and as a Lincoln County Commisioner.

Notes for JESÚSITA DOMINGUEZ:
She divorced Manuel Corona.

Marriage Notes for MANUEL CORONA and JESÚSITA DOMINGUEZ:
Married by: Lincoln Probate Judge, Francisco Gómez.

Child of MANUEL CORONA and JESÚSITA DOMINGUEZ is:
35.   i.   SARA⁶ CORONA, b. December 17, 1905.

Children of MANUEL CORONA and SUSANA TRUJILLO are:
        ii.   MAX⁶ CORONA, b. 1913; d. January 09, 1973, Morenci, Arizona; m. (1) APOLONIA (JUANA) WARNER; m. (2) BRESELIA GONZÁLES.

                More About MAX CORONA:
                Fact 1: January 09, 1973, Died in an automobile accident.

                More About BRESELIA GONZÁLES:
                Fact 1: January 09, 1973, Died in an automobile accident.

        iii.   ANASTACIO CORONA, b. 1917.
        iv.   MANUEL TRUJILLO CORONA.

23. HELENA (ELENA)⁵ CORONA *(MANUELITA⁴ HERRERA, FERNANDO³, PEDRO ALCANTAR² DE HERRERA, JOSÉ JOAQUÍN¹)* was born February 11, 1889 in San Juanito (Ruidoso), Territory of New México, and died March 14, 1928 in San Patricio, New México. She married ROBERTO PRUDENCIO August 20, 1922, son of DAMACIO PRUDENCIO and CLEOFAS MUÑOZ.

Notes for HELENA (ELENA) CORONA:
Born at Gregorio's farm in San Juanito.

More About ROBERTO PRUDENCIO:
Fact 1: September 05, 1901, Baptized.

Children of HELENA CORONA and ROBERTO PRUDENCIO are:
        i.   FELICITA⁶ PRUDENCIO, m. ADAN BARRERA.
        ii.   MARGARITA PRUDENCIO, m. JOSÉ TORRES.

Generation No. 6

24. VIRGINIA⁶ SÁNCHEZ *(JENNIE (JOSEFA)⁵ GILL, MARÍA ALTAGRACIA⁴ HERRERA, FERNANDO³, PEDRO ALCANTAR² DE HERRERA, JOSÉ JOAQUÍN¹)* was born April 13, 1902 in Ruidoso, Territory of New México, and died in Ruidoso, New México. She married JOSÉ CANDELARIO (ANDELARIO) RANDOLPH²⁷ September 14, 1918 in Lincoln, New México²⁸, son of JOSÉ RANDOLPH and CATARINA BRADY.

Children of VIRGINIA SÁNCHEZ and JOSÉ RANDOLPH are:
        i.   JOSEPHINE⁷ RANDOLPH, b. Abt. 1920.
        ii.   AROPAJITA RANDOLPH, b. Abt. 1922.
        iii.   ELMER RANDOLPH, b. Abt. 1926.
        iv.   CATHERINE RANDOLPH, b. Abt. 1928.

25. TELESFORA[6] SÁNCHEZ *(JENNIE (JOSEFA)[5] GILL, MARÍA ALTAGRACIA[4] HERRERA, FERNANDO[3], PEDRO ALCANTAR[2] DE HERRERA, JOSÉ JOAQUÍN[1])* was born November 19, 1903 in Glencoe, Territory of New México. She married TEODORO SÁNCHEZ PEÑA March 01, 1926 in Carrizozo, New México[29], son of LUÍS PEÑA and AMADITA SÁNCHEZ.

Children of TELESFORA SÁNCHEZ and TEODORO PEÑA are:
- i. JOSEPHINE[7] PEÑA, b. Private.
- ii. IDALIA PEÑA.
- iii. LUÍS PEÑA.
- iv. THEODORO (TEODORO) (3) PEÑA.
- v. RAFAEL PEÑA.
- vi. REYES PEÑA.

26. SALOMON GILL[6] SÁNCHEZ *(JENNIE (JOSEFA)[5] GILL, MARÍA ALTAGRACIA[4] HERRERA, FERNANDO[3], PEDRO ALCANTAR[2] DE HERRERA, JOSÉ JOAQUÍN[1])* was born March 17, 1905 in Glencoe, Territory of New México[30]. He married (1) TERESITA SALAS[31] October 11, 1928 in Lincoln, New México. He married (2) RAMONA OTERO November 20, 1932.

Marriage Notes for SALOMON SÁNCHEZ and TERESITA SALAS:
Married by: Padre Reyes.

Children of SALOMON SÁNCHEZ and TERESITA SALAS are:
- i. ORLANDO[7] SÁNCHEZ, b. Private.
- ii. FABIOLA SÁNCHEZ, b. Abt. September 1929.

Children of SALOMON SÁNCHEZ and RAMONA OTERO are:
- iii. MARY OLINDA[7] SÁNCHEZ, b. Private.
- iv. LORENA SÁNCHEZ, b. Private.
- v. ELMON SÁNCHEZ, b. Private.
- vi. ERNEST OTERO SÁNCHEZ, b. Private.

27. ANATALIA (NATALIA)[6] SÁNCHEZ *(JENNIE (JOSEFA)[5] GILL, MARÍA ALTAGRACIA[4] HERRERA, FERNANDO[3], PEDRO ALCANTAR[2] DE HERRERA, JOSÉ JOAQUÍN[1])* was born 1912. She married JULIAN HERRERA April 28, 1934, son of MARTÍN HERRERA and TEODORA MENDOSA.

Children of ANATALIA SÁNCHEZ and JULIAN HERRERA are:
- i. MARTÍN[7] HERRERA, d. October 25, 1954, El Paso, Téxas.
- ii. ANDREW HERRERA.
- iii. ORLIDIA HERRERA.
- iv. VIRGINIA HERRERA.

28. JOSÉ ERNESTO[6] SÁNCHEZ *(FLORINDA[5] SALSBERRY, MANUELITA[4] HERRERA, FERNANDO[3], PEDRO ALCANTAR[2] DE HERRERA, JOSÉ JOAQUÍN[1])* was born April 09, 1928 in San Patricio, New México. He married ORALIA CHÁVEZ March 20, 1948 in Ruidoso, New Mexico, daughter of YSIDRO CHÁVEZ and PAUBLITA SÁNCHEZ.

Children of JOSÉ SÁNCHEZ and ORALIA CHÁVEZ are:
- 36. i. ERNEST JOSEPH[7] SÁNCHEZ, b. July 08, 1951, Long Beach, California.
- 37. ii. JAMES CHARLES SÁNCHEZ, b. October 29, 1953, Long Beach, California.
- iii. STEVE ANTHONY SÁNCHEZ, b. December 24, 1959, Ruidoso, New México; d. January 08, 1978, San Patricio, New México.
- 38. iv. JANICE MARIE SÁNCHEZ, b. August 23, 1968, Ruidoso, New Mexico.

29. DELFINIA OLIDIA[6] SÁNCHEZ *(FLORINDA[5] SALSBERRY, MANUELITA[4] HERRERA, FERNANDO[3], PEDRO ALCANTAR[2] DE HERRERA, JOSÉ JOAQUÍN[1])* was born April 18, 1934 in San Patricio, New México. She married LEANDRO VEGA, son of LEANDRO VEGA and NARCISA RAMIREZ.

Children of DELFINIA SÁNCHEZ and LEANDRO VEGA are:
- i. LEE (LEANDRO)[7] VEGA, b. July 14, 1960, Carrizozo, New México; m. CATHERINE MARIE GARCÍA.

39.   ii.   GARY ANTHONY VEGA, b. June 17, 1961, Carrizozo, New México.

30. FLORA MARÍA⁶ SÁNCHEZ *(FLORINDA⁵ SALSBERRY, MANUELITA⁴ HERRERA, FERNANDO³, PEDRO ALCANTAR² DE HERRERA, JOSÉ JOAQUÍN¹)* was born March 24, 1938 in Capítan, New México. She married RICHARD VEGA.

Children of FLORA SÁNCHEZ and RICHARD VEGA are:
    i.   DEBBI⁷ VEGA, b. Private.
    ii.   JAYLYN VEGA, b. Private.
    iii.   RICHARD SÁNCHEZ VEGA, b. Private.
    iv.   KENNETH VEGA, b. Private.

31. FRED⁶ SÁNCHEZ *(FLORINDA⁵ SALSBERRY, MANUELITA⁴ HERRERA, FERNANDO³, PEDRO ALCANTAR² DE HERRERA, JOSÉ JOAQUÍN¹)* was born May 30, 1940 in Fort Stanton, New México. He married BERTA HERRERA, daughter of VICENTE HERRERA and CIPRIANA GONZÁLES.

Children of FRED SÁNCHEZ and BERTA HERRERA are:
    i.   DAVÍD⁷ SÁNCHEZ, b. Private.
    ii.   ELIZABETH SÁNCHEZ, b. Private.
    iii.   PATRICK SÁNCHEZ, b. Private.
    iv.   JESSICA SÁNCHEZ, b. Private.

32. BREZEL ROBERT⁶ SÁNCHEZ *(FLORINDA⁵ SALSBERRY, MANUELITA⁴ HERRERA, FERNANDO³, PEDRO ALCANTAR² DE HERRERA, JOSÉ JOAQUÍN¹)* was born November 04, 1941 in San Patricio, New México. He married MINNIE ROMERO.

More About BREZEL ROBERT SÁNCHEZ:
Fact 1: Moved to Roswell, New México.

Children of BREZEL SÁNCHEZ and MINNIE ROMERO are:
    i.   RAY⁷ SÁNCHEZ, b. Private.
    ii.   ANTHONY SÁNCHEZ, b. Private.
    iii.   ROSANA SÁNCHEZ, b. Private.
    iv.   VERONICA SÁNCHEZ, b. Private.

33. CINTHIA (CYNTHIA) YOLANDA⁶ SÁNCHEZ *(FLORINDA⁵ SALSBERRY, MANUELITA⁴ HERRERA, FERNANDO³, PEDRO ALCANTAR² DE HERRERA, JOSÉ JOAQUÍN¹)* was born September 10, 1950 in Capítan, New México, and died April 27, 1986 in Rio Rancho, New México. She married BERRY VANDERWALL.

Children of CINTHIA SÁNCHEZ and BERRY VANDERWALL are:
    i.   NEIL SIMON⁷ VANDERWALL, b. Private.
    ii.   MELISSA STEPHANIE VANDERWALL, b. Private.
    iii.   AMANDA DESIREE VANDERWALL, b. Private.
    iv.   AMBER DAWN VANDERWALL, b. Private.

34. ROMÁN⁶ SÁNCHEZ, JR. *(FLORINDA⁵ SALSBERRY, MANUELITA⁴ HERRERA, FERNANDO³, PEDRO ALCANTAR² DE HERRERA, JOSÉ JOAQUÍN¹)* was born March 13, 1954 in San Patricio, New México. He married YOVONNE SALAS.

Children of ROMÁN SÁNCHEZ and YOVONNE SALAS are:
    i.   FELIPÉ⁷ SÁNCHEZ, b. Private, Ruidoso, New México.
    ii.   FABIAN SÁNCHEZ, b. Private, Ruidoso, New México.

35. SARA⁶ CORONA *(MANUEL⁵, MANUELITA⁴ HERRERA, FERNANDO³, PEDRO ALCANTAR² DE HERRERA, JOSÉ JOAQUÍN¹)* was born December 17, 1905. She married JOSÉ MIGUEL ARCHULETA December 22, 1925, son of ANTONIO ARCHULETA and LUZ LUCERO.

More About SARA CORONA:
Fact 1: May 12, 1906, Baptized.

Notes for JOSÉ MIGUEL ARCHULETA:
He was the adopted son of Antonio José Archuleta.

Children of SARA CORONA and JOSÉ ARCHULETA are:

    i.   ANTONIO (TONY)[7] ARCHULETA.
    ii.   GUILLERMO ARCHULETA.
    iii. FRANK ARCHULETA.
    iv. ORLANDO ARCHULETA.
    v.   MELVIN ARCHULETA.
    vi. SERAFIN ARCHULETA.
    vii. FELISITA ARCHULETA.
   viii. JOSEFINA ARCHULETA.
    ix. CECILIA ARCHULETA.
    x.   ARABELA ARCHULETA.

Endnotes

1. 1850 Census Rio Arriba, Page 128, Northern Division, Lists all children born before 1850.
2. *Taos Baptisms 1701-1852, Database Manuscipt*, Page 260, Thomas D. Martinez, July, 2000.
3. *Lincoln County Clerk, Book of Marriages*, Page 254, Book 4, Lists birth date and marriage dates for the bride and groom.
4. *Lincoln County Clerk, Book of Marriages*, Page 136, Book 4, Lists birth dates and marriage date for the bride and groom.
5. *Lincoln County Clerk, Book of Marriages*, Page 4, Book 1 Applications, Lists birth dates for the bride and groom.
6. *LDS Historical Library, Alamogordo*, Fiche # 0017009-3.
7. *Lincoln County Clerk, Book of Marriages*, Page 101, Book 4, Lists birth date and marriage date for the bride and groom.
8. *1900 Census Lincoln County*, Page 13A, Ruidoso, Lists all children born before 1900.
9. *Lincoln County Clerk, Book of Marriages*, Page 227, Book 4, Lists birth dates and marriage date for the bride and groom.
10. *LDS Historical Library, Alamogordo*, Page 140, Fiche # 756.
11. *LDS Historical Library, Alamogordo*, Page 11, Fiche # 754.
12. *Lincoln County Clerk, Book of Marriages*, Page 427, Book 5.
13. *LDS Historical Library, Alamogordo*, Page 6, Fiche # 0017006.
14. *LDS Historical Library, Alamogordo*, Page 17, Fiche # 756.
15. *Lincoln County Clerk, Book of Marriages*, Page 162, Book 1 Applications, Lists birth dates for the bride and groom.
16. 1930 Census Lincoln County, Page 4B, Glencoe, Lists all the children born before 1930.
17. *LDS Historical Library, Alamogordo*, Page 156, Fiche # 754.
18. 1930 Census Lincoln County.
19. *LDS Historical Library, Alamogordo*, Page 5, Fiche # 756.
20. *LDS Historical Library, Alamogordo*, Page 5, Fiche # 0017009.
21. *Lincoln County Clerk, Book of Marriages*, Page 481, Book 5, Lists birth dates and marriage date for the bride and groom.
22. *LDS Historical Library, Alamogordo*, Page 130, Fiche # 754.
23. 1930 Census Lincoln County, Page 2B, Lincoln, Lists all children born before 1930.
24. *LDS Historical Library, Alamogordo*, Page 150, 756.
25. *LDS Historical Library, Alamogordo*, Page 119, Fiche # 754.
26. Lincoln County Clerk, Soldiers Discharge Book, Page 13, Book 1.
27. 1930 Census Lincoln County, Page 3A, Lists all children as of 1930.
28. *Lincoln County Clerk, Book of Marriages*, Page 489, Book 4, Lists birth dates and marriage date for the bride and groom.
29. *Lincoln County Clerk, Book of Marriages*, Book 5, Lists birth dates and marriage date for the bride and groom.
30. *LDS Historical Library, Alamogordo*, Page 48, Fiche # 0017008.
31. 1930 Census Lincoln County, Page 3B, Lincoln, Lists all children born before 1930.

Descendants of Florencio Gonzáles

Generation No. 1

1. SANTIAGO[1] GONZÁLES[1] was born 1801. He married MARÍA MANUELA ARAGÓN.

Notes for SANTIAGO GONZÁLES:
1870 Census showed that he lived in Corrales, New México.

Children of SANTIAGO GONZÁLES and MARÍA ARAGÓN are:
2.   i.   ALTAGRACIA[2] GONZÁLES, b. Abt. 1833, Los Corrales, Nuevo México, República de México.
      ii.   IGNACIO GONZÁLES, b. 1842.
3.   iii. FLORENCIO GONZÁLES, b. November 07, 1843, Corrales, Nuevo México, La República de México; d. December 18, 1897, San Patricio, Territory of New México.

Generation No. 2

2. ALTAGRACIA[2] GONZÁLES *(SANTIAGO[1])* was born Abt. 1833 in Los Corrales, Nuevo México, República de México. She married SERAFÍN POLACO.

Children of ALTAGRACIA GONZÁLES and SERAFÍN POLACO are:
      i.   CRECENSIA[3] POLACO, b. Abt. 1854.
      ii.   ANASTACIA POLACO, b. Abt. 1856.
4.   iii. TRANCITO (FRANCISCO) POLACO, b. Abt. 1858, Corrales,.
      iv.   CANDIDO POLACO, b. Abt. 1860.
5.   v.   ELFIGO POLACO, b. Abt. 1863, Los Corrales, Territory of New México.
      vi.   RUDOLFO POLACO, b. Abt. 1865.
      vii. ALTAGRACIA POLACO, b. Abt. 1867.

3. FLORENCIO[2] GONZÁLES *(SANTIAGO[1])* was born November 07, 1843 in Corrales, Nuevo México, La República de México, and died December 18, 1897 in San Patricio, Territory of New México. He married RAYMUNDA (REIMUNDA) SEGUNDA (CIGISMUNDA) SÁNCHEZ in Manzano, Territory of New México, daughter of MAURICIO SÁNCHEZ and MARÍA GONZÁLES.

Notes for FLORENCIO GONZÁLES:
Corrales is near present day Albuquerque.
1860 Census: Resided in Corrales.
In 1867: he also went by Florencio Gonzáles y Aragón.
1870 Census: Resided in Precinct 1, Fort Stanton
Buried: La Capilla de San Patricio.

Notes for RAYMUNDA (REIMUNDA) SEGUNDA (CIGISMUNDA) SÁNCHEZ:
Buried: La Capilla de San Patricio.

Children of FLORENCIO GONZÁLES and RAYMUNDA SÁNCHEZ are:
      i.   ARISTOTEL[3] GONZÁLES.

            Notes for ARISTOTEL GONZÁLES:
            Died young.

      ii.   ESOILA GONZÁLES, m. FRANK VIGIL, December 05, 1909.
      iii. FILOTEA GONZÁLES.

            Notes for FILOTEA GONZÁLES:
            Died young.

6.	iv.	ESLINDA GONZÁLES, b. 1867, San Patricio, Territory of New México; d. Bef. September 1923.
	v.	JUAN GONZÁLES, b. 1869.
7.	vi.	PROSPERO GONZÁLES, b. July 20, 1871; d. August 20, 1937, San Patricio, New México.
8.	vii.	ALFREDO GONZÁLES, b. 1872; d. 1927, San Patricio, New México.
9.	viii.	LEOPOLDO GONZÁLES, b. April 08, 1875; d. June 10, 1937.
10.	ix.	DOMINGO EPAMINOANDAZ GONZÁLES, b. April 04, 1876; d. February 20, 1970.
11.	x.	MARÍA AURORA (AVRORA) GONZÁLES, b. May 23, 1880; d. 1971.
12.	xi.	AROPAJITA (EROPAJITA) GONZÁLES, b. 1882.
	xii.	AURELIA GONZÁLES, b. May 15, 1883; m. MIGUEL (2ND) LUNA, November 28, 1898, San Patricio, Territory of New México.
13.	xiii.	FLORENCIO SÁNCHEZ GONZÁLES, b. November 24, 1893.

Generation No. 3

4. TRANCITO (FRANCISCO)[3] POLACO *(ALTAGRACIA[2] GONZÁLES, SANTIAGO[1])* was born Abt. 1858 in Corrales,. He married AROPAJITA (EROPAJITA) GONZÁLES November 08, 1900[2], daughter of FLORENCIO GONZÁLES and RAYMUNDA SÁNCHEZ.

More About TRANCITO (FRANCISCO) POLACO:
Fact 1: 1920 Census shows that Francisco was later known as Transito.[3]

Children of TRANCITO POLACO and AROPAJITA GONZÁLES are:

14.	i.	DULCINEA[4] POLACO, b. 1903.
	ii.	TRANSITO GONZÁLES POLACO[4], b. September 01, 1907; d. December 14, 1998.
15.	iii.	ALTAGRACIA POLACO, b. August 24, 1910.
	iv.	ELFIGO GONZÁLES POLACO, b. 1913.

5. ELFIGO[3] POLACO *(ALTAGRACIA[2] GONZÁLES, SANTIAGO[1])[5]* was born Abt. 1863 in Los Corrales, Territory of New México.

Notes for ELFIGO POLACO:
His mother-in-law, Librada Abeyta was living and helping raise the family.

Children of ELFIGO POLACO are:

	i.	SERAFÍN ABEYTA[4] POLACO, b. Abt. 1892.
	ii.	PEDRO POLACO, b. Abt. 1894.
	iii.	TEODORO POLACO, b. Abt. 1898.
	iv.	JULIAN POLACO, b. Abt. 1899.

6. ESLINDA[3] GONZÁLES *(FLORENCIO[2], SANTIAGO[1])* was born 1867 in San Patricio, Territory of New México[6], and died Bef. September 1923. She married RICARDO FRANCISCO (FRANK) CHÁVEZ May 23, 1890[7], son of JOSÉ CHÁVEZ and MARÍA LUNA.

Children of ESLINDA GONZÁLES and RICARDO CHÁVEZ are:

| | i. | FIDEL[4] CHÁVEZ, b. June 30, 1893, San Patricio, Territory of New México; m. DELFINIA PADILLA Y WEST, June 28, 1915, Lincoln, New México[8]. |

> Notes for DELFINIA PADILLA Y WEST:
> Criada y adoptiva de John C. West (Raised and adopted by John C. West). Also known as Delfinia Sánchez y West.
>
> Marriage Notes for FIDEL CHÁVEZ and DELFINIA WEST:
> Married by: Father Girma.
> Padrinos: Candido Chávez and Estela West.

16.	ii.	ERMINDA CHÁVEZ, b. June 22, 1895, San Patricio, Territory of New México; d. November 01, 1956.
	iii.	PALMIRA CHÁVEZ, b. 1896.
	iv.	RAMON CHÁVEZ, b. 1898.
	v.	ENCARNACION CHÁVEZ, b. November 15, 1899.

Notes for ENCARNACION CHÁVEZ:
Died young.

7. PROSPERO[3] GONZÁLES *(FLORENCIO[2], SANTIAGO[1])* was born July 20, 1871[9], and died August 20, 1937 in San Patricio, New México. He married TELESFORA MIRABAL[10] March 28, 1900 in Glencoe, Territory of New México[11], daughter of JUAN MIRABAL and GUADALUPE TRUJILLO.

Notes for PROSPERO GONZÁLES:
Buried: La Capilla de San Patricio.

Notes for TELESFORA MIRABAL:
December 29, 1939: Died in an accident.
Buried in La Capilla de San Ysidro.

More About TELESFORA MIRABAL:
Fact 1: January 28, 1862, Baptized.

Marriage Notes for PROSPERO GONZÁLES and TELESFORA MIRABAL:
Married in La Capilla de San Ysidro.

Children of PROSPERO GONZÁLES and TELESFORA MIRABAL are:

17.   i.   RUBÉN ANDRES[4] GONZÁLES, b. November 02, 1900, Glencoe, Territory of New México; d. Artesia, New Mexico.

18.   ii.   PROSPERO MIRABAL GONZÁLES, b. January 1909; d. January 17, 1960.

          iii.   MARÍA RESENIA (ARCENIA) GONZÁLES, b. February 20, 1898[12]; m. CHARLIE (CHARLES) CURRY, December 20, 1915[13].

                 More About MARÍA RESENIA (ARCENIA) GONZÁLES:
                 Fact 1: May 03, 1898, Baptized.[14]

          iv.   PORFIRIO GONZÁLES, b. August 10, 1903[15]; d. June 13, 1947, San Patricio, New México; m. ANGELINA RUIZ, October 15, 1936.

8. ALFREDO[3] GONZÁLES *(FLORENCIO[2], SANTIAGO[1])*[16] was born 1872, and died 1927 in San Patricio, New México. He married REBECCA SISNEROS SALAZAR February 07, 1904.

Notes for ALFREDO GONZÁLES:
1901-1902: Was elected as Lincoln County Sheriff.
Buried: San Patricio.

Child of ALFREDO GONZÁLES and REBECCA SALAZAR is:
          i.   GODFREY[4] GONZÁLES, b. 1904.

9. LEOPOLDO[3] GONZÁLES *(FLORENCIO[2], SANTIAGO[1])*[17] was born April 08, 1875, and died June 10, 1937. He married REIMUNDA (RAYMUNDA) SEDILLO[18] November 28, 1895, daughter of JUAN SEDILLO and JOSEFA FAJARDO.

Children of LEOPOLDO GONZÁLES and REIMUNDA SEDILLO are:
          i.   JUAN[4] GONZÁLES, b. November 10, 1896[19].

                 Notes for JUAN GONZÁLES:
                 Died young.

          ii.   AROPAJITA GONZÁLES, b. 1900[20]; d. December 05, 1918.

19.   iii.   CRUSITA GONZÁLES, b. May 02, 1904.

20.   iv.   ELISA GONZÁLES, b. February 23, 1912.

10. DOMINGO EPAMINOANDAZ[3] GONZÁLES *(FLORENCIO[2], SANTIAGO[1])* was born April 04, 1876[21], and died February 20, 1970[22]. He married ELVIRA GONZÁLES February 12, 1900[23], daughter of JOSÉ GONZÁLES and MARÍA CHÁVEZ.

More About DOMINGO EPAMINOANDAZ GONZÁLES:
Fact 1: August 04, 1876, Baptized.

Children of DOMINGO GONZÁLES and ELVIRA GONZÁLES are:
          i.   CRECENSIANA[4] GONZÁLES, m. TITO MAÉS.
          ii.   MARÍA GONZÁLES, m. POLO PEÑA.
          iii.   RAFAEL GONZÁLES, m. AVRORA BACA.
          iv.   SIGISMUNDA GONZÁLES, m. ABRAN SÁNCHEZ.
          v.   AGIDA GONZÁLES, b. December 05, 1900[24]; d. October 28, 1941[25]; m. BEN SALAS, December 16, 1921[26].
          vi.   EPAMINOANDAS GONZÁLES GONZÁLES, b. October 21, 1902[27]; m. IGNACIA PRUDENCIO, September 14, 1928, Mescalero, New México[28].
21.   vii.   CIPRIANA GONZÁLES, b. August 21, 1903; d. August 2006, San Patricio, New México.
22.   viii.   FLORENCIO GONZÁLES GONZÁLES, b. September 17, 1907; d. October 11, 1973.
          ix.   BRESELIA GONZÁLES, b. October 10, 1910; d. January 09, 1973, Morenci, Arizona; m. (1) JUAN SÁNCHEZ; m. (2) MAX CORONA.

              More About BRESELIA GONZÁLES:
              Fact 1: January 09, 1973, Died in an automobile accident.

              More About MAX CORONA:
              Fact 1: January 09, 1973, Died in an automobile accident.

          x.   EVA GONZÁLES, b. Private; m. JUAN MONTOYA.

              Notes for JUAN MONTOYA:
              WW II war veteran, Navy.

11. MARÍA AURORA (AVRORA)[3] GONZÁLES *(FLORENCIO[2], SANTIAGO[1])* was born May 23, 1880[29], and died 1971[30]. She married (2) JORGE (GEORGE) ROMERO November 17, 1900[31], son of JUAN ROMERO and CRISTINA CASTILLO.

More About MARÍA AURORA (AVRORA) GONZÁLES:
Fact 1: August 04, 1880, Baptized.
Fact 2: 1920 Census notes that she was divorced.[32]

More About JORGE (GEORGE) ROMERO:
Fact 1: August 03, 1880, Baptized.

Children of MARÍA AURORA (AVRORA) GONZÁLES are:
          i.   ERLINDA[4] GONZÁLES.
          ii.   EMMA GONZÁLES, b. 1915.
          iii.   TRENIDAD GONZÁLES, b. 1919; m. BENINO SÁNCHEZ, April 01, 1934[33].

Children of MARÍA GONZÁLES and JORGE ROMERO are:
23.   iv.   SIGISFREDO[4] ROMERO, b. March 31, 1903.
24.   v.   MELITANA ROMERO, b. February 16, 1902.

12. AROPAJITA (EROPAJITA)[3] GONZÁLES *(FLORENCIO[2], SANTIAGO[1])* was born 1882. She married TRANCITO (FRANCISCO) POLACO November 08, 1900[34], son of SERAFÍN POLACO and ALTAGRACIA GONZÁLES.

More About TRANCITO (FRANCISCO) POLACO:
Fact 1: 1920 Census shows that Francisco was later known as Transito.[35]

Children of AROPAJITA GONZÁLES and TRANCITO POLACO are:
14.   i.   DULCINEA[4] POLACO, b. 1903.
          ii.   TRANSITO GONZÁLES POLACO[36], b. September 01, 1907; d. December 14, 1998.
15.   iii.   ALTAGRACIA POLACO, b. August 24, 1910.
          iv.   ELFIGO GONZÁLES POLACO, b. 1913.

13. FLORENCIO SÁNCHEZ[3] GONZÁLES *(FLORENCIO[2], SANTIAGO[1])* was born November 24, 1893[37]. He married MARÍA AVELINA CHÁVEZ November 09, 1911, daughter of PATROCINIO CHÁVEZ and MARÍA ARCHULETA.

More About FLORENCIO SÁNCHEZ GONZÁLES:
Fact 1: February 10, 1894, Baptized.

More About MARÍA AVELINA CHÁVEZ:
Fact 1: May 07, 1890, Baptized.[38]

Children of FLORENCIO GONZÁLES and MARÍA CHÁVEZ are:
    i.   MIGUEL[4] GONZÁLES, b. July 21, 1918, San Patricio, New México[39]; d. April 08, 1999, San Patricio, New México; m. CRECENCIA YBARRA, May 24, 1935[40].

        Marriage Notes for MIGUEL GONZÁLES and CRECENCIA YBARRA:
        Married by: Justice of the Peace, John Mackey.

25.   ii.   GENEVA GONZÁLES, b. April 11, 1915.
    iii.   JUANITA GONZÁLES, b. Private; m. CHARLIE REYNOLD.
    iv.   DULCINEA GONZÁLES, m. GEORGE REYNOLD.
    v.   ALFEDO GONZÁLES, b. Private.
    vi.   ELOY GONZÁLES.

Generation No. 4

14. DULCINEA[4] POLACO *(TRANCITO (FRANCISCO)[3], ALTAGRACIA[2] GONZÁLES, SANTIAGO[1])*[41] was born 1903. She married GUILLERMO (WILLIAM) (WILLIE) RANDOLPH[42] July 09, 1920 in San Patricio, New México, son of JOSÉ RANDOLPH and CATARINA BRADY.

Marriage Notes for DULCINEA POLACO and GUILLERMO RANDOLPH:
Married by: Reverand Girma.

Children of DULCINEA POLACO and GUILLERMO RANDOLPH are:
    i.   FRANK[5] RANDOLPH, b. Abt. 1921.
    ii.   VIOLA RANDOLPH, b. Abt. 1923.
    iii.   WILLIE POLACO RANDOLPH, b. Abt. 1926.

15. ALTAGRACIA[4] POLACO *(TRANCITO (FRANCISCO)[3], ALTAGRACIA[2] GONZÁLES, SANTIAGO[1])* was born August 24, 1910. She married LEOPOLDO CHÁVEZ[43], son of PABLO CHÁVEZ and JESÚSITA SÁNCHEZ.

Marriage Notes for ALTAGRACIA POLACO and LEOPOLDO CHÁVEZ:
Married by: Justice of the Peace, B.H. Harvey.
Married May 24. The date is unclear but it was sometime in the 1930s.

Children of ALTAGRACIA POLACO and LEOPOLDO CHÁVEZ are:
    i.   ROY[5] CHÁVEZ, m. CRUSITA SILVA.
    ii.   BREZEL CHÁVEZ, m. PABLITA HERRERA.
    iii.   RICHARD CHÁVEZ.
    iv.   LYDIA CHÁVEZ, b. Private; m. BOBBY CHÁVEZ.

16. ERMINDA[4] CHÁVEZ *(ESLINDA[3] GONZÁLES, FLORENCIO[2], SANTIAGO[1])* was born June 22, 1895 in San Patricio, Territory of New México, and died November 01, 1956[44]. She married (1) EPIFANIO ULIBARRÍ November 04, 1915 in Lincoln, New México[45], son of VICENTE ULIBARRÍ and MARÍA SEDILLO. She married (2) JOSÉ JÁQUEZ May 17, 1950[46].

More About ERMINDA CHÁVEZ:
Fact 1: July 20, 1894, Baptized.

Marriage Notes for ERMINDA CHÁVEZ and EPIFANIO ULIBARRÍ:

Padrinos: Florencio Gonzáles, Raymundo Sánchez, Augustín Ulibarrí.

Child of ERMINDA CHÁVEZ and EPIFANIO ULIBARRÍ is:
    i.   DIEGO[5] ULIBARRÍ.

17. RUBÉN ANDRES[4] GONZÁLES *(PROSPERO[3], FLORENCIO[2], SANTIAGO[1])* was born November 02, 1900 in Glencoe, Territory of New México[47], and died in Artesia, New Mexico. He married DOROTEA SALSBERRY February 22, 1918, daughter of JAMES SALSBERRY and MANUELITA HERRERA.

More About RUBÉN ANDRES GONZÁLES:
Fact 1: January 16, 1900, Baptized.

More About DOROTEA SALSBERRY:
Fact 1: July 26, 1902, Baptized.[48]

Children of RUBÉN GONZÁLES and DOROTEA SALSBERRY are:
    i.   OLIVIA[5] GONZÁLES, m. JUAN RODRÍGUEZ.
    ii.   ADELINA GONZÁLES, m. LOLO RODRÍGUEZ.
    iii.   ORALIA GONZÁLES, m. CRISTÓVAL PEREA.
    iv.   VIOLA GONZÁLES, b. Private; m. MANUEL REYES.
    v.   EMILIO GONZÁLES, b. Private; m. RACHEL ALANIS.
    vi.   RUFINA GONZÁLES, b. Private; m. JOSÉ RODRÍGUEZ.
    vii.   FEDELINA GONZÁLES, b. Private; m. COSMÉ GÓMES.
    viii.   RUBÉN GONZÁLES, b. Private; m. MANUELA PAS.
    ix.   REYNER GONZÁLES, b. Private; m. MARY PADILLA.
    x.   TELESFORA (TILLIE) GONZÁLES, m. UNKOWN -----.
    xi.   HELEN GONZÁLES, m. UNKNOWN -----.

18. PROSPERO MIRABAL[4] GONZÁLES *(PROSPERO[3], FLORENCIO[2], SANTIAGO[1])* was born January 1909, and died January 17, 1960[49]. He married AMBROCIA SILVA May 15, 1936[50], daughter of TELESFOR SILVA and ERINEA BENAVIDEZ.

Children of PROSPERO GONZÁLES and AMBROCIA SILVA are:
    i.   LILIA[5] GONZÁLES.
    ii.   FELIX GONZÁLES.
    iii.   DORTHY GONZÁLES.
    iv.   FLOYD GONZÁLES.

19. CRUSITA[4] GONZÁLES *(LEOPOLDO[3], FLORENCIO[2], SANTIAGO[1])* was born May 02, 1904[51]. She married (1) BENITO HERRERA, son of CRUZ HERRERA and REDUCINDA CARDONA. She married (2) CASIMIRO TAFOYA VILLESCAZ 1925 in Lincoln, New México[52], son of CASIMIRO VILLESCAZ and EMILIANA TAFOYA.

Notes for BENITO HERRERA:
Padrinos (baptismal): Ramon Olguín and Lorensa Sedillo.

More About BENITO HERRERA:
Fact 1: April 02, 1890, Baptized.

More About CASIMIRO TAFOYA VILLESCAZ:
Fact 1: January 12, 1895, Baptized.

Marriage Notes for CRUSITA GONZÁLES and CASIMIRO VILLESCAZ:
Another record has them married on February 19, 1928.

Child of CRUSITA GONZÁLES and CASIMIRO VILLESCAZ is:
    i.   ERNESTINA[5] VILLESCAZ.

20. ELISA[4] GONZÁLES *(LEOPOLDO[3], FLORENCIO[2], SANTIAGO[1])* was born February 23, 1912. She married MANUEL HERRERA November 23, 1931[53], son of LUÍS HERRERA and BENJAMIN HERNÁNDEZ.

Children of ELISA GONZÁLES and MANUEL HERRERA are:

> i. LEO[5] HERRERA, m. EMMA ZAMORA.
> ii. FLORIPE HERRERA, m. PORFIRIO SÁNCHEZ.

21. CIPRIANA[4] GONZÁLES *(DOMINGO EPAMINOANDAZ[3], FLORENCIO[2], SANTIAGO[1])* was born August 21, 1903[54], and died August 2006 in San Patricio, New México. She married VICENTE HERRERA August 27, 1932[55], son of CRUZ HERRERA and PETRA DOMINGUEZ.

More About CIPRIANA GONZÁLES:
Fact 1: August 21, 2006, 103 years of age.

Children of CIPRIANA GONZÁLES and VICENTE HERRERA are:
> i. RUFINO[5] HERRERA, b. July 25, 1933, San Patricio, New México; d. January 17, 2006, San Patricio, New México; m. HELENA MONTOYA, April 04, 1957, San Patricio, New México.
>
> Notes for RUFINO HERRERA:
> Korean War Veteran

> 26. ii. BERTA HERRERA, b. Private, San Patricio, New México.

22. FLORENCIO GONZÁLES[4] GONZÁLES *(DOMINGO EPAMINOANDAZ[3], FLORENCIO[2], SANTIAGO[1])* was born September 17, 1907[56], and died October 11, 1973. He married ALBESITA (ALBESA) SÁNCHEZ, daughter of JACOBO SÁNCHEZ and MARÍA TRUJILLO.

Children of FLORENCIO GONZÁLES and ALBESITA SÁNCHEZ are:
> i. JOSÉ[5] GONZÁLES.
> ii. ISAQUIO GONZÁLES, b. Private.
> iii. FRANK GONZÁLES.
> iv. ELVIRA SÁNCHEZ GONZÁLES, b. Private.

23. SIGISFREDO[4] ROMERO *(MARÍA AURORA (AVRORA)[3] GONZÁLES, FLORENCIO[2], SANTIAGO[1])* was born March 31, 1903. He married LUCIA (LUCIANA) YBARRA January 11, 1928, daughter of GREGORIO YBARRA and CATARINA MONTOYA.

Notes for LUCIA (LUCIANA) YBARRA:
Padrinos: Augustín Laguna born in México City, and his wife, Juana María Laguna, born in Polvadera, New México

Children of SIGISFREDO ROMERO and LUCIA YBARRA are:
> i. FLORIPE[5] ROMERO, b. Private.
> ii. FEDELINA ROMERO, b. Private.
> iii. CLEOFAS ROMERO, b. Private; m. JUAN SÁNCHEZ MONTES.
> iv. ISABEL ROMERO, b. Private.
> v. RUBÉN ROMERO, b. Private.
> vi. EDUVIGEN ROMERO, b. Private.
> vii. LEONIRES ROMERO, b. Private.
> viii. FREDO ROMERO, b. Private.
> ix. REBECCA ROMERO, b. Private.

24. MELITANA[4] ROMERO *(MARÍA AURORA (AVRORA)[3] GONZÁLES, FLORENCIO[2], SANTIAGO[1])* was born February 16, 1902. She married PATROCINIO ARCHULETA CHÁVEZ[57] July 13, 1921, son of PATROCINIO CHÁVEZ and MARÍA ARCHULETA.

Children of MELITANA ROMERO and PATROCINIO CHÁVEZ are:
> i. GABRIEL[5] CHÁVEZ.
> ii. AURELIA CHÁVEZ.
> iii. BRIGIDA CHÁVEZ.
> iv. GLORIA CHÁVEZ.
> v. MOISES CHÁVEZ.
> vi. ADAN CHÁVEZ.
> vii. RAY CHÁVEZ.
> viii. VIRGINIA ROMERO CHÁVEZ.
> ix. NORA CHÁVEZ.

25. GENEVA[4] GONZÁLES *(FLORENCIO SÁNCHEZ[3], FLORENCIO[2], SANTIAGO[1])* was born April 11, 1915. She married ERNESTO SILVA February 02, 1933, son of JULIAN SILVA and MARÍA SÁNCHEZ.

Notes for ERNESTO SILVA:
Served with S2 US Navy during WW 2

Children of GENEVA GONZÁLES and ERNESTO SILVA are:

    i.   ERNEST[5] SILVA, b. Private; m. MINNIE SÁNCHEZ.
    ii.   JOSEPHINE SILVA, b. Private; m. WILLIAM GÓMEZ.
    iii. JESUSITA SILVA, b. Private.

Generation No. 5

26. BERTA[5] HERRERA *(CIPRIANA[4] GONZÁLES, DOMINGO EPAMINOANDAZ[3], FLORENCIO[2], SANTIAGO[1])* was born Private in San Patricio, New México. She married FRED SÁNCHEZ, son of ROMÁN SÁNCHEZ and FLORINDA SALSBERRY.

Children of BERTA HERRERA and FRED SÁNCHEZ are:

    i.   DAVÍD[6] SÁNCHEZ, b. Private.
    ii.   ELIZABETH SÁNCHEZ, b. Private.
    iii. PATRICK SÁNCHEZ, b. Private.
    iv. JESSICA SÁNCHEZ, b. Private.

Endnotes

1. 1850 Census, Corrales, Page 14, Lists birth dates of all children born before 1850.
2. *LDS Historical Library, Alamogordo*, Page 138, Fiche # 756.
3. *1920 Census Lincoln County*, Fiche # 1821077-1A.
4. 1930 Census Lincoln County, Birth and death records.
5. *1900 Census Lincoln County*, Fiche # 1241001-16A.
6. *LDS Historical Library, Alamogordo*, Page 11, Fiche # 0017008.
7. *LDS Historical Library, Alamogordo*, Page 63, Fiche # 756.
8. *Lincoln County Clerk, Book of Marriages*, Page 190, Book 4, Lists birth dates and marriage date for the bride and groom.
9. 1930 Census Lincoln County, Both his birth and death records.
10. *1870 Census of Ft. Stanton*, Page 4, Fiche # 0552393.
11. *LDS Historical Library, Alamogordo*, Page 130, Fiche # 756.
12. *LDS Historical Library, Alamogordo*, Page 17, Fiche # 756.
13. *LDS Historical Library, Alamogordo*, Page 60, Fiche # 756.
14. *LDS Historical Library, Alamogordo*, Page 17, Fiche # 754.
15. *LDS Historical Library, Alamogordo*, Page 170, Fiche # 754.
16. *Lincoln County Clerk, Book of Marriages*, Page 277, Book A, Lists birth date and marriage date for bride and groom.
17. 1930 Census Lincoln County, Birth and death records.
18. *1920 Census Lincoln County*, Fiche # 1821077.
19. *LDS Historical Library, Alamogordo*, Page 258, Fiche # 754.
20. *LDS Historical Library, Alamogordo*, Page 28, Fiche # 754.
21. *LDS Historical Library, Alamogordo*, Page 14, Fiche # 754.
22. 1930 Census Lincoln County.
23. *LDS Historical Library, Alamogordo*, Page 127, Fiche # 756.
24. *LDS Historical Library, Alamogordo*, Page 92, Fiche # 754.
25. 1930 Census Lincoln County.
26. *LDS Historical Library, Alamogordo*, Page 112, Fiche # 756.
27. *LDS Historical Library, Alamogordo*, Page 116, Fiche # 754.
28. *LDS Historical Library, Alamogordo*, Page 158, Fiche # 756.
29. *LDS Historical Library, Alamogordo*, Page 13, Fiche 754.
30. 1930 Census Lincoln County.
31. *LDS Historical Library, Alamogordo*, Page 138, Fiche 756.
32. *1920 Census Lincoln County*, Fiche # 21077-1A.
33. *LDS Historical Library, Alamogordo*, Page 8, Fiche # 756.
34. *LDS Historical Library, Alamogordo*, Page 138, Fiche # 756.
35. *1920 Census Lincoln County*, Fiche # 1821077-1A.

36. 1930 Census Lincoln County, Birth and death records.
37. *LDS Historical Library, Alamogordo*, Page 190, Fiche # 754, Lists birth and marriage dates.
38. *LDS Historical Library, Alamogordo*, Page 160, Fiche # 754.
39. 1930 Census Lincoln County.
40. *Lincoln County Clerk, Book of Marriages.*
41. 1930 Census Lincoln County, 3A, Lists all children as of 1930.
42. *Lincoln County Clerk, Book of Marriages*, Page 74, Book 5, Lists birth date and marriage date for bride and groom.
43. *Lincoln County Clerk, Book of Marriages*, Page 133, Lists birthdate and marriage date for the bride and groom.
44. 1930 Census Lincoln County.
45. *Lincoln County Clerk, Book of Marriages*, Page 229, Book 4, Lists birth dates and marriage date for the bride and groom.
46. *LDS Historical Library, Alamogordo*, Fiche # 754.
47. *LDS Historical Library, Alamogordo*, Page 86, Fiche # 754, Birth and marriage dates.
48. *LDS Historical Library, Alamogordo*, Page 130, Fiche # 754.
49. 1930 Census Lincoln County.
50. *LDS Historical Library, Alamogordo*, Page 14, Fiche # 756.
51. *LDS Historical Library, Alamogordo*, Page 172, Fiche # 754.
52. *LDS Historical Library, Alamogordo*, Page 224, Fiche # 754.
53. *LDS Historical Library, Alamogordo*, Page 3, Fiche # 756.
54. *LDS Historical Library, Alamogordo*, Page 167, Fiche # 754.
55. *Lincoln County Clerk, Book of Marriages*, Page 22, Book 1.
56. 1930 Census Lincoln County.
57. *Lincoln County Clerk, Book of Marriages*, Page 153, Book 5, Lists birth date and marriage date for bride and groom.

Descendants of Tranquelino Montoya

Generation No. 1

1. TRANQUELINO[1] MONTOYA was born 1847 in Tomé, Nuevo México, La República de México. He married MARÍA DE JESÚS TRUJILLO.

More About TRANQUELINO MONTOYA:
Fact 1: Abt. 1860, Had migrated to Lincoln County in the 1860s with his wife.

More About MARÍA DE JESÚS TRUJILLO:
Fact 1: Abt. 1860, Had migrated to Lincoln County in the 1860s with her husband.

Children of TRANQUELINO MONTOYA and MARÍA TRUJILLO are:
2.   i.   SARA[2] MONTOYA.
3.   ii.   ESTANISLADO (TANISLAUS) MONTOYA, b. October 29, 1869.
4.   iii.   ARON MONTOYA, b. February 23, 1873.
       iv.   LAZARO MONTOYA, b. June 29, 1879; m. RAMONA MÁRQUEZ, July 20, 1900, San Patricio, New México.
5.   v.   CATARINA MONTOYA, b. 1883; d. 1951.
6.   vi.   ELFIDA MONTOYA, b. October 23, 1883.
7.   vii.   DOROTEO MONTOYA, b. February 06, 1886.
       viii. RICARDO MONTOYA, b. April 03, 1887.
       ix.   GUADALUPE MONTOYA, b. 1888.
       x.   CANDELARIO MONTOYA, b. 1890.

       Notes for CANDELARIO MONTOYA:
       Died at a young age.

       xi.   CANDELARIA MONTOYA, b. February 03, 1890.
8.   xii.   ISABEL MONTOYA, b. November 05, 1895.

Generation No. 2

2. SARA[2] MONTOYA *(TRANQUELINO[1])*. She married CRUZ (GUEVARRA) DEVARA May 24, 1926[1], son of JUAN GUEVARRA and MARÍA MONTAÑO.

Child of SARA MONTOYA and CRUZ DEVARA is:
       i.   CRUZ (2ND)[3] DEVARA.

3. ESTANISLADO (TANISLAUS)[2] MONTOYA *(TRANQUELINO[1])[2]* was born October 29, 1869. He married (1) SARAFINA SOCORRO ULIBARRÍ January 09, 1887 in Carrizo, Territory of New México, daughter of JUAN ULIBARRÍ and ISABEL MONTOYA. He married (2) ELOISA SALAZAR August 27, 1921.

Children of ESTANISLADO MONTOYA and SARAFINA ULIBARRÍ are:
9.   i.   MANUEL[3] MONTOYA, b. 1888, San Patricio, New México; d. Bef. September 1923.
10.   ii.   PABLITA MONTOYA, b. May 02, 1890, San Patricio, New México; d. March 31, 1952, San Patricio, New México.
11.   iii.   TEODORO (THEODORO) MONTOYA, b. January 1893, San Patricio, New México.
       iv.   CANDIDO MONTOYA, b. 1895, San Patricio, New México.
12.   v.   SUSANA (SOCORRO) MONTOYA, b. 1897, San Patricio, New México.
       vi.   ISABEL MONTOYA, b. December 29, 1899, San Patricio, New México; m. (1) CONCHA -----, El Paso, Texas; m. (2) VICTORIA SÁNCHEZ, February 23, 1921.

       More About VICTORIA SÁNCHEZ:
       Fact 1: August 03, 1899, Baptized.

       vii.   DESIDERIO MONTOYA, b. February 11, 1902; m. CATARINA SALAZAR, March 08, 1926.
13.   viii. SENAIDA MONTOYA, b. May 19, 1907; d. July 10, 1944, Roswell, New México.

4. ARON[2] MONTOYA *(TRANQUELINO[1])[3]* was born February 23, 1873. He married (1) BEATRIZ ROMERO January 31, 1898, daughter of DOROTEO ROMERO and AGAPITA GUEBARA. He married (2) PAULITA QUINTANA May 03, 1922.

Notes for ARON MONTOYA:
Padrinos: Gregorio Trujillo and Josefa Fajardo.
1900 Census lists birthdate as: May 1874.
Marriage to Paulita Quintana, church records show his birthdate as July 15, 1873.

More About ARON MONTOYA:
Fact 1: April 25, 1873, Baptized.

Children of ARON MONTOYA and BEATRIZ ROMERO are:
> i.   PAULITA[3] MONTOYA, b. June 12, 1900[4]; m. JOSÉ AMADO CRUZ, August 22, 1918.
>
> Notes for PAULITA MONTOYA:
> Marriage records state that she was born on July 10, 1901.
>
> ii.   DOROTEA MONTOYA, b. June 05, 1902[5]; m. LUPE CASTILLO, November 11, 1921.
> iii.   MANUEL MONTOYA, b. May 04, 1906, Spindle, New México; m. JUANITA BARRERA, August 26, 1931[6].
>
> Notes for MANUEL MONTOYA:
> Spindle is a town just north of Capítan, NM.
>
> iv.   ALTAGRACIA (GRACE) MONTOYA, b. May 07, 1909, San Patricio, Territory of New México; d. September 2006, San Patricio, New México; m. SAMUEL MOYA SÁNCHEZ, May 15, 1939, San Patricio, New México.

5. CATARINA[2] MONTOYA *(TRANQUELINO[1])* was born 1883, and died 1951. She married GREGORIO YBARRA January 22, 1896, son of MAXIMIANO YBARRA and ROBERTA RUIZ.

Children of CATARINA MONTOYA and GREGORIO YBARRA are:
> 14.   i.   PABLO[3] YBARRA, b. 1897.
> 15.   ii.   JULIANITA YBARRA, b. February 16, 1901; d. June 04, 1986.
>   iii.   GENOVEVO YBARRA, b. November 22, 1903; d. February 13, 1975; m. JUANITA SÁNCHEZ[7].
>
> Notes for GENOVEVO YBARRA:
> Raised Manuel Prudencio, son of Roberto Prudencio & Casimira Ybarra Prudencio.
> Buried at the San Ysidro Cemetary.
>
> Notes for JUANITA SÁNCHEZ:
> 1930 Census lists Juanita as a niece.
>
> 16.   iv.   CASIMIRA YBARRA, b. March 03, 1906; d. February 28, 1977.
> 17.   v.   LUCIA (LUCIANA) YBARRA, b. March 17, 1908, San Patricio, New México.
>   vi.   CRUSITA (CRUZ) YBARRA, b. May 03, 1910; m. MAX (MAXIMILIANO) SÁNCHEZ, October 08, 1932, San Patricio, New México.
>
> Marriage Notes for CRUSITA YBARRA and MAX SÁNCHEZ:
> Married by: Father James A. Brady.
>
> vii.   TRANQUELINO YBARRA, b. 1914; m. BESSIE APACHE.
> viii.   WILFREDO YBARRA, b. April 27, 1915; d. July 29, 1951.
>
> Notes for WILFREDO YBARRA:
> WW II veteran. Served with NM PVT 353 Infantry.
>
> ix.   CRECENCIA YBARRA, b. December 06, 1918, San Patricio, New México; m. MIGUEL GONZÁLES, May 24, 1935[8].
>
> Marriage Notes for CRECENCIA YBARRA and MIGUEL GONZÁLES:
> Married by: Justice of the Peace, John Mackey.

6. ELFIDA[2] MONTOYA *(TRANQUELINO*[1]*)* was born October 23, 1883. She married (1) NICOLÁS SILVA May 22, 1898, son of MANUEL SILVA and JOSEFITA ESQUIVEL. She married (2) MACARIO CHÁVEZ December 07, 1904, son of NAVOR CHÁVEZ and GREGORIA TRUJILLO.

More About ELFIDA MONTOYA:
Fact 1: November 30, 1833, Baptized.

Marriage Notes for ELFIDA MONTOYA and MACARIO CHÁVEZ:
Married by: Justice of the Peace Leopoldo Gonzáles

Children of ELFIDA MONTOYA and MACARIO CHÁVEZ are:
18.   i.   PEDRO[3] CHÁVEZ, b. October 23, 1903, Lincoln, New México.
        ii.   MARILLITA CHÁVEZ, m. JULIAN ROMERO Y TORRES.

7. DOROTEO[2] MONTOYA *(TRANQUELINO*[1]*)* was born February 06, 1886. He married ALBINA (VALVINA) SILVA[9] November 22, 1907, daughter of HILARIO SILVA and AMBROSIA ULIBARRÍ.

More About DOROTEO MONTOYA:
Fact 1: February 15, 1886, Baptized.

Children of DOROTEO MONTOYA and ALBINA SILVA are:
19.   i.   LORENSITA[3] MONTOYA, b. February 12, 1912; d. Artesia, New México.
        ii.   SAMUEL MONTOYA, b. 1909; d. 1994; m. EUFRACIA MONTOYA, November 26, 1938[10].
       iii.   COSME MONTOYA, m. AMALIA BENAVIDEZ.
       iv.   JOSEFITA MONTOYA, m. JUAN BACA.
        v.   TRANQUELINO SILVA MONTOYA, m. RUBY SAMORA.

8. ISABEL[2] MONTOYA *(TRANQUELINO*[1]*)* was born November 05, 1895. She married (1) JUAN GALLEGOS ULIBARRÍ May 13, 1889, son of SANTIAGO ULIBARRÍ and JUANA GALLEGOS. She married (2) LUÍS CASTILLO November 04, 1922, son of CRESENCIO CASTILLO and GERTRUDES SOTELA.

Marriage Notes for ISABEL MONTOYA and LUÍS CASTILLO:
Two different marriage dates found, November 04, 1922 and April 15, 1925.

Children of ISABEL MONTOYA and JUAN ULIBARRÍ are:
20.   i.   SARAFINA SOCORRO[3] ULIBARRÍ, b. 1869; d. Bef. August 21.
21.   ii.   VICENTE ULIBARRÍ, b. January 22, 1870.
22.   iii.   MARGARITA ULIBARRÍ.

Generation No. 3

9. MANUEL[3] MONTOYA *(ESTANISLADO (TANISLAUS)*[2]*, TRANQUELINO*[1]*)* was born 1888 in San Patricio, New México, and died Bef. September 1923. He married MARTINA PRUDENCIO October 01, 1911, daughter of JOSÉ PRUDENCIO and VICTORIA FAJARDO.

Children of MANUEL MONTOYA and MARTINA PRUDENCIO are:
        i.   JUANITA[4] MONTOYA.
        ii.   GILBERTO MONTOYA.
       iii.   LUÍS MONTOYA.
       iv.   FELIX MONTOYA.

10. PABLITA[3] MONTOYA *(ESTANISLADO (TANISLAUS)*[2]*, TRANQUELINO*[1]*)* was born May 02, 1890 in San Patricio, New México, and died March 31, 1952 in San Patricio, New México. She married JULIO (2ND) MIRANDA November 15, 1909, son of JULIO MIRANDA and ANTONIA MOLINA.

Marriage Notes for PABLITA MONTOYA and JULIO MIRANDA:
Married by Father Girma.

Children of PABLITA MONTOYA and JULIO MIRANDA are:

23.	i.	EULALIA (ULALIA)⁴ MIRANDA.
	ii.	FRANCISCA MIRANDA, m. ANTONIO HERRERA.
	iii.	CANDIDO MIRANDA.
	iv.	ENRIQUE MIRANDA.
	v.	CARLOS MIRANDA.
	vi.	VIRGINIA MIRANDA, m. ANSELMO SILVA.

11. TEODORO (THEODORO)³ MONTOYA *(ESTANISLADO (TANISLAUS)², TRANQUELINO¹)* was born January 1893 in San Patricio, New México[11]. He married BERSABE SÁNCHEZ December 11, 1919[12], daughter of JUAN SÁNCHEZ and MARÍA SÁNCHEZ.

More About TEODORO (THEODORO) MONTOYA:
Fact 1: June 18, 1893, Baptized.
Fact 2: April 18, 1919, WW I veteran. Discharged from Camp Owen Bierne, Texas.[13]

More About BERSABE SÁNCHEZ:
Fact 1: October 28, 1897, Baptized.

Child of TEODORO MONTOYA and BERSABE SÁNCHEZ is:
        i.   ALVESITA⁴ MONTOYA, m. CARLOS SÁNCHEZ.

12. SUSANA (SOCORRO)³ MONTOYA *(ESTANISLADO (TANISLAUS)², TRANQUELINO¹)* was born 1897 in San Patricio, New México. She married LORENSO MENDOSA September 13, 1915 in Lincoln, New México, son of DIONICIO MENDOSA and ROSENDA MONTOYA.

Notes for LORENSO MENDOSA:
Rosenda's son.

Children of SUSANA MONTOYA and LORENSO MENDOSA are:
        i.   CONSUELO⁴ MENDOSA, m. ERMINIO SÁNCHEZ.
        ii.   SOCORRO MENDOSA.
        iii.   BENJAMIN MENDOSA.
        iv.   DIONICIO (DENNIS) MENDOSA, m. ANA MAE SUTHERLAND.
        v.   ELISA MENDOSA, m. ISMAEL CHÁVEZ.
        vi.   PORFIRIO MENDOSA.
        vii.   ELOY MENDOSA.
        viii. ERNESTO MENDOSA.

13. SENAIDA³ MONTOYA *(ESTANISLADO (TANISLAUS)², TRANQUELINO¹)* was born May 19, 1907[14], and died July 10, 1944 in Roswell, New México[14]. She married EDUARDO BARCELON SÁNCHEZ October 08, 1920 in Carrizozo, New México, son of JUAN SÁNCHEZ and MARÍA SÁNCHEZ.

Children of SENAIDA MONTOYA and EDUARDO SÁNCHEZ are:
        i.   EDUARDO MONTOYA⁴ SÁNCHEZ, b. Abt. August 1921.

                More About EDUARDO MONTOYA SÁNCHEZ:
                Fact 1: July 03, 1943, WW II veteran. Discharged from Camp White, Oregon.[15]

        ii.   CONFERINA MONTOYA SÁNCHEZ, b. Private.
        iii.   ELFIDES SÁNCHEZ, b. Private.
        iv.   MACLOFA SÁNCHEZ, b. Private; m. ARISTEO HERRERA.
        v.   MAGGIE SÁNCHEZ, b. Private.
        vi.   MANUEL MONTOYA SÁNCHEZ, b. Private; m. FLORINDA CARABAJAL Y SÁNCHEZ.
        vii.   RAFAEL MONTOYA SÁNCHEZ, b. Private.
        viii. RUMELIO SÁNCHEZ, b. Private.

14. PABLO³ YBARRA *(CATARINA² MONTOYA, TRANQUELINO¹)* was born 1897. He married SOFIA ULIBARRÍ April 15, 1921 in San Patricio, New México, daughter of VICENTE ULIBARRÍ and MARÍA SEDILLO.

Marriage Notes for PABLO YBARRA and SOFIA ULIBARRÍ:

Married by: Reverand Gremond.

Child of PABLO YBARRA and SOFIA ULIBARRÍ is:
    i.   TIVORCIO (TIVE)⁴ YBARRA.

        Notes for TIVORCIO (TIVE) YBARRA:
        Raised by his grandmother, Catarina Montoya Ybarra.

15. JULIANITA³ YBARRA *(CATARINA² MONTOYA, TRANQUELINO¹)* was born February 16, 1901, and died June 04, 1986. She married JOSÉ PORTIO January 05, 1922, son of MANUELITA HERRERA.

More About JULIANITA YBARRA:
Fact 1: March 17, 1901, Baptized.

Notes for JOSÉ PORTIO:
Born at Gregorio Ybarra's farm.

More About JOSÉ PORTIO:
Fact 1: May 10, 1918, WW I veteran. Discharged from Camp Fremont, California.[16]

Children of JULIANITA YBARRA and JOSÉ PORTIO are:
    i.   RICARDO⁴ PORTIO, m. WANDA PAGE.

        Notes for RICARDO PORTIO:
        He was a WW II veteran.

    ii.   ARON PORTIO, m. ISABEL LUERAS.

        Notes for ARON PORTIO:
        He was a WW II veteran.

    iii.   MANUELITA PORTIO, m. RUBÉN PADILLA.

        Notes for RUBÉN PADILLA:
        He was a WW II veteran.

16. CASIMIRA³ YBARRA *(CATARINA² MONTOYA, TRANQUELINO¹)* was born March 03, 1906, and died February 28, 1977. She married ROBERTO PRUDENCIO July 03, 1929 in San Patricio, New México, son of DAMACIO PRUDENCIO and CLEOFAS MUÑOZ.

More About ROBERTO PRUDENCIO:
Fact 1: September 05, 1901, Baptized.

Marriage Notes for CASIMIRA YBARRA and ROBERTO PRUDENCIO:
Married by: Father Brugere.

Children of CASIMIRA YBARRA and ROBERTO PRUDENCIO are:
    i.   DAMACIO⁴ PRUDENCIO, b. Private.
    ii.   RAMON PRUDENCIO, b. Private.
    iii.   ONESIMO PRUDENCIO, b. Private.
    iv.   CLEOFAS PRUDENCIO, b. Private.

        Notes for CLEOFAS PRUDENCIO:
        Died young.

    v.   MANUEL PRUDENCIO, b. Private.

        Notes for MANUEL PRUDENCIO:
        Raised by Genovevo Ybarra & Juanita Sanchez Ybarra.
        Died young.

17. LUCIA (LUCIANA)³ YBARRA *(CATARINA² MONTOYA, TRANQUELINO¹)* was born March 17, 1908 in San Patricio, New México. She married SIGISFREDO ROMERO January 11, 1928, son of JORGE ROMERO and MARÍA GONZÁLES.

Notes for LUCIA (LUCIANA) YBARRA:
Padrinos: Augustín Laguna born in México City, and his wife, Juana María Laguna, born in Polvadera, New México

Children of LUCIA YBARRA and SIGISFREDO ROMERO are:
    i.   FLORIPE⁴ ROMERO, b. Private.
    ii.   FEDELINA ROMERO, b. Private.
    iii. CLEOFAS ROMERO, b. Private; m. JUAN SÁNCHEZ MONTES.
    iv. ISABEL ROMERO, b. Private.
    v.   RUBÉN ROMERO, b. Private.
    vi. EDUVIGEN ROMERO, b. Private.
    vii. LEONIRES ROMERO, b. Private.
    viii. FREDO ROMERO, b. Private.
    ix. REBECCA ROMERO, b. Private.

18. PEDRO³ CHÁVEZ *(ELFIDA² MONTOYA, TRANQUELINO¹)* was born October 23, 1903 in Lincoln, New México. He married LORENCITA (LORENSA) SILVA TRUJILLO June 13, 1930 in Carrizozo, New México, daughter of BONAFICIO TRUJILLO and LORENSA SILVA.

Notes for PEDRO CHÁVEZ:
Pedro was raised by his half sister's (Elfida Chavez) daughter, Marillita and her husband Julian Romero y Torres in Manzano, NM until he was 16 years old. He was re-united with his mother in Corona, NM.

Children of PEDRO CHÁVEZ and LORENCITA TRUJILLO are:
    i.   MACARIO TRUJILLO⁴ CHÁVEZ, m. TERESA GÓMEZ.
    ii.   RUFINA CHÁVEZ, m. SIGISFREDO MONTOYA.
    iii. ELFIDA TRUJILLO CHÁVEZ, b. Abt. 1884; m. NATIVIDAD PEÑA, June 15, 1921, Corona, New México.

        Marriage Notes for ELFIDA CHÁVEZ and NATIVIDAD PEÑA:
        Married by: Justice of the Peace Ed. Davidson.

    iv. RAYMOND CHÁVEZ.

19. LORENSITA³ MONTOYA *(DOROTEO², TRANQUELINO¹)* was born February 12, 1912, and died in Artesia, New México. She married (1) FERNANDO (FRED) SALSBERRY June 15, 1929 in Carrizozo, New Mexico, son of JAMES SALSBERRY and MANUELITA HERRERA. She married (2) CAMILO SEDILLO May 04, 1940, son of MARTÍN SEDILLO and TOMASA HERRERA.

Notes for LORENSITA MONTOYA:
Burial birthdate states she was born on August 09, 1914.

Notes for FERNANDO (FRED) SALSBERRY:
He died in an automobile accident in Hondo, New México.
Burried: San Patricio, New México.

Children of LORENSITA MONTOYA and FERNANDO SALSBERRY are:
    i.   ANATALIA⁴ SALSBERRY, b. Private; m. MANUEL SOSA.
    ii.   FERNANDO MONTOYA SALSBERRY, b. Private.
    iii. ELOY SALSBERRY, b. Private.

Children of LORENSITA MONTOYA and CAMILO SEDILLO are:
    iv. MARTÍN⁴ SEDILLO.
    v.   DELLA SEDILLO.
    vi. DANNY SEDILLO.
    vii. ELLIE SEDILLO.
    viii. CERINIA SEDILLO.

20. SARAFINA SOCORRO[3] ULIBARRÍ *(ISABEL[2] MONTOYA, TRANQUELINO[1])* was born 1869, and died Bef. August 21. She married ESTANISLADO (TANISLAUS) MONTOYA[17] January 09, 1887 in Carrizo, Territory of New México, son of TRANQUELINO MONTOYA and MARÍA TRUJILLO.

Children of SARAFINA ULIBARRÍ and ESTANISLADO MONTOYA are:

    i.   MANUEL[4] MONTOYA, b. 1888, San Patricio, New México; d. Bef. September 1923; m. MARTINA PRUDENCIO, October 01, 1911.

    ii.   PABLITA MONTOYA, b. May 02, 1890, San Patricio, New México; d. March 31, 1952, San Patricio, New México; m. JULIO (2ND) MIRANDA, November 15, 1909.

        Marriage Notes for PABLITA MONTOYA and JULIO MIRANDA:
        Married by Father Girma.

    iii.   TEODORO (THEODORO) MONTOYA, b. January 1893, San Patricio, New México[18]; m. BERSABE SÁNCHEZ, December 11, 1919[19].

        More About TEODORO (THEODORO) MONTOYA:
        Fact 1: June 18, 1893, Baptized.
        Fact 2: April 18, 1919, WW I veteran. Discharged from Camp Owen Bierne, Texas.[20]

        More About BERSABE SÁNCHEZ:
        Fact 1: October 28, 1897, Baptized.

    iv.   CANDIDO MONTOYA, b. 1895, San Patricio, New México.

    v.   SUSANA (SOCORRO) MONTOYA, b. 1897, San Patricio, New México; m. LORENSO MENDOSA, September 13, 1915, Lincoln, New México.

        Notes for LORENSO MENDOSA:
        Rosenda's son.

    vi.   ISABEL MONTOYA, b. December 29, 1899, San Patricio, New México; m. (1) CONCHA -----, El Paso, Texas; m. (2) VICTORIA SÁNCHEZ, February 23, 1921.

        More About VICTORIA SÁNCHEZ:
        Fact 1: August 03, 1899, Baptized.

    vii.   DESIDERIO MONTOYA, b. February 11, 1902; m. CATARINA SALAZAR, March 08, 1926.

    viii.   SENAIDA MONTOYA, b. May 19, 1907[21]; d. July 10, 1944, Roswell, New México[21]; m. EDUARDO BARCELON SÁNCHEZ, October 08, 1920, Carrizozo, New México.

21. VICENTE[3] ULIBARRÍ *(ISABEL[2] MONTOYA, TRANQUELINO[1])* was born January 22, 1870. He married MARÍA SARAFINA SEDILLO November 06, 1922, daughter of JUAN SEDILLO and JOSEFA FAJARDO.

More About MARÍA SARAFINA SEDILLO:
Fact 1: January 22, 1875, Baptized In Tularosa, Territory of New México

Children of VICENTE ULIBARRÍ and MARÍA SEDILLO are:

24.   i.   PETRA[4] ULIBARRÍ.
      ii.   DOMINGA ULIBARRÍ, b. October 02, 1910; d. June 13, 2001; m. PROFESO (PROCESO) SALCIDO.
25.   iii.   SOFIA ULIBARRÍ, b. 1905; d. October 16, 1941.
26.   iv.   EPIFANIO ULIBARRÍ, b. August 22, 1896, San Patricio, Territory of New México.
27.   v.   AUGUSTINA ULIBARRÍ, b. September 26, 1892; d. April 29, 1970.
      vi.   MARÍA ULIBARRÍ, m. JOSÉ CHÁVEZ, December 02, 1911.

22. MARGARITA[3] ULIBARRÍ *(ISABEL[2] MONTOYA, TRANQUELINO[1])*. She married FRANCISCO ARMERA October 14, 1911.

Child of MARGARITA ULIBARRÍ and FRANCISCO ARMERA is:

28.   i.   FRANCISCO ULIBARRÍ[4] ARMERA, d. December 04, 1927, San Patricio, New México.

Generation No. 4

23. EULALIA (ULALIA)⁴ MIRANDA *(PABLITA³ MONTOYA, ESTANISLADO (TANISLAUS)², TRANQUELINO¹).* She married JOSÉ HERRERA, son of LUÍS HERRERA and BENJAMIN HERNÁNDEZ.

Child of EULALIA MIRANDA and JOSÉ HERRERA is:
    i.   PABLITA⁵ HERRERA, m. BREZEL CHÁVEZ.

24. PETRA⁴ ULIBARRÍ *(VICENTE³, ISABEL² MONTOYA, TRANQUELINO¹).* She married DIEGO SALCIDO November 06, 1922, son of FAUSTINO SALCIDO and MARÍA CHÁVEZ.

Child of PETRA ULIBARRÍ and DIEGO SALCIDO is:
    i.   MONICA⁵ SALCIDO, m. ESTOLANO TRUJILLO SÁNCHEZ.

        More About ESTOLANO TRUJILLO SÁNCHEZ:
        Fact 1: December 21, 1943, WW II veteran. Navy, Discharged from San Diego, California.[22]

25. SOFIA⁴ ULIBARRÍ *(VICENTE³, ISABEL² MONTOYA, TRANQUELINO¹)* was born 1905, and died October 16, 1941. She married PABLO YBARRA April 15, 1921 in San Patricio, New México, son of GREGORIO YBARRA and CATARINA MONTOYA.

Marriage Notes for SOFIA ULIBARRÍ and PABLO YBARRA:
Married by: Reverand Gremond.

Child of SOFIA ULIBARRÍ and PABLO YBARRA is:
    i.   TIVORCIO (TIVE)⁵ YBARRA.

        Notes for TIVORCIO (TIVE) YBARRA:
        Raised by his grandmother, Catarina Montoya Ybarra.

26. EPIFANIO⁴ ULIBARRÍ *(VICENTE³, ISABEL² MONTOYA, TRANQUELINO¹)* was born August 22, 1896 in San Patricio, Territory of New México. He married ERMINDA CHÁVEZ November 04, 1915 in Lincoln, New México[23], daughter of RICARDO CHÁVEZ and ESLINDA GONZÁLES.

More About ERMINDA CHÁVEZ:
Fact 1: July 20, 1894, Baptized.

Marriage Notes for EPIFANIO ULIBARRÍ and ERMINDA CHÁVEZ:
Padrinos: Florencio Gonzáles, Raymundo Sánchez, Augustín Ulibarrí.

Child of EPIFANIO ULIBARRÍ and ERMINDA CHÁVEZ is:
    i.   DIEGO⁵ ULIBARRÍ.

27. AUGUSTINA⁴ ULIBARRÍ *(VICENTE³, ISABEL² MONTOYA, TRANQUELINO¹)* was born September 26, 1892, and died April 29, 1970. She married RAYMUNDO SÁNCHEZ[24] December 17, 1910[25], son of JUAN SÁNCHEZ and MARÍA SÁNCHEZ.

Marriage Notes for AUGUSTINA ULIBARRÍ and RAYMUNDO SÁNCHEZ:
Padrinos: Cosme Sedillos and daughter.

Children of AUGUSTINA ULIBARRÍ and RAYMUNDO SÁNCHEZ are:
    i.   EULALIA⁵ SÁNCHEZ, b. 1913; m. PERFECTO SÁNCHEZ.
    ii.   BENNIE SÁNCHEZ, b. July 26, 1914; m. NICOLÁS TORRES.
    iii. SOFIA SÁNCHEZ, b. 1917.
    iv. ANEDA ULIBARRÍ SÁNCHEZ, b. 1919; m. HERMANDO (ERMANDO) CHÁVEZ[26].
    v.   OLYMPIA SÁNCHEZ, b. 1920; m. EPUNUCENO SÁNCHEZ.
    vi. LUÍS SÁNCHEZ, b. 1928.

28. FRANCISCO ULIBARRÍ[4] ARMERA *(MARGARITA[3] ULIBARRÍ, ISABEL[2] MONTOYA, TRANQUELINO[1])* died December 04, 1927 in San Patricio, New México. He married IGNACIA MONTES August 28, 1901, daughter of ALEJO MONTES and ANGELA SÁNCHEZ.

Notes for FRANCISCO ULIBARRÍ ARMERA:
Buried: Old San Patricio cemetery.

Children of FRANCISCO ARMERA and IGNACIA MONTES are:
   i.   ERMINIA[5] ARMERA, m. SERAPIO NUÑEZ.
   ii. ROMATILDA ARMERA, m. JUAN CHÁVEZ.

Endnotes

1. *LDS Historical Library, Alamogordo*, Microfiche # 756, Page 144.
2. 1910 Census Lincoln County, Page 2B, San Patricio, Lists all children born before 1910.
3. 1910 Census Lincoln County, Page 3A, San Patricio, Lists all children born before 1910.
4. *LDS Historical Library, Alamogordo*, Microfiche #754, Page 72.
5. *LDS Historical Library, Alamogordo*, Microfiche # 754, Page 130.
6. *LDS Historical Library, Alamogordo*, Microfiche # 756, Page 5.
7. 1930 Census Lincoln County, Page 2B, Ruidoso, Lists as a niece.
8. *Lincoln County Clerk, Book of Marriages.*
9. *LDS Historical Library, Alamogordo*, Page 67, Fiche # 0017008.
10. *LDS Historical Library, Alamogordo*, Microfiche #756-25, Page 5.
11. *LDS Historical Library, Alamogordo*, Page 195, Fiche # 754.
12. *Lincoln County Clerk, Book of Marriages*, Page 41, Book 5.
13. Lincoln County Clerk, Soldiers Discharge Book, Page 166, Book 1, Lists date of birth.
14. 1930 Census Lincoln County.
15. Lincoln County Clerk, Soldiers Discharge Book, Page 109, Book 3, Lists date of birth.
16. Lincoln County Clerk, Soldiers Discharge Book, Page 13, Book 1.
17. 1910 Census Lincoln County, Page 2B, San Patricio, Lists all children born before 1910.
18. *LDS Historical Library, Alamogordo*, Page 195, Fiche # 754.
19. *Lincoln County Clerk, Book of Marriages*, Page 41, Book 5.
20. Lincoln County Clerk, Soldiers Discharge Book, Page 166, Book 1, Lists date of birth.
21. 1930 Census Lincoln County.
22. Lincoln County Clerk, Soldiers Discharge Book, Page 158, Book 3, Lists date of birth.
23. *Lincoln County Clerk, Book of Marriages*, Page 229, Book 4, Lists birth dates and marriage date for the bride and groom.
24. *Lincoln County Clerk, Book of Marriages*, Page 352, Book 3, List birthdate and marriage date for the bride and groom.
25. *LDS Historical Library, Alamogordo*, Reel # 756, Page 16.
26. *Lincoln County Clerk, Book of Marriages*, Page 615, Lists birthdate and marriage date for both the bride and groom.

Descendants of Francisco Pacheco

Generation No. 1

1. MANUEL ANTONIO[1] PACHECO was born Abt. 1793. He married PETRA DOMINGA SILVA.

Child of MANUEL PACHECO and PETRA SILVA is:
2.   i.   FRANCISCO[2] PACHECO, b. Abt. 1824; d. February 02, 1892; Stepchild.

Generation No. 2

2. FRANCISCO[2] PACHECO *(MANUEL ANTONIO[1])* was born Abt. 1824, and died February 02, 1892. He married ROMULA ISABELLA SAVEDRA, daughter of JOSÉ SAAVEDRA and ANA GALLEGOS.

Notes for FRANCISCO PACHECO:
His natural father's name was Silva. When his mother re-married, he took on his step-father's name.

Notes for ROMULA ISABELLA SAVEDRA:
Said to be of an unknown Native American tribe, most likely an Apache.

Children of FRANCISCO PACHECO and ROMULA SAVEDRA are:
     i.   NICOLÁSA[3] PACHECO, m. FRANCISCO SEDILLO, July 21, 1871.
     ii.   PROCOPIO PACHECO, m. PIADAD LÓPEZ.
3.   iii.   CORNELIA PACHECO, b. Abt. 1850.
4.   iv.   ANSELMO PACHECO, b. July 1850, Polvadera, Territory of New México; d. Arabela, New México.

Generation No. 3

3. CORNELIA[3] PACHECO *(FRANCISCO[2], MANUEL ANTONIO[1])* was born Abt. 1850. She married ESTOLANO SÁNCHEZ[1] July 21, 1871 in La Plaza del Rio Bonito, Territory of New México[2], son of MAURICIO SÁNCHEZ and MARÍA GONZÁLES.

Notes for ESTOLANO SÁNCHEZ:
1900 US Census lists Estolano and family as living in Reventon, New México.

Children of CORNELIA PACHECO and ESTOLANO SÁNCHEZ are:
5.   i.   FELIPÉ E.[4] SÁNCHEZ, b. January 20, 1874, Placita del Rio Bonito, (Lincoln) New México; d. January 15, 1959, El Paso, Téxas.
6.   ii.   ELUTICIA GAVALDON (LUTISIA) SÁNCHEZ, b. 1875.
     iii.   VALENTÍN (BALENTÍN) SÁNCHEZ, b. April 14, 1881.
7.   iv.   PRESILIANO SÁNCHEZ, b. December 02, 1883, Lincoln, Territory of New México.
8.   v.   AURELIO (AVRELIO) SÁNCHEZ, b. March 12, 1885, Ruidoso, Territory of New México.
9.   vi.   CELIA SÁNCHEZ, b. July 12, 1888, Reventón, Territory of New México.
10.   vii.   ESTOLANO PACHECO SÁNCHEZ, b. 1891.
11.   viii.   ROSARIO SÁNCHEZ, b. August 11, 1896, Reventón,Territory of New México.

4. ANSELMO[3] PACHECO *(FRANCISCO[2], MANUEL ANTONIO[1])* was born July 1850 in Polvadera, Territory of New México, and died in Arabela, New México. He married (1) TERESITA GALLEGOS February 13, 1874. He married (2) ALICE TRAMPTON May 11, 1912 in Lincoln, New México. He married (3) REYES F. SISNEROS September 05, 1919. He married (4) INEZ LUCERO June 26, 1920.

Notes for ANSELMO PACHECO:
1920: Census lists as living in Las Palas.

Children of ANSELMO PACHECO and TERESITA GALLEGOS are:
     i.   ADELIA[4] PACHECO, b. Abt. 1876; m. APOLONIO LUCERO.
     ii.   LEOPOLDO PACHECO, b. Abt. 1878; m. FELISITA LUJÁN, August 15, 1900.

12.   iii.   ROMÁN PACHECO, b. May 16, 1884.
         iv.   DOMINGA PACHECO, b. September 1888; m. JOSÉ CANDELARIA, March 29, 1906.

Children of ANSELMO PACHECO and INEZ LUCERO are:
         v.   ELIZABETH[4] RUE, b. Abt. 1907; Stepchild; m. FERMÍN MARTÍNEZ.

                  Notes for ELIZABETH RUE:
                  Natural father was A. H. Rue.

         vi.   DUDLEY RUE, b. Abt. 1909; Stepchild.

                  Notes for DUDLEY RUE:
                  Natural father was A. H. Rue.

         vii.   CIDRIC RUE, b. Abt. 1911; Stepchild.

                  Notes for CIDRIC RUE:
                  Natural father was A. H. Rue.

         viii.   GEORGE RUE, b. Abt. 1914; Stepchild.

                  Notes for GEORGE RUE:
                  Natural father was A. H. Rue.

Generation No. 4

5. FELIPÉ E.[4] SÁNCHEZ *(CORNELIA[3] PACHECO, FRANCISCO[2], MANUEL ANTONIO[1])* was born January 20, 1874 in Placita del Rio Bonito, (Lincoln) New México[3], and died January 15, 1959 in El Paso, Téxas[4]. He married CANDELARIA PADILLA, daughter of ANDALESIO PADILLA and PAUBLITA MARIÑO.

Notes for FELIPÉ E. SÁNCHEZ:
Ranched on the Río Ruidoso and Reventón.
Migrated to San Elizario, Téxas
Migrated back to Tularosa, New México.

More About FELIPÉ E. SÁNCHEZ:
Fact 1: January 21, 1874, Baptized.[5]

Children of FELIPÉ SÁNCHEZ and CANDELARIA PADILLA are:
13.   i.   ANTONIO[5] SÁNCHEZ, b. May 13, 1897, Tres Ritos, New México; d. February 21, 1984, San Elizario, Texas.
14.   ii.   PAUBLITA (PABLITA) SÁNCHEZ, b. July 30, 1898, Tres Rios, Territory of New México; d. October 13, 1963, Las Vegas, New México.
         iii.   SIPIO SÁNCHEZ, b. 1899; m. LOLA MIRABAL.
15.   iv.   CORNELIA SÁNCHEZ, b. November 16, 1902, Lincoln County, New México.
16.   v.   EMILIANO SÁNCHEZ, b. August 11, 1904, Hondo, Territory of New México.
17.   vi.   ABRAHAM (ABRAN) SÁNCHEZ, b. December 21, 1905, White Oaks, Territory of New México; d. November 18, 1973, El Paso, Téxas.
18.   vii.   REYNALDO SÁNCHEZ, b. Abt. 1906.
         viii.   CELEDONIA SÁNCHEZ, b. Abt. 1909; d. Abt. 1921.

                  Notes for CELEDONIA SÁNCHEZ:
                  Died when she was 12 years old.

19.   ix.   ONECIMO SÁNCHEZ, b. 1915.
20.   x.   BENITO SÁNCHEZ, b. Private.

6. ELUTICIA GAVALDON (LUTISIA)[4] SÁNCHEZ *(CORNELIA[3] PACHECO, FRANCISCO[2], MANUEL ANTONIO[1])[6]* was born 1875. She married (1) ERINELLO FRANCISCO (ERINEO) GAVALDON[7], son of ENCARNACION GAVALDON and ANTONIA DE GAVALDON. She married (2) AUGUSTÍN MIRANDA CHÁVEZ April 12, 1901[8], son of DIONICIA MIRANDA.

Notes for ELUTICIA GAVALDON (LUTISIA) SÁNCHEZ:
1900 Census: Eluticia and her children were living with her parents.

Notes for ERINELLO FRANCISCO (ERINEO) GAVALDON:
1880 Census lists that he lived in Torreón, Valencia County, New México.

Notes for AUGUSTÍN MIRANDA CHÁVEZ:
Had a brother, Rafael Chávez, the son of Maximiano Chávez.

June 28, 1910 to December 19, 1914 and March 2, 1921 to December 7, 1922: Was the Post Master for the Reventón Post Office.

Children of ELUTICIA SÁNCHEZ and ERINELLO GAVALDON are:
  i.   ROSA[5] GAVALDON, b. 1891; m. AVRELIO MARTÍNEZ, December 12, 1910, Patos, New México[9].

        Notes for AVRELIO MARTÍNEZ:
        Raised by Leandro Pacheco.

        Marriage Notes for ROSA GAVALDON and AVRELIO MARTÍNEZ:
        Married at Nuestra Señora de Guadalupe Church in Patos, New México.
        Married by: Father Girma.

  ii.   AVRORA GAVALDON, b. 1895[10]; m. NARCISO MONTOYA[11,12].
  iii. LUPE GAVALDON, b. August 20, 1897, Patos, Territory of New México[13]; m. ELVIRA MÁRQUES, August 13, 1921[14].

        Notes for LUPE GAVALDON:
        Patos, New México is located close to Reventón, New México east of Sierra Capitán. Currently it is inaccesible because it is located on a private farm.

        More About LUPE GAVALDON:
        Fact 1: December 12, 1897, Baptized.

7. PRESILIANO[4] SÁNCHEZ *(CORNELIA[3] PACHECO, FRANCISCO[2], MANUEL ANTONIO[1])*[15] was born December 02, 1883 in Lincoln, Territory of New México. He married (1) LUPITA OROSCO. He married (2) GUADALUPE (LUPITA) MARTÍNEZ October 12, 1905 in Reventón, Territory of New México[16], daughter of ANTONIO MARTÍNEZ and JUANA GUSTAMANTE.

More About PRESILIANO SÁNCHEZ:
Fact 1: September 12, 1896, Church records show that he was in Reventon at the time.

Children of PRESILIANO SÁNCHEZ and LUPITA OROSCO are:
  i.   FIDEL[5] SÁNCHEZ, m. AMALIA TORRES.
  ii.   FERNANDO SÁNCHEZ, m. JOSEFITA TRUJILLO, December 11, 1937[17].
  iii. ESTOLANO OROSCO SÁNCHEZ, m. (1) EMMA PINO; m. (2) UTILIA (EUTILIA) MONTOYA.

Child of PRESILIANO SÁNCHEZ and GUADALUPE MARTÍNEZ is:
  iv.   CORA[5] SÁNCHEZ.

8. AURELIO (AVRELIO)[4] SÁNCHEZ *(CORNELIA[3] PACHECO, FRANCISCO[2], MANUEL ANTONIO[1])*[18] was born March 12, 1885 in Ruidoso, Territory of New México. He married ANASTACIA ARAGÓN[19] October 11, 1907 in Reventón, Territory of New México, daughter of MANUEL ARAGÓN and PORFIRIA GONZÁLES.

More About AURELIO (AVRELIO) SÁNCHEZ:
Fact 1: September 12, 1896, Chgurch records show that he was in Reventon at the time.

Children of AURELIO SÁNCHEZ and ANASTACIA ARAGÓN are:
  i.   EDUARDO (EDWARD)[5] SÁNCHEZ, m. BONNIE -----.
  ii.   IDALIA SÁNCHEZ, m. PETROLINO SEDILLOS[20], February 22, 1926.
  iii. SANTANA SÁNCHEZ, m. MAX CHÁVEZ[21], Reventón, New México.

iv.   EDUMENIO SÁNCHEZ, b. 1916; m. SERIA SÁNCHEZ.
21.   v.   SORAIDA SÁNCHEZ, b. August 27, 1916.
vi.   MACRINA SÁNCHEZ, b. 1920; m. ANDRÉS RICHARDSON.
vii. VICENTE SÁNCHEZ, b. 1922; m. LUISA SALSBERRY.
viii. CLOVIS SÁNCHEZ, b. May 17, 1923, San Patricio, New México; m. CARLOTA PIÑEDA.

More About CLOVIS SÁNCHEZ:
Fact 1: September 07, 1943, WW II veteran. Navy, Discharged from San Diego, California.[22]

ix. BALDAMAR SÁNCHEZ, b. 1924; m. MARGARETTE PENDLEY.
x.   PRESILIANO SÁNCHEZ, b. 1926; m. CECILIA ROMERO.
xi. LUCY SÁNCHEZ, b. 1930; m. ALBERT TELLES.

9. CELIA[4] SÁNCHEZ *(CORNELIA[3] PACHECO, FRANCISCO[2], MANUEL ANTONIO[1])*[23] was born July 12, 1888 in Reventón, Territory of New México. She married JORGE (GEORGE) TORREZ[24] November 12, 1906, son of IGNACIO TORRES and MANUELA LUCERO.

Children of CELIA SÁNCHEZ and JORGE TORREZ are:
i.   ADENAGO[5] TORREZ, b. 1908, Hondo, New México; m. (1) BEATRIZ VIGIL; m. (2) BEATRIZ TORREZ.
ii.   FELIS TORREZ, b. 1909; m. PEDRO SALCIDO, October 24, 1928[25].
iii. GEORGE SÁNCHEZ TORREZ, b. 1911.
iv.   WILFIDO TORREZ, b. 1913; m. JULIA -----.
v.   MIGUEL TORREZ, b. 1917; m. SOCORRO -----.
vi.   MANUELITA TORREZ, b. 1919; m. JUAN JAURIQUE.
vii. JAY TORREZ, b. Aft. 1920; m. EDNA -----.
viii. LORINA TORREZ, b. Aft. 1920; m. ERNESTO OTERO.
ix.   PRESCILIA TORREZ, b. Aft. 1920; m. ERNESTO LÓPEZ.

10. ESTOLANO PACHECO[4] SÁNCHEZ *(CORNELIA[3] PACHECO, FRANCISCO[2], MANUEL ANTONIO[1])* was born 1891. He married (1) ELENA CHÁVEZ, daughter of RAFAEL CHÁVEZ and MARTINA MAÉS. He married (2) BARBARITA TORREZ February 28, 1910, daughter of CRECENCIO TORREZ and MIQUELA MIRANDA.

Children of ESTOLANO SÁNCHEZ and BARBARITA TORREZ are:
i.   AMANDA[5] SÁNCHEZ.
ii.   AMABLE SÁNCHEZ.
iii. FERMÍN SÁNCHEZ, b. October 11, 1915.
iv.   EULALIO (LALO) SÁNCHEZ.

11. ROSARIO[4] SÁNCHEZ *(CORNELIA[3] PACHECO, FRANCISCO[2], MANUEL ANTONIO[1])* was born August 11, 1896 in Reventón,Territory of New México[26]. She married WILLIAM LUCERO BRADY[27] February 19, 1912[28], son of ROBERT BRADY and MANUELA LUCERO.

More About ROSARIO SÁNCHEZ:
Fact 1: September 12, 1896, Baptized.

More About WILLIAM LUCERO BRADY:
Fact 1: March 22, 1892

Marriage Notes for ROSARIO SÁNCHEZ and WILLIAM BRADY:
Rosario's mother, Cornelia gave consent for this marriage.

Children of ROSARIO SÁNCHEZ and WILLIAM BRADY are:
i.   MAX[5] BRADY.
ii.   ORLINDA BRADY, m. ANDREW FRESQUEZ.
iii. BARTOLA BRADY.
iv.   WILLIAM SÁNCHEZ BRADY, m. ORALIA HERRERA.
v.   PRESTINA BRADY.
vi.   LEROY BENNETT BRADY.
vii. BILLY JOE BRADY, b. Private; m. PATSY SALCIDO.
viii. ERMILO BRADY.
ix.   ELMO BRADY, m. JERRY KIMBRELL.

12. ROMÁN[4] PACHECO *(ANSELMO[3], FRANCISCO[2], MANUEL ANTONIO[1])* was born May 16, 1884. He married (1) BONNIE RICHARDSON September 29, 1904, daughter of ANDRÉS RICHARDSON and BENIGNA LUCERO. He married (2) EMILIA GONZÁLES November 02, 1924. He married (3) MARÍA DE JESÚS ARCHULETA May 07, 1927 in Lincoln, New México, daughter of JUAN ARCHULETA.

Notes for ROMÁN PACHECO:
1910: Census lists Román as living in Agua Azul.

Children of ROMÁN PACHECO and BONNIE RICHARDSON are:
22.	i.	FERMÍN[5] PACHECO, b. Abt. 1906.
	ii.	FERNANDO PACHECO, b. Abt. 1906; m. LUCIA GÓMEZ, August 07, 1937.
	iii.	CARLOS PACHECO, b. Abt. 1910.

Generation No. 5

13. ANTONIO[5] SÁNCHEZ *(FELIPÉ E.[4], CORNELIA[3] PACHECO, FRANCISCO[2], MANUEL ANTONIO[1])* was born May 13, 1897 in Tres Ritos, New México, and died February 21, 1984 in San Elizario, Texas[29]. He married (1) MARTINA SALSBERRY October 30, 1915 in Lincoln, Territory of New México[30], daughter of JAMES SALSBERRY and MANUELITA HERRERA. He married (2) JUANITA CABALLERO ALVARADO Aft. December 1917.

Notes for MARTINA SALSBERRY:
She died 8 days after giving birth to a child. Her child also died during birth.
Buried: San Ysidro church cemetary.

Marriage Notes for ANTONIO SÁNCHEZ and MARTINA SALSBERRY:
Married in La Capilla de San Ysidro. James Salsberry, Manuelita Herrera de Salsberry, Felipe Sánchez and Candelaria Padilla de Sánchez gave consent to the marriage.

Children of ANTONIO SÁNCHEZ and JUANITA ALVARADO are:
i.	PAUBLINA[6] SÁNCHEZ.
ii.	CECILIA ALVARADO SÁNCHEZ.
iii.	ELISA SÁNCHEZ.
iv.	LUISA SÁNCHEZ.
v.	TONY SÁNCHEZ, b. Private.
vi.	EFRIN SÁNCHEZ.
vii.	SAMUEL SÁNCHEZ, b. Private.
viii.	LUCILA SÁNCHEZ.
ix.	DAVÍD SÁNCHEZ.
x.	RUFINA SÁNCHEZ.
xi.	BENJAMIN SÁNCHEZ, b. Private.
xii.	EILEEN MARTÍNEZ SÁNCHEZ, b. Private.
xiii.	RAY MARTÍNEZ SÁNCHEZ, b. Private.

14. PAUBLITA (PABLITA)[5] SÁNCHEZ *(FELIPÉ E.[4], CORNELIA[3] PACHECO, FRANCISCO[2], MANUEL ANTONIO[1])* was born July 30, 1898 in Tres Rios, Territory of New México, and died October 13, 1963 in Las Vegas, New México. She married YSIDRO CHÁVEZ[31] August 04, 1913 in Lincoln, New México, son of ROBERTO CHÁVEZ and LUCIA WELDON.

Notes for PAUBLITA (PABLITA) SÁNCHEZ:
Buried: San Patricio, New México.

More About PAUBLITA (PABLITA) SÁNCHEZ:
Fact 1: October 15, 1898, Baptized in Patos Territory of New México.

Notes for YSIDRO CHÁVEZ:
Buried: La Capilla de San Patricio.

More About YSIDRO CHÁVEZ:
Fact 1: May 06, 1892, Baptized.

Marriage Notes for PAUBLITA SÁNCHEZ and YSIDRO CHÁVEZ:
Married by: Father J.H. Girma in La Capilla de San Juan Bautista. Felipe E. Sánchez gave consent to the marriage. Padrinos: Avrora Gavaldon and Antonio Sánchez.

Children of PAUBLITA SÁNCHEZ and YSIDRO CHÁVEZ are:

     i.   ORALIA⁶ CHÁVEZ, b. San Patricio, New México; d. San Patricio, New México.

          Notes for ORALIA CHÁVEZ:
          Died young.

     ii.   SIPIO CHÁVEZ, b. San Patricio, New México; d. San Patricio, New México.

          Notes for SIPIO CHÁVEZ:
          Died young.

     iii. GRESELDA CHÁVEZ, b. May 13, 1914, San Patricio, New México; d. June 09, 1988, Ruidoso, New México; m. FRANCISCO (FRANK) GÓMEZ, February 17, 1934.

          Notes for GRESELDA CHÁVEZ:
          Buried: San Patricio, New México.

     iv. AMARANTE (JACK) CHÁVEZ, b. November 09, 1915, San Patricio, New México; d. Alburquerque, New México; m. DOLORES (LOLA) ROMERO ARCHULETA, September 21, 1936, San Patricio, New México.

          Notes for DOLORES (LOLA) ROMERO ARCHULETA:
          Buried: San Patricio, New México.

     v.   SENON CHÁVEZ, b. March 03, 1917, San Patricio, New México; d. San Patricio, New México.

          Notes for SENON CHÁVEZ:
          WW II veteran, Darby's Rangers, Third battalion. The Battle of Anzio-Cisterna. He was a POW.
          Cremated, Ashes spread on the mountain behind the old Chávez house in San Patricio.

23.   vi. IGNACIA (INES) CHÁVEZ, b. January 23, 1919, San Patricio, New México.
       vii. ADELITA (DELLA) CHÁVEZ, b. July 04, 1920, San Patricio, New México; m. (1) SANTIAGO (JIMMY) LARIOSA; m. (2) GUILLERMO QUIZON; m. (3) MANUEL GÓMEZ.
24.   viii. EMILIANO CHÁVEZ, b. January 11, 1922, San Patricio, New México; d. January 23, 1953, California.
       ix. EFRAÍN CHÁVEZ, b. January 01, 1926, San Patricio, New México; m. LILLIAN MILLER.

          Notes for EFRAÍN CHÁVEZ:
          WW II veteran.
          Died, date unknown.

          More About EFRAÍN CHÁVEZ:
          Fact 1: February 09, 1926, Baptized.

25.   x.   LUVÍN CHÁVEZ, b. November 15, 1929, San Patricio, New México.
26.   xi. ORALIA CHÁVEZ, b. February 18, 1931, San Patricio, New México.
       xii. ONOFRÉ (HUMPHREY) CHÁVEZ, b. August 06, 1932, San Patricio, New México; m. VANGIE -----.

          Notes for ONOFRÉ (HUMPHREY) CHÁVEZ:
          Navy veteran.

      xiii. JOSIE (JOSEPHINE) CHÁVEZ, b. May 18, 1934, San Patricio, New México; m. BENITO HERRERA.
      xiv. MELVIN CHÁVEZ, b. November 06, 1937, San Patricio, New México; m. (1) LORENA ROMERO; m. (2) PRESCILLA GUTIERREZ.
       xv. RAMONA CHÁVEZ, b. April 11, 1939, San Patricio, New México; m. LARRY NUNEZ.
      xvi. DANNY CHÁVEZ, b. December 13, 1940, San Patricio, New México; m. (1) VANGIE MONTES; m. (2) CRUCITA BACA.
     xvii. RAY MARTÍNEZ, b. September 11, 1946.

Notes for RAY MARTÍNEZ:
Was raised by Ysidro and Pablita.

xviii. EILEEN MARTÍNEZ, b. September 25,1947.

Notes for EILEEN MARTÍNEZ:
Was raised by Ysidro and Pablita.

15. CORNELIA⁵ SÁNCHEZ *(FELIPÉ E.⁴, CORNELIA³ PACHECO, FRANCISCO², MANUEL ANTONIO¹)* was born November 16, 1902 in Lincoln County, New México. She married ALFONSO BORREGO, son of ELIJIO BORREGO and FRANCISCA ARIAS.

More About ALFONSO BORREGO:
Fact 1: WW I veteran.

Children of CORNELIA SÁNCHEZ and ALFONSO BORREGO are:
- i. MARIA LYDIA⁶ BORREGO, b. Private.
- ii. LORENZO BORREGO.
- iii. LUIS FILIMON BORREGO.
- iv. RAÚL BORREGO, b. Private.
- v. JOSEPHINA BORREGO, b. Private.
- vi. PEDRO BORREGO.
- vii. ALFONSO (2ND) BORREGO.
- viii. JOE BORREGO.
- ix. MIKE NOMAN BORREGO, b. Private.
- x. TERESA BORREGO, b. Private.
- xi. RAMÓN BORREGO, b. Private.

16. EMILIANO⁵ SÁNCHEZ *(FELIPÉ E.⁴, CORNELIA³ PACHECO, FRANCISCO², MANUEL ANTONIO¹)* was born August 11, 1904 in Hondo, Territory of New México. He married RUBY MARTÍNEZ.

Children of EMILIANO SÁNCHEZ and RUBY MARTÍNEZ are:
- i. EMILIANO JUNIOR⁶ SÁNCHEZ, b. 1927.
- ii. BERNICE SÁNCHEZ, b. Private.
- iii. GLORIA SÁNCHEZ, b. Private.
- iv. LEROY SÁNCHEZ, b. Private.
- v. TERESA SÁNCHEZ, b. Private.
- vi. VIOLA SÁNCHEZ, b. Private.

17. ABRAHAM (ABRAN)⁵ SÁNCHEZ *(FELIPÉ E.⁴, CORNELIA³ PACHECO, FRANCISCO², MANUEL ANTONIO¹)* was born December 21, 1905 in White Oaks, Territory of New México, and died November 18, 1973 in El Paso, Téxas. He married (1) FELIPA RODRÍQUES. He married (2) RAMONSITA GURULÉ.

Notes for ABRAHAM (ABRAN) SÁNCHEZ:
Buried: Carrizozo, New México.

Children of ABRAHAM SÁNCHEZ and FELIPA RODRÍQUES are:
- i. FRANK RODRÍQUES⁶ SÁNCHEZ.
- ii. MARÍA MAGDALENA SÁNCHEZ.
- iii. DAVÍD RODRÍQUES SÁNCHEZ.
- iv. FREDRICK SÁNCHEZ.

Children of ABRAHAM SÁNCHEZ and RAMONSITA GURULÉ are:
- v. PAUBLITA GURULÉ⁶ SÁNCHEZ.
- vi. GEORGE SÁNCHEZ, b. Private.
- vii. RAYNEL SÁNCHEZ, b. Private.
- viii. HERMAN SÁNCHEZ.
- ix. RITA GURULÉ SÁNCHEZ, b. Private.
- x. ROSYLENE SÁNCHEZ, b. Private.
- xi. JOHN GURULÉ SÁNCHEZ, b. Private.

18. REYNALDO[5] SÁNCHEZ *(FELIPÉ E.[4], CORNELIA[3] PACHECO, FRANCISCO[2], MANUEL ANTONIO[1])* was born Abt. 1906. He married SOFIA AGUILAR November 10, 1932.

Children of REYNALDO SÁNCHEZ and SOFIA AGUILAR are:
- i. MARY LILY[6] SÁNCHEZ.
- ii. MABEL SÁNCHEZ.
- iii. JO ANN SÁNCHEZ.

19. ONECIMO[5] SÁNCHEZ *(FELIPÉ E.[4], CORNELIA[3] PACHECO, FRANCISCO[2], MANUEL ANTONIO[1])* was born 1915. He married CLEOTILDE DURÁN, daughter of FRANCISCO DURÁN and HORTENCIA MONTES.

Children of ONECIMO SÁNCHEZ and CLEOTILDE DURÁN are:
- i. YOLANDA[6] SÁNCHEZ, b. Private.
- ii. MAXIMO SÁNCHEZ, b. Private.
- iii. MARY LOU SÁNCHEZ, b. Private.
- iv. DARLENE SÁNCHEZ, b. Private.
- v. HECTOR SÁNCHEZ, b. Private.
- vi. LINDA SÁNCHEZ, b. Private.
- vii. ALEX SÁNCHEZ, b. Private.
- viii. CYNTHIA SÁNCHEZ, b. Private.

20. BENITO[5] SÁNCHEZ *(FELIPÉ E.[4], CORNELIA[3] PACHECO, FRANCISCO[2], MANUEL ANTONIO[1])* was born Private. He married (1) CONCHA RAMÍREZ. He married (2) BEATRICE PINO May 09, 1932 in Tularosa, New México[32].

Children of BENITO SÁNCHEZ and CONCHA RAMÍREZ are:
- i. HOPE[6] SÁNCHEZ.
- ii. ISABEL SÁNCHEZ.
- iii. BENNY SÁNCHEZ.

Children of BENITO SÁNCHEZ and BEATRICE PINO are:
- iv. MARY ALICE[6] SÁNCHEZ.
- v. MARGIE SÁNCHEZ.
- vi. GRACE SÁNCHEZ.
- vii. RAY SÁNCHEZ.

21. SORAIDA[5] SÁNCHEZ *(AURELIO (AVRELIO)[4], CORNELIA[3] PACHECO, FRANCISCO[2], MANUEL ANTONIO[1])* was born August 27, 1916. She married MAXIMILIANO SÁNCHEZ February 11, 1936[33], son of MAURICIO SÁNCHEZ and DELFINIA ROMERO.

More About MAXIMILIANO SÁNCHEZ:
Fact 1: January 05, 1945, WW II veteran. Discharged from Indiana Town Gap, Pennsylvania.[34]

Marriage Notes for SORAIDA SÁNCHEZ and MAXIMILIANO SÁNCHEZ:
Married by: Justice of the Peace, Elerdo Cháves.

Children of SORAIDA SÁNCHEZ and MAXIMILIANO SÁNCHEZ are:
- i. BEATRICE[6] SÁNCHEZ.
- ii. ROSEMARY SÁNCHEZ.

22. FERMÍN[5] PACHECO *(ROMÁN[4], ANSELMO[3], FRANCISCO[2], MANUEL ANTONIO[1])* was born Abt. 1906. He married IGNACIA GÓMEZ August 29, 1932, daughter of FELIPÉ GÓMEZ and BEATRIZ SEDILLO.

Notes for IGNACIA GÓMEZ:

Children of FERMÍN PACHECO and IGNACIA GÓMEZ are:
- i. ROMÁN[6] PACHECO, b. Private.
- ii. ORLANDO PACHECO, b. Private.
- iii. BEATRIZ PACHECO, b. Private.

Generation No. 6

23. IGNACIA (INES)[6] CHÁVEZ *(PAUBLITA (PABLITA)[5] SÁNCHEZ, FELIPÉ E.[4], CORNELIA[3] PACHECO, FRANCISCO[2], MANUEL ANTONIO[1])* was born January 23, 1919 in San Patricio, New México. She married (1) HAROLD STEELE. She married (2) VICTOR BROOKS.

Notes for VICTOR BROOKS:
WW II veteran.

Child of IGNACIA CHÁVEZ and HAROLD STEELE is:
      i.   HAROLD (2ND)[7] STEELE.

24. EMILIANO[6] CHÁVEZ *(PAUBLITA (PABLITA)[5] SÁNCHEZ, FELIPÉ E.[4], CORNELIA[3] PACHECO, FRANCISCO[2], MANUEL ANTONIO[1])* was born January 11, 1922 in San Patricio, New México, and died January 23, 1953 in California. He married MARÍA (MARY) LUCERO, daughter of ANISETO LUCERO and REYNALDA SÁNCHEZ.

Notes for EMILIANO CHÁVEZ:
Served with N.M.2516 Base Unit AAF, and was a WW II veteran.
Buried: San Patricio.

Children of EMILIANO CHÁVEZ and MARÍA LUCERO are:
      i.   BOBBY[7] CHÁVEZ, m. LYDIA CHÁVEZ.
      ii.   ALEX CHÁVEZ.

           Notes for ALEX CHÁVEZ:
           Vietnam War Veteran. Died in Vietnam War.

      iii.   JERRY CHÁVEZ.

           Notes for JERRY CHÁVEZ:
           Died in an accident.

      iv.   LAURENCE CHÁVEZ, b. Private.

25. LUVÍN[6] CHÁVEZ *(PAUBLITA (PABLITA)[5] SÁNCHEZ, FELIPÉ E.[4], CORNELIA[3] PACHECO, FRANCISCO[2], MANUEL ANTONIO[1])* was born November 15, 1929 in San Patricio, New México. He married MARY KAMEES, daughter of SAMUEL MASSAD and TEODORA SILVA.

Notes for LUVÍN CHÁVEZ:
WW II veteran, US Marines.

Child of LUVÍN CHÁVEZ and MARY KAMEES is:
      i.   MARIO[7] CHÁVEZ, b. Private.

26. ORALIA[6] CHÁVEZ *(PAUBLITA (PABLITA)[5] SÁNCHEZ, FELIPÉ E.[4], CORNELIA[3] PACHECO, FRANCISCO[2], MANUEL ANTONIO[1])* was born February 18, 1931 in San Patricio, New México. She married JOSÉ ERNESTO SÁNCHEZ March 20, 1948 in Ruidoso, New Mexico, son of ROMÁN SÁNCHEZ and FLORINDA SALSBERRY.

Children of ORALIA CHÁVEZ and JOSÉ SÁNCHEZ are:
27.	i.	ERNEST JOSEPH[7] SÁNCHEZ, b. July 08, 1951, Long Beach, California.
28.	ii.	JAMES CHARLES SÁNCHEZ, b. October 29, 1953, Long Beach, California.
	iii.	STEVE ANTHONY SÁNCHEZ, b. December 24, 1959, Ruidoso, New México; d. January 08, 1978, San Patricio, New México.
29.	iv.	JANICE MARIE SÁNCHEZ, b. August 23, 1968, Ruidoso, New Mexico.

Generation No. 7

27. ERNEST JOSEPH[7] SÁNCHEZ *(ORALIA[6] CHÁVEZ, PAUBLITA (PABLITA)[5] SÁNCHEZ, FELIPÉ E.[4], CORNELIA[3] PACHECO, FRANCISCO[2], MANUEL ANTONIO[1])* was born July 08, 1951 in Long Beach, California. He married EUGENIE JOYCE HOFF in Carrizozo, New México, daughter of ALFRIED HOFF and PAULINA KUSCHEL.

Children of ERNEST SÁNCHEZ and EUGENIE HOFF are:

	i.	PAUL RAY[8] SÁNCHEZ, b. October 22, 1970, Tularosa, New Mexico.
30.	ii.	ERIK JOSEPH SÁNCHEZ, b. February 19, 1977, Denver, Colorado.

28. JAMES CHARLES[7] SÁNCHEZ *(ORALIA[6] CHÁVEZ, PAUBLITA (PABLITA)[5] SÁNCHEZ, FELIPÉ E.[4], CORNELIA[3] PACHECO, FRANCISCO[2], MANUEL ANTONIO[1])* was born October 29, 1953 in Long Beach, California. He married RUBY ROMO, daughter of PLACIDO ROMO and GENOVEVA CHÁVEZ.

Children of JAMES SÁNCHEZ and RUBY ROMO are:

31.	i.	JAMES MICHAEL[8] SÁNCHEZ.
	ii.	STEPHANIE RAE SÁNCHEZ, b. Socorro, New México.

29. JANICE MARIE[7] SÁNCHEZ *(ORALIA[6] CHÁVEZ, PAUBLITA (PABLITA)[5] SÁNCHEZ, FELIPÉ E.[4], CORNELIA[3] PACHECO, FRANCISCO[2], MANUEL ANTONIO[1])* was born August 23, 1968 in Ruidoso, New Mexico. She married EDDIE BERNAL.

Children of JANICE SÁNCHEZ and EDDIE BERNAL are:

	i.	MONICA[8] BERNAL.
	ii.	EDDIE BERNAL.

Generation No. 8

30. ERIK JOSEPH[8] SÁNCHEZ *(ERNEST JOSEPH[7], ORALIA[6] CHÁVEZ, PAUBLITA (PABLITA)[5] SÁNCHEZ, FELIPÉ E.[4], CORNELIA[3] PACHECO, FRANCISCO[2], MANUEL ANTONIO[1])* was born February 19, 1977 in Denver, Colorado. He married (1) VANESSA -----. He married (2) BRITNEY VIGIL December 01, 2002 in Loveland, Colorado.

Child of ERIK SÁNCHEZ and BRITNEY VIGIL is:

	i.	ALEXA[9] SÁNCHEZ, b. Denver, Colorado.

31. JAMES MICHAEL[8] SÁNCHEZ *(JAMES CHARLES[7], ORALIA[6] CHÁVEZ, PAUBLITA (PABLITA)[5] SÁNCHEZ, FELIPÉ E.[4], CORNELIA[3] PACHECO, FRANCISCO[2], MANUEL ANTONIO[1])*. He married ANGIE.

Children of JAMES SÁNCHEZ and ANGIE are:

	i.	CHAYANNE JADEN[9] SÁNCHEZ, b. Albuquerque, New México.
	ii.	JAMES GEORGE SÁNCHEZ, b. September 28, 2006, Albuquerque, New México.

Endnotes

1. *1900 Census Lincoln County*, Fiche # 1241001-2b, Lincoln County.
2. *LDS Historical Library, Alamogordo*, Page 6, Fiche # 756.
3. *LDS Historical Library, Alamogordo*, Page 54, Fiche # 0017008.
4. *LDS Historical Library, Alamogordo*, Page 12, Fiche # 0017009.
5. *LDS Historical Library, Alamogordo*, Page 22, Fiche # 754, Personal information provided by a descendant of his family.
6. *1900 Census Lincoln County*, Page 2B, Reventón, Lists all the children born before 1900.
7. *1880 Census Lincoln County*, Fiche # 8206107, Census # 77, Lists Erinello, his wife and their children and all of their ages.
8. *Lincoln County Clerk, Book of Marriages*, Page 141, Book B.
9. *Lincoln County Clerk, Book of Marriages*, Page 353, Book 3.
10. *LDS Historical Library, Alamogordo*, Page 206, Fiche # 754.
11. *1920 Census Lincoln County*, Page 3B, White Oaks.
12. *LDS Historical Library, Alamogordo*, Page 207, Fiche # 754.
13. *LDS Historical Library, Alamogordo*, Page 10, Fiche # 754.
14. *LDS Historical Library, Alamogordo*, Page 109, Fiche # 756.
15. *Lincoln County Clerk, Book of Marriages*, Page 25, Book 3, Lists birth date and marriage date for bride and groom.
16. *LDS Historical Library, Alamogordo*, Page 188, Fiche # 188, Marriage location.
17. *LDS Historical Library, Alamogordo*, Page 22 # 5, Fiche # 756.
18. *Lincoln County Clerk, Book of Marriages*, Page 133, Book 3, Lists birthdate and marriage date for bride and groom.
19. 1930 Census Lincoln County, Page 2A, Reventon, Lists all children born before 1930.
20. *Lincoln County Clerk, Book of Marriages*, Page 449, Book 5.
21. *Lincoln County Clerk, Book of Marriages*, Page 547, Book 5.
22. Lincoln County Clerk, Soldiers Discharge Book, Page 129, Book 3, Lists date of birth.
23. *1920 Census Lincoln County*, Fiche # 144157, 5B-Ln 31, Lists husband and children and their respective ages.
24. *Lincoln County Clerk, Book of Marriages*, Page 76, Book 3, Lists birth date and marriage date for bride and groom.
25. *LDS Historical Library, Alamogordo*, Page 160, Fiche # 756.
26. *LDS Historical Library, Alamogordo*, Page 252, Fiche # 754.
27. *1900 Census Lincoln County*, Page 2B, San Patricio.
28. *LDS Historical Library, Alamogordo*, Page 26, Fiche # 756.
29. Martin Funeral Home, El Paso, Téxas.
30. *Lincoln County Clerk, Book of Marriages*, Page 227, Book 4, Lists birth dates and marriage date for the bride and groom.
31. *Lincoln County Clerk, Book of Marriages*, Page 43, Book 4, Lists birth date and marriage dates for the bride and groom.
32. *LDS Historical Library, Alamogordo*, Page 12, Fiche # 0017009.
33. *LDS Historical Library, Alamogordo*, Page 39, Fiche # 756.
34. Lincoln County Clerk, Soldiers Discharge Book, Page 226, Book 3.

Descendants of Ignacio Romero

Generation No. 1

1. IGNACIO[1] ROMERO was born 1796 in El Reyno de Nuevo Méjico. He married RAFAELA (RAFAELITA) ALGERMAN.

Children of IGNACIO ROMERO and RAFAELA ALGERMAN are:

2.	i.	JOSÉ ANTONIO[2] ROMERO, b. Casa Colorada, Nuevo México, La República de México; d. Abt. 1877.
3.	ii.	JUAN ROMERO, b. Casa Colorada, Nuevo México.
4.	iii.	VICENTE ROMERO, b. Casa Colorada, Nuevo México; d. July 19, 1878, Lincoln, Territory of New México.
5.	iv.	FRANCISCO ROMERO, b. 1830, Casa Colorada, Nuevo México, La República de México.

Generation No. 2

2. JOSÉ ANTONIO[2] ROMERO *(IGNACIO[1])* was born in Casa Colorada, Nuevo México, La República de México, and died Abt. 1877. He married (1) CORNELIA DE ROMERO. He married (2) PAULA GALINDO August 25, 1873.

Child of JOSÉ ROMERO and CORNELIA DE ROMERO is:

6.	i.	JUAN DE DÍOS[3] ROMERO, b. March 1859, Casa Colorada, New México; d. 1914, Picacho, New México.

Children of JOSÉ ROMERO and PAULA GALINDO are:

	ii.	LUCIA[3] ROMERO, m. JOSÉ ALVAREZ.

Notes for LUCIA ROMERO:
Was Juan de Díos Romero's half sister.

	iii.	FRANCISCO ROMERO, b. September 14, 1874, Rio Bonito, Territory of New México[1].

3. JUAN[2] ROMERO *(IGNACIO[1])* was born in Casa Colorada, Nuevo México. He married MARÍA GARCÍA.

Children of JUAN ROMERO and MARÍA GARCÍA are:

	i.	PABLO GARCÍA[3] ROMERO.
	ii.	LUIS ROMERO, b. July 07, 1887.

4. VICENTE[2] ROMERO *(IGNACIO[1])* was born in Casa Colorada, Nuevo México, and died July 19, 1878 in Lincoln, Territory of New México. He married MARÍA MARGARITA GONZÁLES.

Notes for VICENTE ROMERO:
July 19, 1878: Was a regulator, killed on the forth day of the Lincoln County War.

Children of VICENTE ROMERO and MARÍA GONZÁLES are:

	i.	MARÍA DEL CARMEL[3] ROMERO, b. June 1873.

More About MARÍA DEL CARMEL ROMERO:
Fact 1: September 01, 1874, Baptized when she was 15 months old.

7.	ii.	PABLO GONZÁLES ROMERO, b. March 26, 1872, Río Bonito, Territory of México.
	iii.	DEMETRIA ROMERO, b. December 27, 1869, San Patricio, Territory of New México[2]; m. JUSTO CHÁVEZ, January 07, 1886.

Notes for JUSTO CHÁVEZ:
Raised Prometiva Romero. The daughter of Pablo Romero & Lucinda Gonzales.

5. FRANCISCO[2] ROMERO *(IGNACIO[1])[3]* was born 1830 in Casa Colorada, Nuevo México, La República de México. He married (1) ANDREA SÁNCHEZ. He married (2) GENOVEVA (VILLESCAS) BILLESCAS March 28, 1890, daughter of CASIMIRO BILLESCAS and DOLORES BALDONADO.

Notes for FRANCISCO ROMERO:
Land patent NMNMMA 010752: 160 acres.
Land patent NMNMMA 010776: 160 acres.

Children of FRANCISCO ROMERO and ANDREA SÁNCHEZ are:
    i.   JUANA[3] ROMERO, b. 1859.
    ii.   PETRA ROMERO, b. 1864; d. Bef. July 1884; m. LUCIANO TRUJILLO, January 09, 1882.

        Marriage Notes for PETRA ROMERO and LUCIANO TRUJILLO:
        Padrinos: George Kimbrell and Paula Romero.

    iii.   FRANCISCA SANCHEZ ROMERO, b. 1868.
    iv.   PABLO ROMERO, b. 1869; m. (1) PETRA; m. (2) JOSEFA SAMORA, June 22, 1897.

Children of FRANCISCO ROMERO and GENOVEVA BILLESCAS are:
8.   v.   PABLITA (PAULITA) (PABLA)[3] ROMERO, b. 1851.
9.   vi.   JUANITA ROMERO, b. 1862.
10.   vii.   FRANCISCA BILLESCAS ROMERO.

Generation No. 3

6. JUAN DE DÍOS[3] ROMERO *(JOSÉ ANTONIO[2], IGNACIO[1])* was born March 1859 in Casa Colorada, New México, and died 1914 in Picacho, New México. He married CRISTINA CASTILLO Abt. 1880, daughter of RAFAEL CASTILLO and MARÍA LUCERO.

Notes for JUAN DE DÍOS ROMERO:
He was raised at La Plaza de San Jose with his grandparents.
Buried in La Capilla de San Patricio.

Notes for CRISTINA CASTILLO:
Raised by her grandparents, José Miguel Lucero & Luciana. She had an aunt, Lola Guerra.

Children of JUAN ROMERO and CRISTINA CASTILLO are:
    i.   MANUEL[4] ROMERO.

        Notes for MANUEL ROMERO:
        Died Young.

11.   ii.   JORGE (GEORGE) ROMERO, b. July 22, 1882, Picacho, Territory of New México.
12.   iii.   MERENCIANA ROMERO, b. August 1883, Picacho, Territory of New México.
13.   iv.   CAROLINA ROMERO, b. January 22, 1884, Picacho, Territory of New México.
14.   v.   DELFINIA ROMERO, b. December 12, 1885, Picacho, Territory of New México; d. November 13, 1926, San Patricio, New México.
15.   vi.   GUADALUPE (LUPITA) ROMERO, b. December 12, 1888, Picacho, Territory of New México.
16.   vii.   ANTONIO ROMERO, b. December 1889, San Patricio, Territory of New México; d. February 06, 1942, San Patricio, New México.
17.   viii.   MARÍA ROMERO, b. March 24, 1893, San Patricio, Territory of New México.
18.   ix.   LUCIA ROMERO, b. December 06, 1895, San Patricio, Territory of New México.
    x.   ARISTOTEL ROMERO, b. 1896, Picacho, Territory of New México; m. FRANCISQUITA CHÁVEZ.
19.   xi.   MANUEL ROMERO, b. October 06, 1899, San Patricio, Territory of New México; d. Silver City, New México.

7. PABLO GONZÁLES[3] ROMERO *(VICENTE[2], IGNACIO[1])* was born March 26, 1872 in Río Bonito, Territory of México[4]. He married (1) LEONIDES CHÁVEZ. He married (2) LUCINDA GONZÁLES, daughter of PERFECTO GONZÁLES and ANTONIA VIGIL.

Children of PABLO ROMERO and LUCINDA GONZÁLES are:

	i.	LOLA[4] ROMERO, b. 1892.
20.	ii.	PROMETIVA ROMERO, b. February 25, 1898, Picacho, Territory of New México.

8. PABLITA (PAULITA) (PABLA)[3] ROMERO *(FRANCISCO[2], IGNACIO[1])* was born 1851. She married GEORGE KIMBRELL 1864.

More About PABLITA (PAULITA) (PABLA) ROMERO:
Fact 1: 1870, Was residing in Plaza de San José

More About GEORGE KIMBRELL:
Fact 1: 1863, Migrated from Las Vegas, NM to Ft. Stanton, Lincoln County, NM.
Fact 2: 1870, Was residing in La Plaza de San José
Fact 3: 1877, Settled in Picacho, NM.

Children of PABLITA ROMERO and GEORGE KIMBRELL are:

21.	i.	JUAN (JOHN) ROMERO[4] KIMBRELL, b. 1867, Picacho, Territory of New México.
	ii.	ELEN KIMBRELL, b. 1869, Picacho, Territory of New México.
	iii.	BEATRIZ KIMBRELL, b. April 18, 1872, Picacho, Territory of New México[4]; m. WALLACE BROCKMAN, May 15, 1889.
	iv.	BONUFANTE (BONIFACIO) KIMBRELL, b. February 22, 1874, Picacho, Territory of New México; m. (1) JESUSITA BARRERA, January 02, 1896; m. (2) FELIZ VIGIL, January 30, 1907.
22.	v.	WILLIAM E. KIMBRELL, b. July 16, 1877, Picacho, Territory of New México.

9. JUANITA[3] ROMERO *(FRANCISCO[2], IGNACIO[1])* was born 1862. She married MARTÍN CHÁVEZ.

More About MARTÍN CHÁVEZ:
Fact 1: 1860, One of the original settlers of Picacho, NM.
Fact 2: Was a Lincoln County Rifleman.
Fact 3: Was a Regulator in the Lincoln County War.

Children of JUANITA ROMERO and MARTÍN CHÁVEZ are:

	i.	DAVÍD[4] VILLESCAZ, b. 1883.
23.	ii.	MODESTO CHÁVEZ, b. 1885.
	iii.	JOSEFITA CHÁVEZ, b. 1887.
	iv.	BENJAMIN CHÁVEZ, b. 1890.

10. FRANCISCA BILLESCAS[3] ROMERO *(FRANCISCO[2], IGNACIO[1]).* She married PERFECTO SANDOVAL, son of ESEQUIEL SANDOVAL and MARIA DOLORES.

Child of FRANCISCA ROMERO and PERFECTO SANDOVAL is:

	i.	PERFECTO (2ND)[4] SANDOVAL, m. VIOLA KIMBRELL.

Generation No. 4

11. JORGE (GEORGE)[4] ROMERO *(JUAN DE DÍOS[3], JOSÉ ANTONIO[2], IGNACIO[1])* was born July 22, 1882 in Picacho, Territory of New México[5]. He married (1) JOSEFITA TORRES, daughter of EUSEVIO TORRES and EMILIA MUÑOZ. He married (2) MARÍA AURORA (AVRORA) GONZÁLES November 17, 1900[6], daughter of FLORENCIO GONZÁLES and RAYMUNDA SÁNCHEZ.

More About JORGE (GEORGE) ROMERO:
Fact 1: August 03, 1880, Baptized.

More About MARÍA AURORA (AVRORA) GONZÁLES:
Fact 1: August 04, 1880, Baptized.
Fact 2: 1920 Census notes that she was divorced.[7]

Children of JORGE ROMERO and JOSEFITA TORRES are:
  i.   GEORGE TORRES⁵ ROMERO, b. June 12, 1914; m. JULIANITA (JUANA) WARNER, October 10, 1934, San Patricio, New México.
  ii. CRISTINA ROMERO, m. ARISTEO CHÁVEZ.
  iii. JUAN ROMERO.
  iv. LUISA ROMERO.
  v.   EMILIA ROMERO.
  vi. EFREN ROMERO.
  vii. BEATRICE ROMERO.
  viii. PATRICIO ROMERO.

       Notes for PATRICIO ROMERO:
       Died young.

Children of JORGE ROMERO and MARÍA GONZÁLES are:
24.   ix. SIGISFREDO⁵ ROMERO, b. March 31, 1903.
25.   x.   MELITANA ROMERO, b. February 16, 1902.

12. MERENCIANA⁴ ROMERO *(JUAN DE DÍOS³, JOSÉ ANTONIO², IGNACIO¹)* was born August 1883 in Picacho, Territory of New México. She married (1) AVESLIN TORRES. She married (2) ALFRED MICKS.

Notes for MERENCIANA ROMERO:
Raised by Jinio and Lola Guerra.

Children of MERENCIANA ROMERO and AVESLIN TORRES are:
  i.   RUBÉN⁵ TORRES.
  ii. MIGUEL ROMERO, b. March 27, 1904, San Patricio, Territory of New México; d. November 19, 1946; m. FRANCISCA TRUJILLO.

       Notes for MIGUEL ROMERO:
       Raised and adopted by his grandmother Cristina Castillo Romero.

13. CAROLINA⁴ ROMERO *(JUAN DE DÍOS³, JOSÉ ANTONIO², IGNACIO¹)* was born January 22, 1884 in Picacho, Territory of New México⁸. She married ANTONIO SÁNCHEZ January 09, 1901⁹, son of FRANCISCO SÁNCHEZ and CONCEPCIÓN TRUJILLO.

Notes for CAROLINA ROMERO:
Raised by Jinio and Lola Guerra.

More About CAROLINA ROMERO:
Fact 1: March 23, 1884, Baptized.¹⁰

Children of CAROLINA ROMERO and ANTONIO SÁNCHEZ are:
  i.   ANEDA ROMERO⁵ SÁNCHEZ.
  ii. ANGELITA ROMERO SÁNCHEZ.
  iii. JESUSITA SÁNCHEZ.
  iv. JOSEFITA ROMERO SÁNCHEZ.
  v.   MARGARITA (MARGARET) SÁNCHEZ, b. August 22, 1903¹¹; m. ROBERTO PÉREZ.
  vi. ISMAEL SÁNCHEZ, b. 1916¹².

14. DELFINIA⁴ ROMERO *(JUAN DE DÍOS³, JOSÉ ANTONIO², IGNACIO¹)* was born December 12, 1885 in Picacho, Territory of New México¹³, and died November 13, 1926 in San Patricio, New México¹⁴. She married MAURICIO SÁNCHEZ January 09, 1901¹⁵, son of FRANCISCO SÁNCHEZ and CONCEPCIÓN TRUJILLO.

Notes for DELFINIA ROMERO:
December 18, 1885: Baptized in San Patricio under the name María Virginia Romero. Padrinos: Román Barragán & Andrea Torres.
Raised by her godparents, Román Barragán & Andrea Torres.
Buried: La Capilla de San Patricio.

Children of DELFINIA ROMERO and MAURICIO SÁNCHEZ are:
26.   i.   JESUSITA ROMERO⁵ SÁNCHEZ, b. San Patricio, New México.

       ii.   JOSÉ SÁNCHEZ, b. San Patricio, New México.

      iii.   JUANITA SÁNCHEZ, b. February 08, 1902, San Patricio, New México; d. December 06, 1975, Ruidoso, New México; m. RAMÓN TORRES, June 13, 1918, Glencoe, New Mexico[16].

           More About JUANITA SÁNCHEZ:
           Fact 1: March 17, 1902, Baptized.
           Fact 2: December 06, 1975, Died in an automobile accident.

           Marriage Notes for JUANITA SÁNCHEZ and RAMÓN TORRES:
           Married by: Justice of the Peace, Wilber Coe. Mauricio Sánchez gave consent to the marriage.

27.   iv.   ROMÁN SÁNCHEZ, b. April 23, 1904, San Patricio, New México; d. February 08, 1973, San Patricio, New México.

28.   v.   MAXIMILIANO SÁNCHEZ, b. August 21, 1911, San Patricio, New México.

      vi.   MABEL SÁNCHEZ, b. Abt. 1914, San Patricio, New México.

29.   vii. MARÍA (MARÍLLITA) SÁNCHEZ, b. May 1919, San Patricio, New México.

15. GUADALUPE (LUPITA)[4] ROMERO *(JUAN DE DÍOS[3], JOSÉ ANTONIO[2], IGNACIO[1])[17]* was born December 12, 1888 in Picacho, Territory of New México. She married GEORGE ORTEGA KIMBRELL[18] January 03, 1920 in Carrizozo, New México, son of JUAN KIMBRELL and DOMISINDA ORTEGA.

Notes for GUADALUPE (LUPITA) ROMERO:
Raised by José Alvarez and Lucia de Alvarez in Socorro, New México.

Children of GUADALUPE ROMERO and GEORGE KIMBRELL are:
      i.   ELSIE[5] KIMBRELL, b. 1922.
      ii.   WILLIAM KIMBRELL, b. 1926.
      iii. ELIZABETH KIMBRELL, b. 1928.
      iv. JOHN ROMERO KIMBRELL, b. Private.

16. ANTONIO[4] ROMERO *(JUAN DE DÍOS[3], JOSÉ ANTONIO[2], IGNACIO[1])* was born December 1889 in San Patricio, Territory of New México, and died February 06, 1942 in San Patricio, New México. He married CAROLINA SILVA June 21, 1916 in Carrizozo, New México[19], daughter of MANUEL GUTIÉRREZ and LEONARDA JIRÓN.

Notes for ANTONIO ROMERO:
Buried in La Capilla de San Patricio.

Children of ANTONIO ROMERO and CAROLINA SILVA are:
      i.   ESTER[5] ROMERO.
      ii.   ARISTOTEL SILVA ROMERO.
      iii. MANUEL SILVA ROMERO.
      iv. PRESILIANA ROMERO.
      v.   PABLO SILVA ROMERO.
      vi. LEONARDA ROMERO.
      vii. DELFINIA SILVA ROMERO.

17. MARÍA[4] ROMERO *(JUAN DE DÍOS[3], JOSÉ ANTONIO[2], IGNACIO[1])* was born March 24, 1893 in San Patricio, Territory of New México. She married HILARIO (YLARIO) GÓMEZ June 25, 1917 in Lincoln, New México[20], son of FELIPÉ GÓMEZ and MIQUELA LUCERO.

Notes for HILARIO (YLARIO) GÓMEZ:
WW I veteran.

Children of MARÍA ROMERO and HILARIO GÓMEZ are:
      i.   ELISEO[5] GÓMEZ, b. January 05, 1919; d. October 06, 1992; m. ROSA CHÁVEZ.

           Notes for ELISEO GÓMEZ:
           WW II veteran.

      ii.   MIQUELA (MICKEY) GÓMEZ, b. October 28, 1924; d. 1983; m. GEORGE MENDOZA, August 28, 1944.

18. LUCIA[4] ROMERO *(JUAN DE DÍOS[3], JOSÉ ANTONIO[2], IGNACIO[1])* was born December 06, 1895 in San Patricio, Territory of New México. She married (1) JOSÉ D. ARCHULETA February 15, 1917. She married (2) JUAN RUBIO July 01, 1925.

Child of LUCIA ROMERO and JOSÉ ARCHULETA is:

     i.   DOLORES (LOLA) ROMERO[5] ARCHULETA, b. February 03, 1916, San Patricio, New México; d. June 07, 1986, San Patricio, New México; m. AMARANTE (JACK) CHÁVEZ, September 21, 1936, San Patricio, New México.

           Notes for DOLORES (LOLA) ROMERO ARCHULETA:
           Buried: San Patricio, New México.

19. MANUEL[4] ROMERO *(JUAN DE DÍOS[3], JOSÉ ANTONIO[2], IGNACIO[1])* was born October 06, 1899 in San Patricio, Territory of New México, and died in Silver City, New México. He married ESTELA GÓMEZ, daughter of FELIPÉ GÓMEZ and BEATRIZ SEDILLO.

Child of MANUEL ROMERO and ESTELA GÓMEZ is:

     i.   LUCILLE[5] ROMERO, Adopted child.

20. PROMETIVA[4] ROMERO *(PABLO GONZÁLES[3], VICENTE[2], IGNACIO[1])* was born February 25, 1898 in Picacho, Territory of New México. She married JUAN (JOHN) ORTEGA KIMBRELL[21] September 14, 1914, son of JUAN KIMBRELL and DOMISINDA ORTEGA.

Marriage Notes for PROMETIVA ROMERO and JUAN KIMBRELL:
John Kimbrell, Domisinda Ortega de Kimbrell, Pablo Romero, and Lucinda Gonzáles gave their consent for the marriage.

Children of PROMETIVA ROMERO and JUAN KIMBRELL are:

     i.   DORA ROMERO[5] KIMBRELL, m. VICTORIANO ROMERO, November 04, 1907.
     ii.   MANUEL ROMERO KIMBRELL, m. PETRA MAÉS, July 14, 1923.
     iii. MANUELA (MELA) KIMBRELL, m. ESTEVAN GARCÍA.

           More About MANUELA (MELA) KIMBRELL:
           Fact 1: Raised by Domisinda Kimbrell.

     iv. ROSE KIMBRELL, m. (1) JULIAN SANDOVAL; m. (2) CARLOS FLORES, November 06, 1922.
     v.   ELISA KIMBRELL, b. 1920; m. ROBERT NUÑEZ SHANK, April 24, 1940.

21. JUAN (JOHN) ROMERO[4] KIMBRELL *(PABLITA (PAULITA) (PABLA)[3] ROMERO, FRANCISCO[2], IGNACIO[1])[22]* was born 1867 in Picacho, Territory of New México. He married DOMISINDA (DOMICINDA) ORTEGA February 04, 1888, daughter of LEANDRO ORTEGA and ROSARIO VIGIL.

Children of JUAN KIMBRELL and DOMISINDA ORTEGA are:

30.   i.   GEORGE ORTEGA[5] KIMBRELL, b. June 15, 1891, Picacho, Territory of New México.
31.   ii.   JUAN (JOHN) ORTEGA KIMBRELL, b. December 09, 1895, Picacho, Territory of New México.
       iii. MANUEL ORTEGA KIMBRELL, b. 1903, Picacho, Territory of New México.
       iv. ROSA KIMBRELL, b. 1905, Picacho, Territory of New México.
       v.   DORA ORTEGA KIMBRELL, b. 1911, Picacho, Territory of New México; m. JULIAN SANDOVAL, October 12, 1935.
       vi. BEATRICE KIMBRELL, b. 1919, Picacho, Territory of New México; m. FRED ROMERO, April 16, 1938.

22. WILLIAM E.[4] KIMBRELL *(PABLITA (PAULITA) (PABLA)[3] ROMERO, FRANCISCO[2], IGNACIO[1])[23]* was born July 16, 1877 in Picacho, Territory of New México. He married VIGINIA ROMERO January 01, 1904, daughter of TRENIDAD ROMERO and EUGENIA GONZÁLES.

Children of WILLIAM KIMBRELL and VIGINIA ROMERO are:

     i.   VIOLA[5] KIMBRELL, b. 1906; m. PERFECTO (2ND) SANDOVAL.
     ii.   RICHARD KIMBRELL, b. 1910.
     iii. ANITA (ANNA) KIMBRELL, b. 1912; m. FRANK T. TWITCHELL, April 14, 1937.
     iv. ANDREA KIMBRELL, b. 1914; m. DANOIS (DAN) SALAS, October 08, 1937.
     v.   MARY JANE KIMBRELL, b. 1916; m. MANUEL ORTIZ, December 25, 1936.
     vi. JOSEPHINE KIMBRELL, b. 1918.

    vii.   PAULINA KIMBRELL, b. 1920; m. STEPHAN A. PIERCE, October 04, 1908.
   viii.   GEORGE KIMBRELL, b. 1926.
    ix.   WILLIE KIMBRELL, b. 1928.

23. MODESTO[4] CHÁVEZ *(JUANITA[3] ROMERO, FRANCISCO[2], IGNACIO[1])[24]* was born 1885. He married TRENIDAD MONTOYA February 26, 1906, daughter of RAFAEL MONTOYA and MAY NORMAN.

Children of MODESTO CHÁVEZ and TRENIDAD MONTOYA are:
    i.   JUANA[5] CHÁVEZ, b. 1910.
    ii.   OLA CHÁVEZ, b. 1914.
   iii.   FRANCISCO CHÁVEZ, b. 1915.
   iv.   OLYMPIA CHÁVEZ, b. 1917.
    v.   MARÍA CHÁVEZ, b. 1919.

Generation No. 5

24. SIGISFREDO[5] ROMERO *(JORGE (GEORGE)[4], JUAN DE DÍOS[3], JOSÉ ANTONIO[2], IGNACIO[1])* was born March 31, 1903. He married LUCIA (LUCIANA) YBARRA January 11, 1928, daughter of GREGORIO YBARRA and CATARINA MONTOYA.

Notes for LUCIA (LUCIANA) YBARRA:
Padrinos: Augustín Laguna born in México City, and his wife, Juana María Laguna, born in Polvadera, New México

Children of SIGISFREDO ROMERO and LUCIA YBARRA are:
    i.   FLORIPE[6] ROMERO, b. Private.
    ii.   FEDELINA ROMERO, b. Private.
   iii.   CLEOFAS ROMERO, b. Private; m. JUAN SÁNCHEZ MONTES.
   iv.   ISABEL ROMERO, b. Private.
    v.   RUBÉN ROMERO, b. Private.
   vi.   EDUVIGEN ROMERO, b. Private.
   vii.   LEONIRES ROMERO, b. Private.
   viii.   FREDO ROMERO, b. Private.
   ix.   REBECCA ROMERO, b. Private.

25. MELITANA[5] ROMERO *(JORGE (GEORGE)[4], JUAN DE DÍOS[3], JOSÉ ANTONIO[2], IGNACIO[1])* was born February 16, 1902. She married PATROCINIO ARCHULETA CHÁVEZ[25] July 13, 1921, son of PATROCINIO CHÁVEZ and MARÍA ARCHULETA.

Children of MELITANA ROMERO and PATROCINIO CHÁVEZ are:
    i.   GABRIEL[6] CHÁVEZ.
    ii.   AURELIA CHÁVEZ.
   iii.   BRIGIDA CHÁVEZ.
   iv.   GLORIA CHÁVEZ.
    v.   MOISES CHÁVEZ.
   vi.   ADAN CHÁVEZ.
   vii.   RAY CHÁVEZ.
   viii.   VIRGINIA ROMERO CHÁVEZ.
   ix.   NORA CHÁVEZ.

26. JESUSITA ROMERO[5] SÁNCHEZ *(DELFINIA[4] ROMERO, JUAN DE DÍOS[3], JOSÉ ANTONIO[2], IGNACIO[1])* was born in San Patricio, New México. She married MAX SILVA.

Notes for MAX SILVA:
Was a WW II veteran.

Children of JESUSITA SÁNCHEZ and MAX SILVA are:
    i.   FRANK[6] SILVA, b. Private.
    ii.   PAT SILVA, b. Private.
   iii.   ANTHONY SILVA, b. Private.
   iv.   RICHARD SILVA.
    v.   JIMMIE SILVA, b. Private.

27. ROMÁN⁵ SÁNCHEZ *(DELFINIA⁴ ROMERO, JUAN DE DÍOS³, JOSÉ ANTONIO², IGNACIO¹)* was born April 23, 1904 in San Patricio, New México²⁶, and died February 08, 1973 in San Patricio, New México. He married FLORINDA SALSBERRY February 20, 1927 in Mescalero, New Mexico²⁷, daughter of JAMES SALSBERRY and MANUELITA HERRERA.

Notes for ROMÁN SÁNCHEZ:
May 29, 1904: Baptized by Román Barragán and his wife Andrea Torres de Barragán in San Patricio.

Died in an automobile accident in Ruidoso Downs.
Buried: La Capilla de San Patricio

Notes for FLORINDA SALSBERRY:
Florinda was born on the Rancho Salsberry by Cañon de Salsberry. The house is no longer standing but a grove of trees is all that remains of their house.

More About FLORINDA SALSBERRY:
Fact 1: June 15, 1910, Baptized. Padrinos: Manuel Corona and Susana Trujillo.²⁸

Children of ROMÁN SÁNCHEZ and FLORINDA SALSBERRY are:
      i.   MADELENA⁶ SÁNCHEZ, b. San Patricio, New México.

              More About MADELENA SÁNCHEZ:
              Fact 1: Died Young

      ii.   MAURICIO SALSBERRY SÁNCHEZ, b. San Patricio, New México.

              More About MAURICIO SALSBERRY SÁNCHEZ:
              Fact 1: Died Young

32.   iii. JOSÉ ERNESTO SÁNCHEZ, b. April 09, 1928, San Patricio, New México.
33.   iv. DELFINIA OLIDIA SÁNCHEZ, b. April 18, 1934, San Patricio, New México.
       v.   ORLANDO SÁNCHEZ, b. April 03, 1936, San Patricio, New México.
34.   vi. FLORA MARÍA SÁNCHEZ, b. March 24, 1938, Capítan, New México.
35.   vii. FRED SÁNCHEZ, b. May 30, 1940, Fort Stanton, New México.
36.   viii. BREZEL ROBERT SÁNCHEZ, b. November 04, 1941, San Patricio, New México.
      ix. GERALDINE (GERALDA) ELSIE SÁNCHEZ, b. January 10, 1945, San Patricio, New México; m. ROBERT MONTES.
      x.   LUVIN SÁNCHEZ, b. October 23, 1947, San Patricio, New México; m. GLORIA BACA.

              More About LUVIN SÁNCHEZ:
              Fact 1: Moved to Roswell, New México.

37.   xi. CINTHIA (CYNTHIA) YOLANDA SÁNCHEZ, b. September 10, 1950, Capítan, New México; d. April 27, 1986, Rio Rancho, New México.
38.   xii. ROMÁN SÁNCHEZ, JR., b. March 13, 1954, San Patricio, New México.

28. MAXIMILIANO⁵ SÁNCHEZ *(DELFINIA⁴ ROMERO, JUAN DE DÍOS³, JOSÉ ANTONIO², IGNACIO¹)* was born August 21, 1911 in San Patricio, New México. He married SORAIDA SÁNCHEZ February 11, 1936²⁹, daughter of AURELIO SÁNCHEZ and ANASTACIA ARAGÓN.

More About MAXIMILIANO SÁNCHEZ:
Fact 1: January 05, 1945, WW II veteran. Discharged from Indiana Town Gap, Pennsylvania.³⁰

Marriage Notes for MAXIMILIANO SÁNCHEZ and SORAIDA SÁNCHEZ:
Married by: Justice of the Peace, Elerdo Cháves.

Children of MAXIMILIANO SÁNCHEZ and SORAIDA SÁNCHEZ are:
      i.   BEATRICE⁶ SÁNCHEZ.
      ii.   ROSEMARY SÁNCHEZ.

29. MARÍA (MARÍLLITA)[5] SÁNCHEZ *(DELFINIA[4] ROMERO, JUAN DE DÍOS[3], JOSÉ ANTONIO[2], IGNACIO[1])* was born May 1919 in San Patricio, New México. She married MANUEL CHÁVEZ.

Children of MARÍA SÁNCHEZ and MANUEL CHÁVEZ are:
- i. WILLIE[6] CHÁVEZ.
- ii. VIRGINIA SÁNCHEZ CHÁVEZ.
- iii. ANDY CHÁVEZ.
- iv. LUISA CHÁVEZ, b. Private.
- v. DENNIS CHÁVEZ, b. Private.
- vi. CLIFFORD CHÁVEZ, b. Private.

30. GEORGE ORTEGA[5] KIMBRELL *(JUAN (JOHN) ROMERO[4], PABLITA (PAULITA) (PABLA)[3] ROMERO, FRANCISCO[2], IGNACIO[1])[31]* was born June 15, 1891 in Picacho, Territory of New México. He married (1) SARA SILVA December 02, 1911, daughter of AUGUSTÍN SILVA and LUCIA GARCÍA. He married (2) GUADALUPE (LUPITA) ROMERO[32] January 03, 1920 in Carrizozo, New México, daughter of JUAN ROMERO and CRISTINA CASTILLO.

Notes for GUADALUPE (LUPITA) ROMERO:
Raised by José Alvarez and Lucia de Alvarez in Socorro, New México.

Children of GEORGE KIMBRELL and SARA SILVA are:
- i. GENEVA[6] KIMBRELL.
- ii. FRED KIMBRELL, m. JULIA TORREZ.

Children of GEORGE KIMBRELL and GUADALUPE ROMERO are:
- iii. ELSIE[6] KIMBRELL, b. 1922.
- iv. WILLIAM KIMBRELL, b. 1926.
- v. ELIZABETH KIMBRELL, b. 1928.
- vi. JOHN ROMERO KIMBRELL, b. Private.

31. JUAN (JOHN) ORTEGA[5] KIMBRELL *(JUAN (JOHN) ROMERO[4], PABLITA (PAULITA) (PABLA)[3] ROMERO, FRANCISCO[2], IGNACIO[1])[33]* was born December 09, 1895 in Picacho, Territory of New México. He married PROMETIVA ROMERO September 14, 1914, daughter of PABLO ROMERO and LUCINDA GONZÁLES.

Marriage Notes for JUAN KIMBRELL and PROMETIVA ROMERO:
John Kimbrell, Domisinda Ortega de Kimbrell, Pablo Romero, and Lucinda Gonzáles gave their consent for the marriage.

Children of JUAN KIMBRELL and PROMETIVA ROMERO are:
- i. DORA ROMERO[6] KIMBRELL, m. VICTORIANO ROMERO, November 04, 1907.
- ii. MANUEL ROMERO KIMBRELL, m. PETRA MAÉS, July 14, 1923.
- iii. MANUELA (MELA) KIMBRELL, m. ESTEVAN GARCÍA.

  More About MANUELA (MELA) KIMBRELL:
  Fact 1: Raised by Domisinda Kimbrell.

- iv. ROSE KIMBRELL, m. (1) JULIAN SANDOVAL; m. (2) CARLOS FLORES, November 06, 1922.
- v. ELISA KIMBRELL, b. 1920; m. ROBERT NUÑEZ SHANK, April 24, 1940.

Generation No. 6

32. JOSÉ ERNESTO[6] SÁNCHEZ *(ROMÁN[5], DELFINIA[4] ROMERO, JUAN DE DÍOS[3], JOSÉ ANTONIO[2], IGNACIO[1])* was born April 09, 1928 in San Patricio, New México. He married ORALIA CHÁVEZ March 20, 1948 in Ruidoso, New Mexico, daughter of YSIDRO CHÁVEZ and PAUBLITA SÁNCHEZ.

Children of JOSÉ SÁNCHEZ and ORALIA CHÁVEZ are:
- 39. i. ERNEST JOSEPH[7] SÁNCHEZ, b. July 08, 1951, Long Beach, California.
- 40. ii. JAMES CHARLES SÁNCHEZ, b. October 29, 1953, Long Beach, California.
- iii. STEVE ANTHONY SÁNCHEZ, b. December 24, 1959, Ruidoso, New México; d. January 08, 1978, San Patricio, New México.
- 41. iv. JANICE MARIE SÁNCHEZ, b. August 23, 1968, Ruidoso, New Mexico.

33. DELFINIA OLIDIA[6] SÁNCHEZ *(ROMÁN[5], DELFINIA[4] ROMERO, JUAN DE DÍOS[3], JOSÉ ANTONIO[2], IGNACIO[1])* was born April 18, 1934 in San Patricio, New México. She married LEANDRO VEGA, son of LEANDRO VEGA and NARCISA RAMIREZ.

Children of DELFINIA SÁNCHEZ and LEANDRO VEGA are:

| | i. | LEE (LEANDRO)[7] VEGA, b. July 14, 1960, Carrizozo, New México; m. CATHERINE MARIE GARCÍA. |
| 42. | ii. | GARY ANTHONY VEGA, b. June 17, 1961, Carrizozo, New México. |

34. FLORA MARÍA[6] SÁNCHEZ *(ROMÁN[5], DELFINIA[4] ROMERO, JUAN DE DÍOS[3], JOSÉ ANTONIO[2], IGNACIO[1])* was born March 24, 1938 in Capítan, New México. She married RICHARD VEGA.

Children of FLORA SÁNCHEZ and RICHARD VEGA are:
- i.   DEBBI[7] VEGA, b. Private.
- ii. JAYLYN VEGA, b. Private.
- iii. RICHARD SÁNCHEZ VEGA, b. Private.
- iv. KENNETH VEGA, b. Private.

35. FRED[6] SÁNCHEZ *(ROMÁN[5], DELFINIA[4] ROMERO, JUAN DE DÍOS[3], JOSÉ ANTONIO[2], IGNACIO[1])* was born May 30, 1940 in Fort Stanton, New México. He married BERTA HERRERA, daughter of VICENTE HERRERA and CIPRIANA GONZÁLES.

Children of FRED SÁNCHEZ and BERTA HERRERA are:
- i.   DAVÍD[7] SÁNCHEZ, b. Private.
- ii. ELIZABETH SÁNCHEZ, b. Private.
- iii. PATRICK SÁNCHEZ, b. Private.
- iv. JESSICA SÁNCHEZ, b. Private.

36. BREZEL ROBERT[6] SÁNCHEZ *(ROMÁN[5], DELFINIA[4] ROMERO, JUAN DE DÍOS[3], JOSÉ ANTONIO[2], IGNACIO[1])* was born November 04, 1941 in San Patricio, New México. He married MINNIE ROMERO.

More About BREZEL ROBERT SÁNCHEZ:
Fact 1: Moved to Roswell, New México.

Children of BREZEL SÁNCHEZ and MINNIE ROMERO are:
- i.   RAY[7] SÁNCHEZ, b. Private.
- ii. ANTHONY SÁNCHEZ, b. Private.
- iii. ROSANA SÁNCHEZ, b. Private.
- iv. VERONICA SÁNCHEZ, b. Private.

37. CINTHIA (CYNTHIA) YOLANDA[6] SÁNCHEZ *(ROMÁN[5], DELFINIA[4] ROMERO, JUAN DE DÍOS[3], JOSÉ ANTONIO[2], IGNACIO[1])* was born September 10, 1950 in Capítan, New México, and died April 27, 1986 in Rio Rancho, New México. She married BERRY VANDERWALL.

Children of CINTHIA SÁNCHEZ and BERRY VANDERWALL are:
- i.   NEIL SIMON[7] VANDERWALL, b. Private.
- ii. MELISSA STEPHANIE VANDERWALL, b. Private.
- iii. AMANDA DESIREE VANDERWALL, b. Private.
- iv. AMBER DAWN VANDERWALL, b. Private.

38. ROMÁN[6] SÁNCHEZ, JR. *(ROMÁN[5], DELFINIA[4] ROMERO, JUAN DE DÍOS[3], JOSÉ ANTONIO[2], IGNACIO[1])* was born March 13, 1954 in San Patricio, New México. He married YOVONNE SALAS.

Children of ROMÁN SÁNCHEZ and YOVONNE SALAS are:
- i.   FELIPÉ[7] SÁNCHEZ, b. Private, Ruidoso, New México.
- ii. FABIAN SÁNCHEZ, b. Private, Ruidoso, New México.

Endnotes

1. *LDS Historical Library, Alamogordo*, Page 55, Fiche # 0017008.

2. *LDS Historical Library, Alamogordo*, Page 44, Fiche # 0017008.

3. *1870 Census of Ft. Stanton*, Page 288, Ft Stanton, Lists all children born before 1870.

4. *LDS Historical Library, Alamogordo*, Page 49, Fiche # 0017008.

5. *LDS Historical Library, Alamogordo*, Page 14, Fiche # 754.

6. *LDS Historical Library, Alamogordo*, Page 138, Fiche 756.

7. *1920 Census Lincoln County*, Fiche # 21077-1A.

8. *LDS Historical Library, Alamogordo*, Page 66, Fiche # 0017008.

9. *LDS Historical Library, Alamogordo*, Page 142, Fiche # 756.

10. *LDS Historical Library, Alamogordo*, Fiche # 0017008-1.

11. *LDS Historical Library, Alamogordo*, Page 161, Fiche # 754.

12. 1920 Census for Lincoln County, Page 1B, San patricio.

13. *LDS Historical Library, Alamogordo*, Page 90, Fiche # 754.

14. 1930 Census Lincoln County.

15. *LDS Historical Library, Alamogordo*, Page 142, Fiche # 756.

16. *Lincoln County Clerk, Book of Marriages*, Page 471, Book 4, Lists birth dates and marriage date for the bride and groom.

17. 1930 Census Lincoln County, Page 1B, Picacho, Lists all children born before 1930.

18. *Lincoln County Clerk, Book of Marriages*, Page 26, Book 1 Applications, Lists birth dates for the bride and groom.

19. *Lincoln County Clerk, Book of Marriages*, Page 116, Book 4, Lists birth dates and marriage date for the bride and groom.

20. *Lincoln County Clerk, Book of Marriages*, Page 386, Book 4, Lists birth dates and marriage date for the bride and groom.

21. *Lincoln County Clerk, Book of Marriages*, Page 110, Book 1 Applications, Lists birth dates for the bride and groom.

22. *1920 Census Lincoln County*, Page 1B, Picacho, Lists all children born before 1920.

23. 1930 Census Lincoln County, Page 1A-2B, Picacho, Lists all children born before 1930.

24. *1920 Census Lincoln County*, Page 2B, Picacho, Lists all children born before 1920.

25. *Lincoln County Clerk, Book of Marriages*, Page 153, Book 5, Lists birth date and marriage date for bride and groom.

26. *LDS Historical Library, Alamogordo*, Page 11, Fiche # 754.

27. *LDS Historical Library, Alamogordo*, Page 150, 756.

28. *LDS Historical Library, Alamogordo*, Page 119, Fiche # 754.

29. *LDS Historical Library, Alamogordo*, Page 39, Fiche # 756.

30. Lincoln County Clerk, Soldiers Discharge Book, Page 226, Book 3.

31. *Lincoln County Clerk, Book of Marriages*, Page 26, Book 1 Applications, Lists birth dates for the bride and groom.

32. 1930 Census Lincoln County, Page 1B, Picacho, Lists all children born before 1930.

33. *Lincoln County Clerk, Book of Marriages*, Page 110, Book 1 Applications, Lists birth dates for the bride and groom.

Descendants of Eugenio Sánchez

Generation No. 1

1. TOMÁS[1] SÁNCHEZ.

Child of TOMÁS SÁNCHEZ is:
2.   i.   FILOMENO[2] SÁNCHEZ.

Generation No. 2

2. FILOMENO[2] SÁNCHEZ *(TOMÁS[1])*. He married VICTORIA DE SÁNCHEZ.

Notes for FILOMENO SÁNCHEZ:
March 02, 1867: A bill was passed abolishing peonage, and Filomeno released his servants. He immediately adopted them as his children.

Children of FILOMENO SÁNCHEZ and VICTORIA DE SÁNCHEZ are:
3.   i.   MANUEL[3] SÁNCHEZ, Adopted child.
        ii.   JULIAN SÁNCHEZ, Adopted child.

            Notes for JULIAN SÁNCHEZ:
            Captured Navajo, who took the Sánchez surname.

        iii. RAFAEL SÁNCHEZ, Adopted child.

            Notes for RAFAEL SÁNCHEZ:
            Captured Navajo, who took the Sánchez surname.

        iv. TOMASITA SÁNCHEZ, Adopted child.

            Notes for TOMASITA SÁNCHEZ:
            Captured Navajo, who took the Sánchez surname.

        v.   MARÍA SÁNCHEZ, Adopted child.

            Notes for MARÍA SÁNCHEZ:
            Captured Navajo, who took the Sánchez surname.

        vi. BARTOLA SÁNCHEZ, Adopted child.

            Notes for BARTOLA SÁNCHEZ:
            Captured Navajo, who took the Sánchez surname.

        vii. CRUZ SÁNCHEZ, Adopted child.

            Notes for CRUZ SÁNCHEZ:
            Captured Navajo, who took the Sánchez surname.

4.   viii. EUGENIO (EUSEVIO) SÁNCHEZ, b. September 1856, Manzano, New México; d. 1936.

Generation No. 3

3. MANUEL[3] SÁNCHEZ *(FILOMENO[2], TOMÁS[1])*.

Notes for MANUEL SÁNCHEZ:
Captured Navajo, who took the Sánchez surname.

Child of MANUEL SÁNCHEZ is:

i.   EUGENIO[4] SÁNCHEZ.

Notes for EUGENIO SÁNCHEZ:
Captured Navajo, who took the Sánchez surname.

4. EUGENIO (EUSEVIO)[3] SÁNCHEZ *(FILOMENO[2], TOMÁS[1])[1]* was born September 1856 in Manzano, New México, and died 1936. He married ROSA GRIEGO 1882 in Manzano, New México.

Notes for EUGENIO (EUSEVIO) SÁNCHEZ:
Adopted by Filomeno (El Patron) Sánchez & his wife, Victoria.
Migrated to Lincoln County.

Children of EUGENIO SÁNCHEZ and ROSA GRIEGO are:

	i.	JOSÉ GRIEGO[4] SÁNCHEZ.
5.	ii.	AVRORA (AURORA) SÁNCHEZ, b. May 1884, Manzano, Territory of New México.
	iii.	TEODORO SÁNCHEZ, b. March 1886.
	iv.	FILOMENO GRIEGO SÁNCHEZ, b. December 1887, Manzano, New México; d. 1937; m. REFUGIA VIGIL, 1915.
	v.	JUAN GRIEGO SÁNCHEZ, b. December 1890.
	vi.	RITA GRIEGO SÁNCHEZ, b. July 1892.
	vii.	GERTRUDES GRIEGO SÁNCHEZ, b. December 1894.
	viii.	MANUEL GRIEGO SÁNCHEZ, b. November 1896.
	ix.	ENRÍQUES SÁNCHEZ, b. May 1898.
	x.	MARÍA AGIDA GRIEGO SÁNCHEZ, b. March 10, 1900.

More About MARÍA AGIDA GRIEGO SÁNCHEZ:
Fact 1: March 28, 1900, Baptized.

xi.   TELESFORO GRIEGO SÁNCHEZ, b. April 21, 1902.

More About TELESFORO GRIEGO SÁNCHEZ:
Fact 1: July 08, 1902, Baptized.

Generation No. 4

5. AVRORA (AURORA)[4] SÁNCHEZ *(EUGENIO (EUSEVIO)[3], FILOMENO[2], TOMÁS[1])* was born May 1884 in Manzano, Territory of New México. She married MAURICIO MARES MONTOYA[2] December 15, 1902 in Capilla de San Ysidro, Las Angusturas, Territory of New México, son of FELIPÉ MONTOYA and PAULA GARCÍA.

Children of AVRORA SÁNCHEZ and MAURICIO MONTOYA are:

	i.	TAVIANA[5] MONTOYA, m. OBSALON SÁNCHEZ.
	ii.	UTILIA (EUTILIA) MONTOYA, m. ESTOLANO OROSCO SÁNCHEZ.
6.	iii.	MASIMIANA (MAXIMIANA) MONTOYA, b. September 09, 1903.
	iv.	FLAVIO MONTOYA, b. 1905; m. GENIVA KIMBRELL.
	v.	JOSÉ SÁNCHEZ MONTOYA, b. 1907.
	vi.	SANTIAGO MONTOYA, b. 1910; d. 1945.

Notes for SANTIAGO MONTOYA:
Died in WW II.

vii.   YSIDRO MONTOYA, b. May 15, 1913; d. December 01, 1960.

Notes for YSIDRO MONTOYA:
Was a WW II veteran.

viii.   MANUEL SÁNCHEZ MONTOYA, b. 1916; m. CELIA SÁNCHEZ.
ix.   ROSA MONTOYA, b. 1918; m. ELISEO GALLEGOS.
x.   JUAN MONTOYA, b. Private; m. EVA GONZÁLES.

Notes for JUAN MONTOYA:
WW II war veteran, Navy.

Generation No. 5

6. MASIMIANA (MAXIMIANA)[5] MONTOYA *(AVRORA (AURORA)[4] SÁNCHEZ, EUGENIO (EUSEVIO)[3], FILOMENO[2], TOMÁS[1])[3]* was born September 09, 1903[4]. She married DELFIDO (ELFIGO) SALAS[5] February 13, 1927[6], son of TEOFILO SALAS and IGENIA GALLEGOS.

More About DELFIDO (ELFIGO) SALAS:
Fact 1: December 31, 1918, WW I veteran. Discharged from Camp Bowie, Texas.[7]

Marriage Notes for MASIMIANA MONTOYA and DELFIDO SALAS:
Marriage license has February 13, 1924.

Children of MASIMIANA MONTOYA and DELFIDO SALAS are:

i.	JUAN[6] SALAS, b. Private.
ii.	MADALENA SALAS, b. Private.
iii.	RAMÓN SALAS, b. Private.
iv.	RAMONA SALAS, b. Private.
v.	TEOFILO MONTOYA SALAS, b. Private.
vi.	TERESA SALAS, b. Private.
vii.	YLARIO SALAS, b. 1925; m. STELLA (JUANA) WARNER.
viii.	PEDRO SALAS, b. 1926.
ix.	REYNALDA SALAS, b. 1929.

Endnotes

1. *1900 Census Lincoln County*, Page 15A, Ruidoso, Lists all the children born before 1900.
2. *1920 Census Lincoln County*, Page 6B, Hondo, Lists all children born before 1920.
3. 1930 Census Lincoln County, Page 8A, Hondo, Lists all children born before 1930.
4. *LDS Historical Library, Alamogordo*, Micrfiche # 754, Page 164.
5. Family information given by Eutilia Montoya Sánchez.
6. *Lincoln County Clerk, Book of Marriages*, Book 5, Page 334.
7. Lincoln County Clerk, Soldiers Discharge Book, Page 2, Book 1.

Descendants of Cosmé Sedillo

Generation No. 1

1. CAMILO[1] SEDILLOS. He married ROSARIA CHÁVEZ.

Child of CAMILO SEDILLOS and ROSARIA CHÁVEZ is:
2.   i.   JUAN[2] SEDILLO, b. 1838, La Joya, Territory of New México.

Generation No. 2

2. JUAN[2] SEDILLO *(CAMILO[1] SEDILLOS)* was born 1838 in La Joya, Territory of New México[1]. He married JOSEFA FAJARDO January 07, 1914.

Marriage Notes for JUAN SEDILLO and JOSEFA FAJARDO:
Married by: Father Girma.

Children of JUAN SEDILLO and JOSEFA FAJARDO are:
      i.   JUANITA[3] SEDILLO.
3.   ii.   RAMONA SEDILLO, d. Bef. December 1913.
4.   iii. COSMÉ SEDILLO, b. 1851, El Berendo, Territory of New México; d. March 05, 1935, San Patricio, New México.
5.   iv. MARÍA SARAFINA SEDILLO, b. January 11, 1875, San Patricio, Territory of New México.
6.   v.   REIMUNDA (RAYMUNDA) SEDILLO, b. 1882.

Generation No. 3

3. RAMONA[3] SEDILLO *(JUAN[2], CAMILO[1] SEDILLOS)* died Bef. December 1913. She married PEDRO SÁNCHEZ.

Children of RAMONA SEDILLO and PEDRO SÁNCHEZ are:
      i.   PEDRO SEDILLO[4] SÁNCHEZ, b. May 15, 1902.
      ii.   YSABEL SÁNCHEZ, b. July 07, 1888, San Patricio, Territory of New México; m. JUAN VALDEZ[2], November 13, 1913, Lincoln, New México.

           Marriage Notes for YSABEL SÁNCHEZ and JUAN VALDEZ:
           Juan was living in Roswell at the time of his marriage. Ysabel was living in Arabela at the time.

      iii. RUFINA SÁNCHEZ, b. February 06, 1896, El Berendo, Territory of New México; m. SANTIAGO GALLEGOS[3], June 01, 1913, Lincoln, New México.

           Notes for SANTIAGO GALLEGOS:
           Both Santiago and Rufina were living in Arabela at the time of their marriage. They were married at La Capilla de San Juan Bautista. Pedro Sánchez and Ramona C. Sánchez gave their consent. Padrinos were Juan Chábes and Saturnina Sánchez.

           Marriage Notes for RUFINA SÁNCHEZ and SANTIAGO GALLEGOS:
           Married in La Capilla de San Juan Bautista.

4. COSMÉ[3] SEDILLO *(JUAN[2], CAMILO[1] SEDILLOS)* was born 1851 in El Berendo, Territory of New México, and died March 05, 1935 in San Patricio, New México. He married MAXIMA SÁNCHEZ November 05, 1873.

Children of COSMÉ SEDILLO and MAXIMA SÁNCHEZ are:
      i.   CATARINA[4] SEDILLO, b. El Berendo, Territory of New México; m. MANUEL FRESQUEZ.
7.   ii.   MARTÍN SEDILLO, b. April 30, 1875, El Berendo, Territory of New México.
8.   iii. FEDERICO SEDILLO, b. February 10, 1880, El Berendo, Territory of New México.
      iv. JUANITA SEDILLO, b. 1885, El Berendo, Territory of New México; m. CANDELARIO CHÁVEZ, February 19, 1898.
      v.   DEMETRIO SEDILLO, b. April 07, 1885, El Berendo, Territory of New México.
      vi. TELESFORA SEDILLO, b. December 24, 1895, El Berendo, New México.

vii.   FILOMENO SEDILLO, b. August 16, 1900.

viii.   SOFIA SEDILLO, b. June 11, 1901.

5. MARÍA SARAFINA[3] SEDILLO *(JUAN[2], CAMILO[1] SEDILLOS)* was born January 11, 1875 in San Patricio, Territory of New México[4]. She married VICENTE ULIBARRÍ November 06, 1922, son of JUAN ULIBARRÍ and ISABEL MONTOYA.

More About MARÍA SARAFINA SEDILLO:
Fact 1: January 22, 1875, Baptized In Tularosa, Territory of New México

Children of MARÍA SEDILLO and VICENTE ULIBARRÍ are:

9.   i.   PETRA[4] ULIBARRÍ.

       ii.   DOMINGA ULIBARRÍ, b. October 02, 1910; d. June 13, 2001; m. PROFESO (PROCESO) SALCIDO.

10.   iii.   SOFIA ULIBARRÍ, b. 1905; d. October 16, 1941.

11.   iv.   EPIFANIO ULIBARRÍ, b. August 22, 1896, San Patricio, Territory of New México.

12.   v.   AUGUSTINA ULIBARRÍ, b. September 26, 1892; d. April 29, 1970.

      vi.   MARÍA ULIBARRÍ, m. JOSÉ CHÁVEZ, December 02, 1911.

6. REIMUNDA (RAYMUNDA)[3] SEDILLO *(JUAN[2], CAMILO[1] SEDILLOS)*[5] was born 1882. She married LEOPOLDO GONZÁLES[6] November 28, 1895, son of FLORENCIO GONZÁLES and RAYMUNDA SÁNCHEZ.

Children of REIMUNDA SEDILLO and LEOPOLDO GONZÁLES are:

      i.   JUAN[4] GONZÁLES, b. November 10, 1896[7].

Notes for JUAN GONZÁLES:
Died young.

      ii.   AROPAJITA GONZÁLES, b. 1900[8]; d. December 05, 1918.

13.   iii.   CRUSITA GONZÁLES, b. May 02, 1904.

14.   iv.   ELISA GONZÁLES, b. February 23, 1912.

Generation No. 4

7. MARTÍN[4] SEDILLO *(COSMÉ[3], JUAN[2], CAMILO[1] SEDILLOS)* was born April 30, 1875 in El Berendo, Territory of New México. He married TOMASA (TOMASITA) HERRERA March 08, 1906, daughter of CRUZ HERRERA and OLOJIA MADRID.

More About MARTÍN SEDILLO:
Fact 1: April 13, 1875, Baptized in San Patricio, Territory of New México.

More About TOMASA (TOMASITA) HERRERA:
Fact 1: January 29, 1885, Baptized.

Children of MARTÍN SEDILLO and TOMASA HERRERA are:

      i.   CARLOS[5] SEDILLO, b. 1908.

      ii.   ROSA SEDILLO, b. 1911.

      iii.   MARIANO SEDILLO, b. 1912.

      iv.   DOMACIO SEDILLO, b. 1913.

      v.   RUFINA SEDILLO, b. 1915.

15.   vi.   CAMILO SEDILLO, b. June 05, 1917; d. Artesia, New México.

      vii.   FRED SEDILLO, b. 1921.

      viii.   CRUZ SEDILLO, b. 1925.

      ix.   KATARINA SEDILLO, b. 1928.

8. FEDERICO[4] SEDILLO *(COSMÉ[3], JUAN[2], CAMILO[1] SEDILLOS)* was born February 10, 1880 in El Berendo, Territory of New México. He married MARÍA LOVE[9] January 19, 1903, daughter of ----- LOVE and ANNA RICE.

Marriage Notes for FEDERICO SEDILLO and MARÍA LOVE:
Married by: Father Girand
Padrinos: Candelario Chávez and Juana Sedillo.

Children of FEDERICO SEDILLO and MARÍA LOVE are:
 i. ADELIDA[5] SEDILLO, b. 1904.
 ii. ELLEN SEDILLO, b. March 1908.

9. PETRA[4] ULIBARRÍ *(MARÍA SARAFINA[3] SEDILLO, JUAN[2], CAMILO[1] SEDILLOS)*. She married DIEGO SALCIDO November 06, 1922, son of FAUSTINO SALCIDO and MARÍA CHÁVEZ.

Child of PETRA ULIBARRÍ and DIEGO SALCIDO is:
 i. MONICA[5] SALCIDO, m. ESTOLANO TRUJILLO SÁNCHEZ.

  More About ESTOLANO TRUJILLO SÁNCHEZ:
  Fact 1: December 21, 1943, WW II veteran. Navy, Discharged from San Diego, California.[10]

10. SOFIA[4] ULIBARRÍ *(MARÍA SARAFINA[3] SEDILLO, JUAN[2], CAMILO[1] SEDILLOS)* was born 1905, and died October 16, 1941. She married PABLO YBARRA April 15, 1921 in San Patricio, New México, son of GREGORIO YBARRA and CATARINA MONTOYA.

Marriage Notes for SOFIA ULIBARRÍ and PABLO YBARRA:
Married by: Reverand Gremond.

Child of SOFIA ULIBARRÍ and PABLO YBARRA is:
 i. TIVORCIO (TIVE)[5] YBARRA.

  Notes for TIVORCIO (TIVE) YBARRA:
  Raised by his grandmother, Catarina Montoya Ybarra.

11. EPIFANIO[4] ULIBARRÍ *(MARÍA SARAFINA[3] SEDILLO, JUAN[2], CAMILO[1] SEDILLOS)* was born August 22, 1896 in San Patricio, Territory of New México. He married ERMINDA CHÁVEZ November 04, 1915 in Lincoln, New México[11], daughter of RICARDO CHÁVEZ and ESLINDA GONZÁLES.

More About ERMINDA CHÁVEZ:
Fact 1: July 20, 1894, Baptized.

Marriage Notes for EPIFANIO ULIBARRÍ and ERMINDA CHÁVEZ:
Padrinos: Florencio Gonzáles, Raymundo Sánchez, Augustín Ulibarrí.

Child of EPIFANIO ULIBARRÍ and ERMINDA CHÁVEZ is:
 i. DIEGO[5] ULIBARRÍ.

12. AUGUSTINA[4] ULIBARRÍ *(MARÍA SARAFINA[3] SEDILLO, JUAN[2], CAMILO[1] SEDILLOS)* was born September 26, 1892, and died April 29, 1970. She married RAYMUNDO SÁNCHEZ[12] December 17, 1910[13], son of JUAN SÁNCHEZ and MARÍA SÁNCHEZ.

Marriage Notes for AUGUSTINA ULIBARRÍ and RAYMUNDO SÁNCHEZ:
Padrinos: Cosme Sedillos and daughter.

Children of AUGUSTINA ULIBARRÍ and RAYMUNDO SÁNCHEZ are:
 i. EULALIA[5] SÁNCHEZ, b. 1913; m. PERFECTO SÁNCHEZ.
 ii. BENNIE SÁNCHEZ, b. July 26, 1914; m. NICOLÁS TORRES.
 iii. SOFIA SÁNCHEZ, b. 1917.
 iv. ANEDA ULIBARRÍ SÁNCHEZ, b. 1919; m. HERMANDO (ERMANDO) CHÁVEZ[14].
 v. OLYMPIA SÁNCHEZ, b. 1920; m. EPUNUCENO SÁNCHEZ.
 vi. LUÍS SÁNCHEZ, b. 1928.

13. CRUSITA[4] GONZÁLES *(REIMUNDA (RAYMUNDA)[3] SEDILLO, JUAN[2], CAMILO[1] SEDILLOS)* was born May 02, 1904[15]. She married (1) BENITO HERRERA, son of CRUZ HERRERA and REDUCINDA CARDONA. She married (2) CASIMIRO TAFOYA VILLESCAZ 1925 in Lincoln, New México[16], son of CASIMIRO VILLESCAZ and EMILIANA TAFOYA.

Notes for BENITO HERRERA:
Padrinos (baptismal): Ramon Olguín and Lorensa Sedillo.

More About BENITO HERRERA:
Fact 1: April 02, 1890, Baptized.

More About CASIMIRO TAFOYA VILLESCAZ:
Fact 1: January 12, 1895, Baptized.

Marriage Notes for CRUSITA GONZÁLES and CASIMIRO VILLESCAZ:
Another record has them married on February 19, 1928.

Child of CRUSITA GONZÁLES and CASIMIRO VILLESCAZ is:
     i.   ERNESTINA⁵ VILLESCAZ.

14. ELISA⁴ GONZÁLES *(REIMUNDA (RAYMUNDA)³ SEDILLO, JUAN², CAMILO¹ SEDILLOS)* was born February 23, 1912. She married MANUEL HERRERA November 23, 1931[17], son of LUÍS HERRERA and BENJAMIN HERNÁNDEZ.

Children of ELISA GONZÁLES and MANUEL HERRERA are:
     i.   LEO⁵ HERRERA, m. EMMA ZAMORA.
    ii.   FLORIPE HERRERA, m. PORFIRIO SÁNCHEZ.

Generation No. 5

15. CAMILO⁵ SEDILLO *(MARTÍN⁴, COSMÉ³, JUAN², CAMILO¹ SEDILLOS)* was born June 05, 1917, and died in Artesia, New México. He married LORENSITA MONTOYA May 04, 1940, daughter of DOROTEO MONTOYA and ALBINA SILVA.

Notes for LORENSITA MONTOYA:
Burial birthdate states she was born on August 09, 1914.

Children of CAMILO SEDILLO and LORENSITA MONTOYA are:
     i.   MARTÍN⁶ SEDILLO.
    ii.   DELLA SEDILLO.
   iii.   DANNY SEDILLO.
   iv.   ELLIE SEDILLO.
    v.   CERINIA SEDILLO.

Endnotes

1. 1910 Census Lincoln County, Page 2A, San Patricio.
2. *Lincoln County Clerk, Book of Marriages*, Page 73, Book 4, Lists birth date and marriage dates for the bride and groom.
3. *Lincoln County Clerk, Book of Marriages*, Page 31, Book 4, Lists birth date and marriage dates for the bride and groom.
4. *LDS Historical Library, Alamogordo*, Page 55, Fiche # 0017008.
5. *1920 Census Lincoln County*, Fiche # 1821077.
6. 1930 Census Lincoln County, Birth and death records.
7. *LDS Historical Library, Alamogordo*, Page 258, Fiche # 754.
8. *LDS Historical Library, Alamogordo*, Page 28, Fiche # 754.
9. 1910 Census Lincoln County, Page 15A, Agua Azul, Lists all children born before 1910.
10. Lincoln County Clerk, Soldiers Discharge Book, Page 158, Book 3, Lists date of birth.
11. *Lincoln County Clerk, Book of Marriages*, Page 229, Book 4, Lists birth dates and marriage date for the bride and groom.
12. *Lincoln County Clerk, Book of Marriages*, Page 352, Book 3, List birth date and marriage date for the bride and groom.
13. *LDS Historical Library, Alamogordo*, Reel # 756, Page 16.
14. *Lincoln County Clerk, Book of Marriages*, Page 615, Lists birth date and marriage date for both the bride and groom.
15. *LDS Historical Library, Alamogordo*, Page 172, Fiche # 754.
16. *LDS Historical Library, Alamogordo*, Page 224, Fiche # 754.
17. *LDS Historical Library, Alamogordo*, Page 3, Fiche # 756.

Descendants of Santiago Ulibarrí

Generation No. 1

1. JOSÉ ENRÍQUES[1] DE LOS REYES[1] was born in San Luís Potosi, Nueva España. He married MARÍA DE YNOJOS.

Children of JOSÉ DE LOS REYES and MARÍA DE YNOJOS are:
2.   i.   JUAN[2] DE ULIBARRÍ, b. 1670, San Luís Potosi, Nueva España; d. Bef. 1718.
        ii.   ANTONIO DE ULIBARRÍ[1], b. Abt. 1680, San Juan de la Paz, Ciudad de México, Nueva España; d. November 02, 1762, Santa Fé, El Reyno de Nuevo Méjico; m. MARÍA DURÁN Y CHÁVEZ, Abt. 1711.

        Notes for ANTONIO DE ULIBARRÍ:
        1714: Was appointed as the Alcalde of the Pueblos of Acoma, Zuñi, and Laguna.
        1731: Was appointed as the Alcalde and the Capitán de Guerra of La Villa de Santa Fé.

Generation No. 2

2. JUAN[2] DE ULIBARRÍ *(JOSÉ ENRÍQUES[1] DE LOS REYES)[1]* was born 1670 in San Luís Potosi, Nueva España, and died Bef. 1718. He married (1) JUANA HURTADO. He married (2) FRANCISCA DE MIZQUIA.

Notes for JUAN DE ULIBARRÍ:
1693: Was a member of the 1693 Vargas reconquest.
1701: Inscribed his name on "Inscription Rock".
1704: Stationed at the Presidio de Santa Fé. He was appointed as the second in command.
1706: Appointed as Procurator of his garrison in the Presidio de Santa Fé.
1706-1707: Liberated the Picurís from their Apache captors.

Children of JUAN DE ULIBARRÍ and JUANA HURTADO are:
3.   i.   JUAN HURTADO[3] DE ULIBARRÍ, b. 1690, San Luís Potosi, Nueva España.
        ii.   ANTONIO HURTADO DE ULIBARRÍ.

Generation No. 3

3. JUAN HURTADO[3] DE ULIBARRÍ *(JUAN[2], JOSÉ ENRÍQUES[1] DE LOS REYES)* was born 1690 in San Luís Potosi, Nueva España. He married ROSALIA DE ARMIJO July 01, 1732 in Alburquerque, El Reyno de Nuevo Méjico, daughter of JOSE DE ARMIJO and MANUELA VELASQUES.

Children of JUAN DE ULIBARRÍ and ROSALIA DE ARMIJO are:
        i.   ANDRES[4] ULIBARRÍ.
        ii.   BERNARDA ULIBARRÍ.
        iii.   JUAN PEDRO CRISOSTOMO ULIBARRÍ, b. Abt. 1733; d. July 24, 1799, San Juan de los Caballeros, El Reyno de Nuevo México.
        iv.   JUANA GETRUDES ULIBARRÍ, b. November 20, 1735, Alburquerque, El Reyno de Nuevo Méjico.
4.   v.   JUAQUÍN SANTA ANA ULIBARRÍ, b. 1742, Belén, El Reyno de Nuevo Méjico.

Generation No. 4

4. JUAQUÍN SANTA ANA[4] ULIBARRÍ *(JUAN HURTADO[3] DE ULIBARRÍ, JUAN[2], JOSÉ ENRÍQUES[1] DE LOS REYES)* was born 1742 in Belén, El Reyno de Nuevo Méjico. He married JUANA MARÍA DURÁN.

Children of JUAQUÍN ULIBARRÍ and JUANA DURÁN are:
        i.   FRANCISCO JUAQUÍN[5] ULIBARRÍ.
        ii.   JOSÉ ANTONIO DE JESÚS ULIBARRÍ.
        iii.   JUAN MIGUEL ANTONIO ULIBARRÍ.
        iv.   MARÍA DOLORES ULIBARRÍ.
        v.   MARÍA GERTRUDES ULIBARRÍ.

vi.   SALVADOR ULIBARRÍ.
vii. URSULA DE JESÚS ULIBARRÍ.
5.   viii. SANTIAGO JOSÉ ULIBARRÍ, b. 1775, Belén, El Reyno de Nuevo Méjico.
ix.   JUAN CRISTÓBAL ULIBARRÍ, b. Abt. 1780.

Generation No. 5

5. SANTIAGO JOSÉ[5] ULIBARRÍ *(JUAQUÍN SANTA ANA[4], JUAN HURTADO[3] DE ULIBARRÍ, JUAN[2], JOSÉ ENRÍQUES[1] DE LOS REYES)* was born 1775 in Belén, El Reyno de Nuevo Méjico. He married MARÍA ENCARNACIÓN LUCERO.

Child of SANTIAGO ULIBARRÍ and MARÍA LUCERO is:
6.   i.   SANTIAGO LUCERO[6] ULIBARRÍ, b. 1805, Belén, El Reyno de Nuevo Méjico.

Generation No. 6

6. SANTIAGO LUCERO[6] ULIBARRÍ *(SANTIAGO JOSÉ[5], JUAQUÍN SANTA ANA[4], JUAN HURTADO[3] DE ULIBARRÍ, JUAN[2], JOSÉ ENRÍQUES[1] DE LOS REYES)* was born 1805 in Belén, El Reyno de Nuevo Méjico. He married JUANA BERNARDINA ROMERO Y GALLEGOS, daughter of JOSE GALLEGOS and JUANA ROMERO.

Children of SANTIAGO ULIBARRÍ and JUANA GALLEGOS are:
7.   i.   JOSÉ ANTONIO[7] ULIBARRÍ, b. 1829, Belén, Nuevo México, República de México.
8.   ii.   JUAN GALLEGOS ULIBARRÍ, b. 1831, Belén, Nuevo México, República de México.
9.   iii. BENITO ULIBARRÍ, b. 1842, Belén, Nuevo México, República de México.

Generation No. 7

7. JOSÉ ANTONIO[7] ULIBARRÍ *(SANTIAGO LUCERO[6], SANTIAGO JOSÉ[5], JUAQUÍN SANTA ANA[4], JUAN HURTADO[3] DE ULIBARRÍ, JUAN[2], JOSÉ ENRÍQUES[1] DE LOS REYES)* was born 1829 in Belén, Nuevo México, República de México. He married MANUELA DE ULIBARRÍ.

Children of JOSÉ ULIBARRÍ and MANUELA DE ULIBARRÍ are:
i.   LORENSA[8] ULIBARRÍ, b. 1857.
ii.   JUANA ULIBARRÍ, b. 1862.
iii. FELIS ULIBARRÍ, b. 1864.
iv.   JUAN ULIBARRÍ, b. 1866.

8. JUAN GALLEGOS[7] ULIBARRÍ *(SANTIAGO LUCERO[6], SANTIAGO JOSÉ[5], JUAQUÍN SANTA ANA[4], JUAN HURTADO[3] DE ULIBARRÍ, JUAN[2], JOSÉ ENRÍQUES[1] DE LOS REYES)* was born 1831 in Belén, Nuevo México, República de México. He married (1) MARÍA CIPRIANA LUCERO January 02, 1865 in Carrizo, Territory of New México. He married (2) ISABEL MONTOYA May 13, 1889, daughter of TRANQUELINO MONTOYA and MARÍA TRUJILLO.

Child of JUAN ULIBARRÍ and MARÍA LUCERO is:
10.   i.   AMBROSIA[8] ULIBARRÍ, b. 1856.

Children of JUAN ULIBARRÍ and ISABEL MONTOYA are:
11.   ii.   SARAFINA SOCORRO[8] ULIBARRÍ, b. 1869; d. Bef. August 21.
12.   iii. VICENTE ULIBARRÍ, b. January 22, 1870.
13.   iv.   MARGARITA ULIBARRÍ.

9. BENITO[7] ULIBARRÍ *(SANTIAGO LUCERO[6], SANTIAGO JOSÉ[5], JUAQUÍN SANTA ANA[4], JUAN HURTADO[3] DE ULIBARRÍ, JUAN[2], JOSÉ ENRÍQUES[1] DE LOS REYES)* was born 1842 in Belén, Nuevo México, República de México. He married JUANITA SÁNCHEZ.

More About BENITO ULIBARRÍ:
Fact 1: 1870, Was residing in Plaza de San José.

More About JUANITA SÁNCHEZ:
Fact 1: 1870, Was residing in Plaza de San José.

Child of BENITO ULIBARRÍ and JUANITA SÁNCHEZ is:
    i.   MARÍA[8] ULIBARRÍ.

Generation No. 8

10. AMBROSIA[8] ULIBARRÍ *(JUAN GALLEGOS[7], SANTIAGO LUCERO[6], SANTIAGO JOSÉ[5], JUAQUÍN SANTA ANA[4], JUAN HURTADO[3] DE ULIBARRÍ, JUAN[2], JOSÉ ENRÍQUES[1] DE LOS REYES)* was born 1856. She married HILARIO (YLARIO) SILVA April 13, 1892, son of MANUEL SILVA and JOSEFITA ESQUIVEL.

Marriage Notes for AMBROSIA ULIBARRÍ and HILARIO SILVA:
Married by: Father Tafoya.

Children of AMBROSIA ULIBARRÍ and HILARIO SILVA are:
14.   i.   ALBINA (VALVINA)[9] SILVA, b. March 19, 1884, San Patricio, Territory of New México.
15.   ii.   TELESFOR (TELESFORO) SILVA, b. April 18, 1885, Tularoso, New México.

11. SARAFINA SOCORRO[8] ULIBARRÍ *(JUAN GALLEGOS[7], SANTIAGO LUCERO[6], SANTIAGO JOSÉ[5], JUAQUÍN SANTA ANA[4], JUAN HURTADO[3] DE ULIBARRÍ, JUAN[2], JOSÉ ENRÍQUES[1] DE LOS REYES)* was born 1869, and died Bef. August 21. She married ESTANISLADO (TANISLAUS) MONTOYA[2] January 09, 1887 in Carrizo, Territory of New México, son of TRANQUELINO MONTOYA and MARÍA TRUJILLO.

Children of SARAFINA ULIBARRÍ and ESTANISLADO MONTOYA are:
16.   i.   MANUEL[9] MONTOYA, b. 1888, San Patricio, New México; d. Bef. September 1923.
17.   ii.   PABLITA MONTOYA, b. May 02, 1890, San Patricio, New México; d. March 31, 1952, San Patricio, New México.
18.   iii.   TEODORO (THEODORO) MONTOYA, b. January 1893, San Patricio, New México.
    iv.   CANDIDO MONTOYA, b. 1895, San Patricio, New México.
19.   v.   SUSANA (SOCORRO) MONTOYA, b. 1897, San Patricio, New México.
    vi.   ISABEL MONTOYA, b. December 29, 1899, San Patricio, New México; m. (1) CONCHA -----, El Paso, Texas; m. (2) VICTORIA SÁNCHEZ, February 23, 1921.

        More About VICTORIA SÁNCHEZ:
        Fact 1: August 03, 1899, Baptized.

    vii.   DESIDERIO MONTOYA, b. February 11, 1902; m. CATARINA SALAZAR, March 08, 1926.
20.   viii.   SENAIDA MONTOYA, b. May 19, 1907; d. July 10, 1944, Roswell, New México.

12. VICENTE[8] ULIBARRÍ *(JUAN GALLEGOS[7], SANTIAGO LUCERO[6], SANTIAGO JOSÉ[5], JUAQUÍN SANTA ANA[4], JUAN HURTADO[3] DE ULIBARRÍ, JUAN[2], JOSÉ ENRÍQUES[1] DE LOS REYES)* was born January 22, 1870. He married MARÍA SARAFINA SEDILLO November 06, 1922, daughter of JUAN SEDILLO and JOSEFA FAJARDO.

More About MARÍA SARAFINA SEDILLO:
Fact 1: January 22, 1875, Baptized In Tularosa, Territory of New México

Children of VICENTE ULIBARRÍ and MARÍA SEDILLO are:
21.   i.   PETRA[9] ULIBARRÍ.
    ii.   DOMINGA ULIBARRÍ, b. October 02, 1910; d. June 13, 2001; m. PROFESO (PROCESO) SALCIDO.
22.   iii.   SOFIA ULIBARRÍ, b. 1905; d. October 16, 1941.
23.   iv.   EPIFANIO ULIBARRÍ, b. August 22, 1896, San Patricio, Territory of New México.
24.   v.   AUGUSTINA ULIBARRÍ, b. September 26, 1892; d. April 29, 1970.
    vi.   MARÍA ULIBARRÍ, m. JOSÉ CHÁVEZ, December 02, 1911.

13. MARGARITA[8] ULIBARRÍ *(JUAN GALLEGOS[7], SANTIAGO LUCERO[6], SANTIAGO JOSÉ[5], JUAQUÍN SANTA ANA[4], JUAN HURTADO[3] DE ULIBARRÍ, JUAN[2], JOSÉ ENRÍQUES[1] DE LOS REYES)*. She married FRANCISCO ARMERA October 14, 1911.

Child of MARGARITA ULIBARRÍ and FRANCISCO ARMERA is:

25. i. FRANCISCO ULIBARRÍ[9] ARMERA, d. December 04, 1927, San Patricio, New México.

Generation No. 9

14. ALBINA (VALVINA)[9] SILVA *(AMBROSIA[8] ULIBARRÍ, JUAN GALLEGOS[7], SANTIAGO LUCERO[6], SANTIAGO JOSÉ[5], JUAQUÍN SANTA ANA[4], JUAN HURTADO[3] DE ULIBARRÍ, JUAN[2], JOSÉ ENRÍQUES[1] DE LOS REYES)[3]* was born March 19, 1884 in San Patricio, Territory of New México. She married DOROTEO MONTOYA November 22, 1907, son of TRANQUELINO MONTOYA and MARÍA TRUJILLO.

More About DOROTEO MONTOYA:
Fact 1: February 15, 1886, Baptized.

Children of ALBINA SILVA and DOROTEO MONTOYA are:

26. i. LORENSITA[10] MONTOYA, b. February 12, 1912; d. Artesia, New México.
     ii. SAMUEL MONTOYA, b. 1909; d. 1994; m. EUFRACIA MONTOYA, November 26, 1938[4].
     iii. COSME MONTOYA, m. AMALIA BENAVIDEZ.
     iv. JOSEFITA MONTOYA, m. JUAN BACA.
     v. TRANQUELINO SILVA MONTOYA, m. RUBY SAMORA.

15. TELESFOR (TELESFORO)[9] SILVA *(AMBROSIA[8] ULIBARRÍ, JUAN GALLEGOS[7], SANTIAGO LUCERO[6], SANTIAGO JOSÉ[5], JUAQUÍN SANTA ANA[4], JUAN HURTADO[3] DE ULIBARRÍ, JUAN[2], JOSÉ ENRÍQUES[1] DE LOS REYES)* was born April 18, 1885 in Tularoso, New México. He married (1) FRANCISCA RODELA UDERO October 27, 1905, daughter of ANDRÉS RODELA and INEZ UDERO. He married (2) ERINEA BENAVIDEZ November 29, 1911, daughter of JUAN BENAVIDEZ and TEOFILA TRUJILLO.

Notes for FRANCISCA RODELA UDERO:
Raised by Andres Rodela.

Child of TELESFOR SILVA and FRANCISCA UDERO is:

27. i. EDUARDO (EDWARDO)[10] SILVA, b. August 10, 1908.

Children of TELESFOR SILVA and ERINEA BENAVIDEZ are:

     ii. BENITO[10] SILVA, m. CONSOLACION (CONSUELO) SÁNCHEZ, February 13, 1932[5].
28. iii. AMBROCIA SILVA, b. April 18, 1914.
     iv. ANSELMO SILVA, m. VIRGINIA MIRANDA.
     v. BONIFACIO SILVA.
     vi. VICTOR SILVA.
     vii. ONESIMA SILVA.
     viii. RAMON SILVA, m. CARMELITA SILVA.

16. MANUEL[9] MONTOYA *(SARAFINA SOCORRO[8] ULIBARRÍ, JUAN GALLEGOS[7], SANTIAGO LUCERO[6], SANTIAGO JOSÉ[5], JUAQUÍN SANTA ANA[4], JUAN HURTADO[3] DE ULIBARRÍ, JUAN[2], JOSÉ ENRÍQUES[1] DE LOS REYES)* was born 1888 in San Patricio, New México, and died Bef. September 1923. He married MARTINA PRUDENCIO October 01, 1911, daughter of JOSÉ PRUDENCIO and VICTORIA FAJARDO.

Children of MANUEL MONTOYA and MARTINA PRUDENCIO are:

     i. JUANITA[10] MONTOYA.
     ii. GILBERTO MONTOYA.
     iii. LUÍS MONTOYA.
     iv. FELIX MONTOYA.

17. PABLITA[9] MONTOYA *(SARAFINA SOCORRO[8] ULIBARRÍ, JUAN GALLEGOS[7], SANTIAGO LUCERO[6], SANTIAGO JOSÉ[5], JUAQUÍN SANTA ANA[4], JUAN HURTADO[3] DE ULIBARRÍ, JUAN[2], JOSÉ ENRÍQUES[1] DE LOS*

REYES) was born May 02, 1890 in San Patricio, New México, and died March 31, 1952 in San Patricio, New México. She married JULIO (2ND) MIRANDA November 15, 1909, son of JULIO MIRANDA and ANTONIA MOLINA.

Marriage Notes for PABLITA MONTOYA and JULIO MIRANDA:
Married by Father Girma.

Children of PABLITA MONTOYA and JULIO MIRANDA are:
29. i.   EULALIA (ULALIA)[10] MIRANDA.
     ii.   FRANCISCA MIRANDA, m. ANTONIO HERRERA.
     iii. CANDIDO MIRANDA.
     iv.   ENRIQUE MIRANDA.
     v.   CARLOS MIRANDA.
     vi.   VIRGINIA MIRANDA, m. ANSELMO SILVA.

18. TEODORO (THEODORO)[9] MONTOYA *(SARAFINA SOCORRO[8] ULIBARRÍ, JUAN GALLEGOS[7], SANTIAGO LUCERO[6], SANTIAGO JOSÉ[5], JUAQUÍN SANTA ANA[4], JUAN HURTADO[3] DE ULIBARRÍ, JUAN[2], JOSÉ ENRÍQUES[1] DE LOS REYES)* was born January 1893 in San Patricio, New México[6]. He married BERSABE SÁNCHEZ December 11, 1919[7], daughter of JUAN SÁNCHEZ and MARÍA SÁNCHEZ.

More About TEODORO (THEODORO) MONTOYA:
Fact 1: June 18, 1893, Baptized.
Fact 2: April 18, 1919, WW I veteran. Discharged from Camp Owen Bierne, Texas.[8]

More About BERSABE SÁNCHEZ:
Fact 1: October 28, 1897, Baptized.

Child of TEODORO MONTOYA and BERSABE SÁNCHEZ is:
       i.   ALVESITA[10] MONTOYA, m. CARLOS SÁNCHEZ.

19. SUSANA (SOCORRO)[9] MONTOYA *(SARAFINA SOCORRO[8] ULIBARRÍ, JUAN GALLEGOS[7], SANTIAGO LUCERO[6], SANTIAGO JOSÉ[5], JUAQUÍN SANTA ANA[4], JUAN HURTADO[3] DE ULIBARRÍ, JUAN[2], JOSÉ ENRÍQUES[1] DE LOS REYES)* was born 1897 in San Patricio, New México. She married LORENSO MENDOSA September 13, 1915 in Lincoln, New México, son of DIONICIO MENDOSA and ROSENDA MONTOYA.

Notes for LORENSO MENDOSA:
Rosenda's son.

Children of SUSANA MONTOYA and LORENSO MENDOSA are:
       i.   CONSUELO[10] MENDOSA, m. ERMINIO SÁNCHEZ.
       ii.   SOCORRO MENDOSA.
       iii. BENJAMIN MENDOSA.
       iv.   DIONICIO (DENNIS) MENDOSA, m. ANA MAE SUTHERLAND.
       v.   ELISA MENDOSA, m. ISMAEL CHÁVEZ.
       vi.   PORFIRIO MENDOSA.
       vii. ELOY MENDOSA.
       viii. ERNESTO MENDOSA.

20. SENAIDA[9] MONTOYA *(SARAFINA SOCORRO[8] ULIBARRÍ, JUAN GALLEGOS[7], SANTIAGO LUCERO[6], SANTIAGO JOSÉ[5], JUAQUÍN SANTA ANA[4], JUAN HURTADO[3] DE ULIBARRÍ, JUAN[2], JOSÉ ENRÍQUES[1] DE LOS REYES)* was born May 19, 1907[9], and died July 10, 1944 in Roswell, New México[9]. She married EDUARDO BARCELON SÁNCHEZ October 08, 1920 in Carrizozo, New México, son of JUAN SÁNCHEZ and MARÍA SÁNCHEZ.

Children of SENAIDA MONTOYA and EDUARDO SÁNCHEZ are:
       i.   EDUARDO MONTOYA[10] SÁNCHEZ, b. Abt. August 1921.

            More About EDUARDO MONTOYA SÁNCHEZ:
            Fact 1: July 03, 1943, WW II veteran. Discharged from Camp White, Oregon.[10]

       ii. CONFERINA MONTOYA SÁNCHEZ, b. Private.

iii. ELFIDES SÁNCHEZ, b. Private.
iv. MACLOFA SÁNCHEZ, b. Private; m. ARISTEO HERRERA.
v. MAGGIE SÁNCHEZ, b. Private.
vi. MANUEL MONTOYA SÁNCHEZ, b. Private; m. FLORINDA CARABAJAL Y SÁNCHEZ.
vii. RAFAEL MONTOYA SÁNCHEZ, b. Private.
viii. RUMELIO SÁNCHEZ, b. Private.

21. PETRA⁹ ULIBARRÍ *(VICENTE⁸, JUAN GALLEGOS⁷, SANTIAGO LUCERO⁶, SANTIAGO JOSÉ⁵, JUAQUÍN SANTA ANA⁴, JUAN HURTADO³ DE ULIBARRÍ, JUAN², JOSÉ ENRÍQUES¹ DE LOS REYES)*. She married DIEGO SALCIDO November 06, 1922, son of FAUSTINO SALCIDO and MARÍA CHÁVEZ.

Child of PETRA ULIBARRÍ and DIEGO SALCIDO is:
i. MONICA¹⁰ SALCIDO, m. ESTOLANO TRUJILLO SÁNCHEZ.

More About ESTOLANO TRUJILLO SÁNCHEZ:
Fact 1: December 21, 1943, WW II veteran. Navy, Discharged from San Diego, California.[11]

22. SOFIA⁹ ULIBARRÍ *(VICENTE⁸, JUAN GALLEGOS⁷, SANTIAGO LUCERO⁶, SANTIAGO JOSÉ⁵, JUAQUÍN SANTA ANA⁴, JUAN HURTADO³ DE ULIBARRÍ, JUAN², JOSÉ ENRÍQUES¹ DE LOS REYES)* was born 1905, and died October 16, 1941. She married PABLO YBARRA April 15, 1921 in San Patricio, New México, son of GREGORIO YBARRA and CATARINA MONTOYA.

Marriage Notes for SOFIA ULIBARRÍ and PABLO YBARRA:
Married by: Reverand Gremond.

Child of SOFIA ULIBARRÍ and PABLO YBARRA is:
i. TIVORCIO (TIVE)¹⁰ YBARRA.

Notes for TIVORCIO (TIVE) YBARRA:
Raised by his grandmother, Catarina Montoya Ybarra.

23. EPIFANIO⁹ ULIBARRÍ *(VICENTE⁸, JUAN GALLEGOS⁷, SANTIAGO LUCERO⁶, SANTIAGO JOSÉ⁵, JUAQUÍN SANTA ANA⁴, JUAN HURTADO³ DE ULIBARRÍ, JUAN², JOSÉ ENRÍQUES¹ DE LOS REYES)* was born August 22, 1896 in San Patricio, Territory of New México. He married ERMINDA CHÁVEZ November 04, 1915 in Lincoln, New México[12], daughter of RICARDO CHÁVEZ and ESLINDA GONZÁLES.

More About ERMINDA CHÁVEZ:
Fact 1: July 20, 1894, Baptized.

Marriage Notes for EPIFANIO ULIBARRÍ and ERMINDA CHÁVEZ:
Padrinos: Florencio Gonzáles, Raymundo Sánchez, Augustín Ulibarrí.

Child of EPIFANIO ULIBARRÍ and ERMINDA CHÁVEZ is:
i. DIEGO¹⁰ ULIBARRÍ.

24. AUGUSTINA⁹ ULIBARRÍ *(VICENTE⁸, JUAN GALLEGOS⁷, SANTIAGO LUCERO⁶, SANTIAGO JOSÉ⁵, JUAQUÍN SANTA ANA⁴, JUAN HURTADO³ DE ULIBARRÍ, JUAN², JOSÉ ENRÍQUES¹ DE LOS REYES)* was born September 26, 1892, and died April 29, 1970. She married RAYMUNDO SÁNCHEZ[13] December 17, 1910[14], son of JUAN SÁNCHEZ and MARÍA SÁNCHEZ.

Marriage Notes for AUGUSTINA ULIBARRÍ and RAYMUNDO SÁNCHEZ:
Padrinos: Cosme Sedillos and daughter.

Children of AUGUSTINA ULIBARRÍ and RAYMUNDO SÁNCHEZ are:
i. EULALIA¹⁰ SÁNCHEZ, b. 1913; m. PERFECTO SÁNCHEZ.
ii. BENNIE SÁNCHEZ, b. July 26, 1914; m. NICOLÁS TORRES.
iii. SOFIA SÁNCHEZ, b. 1917.
iv. ANEDA ULIBARRÍ SÁNCHEZ, b. 1919; m. HERMANDO (ERMANDO) CHÁVEZ[15].
v. OLYMPIA SÁNCHEZ, b. 1920; m. EPUNUCENO SÁNCHEZ.
vi. LUÍS SÁNCHEZ, b. 1928.

25. FRANCISCO ULIBARRÍ[9] ARMERA *(MARGARITA[8] ULIBARRÍ, JUAN GALLEGOS[7], SANTIAGO LUCERO[6], SANTIAGO JOSÉ[5], JUAQUÍN SANTA ANA[4], JUAN HURTADO[3] DE ULIBARRÍ, JUAN[2], JOSÉ ENRÍQUES[1] DE LOS REYES)* died December 04, 1927 in San Patricio, New México. He married IGNACIA MONTES August 28, 1901, daughter of ALEJO MONTES and ANGELA SÁNCHEZ.

Notes for FRANCISCO ULIBARRÍ ARMERA:
Buried: Old San Patricio cematary.

Children of FRANCISCO ARMERA and IGNACIA MONTES are:
    i.   ERMINIA[10] ARMERA, m. SERAPIO NUÑEZ.
    ii. ROMATILDA ARMERA, m. JUAN CHÁVEZ.

Generation No. 10

26. LORENSITA[10] MONTOYA *(ALBINA (VALVINA)[9] SILVA, AMBROSIA[8] ULIBARRÍ, JUAN GALLEGOS[7], SANTIAGO LUCERO[6], SANTIAGO JOSÉ[5], JUAQUÍN SANTA ANA[4], JUAN HURTADO[3] DE ULIBARRÍ, JUAN[2], JOSÉ ENRÍQUES[1] DE LOS REYES)* was born February 12, 1912, and died in Artesia, New México. She married (1) FERNANDO (FRED) SALSBERRY June 15, 1929 in Carrizozo, New Mexico, son of JAMES SALSBERRY and MANUELITA HERRERA. She married (2) CAMILO SEDILLO May 04, 1940, son of MARTÍN SEDILLO and TOMASA HERRERA.

Notes for LORENSITA MONTOYA:
Burial birthdate states she was born on August 09, 1914.

Notes for FERNANDO (FRED) SALSBERRY:
He died in an automobile accident in Hondo, New México.
Burried: San Patricio, New México.

Children of LORENSITA MONTOYA and FERNANDO SALSBERRY are:
    i.   ANATALIA[11] SALSBERRY, b. Private; m. MANUEL SOSA.
    ii. FERNANDO MONTOYA SALSBERRY, b. Private.
    iii. ELOY SALSBERRY, b. Private.

Children of LORENSITA MONTOYA and CAMILO SEDILLO are:
    iv. MARTÍN[11] SEDILLO.
    v.   DELLA SEDILLO.
    vi. DANNY SEDILLO.
    vii. ELLIE SEDILLO.
    viii. CERINIA SEDILLO.

27. EDUARDO (EDWARDO)[10] SILVA *(TELESFOR (TELESFORO)[9], AMBROSIA[8] ULIBARRÍ, JUAN GALLEGOS[7], SANTIAGO LUCERO[6], SANTIAGO JOSÉ[5], JUAQUÍN SANTA ANA[4], JUAN HURTADO[3] DE ULIBARRÍ, JUAN[2], JOSÉ ENRÍQUES[1] DE LOS REYES)* was born August 10, 1908. He married CONSUELO SALAS December 31, 1932, daughter of PEDRO SALAS and TEOFILA BENAVIDEZ.

Marriage Notes for EDUARDO SILVA and CONSUELO SALAS:
Married by: Justice of the Peace, S. W. Land.
Married by the Catholic Church on March 2, 1939 by: Father Savatore.

Child of EDUARDO SILVA and CONSUELO SALAS is:
    i.   CRUSITA[11] SILVA, m. ROY CHÁVEZ.

28. AMBROCIA[10] SILVA *(TELESFOR (TELESFORO)[9], AMBROSIA[8] ULIBARRÍ, JUAN GALLEGOS[7], SANTIAGO LUCERO[6], SANTIAGO JOSÉ[5], JUAQUÍN SANTA ANA[4], JUAN HURTADO[3] DE ULIBARRÍ, JUAN[2], JOSÉ ENRÍQUES[1] DE LOS REYES)* was born April 18, 1914. She married PROSPERO MIRABAL GONZÁLES May 15, 1936[16], son of PROSPERO GONZÁLES and TELESFORA MIRABAL.

Children of AMBROCIA SILVA and PROSPERO GONZÁLES are:

    i.   LILIA[11] GONZÁLES.
    ii.   FELIX GONZÁLES.
   iii. DORTHY GONZÁLES.
   iv. FLOYD GONZÁLES.

29. EULALIA (ULALIA)[10] MIRANDA *(PABLITA[9] MONTOYA, SARAFINA SOCORRO[8] ULIBARRÍ, JUAN GALLEGOS[7], SANTIAGO LUCERO[6], SANTIAGO JOSÉ[5], JUAQUÍN SANTA ANA[4], JUAN HURTADO[3] DE ULIBARRÍ, JUAN[2], JOSÉ ENRÍQUES[1] DE LOS REYES).* She married JOSÉ HERRERA, son of LUÍS HERRERA and BENJAMIN HERNÁNDEZ.

Child of EULALIA MIRANDA and JOSÉ HERRERA is:
    i.   PABLITA[11] HERRERA, m. BREZEL CHÁVEZ.

Endnotes

1. *Fray Angélico Chávez, Origins of New Mexico Families: Revised Edition,* Page 299.
2. 1910 Census Lincoln County, Page 2B, San Patricio, Lists all children born before 1910.
3. *LDS Historical Library, Alamogordo,* Page 67, Fiche # 0017008.
4. *LDS Historical Library, Alamogordo,* Microfiche #756-25, Page 5.
5. *LDS Historical Library, Alamogordo,* Page 17, Fiche # 756.
6. *LDS Historical Library, Alamogordo,* Page 195, Fiche # 754.
7. *Lincoln County Clerk, Book of Marriages,* Page 41, Book 5.
8. Lincoln County Clerk, Soldiers Discharge Book, Page 166, Book 1, Lists date of birth.
9. 1930 Census Lincoln County.
10. Lincoln County Clerk, Soldiers Discharge Book, Page 109, Book 3, Lists date of birth.
11. Lincoln County Clerk, Soldiers Discharge Book, Page 158, Book 3, Lists date of birth.
12. *Lincoln County Clerk, Book of Marriages,* Page 229, Book 4, Lists birth dates and marriage date for the bride and groom.
13. *Lincoln County Clerk, Book of Marriages,* Page 352, Book 3, List birthdate and marriage date for the bride and groom.
14. *LDS Historical Library, Alamogordo,* Reel # 756, Page 16.
15. *Lincoln County Clerk, Book of Marriages,* Page 615, Lists birthdate and marriage date for both the bride and groom.
16. *LDS Historical Library, Alamogordo,* Page 14, Fiche # 756